THE OXFORD

New French
Dictionary

THE OXFORD

New French Dictionary

French—English
English—French

BERKLEY BOOKS, NEW YORK

THE BERKLEY PUBLISHING GROUP
Published by the Penguin Group
Penguin Group (USA) Inc.
375 Hudson Street, New York, New York 10014, USA
Penguin Group (Canada), 90 Eglinton Avenue East, Suite 700, Toronto, Ontario M4P 2Y3, Canada
(a division of Pearson Penguin Canada Inc.)
Penguin Books Ltd., 80 Strand, London WC2R 0RL, England
Penguin Group Ireland, 25 St. Stephen's Green, Dublin 2, Ireland (a division of Penguin Books Ltd.)
Penguin Group (Australia), 250 Camberwell Road, Camberwell, Victoria 3124, Australia
(a division of Pearson Australia Group Pty. Ltd.)
Penguin Books India Pvt. Ltd., 11 Community Centre, Panchsheel Park, New Delhi—110 017, India
Penguin Group (NZ), 67 Apollo Drive, Rosedale, North Shore 0632, New Zealand
(a division of Pearson New Zealand Ltd.)
Penguin Books (South Africa) (Pty.) Ltd., 24 Sturdee Avenue, Rosebank, Johannesburg 2196,
South Africa

Penguin Books Ltd., Registered Offices: 80 Strand, London WC2R 0RL, England

The publisher does not have any control over and does not assume any responsibility for author or
third-party websites or their content.

THE OXFORD NEW FRENCH DICTIONARY, THIRD EDITION

A Berkley Book / published by arrangement with Oxford University Press, Inc.

PRINTING HISTORY
Berkley mass-market first edition /1993
Berkley mass-market second edition / July 2003
Berkley mass-market third edition / July 2009

ISBN: 978-0-425-22861-6

BERKLEY®
Berkley Books are published by The Berkley Publishing Group,
a division of Penguin Group (USA) Inc.,
375 Hudson Street, New York, New York 10014.
BERKLEY is a registered trademark of Penguin Group (USA) Inc.
The "B" design is a trademark of Penguin Group (USA) Inc.

PRINTED IN THE UNITED STATES OF AMERICA

10 9 8 7 6 5 4 3 2

Contents/Table des matières

Contributors/Collaborateurs

Fourth Edition/Quatrième édition

Nicholas Rollin
Jean Benoit Ormal-Grenon

Data capture/Saisie des données
Susan Wilkin

Proofreaders/Correcteurs
Isabelle Stables-Lemoine
Meic Haines
Mary O'Neill

Third Edition/Troisième édition

Isabelle Stables-Lemoine
Marianne Chalmers
Rosalind Combley
Catherine Roux
Laura Wedgeworth

Phrasefinder/Mini guide de conversation
Hélène Haenen
Neil and Roswitha Morris

First and Second Edition/Première et deuxième éditions

Michael Janes
Dora Latiri-Carpenter
Edwin Carpenter

Introduction

The Oxford New French Dictionary has been designed to be a practical reference tool for the student, adult learner, traveller and business professional. It provides user-friendly treatment of core vocabulary across a broad spectrum of written and spoken language.

Enhanced coverage

The wordlist has been revised to reflect recent additions to both languages.

The more complex grammatical words, or *function words*, are given special treatment in highlighted entries to make them easily accessible. All verbs in the French-English section are cross-referenced to the verb tables at the end of the book. Here information is given on regular, irregular and reflexive verbs as well as the translation of French verb tenses.

Easy reference

The dictionary layout has been designed to be clear, streamlined and easy to use. Bullet points separate each new part of speech within an entry. Nuances of meaning or usage are pinpointed by semantic indicators or by typical collocates with which the headword frequently occurs. Extra help is given with symbols to mark the register of language. A boxed exclamation mark ⚠ indicates colloquial language and a cross ✖ indicates slang.

The pronunciation of French is given in the International Phonetic Alphabet. Irregular parts of French verbs appear as headwords with a cross-reference to the main entry of the verb.

Introduction

L'*Oxford New French Dictionary* a été conçue comme un outil de référence pratique destiné aux étudiants, aux touristes et aux professionnels. Il offre un traitement convivial du vocabulaire de base représentatif de la langue écrite et parlée.

Une édition augmentée

La nomenclature a été revisée de façon à refléter les récents apports de vocabulaire dans les deux langues.

Les mots grammaticaux, qui forment les structures de base des deux langues, font l'objet d'une présentation distincte qui les rend rapidement accessibles, les choix de traduction et des exemples étant clairement signalés. De courtes notes d'usage indiquent les pièges éventuels. Une liste de verbes irréguliers anglais se trouve à la fin de l'ouvrage.

Une consulatation facilitée

La présentation du dictionnaire a été conçue de façon à être claire, simplifiée et à faciliter la consultation de l'ouvrage. Des *puces* séparent chaque nouvelle partie du discours à l'intérieur d'une entrée, ce qui facilite leur repérage. Les nuances de sens ou d'usage sont marquées au moyen d'indicateurs sémantiques ou par des collocateurs types avec lesquels le mot s'emploie fréquemment, guidant ainsi rapidement l'utilisateur à la traduction appropriée. Un point d'exclamation ⊞ indique un niveau de langue familier et une croix ⊠ indique un niveau argotique.

Les symboles utilisés pour la prononciation sont ceux de l'Alphabet Phonétique International. Les pluriels irréguliers ainsi que les conjugaisons ou les formes du comparatif et du superlatif irrégulières anglaises sont indiqués entre parenthèses.

Pronunciation of French

Vowels

a	as in	patte	/pat/	ɑ	as in	pâte	/pɑt/
ã		clan	/klã/	e		dé	/de/
ɛ		belle	/bɛl/	ɛ̃		lin	/lɛ̃/
ə		demain	/dəmɛ̃/	i		gris	/gRi/
o		gros	/gRo/	ɔ		corps	/kɔR/
ɔ̃		long	/lɔ̃/	œ		leur	/lœR/
œ̃		brun	/bRœ̃/	ø		deux	/dø/
u		fou	/fu/	y		pur	/pyR/

Semi-Vowels

j	as in	fille	/fij/
ɥ		huit	/ɥit/
w		oui	/wi/

Consonants

Aspiration of 'h'
Where it is impossible to make a liaison this is indicated by /'/ immediately after the slash e.g. *haine* /'ɛn/.

b	as in	bal	/bal/	ŋ	as in	camping	/kãpiŋ/
d		dent	/dã/	p		porte	/pɔRt/
f		foire	/fwaR/	R		rire	/RiR/
g		gomme	/gɔm/	s		sang	/sã/
k		clé	/kle/	ʃ		chien	/ʃjɛ̃/
l		lien	/ljɛ̃/	t		train	/tRɛ̃/
m		mer	/mɛR/	v		voile	/vwal/
n		nage	/naʒ/	z		zèbre	/zɛbR/
ɲ		oignon	/ɲɔ̃/	ʒ		jeune	/ʒœn/

La prononciation de l'anglais

Voyelles et diphtongues

iː	see	ɔː	saw	eɪ	page	ɔɪ	join
ɪ	sit	ʊ	put	əʊ	home	ɪə	near
e	ten	uː	too	aɪ	five	eə	hair
æ	hat	ʌ	cup	aɪə	fire	ʊə	poor
ɑː	arm	ɜː	fur	aʊ	now		
ɒ	got	ə	ago	aʊə	flour		

Consonnes

p	pen	tʃ	chin	s	so	n	no
b	bad	dʒ	June	z	zoo	ŋ	sing
t	tea	f	fall	ʃ	she	l	leg
d	dip	v	voice	ʒ	measure	r	red
k	cat	θ	thin	h	how	j	yes
g	got	ð	then	m	man	w	wet

L'accent d'intensité

L'accent d'intensité est indiqué au moyen du signe / ' /, placé devant la syllabe qu'il affecte.

Aa

a /a/ ➡ AVOIR **5**.

à /a/
● *préposition*

à+le = au
à+les = aux

····▸ (avec verbe de mouvement) to.

····▸ (pour indiquer où l'on se trouve) ~ **la maison** at home; ~ **Nice** in Nice.

····▸ (âge, date, heure) ~ **l'âge de...** at the age of...; **au XIXe siècle** in the 19th century; ~ **deux heures** at two o'clock.

····▸ (description) with; **aux yeux verts** with green eyes.

····▸ (appartenance) ~ **qui est ce stylo?** whose pen is this?; **c'est ~ vous?** is this yours?

····▸ (avec nombre) ~ **90 km/h** at 90 km per hour; ~ **10 minutes d'ici** 10 minutes from here; **des tomates ~ 2 euros le kilo** tomatoes at 2 euros a kilo; **un timbre ~ 2 euros** a 2-euro stamp; **nous avons fait le travail ~ deux** two of us did the work; **mener 5 ~ 4** to lead 5 (to) 4.

····▸ (avec être) **c'est ~ moi** it's my turn; **je suis ~ vous tout de suite** I'll be with you in a minute; **c'est ~ toi de décider** it's up to you to decide.

····▸ (hypothèse) ~ **ce qu'il paraît** apparently; ~ **t'entendre** to hear you talk.

····▸ (exclamatif) ~ **ta santé!** cheers!; ~ **demain/bientôt!** see you tomorrow/soon!

····▸ (moyen) ~ **la main** by hand; ~ **vélo** by bike; ~ **pied** on foot; **chauffage au gaz** gas heating.

abaissement /abɛsmã/ *nm* (de taux, de prix) cut; (de seuil) lowering.

abaisser /abese/ **1** *vt* lower; (levier) pull *ou* push down; (fig) humiliate. ▫ **s'~** *vpr* go down, drop; (fig) demean oneself; **s'~ à** stoop to.

abandon /abãdɔ̃/ *nm* abandonment; (de personne) desertion; (de course) withdrawal; (naturel) abandon; **à l'~** in a state of neglect.

abandonner /abãdɔne/ **1** *vt* abandon; (épouse, cause) desert; (renoncer à) give up, abandon; (céder à to); (course) withdraw from; (Ordinat) abort. ▫ **s'~ à** *vpr* give oneself up to.

abasourdir /abazuʀdiʀ/ **2** *vt* stun.

abat-jour /abaʒuʀ/ *nm inv* lampshade.

abats /aba/ *nmpl* offal.

abattement /abatmã/ *nm* dejection; (faiblesse) exhaustion; (Comm) reduction; ~ **fiscal** tax allowance.

abattre /abatʀ/ **11** *vt* knock down; (arbre) cut down; (animal) slaughter; (avion) shoot down; (affaiblir) weaken; (démoraliser) demoralize; **ne pas se laisser ~** not let things get one down. ▫ **s'~** *vpr* come down, fall (down).

abbaye /abei/ *nf* abbey.

abbé /abe/ *nm* priest; (supérieur d'une abbaye) abbot.

abcès /apsɛ/ *nm* abscess.

abdiquer /abdike/ **1** *vt/i* abdicate.

abdomen /abdɔmɛn/ *nm* abdomen.

abdominal (*pl* **-aux**) /abdɔminal/ *adj* abdominal. **abdominaux** *nmpl* (Sport) stomach exercises.

abeille /abɛj/ *nf* bee.

aberrant, ~e /abɛʀã, -t/ *adj* absurd.

abêtir /abetiʀ/ **2** *vt* turn into a moron.

abîme /abim/ *nm* abyss.

abîmer /abime/ **1** *vt* damage, spoil. ▫ **s'~** *vpr* get damaged *ou* spoilt.

ablation /ablasjɔ̃/ *nf* removal.

aboiement /abwamã/ *nm* bark, barking; ~**s** barking.

abolir /abɔliʀ/ **2** *vt* abolish.

abondance /abɔ̃dãs/ *nf* abundance; (prospérité) affluence. **abondant, ~e** *adj* abundant, plentiful.

abonder /abɔ̃de/ **1** *vi* abound (en in); ~ **dans le sens de qn** agree wholeheartedly with sb.

abonné, ~e /abɔne/ nm, f (lecteur) subscriber; (voyageur, spectateur) season-ticket holder.

abonnement /abɔnmɑ̃/ nm (à un journal) subscription; (de bus, Théât) season-ticket; (au gaz) standing charge.

abonner (s') /(s)abɔne/ **1** vpr subscribe (à to).

abord /abɔr/ nm access; ~s surroundings; **d'**~ first.

abordable /abɔrdabl/ adj (prix) affordable; (personne) approachable; (texte) accessible.

aborder /abɔrde/ **1** vt approach; (lieu) reach; (problème) tackle. ● vi reach land.

aborigène /abɔriʒɛn/ nm aborigine.

aboutir /abutir/ **2** vi succeed, achieve a result; ~ à end (up) in, lead to; **n'**~ **à rien** come to nothing.

aboutissement /abutismɑ̃/ nm outcome; (de carrière, d'évolution) culmination.

aboyer /abwaje/ **31** vi bark.

abrégé /abreʒe/ nm summary.

abréger /abreʒe/ **14 40** vt (texte) shorten, abridge; (mot) abbreviate, shorten; (visite) cut short.

abreuver /abrœve/ **1** vt water; (fig) overwhelm (de with). □ **s'**~ vpr drink.

abréviation /abrevjasjɔ̃/ nf abbreviation.

abri /abri/ nm shelter; **à l'**~ under cover; (en lieu sûr) safe; **à l'**~ **de** sheltered from; **se mettre à l'**~ take shelter.

abricot /abriko/ nm apricot.

abriter /abrite/ **1** vt shelter; (recevoir) house. □ **s'**~ vpr (take) shelter.

abrupt, ~e /abrypt/ adj steep, sheer; (fig) abrupt.

abruti, ~e /abryti/ nm, f **1** idiot.

absence /apsɑ̃s/ nf absence; **il a des** ~s sometimes his mind goes blank.

absent, ~e /apsɑ̃, -t/ adj (personne) absent, away; (chose) missing; **il est toujours** ~ he's still away; **d'un air** ~ absently. ● nm, f absentee.

absenter (s') /(s)apsɑ̃te/ **1** vpr go ou be away; (sortir) go out, leave.

absolu, ~e /apsɔly/ adj absolute.

absorbant, ~e /apsɔrbɑ̃, -t/ adj (travail) absorbing; (matière) absorbent.

absorber /apsɔrbe/ **1** vt absorb; être absorbé par qch be engrossed in sth.

abstenir (s') /(s)apstənir/ **58** vpr abstain; **s'**~ **de** refrain from.

abstrait, ~e /apstrɛ, -t/ adj & nm abstract.

absurde /apsyrd/ adj absurd.

abus /aby/ nm abuse, misuse; (injustice) abuse; ~ **de confiance** breach of trust.

abuser /abyze/ **1** vt deceive. ● vi go too far; ~ **de** abuse, misuse; (profiter de) take advantage of; (alcool) overindulge in. □ **s'**~ vpr be mistaken.

abusif, -ive /abyzif, -v/ adj excessive; (impropre) wrong; (injuste) unfair.

académie /akademi/ nf academy; (circonscription) local education authority.

> **Académie française** A scholarly body composed of 40 life members selected on the basis of their contribution to scholarship or literature. It monitors developments in the French language and rules on French usage, as encoded in the *Dictionnaire de l'Académie française* (which is not always taken seriously by the public at large). *i*

acajou /akaʒu/ nm mahogany.

accablant, ~e /akablɑ̃, -t/ adj (chaleur) oppressive; (fait, témoignage) damning.

accabler /akɑble/ **1** vt overwhelm; ~ **d'impôts** burden with taxes; ~ **d'injures** heap insults upon.

accéder /aksede/ **14** vi ~ **à** (lieu) reach; (pouvoir, trône) accede to; (requête) grant; (Ordinat) access; ~ **à la propriété** become a homeowner.

accélérateur /akseleratœr/ nm accelerator.

accélérer /akselere/ **14** vt/i accelerate. □ **s'**~ vpr speed up.

accent /aksɑ̃/ nm accent; (sur une syllabe) stress, accent; **mettre l'**~ **sur** stress; ~ **aigu/grave/circonflexe** acute/grave/circumflex accent.

accentuer /aksɑ̃tɥe/ **1** vt (lettre, syllabe) accent; (fig) emphasize, accentuate. □ **s'**~ vpr become more pronounced, increase.

accepter /aksɛpte/ **1** vt accept; ~ **de faire** agree to do.

accès /aksɛ/ nm access; (porte) entrance; (de fièvre) bout; (de colère) fit; (d'enthousiasme) burst; (Ordinat) access; **les ~ de** (voies) the approaches to; **facile d'~** easy to get to.

accessoire /akseswaʀ/ adj secondary, incidental. ● nm accessory; (Théât) prop.

accident /aksidɑ̃/ nm accident; ~ **de train/d'avion** train/plane crash; **par ~** by accident. **accidenté, ~e** adj (personne) injured (in an accident); (voiture) damaged; (terrain) uneven, hilly. **accidentel, ~le** adj accidental.

acclamer /aklame/ **1** vt cheer, acclaim.

accommoder /akɔmɔde/ **1** vt adapt (à to); (cuisiner) prepare; (assaisonner) flavour. □ **s'~ de** vpr make the best of.

accompagnateur, -trice /akɔ̃paɲatœʀ, -tʀis/ nm, f (Mus) accompanist; (guide) guide; ~ **d'enfants** accompanying adult.

accompagner /akɔ̃paɲe/ **1** vt accompany. □ **s'~ de** vpr be accompanied by.

accomplir /akɔ̃pliʀ/ **2** vt carry out, fulfil. □ **s'~** vpr take place, happen; (vœu) be fulfilled.

accord /akɔʀ/ nm agreement; (harmonie) harmony; (Mus) chord; **être d'~** agree (**pour** to); **se mettre d'~** come to an agreement, agree; **d'~!** all right **1**, OK!

accorder /akɔʀde/ **1** vt grant; (couleurs) match; (Mus) tune; (attribuer) (valeur, importance) assign. □ **s'~** vpr (se mettre d'accord) agree; (s'octroyer) allow oneself; **s'~ avec** (s'entendre avec) get on with.

accotement /akɔtmɑ̃/ nm verge; ~ **non stabilisé** soft verge.

accouchement /akuʃmɑ̃/ nm childbirth; (travail) labour.

accoucher /akuʃe/ **1** vi give birth (**de** to); (être en travail) be in labour. ● vt deliver. **accoucheur** nm **médecin ~** obstetrician.

accoudoir /akudwaʀ/ nm arm-rest.

accoupler /akuple/ **1** vt (Tech) couple. □ **s'~** vpr mate.

accourir /akuʀiʀ/ **20** vi run up.

accoutumance /akutymɑ̃s/ nf familiarization; (Méd) addiction.

accoutumer /akutyme/ **1** vt accustom. □ **s'~** vpr get accustomed.

accro /akʀo/ nmf **1** (drogué) addict; (amateur) fan.

accroc /akʀo/ nm tear, rip; (fig) hitch.

accrochage /akʀoʃaʒ/ nm hanging; hooking; (Auto) collision; (dispute) clash; (Mil) encounter.

accrocher /akʀoʃe/ **1** vt (suspendre) hang up; (attacher) hook, hitch; (déchirer) catch; (heurter) hit; (attirer) attract. □ **s'~** vpr cling, hang on (**à** to); (se disputer) clash.

accroissement /akʀwasmɑ̃/ nm increase (**de** in).

accroître /akʀwatʀ/ **24** vt increase. □ **s'~** vpr increase.

accroupir (s') /(s)akʀupiʀ/ **2** vpr squat.

accru, ~e /akʀy/ adj increased, greater.

accueil /akœj/ nm reception, welcome.

accueillant, ~e /akœjɑ̃, -t/ adj friendly, welcoming.

accueillir /akœjiʀ/ **25** vt receive, welcome; (film, livre) receive; (prendre en charge) (réfugiés, patients) take care of, cater for.

accumuler /akymyle/ **1** vt (énergie) store up; (capital) accumulate. □ **s'~** vpr (neige, ordures) pile up; (dettes) accrue.

accusation /akyzasjɔ̃/ nf accusation; (Jur) charge; **l'~** (magistrat) the prosecution.

accusé, ~e /akyze/ adj marked. ● nm, f defendant, accused.

accuser /akyze/ **1** vt accuse (**de** of); (blâmer) blame (**de** for); (Jur) charge (**de** with); (fig) emphasize; ~ **réception de** acknowledge receipt of.

acharné, ~e /aʃaʀne/ adj relentless, ferocious. **acharnement** nm (énergie) furious energy; (ténacité) determination.

acharner (s') /(s)aʃaʀne/ **1** vpr persevere; **s'~ sur** set upon; (poursuivre) hound; **s'~ à faire** (s'évertuer) try desperately; (s'obstiner) keep on doing.

achat /aʃa/ nm purchase; ~s shopping; **faire l'~ de** buy; **faire des ~s** do some shopping.

acheminer /aʃ(ə)mine/ **1** vt dispatch, convey; (courrier) handle. □ **s'~ vers** vpr head for.

acheter /aʃ(ə)te/ **6** vt buy; ~ **qch à qn** (pour lui) buy sth for sb; (chez lui) buy sth from sb. **acheteur, -euse** nm, f buyer; (client de magasin) shopper.

achèvement /aʃɛvmã/ nm completion.

achever /aʃ(ə)ve/ **6** vt finish (off). □ **s'~** vpr end.

acide /asid/ adj acid, sharp. ● nm acid.

acier /asje/ nm steel.

acné /akne/ nf acne.

acompte /akɔ̃t/ nm deposit, part-payment.

à-côté (pl ~s) /akote/ nm side issue; ~s (argent) extras.

acoustique /akustik/ nf acoustics (+ sg). ● adj acoustic.

acquéreur /akeRœR/ nm purchaser, buyer.

acquérir /akeRiR/ **7** vt acquire, gain; (biens) purchase, acquire.

acquis, -e /aki, -z/ adj acquired; (fait) established; **tenir qch pour ~** take sth for granted. ● nm experience. **acquisition** nf acquisition; purchase.

acquitter /akite/ **1** vt acquit; (dette) settle. □ **s'~ de** vpr (promesse) fulfil; (devoir) discharge.

âcre /ɑkR/ adj acrid.

acrobatie /akRɔbasi/ nf acrobatics (+ pl); ~ **aérienne** aerobatics (+ pl).

acte /akt/ nm act, action, deed; (Théât) act; (Jur) deed; ~ **de naissance**/ **mariage** birth/marriage certificate; ~s (compte rendu) proceedings; **prendre ~ de** note.

acteur /aktœR/ nm actor.

actif, -ive /aktif, -v/ adj active; (population) working. ● nm (Comm) assets; **avoir à son ~** have to one's credit ou name.

action /aksjɔ̃/ nf action; (Comm) share; (Jur) action; (effet) effect; (initiative) initiative. **actionnaire** nmf shareholder.

activer /aktive/ **1** vt speed up; (feu) boost. □ **s'~** vpr hurry up; (s'affairer) be very busy.

activité /aktivite/ nf activity; **en ~** (volcan) active; (fonctionnaire) working; (usine) in operation.

actrice /aktRis/ nf actress.

actualité /aktɥalite/ nf topicality; **l'~** current affairs; **les ~s** news; **d'~** topical.

actuel, ~le /aktɥɛl/ adj current, present; (d'actualité) topical. **actuellement** adv currently, at the present time.

acupuncture /akypɔ̃ktyR/ nf acupuncture.

adaptateur /adaptatœR/ nm (Électr) adapter.

adapter /adapte/ **1** vt adapt; (fixer) fit. □ **s'~** vpr adapt (oneself); (Tech) fit.

additif /aditif/ nm (note) rider; (substance) additive.

addition /adisjɔ̃/ nf addition; (au café) bill; (US) check. **additionner** **1** vt add; (totaliser) add (up).

adepte /adɛpt/ nmf follower; (d'activité) enthusiast.

adéquat, -e /adekwa, -t/ adj suitable; (suffisant) adequate.

adhérent, ~e /adeRã, -t/ nm, f member.

adhérer /adeRe/ **14** vi adhere, stick (à to); ~ **à** (club) be a member of; (s'inscrire à) join.

adhésif, -ive /adezif, -v/ adj adhesive; **ruban ~** sticky tape.

adhésion /adezjɔ̃/ nf membership; (soutien) support.

adieu (pl ~x) /adjø/ interj & nm goodbye, farewell.

adjectif /adʒɛktif/ nm adjective.

adjoint, ~e /adʒwɛ̃, -t/ nm, f assistant; ~ **au maire** deputy mayor. ● adj assistant.

adjuger /adʒyʒe/ **40** vt award; (aux enchères) auction. □ **s'~** vpr take (for oneself).

ADM abrév fpl (armes de destruction massive) WMD.

admettre /admɛtR/ **42** vt let in, admit; (tolérer) allow; (reconnaître) admit, acknowledge; (candidat) pass.

administrateur, -trice /administRatœR, -tRis/ nm, f administrator, director; (Jur) trustee; ~ **de site Internet** Webmaster.

administratif, -ive /administʀatif, -v/ *adj* administrative; (*document*) official. **administration** *nf* administration; (*gestion*) management; **l'A~** Civil Service.

administrer /administʀe/ **1** *vt* run, manage; (*justice, biens, antidote*) administer.

admirateur, -trice /admiʀatœʀ, -tʀis/ *nm, f* admirer.

admiration /admiʀasjɔ̃/ *nf* admiration.

admirer /admiʀe/ **1** *vt* admire.

admission /admisjɔ̃/ *nf* admission.

ADN *abrév m* (**acide désoxyribonucléique**) DNA.

adolescence /adɔlesɑ̃s/ *nf* adolescence. **adolescent, ~e** *nm, f* adolescent, teenager.

adopter /adɔpte/ **1** *vt* adopt. **adoptif, -ive** *adj* (*enfant*) adopted; (*parents*) adoptive.

adorer /adɔʀe/ **1** *vt* love; (*plus fort*) adore; (Relig) worship, adore.

adosser /adɔse/ **1** *vt* lean (**à, contre** against). **□ s'~** *vpr* lean back (**à, contre** against).

adoucir /adusiʀ/ **2** *vt* soften; (*boisson*) sweeten; (*chagrin*) ease. **□ s'~** *vpr* soften; (*chagrin*) ease; (*temps*) become milder. **adoucissant** *nm* (fabric) softener.

adresse /adʀɛs/ *nf* address; (*habileté*) skill; **~ électronique** email address.

adresser /adʀese/ **1** *vt* send; (écrire l'adresse sur) address; (*remarque*) address; **~ la parole à** speak to. **□ s'~ à** *vpr* address; (aller voir) (*personne*) go and ask *ou* see; (*bureau*) enquire at; (viser, intéresser) be directed at.

adroit, ~e /adʀwa, -t/ *adj* skilful, clever.

ADSL *abrév m* (asymmetrical digital subscriber line) ADSL.

adulte /adylt/ *nmf* adult. ● *adj* adult; (*plante, animal*) fully grown.

adultère /adyltɛʀ/ *adj* adulterous. ● *nm* adultery.

adverbe /advɛʀb/ *nm* adverb.

adversaire /advɛʀsɛʀ/ *nmf* opponent, adversary.

aérer /aeʀe/ **1** *vt* air; (*texte*) space out. **□ s'~** *vpr* get some air.

aérien, ~ne /aeʀjɛ̃, -jɛn/ *adj* air; (*photo*) aerial; (*câble*) overhead.

aérobic /aeʀɔbik/ *nm* aerobics (+ *sg*).

aérogare /aeʀɔgaʀ/ *nf* air terminal.

aéroglisseur /aeʀɔglisœʀ/ *nm* hovercraft.

aérogramme /aeʀɔgʀam/ *nm* airmail letter; (US) aerogram.

aéronautique /aeʀɔnotik/ *adj* aeronautical. ● *nf* aeronautics (+ *sg*).

aéroport /aeʀɔpɔʀ/ *nm* airport.

aérospatial, ~e (*mpl* **-iaux**) /aeʀɔspasjal, -jo/ *adj* aerospace.

affaiblir /afeblir/ **2** *vt* weaken. **□ s'~** *vpr* get weaker.

affaire /afɛʀ/ *nf* affair, matter; (Jur) case; (histoire, aventure) affair; (occasion) bargain; (entreprise) business; (transaction) deal; (question, problème) matter; **~s** (Comm) business; (Pol) affairs; (problèmes personnels) business; (effets personnels) things; **c'est mon ~** that's my business; **avoir ~ à** deal with; **ça fera l'~** that will do the job; **ça fera leur ~** that's just what they need; **tirer qn d'~** help sb out of a tight spot; **se tirer d'~** get out of trouble.

affairé, ~e /afeʀe/ *adj* busy.

affaisser (s') /(s)afese/ **1** *vpr* (*terrain, route*) sink, subside; (*poutre*) sag; (*personne*) collapse.

affamé, ~e /afame/ *adj* starving.

affectation /afɛktasjɔ̃/ *nf* (nomination) (à une fonction) appointment; (dans un lieu) posting; (de matériel, d'argent) allocation; (comportement) affectation.

affecter /afɛkte/ **1** *vt* (feindre) affect; (toucher, affliger) affect; (destiner) assign; (nommer) appoint, post.

affectif, -ive /afɛktif, -v/ *adj* emotional.

affection /afɛksjɔ̃/ *nf* affection; (maladie) complaint.

affectueux, -euse /afɛktɥø, -z/ *adj* affectionate.

affichage /afiʃaʒ/ *nm* billposting; (électronique) display.

affiche /afiʃ/ *nf* (public) notice; (publicité) poster; (Théât) bill; **être à l'~** (*film*) be showing; (*pièce*) be on.

afficher /afiʃe/ **1** *vt* (*annonce*) put up; (*événement*) announce; (*sentiment*) display; (Ordinat) display.

affirmatif, -ive /afiʀmatif, -v/ adj affirmative. **affirmation** nf assertion.

affirmer /afiʀme/ **1** vt assert; (soutenir) maintain.

affligé, ~e /afliʒe/ adj distressed; ~ **de** afflicted with.

affluer /aflye/ **1** vi flood in; (sang) rush.

affolant, ~e /afɔlɑ̃, -t/ adj alarming.

affoler /afɔle/ **1** vt throw into a panic. □ **s'~** vpr panic.

affranchir /afʀɑ̃ʃiʀ/ **2** vt stamp; (à la machine) frank; (esclave) emancipate; (fig) free. **affranchissement** nm (tarif) postage.

affreux, -euse /afʀø, -z/ adj (laid) hideous; (mauvais) awful.

affrontement /afʀɔ̃tmɑ̃/ nm confrontation.

affronter /afʀɔ̃te/ **1** vt confront. □ **s'~** vpr confront each other.

affûter /afyte/ **1** vt sharpen.

afin /afɛ̃/ prép & conj ~ **de faire** in order to do; ~ **que** so that.

africain, ~e /afʀikɛ̃, -ɛn/ adj African. **A~, ~e** nm, f African.

Afrique /afʀik/ nf Africa; ~ **du Sud** South Africa.

agacer /agase/ **10** vt irritate, annoy.

âge /ɑʒ/ nm age; (vieillesse) (old) age; **quel ~ avez-vous?** how old are you?; ~ **adulte** adulthood; ~ **mûr** maturity; **d'un certain ~** middle-aged.

âgé, ~e /ɑʒe/ adj elderly; ~ **de cinq ans** five years old.

agence /aʒɑ̃s/ nf agency, bureau, office; (succursale) branch; ~ **d'interim** employment agency; ~ **de voyages** travel agency; ~ **publicitaire** advertising agency.

agenda /aʒɛ̃da/ nm diary; ~ **électronique** electronic organizer.

agent /aʒɑ̃/ nm agent; (fonctionnaire) official; ~ **(de police)** policeman; ~ **de change** stockbroker; ~ **commercial** sales representative.

agglomération /aglɔmeʀasjɔ̃/ nf town, built-up area.

aggraver /agʀave/ **1** vt aggravate, make worse. □ **s'~** vpr get worse.

agile /aʒil/ adj agile, nimble.

agir /aʒiʀ/ **2** vi act; (se comporter) behave; (avoir un effet) work, take ef-

fect. □ **s'~ de** vpr (être nécessaire) **il s'agit de faire** we/you etc. must do; (être question de) **il s'agit de faire** it is a matter of doing; **dans ce livre il s'agit de** this book is about; **dont il s'agit** in question; **il s'agit de ton fils** it's about your son; **de quoi s'agit-il?** what is it about?

agitation /aʒitasjɔ̃/ nf bustle; (trouble) agitation; (malaise social) unrest.

agité, ~e /aʒite/ adj restless, fidgety; (troublé) agitated; (mer) rough.

agiter /aʒite/ **1** vt (bras, mouchoir) wave; (liquide, boîte) shake; (troubler) agitate; (discuter) debate. □ **s'~** vpr bustle about; (enfant) fidget; (foule, pensées) stir.

agneau (pl ~x) /aɲo/ nm lamb.

agrafe /agʀaf/ nf hook; (pour papiers) staple. **agrafeuse** nf stapler.

agrandir /agʀɑ̃diʀ/ **2** vt enlarge; (maison) extend. □ **s'~** vpr expand, grow. **agrandissement** nm extension; (de photo) enlargement.

agréable /agʀeabl/ adj pleasant.

agréé, ~e /agʀee/ adj (agence) authorized; (nourrice, médecin) registered; (matériel) approved.

agréer /agʀee/ **15** vt accept; ~ **à** please; **veuillez ~, Monsieur, mes salutations distinguées** (personne non nommée) yours faithfully; (personne nommée) yours sincerely.

agrégation /agʀegasjɔ̃/ nf highest examination for recruitment of teachers. **agrégé, ~e** nm, f teacher (who has passed the agrégation).

agrément /agʀemɑ̃/ nm charm; (plaisir) pleasure; (accord) assent.

agresser /agʀese/ **1** vt attack; (pour voler) mug.

agressif, -ive /agʀesif, -v/ adj aggressive. **agression** nf attack; (pour voler) mugging; (Mil) aggression.

agricole /agʀikɔl/ adj agricultural; (ouvrier, produit) farm. **agriculteur, -trice** nm, f farmer. **agriculture** nf agriculture, farming.

agripper /agʀipe/ **1** vt grab. □ **s'~** vpr cling (à to).

agroalimentaire /agʀɔalimɑ̃tɛʀ/ nm food industry.

agrumes /agʀym/ nmpl citrus fruit(s).

ai /e/ ➡**avoir** **5**.

aide /ɛd/ nf help, assistance; (en argent) aid; **à l'~ de** with the help of; **venir en ~ à** help; **~ à domicile** carer, home help; **~ familiale** mother's help; **~ sociale** social security; (US) welfare. ● nmf assistant. **aide-éducateur, -trice** nm, f classroom assistant. **aide-mémoire** nm inv handbook of key facts.

aider /ede/ **1** vt/i help, assist; (subventionner) aid, give aid to; **~ à faire** help to do. □ **s'~ de** vpr use.

aïeul /ajœl/ nm, f grandparent.

aigle /ɛgl/ nm eagle.

aigre /ɛgʀ/ adj sour, sharp; (fig) sharp.

aigrir /egʀiʀ/ **2** vt embitter. □ **s'~** vpr turn sour; (personne) become embittered.

aigu, ~ë /egy/ adj (douleur, problème) acute; (objet) sharp; (voix) shrill; (Mus) high(-pitched); (accent) acute.

aiguille /egɥij/ nf needle; (de montre) hand; (de balance) pointer;- **~ à tricoter** knitting needle.

aiguilleur /egɥijœʀ/ nm pointsman; **~ du ciel** air traffic controller.

aiguiser /eg(ɥ)ize/ **1** vt sharpen; (fig) stimulate.

ail (pl **~s** ou **aulx**) /aj, o/ nm garlic.

aile /ɛl/ nf wing.

ailier /elje/ nm winger; (US) end.

aille /aj/ →ALLER **8**.

ailleurs /ajœʀ/ adv elsewhere, somewhere else; **d'~** besides, moreover; **nulle part ~** nowhere else; **par ~** moreover, furthermore; **partout ~** everywhere else.

aimable /ɛmabl/ adj kind.

aimant /ɛmɑ̃/ nm magnet.

aimer /eme/ **1** vt like; (d'amour) love; **j'aimerais faire** I'd like to do; **~ bien** quite like; **~ mieux** ou **autant** prefer.

aîné, ~e /ene/ adj eldest; (de deux) elder. ● nm, f eldest (child); (premier de deux) elder (child); **~s** elders; **il est mon ~** he is older than me ou my senior.

ainsi /ɛ̃si/ adv like this, thus; (donc) so; **et ~ de suite** and so on; **pour ~ dire** so to speak, as it were; **~ que** as well as; (comme) as.

air /ɛʀ/ nm air; (mine) look, air; (mélodie) tune; **~ conditionné** air-conditioning; **avoir l'~** look, appear;

avoir l'~ de look like; **avoir l'~ de faire** appear to be doing; **en l'~** (up) in the air; (promesses) empty; **prendre l'~** get some fresh air.

aire /ɛʀ/ nf area; **~ d'atterrissage** landing-strip; **~ de pique-nique** picnic area; **~ de repas** rest area; **~ de services** (motorway) services.

aisance /ɛzɑ̃s/ nf ease; (richesse) affluence.

aise /ɛz/ nf joy; **à l'~** (sur un siège) comfortable; (pas gêné) at ease; (fortuné) comfortably off; **mal à l'~** uncomfortable; (ill) at ease; **aimer ses ~s** like one's creature comforts; **mettre qn à l'~** put sb at ease; **se mettre à l'~** make oneself comfortable.

aisé, ~e /eze/ adj easy; (fortuné) well-off.

aisselle /ɛsɛl/ nf armpit.

ait /ɛ/ →AVOIR **5**.

ajourner /aʒuʀne/ **1** vt postpone; (débat, procès) adjourn.

ajout /aʒu/ nm addition.

ajouter /aʒute/ **1** vt add (à to); **~ foi à** lend credence to. □ **s'~** vpr be added.

ajuster /aʒyste/ **1** vt adjust; (cible) aim at; (adapter) fit; **~ son coup** adjust one's aim.

alarme /alaʀm/ nf alarm; **donner l'~** raise the alarm.

alarmer /alaʀme/ **1** vt alarm. □ **s'~** vpr become alarmed (de at).

Albanie /albani/ nf Albania.

alcool /alkɔl/ nm alcohol; (eau de vie) brandy; **~ à brûler** methylated spirit. **alcoolique** adj & nmf alcoholic. **alcoolisé, ~e** adj (boisson) alcoholic. **alcoolisme** nm alcoholism.

alcootest /alkɔtɛst/ nm breath test; (appareil) Breathalyser®.

aléa /alea/ nm hazard. **aléatoire** adj unpredictable, uncertain; (Ordinat) random.

alentours /alɑ̃tuʀ/ nmpl surroundings; **aux ~ de** (de lieu) around; (de chiffre, date) about, around.

alerte /alɛʀt/ adj (personne) alert; (vif) lively. ● nf alert; **~ à la bombe** bomb scare. **alerter** **1** vt alert.

algèbre /alʒɛbʀ/ nf algebra.

Algérie /alʒeʀi/ nf Algeria.

algue /alg/ *nf* seaweed; **les ~s** (Bot) algae.

aliéné, ~e /aljene/ *nm, f* insane person.

aliéner /aljene/ 🔢 *vt* alienate; (céder) give up. □ **s'~** *vpr* alienate.

aligner /aliɲe/ *vt* (objets) line up, make lines of; (chiffres) string together; **~ sur** bring into line with. □ **s'~** *vpr* line up; **s'~ sur** align oneself on.

aliment /alimɑ̃/ *nm* food.

alimentaire /alimɑ̃tɛʀ/ *adj* (industrie) food; (habitudes) dietary; **produits ~s** foodstuffs.

alimentation /alimɑ̃tasjɔ̃/ *nf* feeding, supply(ing); (régime) diet; (aliments) food; **magasin d'~** grocery shop *ou* store.

alimenter /alimɑ̃te/ 🔢 *vt* feed; (fournir) supply; (fig) sustain. □ **s'~** *vpr* eat.

allaiter /alete/ 🔢 *vt* (bébé) breast-feed; (US) nurse; (animal) suckle.

allée /ale/ *nf* path, lane; (menant à une maison) drive(way); (dans un cinéma, magasin) aisle; (rue) road; **~s et venues** comings and goings.

allégé, ~e /aleʒe/ *adj* diet; (beurre, yaourt) low-fat.

alléger /aleʒe/ 🔢 🔢 *vt* make lighter; (fardeau, chargement) lighten; (fig) (souffrance) alleviate.

allégresse /alegʀɛs/ *nf* gaiety, joy.

alléguer /alege/ 🔢 *vt* (exemple) invoke; (prétexter) allege.

Allemagne /almaɲ/ *nf* Germany.

allemand, ~e /almɑ̃, -d/ *adj* German. ● *nm* (Ling) German. **A~, ~e** *nm, f* German.

---

aller /ale/ 🔢

● *verbe auxiliaire*

····▸ **je vais l'appeler** I'm going to call him; **j'allais partir** I was about to leave; **va savoir!** who knows?; **~ en s'améliorant** be improving.

● *verbe intransitif*

····▸ (se déplacer) go; **allons-y!** let's go!; **allez!** come on!

····▸ (se porter) **comment allez-vous?, comment ça va?** how are you?; **ça va (bien)** I'm fine;

---

qu'est-ce qui ne va pas? what's the matter?; **ça ne va pas la tête?** 🔢 are you mad? 🔢.

····▸ (mettre en valeur) **~ à qn** suit sb; **ça te va bien** it really suits you.

····▸ (convenir) **ça va ma coiffure?** is my hair OK?; **ça ne va pas du tout** that's no good at all.

□ **s'en aller** *verbe pronominal*

····▸ go; **va-t'en!** go away!; **ça ne s'en va pas** (tache) it won't come out.

● *nom masculin*

····▸ outward journey; **~ (simple)** single (ticket); (US) one-way (ticket); **~ retour** return (ticket); (US) round trip (ticket); **à l'~** on the way out.

---

allergie /alɛʀʒi/ *nf* allergy. **allergique** *adj* allergic (à to).

alliance /aljɑ̃s/ *nf* alliance; (bague) wedding-ring; (mariage) marriage.

allier /alje/ 🔢 *vt* combine; (Pol) ally. □ **s'~** *vpr* combine; (Pol) form an alliance; (famille) become related (à to).

allô /alo/ *interj* hallo, hello.

allocation /alɔkasjɔ̃/ *nf* allowance; **~ chômage** unemployment benefit; **~s familiales** family allowance.

allonger /alɔ̃ʒe/ 🔢 *vt* lengthen; (bras, jambe) stretch (out); (coucher) lay down. □ **s'~** *vpr* get longer; (s'étendre) lie down; (s'étirer) stretch (oneself) out.

allouer /alwe/ 🔢 *vt* allocate; (prêt) grant.

allumer /alyme/ 🔢 *vt* (bougie, gaz) light; (lampe, appareil) turn on; (pièce) switch the light(s) on in; (fig) arouse. □ **s'~** *vpr* (lumière, appareil) come on.

allumette /alymɛt/ *nf* match.

allure /alyʀ/ *nf* speed, pace; (démarche) walk; (apparence) appearance; **à toute ~** at full speed; **avoir de l'~** have style; **avoir des ~s de** look like; **avoir une drôle d'~** be funny-looking.

allusion /alyzjɔ̃/ *nf* allusion (à to); (implicite) hint (à at); **faire ~ à** allude to; hint at.

alors /alɔʀ/ *adv* (à ce moment-là) then; (de ce fait) so; (dans ce cas-là) then; **ça ~!** well!; **et ~?** so what? ● *conj* **~**

que (pendant que) while; (tandis que) when, whereas.

alouette /alwɛt/ nf lark.

alourdir /aluʀdiʀ/ ② vt weigh down; (rendre plus important) increase.

aloyau (pl ∼x) /alwajo/ nm sirloin.

Alpes /alp/ nfpl **les** ∼ the Alps.

alphabet /alfabɛ/ nm alphabet.
alphabétique adj alphabetical.

alphabétiser /alfabetize/ ① vt teach to read and write.

alpinist /alpinist/ nmf mountaineer.

altérer /alteʀe/ ⑭ vt (fait, texte) distort; (abîmer) spoil; (donner soif à) make thirsty. □ s'∼ vpr deteriorate.

alternance /altɛʀnɑ̃s/ nf alternation; **en** ∼ alternately.

altitude /altityd/ nf altitude, height.

amabilité /amabilite/ nf kindness.

amaigrir /amegʀiʀ/ ② vt make thin(ner).

amande /amɑ̃d/ nf almond; (d'un fruit à noyau) kernel.

amant /amɑ̃/ nm lover.

amarre /amaʀ/ nf (mooring) rope; ∼s moorings.

amas /amɑ/ nm heap, pile.

amasser /amɑse/ ① vt amass, gather; (empiler) pile up. □ s'∼ vpr pile up; (gens) gather.

amateur /amatœʀ/ nm amateur; ∼ **de** lover of; **d'**∼ amateur; (péj) amateurish.

ambassade /ɑ̃basad/ nf embassy. **ambassadeur, -drice** nm, f ambassador.

ambiance /ɑ̃bjɑ̃s/ nf atmosphere. **ambiant, ∼e** adj surrounding.

ambigu, -ë /ɑ̃bigy/ adj ambiguous.

ambitieux, -ieuse /ɑ̃bisjø, -z/ adj ambitious. **ambition** nf ambition.

ambulance /ɑ̃bylɑ̃s/ nf ambulance.

ambulant, ∼e /ɑ̃bylɑ̃, -t/ adj itinerant, travelling.

âme /am/ nf soul; ∼ **sœur** soul mate.

amélioration /ameljɔʀasjɔ̃/ nf improvement.

améliorer /ameljɔʀe/ ① vt improve. □ s'∼ vpr improve.

aménagement /amenaʒmɑ̃/ nm (de magasin) fitting out; (de grenier) conversion; (de territoire) development; (de cuisine) equipping.

aménager /amenaʒe/ ⑩ vt (magasin) fit out; (transformer) convert; (territoire) develop; (cuisine) equip.

amende /amɑ̃d/ nf fine; **faire** ∼ **honorable** make amends.

amener /am(ə)ne/ ⑥ vt bring; (causer) bring about; ∼ **qn à faire** cause sb to do. □ s'∼ vpr ① turn up.

amer, -ère /amɛʀ/ adj bitter.

américain, ∼e /ameʀikɛ̃, -ɛn/ adj American. **A∼, ∼e** nm, f American.

Amérique /ameʀik/ nf America; ∼ **centrale/latine** Central/Latin America; ∼ **du Nord/Sud** North/South America.

amertume /amɛʀtym/ nf bitterness.

ami, ∼e /ami/ nm, f friend; (amateur) lover; **un** ∼ **des bêtes** an animal lover. ● adj friendly.

amiable /amjabl/ adj amicable; **à l'**∼ (divorcer) by mutual consent; (se séparer) on friendly terms; (séparation) amicable.

amical, ∼e (mpl **-aux**) /amikal, -o/ adj friendly.

amiral (pl **-aux**) /amiʀal, -o/ nm admiral.

amitié /amitje/ nf friendship; ∼s (en fin de lettre) kind regards; **prendre qn en** ∼ take a liking to sb.

amnistie /amnisti/ nf amnesty.

amoindrir /amwɛ̃dʀiʀ/ ② vt reduce.

amont: en ∼ /ɑ̃namɔ̃/ loc upstream.

amorcer /amɔʀse/ ⑩ vt start; (hameçon) bait; (pompe) prime; (arme à feu) arm.

amortir /amɔʀtiʀ/ ② vt (choc) cushion; (bruit) deaden; (dette) pay off; ∼ **un achat** make a purchase pay for itself.

amortisseur /amɔʀtisœʀ/ nm shock absorber.

amour /amuʀ/ nm love; **pour l'**∼ **de** for the sake of.

amoureux, -euse /amuʀø, -z/ adj (personne) in love; (relation, regard) loving; (vie) love; ∼ **de qn** in love with sb. ● nm, f lover.

amour-propre /amuʀpʀɔpʀ/ nm self-esteem.

amphithéâtre /ɑ̃fiteatʀ/ nm amphitheatre; (d'université) lecture hall.

ampleur /ɑ̃plœʀ/ nf extent, size; (de vêtement) fullness; **prendre de l'~** spread, grow.

amplifier /ɑ̃plifje/ 45 vt amplify; (fig) expand, develop. □ **s'~** vpr (son) grow; (scandale) intensify.

ampoule /ɑ̃pul/ nf (électrique) bulb; (sur la peau) blister; (Méd) phial, ampoule.

amusant, ~e /amyzɑ̃, -t/ adj (blague) funny; (soirée) enjoyable, entertaining.

amuse-gueule /amyzgœl/ nm inv cocktail snack.

amusement /amyzmɑ̃/ nm amusement; (passe-temps) entertainment.

amuser /amyze/ 1 vt amuse; (détourner l'attention de) distract. □ **s'~** vpr enjoy oneself; (jouer) play.

amygdale /amidal/ nf tonsil.

an /ɑ̃/ nm year; **avoir dix ~s** be ten years old; **un garçon de deux ~s** a two-year-old boy; **à soixante ~s** at the age of sixty; **les moins de dix-huit ~s** under eighteens.

analogie /analɔʒi/ nf analogy.

analogue /analɔg/ adj similar, analogous (à to).

analphabète /analfabɛt/ adj & nmf illiterate.

analyse /analiz/ nf analysis; (Méd) test. **analyser** 1 vt analyse; (Méd) test.

ananas /anana(s)/ nm pineapple.

anarchie /anaʀʃi/ nf anarchy.

anatomie /anatɔmi/ nf anatomy.

ancêtre /ɑ̃sɛtʀ/ nm ancestor.

anchois /ɑ̃ʃwa/ nm anchovy.

ancien, ~ne /ɑ̃sjɛ̃, -jɛn/ adj old; (de jadis) ancient; (meuble) antique; (précédent) former, ex-, old; (dans une fonction) senior; **~ combattant** veteran. ● nm, f senior; (par l'âge) elder. **anciennement** adv formerly. **ancienneté** nf age, seniority.

ancre /ɑ̃kʀ/ nf anchor; **jeter/lever l'~** cast/weigh anchor.

andouille /ɑ̃duj/ nf sausage (filled with chitterlings); (idiot 1) fool; **faire l'~** fool around.

âne /ɑn/ nm donkey, ass; (imbécile 1) dimwit 1.

anéantir /aneɑ̃tiʀ/ 2 vt destroy; (exterminer) annihilate; (accabler) overwhelm.

anémie /anemi/ nf anaemia.

ânerie /ɑnʀi/ nf stupid remark.

anesthésie /anɛstezi/ nf (opération) anaesthetic.

ange /ɑ̃ʒ/ nm angel; **aux ~s** in seventh heaven.

angine /ɑ̃ʒin/ nf throat infection.

anglais, ~e /ɑ̃glɛ, -z/ adj English. ● nm (Ling) English. **A~, ~e** nm, f Englishman, Englishwoman.

angle /ɑ̃gl/ nm angle; (coin) corner.

Angleterre /ɑ̃glətɛʀ/ nf England.

anglophone /ɑ̃glɔfɔn/ adj English-speaking. ● nmf English speaker.

angoissant, ~e /ɑ̃gwasɑ̃, -t/ adj alarming; (effrayant) harrowing.

angoisse /ɑ̃gwas/ nf anxiety. **angoissé, ~e** adj anxious. **angoisser** 1 vi worry.

animal (pl -aux) /animal, -o/ nm animal; **~ familier, ~ de compagnie** pet. ● adj (mpl -aux) animal.

animateur, -trice /animatœʀ, -tʀis/ nm, f organizer, leader; (TV) host, hostess.

animation /animasjɔ̃/ nf liveliness; (affairement) activity; (au cinéma) animation; (activité dirigée) organized activity.

animé, ~e /anime/ adj lively; (affairé) busy; (être) animate.

animer /anime/ 1 vt liven up; (débat, atelier) lead; (spectacle) host; (pousser) drive; (encourager) spur on. □ **s'~** vpr liven up.

anis /ani(s)/ nm (Culin) aniseed; (Bot) anise.

anneau (pl ~x) /ano/ nm ring; (de chaîne) link.

année /ane/ nf year; **~ bissextile** leap year; **~ civile** calendar year.

annexe /anɛks/ adj (document) attached; (question) related; (bâtiment) adjoining. ● nf (bâtiment) annexe; (US) annex; (document) appendix; (électronique) attachment. **annexer** 1 vt annex; (document) attach.

anniversaire /anivɛʀsɛʀ/ nm birthday; (d'un événement) anniversary. ● adj anniversary.

annonce /anɔ̃s/ nf announcement; (publicitaire) advertisement; (indice) sign.

annoncer /anɔse/ **10** vt announce; (prédire) forecast; (être l'indice de) herald. □ **s'~** vpr (crise, tempête) be brewing; **s'~ bien/mal** look good/bad. **annonceur** nm advertiser.

annuaire /anɥɛʀ/ nm year-book; **~ (téléphonique)** (telephone) directory.

annuel, ~le /anɥɛl/ adj annual, yearly.

annulation /anylasjɔ̃/ nf cancellation; (de sanction, loi) repeal; (de mesure) abolition.

annuler /anyle/ **1** vt cancel; (contrat) nullify; (jugement) quash; (loi) repeal. □ **s'~** vpr cancel each other out.

anodin, ~e /anɔdɛ̃, -in/ adj insignificant; (sans risques) harmless, safe.

anonymat /anɔnima/ nm anonymity; **garder l'~** remain anonymous. **anonyme** adj anonymous.

anorexie /anɔʀɛksi/ nf anorexia.

anormal, ~e (mpl **-aux**) /anɔʀmal, -o/ adj abnormal.

anse /ɑ̃s/ nf handle; (baie) cove.

Antarctique /ɑ̃taʀktik/ nm Antarctic.

antenne /ɑ̃tɛn/ nf aerial; (US) antenna; (d'insecte) antenna; (succursale) agency; (Mil) outpost; **à l'~** on the air; **~ chirurgicale** mobile emergency unit; **~ parabolique** satellite dish.

antérieur, ~e /ɑ̃teʀjœʀ/ adj previous, earlier; (placé devant) front; **~ à** prior to.

antiaérien, ~ne /ɑ̃tiaeʀjɛ̃, -ɛn/ adj anti-aircraft; **abri ~** air-raid shelter.

antiatomique /ɑ̃tiatɔmik/ adj **abri ~** nuclear fall-out shelter.

antibiotique /ɑ̃tibjɔtik/ nm antibiotic.

anticipation /ɑ̃tisipasjɔ̃/ nf **d'~** (livre, film) science fiction; **par ~** in advance.

anticiper /ɑ̃tisipe/ **1** vt **~ (sur)** anticipate; (effectuer à l'avance) bring forward.

anticorps /ɑ̃tikɔʀ/ nm antibody.

antidater /ɑ̃tidate/ **1** vt backdate, antedate.

antigel /ɑ̃tiʒɛl/ nm antifreeze.

Antilles /ɑ̃tij/ nfpl **les ~** the West Indies.

antipathique /ɑ̃tipatik/ adj unpleasant.

antiquaire /ɑ̃tikɛʀ/ nmf antique dealer.

antiquité /ɑ̃tikite/ nf (objet) antique; **l'A~** antiquity.

antisémite /ɑ̃tisemit/ adj anti-Semitic.

antiseptique /ɑ̃tisɛptik/ adj & nm antiseptic.

antivirus /ɑ̃tiviʀys/ nm inv (Ordinat) antivirus software.

antivol /ɑ̃tivɔl/ nm anti-theft device; (Auto) steering lock.

anxiété /ɑ̃ksjete/ nf anxiety.

anxieux, -ieuse /ɑ̃ksjø, -z/ adj anxious. ● nm, f worrier.

août /u(t) / nm August.

apaiser /apeze/ **1** vt calm down; (colère, militant) appease; (douleur) soothe; (faim) satisfy. □ **s'~** vpr (tempête) die down.

apathie /apati/ nf apathy. **apathique** adj apathetic.

apercevoir /apɛʀsəvwaʀ/ **52** vt see. □ **s'~ de** vpr notice; **s'~ que** notice ou realize that.

aperçu /apɛʀsy/ nm (échantillon) glimpse, taste; (intuition) insight.

apéritif /apeʀitif/ nm aperitif, drink.

aphte /aft/ nm mouth ulcer.

apitoyer /apitwaje/ **31** vt move (to pity). □ **s'~** vpr **s'~ sur (le sort de) qn** feel sorry for sb.

aplanir /aplaniʀ/ **2** vt level; (fig) iron out.

aplatir /aplatiʀ/ **2** vt flatten (out). □ **s'~** vpr (s'immobiliser) flatten oneself.

aplomb /aplɔ̃/ nm balance; (fig) self-confidence; **d'~** (en équilibre) steady; **je ne suis pas bien d'~** **1** I don't feel very well.

apogée /apɔʒe/ nm peak.

apologie /apɔlɔʒi/ nf panegyric.

apostrophe /apɔstʀɔf/ nf apostrophe; (remarque) remark.

apothéose /apɔteoz/ nf high point; (d'événement) grand finale.

apparaître /apaʀɛtʀ/ **18** vi appear; **il apparaît que** it appears that.

appareil /apaʀɛj/ nm device; (électrique) appliance; (Anat) system; (téléphone) phone; (avion) plane; (Culin) mixture; (système administratif) apparatus; **~ (dentaire)** brace; (dentier) dentures; **~ (photo)** camera; **c'est**

Gabriel à l'~ it's Gabriel on the phone; **~ auditif** hearing aid; **~ électroménager** household electrical appliance.

appareiller /apaʀeje/ **1** vi (navire) cast off, put to sea.

apparemment /apaʀamɑ̃/ adv apparently.

apparence /apaʀɑ̃s/ nf appearance; **en ~** outwardly; (apparemment) apparently.

apparent, ~e /apaʀɑ̃, -t/ adj apparent; (visible) conspicuous.

apparenté, ~e /apaʀɑ̃te/ adj related; (semblable) similar.

apparition /apaʀisjɔ̃/ nf appearance; (spectre) apparition.

appartement /apaʀtəmɑ̃/ nm flat; (US) apartment.

appartenir /apaʀtəniʀ/ **58** vi belong (à to); **il lui appartient de** it is up to him to.

appât /apɑ/ nm bait; (fig) lure.

appauvrir /apovʀiʀ/ **2** vt impoverish. □ **s'~** vpr become impoverished.

appel /apɛl/ nm call; (Jur) appeal; (supplique) appeal, plea; (Mil) call-up; (US) draft; **faire ~** appeal; **faire ~ à** (recourir à) call on; (invoquer) appeal to; (évoquer) call up; (exiger) call for; **faire l'~** (Scol) call the register; (Mil) take a roll-call; **~ d'offres** (Comm) invitation to tender; **faire un ~ de phares** flash one's headlights.

appeler /aple/ **38** vt call; (téléphoner) phone, call; (nécessiter) call for; **en ~ à** appeal to; **appelé à** (destiné) destined for. □ **s'~** vpr be called; **il s'appelle Tim** his name is Tim ou he is called Tim.

appellation /apelasjɔ̃/ nf name, designation.

appendice /apɛ̃dis/ nm appendix. **appendicite** nf appendicitis.

appesantir /apəzɑ̃tiʀ/ **2** vt weigh down. □ **s'~** vpr grow heavier; **s'~ sur** dwell upon.

appétissant, ~e /apetisɑ̃, -t/ adj appetizing.

appétit /apeti/ nm appetite; **bon ~!** enjoy your meal!

applaudir /aplodiʀ/ **2** vt/i applaud. **applaudissements** nmpl applause.

application /aplikasjɔ̃/ nf (soin) care; (de loi) (respect) application; (mise en œuvre) implementation; (Ordinat) application program.

appliqué, ~e /aplike/ adj (travail) painstaking; (sciences) applied; (élève) hard-working.

appliquer /aplike/ **1** vt apply; (loi) enforce. □ **s'~** vpr apply oneself (à to), take great care (à faire to do); **s'~ à** (concerner) apply to.

appoint /apwɛ̃/ nm support; **d'~** extra; **faire l'~** give the correct money.

apport /apɔʀ/ nm contribution.

apporter /apɔʀte/ **1** vt bring; (aide, précision) give; (causer) bring about.

appréciation /apʀesjasjɔ̃/ nf estimate, evaluation; (de monnaie) appreciation; (jugement) assessment.

apprécier /apʀesje/ **45** vt appreciate; (évaluer) assess; (objet) value, appraise.

appréhender /apʀeɑ̃de/ **1** vt dread, fear; (arrêter) apprehend.

apprendre /apʀɑ̃dʀ/ **50** vt learn; (être informé de) hear, learn; (de façon indirecte) hear of; **~ qch à qn** teach sb sth; (informer) tell sb sth; **~ à faire** learn to do; **~ à qn à faire** teach sb to do; **~ que** learn that; (être informé) hear that.

apprenti, ~e /apʀɑ̃ti/ nm, f apprentice. **apprentissage** nm apprenticeship; (d'un sujet) learning.

apprêter /apʀete/ **1** vt prepare; (bois) prime; (mur) size. □ **s'~ à** vpr prepare to.

apprivoiser /apʀivwaze/ **1** vt tame.

approbation /apʀɔbasjɔ̃/ nf approval.

approchant, ~e /apʀɔʃɑ̃, -t/ adj close, similar.

approcher /apʀɔʃe/ **1** vt (objet) move near(er) (de to); (personne) approach; **~ de** get nearer ou closer to. ● vi approach. □ **s'~ de** vpr approach, move near(er) to.

approfondir /apʀɔfɔ̃diʀ/ **2** vt deepen; (fig) (sujet) go into sth in depth; (connaissances) improve.

approprié, ~e /apʀɔpʀije/ adj appropriate.

approprier (s') /(s)apʀɔpʀije/ **45** vpr appropriate.

approuver /apʀuve/ **1** vt approve; (trouver louable) approve of; (soutenir) agree with.

approvisionner /apʀovizjone/ **1** vt supply (**en** with); (compte en banque) pay money into. □ **s'~** vpr stock up.

approximatif, -ive /apʀoksimatif, -v/ adj approximate.

appui /apɥi/ nm support; (de fenêtre) sill; (pour objet) rest; **à l'~ de** in support of; **prendre ~ sur** lean on.

appui-tête (pl **appuis-tête**) /apɥitɛt/ nm headrest.

appuyer /apɥije/ **31** vt lean, rest; (presser) press; (soutenir) support, back. ● vi **~ sur** press (on); (fig) stress. □ **s'~ sur** vpr lean on; (compter sur) rely on.

après /apʀɛ/ prép after; (au-delà de) after, beyond; **~ avoir fait** after doing; **~ tout** after all; **~ coup** after the event; **d'~** (selon) according to; (en imitant) from; (adapté de) based on. ● adv after (wards); (plus tard) later; **le bus d'~** the next bus. ● conj **~ qu'il est parti** after he left. **après-demain** adv the day after tomorrow. **après-guerre** (pl **~s**) nm ou f postwar period. **après-midi** nm ou f inv afternoon. **après-rasage** (pl **~s**) nm aftershave. **après-shampooing** nm conditioner. **après-ski** nm inv moon boot. **après-vente** adj inv after-sales.

a priori /apʀijoʀi/ adv (à première vue) offhand, on the face of it; (sans réfléchir) out of hand. ● nm preconception.

à-propos /apʀopo/ nm timing, timeliness; (fig) presence of mind.

apte /apt/ adj capable (à of); (ayant les qualités requises) suitable (à for); (en état) fit (à for).

aptitude /aptityd/ nf aptitude, ability.

aquarelle /akwaʀɛl/ nf water-colour.

aquatique /akwatik/ adj aquatic; (Sport) water.

arabe /aʀab/ adj Arab; (Ling) Arabic; (désert) Arabian. ● nm (Ling) Arabic. **A~** nmf Arab.

Arabie /aʀabi/ nf **~ Saoudite** Saudi Arabia.

arachide /aʀaʃid/ nf groundnut; **huile d'~** groundnut oil.

araignée /aʀeɲe/ nf spider.

arbitraire /aʀbitʀɛʀ/ adj arbitrary.

arbitre /aʀbitʀ/ nm referee; (au cricket, tennis) umpire; (expert) arbiter; (Jur) arbitrator. **arbitrer** **1** vt (match) referee, umpire; (Jur) arbitrate in.

arbre /aʀbʀ/ nm tree; (Tech) shaft.

arbuste /aʀbyst/ nm shrub.

arc /aʀk/ nm (arme) bow; (courbe) curve; (voûte) arch; **~ de cercle** arc of a circle.

arc-en-ciel (pl **arcs-en-ciel**) /aʀkãsjɛl/ nm rainbow.

arche /aʀʃ/ nf arch; **~ de Noé** Noah's ark.

archéologie /aʀkeoloʒi/ nf archaeology.

archevêque /aʀʃəvɛk/ nm archbishop.

architecte /aʀʃitɛkt/ nmf architect. **architecture** nf architecture.

Arctique /aʀktik/ nm Arctic.

ardent, ~e /aʀdã, -t/ adj burning; (passionné) ardent; (foi) fervent. **ardeur** nf ardour; (chaleur) heat.

ardoise /aʀdwaz/ nf slate; **~ électronique** notepad computer.

arène /aʀɛn/ nf arena; **~s** amphitheatre; (pour corridas) bullring.

arête /aʀɛt/ nf (de poisson) bone; (bord) ridge.

argent /aʀʒã/ nm money; (métal) silver; **~ comptant** cash; **prendre pour ~ comptant** take at face value; **~ de poche** pocket money.

argenté, ~e /aʀʒãte/ adj silver(y); (métal) (silver-)plated.

argenterie /aʀʒãtʀi/ nf silverware.

Argentine /aʀʒãtin/ nf Argentina.

argile /aʀʒil/ nf clay.

argot /aʀgo/ nm slang.

argument /aʀgymã/ nm argument; **~ de vente** selling point. **argumenter** **1** vi argue.

aristocratie /aʀistokʀasi/ nf aristocracy.

arithmétique /aʀitmetik/ nf arithmetic. ● adj arithmetical.

armature /aʀmatyʀ/ nf framework; (de tente) frame.

arme /aʀm/ nf arm, weapon; **~ à feu** firearm; **~s** (blason) coat of arms; **~s**

de destruction massive weapons of mass destruction.

armée /aʀme/ *nf* army; ~ **de l'air** Air Force; ~ **de terre** Army.

armer /aʀme/ **1** *vt* arm; (*fusil*) cock; (*navire*) equip; (*renforcer*) reinforce; (Photo) wind on. □ **s'**~ **de** *vpr* arm oneself with.

armoire /aʀmwaʀ/ *nf* cupboard; (*penderie*) wardrobe; (US) closet; ~ **à pharmacie** medicine cabinet.

armure /aʀmyʀ/ *nf* armour.

arnaque /aʀnak/ *nf* **1** swindling; **c'est de l'**~ it's a swindle **1**.

arobas(e) /aʀɔbas, aʀɔbaz/ *nm* at sign.

aromate /aʀɔmat/ *nm* herb, spice.

aromatisé, ~**e** /aʀɔmatize/ *adj* flavoured.

arôme /aʀom/ *nm* aroma; (*additif*) flavouring.

arpenter /aʀpɑ̃te/ **1** *vt* pace up and down; (*terrain*) survey.

arqué, ~**e** /aʀke/ *adj* arched; (*jambes*) bandy.

arrache-pied: d'~ /daʀaʃpje/ *loc* relentlessly.

arracher /aʀaʃe/ **1** *vt* pull out *ou* off; (*plante*) pull *ou* dig up; (*cheveux, page*) tear *ou* pull out; (*par une explosion*) blow off; ~ **à** (enlever à) snatch from; (fig) force *ou* wrest from. □ **s'**~ **qch** *vpr* fight over sth.

arranger /aʀɑ̃ʒe/ **40** *vt* arrange, fix up; (réparer) put right; (régler) sort out; (convenir à) suit. □ **s'**~ *vpr* (se mettre d'accord) come to an arrangement; (se débrouiller) manage (**pour** to).

arrestation /aʀɛstasjɔ̃/ *nf* arrest.

arrêt /aʀe/ *nm* stopping; (de combats) cessation; (de production) halt; (lieu) stop; (pause) pause; (Jur) ruling; **aux** ~**s** (Mil) under arrest; **à l'**~ (véhicule) stationary; (machine) idle; **faire un** ~ (make a) stop; **sans** ~ (sans escale) nonstop; (sans interruption) constantly; ~ **maladie** sick leave; ~ **de travail** (grève) stoppage; (Méd) sick leave.

arrêté /aʀete/ *nm* order; ~ **municipal** bylaw.

arrêter /aʀete/ **1** *vt* stop; (date) fix; (appareil) turn off; (renoncer à) give up; (appréhender) arrest. ● *vi* stop. □ **s'**~ *vpr* stop; **s'**~ **de faire** stop doing.

arrhes /aʀ/ *nfpl* deposit; **verser des** ~ pay a deposit.

arrière /aʀjɛʀ/ *adj inv* back, rear. ● *nm* back, rear; (football) back; **à l'**~ in *ou* at the back; **en** ~ behind; (marcher, tomber) backwards; **en** ~ **de** behind. **arrière-boutique** (*pl* ~**s**) *nf* back room (of the shop). **arrière-garde** (*pl* ~**s**) *nf* rearguard. **arrière-goût** (*pl* ~**s**) *nm* aftertaste. **arrière-grand-mère** (*pl* **arrière-grands-mères**) *nf* great-grandmother. **arrière-grand-père** (*pl* **arrière-grands-pères**) *nm* great-grandfather. **arrière-pays** (*pl* ~ *inv*) backcountry. **arrière-pensée** (*pl* ~**s**) *nf* ulterior motive. **arrière-plan** *nm* (*pl* ~**s**) background.

arrimer /aʀime/ **1** *vt* secure; (cargaison) stow.

arrivage /aʀivaʒ/ *nm* consignment.

arrivée /aʀive/ *nf* arrival; (Sport) finish.

arriver /aʀive/ **1** *vi* (aux être) arrive, come; (réussir) succeed; (se produire) happen; ~ **à** (atteindre) reach; ~ **à faire** manage to do; **je n'arrive pas à faire** I can't do; **en** ~ **à faire** get to the stage of doing; **il arrive que** it happens that; **il lui arrive de faire** he (sometimes) does.

arriviste /aʀivist/ *nmf* go-getter, self-seeker.

arrondir /aʀɔ̃diʀ/ **2** *vt* (make) round; (somme) round off. □ **s'**~ *vpr* become round(ed).

arrondissement /aʀɔ̃dismɑ̃/ *nm* district.

> **Arrondissement** A subdivision of a *département*. Each *arrondissement* has a *sous-préfet* representing the state administration at local level. In Paris, Lyons and Marseilles, an *arrondissement* is a subdivision of the commune, and has its own *maire* and local council.

arroser /aʀoze/ **1** *vt* water; (repas) wash down (with a drink); (rôti) baste; (victoire) drink to. **arrosoir** *nm* watering can.

art /aʀ/ *nm* art; (don) knack (**de faire** of doing); ~**s et métiers** arts and crafts; ~s **ménagers** home economics (+ sg).

artère /aʀtɛʀ/ nf artery; **(grande)** ~ main road.

arthrite /aʀtʀit/ nf arthritis.

arthrose /aʀtʀoz/ nf osteoarthritis.

artichaut /aʀtiʃo/ nm artichoke.

article /aʀtikl/ nm article; (Comm) item, article; **à l'**~ **de la mort** at death's door; ~ **de fond** feature (article); ~s **de voyage** travel goods.

articulation /aʀtikylasjɔ̃/ nf articulation; (Anat) joint.

articuler /aʀtikyle/ **1** vt articulate; (structurer) structure; (assembler) connect **(sur)** to.

artificiel, ~le /aʀtifisjɛl/ adj artificial.

artisan /aʀtizɑ̃/ nm artisan, craftsman; **l'**~ **de** (fig) the architect of.

artisanal, ~e (mpl ~**aux**) /aʀtizanal/ adj craft; (méthode) traditional; (amateur) home-made; **de fabrication** ~**e** hand-made, hand-crafted.

artiste /aʀtist/ nmf artist. **artistique** adj artistic.

as¹ /a/ ⇒**AVOIR 5**.

as² /as/ nm ace.

ascenseur /asɑ̃sœʀ/ nm lift; (US) elevator.

ascension /asɑ̃sjɔ̃/ nf ascent; **l'A**~ Ascension.

aseptiser /asɛptize/ **1** vt disinfect; (stériliser) sterilize; **aseptisé** (péj) sanitized.

asiatique /azjatik/ adj Asian. **A**~ nmf Asian.

Asie /azi/ nf Asia.

asile /azil/ nm refuge; (Pol) asylum; (pour malades, vieillards) home; ~ **de nuit** night shelter.

aspect /aspɛ/ nm appearance; (facettes) aspect; (perspective) side; **à l'**~ **de** at the sight of.

asperge /aspɛʀʒ/ nf asparagus.

asperger /aspɛʀʒe/ **40** vt spray.

asphyxier /asfiksje/ **45** vt (personne) asphyxiate; (entreprise, réseau) paralyse. □ **s'**~ vpr suffocate; gas oneself; (entreprise, réseau) become paralysed.

aspirateur /aspiʀatœʀ/ nm vacuum cleaner.

aspirer /aspiʀe/ **1** vt inhale; (liquide) suck up. ● vi ~ **à** aspire to.

aspirine® /aspiʀin/ nf aspirin.

assainir /aseniʀ/ **2** vt clean up.

assaisonnement /asɛzɔnmɑ̃/ nm seasoning.

assassin /asasɛ̃/ nm murderer; (Pol) assassin. **assassiner 1** vt murder; (Pol) assassinate.

assaut /aso/ nm assault, onslaught; **donner l'**~ **à, prendre d'**~ storm.

assemblage /asɑ̃blaʒ/ nm assembly; (combinaison) collection; (Tech) joint.

assemblée /asɑ̃ble/ nf meeting; (gens réunis) gathering; (Pol) assembly.

Assemblée nationale The lower house of the French parliament, in which 577 *députés* are elected for a five-year term. *Députés* sit in parties in the semi-circular chamber, with the most left-wing to the extreme left and the most right-wing to the extreme right. The *Assemblée nationale* passes laws, votes on the Budget, and questions ministers.

---

assembler /asɑ̃ble/ **1** vt assemble, put together; (réunir) gather. □ **s'**~ vpr gather, assemble.

asseoir /aswaʀ/ **9** vt sit (down), seat; (bébé, malade) sit up; (affermir) establish; (baser) base. □ **s'**~ vpr sit (down).

assez /ase/ adv (suffisamment) enough; (plutôt) quite, fairly; ~ **grand/rapide** big/fast enough **(pour** to); ~ **de** enough; **j'en ai (**~ **de)** I've had enough (of).

assidu, ~e /asidy/ adj (zélé) assiduous; (régulier) regular; ~ **auprès de** attentive to. **assiduité** nf assiduousness, regularity.

assiéger /asjeʒe/ **14 40** vt besiege.

assiette /asjɛt/ nf plate; (équilibre) seat; ~ **anglaise** assorted cold meats; ~ **creuse/plate** soup-/ dinner-plate; **ne pas être dans son** ~ feel out of sorts.

assigner /asiɲe/ **1** vt assign; (limite) fix.

assimilation /asimilasjɔ̃/ nf assimilation; (comparaison) likening, comparison.

assimiler /asimile/ **1** vt ~ **à** liken to; (classer) class as. □ **s'**~ vpr assimilate;

(être comparable) be comparable (à to).

assis, ~**e** /asi, -z/ adj sitting (down), seated. ● →ASSEOIR 9.

assise /asiz/ nf (base) foundation; ~**s** (tribunal) assizes; (congrès) conference, congress.

assistance /asistãs/ nf audience; (aide) assistance; **l'A~ (publique)** welfare services.

assistant, ~**e** /asistã, -t/ nm, f assistant; (Scol) foreign language assistant; ~**s** (spectateurs) members of the audience; ~**e sociale** social worker; ~ **personnel numérique** personal digital assistant, PDA.

assister /asiste/ 1 vt assist; ~ **à** attend, be (present) at; (accident) witness; **assisté par ordinateur** computer-assisted.

association /asɔsjasjõ/ nf association.

associé, ~**e** /asɔsje/ nm, f partner, associate. ● adj associate.

associer /asɔsje/ 45 vt associate; (mêler) combine (à with); ~ **qn à** (projet) involve sb in; (bénéfices) give sb a share of. □ **s'~** vpr (sociétés, personnes) become associated, join forces (à with); (s'harmoniser) combine (à with); **s'~ à** (joie, opinion de qn) share; (projet) take part in.

assommer /asɔme/ 1 vt knock out; (animal) stun; (fig) overwhelm; (ennuyer 1) bore.

Assomption /asɔpsjõ/ nf Assumption.

assortiment /asɔrtimã/ nm assortment.

assortir /asɔrtir/ 2 vt match (à with, to); ~ **de** accompany with. □ **s'~** vpr match; **s'~ à qch** match sth.

assoupir (s') /(s)asupir/ 2 vpr doze off; (s'apaiser) subside.

assouplir /asuplir/ 2 vt make supple; (fig) make flexible.

assourdir /asurdir/ 2 vt (personne) deafen; (bruit) muffle.

assouvir /asuvir/ 2 vt satisfy.

assujettir /asyʒetir/ 2 vt subjugate, subdue; ~ **à** subject to.

assumer /asyme/ 1 vt assume; (coût) meet; (accepter) come to terms with, accept.

assurance /asyrãs/ nf (self-) assurance; (garantie) assurance; (contrat) insurance; ~**s sociales** social insurance; ~ **automobile/maladie** car/health insurance.

assuré, ~**e** /asyre/ adj certain, assured; (sûr de soi) confident, assured. ● nm, f insured party.

assurer /asyre/ 1 vt ensure; (fournir) provide; (exécuter) carry out; (Comm) insure; (stabiliser) steady; (frontières) make secure; ~ **à qn que** assure sb that; ~ **qn de** assure sb of; ~ **la gestion/défense de** manage/defend. □ **s'~** vpr take out insurance; **s'~ de/que** make sure of/that; **s'~ qch** (se procurer) secure sth. **assureur** nm insurer.

astérisque /asterisk/ nm asterisk.

asthmatique /asmatik/ adj & nmf asthmatic.

asthme /asm/ nm asthma.

asticot /astiko/ nm maggot.

astreindre /astrẽdr/ 22 vt ~ **qn à qch** force sth on sb; ~ **qn à faire** force sb to do.

astrologie /astrɔlɔʒi/ nf astrology. **astrologue** nmf astrologer.

astronaute /astrɔnot/ nmf astronaut.

astronomie /astrɔnɔmi/ nf astronomy.

astuce /astys/ nf smartness; (truc) trick; (plaisanterie) wisecrack.

astucieux, -ieuse /astysjø, -z/ adj smart, clever.

atelier /atəlje/ nm (local) workshop; (de peintre) studio; (séance de travail) workshop.

athée /ate/ nmf atheist. ● adj atheistic.

athlète /atlɛt/ nmf athlete. **athlétisme** nm athletics.

Atlantique /atlãtik/ nm Atlantic (Ocean).

atmosphère /atmɔsfɛr/ nf atmosphere.

atomique /atɔmik/ adj atomic; (énergie, centrale) nuclear.

atomiseur /atɔmizœr/ nm spray.

atout /atu/ nm trump (card); (avantage) asset.

atroce /atrɔs/ adj atrocious.

attabler (s') /(s)atable/ 1 vpr sit down at table.

attachant, ~**e** /ataʃã, -t/ adj charming.

attache /ataʃ/ *nf* (agrafe) fastener; (lien) tie.

attaché, ~e /ataʃe/ *adj* **être ~ à** (aimer) be attached to. ● *nm, f* (Pol) attaché.

attacher /ataʃe/ **1** *vt* tie (up); (ceinture, robe) fasten; (bicyclette) lock; **~ à** (attribuer à) attach to. ● *vi* (Culin) stick. □ **s'~** *vpr* fasten, do up; **s'~ à** (se lier à) become attached to; (se consacrer à) apply oneself to.

attaquant, ~e /atakɑ̃, -t/ *nm, f* attacker; (au football) striker; (au football américain) forward.

attaque /atak/ *nf* attack; **~ (cérébrale)** stroke; **il va en faire une ~** he'll have a fit; **~ à main armée** armed attack.

attaquer /atake/ **1** *vt* attack; (banque) raid. ● *vi* attack. □ **s'~ à** *vpr* attack; (problème, sujet) tackle.

attardé, ~e /ataʀde/ *adj* backward; (idées) outdated; (en retard) late.

attarder (s') /(s)ataʀde/ **1** *vpr* linger.

atteindre /atɛ̃dʀ/ **22** *vt* reach; (blesser) hit; (affecter) affect.

atteint, ~e /atɛ̃, -t/ *adj* **~ de** suffering from.

atteinte /atɛ̃t/ *nf* attack (à on); **porter ~ à** attack; (droit) infringe.

atteler /atle/ **38** *vt* (cheval) harness; (remorque) couple. □ **s'~ à** *vpr* get down to.

attelle /atɛl/ *nf* splint.

attenant, ~e /atnɑ̃, -t/ *adj* **~ (à)** adjoining.

attendant: en ~ /ɑ̃natɑ̃dɑ̃/ *loc* meanwhile.

attendre /atɑ̃dʀ/ **3** *vt* wait for; (bébé) expect; (être le sort de) await; (escompter) expect; **~ que qn fasse** wait for sb to do. ● *vi* wait; (au téléphone) hold. □ **s'~ à** *vpr* expect.

attendrir /atɑ̃dʀiʀ/ **2** *vt* move (to pity). □ **s'~** *vpr* be moved to pity.

attendu¹ /atɑ̃dy/ *prép* given, considering; **~ que** considering that.

attendu², ~e /atɑ̃dy/ *adj* (escompté) expected; (espéré) long-awaited.

attentat /atɑ̃ta/ *nm* assassination attempt; **~ (à la bombe)** (bomb) attack.

attente /atɑ̃t/ *nf* wait(ing); (espoir) expectations (+ *pl*).

attenter /atɑ̃te/ **1** *vi* **~ à** make an attempt on; (fig) violate.

attentif, -ive /atɑ̃tif, -v/ *adj* attentive; (scrupuleux) careful; **~ à** mindful of; (soucieux) careful of.

attention /atɑ̃sjɔ̃/ *nf* attention; (soin) care; **~ (à)!** watch out (for)!; **faire ~ à** (écouter) pay attention to; (prendre garde à) watch out for; (prendre soin de) take care of; **faire ~ à faire** be careful to do. **attentionné, ~e** *adj* considerate.

attentisme /atɑ̃tism/ *nm* wait-and-see policy.

atténuer /atenɥe/ **1** *vt* (violence) reduce; (critique) tone down; (douleur) ease; (faute) mitigate. □ **s'~** *vpr* subside.

atterrir /ateʀiʀ/ **2** *vi* land. **atterrissage** *nm* landing.

attestation /atɛstasjɔ̃/ *nf* certificate.

attester /atɛste/ **1** *vt* testify to; **~ que** testify that.

attirant, ~e /atiʀɑ̃, -t/ *adj* attractive.

attirer /atiʀe/ **1** *vt* draw, attract; (causer) bring. □ **s'~** *vpr* bring upon oneself; (amis) win.

attiser /atize/ **1** *vt* (feu) poke; (sentiment) stir up.

attitré, ~e /atitʀe/ *adj* accredited; (habituel) usual, regular.

attitude /atityd/ *nf* attitude; (maintien) bearing.

attraction /atʀaksjɔ̃/ *nf* attraction.

attrait /atʀɛ/ *nm* attraction.

attraper /atʀape/ **1** *vt* catch; (corde, main) catch hold of; (habitude, accent) pick up; (maladie) catch; **se faire ~** **1** get told off.

attrayant, ~e /atʀɛjɑ̃, -t/ *adj* attractive.

attribuer /atʀibɥe/ **1** *vt* allocate; (prix) award; (imputer) attribute. □ **s'~** *vpr* claim (for oneself). **attribution** *nf* awarding, allocation.

attrouper (s') /(s)atʀupe/ **1** *vpr* gather.

au /o/ **→à**.

aubaine /obɛn/ *nf* godsend, opportunity.

aube /ob/ *nf* dawn, daybreak.

auberge /obɛʀʒ/ *nf* inn; **~ de jeunesse** youth hostel.

aubergine /obɛʀʒin/ nf aubergine; (US) eggplant.

aucun, ~e /okœ̃, okyn/ adj (dans une phrase négative) no, not any; (positif) any. ● pron (dans une phrase négative) none, not any; (positif) any; ~ **des deux** neither of the two; **d'~s** some.
aucunement adv not at all, in no way.

audace /odas/ nf daring; (impudence) audacity.

audacieux, -ieuse /odasjø, -z/ adj daring.

au-delà /od(ə)la/ adv beyond. ● prép ~ **de** beyond.

au-dessous /od(ə)su/ adv below. ● prép ~ **de** below; (couvert par) under.

au-dessus /od(ə)sy/ adv above. ● prép ~ **de** above.

au-devant /od(ə)vɑ̃/ prép aller ~ **de qn** go to meet sb; **aller ~ des désirs de qn** anticipate sb's wishes.

audience /odjɑ̃s/ nf audience; (d'un tribunal) hearing; (succès, attention) success.

audimat® /odimat/ nm **l'~** the TV ratings.

audiovisuel, ~le /odjovizɥɛl/ adj audio-visual.

auditeur, -trice /oditœʀ, -tʀis/ nm, f listener.

audition /odisjɔ̃/ nf hearing; (Théât, Mus) audition.

auditoire /oditwaʀ/ nm audience.

augmentation /ogmɑ̃tasjɔ̃/ nf increase; ~ **(de salaire)** (pay) rise; (US) raise.

augmenter /ogmɑ̃te/ **1** vt/i increase; (employé) give a pay rise ou raise to.

augure /ogyʀ/ nm (devin) oracle; **être de bon/mauvais ~** be a good/ bad sign.

aujourd'hui /oʒuʀdɥi/ adv today.

auparavant /opaʀavɑ̃/ adv (avant) before; (précédemment) previously; (en premier lieu) beforehand.

auprès /opʀɛ/ prép ~ **de** (à côté de) beside, next to; (comparé à) compared with; **s'excuser/se plaindre ~ de** apologize/complain to.

auquel /okɛl/ ➡LEQUEL.

aura, aurait /oʀa, oʀɛ/ ➡AVOIR **5**.

aurore /oʀɔʀ/ nf dawn.

aussi /osi/ adv (également) too, also, as well; (dans une comparaison) as; (si, tellement) so; ~ **bien que** as well as. ● conj (donc) so, consequently.

aussitôt /osito/ adv immediately; ~ **que** as soon as, the moment; ~ **arrivé** as soon as he arrived.

austère /ostɛʀ/ adj austere.

Australie /ostʀali/ nf Australia.

australien, ~ne /ostʀaljɛ̃, -ɛn/ adj Australian. **A~, ~ne** nm, f Australian.

autant /otɑ̃/ adv (travailler, manger) as much (**que** as); ~ **(de)** (quantité) as much (**que** as); (nombre) as many (**que** as); (tant) so much, so many; **faire** one had better do; **d'~ plus que** all the more than; **en faire ~** do the same; **pour ~** for all that.

autel /otɛl/ nm altar.

auteur /otœʀ/ nm author; **l'~ du crime** the perpetrator of the crime.

authentifier /otɑ̃tifje/ **45** vt authenticate.

authentique /otɑ̃tik/ adj authentic.

auto /oto/ nf car; ~ **tamponneuse** dodgem, bumper car.

autobus /otobys/ nm bus.

autocar /otokaʀ/ nm coach.

autochtone /otokton/ nmf native.

autocollant, ~e /otokolɑ̃, -t/ adj self-adhesive. ● nm sticker.

autodidacte /otodidakt/ nmf self-taught person.

auto-école (pl ~s) /otoekol/ nf driving school.

automate /otomat/ nm automaton, robot.

automatique /otomatik/ adj automatic.

automatisation /otomatizasjɔ̃/ nf automation.

automne /oton/ nm autumn; (US) fall.

automobile /otomobil/ adj motor, car; (US) automobile. ● nf (motor) car; **l'~** the motor industry; (Sport) motoring. **automobiliste** nmf motorist.

autonome /otonom/ adj autonomous; (Ordinat) stand-alone.

autoradio /otoʀadjo/ nm car radio.

autorisation /otoʀizasjɔ̃/ nf permission, authorization; (permis) permit.

autorisé, ~e /otoʀize/ adj (opinions) authoritative; (approuvé) authorized.

autoriser /otɔʀize/ **1** vt authorize, permit; (rendre possible) allow (of); (donner un droit) ~ qn à faire entitle sb to do.

autoritaire /otɔʀitɛʀ/ adj authoritarian.

autorité /otɔʀite/ nf authority; **faire** ~ be authoritative.

autoroute /otɔʀut/ nf motorway; (US) highway; ~ **de l'information** (Ordinat) information superhighway.

auto-stop /otostɔp/ nm hitch-hiking; **faire de l'**~ hitch-hike; **prendre qn en** ~ give a lift to sb.

autour /otuʀ/ adv around; **tout** ~ all around. ● prép ~ **de** around.

autre /otʀ/ adj other; **un** ~ **jour/livre** another day/book; ~ **chose/part** something/somewhere else; **quelqu'un/rien d'**~ somebody/nothing else; **quoi d'**~? what else?; **d'**~ **part** on the other hand; (de plus) moreover, besides; **vous** ~s **Anglais** you English. ● pron **un** ~, **une** ~ another (one); **l'**~ the other (one); **les** ~s the others; (autrui) others; **d'**~s (some) others; **l'un l'**~ each other; **l'un et l'**~ both of them; **d'un jour à l'**~ (bientôt) any day now; **entre** ~s among other things.

autrefois /otʀəfwa/ adv in the past; (précédemment) formerly.

autrement /otʀəmã/ adv differently; (sinon) otherwise; (plus **!**) far more; ~ **dit** in other words.

Autriche /otʀiʃ/ nf Austria.

autrichien, ~ne /otʀiʃjɛ̃, -jɛn/ adj Austrian. **A~, ~ne** nm, f Austrian.

autruche /otʀyʃ/ nf ostrich.

autrui /otʀɥi/ pron others, other people.

aux /o/ ➡**À**.

auxiliaire /oksiljɛʀ/ adj auxiliary. ● nmf (assistant) auxiliary. ● nm (Gram) auxiliary.

auxquels, -quelles /okɛl/ ➡**LEQUEL**.

aval: en ~ /ãnaval/ loc downstream.

avaler /avale/ **1** vt swallow.

avance /avãs/ nf advance; (sur un concurrent) lead; ~ **(de fonds)** advance; **à l'**~ in advance; **d'**~ already; **en** ~ early; (montre) fast; **en (**~ **sur)** (menant) ahead (of).

avancement /avãsmã/ nm promotion.

avancé, ~e /avãse/ adj advanced.

avancer /avãse/ **10** vi move forward, advance; (travail) make progress; (montre) be fast; (faire saillie) jut out. ● vt move forward; (dans le temps) bring forward; (argent) advance; (montre) put forward. □ **s'**~ vpr move forward, advance; (se hasarder) commit oneself.

avant /avã/ nm front; (Sport) forward. ● adj inv front. ● prép before; ~ **de faire** before doing; **en** ~ **de** in front of; ~ **peu** shortly; ~ **tout** above all. ● adv (dans le temps) before, beforehand; (d'abord) first; **en** ~ (dans l'espace) forward(s); (dans le temps) ahead; **le bus d'**~ the previous bus. ● conj ~ **que** before; ~ **qu'il (ne) fasse** before he does.

avantage /avãtaʒ/ nm advantage; (Comm) benefit.

avantager /avãtaʒe/ **40** vt favour; (embellir) show off to advantage.

avantageux, -euse /avãtaʒø, -z/ adj advantageous, favourable; (prix) attractive.

avant-bras /avãbʀa/ nm inv forearm.

avant-centre (pl **avants-centres**) /avãsãtʀ/ nm centre forward.

avant-coureur (pl ~s) /avãkuʀœʀ/ adj precursory, foreshadowing.

avant-dernier, -ière (pl ~s) /avãdɛʀnje, -jɛʀ/ adj & nm, f last but one.

avant-goût (pl ~s) /avãgu/ nm foretaste.

avant-hier /avãtjɛʀ/ adv the day before yesterday.

avant-poste (pl ~s) /avãpɔst/ nm outpost.

avant-première (pl ~s) /avãpʀəmjɛʀ/ nf preview.

avant-propos /avãpʀopo/ nm inv foreword.

avare /avaʀ/ adj miserly; ~ **de** sparing with. ● nmf miser.

avarié, ~e /avaʀje/ adj (aliment) spoiled.

avatar /avataʀ/ nm misfortune.

avec /avɛk/ prép with. ● adv **!** with it ou them.

avènement /avɛnmɑ̃/ nm advent; (d'un roi) accession.

avenir /avniʀ/ nm future; **à l'~** in future; **d'~** with (future) prospects.

aventure /avɑ̃tyʀ/ nf adventure; (sentimentale) affair. **aventureux, -euse** adj adventurous; (hasardeux) risky.

avérer (s') /(s)aveʀe/ **14** vpr prove (to be).

averse /avɛʀs/ nf shower.

avertir /avɛʀtiʀ/ **2** vt inform; (mettre en garde, menacer) warn. **avertissement** nm warning.

avertisseur /avɛʀtisœʀ/ nm alarm; (Auto) horn; **~ d'incendie** fire-alarm; **~ lumineux** warning light.

aveu (pl **~x**) /avø/ nm confession; **de l'~ de** by the admission of.

aveugle /avœgl/ adj blind. ● nmf blind man, blind woman.

aviateur, -trice /avjatœʀ, -tʀis/ nm, f aviator.

aviation /avjasjɔ̃/ nf flying; (industrie) aviation; (Mil) air force.

avide /avid/ adj greedy (**de** for); (anxieux) eager (**de** for); **~ de faire** eager to do.

avion /avjɔ̃/ nm plane, aeroplane, aircraft; (US) airplane; **~ à réaction** jet.

aviron /aviʀɔ̃/ nm oar; **l'~** (Sport) rowing.

avis /avi/ nm opinion; (conseil) advice; (renseignement) notification; (Comm) advice; **à mon ~** in my opinion; **changer d'~** change one's mind; **être d'~ que** be of the opinion that; **~ au lecteur** foreword.

avisé, ~e /avize/ adj sensible; **être bien/mal ~ de** be well-/ill-advised to.

aviser /avize/ **1** vt advise, notify. ● vi decide what to do. □ **s'~ de** vpr suddenly realize; **s'~ de faire** take it into one's head to do.

avocat, ~e /avɔka, -t/ nm, f barrister; (US) attorney; (fig) advocate; **~ de la défense** counsel for the defence. ● nm (fruit) avocado (pear).

avoine /avwan/ nf oats (+ pl).

avoir /avwaʀ/ **5**
● verbe auxiliaire
····➤ have; **il nous a appelés hier** he called us yesterday.

● verbe transitif
····➤ (possession) have (got).
····➤ (obtenir) get; (au téléphone) get through to.
····➤ (duper) ⊞ have; **on m'a eu!** I've been had!
····➤ **~ chaud/faim** be hot/hungry.
····➤ **~ dix ans** be ten years old.
● avoir à verbe + préposition
····➤ to have to; **j'ai beaucoup à faire** I have a lot to do; **tu n'as qu'à leur écrire** all you have to do is write to them.
● en avoir pour verbe + préposition
····➤ **j'en ai pour une minute** I will only be a minute; **j'en ai eu pour 100 euros** it cost me 100 euros.
● il y a verbe impersonnel
····➤ there is; (pluriel) there are; **qu'est-ce qu'il y a?** what's the matter?; **il est venu il y a cinq ans** he came here five years ago; **il y a au moins 5 km jusqu'à la gare** it's at least 5 km to the station.
● nom masculin
····➤ (dans un magasin) credit note.
····➤ (biens) asset (+ pl).

avortement /avɔʀtəmɑ̃/ nm (Méd) abortion.

avorter /avɔʀte/ **1** vi (projet) abort; (se faire) **~** have an abortion.

avoué, ~e /avwe/ adj avowed. ● nm solicitor; (US) attorney.

avouer /avwe/ **1** vt (amour, ignorance) confess; (crime) confess to, admit. ● vi confess.

avril /avʀil/ nm April.

axe /aks/ nm axis; (essieu) axle; (d'une politique) main line(s), basis; **~ (routier)** main road.

ayant /ɛjɑ̃/ →AVOIR **5**.

azote /azɔt/ nm nitrogen.

azur /azyʀ/ nm sky-blue.

Bb

baba /baba/ *nm* ~ **(au rhum)** (rum) baba; **en rester** ~ 🆃 be flabbergasted.

babillard /babijaʀ/ *nm* ~ **électronique** (Internet) bulletin board system, BBS.

babines /babin/ *nfpl* **se lécher les** ~ lick one's chops.

babiole /babjɔl/ *nf* trinket.

bâbord /babɔʀ/ *nm* port (side).

baby-foot /babifut/ *nm inv* table football.

bac /bak/ *nm* (Scol) ➔**BACCALAURÉAT**; (bateau) ferry; (récipient) tub; (plus petit) tray.

baccalauréat /bakalɔʀea/ *nm* school leaving certificate.

> **Baccalauréat** Known informally as *le bac*, the *Baccalauréat* is an examination taken in the final year of the *lycée* (*la terminale*). Students sit exams in a broad range of subjects in a particular category: the *bac S* emphasises science subjects, for example, while the *bac L* has a literary bias.

bâche /baʃ/ *nf* tarpaulin.

bachelier, -ière /baʃəlje, -jɛʀ/ *nm, f* holder of the *baccalauréat*.

bachoter /baʃɔte/ 🕐 *vi* cram (for an exam).

bâcler /bɑkle/ 🕐 *vt* botch (up).

bactérie /bakteʀi/ *nf* bacterium; ~**s** bacteria.

badaud, ~e /bado, -d/ *nm, f* onlooker.

badigeonner /badiʒɔne/ 🕐 *vt* whitewash; (barbouiller) daub.

badiner /badine/ 🕐 *vi* banter.

baffe /baf/ *nf* 🆃 slap.

baffle /bafl/ *nm* speaker.

bafouiller /bafuje/ 🕐 *vt/i* stammer.

bagage /bagaʒ/ *nm* bag; (connaissances) knowledge; ~**s** luggage; ~ **à main** hand luggage.

bagarre /bagaʀ/ *nf* fight.

bagatelle /bagatɛl/ *nf* trifle; (somme) trifling amount.

bagnard /baɲaʀ/ *nm* convict.

bagnole /baɲɔl/ *nf* 🆃 car.

bague /bag/ *nf* (bijou) ring.

baguette /bagɛt/ *nf* stick; (de chef d'orchestre) baton; (chinoise) chopstick; (pain) baguette; ~ **magique** magic wand; ~ **de tambour** drumstick.

baie /bɛ/ *nf* (Géog) bay; (fruit) berry; ~ **(vitrée)** picture window; (Ordinat) bay.

baignade /bɛɲad/ *nf* swimming.

baigner /beɲe/ 🕐 *vt* bathe; (enfant) bath. ● *vi* ~ **dans l'huile** swim in grease. □ **se** ~ *vpr* have a swim. **baigneur, -euse** *nm, f* swimmer.

baignoire /bɛɲwaʀ/ *nf* bath(tub).

bail (*pl* **baux**) /baj, bo/ *nm* lease.

bâiller /baje/ 🕐 *vi* yawn; (être ouvert) gape.

bailleur /bajœʀ/ *nm* ~ **de fonds** (Comm) sleeping partner.

bain /bɛ̃/ *nm* bath; (baignade) swim; **prendre un** ~ **de soleil** sunbathe; ~ **de bouche** mouthwash; **être dans le** ~ (fig) be in the swing of things; **se remettre dans le** ~ get back into the swing of things; **prendre un** ~ **de foule** mingle with the crowd.

bain-marie (*pl* **bains-marie**) /bɛ̃maʀi/ *nm* double boiler.

baiser /beze/ 🕐 *vt* (main) kiss; 🆇 screw 🆇. ● *nm* kiss.

baisse /bɛs/ *nf* fall, drop; **être en** ~ be going down.

baisser /bese/ 🕐 *vt* lower; (radio, lampe) turn down. ● *vi* (niveau) go down, fall; (santé, forces) fail. □ **se** ~ *vpr* bend down.

bal (*pl* ~**s**) /bal/ *nm* dance; (habillé) ball; (lieu) dance-hall; ~ **costumé** fancy-dress ball.

balade /balad/ *nf* stroll; (en auto) drive.

balader /balade/ 🕐 *vt* take for a stroll. □ **se** ~ *vpr* (à pied) (go for a) stroll; (en voiture) go for a drive; (voyager) travel.

baladeur /baladœʀ/ *nm* personal stereo.

balafre /balafʀ/ *nf* gash; (cicatrice) scar.

balai /balɛ/ nm broom.

balance /balɑ̃s/ nf scales (+ pl); **la B~** Libra.

balancer /balɑ̃se/ **10** vt swing; (doucement) sway; (lancer **I**) chuck!; (se débarrasser de **I**) chuck out **I**. ● vi sway. □ **se ~** vpr swing; sway; **s'en ~** **I** not to give a damn **I**.

balancier /balɑ̃sje/ nm (d'horloge) pendulum; (d'équilibriste) pole.

balançoire /balɑ̃swaʀ/ nf swing.

balayage /balejaʒ/ nm sweeping; (cheveux) highlights.

balayer /baleje/ **31** vt sweep (up); (vent) sweep away; (se débarrasser de) sweep aside.

balbutiement /balbysimɑ̃/ nm stammering; **les ~s** (fig) the first steps.

balcon /balkɔ̃/ nm balcony; (Théât) dress circle.

baleine /balɛn/ nf whale.

balise /baliz/ nf beacon; (bouée) buoy; (Auto) (road) sign. **baliser** **1** vt mark out (with beacons); (route) signpost; (sentier) mark out.

balivernes /balivɛʀn/ nfpl nonsense.

ballant, ~e /balɑ̃, -t/ adj dangling.

balle /bal/ nf (projectile) bullet; (Sport) ball; (paquet) bale.

ballerine /balʀin/ nf (danseuse) ballerina; (chaussure) ballet pump.

ballet /balɛ/ nm ballet.

ballon /balɔ̃/ nm (Sport) ball; **~ (de baudruche)** balloon; **~ de football** football.

ballonné, ~e /balɔne/ adj bloated.

balnéaire /balneɛʀ/ adj seaside.

balourd, ~e /baluʀ, -d/ nm, f oaf. ● adj uncouth.

balustrade /balystʀad/ nf railing.

ban /bɑ̃/ nm round of applause; **~s** (de mariage) banns; **mettre au ~ de** cast out from.

banal, ~e (mpl **~s**) /banal/ adj commonplace, banal.

banane /banan/ nf banana.

banc /bɑ̃/ nm bench; (de poissons) shoal; **~ des accusés** dock; **~ d'essai** (test) testing ground.

bancaire /bɑ̃kɛʀ/ adj (secteur) banking; (chèque) bank.

bancal, ~e (mpl **~s**) /bɑ̃kal/ adj wobbly; (solution) shaky.

bande /bɑ̃d/ nf (groupe) gang; (de papier) strip; (rayure) stripe; (de film) reel; (pansement) bandage; **~ dessinée** comic strip; **~ (magnétique)** tape; **~ sonore** sound-track.

Bande dessinée More than just a comic book, this form of popular literature (known as the *neuvième art*) plays a significant cultural role in France and is celebrated annually at the Festival d'Angoulême. Cartoon characters such as *Astérix*, *Lucky Luke* and *Tintin* are household names, and older *BD* are often collectors' items.

---

bande-annonce (pl **bandes-annonces**) /bɑ̃danɔ̃s/ nf trailer.

bandeau (pl **~x**) /bɑ̃do/ nm headband; (sur les yeux) blindfold; **~ publicitaire** (Ordinat) banner.

bander /bɑ̃de/ **1** vt bandage; (arc) bend; (muscle) tense; **~ les yeux à** blindfold.

banderole /bɑ̃dʀɔl/ nf banner.

bandit /bɑ̃di/ nm bandit. **banditisme** nm crime.

bandoulière: en ~ /ɑ̃buduljɛʀ/ loc across one's shoulder.

banlieue /bɑ̃ljø/ nf suburbs; **de ~** suburban. **banlieusard, ~e** nm, f (suburban) commuter.

bannir /baniʀ/ **2** vt banish.

banque /bɑ̃k/ nf bank; (activité) banking; **~ de données** databank.

banqueroute /bɑ̃kʀut/ nf bankruptcy.

banquet /bɑ̃kɛ/ nm banquet.

banquette /bɑ̃kɛt/ nf seat.

banquier, -ière /bɑ̃kje, -jɛʀ/ nm, f banker.

baptême /batɛm/ nm baptism, christening. **baptiser** **1** vt baptize, christen; (nommer) call.

bar /baʀ/ nm (lieu) bar.

baragouiner /baʀagwine/ **1** vt/i gabble; (langue) speak a few words of.

baraque /baʀak/ nf hut, shed; (maison **I**) house.

baratin /baʀatɛ̃/ nm **I** sweet ou smooth talk.

barbare /baʀbaʀ/ adj barbaric. ● nmf barbarian.

barbe /baʀb/ nf beard; **~ à papa** candy-floss; (US) cotton candy; **quelle**

~! 🔟 what a drag! 🔟.

barbelé /baʀbəle/ adj fil ~ barbed wire.

barber /baʀbe/ 🔟 vt 🔟 bore.

barboter /baʀbɔte/ 🔟 vi (dans l'eau) paddle, splash. ● vt (voler 🔟) pinch.

barbouiller /baʀbuje/ 🔟 vt (souiller) smear (de with); **tu es tout barbouillé** your face is all dirty; **être barbouillé** feel queasy.

barbu, ~e /baʀby/ adj bearded.

barème /baʀɛm/ nm list, table; (échelle) scale.

baril /baʀil/ nm barrel.

bariolé, ~e /baʀjɔle/ adj multicoloured.

baromètre /baʀɔmɛtʀ/ nm barometer.

baron, ~ne /baʀɔ̃, -ɔn/ nm, f baron, baroness.

barque /baʀk/ nf (small) boat.

barrage /baʀaʒ/ nm dam; (sur route) roadblock.

barre /baʀ/ nf bar; (trait) line, stroke; (Naut) helm; ~ **de boutons** (Ordinat) toolbar.

barreau (pl ~x) /baʀo/ nm bar; (d'échelle) rung; **le** ~ (Jur) the bar.

barrer /baʀe/ 🔟 vt block; (porte) bar; (rayer) cross out; (Naut) steer. □ **se** ~ vpr 🔟 leave.

barrette /baʀɛt/ nf (hair) slide.

barrière /baʀjɛʀ/ nf (porte) gate; (clôture) fence; (obstacle) barrier.

bar-tabac (pl **bars-tabac**) /baʀtaba/ nm café (selling stamps and cigarettes).

bas, basse /ba, bas/ adj (niveau, table) low; (action) base; **au** ~ **mot** at the lowest estimate; **en** ~ **âge** young; ~ **morceaux** (viande) cheap cuts. ● nm bottom; (chaussette) stocking; ~ **de laine** (fig) nest-egg. ● adv low; **en** ~ down below; (dans une maison) downstairs; **en** ~ **de la page** at the bottom of the page; **plus** ~ further ou lower down; **mettre** ~ give birth (to). **bas de casse** nm inv lower case. **bas-côté** (pl ~s) nm (de route) verge; (US) shoulder.

bascule /baskyl/ nf (balance) scales (+ pl); **cheval/fauteuil à** ~ rocking-horse/-chair.

basculer /baskyle/ 🔟 vi topple over; (benne) tip up.

base /baz/ nf base; (fondement) basis; (Pol) rank and file; **de** ~ basic. **base de données** nf database.

baser /baze/ 🔟 vt base. □ **se** ~ **sur** vpr go by.

bas-fonds /bafɔ̃/ nmpl (eau) shallows; (fig) dregs.

basilic /bazilik/ nm basil.

basilique /bazilik/ nf basilica.

basque /bask/ adj Basque. **B~** nmf Basque.

basse /bas/ ➔BAS.

basse-cour (pl **basses-cours**) /baskuʀ/ nf farmyard.

bassesse /bases/ nf baseness; (action) base act.

bassin /basɛ̃/ nm (pièce d'eau) pond; (de piscine) pool; (Géog) basin; (Anat) pelvis; (plat) bowl; ~ **houiller** coalfield.

bassine /basin/ nf bowl.

basson /basɔ̃/ nm bassoon.

bas-ventre (pl ~s) /bavɑ̃tʀ/ nm lower abdomen.

bat /ba/ ➔BATTRE 🔟.

bataille /bataj/ nf battle; (fig) fight.

bâtard, ~e /bataʀ, -d/ adj (solution) hybrid. ● nm, f bastard.

bateau (pl ~x) /bato/ nm boat; ~ **pneumatique** rubber dinghy. **bateau-mouche** (pl **bateaux-mouches**) nm sightseeing boat.

bâti, ~e /bati/ adj bien ~ well-built.

bâtiment /batimɑ̃/ nm building; (industrie) building trade; (navire) vessel.

bâtir /batiʀ/ 🔟 vt build.

bâton /batɔ̃/ nm stick; **conversation à ~s rompus** rambling conversation; ~ **de rouge** lipstick.

battant /batɑ̃/ nm (vantail) flap; **porte à deux ~s** double door.

battement /batmɑ̃/ nm (de cœur) beat(ing); (temps) interval; (Mus) beat.

batterie /batʀi/ nf (Mil, Électr) battery; (Mus) drums; ~ **de cuisine** pots and pans.

batteur /batœʀ/ nm (Mus) drummer; (Culin) whisk.

battre /batʀ/ 🔟 vt/i beat; (cartes) shuffle; (Culin) whisk; (l'emporter sur) beat; ~ **des ailes** flap its wings; ~ **des mains** clap; ~ **des paupières**

blink; ~ **en retraite** beat a retreat; ~ **la semelle** stamp one's feet; ~ **son plein** be in full swing. □ **se** ~ *vpr* fight.

baume /bom/ *nm* balm.

bavard, ~**e** /bavar, -d/ *adj* talkative. ● *nm, f* chatterbox.

bavardage /bavardaʒ/ *nm* chatter, gossip. **bavarder 1** *vi* chat; (jacasser) chatter, gossip.

bave /bav/ *nf* dribble, slobber; (de limace) slime. **baver 1** *vi* dribble, slobber. **baveux, -euse** *adj* dribbling; (omelette) runny.

bavoir /bavwar/ *nm* bib.

bavure /bavyr/ *nf* smudge; (erreur) blunder; ~ **policière** police blunder.

bazar /bazar/ *nm* bazaar; (objets ⓘ) clutter.

BCBG *abrév mf* (**bon chic bon genre**) posh.

BD *abrév f* (**bande dessinée**) comic strip.

béant, ~**e** /beã, -t/ *adj* gaping.

béat, ~**e** /bea, -t/ *adj* (hum) blissful; ~ **d'admiration** wide-eyed with admiration.

beau (**bel** *before vowel or mute h*), **belle** (*mpl* ~**x**) /bo, bɛl/ *adj* beautiful; (*femme*) beautiful; (*homme*) handsome; (*temps*) fine, nice. ● *nm* beauty. ● *adv* **il fait** ~ the weather is nice; **au** ~ **milieu** right in the middle; **bel et bien** well and truly; **de plus belle** more than ever; **faire le** ~ sit up and beg; **on a** ~ **essayer/insister** however much one tries/insists.

beaucoup /boku/ *adv* a lot, very much; ~ **de** (nombre) many; (quantité) a lot of; **pas** ~ (**de**) not many; (quantité) not much; ~ **plus/mieux** much more/better; ~ **trop** far too much; **de** ~ by far.

beau-fils (*pl* **beaux-fils**) /bofis/ *nm* (remariage) stepson.

beau-frère (*pl* **beaux-frères**) /bofrer/ *nm* brother-in-law.

beau-père (*pl* **beaux-pères**) /boper/ *nm* father-in-law; (remariage) stepfather.

beauté /bote/ *nf* beauty; **finir en** ~ end magnificently.

beaux-arts /bozar/ *nmpl* fine arts.

beaux-parents /boparã/ *nmpl* parents-in-law.

bébé /bebe/ *nm* baby. **bébé-éprouvette** (*pl* **bébés-éprouvette**) *nm* test-tube baby.

bec /bɛk/ *nm* beak; (de théière) spout; (de casserole) lip; (bouche ⓘ) mouth; ~ **de gaz** gas street-lamp.

bécane /bekan/ *nf* ⓘ bike.

bêche /bɛʃ/ *nf* spade.

bégayer /begeje/ 31 *vt/i* stammer.

bègue /bɛg/ *nmf* stammerer. ● *adj* **être** ~ stammer.

bégueule /begœl/ *adj* prudish.

beige /bɛʒ/ *adj & nm* beige.

beignet /bɛɲɛ/ *nm* fritter.

bel /bɛl/ →**BEAU**.

bêler /bele/ 1 *vi* bleat.

belette /bəlɛt/ *nf* weasel.

belge /bɛlʒ/ *adj* Belgian. **B**~ *nmf* Belgian.

Belgique /bɛlʒik/ *nf* Belgium.

bélier /belje/ *nm* ram; **le B**~ Aries.

belle /bɛl/ →**BEAU**.

belle-fille (*pl* **belles-filles**) /bɛlfij/ *nf* daughter-in-law; (remariage) stepdaughter.

belle-mère (*pl* **belles-mères**) /bɛlmɛr/ *nf* mother-in-law; (remariage) stepmother.

belle-sœur (*pl* **belles-sœurs**) /bɛlsœr/ *nf* sister-in-law.

belliqueux, -euse /belikø, -z/ *adj* warlike.

bémol /bemɔl/ *nm* (Mus) flat.

bénédiction /benediksjõ/ *nf* blessing.

bénéfice /benefis/ *nm* (gain) profit; (avantage) benefit.

bénéficiaire /benefisjɛr/ *nmf* beneficiary.

bénéficier /benefisje/ 45 *vi* ~ **de** benefit from; (jouir de) enjoy, have.

bénéfique /benefik/ *adj* beneficial.

Bénélux /benelyks/ *nm* Benelux.

bénévole /benevɔl/ *adj* voluntary.

bénin, -igne /benɛ̃, -iɲ/ *adj* minor; (tumeur) benign.

bénir /benir/ 2 *vt* bless. **bénit, ~e** *adj* (eau) holy; (pain) consecrated.

benjamin, ~e /bẽʒamẽ, -in/ *nm, f* youngest child.

benne /bɛn/ *nf* (de grue) scoop; **~ à ordures** (camion) waste disposal truck; (conteneur) skip; **~ (basculante)** dump truck.

béquille /bekij/ *nf* crutch; (de moto) stand.

berceau (*pl* **~x**) /bɛʀso/ *nm* (de bébé, civilisation) cradle.

bercer /bɛʀse/ **10** *vt* (balancer) rock; (apaiser) lull; (leurrer) delude.

béret /beʀɛ/ *nm* beret.

berge /bɛʀʒ/ *nf* (bord) bank.

berger, -ère /bɛʀʒe, -ɛʀ/ *nm, f* shepherd, shepherdess.

berne: en ~ /ũbɛʀn/ *loc* at halfmast.

berner /bɛʀne/ **1** *vt* fool.

besogne /bəzɔɲ/ *nf* task, job.

besoin /bəzwẽ/ *nm* need; **avoir ~ de** need; **au ~** if need be; **dans le ~** in need.

bestiole /bɛstjɔl/ *nf* 🔟 bug.

bétail /betaj/ *nm* livestock.

bête /bɛt/ *adj* stupid. ● *nf* animal; **~ noire** pet hate; **~ sauvage** wild beast; **chercher la petite ~** be overfussy.

bêtise /betiz/ *nf* stupidity; (action) stupid thing.

béton /betɔ̃/ *nm* concrete; **~ armé** reinforced concrete; **en ~** (mur) concrete; (argument 🔟) watertight. **bétonnière** *nf* concrete mixer.

betterave /bɛtʀav/ *nf* beet; **~ rouge** beetroot.

beugler /bøgle/ **1** *vi* bellow; (radio) blare out.

beur /bœʀ/ *nmf & adj* 🔟 second-generation North African living in France.

beurre /bœʀ/ *nm* butter. **beurré, ~e** *adj* buttered; 🔟 drunk. **beurrier** *nm* butter-dish.

bévue /bevy/ *nf* blunder.

biais /bjɛ/ *nm* (moyen) way; **par le ~ de** by means of; **de ~, en ~** at an angle.

bibelot /biblo/ *nm* ornament.

biberon /bibʀɔ̃/ *nm* (feeding) bottle; **nourrir au ~** bottle-feed.

bible /bibl/ *nf* bible; **la B~** the Bible.

bibliographie /biblijɔgʀafi/ *nf* bibliography.

bibliothécaire /biblijɔtekɛʀ/ *nmf* librarian.

bibliothèque /biblijɔtɛk/ *nf* library; (meuble) bookcase.

bic® /bik/ *nm* biro®.

bicarbonate /bikaʀbɔnat/ *nm* **~ (de soude)** bicarbonate (of soda).

biceps /bisɛps/ *nm* biceps.

biche /biʃ/ *nf* doe; **ma ~** darling.

bichonner /biʃɔne/ **1** *vt* pamper.

bicyclette /bisiklɛt/ *nf* bicycle.

bide /bid/ *nm* (ventre 🔟) paunch; (échec 🔟) flop.

bidet /bidɛ/ *nm* bidet.

bidon /bidɔ̃/ *nm* can; (plus grand) drum; (ventre 🔟) belly; **c'est du ~!** it's a load of hogwash 🔟. ● *adj inv* 🔟 phoney.

bidonville /bidɔ̃vil/ *nm* shanty town.

bidule /bidyl/ *nm* 🔟 thing.

Biélorussie /bjelɔʀysi/ *nf* Byelorussia.

bien /bjẽ/ *adv* well; (très) quite, very; **~ des** (nombre) many; **tu as ~ de la chance** you are very lucky; **j'aimerais ~** I would like to; **ce n'est pas ~ de** it is not nice to; **~ sûr** of course. ● *nm* good; (patrimoine) possession; **~s de consommation** consumer goods. ● *adj inv* good; (passable) all right; (en forme) well; (à l'aise) comfortable; (beau) attractive; (respectable) nice, respectable. ● *conj* **~ que** (al-)though; **~ que ce soit** although it is. **bien-aimé, ~e** *adj & nm, f* beloved. **bien-être** *nm* wellbeing.

bienfaisance /bjẽfəzãs/ *nf* charity; **fête de ~** charity event. **bienfaisant, ~e** *adj* beneficial.

bienfait /bjẽfɛ/ *nm* (kind) favour; (avantage) beneficial effect. **bienfaiteur, -trice** *nm, f* benefactor.

bien-pensant, ~e /bjẽpãsã, -t/ *adj* right-thinking.

bienséance /bjẽseãs/ *nf* propriety.

bientôt /bjẽto/ *adv* soon; **à ~** see you soon.

bienveillance /bjẽvɛjãs/ *nf* kind(li)ness.

bienvenu, ~e /bjẽvny/ *adj* welcome. ● *nm, f* **être le ~, être la ~e** be welcome.

bienvenue /bjɛ̃vny/ nf welcome; **souhaiter la ~ à** welcome.

bière /bjɛʀ/ nf beer; (cercueil) coffin; **~ blonde** lager; **~ brune** ≈ stout; **~ pression** draught beer.

bifteck /biftɛk/ nm steak.

bifurquer /bifyʀke/ **1** vi branch off, fork.

bigarré, ~e /bigaʀe/ adj motley.

bigoudi /bigudi/ nm curler.

bijou (pl ~x) /biʒu/ nm jewel; **~x en or** gold jewellery. **bijouterie** nf (boutique) jewellery shop; (Comm) jewellery. **bijoutier, -ière** nm, f jeweller.

bilan /bilɑ̃/ nm outcome; (d'une catastrophe) (casualty) toll; (Comm) balance sheet; **faire le ~ de** assess; **~ de santé** check-up.

bile /bil/ nf bile; **se faire de la ~** 🄸 worry.

bilingue /bilɛ̃g/ adj bilingual.

billard /bijaʀ/ nm billiards (+ pl); (table) billiard-table.

bille /bij/ nf (d'enfant) marble; (de billard) billiard-ball.

billet /bijɛ/ nm ticket; (lettre) note; (article) column; **~ (de banque)** (bank) note; **~ de 50 euros** 50-euro note.

billetterie /bijɛtʀi/ nf cash dispenser.

billion /biljɔ̃/ nm billion; (US) trillion.

bimensuel, ~le /bimɑ̃sɥɛl/ adj fortnightly, bimonthly.

binette /binɛt/ nf hoe; (visage) face; (Internet) smiley.

biochimie /bjoʃimi/ nf biochemistry.

biodégradable /bjodegʀadabl/ adj biodegradable.

biographie /bjɔgʀafi/ nf biography.

biologie /bjɔlɔʒi/ nf biology. **biologique** adj biological; (produit) organic.

bioterrorisme /bjɔtɛʀɔʀism/ nm bioterrorism.

bis /bis/ nm & interj encore.

biscornu, ~e /biskɔʀny/ adj crooked; (bizarre) cranky 🄸.

biscotte /biskɔt/ nf continental toast.

biscuit /biskɥi/ nm biscuit; (US) cookie; **~ salé** cracker; **~ de Savoie** sponge-cake.

bise /biz/ nf 🄸 kiss; (vent) north wind.

bison /bizɔ̃/ nm buffalo.

Bison Futé Devised by the French traffic information service, *Bison Futé* reports on travel conditions nationally and recommends alternative routes (les itinéraires 'bis') for travellers wishing to avoid traffic jams. *Bison Futé* traffic tips are made known through the media and appear on road signs in yellow on a green background.

bisou /bizu/ nm 🄸 kiss.

bistro(t) /bistʀo/ nm 🄸 café, bar.

bit /bit/ nm (Ordinat) bit.

bitume /bitym/ nm asphalt.

bizarre /bizaʀ/ adj odd, strange. **bizarrerie** nf peculiarity.

blafard, ~e /blafaʀ, -d/ adj pale.

blague /blag/ nf 🄸 joke; **sans ~!** no kidding! 🄸.

blaguer /blage/ **1** 🄸 vi joke.

blaireau (pl ~x) /blɛʀo/ nm shaving-brush; (animal) badger.

blâmer /blame/ **1** vt criticize.

blanc, blanche /blɑ̃, blɑ̃ʃ/ adj white; (papier, page) blank. ● nm white; (espace) blank; **~ d'œuf** egg white; **~ de poireau** white part of the leek; **~ (de poulet)** chicken breast; **le ~** (linge) whites; **laisser en ~** leave blank. **B~, Blanche** nm, f white man, white woman. **blanche** nf (Mus) minim.

blanchiment /blɑ̃ʃimɑ̃/ nm (d'argent) laundering.

blanchir /blɑ̃ʃiʀ/ **2** vt whiten; (personne: fig) clear; (argent) launder; (Culin) blanch; **~ (à la chaux)** whitewash. ● vi turn white.

blanchisserie /blɑ̃ʃisʀi/ nf laundry.

blason /blazɔ̃/ nm coat of arms.

blasphème /blasfɛm/ nm blasphemy.

blé /ble/ nm wheat.

blême /blɛm/ adj pallid.

blessant, ~e /blesɑ̃, -t/ adj hurtful.

blessé, ~e /blese/ nm, f casualty, injured person.

blesser /blese/ **1** vt injure, hurt; (par balle) wound; (offenser) hurt. □ **se ~** vpr injure ou hurt oneself. **blessure** nf wound.

bleu, ~e /blø/ adj blue; (Culin) very rare; **~ marine/turquoise** navy blue/turquoise; **avoir une peur ~e** be scared stiff. ● *nm* blue; (contusion) bruise; ~ **(de travail)** overalls (+ *pl*).

bleuet /blœɛ/ *nm* cornflower.

blindé, ~e /blɛ̃de/ *adj* armoured; (fig) immune (**contre** to); **porte** ~e security car. ● *nm* armoured car, tank.

blinder /blɛ̃de/ **1** *vt* armour; (fig) harden.

bloc /blɔk/ *nm* block; (de papier) pad; **serrer à** ~ tighten hard; **en** ~ (matériau) in a block; (nier) outright.

blocage /blɔkaʒ/ *nm* (des prix) freeze, freezing; (des roues) locking; (Psych) block.

bloc-notes (*pl* **blocs-notes**) /blɔknɔt/ *nm* note-pad.

blocus /blɔkys/ *nm* blockade.

blond, ~e /blɔ̃, -d/ *adj* fair, blond. ● *nm, f* fair-haired man, fairhaired woman.

bloquer /blɔke/ **1** *vt* block; (porte, machine) jam; (roues) lock; (prix, crédits) freeze. □ **se** ~ *vpr* jam; (roues) lock; (freins) jam; (ordinateur) crash; **bloqué par la neige** snowbound.

blottir (se) /(sə)blɔtiʀ/ **2** *vpr* snuggle, huddle (**contre** against).

blouse /bluz/ *nf* overall. **blouse blanche** *nf* white coat.

blouson /bluzɔ̃/ *nm* jacket, blouson.

bluffer /blœfe/ **1** *vt/i* bluff.

bobine /bɔbin/ *nf* (de fil, film) reel; (Électr) coil.

bobo /bobo/ *nm* **1** sore, cut; **avoir** ~ have a pain.

bocal (*pl* **-aux**) /bɔkal, -o/ *nm* jar.

bœuf (*pl* ~**s**) /bœf, bø/ *nm* bullock; (US) steer; (viande) beef; ~**s** oxen.

bogue /bɔg/ *nm* (Ordinat) bug.

bohème /bɔɛm/ *adj & nmf* bohemian.

boire /bwaʀ/ **12** *vt/i* (personne, plante) drink; (argile) soak up; ~ **un coup** **1** have a drink.

bois /bwa/ ➡**BOIRE 12**. ● *nm* (matériau, forêt) wood; **de** ~, **en** ~ wooden. ● *nmpl* (de cerf) antlers.

boiseries /bwazʀi/ *nfpl* panelling.

boisson /bwasɔ̃/ *nf* drink.

boit /bwa/ ➡**BOIRE 12**.

boîte /bwat/ *nf* box; (de conserves) tin, can; (entreprise **1**) firm; **en** ~ tinned, canned; ~ **à gants** glove compartment; ~ **aux lettres** letterbox; ~ **aux**

lettres électronique mailbox; ~ **de nuit** night-club; ~ **postale** post-office box; ~ **de vitesses** gear box.

boiter /bwate/ **1** *vi* limp. **boiteux, -euse** *adj* lame; (raisonnement) shaky.

boîtier /bwatje/ *nm* case.

bol /bɔl/ *nm* bowl; ~ **d'air** abreath of fresh air; **avoir du** ~**l** be lucky.

bolide /bɔlid/ *nm* racing car.

Bolivie /bɔlivi/ *nf* Bolivia.

bombardement /bɔ̃baʀdəmɑ̃/ *nm* bombing; shelling.

bombarder /bɔ̃baʀde/ **1** *vt* bomb; (par obus) shell; ~ **qn de** (fig) bombard sb with. **bombardier** *nm* (Aviat) bomber.

bombe /bɔ̃b/ *nf* bomb; (atomiseur) spray, aerosol.

bombé, ~e /bɔ̃be/ *adj* rounded; (route) cambered.

bon, bonne /bɔ̃, bɔn/ *adj* good; (qui convient) right; ~ **à/pour** (approprié) it to/for; **bonne année** happy New Year; ~ **anniversaire** happy birthday; ~ **appétit/voyage** enjoy your meal/ trip; **bonne chance/nuit** good luck/ night; ~ **sens** common sense; **bonne femme** (péj) woman; **de bonne heure** early; **à quoi** ~**?** what's the point? ● *adv* **sentir** ~ smell nice; **tenir** ~ stand firm; **il fait** ~ the weather is mild. ● *interj* right, well. ● *nm* (billet) voucher, coupon; ~ **de commande** order form; **pour de** ~ for good. **bonne** *nf* (domestique) maid.

bonbon /bɔ̃bɔ̃/ *nm* sweet; (US) candy.

bonbonne /bɔ̃bɔn/ *nf* demijohn; (de gaz) cylinder.

bond /bɔ̃/ *nm* leap; **faire un** ~ (de surprise) jump.

bonde /bɔ̃d/ *nf* plug; (trou) plughole.

bondé, ~e /bɔ̃de/ *adj* packed.

bondir /bɔ̃diʀ/ **2** *vi* leap; (de surprise) jump.

bonheur /bɔnœʀ/ *nm* happiness; (chance) (good) luck; **au petit** ~ haphazardly; **par** ~ luckily.

bonhomme (*pl* **bonshommes**) /bɔnɔm, bɔzɔm/ *nm* fellow; ~ **de neige** snowman. ● *adj inv* good hearted.

bonifier (se) /(sə)bɔnifje/ **45** *vpr* improve.

bonjour /bɔ̃ʒuʀ/ nm & interj hallo, hello, good morning ou afternoon.

bon marché /bɔ̃maʀʃe/ adj inv cheap. ● adv cheap (ly)

bonne /bɔn/ ➡BON.

bonne-maman (pl **bonnes-mamans**) /bɔnmamɑ̃/ nf ① granny.

bonnement /bɔnmɑ̃/ adv tout ~ quite simply.

bonnet /bɔnɛ/ nm hat; (de soutien-gorge) cup; ~ **de bain** swimming cap. **bonneterie** nf hosiery.

bonsoir /bɔ̃swaʀ/ nm good evening; (en se couchant) good night.

bonté /bɔ̃te/ nf kindness.

bonus /bɔnys/ nm (Auto) no-claims bonus.

boots /buts/ nmpl ankle boots.

bord /bɔʀ/ nm edge; (rive) bank; à (~ de) on board; **au ~ de la mer** at the seaside; **au ~ des larmes** on the verge of tears; ~ **de la route** road-side.

bordeaux /bɔʀdo/ adj inv maroon. ● nm inv Bordeaux.

bordel /bɔʀdɛl/ nm brothel; (désordre ①) shambles.

border /bɔʀde/ ❶ vt line, border; (tissu) edge; (personne, lit) tuck in.

bordereau (pl ~**x**) /bɔʀdəro/ nm (document) slip.

bordure /bɔʀdyʀ/ nf border; **en ~ de** on the edge of.

borgne /bɔʀɲ/ adj one-eyed.

borne /bɔʀn/ nf boundary marker; (pour barrer le passage) bollard; ~ **(kilométrique)** ≈milestone; ~**s** limits.

borné, ~e /bɔʀne/ adj (esprit) narrow; (personne) narrow minded.

borner (se) /(sə)bɔʀne/ ❶ vpr confine oneself (à to).

bosniaque /bɔsnjak/ adj Bosnian. **B~** nmf Bosnian.

Bosnie /bɔsni/ nf Bosnia.

bosse /bɔs/ nf bump; (de chameau) hump; **avoir la ~ de** ① have a gift for; **avoir roulé sa ~** have been around. **bosselé, ~e** adj dented; (terrain) bumpy.

bosser /bɔse/ ❶ vi ① work (hard).

bossu, ~e /bɔsy/ adj hunchbacked. ● nm, f hunchback.

botanique /bɔtanik/ nf botany.● adj botanical.

botte /bɔt/ nf boot; (de fleurs, légumes) bunch; (de paille) bundle, bale; ~**s de caoutchouc** wellingtons.

botter /bɔte/ ❶ vt ① ça me botte I like the idea.

bottin® /bɔtɛ̃/ nm phone book.

bouc /buk/ nm (billy-)goat; (barbe) goatee; ~ **émissaire** scapegoat.

boucan /bukɑ̃/ nm ①din.

bouche /buʃ/ nf mouth; (lèvres) lips; ~ **bée** open-mouthed; ~ **d'égout** manhole; ~ **d'incendie** (fire)hydrant; ~ **de métro** entrance to the underground ou subway (US). **bouche-à-bouche** nm inv mouth-to-mouth resuscitation. **bouche-à-oreille** nm inv word of mouth.

bouché, ~e /buʃe/ adj (profession, avenir) oversubscribed; (stupide: péj) stupid.

bouchée /buʃe/ nf mouthful.

boucher¹ /buʃe/ ❶ vt block; (bouteille) cork. □ **se ~** vpr get blocked; **se ~ le nez** hold one's nose.

boucher², -ère /buʃe, -ɛʀ/ nm, f butcher. **boucherie** nf butcher's (shop); (carnage) butchery.

bouchon /buʃɔ̃/ nm stopper; (en liège) cork; (de stylo, tube) cap; (de pêcheur) float; (embouteillage) traffic jam; ~ **de cérumen** plug of earwax.

boucle /bukl/ nf (de ceinture) buckle; (de cheveux) curl; (forme) loop; ~ **d'oreille** earring. **bouclé, ~e** adj (cheveux) curly.

boucler /bukle/ ❶ vt fasten; (enfermer ①) shut up; (encercler) seal off; (budget) balance; (terminer) finish off. ● vi curl.

bouclier /buklije/ nm shield.

bouddhiste /budist/ adj & nmf Buddhist.

bouder /bude/ ❶ vi sulk. ● vt stay away from.

boudin /budɛ̃/ nm black pudding.

boue /bu/ nf mud.

bouée /bwe/ nf buoy; ~ **de sauvetage** lifebuoy.

boueux, -euse /buø, -z/ adj muddy.

bouffe /buf/ nf ① food, grub.

bouffée /bufe/ nf puff, whiff; (d'orgueil) fit; ~ **de chaleur** (Méd) hot flush.

bouffi, ~e /bufi/ adj bloated.

bouffon, ~ne /bufɔ̃, -ɔn/ adj farcical. ● nm buffoon.

bougeoir /buʒwaʀ/ nm candlestick.

bougeotte /buʒɔt/ nf **avoir la ~** [T] have the fidgets.

bouger /buʒe/ [40] vt/i move. □ **se ~** vpr [T] move.

bougie /buʒi/ nf candle; (Auto) spark(ing)-plug.

bouillant, ~e /bujɑ̃, -t/ adj boiling; (très chaud) boiling hot.

bouillie /buji/ nf (pour bébé) baby cereal; (péj) mush; **en ~** crushed, mushy.

bouillir /bujiʀ/ [18] vi boil; (fig) seethe; **faire ~** boil.

bouilloire /bujwaʀ/ nf kettle.

bouillon /bujɔ̃/ nm (de cuisson) stock; (potage) broth.

bouillonner /bujɔne/ [1] vi bubble.

bouillotte /bujɔt/ nf hot-water bottle.

boulanger, -ère /bulɑ̃ʒe, -ɛʀ/ nm, f baker. **boulangerie** nf bakery. **boulangerie-pâtisserie** nf bakery (selling cakes and pastries).

boule /bul/ nf ball; ~**s** (jeu) boules; **jouer aux ~s** play boules; **une ~ dans la gorge** a lump in one's throat; ~ **de neige** snowball.

> **Boules** A form of bowls, played on rough, dry ground with metal balls. The aim is to throw the balls to land as near as possible to a smaller target ball called the *cochonnet*. In the South of France, *boules* is often called *pétanque*.

bouleau (pl ~**x**) /bulo/ nm (silver) birch.

boulet /bulɛ/ nm (de forçat) ball and chain; ~ **(de canon)** cannonball; ~ **de charbon** coal nut.

boulette /bulɛt/ nf (de pain, papier) pellet; (bévue) blunder; ~ **de viande** meat ball.

boulevard /bulvaʀ/ nm boulevard.

bouleversant, ~e /bulvɛʀsɑ̃, -t/ adj deeply moving. **bouleversement** nm

upheaval. **bouleverser** [1] vt turn upside down; (pays, plans) disrupt; (émouvoir) upset.

boulimie /bulimi/ nf bulimia.

boulon /bulɔ̃/ nm bolt.

boulot, ~te /bulo, -ɔt/ adj (rond [T]) dumpy. ● nm (travail [T]) work.

boum /bum/ nm & interj bang. ● nf (fête [T]) party.

bouquet /bukɛ/ nm (de fleurs) bunch, bouquet; (d'arbres) clump; **c'est le ~!** [T] that's the last straw!

bouquin /bukɛ̃/ nm [T] book. **bouquiner** [1] vt/i [T] read. **bouquiniste** nmf second-hand bookseller.

bourbier /buʀbje/ nm mire; (fig) tangle.

bourde /buʀd/ nf blunder.

bourdon /buʀdɔ̃/ nm bumble bee. **bourdonnement** nm buzzing.

bourg /buʀ/ nm (market) town (centre), village centre.

bourgeois, ~e /buʀʒwa, -z/ adj & nm,f middle-class (person); (péj) bourgeois. **bourgeoisie** nf middle class(es).

bourgeon /buʀʒɔ̃/ nm bud.

bourgogne /buʀgɔɲ/ nm Burgundy.

bourlinguer /buʀlɛ̃ge/ [1] vi [T] travel about.

bourrage /buʀaʒ/ nm ~ **de crâne** brainwashing.

bourratif, -ive /buʀatif, -v/ adj stodgy.

bourreau (pl ~**x**)/buʀo/ nm executioner; ~ **de travail** (fig) workaholic.

bourrelet /buʀlɛ/ nm weather strip, draught excluder; (de chair) roll of fat.

bourrer /buʀe/ [1] vt cram (de with); (pipe) fill; ~ **de** (nourriture) stuff with; ~ **de coups** thrash; ~ **le crâne à qn** brainwash sb.

bourrique /buʀik/ nf donkey; [T] pigheaded person.

bourru, ~e /buʀy/ adj gruff.

bourse /buʀs/ nf purse; (subvention) grant; **la B~** the Stock Exchange.

boursier, -ière /buʀsje, -jɛʀ/ adj (valeurs) Stock Exchange. ● nm, f grant holder.

boursoufler /buʀsufle/ [1] vt (visage) cause to swell; (peinture) blister.

bousculade /buskylad/ nf crush; (précipitation) rush. **bousculer** [1] vt (pousser) jostle; (presser) rush; (renverser) knock over.

bousiller /buzije/ **1** vt **1** wreck.

boussole /busɔl/ nf compass.

bout /bu/ nm end; (de langue, bâton) piece; (morceau) bit; **à ~** exhausted; **à ~ de souffle** out of breath; **à ~ portant** point-blank; **au ~ de** (après) after; **venir à ~ de** (finir) manage to finish; **d'un ~ à l'autre** throughout; **au ~ du compte** in the end; **~ filtre** filtertip.

bouteille /butɛj/ nf bottle; **~ d'oxygène** oxygen cylinder.

boutique /butik/ nf shop; (de mode) boutique.

bouton /butɔ̃/ nm button; (sur la peau) spot, pimple; (pousse) bud; (de porte, radio) knob; **~ de manchette** cufflink. **boutonner** **1** vt button (up). **boutonnière** nf buttonhole. **bouton-pression** (pl **boutons-pression**) nm press-stud; (US) snap.

bouture /butyʀ/ nf cutting.

bovin, ~e /bɔvɛ̃, -in/ adj bovine. **bovins** nmpl cattle (pl).

box (pl ~ ou **boxes**) /bɔks/ nm lock-up garage; (de dortoir) cubicle; (d'écurie) (loose) box; (Jur) dock.

boxe /bɔks/ nf boxing.

boyau (pl ~x) /bwajo/ nm gut; (corde) catgut; (galerie) gallery; (de bicyclette) tyre; (US) tire.

boycotter /bɔjkɔte/ **1** vt boycott.

BP abrév f (**boîte postale**) PO Box.

bracelet /bʀaslɛ/ nm bracelet; (de montre) watchstrap.

braconnier /bʀakɔnje/ nm poacher.

brader /bʀade/ **1** vt sell off. **braderie** nf clearance sale.

braguette /bʀagɛt/ nf fly.

braille /bʀaj/ nm & adj Braille.

brailler /bʀaje/ **1** vt/i bawl.

braise /bʀɛz/ nf embers (+ pl).

braiser /bʀeze/ **1** vt (Culin) braise.

brancard /bʀɑ̃kaʀ/ nm stretcher; (de charrette) shaft.

branche /bʀɑ̃ʃ/ nf branch.

branché, ~e /bʀɑ̃ʃe/ adj **1** trendy.

branchement /bʀɑ̃ʃmɑ̃/ nm connection. **brancher** **1** vt (prise) plug in; (à un réseau) connect.

brandir /bʀɑ̃diʀ/ **2** vt brandish.

branler /bʀɑ̃le/ **1** vi be shaky.

braquer /bʀake/ **1** vt (arme) aim; (regard) fix; (roue) turn; (banque) **1** hold up; **~ qn contre** turn sb against. ● vi (Auto) turn (the wheel). ❑ **se ~** vpr dig one's heels in.

bras /bʀa/ nm arm; (de rivière) branch; (Tech) arm; **~ dessus ~ dessous** arm in arm; **~ droit** (fig) right hand man; **~ de mer** sound; **en ~ de chemise** in one's shirtsleeves. ● nmpl (fig) labour, hands.

brasier /bʀazje/ nm blaze.

brassard /bʀasaʀ/ nm armband.

brasse /bʀas/ nf breast-stroke; **~ papillon** butterfly (stroke).

brasser /bʀase/ **1** vt mix; (bière) brew; (affaires) handle a lot of. **brasserie** nf brewery; (café) brasserie.

brave /bʀav/ adj (bon) good; (valeureux) brave. **braver** **1** vt defy.

bravo /bʀavo/ interj bravo. ● nm cheer.

bravoure /bʀavuʀ/ nf bravery.

break /bʀɛk/ nm estate car; (US) station-wagon.

brebis /bʀəbi/ nf ewe.

brèche /bʀɛʃ/ nf gap, breach; **être sur la ~** be on the go.

bredouille /bʀəduj/ adj emptyhanded.

bredouiller /bʀəduje/ **1** vt/i mumble.

bref, brève /bʀɛf, -v/ adj short, brief. ● adv in short; **en ~** in short.

Brésil /bʀezil/ nm Brazil.

Bretagne /bʀətaɲ/ nf Brittany.

bretelle /bʀətɛl/ nf (de sac, maillot) strap; (d'autoroute) access road; ~s (pour pantalon) braces; (US) suspenders.

breton, ~ne /bʀətɔ̃, -ɔn/ adj & nm (Ling) Breton. **B~, ~ne** nm, f Breton.

breuvage /bʀœvaʒ/ nm beverage.

brève /bʀɛv/ ➡**BREF.**

brevet /bʀəvɛ/ nm **~ (d'invention)** patent; (diplôme) diploma.

breveté, ~e /bʀəvte/ adj patented.

bribes /bʀib/ nfpl scraps.

bricolage /bʀikɔlaʒ/ nm do-it yourself (jobs).

bricole /bʀikɔl/ nf trifle.

bricoler /bʀikɔle/ **1** vi do DIY; (US) fix things, tinker with.

bricoleur, -euse /bʀikɔlœʀ, -øz/ nm, f handyman, handywoman.

bride /bʀid/ nf bridle.

bridé, ~e /bʀide/ adj **yeux** ~s slanting eyes.

brider /bʀide/ **1** vt (cheval) bridle; (fig) keep in check.

brièvement /bʀijɛvmã/ adv briefly.

brigade /bʀigad/ nf (de police) squad; (Mil) brigade; (fig) team. **brigadier** nm (de gendarmerie) sergeant.

brigand /bʀigã/ nm robber.

brillant, ~e /bʀijã, -t/ adj (couleur) bright; (luisant) shiny; (remarquable) brilliant. ● nm (éclat) shine; (diamant) diamond.

briller /bʀije/ **1** vi shine.

brimade /bʀimad/ nf vexation. **brimer** **1** vt bully, harass; **se sentir brimé** feel put down.

brin /bʀɛ̃/ nm (de muguet) sprig; (d'herbe) blade; (de paille) wisp; **un ~ de** (un peu) a bit of.

brindille /bʀɛ̃dij/ nf twig.

brioche /bʀijɔʃ/ nf brioche, sweet bun; (ventre 🔟) paunch.

brique /bʀik/ nf brick.

briquet /bʀikɛ/ nm (cigarette-)lighter.

brise /bʀiz/ nf breeze.

briser /bʀize/ **1** vt break. □ **se** ~ vpr break.

britannique /bʀitanik/ adj British. B~ nmf Briton; **les B~s** the British.

brocante /bʀɔkãt/ nf bric-à-brac trade; (marché) flea market.

broche /bʀɔʃ/ nf brooch; (Culin) spit; **à la** ~ spit-roasted.

broché, ~e /bʀɔʃe/ adj paperback.

brochet /bʀɔʃɛ/ nm pike.

brochette /bʀɔʃɛt/ nf skewer.

brochure /bʀɔʃyʀ/ nf brochure, booklet.

broder /bʀɔde/ **1** vt/i embroider. **broderie** nf embroidery.

broncher /bʀɔ̃ʃe/ **1** vi **sans** ~ without turning a hair.

bronchite /bʀɔ̃ʃit/ nf bronchitis.

bronze /bʀɔ̃z/ nm bronze.

bronzé, ~e /bʀɔ̃ze/ adj (sun-) tanned.

bronzer /bʀɔ̃ze/ **1** vi (personne) get a (sun-)tan.

brosse /bʀɔs/ nf brush; ~ **à dents** toothbrush; ~ **à habits** clothes brush; **en** ~ (coiffure) in a crew cut.

brosser /bʀɔse/ **1** vt brush; (fig) paint. □ **se** ~ vpr **se** ~ **les dents/les che-**

veux brush one's teeth/hair.

brouette /bʀuɛt/ nf wheelbarrow.

brouhaha /bʀuaa/ nm hubbub.

brouillard /bʀujaʀ/ nm fog.

brouille /bʀuj/ nf quarrel.

brouiller /bʀuje/ **1** vt (vue) blur; (œufs) scramble; (amis) set at odds; ~ **les pistes** cloud the issue. □ **se** ~ vpr (ciel) cloud over; (amis) fall out.

brouillon, ~ne /bʀujɔ̃, -ɔn/ adj untidy. ● nm (rough) draft.

brousse /bʀus/ nf **la** ~ the bush.

brouter /bʀute/ **1** vt/i graze.

broyer /bʀwaje/ **31** vt crush; (moudre) grind.

bru /bʀy/ nf daughter-in-law.

bruine /bʀɥin/ nf drizzle.

bruissement /bʀɥismã/ nm rustling.

bruit /bʀɥi/ nm noise; ~ **de couloir** (fig) rumour.

bruitage /bʀɥitaʒ/ nm sound effects.

brûlant, ~e /bʀylã, -t/ adj burning (hot); (sujet) red-hot; (passion) fiery.

brûlé /bʀyle/ nm burning; **ça sent le** ~ I can smell something burning. ● →BRÛLER **1**.

brûler /bʀyle/ **1** vt/i burn; (essence) use (up); (cierge) light (à to); ~ **un feu (rouge)** jump the lights; ~ **d'envie de faire** be longing to do. □ **se** ~ vpr burn oneself.

brûlure /bʀylyʀ/ nf burn; ~**s d'estomac** heartburn.

brume /bʀym/ nf mist. **brumeux, -euse** adj misty; (esprit) hazy.

brun, ~e /bʀœ̃, -yn/ adj brown, dark. ● nm brown. ● nm, f dark haired person. **brunir** **2** vi turn brown; (bronzer) get a tan.

brushing /bʀœʃiŋ/ nm blow-dry.

brusque /bʀysk/ adj (personne) abrupt; (geste) violent; (soudain) sudden.

brusquer /bʀyske/ **1** vt be abrupt with; (précipiter) rush.

brut, ~e /bʀyt/ adj (diamant) rough; (champagne) dry; (pétrole) crude; (Comm) gross.

brutal, ~e (mpl -aux) /bʀytal, -o/ adj brutal. **brutalité** nf brutality.

brute /bʀyt/ nf brute.

Bruxelles /bʀysɛl/ npr Brussels.

bruyant, ~e /bʀɥijã, -t/ adj noisy.

bruyère /bʀyjɛʀ/ nf heather.

bu /by/ ➡BOIRE 🔟.

bûche /byʃ/ nf log; ~ **de Noël** Christmas log; **ramasser une** ~ 🔟 fall.

bûcher /byʃe/ 🔳 vt/i 🔟 slog away (at) 🔟. ● nm (supplice) stake.

bûcheron /byʃʀɔ̃/ nm lumberjack.

budget /bydʒɛ/ nm budget. **budgétaire** adj budgetary.

buée /bɥe/ nf condensation.

buffet /byfɛ/ nm sideboard; (table garnie) buffet.

buffle /byfl/ nm buffalo.

buisson /bɥisɔ̃/ nm bush.

buissonnière /bɥisɔnjɛʀ/ adj **faire l'école** ~ play truant.

bulbe /bylb/ nm bulb.

bulgare /bylgaʀ/ adj & nm Bulgarian. **B~** nmf Bulgarian.

Bulgarie /bylgaʀi/ nf Bulgaria.

bulldozer /byldozɛʀ/ nm bulldozer.

bulle /byl/ nf bubble.

bulletin /byltɛ̃/ nm bulletin, report; (Scol) report; ~ **d'information** news bulletin; ~ **météorologique** weather report; ~ **(de vote)** ballot-paper; ~ **de salaire** pay-slip.

buraliste /byʀalist/ nmf tobacconist.

bureau (pl ~x) /byʀo/ nm office; (meuble) desk; (comité) board; ~ **d'études** design office; ~ **de poste** post office; ~ **de tabac** tobacconist's (shop); ~ **de vote** polling station.

bureaucrate /byʀokʀat/ nmf bureaucrat. **bureaucratie** nf bureaucracy. **bureaucratique** adj bureaucratic.

bureautique /byʀotik/ nf office automation.

burlesque /byʀlɛsk/ adj (histoire) ludicrous; (film) farcical.

bus /bys/ nm bus.

business /biznɛs/ nm inv (affaires commerciales) business; (affaires privées) affairs.

buste /byst/ nm bust.

but /by(t)/ nm target; (dessein) aim, goal; (football) goal; **avoir pour** ~ **de** aim to; **de** ~ **en blanc** point-blank; **dans le** ~ **de** with the intention of; **aller droit au** ~ go straight to the point.

butane /bytan/ nm butane, Calor gas®.

buté, ~e /byte/ adj obstinate.

buter /byte/ 🔳 vi ~ **contre** knock against; (problème) come up against. ● vt antagonize. ☐ **se** ~ vpr (s'entêter) become obstinate.

buteur /bytœʀ/ nm (au football) striker.

butin /bytɛ̃/ nm booty, loot.

butte /byt/ nf mound; **en** ~ **à** exposed to.

buvard /byvaʀ/ nm blotting-paper.

buvette /byvɛt/ nf (refreshment) bar.

buveur, -euse /byvœʀ, -øz/ nm, f drinker.

Cc

c' /s/ ➡CE.

ça /sa/

● pronom démonstratif

····▸ (sujet) it; that; ~ **flotte** it floats; ~ **suffit!** that's enough!; ~ **y est!** that's it!; ~ **sent le brûlé** there's a smell of burning; ~ **va?** how are things?

····▸ (objet) (proche) this; (plus éloigné) that; **c'est** ~ that's right.

····▸ (dans expressions) **où** ~? where?; **quand** ~? when?; **et avec** ~? anything else?

çà /sa/ adv ~ **et là** here and there.

cabane /kaban/ nf hut; (à outils) shed.

cabaret /kabaʀɛ/ nm cabaret.

cabillaud /kabijo/ nm cod.

cabine /kabin/ nf (à la piscine) cubicle; (de bateau) cabin; (de camion) cab; (d'ascenseur) cage; ~ **d'essayage** fitting room; ~ **de pilotage** cockpit; ~ **de plage** beach hut; ~ **(téléphonique)** phone booth, phone box.

cabinet /kabinɛ/ nm (de médecin) surgery; (US) office; (d'avocat) office; (clientèle) practice; (cabinet collectif) firm; (Pol) Cabinet; (pièce) room; ~**s** (toilettes) toilet; (US) bathroom; ~ **de toilette** bathroom.

câble /kɑbl/ nm cable; (corde) rope; (TV) cable TV. **câbler** vt 🔟 cable; (TV) install cable television in.

cabosser /kabose/ **1** vt dent.

cabotage /kabotaʒ/ nm coastal navigation.

cabrer (se) /(sə)kabʀe/ **1** vpr (cheval) rear; **se ~ contre** rebel against.

cabriole /kabʀijɔl/ nf **faire des ~s** caper about.

cacahuète /kakawɛt/ nf peanut.

cacao /kakao/ nm cocoa.

cachalot /kaʃalo/ nm sperm whale.

cache /kaʃ/ nm mask. ● nf hiding place; **~ d'armes** arms cache.

cache-cache /kaʃkaʃ/ nm inv hide-and-seek.

cache-nez /kaʃne/ nm inv scarf.

cacher /kaʃe/ **1** vt hide, conceal (à from). □ **se ~** vpr hide; (se trouver caché) be hidden.

cachet /kaʃɛ/ nm (de cire) seal; (à l'encre) stamp; (de la poste) postmark; (comprimé) tablet; (d'artiste) fee; (chic) style, cachet.

cachette /kaʃɛt/ nf hiding-place; **en ~** in secret.

cachot /kaʃo/ nm dungeon.

cachottier, -ière /kaʃɔtje, -jɛʀ/ adj secretive.

cacophonie /kakɔfɔni/ nf cacophony.

cactus /kaktys/ nm cactus.

cadavérique /kadaveʀik/ adj (teint) deathly pale.

cadavre /kadavʀ/ nm corpse; (de victime) body.

caddie /kadi/ nm (de supermarché®) trolley; (au golf) caddie.

cadeau (pl ~x) /kado/ nm present, gift; **faire un ~ à qn** give sb a present.

cadenas /kadna/ nm padlock.

cadence /kadɑ̃s/ nf rhythm, cadence; (de travail) rate; **en ~** in time; (marcher) in step.

cadet, ~te /kadɛ, -t/ adj youngest; (entre deux) younger. ● nm, f youngest (child); younger (child).

cadran /kadʀɑ̃/ nm dial; **~ solaire** sundial.

cadre /kadʀ/ nm frame; (lieu) setting; (milieu) surroundings; (limites) scope; (contexte) framework; **dans le ~ de** (à l'occasion de) on the occasion of; (dans le contexte de) in the framework of. ● nm (personne) executive;

les ~s the managerial staff.

cadrer /kadʀe/ **1** vi **~ avec** tally with. ● vt (photo) centre.

cafard /kafaʀ/ nm (insecte) cockroach; **avoir le ~** 1 be down in the dumps.

café /kafe/ nm coffee; (bar) café; **~ crème** espresso with milk; **~ en grains** coffee beans; **~ au lait** white coffee.

cafetière /kaftjɛʀ/ nf coffee-pot; **~ électrique** coffee machine.

cage /kaʒ/ nf cage; **~ d'ascenseur** lift shaft; **~ d'escalier** stairwell; **~ thoracique** rib cage.

cageot /kaʒo/ nm crate.

cagibi /kaʒibi/ nm storage room.

cagneux, -euse /kaɲø, -z/ adj **avoir les genoux ~** be knock-kneed.

cagnotte /kaɲɔt/ nf kitty.

cagoule /kagul/ nf hood; (passe-montagne) balaclava.

cahier /kaje/ nm notebook; (Scol) exercise book; **~ de textes** homework notebook; **~ des charges** (Tech) specifications (+ pl).

cahot /kao/ nm bump, jolt. **cahoteux, -euse** adj bumpy.

caïd /kaid/ nm 1 big shot.

caille /kaj/ nf quail.

cailler /kaje/ **1** vi curdle; **ça caille** 1 it's freezing. □ **se ~** vpr (sang) clot; (lait) curdle. **caillot** nm (blood) clot.

caillou (pl ~x) /kaju/ nm stone; (galet) pebble.

caisse /kɛs/ nf crate, case; (tiroir, machine) till; (guichet) cash desk; (au supermarché) check-out; (bureau) office; (Mus) drum; **~ enregistreuse** cash register; **~ d'épargne** savings bank; **~ de retraite** pension fund. **caissier, -ière** nm, f cashier.

cajoler /kaʒole/ **1** vt coax.

calcaire /kalkɛʀ/ adj (sol) chalky; (eau) hard.

calciné, ~e /kalsine/ adj charred.

calcul /kalkyl/ nm calculation; (Scol) arithmetic; (différentiel) calculus; **~ biliaire** gallstone.

calculatrice /kalkylatʀis/ nf calculator. **calculer** **1** vt calculate. **calculette** nf (pocket) calculator.

cale /kal/ nf wedge; (pour roue) chock; (de navire) hold; **~ sèche** dry dock.

calé, ~e /kale/ adj 1 clever.

caleçon /kalsɔ̃/ *nm* boxer shorts (+ *pl*); underpants (+ *pl*); (de femme) leggings.

calembour /kalɑ̃buʀ/ *nm* pun.

calendrier /kalɑ̃dʀije/ *nm* calendar; (fig) schedule, timetable.

calepin /kalpɛ̃/ *nm* notebook.

caler /kale/ **1** *vt* wedge. ● *vi* stall; (abandonner **2**) give up.

calfeutrer /kalføtʀe/ **1** *vt* (*fissure*) stop up; (*porte*) draught proof.

calibre /kalibʀ/ *nm* calibre; (d'un œuf, fruit) grade.

calice /kalis/ *nm* (Relig) chalice; (Bot) calyx.

califourchon: à ~ /akalifuʀʃɔ̃/ *loc* astride.

câlin, ~e /kalɛ̃, -in/ *adj* (*regard, ton*) affectionate; (*personne*) cuddly.

calmant /kalmɑ̃/ *nm* sedative.

calme /kalm/ *adj* calm. ● *nm* peace; calm; (maîtrise de soi) composure; **du ~!** calm down!

calmer /kalme/ **1** *vt* (*personne*) calm down; (*situation*) defuse; (*douleur*) ease; (*soif*) quench. □ **se ~** *vpr* (*personne, situation*) calm down; (*agitation, tempête*) die down; (*douleur*) ease.

calomnie /kalɔmni/ *nf* (*orale*) slander; (*écrite*) libel. **calomnier** **45** *vt* slander; libel. **calomnieux, -ieuse** *adj* slanderous; libellous.

calorie /kalɔʀi/ *nf* calorie.

calque /kalk/ *nm* tracing; (**papier**) **~** tracing paper; (fig) exact copy.

calquer /kalke/ **1** *vt* trace; (fig) copy; **~ qch sur** model sth on.

calvaire /kalvɛʀ/ *nm* (croix) Calvary; (fig) suffering.

calvitie /kalvisi/ *nf* baldness.

camarade /kamaʀad/ *nmf* friend; (Pol) comrade; **~ de jeu** playmate. **camaraderie** *nf* friendship.

cambouis /kɑ̃bwi/ *nm* dirty oil.

cambrer /kɑ̃bʀe/ **1** *vt* arch. □ **se ~** *vpr* arch one's back.

cambriolage /kɑ̃bʀijɔlaʒ/ *nm* burglary. **cambrioler** **1** *vt* burgle. **cambrioleur, -euse** *nm, f* burglar.

camelot /kamlo/ *nm* **1** street vendor.

camelote /kamlɔt/ *nf* **1** junk.

caméra /kameʀa/ *nf* (cinéma, télévision) camera.

caméscope® /kameskɔp/ *nm* camcorder.

camion /kamjɔ̃/ *nm* lorry, truck. **camion-citerne** (*pl* **camions-citernes**) *nm* tanker. **camionnage** *nm* haulage. **camionnette** *nf* van. **camionneur** *nm* lorry ou truck driver; (entrepreneur) haulage contractor.

camisole /kamizɔl/ *nf* **~ (de force)** straitjacket.

camoufler /kamufle/ **1** *vt* camouflage.

camp /kɑ̃/ *nm* camp; (Sport, Pol) side.

campagnard, ~e /kɑ̃paɲaʀ, -d/ *adj* country. ● *nm, f* countryman, countrywoman.

campagne /kɑ̃paɲ/ *nf* country; countryside; (Mil, Pol) campaign.

campement /kɑ̃pmɑ̃/ *nm* camp, encampment.

camper /kɑ̃pe/ **1** *vi* camp. ● *vt* (esquisser) sketch. □ **se ~** *vpr* plant oneself. **campeur, -euse** *nm, f* camper.

camping /kɑ̃piŋ/ *nm* camping; **faire du ~** go camping; (**terrain de**) **~** campsite. **camping-car** (*pl* **~s**) *nm* camper-van; (US) motorhome. **camping-gaz®** *nm inv* (réchaud) camping stove.

Canada /kanada/ *nm* Canada.

canadien, ~ne /kanadjɛ̃, -ɛn/ *adj* Canadian. **C~, ~ne** *nm, f* Canadian. **canadienne** *nf* (veste) fur-lined jacket; (tente) ridge tent.

canaille /kanɑj/ *nf* rogue.

canal (*pl* **-aux**) /kanal, -o/ *nm* (artificiel) canal; (bras de mer) channel; (Tech, TV) channel; (moyen) channel; **par le ~ de** through. **canalisation** *nf* (tuyaux) mains (+ *pl*). **canaliser** **1** *vt* (*eau*) canalize; (fig) channel.

canapé /kanape/ *nm* sofa.

canard /kanaʀ/ *nm* duck; (journal **1**) rag.

canari /kanaʀi/ *nm* canary.

cancans /kɑ̃kɑ̃/ *nmpl* **1** gossip.

cancer /kɑ̃sɛʀ/ *nm* cancer; **le C~** Cancer. **cancéreux, -euse** *adj* cancerous. **cancérigène** *adj* carcinogenic.

cancre /kɑ̃kʀ/ *nm* dunce.

candeur /kɑ̃dœʀ/ *nf* ingenuousness.

candidat, ~e /kɑ̃dida, -t/ *nm, f* (à un examen, Pol) candidate; (à un poste) applicant, candidate (à for).

candidature /kãdidatyʀ/ nf application; (Pol) candidacy; **poser sa ~ à un poste** apply for a job.

candide /kãdid/ adj ingenuous.

cane /kan/ nf (female) duck. **caneton** nm duckling.

canette /kanɛt/ nf (bouteille) bottle; (boîte) can.

canevas /kanva/ nm canvas; (ouvrage) tapestry; (plan) framework, outline.

caniche /kaniʃ/ nm poodle.

canicule /kanikyl/ nf scorching heat; (vague de chaleur) heatwave.

canif /kanif/ nm penknife.

canine /kanin/ nf canine (tooth).

caniveau (pl ~x) /kanivo/ nm gutter.

cannabis /kanabis/ nm cannabis.

canne /kan/ nf (walking) stick; **~ à pêche** fishing rod; **~ à sucre** sugar cane.

cannelle /kanɛl/ nf cinnamon.

cannibale /kanibal/ adj & nmf cannibal.

canoë /kanɔe/ nm canoe; (Sport) canoeing.

canon /kanɔ̃/ nm (big) gun; (ancien) cannon; (d'une arme) barrel; (principe, règle) canon.

canot /kano/ nm dinghy, (small) boat; **~ de sauvetage** lifeboat; **~ pneumatique** rubber dinghy. **canotier** nm boater.

cantatrice /kãtatʀis/ nf opera singer.

cantine /kãtin/ nf canteen.

cantique /kãtik/ nm hymn.

cantonner /kãtɔne/ **1** vt (Mil) billet. □ **se ~ dans** vpr confine oneself to.

canular /kanylaʀ/ nm hoax.

caoutchouc /kautʃu/ nm rubber; (élastique) rubber band; **~ mousse** foam rubber.

cap /kap/ nm cape, headland; (direction) course; (obstacle) hurdle; **franchir le ~ de la cinquantaine** pass the fifty mark; **mettre le ~ sur** steer a course for.

capable /kapabl/ adj capable (**de** of); **~ de faire** able to do, capable of doing.

capacité /kapasite/ nf ability; (contenance, potentiel) capacity.

cape /kap/ nf cape; **rire sous ~** laugh up one's sleeve.

capillaire /kapilɛʀ/ adj (lotion, soins) hair; **(vaisseau) ~** capillary.

capitaine /kapitɛn/ nm captain.

capital, ~e (mpl -aux) /kapital,-o/ adj key, crucial, fundamental; (peine, lettre) capital. ● nm (pl -aux) (Comm) capital; (fig) stock; **capitaux** (Comm) capital; **~-risque** venture capital; **~-risqueur** venture capitalist. **capitale** nf (ville, lettre) capital.

capitalisme /kapitalism/ nm capitalism.

capitonné, ~e /kapitɔne/ adj padded.

capituler /kapityle/ **1** vi capitulate.

caporal (pl -aux) /kapɔʀal, -o/ nm corporal.

capot /kapo/ nm (Auto) bonnet; (US) hood.

capote /kapɔt/ nf (Auto) hood; (US) top; (préservatif Ⅱ) condom.

capoter /kapɔte/ **1** vi overturn; (fig) collapse.

câpre /kɑpʀ/ nf (Culin) caper.

caprice /kapʀis/ nm whim; (colère) tantrum; **faire un ~** throw a tantrum. **capricieux, -ieuse** adj capricious; (appareil) temperamental.

Capricorne /kapʀikɔʀn/ nm **le ~** Capricorn.

capsule /kapsyl/ nf capsule; (de bouteille) cap.

capter /kapte/ **1** vt (eau) collect; (émission) get; (signal) pick up; (fig) win, capture.

captif, -ive /kaptif, -v/ adj & nm, f captive.

captiver /kaptive/ **1** vt captivate.

capturer /kaptyʀe/ **1** vt capture.

capuche /kapyʃ/ nf hood. **capuchon** nm hood; (de stylo) cap.

car /kaʀ/ conj because, for. ● nm coach; (US) bus.

carabine /kaʀabin/ nf rifle.

caractère /kaʀaktɛʀ/ nm (lettre) character; (nature) nature; **~s d'imprimerie** block letters; **avoir bon/mauvais ~** be good-natured/bad-tempered; **avoir du ~** have character.

caractériel, ~le /kaʀakteʀjɛl/ adj (trait) character; (enfant) disturbed.

caractériser /kaʀakteʀize/ **1** vt characterize. □ **se ~ par** vpr be characterized by. **caractéristique** adj & nf characteristic.

carafe /kaʀaf/ nf carafe.

Caraïbes /kaʀaib/ nfpl **les ~** the Caribbean.

carambolage /kaʀɑ̃bɔlaʒ/ nm pile-up.

caramel /kaʀamɛl/ nm caramel; (bonbon) toffee.

carapace /kaʀapas/ nf shell.

caravane /kaʀavan/ nf (Auto) caravan; (US) trailer; (convoi) caravan.

carbone /kaʀbɔn/ nm carbon; **(papier) ~** carbon (paper). **carboniser** ① vt burn (to ashes).

carburant /kaʀbyʀɑ̃/ nm (motor) fuel.

carburateur /kaʀbyʀatœʀ/ nm carburettor; (US) carburetor.

carcan /kaʀkɑ̃/ nm constraints (+ pl).

carcasse /kaʀkas/ nf (squelette) carcass; (armature) frame; (de voiture) shell.

cardiaque /kaʀdjak/ adj heart. ● nmf heart patient.

cardinal, ~e (mpl **-aux**) /kaʀdinal, -o/ adj & nm cardinal.

Carême /kaʀɛm/ nm le ~ Lent.

carence /kaʀɑ̃s/ nf shortcomings (+ pl); inadequacy; (Méd) deficiency; (absence) lack.

caresse /kaʀɛs/ nf caress; (à un animal) stroke. **caresser** ① vt caress, stroke; (espoir) cherish.

cargaison /kaʀgɛzɔ̃/ nf cargo.

cargo /kaʀgo/ nm cargo boat.

caricature /kaʀikatyʀ/ nf caricature.

carie /kaʀi/ nf (trou) cavity; **la ~ (dentaire)** tooth decay.

carillon /kaʀijɔ̃/ nm chimes (+ pl); (horloge) chiming clock.

caritatif, -ive /kaʀitatif, -v/ adj association caritative charity.

carnage /kaʀnaʒ/ nm carnage.

carnassier, -ière /kaʀnasje, -jɛʀ/ adj carnivorous.

carnaval (pl **~s**) /kaʀnaval/ nm carnival.

carnet /kaʀnɛ/ nm notebook; (detickets, timbres) book; **~ d'adresses** address book; **~ de chèques** chequebook.

carotte /kaʀɔt/ nf carrot.

carpe /kaʀp/ nf carp.

carré, ~e /kaʀe/ adj (forme, mesure) quare; (fig) straightforward; **un mètre ~** one square metre. ● nm square; (de terrain) patch.

carreau (pl **~x**) /kaʀo/ nm (window) pane; (par terre, au mur) tile; (dessin) check; (aux cartes) diamonds (+ pl); **à ~x** (tissu) check(ed); (papier) squared.

carrefour /kaʀfuʀ/ nm crossroads (+ sg).

carrelage /kaʀlaʒ/ nm tiling; (sol) tiles.

carrément /kaʀemɑ̃/ adv (complètement) completely; (stupide, dangereux) downright; (dire) straight out; **elle a ~ démissionné** she went straight ahead and resigned.

carrière /kaʀjɛʀ/ nf career; (terrain) quarry.

carrossable /kaʀɔsabl/ adj suitable for vehicles.

carrosse /kaʀɔs/ nm (horse-drawn) coach.

carrosserie /kaʀɔsʀi/ nf (Auto) body(work).

carrure /kaʀyʀ/ nf shoulders; (fig) necessary qualities, calibre.

cartable /kaʀtabl/ nm satchel.

carte /kaʀt/ nf card; (Géog) map; (Naut) chart; (au restaurant) menu; **~s** (jeu) cards; **à la ~** (manger) à la carte; (horaire) personalized; **donner ~ blanche à** give a free hand to; **~ bleue®** credit card; **~ de crédit** credit card; **~ de fidélité** loyalty card; **~ grise** (car) registration document; **~ d'identité** identity card; **~ magnétique** swipe card; **~ de paiement** debit card; **~ postale** postcard; **~ à puce** smart card; **~ de séjour** resident's permit; **~ SIM** SIM card; **~ des vins** wine list; **~ de visite** (business) card; **~ vitale** social insurance smart card.

Carte d'identité Not to be confused with a passport, this is a proof of identity carried by French citizens. It is issued by the *préfecture* and is valid for ten years. Though not compulsory, it is used to guarantee payments by cheque and is accepted as a travel document within the EU.

cartilage /kaʀtilaʒ/ nm cartilage.

carton /kaʀtɔ̃/ nm cardboard; (boîte) (cardboard) box; **~ à dessin** portfolio; **faire un ~** 🔲 do well.

cartonné, ~e /kaʀtɔne/ adj **livre ~** hardback.

cartouche /kaʀtuʃ/ nf cartridge; (de cigarettes) carton. **cartouchière** nf cartridge-belt.

cas /ka/ nm case; **au ~ où** in case; **~ urgent** emergency; **en aucun ~** on no account; **en ~ de** in the event of, in case of; **en tout ~** in any case; (du moins) at least; **faire ~ de** set great store by; **~ de conscience** moral dilemma.

casanier, -ière /kazanje, -jɛʀ/ adj home-loving.

cascade /kaskad/ nf waterfall; (au cinéma) stunt; (fig) spate, series (+ sg).

cascadeur, -euse /kaskadœʀ,-øz/ nm, f stuntman, stuntwoman.

case /kɑz/ nf hut; (de damier) square; (compartiment) pigeon-hole; (sur un formulaire) box.

caser /kaze/ 🔳 vt 🔲 (mettre) put; (loger) put up; (dans un travail) find a job for; (marier: péj) marry off.

caserne /kazɛʀn/ nf barracks; **~ de sapeurs-pompiers** fire station.

casier /kɑzje/ nm pigeon-hole, compartment; (à chaussures) rack; **~ judiciaire** criminal record.

casque /kask/ nm (de motard) crash helmet; (de cycliste) cycle helmet; (chez le coiffeur) (hair-)drier; **~ (à écouteurs)** headphones; **~ anti-bruit** ear defenders; **~ de protection** safety helmet.

casquette /kaskɛt/ nf cap.

cassant, ~e /kasɑ̃, -t/ adj brittle; (brusque) curt.

cassation /kasasjɔ̃/ nf **cour de ~** appeal court.

casse /kas/ nf (objets) breakages; (lieu) breaker's yard; **mettre à la ~** scrap.

casse-cou /kasku/ nmf inv daredevil.

casse-croûte /kaskʀut/ nm inv snack.

casse-noix /kasnwa/ nm inv nutcrackers (+ pl).

casse-pieds /kaspje/ nmf inv 🔲 pain (in the neck) 🔲.

casser /kase/ 🔳 vt break; (annuler) annul; **~ les pieds à qn** 🔲 annoy sb.

● vi break. □ **se ~** vpr break; (partir 🔲) be off 🔲.

casserole /kasʀɔl/ nf saucepan.

casse-tête /kastɛt/ nm inv (problème) headache; (jeu) brain teaser.

cassette /kasɛt/ nf casket; (de magnétophone) cassette, tape; (de vidéo) video tape; **~ audio numérique ~** digital audio tape.

cassis /kasi(s)/ nm inv blackcurrant.

cassure /kasyʀ/ nf break.

castor /kastɔʀ/ nm beaver.

castration /kastʀasjɔ̃/ nf castration.

catalogue /katalɔg/ nm catalogue.

catalyseur /katalizœʀ/ nm catalyst; (Auto) catalytic convertor.

catastrophe /katastʀɔf/ nf disaster, catastrophe. **catastrophique** adj catastrophic.

catch /katʃ/ nm (all-in) wrestling.

catéchisme /kateʃism/ nm catechism.

catégorie /kategɔʀi/ nf category. **catégorique** adj categorical.

cathédrale /katedʀal/ nf cathedral.

catholique /katɔlik/ adj Catholic; **pas très ~** a bit fishy.

catimini: en ~ /ɑ̃katimini/ loc on the sly.

cauchemar /koʃmaʀ/ nm nightmare.

cause /koz/ nf cause; (raison) reason; (Jur) case; **à ~ de** because of; **en ~** (en jeu, concerné) involved; **pour ~ de** on account of; **mettre en ~** implicate; **remettre en ~** call into question.

causer /koze/ 🔳 vt cause; (discuter de 🔲) **~ travail** talk shop; **~ de** talk about. ● vi chat. **causerie** nf talk.

causette /kozɛt/ nf (Internet) chat; **faire la ~** have a chat.

caution /kosjɔ̃/ nf surety; (Jur) bail; (appui) backing; (garantie) deposit; **libéré sous ~** released on bail. **cautionner** 🔳 vt guarantee; (soutenir) back.

cavalcade /kavalkad/ nf stampede, rush.

cavalier, -ière /kavalje, -jɛʀ/ adj offhand; **allée cavalière** bridle path. ● nm, f rider; (pour danser) partner. ● nm (aux échecs) knight.

cave /kav/ nf cellar. ● adj sunken.

caveau (pl **~x**) /kavo/ nm vault.

caverne /kavɛʀn/ nf cave.

CCP abrév m (**compte chèque postal**) post office account.

CD abrév m (**compact disc**) CD.

CD-ROM abrév m inv (**compact disc read only memory**) CD-ROM.

ce, c', cet, cette (pl **ces**) /sə, s, sɛt, se/

c' before e. cet before vowel or mute h.

● **ce, cet, cette** (pl **ces**) adjectif démonstratif

····▸ this; (plus éloigné) that; **ces** these; (plus éloigné) those; **cette nuit** (passée) last night; (à venir) tonight.

● **ce, c'** pronom démonstratif

····▸ **c'est** it's ou it is; **c'est un policier** he's a policeman; ~ **sont eux qui l'ont fait** they did it; **qui est- ~?** who is it?

····▸ **ce que/qui** what; ~ **que je ne comprends pas** what I don't understand; **elle est venue,** ~ **qui est étonnant** she came, which is surprising; ~ **que tu as de la chance!** how lucky you are! **tout** ~ **qu'elle trouve/peut** everything she finds/can

CE abrév f (**Communauté européenne**) EC.

CEAM abrév f (**Carte européenne d'assurance maladie**) EHIC.

ceci /səsi/ pron this.

cécité /sesite/ nf blindness.

céder /sede/ 14 vt give up; ~ **le passage** give way; (vendre) sell. ● vi (se rompre) give way; (se soumettre) give in.

cédérom /sedeʀɔm/ nm CD-ROM.

cédille /sedij/ nf cedilla.

cèdre /sɛdʀ/ nm cedar.

CEI abrév f (**Communauté des États indépendants**) CIS.

ceinture /sɛ̃tyʀ/ nf belt; (taille) waist; ~ **de sauvetage** lifebelt; ~ **de sécurité** seatbelt.

cela /səla/ pron it, that; (pour désigner) that; ~ **va de soi** it is obvious; ~ **dit/ fait** having said/done that.

célèbre /selɛbʀ/ adj famous. **célébrer** 14 vt celebrate. **célébrité** nf fame; (personne) celebrity.

céleri /sɛlʀi/ nm (en branches) celery. **céleri-rave** (pl **célerisraves**) nm celeriac.

célibat /seliba/ nm celibacy; (état) single status.

célibataire /selibatɛʀ/ adj single. ● nm bachelor. ● nf single woman.

celle, celles /sɛl/ ➡CELUI.

cellulaire /selylɛʀ/ adj cell; **emprisonnement** ~ solitary confinement; **fourgon** ou **voiture** ~ prison van; **téléphone** ~ cellular phone.

cellule /selyl/ nf cell; ~ **souche** stem cell.

celui, celle (pl **ceux, celles**) /səlɥi, sɛl, sə/ pron the one; ~ **de mon ami** my friend's; ~**-ci** this (one); ~**-là** that (one); **ceux-ci** these (ones); **ceux-là** those (ones).

cendre /sɑ̃dʀ/ nf ash.

cendrier /sɑ̃dʀije/ nm ashtray.

censé, ~**e** /sɑ̃se/ adj **être** ~ **faire** be supposed to do.

censeur /sɑ̃sœʀ/ nm censor; (Scol) administrator in charge of discipline.

censure /sɑ̃syʀ/ nf censorship. **censurer** 1 vt censor; (critiquer) censure.

cent /sɑ̃/ adj (a) hundred; **20 pour** ~ 20 per cent.● n (quantité) hundred; ~ **un** a hundred and one;)centième d'euro) cent.

centaine /sɑ̃tɛn/ nf hundred; **une** ~ **(de)** (about) a hundred.

centenaire /sɑ̃tnɛʀ/ nm (anniversaire) centenary.

centième /sɑ̃tjɛm/ adj & nmf hundredth.

centimètre /sɑ̃timɛtʀ/ nm centimetre; (ruban) tape-measure.

central, ~**e** (mpl -**aux**) /sɑ̃tʀal,-o/ adj central. ● nm (pl -**aux**) ~ **(téléphonique)** (telephone) exchange. **centrale** nf power-station.

centre /sɑ̃tʀ/ nm centre; ~ **commercial** shopping centre; (US) mall; ~ **d'appels** call centre; ~ **de formation** training centre; ~ **hospitalier** hospital. **centrer** 1 vt centre. **centreville** (pl **centres-villes**) nm town centre.

centuple /sɑ̃typl/ nm le ~ de a hundred times; **au** ~ a hundredfold.

cep /sɛp/ nm vine stock.

cépage /sepaʒ/ nm grape variety.

cèpe /sɛp/ nm cep.

cependant /səpɑ̃dɑ̃/ adv however.

céramique /seʀamik/ nf ceramic; (art) ceramics (+ sg).

cercle /sɛʀkl/ nm circle; (cerceau) hoop; (association) society, club; ~ **vicieux** vicious circle.

cercueil /sɛʀkœj/ nm coffin.

céréale /seʀeal/ nf cereal; ~**s** (Culin) (breakfast) cereal.

cérébral, ~e (mpl -**aux**) /seʀebʀal, -o/ adj cerebral.

cérémonie /seʀemɔni/ nf ceremony; **sans** ~**s** (repas) informal; (recevoir) informally.

cerf /sɛʀ/ nm stag.

cerfeuil /sɛʀfœj/ nm chervil.

cerf-volant (pl **cerfs-volants**) /sɛʀvɔlɑ̃/ nm kite.

cerise /s(ə)ʀiz/ nf cherry. **cerisier** nm cherry tree.

cerner /sɛʀne/ ⬛ vt surround; (question) define; **avoir les yeux cernés** have rings under one's eyes.

certain, ~e /sɛʀtɛ̃, -ɛn/ adj certain; (sûr) certain, sure (**de** of; **que** that); **d'un** ~ **âge** no longer young; **un** ~ **temps** some time. **certainement** adv (probablement) most probably; (avec certitude) certainly. **certains, -es** pron some people.

certes /sɛʀt/ adv (sans doute) admittedly; (bien sûr) of course.

certificat /sɛʀtifika/ nm certificate.

certifier /sɛʀtifje/ 🔢 vt certify; ~ **qch à qn** assure sb of sth; **copie certifiée conforme** certified true copy.

certitude /sɛʀtityd/ nf certainty.

cerveau (pl ~**x**) /sɛʀvo/ nm brain.

cervelle /sɛʀvɛl/ nf (Anat) brain; (Culin) brains.

ces /se/ ➡CE.

césarienne /sezaʀjɛn/ nf Caesarean (section).

cesse /sɛs/ nf **n'avoir de** ~ **que** have no rest until; **sans** ~ constantly, incessantly.

cesser /sese/ ⬛ vt stop; ~ **de faire** stop doing. ● vi cease; **faire** ~ put an end to.

cessez-le-feu /seselfø/ nm inv ceasefire.

cession /sɛsjɔ̃/ nf transfer.

c'est-à-dire /sɛtadiʀ/ conj that is (to say).

cet, cette /sɛt/ ➡CE.

ceux /sø/ ➡CELUI.

chacun, ~e /ʃakœ̃, -yn/ pron each (one), every one; (tout le monde) everyone; ~ **d'entre nous** each (one) of us.

chagrin /ʃagʀɛ̃/ nm sorrow; **avoir du** ~ be sad.

chahut /ʃay/ nm row, din.

chahuter /ʃayte/ ⬛ vi make a row. ● vt (enseignant) be rowdy with; (orateur) heckle.

chaîne /ʃɛn/ nf chain; (de télévision) channel; ~ (**d'assemblage**) assembly line; ~**s** (Auto) snow chains; ~ **de montagnes** mountain range; ~ **de montage/fabrication** assembly/production line; ~ **hi-fi** hi-fi system; ~ **laser** CD player; **en** ~ (accidents) multiple; (réaction) chain. **chaînette** nf (small) chain. **chaînon** nm link.

chair /ʃɛʀ/ nf flesh; **bien en** ~ plump; **en** ~ **et en os** in the flesh; ~ **à saucisses** sausage meat; **la** ~ **de poule** goose pimples. ● adj inv (couleur) ~ flesh-coloured.

chaire /ʃɛʀ/ nf (d'église) pulpit; (Univ) chair.

chaise /ʃɛz/ nf chair; ~ **longue** deckchair.

châle /ʃɑl/ nm shawl.

chaleur /ʃalœʀ/ nf heat; (moins intense) warmth; (d'un accueil, d'une couleur) warmth. **chaleureux, -euse** adj warm.

chalumeau (pl ~**x**) /ʃalymo/ nm blowtorch.

chalutier /ʃalytje/ nm trawler.

chamailler (se) /(sə)ʃamaje/ ⬛ vpr squabble.

chambre /ʃɑ̃bʀ/ nf (bed) room; (Pol, Jur) chamber; **faire** ~ **à part** sleep in separate rooms; ~ **à air** inner tube; ~ **d'amis** spare ou guest room; ~ **de commerce (et d'industrie)** Chamber of Commerce; ~ **à coucher** bedroom;

~ **à un lit/deux lits** single/twinroom; ~ **pour deux personnes** ~ double room; ~ **forte** strong-room; ~ **d'hôte** bed and breakfast. **chambrer** ◼ *vt* (*vin*) bring to room temperature.

chameau (*pl* ~**x**) /ʃamo/ *nm* camel.

chamois /ʃamwa/ *nm* chamois.

champ /ʃɑ̃/ *nm* field; ~ **de bataille** battlefield; ~ **de courses** racecourse; ~ **de tir** firing range.

champêtre /ʃɑ̃pɛtʀ/ *adj* rural.

champignon /ʃɑ̃piɲɔ̃/ *nm* mushroom; (*moisissure*) fungus; ~ **de Paris** button mushroom.

champion, ~**ne** /ʃɑ̃pjɔ̃, -ɔn/ *nm, f* champion. **championnat** *nm* championship.

chance /ʃɑ̃s/ *nf* (good) luck; (*possibilité*) chance; **avoir de la** ~ be lucky; **quelle** ~! what luck!

chanceler /ʃɑ̃sle/ 38 *vi* stagger; (fig) falter, waver.

chancelier /ʃɑ̃səlje/ *nm* chancellor.

chanceux, -euse /ʃɑ̃sø, -z/ *adj* lucky.

chandail /ʃɑ̃daj/ *nm* sweater.

chandelier /ʃɑ̃dəlje/ *nm* candlestick.

chandelle /ʃɑ̃dɛl/ *nf* candle; **dîner aux** ~**s** candlelight dinner.

change /ʃɑ̃ʒ/ *nm* (foreign) exchange; (taux) exchange rate.

changement /ʃɑ̃ʒmɑ̃/ *nm* change; ~ **climatique** climate change; ~ **de vitesse** (dispositif) ears.

changer /ʃɑ̃ʒe/ 40 *vt* change; ~ **qch de place** move sth; (échanger) change (**pour, contre** for); ~ **de nom/voiture** change one's name/car; ~ **de place/train** change places/trains; ~ **de direction** change direction; ~ **d'avis** *ou* **d'idée** change one's mind; ~ **de vitesse** change gear. □ **se** ~ *vpr* change, get changed.

chanson /ʃɑ̃sɔ̃/ *nf* song.

chant /ʃɑ̃/ *nm* singing; (chanson) song; (Relig) hymn.

chantage /ʃɑ̃taʒ/ *nm* blackmail.

chanter /ʃɑ̃te/ ◼ *vt* sing; **si cela vous chante** ▯ if you feel like it. ● *vi* sing; **faire** ~ (délit) blackmail. **chanteur, -euse** *nm, f* singer.

chantier /ʃɑ̃tje/ *nm* building site; ~ **naval** shipyard; **mettre en** ~ get under way, start.

chaos /kao/ *nm* chaos.

chaparder /ʃapaʀde/ ◼ *vt* ▯ pinch ▯, filch.

chapeau (*pl* ~**x**) /ʃapo/ *nm* hat; ~**!** well done!

chapelet /ʃaplɛ/ *nm* rosary; (fig) string.

chapelle /ʃapɛl/ *nf* chapel.

chapelure /ʃaplyʀ/ *nf* (Culin) breadcrumbs.

chaperonner /ʃapʀɔne/ ◼ *vt* chaperone.

chapiteau (*pl* ~**x**) /ʃapito/ *nm* marquee; (de cirque) big top; (de colonne) capital.

chapitre /ʃapitʀ/ *nm* chapter; (fig) subject.

chaque /ʃak/ *adj* every, each.

char /ʃaʀ/ *nm* (Mil) tank; (de carnaval) float; (charrette) cart; (dans l'antiquité) chariot.

charabia /ʃaʀabja/ *nm* ▯ gibberish.

charade /ʃaʀad/ *nf* riddle.

charbon /ʃaʀbɔ̃/ *nm* coal; (Méd) anthrax; ~ **de bois** charcoal.

charcuterie /ʃaʀkytʀi/ *nf* pork butcher's shop; (aliments) (cooked) pork meats. **charcutier, -ière** *nm, f* pork butcher.

chardon /ʃaʀdɔ̃/ *nm* thistle.

charge /ʃaʀʒ/ *nf* load, burden; (Mil, Électr, Jur) charge; (responsabilité) responsibility; **avoir qn à** ~ be responsible for; ~**s** expenses; (de locataire) service charges; **être à la** ~ **de** (personne) be the responsibility of; (frais) be payable by; ~**s sociales** social security contributions; **prendre en** ~ take charge of.

chargé, ~**e** /ʃaʀʒe/ *adj* (véhicule) loaded; (journée, emploi du temps) busy; (langue) coated. ● *nm, f* ~ **de mission** head of mission; ~ **d'affaires** chargé d'affaires; ~ **de cours** lecturer.

chargement /ʃaʀʒəmɑ̃/ *nm* loading; (objets) load.

charger /ʃaʀʒe/ 40 *vt* load; (Ordinat, Photo) load; (attaquer) charge; (batterie) charge; ~ **qn de** (fardeau) weigh sb down with; (tâche) entrust sb with; ~ **qn de faire** make sb responsible for doing. ● *vi* (attaquer) charge. □ **se** ~ **de** *vpr* take charge *ou* care of.

chariot /ʃaʀjo/ *nm* (à roulettes) rolley; (US) cart; (charrette) cart.

charitable /ʃaʁitabl/ adj charitable.

charité /ʃaʁite/ nf charity; **faire la ~ à** give (money) to.

charlatan /ʃaʁlatɑ̃/ nm charlatan.

charmant, ~e /ʃaʁmɑ̃, -t/ adj charming.

charme /ʃaʁm/ nm charm; (qui envoûte) spell. **charmer** ⬛ vt charm. **charmeur, -euse** nm, f charmer.

charnel, ~le /ʃaʁnɛl/ adj carnal.

charnière /ʃaʁnjɛʁ/ nf hinge; **à la ~ de** at the meeting point between.

charnu, ~e /ʃaʁny/ adj plump, fleshy.

charpente /ʃaʁpɑ̃t/ nf framework; (carrure) build.

charpentier /ʃaʁpɑ̃tje/ nm carpenter.

charrette /ʃaʁɛt/ nf cart.

charrue /ʃaʁy/ nf plough.

chasse /ʃas/ nf hunting; (au fusil) shooting; (faire partir) chase; (recherche) hunt(ing); **~ (d'eau)** (toilet) flush; **~ sous-marine** harpoon fishing.

chasse-neige /ʃasnɛʒ/ nm inv snow-plough.

chasser /ʃase/ ⬛ vt hunt; (au fusil) shoot; (faire partir) chase away; (odeur, employé) get rid of. ● vi go hunting; (au fusil) go shooting.

chasseur, -euse /ʃasœʁ, -øz/ nm, f hunter. ● nm bellboy; (US) bellhop; (avion) fighter plane.

châssis /ʃɑsi/ nm frame; (Auto) chassis.

chasteté /ʃastəte/ nf chastity.

chat¹ /ʃa/ nm cat; (mâle) tomcat.

chat² /tʃat/ nm (Internet) chat.

châtaigne /ʃatɛɲ/ nf chestnut. **châtaignier** nm chestnut tree. **châtain** adj inv chestnut (brown).

château (pl ~x) /ʃato/ nm castle; (manoir) manor; **~ d'eau** water tower; **~ fort** fortified castle.

châtiment /ʃatimɑ̃/ nm punishment.

chaton /ʃatɔ̃/ nm (chat) kitten.

chatouillement /ʃatujmɑ̃/ nm tickling. **chatouiller** ⬛ vt tickle. **chatouilleux, -euse** adj ticklish; (susceptible) touchy.

châtrer /ʃatʁe/ ⬛ vt castrate; (chat) neuter.

chatte /ʃat/ nf female cat.

chaud, ~e /ʃo, -d/ adj warm; (brûlant) hot; (vif: fig) warm. ● nm heat; **au ~**

in the warm(th); **avoir ~** be warm; be hot; **il fait ~** it is warm; it is hot; **pour te tenir ~** to keep you warm. **chaudement** adv warmly; (disputé) hotly.

chaudière /ʃodjɛʁ/ nf boiler.

chaudron /ʃodʁɔ̃/ nm cauldron.

chauffage /ʃofaʒ/ nm heating; **~ central** central heating.

chauffard /ʃofaʁ/ nm (péj) reckless driver.

chauffer /ʃofe/ ⬛ vt/i heat (up); (moteur, appareil) overheat. ◻ **se ~** vpr warm oneself (up).

chauffeur /ʃofœʁ/ nm driver; (aux gages de qn) chauffeur.

chaume /ʃom/ nm (de toit) thatch.

chaussée /ʃose/ nf road (way).

chausse-pied /ʃospje/ (pl ~s) /ʃospje/ nm shoehorn.

chausser /ʃose/ ⬛ vt (chaussures) put on; (enfant) put shoes on (to). ● vi **~ bien** (aller) fit well; **~ du 35** take a size 35 shoe. ◻ **se ~** vpr put one's shoes on.

chaussette /ʃosɛt/ nf sock.

chausson /ʃosɔ̃/ nm slipper; (de bébé) bootee; **~ de danse** ballet shoe; **~ aux pommes** apple turnover.

chaussure /ʃosyʁ/ nf shoe; **~ de ski** ski boot; **~ de marche** hiking boot.

chauve /ʃov/ adj bald.

chauve-souris (pl chauves-souris) /ʃovsuʁi/ nf bat.

chauvin, ~e /ʃovɛ̃, -in/ adj chauvinistic. ● nm, f chauvinist.

chavirer /ʃaviʁe/ ⬛ vt (bateau) capsize; (objets) tip over.

chef /ʃɛf/ nm leader, head; (supérieur) boss, superior; (Culin) chef; (de tribu) chief; **architecte en ~** chief ou head architect; **~ d'accusation** (Jur) charge; **~ d'équipe** foreman; (Sport) captain; **~ d'État** head of State; **~ de famille** head of the family; **~ de file** (Pol) leader; **~ de gare** stationmaster; **~ d'orchestre** conductor; **~ de service** department head; **~ de train** guard; (US) conductor.

chef-d'œuvre (pl chefs-d'œuvre) /ʃɛdœvʁ/ nm masterpiece.

chef-lieu (pl chefs-lieux) /ʃɛfljø/ nm county town, administrative centre.

chemin /ʃəmɛ̃/ nm road; (étroit) lane; (de terre) track; (pour piétons) path; (passage) way; (direction, trajet) way; **avoir du ~ à faire** have a long way to go; **~ de fer** railway; **par ~ de fer** by rail; **~ de halage** towpath; **~ vicinal** country lane.

cheminée /ʃəmine/ nf chimney; (intérieure) fireplace; (encadrement) mantelpiece; (de bateau) funnel.

cheminot /ʃəmino/ nm railwayman; (US) railroad man.

chemise /ʃəmiz/ nf shirt; (dossier) folder; (de livre) jacket; **~ de nuit** nightdress. **chemisette** nf short-sleeved shirt. **chemisier** nm blouse.

chêne /ʃɛn/ nm oak.

chenil /ʃəni(l)/ nm (pension) kennels (+ sg).

chenille /ʃənij/ nf caterpillar; **véhicule à ~s** tracked vehicle.

cheptel /ʃɛptɛl/ nm livestock.

chèque /ʃɛk/ nm cheque; **~ sans provision** bad cheque; **~ de voyage** traveller's cheque. **chéquier** nm chequebook.

cher, chère /ʃɛr/ adj (coûteux) dear, expensive; (aimé) dear; (dans la correspondance) dear. ● adv (coûter, payer) a lot (of money); (en importance) dearly. ● nm, f **mon ~, ma chère** my dear.

chercher /ʃɛrʃe/ ◼ vt look for; (aide, paix, gloire) seek; **aller ~** go and ou fetch, go for; **~ à faire** attempt to do; **~ la petite bête** be finicky.

chercheur, -euse /ʃɛrʃœr, -øz/ nm, f research worker.

chèrement /ʃɛrmɑ̃/ adv dearly.

chéri, ~e /ʃeri/ adj beloved. ● nm, f darling.

chérir /ʃerir/ ◻ vt cherish.

chétif, -ive /ʃetif, -v/ adj puny.

cheval (pl **-aux**) /ʃəval, -o/ nm horse; **à ~** on horseback; **à ~ sur** astride, straddling; **faire du ~** ride, go horse-riding.

chevalerie /ʃəvalri/ nf chivalry.

chevalet /ʃəvalɛ/ nm easel; (de menuisier) trestle.

chevalier /ʃəvalje/ nm knight.

chevalière /ʃəvaljɛr/ nf signet ring.

cheval-vapeur (pl **chevaux-vapeur**) /ʃəvalvapœr/ nm horsepower.

chevaucher /ʃəvoʃe/ ◼ vt sit astride. ◻ **se ~** vpr overlap.

chevelu, ~e /ʃəvly/ adj (péj) long-haired; (Bot) hairy.

chevelure /ʃəvlyr/ nf hair.

chevet /ʃəvɛ/ nm **au ~ de** at the bedside of; **livre de ~** bedside book.

cheveu (pl **~x**) /ʃəvø/ nm (poil) air; **~x** (chevelure) hair; **avoir les ~x longs** have long hair.

cheville /ʃəvij/ nf ankle; (fiche) peg, pin; (pour mur) (wall) plug.

chèvre /ʃɛvr/ nf goat.

chevreuil /ʃəvrœj/ nm roe (deer); (Culin) venison.

chevron /ʃəvrɔ̃/ nm (poutre) rafter; **à ~s** herringbone.

chez /ʃe/ prép (au domicile de) at the house of; (parmi) among; (dans le caractère ou l'œuvre de) in; **aller ~ qn** go to sb's house; **~ le boucher** at ou to the butcher's; **~ soi** at home; **rentrer ~ soi** go home. **chez-soi** nm inv home.

chic /ʃik/ adj inv smart; (gentil) kind. ● nm style; **avoir le ~ pour** have a knack for; **~ (alors)!** great!

chicane /ʃikan/ nf double bend; **chercher ~ à qn** pick a quarrel with sb.

chiche /ʃiʃ/ adj mean (de with); **~ que je le fais!** ◻ I bet you I can do it.

chichis /ʃiʃi/ nmpl ◻ fuss.

chicorée /ʃikɔre/ nf (frisée) endive; (à café) chicory.

chien /ʃjɛ̃/ nm dog; **~ d'aveugle** guide dog; **~ de garde** watch-dog. **chienne** nf dog, bitch.

chiffon /ʃifɔ̃/ nm rag; (pour nettoyer) duster; **~ humide** damp cloth. **chiffonner** ◼ vt crumple; (préoccuper ◻) bother.

chiffre /ʃifr/ nm figure; (numéro) number; (code) code; **~s arabes/romains** Arabic/Roman numerals; **~s (statistiques)** statistics; **~ d'affaires** turnover.

chiffrer /ʃifre/ ◼ vt put a figure on, assess; (texte) encode. ◻ **se ~ à** vpr come to.

chignon /ʃiɲɔ̃/ nm bun, chignon.

Chili /ʃili/ nm Chile.

chimère /ʃimɛr/ nf fantasy.

chimie /ʃimi/ nf chemistry. **chimique** adj chemical. **chimiste** nmf chemist.

chimpanzé /ʃɛ̃pɑ̃ze/ nm chimpanzee.

Chine /ʃin/ nf China.

chinois, ~e /ʃinwa, -z/ adj Chinese.
● nm (Ling) Chinese. **C~, ~e** nm, f
Chinese.

chiot /ʃjo/ nm pup(py).

chipoter /ʃipote/ **1** vi (manger) pick
at one's food; (discuter) quibble.

chips /ʃips/ nf inv crisp; (US) chip.

chirurgie /ʃiʀyʀʒi/ nf surgery; **~ esthétique** plastic surgery. **chirurgien**
nm surgeon.

chlore /klɔʀ/ nm chlorine.

choc /ʃɔk/ nm (heurt) impact, shock;
(émotion) shock; (collision) crash; (affrontement) clash; (Méd) shock; **sous
le ~** in shock.

chocolat /ʃɔkɔla/ nm chocolate; (à
boire) drinking chocolate; **~ au lait**
milk chocolate; **~ chaud** hot chocolate; **~ noir** dark chocolate.

chœur /kœʀ/ nm (antique) chorus;
(chanteurs, nef) choir; **en ~** in chorus.

choisir /ʃwaziʀ/ **2** vt choose, select.

choix /ʃwa/ nm choice, selection; **fromage ou dessert au ~** a choice of
cheese or dessert; **de ~** choice; **de
premier ~** top quality.

chômage /ʃomaʒ/ nm unemployment;
au ~, en ~ unemployed; **mettre en
~ technique** lay off.

chômeur, -euse /ʃomœʀ, -øz/ nm, f
unemployed person; **les ~s** the unemployed.

choquer /ʃɔke/ **1** vt shock; (commo-
tionner) shake.

choral, ~e (mpl ~s) /kɔʀal/ adj choral.
chorale nf choir, choral society.

chorégraphie /kɔʀegʀafi/ nf chore-
ography.

choriste /kɔʀist/ nmf (à l'église) chor-
ister; (à l'opéra) member of the
chorus ou choir.

chose /ʃoz/ nf thing; **(très) peu de ~**
nothing much; **pas grand ~**
not much.

chou (pl ~x) /ʃu/ nm cabbage; **~ (à la
crème)** cream puff; **~ de Bruxelles**
Brussels sprout; **mon petit ~** **1**
my dear.

chouchou, ~te /ʃuʃu, -t/ nm, f (de
professeur) pet; (du public) darling.

choucroute /ʃukʀut/ nf sauerkraut.

chouette /ʃwɛt/ nf owl. ● adj **1** super.

chou-fleur (pl **choux-fleurs**) /ʃuflœʀ/
nm cauliflower.

choyer /ʃwaje/ **31** vt pamper.

chrétien, ~ne /kʀetjɛ̃, -jɛn/ adj & nm,
f Christian.

Christ /kʀist/ nm **le ~** Christ.

chrome /kʀom/ nm chromium,
chrome.

chromosome /kʀɔmozom/ nm
chromosome.

chronique /kʀɔnik/ adj chronic. ● nf
(rubrique) column; (nouvelles) news;
(annales) chronicle.

chronologique /kʀɔnɔlɔʒik/ adj
chronological.

chronomètre /kʀɔnɔmɛtʀ/ nm stop-
watch. **chronométrer** **14** vt time.

chrysanthème /kʀizɑ̃tɛm/ nm chrysanthemum.

chuchoter /ʃyʃɔte/ **1** vt/i whisper.

chut /ʃyt/ interj shh, hush.

chute /ʃyt/ nf fall; (déchet) offcut; **~
(d'eau)** waterfall; **~ de pluie** rainfall;
~ des cheveux hair loss; **~ des ventes** ~ drop in sales; **~ de 5%** 5%
drop. **chuter** **1** vi fall.

Chypre /ʃipʀ/ nf Cyprus.

ci /si/ adv here; **~-gît** here lies; **cet
homme-~** this man; **ces maisons-~**
these houses.

ci-après /siapʀɛ/ adv below.

cible /sibl/ nf target.

ciboulette /sibulɛt/ nf (Culin) chives
(+ pl).

cicatrice /sikatʀis/ nf scar.

cicatriser /sikatʀize/ **1** vt heal. □ **se
~** vpr heal.

ci-dessous /sidəsu/ adv below.

ci-dessus /sidəsy/ adv above.

cidre /sidʀ/ nm cider.

ciel (pl **cieux, ciels**) /sjɛl, sjø/ nm sky;
(Relig) heaven; **cieux** (Relig) heaven.

cierge /sjɛʀʒ/ nm (church) candle.

cigale /sigal/ nf cicada.

cigare /sigaʀ/ nm cigar.

cigarette /sigaʀɛt/ nf cigarette.

cigogne /sigɔɲ/ nf stork.

ci-joint /siʒwɛ̃/ adv enclosed.

cil /sil/ nm eyelash.

cime /sim/ nf peak, tip.

ciment /simɑ̃/ nm cement.

cimetière /simtjɛʀ/ nm cemetery, graveyard; ~ **de voitures** breaker's yard.

cinéaste /sineast/ nmf film-maker.

cinéma /sinema/ nm cinema; (US) movie theater. **cinémathèque** nf film archive; (salle) film theatre. **cinématographique** adj cinema.

cinéphile /sinefil/ nmf film lover.

cinglant, ~e /sɛ̃glɑ̃, -t/ adj (vent) biting; (remarque) scathing.

cinglé, ~e /sɛ̃gle/ adj 1 crazy.

cinq /sɛ̃k/ adj & nm five.

cinquante /sɛ̃kɑ̃t/ adj & nm fifty.

cinquième /sɛ̃kjɛm/ adj & nmf fifth.

> **Cinquième République** As established by the constitution of 1958 and still in force today, the Cinquième République refers to the system of government established by Charles de Gaulle, enshrining a strong executive and institutions to guarantee stability.

---

cintre /sɛ̃tʀ/ nm coat-hanger; (Archit) curve.

cirage /siʀaʒ/ nm polish.

circoncision /siʀkɔ̃sizjɔ̃/ nf circumcision.

circonflexe /siʀkɔ̃flɛks/ adj circumflex.

circonscription /siʀkɔ̃skʀipsjɔ̃/ nf district; ~ **électorale** constituency; (US) district; (de conseiller, maire) ward.

circonscrire /siʀkɔ̃skʀiʀ/ 30 vt (incendie, épidémie) contain; (sujet) define.

circonspect, ~e /siʀkɔ̃spɛkt/ adj circumspect.

circonstance /siʀkɔ̃stɑ̃s/ nf circumstance; (situation) situation; (occasion) occasion; ~s **atténuantes** mitigating circumstances.

circuit /siʀkɥi/ nm circuit; (trajet) tour, trip.

circulaire /siʀkylɛʀ/ adj & nf circular.

circulation /siʀkylasjɔ̃/ nf circulation; (de véhicules) traffic.

circuler /siʀkyle/ 1 vi (se répandre, être distribué) circulate; (aller d'un lieu à un autre) get around; (en voiture) travel; (piéton) walk; (être en service) (bus, train) run; **faire** ~ (badauds)

move on; (rumeur) spread.

cire /siʀ/ nf wax.

ciré /siʀe/ nm oilskin.

cirer /siʀe/ 1 vt polish.

cirque /siʀk/ nm circus; (arène) amphitheatre; (désordre: fig) chaos; **faire le** ~**!** make a racket 1.

ciseau (pl ~x) /sizo/ nm chisel; ~x scissors.

ciseler /sizle/ 6 vt chisel.

citadelle /sitadɛl/ nf citadel.

citadin, ~e /sitadɛ̃, -in/ nm, f city-dweller. ● adj city.

citation /sitasjɔ̃/ nf quotation; (Jur) summons.

cité /site/ nf city; (logements) housing estate; ~ **universitaire** (university) halls of residence.

citer /site/ 1 vt quote, cite; (Jur) summon.

citerne /sitɛʀn/ nf tank.

citoyen, ~ne /sitwajɛ̃, -ɛn/ nm, f citizen.

citron /sitʀɔ̃/ nm lemon; ~ **vert** lime. **citronnade** nf lemon squash, (still) lemonade.

citrouille /sitʀuj/ nf pumpkin.

civet /sivɛ/ nm stew; ~ **de lièvre** jugged hare.

civière /sivjɛʀ/ nf stretcher.

civil, ~e /sivil/ adj civil; (non militaire) civilian; (poli) civil. ● nm civilian; **dans le** ~ in civilian life; **en** ~ in plain clothes.

civilisation /sivilizasjɔ̃/ nf civilization.

civiliser /sivilize/ 1 vt civilize. □ **se** ~ vpr become civilized.

civique /sivik/ adj civic.

clair, ~e /klɛʀ/ adj clear; (éclairé) light, bright; (couleur) light; **le plus** ~ **de** most of. ● adv clearly; **il faisait** ~ it was already light. ● nm ~ **de lune** moonlight; **tirer une histoire au** ~ get to the bottom of things. **clairement** adv clearly.

clairière /klɛʀjɛʀ/ nf clearing.

clairsemé, ~e /klɛʀsəme/ adj sparse.

clamer /klame/ 1 vt proclaim.

clameur /klamœʀ/ nf clamour.

clan /klɑ̃/ nm clan.

clandestin, ~e /klɑ̃dɛstɛ̃, -in/ adj secret; (journal) underground; (immigra-

tion, travail) illegal; **passager** ∼ stowaway.

clapier /klapje/ *nm* (rabbit) utch.

clapoter /klapɔte/ ◻ *vi* lap.

claquage /klaka3/ *nm* strained muscle; **se faire un** ∼ pull a muscle.

claque /klak/ *nf* slap.

claquer /klake/ ◻ *vi* bang; (*porte*) slam, bang; (*fouet*) crack; (se casser ◻) conk out; (mourir ◻) snuff it!; ∼ **des doigts** snap one's fingers; ∼ **des mains** clap one's hands; **il claque des dents** his teeth are chattering. ● *vt* (*porte*) slam, bang; (*dépenser* ◻) blow; (*fatiguer* ◻) tire out.

claquettes /klakɛt/ *nfpl* tapdancing.

clarifier /klaʀifje/ ◻ *vt* clarify.

clarinette /klaʀinɛt/ *nf* clarinet.

clarté /klaʀte/ *nf* light, brightness; (netteté) clarity.

classe /klas/ *nf* class; (salle: Scol) class-room; (cours) class, lesson; **aller en** ∼ go to school; **faire la** ∼ teach; ∼ **ouvrière/moyenne** working/middle class.

classement /klasmã/ *nm* classification; (d'élèves) grading; (de documents) filing; (rang) place, grade; (de coureur) placing.

classer /klase/ ◻ *vt* classify; (par mérite) grade; (*papiers*) file; (Jur) (*affaire*) close. ◻ **se** ∼ *vpr* rank.

classeur /klasœʀ/ *nm* (meuble) filing cabinet; (chemise) file; (à anneaux) ring binder.

classification /klasifikasjɔ̃/ *nf* classification.

classique /klasik/ *adj* classical; (de qualité) classic; (habituel) classic, standard. ● *nm* classic; (auteur) classical author.

clavecin /klavsɛ̃/ *nm* harpsichord.

clavicule /klavikyl/ *nf* collarbone.

clavier /klavje/ *nm* keyboard; ∼ **numérique** keypad.

clé, clef /kle/ *nf* key; (outil) spanner; (Mus) clef; ∼ **anglaise** (monkey-)wrench; ∼ **de contact** ignition key; ∼ **à molette** adjustable spanner; ∼ **de voûte** keystone.● *adj inv* key.

clémence /klemãs/ *nf* (de climat) mildness; (indulgence) leniency.

clergé /klɛʀ3e/ *nm* clergy.

clérical, ∼e (*mpl* **-aux**) /kleʀikal, -o/ *adj* clerical.

clic /klik/ *nm* (Ordinat) click.

cliché /kliʃe/ *nm* cliché; (Photo) negative.

client, ∼e /klijã, -t/ *nm, f* customer; (d'un avocat) client; (d'un médecin) patient; (d'hôtel) guest; (de taxi) passenger.

clientèle /klijãtɛl/ *nf* customers, clientele; (d'un avocat) clients, practice; (d'un médecin) patients, practice; (soutien) custom.

cligner /kliɲe/ ◻ *vi* ∼ **des yeux** blink; ∼ **de l'œil** wink.

clignotant /kliɲɔtã/ *nm* (Auto) indicator, turn.

clignoter /kliɲɔte/ ◻ *vi* blink; (lumière) flicker; (comme signal) flash.

climat /klima/ *nm* climate.

climatisation /klimatizasjɔ̃/ *nf* air-conditioning.

clin d'œil /klɛ̃dœj/ *nm* wink; **en un** ∼ in a flash.

clinique /klinik/ *adj* clinical. ● *nf* (private) clinic.

clinquant, ∼e /klɛ̃kã, -t/ *adj* showy.

clip /klip/ *nm* video.

cliquer /klike/ ◻ *vi* (Ordinat) click (sur on).

cliqueter /klikte/ ◻ *vi* (couverts) clink; (clés, monnaie) jingle; (ferraille) rattle. **cliquetis** *nm* clink(ing), jingle, rattle.

clivage /kliva3/ *nm* divide.

clochard, ∼e /klɔʃaʀ, -d/ *nm, f* tramp.

cloche /klɔʃ/ *nf* bell; (imbécile ◻) idiot; ∼ **à fromage** cheese-cover.

cloche-pied: à ∼ /aklɔʃpje/ *loc* **sauter à** ∼ hop on one leg.

clocher /klɔʃe/ *nm* bell-tower; (pointu) steeple; **de** ∼ parochial.

cloison /klwazɔ̃/ *nf* partition; (fig) barrier.

cloître /klwatʀ/ *nm* cloister. **cloîtrer (se)** ◻ *vpr* shut oneself away.

clonage /klɔna3/ *nm* clonage.

cloner /klone/ ◻ *vt* clone.

cloque /klɔk/ *nf* blister.

clos, ∼e /klo, -z/ *adj* closed.

clôture /klotyʀ/ *nf* fence; (fermeture) closure; (de magasin, bureau) closing; (de débat, liste) close; (en Bourse) close of trading. **clôturer** ◻ *vt* en-

clou | colique

close, fence in; (*festival, séance*) close.

clou /klu/ *nm* nail; (furoncle) boil; (de spectacle) star attraction; **les ~s** (passage) pedestrian crossing; (US) crosswalk.

clouer /klue/ **1** *vt* nail down; (fig) nail down; **être cloué au lit** be confined to one's bed; **~ le bec à qn** shut sb up.

clouté, **~e** /klute/ *adj* studded; **passage ~** pedestrian crossing; (US) crosswalk.

CMU *abrév f* free health care for people on low incomes.

coaliser (se) /(sə)kɔalize/ **1** *vpr* join forces.

coalition /kɔalisjɔ̃/ *nf* coalition.

cobaye /kɔbaj/ *nm* guinea-pig.

cocaïne /kɔkain/ *nf* cocaine.

cocasse /kɔkas/ *adj* comical.

coccinelle /kɔksinɛl/ *nf* ladybird; (US) ladybug.

cocher /kɔʃe/ **1** *vt* tick (off), check. ● *nm* coachman.

cochon, **~ne** /kɔʃɔ̃, -ɔn/ *nm, f* (personne ⚠) pig. ● *adj* ⚠ filthy. ● *nm* pig. **cochonnerie** *nf* (saleté ⚠) filth; (marchandise ⚠) rubbish, junk.

cocon /kɔkɔ̃/ *nm* cocoon.

cocorico /kɔkɔʀikɔ/ *nm* cock-a-doodle-doo.

cocotier /kɔkɔtje/ *nm* coconut palm.

cocotte /kɔkɔt/ *nf* (marmite) casserole; **~ minute®** pressure-cooker; **ma ~** ⚠ my dear.

cocu, **~e** /kɔky/ *nm, f* ⚠ deceived husband, deceived wife.

code /kɔd/ *nm* code; **~s** dipped headlights; **se mettre en ~s** dip one's headlights; **~ (à) barres** bar code; **~ confidentiel (d'identification)** PIN number; **~ postal** post code; (US) zip code; **~ de la route** Highway Code. **coder** **1** *vt* code, encode.

coéquipier, -ière /kɔekipje, -jɛʀ/ *nm, f* team mate.

cœur /kœʀ/ *nm* heart; (aux cartes) hearts (+ *pl*); **~ d'artichaut** artichoke heart; **~ de palmier** palm heart; **à ~ ouvert** (*opération*) open-heart; (*parler*) freely; **avoir bon ~** be kind-hearted; **de bon ~** willingly; (*rire*) heartily; **par ~** by heart; **avoir mal au ~** feel sick *ou* nauseous; **je veux en avoir le ~**

net I want to be clear in my own mind (about it).

coffre /kɔfʀ/ *nm* chest; (pour argent) safe; (Auto) boot; (US) trunk. **coffre-fort** (*pl* **coffres-forts**) *nm* safe.

coffret /kɔfʀɛ/ *nm* casket, box; (de livres, cassettes) boxed set.

cogner /kɔɲe/ **1** *vt/i* knock. □ **se ~** *vpr* knock oneself; **se ~ la tête** bump one's head.

cohabiter /kɔabite/ **1** *vi* live together.

cohérent, **~e** /kɔeʀã, -t/ *adj* coherent; (homogène) consistent.

cohue /kɔy/ *nf* crowd.

coi, **~te** /kwa, -t/ *adj* silent.

coiffe /kwaf/ *nf* headgear.

coiffer /kwafe/ **1** *vt* do the hair of; (*chapeau*) put on; (surmonter) cap; **~ qn d'un chapeau** put a hat on sb; **coiffé de** wearing; **être bien/mal coiffé** have tidy/untidy hair. □ **se ~** *vpr* do one's hair.

coiffeur, -euse /kwafœʀ, -øz/ *nm, f* hairdresser. **coiffeuse** *nf* dressing-table.

coiffure /kwafyʀ/ *nf* hairstyle; (métier) hairdressing; (chapeau) hat.

coin /kwɛ̃/ *nm* corner; (endroit) spot; (cale) wedge; **au ~ du feu** by the fireside; **dans le ~** locally; **du ~** local.

coincer /kwɛ̃se/ **10** *vt* jam; (caler) wedge; (attraper ⚠) catch. □ **se ~** *vpr* get jammed.

coïncidence /kɔɛ̃sidɑ̃s/ *nf* coincidence.

coing /kwɛ̃/ *nm* quince.

coït /kɔit/ *nm* intercourse.

col /kɔl/ *nm* collar; (de bouteille) neck; (de montagne) pass; **~ blanc** white-collar worker; **~ roulé** polo-neck; (US) turtle-neck; **~ de l'utérus** cervix; **se casser le ~ du fémur** break one's hip.

colère /kɔlɛʀ/ *nf* anger; (accès) fit of anger; **en ~** angry; **se mettre en ~** lose one's temper; **faire une ~** throw a tantrum.

coléreux, -euse /kɔleʀø, -z/ *adj* quick-tempered.

colin /kɔlɛ̃/ *nm* (merlu) hake; (lieu noir) coley.

colique /kɔlik/ *nf* diarrhoea; (Méd) colic.

colis /kɔli/ *nm* parcel.

collaborateur, -trice /kɔlabɔʀatœʀ, -tʀis/ *nm, f* collaborator; (journaliste) contributor; (collègue) colleague.

collaboration /kɔlabɔʀasjɔ̃/ *nf* collaboration (à on); (à ouvrage, projet) contribution (à to).

collaborer /kɔlabɔʀe/ **1** *vi* collaborate (à on); ~ **à** (*journal*) contribute to.

collant, ~e /kɔlɑ̃, -t/ *adj* (moulant) kin-tight; (poisseux) sticky. ● *nm* (bas) tights; (US) panty hose.

colle /kɔl/ *nf* glue; (en pâte) paste; (problème 🄸) poser; (Scol 🄸) detention.

collecter /kɔlɛkte/ **1** *vt* collect.

collectif, -ive /kɔlɛktif, -v/ *adj* collective; (billet, voyage) group.

collection /kɔlɛksjɔ̃/ *nf* collection; (ouvrages) series (+ *sg*); (du même auteur) set. **collectionner** **1** *vt* collect. **collectionneur, -euse** *nm, f* collector.

collectivité /kɔlɛktivite/ *nf* community; ~ **locale** local authority.

collège /kɔlɛʒ/ *nm* secondary school (*up to age 15*); (US) junior high school; (assemblée) college. **collégien, ~ne** *nm, f* schoolboy, schoolgirl.

collègue /kɔlɛg/ *nmf* colleague.

coller /kɔle/ **1** *vt* stick; (avec colle liquide) glue; (affiche) stick up; (mettre 🄸) stick; (par une question 🄸) stump; (Scol 🄸) **se faire ~** get a detention; **je me suis fait ~ en maths** I failed ou flunked maths. ● *vi* stick (à to); (être collant) be sticky; ~ **à** (convenir à) fit, correspond to.

collet /kɔlɛ/ *nm* (piège) snare; ~ **monté** prim and proper; **mettre la main au ~ de qn** collar sb.

collier /kɔlje/ *nm* necklace; (de chien) collar.

colline /kɔlin/ *nf* hill.

collision /kɔlizjɔ̃/ *nf* (choc) collision; (lutte) clash; **entrer en ~ (avec)** collide (with).

collyre /kɔliʀ/ *nm* eye drops (+ *pl*).

colmater /kɔlmate/ **1** *vt* plug, seal.

colombe /kɔlɔ̃b/ *nf* dove.

Colombie /kɔlɔ̃bi/ *nf* Colombia.

colon /kɔlɔ̃/ *nm* settler.

colonel /kɔlɔnɛl/ *nm* colonel.

colonie /kɔlɔni/ *nf* colony; ~ **de vacances** children's holiday camp.

Colonie de vacances A holiday village or summer camp where children take part in a variety of outdoor activities. Originally set up to give poorer children a means of getting out into the countryside, they are still largely state-subsidized. Colloquially they are referred to as *la/une colo*.

colonne /kɔlɔn/ *nf* column; ~ **vertébrale** spine; **en ~ par deux** in double file.

colorant /kɔlɔʀɑ̃/ *nm* colouring.

colorier /kɔlɔʀje/ 🄴🄵 *vt* colour (in).

colosse /kɔlɔs/ *nm* giant.

colza /kɔlza/ *nm* rape(-seed).

coma /kɔma/ *nm* coma; **dans le ~** in a coma.

combat /kɔ̃ba/ *nm* fight; (Sport) match; ~**s** fighting. **combatif, -ive** *adj* eager to fight; (*esprit*) fighting.

combattre /kɔ̃batʀ/ **1** *vt/i* fight.

combien /kɔ̃bjɛ̃/ *adv* ~ **(de)** quantité) how much; (nombre) how many; (temps) how long; ~ **il a changé!** (comme) how he has changed!; ~ **y a-t-il d'ici à...?** how far is it to...?; **on est le ~ aujourd'hui?** what's the date today?

combinaison /kɔ̃binezɔ̃/ *nf* combination; (de femme) slip; (bleu de travail) boiler suit; (US) overalls; ~ **d'aviateur** flying-suit; ~ **de plongée** wetsuit.

combine /kɔ̃bin/ *nf* trick; (fraude) fiddle; (intrigue) scheme.

combiné /kɔ̃bine/ *nm* (de téléphone) receiver, handset.

combiner /kɔ̃bine/ **1** *vt* (réunir) combine; (calculer) devise; ~ **de faire** plan to do.

comble /kɔ̃bl/ *adj* packed. ● *nm* height; ~**s** (mansarde) attic, loft; **c'est le ~!** that's the (absolute) limit!

combler /kɔ̃ble/ **1** *vt* fill; (perte, déficit) make good; (désir) fulfil; ~ **qn de cadeaux** lavish gifts on sb.

combustible /kɔ̃bystibl/ *nm* fuel.

comédie /kɔmedi/ *nf* comedy; (histoire🄸) fuss; ~ **musicale** musical; **jouer la ~** put on an act. **comédien,**

~**ne** *nm, f* actor,actress.

comestible /kɔmɛstibl/ *adj* edible.

comète /kɔmɛt/ *nf* comet.

comique /kɔmik/ *adj* comical, funny; (*genre*) comic. ● *nm* (acteur) comic; (comédie) comedy; (côté drôle) comical aspect.

commandant /kɔmɑ̃dɑ̃/ *nm* commander; (dans l'armée de terre) major; ~ **(de bord)** captain; ~ **en chef** Commander-in-Chief.

commande /kɔmɑ̃d/ *nf* (Comm) order; (Tech) control; ~**s** (d'avion) controls.

commandement /kɔmɑ̃dmɑ̃/ *nm* command; (Relig) commandment.

commander /kɔmɑ̃de/ **1** *vt* command; (acheter) order; (*étude, œuvre d'art*) commission; ~ **à** (maîtriser) control; ~ **à qn de** command sb to. ● *vi* be in command.

comme /kɔm/ *adv* ~ **c'est bon!** it's so good!; ~ **il est mignon!** isn't he sweet! ● *conj* (dans une comparaison) as; (dans une équivalence, illustration) like; (en tant que) as; (puisque) as, since; (au moment où) as; **vif ~ l'éclair** as quick as a flash; **travailler ~ sage-femme** work as a midwife; ~ **ci ~ ça** so-so; ~ **il faut** properly; ~ **pour faire** as if to do; **jolie ~ tout** as pretty as anything; **qu'est-ce qu'il y a ~ légumes?** what is there in the way of vegetables?

commencer /kɔmɑ̃se/ **10** *vt/i* begin, start; ~ **à faire** begin *ou* start to do.

comment /kɔmɑ̃/ *adv* how; ~**?** (répétition) pardon?; (surprise) what?; ~ **est-il?** what is he like?; **le ~ et le pourquoi** the whys and wherefores.

commentaire /kɔmɑ̃tɛʀ/ *nm* comment; (d'un texte, événement) commentary. **commentateur, -trice** *nm, f* commentator.

commenter /kɔmɑ̃te/ **1** *vt* comment on; (*film, visite*) provide a commentary for; (radio,TV) commentate.

commérages /kɔmeʀaʒ/ *nmpl* gossip.

commerçant, ~**e** /kɔmɛʀsɑ̃, -t/ *adj* (*rue*) shopping; (*personne*) business-minded. ● *nm, f* shopkeeper.

commerce /kɔmɛʀs/ *nm* trade, commerce; (magasin) business; **faire du ~** be in business; ~ **électrique** e-commerce; ~ **équitable** fair trade.

commercial, ~**e** (*mpl* **-iaux**) kɔmɛʀsjal, -jo/ *adj* commercial. **commercialiser** **1** *vt* market.

commettre /kɔmɛtʀ/ **42** *vt* commit.

commis /kɔmi/ *nm* (de magasin) assistant; (de bureau) clerk.

commissaire /kɔmisɛʀ/ *nm* commissioner; (Sport) steward; ~ **(de police)** (police) superintendent. **commissaire-priseur** (*pl* **commissaires-priseurs**) *nm* auctioneer.

commissariat /kɔmisaʀja/ *nm* ~ **(de police)** police station.

commission /kɔmisjɔ̃/ *nf* commission; (course) errand; (message) message; ~**s** shopping.

commode /kɔmɔd/ *adj* handy; (facile) easy; **il n'est pas ~** he's a difficult customer. ● *nf* chest (of drawers). **commodité** *nf* convenience.

commotion /kɔmosjɔ̃/ *nf* ~ **(cérébrale)** concussion.

commun, ~**e** /kɔmœ̃, -yn/ *adj* common; (*effort, action*) joint; (*frais, pièce*) shared; **en ~** jointly; **avoir** *ou* **mettre en ~** share; **le ~ des mortels** ordinary mortals. **communal,** ~**e** (*mpl* **-aux**) *adj* of the commune, local.

communauté /kɔmynote/ *nf* community.

commune /kɔmyn/ *nf* (circonscription, collectivité) commune.

> **Commune** The smallest administrative unit in France, headed by a *maire* and a *conseil municipal*. Each village, town and city is a *commune*, of which there are 36,000 throughout the country.

---

communicatif, -ive /kɔmynikatif, -v/ *adj* (*personne*) talkative; (*gaieté*) infectious.

communication /kɔmynikasjɔ̃/ *nf* communication; (téléphonique) call; ~**s** (relations) communications (+ *pl*); **voies** *ou* **moyens de ~** communications (+ *pl*).

communier /kɔmynje/ **45** *vi* (Relig) receive communion; (fig) commune.

communiqué /kɔmynike/ *nm* statement; (de presse) communiqué.

communiquer /kɔmynike/ **1** *vt* pass on, communicate; (*date, décision*) an-

nounce. ● *vi* communicate. ☐ **se ~ à**
vpr spread to.

communiste /kɔmynist/ *adj & nmf*
communist.

commutateur /kɔmytatœʀ/ *nm*
(Électr) switch.

compagne /kɔ̃paɲ/ *nf* companion.

compagnie /kɔ̃paɲi/ *nf* company;
tenir ~ à keep company; **en ~ de**
together with; **~ aérienne** airline.

compagnon /kɔ̃paɲɔ̃/ *nm* companion.

comparable /kɔ̃paʀabl/ *adj* comparable (à to). **comparaison** *nf* comparison; (littéraire) simile.

comparaître /kɔ̃paʀɛtʀ/ 18 *vi* (Jur)
appear (**devant** before).

comparatif, -ive /kɔ̃paʀatif, -v/ *adj &*
nm comparative.

comparer /kɔ̃paʀe/ 1 *vt* compare (à
with). ☐ **se ~** *vpr* compare oneself;
(être comparable) be comparable.

compartiment /kɔ̃paʀtimɑ̃/ *nm* compartment.

comparution /kɔ̃paʀysjɔ̃/ *nf* (Jur) appearance.

compas /kɔ̃pa/ *nm* (pair of) compasses; (boussole) compass.

compassion /kɔ̃pasjɔ̃/ *nf* compassion.

compatible /kɔ̃patibl/ *adj* compatible.

compatir /kɔ̃patiʀ/ 2 *vi* sympathize;
~ à share in.

compatriote /kɔ̃patʀijɔt/ *nmf* compatriot.

compensation /kɔ̃pɑ̃sasjɔ̃/ *nf* compensation. **compenser** 1 *vt* compensate for, make up for.

compère /kɔ̃pɛʀ/ *nm* accomplice.

compétence /kɔ̃petɑ̃s/ *nf* competence; (fonction) domain, sphere; **entrer dans les ~s de qn** come in sb's domain. **compétent, ~e** *adj* competent.

compétition /kɔ̃petisjɔ̃/ *nf* competition; (sportive) event; **de ~** competitive.

complaire (se) /(sə)kɔ̃plɛʀ/ 47 *vpr* **se
~ dans** delight in.

complaisance /kɔ̃plɛzɑ̃s/ *nf* kindness;
(indulgence) indulgence.

complément /kɔ̃plemɑ̃/ *nm* supplement; (Gram) complement; **~ (d'objet)** (Gram) object; **~ d'information** further information. **complémentaire** *adj* complementary; (renseignements) supplementary.

complet, -ète /kɔ̃plɛ, -t/ *adj* complete;
(train, hôtel) full. ● *nm* suit.

compléter /kɔ̃plete/ 14 *vt* complete;
(agrémenter) complement. ☐ **se ~** *vpr*
complement each other.

complexe /kɔ̃plɛks/ *adj* complex. ●
nm (sentiment, bâtiments) complex.

complexé, ~e /kɔ̃plekse/ *adj* être **~**
have a lot of hang-ups.

complice /kɔ̃plis/ *nm* accomplice.

compliment /kɔ̃plimɑ̃/ *nm* compliment; **~s** (félicitations) compliments,
congratulations.

compliquer /kɔ̃plike/ 1 *vt* complicate. ☐ **se ~** *vpr* become complicated.

complot /kɔ̃plo/ *nm* plot.

comportement /kɔ̃pɔʀtəmɑ̃/ *nm* behaviour; (de joueur, voiture) performance.

comporter /kɔ̃pɔʀte/ 1 *vt* (être composé de) comprise; (inclure) include;
(risque) entail. ☐ **se ~** *vpr* behave;
(joueur, voiture) perform.

composant /kɔ̃pozɑ̃/ *nm* component.

composé, ~e /kɔ̃poze/ *adj* composite;
(salade) mixed; (guindé) affected.
● *nm* compound.

composer /kɔ̃poze/ 1 *vt* make up,
compose; (chanson, visage) compose;
(numéro) dial; (page) typeset. ● *vi*
(transiger) compromise. ☐ **se ~ de**
vpr be made up ou composed of.
compositeur, -trice *nm, f* (Mus)
composer.

composter /kɔ̃pɔste/ 1 *vt* (billet)
punch.

compote /kɔ̃pɔt/ *nf* stewed fruit; **~
de pommes** stewed apples.

compréhensible /kɔ̃pʀeɑ̃sibl/ *adj*
understandable; (intelligible) comprehensible.

compréhensif, -ive /kɔ̃pʀeɑ̃sif, -v/
adj understanding.

compréhension /kɔ̃pʀeɑ̃sjɔ̃/ *nf*
understanding, comprehension.

comprendre /kɔ̃pʀɑ̃dʀ/ 50 *vt* understand; (comporter) comprise, be made
up of. ☐ **se ~** *vpr* (personnes) understand each other; **ça se comprend**
that is understandable.

compresse /kɔ̃pʀɛs/ *nf* compress.

comprimé /kɔ̃pʀime/ *nm* tablet.

comprimer /kɔ̃pʀime/ 1 *vt* compress; (réduire) reduce.

compris, ~e /kɔ̃pʀi, -z/ *adj* included; (d'accord) agreed; **~ entre** (contained) between; **service (non) ~** service (not) included; **tout ~** (all) inclusive; **y ~** including.

compromettre /kɔ̃pʀɔmɛtʀ/ 42 *vt* compromise. **compromis** *nm* compromise.

comptabilité /kɔ̃patibilite/ *nf* accountancy; (comptes) accounts; (service) accounts department.

comptable /kɔ̃tabl/ *adj* accounting. ● *nmf* accountant.

comptant /kɔ̃tɑ̃/ *adv* (payer) (in) cash; (acheter) for cash.

compte /kɔ̃t/ *nm* count; (facture, comptabilité) account; (nombre exact) right number; **~ bancaire, ~ en banque** bank account; **prendre qch en ~, tenir ~ de qch** take sth into account; **se rendre ~ de** realize; **demander/rendre des ~s** ask for/ give an explanation; **à bon ~** cheaply; **s'en tirer à bon ~** get off lightly; **travailler à son ~** be self-employed; **faire le ~ de** count; **pour le ~ de** on behalf of; **sur le ~ de** about; **au bout du ~** all things considered; **à rebours** countdown.

compte-gouttes /kɔ̃tgut/ *nm inv* (Méd) dropper; **au ~** (fig) in dribs and drabs.

compter /kɔ̃te/ 1 *vt* count; (prévoir) allow, reckon on; (facturer) charge for; (avoir) have; (classer) consider; **~ faire** intend to do. ● *vi* (calculer, importer) count; **~ avec** reckon with; **~ parmi** (figurer) be considered among; **~ sur** rely on, count on.

compte(-)rendu /kɔ̃tʀɑ̃dy/ *nm* report; (de film, livre) review.

compteur /kɔ̃tœʀ/ *nm* meter; **~ de vitesse** speedometer.

comptine /kɔ̃tin/ *nf* nursery rhyme.

comptoir /kɔ̃twaʀ/ *nm* counter; (de café) bar.

comte /kɔ̃t/ *nm* count.

comté /kɔ̃te/ *nm* county.

comtesse /kɔ̃tɛs/ *nf* countess.

con, ~ne /kɔ̃, kɔn/ *adj* 🅧 bloody stupid 🅧. ● *nm, f* 🅧 bloody fool 🅧.

concentrer /kɔ̃sɑ̃tʀe/ 1 *vt* concentrate. □ **se ~** *vpr* be concentrated.

concept /kɔ̃sɛpt/ *nm* concept.

concerner /kɔ̃sɛʀne/ 1 *vt* concern; **en ce qui me concerne** as far as I am concerned.

concert /kɔ̃sɛʀ/ *nm* concert; **de ~** in unison.

concerter /kɔ̃sɛʀte/ 1 *vt* organize, prepare. □ **se ~** *vpr* confer.

concession /kɔ̃sesjɔ̃/ *nf* concession; (terrain) plot.

concevoir /kɔ̃svwaʀ/ 52 *vt* (imaginer, engendrer) conceive; (comprendre) understand; (élaborer) design.

concierge /kɔ̃sjɛʀʒ/ *nmf* caretaker.

concilier /kɔ̃silje/ 45 *vt* reconcile. □ **se ~** *vpr* (s'attirer) win (over).

concis, ~e /kɔ̃si, -z/ *adj* concise.

conclure /kɔ̃klyʀ/ 16 *vt* conclude; **~ en faveur de** conclude in favour of. ● *vi* **~ en faveur de/contre** find in favour of/against. **conclusion** *nf* conclusion.

concombre /kɔ̃kɔ̃bʀ/ *nm* cucumber.

concordance /kɔ̃kɔʀdɑ̃s/ *nf* agreement.

concourir /kɔ̃kuʀiʀ/ 20 *vi* compete. ● *vt* **~ à** contribute towards.

concours /kɔ̃kuʀ/ *nm* competition; (examen) competitive examination; (aide) help; (de circonstances) combination.

concret, -ète /kɔ̃kʀɛ, -t/ *adj* concrete.

concrétiser /kɔ̃kʀetize/ 1 *vt* give concrete form to. □ **se ~** *vpr* materialize.

conçu, ~e /kɔ̃sy/ *adj* **bien/mal ~** well/badly designed.

concubinage /kɔ̃kybinaʒ/ *nm* cohabitation; **vivre en ~** live together, cohabit.

concurrence /kɔ̃kyʀɑ̃s/ *nf* competition; **faire ~ à** compete with; **jusqu'à ~ de** up to a limit of.

concurrencer /kɔ̃kyʀɑ̃se/ 10 *vt* compete with.

concurrent, ~e /kɔ̃kyʀɑ̃, -t/ *nm, f* competitor; (Scol) candidate. ● *adj* rival.

condamnation /kɔ̃danasjɔ̃/ *nf* condemnation; (peine) sentence; **~ centralisée des portières** central locking. **condamné, ~e** *nm, f* condemned man, condemned woman. **condamner** 1 *vt* (censurer, obliger) condemn; (Jur) sentence; (porte) block up.

condition /kɔ̃disjɔ̃/ nf condition; ~s
(prix) terms; à ~ de ou que provided
(that); sans ~ unconditional(ly); sous
~ conditionally.
conditionnel, ~le /kɔ̃disjɔnɛl/ adj
conditional. ● nm conditional (tense).
conditionnement /kɔ̃disjɔnmā/ nm
conditioning; (emballage) packaging.
condoléances /kɔ̃dɔleās/ nfpl condolences.
conducteur, -trice /kɔ̃dyktœr, -tris/
nm, f driver.
conduire /kɔ̃dɥiʀ/ 17 vt take (à to);
(guider) lead; (Auto) drive; (affaire)
conduct; ~ à (faire aboutir) lead to.
● vi drive. □ se ~ vpr behave.
conduit /kɔ̃dɥi/ nm duct.
conduite /kɔ̃dɥit/ nf conduct, behaviour; (Auto) driving; (tuyau) pipe; voiture avec ~ à droite right-hand
drive car.
confection /kɔ̃fɛksjɔ̃/ nf making; de
~ ready-made; la ~ the clothing industry.
conférence /kɔ̃feʀās/ nf conference;
(exposé) lecture; ~ au sommet summit meeting. **conférencier, -ière** nm, f
lecturer.
confesser /kɔ̃fese/ 1 vt confess. □ se
~ vpr go to confession.
confiance /kɔ̃fjās/ nf trust; avoir ~
en trust.
confiant, ~e /kɔ̃fjā, -t/ adj (assuré)
confident; (sans défiance) trusting.
confidence /kɔ̃fidās/ nf confidence.
confidentiel, ~le /kɔ̃fidāsjɛl/ adj
confidential.
confier /kɔ̃fje/ 45 vt ~ à qn entrust sb
with; ~ un secret à qn tell sb a secret. □ se ~ à vpr confide in.
configuration /kɔ̃figyʀasjɔ̃/ nf configuration.
configurer /kɔ̃figyʀe/ vt configure.
confiner /kɔ̃fine/ 1 vt confine; ~ à
border on. □ se ~ vpr confine oneself
(à, dans to).
confirmation /kɔ̃fiʀmasjɔ̃/ nf confirmation. **confirmer** 1 vt confirm.
confiserie /kɔ̃fizʀi/ nf sweet shop; ~s
confectionery.
confisquer /kɔ̃fiske/ 1 vt confiscate.
confit, ~e /kɔ̃fi, -t/ adj candied;
(fruits) crystallized. ● nm ~ de ca-

nard confit of duck.
confiture /kɔ̃fityʀ/ nf jam.
conflit /kɔ̃fli/ nm conflict.
confondre /kɔ̃fɔ̃dʀ/ 3 vt confuse, mix
up; (étonner) confound. □ se ~ vpr
merge; se ~ en excuses apologize
profusely.
conforme /kɔ̃fɔʀm/ adj être ~ à
comply with; (être en accord) be in
keeping with.
conformer /kɔ̃fɔʀme/ 1 vt adapt.
□ se ~ à vpr conform to.
conformité /kɔ̃fɔʀmite/ nf compliance, conformity; agir en ~ avec act
in accordance with.
confort /kɔ̃fɔʀ/ nm comfort; tout ~
with all mod cons. **confortable** adj
comfortable.
confrère /kɔ̃fʀɛʀ/ nm colleague.
confronter /kɔ̃fʀɔ̃te/ 1 vt confront;
(textes) compare. □ se ~ à vpr be
confronted with.
confus, ~e /kɔ̃fy, -z/ adj confused;
(gêné) embarrassed.
congé /kɔ̃ʒe/ nm holiday; (arrêt momentané) time off, leave; (avis de départ) notice; en ~ on holiday ou
leave; ~ de maladie/maternité sick/
maternity leave; jour de ~ day off;
prendre ~ de take one's leave of.
congédier /kɔ̃ʒedje/ 45 vt dismiss.
congélateur /kɔ̃ʒelatœʀ/ nm freezer.
congeler /kɔ̃ʒle/ 6 vt freeze.
congère /kɔ̃ʒɛʀ/ nf snowdrift.
congrès /kɔ̃gʀɛ/ nm conference; (Pol)
congress.
conjoint, ~e /kɔ̃ʒwɛ̃, -t/ nm, f spouse.
● adj joint.
conjonctivite /kɔ̃ʒɔ̃ktivit/ nf conjunctivitis.
conjoncture /kɔ̃ʒɔ̃ktyʀ/ nf situation;
(économique) economic climate.
conjugaison /kɔ̃ʒygɛzɔ̃/ nf conjugation.
conjugal, ~e (mpl -aux) /kɔ̃ʒygal, -o/
adj conjugal, married.
conjuguer /kɔ̃ʒyge/ 1 vt (Gram) conjugate; (efforts) combine. □ se ~ vpr
(Gram) be conjugated; (facteurs) be
combined.
conjurer /kɔ̃ʒyʀe/ 1 vt (éviter) avert;
(implorer) beg.

connaissance /kɔnɛsɑ̃s/ nf knowledge; (personne) acquaintance; ~s (science) knowledge; **faire la ~ de** meet; (apprécier une personne) get to know; **perdre/reprendre ~** lose/regain consciousness; **sans ~** unconscious.

connaisseur /kɔnɛsœʀ/ nm expert, connoisseur.

connaître /kɔnɛtʀ/ 18 vt know; (difficultés, faim, succès) experience; **faire ~** make known. □ **se ~** vpr (se rencontrer) meet; **s'y ~ en** know (all) about.

connecter /kɔnɛkte/ 1 vt connect; **être/ne pas être connecté** be on-/off-line. □ **se ~ à** vpr (Ordinat) log on to.

connerie /kɔnʀi/ nf ⊠ **faire une ~** do something stupid; **dire des ~s** talk rubbish.

connexion /kɔnɛksjɔ̃/ nf (Ordinat) connection.

connu, ~e /kɔny/ adj well-known.

conquérant, ~e /kɔ̃keʀɑ̃, -t/ nm, f conqueror.

conquête /kɔ̃kɛt/ nf conquest.

consacrer /kɔ̃sakʀe/ 1 vt devote; (Relig) consecrate; (sanctionner) sanction. □ **se ~ à** vpr devote oneself to.

conscience /kɔ̃sjɑ̃s/ nf conscience; (perception) awareness; (de collectivité) consciousness; **avoir/prendre ~ de** be/become aware of; **perdre/reprendre ~** lose/regain consciousness; **avoir bonne/mauvaise ~** have a clear/guilty conscience.

conscient, ~e /kɔ̃sjɑ̃, -t/ adj conscious; **~ de** aware ou conscious of.

conseil /kɔ̃sɛj/ nm (piece of) advice; (assemblée) council, committee; (séance) meeting; (personne) consultant; **~ d'administration** board of directors; **~ en gestion** management consultant; **~ des ministres** Cabinet; **~ municipal** town council.

conseiller[1] /kɔ̃seje/ 1 vt advise; **~ à qn de** advise sb to; **~ qch à qn** recommend sth to sb.

conseiller,[2] **-ère** /kɔ̃seje, -jɛʀ/ nm, f adviser, counsellor; **~ municipal** town councillor; **~ d'orientation** careers adviser.

consentement /kɔ̃sɑ̃tmɑ̃/ nm consent.

conséquence /kɔ̃sekɑ̃s/ nf consequence; **en ~** (comme il convient) accordingly; **en ~ (de quoi)** as a result of which.

conséquent, ~e /kɔ̃sekɑ̃, -t/ adj consistent, logical; (important) substantial; **par ~** consequently, therefore.

conservateur, -trice /kɔ̃sɛʀvatœʀ, -tʀis/ adj conservative. ● nm, f (Pol) conservative; (de musée) curator. ● nm preservative.

conservation /kɔ̃sɛʀvasjɔ̃/ nf preservation; (d'espèce, patrimoine) conservation.

conservatoire /kɔ̃sɛʀvatwaʀ/ nm academy.

conserve /kɔ̃sɛʀv/ nf tinned ou canned food; **en ~** tinned, canned; **boîte de ~** tin, can.

conserver /kɔ̃sɛʀve/ 1 vt keep; (en bon état) preserve; (Culin) preserve. □ **se ~** vpr (Culin) keep.

considérer /kɔ̃sideʀe/ 14 vt consider; (respecter) esteem; **~ comme** consider to be.

consigne /kɔ̃siɲ/ nf (de gare) left-luggage office; (US) baggage checkroom; (somme) deposit; (ordres) orders; **~ automatique** left-luggage lockers; (US) baggage lockers.

consistance /kɔ̃sistɑ̃s/ nf consistency; (fig) substance, weight. **consistant, ~e** adj solid; (épais) thick.

consister /kɔ̃siste/ 1 vi ~ **en/dans** consist of/in; **~ à faire** consist in doing.

consoler /kɔ̃sɔle/ 1 vt console. □ **se ~** vpr find consolation; **se ~ de qch** get over sth.

consolider /kɔ̃sɔlide/ 1 vt strengthen; (fig) consolidate.

consommateur, -trice /kɔ̃sɔmatœʀ, -tʀis/ nm, f (Comm) consumer; (dans un café) customer.

consommation /kɔ̃sɔmasjɔ̃/ nf consumption; (accomplissement) consummation; (boisson) drink; **de ~** (Comm) consumer.

consommer /kɔ̃sɔme/ 1 vt consume, use; (manger) eat; (boire) drink; (mariage) consummate. □ **se ~** vpr (être mangé) be eaten; (être utilisé) be used.

consonne /kɔ̃sɔn/ nf consonant.

constat /kɔ̃sta/ nm (official) report; ~ (à l')amiable accident report drawn up by those involved.

constatation /kɔ̃statasjɔ̃/ nf observation, statement of fact. **constater 1** vt note, notice; (certifier) certify.

consternation /kɔ̃stɛʀnasjɔ̃/ nf dismay.

constipé, ~e /kɔ̃stipe/ adj constipated; (fig) uptight.

constituer /kɔ̃stitɥe/ **1** vt (composer) make up, constitute; (organiser) form; (être) constitute; **constitué de** made up of. □ se ~ vpr se ~ **prisonnier** give oneself up.

constitution /kɔ̃stitysjɔ̃/ nf formation, setting up; (Pol, Méd) constitution.

constructeur /kɔ̃stʀyktœʀ/ nm manufacturer, builder.

construction /kɔ̃stʀyksjɔ̃/ nf building; (structure, secteur) construction; (fabrication) manufacture.

construire /kɔ̃stʀɥiʀ/ **17** vt build; (système, phrase) construct.

consulat /kɔ̃syla/ nm consulate.

consultation /kɔ̃syltasjɔ̃/ nf consultation; (réception: Méd) surgery; (US) office; **heures de** ~ surgery ou office (US) hours.

consulter /kɔ̃sylte/ **1** vt consult. ● vi (médecin) hold surgery, see patients. □ se ~ vpr consult together.

contact /kɔ̃takt/ nm contact; (toucher) touch; **au** ~ **de** on contact with; (personne) by contact with, by seeing; **mettre/couper le** ~ (Auto) switch on/off the ignition; **prendre** ~ **avec** get in touch with. **contacter 1** vt contact.

contagieux, -ieuse /kɔ̃taʒjø, -z/ adj contagious.

conte /kɔ̃t/ nm tale; ~ **de fées** fairy tale.

contempler /kɔ̃tɑ̃ple/ **1** vt contemplate.

contemporain, ~e /kɔ̃tɑ̃pɔʀɛ̃, -ɛn/ adj & nm,f contemporary.

contenance /kɔ̃t(ə)nɑ̃s/ nf (volume) capacity; (allure) bearing; **perdre** ~ lose one's composure.

contenir /kɔ̃t(ə)niʀ/ **58** vt contain; (avoir une capacité de) hold. □ se ~ vpr contain oneself.

content, ~e /kɔ̃tɑ̃, -t/ adj pleased, happy (**de** with); ~ **de faire** pleased ou happy to do.

contenter /kɔ̃tɑ̃te/ **1** vt satisfy. □ se ~ **de** vpr content oneself with.

contenu /kɔ̃t(ə)ny/ nm (de récipient) contents (+ pl); (de texte) content.

conter /kɔ̃te/ **1** vt tell, relate.

contestation /kɔ̃tɛstasjɔ̃/ nf dispute; (opposition) protest.

contester /kɔ̃tɛste/ **1** vt question, dispute; (s'opposer) protest against. ● vi protest.

conteur, -euse /kɔ̃tœʀ, -øz/ nm, f storyteller.

contigu, ~ë /kɔ̃tigy/ adj adjacent (à to).

continent /kɔ̃tinɑ̃/ nm continent.

continu, ~e /kɔ̃tiny/ adj continuous.

continuer /kɔ̃tinɥe/ **1** vt continue. ● vi continue, go on; ~ **à** ou **de faire** carry on ou go on ou continue doing.

contorsionner (se) /(sə) kɔ̃tɔʀsjɔne/ vpr wriggle.

contour /kɔ̃tuʀ/ nm outline, contour; ~s (d'une route) twists and turns, bends.

contourner /kɔ̃tuʀne/ **1** vt go round, by-pass; (difficulté) get round.

contraceptif, -ive /kɔ̃tʀasɛptif, -v/ adj contraceptive. ● nm contraceptive. **contraception** nf contraception.

contracter /kɔ̃tʀakte/ **1** vt (maladie) contract; (dette) incur; (muscle) tense; (assurance) take out. □ se ~ vpr contract.

contractuel, ~le /kɔ̃tʀaktɥɛl/ nm, f (agent) traffic warden.

contradictoire /kɔ̃tʀadiktwaʀ/ adj contradictory; (débat) open.

contraignant, ~e /kɔ̃tʀɛɲɑ̃, -t/ adj restricting.

contraindre /kɔ̃tʀɛ̃dʀ/ **22** vt force, compel (à faire to do).

contrainte /kɔ̃tʀɛ̃t/ nf constraint.

contraire /kɔ̃tʀɛʀ/ adj opposite; ~ **à** contrary to. ● nm opposite; **au** ~ on the contrary; **au** ~ **de** unlike.

contrarier /kɔ̃tʀaʀje/ **45** vt annoy; (projet, volonté) frustrate; (chagriner) upset.

contraste /kɔ̃tʀast/ nm contrast.

contrat /kɔ̃tʀa/ nm contract.

contravention /kɔ̃tʀavɑ̃sjɔ̃/ nf (parking) ticket; **en ~** in breach (**à** of).

contre /kɔ̃tʀ(ə)/ prép against; (en échange de) for; **par ~** on the other hand; **tout ~** close by. **contreattaque** (pl **~s**) nf counterattack. **contre-attaquer** ① vt counter-attack. **contre-balancer** ⑩ vt counter-balance.

contrebande /kɔ̃tʀəbɑ̃d/ nf contraband; **faire la ~ de** smuggle.

contrebas: en ~ /ɑ̃kɔ̃tʀəba/ loc below.

contrebasse /kɔ̃tʀəbas/ nf double bass.

contrecœur: à ~ /akɔ̃tʀəkœr/ loc reluctantly.

contrecoup /kɔ̃tʀəku/ nm effects, repercussions.

contredire /kɔ̃tʀədiʀ/ ㊲ vt contradict. □ **se ~** vpr contradict oneself.

contrée /kɔ̃tʀe/ nf region; (pays) land.

contrefaçon /kɔ̃tʀəfasɔ̃/ nf (objet imité, action) forgery.

contre-indiqué, ~e /kɔ̃tʀɛ̃dike/ adj (Méd) contra-indicated; (déconseillé) not recommended.

contre-jour: à ~ /akɔ̃tʀəʒuʀ/ loc against the light.

contrepartie /kɔ̃tʀəpaʀti/ nf compensation; **en ~** in exchange, in return.

contreplaqué /kɔ̃tʀəplake/ nm plywood.

contresens /kɔ̃tʀəsɑ̃s/ nm misinterpretation; (absurdité) nonsense; **à ~** the wrong way.

contretemps /kɔ̃tʀətɑ̃/ nm hitch; **à ~** (fig) at the wrong time.

contribuable /kɔ̃tʀibɥabl/ nmf taxpayer.

contribuer /kɔ̃tʀibɥe/ ① vt contribute (**à** to, towards).

contrôle /kɔ̃tʀol/ nm (maîtrise) control; (vérification) check; (des prix) control; (poinçon) hallmark; (Scol) test; **~ continu** continuous assessment; **~ des changes** exchange control; **~ des naissances** birth control; **~ de soi-même** self-control; **~ technique** (des véhicules) MOT (test).

contrôler /kɔ̃tʀole/ ① vt (vérifier) check; (surveiller, maîtriser) control. □ **se ~** vpr control oneself.

contrôleur, -euse /kɔ̃tʀolœʀ, -øz/ nm, f inspector.

convaincre /kɔ̃vɛ̃kʀ/ ㊾ vt convince; **~ qn de faire** persuade sb to do.

convalescence /kɔ̃valesɑ̃s/ nf convalescence; **être en ~** be convalescing.

convenable /kɔ̃vnabl/ adj (correct) decent, proper; (approprié) suitable; (acceptable) reasonable, acceptable.

convenance /kɔ̃vnɑ̃s/ nf **à ma ~** to my satisfaction; **les ~s** convention.

convenir /kɔ̃vniʀ/ ㊳ vt/i be suitable; **~ à** suit; **~ que** admit that; **~ de qch** (avouer) admit sth; (s'accorder sur) agree on sth; **~ de faire** agree to do; **il convient de** it is advisable to; (selon les bienséances) it would be right to.

convention /kɔ̃vɑ̃sjɔ̃/ nf agreement, convention; (clause) article, clause; **~s** (convenances) convention; **de ~** conventional; **~ collective** industrial agreement.

convenu, ~e /kɔ̃vny/ adj agreed.

conversation /kɔ̃vɛʀsasjɔ̃/ nf conversation.

convertir /kɔ̃vɛʀtiʀ/ ② vt convert (**à** to; **en** into). □ **se ~** vpr be converted, convert.

conviction /kɔ̃viksjɔ̃/ nf conviction; **avoir la ~ que** be convinced that.

convivial, ~e (mpl **-iaux**) /kɔ̃vivjal, -jo/ adj convivial; (Ordinat) user-friendly.

convocation /kɔ̃vɔkasjɔ̃/ nf (Jur) summons; (d'une assemblée) convening; (document) notification to attend.

convoi /kɔ̃vwa/ nm convoy; (train) train; **~ (funèbre)** funeral procession.

convoquer /kɔ̃vɔke/ ① vt (assemblée) convene; (personne) summon; **être convoqué pour un entretien** be called for interview.

coopération /kɔɔpeʀasjɔ̃/ nf cooperation; (Mil) civilian national service abroad.

coordination /kɔɔʀdinasjɔ̃/ nf coordination. **coordonnées** nfpl coordinates; (adresse) address and telephone number.

copain /kɔpɛ̃/ nm friend; (petit ami) boyfriend.

copie /kɔpi/ nf copy; (Scol) paper; **~ d'examen** exam paper ou script; **~**

de sauvegarde back-up copy.

copier /kɔpje/ 🔢 *vt/i* copy; ~ **sur** (Scol) copy *ou* crib from.

copieux, -ieuse /kɔpjø, -z/ *adj* copious.

copine /kɔpin/ *nf* friend; (petite amie) girlfriend.

coq /kɔk/ *nm* cockerel.

coque /kɔk/ *nf* shell; (de bateau) hull.

coquelicot /kɔkliko/ *nm* poppy.

coqueluche /kɔklyʃ/ *nf* whooping cough.

coquet, -te /kɔkɛ, -t/ *adj* flirtatious; (élégant) pretty; (somme 🔢) tidy.

coquetier /kɔktje/ *nm* eggcup.

coquillage /kɔkijaʒ/ *nm* shellfish; (coquille) shell.

coquille /kɔkij/ *nf* shell; (faute) misprint; ~ **Saint-Jacques** scallop.

coquin, -in /kɔkɛ̃, -in/ *adj* mischievous. ● *nm, f* rascal.

cor /kɔʀ/ *nm* (Mus) horn; (au pied) corn.

corail (*pl* **-aux**) /kɔʀaj, -o/ *nm* coral.

corbeau (*pl* **~x**) /kɔʀbo/ *nm* (oiseau) crow.

corbeille /kɔʀbɛj/ *nf* basket; ~ **à papier** waste-paper basket.

corbillard /kɔʀbijaʀ/ *nm* hearse.

cordage /kɔʀdaʒ/ *nm* rope; ~s (Naut) rigging.

corde /kɔʀd/ *nf* rope; (d'arc, de violon) string; ~ **à linge** washing line; ~ **à sauter** skipping-rope; ~ **raide** tightrope; ~s **vocales** vocal cords.

cordon /kɔʀdɔ̃/ *nm* string, cord; ~ **de police** police cordon.

cordonnier /kɔʀdɔnje/ *nm* cobbler.

Corée /kɔʀe/ *nf* Korea.

coriace /kɔʀjas/ *adj* tough.

corne /kɔʀn/ *nf* horn.

corneille /kɔʀnɛj/ *nf* crow.

cornemuse /kɔʀnəmyz/ *nf* bagpipes (+ *pl*).

corner /kɔʀne/ 🔢 *vt* (page) turn down the corner of; **page cornée** dog-eared page. ● *vi* (Auto) hoot, honk.

cornet /kɔʀnɛ/ *nm* (paper) cone; (crème glacée) cornet, cone.

corniche /kɔʀniʃ/ *nf* cornice; (route) cliff road.

cornichon /kɔʀniʃɔ̃/ *nm* gherkin.

corporel, ~le /kɔʀpɔʀɛl/ *adj* bodily; (châtiment) corporal.

corps /kɔʀ/ *nm* body; (Mil) corps; **combat** ~ **à** ~ hand-to-hand combat; ~ **électoral** electorate; ~ **enseignant** teaching profession.

correct, ~e /kɔʀɛkt/ *adj* proper, correct; (exact) correct.

correcteur, -trice /kɔʀɛktœʀ, -tʀis/ *nm, f* (d'épreuves) proofreader; (Scol) examiner; ~ **liquide** correction fluid; ~ **d'orthographe** spell-checker.

correction /kɔʀɛksjɔ̃/ *nf* correction; (d'examen) marking, grading; (punition) beating.

correspondance /kɔʀɛspɔ̃dɑ̃s/ *nf* correspondence; (de train, d'autobus) connection; **vente par** ~ mail order; **faire des études par** ~ do a correspondence course.

correspondant, ~e /kɔʀɛspɔ̃dɑ̃, -t/ *adj* corresponding. ● *nm, f* correspondent; penfriend; (au téléphone) **votre** ~ the person you are calling.

correspondre /kɔʀɛspɔ̃dʀ/ 🔢 *vi* (s'accorder, écrire) correspond; (chambres) communicate. ● *v + prép* ~ **à** (être approprié à) match, suit; (équivaloir à) correspond to. ▫ **se** ~ *vpr* correspond.

corrida /kɔʀida/ *nf* bullfight.

corriger /kɔʀiʒe/ 🔢 *vt* correct; (devoir) mark, grade, correct; (punir) beat; (guérir) cure.

corsage /kɔʀsaʒ/ *nm* bodice; (chemisier) blouse.

corsaire /kɔʀsɛʀ/ *nm* pirate.

Corse /kɔʀs/ *nf* Corsica. ● *nmf* Corsican. **corse** *adj* Corsican.

corsé, ~e /kɔʀse/ *adj* (vin) full-bodied; (café) strong; (scabreux) racy; (problème) tough.

cortège /kɔʀtɛʒ/ *nm* procession; ~ **funèbre** funeral procession.

corvée /kɔʀve/ *nf* chore.

cosmonaute /kɔsmɔnot/ *nmf* cosmonaut.

cosmopolite /kɔsmɔpɔlit/ *adj* cosmopolitan.

cosse /kɔs/ *nf* (de pois) pod.

cossu, ~e /kɔsy/ *adj* (gens) well-to-do; (demeure) opulent.

costaud, ~e /kɔsto, -d/ 🔢 *adj* strong. ● *nm* strong man.

costume /kɔstym/ *nm* suit; (Théât) costume.

cote /kɔt/ nf (classification) mark; (en Bourse) quotation; (de cheval) odds (**de** on); (de candidat, acteur) rating; ~ **d'alerte** danger level; **avoir la ~** be popular.

côte /kot/ nf (littoral) coast; (pente) hill; (Anat) rib; (Culin) chop; ~ **à ~** side by side; **la C~ d'Azur** the (French) Riviera.

côté /kote/ nm side; (direction) way; **à ~** nearby; **voisin d'à ~** next-door neighbour; **à ~ de** next to; (comparé à) compared to; **à ~ de la cible** wide of the target; **aux ~s de** by the side of; **de ~** (regarder) sideways; (sauter) to one side; **mettre de ~** put aside; **de ce ~** this way; **de chaque ~** on each side; **de tous les ~s** on every side; (partout) everywhere; **du ~ de** (vers) towards; (proche de) near.

côtelette /kotlɛt/ nf chop.

coter /kote/ **1** vt (Comm) quote; **coté en Bourse** listed on the Stock Exchange; **très coté** highly rated.

cotiser /kɔtize/ **1** vi pay one's contributions (**à** to); (à un club) pay one's subscription. □ **se ~** vpr club together.

coton /kɔtɔ̃/ nm cotton; ~ **hydrophile** cotton wool.

cou /ku/ nm neck.

couchant /kuʃɑ̃/ nm sunset.

couche /kuʃ/ nf layer; (de peinture) coat; (de bébé) nappy; (US) diaper; ~**s** (Méd) childbirth; ~**s sociales** social strata.

coucher /kuʃe/ **1** vt put to bed; (loger) put up; (étendre) lay down; ~ **(par écrit)** set down. ● vi sleep. □ **se ~** vpr go to bed; (s'étendre) lie down; (soleil) set. ● nm ~ **de soleil** sunset.

couchette /kuʃɛt/ nf (de train) couchette; (Naut) berth.

coude /kud/ nm elbow; (de rivière, chemin) bend; ~ **à ~** side by side.

cou-de-pied (pl **cous-de-pied**) /kudpje/ nm instep.

coudre /kudʀ/ **19** vt/i sew.

couette /kwɛt/ nf duvet, quilt.

couler /kule/ **1** vi flow, run; (fromage, nez) run; (fuir) leak; (bateau) sink; (entreprise) go under; **faire ~ un bain** run a bath. ● vt (bateau) sink; (sculp-

ture, métal) cast. □ **se ~** vpr slip (**dans** into).

couleur /kulœʀ/ nf colour; (peinture) paint; (aux cartes) suit; ~**s** (teint) colour; **de ~** (homme, femme) coloured; **en ~s** (télévision, film) colour.

couleuvre /kulœvʀ/ nf grass snake.

coulisse /kulis/ nf (de tiroir) runner; **à ~** (porte, fenêtre) sliding; ~**s** (Théât) wings; **dans les ~s** (fig) behind the scenes.

couloir /kulwaʀ/ nm corridor; (Sport) lane; ~ **de bus** bus lane.

coup /ku/ nm blow; (choc) knock; (Sport) stroke; (de crayon, chance, cloche) stroke; (de fusil, pistolet) shot; (fois) time; (aux échecs) move; **donner un ~ de pied/poing** à kick/punch; **à ~ sûr** definitely; **après ~** after the event; **boire un ~** 🔟 have a drink; ~ **sur ~** in rapid succession; **du ~** as a result; **d'un seul ~** in one go; **du premier ~** first go; **sale ~** dirty trick; **sous le ~ de la fatigue/colère** out of tiredness/anger; **sur le ~** instantly; **tenir le ~** hold out; **manquer son ~** 🔟 blow it!; ~ **de chiffon** wipe (with a rag); ~ **de coude** nudge; ~ **de couteau** stab; ~ **d'envoi** kick-off; ~ **d'État** (Pol) coup; ~ **franc** free kick; ~ **de main** helping hand; ~ **d'oeil** glance; ~ **de soleil** sunburn; ~ **de téléphone** telephone call; ~ **de vent** gust of wind.

coupable /kupabl/ adj guilty.

coupe /kup/ nf cup; (de champagne) goblet; (à fruits) dish; (de vêtement) cut; (dessin) section; ~ **de cheveux** haircut.

couper /kupe/ **1** vt cut; (arbre) cut down; (arrêter) cut off; (voyage) break up; (appétit) take away; (vin) water down; ~ **par** take a short cut via; ~ **la parole à qn** cut sb short. ● vi cut. □ **se ~** vpr cut oneself; **se ~ le doigt** cut one's finger; (routes) intersect; **se ~ de** cut oneself off from.

couple /kupl/ nm couple; (d'animaux) pair.

coupure /kupyʀ/ nf cut; (billet de banque) note; (de presse) cutting; (pause, rupture) break; (~ **de courant**) power cut.

cour /kuʀ/ nf (court) yard; (du roi) court; (tribunal) court; (~ **de récréa-**

tion) playground; ~ **martiale** court-martial; **faire la ~ à** court.

courageux, -euse /kuraʒø, -z/ adj courageous.

couramment /kuramã/ adv frequently; (parler) fluently.

courant, ~e /kurã, -t/ adj standard, ordinary; (en cours) current. ● nm current; (de mode, d'idées) trend; ~ **d'air** draught; **dans le ~ de** in the course of; **être/mettre au ~ de** know/tell about; (à jour) be/bring up to date on.

courbature /kurbatyr/ nf ache; **avoir des ~s** be stiff, ache.

courber /kurbe/ **1** vt bend.

coureur, -euse /kurœr, -øz/ nm, f (Sport) runner; ~ **automobile** racing driver; ~ **cycliste** racing cyclist. ● nm womanizer.

courgette /kurʒɛt/ nf courgette; (US) zucchini.

courir /kurir/ **20** vi run; (se hâter) rush; (nouvelles) go round; ~ **après qn/qch** chase after sb/ sth. ● vt (risque) run; (danger) face; (épreuve sportive) run ou compete in; (fréquenter) do the rounds of; (filles) chase (after).

couronne /kurɔn/ nf crown; (de fleurs) wreath.

couronnement /kurɔnmã/ nm coronation, crowning; (fig) crowning achievement.

courriel /kurjɛl/ nm email.

courrier /kurje/ nm post, mail; (à écrire) letters; ~ **du cœur** problem page; ~ **électronique** email.

cours /kur/ nm (leçon) class; (série de leçons) course; (prix) price; (cote) (de valeur, denrée) price; (de devises) exchange rate; (déroulement, d'une rivière) course; (allée) avenue; **au ~ de** in the course of; **avoir ~** (monnaie) be legal tender; (fig) be current; (Scol) have a lesson; ~ **d'eau** river, stream; ~ **du soir** evening class; ~ **particulier** private lesson; ~ **magistral** (Univ) lecture; **en ~** current; (travail) in progress; **en ~ de route** along the way.

course /kurs/ nf running; (épreuve de vitesse) race; (activité) racing; (entre rivaux: fig) race; (de projectile) flight; (voyage) journey; (commission) errand; ~s (achats) shopping; (de che-

vaux) races; **faire la ~ avec qn** race sb.

coursier, -ière /kursje, -jɛr/ nm, f messenger.

court, ~e /kur, -t/ adj short. ● adv short; **à ~ de** short of; **pris de ~** caught unawares. ● nm ~ **(de tennis)** (tennis) court.

courtier, -ière /kurtje, -jɛr/ nm, f broker.

courtiser /kurtize/ **1** vt woo, court.

courtois, ~e /kurtwa, -z/ adj courteous. **courtoisie** nf courtesy.

cousin, ~e /kuzɛ̃, -in/ nm, f cousin; ~ **germain** first cousin.

coussin /kusɛ̃/ nm cushion.

coût /ku/ nm cost; **le ~ de la vie** the cost of living.

couteau (pl ~x) /kuto/ nm knife; ~ **à cran d'arrêt** flick knife.

coûter /kute/ **1** vt/i cost; **coûte que coûte** at all costs; **au prix coûtant** at cost (price).

coutume /kutym/ nf custom.

couture /kutyr/ nf sewing; (métier) dressmaking; (points) seam. **couturier** nm fashion designer. **couturière** nf dressmaker.

couvée /kuve/ nf brood.

couvent /kuvã/ nm convent.

couver /kuve/ **1** vt (œufs) hatch; (personne) overprotect, pamper; (maladie) be coming down with, be sickening for. ● vi (feu) smoulder; (mal) be brewing.

couvercle /kuvɛrkl/ nm (de marmite, boîte) lid; (qui se visse) screwtop.

couvert, ~e /kuvɛr, -t/ adj covered (de with); (habillé) covered up; (ciel) overcast. ● nm (à table) place setting; (prix) cover charge; ~s (couteaux etc.) cutlery; **mettre le ~** lay the table; (abri) cover; **à ~** (Mil) under cover; **à ~ de** (fig) safe from.

couverture /kuvɛrtyr/ nf cover; (de lit) blanket; (toit) roofing; (dans la presse) coverage; ~ **chauffante** electric blanket.

couvre-feu (pl ~x) /kuvrəfø/ nm curfew.

couvre-lit (pl ~s) /kuvrəli/ nm bedspread.

couvrir /kuvrir/ **21** vt cover. □ **se ~** vpr (s'habiller) wrap up; (se coiffer) put

one's hat on; (*ciel*) become overcast.
covoiturage /kɔvwatyʀaʒ/ *nm* car
sharing.
cracher /kʀaʃe/ ◘ *vi* spit; (*radio*)
crackle. ● *vt* spit (out); (*fumée*)
belch out.
crachin /kʀaʃɛ̃/ *nm* drizzle.
craie /kʀɛ/ *nf* chalk.
craindre /kʀɛ̃dʀ/ ◙ *vt* be afraid of,
fear; (être sensible à) be easily damaged by.
crainte /kʀɛ̃t/ *nf* fear (**pour** for); **de ∼**
de/que for fear of/that. **craintif, -ive**
adj timid.
crampon /kʀɑ̃pɔ̃/ *nm* (de chaussure) stud.
cramponner (se) /(sə)kʀɑ̃pɔne/ ◘
vpr **se ∼ à** cling to.
cran /kʀɑ̃/ *nm* (entaille) notch; (trou)
hole; (courage ▣) guts ▣, courage;
∼ de sûreté safety catch.
crâne /kʀɑn/ *nm* skull.
crapaud /kʀapo/ *nm* toad.
craquer /kʀake/ ◘ *vi* crack, snap;
(*plancher*) creak; (*couture*) split; (fig)
(*personne*) break down; (céder) give
in. ● *vt* (allumette) strike; (vêtement)
split.
crasse /kʀas/ *nf* grime.
cravache /kʀavaʃ/ *nf* (horse) whip.
cravate /kʀavat/ *nf* tie.
crayon /kʀɛjɔ̃/ *nm* pencil; **∼ de couleur** coloured pencil; **∼ à bille** ball-
point pen; **∼ optique** light pen.
créateur, -trice /kʀeatœʀ, -tʀis/ *adj*
creative. ● *nm, f* creator, designer.
crèche /kʀɛʃ/ *nf* day nursery, crèche;
(Relig) crib.
crédit /kʀedi/ *nm* credit; (somme al-
louée) funds; **à ∼** on credit; **faire ∼**
give credit (**à** to).
créer /kʀee/ ▣ *vt* create; (*produit*) design; (société) set up.
crémaillère /kʀemajɛʀ/ *nf* **pendre la
∼** have a housewarming party.
crème /kʀɛm/ *adj inv* cream. ● *nm*
(café) **∼** espresso with milk. ● *nf*
cream; (dessert) cream dessert; **∼ anglaise** egg custard; **∼ fouettée**
whipped cream; **∼ pâtissière** confectioner's custard. **crémerie** *nf* dairy.
crémeux, -euse *adj* creamy. **crémier,
-ière** *nm, f* dairyman, dairywoman.

créneau (*pl* **∼x**) /kʀeno/ *nm* (trou,
moment) slot, window; (dans le marché) gap; **faire un ∼** to parallel-park.
crêpe /kʀɛp/ *nf* (galette) pancake. ● *nm*
(tissu) crêpe; (matière) crêpe (rubber).
crépitement /kʀepitmɑ̃/ *nm* crack-
ling; (d'huile) sizzling.
crépuscule /kʀepyskyl/ *nm* twilight, dusk.
cresson /kʀɛsɔ̃/ *nm* (water) cress.
crête /kʀɛt/ *nf* crest; (de coq) comb.
crétin, ∼e /kʀetɛ̃, -in/ *nm, f* ▣
moron ▣.
creuser /kʀøze/ ◘ *vt* dig; (évider) hollow out; (fig) go into in depth. ▫ **se
∼** *vpr* (écart) widen; **se ∼ (la cervelle)**
▣ rack one's brains.
creux, -euse /kʀø, -z/ *adj* hollow; (heures) off-peak. ● *nm* hollow; (de l'estomac) pit; **dans le ∼ de la main** in the
palm of the hand.
crevaison /kʀəvɛzɔ̃/ *nf* puncture.
crevasse /kʀəvas/ *nf* crack; (de glacier) crevasse; (de la peau) chap.
crevé, ∼e /kʀəve/ *adj* ▣ worn out.
crever /kʀəve/ ◘ *vt* burst; (*pneu*)
puncture, burst; (exténuer ▣) exhaust; (œil) put out. ● *vi* (*pneu, sac*)
burst; (mourir ▣) die.
crevette /kʀəvɛt/ *nf* **∼ grise** shrimp;
∼ rose prawn.
cri /kʀi/ *nm* cry; (de douleur) scream,
cry; **pousser un ∼** cry out, scream.
criard, ∼e /kʀijaʀ, -d/ *adj* (couleur)
garish; (voix) shrill.
crier /kʀije/ ◙ *vi* (fort) shout, cry
(out); (de douleur) scream; (grincer)
creak. ● *vt* (ordre) shout (out).
crime /kʀim/ *nm* crime; (meurtre)
murder.
criminel, ∼le /kʀiminɛl/ *adj* criminal.
● *nm, f* criminal; (assassin) murderer.
crinière /kʀinjɛʀ/ *nf* mane.
crise /kʀiz/ *nf* crisis; (Méd) attack; (de
colère) fit; **∼ cardiaque** heart attack;
∼ de foie bilious attack; **∼ de nerfs**
hysterics (+ *pl*).
crisper /kʀispe/ ◘ *vt* tense; (énerver
▣) irritate. ▫ **se ∼** *vpr* tense; (mains)
clench.
critère /kʀitɛʀ/ *nm* criterion.
critique /kʀitik/ *adj* critical. ● *nf* criticism; (article) review; (commentateur)

critic; **la** ~ (personnes) the critics. **critiquer** 🔟 vt criticize.

Croate /kʀɔat/ adj Croatian. **C**~ nmf Croatian.

Croatie /kʀɔasi/ nf Croatia.

croche /kʀɔʃ/ nf quaver.

croche-pied (pl ~s) /kʀɔʃpje/ nm 🔟 **faire un** ~ **à** trip up.

crochet /kʀɔʃɛ/ nm hook; (détour) detour; (signe) (square) bracket; (tricot) crochet; **faire au** ~ crochet.

crochu, ~e /kʀɔʃy/ adj hooked.

crocodile /kʀɔkɔdil/ nm crocodile.

croire /kʀwaʀ/ 🔢 vt believe (à, en in); (estimer) think, believe (**que** that). ● vi believe.

croisade /kʀwazad/ nf crusade.

croisement /kʀwazmɑ̃/ nm crossing; (fait de passer à côté de) passing; (carrefour) crossroads.

croiser /kʀwaze/ 🔟 vi (bateau) cruise. ● vt cross; (passant, véhicule) pass; ~ **les bras** fold one's arms; ~ **les jambes** cross one's legs; (animaux) crossbreed. ☐ **se** ~ vpr (véhicules, piétons) pass each other; (lignes) cross. **croisière** nf cruise.

croissance /kʀwasɑ̃s/ nf growth.

croissant, ~e /kʀwasɑ̃, -t/ adj growing. ● nm crescent; (pâtisserie) croissant.

croix /kʀwa/ nf cross; ~ **gammée** swastika; **C**~-**Rouge** Red Cross.

croquant, ~e /kʀɔkɑ̃, -t/ adj crunchy.

croque-monsieur /kʀɔkməsjø/ nm inv toasted ham and cheese sandwich.

croque-mort (pl ~s) /kʀɔkmɔʀ/ nm 🔟 undertaker.

croquer /kʀɔke/ 🔟 vt crunch; (dessiner) sketch; **chocolat à** ~ plain chocolate. ● vi be crunchy.

croquis /kʀɔki/ nm sketch.

crotte /kʀɔt/ nf dropping.

crotté, ~e /kʀɔte/ adj muddy.

crottin /kʀɔtɛ̃/ nm (horse) dropping.

croupir /kʀupiʀ/ 🔢 vi stagnate.

croustillant, ~e /kʀustijɑ̃, -t/ adj crispy; (pain) crusty; (fig) spicy.

croûte /kʀut/ nf crust; (de fromage) rind; (de plaie) scab; **en** ~ (Culin) in pastry.

croûton /kʀutɔ̃/ nm (bout de pain) crust; (avec potage) croûton.

CRS abrév m (**Compagnie républicaine de sécurité**) French riot police; **un** ~ a member of the French riot police.

cru¹ /kʀy/ ➡**CROIRE** 🔢.

cru², ~e /kʀy/ adj raw; (lumière) harsh; (propos) crude. ● nm vineyard; (vin) vintage wine.

crû /kʀy/ ➡**CROÎTRE** 🔢.

cruauté /kʀyote/ nf cruelty.

cruche /kʀyʃ/ nf jug, pitcher.

crucial, ~e (mpl -**iaux**) /kʀysjal, -jo/ adj crucial.

crudité /kʀydite/ nf (de langage) crudeness; ~s (Culin) raw vegetables.

crue /kʀy/ nf rise in water level; **en** ~ in spate.

crustacé /kʀystase/ nm shellfish.

cube /kyb/ nm cube. ● adj (mètre) cubic.

cueillir /kœjiʀ/ 🔢 vt pick, gather; (personne 🔟) pick up.

cuiller, cuillère /kɥijɛʀ/ nf spoon; ~ **à soupe** soup spoon; (mesure) tablespoonful.

cuir /kɥiʀ/ nm leather; ~ **chevelu** scalp.

cuire /kɥiʀ/ 🔢 vt cook; ~ (**au four**) bake. ● vi cook; **faire** ~ cook.

cuisine /kɥizin/ nf kitchen; (art) cookery, cooking; (aliments) food; **faire la** ~ cook.

cuisiner /kɥizine/ 🔟 vt cook; (interroger 🔟) grill. ● vi cook.

cuisinier, -ière /kɥizinje, -jɛʀ/ nm, f cook. **cuisinière** nf (appareil) cooker, stove.

cuisse /kɥis/ nf thigh; (de poulet) thigh; (de grenouille) leg.

cuisson /kɥisɔ̃/ nf cooking.

cuit, ~e /kɥi, -t/ adj cooked; **bien** ~ well done ou cooked; **trop** ~ overdone.

cuivre /kɥivʀ/ nm copper; ~ (**jaune**) brass; ~s (Mus) brass.

cul /ky/ nm (derrière 🗷) backside, bottom, arse 🗷.

culbuter /kylbyte/ 🔟 vi (personne) tumble; (objet) topple (over). ● vt knock over.

culminer /kylmine/ 🔟 vi reach its highest point ou peak.

culot /kylo/ nm (audace 🔟) nerve, cheek; (Tech) base.

culotte /kylɔt/ nf (de femme) pants (+ pl), knickers (+ pl); (US) panties (+ pl); ~ **de cheval** riding breeches; **en ~ courte** in short trousers.

culpabilité /kylpabilite/ nf guilt.

culte /kylt/ nm cult, worship; (religion) religion; (office protestant) service.

cultivateur, -trice /kyltivatœr, -tris/ nm, f farmer.

cultiver /kyltive/ **1** vt cultivate; (plantes) grow.

culture /kyltyr/ nf cultivation; (de plantes) growing; (agriculture) farming; (éducation) culture; (connaissances) knowledge; ~**s** (terrains) lands under cultivation; ~ **physique** physical training.

culturel, ~le /kyltyrɛl/ adj cultural.

cumuler /kymyle/ **1** vt accumulate; (fonctions) hold concurrently.

cure /kyr/ nf (course of) treatment.

curé /kyre/ nm (parish) priest.

cure-dent (pl ~s) /kyrdɑ̃/ nm toothpick.

curer /kyre/ **1** vt clean. □ se ~ vpr se ~ **les dents/ongles** clean one's teeth/nails.

curieux, -ieuse /kyrjø, -z/ adj curious. ● nm, f (badaud) onlooker.

curiosité /kyrjozite/ nf curiosity; (objet) curio; (spectacle) unusual sight.

curriculum vitae /kyrikylɔm vite/ nm inv curriculum vitae; (US) résumé.

curseur /kyrsœr/ nm cursor.

cutané, ~e /kytane/ adj skin.

cuve /kyv/ nf vat; (à mazout, eau) tank.

cuvée /kyve/ nf (de vin) vintage.

cuvette /kyvɛt/ nf bowl; (de lavabo) (wash) basin; (des cabinets) pan, bowl.

CV abrév m (**curriculum vitae**) CV.

cyberbranché, ~e /sibɛrbrɑ̃ʃe/ adj cyberwired.

cybercafé /sibɛrkafe/ nm cybercafe.

cyberespace /sibɛrsɛpas/ nm cyberspace.

cybernaute /sibɛrnot/ nmf Netsurfer.

cybernétique /sibɛrnetik/ nf cybernetics (+ pl).

cyclisme /siklism/ nm cycling.

cycliste /siklist/ nmf cyclist. ● nm cycling shorts. ● adj cycle.

cyclone /siklon/ nm cyclone.

cygne /siɲ/ nm swan.

cynique /sinik/ adj cynical. ● nm cynic.

Dd

d' /d/ ➡DE.

d'abord /dabɔr/ adv first; (au début) at first.

dactylo /daktilo/ nf typist. **dactylographier** 45 vt type.

dada /dada/ nm hobby-horse.

daim /dɛ̃/ nm (fallow) deer; (cuir) suede.

dallage /dalaʒ/ nm paving. **dalle** nf slab.

daltonien, ~ne /daltɔnjɛ̃, -ɛn/ adj colour-blind.

dame /dam/ nf lady; (cartes, échecs) queen; ~**s** (jeu) draughts; (US) checkers.

damier /damje/ nm draught board; (US) checker-board; **à ~** chequered.

damner /dane/ **1** vt damn.

dandiner (se) /(sə)dɑ̃dine/ **1** vpr waddle.

Danemark /danmark/ nm Denmark.

danger /dɑ̃ʒe/ nm danger; **en ~** in danger; **mettre en ~** endanger.

dangereux, -euse /dɑ̃ʒ(ə)rø, -z/ adj dangerous.

danois, ~e /danwa, -z/ adj Danish. ● nm (Ling) Danish. **D~, ~e** nm, f Dane.

dans /dɑ̃/ prép in; (mouvement) into; (à l'intérieur de) inside, in; **être ~ un avion** be on a plane; **~ dix jours** in ten days' time; **boire ~ un verre** drink out of a glass; **~ les 10 euros** about 10 euros.

danse /dɑ̃s/ nf dance; (art) dancing.

danser /dɑ̃se/ **1** vt/i dance. **danseur, -euse** nm, f dancer.

darne /darn/ nf steak (of fish).

date /dat/ nf date; ~ **limite** deadline; ~ **limite de vente** sell-by date; ~ **de**

péremption use-by date.

dater /date/ **1** vt/i date; **à ~ de** as from.

datte /dat/ nf (fruit) date.

daube /dob/ nf casserole.

dauphin /dofɛ̃/ nm (animal) dolphin.

davantage /davɑ̃taʒ/ adv more; (plus longtemps) longer; **~ de** more; **je n'en sais pas ~** that's as much as I know.

---

de, **d'** /də, d/

d' before vowel or mute h.

● préposition

····▸ of; **le livre ~ mon ami** my friend's book; **un pont ~ fer** an iron bridge.

····▸ (provenance) from.

····▸ (temporel) from; **~ 8 heures à 10 heures** from 8 till 10.

····▸ (mesure, manière) **dix mètres ~ haut** ten metres high; **pleurer ~ rage** cry with rage.

····▸ (agent) by; **un livre ~ Marcel Aymé** a book by Marcel Aymé.

● **de, de l', de la, du,** (pl **des**) déterminant

····▸ some; **du pain** (some) bread; **des fleurs** (some) flowers; **je ne bois jamais ~ vin** I never drink wine.

de + le = du
de + les = des

---

dé /de/ nm (à jouer) dice; (à coudre) thimble; **~s** (jeu) dice.

débâcle /debɑkl/ nf (Géog) breaking up; (Mil) rout.

déballer /debale/ **1** vt unpack; (révéler) spill out.

débarbouiller /debaʀbuje/ vt wash the face of. □ **se ~** vpr wash one's face.

débarcadère /debaʀkadɛʀ/ nm landing-stage.

débardeur /debaʀdœʀ/ nm (vêtement) tank top.

débarquement /debaʀkəmɑ̃/ nm disembarkation. **débarquer** **1** vt/i disembark, land; (arriver **1**) turn up.

débarras /debaʀa/ nm junk room; **bon ~!** good riddance!

débarrasser /debaʀase/ **1** vt clear (**de** of); **~ qn de** relieve sb of; (défaut, ennemi) rid sb of. □ **se ~ de** vpr get rid of.

débat /deba/ nm debate.

débattre /debatʀ/ **11** vt debate. ● vi **~ de** discuss. □ **se ~** vpr struggle (to get free).

débauche /deboʃ/ nf debauchery; (fig) profusion.

débaucher /deboʃe/ **1** vt (licencier) lay off; (distraire) tempt away.

débile /debil/ adj weak; (**1**) stupid. ● nmf moron **1**.

débit /debi/ nm (rate of) flow; (élocution) delivery; (de compte) debit; **~ de tabac** tobacconist's shop; **~ de boissons** bar; **haut ~** broadband.

débiter /debite/ **1** vt (compte) debit; (fournir) produce; (vendre) sell; (dire: péj) spout; (couper) cut up.

débiteur, -trice /debitœʀ, -tʀis/ nm, f debtor. ● adj (compte) in debit.

déblayer /debleje/ **31** vt clear.

déblocage /deblɔkaʒ/ nm (de prix) deregulating. **débloquer** **1** vt (prix, salaires) unfreeze.

déboiser /debwaze/ **1** vt clear (of trees).

déboîter /debwate/ **1** vi (véhicule) pull out. ● vt (membre) dislocate.

débordement /debɔʀdəmɑ̃/ nm (de joie) excess.

déborder /debɔʀde/ **1** vi overflow. ● vt (dépasser) extend beyond; **~ de** (joie etc.) be brimming over with.

débouché /debuʃe/ nm opening; (carrière) prospect; (Comm) outlet; (sortie) end, exit.

déboucher /debuʃe/ **1** vt (bouteille) uncork; (évier) unblock. ● vi come out (**de** from); **~ sur** (rue) lead into.

débourser /debuʀse/ **1** vt pay out.

debout /dəbu/ adv standing; (levé, éveillé) up; **être ~, se tenir ~** be standing, stand; **se mettre ~** stand up.

déboutonner /debutɔne/ **1** vt unbutton. □ **se ~** vpr unbutton oneself; (vêtement) come undone.

débrancher /debʀɑ̃ʃe/ **1** vt (prise) unplug; (système) disconnect.

débrayer /debʀeje/ **31** vi (Auto) declutch; (faire grève) stop work.

débris /debʀi/ nmpl fragments; (détritus) rubbish (+ sg); debris.

débrouillard, ~e /debʀujaʀ, -d/ adj 🔟 resourceful.

débrouiller /debʀuje/ 🔟 vt disentangle; (problème) solve. □ se ~ vpr manage.

début /deby/ nm beginning; **faire ses** ~s (en public) make one's début; **à mes** ~s when I started out. **débutant,** ~e nm, f beginner. **débuter** 🔟 vi begin; (dans un métier etc.) start out.

déca /deka/ nm 🔟 decaf.

deçà: en ~ /ɑ̃dəsa/ loc this side. ● prép en ~ de this side of.

décacheter /dekaʃte/ 🔟 vt open.

décade /dekad/ nf ten days; (décennie) decade.

décadent, ~e /dekadɑ̃, -t/ adj decadent.

décalage /dekalaʒ/ nm (écart) gap; ~ horaire time difference. **décaler** 🔟 vt shift.

décalquer /dekalke/ 🔟 vt trace.

décamper /dekɑ̃pe/ 🔟 vi clear off.

décanter /dekɑ̃te/ vt allow to settle. □ se ~ vpr settle.

décapant /dekapɑ̃/ nm chemical agent; (pour peinture) paint stripper. ● adj (humour) caustic.

décapotable /dekapɔtabl/ adj convertible.

décapsuleur /dekapsylœʀ/ nm bottle-opener.

décédé, ~e /desede/ adj deceased. **décéder** 🔟 vi die.

déceler /desle/ 🔟 vt detect; (démontrer) reveal.

décembre /desɑ̃bʀ/ nm December.

décemment /desamɑ̃/ adv decently. **décence** nf decency. **décent,** ~e adj decent.

décennie /deseni/ nf decade.

décentralisation /desɑ̃tʀalizasjɔ̃/ nf decentralization. **décentraliser** 🔟 vt decentralize.

déception /desɛpsjɔ̃/ nf disappointment.

décerner /desɛʀne/ 🔟 vt award.

décès /desɛ/ nm death.

décevant, ~e /des(ə)vɑ̃, -t/ adj disappointing. **décevoir** 🔟 vt disappoint.

déchaîner /deʃene/ 🔟 vt (enthousiasme) rouse. □ se ~ vpr go wild.

décharge /deʃaʀʒ/ nf (de fusil) discharge; ~ **électrique** electric shock; ~ **publique** municipal dump.

décharger /deʃaʀʒe/ 🔟 vt unload; ~ **qn de** relieve sb from. □ se ~ vpr (batterie, pile) go flat.

déchausser (se) /(sə)deʃose/ 🔟 vpr take off one's shoes; (dent) work loose.

dèche /dɛʃ/ nf 🔟 **dans la** ~ broke.

déchéance /deʃeɑ̃s/ nf decay.

déchet /deʃɛ/ nm (reste) scrap; (perte) waste; ~s (ordures) refuse.

déchiffrer /deʃifʀe/ 🔟 vt decipher.

déchiqueter /deʃikte/ 🔟 vt tear to shreds.

déchirement /deʃiʀmɑ̃/ nm heartbreak; (conflit) split.

déchirer /deʃiʀe/ 🔟 vt (par accident) tear; (lacérer) tear up; (arracher) tear off ou out; (diviser) tear apart. □ se ~ vpr tear. **déchirure** nf tear.

décibel /desibɛl/ nm decibel.

décidément /desidemɑ̃/ adv really.

décider /deside/ 🔟 vt decide on; (persuader) persuade; ~ **que/de** decide that/to; ~ **de qch** decide on sth. □ se ~ vpr make up one's mind (à to).

décimal, ~e (mpl ~aux) /desimal, -o/ adj & nf decimal.

décisif, -ive /desizif, -v/ adj decisive.

décision /desizjɔ̃/ nf decision.

déclaration /deklaʀasjɔ̃/ nf declaration; (commentaire politique) statement; ~ **d'impôts** tax return.

déclarer /deklaʀe/ 🔟 vt declare; (naissance) register; **déclaré coupable** found guilty; ~ **forfait** (Sport) withdraw. □ se ~ vpr (feu) break out.

déclencher /deklɑ̃ʃe/ 🔟 vt (Tech) set off; (conflit) spark off; (avalanche) start; (rire) provoke. □ se ~ vpr (Tech) go off. **déclencheur** nm (Photo) shutter release.

déclic /deklik/ nm click.

déclin /deklɛ̃/ nm decline.

déclinaison /deklinɛzɔ̃/ nf (Ling) declension.

décliner /dekline/ 🔟 vt (refuser) decline; (dire) state; (Ling) decline.

décocher /dekɔʃe/ 🔟 vt (coup) fling; (regard) shoot.

décollage /dekɔlaʒ/ nm take-off.

décoller /dekɔle/ **1** vt unstick. • vi (avion) take off. □ se ~ vpr come off.

décolleté, ~e /dekɔlte/ adj lowcut. • nm low neckline.

décolorer /dekɔlɔʀe/ **1** vt fade; (cheveux) bleach. □ se ~ vpr fade.

décombres /dekɔ̃bʀ/ nmpl rubble.

décommander /dekɔmɑ̃de/ **1** vt cancel.

décomposer /dekɔ̃poze/ **1** vt break up; (substance) decompose. □ se ~ vpr (pourrir) decompose.

décompte /dekɔ̃t/ nm deduction; (détail) breakdown.

décongeler /dekɔ̃ʒle/ **6** vt thaw.

déconseillé, ~e /dekɔ̃seje/ adj not recommended, inadvisable.

déconseiller /dekɔ̃seje/ **1** vt ~ qch à qn advise sb against sth.

décontracté, ~e /dekɔ̃tʀakte/ adj relaxed.

déconvenue /dekɔ̃vny/ nf disappointment.

décor /dekɔʀ/ nm (paysage) scenery; (de cinéma, théâtre) set; (cadre) setting; (de maison) décor.

décoratif, -ive /dekɔʀatif, -v/ adj decorative.

décorateur, -trice /dekɔʀatœʀ, -tʀis/ nm, f (de cinéma) set designer. **décoration** nf decoration. **décorer** **1** vt decorate.

décortiquer /dekɔʀtike/ **1** vt shell; (fig) dissect.

découdre (se) /(sə)dekudʀ/ **19** vpr come unstitched.

découler /dekule/ **1** vi ~ de follow from.

découper /dekupe/ **1** vt cut up; (viande) carve; (détacher) cut out.

découragement /dekuʀaʒmɑ̃/ nm discouragement.

décourager /dekuʀaʒe/ **40** vt discourage. □ se ~ vpr become discouraged.

décousu, ~e /dekuzy/ adj (vêtement) which has come unstitched; (idées) disjointed.

découvert, ~e /dekuvɛʀ, -t/ adj (tête) bare; (terrain) open. • nm (de compte) overdraft; à ~ exposed; (fig) openly.

découverte /dekuvɛʀt/ nf discovery; à la ~ de in search of.

découvrir /dekuvʀiʀ/ **21** vt discover; (voir) see; (montrer) reveal. □ se ~ vpr (se décoiffer) take one's hat off; (ciel) clear.

décrasser /dekʀase/ **1** vt clean.

décrépit, ~e /dekʀepi, -t/ adj decrepit. **décrépitude** nf decay.

décret /dekʀɛ/ nm decree. **décréter** **14** vt order; (dire) declare.

décrié, ~e /dekʀije/ adj criticized.

décrire /dekʀiʀ/ **30** vt describe.

décroché, ~e /dekʀɔʃe/ adj (téléphone) off the hook.

décrocher /dekʀɔʃe/ **1** vt unhook; (obtenir **1**) get. • vi (abandonner **1**) give up; ~ (le téléphone) pick up the phone.

décroître /dekʀwatʀ/ **24** vi decrease.

déçu, ~e /desy/ adj disappointed.

décupler /dekyple/ **1** vt/i increase tenfold.

dédaigner /dedɛɲe/ **1** vt scorn.

dédain /dedɛ̃/ nm scorn.

dédale /dedal/ nm maze.

dedans /dədɑ̃/ adv & nm inside; en ~ on the inside.

dédicacer /dedikase/ **10** vt dedicate; (signer) sign.

dédier /dedje/ **45** vt dedicate.

dédommagement /dedɔmaʒmɑ̃/ nm compensation. **dédommager** **40** vt compensate (de for).

déduction /dedyksjɔ̃/ nf deduction; ~ d'impôts tax deduction.

déduire /deduiʀ/ **17** vt deduct; (conclure) deduce.

déesse /deɛs/ nf goddess.

défaillance /defajɑ̃s/ nf (panne) failure; (évanouissement) blackout. **défaillant, ~e** adj (système) faulty; (personne) faint.

défaire /defɛʀ/ **33** vt undo; (valise) unpack; (démonter) take down. □ se ~ vpr come undone; se ~ de rid oneself of.

défait, ~e /defɛ, -t/ adj (cheveux) ruffled; (visage) haggard; (nœud) undone. **défaite** nf defeat.

défaitiste /defetist/ adj & nmf defeatist.

défalquer /defalke/ **1** vt (somme) deduct.

défaut /defo/ nm fault, defect; (d'un verre, diamant, etc.) flaw; (pénurie) shortage; **à ~ de** for lack of; **pris en ~** caught out; **faire ~** (*argent etc.*) be lacking; **par ~** (Jur) in one's absence; **~ de paiement** non-payment.

défavorable /defavɔʀabl/ *adj* unfavourable.

défavoriser /defavɔʀize/ **1** *vt* discriminate against.

défectueux, -euse /defɛktɥø, -z/ *adj* faulty, defective.

défendre /defɑ̃dʀ/ **3** *vt* defend; (interdire) forbid; **~ à qn de** forbid sb to. □ **se ~** *vpr* defend oneself; (se protéger) protect oneself; (se débrouiller) manage; **se ~ de** (refuser) refrain from.

défense /defɑ̃s/ *nf* defence; **~ de fumer** no smoking; (d'éléphant) tusk. **défenseur** *nm* defender. **défensif, -ive** *adj* defensive.

déferler /defɛʀle/ **1** *vi* (vagues) break; (violence) erupt.

défi /defi/ *nm* challenge; (provocation) defiance; **mettre au ~** challenge.

déficience /defisjɑ̃s/ *nf* deficiency. **déficient, ~e** *adj* deficient.

déficit /defisit/ *nm* deficit. **déficitaire** *adj* in deficit.

défier /defje/ **45** *vt* challenge; (braver) defy.

défilé /defile/ *nm* procession; (Mil) parade; (fig) (continual) stream; (Géog) gorge; **~ de mode** fashion parade.

défiler /defile/ **1** *vi* march; (visiteurs) stream; (images) flash by; (chiffres, minutes) add up. □ **se ~** *vpr* **1** sneak off.

défini, ~e /defini/ *adj* (Ling) definite.

définir /definiʀ/ **2** *vt* define.

définitif, -ive /definitif, -v/ *adj* final, definitive; **en définitive** in the end.

définition /definisjɔ̃/ *nf* definition; (de mots croisés) clue.

définitivement /definitivmɑ̃/ *adv* definitively, permanently.

déflagration /deflagʀasjɔ̃/ *nf* explosion.

déflation /deflasjɔ̃/ *nf* deflation. **déflationniste** *adj* deflationary.

défoncé, ~e /defɔ̃se/ *adj* (terrain) full of potholes; (siège) broken; (drogué: **1**) high.

défoncer /defɔ̃se/ **10** *vt* (porte) break down; (mâchoire) break. □ **se ~** *vpr* **1** to give one's all.

déformation /defɔʀmasjɔ̃/ *nf* distortion. **déformer** **1** *vt* put out of shape; (faits, pensée) distort.

défouler (se) /(sə)defule/ **1** *vpr* let off steam.

défrayer /defʀeje/ **31** *vt* (payer) pay the expenses of; **~ la chronique** be the talk of the town.

défricher /defʀiʃe/ **1** *vt* clear.

défroisser /defʀwase/ **1** *vt* smooth out.

défunt, ~e /defœ̃, -t/ *adj* (mort) late. ● *nm, f* deceased.

dégagé, ~e /degaʒe/ *adj* (ciel) clear; (front) bare; **d'un ton ~** casually.

dégagement /degaʒmɑ̃/ *nm* clearing; (football) clearance.

dégager /degaʒe/ **40** *vt* (exhaler) give off; (désencombrer) clear; (faire ressortir) bring out; (ballon) clear. □ **se ~** *vpr* free oneself; (ciel, rue) clear; (odeur) emanate.

dégarnir (se) /(sə)degaʀniʀ/ **2** *vpr* clear, empty; (personne) be going bald.

dégâts /dega/ *nmpl* damage (+ sg).

dégel /deʒɛl/ *nm* thaw. **dégeler** **6** *vi* thaw (out).

dégénéré, ~e /deʒeneʀe/ *adj & nm,f* degenerate.

dégivrer /deʒivʀe/ **1** *vt* (Auto) de-ice; (réfrigérateur) defrost.

déglinguer /deglɛ̃ge/ **1** *vt* bust. □ **se ~** *vpr* break down.

dégonflé, ~e /degɔ̃fle/ *adj* (pneu) flat; (lâche **1**) yellow.

dégonfler /degɔ̃fle/ **1** *vt* deflate. ● *vi* (blessure) go down. □ **se ~** *vpr* **1** chicken out.

dégouliner /deguline/ **1** *vi* trickle.

dégourdi, ~e /degurdi/ *adj* smart.

dégourdir /deguʀdiʀ/ **2** *vt* (membre, liquide) warm up. □ **se ~** *vpr* **se ~ les jambes** stretch one's legs.

dégoût /degu/ *nm* disgust.

dégoûtant, ~e /degutɑ̃, -t/ *adj* disgusting.

dégoûter /degute/ **1** *vt* disgust; **~ qn de qch** put sb off sth.

dégradant, ~e /degʀadɑ̃, -t/ *adj* degrading.

dégradation /degʀadasjɔ̃/ nf damage; **commettre des ~s** cause damage.

dégrader /degʀade/ **1** vt (abîmer) damage. □ **se ~** vpr (se détériorer) deteriorate.

dégrafer /degʀafe/ **1** vt unhook.

degré /dəgʀe/ nm degree; (d'escalier) step.

dégressif, -ive /degʀesif, -v/ adj graded; **tarif ~** tapering charge.

dégrèvement /degʀɛvmɑ̃/ nm ~ **fiscal** ou **d'impôts** tax reduction.

dégringolade /degʀɛ̃gɔlad/ nf tumble.

dégrossir /degʀosiʀ/ **2** vt (bois) trim; (projet) rough out.

déguerpir /degɛʀpiʀ/ **2** vi clear off.

dégueulasse /degœlas/ adj 🗷 disgusting, lousy.

dégueuler /degœle/ **1** vt 🗷 throw up.

déguisement /degizmɑ̃/ nm (de carnaval) fancy dress; (pour duper) disguise.

déguiser /degize/ **1** vt dress up; (pour duper) disguise. □ **se ~** vpr (au carnaval etc.) dress up; (pour duper) disguise oneself.

déguster /degyste/ **1** vt taste, sample; (savourer) enjoy.

dehors /dəɔʀ/ adv **en ~ de** outside; (hormis) apart from; **jeter/ mettre ~** throw/put out. ● nm outside. ● nmpl (aspect de qn) exterior.

déjà /deʒa/ adv already; (avant) before, already.

déjeuner /deʒœne/ **1** vi have lunch; (le matin) have breakfast. ● nm lunch; **petit ~** breakfast.

delà /dəla/ adv & prép **au ~ (de) par ~** beyond.

délai /delɛ/ nm time-limit; (attente) wait; (sursis) extension (of time); **sans ~** immediately; **dans un ~ de 2 jours** within 2 days; **finir dans les ~s** finish within the deadline; **dans les plus brefs ~s** as soon as possible.

délaisser /delese/ **1** vt (négliger) neglect.

délassement /delasmɑ̃/ nm relaxation.

délation /delasjɔ̃/ nf informing.

délavé, ~e /delave/ adj faded.

délayer /deleje/ **31** vt mix (with liquid); (idée) drag out.

délecter (se) /(sə)delɛkte/ **1** vpr **se ~ de** delight in.

délégué, ~e /delege/ nm, f delegate.

délibéré, ~e /delibeʀe/ adj deliberate; (résolu) determined.

délicat, ~e /delika, -t/ adj delicate; (plein de tact) tactful. **délicatesse** nf delicacy; (tact) tact. **délicatesses** nfpl (kind) attentions.

délice /delis/ nm delight. **délicieux, -ieuse** adj (au goût) delicious; (charmant) delightful.

délier /delje/ **45** vt untie; (délivrer) free. □ **se ~** vpr come untied.

délimiter /delimite/ **1** vt determine, demarcate.

délinquance /delɛ̃kɑ̃s/ nf delinquency. **délinquant, ~e** adj & nm, f delinquent.

délirant, ~e /deliʀɑ̃, -t/ adj delirious; (frénétique) frenzied; 🗓 wild.

délire /deliʀ/ nm delirium; (fig) frenzy. **délirer** **1** vi be delirious (**de** with); 🗓 be off one's rocker 🗓.

délit /deli/ nm offence.

délivrance /delivʀɑ̃s/ nf release; (soulagement) relief; (remise) issue. **délivrer** **1** vt free, release; (pays) liberate; (remettre) issue.

déloyal, ~e (mpl **-aux**) /delwajal, -jo/ adj disloyal; (procédé) unfair.

deltaplane /dɛltaplan/ nm hangglider.

déluge /delyʒ/ nm downpour; **le D~** the Flood.

démagogie /demagɔʒi/ nf demagogy. **démagogue** nmf demagogue.

demain /dəmɛ̃/ adv tomorrow.

demande /dəmɑ̃d/ nf request; ~ **d'emploi** job application; ~ **en mariage** marriage proposal.

demander /dəmɑ̃de/ **1** vt ask for; (chemin, heure) ask; (nécessiter) require; ~ **que/si** ask that/if; ~ **qch à qn** ask sb sth; ~ **à qn de** ask sb to; ~ **en mariage** propose to. □ **se ~** vpr **se ~ si/où** wonder if/where.

demandeur, -euse /dəmɑ̃dœʀ, -øz/ nm, f ~ **d'emploi** job seeker; ~ **d'asile** asylum-seeker.

démangeaison /demɑ̃ʒezɔ̃/ nf itch(ing).

démanteler /demɑ̃tle/ **6** vt break up.

démaquillant /demakijɑ̃/ nm make-up remover. **démaquiller (se)** 1 vpr remove one's make-up.

démarchage /demaʁʃaʒ/ nm door-to-door selling.

démarche /demaʁʃ/ nf walk, gait; (procédé) step.

démarcheur, -euse /demaʁʃœʁ, -øz/ nm, f (door-to-door) canvasser.

démarrage /demaʁaʒ/ nm start.

démarrer /demaʁe/ 1 vi (moteur) start (up); (partir) move off; (fig) get moving. ● vt 1 get moving.

démarreur /demaʁœʁ/ nm starter.

démêlant /demelɑ̃/ nm conditioner. **démêler** 1 vt disentangle.

déménagement /demenaʒmɑ̃/ nm move; (transport) removal.

déménager /demenaʒe/ 40 vi move (house). ● vt (meubles) remove.

déménageur /demenaʒœʁ/ nm removal man.

démence /demɑ̃s/ nf insanity.

démener (se) /(sə)demne/ 6 vpr move about wildly; (fig) put oneself out.

dément, -e /demɑ̃, -t/ adj insane. ● nm, f lunatic.

démenti /demɑ̃ti/ nm denial.

démentir /demɑ̃tiʁ/ 46 vt deny; (contredire) refute; ~ **que** deny that.

démerder (se) /(sə)demɛʁde/ 1 vpr ⊠ manage.

démettre /demɛtʁ/ 42 vt (poignet etc.) dislocate; ~ **qn de** relieve sb of. □ **se** ~ vpr resign (**de** from).

demeure /dəmœʁ/ nf residence; **mettre en** ~ **de** order to.

demeurer /dəmœʁe/ 1 vi live; (rester) remain.

demi, ~e /dəmi/ adj half(-). ● nm, f half. ● nm (bière) (half-pint) glass of beer; (football) half-back. ● adv **à** ~ half; (ouvrir, fermer) halfway; **à la** ~**e** at half past; **une heure et** ~**e** an hour and a half; (à l'horloge) half past one; **une** ~-**journée/-livre** half a day/ pound. **demi-cercle** (pl ~s) nm semicircle. **demi-finale** (pl ~s) nf semifinal. **demi-frère** (pl ~s) nm half-brother, stepbrother. **demi-heure** (pl ~s) nf half-hour, half an hour. **demi-litre** (pl ~s) nm half a litre. **demi-mesure** (pl ~s) nf half-measure.

à demi mot adv without having to express every word. **demi-pension** nf half-board. **demi-queue** nm boudoir grand piano.

demi-sel adj inv slightly salted.

demi-sœur (pl ~s) nf half-sister, stepsister.

démission /demisjɔ̃/ nf resignation.

demi-tarif (pl ~s) /dəmitaʁif/ nm half-fare.

demi-tour (pl ~s) /dəmituʁ/ nm about turn; (Auto) U-turn; **faire** ~ turn back.

démocrate /demɔkʁat/ nmf democrat. ● adj democratic. **démocratie** nf democracy.

démodé, ~e /demɔde/ adj old-fashioned.

demoiselle /dəmwazɛl/ nf young lady; (célibataire) single lady; ~ **d'honneur** bridesmaid.

démolir /demɔliʁ/ 2 vt demolish.

démon /demɔ̃/ nm demon; **le D~** the Devil. **démoniaque** adj fiendish.

démonstration /demɔ̃stʁasjɔ̃/ nf demonstration; (de force) show.

démonter /demɔ̃te/ 1 vt take apart, dismantle; (installation) take down; (fig) disconcert. □ **se** ~ vpr come apart.

démontrer /demɔ̃tʁe/ 1 vt demonstrate; (indiquer) show.

démoraliser /demɔʁalize/ 1 vt demoralize.

démuni, ~e /demyni/ adj impoverished; ~ **de** without.

démunir /demyniʁ/ 2 vt ~ **de** deprive of. □ **se** ~ **de** vpr part with.

dénaturer /denatyʁe/ 1 vt (faits) distort.

dénigrement /deniɡʁəmɑ̃/ nm denigration.

dénivellation /denivɛlasjɔ̃/ nf (pente) slope.

dénombrer /denɔ̃bʁe/ 1 vt count.

dénomination /denɔminasjɔ̃/ nf designation.

dénommé, ~e /denɔme/ nm, f **le** ~ **X** the said X.

dénoncer /denɔ̃se/ 10 vt denounce. □ **se** ~ vpr give oneself up. **dénonciateur, -trice** nm, f informer.

dénouement /denumɑ̃/ nm outcome; (Théât) dénouement.

dénouer /denwe/ **1** vt undo. ◻ **se ~** vpr (nœud) come undone.

dénoyauter /denwajote/ **1** vt stone.

denrée /dɑ̃ʀe/ nf **~ alimentaire** foodstuff.

dense /dɑ̃s/ adj dense. **densité** nf density.

dent /dɑ̃/ nf tooth; **faire ses ~s** teethe; **~ de lait** milk tooth; **~ de sagesse** wisdom tooth; (de roue) cog. **dentaire** adj dental.

denté, ~e /dɑ̃te/ adj (roue) toothed

dentelé, ~e /dɑ̃tle/ adj jagged.

dentelle /dɑ̃tɛl/ nf lace.

dentier /dɑ̃tje/ nm dentures (+ pl), false teeth (+ pl).

dentifrice /dɑ̃tifʀis/ nm toothpaste.

dentiste /dɑ̃tist/ nmf dentist.

dentition /dɑ̃tisjɔ̃/ nf teeth, dentition.

dénudé, ~e /denyde/ adj bare.

dénué, ~e /denɥe/ adj **~ de** devoid of.

dénuement /denymɑ̃/ nm destitution.

déodorant /deɔdɔʀɑ̃/ nm deodorant.

dépannage /depanaʒ/ nm repair; (Ordinat) troubleshooting. **dépanner 1** vt repair; (fig) help out. **dépanneuse** nf breakdown lorry.

dépareillé, ~e /depaʀeje/ adj odd, not matching.

départ /depaʀ/ nm departure; (Sport) start; **au ~ de Nice** from Nice; **au ~** (d'abord) at first.

département /depaʀtəmɑ̃/ nm department.

> **Département** An administrative unit, of which there are 96 in Metropolitan France, most are named after rivers or mountains within their borders. Each *département* has a number which appears as the first two digits in postcodes for addresses within the *département* and as the final two-digit number in vehicle registration numbers. See ▸RÉGION.

dépassé, ~e /depɑse/ adj outdated.

dépasser /depɑse/ **1** vt go past, pass; (véhicule) overtake; (excéder) exceed; (rival) surpass; **ça me dépasse** it's beyond me. ● vi stick out.

dépaysement /depeizmɑ̃/ nm change of scenery; (désagréable) disorientation.

dépêche /depɛʃ/ nf dispatch.

dépêcher /depeʃe/ **1** vt dispatch. ◻ **se ~** vpr hurry (up).

dépendance /depɑ̃dɑ̃s/ nf dependence; (à une drogue) dependency; (bâtiment) outbuilding.

dépendre /depɑ̃dʀ/ **3** vt take down. ● vi depend (**~ de** on); **~ de** (appartenir à) belong to.

dépens /depɑ̃/ nmpl **aux ~ de** at the expense of.

dépense /depɑ̃s/ nf expense; expenditure.

dépenser /depɑ̃se/ **1** vt/i spend; (énergie etc.) use up. ◻ **se ~** vpr get some exercise.

dépérir /depeʀiʀ/ **2** vi wither.

dépêtrer (se) /(sə)depetʀe/ **1** vpr get oneself out (**de** of).

dépeupler /depœple/ **1** vt depopulate. ◻ **se ~** vpr become depopulated.

déphasé, ~e /defɑze/ adj out of step.

dépilatoire /depilatwaʀ/ adj & nm depilatory.

dépistage /depistaʒ/ nm screening. **dépister 1** vt detect; (criminel) track down.

dépit /depi/ nm resentment; **par ~** out of pique; **en ~ de** despite; **en ~ du bon sens** in a very illogical way. **dépité, ~e** adj vexed.

déplacé, ~e /deplase/ adj (remarque) uncalled for.

déplacement /deplasmɑ̃/ nm (voyage) trip.

déplacer /deplase/ **10** vt move. ◻ **se ~** vpr move; (voyager) travel.

déplaire /deplɛʀ/ **47** vi **~ à** (irriter) displease; **ça me déplaît** I don't like it.

déplaisant, ~e /deplɛzɑ̃, -t/ adj unpleasant, disagreeable.

dépliant /deplijɑ̃/ nm leaflet.

déplier /deplije/ **45** vt unfold.

déploiement /deplwamɑ̃/ nm (démonstration) display; (militaire) deployment.

déplorable /deplɔʀabl/ adj deplorable. **déplorer 1** vt (trouver regrettable) deplore; (mort) lament.

déployer /deplwaje/ [31] vt (ailes, carte) spread; (courage) display; (armée) deploy.

déportation /depɔʀtasjɔ̃/ nf (en 1940) internment in a concentration camp.

déposer /depoze/ [1] vt put down; (laisser) leave; (passager) drop; (argent) deposit; (plainte) lodge; (armes) lay down. ● vi (Jur) testify. □ se ~ vpr settle.

dépositaire /depozitɛʀ/ nmf (Comm) agent.

déposition /depozisjɔ̃/ nf (Jur) statement.

dépôt /depo/ nm (entrepôt) warehouse; (d'autobus) depot; (particules) deposit; (garantie) deposit; **laisser en ~** give for safe keeping; **~ légal** formal deposit of a publication with an institution.

dépouille /depuj/ nf skin, hide; (~ **mortelle**) mortal remains.

dépouiller /depuje/ [1] vt (courrier) open; (scrutin) count; (écorcher) skin; **~ qn de** strip sb of.

dépourvu, ~e /depuʀvy/ adj **~ de** devoid of; **prendre au ~** catch unawares.

déprécier /depʀesje/ [45] vt depreciate. □ se ~ vpr depreciate.

déprédations /depʀedasjɔ̃/ nfpl damage (+ sg).

dépression /depʀesjɔ̃/ nf depression; **~ nerveuse** nervous breakdown.

déprimer /depʀime/ [1] vt depress.

---

depuis /dəpɥi/

● préposition

····▸ (point de départ) since; **~ quand attendez-vous?** how long have you been waiting?

····▸ (durée) for; **~ toujours** always; **~ peu** recently.

● adverbe

····▸ since; **il a eu une attaque le mois dernier, ~ nous sommes inquiets** he had a stroke last month and we've been worried ever since.

● depuis que conjonction

····▸ since, ever since; **Sophie a beaucoup changé depuis que Camille est née** Sophie has

---

changed a lot since Camille was born.

député /depyte/ nm ≈ Member of Parliament.

déraciné, -e /deʀasine/ nm, f rootless person.

déraillement /deʀajmɑ̃/ nm derailment.

dérailler /deʀaje/ [1] vi be derailed; (fig [1]) be talking nonsense; **faire ~** derail. **dérailleur** nm (de vélo) derailleur.

déraisonnable /deʀɛzɔnabl/ adj unreasonable.

dérangement /deʀɑ̃ʒmɑ̃/ nm bother; (désordre) disorder, upset; **en ~** out of order; **les ~s** the fault reporting service.

déranger /deʀɑ̃ʒe/ [40] vt (gêner) bother, disturb; (dérégler) upset, disrupt. □ se ~ vpr (aller) go; (fig) put oneself out; **ça te dérangerait de...?** would you mind...?

dérapage /deʀapaʒ/ nm skid. **déraper** [1] vi skid; (fig) (prix) get out of control.

déréglé, ~e /deʀegle/ adj (vie) dissolute; (estomac) upset; (mécanisme) (that is) not running properly.

dérégler /deʀegle/ [14] vt make go wrong. □ se ~ vpr go wrong.

dérision /deʀizjɔ̃/ nf mockery; **tourner en ~** ridicule.

dérive /deʀiv/ nf **aller à la ~** drift.

dérivé /deʀive/ nm by-product.

dériver /deʀive/ [1] vi (bateau) drift; **~ de** stem from.

dermatologie /dɛʀmatɔlɔʒi/ nf dermatology.

dernier, -ière /dɛʀnje, -jɛʀ/ adj last; (nouvelles, mode) latest; (étage) top. ● nm, f last (one); **ce ~** the latter; **le ~ de mes soucis** the least of my worries.

dernièrement /dɛʀnjɛʀmɑ̃/ adv recently.

dérober /deʀɔbe/ [1] vt steal. □ se ~ vpr slip away; **se ~ à** (obligation) shy away from.

dérogation /deʀɔgasjɔ̃/ nf special authorization.

déroger /deʀɔʒe/ [40] vi **~ à** depart from.

déroulement /deʀulmã/ nm (d'une action) development.

dérouler /deʀule/ ❶ vt (fil etc.) unwind. □ se ~ vpr unwind; (avoir lieu) take place; (récit, paysage) unfold.

déroute /deʀut/ nf (Mil) rout.

dérouter /deʀute/ ❶ vt disconcert.

derrière /dɛʀjɛʀ/ prép & adv behind. ● nm back, rear; (postérieur 🆃) behind 🆃; **de** ~ (fenêtre) back, rear; (pattes) hind.

des /de/ ➡DE.

dès /dɛ/ prép (right) from; ~ **lors** from then on; ~ **que** as soon as.

désabusé, ~e /dezabyze/ adj disillusioned.

désaccord /dezakɔʀ/ nm disagreement.

désaffecté, ~e /dezafɛkte/ adj disused.

désagréable /dezagʀeabl/ adj unpleasant.

désagrément /dezagʀemã/ nm annoyance, inconvenience.

désaltérer (se) /(sə)dezalteʀe/ 🄸🄸 vpr quench one's thirst.

désamorcer /dezamɔʀse/ 🄸🄾 vt (situation, obus) defuse.

désapprobation /dezapʀɔbasjõ/ nf disapproval. **désapprouver** ❶ vt disapprove of.

désarçonner /dezaʀsɔne/ ❶ vt throw.

désarmement /dezaʀmǝmã/ nm (Pol) disarmament.

désarroi /dezaʀwa/ nm distress.

désastre /dezastʀ/ nm disaster. **désastreux, -euse** adj disastrous.

désavantage /dezavãtaʒ/ nm disadvantage. **désavantager** 🄸🄾 vt put at a disadvantage.

désaveu (pl ~x) /dezavø/ nm denial. **désavouer** ❶ vt deny.

descendance /desãdãs/ nf descent; (enfants) descendants (+ pl). **descendant**, ~e nm, f descendant.

descendre /desãdʀ/ 🄸 vi (aux être) go down; (venir) come down; (passager) get off ou out; (nuit) fall; ~ **à pied** walk down; ~ **par l'ascenseur** take the lift down; ~ **de** (être issu de) be descended from; ~ **à l'hôtel** go to a hotel; ~ **dans la rue** (Pol) take to the streets. ● vt (aux avoir) (escalier etc.) go ou come down; (objet) take

down; (abattre 🆃) shoot down.

descente /desãt/ nf descent; (à ski) downhill; (raid) raid; **dans la** ~ going downhill; ~ **de lit** bedside rug.

descriptif, -ive /dɛskʀiptif, -v/ adj descriptive. **description** nf description.

désemparé, ~e /dezãpaʀe/ adj distraught.

désendettement /dezãdɛtmã/ nm reduction of the debt.

déséquilibré, ~e /dezekilibʀe/ adj unbalanced; 🆃 crazy. ● nm, f lunatic. **déséquilibrer** ❶ vt throw off balance.

désert, ~e /dezɛʀ, -t/ adj deserted. ● nm desert.

déserter /dezɛʀte/ ❶ vt/i desert. **déserteur** nm deserter.

désertique /dezɛʀtik/ adj desert.

désespérant, ~e /dezɛspeʀã, -t/ adj utterly disheartening.

désespéré, ~e /dezɛspeʀe/ adj in despair; (état, cas) hopeless; (effort) desperate.

désespérer /dezɛspeʀe/ 🄸🄸 vt drive to despair. ● vi despair, lose hope; ~ **de** despair of. □ se ~ vpr despair.

désespoir /dezɛspwaʀ/ nm despair; **en** ~ **de cause** as a last resort.

déshabillé, ~e /dezabije/ adj undressed. ● nm négligee.

déshabiller /dezabije/ ❶ vt undress. □ se ~ vpr get undressed.

désherbant /dezɛʀbã/ nm weedkiller.

déshérité, ~e /dezeʀite/ adj (région) deprived; (personne) the underprivileged.

déshériter /dezeʀite/ ❶ vt disinherit.

déshonneur /dezɔnœʀ/ nm disgrace.

déshonorer /dezɔnɔʀe/ ❶ vt dishonour.

déshydrater /dezidʀate/ ❶ vt dehydrate. □ se ~ vpr get dehydrated.

désigner /dezine/ ❶ vt (montrer) point to ou out; (élire) appoint; (signifier) designate.

désillusion /dezilyzjõ/ nf disillusionment.

désinence /dezinãs/ nf (Gram) ending.

désinfectant /dezɛ̃fɛktã/ nm disinfectant. **désinfecter** ❶ vt disinfect.

désintéressé, ~e /dezɛ̃teʀese/ adj (personne, acte) selfless.

désintéresser (se) | détachant

désintéresser (se) /(sə)dezɛ̃teʀese/ **1** *vpr* **se ~ de** lose interest in.

désintoxiquer /dezɛ̃tɔksike/ **1** *vt* detoxify; **se faire ~** to undergo detoxification.

désinvolte /dezɛ̃vɔlt/ *adj* casual. **désinvolture** *nf* casualness.

désir /deziʀ/ *nm* wish, desire; (convoitise) desire.

désirer /deziʀe/ **1** *vt* want; (sexuellement) desire; **vous désirez?** what would you like?

désireux, -euse /deziʀø, -z/ *adj* **~ de faire** anxious to do.

désistement /dezistəmɑ̃/ *nm* withdrawal.

désobéir /dezɔbeiʀ/ **2** *vi* **(~ à)** disobey. **désobéissant, ~e** *adj* disobedient.

désobligeant, ~e /dezɔbliʒɑ̃, -t/ *adj* disagreeable, unkind.

désodorisant /dezɔdɔʀizɑ̃/ *nm* air freshener.

désodoriser /dezɔdɔʀize/ **1** *vt* freshen up.

désœuvré, ~e /dezœvʀe/ *adj* at a loose end. **désœuvrement** *nm* lack of anything to do.

désolation /dezɔlasjɔ̃/ *nf* distress.

désolé, ~e /dezɔle/ *adj* (au regret) sorry; (région) desolate.

désoler /dezɔle/ **1** *vt* distress. □ **se ~** *vpr* be upset (**de qch** about sth).

désopilant, ~e /dezɔpilɑ̃, -t/ *adj* hilarious.

désordonné, ~e /dezɔʀdɔne/ *adj* untidy; (mouvements) uncoordinated.

désordre /dezɔʀdʀ/ *nm* untidiness; (Pol) disorder; **en ~** untidy.

désorganiser /dezɔʀganize/ **1** *vt* disorganize.

désorienter /dezɔʀjɑ̃te/ **1** *vt* disorient.

désormais /dezɔʀmɛ/ *adv* from now on.

desquels, desquelles /dekɛl/ ⇒LEQUEL.

dessécher /deseʃe/ **1** *vt* dry out. □ **se ~** *vpr* dry out, become dry; (plante) wither.

dessein /desɛ̃/ *nm* intention; **à ~** intentionally.

desserrer /deseʀe/ **1** *vt* loosen; **il n'a pas desserré les dents** he never once

opened his mouth. □ **se ~** *vpr* come loose.

dessert /desɛʀ/ *nm* dessert; **en ~** for dessert.

desservir /desɛʀviʀ/ **46** *vt/i* (débarrasser) clear away; (autobus) serve.

dessin /desɛ̃/ *nm* drawing; (motif) design; (discipline) art; (contour) outline; **professeur de ~** art teacher; **~ animé** (cinéma) cartoon; **~ humoristique** cartoon.

dessinateur, -trice /desinatœʀ, -tʀis/ *nm, f* artist; (industriel) draughtsman.

dessiner /desine/ **1** *vt/i* draw; (fig) outline. □ **se ~** *vpr* appear, take shape.

dessoûler /desule/ **1** *vt/i* sober up.

dessous /dəsu/ *adv* underneath. ● *nm* underside, underneath. ● *nmpl* underwear; **les ~ d'une histoire** what is behind a story; **du ~** bottom; (voisins) downstairs; **en ~, par-~** underneath. **dessous-de-plat** *nm inv* (heat resistant) table-mat. **dessous-de-table** *nm inv* backhander. **dessous-de-verre** *nm inv* coaster.

dessus /dəsy/ *adv* on top (of it), on it. ● *nm* top; **du ~** top; (voisins) upstairs; **avoir le ~** get the upper hand. **dessus-de-lit** *nm inv* bedspread.

destabiliser /destabilize/ **1** *vt* destabilize, unsettle.

destin /dɛstɛ̃/ *nm* (sort) fate; (avenir) destiny.

destinataire /dɛstinatɛʀ/ *nmf* addressee.

destination /dɛstinasjɔ̃/ *nf* destination; (fonction) purpose; **vol à ~ de** flight to.

destinée /dɛstine/ *nf* destiny.

destiner /dɛstine/ **1** *vt* **~ à** intend for; (vouer) destine for; **le commentaire m'est destiné** this comment is aimed at me; **être destiné à faire** be intended to do; (obligé) be destined to do. □ **se ~ à** *vpr* (carrière) intend to take up.

destituer /dɛstitɥe/ **1** *vt* discharge.

destructeur, -trice /dɛstʀyktœʀ, -tʀis/ *adj* destructive. **destruction** *nf* destruction.

désuet, -ète /dezɥɛ, -t/ *adj* outdated.

détachant /detaʃɑ̃/ *nm* stain remover.

détacher /detaʃe/ **1** vt untie; (ôter) remove, detach; (déléguer) second. □ se ~ vpr come off, break away; (nœud etc.) come undone; (ressortir) stand out.

détail /detaj/ nm detail; (de compte) breakdown; (Comm) retail; **au** ~ (vendre etc.) retail; **de** ~ (prix etc.) retail; **en** ~ in detail; **entrer dans les** ~s go into detail.

détaillant, ~e /detajɑ̃, -t/ nm, f retailer.

détaillé, ~e /detaje/ adj detailed.

détailler /detaje/ **1** vt (rapport) detail; ~ **ce que qn fait** scrutinize what sb does.

détaler /detale/ **1** vi 🔟 bolt.

détartrant /detartrɑ̃/ nm descaler.

détecter /detɛkte/ **1** vt detect. **détecteur** nm detector.

détective /detɛktiv/ nm detective.

déteindre /detɛ̃dʀ/ 🔢 vi (dans l'eau) run (sur on to); (au soleil) fade; ~ **sur** (fig) rub off on.

détendre /detɑ̃dʀ/ **3** vt slacken; (ressort) release; (personne) relax. □ se ~ vpr (ressort) slacken; (personne) relax. **détendu,** ~e adj (calme) relaxed.

détenir /det(ə)niʀ/ 🔢 vt hold; (secret, fortune) possess.

détente /detɑ̃t/ nf relaxation; (Pol) détente; (saut) spring; (gâchette) trigger; **être lent à la** ~ 🔟 be slow on the uptake.

détenteur, -trice /detɑ̃tœʀ, -tʀis/ nm, f holder.

détention /detɑ̃sjɔ̃/ nf detention; ~ **provisoire** custody.

détenu, ~e /detny/ nm, f prisoner.

détergent /detɛʀʒɑ̃/ nm detergent.

détérioration /deteʀjɔʀasjɔ̃/ nf deterioration; (dégât) damage.

détériorer /deteʀjɔʀe/ **1** vt damage. □ se ~ vpr deteriorate.

détermination /detɛʀminasjɔ̃/ nf determination. **déterminé,** ~e adj (résolu) determined; (précis) definite. **déterminer** **1** vt determine.

déterrer /detɛʀe/ **1** vt dig up.

détestable /detɛstabl/ adj (caractère, temps) foul.

détester /detɛste/ **1** vt hate. □ se ~ vpr hate each other.

détonation /detɔnasjɔ̃/ nf explosion, detonation.

détour /detuʀ/ nm (crochet) detour; (fig) roundabout means; (virage) bend.

détournement /detuʀnəmɑ̃/ nm hijack(ing); (de fonds) embezzlement.

détourner /detuʀne/ **1** vt (attention) divert; (tête, yeux) turn away; (avion) hijack; (argent) embezzle. □ se ~ de vpr stray from.

détraquer /detʀake/ **1** vt make go wrong; (estomac) upset. □ se ~ vpr (machine) go wrong.

détresse /detʀɛs/ nf distress; **dans la** ~, **en** ~ in distress.

détritus /detʀity(s)/ nmpl rubbish (+ sg).

détroit /detʀwa/ nm strait.

détromper /detʀɔ̃pe/ **1** vt set straight. □ se ~ vpr **détrompe-toi!** you'd better think again!

détruire /detʀɥiʀ/ 🔢 vt destroy.

dette /dɛt/ nf debt.

deuil /dœj/ nm (période) mourning; (décès) bereavement; **porter le** ~ be in mourning; **faire son** ~ **de qch** give sth up as lost.

deux /dø/ adj & nm two; ~ **fois** twice; **tous (les** ~) both. **deuxième** adj & nmf second. **deux-pièces** nm inv (maillot de bain) two-piece; (logement) two-room flat. **deux-points** nm inv (Gram) colon. **deux-roues** nm inv two-wheeled vehicle.

dévaliser /devalize/ **1** vt rob, clean out.

dévalorisant, ~e /devalɔʀizɑ̃, -t/ adj demeaning.

dévaloriser /devalɔʀize/ **1** vt (monnaie) devalue. □ se ~ vpr (personne) put oneself down.

dévaluation /devalɥasjɔ̃/ nf devaluation.

dévaluer /devalɥe/ **1** vt devalue. □ se ~ vpr devalue.

devancer /dəvɑ̃se/ 🔟 vt be ou go ahead of; (arriver) arrive ahead of; (prévenir) anticipate.

devant /d(ə)vɑ̃/ prép in front of; (distance) ahead of; (avec mouvement) past; (en présence de) in front of; (face à) in the face of; **avoir du temps** ~ **soi** have plenty of time. ● adv in front; (à distance) ahead; **de**

~ front. ● nm front; **prendre les ~s** take the initiative.

devanture /dəvãtyʀ/ nf shop front; (vitrine) shop window.

développement /devlɔpmã/ nm development; (de photos) developing.

développer /devlɔpe/ **1** vt develop. □ **se ~** vpr (corps, talent) develop; (entreprise) grow, expand.

devenir /dəvniʀ/ **58** vi (aux être) become; **qu'est-il devenu?** what has become of him?

dévergondé, ~e /devɛʀgɔ̃de/ adj & nm,f shameless (person).

déverser /devɛʀse/ **1** vt (liquide) pour; (ordures, pétrole) dump. □ **se ~** vpr (rivière) flow; (égout, foule) pour.

dévêtir /devetiʀ/ **61** vt undress. □ **se ~** vpr get undressed.

déviation /devjasjɔ̃/ nf diversion.

dévier /devje/ **45** vt divert; (coup) deflect. ● vi (ballon, balle) veer; (personne) deviate.

devin /dəvɛ̃/ nm soothsayer.

deviner /dəvine/ **1** vt guess; (apercevoir) distinguish.

devinette /dəvinɛt/ nf riddle.

devis /dəvi/ nm estimate, quote.

dévisager /deviza3e/ **40** vt stare at.

devise /dəviz/ nf motto; **~s** (monnaie) (foreign) currency.

dévisser /devise/ **1** vt unscrew.

dévitaliser /devitalize/ **1** vt (dent) carry out root canal treatment on.

dévoiler /devwale/ **1** vt reveal.

---

devoir /dəvwaʀ/ **26**

● verbe auxiliaire

····▸ ~ **faire** (obligation, hypothèse) must do; (nécessité) have got to do; **je dois dire que...** I have to say that...; **il a dû partir** (nécessité) he had to leave; (hypothèse) he must have left.

····▸ (prévision) **je devais lui dire** I was to tell her; **elle doit rentrer bientôt** she's due back soon.

····▸ (conseil) **tu devrais** you should.

● verbe transitif

····▸ (argent, excuses) owe; **combien je vous dois?** (en achetant) how much is it?

□ **se devoir** verbe pronominal

····▸ **je me dois de le faire** it's my duty to do it.

● nom masculin

····▸ duty; **faire son ~** do one's duty.

····▸ (Scol) ~ **(surveillé)** test; **les ~s** homework (+ sg); **faire ses ~s** do one's homework.

dévorer /devɔʀe/ **1** vt devour.

dévot, ~e /devo, -ɔt/ adj devout.

dévoué, ~e /devwe/ adj devoted. **dévouement** nm devotion.

dévouer (se) /(sə)devwe/ **1** vpr devote oneself (à to); (se sacrifier) sacrifice oneself.

dextérité /dɛksteʀite/ nf skill.

diabète /djabɛt/ nm diabetes. **diabétique** adj & nmf diabetic.

diable /djɑbl/ nm devil.

diagnostic /djagnɔstik/ nm diagnosis. **diagnostiquer** **1** vt diagnose.

diagonal, ~e (mpl -aux) /djagɔnal, -o/ adj diagonal. **diagonale** nf diagonal; **en ~e** diagonally.

diagramme /djagʀam/ nm diagram; (graphique) graph.

dialecte /djalɛkt/ nm dialect.

dialogue /djalɔg/ nm dialogue. **dialoguer** **1** vi have talks, enter into a dialogue.

diamant /djamã/ nm diamond.

diamètre /djamɛtʀ/ nm diameter.

diapositive /djapozitiv/ nf slide.

diarrhée /djaʀe/ nf diarrhoea.

dictateur /diktatœʀ/ nm dictator.

dicter /dikte/ **1** vt dictate. **dictée** nf dictation.

dictionnaire /diksjɔnɛʀ/ nm dictionary.

dicton /diktɔ̃/ nm saying.

dièse /djɛz/ nm (Mus) sharp.

diesel /djezɛl/ nm & adj inv diesel.

diète /djɛt/ nf restricted diet.

diététicien, ~ne /djetetisjɛ̃, -ɛn/ nm, f dietician.

diététique /djetetik/ nf dietetics. ● adj **produit** ou **aliment ~** dietary product; **magasin ~** health food shop ou store.

dieu (pl ~x) /djø/ nm god; **D~** God.

diffamation /difamasjɔ̃/ nf slander; (par écrit) libel. **diffamer** **1** vt slan-

der; (par écrit) libel.
différé: en ~ /ãdifeRe/ *loc* (*émission*) pre-recorded.
différemment /diferamã/ *adv* differently.
différence /difeRãs/ *nf* difference; **à la ~ de** unlike.
différencier /difeRãsje/ [45] *vt* differentiate. □ **se ~** *vpr* differentiate oneself; **se ~ de** (différer de) differ from.
différend /difeRã/ *nm* difference (of opinion).
différent, ~e /difeRã, -t/ *adj* different (de from).
différer /difeRe/ [14] *vt* postpone. ● *vi* differ (de from).
difficile /difisil/ *adj* difficult; (exigeant) fussy. **difficilement** *adv* with difficulty.
difficulté /difikylte/ *nf* difficulty; **faire des ~s** raise objections.
diffus, ~e /dify, -z/ *adj* diffuse.
diffuser /difyze/ [1] *vt* (*émission*) broadcast; (*nouvelle*) spread; (*lumière, chaleur*) diffuse; (Comm) distribute. **diffusion** *nf* broadcasting; diffusion; distribution.
digérer /diʒeRe/ [14] *vt* digest; (endurer [1]) stomach. **digeste** *adj* digestible.
digestif, -ive /diʒɛstif, -v/ *adj* digestive. ● *nm* after-dinner liqueur.
digital, ~e (*mpl* **-aux**) /diʒital, -o/ *adj* digital.
digne /diɲ/ *adj* (noble) dignified; (approprié) worthy; **~ de** worthy of; **~ de foi** trustworthy.
digue /dig/ *nf* dyke; (US) dike.
dilater /dilate/ [1] *vt* dilate. □ **se ~** *vpr* dilate; (*estomac*) distend.
dilemme /dilɛm/ *nm* dilemma.
dilettante /diletãt/ *nmf* amateur.
diluant /dilɥã/ *nm* thinner.
diluer /dilɥe/ [1] *vt* dilute.
dimanche /dimãʃ/ *nm* Sunday.
dimension /dimãsjõ/ *nf* (taille) size; (mesure) dimension; (aspect) dimension.
diminuer /diminɥe/ [1] *vt* reduce, decrease; (*plaisir, courage*) dampen; (dénigrer) diminish. ● *vi* (se réduire) decrease; (faiblir) (*bruit, flamme*) die down; (*ardeur*) cool. **diminutif** *nm* diminutive; (surnom) pet name. **diminution** *nf* decrease (de in); (réduction)

reduction; (affaiblissement) diminishing.
dinde /dɛd/ *nf* turkey.
dîner /dine/ [1] *vi* have dinner. ● *nm* dinner.
dingue /dɛg/ *adj* [1] crazy.
dinosaure /dinozɔR/ *nm* dinosaur.
diphtongue /diftɔ̃g/ *nf* diphthong.
diplomate /diplɔmat/ *nmf* diplomat. ● *adj* diplomatic. **diplomatique** *adj* diplomatic.
diplôme /diplom/ *nm* certificate, diploma; (Univ) degree. **diplômé, ~e** *adj* qualified.
dire /diR/ [27] *vt* say; (secret, vérité, heure) tell; (penser) think; **~ que** say that; **~ à qn que** tell sb that; **~ à qn de** tell sb to; **ça me dit de faire** I feel like doing; **on dirait que** it would seem that, it seems that; **dis/dites donc!** hey! □ **se ~** *vpr* (*mot*) be said; (penser) tell oneself; (se prétendre) claim to be. ● *nm* **au ~ de, selon les ~s de** according to.
direct, ~e /diRɛkt/ *adj* direct. ● *nm* (train) express train; **en ~** (*émission*) live.
directeur, -trice /diRɛktœR, -tRis/ *nm, f* director; (chef de service) manager, manageress; (de journal) editor; (d'école) headteacher; (US) principal; **~ de banque** bank manager; **~ commercial** sales manager; **~ des ressources humaines** human resources manager.
direction /diRɛksjõ/ *nf* (sens) direction; (de société) management; (Auto) steering; **en ~ de** (going) to.
dirigeant, ~e /diRiʒã, -t/ *nm, f* (Pol) leader; (Comm) manager. ● *adj* (classe) ruling.
diriger /diRiʒe/ [40] *vt* (service, école, parti, pays) run; (entreprise, usine) manage; (travaux) supervise; (véhicule) steer; (orchestre) conduct; (braquer) aim; (tourner) turn. □ **se ~** *vpr* (s'orienter) find one's way; **se ~ vers** head for, make for.
dis /di/ →**DIRE** [27].
discernement /disɛRnəmã/ *nm* discernment.
disciplinaire /disiplinɛR/ *adj* disciplinary. **discipline** *nf* discipline.

discontinu, ~e /diskɔ̃tiny/ adj intermittent.

discordant, ~e /diskɔʀdɑ̃, -t/ adj discordant.

discothèque /diskɔtɛk/ nf record library; (boîte de nuit) disco- (thèque).

discours /diskuʀ/ nm speech; (propos) views.

discret, -ète /diskʀɛ, -t/ adj discreet.

discrétion /diskʀesjɔ̃/ nf discretion; à ~ (vin) unlimited; (manger, boire) as much as one desires.

discrimination /diskʀiminasjɔ̃/ nf discrimination. **discriminatoire** adj discriminatory.

disculper /diskylpe/ 🔳 vt exonerate. ⬜ se ~ vpr vindicate oneself.

discussion /diskysjɔ̃/ nf discussion; (querelle) argument.

discutable /diskytabl/ adj debatable; (critiquable) questionable.

discuter /diskyte/ 🔳 vt discuss; (contester) question. ● vi (parler) talk; (répliquer) argue; ~ de discuss.

disette /dizɛt/ nf food shortage.

disgrâce /disgʀɑs/ nf disgrace.

disgracieux, -ieuse /disgʀasjø, -z/ adj ugly, unsightly.

disjoindre /disʒwɛ̃dʀ/ 🄢 vt take apart. ⬜ se ~ vpr come apart.

disloquer /dislɔke/ 🔳 vt (membre) dislocate; (machine) break (apart). ⬜ se ~ vpr (parti, cortège) break up; (meuble) come apart.

disparaître /dispaʀɛtʀ/ 🄳 vi disappear; (mourir) die; **faire ~** get rid of. **disparition** nf disappearance; (mort) death.

disparate /dispaʀat/ adj illassorted.

disparu, ~e /dispaʀy/ adj missing. ● nm, f missing person; (mort) dead person.

dispensaire /dispɑ̃sɛʀ/ nm clinic.

dispense /dispɑ̃s/ nf exemption.

dispenser /dispɑ̃se/ 🔳 vt exempt (de from). ⬜ se ~ de vpr avoid.

disperser /dispɛʀse/ 🔳 vt (éparpiller) scatter; (répartir) disperse. ⬜ se ~ vpr disperse.

disponibilité /disponibilite/ nf availability. **disponible** adj available.

dispos, ~e /dispo, -z/ adj **frais et ~** fresh and alert.

disposé, ~e /dispoze/ adj **bien/mal ~** in a good/bad mood; ~ **à** prepared to; ~ **envers** disposed towards.

disposer /dispoze/ 🔳 vt arrange; ~ **à** (engager à) incline to. ● vi ~ **de** have at one's disposal. ⬜ **se ~ à** vpr prepare to.

dispositif /dispozitif/ nm device; (ensemble de mesures) operation.

disposition /dispozisjɔ̃/ nf arrangement, layout; (tendance) tendency; ~s (humeur) mood; (préparatifs) arrangements; (mesures) measures; (aptitude) aptitude; **mettre à la ~ de** place ou put at the disposal of.

disproportionné, ~e /dispʀopɔʀsjone/ adj disproportionate; ~ **à** out of proportion with.

dispute /dispyt/ nf quarrel.

disputer /dispyte/ 🔳 vt (match) play; (course) run in; (prix) fight for; (gronder 🔳) tell off. ⬜ **se ~** vpr quarrel; (se battre pour) fight over; (match) be played.

disquaire /diskɛʀ/ nmf record dealer.

disque /disk/ nm (Mus) record; (Sport) discus; (cercle) disc, disk; (Ordinat) disk; ~ **compact** compact disc; ~ **dur** hard disk; ~ **optique compact** CD-ROM; ~ **souple** floppy disk.

disquette /diskɛt/ nf floppy disk, diskette; ~ **de sauvegarde** back-up disk.

disséminer /disemine/ 🔳 vt spread, scatter.

dissertation /disɛʀtasjɔ̃/ nf essay, paper.

disserter /disɛʀte/ 🔳 vi ~ **sur** speak about; (par écrit) write about.

dissident, ~e /disidɑ̃, -t/ adj & nm, f dissident.

dissimulation /disimylasjɔ̃/ nf concealment; (fig) deceit.

dissimuler /disimyle/ 🔳 vt conceal (à from). ⬜ **se ~** vpr conceal oneself.

dissipé, ~e /disipe/ adj (élève) unruly.

dissiper /disipe/ 🔳 vt (fumée, crainte) dispel; (fortune) squander; (personne) distract. ⬜ **se ~** vpr disappear; (élève) grow restless.

dissolvant /disolvɑ̃/ nm solvent; (pour ongles) nail polish remover.

dissoudre /disudʀ/ 🄳 vt dissolve. ⬜ **se ~** vpr dissolve.

dissuader /disɥade/ **1** vt dissuade
(de from).

dissuasion /disɥazjɔ̃/ nf dissuasion;
force de ~ deterrent force.

distance /distɑ̃s/ nf distance; (écart)
gap; à ~ at ou from a distance.

distancer /distɑ̃se/ **10** vt outdistance.

distendre /distɑ̃dʀ/ **3** vt (estomac)
distend; (corde) stretch.

distinct, ~e /distɛ̃(kt)/ , -ɛ̃kt/ adj
distinct.

distinctif, -ive /distɛ̃ktif, -v/ adj (trait)
distinctive; (signe, caractère) distin-
guishing.

distinction /distɛ̃ksjɔ̃/ nf distinction;
(récompense) honour.

distinguer /distɛ̃ge/ **1** vt distinguish.

distraction /distʀaksjɔ̃/ nf absent-
mindedness; (passe-temps) entertainment, leisure; (détente) recreation.

distraire /distʀɛʀ/ **29** vt amuse; (rendre inattentif) distract; ~ qn de qch
take sb's mind off sth. □ se ~ vpr
amuse oneself.

distrait, ~e /distʀɛ, -t/ adj absent-
minded; (élève) inattentive.

distrayant, ~e /distʀɛjɑ̃, -t/ adj entertaining.

distribuer /distʀibɥe/ **1** vt hand out,
distribute; (répartir) distribute; (tâches,
rôles) allocate; (cartes) deal; (courrier)
deliver.

distributeur /distʀibytœʀ/ nm (Auto,
Comm) distributor; ~ (automatique)
vending-machine; ~ de billets (de
banque) cash dispenser. **distribution**
nf distribution; (du courrier) delivery;
(acteurs) cast; (secteur) retailing.

district /distʀikt/ nm district.

dit¹, dites /di, dit/ ➡DIRE **27**.

dit², ~e /di, dit/ adj (décidé) agreed;
(surnommé) known as.

diurne /djyʀn/ adj diurnal; (activité)
daytime.

divagations /divagasjɔ̃/ nfpl ravings.

divergence /divɛʀʒɑ̃s/ nf divergence.
divergent, ~e adj divergent. **diverger** **40** vi diverge.

divers, ~e /divɛʀ, -s/ adj (varié) diverse; (différent) various; (frais) miscellaneous; **dépenses ~es** sundries.
diversifier **45** vt diversify.

diversité /divɛʀsite/ nf diversity,
variety.

divertir /divɛʀtiʀ/ **2** vt amuse, entertain. □ se ~ vpr amuse oneself; (passer du bon temps) enjoy oneself. **divertissement** nm amusement,
entertainment.

dividende /dividɑ̃d/ nm dividend.

divin, ~e /divɛ̃, -in/ adj divine. **divi-
nité** nf divinity.

diviser /divize/ **1** vt divide. □ se ~
vpr become divided; **se ~ par sept** be
divisible by seven. **division** nf division.

divorce /divɔʀs/ nm divorce.

divorcé, ~e /divɔʀse/ adj divorced.
● nm, f divorcee.

divorcer /divɔʀse/ **10** vi (d'avec)
divorce.

dix /dis/ /di/ before consonant, /diz/
before vowel) adj & nm ten.

dix-huit /dizɥit/ adj & nm eighteen.

dixième /dizjɛm/ adj & nmf tenth.

dix-neuf /diznœf/ adj & nm nineteen.

dix-sept /disɛt/ adj & nm seventeen.

docile /dɔsil/ adj docile.

docteur /dɔktœʀ/ nm doctor.

doctorat /dɔktɔʀa/ nm doctorate, PhD.

document /dɔkymɑ̃/ nm document.
documentaire adj & nm documentary.

documentaliste /dɔkymɑ̃talist/ nmf
information officer; (Scol) librarian.

documentation /dɔkymɑ̃tasjɔ̃/ nf
information, literature; **centre de ~**
resource centre.

documenté, ~e /dɔkymɑ̃te/ adj well-
documented.

documenter /dɔkymɑ̃te/ **1** vt provide with information. □ se ~ vpr collect information.

dodo /dodo/ nm faire ~ (langage enfantin) sleep.

dodu, ~e /dɔdy/ adj plump.

dogmatique /dɔgmatik/ adj dogmatic. **dogme** nm dogma.

doigt /dwa/ nm finger; **un ~ de** a drop
of; **montrer qch du ~** point at sth; **à
deux ~s de** a hair's breadth away
from; ~ **de pied** toe. **doigté** nm
(Mus) fingering, touch; (diplomatie) tact.

dois, doit /dwa/ ➡DEVOIR **26**.

doléances /dɔleɑ̃s/ nfpl grievances.

dollar /dɔlaʀ/ *nm* dollar.

domaine /dɔmɛn/ *nm* estate, domain; (fig) domain, field.

domestique /dɔmɛstik/ *adj* domestic. ● *nmf* servant. **domestiquer** **1** *vt* domesticate.

domicile /dɔmisil/ *nm* home; **à** ~ at home; (*livrer*) to the home.

domicilié, ~e /dɔmisilje/ *adj* resident; **être** ~ **à Paris** live *ou* be resident in Paris.

dominant, ~e /dɔminɑ̃, -t/ *adj* dominant. **dominante** *nf* dominant feature.

dominer /dɔmine/ **1** *vt* dominate; (*surplomber*) tower over, dominate; (*sujet*) master; (*peur*) overcome. ● *vi* dominate; (*équipe*) be in the lead; (*prévaloir*) stand out.

domino /dɔmino/ *nm* domino.

dommage /dɔmaʒ/ *nm* (*tort*) harm; (~s) (*dégâts*) damage; **c'est** ~ it's a pity *ou* shame; **quel** ~ what a pity *ou* shame. **dommages-intérêts** *nmpl* (Jur) damages.

dompter /dɔ̃te/ **1** *vt* tame. **dompteur, -euse** *nm, f* tamer.

DOM-TOM /dɔmtɔm/ *abrév mpl* (**départements et territoires d'outre-mer**) French overseas departments and territories.

don /dɔ̃/ *nm* (*cadeau, aptitude*) gift. **donateur, -trice** *nm, f* donor. **donation** *nf* donation.

donc /dɔ̃k/ *conj* so, then; (*par conséquent*) so, therefore; **quoi** ~? what did you say?; **tiens** ~! fancy that!

donjon /dɔ̃ʒɔ̃/ *nm* (tour) keep.

donné, ~e /dɔne/ *adj* (*fixé*) given; (*pas cher* **1**) dirt cheap; **étant** ~ **que** given that.

donnée /dɔne/ *nf* (élément d'information) fact; ~s data.

donner /dɔne/ **1** *vt* give; (*vieilles affaires*) give away; (*distribuer*) give out; (*fruits, résultats*) produce; (*film*) show; (*pièce*) put on; **ça donne soif/faim** it makes one thirsty/hungry; ~ **qch à réparer** take sth to be repaired; ~ **lieu à** give rise to. ● *vi* ~ **sur** look out on to; ~ **dans** tend towards. □ **se** ~ **à** *vpr* devote oneself to; **se** ~ **du mal** go to a lot of trouble (**pour faire** to do).

dont /dɔ̃/

● *pronom*

····▸ (personne) **la fille** ~ **je te parlais** the girl I was telling you about; **l'homme** ~ **la fille a dit…** the man whose daughter said…

····▸ (chose) which, **l'affaire** ~ **il parle** the matter which he is referring to; **la manière** ~ **elle parle** the way she speaks; **ce** ~ **il parle** what he's talking about

····▸ (provenance) from which.

····▸ (parmi lesquels) **deux personnes** ~ **toi** two people, one of whom is you; **plusieurs thèmes** ~ **l'identité et le racisme** several topics including identity and racism.

dopage /dɔpaʒ/ *nm* (de cheval) doping; (d'athlète) illegal drug-use.

doper /dɔpe/ **1** *vt* dope. □ **se** ~ *vpr* take drugs.

doré, ~e /dɔʀe/ *adj* (couleur d'or) golden; (qui rappelle de l'or) gold; (avec de l'or) gilt; **la jeunesse** ~e gilded youth.

dorénavant /dɔʀenavɑ̃/ *adv* henceforth.

dorer /dɔʀe/ **1** *vt* gild; (Culin) brown.

dormir /dɔʀmiʀ/ **46** *vi* sleep; (être endormi) be asleep; ~ **debout** be asleep on one's feet; **une histoire à** ~ **debout** a cock-and-bull story.

dortoir /dɔʀtwaʀ/ *nm* dormitory.

dorure /dɔʀyʀ/ *nf* gilding.

dos /do/ *nm* back; (de livre) spine; **à** ~ **de** riding on; **au** ~ **de** (*chèque*) on the back of; **de** ~ from behind; ~ **crawlé** backstroke.

dosage /dozaʒ/ *nm* (mélange) mixture; (quantité) amount, proportions. **dose** *nf* dose. **doser** **1** *vt* measure out; (contrôler) use in a controlled way.

dossier /dosje/ *nm* (documents) file; (Jur) case; (de chaise) back; (TV, presse) special feature.

dot /dɔt/ *nf* dowry.

douane /dwan/ *nf* customs.

douanier, -ière /dwanje, -jɛʀ/ *adj* customs. ● *nm* customs officer.

double /dubl/ *adj & adv* double. ● *nm* (copie) duplicate; (sosie) double; **le** ~ **(de)** twice as much *ou* as many (as);

le ~ **messieurs** the men's doubles.

double-cliquer /dublklike/ **1** *vt* double-click.

doubler /duble/ **1** *vt* double; (*dépasser*) overtake; (*vêtement*) line; (*film*) dub; (*classe*) repeat; (*cap*) round. ● *vi* double.

doublure /dublyʀ/ *nf* (étoffe) lining; (acteur) understudy.

douce /dus/ ➡**DOUX.**

doucement /dusmã/ *adv* gently; (sans bruit) quietly; (lentement) slowly.

douceur /dusœʀ/ *nf* (mollesse) softness; (de climat) mildness; (de personne) gentleness; (friandise) sweet; (US) candy; **en ~** smoothly.

douche /duʃ/ *nf* shower.

doucher (se) /duʃe/ **1** *vpr* have ou take a shower.

doudoune /dudun/ *nf* Ⓘ down jacket.

doué, ~e /dwe/ *adj* gifted; **~ de** endowed with.

douille /duj/ *nf* (Électr) socket.

douillet, ~te /duje, -t/ *adj* cosy, comfortable; (*personne*: péj) soft.

douleur /dulœʀ/ *nf* pain; (chagrin) sorrow, grief. **douloureux, -euse** *adj* painful.

doute /dut/ *nm* doubt; **sans ~** no doubt; **sans aucun ~** without doubt.

douter /dute/ **1** *vt* **~ de** doubt; **~ que** doubt that. ● *vi* doubt. □ **se ~ de** *vpr* suspect; **je m'en doutais** I thought so.

douteux, -euse /dutø, -z/ *adj* dubious, doubtful.

Douvres /duvʀ/ *npr* Dover.

doux, douce /du, dus/ *adj* (moelleux) soft; (sucré) sweet; (clément, pas fort) mild; (pas brusque, bienveillant) gentle.

douzaine /duzɛn/ *nf* about twelve; (douze) dozen; **une ~ d'œufs** a dozen eggs.

douze /duz/ *adj & nm* twelve. **douzième** *adj & nmf* twelfth.

doyen, ~ne /dwajɛ̃, -ɛn/ *nm, f* dean; (en âge) most senior person.

dragée /dʀaʒe/ *nf* sugared almond.

draguer /dʀage/ **1** *vt* (rivière) dredge; (filles Ⓘ) chat up.

drainer /dʀene/ **1** *vt* drain.

dramatique /dʀamatik/ *adj* dramatic; (tragique) tragic. ● *nf* (television) drama.

dramatiser /dʀamatize/ **1** *vt* dramatize.

dramaturge /dʀamatyʀʒ/ *nmf* dramatist.

drame /dʀam/ *nm* (genre) drama; (pièce) play; (événement tragique) tragedy.

drap /dʀa/ *nm* sheet; (tissu) (woollen) cloth.

drapeau (*pl* **~x**) /dʀapo/ *nm* flag.

drap-housse (*pl* **draps-housses**) /dʀaus/ *nm* fitted sheet.

dressage /dʀesaʒ/ *nm* training; (compétition équestre) dressage.

dresser /dʀese/ **1** *vt* put up, erect; (tête) raise; (animal) train; (liste, plan) draw up; **~ l'oreille** prick up one's ears. □ **se ~** *vpr* (bâtiment) stand; (personne) draw oneself up. **dresseur, -euse** *nm, f* trainer.

dribbler /dʀible/ **1** *vi* (Sport) dribble.

drive /dʀajv/ *nm* (Ordinat) drive.

drogue /dʀɔg/ *nf* drug; **la ~** drugs.

drogué, ~e /dʀɔge/ *nm, f* drug addict.

droguer /dʀɔge/ **1** *vt* (malade) drug heavily; (victime) drug. □ **se ~** *vpr* take drugs.

droguerie /dʀɔgʀi/ *nf* hardware shop. **droguiste** *nmf* owner of a hardware shop.

droit, ~e /dʀwa, -t/ *adj* (contraire de gauche) right; (non courbe) straight; (loyal) upright; **angle ~** right angle. ● *adv* straight. ● *nm* right; **~(s)** (taxe) duty; **le ~** (Jur) law; **avoir ~ à** be entitled to; **avoir le ~ de** be allowed to; **être dans son ~** be in the right; **~ d'auteur** copyright; **~ d'inscription** registration fee; **~s d'auteur** royalties.

droite /dʀwat/ *nf* (contraire de gauche) right; **à ~** on the right; (direction) (to the) right; **la ~** the right (side); (Pol) the right (wing); (ligne) straight line. **droitier, -ière** *adj* right-handed.

drôle /dʀol/ *adj* (amusant) funny; (bizarre) funny, odd. **drôlement** *adv* funnily; (très Ⓘ) really.

dru, ~e /dʀy/ *adj* thick; **tomber ~** fall thick and fast.

drugstore /dʀœgstɔʀ/ *nm* drugstore.

DTD *abrév m* (**document type definition**) DTD.

du /dy/ →DE.

dû, due /dy/ *adj* due. ● *nm* due; (argent) dues; ~ **à** due to. ● →DE· **VOIR** 26.

duc, duchesse /dyk, dyʃɛs/ *nm, f* duke, duchess.

duo /dɥo/ *nm* (Mus) duet; (fig) duo.

dupe /dyp/ *nf* dupe.

duplex /dyplɛks/ *nm* split-level apartment; (US) duplex; (émission) link-up.

duplicata /dyplikata/ *nm inv* duplicate.

duquel /dykɛl/ →LEQUEL.

dur, ~e /dyʀ/ *adj* hard; (sévère) harsh, hard; (viande) tough; (col, brosse) stiff; ~ **d'oreille** hard of hearing. ● *adv* hard. ● *nm, f* tough nut 1; (Pol) hardliner.

durable /dyʀabl/ *adj* lasting.

durant /dyʀɑ̃/ *prép* (au cours de) during; (avec mesure de temps) for; ~ **des heures** for hours; **des heures** ~ for hours and hours.

durcir /dyʀsiʀ/ 2 *vt* harden. ● *vi* (terre) harden; (ciment) set; (pain) go hard. □ **se** ~ *vpr* harden.

durée /dyʀe/ *nf* length; (période) duration; **de courte** ~ short-lived; **pile longue** ~ long-life battery.

durer /dyʀe/ 1 *vi* last.

dureté /dyʀte/ *nf* hardness; (sévérité) harshness.

duvet /dyvɛ/ *nm* down; (sac) sleeping-bag.

DVD *abrév m* (**digital versatile disc**) DVD.

dynamique /dinamik/ *adj* dynamic.

dynamite /dinamit/ *nf* dynamite.

dynamo /dinamo/ *nf* dynamo.

Ee

eau (*pl* ~**x**) /o/ *nf* water; ~ **courante** running water; ~ **de mer** seawater; ~ **de source** spring water; ~ **douce/ salée** fresh/salt water; ~ **de pluie** rainwater; ~ **potable** drinking water; ~ **de Javel** bleach; ~ **minérale** min-

eral water; ~ **gazeuse** sparkling water; ~ **plate** still water; ~ **de toilette** eau de toilette; ~**x usées** dirty water; ~**x et forêts** forestry commission (+ *sg*); **tomber à l'~** (fig) fall through; **prendre l'~** take in water. **eau-de-vie** (*pl* **eaux-de-vie**) *nf* brandy.

ébahi, ~e /ebai/ *adj* dumbfounded.

ébauche /eboʃ/ *nf* (dessin) sketch; (fig) attempt.

ébéniste /ebenist/ *nm* cabinet-maker.

éblouir /ebluiʀ/ 2 *vt* dazzle.

éboueur /ebwœʀ/ *nm* dustman.

ébouillanter /ebujɑ̃te/ 1 *vt* scald.

éboulement /ebulmɑ̃/ *nm* landslide.

ébouriffé, ~e /eburife/ *adj* dishevelled.

ébrécher /ebreʃe/ 14 *vt* chip.

ébruiter /ebruite/ 1 *vt* spread about. □ **s'~** *vpr* get out.

ébullition /ebylisjɔ̃/ *nf* boiling; **en** ~ boiling.

écaille /ekaj/ *nf* (de poisson) scale; (de peinture, roc) flake; (matière) tortoiseshell.

écarlate /ekaʀlat/ *adj* scarlet.

écarquiller /ekaʀkije/ 1 *vt* ~ **les yeux** open one's eyes wide.

écart /ekaʀ/ *nm* gap; (de prix) difference; (embardée) swerve; ~ **de conduite** lapse in behaviour; **être à l'~** be isolated; **se tenir à l'~ de** stand apart from; (fig) keep out of the way of.

écarté, ~e /ekaʀte/ *adj* (lieu) remote; **les jambes ~es** (with) legs apart; **les bras ~s** with one's arms out.

écarter /ekaʀte/ 1 *vt* (séparer) move apart; (membres) spread; (branches) part; (éliminer) dismiss; ~ **qch de** move sth away from; ~ **qn de** keep sb away from. □ **s'~** *vpr* (s'éloigner) move away; (quitter son chemin) move aside; **s'~ de** stray from.

ecchymose /ekimoz/ *nf* bruise.

écervelé, ~e /esɛʀvale/ *adj* scatterbrained. ● *nm, f* scatterbrain.

échafaudage /eʃafodaʒ/ *nm* scaffolding; (amas) heap.

échalote /eʃalot/ *nf* shallot.

échancré, ~e /eʃɑ̃kʀe/ *adj* lowcut.

échange /eʃɑ̃ʒ/ *nm* exchange; **en** ~ **(de)** in exchange (for). **échanger** 40 *vt* exchange (**contre** for).

échangeur /eʃɑ̃ʒœʀ/ *nm* (Auto) interchange.

échantillon /eʃɑ̃tijɔ̃/ *nm* sample.

échappatoire /eʃapatwaʀ/ *nf* way out.

échappement /eʃapmɑ̃/ *nm* exhaust.

échapper /eʃape/ **1** *vi* ~ **à** escape; (en fuyant) escape (from); ~ **des mains de** slip out of the hands of; **ça m'a échappé** (fig) it just slipped out; **l'~ belle** have a narrow *ou* lucky escape. □ **s'~** *vpr* escape.

écharde /eʃaʀd/ *nf* splinter.

écharpe /eʃaʀp/ *nf* scarf; (de maire) sash; **en ~** (bras) in a sling.

échasse /eʃas/ *nf* stilt.

échauffement /eʃofmɑ̃/ *nm* (Sport) warm-up.

échauffer /eʃofe/ **1** *vt* heat; (fig) excite. □ **s'~** *vpr* warm up.

échéance /eʃeɑ̃s/ *nf* due date (for payment); (délai) deadline; (obligation) (financial) commitment.

échéant: le cas ~ /ləkazeʃeɑ̃/ *loc* if need be.

échec /eʃɛk/ *nm* failure; ~**s** (jeu) chess; ~ **et mat** checkmate.

échelle /eʃɛl/ *nf* ladder; (dimension) scale.

échelon /eʃlɔ̃/ *nm* rung; (hiérarchique) grade; (niveau) level.

échevelé, ~e /eʃəvle/ *adj* dishevelled.

écho /eko/ *nm* echo; ~**s** (dans la presse) gossip.

échographie /ekɔgʀafi/ *nf* (ultrasound) scan.

échouer /eʃwe/ **1** *vi* (bateau) run aground; (ne pas réussir) fail; ~ **à un examen** fail an exam. ● *vt* (bateau) ground. □ **s'~** *vpr* run aground.

échu, ~e /eʃy/ *adj* (délai) expired.

éclabousser /eklabuse/ **1** *vt* splash.

éclair /eklɛʀ/ *nm* (flash of) lightning; (fig) flash; (gâteau) éclair. ● *adj inv* (visite) brief.

éclairage /eklɛʀaʒ/ *nm* lighting.

éclaircie /eklɛʀsi/ *nf* sunny interval.

éclaircir /eklɛʀsiʀ/ **2** *vt* lighten; (mystère) clear up. □ **s'~** *vpr* (ciel) clear; (mystère) become clearer. **éclaircissement** *nm* clarification.

éclairer /eklere/ **1** *vt* light (up); (personne) (fig) enlighten; (situation) throw light on. ● *vi* give light. □ **s'~** *vpr* become clearer.

éclaireur, -euse /eklɛʀœʀ, -øz/ *nm, f* (boy) scout, (girl) guide.

éclat /ekla/ *nm* fragment; (de lumière) brightness; (splendeur) brilliance; ~ **de rire** burst of laughter.

éclatant, ~e /eklatɑ̃, -t/ *adj* brilliant; (soleil) dazzling.

éclater /eklate/ **1** *vi* burst; (exploser) go off; (verre) shatter; (guerre) break out; (groupe) split up; ~ **de rire** burst out laughing.

éclipse /eklips/ *nf* eclipse.

éclosion /eklozjɔ̃/ *nf* hatching, opening.

écluse /eklyz/ *nf* (de canal) lock.

écœurant, ~e /ekœʀɑ̃, -t/ *adj* (gâteau) sickly; (fig) disgusting. **écœurer** **1** *vt* sicken.

éco-guerrier, -ière /ekogɛʀje, jɛʀ/ *nmf* eco-warrior.

école /ekɔl/ *nf* school; ~ **maternelle/primaire/secondaire** nursery/primary/secondary school; ~ **normale** teachers' training college. **écolier, -ière** *nm, f* schoolboy, schoolgirl.

écologie /ekɔlɔʒi/ *nf* ecology. **écologique** *adj* ecological, green. **écologiste** *nmf* (chercheur) ecologist; (dans l'âme) environmentalist; (Pol) Green.

économie /ekɔnɔmi/ *nf* economy; (discipline) economics; ~**s** (argent) savings; **une ~ de** (gain) a saving of. **économique** *adj* (Pol) economic; (bon marché) economical.

économiser /ekɔnɔmize/ **1** *vt/i* save.

écorce /ekɔʀs/ *nf* bark; (de fruit) peel.

écorcher /ekɔʀʃe/ **1** *vt* (genou) graze; (animal) skin. □ **s'~** *vpr* graze oneself. **écorchure** *nf* graze.

écossais, ~e /ekɔsɛ, -z/ *adj* Scottish. **É~, ~e** *nm, f* Scot.

Écosse /ekɔs/ *nf* Scotland.

écoulement /ekulmɑ̃/ *nm* flow.

écouler /ekule/ **1** *vt* dispose of, sell. □ **s'~** *vpr* (liquide) flow; (temps) pass.

écourter /ekuʀte/ **1** *vt* shorten.

écoute /ekut/ *nf* listening; **à l'~ (de)** listening in (to); **heures de grande ~** prime time; ~**s téléphoniques** phone tapping.

écouter /ekute/ **1** vt listen to. ● vi listen; ~ **aux portes** eavesdrop. **écouteur** nm earphones (+ pl); (de téléphone) receiver.

écran /ekrɑ̃/ nm screen; ~ **total** sunblock.

écraser /ekrɑze/ **1** vt crush; (piéton) run over; (cigarette) stub out. □ **s'~** vpr crash (contre into).

écrémé, ~e /ekreme/ adj skimmed; **demi-~** semi-skimmed.

écrevisse /ekrəvis/ nf crayfish.

écrier (s') /(s)ekrije/ **45** vpr exclaim.

écrin /ekrɛ̃/ nm case.

écrire /ekrir/ **30** vt/i write; (orthographier) spell. □ **s'~** vpr (mot) be spelt.

écrit /ekri/ nm document; (examen) written paper; **par ~** in writing.

écriteau (pl ~x) /ekrito/ nm notice.

écriture /ekrityr/ nf writing; ~s (Comm) accounts.

écrivain /ekrivɛ̃/ nm writer.

écrou /ekru/ nm (Tech) nut.

écrouler (s') /(s)ekrule/ **1** vpr collapse.

écru, ~e /ekry/ adj (couleur) natural; (tissu) raw.

écueil /ekœj/ nm reef; (fig) danger.

éculé, ~e /ekyle/ adj (soulier) worn at the heel; (fig) well-worn.

écume /ekym/ nf foam; (Culin) scum.

écumer /ekyme/ **1** vt skim. ● vi foam.

écureuil /ekyrœj/ nm squirrel.

écurie /ekyri/ nf stable.

écuyer, -ère /ekɥije, -jɛr/ nm, f (horse) rider.

eczéma /ɛgzema/ nm eczema.

EDF abrév f (**Électricité de France**) French electricity board.

édifice /edifis/ nm building.

édifier /edifje/ **45** vt construct; (porter à la vertu) edify.

Édimbourg /edɛ̃bur/ npr Edinburgh.

édit /edi/ nm edict.

éditer /edite/ **1** vt publish; (annoter) edit. **éditeur, -trice** nm, f publisher; (réviseur) editor.

édition /edisjɔ̃/ nf (activité) publishing; (livre, disque) edition.

éditique /editik/ nf electronic publishing.

éditorial, ~e (pl -iaux) /editɔrjal, -jo/ adj & nm editorial.

édredon /edrədɔ̃/ nm eiderdown.

éducateur, -trice /edykatœr, -tris/ nm, f youth worker.

éducatif, -ive /edykatif, -v/ adj educational.

éducation /edykasjɔ̃/ nf (façon d'élever) upbringing; (enseignement) education; (manières) manners; ~ **physique** physical education.

éduquer /edyke/ **1** vt (élever) bring up; (former) educate.

effacé, ~e /efase/ adj (modeste) unassuming.

effacer /efase/ **10** vt (gommer) rub out; (à l'écran) delete; (souvenir) erase. □ **s'~** vpr fade; (s'écarter) step aside.

effarer /efare/ **1** vt alarm; **être effaré** be astounded.

effaroucher /efaruʃe/ **1** vt scare away.

effectif, -ive /efɛktif, -v/ adj effective. ● nm (d'école) number of pupils; ~s numbers. **effectivement** adv effectively; (en effet) indeed.

effectuer /efɛktɥe/ **1** vt carry out, make.

efféminé, ~e /efemine/ adj effeminate.

effervescent, ~e /efɛrvesɑ̃, -t/ adj **comprimé ~** effervescent tablet.

effet /efɛ/ nm effect; (impression) impression; ~s (habits) clothes, things; **sous l'~ d'une drogue** under the influence of drugs; **en ~** indeed; **faire de l'~** have an effect, be effective; **faire bon/ mauvais ~** make a good/ bad impression; **ça fait un drôle d'~** it feels strange.

efficace /efikas/ adj effective; (personne) efficient. **efficacité** nf effectiveness; (de personne) efficiency.

effleurer /eflœre/ **1** vt touch lightly; (sujet) touch on; **ça ne m'a pas effleuré** it did not cross my mind.

effondrement /efɔ̃drəmɑ̃/ nm collapse. **effondrer (s')** **1** vpr collapse.

efforcer (s') /(s)efɔrse/ **10** vpr try (hard) (de to).

effort /efɔr/ nm effort.

effraction /efraksjɔ̃/ nf **entrer par ~** break in.

effrayant, ~e /efrejɑ̃, -t/ adj frightening; (fig) frightful.

effrayer /efʀeje/ 🔢 vt frighten; (décourager) put off. □ **s'~** vpr be frightened.

effréné, ~e /efʀene/ adj wild.

effriter (s') /(s)efʀite/ 🔢 vpr crumble.

effroi /efʀwa/ nm dread.

effronté, ~e /efʀɔ̃te/ adj cheeky. ● nm, f cheeky boy, cheeky girl.

effroyable /efʀwajabl/ adj dreadful.

égal, ~e (mpl **-aux**) /egal, -o/ adj equal; (surface, vitesse) even. ● nm, f equal; **ça m'est/lui est ~** it is all the same to me/him; **sans ~** matchless; **d'~ à ~** between equals. **également** adv equally; (aussi) as well. **égaler** 🔢 vt equal.

égaliser /egalize/ 🔢 vt/i (Sport) equalize; (niveler) level out; (cheveux) trim.

égalitaire /egaliteʀ/ adj egalitarian.

égalité /egalite/ nf equality; (de surface) evenness; **être à ~** be level.

égard /egaʀ/ nm consideration; **~s** respect (+ sg); **par ~ pour** out of consideration for; **à cet ~** in this respect; **à l'~ de** with regard to; (envers) towards.

égarer /egaʀe/ 🔢 vt mislay; (tromper) lead astray. □ **s'~** vpr get lost; (se tromper) go astray.

égayer /egeje/ 🔢 vt (personne) cheer up; (pièce) brighten up.

église /egliz/ nf church.

égoïsme /egɔism/ nm selfishness, egoism.

égoïste /egɔist/ adj selfish. ● nmf egoist.

égorger /egɔʀʒe/ 🔢 vt slit the throat of.

égout /egu/ nm sewer.

égoutter /egute/ 🔢 vt drain. □ **s'~** vpr (vaisselle) drain; (lessive) drip dry. **égouttoir** nm draining-board.

égratigner /egʀatiɲe/ 🔢 vt scratch. **égratignure** nf scratch.

Égypte /eʒipt/ nf Egypt.

éjecter /eʒɛkte/ 🔢 vt eject.

élaboration /elabɔʀasjɔ̃/ nf elaboration. **élaborer** 🔢 vt elaborate.

élan /elɑ̃/ nm (animal) moose; (Sport) run-up; (vitesse) momentum; (fig) surge.

élancé, ~e /elɑ̃se/ adj slender.

élancement /elɑ̃smɑ̃/ nm twinge.

élancer (s') /(s)elɑ̃se/ 🔢 vpr leap forward, dash; (arbre, édifice) soar.

élargir /elaʀʒiʀ/ 🔢 vt (route) widen; (connaissances) broaden. □ **s'~** vpr (famille) expand; (route) widen; (écart) increase; (vêtement) stretch.

élastique /elastik/ adj elastic. ● nm elastic band; (tissu) elastic.

électeur, -trice /elɛktœʀ, -tʀis/ nm, f voter. **élection** nf election. **électoral, ~e** (mpl **-aux**) adj (réunion) election. **électorat** nm electorate, voters (+ pl).

électricien, ~ne /elɛktʀisjɛ̃, ɛn/ nm, f electrician. **électricité** nf electricity.

électrifier /elɛktʀifje/ 🔢 vt electrify.

électrique /elɛktʀik/ adj electric; (installation) electrical.

électrocuter /elɛktʀɔkyte/ 🔢 vt electrocute.

électroménager /elɛktʀɔmenaʒe/ nm **l'~** household appliances (+ pl).

électron /elɛktʀɔ̃/ nm electron. **électronicien, ~ne** nm, f electronics engineer.

électronique /elɛktʀɔnik/ adj electronic. ● nf electronics.

élégance /elegɑ̃s/ nf elegance. **élégant, ~e** adj elegant.

élément /elemɑ̃/ nm element; (meuble) unit. **élémentaire** adj elementary.

éléphant /elefɑ̃/ nm elephant.

élevage /ɛlvaʒ/ nm (stock-) breeding.

élévation /elevasjɔ̃/ nf rise; (hausse) rise; (plan) elevation; **~ de terrain** rise in the ground.

élève /elɛv/ nmf pupil.

élevé, ~e /ɛlve/ adj high; (noble) elevated; **bien ~** well-mannered.

élever /ɛlve/ 🔢 vt (lever) raise; (enfants) bring up, raise; (animal) breed. □ **s'~** vpr rise; (dans le ciel) soar up; **s'~ à** amount to. **éleveur, -euse** nm, f (stock-)breeder.

éligible /eliʒibl/ adj eligible.

élimination /eliminasjɔ̃/ nf elimination.

éliminatoire /eliminatwaʀ/ adj qualifying. ● nf (Sport) heat.

éliminer /elimine/ 🔢 vt eliminate.

élire /eliʀ/ 🔢 vt elect.

elle /ɛl/ pron she; (complément) her; (chose) it. **elle-même** pron herself; itself. **elles** pron they; (complément) them. **elles-mêmes** *pron* themselves.

élocution /elɔkysjɔ̃/ *nf* diction.

éloge /elɔʒ/ *nm* praise; **faire l'~ de**
praise; **~s** praise (+ *sg*).

éloigné, ~e /elwaɲe/ *adj* distant; **~**
de far away from; **parent ~** distant
relative.

éloigner /elwaɲe/ **1** *vt* take away *ou*
remove (**de** from); (*danger*) ward off;
(*visite*) put off. **□ s'~** *vpr* go *ou* move
away (**de** from); (*affectivement*) become estranged (**de** from).

élongation /elɔ̃gasjɔ̃/ *nf* strained
muscle.

éloquent, ~e /elɔkã, -t/ *adj* eloquent.

élu, ~e /ely/ *adj* elected. **●** *nm, f* (Pol)
elected representative.

élucider /elyside/ **1** *vt* elucidate.

éluder /elyde/ **1** *vt* evade.

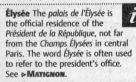

Élysée The *palais de l'Élysée* is
the official residence of the
Président de la République, not far
from the *Champs Élysées* in central
Paris. The word *Élysée* is often used
to refer to the president's office.
See ▷**MATIGNON**.

émacié, ~e /emasje/ *adj* emaciated.

e-mail /imɛl/ *nm* email; **envoyer un ~**
a qn email sb.

émail (*pl* **-aux**) /emaj, -o/ *nm* enamel.

émanciper /emãsipe/ **1** *vt* emancipate. **□ s'~** *vpr* become emancipated.

émaner /emane/ **1** *vi* emanate.

emballage /ãbalaʒ/ *nm* (dur) packaging; (souple) wrapping.

emballer /ãbale/ **1** *vt* pack; (en papier) wrap; **ça ne m'emballe pas** **1**
I'm not really taken by it. **□ s'~** *vpr*
(moteur) race; (cheval) bolt; (personne)
get carried away; (prices) shoot up.

embarcadère /ãbaʀkadɛʀ/ *nm*
landing-stage.

embarcation /ãbaʀkasjɔ̃/ *nf* boat.

embardée /ãbaʀde/ *nf* swerve.

embarquement /ãbaʀkəmã/ *nm* (de
passagers) boarding; (de fret) loading.

embarquer /ãbaʀke/ **1** *vt* take on
board; (frêt) load; (emporter **1**) cart
off. **●** *vi* board. **□ s'~** *vpr* board; **s'~**
dans embark upon.

embarras /ãbaʀa/ *nm* (gêne) embarrassment; (difficulté) difficulty.

embarrasser /ãbaʀase/ **1** *vt* (encombrer) clutter (up); (fig) embarrass.
□ s'~ de *vpr* burden oneself with.

embauche /ãboʃ/ *nf* hiring. **embau-**
cher **1** *vt* hire, take on.

embaumer /ãbome/ **1** *vt* (pièce) fill;
(cadavre) embalm. **●** *vi* be fragrant.

embellir /ãbeliʀ/ **2** *vt* make more attractive; (récit) embellish.

embêtant, ~e /ãbɛtã, -t/ *adj* **1** annoying.

embêter /ãbete/ **1** *vt* bother. **□ s'~**
vpr be bored.

emblée: d'~ /dãble/ *loc* right away.

emblème /ãblɛm/ *nm* emblem.

emboîter /ãbwate/ **1** *vt* fit together;
~ le pas à qn (imiter) follow suit.
□ s'~ *vpr* fit together; (s')**~ dans**
fit into.

embonpoint /ãbɔ̃pwɛ̃/ *nm* stoutness.

embourber (s') /(s)ãbuʀbe/ **1** *vpr*
get stuck in the mud; (fig) get
bogged down.

embouteillage /ãbutɛjaʒ/ *nm* traffic jam.

emboutir /ãbutiʀ/ **2** *vt* (Auto)
crash into.

embraser (s') /(s)ãbʀaze/ **1** *vpr*
catch fire.

embrasser /ãbʀase/ **1** *vt* kiss; (adopter, contenir) embrace. **□ s'~** *vpr* kiss.

embrayage /ãbʀejaʒ/ *nm* clutch. **em-**
brayer **31** *vi* engage the clutch.

embrouiller /ãbʀuje/ **1** *vt* confuse;
(fils) tangle. **□ s'~** *vpr* become
confused.

embryon /ãbʀijɔ̃/ *nm* embryo.

embûches /ãbyʃ/ *nfpl* traps.

embuer(s') /(s)ãbɥe/ **1** *vpr* mist up.

embuscade /ãbyskad/ *nf* ambush.

émeraude /ɛmʀod/ *nf* emerald.

émerger /emɛʀʒe/ **40** *vi* emerge; (fig)
stand out.

émeri /ɛmʀi/ *nm* emery.

émerveillement /emɛʀvɛjmã/ *nm*
amazement, wonder.

émerveiller /emɛʀveje/ **1** *vt* fill with
wonder. **□ s'~** *vpr* marvel at.

émetteur /emetœʀ/ *nm* transmitter.

émettre /emɛtʀ/ **42** *vt* (son) produce;
(message) send out; (timbre, billet)
issue; (opinion) express.

émeute /emøt/ nf riot.

émietter /emjete/ **1** vt crumble. □ **s'**~ vpr crumble.

émigrant, ~e /emigʀɑ̃, -t/ nm, f emigrant. **émigration** nf emigration. **émigrer** **1** vi emigrate.

émincer /emɛ̃se/ **10** vt cut into thin slices.

éminent, ~e /eminɑ̃, -t/ adj eminent.

émissaire /emisɛʀ/ nm emissary.

émission /emisjɔ̃/ nf (programme) programme; (de chaleur, gaz) emission; (de timbre) issue.

emmagasiner /ɑ̃magazine/ **1** vt store.

emmanchure /ɑ̃mɑ̃ʃyʀ/ nf armhole.

emmêler /ɑ̃mele/ **1** vt tangle. □ **s'**~ vpr get mixed up.

emménager /ɑ̃menaʒe/ **40** vi move in; ~ **dans** move into.

emmener /ɑ̃mne/ **6** vt take; (comme prisonnier) take away.

emmerder /ɑ̃mɛʀde/ **1** ☒ vt ~ **qn** get on sb's nerves. □ **s'**~ vpr be bored.

emmitoufler /ɑ̃mitufle/ **1** vt wrap up warmly. □ **s'**~ vpr wrap oneself up warmly.

émoi /emwa/ nm turmoil; (plaisir) excitement.

émotif, **-ive** /emɔtif, -v/ adj emotional. **émotion** nf emotion; (peur) fright. **émotionnel**, ~**le** adj emotional.

émousser /emuse/ **1** vt blunt.

émouvant, ~e /emuvɑ̃, -t/ adj moving.

empailler /ɑ̃paje/ **1** vt stuff.

empaqueter /ɑ̃pakte/ **38** vt package.

emparer (s') /(s)ɑ̃paʀe/ **1** vpr **s'**~ **de** get hold of.

empêchement /ɑ̃pɛʃmɑ̃/ nm **avoir un** ~ to be held up.

empêcher /ɑ̃peʃe/ **1** vt prevent; ~ **de faire** prevent ou stop (from) doing; **(il) n'empêche que** still. □ **s'**~ vpr **il ne peut pas s'en** ~ he cannot help it.

empereur /ɑ̃pʀœʀ/ nm emperor.

empester /ɑ̃pɛste/ **1** vt stink out; (essence) stink of. ● vi stink.

empêtrer (s') /(s)ɑ̃petʀe/ **1** vpr become entangled.

empiéter /ɑ̃pjete/ **14** vi ~ **sur** encroach upon.

empiffrer (s') /(s)ɑ̃pifʀe/ **1** vpr **1** stuff oneself.

empiler /ɑ̃pile/ **1** vt pile up. □ **s'**~ vpr pile up.

empire /ɑ̃piʀ/ nm empire.

emplacement /ɑ̃plasmɑ̃/ nm site.

emplâtre /ɑ̃plɑtʀ/ nm (Méd) plaster.

emploi /ɑ̃plwa/ nm (travail) job; (embauche) employment; (utilisation) use; **un** ~ **de chauffeur** a job as a driver; ~ **du temps** timetable. **employé**, ~**e** nm, f employee.

employer /ɑ̃plwaje/ **31** vt (personne) employ; (utiliser) use. □ **s'**~ vpr be used; **s'**~ **à** devote oneself to. **employeur**, **-euse** nm, f employer.

empoigner /ɑ̃pwaɲe/ **1** vt grab. □ **s'**~ vpr come to blows.

empoisonnement /ɑ̃pwazɔnmɑ̃/ nm poisoning.

empoisonner /ɑ̃pwazɔne/ **1** vt poison; (embêter **1**) annoy. □ **s'**~ vpr to poison oneself.

emporter /ɑ̃pɔʀte/ **1** vt take (away); (entraîner) sweep away; (arracher) tear off. □ **s'**~ vpr lose one's temper; **l'**~ get the upper hand (**sur** of); **plat à** ~ take-away.

empoté, ~**e** /ɑ̃pɔte/ adj clumsy.

empreinte /ɑ̃pʀɛ̃t/ nf mark; ~ **(digitale)** fingerprint; ~ **écologique** carbon footprint; ~ **de pas** footprint.

empressé, ~**e** /ɑ̃pʀese/ adj attentive.

empresser (s') /(s)ɑ̃pʀese/ **1** vpr **s'**~ **de** hasten to; **s'**~ **auprès de** be attentive to.

emprise /ɑ̃pʀiz/ nf influence.

emprisonnement /ɑ̃pʀizɔnmɑ̃/ nm imprisonment. **emprisonner** **1** vt imprison.

emprunt /ɑ̃pʀœ̃/ nm loan; **faire un** ~ take out a loan.

emprunté, ~**e** /ɑ̃pʀœ̃te/ adj awkward.

emprunter /ɑ̃pʀœ̃te/ **1** vt borrow (à from); (route) take; (fig) assume. **emprunteur**, **-euse** nm, f borrower.

ému, ~**e** /emy/ adj moved; (intimidé) nervous.

émule /emyl/ nmf imitator.

en /ã/

Pour les expressions comme **en principe, en train de, s'en aller**, etc. →**principe, train, aller**, etc.

● *préposition*

····▸ (lieu) in.

····▸ (avec mouvement) to.

····▸ (temps) in.

····▸ (manière, état) in; ~ **faisant** by *ou* while doing; **je t'appelle ~ rentrant** I will call you when I get back.

····▸ (en qualité de) as.

····▸ (transport) by.

····▸ (composition) made of; **table ~ bois** wooden table.

● *pronom*

····▸ **en avoir/vouloir** have/want some; **ne pas ~ avoir/vouloir** not have/want any; **j'~ ai deux** I've got two; **prends-~ plusieurs** take several; **il m'~ reste un** I have one left; **j'~ suis content** I am pleased with him/her/it/them; **je m'~ souviens** I remember it.

····▸ ~ **êtes-vous sûr?** are you sure?

encadrement /ãkadRəmã/ *nm* framing; (de porte) frame. **encadrer** [1] *vt* frame; (entourer d'un trait) circle; (superviser) supervise.

encaisser /ãkese/ [1] *vt* (argent) collect; (chèque) cash; (coups [1]) take.

encart /ãkaR/ *nm* ~ **publicitaire** (advertising) insert.

en-cas /ãkɑ/ *nm* (stand-by) snack.

encastré, ~e /ãkastRe/ *adj* built-in.

encaustique /ãkostik/ *nf* wax polish.

enceinte /ãsɛ̃t/ *adj f* pregnant; ~ **de 3 mois** 3 months pregnant. ● *nf* enclosure; ~ **(acoustique)** speaker.

encens /ãsã/ *nm* incense.

encercler /ãsɛRkle/ [1] *vt* surround.

enchaînement /ãʃɛnmã/ *nm* (suite) chain; (d'idées) sequence.

enchaîner /ãʃene/ [1] *vt* chain (up); (phrases) link (up). ● *vi* continue. □ **s'~** *vpr* follow on.

enchanté, ~e /ãʃãte/ *adj* (ravi) delighted. **enchanter** [1] *vt* delight; (ensorceler) enchant.

enchère /ãʃɛR/ *nf* bid; **mettre** *ou* **vendre aux ~s** sell by auction.

enchevêtrer /ãʃəvetRe/ [1] *vt* tangle. □ **s'~** *vpr* become tangled.

enclave /ãklav/ *nf* enclave.

enclencher /ãklãʃe/ [1] *vt* engage.

enclin, ~e /ãklɛ̃, -in/ *adj* ~ **à** inclined to.

enclos /ãklo/ *nm* enclosure.

enclume /ãklym/ *nf* anvil.

encoche /ãkɔʃ/ *nf* notch.

encolure /ãkɔlyR/ *nf* neck.

encombrant, ~e /ãkɔ̃bRã, -t/ *adj* cumbersome.

encombre /ãkɔ̃bR/ *nm* **sans ~** without any problems.

encombrement /ãkɔ̃bRəmã/ *nm* (Auto) traffic congestion; (volume) bulk.

encombrer /ãkɔ̃bRe/ [1] *vt* clutter (up); (obstruer) obstruct. □ **s'~ de** *vpr* burden oneself with.

encontre: à l'~ de /alãkɔ̃tRədə/ *loc* against.

encore /ãkɔR/ *adv* (toujours) still; (de nouveau) again; (de plus) more; (aussi) also; ~ **plus grand** even larger; ~ **un café** another coffee; **pas ~** not yet; **si ~** if only; **et puis quoi ~?** [1] what next?

encouragement /ãkuRaʒmã/ *nm* encouragement. **encourager** [40] *vt* encourage.

encourir /ãkuRiR/ [20] *vt* incur.

encrasser /ãkRase/ [1] *vt* clog up (with dirt).

encre /ãkR/ *nf* ink. **encrier** *nm* ink-well.

encyclopédie /ãsiklɔpedi/ *nf* encyclopaedia.

endettement /ãdɛtmã/ *nm* debt.

endetter /ãdete/ [1] *vt* put into debt. □ **s'~** *vpr* get into debt.

endiguer /ãdige/ [1] *vt* dam; (fig) curb.

endimanché, ~e /ãdimãʃe/ *adj* in one's Sunday best.

endive /ãdiv/ *nf* chicory.

endoctriner /ãdɔktRine/ [1] *vt* indoctrinate.

endommager /ãdɔmaʒe/ [40] *vt* damage.

endormi, ~e /ãdɔRmi/ *adj* asleep; (apathique) sleepy.

endormir /ɑ̃dɔʀmiʀ/ 46 *vt* send to sleep; (médicalement) put to sleep; (duper) dupe (**avec** with). □ **s'~** *vpr* fall asleep.

endosser /ɑ̃dɔse/ 1 *vt* (*vêtement*) put on; (assumer) take on; (Comm) endorse.

endroit /ɑ̃dʀwa/ *nm* place; (de tissu) right side; **à l'~** the right way round; **par ~s** in places.

enduire /ɑ̃dμiʀ/ 17 *vt* coat. **enduit** *nm* coating.

endurance /ɑ̃dyʀɑ̃s/ *nf* endurance. **endurant, ~e** *adj* tough.

endurcir /ɑ̃dyʀsiʀ/ 2 *vt* strengthen. □ **s'~** *vpr* become hard (hardened).

endurer /ɑ̃dyʀe/ 1 *vt* endure.

énergétique /enɛʀʒetik/ *adj* energy; (*food*) high-calorie. **énergie** *nf* energy; (Tech) power. **énergique** *adj* energetic.

énervant, ~e /enɛʀvɑ̃, -t/ *adj* irritating, annoying.

énerver /enɛʀve/ 1 *vt* irritate. □ **s'~** *vpr* get worked up.

enfance /ɑ̃fɑ̃s/ *nf* childhood; **la petite ~** infancy.

enfant /ɑ̃fɑ̃/ *nmf* child. **enfantillage** *nm* childishness. **enfantin, ~e** *adj* simple, easy; (puéril) childish; (*jeu, langage*) children's.

enfer /ɑ̃fɛʀ/ *nm* (Relig) Hell; (fig) hell.

enfermer /ɑ̃fɛʀme/ 1 *vt* shut up. □ **s'~** *vpr* shut oneself up.

enfiler /ɑ̃file/ 1 *vt* (aiguille) thread; (vêtement) slip on; (rue) take.

enfin /ɑ̃fɛ̃/ *adv* (de soulagement) at last; (en dernier lieu) finally; (résignation, conclusion) well; **~ presque** well nearly.

enflammé, ~e /ɑ̃flame/ *adj* (Méd) inflamed; (discours) fiery; (lettre) passionate.

enflammer /ɑ̃flame/ 1 *vt* set fire to. □ **s'~** *vpr* catch fire.

enfler /ɑ̃fle/ 1 *vt* (histoire) exaggerate. ● *vi* (partie du corps) swell (up); (mer) swell; (rumeur, colère) spread. □ **s'~** *vpr* (colère) mount; (rumeur) grow.

enfoncer /ɑ̃fɔ̃se/ 10 *vt* (épingle) push *ou* drive in; (chapeau) push down; (porte) break down. ● *vi* sink. □ **s'~** *vpr* sink (**dans** into).

enfouir /ɑ̃fwiʀ/ 2 *vt* bury.

enfourcher /ɑ̃fuʀʃe/ 1 *vt* mount.

enfreindre /ɑ̃fʀɛ̃dʀ/ 22 *vt* infringe, break.

enfuir (s') /(s)ɑ̃fμiʀ/ 35 *vpr* run away.

enfumé, ~e /ɑ̃fyme/ *adj* filled with smoke.

engagé, ~e /ɑ̃ɡaʒe/ *adj* committed.

engagement /ɑ̃ɡaʒmɑ̃/ *nm* (promesse) promise; (Pol, Comm) commitment.

engager /ɑ̃ɡaʒe/ 40 *vt* (lier) bind, commit; (embaucher) take on; (commencer) start; (introduire) insert; (investir) invest. □ **s'~** *vpr* (promettre) commit oneself; (commencer) start; (soldat) enlist; (concurrent) enter; **s'~ à faire** undertake to do; **s'~ dans** (voie) enter.

engelure /ɑ̃ʒlyʀ/ *nf* chilblain.

engendrer /ɑ̃ʒɑ̃dʀe/ 1 *vt* (causer) generate.

engin /ɑ̃ʒɛ̃/ *nm* device; (véhicule) vehicle; (missile) missile.

engloutir /ɑ̃ɡlutiʀ/ 2 *vt* swallow (up).

engouement /ɑ̃ɡumɑ̃/ *nm* passion.

engouffrer /ɑ̃ɡufʀe/ 1 *vt* 1 gobble up. □ **s'~ dans** *vpr* rush in.

engourdir /ɑ̃ɡuʀdiʀ/ 2 *vt* numb. □ **s'~** *vpr* go numb.

engrais /ɑ̃ɡʀɛ/ *nm* manure; (chimique) fertilizer.

engrenage /ɑ̃ɡʀənaʒ/ *nm* gears (+ *pl*); (fig) spiral.

engueuler /ɑ̃ɡœle/ 1 ⊠ *vt* shout at. □ **s'~** *vpr* have a row.

enhardir (s') /(s)ɑ̃aʀdiʀ/ 2 *vpr* become bolder.

énième /ɛnjɛm/ *adj* umpteenth.

énigmatique /enigmatik/ *adj* enigmatic. **énigme** *nf* enigma; (devinette) riddle.

enivrer /ɑ̃nivʀe/ 1 *vt* intoxicate. □ **s'~** *vpr* get intoxicated.

enjambée /ɑ̃ʒɑ̃be/ *nf* stride. **enjamber** 1 *vt* step over; (pont) span.

enjeu (*pl* **~x**) /ɑ̃ʒø/ *nm* stake.

enjoué, ~e /ɑ̃ʒwe/ *adj* cheerful.

enlacer /ɑ̃lase/ 10 *vt* entwine.

enlèvement /ɑ̃lɛvmɑ̃/ *nm* (de colis) removal; (d'ordures) collection; (rapt) kidnapping.

enlever /ɑ̃lve/ 6 *vt* remove (**à** from); (vêtement) take off; (tache, organe) take out, remove; (kidnapper) kidnap; (gagner) win.

enliser (s') /(s)ālize/ **1** vpr get bogged down.

enneigé, ~e /āneʒe/ adj snow-covered.

ennemi, ~e /ɛnmi/ adj & nm enemy; **~ de** (fig) hostile to.

ennui /ānɥi/ nm problem; (tracas) boredom; **s'attirer des ~s** run into trouble.

ennuyer /ānɥije/ **31** vt bore; (irriter) annoy; (préoccuper) worry; **si cela ne t'ennuie pas** if you don't mind. □ **s'~** vpr get bored.

ennuyeux, -euse /ānɥijø, -z/ adj boring; (fâcheux) annoying.

énoncé /enɔse/ nm wording, text; (Gram) utterance.

énoncer /enɔse/ **10** vt express, state.

enorgueillir (s') /(s)ānɔʀɡœjir/ **2** vpr **s'~ de** pride oneself on.

énorme /enɔʀm/ adj enormous.

enquête /āket/ nf (Jur) investigation, inquiry; (sondage) survey; **mener l'~** lead the inquiry. **enquêter 1** vi **~ (sur)** investigate. **enquêteur, -euse** nm, f investigator.

enquiquinant, ~e /ākikinā, -t/ adj **1** irritating.

enraciné, ~e /āʀasine/ adj deep rooted.

enragé, ~e /āʀaʒe/ adj furious; (chien) rabid; (fig) fanatical.

enrager /āʀaʒe/ **40** vi be furious; **faire ~ qn** annoy sb.

enregistrement /āʀ(ə)ʒistʀəmā/ nm recording; (des bagages) check-in. **enregistrer 1** vt (Mus, TV) record; (mémoriser) take in; (bagages) check in.

enrhumer (s') /(s)āʀyme/ **1** vpr catch a cold.

enrichir /āʀiʃiʀ/ **2** vt enrich. □ **s'~** vpr grow rich(er). **enrichissant, ~e** adj (expérience) rewarding.

enrober /āʀɔbe/ **1** vt coat (**de** with).

enrôler /āʀole/ **1** vt recruit. □ **s'~** vpr enlist, enrol.

enroué, ~e /āʀwe/ adj hoarse.

enrouler /āʀule/ **1** vt wind, wrap. □ **s'~** vpr wind; **s'~ dans une couverture** roll oneself up in a blanket.

ensanglanté, ~e /āsāɡlāte/ adj bloodstained.

enseignant, ~e /āsɛɲā, -t/ nm, f teacher. ● adj teaching.

enseigne /āsɛɲ/ nf sign.

enseignement /āsɛɲəmā/ nm (profession) teaching; (instruction) education.

enseigner /āsɛɲe/ **1** vt/i teach; **~ qch à qn** teach sb sth.

ensemble /āsābl/ adv together. ● nm group; (Mus) ensemble; (vêtements) outfit; (cohésion) unity; (maths) set; **dans l'~** on the whole; **d'~** (idée) general; **l'~ de** (totalité) all of, the whole of.

ensevelir /āsəvliʀ/ **2** vt bury.

ensoleillé, ~e /āsɔleje/ adj sunny.

ensorceler /āsɔʀsəle/ **38** vt bewitch.

ensuite /āsɥit/ adv next, then; (plus tard) later.

ensuivre (s') /(s)āsɥivʀ/ **57** vpr follow; **et tout ce qui s'ensuit** and all the rest of it.

entaille /ātaj/ nf cut; (profonde) gash; (encoche) notch.

entamer /ātame/ **1** vt start; (inciser) cut into; (ébranler) shake.

entasser /ātase/ **1** vt (livres) pile; (argent) hoard; (personnes) cram (**dans** into). □ **s'~** vpr (objets) pile up (**dans** into); (personnes) squeeze (**dans** into).

entendement /ātādmā/ nm understanding; **ça dépasse l'~** it's beyond belief.

entendre /ātādʀ/ **3** vt hear; (comprendre) understand; (vouloir dire) mean; **~ parler de** hear of; **~ dire que** hear that. □ **s'~** vpr (être d'accord) agree; **s'~ (bien)** get on (**avec** with); **cela s'entend** of course.

entendu, ~e /ātādy/ adj (convenu) agreed; (sourire, air) knowing; **bien ~** of course; **(c'est) ~!** all right!

entente /ātāt/ nf understanding; **bonne ~** good relationship.

enterrement /āteʀmā/ nm funeral.

enterrer /āteʀe/ **1** vt bury.

en-tête /ātet/ nm heading; **à ~** headed.

entêté, ~e /ātete/ adj stubborn. **entêtement** nm stubbornness. **entêter (s')** **1** vpr persist (**à**, **dans** in).

enthousiasme /ātuzjasm/ nm enthusiasm. **enthousiasmer 1** vt fill with enthusiasm. **enthousiaste** adj enthusiastic.

enticher (s') /(s)ātiʃe/ **1** vpr s'~ de become infatuated with.

entier, -ière /ātje, -jɛʀ/ adj whole; (absolu) absolute; (entêté) unyielding. ● nm whole; **en ~** entirely.

entonnoir /ātɔnwaʀ/ nm funnel; (trou) crater.

entorse /ātɔʀs/ nf sprain; (fig) ~ à (loi) infringement of.

entortiller /ātɔʀtije/ **1** vt wind, wrap (**autour** around); (duper **1**) get round.

entourage /ātuʀaʒ/ nm circle of family and friends; (bordure) surround.

entouré, ~e /ātuʀe/ adj (personne) supported.

entourer /ātuʀe/ **1** vt surround (de with); (réconforter) rally round; **~ qch de mystère** shroud sth in mystery.

entracte /ātʀakt/ nm interval.

entraide /ātʀɛd/ nf mutual aid. **entraider (s')** **1** vpr help each other.

entrain /ātʀɛ̃/ nm zest, spirit.

entraînement /ātʀɛnmā/ nm (Sport) training.

entraîner /ātʀene/ **1** vt (emporter) carry away; (provoquer) lead to; (Sport) train; (actionner) drive. □ **s'~** vpr train. **entraîneur** nm trainer.

entrave /ātʀav/ nf hindrance. **entraver** **1** vt hinder.

entre /ātʀ(ə)/ prép between; (parmi) among(st); **~ autres** among other things; **l'un d'~ nous/eux** one of us/them.

entrebâillé, ~e /ātʀəbaje/ adj ajar, half-open.

entrechoquer (s') /(s)ātʀəʃɔke/ **1** vpr knock against each other.

entrecôte /ātʀəkot/ nf rib steak.

entrecouper /ātʀəkupe/ **1** vt ~ de intersperse with.

entrecroiser (s') /(s)ātʀəkʀwaze/ **1** vpr (routes) intertwine.

entrée /ātʀe/ nf entrance; (vestibule) hall; (accès) admission, entry; (billet) ticket; (Culin) starter; (Ordinat) **tapez sur E~** press Enter; **'~ interdite'** 'no entry'.

entrejambes /ātʀəʒāb/ nm crotch.

entremets /ātʀəmɛ/ nm dessert.

entremise /ātʀəmiz/ nf intervention; **par l'~ de** through.

entreposer /ātʀəpoze/ **1** vt store.

entrepôt /ātʀəpo/ nm warehouse.

entreprenant, ~e /ātʀəpʀənā, -t/ adj (actif) enterprising; (séducteur) forward.

entreprendre /ātʀəpʀādʀ/ **50** vt start on, undertake; (personne) buttonhole; **~ de faire** undertake to do.

entrepreneur /ātʀəpʀənœʀ/ nm (de bâtiment) contractor; (chef d'entreprise) firm manager.

entreprise /ātʀəpʀiz/ nf (projet) undertaking; (société) firm, business, company.

entrer /ātʀe/ **1** vi (aux être) go in, enter; (venir) come in, enter; **~ dans** go ou come into, enter; (club) join; **~ en collision** collide (**avec** with); **faire ~** (personne) show in; **laisser ~** let in; **~ en guerre** go to war. ● vt (données) enter.

entre-temps /ātʀətā/ adv meanwhile.

entretenir /ātʀət(ə)niʀ/ **58** vt (appareil) maintain; (vêtement) look after; (alimenter) (feu) keep going; (amitié) keep alive; **~ qn de** converse with sb about. □ **s'~** vpr speak (**de** about; **avec** to). **entretien** nm maintenance; (discussion) talk; (pour un emploi) interview.

entrevoir /ātʀəvwaʀ/ **63** vt make out; (brièvement) glimpse.

entrevue /ātʀəvy/ nf meeting.

entrouvert, ~e /ātʀuvɛʀ, -t/ adj ajar, half-open.

énumération /enymeʀasjō/ nf enumeration. **énumérer** **14** vt enumerate.

envahir /āvaiʀ/ **2** vt invade, overrun; (douleur, peur) overcome.

enveloppe /āvlɔp/ nf envelope; (emballage) wrapping; **~ budgétaire** budget. **envelopper** **1** vt wrap (up); (fig) envelop.

envergure /āvɛʀgyʀ/ nf wingspan; (importance) scope; (qualité) calibre.

envers /āvɛʀ/ prép toward(s), to. ● nm (de tissu) wrong side; **à l'~** (tableau) upside down; (devant derrière) back to front; (chaussette) inside out.

envie /āvi/ nf (jalousie) envy; **avoir ~ de qch** feel like sth; **avoir ~ de faire** want to do; (moins urgent) feel like doing; **faire ~ à qn** make sb envious.

envier /ãvje/ 45 *vt* envy. **envieux, -ieuse** *adj* envious.

environ /ãviRɔ̃/ *adv* about.

environnant, ~e /ãviRɔnã, -t/ *adj* surrounding.

environnement /ãviRɔnmã/ *nm* environment.

environs /ãviRɔ̃/ *nmpl* vicinity; **aux ~ de** (*lieu*) in the vicinity of; (*heure*) round about.

envisager /ãvizaʒe/ 40 *vt* consider; (*imaginer*) envisage; **~ de faire** consider doing.

envoi /ãvwa/ *nm* dispatch; (*paquet*) consignment; **faire un ~** send; **coup d'~** (Sport) kick-off.

envoler (s') /(s)ãvɔle/ 1 *vpr* fly away; (*avion*) take off; (*papiers*) blow away.

envoyé, ~e /ãvwaje/ *nm, f* envoy; **~ spécial** special correspondent.

envoyer /ãvwaje/ 32 *vt* send; (*lancer*) throw.

éolienne /eɔljɛn/ *nf* windmill; **ferme d'~s** wind farm.

épais, ~se /epɛ, -s/ *adj* thick. **épaisseur** *nf* thickness.

épaissir /epesiR/ 2 *vt/i* thicken. □ **s'~** *vpr* thicken; (*mystère*) deepen.

épanoui, ~e /epanwi/ *adj* (*personne*) beaming, radiant.

épanouir (s') /(s)epanwiR/ 2 *vpr* (*fleur*) open out; (*visage*) beam; (*personne*) blossom. **épanouissement** *nm* (*éclat*) blossoming, full bloom.

épargne /epaRɲ/ *nf* savings.

épargner /epaRɲe/ 1 *vt/i* save; (*ne pas tuer*) spare; **~ qch à qn** spare sb sth.

éparpiller /epaRpije/ 1 *vt* scatter. □ **s'~** *vpr* scatter; (*fig*) dissipate one's efforts.

épars, ~e /epaR, -s/ *adj* scattered.

épatant, ~e /epatã, -t/ *adj* 1 amazing.

épaule /epol/ *nf* shoulder.

épave /epav/ *nf* wreck.

épée /epe/ *nf* sword.

épeler /ɛple/ 6 *vt* spell.

éperdu, ~e /epɛRdy/ *adj* wild, frantic.

éperon /epRɔ̃/ *nm* spur.

éphémère /efemɛR/ *adj* ephemeral.

épi /epi/ *nm* (de blé) ear; (*mèche*) tuft of hair; **~ de maïs** corn cob.

épice /epis/ *nf* spice. **épicé, ~e** *adj* spicy.

épicerie /episRi/ *nf* grocery shop; (*produits*) groceries. **épicier, -ière** *nm, f* grocer.

épidémie /epidemi/ *nf* epidemic.

épiderme /epidɛRm/ *nm* skin.

épier /epje/ 45 *vt* spy on.

épilepsie /epilɛpsi/ *nf* epilepsy. **épileptique** *adj & nmf* epileptic.

épiler /epile/ 1 *vt* remove unwanted hair from; (*sourcils*) pluck.

épilogue /epilɔg/ *nm* epilogue; (*fig*) outcome.

épinard /epinaR/ *nm* **~s** spinach (+ *sg*).

épine /epin/ *nf* thorn, prickle; (*d'animal*) prickle, spine; **~ dorsale** backbone. **épineux, -euse** *adj* thorny.

épingle /epɛ̃gl/ *nf* pin; **~ de nourrice, ~ de sûreté** safety-pin.

épisode /epizɔd/ *nm* episode; **à ~s** serialized.

épitaphe /epitaf/ *nf* epitaph.

épluche-légumes /eplyʃlegym/ *nm inv* (potato) peeler.

éplucher /eplyʃe/ 1 *vt* peel; (*examiner:* fig) scrutinize.

épluchure /eplyʃyR/ *nf* **~s** peelings.

éponge /epɔ̃ʒ/ *nf* sponge. **éponger** 40 *vt* (*liquide*) mop up; (*surface, front*) mop; (*fig*) (*dettes*) wipe out.

épopée /epɔpe/ *nf* epic.

époque /epɔk/ *nf* time, period; **à l'~** at the time; **d'~** period.

épouse /epuz/ *nf* wife.

épouser /epuze/ 1 *vt* marry; (*forme, idée*) adopt.

épousseter /epuste/ 38 *vt* dust.

épouvantable /epuvãtabl/ *adj* appalling.

épouvantail /epuvãtaj/ *nm* scarecrow.

épouvante /epuvãt/ *nf* terror. **épouvanter** 1 *vt* terrify.

époux /epu/ *nm* husband; **les ~** the married couple.

éprendre (s') /(s)epRãdR/ 50 *vpr* **s'~ de** fall in love with.

épreuve /epRœv/ *nf* test; (Sport) event; (*malheur*) ordeal; (Photo, d'imprimerie) proof; **mettre à l'~** put to the test.

éprouver /epʀuve/ **1** vt (ressentir) experience; (affliger) distress; (tester) test.

éprouvette /epʀuvɛt/ nf test tube.

EPS abrév f (**éducation physique et sportive**) PE.

épuisé, ~e /epɥize/ adj exhausted; (livre) out of print. **épuisement** nm exhaustion.

épuiser /epɥize/ **1** vt (fatiguer, user) exhaust. □ **s'~** vpr become exhausted.

épuration /epyʀasjɔ̃/ nf purification; (Pol) purge. **épurer** **1** vt purify; (Pol) purge.

équateur /ekwatœʀ/ nm equator.

équilibre /ekilibʀ/ nm balance; **être ou se tenir en ~** (personne) balance; (objet) be balanced. **équilibré**, ~e adj well-balanced.

équilibrer /ekilibʀe/ **1** vt balance. □ **s'~** vpr balance each other.

équilibriste /ekilibʀist/ nmf acrobat.

équipage /ekipaʒ/ nm crew.

équipe /ekip/ nf team; **~ de nuit/jour** night/day shift.

équipé, ~e /ekipe/ adj equipped; **cuisine** ~e fitted kitchen.

équipement /ekipmɑ̃/ nm equipment; ~s (installations) amenities, facilities.

équiper /ekipe/ **1** vt equip (de with). □ **s'~** vpr equip oneself.

équipier, -ière /ekipje, -jɛʀ/ nm, f team member.

équitable /ekitabl/ adj fair.

équitation /ekitasjɔ̃/ nf (horse-) riding.

équivalence /ekivalɑ̃s/ nf equivalence. **équivalent**, ~e adj equivalent.

équivaloir /ekivalwaʀ/ **60** vi ~ **à** be equivalent to.

équivoque /ekivɔk/ adj equivocal; (louche) questionable. ● nf ambiguity.

érable /eʀabl/ nm maple.

érafler /eʀafle/ **1** vt scratch. **éraflure** nf scratch.

éraillé, ~e /eʀaje/ adj (voix) raucous.

ère /ɛʀ/ nf era.

éreintant, ~e /eʀɛ̃tɑ̃, -t/ adj exhausting. **éreinter (s')** **1** vpr wear oneself out.

ériger /eʀiʒe/ **40** vt erect. □ **s'~ en** vpr set (oneself) up as.

éroder /eʀɔde/ **1** vt erode. **érosion** nf erosion.

errer /ɛʀe/ **1** vi wander.

erreur /ɛʀœʀ/ nf mistake, error; **dans l'~** mistaken; **par ~** by mistake; ~ **judiciaire** miscarriage of justice.

erroné, ~e /ɛʀɔne/ adj erroneous.

érudit, ~e /eʀydi, -t/ adj scholarly. ● nm, f scholar.

éruption /eʀypsjɔ̃/ nf eruption; (Méd) rash.

es /ɛ/ ➡ÊTRE **4**.

escabeau (pl ~x) /ɛskabo/ nm stepladder.

escadron /ɛskadʀɔ̃/ nm (Mil) company.

escalade /ɛskalad/ nf climbing; (Pol, Comm) escalation. **escalader** **1** vt climb.

escale /ɛskal/ nf (d'avion) stopover; (port) port of call; **faire ~ à** (avion, passager) stop over at; (navire, passager) put in at.

escalier /ɛskalje/ nm stairs (+ pl); ~ **mécanique** ou **roulant** escalator.

escalope /ɛskalɔp/ nf escalope.

escargot /ɛskaʀgo/ nm snail.

escarpé, ~e /ɛskaʀpe/ adj steep.

escarpin /ɛskaʀpɛ̃/ nm court shoe; (US) pump.

escient: à bon ~ /abɔnesjɑ̃/ loc wisely.

esclandre /ɛsklɑ̃dʀ/ nm scene.

esclavage /ɛsklavaʒ/ nm slavery. **esclave** nmf slave.

escompte /ɛskɔ̃t/ nm discount. **escompter** **1** vt expect; (Comm) discount.

escorte /ɛskɔʀt/ nf escort.

escrime /ɛskʀim/ nf fencing.

escroc /ɛskʀo/ nm swindler.

escroquer /ɛskʀɔke/ **1** vt swindle; ~ **qch à qn** swindle sb out of sth. **escroquerie** nf swindle.

espace /ɛspas/ nm space; ~s **verts** gardens and parks.

espacer /ɛspase/ **10** vt space out. □ **s'~** vpr become less frequent.

espadrille /ɛspadʀij/ nf rope sandal.

Espagne /ɛspaɲ/ nf Spain.

espagnol, ~e /ɛspaɲɔl/ adj Spanish. ● nm (Ling) Spanish. **E~, ~e** nm, f Spaniard.

espèce /ɛspɛs/ nf kind, sort; (race) species; **en ~s** (argent) in cash; **~ d'idiot!** [!] you idiot! [!].

espérance /ɛspeʀɑ̃s/ nf hope.

espérer /ɛspeʀe/ [14] vt hope for; **~ faire/que** hope to do/that. ● vi hope.

espiègle /ɛspjɛgl/ adj mischievous.

espion, ~ne /ɛspjɔ̃, -ɔn/ nm, f spy. **espionnage** nm espionage, spying. **espionner** [1] vt spy (on).

espoir /ɛspwaʀ/ nm hope; **reprendre ~** feel hopeful again.

esprit /ɛspʀi/ nm (intellect) mind; (humour) wit; (fantôme) spirit; (ambiance) atmosphere; **perdre l'~** lose one's mind; **reprendre ses ~s** come to; **faire de l'~** try to be witty.

esquimau, ~de (mpl **~x**) /ɛskimo, -d/ nm, f Eskimo.

esquinter /ɛskɛ̃te/ [1] vt [!] ruin.

esquisse /ɛskis/ nf sketch; (fig) outline.

esquiver /ɛskive/ [1] vt dodge. □ **s'~** vpr slip away.

essai /esɛ/ nm (épreuve) test, trial; (tentative) try; (article) essay; (au rugby) try; **~s** (Auto) qualifying round (+ sg); **à l'~** on trial.

essaim /esɛ̃/ nm swarm.

essayage /esɛjaʒ/ nm fitting; **salon d'~** fitting room.

essayer /eseje/ [31] vt/i try; (vêtement) try (on); (voiture) try (out); **~ de faire** try to do.

essence /esɑ̃s/ nf (carburant) petrol; (nature, extrait) essence; **~ sans plomb** unleaded petrol.

essentiel, ~le /esɑ̃sjɛl/ adj essential. ● nm **l'~** the main thing; (quantité) the main part.

essieu (pl **~x**) /esjø/ nm axle.

essor /esɔʀ/ nm expansion; **prendre son ~** expand.

essorage /esɔʀaʒ/ nm spin drying. **essorer** [1] vt (linge) spin-dry; (en tordant) wring.

essoreuse /esɔʀøz/ nf spin-drier; **~ à salade** salad spinner.

essoufflé, ~e /esufle/ adj out of breath.

essuie-glace /esɥiglas/ nm inv windscreen wiper.

essuie-mains /esɥimɛ̃/ nm inv handtowel.

essuie-tout /esɥitu/ nm inv kitchen paper.

essuyer /esɥije/ [31] vt wipe; (subir) suffer. □ **s'~** vpr dry ou wipe oneself.

est¹ /ɛ/ ➡ÊTRE [4].

est² /ɛst/ nm east. ● adj inv east; (partie) eastern; (direction) easterly.

estampe /ɛstɑ̃p/ nf print.

esthète /ɛstɛt/ nmf aesthete.

esthéticienne /ɛstetisjɛn/ nf beautician.

esthétique /ɛstetik/ adj aesthetic.

estimation /ɛstimasjɔ̃/ nf (de coûts) estimate; (valeur) valuation.

estime /ɛstim/ nf esteem.

estimer /ɛstime/ [1] vt (tableau) value; (calculer) estimate; (respecter) esteem; (considérer) consider (**que** that).

estival, ~e (mpl **-aux**) /ɛstival, -o/ adj summer. **estivant, ~e** nm, f summer visitor.

estomac /ɛstɔma/ nm stomach.

estomaqué, ~e /ɛstɔmake/ adj [!] stunned.

Estonie /ɛstɔni/ nf Estonia.

estrade /ɛstʀad/ nf platform.

estragon /ɛstʀagɔ̃/ nm tarragon.

estropié, ~e /ɛstʀɔpje/ nm, f cripple. ● adj crippled.

estuaire /ɛstɥɛʀ/ nm estuary.

et /e/ conj and; **~ moi?** what about me?; **~ alors?** so what?

étable /etabl/ nf cow-shed.

établi, ~e /etabli/ adj established; **un fait bien ~** a well-established fact. ● nm work-bench.

établir /etabliʀ/ [2] vt establish; (liste, facture) draw up; (personne, camp, record) set up. □ **s'~** vpr (personne) settle; **s'~ à son compte** set up on one's own.

établissement /etablismɑ̃/ nm (entreprise) organization; (institution) establishment; **~ scolaire** school.

étage /etaʒ/ nm floor, storey; (de fusée) stage; **à l'~** upstairs; **au premier ~** on the first floor.

étagère /etaʒɛʀ/ nf shelf; (meuble) shelving unit.

étain /etɛ̃/ nm pewter.

étais, était /etɛ/ ➡ÊTRE **4**.

étalage /etalaʒ/ nm display; (vitrine) shop-window; **faire ~ de** flaunt. **étalagiste** nmf window-dresser.

étaler /etale/ **1** vt spread; (journal) spread (out); (pâte) roll out; (exposer) display; (richesse) flaunt. □ **s'~** vpr (prendre de la place) spread out; (tomber **1**) fall flat; **s'~ sur** (paiement) be spread over.

étalon /etalɔ̃/ nm (cheval) stallion; (modèle) standard.

étanche /etɑ̃ʃ/ adj watertight; (montre) waterproof.

étancher /etɑ̃ʃe/ **1** vt (soif) quench.

étang /etɑ̃/ nm pond.

étant /etɑ̃/ ➡ÊTRE **4**.

étape /etap/ nf stage; (lieu d'arrêt) stopover; (fig) stage.

état /eta/ nm state; (liste) statement; (métier) profession; **en bon/mauvais ~** in good/bad condition; **en ~ de** in a position to; **en ~ de marche** in working order; **faire ~ de** (citer) mention; **être dans tous ses ~s** be in a state; **~ civil** civil status; **~ des lieux** inventory of fixtures. **État** nm State.

état-major (pl **états-majors**) /etamaʒɔʀ/ nm (officiers) staff (+ pl).

États-Unis /etazyni/ nmpl **~ (d'Amérique)** United States (of America).

étau (pl **~x**) /eto/ nm vice.

étayer /eteje/ **31** vt prop up.

été[1] /ete/ ➡ÊTRE **4**.

été[2] /ete/ nm summer.

éteindre /etɛ̃dʀ/ **22** vt (feu) put out; (lumière, radio) turn off. □ **s'~** vpr (feu, lumière) go out; (appareil) go off; (mourir) die. **éteint, ~e** adj (feu) out; (volcan) extinct.

étendard /etɑ̃daʀ/ nm standard.

étendre /etɑ̃dʀ/ **3** vt (nappe) spread (out); (bras, jambes) stretch (out); (linge) hang out; (agrandir) extend. □ **s'~** vpr (s'allonger) lie down; (se propager) spread; (plaine) stretch; **s'~ sur** (sujet) dwell on.

étendu, ~e /etɑ̃dy/ adj extensive. **étendue** nf area; (d'eau) stretch; (importance) extent.

éternel, ~le /etɛʀnɛl/ adj (vie) eternal; (fig) endless.

éterniser (s') /(s)etɛʀnize/ **1** vpr (durer) drag on.

éternité /etɛʀnite/ nf eternity.

éternuement /etɛʀnymɑ̃/ nm sneeze. **éternuer** **1** vi sneeze.

êtes /ɛt/ ➡ÊTRE **4**.

éthique /etik/ adj ethical. ● nf ethics (+ sg).

ethnie /ɛtni/ nf ethnic group. **ethnique** adj ethnic.

étincelant, ~e /etɛ̃slɑ̃, -t/ adj sparkling. **étinceler** **38** vi sparkle. **étincelle** nf spark.

étiqueter /etikte/ **38** vt label. **étiquette** nf label; (protocole) etiquette.

étirer /etire/ **1** vt stretch. □ **s'~** vpr stretch.

étoffe /etɔf/ nf fabric.

étoffer /etɔfe/ **1** vt expand. □ **s'~** vpr fill out.

étoile /etwal/ nf star; **à la belle ~** in the open; **~ filante** shooting star; **~ de mer** starfish.

étonnant, ~e /etɔnɑ̃, -t/ adj (curieux) surprising; (formidable) amazing. **étonnement** nm surprise; (plus fort) amazement.

étonner /etɔne/ **1** vt amaze. □ **s'~** vpr be amazed (**de** at).

étouffant, ~e /etufɑ̃, -t/ adj stifling.

étouffer /etufe/ **1** vt/i suffocate; (sentiment, révolte) stifle; (feu) smother; (bruit) muffle; **on étouffe** it is stifling. □ **s'~** vpr suffocate; (en mangeant) choke.

étourderie /eturdəri/ nf thoughtlessness; (acte) careless mistake.

étourdi, ~e /eturdi/ adj absent-minded. ● nm, f scatterbrain.

étourdir /eturdir/ **2** vt stun; (fatiguer) make sb's head spin. **étourdissant, ~e** adj stunning.

étourneau (pl **~x**) /eturno/ nm starling.

étrange /etʀɑ̃ʒ/ adj strange.

étranger, -ère /etʀɑ̃ʒe, -ɛʀ/ adj (inconnu) strange, unfamiliar; (d'un autre pays) foreign. ● nm, f foreigner; (inconnu) stranger; **à l'~** abroad; **de l'~** from abroad.

étrangler /etʀɑ̃gle/ **1** vt strangle; (col) throttle. □ **s'~** vpr choke.

être /ɛtʀ/ **4**
● *verbe auxiliaire*
····▸ (du passé) have; **elle est partie/venue hier** she left/came yesterday.
····▸ (de la voix passive) be.
● *verbe intransitif (aux avoir)*
····▸ be; **~ médecin** be a doctor; **je suis à vous** I'm all yours; **j'en suis à me demander si...** I'm beginning to wonder whether...; **qu'en est-il de...?** what's the news about...?
····▸ (appartenance) be, belong to.
····▸ (heure, date) be; **nous sommes le 3 mars** it's March 3.
····▸ (aller) be; **je n'y ai jamais été** I've never been; **il a été le voir** he went to see him.
····▸ **c'est** it is *or* it's; **c'est moi qui l'ai fait** I did it; **est-ce que tu veux du thé?** do you want some tea?
● *nom masculin*
····▸ being; **~ humain** human being.
····▸ (personne) person; **un ~ cher** a loved one.

étreindre /etʀɛ̃dʀ/ **22** *vt* embrace. **étreinte** *nf* embrace.
étrennes /etʀɛn/ *nfpl* (New Year's) gift (+ *sg*); (argent) money.
étrier /etʀije/ *nm* stirrup.
étriqué, ~e /etʀike/ *adj* tight.
étroit, ~e /etʀwa, -t/ *adj* narrow; (vêtement) tight; (liens, surveillance) close; **à l'~** cramped. **étroitement** *adv* closely. **étroitesse** *nf* narrowness.
étude /etyd/ *nf* study; (enquête) survey; (bureau) office; **(salle d')~** (Scol) prep room; **à l'~** under consideration; **faire des ~s (de)** study; **il n'a pas fait d'~s** he didn't go to university; **~ de marché** market research.
étudiant, ~e /etydjɑ̃, -t/ *nm, f* student.
étudier /etydje/ **45** *vt/i* study.
étui /etɥi/ *nm* case.
étuve /etyv/ *nf* steam room.
eu, ~e /y/ →AVOIR **5**.
euro /øʀo/ *nm* euro.
Europe /øʀɔp/ *nf* Europe.

européen, ~ne /øʀɔpeɛ̃, -ɛɛn/ *adj* European. **E~, ~ne** *nm, f* European.
euthanasie /øtanazi/ *nf* euthanasia.
eux /ø/ *pron* they; (complément) them. **eux-mêmes** *pron* themselves.
évacuation /evakɥasjɔ̃/ *nf* evacuation; (d'eaux usées) discharge. **évacuer** **1** *vt* evacuate.
évadé, ~e /evade/ *adj* escaped. ● *nm, f* escaped prisoner. **évader (s')** **1** *vpr* escape.
évaluation /evalɥasjɔ̃/ *nf* assessment. **évaluer** **1** *vt* assess.
évangile /evɑ̃ʒil/ *nm* gospel; **l'É~** the Gospel.
évanouir (s') /(s)evanwiʀ/ **2** *vpr* faint; (disparaître) vanish.
évaporation /evapɔʀasjɔ̃/ *nf* evaporation. **évaporer (s')** **1** *vpr* evaporate.
évasif, -ive /evazif, -v/ *adj* evasive.
évasion /evazjɔ̃/ *nf* escape.
éveil /evɛj/ *nm* awakening; **en ~** alert.
éveillé, ~e /eveje/ *adj* awake; (intelligent) alert.
éveiller /eveje/ **1** *vt* awake(n); (susciter) arouse. □ **s'~** *vpr* awake.
événement /evenmɑ̃/ *nm* event.
éventail /evɑ̃taj/ *nm* fan; (gamme) range.
éventrer /evɑ̃tʀe/ **1** *vt* (sac) rip open.
éventualité /evɑ̃tɥalite/ *nf* possibility; **dans cette ~** in that event.
éventuel, ~le /evɑ̃tɥɛl/ *adj* possible. **éventuellement** *adv* possibly.
évêque /evɛk/ *nm* bishop.
évertuer (s') /(s)evɛʀtɥe/ **1** *vpr* **s'~ à** struggle hard to.
éviction /eviksjɔ̃/ *nf* eviction.
évidemment /evidamɑ̃/ *adv* obviously; (bien sûr) of course.
évidence /evidɑ̃s/ *nf* obviousness; (fait) obvious fact; **être en ~** be conspicuous; **mettre en ~** (fait) highlight. **évident, ~e** *adj* obvious, evident.
évier /evje/ *nm* sink.
évincer /evɛ̃se/ **10** *vt* oust.
éviter /evite/ **1** *vt* avoid (de faire doing); **~ qch à qn** (dérangement) save sb sth.
évocateur, -trice /evɔkatœʀ, -tʀis/ *adj* evocative. **évocation** *nf* evocation.

évolué, ~e /evɔlɥe/ adj highly developed.

évoluer /evɔlɥe/ **1** vi evolve; (situation) develop; (se déplacer) glide. **évolution** nf evolution; (d'une situation) development.

évoquer /evɔke/ **1** vt call to mind, evoke.

exacerber /ɛgzasɛʀbe/ **1** vt exacerbate.

exact, ~e /ɛgza(kt), -akt/ adj (précis) exact, accurate; (juste) correct; (personne) punctual. **exactement** adv exactly. **exactitude** nf exactness; punctuality.

ex æquo /ɛgzeko/ adv être ~ tie (avec qn with sb).

exagération /ɛgzaʒeʀasjɔ̃/ nf exaggeration. **exagéré, ~e** adj excessive.

exagérer /ɛgzaʒeʀe/ **14** vt/i exaggerate; (abuser) go too far.

exalté, ~e /ɛgzalte/ nm, f fanatic. **exalter** **1** vt excite; (glorifier) exalt.

examen /ɛgzamɛ̃/ nm examination; (Scol) exam. **examinateur, -trice** nm, f examiner. **examiner** **1** vt examine.

exaspération /ɛgzaspeʀasjɔ̃/ nf exasperation. **exaspérer** **14** vt exasperate.

exaucer /ɛgzose/ **10** vt grant; (personne) grant the wish(es) of.

excédent /ɛksedã/ nm surplus; ~ de bagages excess luggage; ~ de la balance commerciale trade surplus. **excédentaire** adj excess, surplus.

excéder /ɛksede/ **14** vt (dépasser) exceed; (agacer) irritate.

excellence /ɛksɛlãs/ nf excellence. **excellent, ~e** adj excellent. **exceller** **1** vi excel (dans in).

excentricité /ɛksãtʀisite/ nf eccentricity. **excentrique** adj & nmf eccentric.

excepté, ~e /ɛksɛpte/ adj & prép except.

excepter /ɛksɛpte/ **1** vt except.

exception /ɛksɛpsjɔ̃/ nf exception; à l'~ de except for; d'~ exceptional; faire ~ be an exception. **exceptionnel, ~le** adj exceptional. **exceptionnellement** adv exceptionally.

excès /ɛksɛ/ nm excess; ~ de vitesse speeding.

excessif, -ive /ɛksesif, -v/ adj excessive.

excitant, ~e /ɛksitã, -t/ adj stimulating; (palpitant) exciting. ● nm stimulant.

exciter /ɛksite/ **1** vt excite; (irriter) get excited. □ s'~ vpr get excited.

exclamer (s') /(s)ɛksklame/ **1** vpr exclaim.

exclure /ɛksklyʀ/ **16** vt exclude; (expulser) expel; (empêcher) preclude.

exclusif, -ive /ɛksklyzif, -v/ adj exclusive.

exclusion /ɛksklyzjɔ̃/ nf exclusion.

exclusivité /ɛksklyzivite/ nf (Comm) exclusive rights (+ pl); projeter en ~ show exclusively.

excursion /ɛkskyʀsjɔ̃/ nf excursion; (à pied) hike.

excuse /ɛkskyz/ nf excuse; ~s apology (+ sg); faire des ~s apologize.

excuser /ɛkskyze/ **1** vt excuse; excusez-moi excuse me. □ s'~ vpr apologize (de for).

exécrable /ɛgzekʀabl/ adj dreadful. **exécrer** **14** vt loathe.

exécuter /ɛgzekyte/ **1** vt carry out, execute; (Mus) perform; (tuer) execute.

exécutif, -ive /ɛgzekytif, -v/ adj & nm (Pol) executive.

exécution /ɛgzekysjɔ̃/ nf execution; (Mus) performance.

exemplaire /ɛgzãplɛʀ/ adj exemplary. ● nm copy.

exemple /ɛgzãpl/ nm example; par ~ for example; donner l'~ set an example.

exempt, ~e /ɛgzã, -t/ adj ~ de exempt (de from).

exempter /ɛgzãte/ **1** vt exempt (de from). **exemption** nf exemption.

exercer /ɛgzɛʀse/ **10** vt exercise; (influence, contrôle) exert; (former) train, exercise; ~ un métier have a job; ~ le métier de... work as a... □ s'~ vpr practise.

exercice /ɛgzɛʀsis/ nm exercise; (de métier) practice; en ~ in office; (médecin) in practice.

exhaler /ɛgzale/ **1** vt emit.

exhaustif, -ive /ɛgzostif, -v/ adj exhaustive.

exhiber /ɛgzibe/ **1** vt exhibit.

exhorter /ɛgzɔʀte/ **1** vt exhort (à to).

exigeant, ∼e /ɛgziʒɑ̃, -t/ adj demanding; **être ∼ avec qn** demand a lot of sb. **exigence** nf demand. **exiger** 40 vt demand.

exigu, ∼ë /ɛgzigy/ adj tiny.

exil /ɛgzil/ nm exile. **exilé,** ∼e nm, f exile.

exiler /ɛgzile/ 1 vt exile. □ **s'∼** vpr go into exile.

existence /ɛgzistɑ̃s/ nf existence. **exister** 1 vi exist.

exode /ɛgzɔd/ nm exodus.

exonérer /ɛgzɔneʀe/ 14 vt exempt (de from).

exorbitant, ∼e /ɛgzɔʀbitɑ̃, -t/ adj exorbitant.

exorciser /ɛgzɔʀsize/ 1 vt exorcize.

exotique /ɛgzɔtik/ adj exotic.

expansé, ∼e /ɛkspɑ̃se/ adj (Tech) expanded.

expansif, -ive /ɛkspɑ̃sif, -v/ adj expansive. **expansion** nf expansion.

expatrié, ∼e /ɛkspatʀije/ nm, f expatriate.

expectative /ɛkspɛktativ/ nf **être dans l'∼** wait and see.

expédient /ɛkspedjɑ̃/ nm expedient; **vivre d'∼s** live by one's wits; **user d'∼s** resort to expedients.

expédier /ɛkspedje/ 45 vt send, dispatch; (tâche 1) polish off. **expéditeur, -trice** nm, f sender.

expéditif, -ive /ɛkspeditif, -v/ adj quick.

expédition /ɛkspedisjɔ̃/ nf (envoi) dispatching; (voyage) expedition.

expérience /ɛkspeʀjɑ̃s/ nf experience; (scientifique) experiment.

expérimental, ∼e (mpl **-aux**) /ɛkspeʀimɑ̃tal, o/ adj experimental. **expérimentation** nf experimentation. **expérimenté,** ∼e adj experienced. **expérimenter** 1 vt test, experiment with.

expert, ∼e /ɛkspɛʀ, -t/ adj expert. ● nm expert; (d'assurances) adjuster. **expert-comptable** (pl **experts-comptables**) nm accountant.

expertise /ɛkspɛʀtiz/ nf valuation; (de dégâts) assessment. **expertiser** 1 vt value; (dégâts) assess.

expier /ɛkspje/ 45 vt atone for.

expiration /ɛkspiʀasjɔ̃/ nf expiry.

expirer /ɛkspiʀe/ 1 vi breathe out; (finir, mourir) expire.

explicatif, -ive /ɛksplikatif, -v/ adj explanatory.

explication /ɛksplikasjɔ̃/ nf explanation; (fig) discussion; **∼ de texte** (Scol) literary commentary.

explicite /ɛksplisit/ adj explicit.

expliquer /ɛksplike/ 1 vt explain. □ **s'∼** vpr explain oneself; (discuter) discuss things; (être explicable) be understandable.

exploit /ɛksplwa/ nm exploit.

exploitant, ∼e /ɛksplwatɑ̃, -t/ nm, f **∼ (agricole)** farmer.

exploitation /ɛksplwatasjɔ̃/ nf exploitation; (d'entreprise) running; (ferme) farm.

exploiter /ɛksplwate/ 1 vt exploit; (ferme) run; (mine) work.

explorateur, -trice /ɛksplɔʀatœʀ, -tʀis/ nm, f explorer. **exploration** nf exploration. **explorer** 1 vt explore.

exploser /ɛksploze/ 1 vi explode; **faire ∼** explode; (bâtiment) blow up.

explosif, -ive /ɛksplozif, -v/ adj & nm explosive. **explosion** nf explosion.

exportateur, -trice /ɛkspɔʀ- tatœʀ, -tʀis/ nm, f exporter. ● adj exporting. **exportation** nf export. **exporter** 1 vt export.

exposant, ∼e /ɛks
pozɑ̃, -t/ nm, f exhibitor.

exposé, ∼e /ɛkspoze/ nm talk (sur on); (d'une action) account; **faire l'∼ de la situation** give an account of the situation. ● adj **∼ au nord** facing north.

exposer /ɛkspoze/ 1 vt display, show; (expliquer) explain; (soumettre, mettre en danger) expose (à to); (vie) endanger. □ **s'∼ à** vpr expose oneself to.

exposition /ɛkspozisjɔ̃/ nf (d'art) exhibition; (de faits) exposition; (géographique) aspect.

exprès[1] /ɛkspʀɛ/ adv specially; (délibérément) on purpose.

exprès[2], **-esse** /ɛkspʀɛs/ adj express.

express /ɛkspʀɛs/ adj & nm inv **(café)** ∼ espresso; **(train)** ∼ fast train.

expressif, -ive /ɛkspʀesif, -v/ adj expressive. **expression** nf expression.

exprimer /ɛkspʀime/ 1 vt express. □ **s'∼** vpr express oneself.

expulser /ɛkspylse/ ◼ *vt* expel; (*locataire*) evict; (*joueur*) send off. **expulsion** *nf* (d'élève) expulsion; (de locataire) eviction; (d'immigré) deportation.

exquis, ~e /ɛkski, -z/ *adj* exquisite.

extase /ɛkstaz/ *nf* ecstasy.

extasier (s') /(s)ɛkstazje/ ◾ *vpr* s'~ sur be ecstatic about.

extensible /ɛkstɑ̃sibl/ *adj* (*tissu*) stretch.

extension /ɛkstɑ̃sjɔ̃/ *nf* extension; (expansion) expansion.

exténuer /ɛkstenɥe/ ◼ *vt* exhaust.

extérieur, ~e /ɛksterjœr/ *adj* outside; (*signe, gaieté*) outward; (*politique*) foreign. ● *nm* outside, exterior; (de personne) exterior; à l'~ (de) outside. **extérioriser** ◼ *vt* show, externalize.

extermination /ɛkstɛrminasjɔ̃/ *nf* extermination. **exterminer** ◼ *vt* exterminate.

externe /ɛkstɛrn/ *adj* external. ● *nmf* (Scol) day pupil.

extincteur /ɛkstɛ̃ktœr/ *nm* fire extinguisher.

extinction /ɛkstɛ̃ksjɔ̃/ *nf* extinction; **avoir une ~ de voix** have lost one's voice.

extorquer /ɛkstɔrke/ ◼ *vt* extort.

extra /ɛkstra/ *adj inv* first-rate. ● *nm inv* (repas) (special) treat.

extraction /ɛkstraksjɔ̃/ *nf* extraction.

extrader /ɛkstrade/ ◼ *vt* extradite.

extraire /ɛkstrɛr/ ◼ *vt* extract. **extrait** *nm* extract.

extraordinaire /ɛkstraɔrdinɛr/ *adj* extraordinary.

extravagance /ɛkstravagɑ̃s/ *nf* extravagance. **extravagant, ~e** *adj* extravagant.

extraverti, ~e /ɛkstravɛrti/ *nm, f* extrovert.

extrême /ɛkstrɛm/ *adj & nm* extreme. **extrêmement** *adv* extremely.

Extrême-Orient /ɛkstrɛmɔrjɑ̃/ *nm* Far East.

extrémiste /ɛkstremist/ *nmf* extremist.

extrémité /ɛkstremite/ *nf* end; (mains, pieds) extremity.

exubérance /ɛgzyberɑ̃s/ *nf* exuberance. **exubérant, ~e** *adj* exuberant.

F *abrév* f (**franc, francs**) franc, francs.

fabricant, ~e /fabrikɑ̃, -t/ *nm, f* manufacturer. **fabrication** *nf* making; manufacture.

fabrique /fabrik/ *nf* factory. **fabriquer** ◼ *vt* make; (industriellement) manufacture; (fig) make up.

fabuler /fabyle/ ◼ *vi* fantasize.

fabuleux, -euse /fabylø, -z/ *adj* fabulous.

fac /fak/ *nf* 🆎 university.

façade /fasad/ *nf* front; (fig) façade.

face /fas/ *nf* face; (d'un objet) side; **en (~ de), d'en ~** opposite; **en ~ de** (fig) faced with; **~ à** facing; (fig) faced with; **faire ~ à** face. **face-à-face** *nm inv* (débat) one-to-one debate.

fâcher /faʃe/ ◼ *vt* anger; **fâché** angry; (désolé) sorry. ◻ **se ~** *vpr* get angry; (se brouiller) fall out.

facile /fasil/ *adj* easy; (caractère) easygoing.

facilité /fasilite/ *nf* easiness; (aisance) ease; (aptitude) ability; **~s** (possibilités) facilities, opportunities; **~s d'importation** import opportunities; **~s de paiement** easy terms.

faciliter /fasilite/ ◼ *vt* facilitate, make easier.

façon /fasɔ̃/ *nf* way; (de vêtement) cut; **de cette ~** in this way; **de ~ à** so as to; **de toute ~** anyway; **~s** (chichis) fuss; **faire des ~s** stand on ceremony; **sans ~s** (repas) informal; (personne) unpretentious. **façonner** ◼ *vt* shape; (faire) make.

fac-similé (*pl* **~s**) /faksimile/ *nm* facsimile.

facteur, -trice /faktœr, -tris/ *nm, f* postman, postwoman. ● *nm* (élément) factor.

facture /faktyr/ *nf* bill; (Comm) invoice; **~ détaillée** itemized bill. **facturer** ◼ *vt* invoice. **facturette** *nf* credit card slip.

facultatif, -ive /fakyltatif, -v/ *adj* optional.

faculté /fakylte/ nf faculty; (possibilité) power; (Univ) faculty.

fade /fad/ adj insipid.

faible /fɛbl/ adj weak; (espoir, quantité, écart) slight; (revenu, intensité) low; ~ **d'esprit** feeble-minded. ● nm (personne) weakling; (penchant) weakness. **faiblesse** nf weakness. **faiblir** ② vi weaken.

faïence /fajɑ̃s/ nf earthenware.

faillir /fajiʀ/ ② vi **j'ai failli acheter** I almost bought.

faillite /fajit/ nf bankruptcy; (fig) collapse.

faim /fɛ̃/ nf hunger; **avoir** ~ be hungry; **rester sur sa** ~ (fig) be left wanting more.

fainéant, ~e /feneɑ̃, -t/ adj idle. ● nm, f idler.

---

faire /fɛʀ/ ③③

➡ Pour les expressions comme **faire attention**, **faire la cuisine**, etc. ➡ **attention, cuisine** etc.

● verbe transitif

····▶ (préparer, créer) make; ~ **une tarte/une erreur** make a tart/a mistake.

····▶ (se livrer à une activité) do; ~ **du droit** do law; ~ **du foot/du violon** play football/the violin; **qu'est-ce qu'elle fait?** (dans la vie) what does she do?; (en ce moment précis) what is she doing?

····▶ (dans les calculs, mesures, etc.) **10 et 10 font 20** 10 and 10 make 20; **ça fait 25 euros** that's 25 euros; ~ **60 kilos** weigh 60 kilos; **il fait 1,75 m** he's 1.75 m tall.

····▶ (dans les expressions de temps) **ça fait une heure que j'attends** I have been waiting for an hour.

····▶ (imiter) ~ **le clown** act the clown; **faire le malade** pretend to be ill.

····▶ (parcourir) ~ **10 km** do ou cover 10 km; ~ **les musées** go round the museums.

····▶ (entraîner, causer) **ça ne fait** rien it doesn't matter; **l'accident a fait 8 morts** 8 people died in the accident.

····▶ (dire) say; **'excusez-moi', fit-elle** 'excuse me', she said.

● verbe auxiliaire

····▶ (faire + infinitif + qn) make; ~ **pleurer qn** make sb cry.

····▶ (faire + infinitif + qch) have, get; ~ **réparer sa voiture** have ou get one's car mended.

····▶ (ne faire que + infinitif) (continuellement) **ne** ~ **que pleurer** do nothing but cry; (seulement) **je ne fais qu'obéir** I'm only following orders.

● verbe intransitif

····▶ (agir) do, act; ~ **vite** act quickly; **fais comme tu veux** do as you please; **fais comme chez toi** make yourself at home.

····▶ (paraître) look; ~ **joli** look pretty; **ça fait cher** it's expensive.

····▶ (en parlant du temps) **il fait chaud/gris** it's hot/overcast.

□ **se faire** verbe pronominal

····▶ (obtenir, confectionner) make; **se** ~ **des amis** make friends; **se** ~ **un thé** make (oneself) a cup of tea.

····▶ (se faire + infinitif) **se** ~ **gronder** be scolded; **se** ~ **couper les cheveux** have one's hair cut.

····▶ (devenir) **il se fait tard** it's getting late.

····▶ (être d'usage) **ça ne se fait pas** it's not the done thing.

····▶ (emploi impersonnel) **comment se fait-il que tu sois ici?** how come you're here?

····▶ □ **se faire à** get used to; **je ne m'y fais pas** I can't get used to it.

····▶ □ **s'en faire** worry; **ne t'en fais pas** don't worry.

❶ Lorsque **faire** remplace un verbe plus précis, on traduira quelquefois par ce dernier: **faire une visite** pay a visit, **faire un nid** build a nest.

---

faire-part /fɛʀpaʀ/ nm inv announcement.

fais /fɛ/ ➡ **FAIRE** ③③.

faisan /fəzɑ̃/ nm pheasant.

faisceau (pl ~x) /fɛso/ nm (rayon) beam; (fagot) bundle.

fait, ~e /fɛ, fɛt/ adj done; (fromage) ripe; ~ **pour** made for; **tout** ~ ready made; **c'est bien** ~ **pour toi** it serves you right. ● nm fact; (événement) event; **au** ~ **(de)** informed (of); **de ce** ~ therefore; **du** ~ **de** on account of; ~ **divers** (trivial) news item; ~ **nouveau** new development; **prendre qn sur le** ~ catch sb in the act. ● ➡**FAIRE** 33.

faîte /fɛt/ nm top; (fig) peak.

faites /fɛt/ ➡**FAIRE** 33.

falaise /falɛz/ nf cliff.

falloir /falwaʀ/ 34 vi **il faut qch/qn** we/you etc. need sth/sb; **il lui faut du pain** he needs bread; **il faut rester** we/you etc. have to ou must stay; **il faut que j'y aille** I have to ou must go; **il faudrait que tu partes** you should leave; **il aurait fallu le faire** we/you etc. should have done it; **comme il faut** (manger, se tenir) properly; (personne) respectable, proper. □ **s'en** ~ vpr **il s'en est fallu de peu qu'il gagne** he nearly won; **il s'en faut de beaucoup que je sois** I am far from being.

falsifier /falsifje/ 45 vt falsify; (signature, monnaie) forge.

famé, ~e /fame/ adj **mal** ~ disreputable, seedy.

fameux, -**euse** /famø, -z/ adj famous; (excellent 1) first-rate.

familial, ~e (mpl -**iaux**) /familjal, -jo/ adj family.

familiale /familjal/ nf estate car; (US) station wagon.

familiariser /familjaʀize/ 1 vt familiarize (**avec** with). □ **se** ~ vpr familiarize oneself.

familier, -**ière** /familje, -jɛʀ/ adj familiar; (amical) informal.

famille /famij/ nf family; **en** ~ with one's family.

famine /famin/ nf famine.

fanatique /fanatik/ adj fanatical. ● nmf fanatic.

fanfare /fɑ̃faʀ/ nf brass band; (musique) fanfare.

fantaisie /fɑ̃tezi/ nf imagination, fantasy; (caprice) whim; **(de)** ~ (boutons etc.) fancy. **fantaisiste** adj unorthodox; (personne) eccentric.

fantasme /fɑ̃tasm/ nm fantasy.

fantastique /fɑ̃tastik/ adj fantastic.

fantôme /fɑ̃tom/ nm ghost; **cabinet(-)**~ (Pol) shadow cabinet.

faon /fɑ̃/ nm fawn.

FAQ abrév f (**Foire aux questions**) (Internet) FAQ, Frequently Asked Questions.

farce /faʀs/ nf (practical) joke; (Théât) farce; (hachis) stuffing.

farcir /faʀsiʀ/ 2 vt stuff.

fard /faʀ/ nm make-up; ~ **à paupières** eye-shadow; **piquer un** ~ blush.

fardeau (pl ~x) /faʀdo/ nm burden.

farfelu, ~e /faʀfǝly/ adj & nm,f eccentric.

farine /faʀin/ nf flour. **farineux**, -**euse** adj floury. **farineux** nmpl starchy food.

farouche /faʀuʃ/ adj shy; (peu sociable) unsociable; (violent) fierce.

fascicule /fasikyl/ nm (brochure) booklet; (partie d'un ouvrage) fascicule.

fasciner /fasine/ 1 vt fascinate.

fascisme /faʃism/ nm fascism.

fasse /fas/ ➡**FAIRE** 33.

fast-food /fastfud/ nm fast-food place.

fastidieux, -**ieuse** /fastidjø, -z/ adj tedious.

fatal, ~e (mpl ~s) /fatal/ adj inevitable; (mortel) fatal. **fatalité** nf (destin) fate.

fatigant, ~e /fatigɑ̃, -t/ adj tiring; (ennuyeux) tiresome.

fatigue /fatig/ nf fatigue, tiredness.

fatigué, ~e /fatige/ adj tired.

fatiguer /fatige/ 1 vt tire; (yeux, moteur) strain. ● vi (moteur) labour. □ **se** ~ vpr get tired, tire (**de** of).

faubourg /fobuʀ/ nm suburb.

faucher /foʃe/ 1 vt (herbe) mow; (voler 1) pinch; ~ **qn** (véhicule, tir) mow sb down.

faucon /fokɔ̃/ nm falcon, hawk.

faudra, **faudrait** /fodʀa, fodʀɛ/ ➡**FALLOIR** 34.

faufiler (se) /(sǝ)fofile/ 1 vpr edge one's way, squeeze.

faune /fon/ nf wildlife, fauna.

faussaire /fosɛʀ/ nmf forger.

fausse /fos/ ➡**FAUX**².

fausser /fose/ **1** vt buckle; (fig) distort; ~ **compagnie à qn** give sb the slip.

faut /fo/ ➔FALLOIR **34**.

faute /fot/ nf mistake; (responsabilité) fault; (délit) offence; (péché) sin; **en** ~ at fault; ~ **de** for want of; ~ **de quoi** failing which; **sans** ~ without fail; ~ **de frappe** typing error; ~ **de goût** bad taste; ~ **professionnelle** professional misconduct.

fauteuil /fotœj/ nm armchair; (de président) chair; (Théât) seat; ~ **roulant** wheelchair.

fautif, -ive /fotif, -v/ adj guilty; (faux) faulty. ● nm, f guilty party.

fauve /fov/ adj (couleur) fawn, tawny. ● nm wild cat.

faux¹ /fo/ nf scythe.

faux², fausse /fo, fos/ adj false; (falsifié) fake, forged; (numéro, calcul) wrong; (voix) out of tune; **c'est ~!** that is wrong!; ~ **témoignage** perjury; **faire** ~ **bond à qn** stand sb up; **fausse couche** miscarriage; ~ **frais** incidental expenses. ● adv (chanter) out of tune. ● nm forgery. **faux-filet** (pl ~s) nm sirloin.

faveur /favœR/ nf favour; **de** ~ (régime) preferential; **en** ~ **de** in favour of.

favorable /favoRabl/ adj favourable.

favori, ~te /favoRi, -t/ adj & nm,f favourite. **favoriser 1** vt favour.

fax /faks/ nm fax. **faxer 1** vt fax.

fébrile /febRil/ adj feverish.

fécond, ~e /fekɔ̃, -d/ adj fertile. **féconder 1** vt fertilize. **fécondité** nf fertility.

fédéral, ~e (mpl **-aux**) /fedeRal, -o/ adj federal. **fédération** nf federation.

fée /fe/ nf fairy. **féerie** nf magical spectacle. **féerique** adj magical.

feindre /fɛ̃dR/ **22** vt feign; ~ **de** pretend to.

fêler /fele/ **1** vt crack. ☐ **se** ~ vpr crack.

félicitations /felisitasjɔ̃/ nfpl congratulations (**pour** on). **féliciter 1** vt congratulate (**de** on).

félin, ~e /felɛ̃, -in/ adj & nm feline.

femelle /fəmɛl/ adj & nf female.

féminin, ~e /feminɛ̃, -in/ adj feminine; (sexe) female; (mode, équipe) women's. ● nm feminine. **féministe** nmf feminist.

femme /fam/ nf woman; (épouse) wife; ~ **au foyer** housewife; ~ **de chambre** chambermaid; ~ **de ménage** cleaning lady.

fémur /femyR/ nm thigh-bone.

fendre /fɑ̃dR/ **3** vt (couper) split; (fissurer) crack. ☐ **se** ~ vpr crack.

fenêtre /fənɛtR/ nf window.

fenouil /fənuj/ nm fennel.

fente /fɑ̃t/ nf (ouverture) slit, slot; (fissure) crack.

féodal, ~e (mpl **-aux**) /feodal, -o/ adj feudal.

fer /fɛR/ nm iron; ~ **(à repasser)** iron; ~ **à cheval** horseshoe; ~ **de lance** spearhead; ~ **forgé** wrought iron.

fera, ferait /fəRa, fəRɛ/ ➔FAIRE **33**.

férié, ~e /feRje/ adj **jour** ~ public holiday.

ferme /fɛRm/ nf farm; (maison) farm-(house); ~ **éolienne** wind farm. ● adj firm. ● adv (travailler) hard.

fermé, ~e /fɛRme/ adj closed; (gaz, radio) off.

fermenter /fɛRmɑ̃te/ **1** vi ferment.

fermer /fɛRme/ **1** vt/i close, shut; (cesser d'exploiter) close ou shut down; (gaz, robinet) turn off. ☐ **se** ~ vpr close, shut.

fermeté /fɛRməte/ nf firmness.

fermeture /fɛRmətyR/ nf closing; (dispositif) catch; ~ **annuelle** annual closure; ~ **éclair®** zip(-fastener); (US) zipper.

fermier, -ière /fɛRmje, -jɛR/ adj farm. ● nm farmer. **fermière** nf farmer's wife.

féroce /feRɔs/ adj ferocious.

ferraille /fɛRaj/ nf scrap-iron.

ferrer /feRe/ **1** vt (cheval) shoe.

ferroviaire /feRɔvjɛR/ adj rail(way).

ferry /feRi/ nm ferry.

fertile /fɛRtil/ adj fertile; ~ **en** (fig) rich in. **fertiliser 1** vt fertilize. **fertilité** nf fertility.

fervent, ~e /fɛRvɑ̃, -t/ adj fervent. ● nm, f enthusiast (**de** of).

fesse /fɛs/ nf buttock. **fessée** nf spanking, smack.

festin /fɛstɛ̃/ nm feast.

festival (pl ~s) /fɛstival/ nm festival.

fêtard, ~e /fetaʀ, -d/ *nm, f* 🔟 party
animal.

fête /fɛt/ *nf* holiday; (religieuse) feast;
(du nom) name-day; (réception) party;
(en famille) celebration; (foire) fair;
(folklorique) festival; ~ **des Mères**
Mother's Day; ~ **foraine** fun-fair;
faire la ~ live it up; **les ~s (de fin
d'année)** the Christmas season. **fêter**
🔟 *vt* celebrate; (*personne*) give a celebration for.

fétiche /fetiʃ/ *nm* fetish; (fig) mascot.

feu¹ (*pl* ~**x**) /fø/ *nm* fire; (lumière)
light; (de réchaud) burner; **à ~ doux/
vif** on a low/high heat; ~ **rouge/
vert/orange** red/green/amber light;
aux ~x, tournez à droite turn right
at the traffic lights; **avez-vous du ~?**
(pour cigarette) have you got a light?;
au ~! fire!; **mettre le ~ à** set fire to;
prendre ~ catch fire; **jouer avec le
~** play with fire; **ne pas faire long ~**
not last; ~ **d'artifice** firework display;
~ **de joie** bonfire; ~ **de position**
sidelight.

feu² /fø/ *adj inv* (mort) late.

feuillage /fœjaʒ/ *nm* foliage.

feuille /fœj/ *nf* leaf; (de papier) sheet;
(formulaire) form; ~ **d'impôts** tax return; ~ **de paie** payslip.

feuilleté, ~e /fœjte/ *adj* **pâte ~e** puff
pastry. ● *nm* savoury pasty.

feuilleter /fœjte/ 🔟 *vt* leaf through.

feuilleton /fœjtɔ̃/ *nm* (à suivre) serial;
(histoire complète) series.

feutre /føtʀ/ *nm* felt; (chapeau) felt
hat; (crayon) felt-tip (pen).

fève /fɛv/ *nf* broad bean.

février /fevʀije/ *nm* February.

fiable /fjabl/ *adj* reliable.

fiançailles /fjɑ̃saj/ *nfpl* engagement.

fiancé, ~e /fjɑ̃se/ *adj* engaged. ● *nm*
fiancé. *nf* fiancée. **fiancer (se)**
🔟 *vpr* become engaged (**avec** to).

fibre /fibʀ/ *nf* fibre; ~ **de verre**
fibreglass.

ficeler /fisle/ 🔟 *vt* tie up.

ficelle /fisɛl/ *nf* string.

fiche /fiʃ/ *nf* (index) card; (formulaire)
form, slip; (Électr) plug.

ficher¹ /fiʃe/ 🔟 *vt* (enfoncer) drive
(**dans** into).

ficher² /fiʃe/ 🔟 🔟 *vt* (faire) do; (donner) give; (mettre) put; ~ **le camp**

clear off. □ **se ~ de** *vpr* make fun of;
il s'en fiche he couldn't care less.

fichier /fiʃje/ *nm* file.

fichu, ~e /fiʃy/ *adj* 🔟 (mauvais) rotten; (raté) done for; **mal ~** terrible.

fictif, -ive /fiktif, -v/ *adj* fictitious. **fiction** *nf* fiction.

fidèle /fidɛl/ *adj* faithful. ● *nmf* (client)
regular; (Relig) believer; ~**s** (à l'église)
congregation. **fidélité** *nf* fidelity.

fier¹, fière /fjɛʀ/ *adj* proud (**de** of).

fier²(se) /(sə)fje/ 🔟 *vpr* **se ~ à** trust.

fierté /fjɛʀte/ *nf* pride.

fièvre /fjɛvʀ/ *nf* fever; **avoir de la ~**
have a temperature; ~ **aphteuse** foot-
and-mouth disease. **fiévreux, -euse**
adj feverish.

figer /fiʒe/ 🔟 *vi* (graisse) congeal;
(sang) clot; **figé sur place** frozen to
the spot. □ **se ~** *vpr* (personne, sourire) freeze; (graisse) congeal;
(sang) clot.

figue /fig/ *nf* fig.

figurant, ~e /figyʀɑ̃, -t/ *nm, f* (au cinéma) extra.

figure /figyʀ/ *nf* face; (forme, personnage) figure; (illustration) picture.

figuré, ~e /figyʀe/ *adj* (sens) fig-
urative.

figurer /figyʀe/ 🔟 *vi* appear. ● *vt* represent. □ **se ~** *vpr* imagine.

fil /fil/ *nm* thread; (métallique, électrique) wire; (de couteau) edge; (à coudre) cotton; **au ~ de** with the passing
of; **au ~ de l'eau** with the current; ~
de fer wire; **au bout du ~** 🔟 on the
phone.

file /fil/ *nf* line; (voie: Auto) lane; ~
(d'attente) queue; (US) line; **en ~ indienne** in single file.

filer /file/ 🔟 *vt* spin; (suivre) shadow;
~ **qch à qn** 🔟 slip sb sth. ● *vi* (bas)
ladder, run; (liquide) run; (aller vite 🔟)
speed along, fly by; (partir 🔟) dash
off; (disparaître 🔟) ~ **entre les
mains** slip through one's fingers; ~
doux do as one's told.

filet /filɛ/ *nm* net; (d'eau) trickle; (de
viande) fillet; ~ **(à bagages)** (luggage) rack; ~ **à provisions** string bag
(for shopping).

filiale /filjal/ *nf* subsidiary (company).

filière /filjɛʀ/ *nf* (official) channels; (de
trafiquants) network; **passer par** ou

suivre la ~ (*employé*) work one's way up.

fille /fij/ *nf* girl; (opposé à fils) daughter. **fillette** *nf* little girl.

filleul /fijœl/ *nm* godson.

filleule /fijœl/ *nf* god-daughter.

film /film/ *nm* film; **~ d'épouvante/ muet/parlant** horror/silent/talking film; **~ dramatique** drama. **filmer** [1] *vt* film.

filon /filɔ̃/ *nm* (Géol) seam; (travail lucratif [1]) money spinner; **avoir trouvé le bon ~** be onto a good thing.

fils /fis/ *nm* son.

filtre /filtʀ/ *nm* filter. **filtrer** [1] *vt/i* filter; (*personne*) screen.

fin[1] /fɛ̃/ *nf* end; **à la ~** finally; **en ~ de compte** all things considered; **~ de semaine** weekend; **mettre ~ à** put an end to; **prendre ~** come to an end.

fin[2], **~e** /fɛ̃, fin/ *adj* fine; (*tranche, couche*) thin; (*taille*) slim; (*plat*) exquisite; (*esprit, vue*) sharp; **~es herbes** mixed herbs. ● *adv* (*couper*) finely.

final, ~e (*mpl* **-aux**) /final, -o/ *adj* final.

finale /final/ *nm* (Mus) finale. ● *nf* (Sport) final; (Gram) final syllable. **finalement** *adv* finally; (*somme toute*) after all. **finaliste** *nmf* finalist.

finance /finɑ̃s/ *nf* finance. **financer** [10] *vt* finance.

financier, -ière /finɑ̃sje, -jɛʀ/ *adj* financial. ● *nm* financier.

finesse /fines/ *nf* fineness; (de taille) slimness; (acuité) sharpness; **~s** (de langue) niceties.

finir /finiʀ/ [2] *vt/i* finish, end; (*arrêter*) stop; (*manger*) finish (up); **en ~ avec** have done with; **~ par faire** end up doing; **ça va mal ~** it will turn out badly.

finlandais, ~e /fɛ̃lɑ̃dɛ, -z/ *adj* Finnish. **F~, ~e** *nm, f* Finn.

Finlande /fɛ̃lɑ̃d/ *nf* Finland.

finnois, ~e /finwa/ *adj* Finnish. ● *nm* (Ling) Finnish.

firme /fiʀm/ *nf* firm.

fisc /fisk/ *nm* tax authorities. **fiscal, ~e** (*mpl* **-aux**) *adj* tax, fiscal. **fiscalité** *nf* tax system.

fissure /fisyʀ/ *nf* crack.

FIV *abrév f* (**fécondation in vitro**) IVF.

fixe /fiks/ *adj* fixed; (*stable*) steady; **à heure ~** at a set time; **menu à prix ~** set menu. ● *nm* basic pay.

fixer /fikse/ [1] *vt* fix; **~ (du regard)** stare at; **être fixé** (*personne*) have made up one's mind. □ **se ~** *vpr* (s'attacher) be attached; (s'installer) settle down.

flacon /flakɔ̃/ *nm* bottle.

flagrant, ~e /flagʀɑ̃, -t/ *adj* flagrant, blatant; **en ~ délit** in the act.

flair /flɛʀ/ *nm* (sense of) smell; (fig) intuition.

flamand, ~e /flamɑ̃, -d/ *adj* Flemish. ● *nm* (Ling) Flemish. **F~, ~e** *nm, f* Fleming.

flamant /flamɑ̃/ *nm* flamingo.

flambeau (*pl* **~x**) /flɑ̃bo/ *nm* torch.

flambée /flɑ̃be/ *nf* blaze; (fig) explosion.

flamber /flɑ̃be/ [1] *vi* blaze; (*prix*) shoot up. ● *vt* (*aiguille*) sterilize; (*volaille*) singe.

flamme /flam/ *nf* flame; (fig) ardour; **en ~s** ablaze.

flan /flɑ̃/ *nm* custard tart.

flanc /flɑ̃/ *nm* side; (d'animal, d'armée) flank.

flâner /flɑne/ [1] *vi* stroll. **flânerie** *nf* stroll.

flanquer /flɑ̃ke/ [1] *vt* flank; (jeter [1]) chuck; (donner [1]) give; **~ à la porte** kick out.

flaque /flak/ *nf* (d'eau) puddle; (de sang) pool.

flash (*pl* **~es**) /flaʃ/ *nm* (Photo) flash; (information) news flash; **~ publicitaire** commercial.

flatter /flate/ [1] *vt* flatter. □ **se ~ de** *vpr* pride oneself on.

flatteur, -euse /flatœʀ, -øz/ *adj* flattering. ● *nm, f* flatterer.

fléau (*pl* **~x**) /fleo/ *nm* (désastre) scourge; (personne) pest.

flèche /flɛʃ/ *nf* arrow; (de clocher) spire; **monter en ~** spiral; **partir en ~** shoot off.

flécher /fleʃe/ [14] *vt* mark *ou* signpost (with arrows). **fléchette** *nf* dart.

fléchir /fleʃiʀ/ [2] *vt* bend; (*personne*) move, sway. ● *vi* (faiblir) weaken; (*prix*) fall; (*poutre*) sag, bend.

flemme /flɛm/ *nf* [1] laziness; **j'ai la ~ de faire** I can't be bothered doing.

flétrir (se) /(sə)fletʀiʀ/ **2** vpr (plante) wither; (fruit) shrivel; (beauté) fade.

fleur /flœʀ/ nf flower; **à ~ de terre/ d'eau** just above the ground/water; **à ~s** flowery; **~ de l'âge** prime of life; **en ~s** in flower.

fleurir /flœʀiʀ/ **2** vi flower; (arbre) blossom; (fig) flourish. ● vt decorate with flowers. **fleuriste** nmf florist.

fleuve /flœv/ nm river.

flic /flik/ nm **1** cop.

flipper /flipœʀ/ nm pinball (machine).

flirter /flœʀte/ **1** vi flirt.

flocon /flɔkɔ̃/ nm flake.

flore /flɔʀ/ nf flora.

florissant, ~e /flɔʀisã, -t/ adj flourishing.

flot /flo/ nm flood, stream; **être à ~** be afloat; **les ~s** the waves.

flottant, ~e /flɔtã, -t/ adj (vêtement) loose; (indécis) indecisive.

flotte /flɔt/ nf fleet; (pluie **1**) rain; (eau **1**) water.

flottement /flɔtmã/ nm (incertitude) indecision.

flotter /flɔte/ **1** vi float; (drapeau) flutter; (nuage, parfum, pensées) drift; (pleuvoir **1**) rain. **flotteur** nm float.

flou, ~e /flu/ adj out of focus; (fig) vague.

fluctuer /flyktɥe/ **1** vi fluctuate.

fluet, ~te /flyɛ, -t/ adj thin.

fluide /flɥid/ adj & nm fluid.

fluor /flyɔʀ/ nm (pour les dents) fluoride.

fluorescent, ~e /flyɔʀesã, -t/ adj fluorescent.

flûte /flyt/ nf flute; (verre) champagne glass.

fluvial, ~e (mpl -iaux) /flyvjal, -jo/ adj river.

flux /fly/ nm flow; **~ et reflux** ebb and flow.

FM abrév f (**frequency modulation**) FM.

fœtus /fetys/ nm foetus.

foi /fwa/ nf faith; **être de bonne/ mauvaise ~** be acting in good/bad faith; **ma ~!** well (indeed)!

foie /fwa/ nm liver.

foin /fwɛ̃/ nm hay.

foire /fwaʀ/ nf fair; **faire la ~ 1** live it up.

fois /fwa/ nf time; **une ~** once; **deux ~** twice; **à la ~** at the same time; **des ~** (parfois) sometimes; **une ~ pour toutes** once and for all.

fol /fɔl/ ➡**FOU**.

folie /fɔli/ nf madness; (bêtise) foolish thing, folly; **faire une ~, faire des ~s** be extravagant.

folklore /fɔlklɔʀ/ nm folklore. **folklorique** adj folk; **1** eccentric.

folle /fɔl/ ➡**FOU**.

foncé, ~e /fɔ̃se/ adj dark.

foncer /fɔ̃se/ **10** vt darken. ● vi (s'assombrir) darken; (aller vite **1**) dash along; **~ sur 1** charge at.

foncier, -ière /fɔ̃sje, -jɛʀ/ adj fundamental; (Comm) real estate.

fonction /fɔ̃ksjɔ̃/ nf function; (emploi) position; **~s** (obligations) duties; **en ~ de** according to; **~ publique** civil service; **voiture de ~** company car. **fonctionnaire** nmf civil servant. **fonctionnement** nm working.

fonctionner /fɔ̃ksjɔne/ **1** vi work; **faire ~** work.

fond /fɔ̃/ nm bottom; (de salle, magasin, etc.) back; (essentiel) basis; (contenu) content; (plan) background; (Sport) long-distance running; **à ~** thoroughly; **au ~** basically; **de ~** (bruit) background; **de ~ en comble** from top to bottom; **au ou dans le ~** really; **~ de teint** foundation, make-up base.

fondamental, ~e (mpl -aux) /fɔ̃damãtal, -o/ adj fundamental.

fondateur, -trice /fɔ̃datœʀ, -tʀis/ nm, f founder. **fondation** nf foundation.

fonder /fɔ̃de/ **1** vt found; (baser) base (**sur** on); (**bien**) **fondé** wellfounded. □ **se ~ sur** vpr be guided by, be based on.

fonderie /fɔ̃dʀi/ nf foundry.

fondre /fɔ̃dʀ/ **3** vt/i melt; (dans l'eau) dissolve; (mélanger) merge; **faire ~** melt; dissolve; **~ en larmes** burst into tears; **~ sur** swoop on. □ **se ~** vpr merge.

fonds /fɔ̃/ nm fund; **~ de commerce** business. ● nmpl (capitaux) funds.

fondu, ~e /fɔ̃dy/ adj melted; (métal) molten.

font /fɔ̃/ ➡**FAIRE** **33**.

fontaine /fɔ̃tɛn/ nf fountain; (source) spring.

fonte /fɔ̃t/ nf melting; (fer) cast iron; ~ **des neiges** thaw.

foot /fut/ nm Ⓕ football.

football /futbol/ nm football.

footing /futiŋ/ nm jogging.

forain /fɔʀɛ̃/ nm fairground entertainer; **marchand ~** stallholder.

forçat /fɔʀsa/ nm convict.

force /fɔʀs/ nf force; (physique) strength; (hydraulique etc.) power; ~**s** (physiques) strength; **à ~ de** by sheer force of; **de ~, par la ~** by force; ~ **de dissuasion** deterrent; ~ **de frappe** strike force, deterrent; ~ **de l'âge** prime of life; ~**s de l'ordre** police (force) ; ~**s de marché** market forces.

forcé, ~e /fɔʀse/ adj forced; (inévitable) inevitable; **c'est ~ qu'il fasse** Ⓕ he's bound to do. **forcément** adv necessarily; (évidemment) obviously.

forcené, ~e /fɔʀsəne/ adj frenzied. ● nm, f maniac.

forcer /fɔʀse/ Ⓘ vt force (**à faire** to do); (voix) strain; ~ **la dose** Ⓕ overdo it. ● vi force; (exagérer) overdo it. □ **se ~** vpr force oneself.

forer /fɔʀe/ Ⓘ vt drill.

forestier, -ière /fɔʀɛstje, -jɛʀ/ adj forest. ● nm, f forestry worker.

forêt /fɔʀɛ/ nf forest.

forfait /fɔʀfɛ/ nm (Comm) (prix fixe) fixed price; (offre promotionnelle) package. **forfaitaire** adj (prix) fixed.

forger /fɔʀʒe/ Ⓜ vt forge; (inventer) make up.

forgeron /fɔʀʒəʀɔ̃/ nm blacksmith.

formaliser (se) /(sə)fɔʀmalize/ Ⓘ vpr take offence (**de** at).

formalité /fɔʀmalite/ nf formality.

format /fɔʀma/ nm format. **formater** Ⓘ vt (Ordinat) format.

formation /fɔʀmasjɔ̃/ nf formation; (professionnelle) training; (culture) education; ~ **permanente** ou **continue** continuing education.

forme /fɔʀm/ nf form; (contour) shape, form; ~**s** (de femme) figure; **être en ~** be in good shape, be on form; **en ~ de** in the shape of; **en bonne et due ~** in due form.

formel, ~le /fɔʀmɛl/ adj formal; (catégorique) positive.

former /fɔʀme/ Ⓘ vt form; (instruire) train. □ **se ~** vpr form.

formidable /fɔʀmidabl/ adj fantastic.

formulaire /fɔʀmylɛʀ/ nm form.

formule /fɔʀmyl/ nf formula; (expression) expression; (feuille) form; ~ **de politesse** polite phrase, letter ending. **formuler** Ⓘ vt formulate.

fort, ~e /fɔʀ, -t/ adj strong; (grand) big; (pluie) heavy; (bruit) loud; (pente) steep; (élève) clever; **au plus ~ de** at the height of; **c'est une ~e tête** she's headstrong. ● adv (frapper) hard; (parler) loud; (très) very; (beaucoup) very much. ● nm (atout) strong point; (Mil) fort.

fortifiant /fɔʀtifjɑ̃/ nm tonic. **fortifier** Ⓜ vt fortify.

fortune /fɔʀtyn/ nf fortune; **de ~** (improvisé) makeshift; **faire ~** make one's fortune.

forum /fɔʀɔm/ nm forum; ~ **de discussion** (Internet) newsgroup.

fosse /fos/ nf pit; (tombe) grave; ~ **d'orchestre** orchestra pit; ~ **septique** septic tank.

fossé /fose/ nm ditch; (fig) gulf; ~ **numérique** digital divide.

fossette /fosɛt/ nf dimple.

fossile /fosil/ nm fossil.

fou (fol before vowel or mute h) , **folle** /fu, fɔl/ adj mad; (course, regard) wild; (énorme Ⓕ) tremendous; ~ **de** crazy about; **le ~ rire** the giggles. ● nm madman; (bouffon) jester. **folle** nf madwoman.

foudre /fudʀ/ nf lightning.

foudroyant, ~e /fudʀwajɑ̃, -t/ adj (mort, maladie) violent.

foudroyer /fudʀwaje/ Ⓢ vt (orage) strike; (maladie etc.) strike down; ~ **qn du regard** look daggers at sb.

fouet /fwɛ/ nm whip; (Culin) whisk.

fougère /fuʒɛʀ/ nf fern.

fougue /fug/ nf ardour. **fougueux, -euse** adj ardent.

fouille /fuj/ nf search; (Archéol) excavation.

fouiller /fuje/ Ⓘ vt/i search; (creuser) dig; ~ **dans** (tiroir) rummage through.

fouillis /fuji/ nm jumble.

foulard /fulaʀ/ nm scarf.

foule /ful/ nf crowd; **une ~ de** (fig) a mass of.

foulée /fule/ *nf* stride; **il l'a fait dans la** ~ he did it while he was at *ou* about it.

fouler /fule/ **1** *vt* (*raisin*) press; (*sol*) set foot on; ~ **qch aux pieds** trample sth underfoot; (*fig*) ride roughshod over sth. □ **se** ~ *vpr* **se** ~ **le poignet/ le pied** sprain one's wrist/foot; **ne pas se** ~ **1** not strain oneself.

four /fuR/ *nm* oven; (*de potier*) kiln; (Théât) flop; ~ **à micro-ondes** microwave oven; ~ **crématoire** crematorium.

fourbe /fuRb/ *adj* deceitful.

fourche /fuRʃ/ *nf* fork; (à foin) pitchfork. **fourchette** *nf* fork; (Comm) bracket, range.

fourgon /fuRgɔ̃/ *nm* van.

fourmi /fuRmi/ *nf* ant; **avoir des** ~s have pins and needles.

fourmiller /fuRmije/ **1** *vi* swarm (**de** with).

fourneau (*pl* ~**x**) /fuRno/ *nm* stove.

fourni, ~e /fuRni/ *adj* (épais) thick.

fournir /fuRniR/ **2** *vt* supply, provide; (*client*) supply; (*effort*) put in; ~ **à qn** supply sb with. □ **se** ~ **chez** *vpr* shop at.

fournisseur /fuRnisœR/ *nm* supplier; ~ **d'accès à l'Internet** Internet service provider.

fourniture /fuRnityR/ *nf* supply.

fourrage /fuRaʒ/ *nm* fodder.

fourré, ~e /fuRe/ *adj* (vêtement) furlined; (gâteau etc.) filled (with jam, cream, etc.). ● *nm* thicket.

fourre-tout /fuRtu/ *nm inv* (sac) holdall.

fourreur /fuRœR/ *nm* furrier.

fourrière /fuRjɛR/ *nf* (lieu) pound.

fourrure /fuRyR/ *nf* fur.

foutre /futR/ **3** *vt* 🔲= **ficher² 1**.

foutu, ~e /futy/ *adj* 🔲 = **fichu**.

foyer /fwaje/ *nm* home; (âtre) hearth; (club) club; (d'étudiants) hostel; (Théât) foyer; (Photo) focus; (centre) centre.

fracas /fRaka/ *nm* din; (de train) roar; (d'objet qui tombe) crash. **fracassant, ~e** *adj* (bruyant) deafening; (violent) shattering.

fraction /fRaksjɔ̃/ *nf* fraction.

fracture /fRaktyR/ *nf* fracture; ~ **du poignet** fractured wrist.

fragile /fRaʒil/ *adj* fragile; (peau) sensitive; (cœur) weak. **fragilité** *nf* fragility.

fragment /fRagmɑ̃/ *nm* bit, fragment. **fragmenter** **1** *vt* split, fragment.

fraîchement /fRɛʃmɑ̃/ *adv* (récemment) freshly; (avec froideur) coolly. **fraîcheur** *nf* coolness; (nouveauté) freshness. **fraîchir** **2** *vi* freshen, become colder.

frais¹, fraîche /fRɛ, -ʃ/ *adj* fresh; (temps, accueil) cool; (peinture) wet; ~ **et dispos** fresh; **il fait** ~ it is cool. ● *adv* (récemment) newly, freshly. ● *nm* **mettre au** ~ put in a cool place; **prendre le** ~ get some fresh air.

frais² /fRɛ/ *nmpl* expenses; (droits) fees; **aux** ~ **de** at the expense of; **faire des** ~ spend a lot of money; ~ **généraux** (Comm) overheads, running expenses; ~ **de scolarité** school fees.

fraise /fRɛz/ *nf* strawberry. **fraisier** *nm* strawberry plant; (gâteau) strawberry gateau.

framboise /fRɑ̃bwaz/ *nf* raspberry. **framboisier** *nm* raspberry bush.

franc, franche /fRɑ̃, -ʃ/ *adj* frank; (regard) frank, candid; (cassure) clean; (net) clear; (libre) free; (véritable) downright. ● *nm* franc.

français, ~e /fRɑ̃sɛ, -z/ *adj* French. ● *nm* (Ling) French. **F~, ~e** *nm, f* Frenchman, Frenchwoman.

France /fRɑ̃s/ *nf* France.

franchement /fRɑ̃ʃmɑ̃/ *adv* frankly; (nettement) clearly; (tout à fait) really.

franchir /fRɑ̃ʃiR/ **2** *vt* (obstacle) get over; (distance) cover; (limite) exceed; (traverser) cross.

franchise /fRɑ̃ʃiz/ *nf* (qualité) frankness; (Comm) franchise; (exemption) exemption; ~ **douanière** exemption from duties.

franc-maçon (*pl* **francs-maçons**) /fRɑ̃masɔ̃/ *nm* Freemason. **franc-maçonnerie** *nf* Freemasonry.

franco /fRɑ̃ko/ *adv* postage paid.

francophone /fRɑ̃kɔfɔn/ *adj* French-speaking. ● *nmf* French speaker.

franc-parler /fRɑ̃paRle/ *nm inv* outspokenness.

frange /fRɑ̃ʒ/ *nf* fringe.

frappe /fRap/ *nf* (de texte) typing.

frappé, ~e /fRape/ *adj* chilled.

frapper /fʀape/ ❶ vt/i strike; (battre) hit, strike; (monnaie) mint; (à la porte) knock, bang; **frappé de panique** panic-stricken.

fraternel, ~le /fʀatɛʀnɛl/ adj brotherly. **fraternité** nf brotherhood.

fraude /fʀod/ nf fraud; (à un examen) cheating; **passer qch en ~** smuggle sth in. **frauder** ❶ vt/i cheat. **frauduleux, -euse** adj fraudulent.

frayer /fʀeje/ ❸❶ vt open up. □ se ~ vpr se ~ **un passage** force one's way (à travers, dans through).

frayeur /fʀejœʀ/ nf fright.

fredonner /fʀədɔne/ ❶ vt hum.

free-lance /fʀilɑ̃s/ adj & nmf freelance.

freezer /fʀizœʀ/ nm freezer.

frein /fʀɛ̃/ nm brake; **mettre un ~ à** curb; **~ à main** hand brake.

freiner /fʀene/ ❶ vt slow down; (modérer, enrayer) curb. ● vi (Auto) brake.

frêle /fʀɛl/ adj frail.

frelon /fʀəlɔ̃/ nm hornet.

frémir /fʀemiʀ/ ❷ vi shudder, shake; (feuille, eau) quiver.

frêne /fʀɛn/ nm ash.

frénésie /fʀenezi/ nf frenzy. **frénétique** adj frenzied.

fréquemment /fʀekamɑ̃/ adv frequently. **fréquence** nf frequency. **fréquent, ~e** adj frequent. **fréquentation** nf frequenting.

fréquentations /fʀekɑ̃tasjɔ̃/ nfpl acquaintances; **avoir de mauvaises ~** keep bad company.

fréquenter /fʀekɑ̃te/ ❶ vt frequent; (école) attend; (personne) see.

frère /fʀɛʀ/ nm brother.

fret /fʀɛt/ nm freight.

friand, ~e /fʀijɑ̃, -d/ adj ~ **de** very fond of.

friandise /fʀijɑ̃diz/ nf sweet; (US) candy; (gâteau) cake.

fric /fʀik/ nm ① money.

friction /fʀiksjɔ̃/ nf friction; (massage) rub-down.

frigidaire ® /fʀiʒidɛʀ/ nm refrigerator.

frigo /fʀigo/ nm ① fridge. **frigorifique** adj (vitrine etc.) refrigerated.

frileux, -euse /fʀilø, -z/ adj sensitive to cold.

frime /fʀim/ nf ① **c'est de la ~** it's all pretence; **pour la ~** for show.

frimousse /fʀimus/ nf face.

fringale /fʀɛ̃gal/ nf ① ravenous appetite.

fringant, ~e /fʀɛ̃gɑ̃, -t/ adj dashing.

fringues /fʀɛ̃g/ nfpl ① gear.

friper /fʀipe/ ❶ vt crumple, crease. □ se ~ vpr crumple, crease.

fripon, ~ne /fʀipɔ̃, -ɔn/ nm, f rascal. ● adj mischievous.

fripouille /fʀipuj/ nf rogue.

frire /fʀiʀ/ ❺❻ vt/i fry; **faire ~** fry.

frise /fʀiz/ nf frieze.

friser /fʀize/ ❶ vt/i (cheveux) curl; (personne) curl the hair of; **frisé** curly.

frisson /fʀisɔ̃/ nm (de froid) shiver; (de peur) shudder. **frissonner** ❶ vi shiver; shudder.

frit, ~e /fʀi, -t/ adj fried.

frite /fʀit/ nf chip; **avoir la ~** ① feel good.

friteuse /fʀitøz/ nf chip pan; (électrique) (deep) fryer.

friture /fʀityʀ/ nf fried fish; (huile) (frying) oil ou fat.

frivole /fʀivɔl/ adj frivolous.

froid, ~e /fʀwa, -d/ adj & nm cold; **avoir/prendre ~** be/catch cold; **il fait ~** it is cold. **froidement** adv coldly; (calculer) coolly. **froideur** nf coldness.

froisser /fʀwase/ ❶ vt crumple; (fig) offend. □ se ~ vpr crumple; (fig) take offence; **se ~ un muscle** strain a muscle.

frôler /fʀole/ ❶ vt brush against; skim; (fig) come close to.

fromage /fʀɔmaʒ/ nm cheese.

fromager, -ère /fʀɔmaʒe, -ɛʀ/ adj cheese. ● nm, f (fabricant) cheesemaker; (marchand) cheesemonger.

froment /fʀɔmɑ̃/ nm wheat.

froncer /fʀɔ̃se/ ❿ vt gather; ~ **les sourcils** frown.

front /fʀɔ̃/ nm forehead; (Mil, Pol) front; **de ~** at the same time; (de face) head-on; (côte à côte) abreast; **faire ~ à** face up to. **frontal, ~e** (mpl -aux) adj frontal; (Ordinat) front-end.

frontalier, -ière /fʀɔ̃talje, -jɛʀ/ adj border; **travailleur ~** commuter from across the border.

frontière /fʀɔ̃tjɛʀ/ nf border, frontier.

frottement /frɔtmɑ̃/ nm rubbing; (Tech) friction. **frotter 1** vt/i rub; (allumette) strike.

frottis /frɔti/ nm ~ **vaginal** cervical smear.

frousse /frus/ nf 1 fear; **avoir la** ~ 1 be scared.

fructifier /fryktifje/ 45 vi **faire** ~ put to work.

fructueux, -euse /fryktɥø, -z/ adj fruitful.

frugal, ~e (mpl -aux) /frygal, -o/ adj frugal.

fruit /frɥi/ nm fruit; **des** ~s (some) fruit; ~s **de mer** seafood. **fruité, ~e** adj fruity.

frustrant, ~e /frystrɑ̃, -t/ adj frustrating. **frustrer 1** vt frustrate.

fuel /fjul/ nm fuel oil.

fugitif, -ive /fyʒitif, -v/ adj (passager) fleeting. ● nm, f fugitive.

fugue /fyg/ nf (Mus) fugue; **faire une** ~ run away.

fuir /fɥir/ 35 vi flee, run away; (eau, robinet, etc.) leak. ● vt (quitter) flee; (éviter) shun.

fuite /fɥit/ nf flight; (de liquide, d'une nouvelle) leak; **en** ~ on the run; **mettre en** ~ put to flight; **prendre la** ~ take flight.

fulgurant, ~e /fylgyrɑ̃, -t/ adj (vitesse) lightning.

fumé, ~e /fyme/ adj (poisson, verre) smoked.

fumée /fyme/ nf smoke; (vapeur) steam.

fumer /fyme/ 1 vt/i smoke.

fumeur, -euse /fymœr, -øz/ nm, f smoker; **zone non-**~s no smoking area.

fumier /fymje/ nm manure.

funambule /fynɑ̃byl/ nmf tightrope walker.

funèbre /fynɛbr/ adj funeral; (fig) gloomy.

funérailles /fyneraj/ nfpl funeral.

funéraire /fynerɛr/ adj funeral.

funeste /fynɛst/ adj fatal.

fur: au ~ **et à mesure** /ofyreaməzyr/ loc as one goes along, progressively; **au** ~ **et à mesure que** as.

furet /fyrɛ/ nm ferret.

fureur /fyrœr/ nf fury; (passion) passion; **avec** ~ furiously; passionately; **mettre en** ~ infuriate; **faire** ~ be all the rage.

furieux, -ieuse /fyrjø, -z/ adj furious.

furoncle /fyrɔ̃kl/ nm boil.

furtif, -ive /fyrtif, -v/ adj furtive.

fuseau (pl ~x) /fyzo/ nm ski trousers; (pour filer) spindle; ~ **horaire** time zone.

fusée /fyze/ nf rocket.

fusible /fyzibl/ nm fuse.

fusil /fyzi/ nm rifle, gun; (de chasse) shotgun; ~ **mitrailleur** machine-gun.

fusion /fyzjɔ̃/ nf fusion; (Comm) merger. **fusionner 1** vt/i merge.

fut /fy/ ➔ÊTRE 5.

fût /fy/ nm (tonneau) barrel; (d'arbre) trunk.

futé, ~e /fyte/ adj cunning.

futile /fytil/ adj futile.

futur, ~e /fytyr/ adj future; ~**e femme/maman** wife-/mother-to-be. ● nm future.

fuyant, ~e /fɥijɑ̃, -t/ adj (front, ligne) receding; (personne) evasive.

fuyard, ~e /fɥijar, -d/ nm, f runaway.

Gg

gabardine /gabardin/ nf raincoat.

gabarit /gabari/ nm size; (patron) template; (fig) calibre.

gâcher /gɑʃe/ 1 vt (gâter) spoil; (gaspiller) waste.

gâchette /gɑʃɛt/ nf trigger.

gâchis /gɑʃi/ nm waste.

gaffe /gaf/ nf 1 blunder; **faire** ~ be careful (à of).

gage /gaʒ/ nm security; (de bonne foi) pledge; (de jeu) forfeit; ~s (salaire) wages; **en** ~ **de** as a token of; **mettre en** ~ pawn; **tueur à** ~s hired killer.

gageure /gaʒyr/ nf challenge.

gagnant, ~e /gaɲɑ̃, -t/ adj winning. ● nm, f winner.

gagne-pain /gaɲpɛ̃/ nm inv job.

gagner /gaɲe/ 1 vt (match, prix) win; (argent, pain) earn; (terrain) gain;

(*temps*) save; (atteindre) reach; (convaincre) win over; ~ **sa vie** earn one's living. ● *vi* win; (fig) gain.

gai, ~e /ge/ *adj* cheerful; (ivre) merry. **gaiement** *adv* cheerfully. **gaieté** *nf* cheerfulness.

gain /gɛ̃/ *nm* (salaire) earnings; (avantage) gain; (économie) saving; ~**s** (Comm) profits; (au jeu) winnings.

gaine /gɛn/ *nf* (corset) girdle; (étui) sheath.

galant, ~e /galɑ̃, -t/ *adj* courteous; (amoureux) romantic.

galaxie /galaksi/ *nf* galaxy.

gale /gal/ *nf* (de chat etc.) mange.

galère /galɛʀ/ *nf* (navire) galley; **c'est la ~!** 🔢 what an ordeal!

galérer /galeʀe/ 🔢 *vi* 🔢 (peiner) have a hard time.

galerie /galʀi/ *nf* gallery; (Théât) circle; (de voiture) roof-rack; ~ **marchande** shopping arcade.

galet /galɛ/ *nm* pebble.

galette /galɛt/ *nf* flat cake; ~ **des Rois** Twelfth Night cake.

Galles /gal/ *nfpl* **le pays de ~** Wales.

gallois, ~e /galwa, -z/ *adj* Welsh. ● *nm* (Ling) Welsh. **G~, ~e** *nm, f* Welshman, Welshwoman.

galon /galɔ̃/ *nm* braid; (Mil) stripe; **prendre du ~** be promoted.

galop /galo/ *nm* canter; **aller au ~** canter; **grand ~** gallop; ~ **d'essai** trial run. **galoper** 🔢 *vi* (cheval) canter; (au grand galop) gallop; (personne) run.

galopin /galɔpɛ̃/ *nm* 🔢 rascal.

gambader /gɑ̃bade/ 🔢 *vi* leap about.

gamelle /gamɛl/ *nf* (de soldat) mess kit; (d'ouvrier) lunch-box.

gamin, ~e /gamɛ̃, -in/ *adj* childish; (air) youthful. ● *nm, f* 🔢 kid.

gamme /gam/ *nf* (Mus) scale; (série) range; **haut de ~** up-market, top of the range; **bas de ~** down-market, bottom of the range.

gang /gɑ̃g/ *nm* 🔢 gang.

ganglion /gɑ̃glijɔ̃/ *nm* ganglion.

gangster /gɑ̃gstɛʀ/ *nm* gangster; (escroc) crook.

gant /gɑ̃/ *nm* glove; ~ **de ménage** rubber glove; ~ **de toilette** face-flannel, face-cloth.

garage /gaʀaʒ/ *nm* garage. **garagiste** *nmf* garage owner; (employé) car mechanic.

garant, ~e /gaʀɑ̃, -t/ *nm, f* guarantor. ● *adj* **se porter ~ de** vouch for.

garanti, ~e /gaʀɑ̃ti/ *adj* guaranteed.

garantie /gaʀɑ̃ti/ *nf* guarantee; ~**s** (de police d'assurance) cover. **garantir** 🔢 *vt* guarantee; (protéger) protect (de from).

garçon /gaʀsɔ̃/ *nm* boy; (jeune homme) young man; (célibataire) bachelor; ~ **(de café)** waiter; ~ **d'honneur** best man. **garçonnière** *nf* bachelor flat.

garde[1] /gaʀd/ *nf* guard; (d'enfants, de bagages) care; (service) guard (duty); (infirmière) nurse; **de ~** on duty; ~ **à vue** (police) custody; **mettre en ~** warn; **prendre ~** be careful (à of); **(droit de) ~** custody (de of).

garde[2] /gaʀd/ *nm* guard; (de propriété, parc) warden; ~ **champêtre** village policeman; ~ **du corps** bodyguard.

garde-à-vous /gaʀdavu/ *nm inv* (Mil) **se mettre au ~** stand to attention.

garde-chasse (*pl* ~**s**) /gaʀdə- ʃas/ *nm* gamekeeper.

garde-manger /gaʀdmɑ̃ʒe/ *nm inv* meat safe; (placard) larder.

garder /gaʀde/ 🔢 *vt* (conserver, maintenir) keep; (vêtement) keep on; (surveiller) look after; (défendre) guard; ~ **le lit** stay in bed. □ **se ~** *vpr* (denrée) keep; **se ~ de faire** be careful not to do.

garderie /gaʀdəʀi/ *nf* day nursery.

garde-robe (*pl* ~**s**) /gaʀdəʀɔb/ *nf* wardrobe.

gardien, ~ne /gaʀdjɛ̃, -ɛn/ *nm, f* (de locaux) security guard; (de prison, réserve) warden; (d'immeuble) caretaker; (de musée) attendant; (de zoo) keeper; (de traditions) guardian; ~ **de but** goalkeeper; ~ **de la paix** policeman; ~ **de nuit** watchman; **gardienne d'enfants** childminder.

gare /gaʀ/ *nf* (Rail) station; ~ **routière** coach station; (US) bus station. ● *interj* ~ **(à toi)** watch out!

garer /gaʀe/ 🔢 *vt* park. □ **se ~** *vpr* park; (s'écarter) move out of the way.

gargouille /gaʀguj/ *nf* waterspout; (sculptée) gargoyle. **gargouiller** 🔢 *vi*

garni, ~e /gaʀni/ adj (plat) served with vegetables; **bien ~** (rempli) well-filled.

garnir /gaʀniʀ/ ② vt (remplir) fill; (décorer) decorate; (couvrir) cover; (doubler) line; (Culin) garnish. **garniture** nf (légumes) vegetables; (ornement) trimming; (de voiture) trim.

gars /gɑ/ nm ① lad; (adulte) guy, bloke.

gas-oil /gazwal/ nm diesel (oil).

gaspillage /gaspijaʒ/ nm waste. **gaspiller** ① vt waste.

gastrique /gastʀik/ adj gastric.

gastronome /gastʀɔnɔm/ nmf gourmet.

gâteau (pl ~x) /gato/ nm cake; ~ **sec** biscuit; (US) cookie; **un papa ~** a doting dad.

gâter /gate/ ① vt spoil. □ **se ~** vpr (viande) go bad; (dent) rot; (temps) get worse.

gâterie /gatʀi/ nf little treat.

gâteux, -euse /gatø, -z/ adj senile.

gauche /goʃ/ adj left; (maladroit) awkward. ● nf left; **à ~** on the left; (direction) (to the) left; **la ~** the left (side); (Pol) the left (wing).

gaucher, -ère /goʃe, -ɛʀ/ adj left handed.

gaufre /gofʀ/ nf waffle. **gaufrette** nf wafer.

gaulois, ~e /golwa, -z/ adj Gallic; (fig) bawdy. **G~, ~e** nm, f Gaul.

gaver /gave/ ① vt force-feed; (fig) cram. □ **se ~ de** vpr gorge oneself with; (fig) devour.

gaz /gaz/ nm inv gas; ~ **d'échappement** exhaust fumes; ~ **lacrymogène** tear-gas.

gaze /gaz/ nf gauze.

gazer /gaze/ ① vi ① **ça gaze?** how's things?

gazette /gazɛt/ nf newspaper.

gazeux, -euse /gazø, -z/ adj (boisson) fizzy; (eau) sparkling.

gazoduc /gazɔdyk/ nm gas pipeline.

gazon /gazɔ̃/ nm lawn, grass.

gazouiller /gazuje/ ① vi (oiseau) chirp; (bébé) babble.

GDF abrév m (**Gaz de France**) French gas board.

géant, ~e /ʒeɑ̃, -t/ adj giant. ● nm giant. **géante** nf giantess.

geindre /ʒɛ̃dʀ/ ㉒ vi groan, moan.

gel /ʒɛl/ nm frost; (produit) gel; (Comm) freeze; ~ **coiffant** hair gel.

gelée /ʒ(ə)le/ nf frost; (Culin) jelly; ~ **blanche** hoarfrost.

geler /ʒəle/ ⑥ vt/i freeze; **on gèle** (on a froid) it's freezing; **il ou ça gèle** (il fait froid) it's freezing.

gélule /ʒelyl/ nf (Méd) capsule.

Gémeaux /ʒemo/ nmpl Gemini.

gémir /ʒemiʀ/ ② vi groan.

gênant, ~e /ʒenɑ̃, -t/ adj embarrassing; (irritant) annoying; (incommode) cumbersome.

gencive /ʒɑ̃siv/ nf gum.

gendarme /ʒɑ̃daʀm/ nm policeman, gendarme. **gendarmerie** nf police force; (local) police station.

> **Gendarmerie nationale** A section of the military, which provides the police service outside major towns.

gendre /ʒɑ̃dʀ/ nm son-in-law.

gène /ʒɛn/ nm gene.

gêne /ʒɛn/ nf discomfort; (confusion) embarrassment; (dérangement) trouble, inconvenience; (pauvreté) poverty.

gêné, ~e /ʒene/ adj embarrassed; (désargenté) short of money.

généalogie /ʒenealɔʒi/ nf genealogy.

gêner /ʒene/ ① vt bother, disturb; (troubler) embarrass; (entraver) block; (faire mal) hurt.

général, ~e (mpl **-aux**) /ʒeneʀal, -o/ adj general; **en ~** in general. ● nm (pl **-aux**) general.

généralement /ʒeneʀalmɑ̃/ adv generally.

généraliser /ʒeneʀalize/ ① vt make general. ● vi generalize. □ **se ~** vpr become widespread ou general.

généraliste /ʒeneʀalist/ nmf general practitioner, GP.

généralité /ʒeneʀalite/ nf general point.

génération /ʒeneʀasjɔ̃/ nf generation.

généreux, ~euse /ʒeneʀø, -z/ adj generous.

générique /ʒeneʀik/ nm (au cinéma) credits. ● adj generic.

générosité /ʒeneʀozite/ nf generosity.

génétique /ʒenetik/ adj genetic. ● nf genetics.

Genève /ʒɔnɛv/ npr Geneva.

génial, ~e (mpl **-iaux**) /ʒenjal, -jo/ adj brilliant; (fantastique 🗓) fantastic.

génie /ʒeni/ nm genius; ~ **civil** civil engineering.

génital, ~e (mpl **-aux**) /ʒenital, -o/ adj genital.

génocide /ʒenɔsid/ nm genocide.

génoise /ʒenwaz/ nf sponge (cake).

génome /ʒenom/ nm genome.

génothèque /ʒenɔtɛk/ nf gene bank.

genou (pl **~x**) /ʒɔnu/ nm knee; **être à ~x** be kneeling.

genre /ʒɑ̃ʀ/ nm sort, kind; (Gram) gender; (allure) **avoir bon/mauvais ~** to look nice/disreputable; (comportement) **c'est bien son ~** it's just like him/her.

gens /ʒɑ̃/ nmpl people.

gentil, ~le /ʒɑ̃ti, -j/ adj kind, nice; (sage) good. **gentillesse** nf kindness. **gentiment** adv kindly.

géographie /ʒeɔgʀafi/ nf geography.

geôlier, -ière /ʒolje, -jɛʀ/ nm, f gaoler, jailer.

géologie /ʒeɔlɔʒi/ nf geology.

géomètre /ʒeɔmɛtʀ/ nm surveyor.

géométrie /ʒeɔmetʀi/ nf geometry. **géométrique** adj geometric.

gérance /ʒeʀɑ̃s/ nf management.

gérant, ~e /ʒeʀɑ̃, -t/ nm, f manager, manageress; ~ **d'immeuble** landlord's agent.

gerbe /ʒɛʀb/ nf (de fleurs) bunch, bouquet; (d'eau) spray; (de blé) sheaf.

gercer /ʒɛʀse/ 🔟 vt chap; **avoir les lèvres gercées** have chapped lips. ● vi become chapped. **gerçure** nf crack, chap.

gérer /ʒeʀe/ 🔢 vt manage, run; (traiter: fig) (crise, situation) handle.

germe /ʒɛʀm/ nm germ; ~**s de soja** bean sprouts.

germer /ʒɛʀme/ 🔟 vi germinate.

gestation /ʒɛstasjɔ̃/ nf gestation.

geste /ʒɛst/ nm gesture.

gesticuler /ʒɛstikyle/ 🔟 vi gesticulate.

gestion /ʒɛstjɔ̃/ nf management. **gestionnaire** nmf administrator.

ghetto /gɛto/ nm ghetto.

gibier /ʒibje/ nm (animaux) game.

giboulée /ʒibule/ nf shower.

gicler /ʒikle/ 🔟 vi squirt; **faire ~** squirt.

gifle /ʒifl/ nf slap in the face. **gifler** 🔟 vt slap.

gigantesque /ʒigɑ̃tɛsk/ adj gigantic.

gigot /ʒigo/ nm leg (of lamb).

gigoter /ʒigɔte/ 🔟 vi wriggle; (nerveusement) fidget.

gilet /ʒilɛ/ nm waistcoat; (cardigan) cardigan; ~ **de sauvetage** life jacket.

gingembre /ʒɛ̃ʒɑ̃bʀ/ nm ginger.

girafe /ʒiʀaf/ nf giraffe.

giratoire /ʒiʀatwaʀ/ adj **sens ~** roundabout.

girofle /ʒiʀɔfl/ nm **clou de ~** clove.

girouette /ʒiʀwɛt/ nf weathercock, weathervane.

gisement /ʒizmɑ̃/ nm deposit.

gitan, ~e /ʒitɑ̃, -an/ nm, f gypsy.

gîte /ʒit/ nm (maison) home; (abri) shelter; ~ **rural** holiday cottage.

givre /ʒivʀ/ nm frost; (sur parebrise) ice.

givré, ~e /ʒivʀe/ adj 🗓 crazy.

glace /glas/ nf ice; (crème) icecream; (vitre) window; (miroir) mirror; (verre) glass.

glacé, ~e /glase/ adj (vent, accueil) icy; (hands) frozen; (gâteau) iced.

glacer /glase/ 🔟 vt freeze; (gâteau, boisson) chill; (pétrifier) chill. ▢ **se ~** vpr freeze.

glacier /glasje/ nm (Géog) glacier; (vendeur) ice-cream seller. **glacière** nf coolbox. **glaçon** nm ice-cube.

glaïeul /glajœl/ nm gladiolus.

glaise /glɛz/ nf clay.

gland /glɑ̃/ nm acorn; (ornement) tassel.

glande /glɑ̃d/ nf gland.

glander /glɑ̃de/ 🔟 vi 🗓 laze around.

glaner /glane/ 🔟 vt glean.

glauque /glok/ adj (fig) murky; (street) squalid.

glissade /glisad/ nf (jeu) slide; (dérapage) skid.

glissant, ~e /glisɑ̃, -t/ adj slippery.

glissement /glismã/ nm sliding; gliding; (fig) shift; ~ **de terrain** landslide.

glisser /glise/ **1** vi slide; (être glissant) be slippery; (sur l'eau) glide; (déraper) slip; (véhicule) skid. ● vt (objet) slip (**dans** into); (remarque) slip in. □ **se ~** vpr slip (**dans** into).

glissière /glisjɛʀ/ nf slide; **porte à ~** sliding door; ~ **de sécurité** (Auto) crash-barrier; **fermeture à ~** zip.

global, **~e** (mpl **-aux**) /glɔbal, -o/ adj (entier, général) overall. **globalement** adv as a whole.

globe /glɔb/ nm globe; ~ **oculaire** eyeball; ~ **terrestre** globe.

globule /glɔbyl/ nm (du sang) corpuscle.

gloire /glwaʀ/ nf glory, fame. **glorieux**, **-ieuse** adj glorious. **glorifier** **45** vt glorify.

glose /gloz/ nf gloss.

glossaire /glɔsɛʀ/ nm glossary.

gloussement /glusmã/ nm chuckle; (de poule) cluck.

glouton, **~ne** /glutõ, -ɔn/ adj gluttonous. ● nm, f glutton.

gluant, **~e** /glyã, -t/ adj sticky.

glucose /glykoz/ nm glucose.

glycérine /glisexin/ nf glycerin(e).

GO abrév fpl (**grandes ondes**) long wave.

goal /gol/ nm **🇹** goalkeeper.

gobelet /gɔblɛ/ nm cup; (en verre) tumbler.

gober /gɔbe/ **1** vt swallow (whole); **je ne peux pas le ~** **🇹** I can't stand him.

goéland /gɔelã/ nm (sea)gull.

gogo: **à ~** /agogo/ loc **🇹** galore, in abundance.

goinfre /gwɛ̃fʀ/ nm (glouton **🇹**) pig. **goinfrer (se)** **1** vpr **🇹** stuff oneself (**de** with).

golf /gɔlf/ nm golf; (terrain) golf course.

golfe /gɔlf/ nm gulf.

gomme /gɔm/ nf rubber; (US) eraser; (résine) gum. **gommer** **1** vt rub out.

gond /gõ/ nm hinge; **sortir de ses ~s** **🇹** go mad.

gondoler (se) /(sə)gõdɔle/ **1** vpr (bois) warp; (métal) buckle.

gonflé, **~e** /gõfle/ adj swollen; **il est ~** **🇹** he's got a nerve.

gonflement /gõfləmã/ nm swelling.

gonfler /gõfle/ **1** vt (ballon, pneu) pump up, blow up; (augmenter) increase; (exagérer) inflate. ● vi swell.

gorge /gɔʀʒ/ nf throat; (poitrine) breast; (vallée) gorge.

gorgée /gɔʀʒe/ nf sip, gulp.

gorger /gɔʀʒe/ **40** vt fill (**de** with); **gorgé de** full of. □ **se ~** vpr gorge oneself (**de** with).

gorille /gɔʀij/ nm gorilla; (garde **🇹**) bodyguard.

gosier /gozje/ nm throat.

gosse /gɔs/ nmf **🇹** kid.

gothique /gɔtik/ adj Gothic.

goudron /gudʀõ/ nm tar. **goudronner** **1** vt tarmac.

gouffre /gufʀ/ nm abyss, gulf.

goujat /guʒa/ nm lout, boor.

goulot /gulo/ nm neck; **boire au ~** drink from the bottle.

goulu, **~e** /guly/ adj gluttonous. ● nm, f glutton.

gourde /guʀd/ nf (à eau) flask; (idiot **🇹**) fool.

gourer (se) /(sə)guʀe/ **1** vpr **🇹** make a mistake.

gourmand, **~e** /guʀmã, -d/ adj greedy. ● nm, f glutton.

gourmandise /guʀmãdiz/ nf greed; **~s** sweets.

gourmet /guʀmɛ/ nm gourmet.

gourmette /guʀmɛt/ nf chain bracelet.

gousse /gus/ nf ~ **d'ail** clove of garlic.

goût /gu/ nm taste; (gré) liking; **prendre ~ à** develop a taste for; **avoir bon ~** (aliment) taste nice; (personne) have good taste; **donner du ~ à** give flavour.

goûter /gute/ **1** vt taste; (apprécier) enjoy; ~ **à** ou **de** taste. ● vi have tea. ● nm tea, snack.

goutte /gut/ nf drop; (Méd) gout. **goutte-à-goutte** nm inv drip. **goutter** **1** vi drip.

gouttière /gutjɛʀ/ nf gutter.

gouvernail /guvɛʀnaj/ nm rudder; (barre) helm.

gouvernement /guvɛʀnəmã/ nm government.

gouverner /guvɛʀne/ **1** vt/i govern; (dominer) control. **gouverneur** nm governor.

GPS abrév m (**global positioning system**) GPS.

grâce /gʀɑs/ nf (charme) grace; (faveur) favour; (volonté) grace; (Jur) pardon; (Relig) grace; ~ **à** thanks to; **rendre (~s) à** give thanks to.

gracier /gʀasje/ **45** vt pardon.

gracieusement /gʀasjøzmɑ̃/ adv gracefully; (gratuitement) free (of charge).

gracieux, -ieuse /gʀasjø, -z/ adj graceful.

grade /gʀad/ nm rank; **monter en ~** be promoted.

gradin /gʀadɛ̃/ nm tier, step; **en ~s** terraced; **les ~s** terraces.

gradué, ~e /gʀadɥe/ adj graded, graduated; **verre ~** measuring jug.

graffiti /gʀafiti/ nmpl graffiti.

grain /gʀɛ̃/ nm grain; (Naut) squall; ~ **de beauté** beauty spot; ~ **de café** coffee bean; ~ **de poivre** pepper corn; ~ **de raisin** grape.

graine /gʀɛn/ nf seed.

graisse /gʀɛs/ nf fat; (lubrifiant) grease. **graisser** **1** vt grease. **graisseux, -euse** adj greasy.

grammaire /gʀam(m)ɛʀ/ nf grammar.

gramme /gʀam/ nm gram.

grand, ~e /gʀɑ̃, -d/ adj big, large; (haut) tall; (intense, fort) great; (brillant) great; (principal) main; (plus âgé) big, elder; (adulte) grown-up; **au ~ air** in the open air; **au ~ jour** in broad daylight; (fig) in the open; **~e partie** largely; **~e banlieue** outer suburbs; ~ **ensemble** housing estate; **~es lignes** (Rail) main lines; ~ **magasin** department store; **~e personne** grown-up; ~ **public** general public; **~e surface** hypermarket; **~es vacances** summer holidays. ● adv (ouvrir) wide; ~ **ouvert** wide open; **voir ~** think big. ● nm, f (adulte) grown-up; (enfant) big boy, big girl; (Scol) senior.

grand-chose /gʀɑ̃ʃoz/ pron **pas ~** not much, not a lot.

Grande-Bretagne /gʀɑ̃dbʀətaɲ/ nf Great Britain.

grandeur /gʀɑ̃dœʀ/ nf greatness; (dimension) size; **folie des ~s** delusions of grandeur.

grandir /gʀɑ̃diʀ/ **2** vi grow; (bruit) grow louder. ● vt (talons) make taller; (loupe) magnify.

grand-mère (pl **grands-mères**) /gʀɑ̃mɛʀ/ nf grandmother.

grand-père (pl **grands-pères**) /gʀɑ̃pɛʀ/ nm grandfather.

grands-parents /gʀɑ̃paʀɑ̃/ nmpl grandparents.

grange /gʀɑ̃ʒ/ nf barn.

granulé /gʀanyle/ nm granule.

graphique /gʀafik/ adj graphic; (Ordinat) graphics; **informatique ~** computer graphics. ● nm graph.

graphologie /gʀafɔlɔʒi/ nf graphology.

grappe /gʀap/ nf cluster; ~ **de raisin** bunch of grapes.

gras, ~se /gʀɑ, -s/ adj (gros) fat; (aliment) fatty; (surface, peau, cheveux) greasy; (épais) thick; (caractères) bold; **faire la ~se matinée** sleep late. ● nm (Culin) fat.

gratifiant, ~e /gʀatifjɑ̃, -t/ adj gratifying; (travail) rewarding.

gratifier /gʀatifje/ **45** vt favour, reward (de with).

gratin /gʀatɛ̃/ nm gratin (baked dish with cheese topping); (élite **1**) upper crust.

gratis /gʀatis/ adv free.

gratitude /gʀatityd/ nf gratitude.

gratte-ciel /gʀatsjɛl/ nm inv skyscraper.

gratter /gʀate/ **1** vt/i scratch; (avec un outil) scrape; **ça me gratte 1** it itches. □ **se ~** vpr scratch oneself; **se ~ la tête** scratch one's head.

gratuiciel /gʀatɥisjɛl/ *nm* (Internet) freeware.

gratuit, ~e /gʀatɥi, -t/ *adj* free; (*acte*) gratuitous. **gratuitement** *adv* free (of charge).

grave /gʀav/ *adj* (*maladie, accident, problème*) serious; (*solennel*) grave; (*voix*) deep; (*accent*) grave. **gravement** *adv* seriously; gravely.

graver /gʀave/ **1** *vt* engrave; (*sur bois*) carve; (*Ordinat*) burn.

graveur /gʀavœʀ/ *nm* (Ordinat) burner.

gravier /gʀavje/ *nm* du ~ gravel.

gravité /gʀavite/ *nf* gravity.

graviter /gʀavite/ **1** *vi* revolve.

gravure /gʀavyʀ/ *nf* engraving; (*de tableau, photo*) print, plate.

gré /gʀe/ *nm* (*volonté*) will; (*goût*) taste; **à son ~** (*agir*) as one likes; **de bon ~** willingly; **bon ~ mal ~** like it or not; **je vous en saurais ~** I'd be grateful for that.

grec, ~que /gʀɛk/ *adj* Greek. ● *nm* (Ling) Greek. **G~, ~que** *nm, f* Greek.

Grèce /gʀɛs/ Greece.

greffe /gʀɛf/ *nf* graft; (*d'organe*) transplant. **greffer** **1** *vt* graft; transplant.

greffier, -ière /gʀefje, -jɛʀ/ *nm, f* clerk of the court.

grêle /gʀɛl/ *adj* (*maigre*) spindly; (*voix*) shrill. ● *nf* hail.

grêler /gʀele/ **1** *vi* hail; **il grêle** it's hailing. **grêlon** *nm* hailstone.

grelot /gʀəlo/ *nm* (little) bell.

grelotter /gʀəlɔte/ **1** *vi* shiver.

grenade /gʀənad/ *nf* (*fruit*) pomegranate; (*explosif*) grenade.

grenat /gʀəna/ *adj inv* dark red.

grenier /gʀənje/ *nm* attic; (*pour grain*) loft.

grenouille /gʀənuj/ *nf* frog.

grès /gʀɛ/ *nm* sandstone; (*poterie*) stoneware.

grésiller /gʀezije/ **1** *vi* sizzle; (*radio*) crackle.

grève /gʀɛv/ *nf* (*rivage*) shore; (*cessation de travail*) strike; **faire ~, être en ~** be on strike; **se mettre en ~** go on strike. **gréviste** *nmf* striker.

gribouiller /gʀibuje/ **1** *vt/i* scribble.

grief /gʀijɛf/ *nm* grievance.

grièvement /gʀijɛvmɑ̃/ *adv* seriously.

griffe /gʀif/ *nf* claw; (*de couturier*) label; **coup de ~** scratch.

griffé, ~e /gʀife/ *adj* (*vêtement, article*) designer.

griffer /gʀife/ **1** *vt* scratch, claw.

grignoter /gʀiɲɔte/ **1** *vt/i* nibble.

gril /gʀil/ *nm* (de cuisinière) grill; (plaque) grill pan.

grillade /gʀijad/ *nf* (viande) grill.

grillage /gʀijaʒ/ *nm* wire netting.

grille /gʀij/ *nf* railings; (*portail*) (metal) gate; (de fenêtre) bars; (de cheminée) grate; (fig) grid. **grille-pain** *nm inv* toaster.

griller /gʀije/ **1** *vt* (*pain*) toast; (*viande*) grill; (*ampoule*) blow; (*feu rouge*) go through; (*appareil*) burn out. ● *vi* (*ampoule*) blow; (Culin) **faire ~** (*viande*) grill; (*pain*) toast.

grillon /gʀijɔ̃/ *nm* cricket.

grimace /gʀimas/ *nf* (funny) face; (de douleur, dégoût) grimace; **faire des ~s** make faces; **faire la ~** pull a face, grimace.

grimper /gʀɛ̃pe/ **1** *vt* climb. ● *vi* climb; ~ **sur** *ou* **dans un arbre** climb a tree.

grincement /gʀɛ̃smɑ̃/ *nm* creak-(ing).

grincer /gʀɛ̃se/ **10** *vi* creak; ~ **des dents** grind one's teeth.

grincheux, -euse /gʀɛ̃ʃø, -z/ *adj* grumpy.

grippe /gʀip/ *nf* influenza, flu.

grippé, ~e /gʀipe/ *adj* **être ~** have (the) flu; (*mécanisme*) be seized up *ou* jammed.

gris, ~e /gʀi, -z/ *adj* grey; (*saoul*) tipsy.

grivois, ~e /gʀivwa, -z/ *adj* bawdy.

grog /gʀɔg/ *nm* hot toddy.

grogner /gʀɔɲe/ **1** *vi* (*animal*) growl; (*personne*) grumble.

grognon /gʀɔɲɔ̃/ *adj* grumpy.

groin /gʀwɛ̃/ *nm* snout.

gronder /gʀɔ̃de/ **1** *vi* (*tonnerre, volcan*) rumble; (*chien*) growl; (*conflit*) be brewing. ● *vt* scold.

groom /gʀum/ *nm* bellboy.

gros, ~se /gʀo, -s/ *adj* big, large; (*gras*) fat; (*important*) big; (*épais*) thick;

(lourd) heavy; (*buveur, fumeur*) heavy; ~ **bonnet** 🄻 bigwig; ~ **lot** jackpot; . ~ **mot** swear word; ~ **plan** close-up; ~**se caisse** bass drum; ~ **titre** headline. ● *nm, f* fat man, fat woman. ● *adv* (écrire) big; (*risquer, gagner*) a lot. ● *nm* **le** ~ **de** the bulk of; **de** ~ (Comm) wholesale; **en** ~ roughly; (Comm) wholesale.

groseille /grozɛj/ *nf* redcurrant; ~ **à maquereau** gooseberry.

grossesse /grosɛs/ *nf* pregnancy.

grosseur /grosœr/ *nf* (volume) size; (enflure) lump.

grossier, -ière /grosje, -jɛr/ *adj* (sans finesse) coarse, rough; (rudimentaire) crude; (vulgaire) coarse; (impoli) rude; (erreur) gross. **grossièrement** *adv* (sommairement) roughly; (vulgairement) coarsely. **grossièreté** *nf* coarseness; crudeness; rudeness; (mot) rude word.

grossir /grosir/ 🄻 *vt* (faire augmenter) increase, boost; (agrandir) enlarge; (exagérer) exaggerate; ~ **les rangs** *ou* **la foule** swell the ranks. ● *vi* (personne) put on weight; (augmenter) grow.

grossiste /grosist/ *nmf* wholesaler.

grosso modo /grosomodo/ *adv* roughly.

grotesque /grotɛsk/ *adj* grotesque; (ridicule) ludicrous.

grotte /grot/ *nf* cave; grotto.

grouiller /gruje/ 🄻 *vi* swarm; ~ **de** be swarming with.

groupe /grup/ *nm* group; (Mus) group, band; ~ **électrogène** generating set; ~ **scolaire** school; ~ **de travail** working party.

groupement /grupmɑ̃/ *nm* grouping.

grouper /grupe/ 🄻 *vt* put together. □ **se** ~ *vpr* group (together).

grue /gry/ *nf* (machine, oiseau) crane.

gruyère /gryjɛr/ *nm* gruyère (cheese).

gué /ge/ *nm* ford; **passer** *ou* **traverser à** ~ ford.

guenon /gənɔ̃/ *nf* female monkey.

guépard /gepar/ *nm* cheetah.

guêpe /gɛp/ *nf* wasp.

guère /gɛr/ *adv* **ne** ~ hardly; **il n'y a** ~ **d'espoir** there is no hope; **elle n'a**

~ **dormi** she didn't sleep much, she hardly slept.

guérilla /gerija/ *nf* guerrilla warfare; (groupe) guerillas.

guérir /gerir/ 🄻 *vt* (personne, maladie, mal) cure (**de** of); (plaie, membre) heal. ● *vi* get better; (blessure) heal; ~ **de** recover from. **guérison** *nf* curing; healing; (de personne) recovery.

guerre /gɛr/ *nf* war; **en** ~ at war; **faire la** ~ wage war (**à** against); ~ **civile** civil war; ~ **mondiale** world war.

guerrier, -ière /gɛrje, -jɛr/ *adj* warlike. ● *nm, f* warrior.

guet /gɛ/ *nm* watch; **faire le** ~ be on the watch. **guet-apens** (*pl* **guets-apens**) *nm* ambush.

guetter /gete/ 🄻 *vt* watch; (attendre) watch out for.

gueule /gœl/ *nf* mouth; (figure 🄻) face; **ta** ~**!** shut up!; ~ **de bois** 🄻 hangover.

gueuleton /gœltɔ̃/ *nm* 🄻 blowout, slap-up meal.

gui /gi/ *nm* mistletoe.

guichet /giʃɛ/ *nm* window, counter; (de gare) ticket-office; (Théât) box-office; **jouer à** ~**s fermés** (pièce) be sold out; ~ **automatique** cash dispenser.

guide /gid/ *nm* guide. ● *nf* (fille scout) girl guide.

guider /gide/ 🄻 *vt* guide.

guidon /gidɔ̃/ *nm* handlebars.

guignol /giɲɔl/ *nm* puppet; (personne) clown; (spectacle) puppet-show.

guillemets /gijmɛ/ *nmpl* quotation marks, inverted commas; **entre** ~ in inverted commas.

guillotine /gijotin/ *nf* guillotine.

guimauve /gimov/ *nf* marshmallow; **c'est de la** ~ 🄻 it's slushy *ou* schmaltzy 🄻.

guindé, ~e /gɛ̃de/ *adj* stiff, formal; (style) stilted.

guirlande /girlɑ̃d/ *nf* garland; tinsel.

guitare /gitar/ *nf* guitar.

gym /ʒim/ *nf* gymnastics; (Scol) physical education, PE.

gymnase /ʒimnɑz/ *nm* gym(nasium). **gymnastique** *nf* gymnastics.

gynécologie /ʒinekɔlɔʒi/ *nf* gynaecology.

Hh

habile /abil/ *adj* skilful, clever.

habillé, ~e /abije/ *adj* (*vêtement*) smart; (*soirée*) formal.

habillement /abijmã/ *nm* clothing.

habiller /abije/ **1** *vt* dress (**de** in); (*équiper*) clothe; (*recouvrir*) cover (**de** with). □ **s'~** *vpr* get dressed; (*élégamment*) dress up.

habit /abi/ *nm* (*de personnage*) outfit; (*de cérémonie*) tails; **~s** clothes.

habitant, ~e /abitã, -t/ *nm, f* (*de maison, quartier*) resident; (*de pays*) inhabitant.

habitat /abita/ *nm* (*mode de peuplement*) settlement; (*conditions*) housing.

habitation /abitasjõ/ *nf* (*logement*) house.

habité, ~e /abite/ *adj* (*terre*) inhabited.

habiter /abite/ **1** *vi* live. ● *vt* live in.

habitude /abityd/ *nf* habit; **avoir l'~ de** be used to; **d'~** usually; **comme d'~** as usual.

habitué, ~e /abitue/ *nm, f* (*client*) regular.

habituel, ~le /abituɛl/ *adj* usual. **habituellement** *adv* usually.

habituer /abitue/ **1** *vt* ~ **qn à** get sb used to. □ **s'~ à** *vpr* get used to.

hache /'aʃ/ *nf* axe.

haché, ~e /'aʃe/ *adj* (*viande*) minced; (*phrases*) jerky.

hacher /'aʃe/ **1** *vt* mince; (*au couteau*) chop.

hachis /'aʃi/ *nm* minced meat; (US) ground meat; **~ Parmentier** ≈ *shepherd's pie.*

hachisch /'aʃiʃ/ *nm* hashish.

hachoir /'aʃwaʀ/ *nm* (*appareil*) mincer; (*couteau*) chopper; (*planche*) chopping board.

haie /'ɛ/ *nf* hedge; **course de ~s** hurdle race.

haillon /'ajõ/ *nm* rag.

haine /'ɛn/ *nf* hatred.

haïr /'aiʀ/ **36** *vt* hate.

hâlé /'ɑle/ *adj* (sun-)tanned.

haleine /alɛn/ *nf* breath; **travail de longue ~** long job.

haleter /'alte/ **6** *vi* pant.

hall /'ol/ *nm* hall; (*de gare*) concourse.

halle /'al/ *nf* market hall; **~s** covered market.

halte /'alt/ *nf* stop; **faire ~** stop. ● *interj* stop; (Mil) halt.

haltère /altɛʀ/ *nm* dumbbell; **faire des ~s** to do weightlifting.

hameau (*pl* ~**x**) /'amo/ *nm* hamlet.

hameçon /amsõ/ *nm* hook.

hanche /'ãʃ/ *nf* hip.

handicap /'ãdikap/ *nm* handicap. **handicapé,** ~e *adj* & *nm, f* disabled (person).

hangar /'ãgaʀ/ *nm* shed; (*pour avions*) hangar.

hanter /'ãte/ **1** *vt* haunt.

hantise /'ãtiz/ *nf* dread; **avoir la ~ de** dread.

haras /'aʀɑ/ *nm* stud-farm.

harasser /'aʀase/ **1** *vt* exhaust.

harcèlement /'aʀsɛlmã/ *nm* ~ **sexuel** sexual harassment.

harceler /'aʀsəle/ **6** *vt* harass.

hardi, ~e /'aʀdi/ *adj* bold.

hareng /'aʀã/ *nm* herring.

hargne /'aʀɲ/ *nf* (aggressive) bad temper.

haricot /'aʀiko/ *nm* bean; **~ vert** French bean; (US) green bean.

harmonie /aʀmɔni/ *nf* harmony. **harmonieux, -ieuse** *adj* harmonious.

harmoniser /aʀmɔnize/ **1** *vt* harmonize. □ **s'~** *vpr* harmonize.

harnacher /'aʀnaʃe/ **1** *vt* harness.

harnais /'aʀnɛ/ *nm* harness.

harpe /'aʀp/ *nf* harp.

harpon /'aʀpõ/ *nm* harpoon.

hasard /'azaʀ/ *nm* chance; (*coïncidence*) coincidence; **les ~s de** the fortunes of; **au ~** (*choisir etc.*) at random; (*flâner*) aimlessly. **hasardeux, -euse** *adj* risky.

hasarder /'azaʀde/ **1** *vt* risk; (*remarque*) venture.

hâte /'ɑt/ *nf* haste; **à la ~, en ~** hurriedly; **avoir ~ de** look forward to.

hâter /'ɑte/ **1** *vt* hasten. □ **se ~** *vpr* hurry (**de** to).

hâtif, -ive /'ɑtif, -v/ adj hasty; (précoce) early.

hausse /'os/ nf rise (de in); ~ **des prix** price rise; **en** ~ rising.

hausser /'ose/ **1** vt raise; (épaules) shrug.

haut, ~e /'o, 'ot/ adj high; (de taille) tall; **à voix ~e** aloud; ~ **en couleur** colourful; **plus** ~ higher up; (dans un texte) above; **en** ~ **lieu** in high places. ● adv high; **tout** ~ out loud. ● nm top; **des** ~**s et des bas** ups and downs; **en** ~ (regarder) up; (à l'étage) upstairs; **en** ~ **de**) at the top (of).

hautbois /'obwa/ nm oboe.

haut-de-forme /'odfɔʀm/ (pl **hauts-de-forme**) nm top hat.

hauteur /'otœʀ/ nf height; (colline) hill; (arrogance) haughtiness; **être à la** ~ be up to it; **à la** ~ **de** (ville) near; **être à la** ~ **de la situation** be equal to the situation.

haut-le-cœur /'olkœʀ/ nm inv nausea.

haut-parleur (pl ~**s**) /'opaʀlœʀ/ nm loudspeaker.

havre /'ɑvʀ/ nm haven (de of).

hayon /'ɑjɔ̃/ nm (Auto) hatchback.

hebdomadaire /ɛbdɔmadɛʀ/ adj & nm weekly.

hébergement /ebɛʀʒəmɑ̃/ nm accommodation.

héberger /ebɛʀʒe/ **40** vt (ami) put up; (réfugiés) take in.

hébreu (pl ~**x**) /ebʀø/ am Hebrew. ● nm (Ling) Hebrew; **c'est de l'~!** it's all Greek to me!

Hébreu (pl ~**x**) /ebʀø/ nm Hebrew; **les** ~**x** the Hebrews.

hécatombe /ekatɔ̃b/ nf slaughter.

hectare /ɛktaʀ/ nm hectare (= 10,000 square metres).

hélas /'elɑs/ interj alas. ● adv sadly.

hélice /elis/ nf propeller.

hélicoptère /elikɔptɛʀ/ nm helicopter.

helvétique /ɛlvetik/ adj Swiss.

hématome /ematom/ nm bruise.

hémorragie /emɔʀaʒi/ nf haemorrhage.

hémorroïdes /emɔʀɔid/ nfpl piles, haemorrhoids.

hennir /'eniʀ/ **2** vi neigh.

hépatite /epatit/ nf hepatitis.

herbe /ɛʀb/ nf grass; (Méd, Culin) herb; **en** ~ in the blade; (fig) budding.

héréditaire /eʀeditɛʀ/ adj hereditary.

hérédité /eʀedite/ nf heredity.

hérisser /'eʀise/ **1** vt bristle; ~ **qn** (fig) ruffle sb. □ **se** ~ vpr bristle.

hérisson /'eʀisɔ̃/ nm hedgehog.

héritage /eʀitaʒ/ nm inheritance; (spirituel) heritage.

hériter /eʀite/ **1** vt/i inherit (de from); ~ **de qch** inherit sth. **héritier, -ière** nm, f heir, heiress.

hermétique /ɛʀmetik/ adj airtight; (fig) unfathomable.

hernie /'ɛʀni/ nf hernia.

héroïne /eʀɔin/ nf (femme) heroine; (drogue) heroin.

héroïque /eʀɔik/ adj heroic.

héros /'eʀo/ nm hero.

hésiter /ezite/ **1** vi hesitate (à to); **j'hésite** I'm not sure.

hétérogène /eteʀɔʒɛn/ adj heterogeneous.

hétérosexuel, ~le /eteʀɔsɛksɥɛl/ nm/ f & adj heterosexual.

hêtre /'ɛtʀ/ nm beech.

heure /œʀ/ nf time; (soixante minutes) hour; **quelle** ~ **est-il?** what time is it?; **il est dix** ~**s** it is ten o'clock; **à l'**~ (venir, être) on time; **d'**~ **en** ~ by the hour; **toutes les deux** ~**s** every two hours; ~ **de pointe** rush-hour; ~ **de cours** (Scol) period; ~ **indue** ungodly hour; ~**s creuses** off peak periods; ~**s supplémentaires** overtime.

heureusement /œʀøzmɑ̃/ adv fortunately, luckily.

heureux, -euse /œʀø, -z/ adj happy; (chanceux) lucky, fortunate.

heurt /'œʀ/ nm collision; (conflit) clash; **sans** ~ smoothly.

heurter /'œʀte/ **1** vt (cogner) hit; (mur) bump into, hit; (choquer) offend. □ **se** ~ **à** vpr bump into, hit; (fig) come up against.

hexagone /ɛgzagon/ nm hexagon; **l'**~ France.

hiberner /ibɛʀne/ **1** vi hibernate.

hibou (pl ~**x**) /'ibu/ nm owl.

hier /jɛʀ/ adv yesterday; ~ **soir** last night, yesterday evening.

hiérarchie /'jeʀaʀʃi/ nf hierarchy.

hilare /ilaʀ/ adj (visage) merry; **être ~** be laughing.

hindou, ~e /ɛ̃du/ adj & nm, f Hindu. **H~, ~e** nm, f Hindu.

hippique /ipik/ adj equestrian; **le concours ~** showjumping.

hippodrome /ipɔdʀom/ nm racecourse.

hippopotame /ipopotam/ nm hippopotamus.

hirondelle /iʀɔ̃dɛl/ nf swallow.

hisser /'ise/ **1** vt hoist, haul. □ **se ~** vpr heave oneself up.

histoire /istwaʀ/ nf (récit) story; (étude) history; (affaire) business; **~(s)** (chichis) fuss; (ennuis) trouble. **historique** adj historical.

hiver /iveʀ/ nm winter. **hivernal, ~e** (mpl **-aux**) adj winter; (glacial) wintry.

H.L.M. abbrév m ou f (**habitation à loyer modéré**) block of council flats; (US) low-rent apartment building.

hocher /'ɔʃe/ **1** vt **~ la tête** (pour dire oui) nod; (pour dire non) shake one's head.

hochet /'ɔʃɛ/ nm rattle.

hockey /'ɔkɛ/ nm hockey; **~ sur glace** ice hockey.

hollandais, ~e /'ɔlɑ̃dɛ, -z/ adj Dutch. ● nm (Ling) Dutch. **H~, ~e** nm, f Dutchman, Dutchwoman.

Hollande /'ɔlɑ̃d/ nf Holland.

homard /'ɔmaʀ/ nm lobster.

homéopathie /ɔmeopati/ nf homoeopathy.

homicide /ɔmisid/ nm homicide; **~ involontaire** manslaughter.

hommage /ɔmaʒ/ nm tribute; **~s** (salutations) respects; **rendre ~ à** pay tribute to.

homme /ɔm/ nm man; (espèce) man (kind); **~ d'affaires** businessman; **~ de la rue** man in the street; **~ d'État** statesman; **~ politique** politician.

homogène /ɔmɔʒɛn/ adj homogeneous.

homonyme /ɔmɔnim/ nm (personne) namesake.

homosexualité /ɔmɔsɛksɥalite/ nf homosexuality.

homosexuel, ~le /ɔmɔsɛksɥɛl/ adj & nm, f homosexual.

Hongrie /'ɔ̃gʀi/ nf Hungary.

hongrois, ~e /'ɔ̃gʀwa, -z/ adj Hungarian. ● nm (Ling) Hungarian. **H~, ~e** nm, f Hungarian.

honnête /ɔnɛt/ adj honest; (juste) fair. **honnêteté** nf honesty.

honneur /ɔnœʀ/ nm honour; (mérite) credit; **d'~** (invité, place) of honour; **en l'~ de** in honour of; **en quel ~?** ⊞ why?; **faire ~ à** (équipe, famille) bring credit to.

honorable /ɔnɔʀabl/ adj honourable; (convenable) respectable.

honoraire /ɔnɔʀɛʀ/ adj honorary. **honoraires** nmpl fees.

honorer /ɔnɔʀe/ **1** vt honour; (faire honneur à) do credit to.

honte /'ɔ̃t/ nf shame; **avoir ~** be ashamed (**de** of); **faire ~ à** make ashamed. **honteux, -euse** adj (personne) ashamed (**de** of); (action) shameful.

hôpital (pl **-aux**) /ɔpital, -o/ nm hospital.

hoquet /'ɔkɛ/ nm **le ~** (the) hiccups.

horaire /ɔʀɛʀ/ adj hourly. ● nm timetable; **~s libres** flexitime.

horizon /ɔʀizɔ̃/ nm horizon; (Fig) outlook.

horizontal, ~e (mpl **-aux**) /ɔʀi zɔ̃tal, -o/ adj horizontal.

horloge /ɔʀlɔʒ/ nf clock.

hormis /'ɔʀmi/ prép save.

hormonal, ~e (mpl **-aux**) /ɔʀmonal, -o/ adj hormonal, hormone.

hormone /ɔʀmon/ nf hormone.

horreur /ɔʀœʀ/ nf horror; **avoir ~ de** hate.

horrible /ɔʀibl/ adj horrible.

horrifier /ɔʀifje/ **45** vt horrify.

hors /'ɔʀ/ prép **~ de** outside, (avec mouvement) out of; **~ d'atteinte** out of reach; **~ d'haleine** out of breath; **~ de prix** extremely expensive; **~ pair** outstanding; **~ de soi** beside oneself. **hors-bord** nm inv speedboat. **hors-d'œuvre** nm inv hors-d'œuvre. **hors-jeu** adj inv offside. **hors-la-loi** nm inv outlaw. **hors-piste** nm off-piste skiing. **hors-taxe** adj inv duty-free.

horticulteur, -trice /ɔʀtikyltœʀ, -tʀis/ nm, f horticulturist.

hospice /ɔspis/ nm home.

hospitalier, -ière /ɔspitalje, -jɛʀ/ adj hospitable; (Méd) hospital. **hospitali-**

ser 🔟 vt take to hospital. **hospitalité** nf hospitality.

hostile /ɔstil/ adj hostile. **hostilité** nf hostility.

hôte /ot/ nm (maître) host; (invité) guest.

hôtel /otɛl/ nm hotel; ~ **(particulier)** (private) mansion; ~ **de ville** town hall.

hôtelier, -ière /otəlje, -jɛR/ adj hotel. ● nm, f hotel keeper. **hôtellerie** nf hotel business.

hôtesse /otɛs/ nf hostess; ~ **de l'air** stewardess.

hotte /'ɔt/ nf basket; ~ **aspirante** extractor (hood), (US) ventilator.

houblon /'ublɔ̃/ nm le ~ hops.

houille /'uj/ nf coal; ~ **blanche** hydroelectric power.

houle /'ul/ nf swell. **houleux, -euse** adj (mer) rough; (débat) stormy.

housse /'us/ nf cover; ~ **de siège** seat cover.

houx /'u/ nm holly.

huées /'ɥe/ nfpl boos. **huer** 🔟 vt boo.

huile /ɥil/ nf oil; (personne 🔟) bigwig. **huiler** 🔟 vt oil. **huileux, -euse** adj oily.

huis /'ɥi/ nm à ~ **clos** in camera.

huissier /ɥisje/ nm (Jur) bailiff; (portier) usher.

huit /'ɥi(t)/ adj eight; ~ **jours** a week; **lundi en** ~ a week on Monday. ● nm eight. **huitième** adj & nmf eighth.

huître /ɥitR/ nf oyster.

humain, -e /ymɛ̃, -ɛn/ adj human; (compatissant) humane. **humanitaire** adj humanitarian. **humanité** nf humanity.

humble /œbl/ adj humble.

humeur /ymœR/ nf mood; (tempérament) temper; **de bonne/ mauvaise** ~ in a good/bad mood.

humide /ymid/ adj damp; (chaleur, climat) humid; (lèvres, yeux) moist. **humidité** nf humidity.

humilier /ymilje/ 🔢 vt humiliate.

humoristique /ymɔRistik/ adj humorous.

humour /ymuR/ nm humour; **avoir de l'**~ have a sense of humour.

hurlement /'yRləmɑ̃/ nm howl (ing). **hurler** 🔟 vt/i howl.

hutte /'yt/ nf hut.

hydratant, ~e /idRatɑ̃, -t/ adj (lotion) moisturizing.

hydravion /idRavjɔ̃/ nm seaplane.

hydroélectrique /idRɔelɛktRik/ adj hydroelectric.

hydrogène /idRɔʒɛn/ nm hydrogen.

hygiène /iʒjɛn/ nf hygiene. **hygiénique** adj hygienic.

hymne /imn/ nm hymn; ~ **national** national anthem.

hyperlien /ipɛrljɛ̃/ nm (Internet) hyperlink.

hypermarché /ipɛRmaRʃe/ nm (supermarché) hypermarket.

hypertension /ipɛRtɑ̃sjɔ̃/ nf high blood-pressure.

hypertexte /ipɛRtɛkst/ nm (Internet) hypertext.

hypnotiser /ipnɔtize/ 🔟 vt hypnotize.

hypocrisie /ipɔkRizi/ nf hypocrisy.

hypocrite /ipɔkRit/ adj hypocritical. ● nmf hypocrite.

hypothèque /ipɔtɛk/ nf mortgage.

hypothèse /ipɔtɛz/ nf hypothesis.

hystérie /isteRi/ nf hysteria.

Ii

ici /isi/ adv (dans l'espace) here; (dans le temps) now; **d'**~ **demain** by tomorrow; **d'**~ **là** in the meantime; **d'**~ **peu** shortly; ~ **même** in this very place; **jusqu'**~ until now; (dans le passé) until then.

idéal, ~e (mpl -aux) /ideal, -o/ adj & nm ideal. **idéaliser** 🔟 vt idealize.

idée /1de/ nf idea; (esprit) mind; **avoir dans l'**~ **de faire** plan to do; **il ne me viendrait jamais à l'**~ **de faire** it would never occur to me to do; ~ **fixe** obsession; ~ **reçue** conventional opinion.

identification /idɑ̃tifikasjɔ̃/ nf identification. **identifier** 🔢 vt, **s'identifier** vpr identify (à with).

identique /idɑ̃tik/ adj identical.

identité /idɑ̃tite/ nf identity.

idéologie /ideɔlɔʒi/ nf ideology.

idiome /idjom/ nm idiom.

idiot, ~e /idjo, -ɔt/ adj idiotic. ● nm, f idiot. **idiotie** nf idiocy; (acte, parole) idiotic thing.

idole /idɔl/ nf idol.

if /if/ nm yew.

ignare /iɲaʀ/ adj ignorant. ● nmf ignoramus.

ignoble /iɲɔbl/ adj vile.

ignorance /iɲɔʀɑ̃s/ nf ignorance.

ignorant, ~e /iɲɔʀɑ̃, -t/ adj ignorant. ● nm, f ignoramus.

ignorer /iɲɔʀe/ **1** vt not know; **je l'ignore** I don't know; (personne) ignore.

il /il/ pron (personne, animal familier) he; (chose, animal) it; (impersonnel) it; ~ **est vrai que** it is true that; ~ **neige/pleut** it is snowing/raining; ~ **y a** there is; (pluriel) there are; (temps) ago; (durée) for; ~ **y a 2 ans** 2 years ago; ~ **y a plus d'une heure que j'attends** I've been waiting for over an hour.

île /il/ nf island; ~ **déserte** desert island; ~**s anglo-normandes** Channel Islands; ~**s Britanniques** British Isles.

illégal, ~e (mpl ~aux) /ilegal, -o/ adj illegal.

illégitime /ileʒitim/ adj illegitimate.

illettré, ~e /iletʀe/ adj & nm, f illiterate.

illicite /ilisit/ adj illicit; (Jur) unlawful.

illimité, ~e /ilimite/ adj unlimited.

illisible /ilizibl/ adj illegible; (livre) unreadable.

illogique /ilɔʒik/ adj illogical.

illuminé, ~e /ilymine/ adj lit up; (monument) floodlit.

illusion /ilyzjɔ̃/ nf illusion; **se faire des** ~**s** delude oneself. **illusoire** adj illusory.

illustre /ilystʀ/ adj illustrious.

illustré, ~e /ilystʀe/ adj illustrated. ● nm comic.

illustrer /ilystʀe/ **1** vt illustrate. □ **s'**~ vpr become famous.

îlot /ilo/ nm islet; (de maisons) block.

ils /il/ pron they.

image /imaʒ/ nf picture; (métaphore) image; (reflet) reflection. **imagé,** ~e adj full of imagery.

imaginaire /imaʒinɛʀ/ adj imaginary. **imaginatif, -ive** adj imaginative. **imagination** nf imagination.

imaginer /imaʒine/ **1** vt imagine; (inventer) think up. □ **s'**~ vpr (se représenter) imagine (que that); (croire) think (que that).

imbécile /ɛbesil/ adj idiotic. ● nmf idiot.

imbiber /ɛbibe/ **1** vt soak (de with). □ **s'**~ vpr become soaked (de with).

imbriqué, ~e /ɛbʀike/ adj (lié) interlinked; (tuiles) overlapping.

imbu, ~e /ɛby/ adj ~ **de** full of.

IMC abrév m (**indice de masse corporelle**) BMI.

imitateur, -trice /imitatœʀ, -tʀis/ nm, f imitator; (comédien) impersonator. **imiter** **1** vt imitate; (personnage) impersonate; (signature) forge; (faire comme) do the same as.

immatriculation /imatʀikylasjɔ̃/ nf registration.

immatriculer /imatʀikyle/ **1** vt register; **se faire** ~ register; **faire** ~ **une voiture** have a car registered.

immédiat, ~e /imedja, -t/ adj immediate. ● nm **dans l'**~ for the time being.

immense /imɑ̃s/ adj huge.

immerger /imɛʀʒe/ **40** vt immerse. □ **s'**~ vpr immerse oneself (dans in).

immeuble /imœbl/ nm block of flats, building; ~ **de bureaux** office building ou block.

immigrant, ~e /imigʀɑ̃, -t/ adj & nm, f immigrant. **immigration** nf immigration. **immigré,** ~e adj & nm, f immigrant. **immigrer** **1** vi immigrate.

imminent, ~e /iminɑ̃, -t/ adj imminent.

immobile /imɔbil/ adj still, motionless.

immobilier, -ière /imɔbilje, -jɛʀ/ adj property; **agence immobilière** estate agent's office; (US) real estate office; **agent** ~ estate agent; (US) real estate agent. ● nm **l'**~ property; (US) real estate.

immobiliser /imɔbilize/ **1** vt immobilize; (stopper) stop. □ **s'**~ vpr stop.

immonde /imɔ̃d/ adj filthy.

immoral, ~e (mpl -aux) /imɔʀal, -o/ adj immoral.

immortel, ~le /imɔʀtɛl/ adj immortal.

immuable /imɥabl/ adj unchanging.

immuniser /imynize/ **1** vt immunize; **immunisé contre** (à l'abri de) immune to. **immunité** nf immunity.

impact /ɛ̃pakt/ nm impact.

impair, ~e /ɛ̃pɛʀ/ adj (numéro) odd. ● nm blunder, faux pas.

imparfait, ~e /ɛ̃paʀfɛ, -t/ adj & nm imperfect.

impasse /ɛ̃pɑs/ nf (rue) dead end; (situation) deadlock.

impatient, ~e /ɛ̃pasjɑ̃, -t/ adj impatient.

impatienter /ɛ̃pasjɑ̃te/ **1** vt annoy. □ **s'~** vpr get impatient (**contre qn** with sb).

impayé, ~e /ɛ̃peje/ adj unpaid.

impeccable /ɛ̃pekabl/ adj (propre) impeccable, spotless; (soigné) perfect.

impensable /ɛ̃pɑ̃sabl/ adj unthinkable.

impératif, -ive /ɛ̃peʀatif, -v/ adj imperative. ● nm (Gram) imperative; (contrainte) imperative; **~s** (exigences) requirements, demands (**de** of).

impératrice /ɛ̃peʀatʀis/ nf empress.

impérial, ~e (mpl **-iaux**) /ɛ̃peʀjal, -jo/ adj imperial.

impérieux, -ieuse /ɛ̃peʀjø, -z/ adj imperious; (pressant) pressing.

imperméable /ɛ̃pɛʀmeabl/ adj impervious (**à** to); (manteau, tissu) waterproof. ● nm raincoat.

impersonnel, ~le /ɛ̃pɛʀsɔnɛl/ adj impersonal.

impertinent, ~e /ɛ̃pɛʀtinɑ̃, -t/ adj impertinent.

imperturbable /ɛ̃pɛʀtyʀbabl/ adj unshakeable, unruffled.

impétueux, -euse /ɛ̃petɥø, -z/ adj impetuous.

impitoyable /ɛ̃pitwajabl/ adj merciless.

implant /ɛ̃plɑ̃/ nm implant.

implanter /ɛ̃plɑ̃te/ **1** vt establish, set up. □ **s'~** vpr become established.

implication /ɛ̃plikasjɔ̃/ nf (conséquence) implication; (participation) involvement.

impliquer /ɛ̃plike/ **1** vt (mêler) implicate (**dans** in); (signifier) imply, mean

(**que** that); (nécessiter) involve (**de faire** doing).

implorer /ɛ̃plɔʀe/ **1** vt implore, beg for.

impoli, ~e /ɛ̃pɔli/ adj impolite, rude.

importance /ɛ̃pɔʀtɑ̃s/ nf importance; (taille) size; (ampleur) extent; **sans ~** unimportant.

important, ~e /ɛ̃pɔʀtɑ̃, -t/ adj important; (en quantité) considerable, sizeable, big; (air) self-important. ● nm **l'~** the important thing.

importateur, -trice /ɛ̃pɔʀtatœʀ, -tʀis/ nm, f importer. ● adj importing. **importation** nf import.

importer /ɛ̃pɔʀte/ **1** vt (Comm) import. ● vi matter, be important (**à** to); **il importe que** it is important that; **n'importe, peu importe** it does not matter; **n'importe comment** anyhow; **n'importe où** anywhere; **n'importe qui** anybody; **n'importe quoi** anything.

importun, ~e /ɛ̃pɔʀtœ̃, -yn/ adj troublesome. ● nm, f nuisance.

imposer /ɛ̃poze/ **1** vt impose (**à** on); (taxer) tax; **en ~ à qn** impress sb. □ **s'~** vpr (action) be essential; (se faire reconnaître) stand out; (s'astreindre à) **s'~ de faire** force oneself to do.

imposition /ɛ̃pozisjɔ̃/ nf taxation; **~ des mains** laying-on of hands.

impossible /ɛ̃posibl/ adj impossible. ● nm faire **l'~** do one's utmost.

impôt /ɛ̃po/ nm tax; **~s** (contributions) tax(ation), taxes; **~ sur le revenu** income tax.

impotent, ~e /ɛ̃potɑ̃, -t/ adj disabled.

imprécis, ~e /ɛ̃pʀesi, -z/ adj imprecise.

imprégner /ɛ̃pʀeɲe/ **14** vt fill (**de** with); (imbiber) impregnate (**de** with). □ **s'~ de** vpr (fig) immerse oneself in.

impression /ɛ̃pʀesjɔ̃/ nf impression; (de livre) printing. **impressionnant, ~e** adj impressive; (choquant) disturbing. **impressionner** **1** vt impress; (choquer) disturb.

imprévisible /ɛ̃pʀevizibl/ adj unpredictable.

imprévu, ~e /ɛ̃pʀevy/ adj unexpected. ● nm unexpected incident;

sauf ~ unless anything unexpected happens.

imprimante /ɛ̃pʀimɑ̃t/ *nf* (Ordinat) printer; **~ à jet d'encre** ink-jet printer; **~ (à) laser** laser printer.

imprimé, ~e /ɛ̃pʀime/ *adj* printed. ● *nm* printed form.

imprimer /ɛ̃pʀime/ 1 *vt* print; (marquer) imprint. **imprimerie** *nf* (art) printing; (lieu) printing works. **imprimeur** *nm* printer.

improbable /ɛ̃pʀɔbabl/ *adj* unlikely, improbable.

impropre /ɛ̃pʀɔpʀ/ *adj* incorrect; **~ à** unfit for.

improviste: à l'~ /alɛ̃pʀɔvist/ *loc* unexpectedly.

imprudence /ɛ̃pʀydɑ̃s/ *nf* carelessness; (acte) careless action.

imprudent, ~e /ɛ̃pʀydɑ̃, -t/ *adj* careless; **il est ~ de** it is unwise to.

impudent, ~e /ɛ̃pydɑ̃, -t/ *adj* impudent.

impuissant, ~e /ɛ̃pɥisɑ̃, -t/ *adj* helpless; (Méd) impotent; **~ à faire** powerless to do.

impulsif, -ive /ɛ̃pylsif, -v/ *adj* impulsive. **impulsion** *nf* (poussée, influence) impetus; (instinct, mouvement) impulse.

impur, ~e /ɛ̃pyʀ/ *adj* impure.

imputer /ɛ̃pyte/ 1 *vt* **~ à** attribute to, impute to.

inabordable /inabɔʀdabl/ *adj* (*prix*) prohibitive.

inacceptable /inaksɛptabl/ *adj* unacceptable.

inactif, -ive /inaktif, -v/ *adj* inactive.

inadapté, ~e /inadapte/ *adj* maladjusted. ● *nm, f* (Psych) maladjusted person.

inadmissible /inadmisibl/ *adj* unacceptable.

inadvertance /inadvɛʀtɑ̃s/ *nf* **par ~** by mistake.

inanimé, ~e /inanime/ *adj* (évanoui) unconscious; (mort) lifeless; (*matière*) inanimate.

inaperçu, ~e /inapɛʀsy/ *adj* unnoticed.

inapte /inapt/ *adj* unsuited (**à** to); **~ à faire** incapable of doing; **~ au service militaire** unfit for military service.

inattendu, ~e /inatɑ̃dy/ *adj* unexpected.

inaugurer /inogyʀe/ 1 *vt* inaugurate.

incapable /ɛ̃kapabl/ *adj* incapable (**de qch** of sth); **~ de faire** unable to do, incapable of doing. ● *nmf* incompetent.

incapacité /ɛ̃kapasite/ *nf* inability, incapacity; **être dans l'~ de faire** be unable to do.

incarcérer /ɛ̃kaʀseʀe/ 14 *vt* imprison, incarcerate.

incarnation /ɛ̃kaʀnasjɔ̃/ *nf* embodiment, incarnation. **incarné, ~e** *adj* (*ongle*) ingrowing.

incassable /ɛ̃kɑsabl/ *adj* unbreakable.

incendiaire /ɛ̃sɑ̃djɛʀ/ *adj* incendiary; (*propos*) inflammatory. ● *nmf* arsonist.

incendie /ɛ̃sɑ̃di/ *nm* fire; **~ criminel** arson. **incendier** 45 *vt* set fire to.

incertain, ~e /ɛ̃sɛʀtɛ̃, -ɛn/ *adj* uncertain; (*contour*) vague; (*temps*) unsettled. **incertitude** *nf* uncertainty.

inceste /ɛ̃sɛst/ *nm* incest.

incidence /ɛ̃sidɑ̃s/ *nf* effect.

incident /ɛ̃sidɑ̃/ *nm* incident; **~ technique** technical hitch.

incinérer /ɛ̃sineʀe/ 14 *vt* incinerate; (*mort*) cremate.

inciser /ɛ̃size/ 1 *vt* make an incision in; (*abcès*) lance. **incisif, -ive** *adj* incisive. **incision** *nf* incision; (d'abcès) lancing.

incitation /ɛ̃sitasjɔ̃/ *nf* (Jur) incitement (**à** to); (encouragement) incentive. **inciter** 1 *vt* incite (**à** to); (encourager) encourage.

inclinaison /ɛ̃klinɛzɔ̃/ *nf* incline; (de la tête) tilt.

inclination /ɛ̃klinasjɔ̃/ *nf* (penchant) inclination; (geste) (du buste) bow; (de la tête) nod.

incliner /ɛ̃kline/ 1 *vt* tilt, lean; (courber) bend; (inciter) encourage (**à** to); **~ la tête** (approuver) nod; (révérence) bow. ● *vi* **~ à** be inclined to. □ **s'~** *vpr* lean forward; (se courber) bow down (**devant** before); (céder) give in, yield (**devant** to); (*chemin*) slope.

inclure /ɛ̃klyʀ/ 16 *vt* include; (enfermer) enclose; **jusqu'au lundi inclus** up to and including Monday.

incohérence /ɛ̃kɔeRɑ̃s/ nf incoherence; (contradiction) discrepancy. **incohérent, ∼e** adj incoherent, inconsistent.

incolore /ɛ̃kɔlɔR/ adj colourless; (verre) clear.

incommoder /ɛ̃kɔmɔde/ **1** vt inconvenience, bother.

incompatible /ɛ̃kɔ̃patibl/ adj incompatible.

incompétent, ∼e /ɛ̃kɔ̃petɑ̃, -t/ adj incompetent.

incomplet, -ète /ɛ̃kɔ̃plɛ, -t/ adj incomplete.

incompréhension /ɛ̃kɔ̃pReɑ̃sjɔ̃/ nf lack of understanding.

incompris, ∼e /ɛ̃kɔ̃pRi, -z/ adj misunderstood.

inconcevable /ɛ̃kɔ̃svabl/ adj inconceivable.

incongru, ∼e /ɛ̃kɔ̃gRy/ adj unseemly.

inconnu, ∼e /ɛ̃kɔny/ adj unknown (à to). ● nm, f stranger. ● nm l'∼ the unknown.

inconscience /ɛ̃kɔ̃sjɑ̃s/ nf unconsciousness; (folie) madness.

inconscient, ∼e /ɛ̃kɔ̃sjɑ̃, -t/ adj unconscious (de of); (fou) mad. ● nm (Psych) subconscious.

incontestable /ɛ̃kɔ̃tɛstabl/ adj indisputable.

incontrôlable /ɛ̃kɔ̃tRolabl/ adj unverifiable; (non maîtrisé) uncontrollable.

inconvenant, ∼e /ɛ̃kɔ̃vnɑ̃, -t/ adj improper.

inconvénient /ɛ̃kɔ̃venjɑ̃/ nm disadvantage, drawback; (objection) objection.

incorporer /ɛ̃kɔRpɔRe/ **1** vt incorporate; (Culin) blend (à into); (Mil) enlist.

incorrect, ∼e /ɛ̃kɔRɛkt/ adj (faux) incorrect; (malséant) improper; (impoli) impolite; (déloyal) unfair.

incrédule /ɛ̃kRedyl/ adj incredulous.

incriminer /ɛ̃kRimine/ **1** vt (personne) incriminate; (conduite, action) attack.

incroyable /ɛ̃kRwajabl/ adj incredible.

incruster /ɛ̃kRyste/ **1** vt inlay (de with).

incubateur /ɛ̃kybatœR/ nm incubator.

inculpation /ɛ̃kylpasjɔ̃/ nf charge (de, pour of). **inculpé, ∼e** nm, f accused.

inculper **1** vt charge (de with).

inculquer /ɛ̃kylke/ **1** vt instil (à into).

inculte /ɛ̃kylt/ adj uncultivated; (personne) uneducated.

incurver /ɛ̃kyRve/ **1** vt curve, bend. □ s'∼ vpr curve, bend.

Inde /ɛ̃d/ nf India.

indécent, ∼e /ɛ̃desɑ̃, -t/ adj indecent.

indécis, ∼e /ɛ̃desi, -z/ adj (de nature) indecisive; (temporairement) undecided.

indéfini, ∼e /ɛ̃defini/ adj (Gram) indefinite; (vague) undefined; (sans limites) indeterminate.

indemne /ɛ̃dɛmn/ adj unharmed.

indemniser /ɛ̃dɛmnize/ **1** vt compensate (de for).

indemnité /ɛ̃dɛmnite/ nf indemnity, compensation; (allocation) allowance; ∼s de licenciement redundancy payment.

indépendance /ɛ̃depɑ̃dɑ̃s/ nf independence. **indépendant, ∼e** adj independent.

indéterminé, ∼e /ɛ̃detɛRmine/ adj unspecified.

index /ɛ̃dɛks/ nm forefinger; (liste) index.

indicateur, -trice /ɛ̃dikatœR, -tRis/ nm, f (police) informer. ● nm (livre) guide; (Tech) indicator.

indicatif, -ve /ɛ̃dikatif, -v/ adj indicative (de of). ● nm (à la radio) signature tune; (téléphonique) dialling code; (Gram) indicative.

indication /ɛ̃dikasjɔ̃/ nf indication; (renseignement) information; (directive) instruction.

indice /ɛ̃dis/ nm sign; (dans une enquête) clue; (des prix) index; (évaluation) rating; ∼ d'écoute audience ratings.

indifférence /ɛ̃difeRɑ̃s/ nf indifference.

indifférent, ∼e /ɛ̃difeRɑ̃, -t/ adj indifferent (à to); ça m'est ∼ it makes no difference to me.

indigène /ɛ̃diʒɛn/ adj & nmf native, indigenous; (du pays) local. ● nmf native.

indigent, ∼e /ɛ̃diʒɑ̃, -t/ adj destitute.

indigeste /ɛ̃diʒɛst/ adj indigestible. **indigestion** nf indigestion.

indigne /ɛ̃diɲ/ *adj* unworthy (**de** of); (*acte*) vile. **indigner (s')** ◾ *vpr* become indignant (**de** at).

indiqué, ~e /ɛ̃dike/ *adj* (*heure*) appointed; (*opportun*) appropriate; (*conseillé*) recommended.

indiquer /ɛ̃dike/ ◾ *vt* (*montrer*) show, indicate; (*renseigner sur*) point out, tell; (*déterminer*) give, state, appoint; **~ du doigt** point to *ou* out *ou* at.

indirect, ~e /ɛ̃diʀɛkt/ *adj* indirect.

indiscipliné, ~e /ɛ̃disipline/ *adj* unruly.

indiscret, -ète /ɛ̃diskʀɛ, -t/ *adj* (*personne*) inquisitive; (*question*) indiscreet.

indiscutable /ɛ̃diskytabl/ *adj* unquestionable.

indispensable /ɛ̃dispɑ̃sabl/ *adj* indispensable; **il est ~ qu'il vienne** it is essential that he comes.

individu /ɛ̃dividy/ *nm* individual.

individuel, ~le /ɛ̃dividɥɛl/ *adj* (pour une personne) individual; (qui concerne l'individu) personal; **chambre ~le** single room; **maison ~le** detached house.

indolore /ɛ̃dɔlɔʀ/ *adj* painless.

Indonésie /ɛ̃dɔnezi/ *nf* Indonesia.

indu, ~e /ɛ̃dy/ *adj* **à une heure ~e** at some ungodly hour.

induire /ɛ̃dɥiʀ/ ◾ *vt* infer (**de** from); (*inciter*) induce (**à faire** to do); **~ en erreur** mislead.

indulgence /ɛ̃dylʒɑ̃s/ *nf* indulgence; (*de jury*) leniency. **indulgent, ~e** *adj* indulgent; (*clément*) lenient.

industrialisé, ~e /ɛ̃dystʀijalize/ *adj* industrialized.

industrie /ɛ̃dystʀi/ *nf* industry.

industriel, ~le /ɛ̃dystʀijɛl/ *adj* industrial. ● *nm* industrialist.

inédit, ~e /inedi, -t/ *adj* unpublished; (*fig*) original.

inefficace /inefikas/ *adj* (*remède, mesure*) ineffective; (*appareil, système*) inefficient.

inégal, ~e (*mpl* **-aux**) /inegal, -o/ *adj* unequal; (*irrégulier*) uneven. **inégalable** *adj* matchless. **inégalité** *nf* (*injustice*) inequality; (*irrégularité*) unevenness; (*disproportion*) disparity.

inéluctable /inelyktabl/ *adj* inescapable.

inepte /inɛpt/ *adj* inept, absurd.

inerte /inɛʀt/ *adj* inert; (*immobile*) lifeless; (*sans énergie*) apathetic. **inertie** *nf* inertia; (*fig*) apathy.

inespéré, ~e /inɛspeʀe/ *adj* unhoped for.

inestimable /inɛstimabl/ *adj* priceless; (*aide*) invaluable.

inexact, ~e /inɛgza(kt), . -kt/ *adj* (*imprécis*) inaccurate; (*incorrect*) incorrect.

in extremis /inɛkstʀemis/ *adv* (*par nécessité*) as a last resort; (*au dernier moment*) at the last minute. ● *adj* last-minute.

infaillible /ɛ̃fajibl/ *adj* infallible.

infâme /ɛ̃fɑm/ *adj* vile.

infantile /ɛ̃fɑ̃til/ *adj* (*puéril*) infantile; (*maladie*) childhood; (*mortalité*) infant.

infarctus /ɛ̃faʀktys/ *nm* coronary, heart attack.

infatigable /ɛ̃fatigabl/ *adj* tireless.

infect, ~e /ɛ̃fɛkt/ *adj* revolting.

infecter /ɛ̃fɛkte/ ◾ *vt* infect. □ **s'~** *vpr* become infected. **infectieux, -ieuse** *adj* infectious. **infection** *nf* infection.

inférieur, ~e /ɛ̃feʀjœʀ/ *adj* (*plus bas*) lower; (*moins bon*) inferior (**à** to); **~ à** (*plus petit que*) smaller than; (*plus bas que*) lower than. ● *nm*, *f* inferior. **infériorité** *nf* inferiority.

infernal, ~e (*mpl* **-aux**) /ɛ̃fɛʀnal, -o/ *adj* infernal.

infester /ɛ̃fɛste/ ◾ *vt* infest.

infidèle /ɛ̃fidɛl/ *adj* unfaithful (**à** to). **infidélité** *nf* unfaithfulness; (*acte*) infidelity.

infiltrer (s') /sɛ̃filtʀe/ ◾ *vpr* **s'~** (**dans**) (*personnes, idées*) infiltrate; (*liquide*) seep through.

infime /ɛ̃fim/ *adj* tiny, minute.

infini, ~e /ɛ̃fini/ *adj* infinite. ● *nm* infinity; **à l'~** endlessly.

infinité /ɛ̃finite/ *nf* **l'~** infinity; **une ~ de** an endless number of.

infinitif /ɛ̃finitif/ *nm* infinitive.

infirme /ɛ̃fiʀm/ *adj* disabled. ● *nmf* disabled person. **infirmerie** *nf* sickbay, infirmary. **infirmier** *nm* (*male*) nurse. **infirmière** *nf* nurse. **infirmité** *nf* disability.

inflammable /ɛ̃flamabl/ *adj* inflammable.

inflation /ɛ̃flasjɔ̃/ *nf* inflation.

infliger /ɛ̃fliʒe/ 40 vt inflict; (*sanction*) impose.

influence /ɛ̃flyɑ̃s/ nf influence. **influencer** 10 vt influence. **influent, ∼e** adj influential.

influer /ɛ̃flye/ 1 vi ∼ **sur** influence.

informateur, -trice /ɛ̃fɔʀmatœʀ, -tʀis/ nm, f informant; (pour la police) informer.

informaticien, ∼ne /ɛ̃fɔʀmatisjɛ̃, -ɛn/ nm, f computer scientist.

information /ɛ̃fɔʀmasjɔ̃/ nf information; (Jur) inquiry; **une ∼** (some) information; **(nouvelle)** (some) news; **les ∼s** the news.

informatique /ɛ̃fɔʀmatik/ nf computer science; (techniques) information technology. **informatiser** 1 vt computerize.

informer /ɛ̃fɔʀme/ 1 vt inform (**de** about, of). □ **s'∼** vpr enquire (**de** about).

inforoute /ɛ̃fɔʀut/ nf (Ordinat) information highway.

infortune /ɛ̃fɔʀtyn/ nf misfortune.

infraction /ɛ̃fʀaksjɔ̃/ nf offence; **∼ à** (*loi, règlement*) breach of.

infrastructure /ɛ̃fʀastʀyktyʀ/ nf infrastructure; (équipements) facilities.

infructueux, -euse /ɛ̃fʀyktɥø, -z/ adj fruitless.

infuser /ɛ̃fyze/ 1 vt/i infuse, brew. **infusion** nf herbal tea, infusion.

ingénier (s') /(s)ɛ̃ʒenje/ 45 vpr **s'∼ à** strive to.

ingénieur /ɛ̃ʒenjœʀ/ nm engineer.

ingénieux, -ieuse /ɛ̃ʒenjø, -z/ adj ingenious. **ingéniosité** nf ingenuity.

ingénu, ∼e /ɛ̃ʒeny/ adj naïve.

ingérence /ɛ̃ʒeʀɑ̃s/ nf interference.

ingérer (s') /sɛ̃ʒeʀe/ 14 vpr **s'∼ dans** interfere in.

ingrat, ∼e /ɛ̃gʀa, -t/ adj (*personne*) ungrateful; (*travail*) unrewarding, thankless; (*visage*) unattractive.

ingrédient /ɛ̃gʀedjɑ̃/ nm ingredient.

ingurgiter /ɛ̃gyʀʒite/ 1 vt swallow.

inhabité, ∼e /inabite/ adj uninhabited.

inhabituel, ∼le /inabitɥɛl/ adj unusual.

inhumain, ∼e /inymɛ̃, -ɛn/ adj inhuman.

inhumation /inymasjɔ̃/ nf burial.

initial, ∼e (*mpl* **-iaux**) /inisjal, -jo/ adj initial. **initiale** nf initial.

initialisation /inisjalizasjɔ̃/ nf (Ordinat) formatting. **initialiser** 1 vt format.

initiation /inisjasjɔ̃/ nf initiation; (formation) introduction (**à** to); **cours d'∼** introductory course.

initiative /inisjativ/ nf initiative.

initier /inisje/ 45 vt initiate (**à** into); (faire découvrir) introduce (**à** to). □ **s'∼** vpr **s'∼ à qch** learn sth.

injecter /ɛ̃ʒɛkte/ 1 vt inject; **injecté de sang** bloodshot. **injection** nf injection.

injure /ɛ̃ʒyʀ/ nf insult. **injurier** 45 vt insult. **injurieux, -ieuse** adj insulting.

injuste /ɛ̃ʒyst/ adj unjust, unfair. **injustice** nf injustice.

inné, ∼e /inne/ adj innate, inborn.

innocence /inɔsɑ̃s/ nf innocence. **innocent, ∼e** adj & nm, f innocent. **innocenter** 1 vt clear, prove innocent.

innombrable /inɔ̃bʀabl/ adj countless.

innovateur, -trice /inɔvatœʀ, -tʀis/ nm, f innovator. **innovation** nf innovation. **innover** 1 vi innovate.

inodore /inɔdɔʀ/ adj odourless.

inoffensif, -ive /inɔfɑ̃sif, -v/ adj harmless.

inondation /inɔ̃dasjɔ̃/ nf flood; (action) flooding.

inonder /inɔ̃de/ 1 vt flood; (mouiller) soak; (envahir) inundate (**de** with); **inondé de soleil** bathed in sunlight.

inopiné, ∼e /inɔpine/ adj unexpected; (*mort*) sudden.

inopportun, ∼e /inɔpɔʀtœ̃, -yn/ adj inopportune, ill-timed.

inoubliable /inublijabl/ adj unforgettable.

inouï, ∼e /inwi/ adj incredible; (événement) unprecedented.

inox® /inɔks/ nm stainless steel.

inoxydable /inɔksidabl/ adj **acier ∼** stainless steel.

inqualifiable /ɛ̃kalifjabl/ adj unspeakable.

inquiet, -iète /ɛ̃kjɛ, -t/ adj worried. **inquiétant, ∼e** adj worrying.

inquiéter /ɛ̃kjete/ **14** vt worry. □ s'~ vpr worry (de about). **inquiétude** nf anxiety, worry.

insaisissable /ɛ̃sezisabl/ adj (personne) elusive; (nuance) indefinable.

insalubre /ɛ̃salybʀ/ adj unhealthy.

insatisfaisant, ~e /ɛ̃satisfəzɑ̃, -t/ adj unsatisfactory. **insatisfait,** ~e adj (mécontent) dissatisfied; (frustré) unfulfilled.

inscription /ɛ̃skʀipsjɔ̃/ nf inscription; (immatriculation) enrolment.

inscrire /ɛ̃skʀiʀ/ **30** vt write (down); (graver, tracer) inscribe; (personne) enrol; (sur une liste) put down. □ s'~ vpr put one's name down; s'~ à (école) enrol at; (club, parti) join; (examen) enter for.

insecte /ɛ̃sɛkt/ nm insect.

insécurité /ɛ̃sekyʀite/ nf insecurity.

insensé, ~e /ɛ̃sɑ̃se/ adj mad.

insensibilité /ɛ̃sɑ̃sibilite/ nf insensitivity. **insensible** adj insensitive (à to); (graduel) imperceptible.

insérer /ɛ̃seʀe/ **14** vt insert. □ s'~ vpr be inserted; s'~ dans be part of.

insigne /ɛ̃siɲ/ nm badge; ~s (d'une fonction) insignia.

insignifiant, ~e /ɛ̃siɲifjɑ̃, -t/ adj insignificant.

insinuation /ɛ̃sinɥasjɔ̃/ nf insinuation.

insinuer /ɛ̃sinɥe/ **1** vt insinuate.
□ s'~ vpr (socialement) ingratiate oneself (auprès de qn with sb); s'~ dans (se glisser) slip into; (idée, nuance) creep into.

insipide /ɛ̃sipid/ adj insipid.

insistance /ɛ̃sistɑ̃s/ nf insistence. **insistant,** ~e adj insistent.

insister /ɛ̃siste/ **1** vi insist (pour faire on doing); ~ sur stress.

insolation /ɛ̃sɔlasjɔ̃/ nf (Méd) sunstroke.

insolent, ~e /ɛ̃sɔlɑ̃, -t/ adj insolent.

insolite /ɛ̃sɔlit/ adj unusual.

insolvable /ɛ̃sɔlvabl/ adj insolvent.

insomnie /ɛ̃sɔmni/ nf insomnia.

insonoriser /ɛ̃sɔnɔʀize/ **1** vt soundproof.

insouciance /ɛ̃susjɑ̃s/ nf lack of concern. **insouciant,** ~e adj carefree.

insoutenable /ɛ̃sutnabl/ adj unbearable; (argument) untenable.

inspecter /ɛ̃spɛkte/ **1** vt inspect. **inspecteur, -trice** nm, f inspector. **inspection** nf inspection.

inspiration /ɛ̃spiʀasjɔ̃/ nf inspiration; (respiration) breath.

inspirer /ɛ̃spiʀe/ **1** vt inspire; ~ la méfiance à qn inspire distrust in sb. ● vi breathe in. □ s'~ de vpr be inspired by.

instabilité /ɛ̃stabilite/ nf instability; unsteadiness. **instable** adj unstable; (temps) unsettled.

installation /ɛ̃stalasjɔ̃/ nf installation; (de local) fitting out; (de locataire) settling in. **installations** nfpl facilities.

installer /ɛ̃stale/ **1** vt install; (meuble) put in; (étagère) put up; (gaz, téléphone) connect; (équiper) fit out.
□ s'~ vpr settle (down); (emménager) settle in; s'~ comme set oneself up as.

instance /ɛ̃stɑ̃s/ nf authority; (prière) entreaty; avec ~ with insistence; en ~ pending; en ~ de in the course of, on the point of.

instant /ɛ̃stɑ̃/ nm moment, instant; à l'~ this instant.

instantané, ~e /ɛ̃stɑ̃tane/ adj instantaneous; (café) instant.

instar: à l'~ de /alɛstaʀdə/ loc like.

instaurer /ɛ̃stɔʀe/ **1** vt institute.

instigateur, -trice /ɛ̃stigatœʀ, -tʀis/ nm, f instigator.

instinct /ɛ̃stɛ̃/ nm instinct; d'~ instinctively. **instinctif, -ive** adj instinctive.

instituer /ɛ̃stitɥe/ **1** vt establish.

institut /ɛ̃stity/ nm institute; ~ de beauté beauty parlour.

instituteur, -trice /ɛ̃stitytœʀ, -tʀis/ nm, f primary-school teacher.

institution /ɛ̃stitysjɔ̃/ nf institution; (école) private school.

instructif, -ive /ɛ̃stʀyktif, -v/ adj instructive.

instruction /ɛ̃stʀyksjɔ̃/ nf (formation) education; (Mil) training; (document) directive; ~s (ordres, mode d'emploi) instructions; (Ordinat) (énoncé) instruction; (pas de séquence) statement.

instruire /ɛ̃stʀɥiʀ/ **17** vt teach, educate; ~ de inform of. □ s'~ vpr learn, educate oneself; s'~ de enquire about. **instruit, ~e** adj educated.

instrument /ɛ̃stʀymɑ̃/ nm instrument; (outil) tool; (moyen: fig) instrument; **~ de gestion** management tool; **~s de bord** (Aviat) controls.

insu: à l'**~ de** /alɛ̃sydə/ loc without the knowledge of.

insuffisance /ɛ̃syfizɑ̃s/ nf (pénurie) shortage; (médiocrité) inadequacy. **insuffisant, ~e** adj inadequate; (en nombre) insufficient.

insulaire /ɛ̃sylɛʀ/ adj island. ● nmf islander.

insuline /ɛ̃sylin/ nf insulin.

insulte /ɛ̃sylt/ nf insult. **insulter** 1 vt insult.

insupportable /ɛ̃sypɔʀtabl/ adj unbearable.

insurger (s') /(s)ɛ̃syʀʒe/ 40 vpr rebel.

intact, ~e /ɛ̃takt/ adj intact.

intangible /ɛ̃tɑ̃ʒibl/ adj intangible; (principe) inviolable.

intarissable /ɛ̃taʀisabl/ adj inexhaustible.

intégral, ~e (mpl **-aux**) /ɛ̃tegʀal, -o/ adj complete; (texte, édition) unabridged; (paiement) full, in full. **intégralement** adv in full. **intégralité** nf whole.

intègre /ɛ̃tɛgʀ/ adj upright.

intégrer /ɛ̃tegʀe/ 14 vt integrate. □ **s'~** vpr (personne) integrate; (maison) fit in.

intégriste /ɛ̃tegʀist/ nmf fundamentalist.

intégrité /ɛ̃tegʀite/ nf integrity.

intellect /ɛ̃telɛkt/ nm intellect. **intellectuel, ~le** adj & nm, f intellectual.

intelligence /ɛ̃teliʒɑ̃s/ nf intelligence; (compréhension) understanding; (complicité) agreement; **agir d'~ avec qn** act in agreement with sb. **intelligent, ~e** adj intelligent.

intempéries /ɛ̃tɑ̃peʀi/ nfpl severe weather.

intempestif, -ive /ɛ̃tɑ̃pɛstif, -v/ adj untimely.

intenable /ɛ̃tnabl/ adj unbearable; (enfant) impossible.

intendance /ɛ̃tɑ̃dɑ̃s/ nf (Scol) bursar's office.

intendant, ~e /ɛ̃tɑ̃dɑ̃, -t/ nm (Mil) quartermaster. ● nm, f (Scol) bursar.

intense /ɛ̃tɑ̃s/ adj intense; (circulation) heavy. **Intensif, -ive** adj intensive. **intensité** nf intensity.

intenter /ɛ̃tɑ̃te/ 1 vt **~ un procès** ou **une action** institute proceedings (à, contre against).

intention /ɛ̃tɑ̃sjɔ̃/ nf intention (de faire of doing); à l'**~ de qn** for sb. **intentionnel, ~le** adj intentional.

interactif, -ive /ɛ̃teʀaktif, -v/ adj (TV, vidéo) interactive.

interaction /ɛ̃teʀaksjɔ̃/ nf interaction.

intercaler /ɛ̃teʀkale/ 1 vt insert.

intercéder /ɛ̃teʀsede/ 14 vi intercede (en faveur de on behalf of).

intercepter /ɛ̃teʀsɛpte/ 1 vt intercept.

interdiction /ɛ̃teʀdiksjɔ̃/ nf ban; **~ de fumer** no smoking.

interdire /ɛ̃teʀdiʀ/ 37 vt forbid; (officiellement) ban, prohibit; **~ à qn de faire** forbid sb to do.

interdit, ~e /ɛ̃teʀdi, -t/ adj prohibited, forbidden; (étonné) dumbfounded.

intéressant, ~e /ɛ̃teʀesɑ̃, -t/ adj interesting; (avantageux) attractive.

intéressé, ~e /ɛ̃teʀese/ adj (en cause) concerned; (pour profiter) self-interested. ● nm, f person concerned.

intéresser /ɛ̃teʀese/ 1 vt interest; (concerner) concern. □ **s'~ à** vpr be interested in.

intérêt /ɛ̃teʀɛ/ nm interest; (égoïsme) self-interest; (~s) (Comm) interest; **vous avez ~ à** it is in your interest to.

interface /ɛ̃teʀfas/ nf (Ordinat) interface.

intérieur, ~e /ɛ̃teʀjœʀ/ adj inner, inside; (mur, escalier) internal; (vol, politique) domestic; (vie, calme) inner. ● nm interior; (de boîte, tiroir) inside; à l'**~ (de)** inside; (fig) within. **intérieurement** adv inwardly.

intérim /ɛ̃teʀim/ nm interim; **assurer l'~** deputize (de for); **par ~** on an interim basis; **président par ~** acting president; **faire de l'~** temp.

intérimaire /ɛ̃teʀimɛʀ/ adj temporary, interim. ● nmf (secrétaire) temp; (médecin) locum.

interjection /ɛ̃teʀʒɛksjɔ̃/ nf interjection.

125

interlocuteur | introverti

interlocuteur, -trice /ɛ̃tɛʀlɔkytœʀ, -tʀis/ *nm, f* **son** ~ the person one is speaking to.

interloqué, ~e /ɛ̃tɛʀlɔke/ *adj* **être** ~ be taken aback.

intermède /ɛ̃tɛʀmɛd/ *nm* interlude.

intermédiaire /ɛ̃tɛʀmedjɛʀ/ *adj* intermediate. ● *nmf* intermediary. ● *nm* **sans** ~ without an intermediary, direct; **par l'**~ **de** through.

interminable /ɛ̃tɛʀminabl/ *adj* endless.

intermittence /ɛ̃tɛʀmitɑ̃s/ *nf* **par** ~ intermittently.

internat /ɛ̃tɛʀna/ *nm* boardingschool.

international, ~e (*mpl* **-aux**) /ɛ̃tɛʀnasjɔnal, -o/ *adj* international.

internaute /ɛ̃tɛʀnot/ *nmf* (Ordinat) Netsurfer, Internet user.

interne /ɛ̃tɛʀn/ *adj* internal; (*cours, formation*) in-house. ● *nmf* (Scol) boarder; (Méd) house officer; (US) intern.

internement /ɛ̃tɛʀnəmɑ̃/ *nm* (Pol) internment. **interner** 🛈 *vt* (Pol) intern; (Méd) commit.

Internet /ɛ̃tɛʀnɛt/ *nm* Internet; **sur** ~ on the Internet.

interpellation /ɛ̃tɛʀpelasjɔ̃/ *nf* (Pol) questioning. **interpeller** 🛈 *vt* shout to; (*apostropher*) shout at; (*interroger*) question.

interphone /ɛ̃tɛʀfɔn/ *nm* intercom; (d'immeuble) entry phone.

interposer (s') /(s)ɛ̃tɛʀpoze/ 🛈 *vpr* intervene.

interprétariat /ɛ̃tɛʀpretaʀja/ *nm* interpreting. **interprétation** *nf* interpretation; (d'artiste) performance. **interprète** *nmf* interpreter; (artiste) performer. **interpréter** 🛈 *vt* interpret; (jouer) play; (chanter) sing.

interrogateur, -trice /ɛ̃tɛʀɔgatœʀ, -tʀis/ *adj* questioning. **interrogatif, -ive** *adj* interrogative. **interrogation** *nf* question; (action) questioning; (épreuve) test. **interrogatoire** *nm* interrogation. **interroger** 🛈 *vt* question; (élève) test.

interrompre /ɛ̃tɛʀɔ̃pʀ/ 🛈 *vt* break off, interrupt; (personne) interrupt. □ **s'**~ *vpr* break off. **interrupteur** *nm* switch. **interruption** *nf* interruption; (arrêt) break.

interurbain, ~e /ɛ̃tɛʀyʀbɛ̃, -ɛn/ *adj* long-distance, trunk.

intervalle /ɛ̃tɛʀval/ *nm* space; (temps) interval; **dans l'**~ in the meantime.

intervenir /ɛ̃tɛʀvəniʀ/ 🛈 *vi* (agir) intervene (**auprès de qn** with sb); (survenir) occur, take place; (Méd) operate. **intervention** *nf* intervention; (Méd) operation.

intervertir /ɛ̃tɛʀvɛʀtiʀ/ 🛈 *vt* invert; (rôles) reverse.

interview /ɛ̃tɛʀvju/ *nf* interview. **interviewer** 🛈 *vt* interview.

intestin /ɛ̃tɛstɛ̃/ *nm* intestine.

intime /ɛ̃tim/ *adj* intimate; (fête, vie) private; (dîner) quiet. ● *nmf* intimate friend.

intimider /ɛ̃timide/ 🛈 *vt* intimidate.

intimité /ɛ̃timite/ *nf* intimacy; (vie privée) privacy.

intituler /ɛ̃tityle/ 🛈 *vt* call, entitle. □ **s'**~ *vpr* be called *ou* entitled.

intolérable /ɛ̃tɔleʀabl/ *adj* intolerable. **intolérance** *nf* intolerance. **intolérant, ~e** *adj* intolerant.

intonation /ɛ̃tɔnasjɔ̃/ *nf* intonation.

intox /ɛ̃tɔks/ *nf* 🛈 brainwashing.

intoxication /ɛ̃tɔksikasjɔ̃/ *nf* poisoning; (fig) brainwashing; ~ **alimentaire** food poisoning. **intoxiquer** 🛈 *vt* poison; (fig) brainwash.

intraitable /ɛ̃tʀɛtabl/ *adj* inflexible.

Intranet /ɛ̃tʀanɛt/ *nm* Intranet.

intransigeant, ~e /ɛ̃tʀɑ̃ziʒɑ̃, -t/ *adj* intransigent.

intransitif, -ive /ɛ̃tʀɑ̃zitif, -v/ *adj* intransitive.

intraveineux, -euse /ɛ̃tʀavɛnø, -z/ *adj* intravenous.

intrépide /ɛ̃tʀepid/ *adj* fearless.

intrigue /ɛ̃tʀig/ *nf* intrigue; (scénario) plot.

intrinsèque /ɛ̃tʀɛ̃sɛk/ *adj* intrinsic.

introduction /ɛ̃tʀɔdyksjɔ̃/ *nf* introduction; (insertion) insertion.

introduire /ɛ̃tʀɔdɥiʀ/ 🛈 *vt* introduce, bring in; (insérer) put in, insert; ~ **qn** show sb in. □ **s'**~ *vpr* get in; **s'**~ **dans** get into, enter.

introuvable /ɛ̃tʀuvabl/ *adj* that cannot be found.

introverti, ~e /ɛ̃tʀɔvɛʀti/ *nm, f* introvert. ● *adj* introverted.

intrus, ~e /ɛ̃tʀy, -z/ nm, f intruder. **intrusion** nf intrusion.

intuitif, -ive /ɛ̃tɥitif, -iv/ adj intuitive. **intuition** nf intuition.

inusable /inyzabl/ adj hardwearing.

inusité, ~e /inyzite/ adj little used.

inutile /inytil/ adj useless; (vain) needless. **inutilement** adv needlessly. **inutilisable** adj unusable.

invalide /ɛ̃valid/ adj & nmf disabled (person).

invariable /ɛ̃vaʀjabl/ adj invariable.

invasion /ɛ̃vɑzjɔ̃/ nf invasion.

invectiver /ɛ̃vɛktive/ **1** vt abuse.

inventaire /ɛ̃vɑ̃tɛʀ/ nm inventory; (Comm) stocklist; **faire l'~** draw up an inventory; (Comm) do a stocktake.

inventer /ɛ̃vɑ̃te/ **1** vt invent. **inventeur, -trice** nm, f inventor. **inventif, -ive** adj inventive. **invention** nf invention.

inverse /ɛ̃vɛʀs/ adj opposite; (ordre) reverse; **en sens ~** in ou from the opposite direction. ● nm reverse; **c'est l'~** it's the other way round. **inversement** adv conversely. **inverser** **1** vt reverse, invert.

investir /ɛ̃vɛstiʀ/ **2** vt invest. **investissement** nm investment.

investiture /ɛ̃vɛstityʀ/ nf (de candidat) nomination; (de président) investiture.

invétéré, ~e /ɛ̃vetere/ adj inveterate; (menteur) compulsive; (enraciné) deep-rooted.

invisible /ɛ̃vizibl/ adj invisible.

invitation /ɛ̃vitasjɔ̃/ nf invitation. **invité, ~e** nm, f guest. **inviter** **1** vt invite (à to).

involontaire /ɛ̃vɔlɔ̃tɛʀ/ adj involuntary; (témoin, héros) unwitting.

invoquer /ɛ̃vɔke/ **1** vt call upon, invoke.

invraisemblable /ɛ̃vʀɛsɑ̃blabl/ adj improbable, unlikely; (incroyable) incredible. **invraisemblance** nf improbability.

iode /jɔd/ nm iodine.

ira, irait /iʀa, iʀɛ/ ➡ALLER **8**.

Irak /iʀak/ nm Iraq.

Iran /iʀɑ̃/ nm Iran.

iris /iʀis/ nm iris.

irlandais, ~e /iʀlɑ̃dɛ, -z/ adj Irish. **I~, ~e** nm, f Irishman, Irishwoman.

Irlande /iʀlɑ̃d/ nf Ireland.

IRM abrév m (imagerie par résonance magnétique) magnetic resonance imaging.

ironie /iʀɔni/ nf irony. **ironique** adj ironic.

irrationnel, ~le /iʀasjɔnɛl/ adj irrational.

irréalisable /iʀealizabl/ adj (idée, rêve) unachievable; (projet) unworkable.

irrécupérable /iʀekypeʀabl/ adj irretrievable; (capital) irrecoverable.

irréel, ~le /iʀeɛl/ adj unreal.

irréfléchi, ~e /iʀefleʃi/ adj thoughtless.

irrégulier, -ière /iʀegylje, -jɛʀ/ adj irregular.

irrémédiable /iʀemedjabl/ adj irreparable.

irremplaçable /iʀɑ̃plasabl/ adj irreplaceable.

irréparable /iʀepaʀabl/ adj (objet) beyond repair; (tort, dégâts) irreparable.

irréprochable /iʀepʀɔʃabl/ adj flawless.

irrésistible /iʀezistibl/ adj irresistible; (drôle) hilarious.

irrésolu, ~e /iʀezɔly/ adj indecisive; (problème) unsolved.

irrespirable /iʀɛspiʀabl/ adj stifling.

irresponsable /iʀɛspɔ̃sabl/ adj irresponsible.

irrigation /iʀigasjɔ̃/ nf irrigation. **irriguer** **1** vt irrigate.

irritable /iʀitabl/ adj irritable.

irriter /iʀite/ **1** vt irritate. □ **s'~** vpr get annoyed (de at).

irruption /iʀypsjɔ̃/ nf faire ~ dans burst into.

Islam /islam/ nm Islam. **islamique** adj Islamic.

islamiste /islamist/ adj Islamist, Islamic; n m,f Islamist.

islandais, ~e /islɑ̃dɛ, -z/ adj Icelandic. ● nm (Ling) Icelandic. **I~, ~e** nm, f Icelander.

Islande /islɑ̃d/ nf Iceland.

isolant /izɔlɑ̃/ nm insulating material. **isolation** nf insulation.

isolé, ~e /izɔle/ adj isolated. **isolement** nm isolation.

isoler /izɔle/ **1** vt isolate; (Électr) insulate. □ **s'~** vpr isolate oneself.

isoloir /izɔlwar/ nm polling booth.

Isorel ® /izɔrɛl/ nm hardboard.

Israël /israɛl/ nm Israel. **israélien, ~ne** adj Israeli.

israélite /israelit/ adj Jewish. ● nmf Jew.

issu, ~e /isy/ adj être ~ de (personne) come from; (résulter de) result ou stem from.

issue /isy/ nf (sortie) exit; (résultat) outcome; (fig) solution; **à l'~ de** at the conclusion of; **~ de secours** emergency exit; **rue** ou **voie sans ~** dead end.

Italie /itali/ nf Italy.

italien, ~ne /italjɛ̃, -ɛn/ adj Italian. ● nm (Ling) Italian. **I~, ~ne** nm, f Italian.

italique /italik/ nm italics.

itinéraire /itinerɛr/ nm itinerary, route.

I.U.T. abrév m (**Institut universitaire de technologie**) university institute of technology.

I.V.G. abrév f (**interruption volontaire de grossesse**) abortion.

ivoire /ivwar/ nm ivory.

ivre /ivr/ adj drunk. **ivresse** nf drunkenness; (fig) exhilaration. **ivrogne** nmf drunk(ard).

. . . .

Jj

. . . .

j' /ʒ/ ➞JE.

jacinthe /ʒasɛt/ nf hyacinth.

jadis /ʒadis/ adv long ago.

jaillir /ʒajir/ **2** vi (liquide) spurt (out); (lumière) stream out; (apparaître) burst forth, spring out.

jalonner /ʒalɔne/ **1** vt mark (out).

jalousie /ʒaluzi/ nf jealousy; (store) (venetian) blind. **jaloux, -ouse** adj jealous.

jamais /ʒamɛ/ adv ever; **ne ~** never; **il ne boit ~** he never drinks; **à ~** for ever; **si ~** if ever.

jambe /ʒɑ̃b/ nf leg.

jambon /ʒɑ̃bɔ̃/ nm ham. **jambonneau** (pl ~x) nm knuckle of ham.

janvier /ʒɑ̃vje/ nm January.

Japon /ʒapɔ̃/ nm Japan.

japonais, ~e /japɔnɛ, -z/ adj Japanese. ● nm (Ling) Japanese. **J~, ~e** nm, f Japanese.

japper /ʒape/ **1** vi yap.

jaquette /ʒakɛt/ nf (de livre, femme) jacket; (d'homme) morning coat.

jardin /ʒardɛ̃/ nm garden; **~ d'enfants** nursery (school); **~ public** public park. **jardinage** nm gardening. **jardiner** **1** vi do some gardening, garden. **jardinier, -ière** nm, f gardener.

jardinière /ʒardinjɛr/ nf (meuble) plant-stand; **~ de légumes** mixed vegetables.

jarretelle /ʒartɛl/ nf suspender; (US) garter.

jarretière /ʒartjɛr/ nf garter.

jatte /ʒat/ nf bowl.

jauge /ʒoʒ/ nf capacity; (de navire) tonnage; (compteur) gauge; **~ d'huile** dipstick.

jaune /ʒon/ adj & nm yellow; (péj) scab; **~ d'œuf** (egg) yolk; **rire ~** give a forced laugh. **jaunir** **2** vt/i turn yellow. **jaunisse** nf jaundice.

javelot /ʒavlo/ nm javelin.

jazz /dʒaz/ nm jazz.

J.C. abrév m (**Jésus-Christ**) 500 avant/ après ~ 500 B.C./A.D.

je, j' /ʒə, ʒ/ pron I.

jean /dʒin/ nm jeans; **un ~** a pair of jeans.

jet¹ /ʒɛ/ nm throw; (de liquide, vapeur) jet; **~ d'eau** fountain.

jet² /dʒɛt/ nm (avion) jet.

jetable /ʒətabl/ adj disposable.

jetée /ʒəte/ nf pier.

jeter /ʒəte/ **38** vt throw; (au rebut) throw away; (regard, ancre, lumière) cast; (cri) utter; (bases) lay; **~ un coup d'œil** have ou take a look (**à** at). □ **se ~ contre** vpr crash ou bash into; **se ~ dans** (fleuve) flow into; **se ~ sur** (se ruer sur) rush at.

jeton /ʒətɔ̃/ nm token; (pour compter) counter; (au casino) chip.

jeu (pl ~x) /ʒø/ nm game; (amusement) play; (au casino) gambling; (Théât) acting; (série) set; (de lumière, ressort) play; **en ~** (*honneur*) at stake; (*forces*) at work; **~ de cartes** (paquet) pack of cards; **~d'échecs** (boîte) chess set; **~ de mots** pun; **~ télévisé** tv game show; **~ vidéo** video game; **~x de grattage** scratch cards; **les ~x olympiques/ paralympiques** the Olympic Games/ Paralympic Games.

jeudi /ʒødi/ *nm* Thursday.

jeun: à ~ /aʒœ̃/ *loc* on an empty stomach.

jeune /ʒœn/ *adj* young; **~ fille** girl; **~ pousse** (Comm) start-up; **~s mariés** newlyweds. ● *nmf* young person; **les ~s** young people.

jeûne /ʒøn/ *nm* fast.

jeunesse /ʒœnɛs/ *nf* youth; (apparence) youthfulness; **la ~** (jeunes) the young.

joaillerie /ʒɔajʀi/ *nf* jewellery; (magasin) jeweller's shop.

joie /ʒwa/ *nf* joy.

joindre /ʒwɛ̃dʀ/ **22** *vt* join (à to); (*mains, pieds*) put together; (*efforts*) combine; (contacter) contact; (dans une enveloppe) enclose. □ **se ~ à** *vpr* join.

joint, ~e /ʒwɛ̃, -t/ *adj* (*efforts*) joint; (*pieds*) together. ● *nm* joint; (de robinet) washer.

joli, ~e /ʒɔli/ *adj* pretty, nice; (somme, profit) nice; **c'est du ~!** (ironique) charming! **c'est bien ~ mais** that is all very well but.

joncher /ʒɔ̃ʃe/ **1** *vt* litter, be strewn over; **jonché de** littered with.

jonction /ʒɔ̃ksjɔ̃/ *nf* junction.

jongleur, -euse /ʒɔ̃glœʀ, øz/ *nm, f* juggler.

jonquille /ʒɔ̃kij/ *nf* daffodil.

joue /ʒu/ *nf* cheek.

jouer /ʒwe/ **1** *vt/i* play; (Théât) act; (au casino) gamble; (fonctionner) work; (*film, pièce*) put on; (*cheval*) back; (être important) count; **~ à** (*jeu*, Sport) play; **~ de** (Mus) play; **~ la comédie** put on an act; **bien joué!** well done!

jouet /ʒwɛ/ *nm* toy; (personne: fig) plaything; (victime) victim.

joueur, -euse /ʒwœʀ, -øz/ *nm, f* player; (parieur) gambler.

jouffflu, ~e /ʒufly/ *adj* chubby-cheeked; (visage) chubby.

jouir /ʒwiʀ/ **2** *vi* (sexe) come; **~ de** (*droit, avantage*) enjoy; (*bien, concession*) enjoy the use of. **jouissance** *nf* pleasure; (usage) use (**de qch** of sth).

joujou (*pl* ~x) /ʒuʒu/ *nm* **1** toy.

jour /ʒuʀ/ *nm* day; (opposé à nuit) day (time); (lumière) daylight; (aspect) light; (ouverture) gap; **de nos ~s** nowadays; **du ~ au lendemain** overnight; **il fait ~** it is daylight; **~ chômé** ou **férié** public holiday; **~ de fête** holiday; **~ ouvrable, ~ de travail** working day; **mettre à ~** update; **mettre au ~** uncover; **au grand ~** in the open; **donner le ~** give birth; **voir le ~** be born; **vivre au ~ le jour** live from day to day.

journal (*pl* -aux) /ʒuʀnal, -o/ *nm* (news)paper; (spécialisé) journal; (intime) diary; (à la radio) news; **~ de bord** log-book.

journalier, -ière /ʒuʀnalje, -jɛʀ/ *adj* daily.

journalisme /ʒuʀnalism/ *nm* journalism. **journaliste** *nmf* journalist.

journée /ʒuʀne/ *nf* day.

jovial, ~e (*mpl* -iaux) /ʒɔvjal, -jo/ *adj* jovial.

joyau (*pl* ~x) /ʒwajo/ *nm* gem.

joyeux, -euse /ʒwajø, -z/ *adj* merry, joyful; **~ anniversaire** happy birthday.

jubiler /ʒybile/ **1** *vi* be jubilant.

jucher /ʒyʃe/ **1** *vt* perch. □ **se ~** *vpr* perch.

judaïsme /ʒydaism/ *nm* Judaism.

judiciaire /ʒydisjɛʀ/ *adj* judicial.

judicieux, -ieuse /ʒydisjø, -z/ *adj* judicious.

judo /ʒydo/ *nm* judo.

juge /ʒyʒ/ *nm* judge; (arbitre) referee; **~ de paix** Justice of the Peace; **~ de touche** linesman.

jugé: au ~ /oʒyʒe/ *loc* by guesswork.

jugement /ʒyʒmã/ *nm* judgement; (criminel) sentence.

juger /ʒyʒe/ **40** *vt/i* judge; (estimer) consider (**que** that); **~ de** judge.

juguler /ʒygyle/ **1** *vt* stamp out; curb.

juif, -ive /ʒyif, -v/ *adj* Jewish. ● *nm, f* Jew.

juillet /ʒyijɛ/ *nm* July.

juin /ʒɥɛ̃/ *nm* June.

jumeau, -elle (*mpl* ~**x**) /ʒymo, -ɛl/ *adj* & *nm, f* twin. **jumeler** 🔲 *vt* (*villes*) twin.

jumelles /ʒymɛl/ *nfpl* binoculars.

jument /ʒymɑ̃/ *nf* mare.

junior /ʒynjɔʀ/ *adj* & *nmf* junior.

jupe /ʒyp/ *nf* skirt.

jupon /ʒypɔ̃/ *nm* slip, petticoat.

juré, ~e /ʒyʀe/ *nm, f* juror. ● *adj* sworn.

jurer /ʒyʀe/ 🔲 *vt* swear (**que** that). ● *vi* (*pester*) swear; (*contraster*) clash (**avec** with).

juridiction /ʒyʀidiksjɔ̃/ *nf* jurisdiction; (*tribunal*) court of law.

juridique /ʒyʀidik/ *adj* legal.

juriste /ʒyʀist/ *nmf* legal expert.

juron /ʒyʀɔ̃/ *nm* swearword.

jury /ʒyʀi/ *nm* (Jur) jury; (*examinateurs*) panel of judges.

jus /ʒy/ *nm* juice; (*de viande*) gravy; ~ **de fruit** fruit juice.

jusque /ʒysk(ə)/ *prép* **jusqu'à** (up) to, as far as; (*temps*) until, till; (*limite*) up to; (*y compris*) even; **jusqu'à ce que** until; **jusqu'à présent** until now; **jusqu'en** until; **jusqu'où?** how far?; ~ **dans**, ~ **sur** as far as.

juste /ʒyst/ *adj* fair, just; (*légitime*) just; (*correct, exact*) right; (*vrai*) true; (*vêtement*) tight; (*quantité*) on the short side; **le ~ milieu** the happy medium. ● *adv* rightly, correctly; (*chanter*) in tune; (*seulement, exactement*) just; (**un peu**) ~ (*calculer, mesurer*) a bit fine *ou* close; **au ~** exactly; **c'était ~** (*presque raté*) it was a close thing. **justement** *adv* (*précisément*) precisely; (*à l'instant*) just; (*avec justesse*) correctly; (*légitimement*) justifiably.

justesse /ʒystɛs/ *nf* accuracy; **de ~** just, narrowly.

justice /ʒystis/ *nf* justice; (*autorités*) law; (*tribunal*) court.

justifier /ʒystifje/ 🔲 *vt* justify. ● *vi* ~ **de** prove. ▫ **se** ~ *vpr* justify oneself.

juteux, -euse /ʒytø, -z/ *adj* juicy.

juvénile /ʒyvenil/ *adj* youthful; (*délinquance, mortalité*) juvenile.

Kk

kaki /kaki/ *adj inv* & *nm* khaki.

kangourou /kɑ̃guʀu/ *nm* kangaroo.

karaté /kaʀate/ *nm* karate.

kart /kaʀt/ *nm* go-cart.

kascher /kaʃɛʀ/ *adj inv* kosher.

kayak /kajak/ *nm* kayak.

képi /kepi/ *nm* kepi.

kermesse /kɛʀmɛs/ *nf* fête.

kidnapper /kidnape/ 🔲 *vt* kidnap.

kilo /kilo/ *nm* kilo.

kilogramme /kilogʀam/ *nm* kilogram.

kilométrage /kilɔmetʀaʒ/ *nm* ≈ mileage. **kilomètre** *nm* kilometre.

kinésithérapeute /kineziteʀapø t/ *nmf* physiotherapist. **kinésithérapie** *nf* physiotherapy.

kiosque /kjɔsk/ *nm* kiosk; ~ **à musique** bandstand.

kit /kit/ *nm* kit; ~ **mains libres conducteur** hands-free kit.

klaxon® /klaksɔn/ *nm* (Auto) horn. **klaxonner** 🔲 *vi* sound one's horn.

Ko *abrév m* (**kilo-octet**) (Ordinat) KB.

KO *abrév m* (**knock-out**) KO 🔲.

K-way® /kawɛ/ *nm inv* windcheater.

kyste /kist/ *nm* cyst.

Ll

l', la /l, la/ ➡**le.**

là /la/
● *adverbe*
····▸ (*dans ce lieu*) there; (*ici*) here; (*chez soi*) in; **c'est ~ que** this is where; ~ **où** where; **par ~** (*dans cette direction*) this way; (*dans cette zone*) around there; **de ~** hence.
····▸ (*à ce moment*) then; **c'est ~ que** that's when.

····> **cet homme-~** that man; **ces maisons-~** those houses.
● *interjection*
····> **~** 🔟 **c'est fini** there (now), it's all over!

là-bas /labɑ/ *adv* there; (à l'endroit que l'on indique) over there.

label /labɛl/ *nm* seal, label.

laboratoire /labɔʀatwaʀ/ *nm* laboratory.

laborieux, -ieuse /labɔʀjø, -z/ *adj* laborious; (*personne*) industrious; **classes laborieuses** working classes.

labour /labuʀ/ *nm* ploughing; (US) plowing. **labourer** 🔟 *vt* plough; (US) plow; (déchirer) rip at.

labyrinthe /labiʀɛ̃t/ *nm* maze, labyrinth.

lac /lak/ *nm* lake.

lacer /lase/ 🔟 *vt* lace up.

lacet /lasɛ/ *nm* (de chaussure) (shoe-)lace; (de route) sharp bend.

lâche /lɑʃ/ *adj* cowardly; (détendu) loose; (sans rigueur) lax. ● *nmf* coward.

lâcher /lɑʃe/ 🔟 *vt* let go of; (laisser tomber) drop; (abandonner) give up; (laisser) leave; (libérer) release; (*flèche, balle*) fire; (*juron, phrase*) come out with; (desserrer) loosen; **~ prise** let go. ● *vi* give way.

lâcheté /lɑʃte/ *nf* cowardice.

lacrymogène /lakʀimɔʒɛn/ *adj* **gaz ~** tear gas.

lacune /lakyn/ *nf* gap.

là-dedans /lad(ə)dɑ̃/ *adv* (près) in here; (plus loin) in there.

là-dessous /lad(ə)su/ *adv* (près) under here; (plus loin) under there.

là-dessus /lad(ə)sy/ *adv* (sur une surface) on here; (plus loin) on there; (sur ce) with that; (quelque temps après) after that; **qu'avez-vous à dire ~?** what have you got to say about it?

ladite /ladit/ →**ledit.**

lagune /lagyn/ *nf* lagoon.

là-haut /lao/ *adv* (en hauteur) up here; (plus loin) up there; (à l'étage) upstairs.

laïc /laik/ *nm* layman.

laid, ~e /lɛ, lɛd/ *adj* ugly; (action) vile. **laideur** *nf* ugliness.

lainage /lɛnaʒ/ *nm* woollen garment.

laine /lɛn/ *nf* wool; **de ~** woollen.

laïque /laik/ *adj* (état, loi) secular; (habit, personne) lay; (école) nondenominational. ● *nmf* layman, laywoman.

laisse /lɛs/ *nf* lead, leash; **tenir en ~** keep on a lead.

laisser /lese/ 🔟 *vt* (déposer) leave, drop off; (confier) leave (**à qn** with sb); (abandonner) leave; (rendre) **~ qn perplexe/froid** leave sb puzzled/cold; **~ qch à qn** (céder, prêter) let sb have sth; (donner) (choix, temps) give sb sth. □ **se ~** *vpr* **se ~ persuader/insulter** let oneself be persuaded/insulted; **elle ne se laisse pas faire** she won't be pushed around; **laisse-toi faire** leave it to me/him/her etc.; **se ~ aller** let oneself go. ● *v aux* **~ qn/qch faire** let sb/sth do; **laisse-moi faire** (ne m'aide pas) let me do it; (je m'en occupe) leave it to me; **laisse faire!** so what! **laisser-aller** *nm inv* carelessness; (dans la tenue) scruffiness. **laissez-passer** *nm inv* pass.

lait /lɛ/ *nm* milk; **~ longue conservation** long-life ou UHT milk; **frère/sœur de ~** foster-brother/-sister. **laitage** *nm* milk product. **laiterie** *nf* dairy. **laiteux, -euse** *adj* milky.

laitier, -ière /letje, -jɛʀ/ *adj* dairy. ● *nm, f* (livreur) milkman, milkwoman.

laiton /lɛtɔ̃/ *nm* brass.

laitue /lety/ *nf* lettuce.

lama /lama/ *nm* llama.

lambeau (*pl* **~x**) /lɑ̃bo/ *nm* shred; **en ~x** in shreds.

lame /lam/ *nf* blade; (lamelle) strip; (vague) wave; **~ de fond** ground swell; **~ de rasoir** razor blade.

lamentable /lamɑ̃tabl/ *adj* deplorable. **lamenter (se)** 🔟 *vpr* moan (**sur** about, over).

lampadaire /lɑ̃padɛʀ/ *nm* standard lamp; (de rue) street lamp.

lampe /lɑ̃p/ *nf* lamp; (ampoule) bulb; (de radio) valve; **~ (de poche)** torch; (US) flashlight; **~ à souder** blowlamp; **~ de chevet** bedside lamp; **~ solaire, ~ à bronzer** sunlamp.

lance /lɑ̃s/ *nf* spear; (de tournoi) lance; (tuyau) hose; **~ d'incendie** fire hose.

lancement /lɑ̃smɑ̃/ *nm* throwing; (de navire, de missile, mise sur le marché) launch.

lance-missiles /lɑ̃smisil/ nm inv missile launcher.

lance-pierres /lɑ̃spjɛʀ/ nm inv catapult.

lancer /lɑ̃se/ **10** vt throw; (avec force) hurl; (navire, idée, artiste) launch; (émettre) give out; (regard) cast; (moteur) start. □ **se** ~ vpr (Sport) gain momentum; (se précipiter) rush; **se** ~ **dans** (explication) launch into; (passe-temps) take up. ● nm throw; (action) throwing.

lancinant, ~**e** /lɑ̃sinɑ̃, -t/ adj (douleur) shooting; (problème) nagging.

landau /lɑ̃do/ nm pram; (US) baby carriage.

lande /lɑ̃d/ nf heath, moor.

langage /lɑ̃gaʒ/ nm language; ~ **machine/de programmation** machine/programming language.

langouste /lɑ̃gust/ nf spiny lobster. **langoustine** nf Dublin Bay prawn.

langue /lɑ̃g/ nf (Anat) tongue; (Ling) language; **il m'a tiré la** ~ he stuck his tongue out at me; **de** ~ **anglaise** (personne) English-speaking; (journal) English-language; ~ **maternelle** mother tongue; ~ **vivante** modern language.

lanière /lanjɛʀ/ nf strap.

lanterne /lɑ̃tɛʀn/ nf lantern; (électrique) lamp; (de voiture) sidelight.

lapin /lapɛ̃/ nm rabbit; **poser un** ~ **à qn** **1** stand sb up; **le coup du** ~ rabbit punch; (en voiture) whiplash injury.

lapsus /lapsys/ nm slip (of the tongue).

laque /lak/ nf lacquer; (pour cheveux) hairspray; (peinture) gloss paint.

laquelle /lakɛl/ pron →LEQUEL.

lard /laʀ/ nm streaky bacon.

large /laʀʒ/ adj wide, broad; (grand) large; (généreux) generous; **avoir les idées** ~**s** be broad-minded; ~ **d'esprit** broad-minded. ● adv (calculer, mesurer) on the generous side; **voir** ~ think big. ● nm **faire 10 cm de** ~ be 10 cm wide; **le** ~ (mer) the open sea; **au** ~ **de** (Naut) off. **largement** adv widely; (ouvrir) wide; (amplement) amply; (généreusement) generously; (au moins) easily.

largesse /laʀʒɛs/ nf generous gift.

largeur /laʀʒœʀ/ nf width, breadth; ~ **d'esprit** broad-mindedness.

larguer /laʀge/ **1** vt drop; ~ **les amarres** cast off.

larme /laʀm/ nf tear; (goutte **1**) drop; **en** ~**s** in tears.

larmoyant, ~**e** /laʀmwajɑ̃, -t/ adj full of tears. **larmoyer** **31** vi (yeux) water; (pleurnicher) whine.

larynx /laʀɛ̃ks/ nm larynx.

las, ~**se** /lɑ, lɑs/ adj weary.

lasagnes /lazaɲ/ nfpl lasagna.

laser /lazɛʀ/ nm laser.

lasser /lɑse/ **1** vt weary. □ **se** ~ vpr grow tired, get weary (**de** of).

latéral, ~**e** (mpl -**aux**) /lateʀal, -o/ adj lateral.

latin, ~**e** /latɛ̃, -in/ adj Latin. ● nm (Ling) Latin.

latte /lat/ nf lath; (de plancher) board; (de siège) slat; (de mur, plafond) lath.

lauréat, ~**e** /loʀea, -t/ adj prizewinning. ● nm, f prize-winner.

laurier /loʀje/ nm (Bot) laurel; (Culin) bay-leaves.

lavable /lavabl/ adj washable.

lavabo /lavabo/ nm wash-basin; ~**s** toilet(s).

lavage /lavaʒ/ nm washing; ~ **de cerveau** brainwashing.

lavande /lavɑ̃d/ nf lavender.

lave /lav/ nf lava.

lave-glace (pl ~**s**) /lavglas/ nm windscreen washer.

lave-linge /lavlɛ̃ʒ/ nm inv washing machine.

laver /lave/ **1** vt wash; ~ **qn de** (fig) clear sb of. □ **se** ~ vpr wash (oneself); **se** ~ **les mains** wash one's hands.

laverie /lavʀi/ nf ~ **(automatique)** launderette; (US) laundromat.

lave-vaisselle /lavvɛsɛl/ nm inv dishwasher.

laxatif, -ive /laksatif, -v/ adj & nm laxative.

layette /lɛjɛt/ nf baby clothes.

---

le, la, l' (pl **les**) /lə, la, l, le/

l' before vowel or mute h.

● déterminant

····➤ the.

····➤ (notion générale) **aimer la**

musique like music; **l'amour** love.

····➤ (possession) **avoir les yeux verts** have green eyes; **il s'est cassé la jambe** he broke his leg.

····➤ (prix) **10 euros ∼ kilo** 10 euros a kilo.

····➤ (temps) **∼ lundi** on Mondays; **tous les mardis** every Tuesday.

····➤ (avec nom propre) **les Dury** the Durys; **la reine Margot** Queen Margot; **la Belgique** Belgium.

····➤ (avec adjectif) the; **je veux la rouge** I want the red one; **les riches** the rich.

● pronom

····➤ (homme) him; (femme) her; (chose, animal) it; (au pluriel) them.

····➤ (remplaçant une phrase) **je te l'avais bien dit** I told you so; **je ∼ croyais aussi** I thought so too.

lécher /leʃe/ **14** vt lick; (flamme) lick; (mer) lap.

lèche-vitrines /lɛʃvitʀin/ nm inv **faire du ∼** go window-shopping.

leçon /ləsɔ̃/ nf lesson; **faire la ∼ à** lecture sb; **∼ particulière** private lesson; **∼s de conduite** driving lessons.

lecteur, -trice /lɛktœʀ, -tʀis/ nm, f reader; (Univ) foreign language assistant; **∼ de cassettes** cassette player; **∼ de disquettes** (disk) drive; **∼ laser** CD player; **∼ optique** optical scanner.

lecture /lɛktyʀ/ nf reading.

ledit, ladite (pl **lesdit(e)s**) /lədi, ladit, ledi(t)/ adj the aforementioned.

légal, ∼e (mpl **-aux**) /legal, -o/ adj legal. **légaliser** **1** vt legalize. **légalité** nf legality; (loi) law.

légendaire /leʒɑ̃dɛʀ/ adj legendary. **légende** nf (histoire, inscription) legend; (de carte) key; (d'illustration) caption.

léger, -ère /leʒe, -ɛʀ/ adj light; (bruit, faute, maladie) slight; (café, argument) weak; (imprudent) thoughtless; (frivole) fickle; **à la légère** thoughtlessly. **légèrement** adv lightly; (agir) thoughtlessly; (un peu) slightly. **légèreté** nf lightness; thoughtlessness.

légion /leʒjɔ̃/ nf legion.

> **Légion d'honneur** The system of honours awarded by the state for meritorious achievement. The Président de la République is the Grand maître. The basic rank is Chevalier. Holders of the Légion d'honneur are entitled to wear une rosette (a small red lapel ribbon).

légionellose /leʒjɔnɛloz/ nf (Méd) legionnaire's disease.

législatif, -ive /leʒislatif, -v/ adj legislative; **élections législatives** general election.

législature /leʒislatyʀ/ nf term of office.

légitime /leʒitim/ adj (Jur) legitimate; (fig) rightful; **agir en état de ∼ défense** act in self-defence. **légitimité** nf legitimacy.

legs /lɛg/ nm legacy; (d'effets personnels) bequest.

léguer /lege/ **14** vt bequeath.

légume /legym/ nm vegetable.

lendemain /lɑ̃dmɛ̃/ nm **le ∼** the next day; (fig) the future; **le ∼ de** the day after; **le ∼ matin/soir** the next morning/evening; **du jour au ∼** from one day to the next.

lent, ∼e /lɑ̃, -t/ adj slow. **lentement** adv slowly. **lenteur** nf slowness.

lentille /lɑ̃tij/ nf (Culin) lentil; (verre) lens; **∼s de contact** contact lenses.

léopard /leɔpaʀ/ nm leopard.

lèpre /lɛpʀ/ nf leprosy.

---

lequel, laquelle (pl **les-quel-(le)s**), **auquel** (pl **auxquel(le)s**), **duquel** (pl **desquel(le)s**) /ləkɛl, lakɛl, lekɛl, okɛl, dykɛl, dekɛl/

à + lequel = auquel,
à + lesquel(le)s = auxquel(le)s;
de + lequel = duquel,
de + lesquel(le)s = desquel(le)s

● pronom

····➤ (relatif) (personne) who; (complément indirect) whom; (autres cas) which; **l'ami auquel tu as écrit** the friend to whom you wrote; **les voisins chez lesquels Sophie est allée** the neighbours whose house Sophie went to.

····➤ (interrogatif) which; **∼ tu**

veux? which one do you want?
● *adjectif*
····▸ **auquel cas** in which case.

les /le/ ➠**le.**

lesbienne /lɛsbjɛn/ *nf* lesbian.

léser /leze/ **14** *vt* wrong.

lésiner /lezine/ **1** *vi* **ne pas ~ sur** not stint on.

lesquels, lesquelles /lekɛl/ ➠**lequel.**

lessive /lesiv/ *nf* (poudre) washing-powder; (liquide) washing liquid; (linge, action) washing.

leste /lɛst/ *adj* agile, nimble; (grivois) coarse.

Lettonie /letɔni/ *nf* Latvia.

lettre /lɛtʀ/ *nf* letter; **à la ~, au pied de la ~** literally; **en toutes ~s** in full; **les ~s** (Univ) (the) arts.

leucémie /løsemi/ *nf* leukaemia.

leur (*pl* **~s**) /lœʀ/
● *pronom personnel invariable*
····▸ them; **donne-le ~** give it to them; **je ~ fais confiance** I trust them.
● *adjectif possessif*
····▸ their; **~s enfants** their children; **à ~ arrivée** when they arrived.
● **le leur, la leur,** (*pl* **les leurs**) *pronom possessif*
····▸ theirs; **chacun le ~** one each; **je suis des ~s** I am one of them.

levain /ləvɛ̃/ *nm* leaven.

levé, ~e /ləve/ *adj* (debout) up.

levée /ləve/ *nf* (de peine, de sanctions) lifting; (de courrier) collection; (de troupes, d'impôts) levying.

lever /ləve/ **6** *vt* lift (up), raise; (interdiction) lift; (séance) close; (armée, impôts) levy. ● *vi* (pâte) rise. □ **se ~** *vpr* get up; (soleil, rideau) rise; (jour) break. ● *nm* **au ~** on getting up; **~ du jour** daybreak; **~ de rideau** (Théât) curtain (up); **~ du soleil** sunrise.

levier /ləvje/ *nm* lever; **~ de changement de vitesse** gear lever.

lèvre /lɛvʀ/ *nf* lip.

lévrier /levʀije/ *nm* greyhound.

levure /ləvyʀ/ *nf* yeast; **~ chimique** baking powder.

lexique /lɛksik/ *nm* vocabulary; (glossaire) lexicon.

lézard /lezaʀ/ *nm* lizard.

lézarde /lezaʀd/ *nf* crack.

liaison /ljezɔ̃/ *nf* connection; (transport, Ordinat) link; (contact) contact; (Gram, Mil) liaison; (amoureuse) affair; **être en ~ avec** be in contact with; **assurer la ~ entre** liaise between.

liane /ljan/ *nf* creeper.

Liban /libã/ *nm* Lebanon.

libeller /libele/ **1** *vt* (chèque) write; (contrat) draw up; **libellé à l'ordre de** made out to.

libellule /libelyl/ *nf* dragonfly.

libéral, ~e (*mpl* **-aux**) /liberal, -o/ *adj* liberal; **les professions ~es** the professions.

libérateur, -trice /liberatœʀ, -tʀis/ *adj* liberating. ● *nm, f* liberator. **libération** *nf* release; (de pays) liberation.

libérer /libere/ **14** *vt* (personne) free, release; (pays) liberate, free; (bureau, lieux) vacate; (gaz) release. □ **se ~** *vpr* free oneself.

liberté /libɛʀte/ *nf* freedom, liberty; (loisir) free time; **être/mettre en ~** be/set free; **~ conditionnelle** parole; **~ provisoire** provisional release (pending trial); **~ surveillée** probation; **~s publiques** civil liberties.

Libertel /libɛʀtɛl/ *nm* (Internet) Freenet.

libraire /libʀɛʀ/ *nmf* bookseller. **librairie** *nf* bookshop.

libre /libʀ/ *adj* free; (place, pièce) vacant, free; (passage) clear; (école) private (usually religious); **~ de qch/de faire** free from sth/to do. **libre-échange** *nm* free trade. **libre-service** (*pl* **libres-services**) *nm* (magasin) self-service shop; (restaurant) self-service restaurant.

licence /lisãs/ *nf* licence; (Univ) degree.

licencié, ~e /lisãsje/ *nm, f* graduate; **~ ès lettres/sciences** Bachelor of Arts/Science.

licenciements /lisãsimã/ *nm* redundancy; (pour faute) dismissal. **licencier** **45** *vt* make redundant; (pour faute) dismiss.

licorne /likɔʀn/ *nf* unicorn.

liège /ljeʒ/ *nm* cork.

lien /ljɛ̃/ nm (rapport) link; (attache) bond, tie; (corde) rope; ~s affectifs/ de parenté emotional/family ties.

lier /lje/ 45 vt tie (up), bind; (relier) link; (engager, unir) bind; ~ conversation strike up a conversation; ils sont très liés they are very close. □ se ~ avec vpr make friends with.

lierre /ljɛʀ/ nm ivy.

lieu (pl ~x) /ljø/ nm place; ~x (locaux) premises; (d'un accident) scene; sur les ~x at the scene; au ~ de instead of; avoir ~ take place; donner ~ à give rise to; tenir ~ de serve as; s'il y a ~ if necessary; en premier ~ firstly; en dernier ~ lastly; ~ commun commonplace; ~ de rencontre meeting place.

lièvre /ljɛvʀ/ nm hare.

lifting /liftiŋ/ nm face-lift.

ligne /liɲ/ nf line; (trajet) route; (de métro, train) line; (formes) lines; (de femme) figure; en ~ (joueurs) lined up; (au téléphone) on the phone; (Ordinat) on line; ~ spécialisée (Internet) dedicated line.

ligoter /ligɔte/ 1 vt tie up.

ligue /lig/ nf league. **liguer (se)** 1 vpr join forces (contre against).

lilas /lila/ nm & a inv lilac.

limace /limas/ nf slug.

limande /limɑ̃d/ nf (poisson) dab.

lime /lim/ nf file; ~ à ongles nail file.

limitation /limitasjɔ̃/ nf limitation; ~ de vitesse speed limit.

limite /limit/ nf limit; (de jardin, champ) boundary; à la ~ de (fig) verging on, bordering on; à la ~ if it comes to it, at a pinch; dans une certaine ~ up to a point; dans la ~ du possible as far as possible. ● adj (vitesse, âge) maximum; cas ~ borderline case; date ~ deadline; date ~ de vente sell-by date.

limiter /limite/ 1 vt limit; (délimiter) form the border of. □ se ~ vpr limit oneself (à to).

limonade /limɔnad/ nf lemonade.

limpide /lɛ̃pid/ adj limpid, clear.

lin /lɛ̃/ nm (tissu) linen.

linge /lɛ̃ʒ/ nm linen; (lessive) washing; (torchon) cloth; ~ (de corps) underwear. **lingerie** nf underwear. **lingette** nf wipe.

lingot /lɛ̃go/ nm ingot.

linguistique /lɛ̃gɥistik/ adj linguistic. ● nf linguistics.

lion /ljɔ̃/ nm lion; le L~ Leo. **lionceau** (pl ~x) nm lion cub. **lionne** nf lioness.

liquidation /likidasjɔ̃/ nf liquidation; (vente) (clearance) sale; entrer en ~ go into liquidation.

liquide /likid/ adj liquid. ● nm (argent) ~ ready money; payer en ~ pay cash; ~ de frein brake fluid.

liquider /likide/ 1 vt liquidate; (vendre) sell.

lire /liʀ/ 39 vt/i read. ● nf lira.

lis[1] /li/ →LIRE 39.

lis[2] /lis/ nm (fleur) lily.

lisible /lizibl/ adj legible; (roman) readable.

lisière /lizjɛʀ/ nf edge.

lisse /lis/ adj smooth.

liste /list/ nf list; ~ d'attente waiting list; ~ électorale register of voters; être sur (la) ~ rouge be ex-directory.

listing /listiŋ/ nm printout.

lit /li/ nm bed; se mettre au ~ get into bed; ~ de camp camp-bed; ~ d'enfant cot; ~ d'une personne single bed; ~ de deux personnes, grand ~ double bed.

literie /litʀi/ nf bedding.

litière /litjɛʀ/ nf litter.

litige /litiʒ/ nm dispute.

litre /litʀ/ nm litre.

littéraire /liteʀɛʀ/ adj literary; (études, formation) arts.

littéral, ~e (mpl -aux) /liteʀal, -o/ adj literal.

littérature /liteʀatyʀ/ nf literature.

littoral (pl -aux) /litɔʀal, -o/ nm coast.

Lituanie /litɥani/ nf Lithuania.

livide /livid/ adj deathly pale.

livraison /livʀɛzɔ̃/ nf delivery.

livre /livʀ/ nf (monnaie, poids) pound. ● nm book; ~ de bord log-book; ~ de compte books; ~ de poche paperback.

livrer /livʀe/ 1 vt (Comm) deliver; (abandonner) give over (à to); (remettre) (coupable, document) hand over (à to); livré à soi-même left to oneself. □ se ~ vpr (se rendre) give oneself up (à to); se ~ à (boisson, actes) indulge in; (ami) confide in.

livret /livʀɛ/ *nm* book; (Mus) libretto; **~ de caisse d'épargne** savings book; **~ scolaire** school report (book).

livreur, -euse /livʀœʀ, -øz/ *nm, f* delivery man, delivery woman.

local¹, ~e (*mpl* **-aux**) /lɔkal, -o/ *adj* local.

local² (*pl* **-aux**) /lɔkal, -o/ *nm* premises; **locaux** premises.

localement /lɔkalmã/ *adv* locally.

localisation /lɔkalizasjɔ̃/ *nf* localization.

localiser /lɔkalize/ **1** *vt* (repérer) locate; (circonscrire) localize.

locataire /lɔkatɛʀ/ *nmf* tenant; (de chambre) lodger.

location /lɔkasjɔ̃/ *nf* (de maison) renting; (de voiture, de matériel) hire, rental; (de place) booking, reservation; (par propriétaire) renting out; hiring out; **en ~** (*voiture*) on hire, rented; (*habiter*) in rented accommodation.

locomotive /lɔkɔmɔtiv/ *nf* engine, locomotive.

locution /lɔkysjɔ̃/ *nf* phrase.

loft /lɔft/ *nm* loft (apartment).

loge /lɔʒ/ *nf* (de concierge, de francmaçons) lodge; (d'acteur) dressing-room; (de spectateur) box.

logement /lɔʒmã/ *nm* accommodation; (appartement) flat; (habitat) housing.

loger /lɔʒe/ **40** *vt* (réfugié, famille) house; (*ami*) put up; (*client*) accommodate. ● *vi* live. □ **se ~** *vpr* live; **trouver à se ~** find accommodation; **se ~ dans** (*balle*) lodge itself in.

logiciel /lɔʒisjɛl/ *nm* software; **~ contributif** shareware; **~ d'application** application software; **~ de groupe** groupware; **~ de jeux** games software; **~ de navigation** browser; **~ public** freeware.

logique /lɔʒik/ *adj* logical. ● *nf* logic.

logis /lɔʒi/ *nm* dwelling.

logistique /lɔʒistik/ *nf* logistics.

loi /lwa/ *nf* law.

loin /lwɛ̃/ *adv* far (away); **au ~** far away; **de ~** from far away; (de beaucoup) by far; **de là ~** far from it; **plus ~** further; **il revient de ~** (fig) he had a close shave.

lointain, ~e /lwɛ̃tɛ̃, -ɛn/ *adj* distant. ● *nm* distance; **dans le ~** in the distance.

loisir /lwaziʀ/ *nm* (spare) time; **~s** (temps libre) leisure, spare time; (distractions) leisure activities; **à ~** at one's leisure; **avoir le ~ de faire** have time to do.

londonien, ~ne /lɔ̃dɔnjɛ̃, -ɛn/ *adj* London. **L~, ~e** *nm, f* Londoner.

Londres /lɔ̃dʀ/ *npr* London.

long, longue /lɔ̃, lɔ̃g/ *adj* long; **à ~ terme** long-term; **être ~ à faire** be a long time doing. ● *nm* **de ~** (mesure) long; **de ~ en large** back and forth; **(tout) le ~ de** (all) along. ● *adv* **en dire ~ sur qn/qch** say a lot about sb/sth; **en savoir plus ~ sur** know more about.

longer /lɔ̃ʒe/ **40** *vt* go along; (limiter) border.

longitude /lɔ̃ʒityd/ *nf* longitude.

longtemps /lɔ̃tã/ *adv* a long time; **avant ~** before long; **trop ~** too long; **ça prendra ~** it will take a long time; **prendre plus ~ que prévu** take longer than anticipated.

longuement /lɔ̃gmã/ *adv* (longtemps) for a long time; (en détail) at length.

longueur /lɔ̃gœʀ/ *nf* length; **~s** (de texte) over-long parts; **à ~ de journée** all day long; **en ~** lengthwise; **~ d'onde** wavelength.

lopin /lɔpɛ̃/ *nm* **~ de terre** patch of land.

loque /lɔk/ *nf* **~s** rags; **~ (humaine)** (human) wreck.

loquet /lɔkɛ/ *nm* latch.

lors de /lɔʀdə/ *prép* (au moment de) at the time of; (pendant) during.

lorsque /lɔʀsk(ə)/ *conj* when.

losange /lɔzɑ̃ʒ/ *nm* diamond.

lot /lo/ *nm* (portion) share; (aux enchères) lot; (Ordinat) batch; (destin) lot; **gagner le gros ~** hit the jackpot.

loterie /lɔtʀi/ *nf* lottery.

lotion /losjɔ̃/ *nf* lotion.

lotissement /lɔtismã/ *nm* (à construire) building plot; (construit) (housing) development.

louable /luabl/ *adj* praiseworthy.

louange *nf* praise.

louche /luʃ/ *adj* shady, dubious. ● *nf* ladle.

loucher /luʃe/ **1** *vi* squint.

louer /lwe/ **1** *vt* (approuver) praise (**de** for); (prendre en location) (*maison*) rent; (*voiture, matériel*) hire, rent; (*place*) book, reserve; (donner en location) (*maison*) rent out; (*matériel*) rent out, hire out; **à ~** to let, for rent (US).

loufoque /lufɔk/ *adj* **1** crazy.

loup /lu/ *nm* wolf.

loupe /lup/ *nf* magnifying glass.

louper /lupe/ **1** *vt* **1** miss; (*examen*) flunk **1**.

lourd, ~e /luʀ, -d/ *adj* heavy; (*faute*) serious; **~ de dangers** fraught with danger; **il fait ~** it's close *ou* muggy.

loutre /lutʀ/ *nf* otter.

louveteau (*pl* **~x**) /luvto/ *nm* wolf cub; (scout) Cub (Scout).

loyal, ~e (*mpl* **-aux**) /lwajal, -o/ *adj* loyal, faithful; (honnête) fair. **loyauté** *nf* loyalty; fairness.

loyer /lwaje/ *nm* rent.

lu /ly/ ⇒ **LIRE** 39.

lubrifiant /lybʀifjɑ̃/ *nm* lubricant.

lucide /lysid/ *adj* lucid. **lucidité** *nf* lucidity.

lucratif, -ive /lykʀatif, -v/ *adj* lucrative; **à but non ~** non-profitmaking.

ludiciel /lydisjɛl/ *nm* (Ordinat) games software.

lueur /lɥœʀ/ *nf* (faint) light, glimmer; (fig) glimmer, gleam.

luge /lyʒ/ *nf* toboggan.

lugubre /lygybʀ/ *adj* gloomy.

---

lui /lɥi/

● *pronom*

····▸ (masculin) (sujet) he; **~, il est à l'étranger** he's abroad; **c'est ~!** it's him!; (objet) him; (animal) it; **c'est à ~** it's his; **elle conduit mieux que ~** she's a better driver than he is.

····▸ (féminin) her; **je ~ ai annoncé** I told her.

····▸ (masculin/féminin) **donne-le-~** give it to him/her.

---

lui-même /lɥimɛm/ *pron* himself; (animal) itself.

luire /lɥiʀ/ **17** *vi* shine; (reflet humide) glisten; (reflet chaud, faible) glow.

lumière /lymjɛʀ/ *nf* light; **~s** (connaissances) knowledge; **faire (toute)**

la ~ sur une affaire clear a matter up.

luminaire /lyminɛʀ/ *nm* lamp.

lumineux, -euse /lyminø, -z/ *adj* luminous; (éclairé) illuminated; (*rayon*) of light; (radieux) radiant; **source lumineuse** light source.

lunaire /lynɛʀ/ *adj* lunar.

lunatique /lynatik/ *adj* temperamental.

lunch /lœnʃ/ *nm* buffet lunch.

lundi /lœdi/ *nm* Monday.

lune /lyn/ *nf* moon; **~ de miel** honeymoon.

lunettes /lynɛt/ *nfpl* glasses; (de protection) goggles; **~ de ski/natation** ski/swimming goggles; **~ noires** dark glasses; **~ de soleil** sun-glasses.

lustre /lystʀ/ *nm* (éclat) lustre; (objet) chandelier.

lutin /lytɛ̃/ *nm* goblin.

lutte /lyt/ *nf* fight, struggle; (Sport) wrestling. **lutter** **1** *vi* fight, struggle; (Sport) wrestle. **lutteur, -euse** *nm, f* fighter; (Sport) wrestler.

luxe /lyks/ *nm* luxury; **de ~** luxury; (*produit*) de luxe.

Luxembourg /lyksɑ̃buʀ/ *nm* Luxemburg.

luxer (se) /(sə)lykse/ **1** *vpr* **se ~ le genou** dislocate one's knee.

luxueux, -euse /lyksɥø, -z/ *adj* luxurious.

lycée /lise/ *nm* (secondary) school. **lycéen, ~ne** *nm, f* pupil (at secondary school).

lyophilisé, ~e /ljɔfilize/ *adj* freeze-dried.

lyrique /liʀik/ *adj* (poésie) lyric; (passionné) lyrical; **artiste/théâtre ~** opera singer/house.

lys /lis/ *nm* lily.

Mm

m¹ /m/ ➡ME.

ma /ma/ ➡MON.

macabre /makabʀ/ adj macabre.

macadam /makadam/ nm Tarmac®.

macaron /makaʀɔ̃/ nm (gâteau) macaroon; (insigne) badge.

macédoine /masedwan/ nf mixed diced vegetables; ~ **de fruits** fruit salad.

macérer /maseʀe/ **14** vt/i soak; (dans du vinaigre) pickle.

mâcher /mɑʃe/ **1** vt chew; **ne pas ~ ses mots** not mince one's words.

machin /maʃɛ̃/ nm **1** (chose) thing; (dont on ne trouve pas le nom) whatsit **1**.

machinal, ~e (mpl **-aux**) /maʃinal, -o/ adj automatic. **machinalement** adv mechanically, automatically.

machination /maʃinasjɔ̃/ nf plot; **des ~s** machinations.

machine /maʃin/ nf machine; (d'un train, navire) engine; ~ **à écrire** typewriter; ~ **à laver/coudre** washing-/sewing-machine; ~ **à sous** fruit machine; (US) slot machine.
machine-outil (pl **machines-outils**) nf machine tool. **machinerie** nf machinery.

machiniste /maʃinist/ nm (Théât) stage-hand; (conducteur) driver.

mâchoire /mɑʃwaʀ/ nf jaw.

mâchonner /mɑʃɔne/ **1** vt chew.

maçon /masɔ̃/ nm (entrepreneur) builder; (poseur de briques) bricklayer; (qui construit en pierre) mason. **maçonnerie** nf (briques) brickwork; (pierres) stonework, masonry; (travaux) building.

madame (pl **mesdames**) /madam, medam/ nf (à une inconnue) (dans une lettre) M~ Dear Madam; **bonjour**, ~ good morning; **mesdames et messieurs** ladies and gentlemen; (à une femme dont on connaît le nom) (dans une lettre) **Chère M~** Dear Mrs ou Ms X; **bonjour**, ~ good morning Mrs ou Ms X; **oui M ~ le Ministre**

yes Minister; (formule de respect) **oui M~** yes madam.

mademoiselle (pl **mesdemoiselles**) /madmwazɛl, medmwazɛl/ nf (à une inconnue) (dans une lettre) M~ Dear Madam; **bonjour**, ~ good morning; **entrez mesdemoiselles** come in (ladies); (à une jeune fille dont on connaît le nom) (dans une lettre) **Chère M~** Dear Ms ou Miss X; **bonjour**, ~ good morning Miss ou Ms X.

magasin /magazɛ̃/ nm shop, store; (entrepôt) warehouse; (d'une arme) magazine; **en ~** in stock.

magazine /magazin/ nm magazine; (émission) programme.

Maghreb /magʀɛb/ nm North Africa.

magicien, ~ne /maʒisjɛ̃, -ɛn/ nm, f magician.

magie /maʒi/ nf magic. **magique** adj magic; (mystérieux) magical.

magistral, ~e (mpl **-aux**) /maʒistʀal, -o/ adj masterly; (grand: hum) tremendous; **cours ~** lecture.

magistrat /maʒistʀa/ nm magistrate.

magistrature /maʒistʀatyʀ/ nf judiciary; (fonction) public office.

magner (se) /(sə)maɲe/ **1** vpr ✖ get a move on.

magnétique /maɲetik/ adj magnetic. **magnétiser 1** vt magnetize. **magnétisme** nm magnetism.

magnétophone /maɲetɔfɔn/ nm tape recorder; (à cassettes) cassette recorder.

magnétoscope /maɲetɔskɔp/ nm video recorder.

magnificence /maɲifisɑ̃s/ nf magnificence. **magnifique** adj magnificent.

magot /mago/ nm **1** hoard (of money).

magouille /maguj/ nf **1** scheming, skulduggery.

magret /magʀɛ/ nm ~ **de canard** duck breast.

mai /mɛ/ nm May.

maigre /mɛgʀ/ adj thin; (viande) lean; (yaourt) low-fat; (fig) poor, meagre; **faire ~** abstain from meat. **maigreur** nf thinness; leanness; (fig) meagreness.

maigrir /megʀiʀ/ **2** vi get thin(ner); (en suivant un régime) slim. ● vt make thin(ner).

maille /mɑj/ nf stitch; (de filet) mesh; ~ **qui file** ladder, run; **avoir** ~ **à partir avec qn** have a brush with sb.

maillet /majɛ/ nm mallet.

maillon /mɑjɔ̃/ nm link.

maillot /majo/ nm (Sport) shirt, jersey; (~ **de corps**) vest; (US) undershirt; (~ **de bain**) (swimming) costume.

main /mɛ̃/ nf hand; **donner la** ~ **à qn** hold sb's hand; **se donner la** ~ hold hands; **en** ~**s propres** in person; **en bonnes** ~**s** in good hands; ~ **courante** handrail; **se faire la** ~ get the hang of it; **perdre la** ~ lose one's touch; **sous la** ~ to hand; **vol à** ~ **armée** armed robbery; **fait (à la)** ~ handmade; **haut les** ~**s!** hands up! **main-d'œuvre** (pl **mains-d'œuvre**) nf labour; (ouvriers) labour force.

main-forte /mɛ̃fɔʀt/ nf inv **prêter** ~ **à qn** come to sb's aid.

maint, ~**e** /mɛ̃, mɛ̃t/ adj many a (+ sg); ~**s** many; **à** ~**es reprises** many times.

maintenant /mɛ̃t(ə)nɑ̃/ adv now; (de nos jours) nowadays; (l'époque actuelle) today.

maintenir /mɛ̃t(ə)niʀ/ 58 vt keep, maintain; (soutenir) support, hold up; (affirmer) maintain; (decision) stand by. □ **se** ~ vpr (tendance) persist; (prix, malade) remain stable.

maintien /mɛ̃tjɛ̃/ nm (attitude) bearing; (conservation) maintenance.

maire /mɛʀ/ nm mayor.

mairie /meʀi/ nf town hall; (administration) town council.

mais /mɛ/ conj but; ~ **oui** of course; ~ **non** of course not.

maïs /mais/ nm maize, corn; (Culin) sweetcorn.

maison /mɛzɔ̃/ nf house; (foyer) home; (immeuble) building; (~ **de commerce**) firm; **à la** ~ at home; **rentrer ou aller à la** ~ go home; ~ **des jeunes (et de la culture)** youth club; ~ **de repos** rest home; ~ **de convalescence** convalescent home; ~ **de retraite** old people's home; ~ **mère** parent company. ● adj inv (Culin) home-made.

Maison des jeunes et de la culture The *Maison des jeunes et de la culture (MJC)* is an organization which provides community arts, sports and leisure activities for young people. Attached to the Ministry of Sport, the *MJC* was founded in 1964 to enable young people in rural communities to take part in cultural activities in winter.

maître, -esse /mɛtʀ, -ɛs/ adj (qui contrôle) **être** ~ **de soi** be one's own master; ~ **de la situation** in control of the situation; (principal) (idée, qualité) key, main. ● nm, f (Scol) teacher; (d'animal) owner, master. ● nm (expert, guide) master; (dirigeant) leader; ~ **de conférences** senior lecturer; ~ **d'hôtel** head waiter; (domestique) butler. **maître-assistant**, ~ **e** (pl **maîtres-assistants**) nm, f lecturer. **maître-chanteur** (pl **maîtres-chanteurs**) nm blackmailer. **maître-nageur** (pl **maîtres-nageurs**) nm swimming instructor. **maîtresse** nf (amante) mistress.

maîtrise /metʀiz/ nf mastery; (contrôle) control; (Mil) supremacy; (Univ) master's degree; (~ **de soi**) self-control.

maîtriser /metʀize/ 1 vt (sujet, technique) master; (incendie, sentiment, personne) control. □ **se** ~ vpr have self-control.

maïzena® /maizena/ nf cornflour.

majesté /maʒeste/ nf majesty.

majestueux, -euse /maʒestɥø, z/ adj majestic.

majeur, ~**e** /maʒœʀ/ adj major, main; (Jur) of age; **en** ~**e partie** mostly; **la** ~**e partie de** most of. ● nm middle finger.

majoration /maʒɔʀasjɔ̃/ nf increase (de in). **majorer** 1 vt increase.

majoritaire /maʒɔʀitɛʀ/ adj majority; **être** ~ be in the majority. **majorité** nf majority; **en** ~ chiefly.

Majorque /maʒɔʀk/ nf Majorca.

majuscule /maʒyskyl/ adj capital. ● nf capital letter.

mal¹ /mal/ adv badly; (incorrectement) wrong(ly); **aller** ~ (personne) be unwell; (affaires) go badly; ~ **entendre/ comprendre** not hear/understand properly; ~ **en point** in a bad state; **pas** ~ quite a lot. ● adj inv bad, wrong; **c'est ~ de** it is wrong ou bad to; **ce n'est pas ~** 🛈 it's not bad; **Nick n'est pas ~** 🛈Nick is not bad-looking.

mal² (*pl* **maux**) /mal, mo/ *nm* evil; (douleur) pain, ache; (maladie) disease; (effort) trouble; (dommage) harm; (malheur) misfortune; **avoir ~ à la tête/à la gorge** have a headache/ a sore throat; **avoir le ~ de mer/du pays** be seasick/ homesick; **faire ~** hurt; **se faire ~** hurt oneself; **j'ai ~** it hurts; **faire du ~ à** hurt, harm; **se donner du ~ pour faire qch** go to a lot of trouble to do sth.

malade /malad/ *adj* sick, ill; (*bras, œil*) bad; (*plante, poumons, côlon*) diseased; **tomber ~** fall ill; (*fou* 🛈) mad. ● *nmf* sick person; (d'un médecin) patient; **~ mental** mentally ill person.

maladie /maladi/ *nf* illness, disease; (manie 🛈) mania.

maladif, -ive /maladif, -v/ *adj* sickly; (*jalousie, peur*) pathological.

maladresse /maladʀɛs/ *nf* clumsiness; (erreur) blunder.

maladroit, ~e /maladʀwa, -t/ *adj* clumsy; (sans tact) tactless.

malaise /malɛz/ *nm* feeling of faintness; (gêne) uneasiness; (état de crise) unrest.

malaisé, ~e /maleze/ *adj* difficult.

Malaisie /malɛzi/ *nf* Malaysia.

malaria /malaʀja/ *nf* malaria.

malaxer /malakse/ 🛈 *vt* (pétrir) knead; (mêler) mix.

malchance /malʃɑ̃s/ *nf* misfortune. **malchanceux, -euse** *adj* unlucky.

mâle /mɑl/ *adj* male; (viril) manly. ● *nm* male.

malédiction /malediksjɔ̃/ *nf* curse. **maléfice** /malefis/ *nm* evil spell. **maléfique** *adj* evil.

malentendant, ~e /malɑ̃tɑ̃dɑ̃, -t/ *adj* hard of hearing.

malentendu /malɑ̃tɑ̃dy/ *nm* misunderstanding.

malfaçon /malfasɔ̃/ *nf* defect.

malfaisant, ~e /malfəzɑ̃, -t/ *adj* harmful; (personne) evil.

malfaiteur /malfɛtœʀ/ *nm* criminal.

malformation /malfɔʀmasjɔ̃/ *nf* malformation.

malgré /malgʀe/ *prép* in spite of, despite; **~ tout** nevertheless.

malheur /malœʀ/ *nm* misfortune; (accident) accident; **par ~** unfortunately; **faire un ~** 🛈 be a big hit; **porter ~** be ou bring bad luck.

malheureusement /malœ ʀøzmɑ̃/ *adv* unfortunately.

malheureux, -euse /malœʀø, -z/ *adj* unhappy; (regrettable) unfortunate; (sans succès) unlucky; (insignifiant) paltry, pathetic. ● *nm, f* (poor) wretch.

malhonnête /malɔnɛt/ *adj* dishonest. **malhonnêteté** *nf* dishonesty.

malice /malis/ *nf* mischief; **sans ~** harmless; **avec ~** mischievously. **malicieux, -ieuse** *adj* mischievous.

malignité /maliɲite/ *nf* malignancy. **malin, -igne** *adj* clever, smart; (méchant) malicious; (tumeur) malignant; (difficile 🛈) difficult.

malingre /malɛ̃gʀ/ *adj* puny.

malle /mal/ *nf* (valise) trunk; (Auto) boot; (US) trunk.

mallette /malɛt/ *nf* (small) suitcase; (pour le bureau) briefcase.

malmener /malməne/ 🛈 *vt* manhandle; (fig) give a rough ride to.

malnutrition /malnytʀisjɔ̃/ *nf* malnutrition.

malodorant, ~e /malɔdɔʀɑ̃, -t/ *adj* smelly, foul-smelling.

malpoli, ~e /malpɔli/ *adj* rude, impolite.

malpropre /malpʀɔpʀ/ *adj* dirty.

malsain, ~e /malsɛ̃, -ɛn/ *adj* unhealthy.

malt /malt/ *nm* malt.

Malte /malt/ *nf* Malta.

maltraiter /maltʀete/ 🛈 *vt* illtreat.

malveillance /malvejɑ̃s/ *nf* malice. **malveillant, ~e** *adj* malicious.

maman /mamɑ̃/ *nf* mum(my), mother; (US) mom(my).

mamelle /mamɛl/ *nf* teat.

mamelon /mamlɔ̃/ *nm* (Anat) nipple; (colline) hillock.

mamie /mami/ *nf* 🛈 granny.

mammifère /mamifɛʀ/ *nm* mammal.

manche /mɑ̃ʃ/ *nf* sleeve; (Sport, Pol) round. ● *nm* (d'un instrument) handle; **~ à balai** broomstick; (Aviat) joystick. **M~** *nf* **la M~** the Channel; **le tunnel**

sous la **M~** the Channel tunnel.

manchette /mɑ̃ʃɛt/ *nf* cuff; (de journal) headline.

manchot, ~te /mɑ̃ʃo, -ɔt/ *nm, f* one-armed person; (sans bras) armless person. ● *nm* (oiseau) penguin.

mandarine /mɑ̃daRin/ *nf* tangerine, mandarin (orange).

mandat /mɑ̃da/ *nm* (postal) money order; (Pol) mandate; (procuration) proxy; (de police) warrant; **~ d'arrêt** arrest warrant.

mandataire /mɑ̃datɛR/ *nm* representative; (Jul) proxy.

manège /manɛʒ/ *nm* riding school; (à la foire) merry-go-round; (manœuvre) trick, ploy.

manette /manɛt/ *nf* lever; (de jeu) joystick.

mangeable /mɑ̃ʒabl/ *adj* edible.

mangeoire /mɑ̃ʒwaR/ *nf* trough; (pour oiseaux) feeder.

manger /mɑ̃ʒe/ 🔟 *vt* eat; (fortune) go through; (profits) eat away at; (économies) use up; (ronger) eat into. ● *vi* eat; **donner à ~ à** feed. ● *nm* food.

mangue /mɑ̃g/ *nf* mango.

maniable /manjabl/ *adj* easy to handle.

maniaque /manjak/ *adj* fussy. ● *nmf* fusspot; (fou) maniac; (fanatique) fanatic; **un ~ de l'ordre** a stickler for tidiness.

manie /mani/ *nf* habit; (marotte) obsession.

maniement /manimɑ̃/ *nm* handling. **manier** 🔢 *vt* handle.

manière /manjɛR/ *nf* way, manner; **~s** (politesse) manners; (chichis) fuss; **à la ~ de** in the style of; **de ~ à** so as to; **de toute ~** anyway, in any case.

maniéré, ~e /manjeRe/ *adj* affected.

manif /manif/ *nf* 🔟 demo.

manifestant, ~e /manifɛstɑ̃, -t/ *nm, f* demonstrator.

manifestation /manifɛstasjɔ̃/ *nf* expression, manifestation; (de maladie, phénomène) appearance; (Pol) demonstration; (événement) event; **~ culturelle** cultural event.

manifeste /manifɛst/ *adj* obvious. ● *nm* manifesto.

manifester /manifɛste/ 🔟 *vt* show, manifest; (désir, crainte) express. ● *vi*

(Pol) demonstrate. □ **se ~** *vpr* (sentiment) show itself; (apparaître) appear; (répondre à un appel) come forward.

manigance /manigɑ̃s/ *nf* little plot. **manigancer** 🔟 *vt* plot.

manipulation /manipylasjɔ̃/ *nf* handling; (péj) manipulation.

manivelle /manivɛl/ *nf* handle, crank.

mannequin /mankɛ̃/ *nm* (personne) model; (statue) dummy.

manœuvrer /manœvRe/ 🔟 *vt* manoeuvre; (machine) operate. ● *vi* manoeuvre.

manoir /manwaR/ *nm* manor.

manque /mɑ̃k/ *nm* lack (de of); (lacune) gap; **~ à gagner** loss of earnings; **en (état de) ~** having withdrawal symptoms.

manqué, ~e /mɑ̃ke/ *adj* (écrivain) failed; **garçon ~** tomboy.

manquement /mɑ̃kmɑ̃/ *nm* **~ à** breach of.

manquer /mɑ̃ke/ 🔟 *vt* miss; (gâcher) spoil; **~ à** (devoir) fail in; **~ de** be short of, lack; **il/ça lui manque** he misses him/it; **~ (de) faire** (faillir) nearly do; **ne manquez pas de** be sure to; **~ à sa parole** break one's word. ● *vi* be short ou lacking; (être absent) be absent; (en moins, disparu) be missing; **il me manque 20 euros** I'm 20 euros short.

mansarde /mɑ̃saRd/ *nf* attic (room).

manteau (pl **~x**) /mɑ̃to/ *nm* coat.

manucure /manykyR/ *nmf* manicurist. ● *nf* (soins) manicure.

manuel, ~le /manɥɛl/ *adj* manual. ● *nm* (livre) manual; (Scol) textbook.

manufacture /manyfaktyR/ *nf* factory; (fabrication) manufacture. **manufacturer** 🔟 *vt* manufacture.

manuscrit, ~e /manyskRi, -t/ *adj* handwritten. ● *nm* manuscript.

mappemonde /mapmɔ̃d/ *nf* world map; (sphère) globe.

maquereau (pl **~x**) /makRo/ *nm* (poisson) mackerel; 🔟 pimp.

maquette /makɛt/ *nf* (scale) model; **~ (de mise en page)** paste-up.

maquillage /makijaʒ/ *nm* make-up.

maquiller /makije/ 🔟 *vt* make up; (truquer) doctor, fake. □ **se ~** *vpr* make (oneself) up.

maquis /maki/ nm (paysage) scrub; (Mil) Maquis, underground.

maraîcher, -ère /maʀeʃe, -ɛʀ/ nm, f market gardener; (US) truck farmer.

marais /maʀɛ/ nm marsh.

marasme /maʀasm/ nm slump, stagnation; **dans le ~** in the doldrums.

marbre /maʀbʀ/ nm marble.

marc /maʀ/ nm (eau-de-vie) marc; **~ de café** coffee grounds.

marchand, ~e /maʀʃɑ̃, -d/ adj (valeur) market. ● nm, f trader; (de charbon, vins) merchant; **~ de couleurs** ironmonger; (US) hardware merchant; **~ de journaux** newsagent; **~ de légumes** greengrocer; **~ de poissons** fishmonger.

marchander /maʀʃɑ̃de/ **1** vt haggle over. ● vi haggle.

marchandise /maʀʃɑ̃diz/ nf goods.

marche /maʀʃ/ nf (démarche, trajet) walk; (rythme) pace; (Mil, Mus, Pol) march; (d'escalier) step; (Sport) walking; (de machine) operation, working; (de véhicule) running; **en ~** (train) moving; (moteur, machine) running; **faire ~ arrière** (véhicule) reverse; **mettre en ~** start (up); **se mettre en ~** start moving.

marché /maʀʃe/ nm market; (contrat) deal; **faire son ~** do one's shopping; **~ aux puces** flea market; **~ noir** black market.

marchepied /maʀʃəpje/ nm (de train, camion) step.

marcher /maʀʃe/ **1** vi walk; (poser le pied) tread (**sur** on); (aller) go; (fonctionner) work, run; (prospérer) go well; (film, livre) do well; (consentir **1**) agree; **faire ~ qn 1** pull sb's leg.

mardi /maʀdi/ nm Tuesday; **M ~ gras** Shrove Tuesday.

mare /maʀ/ nf (étang) pond; (flaque) pool.

marécage /maʀekaʒ/ nm marsh; (sous les tropiques) swamp.

maréchal (pl **-aux**) /maʀeʃal, -o/ nm field marshal.

maréchal-ferrant (pl **-aux-ferrants** /maʀeʃalferɑ̃/ nm blacksmith.

marée /maʀe/ nf tide; (poissons) fresh fish; **~ haute/basse** high/ low tide; **~ noire** oil slick.

marelle /maʀɛl/ nf hopscotch.

margarine /maʀgaʀin/ nf margarine.

marge /maʀʒ/ nf margin; **en ~ de** (à l'écart de) on the fringe(s) of; **~ bénéficiaire** profit margin.

marginal, ~e (mpl **-aux**) /maʀʒinal, -o/ adj marginal. ● nm, f drop-out.

marguerite /maʀgəʀit/ nf daisy; (qui imprime) daisy-wheel.

mari /maʀi/ nm husband.

mariage /maʀjaʒ/ nm marriage; (cérémonie) wedding.

marié, ~e /maʀje/ adj married. ● nm, f (bride) groom, bride; **les ~s** the bride and groom.

> **Marianne** The symbolic female figure often used to represent the French Republic. There are statues of her in public places all over France, always wearing the Phrygian bonnet, a pointed cap which became a symbol of liberty as represented by the 1789 Revolution. She also appears on the standard French postage stamp.

marier /maʀje/ **45** vt marry. □ **se ~** vpr get married, marry; **se ~ avec** marry, get married to.

marin, ~e /maʀɛ̃, -in/ adj sea. ● nm sailor.

marine /maʀin/ nf navy; **~ marchande** merchant navy. ● adj inv navy (blue).

marionnette /maʀjɔnɛt/ nf puppet; (à fils) marionette.

maritalement /maʀitalmɑ̃/ adv (vivre) as husband and wife.

maritime /maʀitim/ adj maritime, coastal; (agent, compagnie) shipping.

marmaille /maʀmaj/ nf **1** brats.

marmelade /maʀməlad/ nf stewed fruit; **~ d'oranges** (orange) marmalade.

marmite /maʀmit/ nf (cooking-)pot.

marmonner /maʀmɔne/ **1** vt mumble.

marmot /maʀmo/ nm **1** kid.

Maroc /maʀɔk/ nm Morocco.

maroquinerie /maʀɔkinʀi/ nf (magasin) leather goods shop.

marquant, ~e /maʀkɑ̃, -t/ adj (remarquable) outstanding; (qu'on n'oublie pas) memorable.

marque /mark/ *nf* mark; (de produits) brand, make; (décompte) score; **à vos ~s!** (Sport) on your marks!; **de ~** (Comm) brand name; (fig) important; **~ de fabrique** trademark; **~ déposée** registered trademark.

marquer /marke/ **1** *vt* mark; (indiquer) show, say; (écrire) note down; (point, but) score; (joueur) mark; (influencer) leave its mark on; (exprimer) (volonté, sentiment) show. ● *vi* (laisser une trace) leave a mark; (événement) stand out; (Sport) score.

marquis, ~e /marki, -z/ *nm, f* marquis, marchioness.

marraine /marɛn/ *nf* godmother.

marrant, ~e /marɑ̃, -t/ *adj* **1** funny.

marre /mar/ *adv* **en avoir ~** **1** be fed up (de with).

marrer (se) /(sə)mare/ **1** *vpr* **1** laugh, have a (good) laugh.

marron /marɔ̃/ *nm* chestnut; (couleur) brown; (coup **1**) thump; **~ d'Inde** horse chestnut. ● *adj inv* brown.

mars /mars/ *nm* March.

> **Marseillaise, la** The popular name of the French national anthem, composed by Claude-Joseph Rouget de Lisle in 1792. It was adopted as a marching song by a group of Republican volunteers from Marseilles and became famous as they sang it on entering Paris.

marteau (*pl* **~x**) /marto/ *nm* hammer; **~ (de porte)** (door) knocker; **~ piqueur** *ou* **pneumatique** pneumatic drill; **être ~ 1** be mad.

marteler /martəle/ **6** *vt* hammer; (poings, talons) pound; (scander) rap out.

martial, ~e (*mpl* **-iaux**) /marsjal, -jo/ *adj* military; (art) martial.

martien, ~ne /marsjɛ̃, -ɛn/ *adj & nm, f* Martian.

martyr, ~e /martir/ *nm, f* martyr. ● *adj* martyred; (enfant) battered.

martyre /martir/ *nm* (Relig) martyrdom; (fig) agony, suffering.

martyriser /martirize/ **1** *vt* (Relig) martyr; (torturer) torture; (enfant) batter.

marxisme /marksism/ *nm* Marxism. **marxiste** *adj & nmf* Marxist.

masculin, ~e /maskylɛ̃, -in/ *adj* masculine; (sexe) male; (mode, équipe) men's. ● *nm* masculine.

masochisme /mazoʃism/ *nm* masochism.

masochiste /mazoʃist/ *nmf* masochist. ● *adj* masochistic.

masque /mask/ *nm* mask; **~ de beauté** face pack. **masquer** **1** *vt* (cacher) hide, conceal (à from); (lumière) block (off).

massacre /masakr/ *nm* massacre. **massacrer** **1** *vt* massacre; (abîmer **1**) ruin.

massage /masaʒ/ *nm* massage.

masse /mas/ *nf* (volume) mass; (gros morceau) lump, mass; (outil) sledgehammer; **en ~** (vendre) in bulk; (venir) in force; **produire en ~** mass-produce; **la ~** (foule) the masses; **une ~ de 1** masses of; **la ~ de** the majority of.

masser /mase/ **1** *vt* (assembler) assemble; (pétrir) massage. □ **se ~** *vpr* (gens, foule) mass.

massif, -ive /masif, -v/ *adj* massive; (or, argent) solid. ● *nm* (de fleurs) clump; (parterre) bed; (Géog) massif. **massivement** *adv* (en masse) in large numbers.

massue /masy/ *nf* club, bludgeon.

mastic /mastik/ *nm* putty; (pour trous) filler.

mastiquer /mastike/ **1** *vt* (mâcher) chew.

mat /mat/ *adj* (couleur) matt; (bruit) dull; (teint) olive; **être ~** (aux échecs) be in checkmate.

mât /mɑ/ *nm* mast; (pylône) pole; **~ de drapeau** flagpole.

match /matʃ/ *nm* match; (US) game; **faire ~ nul** tie, draw; **~ aller** first leg; **~ retour** return match.

matelas /matla/ *nm* mattress; **~ pneumatique** air bed.

matelassé, ~e /matlase/ *adj* padded; (tissu) quilted.

matelot /matlo/ *nm* sailor.

mater /mate/ **1** *vt* (révolte) put down; (personne) bring into line.

matérialiser (se) /(sə)materjalize/ **1** *vpr* materialize.

matérialiste /materjalist/ *adj* materialistic. ● *nmf* materialist.

matériau (*pl* ~**x**) /materjo/ *nm* material.

matériel, ~**le** /materjɛl/ *adj* material. ● *nm* equipment, materials; ~ **informatique** hardware.

maternel, ~**le** /matɛrnɛl/ *adj* maternal; (comme d'une mère) motherly. **maternelle** *nf* nursery school.

maternité /matɛrnite/ *nf* maternity hospital; (état de mère) motherhood; **de** ~ maternity.

mathématicien, ~**ne** /matematisjɛ̃, -ɛn/ *nm, f* mathematician.

mathématique /matematik/ *adj* mathematical. **mathématiques** *nfpl* mathematics (+ *sg*).

maths /mat/ *nfpl* 🔢 maths (+ *sg*).

matière /matjɛr/ *nf* matter; (produit) material; (sujet) subject; **en** ~ **de** as regards; ~ **plastique** plastic; ~**s grasses** fat content; ~**s premières** raw materials.

matin /matɛ̃/ *nm* morning; **de bon** ~ early in the morning.

matinal, ~**e** (*mpl* -**aux**) /matinal, -o/ *adj* morning; (de bonne heure) early; **être** ~ be up early; (d'habitude) be an early riser.

matinée /matine/ *nf* morning; (spectacle) matinée.

matou /matu/ *nm* tomcat.

matraque /matrak/ *nf* (de police) truncheon; (US) billy (club). **matraquer** 🔢 *vt* club, beat; (produit, chanson) plug.

matrimonial, ~**e** (*mpl* -**iaux**) /matrimɔnjal, -jo/ *adj* matrimonial; **agence** ~**e** marriage bureau.

maturité /matyrite/ *nf* maturity.

maudire /modir/ 🔢 *vt* curse.

maudit, ~**e** /modi, -t/ *adj* 🔢 blasted, damned.

maugréer /mogree/ 🔢 *vi* grumble.

mausolée /mozole/ *nm* mausoleum.

maussade /mosad/ *adj* gloomy.

mauvais, ~**e** /mɔvɛ, -z/ *adj* bad; (erroné) wrong; (malveillant) evil; (désagréable) nasty, bad; (mer) rough; **le** ~ **moment** the wrong time; ~**e herbe** weed; ~**e langue** gossip; ~**e passe** tight spot; ~ **traitements** ill-treatment. ● *adv* (sentir) bad; **il fait** ~ the weather is bad. ● *nm* **le bon et le** ~ the good and the bad.

mauve /mov/ *adj & nm* mauve.

mauviette /movjɛt/ *nf* weakling, wimp.

maux /mo/ ➡**MAL**[2].

maximal, ~**e** (*mpl* -**aux**) /maksimal, -o/ *adj* maximum.

maxime /maksim/ *nf* maxim.

maximum /maksimɔm/ *adj* maximum. ● *nm* maximum; **au** ~ as much as possible; (tout au plus) at most; **faire le** ~ do one's utmost.

mazout /mazut/ *nm* (fuel) oil.

me, m' /mə, m/ *pron* me; (indirect) (to) me; (réfléchi) myself.

méandre /meɑ̃dr/ *nm* meander.

mec /mɛk/ *nm* 🔢 bloke, guy.

mécanicien, ~**ne** /mekanisjɛ̃, -jɛn/ *nm, f* mechanic. ● *nm* train driver.

mécanique /mekanik/ *adj* mechanical; (jouet) clockwork; **problème** ~ engine trouble. ● *nf* mechanics (+ *sg*); (mécanisme) mechanism. **mécaniser** 🔢 *vt* mechanize.

mécanisme /mekanism/ *nm* mechanism.

méchamment /meʃamɑ̃/ *adv* spitefully. **méchanceté** *nf* nastiness; (action) wicked action.

méchant, ~**e** /meʃɑ̃, -t/ *adj* (cruel) wicked; (désagréable, grave) nasty; (enfant) naughty; (chien) vicious; (sensationnel 🔢) terrific. ● *nm, f* (enfant) naughty child.

mèche /mɛʃ/ *nf* (de cheveux) lock; (de bougie) wick; (d'explosif) fuse; (outil) drill bit; **de** ~ **avec** in league with.

méconnaissable /mekɔnɛsabl/ *adj* unrecognizable.

méconnaître /mekɔnɛtr/ 🔢 *vt* misunderstand, misread; (mésestimer) underestimate.

méconnu, ~**e** /mekɔny/ *adj* unrecognized; (artiste) neglected.

mécontent, ~**e** /mekɔ̃tɑ̃, -t/ *adj* dissatisfied (**de** with); (irrité) annoyed (de at, with). **mécontentement** nm dissatisfaction; annoyance. **mécontenter** ⬛ vt dissatisfy; (irriter) annoy.

médaille /medaj/ nf medal; (insigne) badge; (bijou) medallion. **médaillé, ∼e** nm, f medallist.

médaillon /medajɔ̃/ nm medallion; (bijou) locket.

médecin /mɛdsɛ̃/ nm doctor.

médecine /mɛdsin/ nf medicine.

média /medja/ nm medium; **les ∼s** the media.

médiateur, -trice /medjatœr, -tris/ nm, f mediator.

médiatique /medjatik/ adj (événement, personnalité) media.

médical, ∼e (mpl -aux) /medikal, -o/ adj medical.

médicament /medikamɑ̃/ nm medicine, drug.

médico-légal, ∼e (mpl -aux) /medikolegal, -o/ adj forensic.

médiéval, ∼e (mpl -aux) /medjeval, -o/ adj medieval.

médiocre /medjɔkr/ adj mediocre, poor. **médiocrité** nf mediocrity.

médire /medir/ ⬛ vi ∼ de speak ill of, malign.

médisance /medizɑ̃s/ nf ∼(s) malicious gossip.

méditer /medite/ ⬛ vi meditate (sur on). ● vt contemplate; (paroles, conseils) mull over; ∼ de plan to.

Méditerranée /mediterane/ nf la ∼ the Mediterranean.

méditerranéen, ∼ne /mediteraneɛ̃, -ɛn/ adj Mediterranean.

médium /medjɔm/ nm (personne) medium.

méduse /medyz/ nf jellyfish.

meeting /mitiŋ/ nm meeting.

méfait /mefɛ/ nm misdeed; **les ∼s de** (conséquences) the ravages of.

méfiance /mefjɑ̃s/ nf suspicion, distrust. **méfiant, ∼e** adj suspicious, distrustful.

méfier (se) /(sə)mefje/ ⬛ vpr be wary ou careful; **se ∼ de** distrust, be wary of.

mégaoctet /megaɔkte/ nm (Ordinat) megabyte.

mégère /meʒɛr/ nf (femme) shrew.

mégot /mego/ nm cigarette end.

meilleur, ∼e /mɛjœr/ adj (comparatif) better (que than); (superlatif) best; **le ∼ livre** the best book; **mon ∼ ami** my best friend; **∼ marché** cheaper. ● nm, f le ∼, la ∼e the best (one). ● adv (sentir) better; **il fait ∼** the weather is better.

mél /mel/ nm email; **envoyer un ∼** send an email.

mélancolie /melɑ̃kɔli/ nf melancholy.

mélange /melɑ̃ʒ/ nm mixture, blend.

mélanger /melɑ̃ʒe/ ⬛ vt mix; (thés, parfums) blend. ▫ **se ∼** vpr mix; (thés, parfums) blend; (idées) get mixed up.

mélasse /melas/ nf black treacle; (US) molasses.

mêlée /mele/ nf free for all; (au rugby) scrum.

mêler /mele/ ⬛ vt mix (à with); (qualités) combine; (embrouiller) mix up; ∼ **qn à** (impliquer dans) involve sb in. ▫ **se ∼** vpr mix; combine; **se ∼ à** (se joindre à) mingle with; (participer à) join in; **se ∼ de** meddle in; **mêle-toi de ce qui te regarde** mind your own business.

méli-mélo (pl **mélis-mélos**) /melimelo/ nm jumble.

mélo /melo/ ⬛ nm melodrama. ● adj inv slushy, schmaltzy ⬛.

mélodie /melɔdi/ nf melody. **mélodieux, -ieuse** adj melodious. **mélodique** adj melodic.

mélodramatique /melɔdramatik/ adj melodramatic. **mélodrame** nm melodrama.

mélomane /meloman/ nmf music lover.

melon /məlɔ̃/ nm melon; (chapeau) ∼ bowler (hat).

membrane /mɑ̃bran/ nf membrane.

membre /mɑ̃br/ nm (Anat) limb; (adhérent) member.

même /mɛm/ adj same; **ce livre ∼** this very book; **la bonté ∼** kindness itself; **en ∼ temps** at the same time. ● pron **le ∼, la ∼** the same (one). ● adv even; **à ∼** (sur) directly on; **à ∼ de** in a position to; **de ∼** (aussi) too; (de la même façon) likewise; **de ∼ que** just as; ∼ **si** even if.

mémé /meme/ nf ⬛ granny.

mémo /memo/ nm note, memo.

mémoire /memwaʀ/ nm (rapport) memorandum; (Univ) dissertation; ∼s (souvenirs écrits) memoirs. ● nf memory; **à la** ∼ **de** to the memory of; **de** ∼ from memory; ∼ **morte/vive** (Ordinat) ROM/RAM.

mémorable /memɔʀabl/ adj memorable.

menace /mənas/ nf threat. **menacer** ⑩ vt threaten (**de faire** to do).

ménage /menaʒ/ nm (couple) couple; (travail) housework; (famille) household; **se mettre en** ∼ set up house.

ménagement /menaʒmã/ nm **avec** ∼s gently; **sans** ∼s (dire) bluntly; (jeter, pousser) roughly.

ménager¹, **-ère** /menaʒe, -ɛʀ/ adj household, domestic; **travaux** ∼s housework.

ménager² /menaʒe/ ⑩ vt be gentle with, handle carefully; (utiliser) be careful with; (organiser) prepare (carefully); **ne pas** ∼ **ses efforts** spare no effort.

ménagère /menaʒɛʀ/ nf housewife.

ménagerie /menaʒʀi/ nf menagerie.

mendiant, ∼e /mãdjã, -t/ nm, f beggar.

mendier /mãdje/ ㊺ vt beg for. ● vi beg.

mener /məne/ ⑥ vt lead; (entreprise, pays) run; (étude, enquête) carry out; (politique) pursue; ∼ **à** (accompagner à) take to; (faire aboutir) lead to; ∼ **à bien** see through. ● vi lead.

méningite /menɛ̃ʒit/ nf meningitis.

menotte /mənɔt/ nf ① hand; ∼s handcuffs.

mensonge /mãsɔ̃ʒ/ nm lie; (action) lying. **mensonger**, **-ère** adj untrue, false.

mensualité /mãsɥalite/ nf monthly payment.

mensuel, ∼le /mãsɥɛl/ adj monthly. ● nm monthly (magazine). **mensuellement** adv monthly.

mensurations /mãsyʀasjɔ̃/ nfpl measurements.

mental, ∼e (mpl -aux) /mãtal, -o/ adj mental; **malade** ∼ mentally ill person; **handicapé** ∼ mentally handicapped person.

mentalité /mãtalite/ nf mentality.

menteur, **-euse** /mãtœʀ, -øz/ nm, f liar. ● adj untruthful.

menthe /mãt/ nf mint.

mention /mãsjɔ̃/ nf mention; (annotation) note; (Scol) grade; **rayer la** ∼ **inutile** delete as appropriate. **mentionner** ① vt mention.

mentir /mãtiʀ/ ㊻ vi lie.

menton /mãtɔ̃/ nm chin.

menu, ∼e /məny/ adj (petit) tiny; (fin) fine; (insignifiant) minor. ● adv (couper) fine. ● nm (carte) menu; (repas) meal; (Ordinat) menu; ∼ **déroulant** pull-down menu.

menuiserie /mənɥizʀi/ nf carpentry, joinery. **menuisier** nm carpenter, joiner.

méprendre (se) /(sə)mepʀãdʀ/ ㊿ vpr **se** ∼ **sur** be mistaken about.

mépris /mepʀi/ nm contempt, scorn (**de** for); **au** ∼ **de** regardless of.

méprisable /mepʀizabl/ adj contemptible, despicable.

méprise /mepʀiz/ nf mistake.

méprisant, ∼e /mepʀizã, -t/ adj scornful. **mépriser** ① vt scorn, despise.

mer /mɛʀ/ nf sea; (marée) tide; **en pleine** ∼ out at sea.

mercenaire /mɛʀsənɛʀ/ nm & a mercenary.

mercerie /mɛʀs(ə)ʀi/ nf haberdashery; (US) notions store. **mercier**, **-ière** nm, f haberdasher; (US) notions seller.

merci /mɛʀsi/ interj thank you, thanks (**de**, **pour** for); ∼ **beaucoup**, ∼ **bien** thank you very much. ● nm thank you. ● nf mercy.

mercredi /mɛʀkʀədi/ nm Wednesday; ∼ **des Cendres** Ash Wednesday.

merde /mɛʀd/ nf ⊠ shit ⊠.

mère /mɛʀ/ nf mother; ∼ **de famille** mother.

méridional, ∼e (mpl -aux) /meʀidjɔnal, -o/ adj southern. ● nm, f Southerner.

mérite /meʀit/ nm merit; **avoir du** ∼ **à faire** deserve credit for doing.

mériter /meʀite/ ① vt deserve; ∼ **d'être lu** be worth reading.

méritoire /meʀitwaʀ/ adj commendable.

merlan /mɛʀlã/ nm whiting.

merle /mɛʀl/ nm blackbird.

merveille /mɛʀvɛj/ nf wonder, marvel; **à ~** wonderfully; **faire des ~s** work wonders.

merveilleux, -euse /mɛʀvɛjø, -z/ adj wonderful, marvellous.

mes /me/ ➡MON.

mésange /mezɑ̃ʒ/ nf tit(mouse).

mésaventure /mezavɑ̃tyʀ/ nf misadventure; **par ~** by some misfortune.

mesdames /medam/ ➡MADAME.

mesdemoiselles /medmwazɛl/ ➡MADEMOISELLE.

mésentente /mezɑ̃tɑ̃t/ nf disagreement.

mesquin, ~e /mɛskɛ̃, -in/ adj meanminded, petty; (chiche) mean. **mesquinerie** nf meanness.

message /mesaʒ/ nm message; **un ~ électronique** an email; **~ texte** text message.

messager, -ère /mesaʒe, -ɛʀ/ nm, f messenger. ● nm **~ de poche** pager.

messagerie /mesaʒʀi/ nf (transports) freight forwarding; (télécommunications) messaging; **~ électronique** electronic mail; **~ vocale** voice mail.

messe /mɛs/ nf (Relig) mass.

messieurs /mesjø/ ➡MONSIEUR.

mesure /məzyʀ/ nf measurement; (quantité, unité) measure; (disposition) measure, step; (cadence) time; **en ~** in time; (modération) moderation; **à ~ que** as; **dans la ~ où** in so far as; **dans une certaine ~** to some extent; **en ~ de** in a position to; **sans ~** to excess; **(fait) sur ~** made-to-measure.

mesuré, ~e /məzyʀe/ adj measured; (attitude) moderate.

mesurer /məzyʀe/ **1** vt measure; (juger) assess; (argent, temps) ration. ● vi **~ 15 mètres de long** be 15 metres long. □ **se ~ avec** vpr pit oneself against.

met /mɛ/ ➡METTRE **42**.

métal (pl **-aux**) /metal, -o/ nm metal. **métallique** adj (objet) metal; (éclat) metallic.

métallurgie /metalyʀʒi/ nf (industrie) metalworking industry.

métamorphoser /metamɔʀfoze/ **1** vt transform. □ **se ~** vpr be transformed; **se ~ en** metamorphose into.

métaphore /metafɔʀ/ nf metaphor.

météo /meteo/ nf (bulletin) weather forecast.

météore /meteɔʀ/ nm meteor.

météorologie /meteɔʀɔlɔʒi/ nf meteorology.

météorologique /meteɔʀɔlɔʒik/ adj meteorological; **conditions ~s** weather conditions.

méthode /metɔd/ nf method; (ouvrage) course, manual. **méthodique** adj methodical.

méticuleux, -euse /metikylø, -z/ adj meticulous.

métier /metje/ nm job; (manuel) trade; (intellectuel) profession; (expérience) experience, skill; **~ (à tisser)** loom; **remettre qch sur le ~** rework sth.

métis, ~se /metis/ adj mixed race. ● nm, f person of mixed race.

métrage /metʀaʒ/ nm length; **court ~** short (film); **long ~** feature-length film.

mètre /mɛtʀ/ nm metre; (règle) rule; **~ ruban** tape-measure.

métreur, -euse /metʀœʀ, -øz/ nm, f quantity surveyor.

métrique /metʀik/ adj metric.

métro /metʀo/ nm underground; (US) subway.

métropole /metʀɔpɔl/ nf metropolis; (pays) mother country. **métropolitain, ~e** adj metropolitan.

mets /mɛ/ nm dish. ● ➡METTRE **42**.

mettable /mɛtabl/ adj wearable.

metteur /mɛtœʀ/ nm **~ en scène** director.

mettre /mɛtʀ/ **42** vt put; (radio, chauffage) put ou switch on; (réveil) set; (installer) put in; (revêtir) put on; (porter habituellement) (vêtement, lunettes) wear; (prendre) take; (investir, dépenser) put; (écrire) write, say; **elle a mis deux heures** it took her two hours; **~ la table** lay the table; **~ en question** question; **~ en valeur** highlight; (terrain) develop; **mettons que** let's suppose that. ● vi **~ bas** (animal) give birth. □ **se ~** vpr (vêtement, maquillage) put on; (se placer) (objet) go; (personne) (debout) stand; (assis) sit; (couché) lie; **se ~ en short** put shorts on; **se ~ debout** stand up; **se ~ au lit** go to bed; **se ~ à table** sit down at table; **se ~ en ligne** line up; **se ~ du sable dans les yeux** get sand in one's eyes; **se ~ au chinois/tennis** take up Chinese/tennis; **se ~ au travail** set to work; **se ~ à faire** start to do.

meuble /mœbl/ *nm* piece of furniture; **~s** furniture.

meublé /møble/ *nm* furnished flat.

meubler /møble/ **1** *vt* furnish; (fig) fill. □ **se ~** *vpr* buy furniture.

meugler /møgle/ *vi* moo.

meule /møl/ *nf* millstone; **~ de foin** haystack.

meunier, -ière /mønje, -jɛR/ *nm, f* miller.

meurs, meurt /mœR/ →**MOURIR** **43**.

meurtre /mœRtR/ *nm* murder.

meurtrier, -ière /mœRtRije, -jɛR/ *adj* deadly. ● *nm, f* murderer.

meurtrir /mœRtRiR/ **2** *vt* bruise.

meute /møt/ *nf* pack of hounds.

Mexique /mɛksik/ *nm* Mexico.

mi- /mi/ *préf* mid-, half-; **à mi-chemin** half-way; **à mi-pente** half-way up the hill; **à la mi-juin** in mid-June.

miauler /mjole/ **1** *vi* miaow.

micro /mikRo/ *nm* microphone, mike; (Ordinat) micro.

microbe /mikRɔb/ *nm* germ.

microfilm /mikRɔfilm/ *nm* microfilm.

micro-onde /mikRoõd/ *nf* microwave; **un four à ~s** microwave (oven). **micro-ondes** *nm inv* microwave (oven).

micro-ordinateur (*pl* **~s**) /mikRɔɔRdinatœR/ *nm* personal computer.

microphone /mikRɔfɔn/ *nm* microphone.

microprocesseur /mikRɔpRɔsesœR/ *nm* microprocessor.

microscope /mikRɔskɔp/ *nm* microscope.

midi /midi/ *nm* twelve o'clock, midday, noon; (déjeuner) lunch-time; (sud) south. **Midi** *nm* **le M~** the South of France.

mie /mi/ *nf* soft part (of the loaf); **un pain de ~** a sandwich loaf.

miel /mjɛl/ *nm* honey.

mielleux, -euse /mjɛlø, -z/ *adj* unctuous.

mien, ~ne /mjɛ̃, -ɛn/ *pron* **le ~, la ~ne, les ~(ne)s** mine.

miette /mjɛt/ *nf* crumb; (fig) scrap; **en ~s** in pieces.

mieux /mjø/ *adj inv* better (**que** than); **le** *ou* **la** *ou* **les ~** (the) best. ● *nm* best; (progrès) improvement; **faire de son ~** do one's best; **le ~ serait de** the best thing would be to. ● *adv* better; **le** *ou* **la** *ou* **les ~** (de deux) the better; (de plusieurs) the best; **elle va ~** she is better; **j'aime ~ rester** I'd rather stay; **il vaudrait ~ partir** it would be best to leave; **tu ferais ~ de faire** you would be best to do.

mièvre /mjɛvR/ *adj* insipid.

mignon, ~ne /miɲõ, -ɔn/ *adj* cute; (gentil) kind.

migraine /migRɛn/ *nf* headache; (plus fort) migraine.

migrant /migRã/ *nm, f* migrant.

migration /migRasjõ/ *nf* migration.

mijoter /miʒote/ **1** *vt/i* simmer; (tramer **1**) cook up.

mil /mil/ *nm* a thousand.

milice /milis/ *nf* militia.

milieu (*pl* **~x**) /miljø/ *nm* middle; (environnement) environment; (appartenance sociale) background; (groupe) circle; (voie) middle way; (criminel) underworld; **au ~ de** in the middle of; **en plein** *ou* **au beau ~ de** right in the middle (of).

militaire /militɛR/ *adj* military. ● *nm* soldier, serviceman.

militant, ~e /militã, -t/ *nm, f* militant.

militer /milite/ **1** *vi* be a militant; **~ pour** militate in favour of.

mille[1] /mil/ *adj & nm inv* a thousand; **deux ~** two thousand; **mettre dans le ~** (fig) hit the nail on the head.

mille[2] /mil/ *nm* **~ (marin)** (nautical) mile.

millénaire /milenɛR/ *nm* millennium. ● *adj* a thousand years old.

mille-pattes /milpat/ *nm inv* centipede.

millésime /milezim/ *nm* date; (de vin) vintage.

millet /mijɛ/ *nm* millet.

milliard /miljaR/ *nm* thousand million, billion. **milliardaire** *nmf* multimillionaire.

millième /miljɛm/ adj & nmf thousandth.

millier /milje/ nm thousand; **un ~ (de)** about a thousand.

millimètre /milimɛtr/ nm millimetre.

million /miljɔ̃/ nm million; **deux ~s (de)** two million. **millionnaire** nmf millionaire.

mime /mim/ nmf mime-artist. ● nm (art) mime. **mimer** [1] vt mime; (imiter) mimic.

mimique /mimik/ nf expressions and gestures.

minable /minabl/ adj [1] (logement) shabby; (médiocre) pathetic, crummy.

minauder /minode/ [1] vi simper.

mince /mɛ̃s/ adj thin; (svelte) slim; (faible) (espoir, majorité) slim. ● interj [1] blast [1], darn it [1]. **minceur** nf thinness; slimness.

mincir /mɛ̃sir/ [2] vi get slimmer; **ça te mincit** it makes you look slimmer.

mine /min/ nf expression; (allure) appearance; **avoir bonne ~** look well; **faire ~ de** make as if to; (exploitation, explosif) mine; (de crayon) lead; **~ de charbon** coalmine.

miner /mine/ [1] vt (saper) undermine; (garnir d'explosifs) mine.

minerai /minrɛ/ nm ore.

minéral, ~e (mpl **-aux**) /mineral, -o/ adj mineral. ● nm (pl **-aux**) mineral.

minéralogique /mineralɔʒik/ adj **plaque ~** numberplate; (US) license plate.

minet, ~te /minɛ, -t/ nm, f (chat [1]) pussy(cat).

mineur, ~e /minœr/ adj minor; (Jur) under age. ● nm, f (Jur) minor. ● nm (ouvrier) miner.

miniature /minjatyr/ nf & adj miniature.

minier, -ière /minje, -jɛr/ adj mining.

minimal, ~e (mpl **-aux**) /minimal, o/ adj minimal, minimum.

minime /minim/ adj minimal, minor. ● nmf (Sport) junior.

minimum /minimɔm/ adj minimum. ● nm minimum; **au ~** (pour le moins) at the very least; **en faire un ~** do as little as possible.

ministère /ministɛr/ nm ministry; (gouvernement) government; **~ public** public prosecutor's office. **minis-**

tériel, ~le adj ministerial, government.

ministre /ministr/ nm minister; (au Royaume-Uni) Secretary of State; (US) Secretary.

Minitel® /minitɛl/ nm Minitel (telephone videotext system).

minorer /minɔre/ [1] vt reduce.

minoritaire /minɔritɛr/ adj minority; **être ~** be in the minority. **minorité** nf minority.

minuit /minɥi/ nm midnight.

minuscule /minyskyl/ adj minute. ● nf **(lettre) ~** lower case.

minute /minyt/ nf minute; **'talons ~'** 'heels repaired while you wait'.

minuterie /minytri/ nf time-switch.

minutie /minysi/ nf meticulousness. **minutieux, -ieuse** /minysjø, -z/ adj meticulous.

mioche /mjɔʃ/ nm, f [1] kid.

mirabelle /mirabɛl/ nf (mirabelle) plum.

miracle /mirakl/ nm miracle; **par ~** miraculously. **miraculeux, -euse** /mirakylø, -z/ adj miraculous.

mirage /miraʒ/ nm mirage.

mire /mir/ nf (fig) centre of attraction; (TV) test card.

mirobolant, ~e /mirɔbɔlɑ̃, -t/ adj [1] marvellous.

miroir /mirwar/ nm mirror.

miroiter /mirwate/ [1] vi shimmer, sparkle.

mis, ~e /mi, miz/ adj **bien ~** well-dressed. ● **→METTRE** [42].

mise /miz/ nf (argent) stake; (tenue) attire; **~ à feu** blast-off; **~ au point** adjustment; (fig) clarification; **~ de fonds** capital outlay; **~ en garde** warning; **~ en plis** set; **~ en scène** direction.

miser /mize/ [1] vt (argent) bet, stake (sur on). ● vi **~ sur** (parier) place a bet on; (compter sur) bank on.

misérable /mizerabl/ adj miserable, wretched; (indigent) destitute; (minable) seedy, squalid.

misère /mizɛr/ nf destitution; (malheur) trouble, woe. **miséreux, -euse** nm, f destitute person.

miséricorde /mizerikɔrd/ nf mercy.

missel /misɛl/ nm missal.

missile /misil/ nm missile.

mission /misjɔ̃/ nf mission. **missionnaire** nmf missionary.

missive /misiv/ nf missive.

mistral /mistral/ nm (vent) mistral.

mitaine /mitɛn/ nf fingerless mitt.

mite /mit/ nf (clothes-)moth.

mi-temps /mitɑ̃/ nf inv (arrêt) half-time; (période) half. ● nm inv part-time work; à ~ part-time.

miteux, -euse /mitø, -z/ adj shabby.

mitigé, ~e /mitiʒe/ adj (modéré) luke-warm; (succès) qualified.

mitonner /mitɔne/ 1 vt cook slowly with care; (fig) cook up.

mitoyen, ~ne /mitwajɛ̃, -ɛn/ adj mur ~ party wall.

mitrailler /mitraje/ 1 vt machine-gun; (fig) bombard.

mitraillette /mitrajɛt/ nf submachine gun. **mitrailleuse** nf machine gun.

mi-voix: à ~ /amivwa/ loc in a low voice.

mixeur /miksœr/ nm liquidizer, blender; (batteur) mixer.

mixte /mikst/ adj mixed; (commission) joint; (école) coeducational; (peau) combination.

mobile /mɔbil/ adj mobile; (pièce) moving; (feuillet) loose. ● nm (art) mobile; (raison) motive.

mobilier /mɔbilje/ nm furniture.

mobilisation /mɔbilizasjɔ̃/ nf mobilization. **mobiliser** 1 vt mobilize.

mobilité /mɔbilite/ nf mobility.

mobylette® /mɔbilɛt/ nf moped.

moche /mɔʃ/ adj 1 (laid) ugly; (mauvais) lousy.

modalités /mɔdalite/ nfpl (conditions) terms; (façon de fonctionner) practical details.

mode /mɔd/ nf fashion; (coutume) custom; à la ~ fashionable. ● nm method, mode; (genre) way; ~ d'emploi directions (for use).

modèle /mɔdɛl/ adj model. ● nm model; (exemple) example; (Comm) (type) model; (taille) size; (style) style; ~ familial family size; ~ réduit (small-scale) model.

modeler /mɔdle/ 6 vt model (sur on). □ se ~ sur vpr model oneself on.

modem /mɔdɛm/ nm modem.

modérateur, -trice /mɔderatœr, -tris/ adj moderating. **modération** nf moderation.

modéré, ~e /mɔdere/ adj & nm, f moderate.

modérer /mɔdere/ 14 vt (propos) moderate; (désirs, sentiments) curb. □ se ~ vpr restrain oneself.

moderne /mɔdɛrn/ adj modern. **moderniser** 1 vt modernize.

modeste /mɔdɛst/ adj modest. **modestie** nf modesty.

modification /mɔdifikasjɔ̃/ nf modification.

modifier /mɔdifje/ 45 vt change, modify. □ se ~ vpr change, alter.

modique /mɔdik/ adj modest.

modiste /mɔdist/ nf milliner.

moduler /mɔdyle/ 1 vt modulate; (adapter) adjust.

moelle /mwal/ nf marrow; ~ épinière spinal cord; ~ osseuse bone marrow.

moelleux, -euse /mwalø, -z/ adj soft; (onctueux) smooth.

mœurs /mœr(s)/ nfpl (morale) morals; (usages) customs; (manières) habits, ways.

moi /mwa/ pron me; (indirect) (to) me; (sujet) I. ● nm self.

moignon /mwaɲɔ̃/ nm stump.

moi-même /mwamɛm/ pron myself.

moindre /mwɛ̃dr/ adj (moins grand) lesser; le ou la ~, les ~s the slightest, the least.

moine /mwan/ nm monk.

moineau (pl ~x) /mwano/ nm sparrow.

moins /mwɛ̃/ prép minus; (pour dire l'heure) to; une heure ~ dix ten to one. ● adv less (que than); le ou la ou les ~ the least; le ~ grand/haut the smallest/lowest; ~ de (avec un nom non dénombrable) less (que than); ~ de dix euros less than ten euros; ~ de livres fewer books; au ~, du ~ at least; à ~ que unless; de ~ less; de ~ en ~ less and less; en ~ less; (manquant) missing.

mois /mwa/ nm month.

moisi, ~e /mwazi/ adj mouldy. ● nm mould; de ~ (odeur) musty. **moisir** 2 vi go mouldy. **moisissure** nf mould.

moisson /mwasɔ̃/ nf harvest.

moissonner /mwasɔne/ **1** vt harvest, reap. **moissonneur, -euse** nm, f harvester.

moite /mwat/ adj sticky, clammy.

moitié /mwatje/ nf half; (milieu) halfway mark; **s'arrêter à la ~** stop halfway through; **à ~ vide** half empty; **à ~ prix** (at) half-price; **la ~ de** half (of). **moitié-moitié** adv half-and-half.

mol /mɔl/ ➡MOU.

molaire /mɔlɛR/ nf molar.

molécule /mɔlekyl/ nf molecule.

molester /mɔlɛste/ **1** vt manhandle, rough up.

molle /mɔl/ ➡MOU.

mollement /mɔlmɑ̃/ adv softly; (faiblement) feebly. **mollesse** nf softness; (faiblesse) feebleness; (apathie) listlessness.

mollet /mɔlɛ/ nm (de jambe) calf.

mollir /mɔliR/ **2** vi soften; (céder) yield.

môme /mom/ nmf **1** kid.

moment /mɔmɑ̃/ nm moment; (période) time; **(petit) ~** short while; **au ~ où** when; **par ~s** now and then; **du ~ où** ou **que** (pourvu que) as long as, provided that; (puisque) since; **en ce ~** at the moment.

momentané, ~e /mɔmɑ̃tane/ adj momentary. **momentanément** adv momentarily; (en ce moment) at present.

momie /mɔmi/ nf mummy.

mon, ma (**mon** before vowel or mute h) (pl **mes**) /mɔ̃, ma, mɔ̃n, me/ adj my.

Monaco /mɔnako/ npr Monaco.

monarchie /mɔnaRʃi/ nf monarchy.

monarque /mɔnaRk/ nm monarch.

monastère /mɔnastɛR/ nm monastery.

monceau (pl **~x**) /mɔ̃so/ nm heap, pile.

mondain, ~e /mɔ̃dɛ̃, -ɛn/ adj society, social.

monde /mɔ̃d/ nm world; **du ~** (a lot of) people; (quelqu'un) somebody; **le (grand) ~** (high) society; **se faire (tout) un ~ de qch** make a great deal of fuss about sth; **pas le moins du ~** not in the least.

mondial, ~e (mpl **-iaux**) /mɔ̃djal, -jo/ adj world; (influence) worldwide. **mondialement** adv the world over.

mondialisation /mɔ̃djalizasjɔ̃/ nf globalisation.

monétaire /mɔnetɛR/ adj monetary.

moniteur, -trice /mɔnitœR, -tRis/ nm, f instructor; (de colonie de vacances) group leader; (US) (camp) counselor.

monnaie /mɔnɛ/ nf currency; (pièce) coin; (appoint) change; **faire la ~ de** get change for; **faire de la ~ à qn** give sb change; **menue** ou **petite ~** small change.

monnayer /mɔneje/ **31** vt convert into cash.

monologue /mɔnɔlɔg/ nm monologue.

monoparental, ~e /mɔnɔpaRɑ̃tal/ adj **famille ~e** single-parent family.

monopole /mɔnɔpɔl/ nm monopoly. **monopoliser** **1** vt monopolize.

monospace /mɔnɔspas/ nm (Auto) people carrier.

monotone /mɔnɔtɔn/ adj monotonous. **monotonie** nf monotony.

Monseigneur (pl **Messeigneurs**) /mɔ̃sɛɲœR/ nm (à un duc, archevêque) Your Grace; (à un prince) Your Highness.

monsieur (pl **messieurs**) /məsjø, mesjø/ nm (à un inconnu) (dans une lettre) **M~** Dear Sir; **bonjour, ~** good morning; **mesdames et messieurs** ladies and gentlemen; (à un homme dont on connaît le nom) (dans une lettre) **Cher M~** Dear Mr X; **bonjour, ~** good morning Mr X; **M~ le curé** Father X; **oui M~ le ministre** yes Minister; (homme) man; (formule de respect) sir.

monstre /mɔ̃stR/ nm monster. ● adj **1** colossal.

monstrueux, -euse /mɔ̃stRyø, -z/ adj monstrous. **monstruosité** nf monstrosity.

mont /mɔ̃/ nm mountain; **le ~ Everest** Mount Everest; **être toujours par ~s et par vaux** be always on the move.

montage /mɔ̃taʒ/ nm (assemblage) assembly; (au cinéma) editing.

montagne /mɔ̃taɲ/ nf mountain; (région) mountains; **~s russes** rollercoaster. **montagneux, -euse** adj mountainous.

montant, ~e /mɔ̃tɑ̃, -t/ adj rising; (col) high; (chemin) uphill. ● nm amount; (pièce de bois) upright.

mont-de-piété (pl **monts-de-piété**) /mɔ̃dpjete/ nm pawnshop.

monte-charge /mɔ̃tʃaʀʒ/ nm inv goods lift.

montée /mɔ̃te/ nf ascent, climb; (de prix) rise; (de coûts, risques) increase; (côte) hill.

monter /mɔ̃te/ **1** vt (aux. avoir) take up; (à l'étage) take upstairs; (escalier, rue, pente) go up; (assembler) assemble; (tente, échafaudage) put up; (col, manche) set in; (organiser) (pièce) stage; (société) set up; (attaque, garde) mount. ● vi (aux. être) go ou come up; (à l'étage) go ou come upstairs; (avion) climb; (route) go uphill, climb; (augmenter) rise; (marée) come up; ~ **sur** (trottoir, toit) get up on; (cheval, bicyclette) get on; ~ **à l'échelle/ l'arbre** climb the ladder/tree; ~ **dans** (voiture) get in; (train, bus, avion) get on; ~ **à bord** climb on board; ~ **(à cheval)** ride; ~ **à bicyclette/moto** ride a bike/motorbike.

monteur, -euse /mɔ̃tœʀ, -øz/ nm, f (Tech) fitter; (au cinéma) editor.

montre /mɔ̃tʀ/ nf watch; **faire ~ de** show.

montrer /mɔ̃tʀe/ **1** vt show (à to); ~ **du doigt** point to. □ **se ~** vpr show oneself; (être) be; (s'avérer) prove to be.

monture /mɔ̃tyʀ/ nf (cheval) mount; (de lunettes) frames (+ pl); (de bijou) setting.

monument /mɔnymɑ̃/ nm monument; ~ **aux morts** war memorial. **monumental** (mpl **-aux**) adj monumental.

moquer (se) /(sə)mɔke/ **1** vpr **se ~ de** make fun of; **je m'en moque** **1** I couldn't care less. **moquerie** nf mockery. **moqueur, -euse** adj mocking.

moquette /mɔket/ nf fitted carpet; (US) wall-to-wall carpeting.

moral, ~e (mpl **-aux**) /mɔʀal, -o/ adj moral. ● nm (pl **-aux**) morale; **ne pas avoir le ~** feel down; **avoir le ~** be in good spirits; **ça m'a remonté le ~** it gave me a boost.

morale /mɔʀal/ nf moral code; (mœurs) morals; (de fable) moral; **faire la ~ à** lecture. **moralité** nf (de personne) morals (+ pl); (d'action,

œuvre) morality; (de fable) moral.

moralisateur, -trice /mɔʀalizatœʀ, -tʀis/ adj moralizing.

morbide /mɔʀbid/ adj morbid.

morceau (pl **~x**) /mɔʀso/ nm piece, bit; (de sucre) lump; (de viande) cut; (passage) passage; **manger un ~** **1** have a bite to eat; **mettre en ~x** smash ou tear to bits.

morceler /mɔʀsəle/ **6** vt divide up.

mordant, ~e /mɔʀdɑ̃, -t/ adj scathing; (froid) biting. ● nm vigour, energy.

mordiller /mɔʀdije/ **1** vt nibble at.

mordre /mɔʀdʀ/ **3** vi bite (**dans** into); ~ **sur** (ligne) go over; (territoire) encroach on; ~ **à l'hameçon** bite. ● vt bite.

mordu, ~e /mɔʀdy/ **1** nm, f fan. ● adj smitten; ~ **de** crazy about.

morfondre (se) /(sə)mɔʀfɔ̃dʀ/ **3** vpr wait anxiously; (languir) mope.

morgue /mɔʀg/ nf morgue, mortuary; (attitude) arrogance.

moribond, ~e /mɔʀibɔ̃, -d/ adj dying.

morne /mɔʀn/ adj dull.

morphine /mɔʀfin/ nf morphine.

mors /mɔʀ/ nm (de cheval) bit.

morse /mɔʀs/ nm (animal) walrus; (code) Morse code.

morsure /mɔʀsyʀ/ nf bite.

mort¹ /mɔʀ/ nf death.

mort², ~e /mɔʀ, -t/ adj dead; ~ **de fatigue** dead tired. ● nm, f dead man, dead woman; **les ~s** the dead.

mortalité /mɔʀtalite/ nf mortality; **(taux de) ~** death rate.

mortel, ~le /mɔʀtɛl/ adj mortal; (accident) fatal; (poison, silence) deadly. ● nm, f mortal. **mortellement** adv mortally.

mortifié, ~e /mɔʀtifje/ adj mortified.

mort-né, ~e /mɔʀne/ adj stillborn.

mortuaire /mɔʀtɥeʀ/ adj (cérémonie) funeral.

morue /mɔʀy/ nf cod.

mosaïque /mɔzaik/ nf mosaic.

mosquée /mɔske/ nf mosque.

mot /mo/ nm word; (lettre, message) note; ~ **d'ordre** watchword; ~ **de passe** password; **~s croisés** crossword (puzzle).

motard /mɔtaʀ/ nm biker; (policier) police motorcyclist.

moteur, -trice /mɔtœʀ, -tʀis/ *adj* (Méd) motor; (*force*) driving; **à 4 roues motrices** 4-wheel drive. ● *nm* engine, motor; **barque à ~** motor launch; **~ de recherche** (Internet) search engine.

motif /mɔtif/ *nm* (raisons) grounds (+ *pl*); (cause) reason; (Jur) motive; (dessin) pattern.

motion /mosjɔ̃/ *nf* motion.

motivation /mɔtivasjɔ̃/ *nf* motivation. **motiver** 1 *vt* motivate.

moto /mɔto/ *nf* motor cycle. **motocycliste** *nmf* motorcyclist.

motorisé, ~e /mɔtɔʀize/ *adj* motorized.

motrice /mɔtʀis/ →MOTEUR.

motte /mɔt/ *nf* lump; (de beurre) slab; (de terre) clod; **~ de gazon** turf.

mou (**mol** *before vowel or mute h*), **molle** /mu, mɔl/ *adj* soft; (*ventre*) flabby; (sans conviction) feeble; (apathique) sluggish, listless. ● *nm* slack; **avoir du ~** be slack.

mouchard, ~e /muʃaʀ, -d/ *nm, f* informer; (Scol) sneak.

mouche /muʃ/ *nf* fly; (de cible) bull's eye.

moucher (se) /(sə)muʃe/ 1 *vpr* blow one's nose.

moucheron /muʃʀɔ̃/ *nm* midge.

moucheté, ~e /muʃte/ *adj* speckled.

mouchoir /muʃwaʀ/ *nm* handkerchief, hanky; **~ en papier** tissue.

moue /mu/ *nf* pout; **faire la ~** pout.

mouette /mwɛt/ *nf* (sea)gull.

moufle /mufl/ *nf* (gant) mitten.

mouillé, ~e /muje/ *adj* wet.

mouiller /muje/ 1 *vt* wet, make wet; **~ l'ancre** drop anchor. □ **se ~** *vpr* get (oneself) wet.

moulage /mulaʒ/ *nm* cast.

moule /mul/ *nf* (coquillage) mussel. ● *nm* mould; **~ à gâteau** cake tin; **~ à tarte** flan dish. **mouler** 1 *vt* mould; (statue) cast.

moulin /mulɛ̃/ *nm* mill; **~ à café** coffee grinder; **~ à poivre** pepper mill; **~ à vent** windmill.

moulinet /mulinɛ/ *nm* (de canne à pêche) reel; **faire des ~s avec qch** twirl sth around.

moulinette® /mulinɛt/ *nf* vegetable mill.

moulu, ~e /muly/ *adj* ground; (fatigué 1) worn out.

moulure /mulyʀ/ *nf* moulding.

mourant, ~e /muʀã, -t/ *adj* dying. ● *nm, f* dying person.

mourir /muʀiʀ/ 48 *vi* (*aux. être*) die; **~ d'envie de** be dying to; **~ de faim** be starving; **~ d'ennui** be dead bored.

mousquetaire /muskətɛʀ/ *nm* musketeer.

mousse /mus/ *nf* moss; (écume) froth, foam; (de savon) lather; (dessert) mousse; **~ à raser** shaving foam. ● *nm* ship's boy.

mousseline /muslin/ *nf* muslin; (de soie) chiffon.

mousser /muse/ 1 *vi* froth, foam; (savon) lather.

mousseux, -euse /musø, -z/ *adj* frothy. ● *nm* sparkling wine.

mousson /musɔ̃/ *nf* monsoon.

moustache /mustaʃ/ *nf* moustache; **~s** (d'animal) whiskers.

moustique /mustik/ *nm* mosquito.

moutarde /mutaʀd/ *nf* mustard.

mouton /mutɔ̃/ *nm* sheep; (peau) sheepskin; (viande) mutton.

mouvant, ~e /muvã, -t/ *adj* changing; (terrain) shifting, unstable.

mouvement /muvmã/ *nm* movement; (agitation) bustle; (en gymnastique) exercise; (impulsion) impulse; (tendance) tend, tendency; **en ~** in motion.

mouvementé, ~e /muvmãte/ *adj* eventful.

moyen, ~ne /mwajɛ̃, -ɛn/ *adj* average; (médiocre) poor; **de taille moyenne** medium-sized. ● *nm* means, way; **~s** means; (dons) ability; **au ~ de** by means of; **il n'y a pas ~ de** it is not possible to. **Moyen Âge** *nm* Middle Ages (+ *pl*).

moyennant /mwajɛnã/ *prép* (pour) for; (grâce à) with.

moyenne /mwajɛn/ *nf* average; (Scol) pass-mark; **en ~** on average; **~ d'âge** average age. **moyennement** *adv* moderately.

Moyen-Orient /mwajɛnɔʀjã/ *nm* Middle East.

moyeu (*pl* ~**x**) /mwajø/ *nm* hub.

mû, mue /my/ *adj* driven (**par** by).

mucoviscidose /mykɔvisidoz/ *nf* cystic fibrosis.

mue /my/ *nf* moulting; (de voix) breaking of the voice.

muer /mɥe/ **1** *vi* moult; (*voix*) break. □ **se** ~ **en** *vpr* change into.

muet, ~**te** /mɥɛ, -t/ *adj* (Méd) dumb; (fig) speechless (**de** with); (silencieux) silent. ● *nm, f* mute.

mufle /myfl/ *nm* nose, muzzle; (personne 🔟) boor, lout.

mugir /myʒiʀ/ **2** *vi* (*vache*) moo; (*bœuf*) bellow; (fig) howl.

muguet /mygɛ/ *nm* lily of the valley.

mule /myl/ *nf* (female) mule; (pantoufle) mule.

mulet /mylɛ/ *nm* (male) mule.

multicolore /myltikɔlɔʀ/ *adj* multicoloured.

multimédia /myltimedja/ *adj & nm* multimedia.

multinational, ~**e** (*mpl* -**aux**) /myltinasjɔnal, -o/ *adj* multinational. **multinationale** *nf* multinational (company).

multiple /myltipl/ *nm* multiple. ● *adj* numerous, many; (naissances) multiple.

multiplication /myltiplikasjɔ̃/ *nf* multiplication.

multiplicité /myltiplisite/ *nf* multiplicity.

multiplier /myltiplije/ **45** *vt* multiply; (*risques*) increase. □ **se** ~ *vpr* multiply; (*accidents*) be on the increase; (*difficultés*) increase.

multitude /myltityd/ *nf* multitude, mass.

municipal, ~**e** (*mpl* -**aux**) /mynisipal, -o/ *adj* municipal; **conseil** ~ town council. **municipalité** *nf* (ville) municipality; (conseil) town council.

munir /myniʀ/ **2** *vt* ~ **de** provide with. □ **se** ~ **de** *vpr* (apporter) bring; (emporter) take.

munitions /mynisjɔ̃/ *nfpl* ammunition.

mur /myʀ/ *nm* wall; ~ **du son** sound barrier.

mûr, ~**e** /myʀ/ *adj* ripe; (*personne*) mature.

muraille /myʀɑj/ *nf* (high) wall.

mural, ~**e** (*mpl* -**aux**) /myʀal, -o/ *adj* wall; **peinture** ~**e** mural.

mûre /myʀ/ *nf* blackberry.

mûrir /myʀiʀ/ **2** *vi* ripen; (*abcès*) come to a head; (*personne, projet*) mature. ● *vt* (*fruit*) ripen; (*personne*) mature.

murmure /myʀmyʀ/ *nm* murmur.

muscade /myskad/ *nf* **noix** ~ nutmeg.

muscle /myskl/ *nm* muscle. **musclé,** ~**e** *adj* muscular. **musculaire** *adj* muscular.

musculation /myskylasjɔ̃/ *nf* bodybuilding.

musculature /myskylatyʀ/ *nf* muscles (+ *pl*).

museau (*pl* ~**x**) /myzo/ *nm* muzzle; (de porc) snout.

musée /myze/ *nm* museum; (de peinture) art gallery.

muselière /myzəljɛʀ/ *nf* muzzle.

musette /myzɛt/ *nf* haversack.

muséum /myzeɔm/ *nm* natural history museum.

musical, ~**e** (*mpl* -**aux**) /myzikal, -o/ *adj* musical.

musicien, ~**ne** /myzisjɛ̃, -ɛn/ *adj* musical. ● *nm, f* musician.

musique /myzik/ *nf* music; (orchestre) band.

must /myst/ *nm* 🔟 must.

musulman, ~**e** /myzylmɑ̃, -an/ *adj & nm, f* Muslim.

mutation /mytasjɔ̃/ *nf* change; (biologique) mutation; (d'un employé) transfer.

muter /myte/ **1** *vt* transfer. ● *vi* mutate.

mutilation /mytilasjɔ̃/ *nf* mutilation. **mutiler** **1** *vt* mutilate. **mutilé,** ~**e** *nm, f* disabled person.

mutin, ~**e** /mytɛ̃, -in/ *adj* mischievous. ● *nm* mutineer; (prisonnier) rioter.

mutinerie /mytinʀi/ *nf* mutiny; (de prisonniers) riot.

mutisme /mytism/ *nm* silence.

mutuel, ~**le** /mytɥɛl/ *adj* mutual. **mutuelle** *nf* mutual insurance company. **mutuellement** *adv* mutually; (l'un l'autre) each other.

myope /mjɔp/ adj short-sighted. **myopie** nf short-sightedness.

myosotis /mjozɔtis/ nm forget-me-not.

myrtille /miʀtij/ nf bilberry, blueberry.

mystère /mistɛʀ/ nm mystery.

mystérieux, -ieuse /misteʀjø, -z/ adj mysterious.

mystification /mistifikasjɔ̃/ nf hoax.

mysticisme /mistisism/ nm mysticism.

mystique /mistik/ adj mystic(al). ● nmf mystic. ● nf mystique.

mythe /mit/ nm myth. **mythique** adj mythical.

mythologie /mitɔlɔʒi/ nf mythology.

Nn

n' /n/ →NE.

nacre /nakʀ/ nf mother-of-pearl.

nage /naʒ/ nf swimming; (manière) stroke; **traverser à la** ∼ swim across; **en** ∼ sweating.

nageoire /naʒwaʀ/ nf fin; (de mammifère) flipper.

nager /naʒe/ 40 vt/i swim. **nageur, -euse** nm, f swimmer.

naguère /nagɛʀ/ adv (autrefois) formerly.

naïf, -ive /naif, -v/ adj naïve.

nain, ∼e /nɛ̃, nɛn/ nm, f & adj dwarf.

naissance /nɛsɑ̃s/ nf birth; **donner** ∼ **à** give birth to; (fig) give rise to.

naître /nɛtʀ/ 44 vi be born; (résulter) arise (**de** from); **faire** ∼ (susciter) give rise to.

naïveté /naivte/ nf naïvety.

nappe /nap/ nf tablecloth; (de pétrole, gaz) layer; ∼ **phréatique** ground water.

napperon /napʀɔ̃/ nm (cloth) tablemat.

narco-dollars /naʀkodɔlaʀ/ nmpl drug money.

narcotique /naʀkɔtik/ adj & nm narcotic. **narco(-)trafiquant, ∼e** (pl ∼s) nm, f drug trafficker.

narguer /naʀge/ 1 vt taunt; (autorité) flout.

narine /naʀin/ nf nostril.

nasal, ∼e (mpl **-aux**) /nazal, -o/ adj nasal.

naseau (pl ∼**x**) /nazo/ nm nostril.

natal, ∼e (mpl ∼**s**) /natal/ adj native.

natalité /natalite/ nf birth rate.

natation /natasjɔ̃/ nf swimming.

natif, -ive /natif, -v/ adj native.

nation /nasjɔ̃/ nf nation.

national, ∼e (mpl **-aux**) /nasjɔnal, -o/ adj national. **nationale** nf A road; (US) highway. **nationaliser** 1 vt nationalize.

nationalité /nasjɔnalite/ nf nationality.

natte /nat/ nf (de cheveux) plait; (US) braid; (tapis de paille) mat.

nature /natyʀ/ nf nature; ∼ **morte** still life; **de** ∼ **à** likely to; **payer en** ∼ pay in kind. ● adj inv plain; (yaourt) natural; (thé) black.

naturel, ∼le /natyʀɛl/ adj natural. ● nm nature; (simplicité) naturalness; (Culin) **au** ∼ plain; (thon) in brine. **naturellement** adv naturally; (bien sûr) of course.

naufrage /nofʀaʒ/ nm shipwreck; **faire** ∼ be shipwrecked; (bateau) be wrecked.

nauséabond, ∼e /nozeabɔ̃, -d/ adj nauseating.

nausée /noze/ nf nausea.

nautique /notik/ adj nautical; **sports** ∼**s** water sports.

naval, ∼e (mpl ∼**s**) /naval/ adj naval; **chantier** ∼ shipyard.

navet /navɛ/ nm turnip; (film: péj) flop; (US) turkey.

navette /navɛt/ nf shuttle (service); **faire la** ∼ shuttle back and forth.

navigateur, -trice /navigatœʀ, -tʀis/ nm, f sailor; (qui guide) navigator; (Internet) browser. **navigation** nf navigation; (trafic) shipping; (Internet) browsing.

naviguer /navige/ 1 vi sail; (piloter) navigate; (Internet) browse; ∼ **dans l'Internet** surf the Internet.

navire /naviʀ/ nm ship.

navré, ∼e /navʀe/ adj sorry (**de** to).

ne, n' /nə, n/

n' before vowel or mute h.

● *adverbe*

⋯▸ **je n'ai que 10 euros** I've only got 10 euros.

⋯▸ **tu n'avais qu'à le dire!** you only had to say so!

⋯▸ **je crains qu'il ~ parte** I am afraid he will leave.

➡️ Pour les expressions comme **ne... guère, ne... jamais, ne... pas, ne... plus,** etc. ➡**guère, jamais, pas, plus,** etc.

né, ~e /ne/ adj born; ~e **Martin** née Martin; (dans composés) **dernier-~** last-born. ● ➡**NAÎTRE 44**.

néanmoins /neɑ̃mwɛ̃/ adv nevertheless.

néant /neɑ̃/ nm nothingness; **réduire à** ~ (effet, efforts) negate, nullify; (espoir) dash; '**revenus: ~**' 'income: nil'.

nécessaire /nesesɛʀ/ adj necessary. ● nm (sac) bag; (trousse) kit; **le** ~ (l'indispensable) the necessities ou essentials; **faire le** ~ do what is necessary.

nécessité /nesesite/ nf necessity; **de première** ~ vital.

nécessiter /nesesite/ **1** vt necessitate.

néerlandais, ~e /neɛʀlɑ̃dɛ, -z/ adj Dutch. ● nm (Ling) Dutch. **N~,** ~**e** nm, f Dutchman, Dutchwoman.

néfaste /nefast/ adj harmful (à to).

négatif, -ive /negatif, -v/ adj & nm negative.

négligé, ~e /negliʒe/ adj (travail) careless; (tenue) scruffy. ● nm (tenue) negligee.

négligent, ~e /negliʒɑ̃, -t/ adj careless, negligent.

négliger /negliʒe/ **40** vt neglect; (ne pas tenir compte de) ignore, disregard; ~ **de faire** fail to do. □ **se** ~ vpr neglect oneself.

négoce /negɔs/ nm business, trade. **négociant,** ~e nm, f merchant.

négociation /negɔsjasjɔ̃/ nf negotiation. **négocier 45** vt/i negotiate.

nègre /nɛgʀ/ adj (musique, art) Negro. ● nm (écrivain) ghost writer.

neige /nɛʒ/ nf snow. **neiger 40** vi snow.

nénuphar /nenyfaʀ/ nm waterlily.

nerf /nɛʀ/ nm nerve; (vigueur) stamina; **être sur les ~s** be on edge.

nerveux, -euse /nɛʀvø, -z/ adj nervous; (irritable) nervy; (centre, cellule) nerve; (voiture) responsive. **nervosité** nf nervousness; (irritabilité) touchiness.

net, ~te /nɛt/ adj (clair, distinct) clear; (propre) clean; (notable) marked; (soigné) neat; (prix, poids) net. ● **N~** nm (Ordinat) net. ● adv (s'arrêter) dead; (refuser) flatly; (parler) plainly; (se casser) cleanly; (tuer) outright. **nettement** adv (expliquer) clearly; (augmenter, se détériorer) markedly; (indiscutablement) distinctly, decidedly. **netteté** nf clearness.

netéconomie /nɛtekɔnɔmi/ nf e-economy.

nétiquette /netikɛt/ nf netiquette.

nettoyage /nɛtwajaʒ/ nm cleaning; ~ **à sec** dry-cleaning; **produit de** ~ cleaner; ~ **ethnique** ethnic cleansing.

nettoyer /nɛtwaje/ **81** vt clean.

neuf¹ /nœf/ (/nœv/ before vowels and mute h) adj inv & nm nine.

neuf², -euve /nœf, -v/ adj new; **tout** ~ brand new. ● nm new; **remettre à** ~ brighten up; **du** ~ a new development; **quoi de ~?** what's new?

neutre /nøtʀ/ adj neutral; (Gram) neuter. ● nm (Gram) neuter.

neuve /nœv/ ➡**NEUF²**.

neuvième /nœvjɛm/ adj & nm, f ninth.

neveu (pl ~**x**) /nəvø/ nm nephew.

névrose /nevʀoz/ nf neurosis. **névrosé,** ~e adj & nm, f neurotic.

nez /ne/ nm nose; ~ **à** ~ face to face; ~ **retroussé** turned-up nose.

ni /ni/ conj neither, nor; ~ **grand** ~ **petit** neither big nor small; ~ **l'un** ~ **l'autre ne fument** neither (one nor the other) smokes; **sortir sans manteau** ~ **chapeau** go without a coat or hat; **elle n'a dit** ~ **oui** ~ **non** she didn't say either yes or no.

niais, ~e /njɛ, -z/ adj silly.

niche /niʃ/ nf (de chien) kennel; (cavité) niche.

nicher /niʃe/ **1** vi nest. □ **se** ~ vpr nest; (se cacher) hide.

nicotine /nikɔtin/ nf nicotine.

nid /ni/ nm nest; **faire un ~** build a nest. **nid-de-poule** (pl **nids-de-poule**) nm pot-hole.

nièce /njɛs/ nf niece.

nier /nje/ [45] vt deny.

nigaud, ~e /nigo, -d/ nm, f fool.

nippon, ~ne /nipɔ̃, -ɔn/ adj Japanese. **N~, ~ne** nm, f Japanese.

niveau (pl **~x**) /nivo/ nm level; (compétence) standard; (étage) storey; (US) story; **au ~** up to standard; **mettre à ~** (Ordinat) upgrade; **~ à bulle** (d'air) spirit level; **~ de vie** standard of living.

niveler /nivle/ [6] vt level.

noble /nɔbl/ adj noble. ● nm, f nobleman, noblewoman. **noblesse** nf nobility.

noce /nɔs/ nf (fête [1]) party; (invités) wedding guests; **~s** wedding; **faire la ~** [1] live it up.

nocif, -ive /nɔsif, -v/ adj harmful.

nocturne /nɔktyʀn/ adj nocturnal. ● nm (Mus) nocturne. ● nf (Sport) evening fixture; (de magasin) late-night opening.

Noël /nɔɛl/ nm Christmas.

nœud /nø/ nm (Naut) knot; (pour lier) knot; (pour orner) bow; **~s** (fig) ties; **~ coulant** slipknot, noose; **~ papillon** bow-tie.

noir, ~e /nwaʀ/ adj black; (obscur, sombre) dark; (triste) gloomy. ● nm black; (obscurité) dark; **travail au ~** moonlighting. ● nm, f (personne) Black.

noircir /nwaʀsiʀ/ [2] vt blacken; **~ la situation** paint a black picture of the situation. ● vi (banane) go black; (mur) get dirty; (métal) tarnish. □ **se ~** vpr (ciel) darken.

noire /nwaʀ/ nf (Mus) crotchet.

noisette /nwazɛt/ nf hazelnut; (de beurre) knob.

noix /nwa/ nf nut; (du noyer) walnut; (de beurre) knob; **~ de cajou** cashew nut; **~ de coco** coconut; **à la ~** [1] useless.

nom /nɔ̃/ nm name; (Gram) noun; **au ~ de** on behalf of; **~ et prénom** full name; **~ déposé** registered trademark; **~ de famille** surname; **~ de jeune fille** maiden name; **~ de plume** pen name; **~ propre** proper noun; **~ d'utilisateur** username.

nomade /nɔmad/ adj nomadic; (worker) mobile. ● nmf nomad.

nombre /nɔ̃bʀ/ nm number; **au ~ de** (parmi) among; (l'un de) one of; **en (grand) ~** in large numbers; **sans ~** countless.

nombreux, -euse /nɔ̃bʀø, -z/ adj (en grand nombre) many, numerous; (important) large; **de ~ enfants** many children; **nous étions très ~** there were a great many of us.

nombril /nɔ̃bʀil/ nm navel.

nomination /nɔminasjɔ̃/ nf appointment.

nommer /nɔme/ [1] vt name; (élire) (à un poste) appoint; (à un lieu) post. □ **se ~** vpr (s'appeler) be called.

non /nɔ̃/ adv no; (pas) not; **~ (pas) que** not that; **il vient, ~?** he is coming, isn't he?; **moi ~ plus** neither am/do/can/etc. I. ● nm inv no.

non- /nɔ̃/ préf non-; **~-fumeur** non-smoker.

nonante /nɔnɑ̃t/ adj & nm ninety.

non-sens /nɔ̃sɑ̃s/ nm inv absurdity.

nord /nɔʀ/ adj inv (façade, côte) north; (frontière, zone) northern. ● nm north; **le ~ de l'Europe** northern Europe; **vent de ~** northerly (wind); **aller vers le ~** go north; **le Nord** the North; **du Nord** northern. **nord-est** nm north-east.

nordique /nɔʀdik/ adj Scandinavian.

nord-ouest /nɔʀwɛst/ nm north-west.

normal, ~e (mpl **-aux**) /nɔʀmal, -o/ adj normal. **normale** nf normality; (norme) norm; (moyenne) average.

normand, ~e /nɔʀmɑ̃, -d/ adj Norman. **N~, ~e** nm, f Norman.

Normandie /nɔʀmɑ̃di/ nf Normandy.

norme /nɔʀm/ nf norm; (de production) standard; **~s de sécurité** safety standards.

Norvège /nɔʀvɛʒ/ nf Norway.

norvégien, ~ne /nɔʀveʒjɛ̃, -ɛn/ adj Norwegian. **N~, ~ne** nm, f Norwegian.

nos /no/ ⇒NOTRE.

nostalgie /nɔstalʒi/ nf nostalgia; **avoir la ~ de son pays** be homesick. **nostalgique** adj nostalgic.

notaire /nɔtɛʀ/ nm notary public.

notamment /nɔtamɑ̃/ adv notably.

note /nɔt/ *nf* (remarque) note; (chiffrée) mark, grade; (facture) bill; (Mus) note; ∼ **(de service)** memorandum.

noter /nɔte/ **1** *vt* note, notice; (écrire) note (down); (devoir) mark; (US) grade; **bien/mal noté** (employé) highly/poorly rated.

notice /nɔtis/ *nf* note; (mode d'emploi) instructions, directions.

notifier /nɔtifje/ **45** *vt* notify (à to).

notion /nɔsjɔ̃/ *nf* notion; **avoir des** ∼**s de** have a basic knowledge of.

notoire /nɔtwaʀ/ *adj* well-known; (criminel) notorious.

notre (*pl* **nos**) /nɔtʀ, no/ *adj* our.

nôtre /nɔtʀ/ *pron* **le** *ou* **la** ∼, **les** ∼**s** ours.

nouer /nwe/ **1** *vt* tie, knot; (relations) strike up.

nouille /nuj/ *nf* (Culin) noodle; **des** ∼**s** noodles, pasta; (idiot **1**) idiot.

nounours /nunuʀs/ *nm* **1** teddy bear.

nourri, ∼**e** /nuʀi/ *adj* **être logé** ∼ have bed and board; ∼ **au sein** breastfed.

nourrice /nuʀis/ *nf* childminder.

nourrir /nuʀiʀ/ **2** *vt* feed; (espoir, crainte) harbour; (projet) nurture; (passion) fuel. ● *vi* be nourishing. □ **se** ∼ *vpr* eat; **se** ∼ **de** feed on. **nourrissant,** ∼**e** *adj* nourishing.

nourrisson /nuʀisɔ̃/ *nm* infant.

nourriture /nuʀityʀ/ *nf* food.

nous /nu/ *pron* (sujet) we; (complément) us; (indirect) (to) us; (réfléchi) ourselves; (l'un l'autre) each other; **la voiture est à** ∼ the car is ours. **nous-mêmes** *pron* ourselves.

nouveau (**nouvel** before vowel or mute h), **nouvelle** (*mpl* ∼**x**) /nuvo, nuvɛl/ *adj* new; **nouvel an** new year; ∼**x mariés** newly-weds; ∼ **venu, nouvelle venue** newcomer. ● *nm, f* (élève) new boy, new girl. ● *nm* **du** ∼ (fait nouveau) a new development; **de** ∼, **à** ∼ again. **nouveau-né** (*pl* ∼**s**) *nm* newborn baby.

nouveauté /nuvote/ *nf* novelty; (chose) new thing; (livre) new publication; (disque) new release.

nouvelle /nuvɛl/ *nf* (piece of) news; (récit) short story; ∼**s** news.

Nouvelle-Zélande /nuvɛlzelɑ̃d/ *nf* New Zealand.

novembre /nɔvɑ̃bʀ/ *nm* November.

noyade /nwajad/ *nf* drowning.

noyau (*pl* ∼**x**) /nwajo/ *nm* (de fruit) stone; (US) pit; (de cellule) nucleus; (groupe) group; (centre: fig) core.

noyer /nwaje/ **31** *vt* drown; (inonder) flood. □ **se** ∼ *vpr* drown; (volontairement) drown oneself; **se** ∼ **dans un verre d'eau** make a mountain out of a molehill. ● *nm* walnut-tree.

nu, ∼**e** /ny/ *adj* (corps, personne) naked; (mains, mur, fil) bare; **à l'œil** ∼ to the naked eye. ● *nm* nude; **mettre à** ∼ expose.

nuage /nyaʒ/ *nm* cloud.

nuance /nyɑ̃s/ *nf* shade; (de sens) nuance; (différence) difference. **nuancer** **10** *vt* (opinion) qualify.

nucléaire /nykleɛʀ/ *adj* nuclear. ● *nm* **le** ∼ nuclear energy.

nudisme /nydism/ *nm* nudism.

nudité /nydite/ *nf* nudity; (de lieu) bareness.

nuée /nɥe/ *nf* swarm, host.

nues /ny/ *nfpl* **tomber des** ∼ be amazed; **porter qn aux** ∼ praise sb to the skies.

nuire /nɥiʀ/ **17** *vi* ∼ **à** harm.

nuisible /nɥizibl/ *adj* harmful (à to).

nuit /nɥi/ *nf* night; **cette** ∼ tonight; (hier) last night; **il fait** ∼ it is dark; ∼ **blanche** sleepless night; **la** ∼, **de** ∼ at night; ∼ **de noces** wedding night.

nul, ∼**le** /nyl/ *adj* (aucun) no; (zéro) nil; (qui ne vaut rien) useless; (non valable) null; (contrat) void; (testament) invalid; **match** ∼ draw; ∼ **en sciences** no good at science; **nulle part** nowhere; ∼ **autre** no one else. ● *pron* no one. **nullement** *adv* not at all. **nullité** *nf* uselessness; (personne) nonentity.

numérique /nymeʀik/ *adj* numerical; (montre, horloge) digital.

numériser /nymeʀize/ *vt* digitize.

numéro /nymeʀo/ *nm* number; (de journal) issue; (spectacle) act; ∼ **de téléphone** telephone number; ∼ **vert** freephone number. **numéroter** **1** *vt* number.

nuque /nyk/ *nf* nape (of the neck).

nurse /nœʀs/ *nf* nanny.

nutritif, -ive /nytʀitif, -v/ *adj* nutritious; (valeur) nutritional.

Oo

oasis /ɔazis/ nf oasis.

obéir /ɔbeiʀ/ 2 vt ~ à obey. ● vi obey. **obéissance** nf obedience. **obéissant**, ~e adj obedient.

obèse /ɔbɛz/ adj obese.

objecter /ɔbʒɛkte/ 1 vt object.

objectif, -ive /ɔbʒɛktif, -v/ adj objective. ● nm objective; (Photo) lens.

objection /ɔbʒɛksjɔ̃/ nf objection; **soulever des** ~s raise objections.

objet /ɔbʒɛ/ nm (chose) object; (sujet) subject; (but) purpose, object; **être** ou **faire l'**~ **de** be the subject of; ~ **d'art** objet d'art; ~s **trouvés** lost property; (US) lost and found.

obligation /ɔbligasjɔ̃/ nf obligation; (Comm) bond; **être dans l'**~ **de** be under obligation to.

obligatoire /ɔbligatwaʀ/ adj compulsory. **obligatoirement** adv (par règlement) of necessity; (inévitablement) inevitably.

obligeance /ɔbliʒɑ̃s/ nf **avoir l'**~ **de faire** be kind enough to do.

obliger /ɔbliʒe/ 40 vt compel, force (à faire to do); (aider) oblige; **être obligé de** have to (de for).

oblique /ɔblik/ adj oblique; **regard** ~ sidelong glance; **en** ~ at an angle.

oblitérer /ɔblitere/ 14 vt (timbre) cancel.

obnubilé, ~e /ɔbnybile/ adj obsessed.

obscène /ɔpsɛn/ adj obscene.

obscur, ~e /ɔpskyʀ/ adj dark; (confus, humble) obscure; (vague) vague.

obscurcir /ɔpskyʀsiʀ/ 2 vt make dark; (fig) obscure. □ **s'**~ vpr (ciel) darken.

obscurité /ɔpskyʀite/ nf dark(-ness); (de passage, situation) obscurity.

obsédant, ~e /ɔpsedɑ̃, -t/ adj (problème) nagging; (musique, souvenir) haunting.

obsédé, ~e /ɔpsede/ nm, f ~ (sexuel) sex maniac; ~ **du ski/jazz** ski/jazz freak.

obséder /ɔpsede/ 14 vt obsess.

obsèques /ɔpsɛk/ nfpl funeral.

observateur, -trice /ɔpsɛʀ-vatœʀ, -tʀis/ adj observant. ● nm, f observer.

observation /ɔpsɛʀvasjɔ̃/ nf observation; (remarque) remark, comment; (reproche) criticism; (obéissance) observance; **en** ~ under observation.

observer /ɔpsɛʀve/ 1 vt (regarder) observe; (surveiller) watch, observe; (remarquer) notice, observe; **faire** ~ **qch** point sth out (à to).

obsession /ɔpsesjɔ̃/ nf obsession.

obstacle /ɔpstakl/ nm obstacle; (pour cheval) fence, jump; (pour athlète) hurdle; **faire** ~ **à** stand in the way of, obstruct.

obstétrique /ɔpstetʀik/ nf obstetrics (+ sg).

obstiné, ~e /ɔpstine/ adj obstinate.

obstiner (s') /(s)ɔpstine/ 1 vpr persist (à in).

obstruction /ɔpstʀyksjɔ̃/ nf obstruction; (de conduit) blockage.

obstruer /ɔpstʀye/ 1 vt obstruct.

obtenir /ɔptəniʀ/ 58 vt get, obtain. **obtention** nf obtaining.

obus /ɔby/ nm shell.

occasion /ɔkazjɔ̃/ nf opportunity (de faire of doing); (circonstance) occasion; (achat) bargain; (article non neuf) second-hand buy; **à l'**~ sometimes; **d'**~ second-hand. **occasionnel**, ~le adj occasional.

occasionner /ɔkazjɔne/ 1 vt cause.

occident /ɔksidɑ̃/ nm (direction) west; **l'O**~ the West.

occidental, ~e (mpl -aux) /ɔksidɑ̃tal, -o/ adj western. **O**~, ~e (mpl -aux) nm, f westerner.

occulte /ɔkylt/ adj occult.

occupant, ~e /ɔkypɑ̃, -t/ nm, f occupant. ● nm (Mil) forces of occupation.

occupation /ɔkypasjɔ̃/ nf occupation.

occupé, ~e /ɔkype/ adj busy; (place, pays) occupied; (téléphone) engaged, busy; (toilettes) engaged.

occuper /ɔkype/ 1 vt occupy; (poste) hold; (espace, temps) take up. □ **s'**~ vpr (s'affairer) keep busy (à faire doing); **s'**~ **de** (personne, problème) take care of; (bureau, firme) be in charge of; (se mêler) **occupe-toi de tes affaires** mind your own business.

occurrence: en l'~ /ãlɔkyRãs/ *loc* in this case.

océan /ɔseã/ *nm* ocean.

Océanie /ɔseani/ *nf* Oceania.

ocre /ɔkR/ *adj inv* ochre.

octante /ɔktãt/ *adj* eighty.

octet /ɔktɛ/ *nm* byte.

octobre /ɔktɔbR/ *nm* October.

octogone /ɔktɔgɔn/ *nm* octagon.

octroyer /ɔktRwaje/ 🔢 *vt* grant.

oculaire /ɔkylɛR/ *adj* **témoin ~** eye-witness; **troubles ~s** eye trouble.

oculiste /ɔkylist/ *nmf* ophthalmologist.

odeur /ɔdœR/ *nf* smell.

odieux, -ieuse /ɔdjø, -z/ *adj* odious.

odorant, ~e /ɔdɔRã, -t/ *adj* sweet-smelling.

odorat /ɔdɔRa/ *nm* sense of smell.

œil (*pl* **yeux**) /œj, jø/ *nm* eye; **à l'~** 🔢 for free; **à mes yeux** in my view; **faire de l'~ à** make eyes at; **faire les gros yeux** à to glare at; **ouvrir l'~** keep one's eyes open; **~ poché** black eye; **fermer les yeux** shut one's eyes; (fig) turn a blind eye.

œillères /œjɛR/ *nfpl* blinkers.

œillet /œjɛ/ *nm* (plante) carnation; (trou) eyelet.

œuf (*pl* **~s**) /œf, ø/ *nm* egg; **~ à la coque/dur/sur le plat** boiled/ hard-boiled/fried egg.

œuvre /œvR/ *nf* (ouvrage, travail) work; **~ d'art** work of art; (**~ de bienfaisance**) charity; **être à l'~** be at work; **mettre en ~** (*réforme, moyens*) implement; **mise en ~** implementation. ● *nm* (ensemble spécifié) **l'~ entier de Beethoven** the complete works of Beethoven.

œuvrer /œvRe/ 🔢 *vi* work.

offense /ɔfãs/ *nf* insult.

offenser /ɔfãse/ 🔢 *vt* offend. ◻ **s'~** *vpr* take offence (**de** at).

offensive /ɔfãsiv/ *nf* offensive.

offert, ~e /ɔfɛR, -t/ ➡**OFFRIR** 🔢.

office /ɔfis/ *nm* office; (Relig) service; (de cuisine) pantry; **faire ~ de** act as; **d'~** without consultation, automatically; **~ du tourisme** tourist information office.

officiel, ~le /ɔfisjɛl/ *adj* official. ● *nm* official.

officier /ɔfisje/ 🔢 *vi* (Relig) officiate. ● *nm* officer.

officieux, -ieuse /ɔfisjø, -z/ *adj* unofficial.

offre /ɔfR/ *nf* offer; (aux enchères) bid; **l'~ et la demande** supply and demand; **'~s d'emploi**' 'situations vacant'.

offrir /ɔfRiR/ 🔢 *vt* offer (**de faire** to do); (*cadeau*) give; (acheter) buy; **~ à boire à** (chez soi) give a drink to; (au café) buy a drink for. ◻ **s'~** *vpr* (se proposer) offer oneself (**comme** as); (*solution*) present itself; (s'acheter) treat oneself to.

ogive /ɔʒiv/ *nf* **~ nucléaire** nuclear warhead.

OGM (organisation génétiquement modifiée) genetically modified organism.

oie /wa/ *nf* goose.

oignon /ɔɲɔ̃/ *nm* (légume) onion; (de fleur) bulb.

oiseau (*pl* **~x**) /wazo/ *nm* bird.

oisif, -ive /wazif, -v/ *adj* idle.

olive /ɔliv/ *nf & adj inv* olive. **olivier** *nm* olive tree.

olympique /ɔlɛ̃pik/ *adj* Olympic.

ombrage /ɔ̃bRaʒ/ *nm* shade; **pren-dre ~ de** take offence at. **ombragé, ~e** *adj* shady.

ombre /ɔ̃bR/ *nf* (pénombre) shade; (contour) shadow; (soupçon: fig) hint, shadow; **dans l'~** (*agir, rester*) behind the scenes; **faire de l'~ à qn** be in sb's light.

ombrelle /ɔ̃bRɛl/ *nf* parasol.

omelette /ɔmlɛt/ *nf* omelette.

omettre /ɔmɛtR/ 🔢 *vt* omit, leave out.

omnibus /ɔmnibys/ *nm* stopping *ou* local train.

omoplate /ɔmɔplat/ *nf* shoulder blade.

on /ɔ̃/ *pron* (tu, vous) you; (nous) we; (ils, elles) they; (les gens) people, they; (quelqu'un) someone; (indéterminé) one, you; **~ dit** people say, they say, it is said; **~ m'a demandé mon avis** I was asked for my opinion.

oncle /ɔ̃kl/ *nm* uncle.

onctueux, -euse /ɔktɥø, -z/ *adj* smooth.

onde /ɔ̃d/ *nf* wave; ~**s courtes/ longues** short/long wave; **sur les** ~**s** on the air.

on-dit /ɔ̃di/ *nm inv* **les** ~ hearsay.

onduler /ɔ̃dyle/ **1** *vi* undulate; (*cheveux*) be wavy.

onéreux, -euse /ɔneRø, -z/ *adj* costly.

ONG *abrév f* (**organisation non gouvernmentale**) NGO, non-governmental organization.

ongle /ɔ̃gl/ *nm* (finger) nail; ~ **de pied** toenail; **se faire les** ~**s** do one's nails.

ont /ɔ̃/ →AVOIR **5**.

ONU *abrév f* (**Organisation des Nations unies**) UN.

onze /ɔ̃z/ *adj & nm* eleven. **onzième** *adj & nmf* eleventh.

OPA *abrév f* (**offre publique d'achat**) takeover bid.

opéra /ɔpeRa/ *nm* opera; (*édifice*) opera house. **opéra-comique** (*pl* **opéras-comiques**) *nm* light opera.

opérateur, -trice /ɔpeRatœr, -tRis/ *nm, f* operator.

opération /ɔperasjɔ̃/ *nf* operation; (Comm) deal; (*calcul*) calculation; ~ **escargot** slow-moving protest convoy.

opératoire /ɔperatwaR/ *adj* (Méd) surgical; **bloc** ~ operating suite.

opérer /ɔpeRe/ **14** *vt* (*personne*) operate on; (*exécuter*) carry out, make; ~ **qn d'une tumeur** operate on sb to remove a tumour; **se faire** ~ have surgery *ou* an operation. ● *vi* (Méd) operate; (faire effet) work. □ **s'**~ *vpr* (se produire) occur.

opiniâtre /ɔpinjɑtR/ *adj* tenacious.

opinion /ɔpinjɔ̃/ *nf* opinion.

opportuniste /ɔpɔRtynist/ *nmf* opportunist.

opposant, ~e /ɔpozɑ̃, -t/ *nm, f* opponent.

opposé, ~e /ɔpoze/ *adj* (*sens, angle, avis*) opposite; (*factions*) opposing; (*intérêts*) conflicting; **être** ~ **à** be opposed to. ● *nm* opposite; **à l'**~ **de** (contrairement à) contrary to, unlike.

opposer /ɔpoze/ **1** *vt* (*objets*) place opposite each other; (*personnes*) match, oppose; (*contraster*) contrast; (*résistance, argument*) put up. □ **s'**~ *vpr* (*personnes*) confront each other; (*styles*) contrast; **s'**~ **à** oppose.

opposition /ɔpozisjɔ̃/ *nf* opposition; **par** ~ **à** in contrast with; **entrer en** ~ **avec** come into conflict with; **faire** ~ **à un chèque** stop a cheque.

oppressant, ~e /ɔpResɑ̃, -t/ *adj* oppressive.

opprimer /ɔpRime/ **1** *vt* oppress.

opter /ɔpte/ **1** *vi* ~ **pour** opt for.

opticien, ~ne /ɔptisjɛ̃, -ɛn/ *nm, f* optician.

optimisme /ɔptimism/ *nm* optimism.

optimiste /ɔptimist/ *nmf* optimist. ● *adj* optimistic.

option /ɔpsjɔ̃/ *nf* option.

optique /ɔptik/ *adj* (*verre*) optical. ● *nf* (science) optics (+ *sg*); (*perspective*) perspective.

or¹ /ɔR/ *nm* gold; **d'**~ golden; **en** ~ gold; (*occasion*) golden.

or² /ɔR/ *conj* now, well; (indiquant une opposition) and yet.

orage /ɔRaʒ/ *nm* (thunder)storm. **orageux, -euse** *adj* stormy.

oral, ~e (*mpl* **-aux**) /ɔRal, -o/ *adj* oral. ● *nm* (*pl* **-aux**) oral.

orange /ɔRɑ̃ʒ/ *adj inv* orange; (Aut) (*feu*) amber; (US) yellow. ● *nf* orange. **orangeade** *nf* orangeade. **oranger** *nm* orange tree.

orateur, -trice /ɔRatœr, -tRis/ *nm, f* speaker.

orbite /ɔRbit/ *nf* orbit; (d'œil) socket.

orchestre /ɔRkɛstR/ *nm* orchestra; (de jazz) band; (parterre) stalls.

ordinaire /ɔRdinɛR/ *adj* ordinary; (habituel) usual; (*qualité*) standard; (médiocre) very average. ● *nm* **l'**~ the ordinary; (nourriture) the standard fare; **d'**~, **à l'**~ usually. **ordinairement** *adv* usually.

ordinateur /ɔRdinatœr/ *nm* computer; ~ **personnel/de bureau** personal/desktop computer; ~ **portable** laptop (computer); ~ **hôte** (Internet) host.

ordonnance /ɔRdɔnɑ̃s/ *nf* (ordre, décret) order; (de médecin) prescription.

ordonné, ~e /ɔRdɔne/ *adj* tidy.

ordonner /ɔRdɔne/ **1** *vt* order (**à qn de** sb to); (agencer) arrange; (Méd) prescribe; (prêtre) ordain.

ordre /ɔRdR/ *nm* order; (propreté) tidiness; **aux** ~**s de qn** at sb's disposal; **avoir de l'**~ be tidy; **en** ~ tidy, in order; **de premier** ∼ first-rate; **d'∼ officiel** of an official nature; **l'∼ du jour** (programme) agenda; **mettre de l'∼ dans** tidy up; **jusqu'à nouvel** ∼ until further notice; **un** ∼ **de grandeur** an approximate idea.

ordure /ɔʀdyʀ/ nf filth; ∼**s** (détritus) rubbish; (US) garbage; ∼**s ménagères** household refuse.

oreille /ɔʀɛj/ nf ear.

oreiller /ɔʀeje/ nm pillow.

oreillons /ɔʀejɔ̃/ nmpl mumps.

orfèvre /ɔʀfɛvʀ/ nm goldsmith.

organe /ɔʀgan/ nm organ.

organigramme /ɔʀganigʀam/ nm organization chart; (Ordinat) flowchart.

organique /ɔʀganik/ adj organic.

organisateur, -trice /ɔʀganizatœʀ, -tʀis/ nm, f organizer.

organisation /ɔʀganizasjɔ̃/ nf organization.

organiser /ɔʀganize/ **1** vt organize. □ **s'**∼ vpr organize oneself, get organized.

organisme /ɔʀganism/ nm body, organism.

orge /ɔʀʒ/ nf barley.

orgelet /ɔʀʒəlɛ/ nm sty.

orgue /ɔʀg/ nm organ; ∼ **de Barbarie** barrel-organ. **orgues** nfpl organ.

orgueil /ɔʀgœj/ nm pride. **or-gueilleux, -euse** adj proud.

orient /ɔʀjɑ̃/ nm (direction) east; **l'O**∼ the Orient.

oriental, ∼e (mpl **-aux**) /ɔʀjɑ̃tal, -o/ adj eastern; (de l'Orient) oriental. **O**∼, ∼**e** (mpl **-aux**) nm, f Asian.

orientation /ɔʀjɑ̃tasjɔ̃/ nf direction; (tendance politique) leanings (+ pl); (de maison) aspect; (Sport) orienteering; ∼ **professionnelle** careers advice; ∼ **scolaire** curriculum counselling.

orienter /ɔʀjɑ̃te/ **1** vt position; (personne) direct. □ **s'**∼ vpr (se repérer) find one's bearings; **s'**∼ **vers** turn towards.

origan /ɔʀigɑ̃/ nm oregano.

originaire /ɔʀiʒinɛʀ/ adj **être** ∼ **de** be a native of.

original, ∼e (mpl **-aux**) /ɔʀiʒinal, -o/ adj original; (curieux) eccentric. ● nm (œuvre) original. ● nm, f eccentric. **originalité** nf originality; eccentricity.

origine /ɔʀiʒin/ nf origin; **à l'**∼ originally; **d'**∼ (pièce, pneu) original; **être d'**∼ **noble** come from a noble background.

originel, ∼le /ɔʀiʒinɛl/ adj original.

orme /ɔʀm/ nm elm.

ornement /ɔʀnəmɑ̃/ nm ornament.

orner /ɔʀne/ **1** vt decorate.

orphelin, ∼e /ɔʀfəlɛ̃, -in/ nm, f orphan. ● adj orphaned. **orphelinat** nm orphanage.

orteil /ɔʀtɛj/ nm toe.

orthodoxe /ɔʀtɔdɔks/ adj orthodox.

orthographe /ɔʀtɔgʀaf/ nf spelling.

ortie /ɔʀti/ nf nettle.

os /ɔs, o/ nm inv bone.

OS abrév m ➙**OUVRIER SPÉCIALISÉ**.

osciller /ɔsile/ **1** vi sway; (Tech) oscillate; (hésiter) waver; (fluctuer) fluctuate.

osé, ∼e /oze/ adj daring.

oseille /ozɛj/ nf (plante) sorrel.

oser /oze/ **1** vi dare.

osier /ozje/ nm wicker.

ossature /ɔsatyʀ/ nf skeleton, frame.

ossements /ɔsmɑ̃/ nmpl bones, remains.

osseux, -euse /ɔsø, -z/ adj bony; (Méd) bone.

otage /ɔtaʒ/ nm hostage.

OTAN /ɔtɑ̃/ abrév f (**Organisation du traité de l'Atlantique Nord**) NATO.

otarie /ɔtaʀi/ nf eared seal.

ôter /ote/ **1** vt remove (**à qn** from sb); (déduire) take away.

otite /ɔtit/ nf ear infection.

ou /u/ conj or; ∼ **bien** or else; ∼ **(bien)...** ∼ **(bien)...** either... or...; **vous** ∼ **moi** either you or me.

où /u/ pron where; (dans lequel) in which; (sur lequel) on which; (auquel) at which; **d'**∼ from which; (pour cette raison) hence; **par** ∼ through which; ∼ **qu'il soit** wherever he may be; **juste au moment** ∼ just as; **le jour** ∼ the day when. ● adv where; **d'**∼**?** where from?

ouate /wat/ nf cotton wool; (US) absorbent cotton.

oubli /ubli/ nm forgetfulness; (trou de mémoire) lapse of memory; (négligence) oversight; **tomber dans l'**∼ sink into oblivion.

oublier /ublije/ 45 vt forget; (omettre) leave out, forget. □ **s'~** vpr (chose) be forgotten.

ouest /wɛst/ adj inv (façade, côte) west; (frontière, zone) western. ● nm west; **l'~ de l'Europe** western Europe; **vent d'~** westerly (wind); **aller vers l'~** go west; **l'O~** the West; **de l'O~** western.

oui /wi/ adv & nm inv yes.

ouï-dire: par ~ /parwidir/ loc by hearsay.

ouïe /wi/ nf hearing; (de poisson) gill.

ouragan /uragɑ̃/ nm hurricane.

ourlet /urlɛ/ nm hem.

ours /urs/ nm bear; **~ blanc** polar bear; **~ en peluche** teddy bear.

outil /uti/ nm tool. **outillage** nm tools (+ pl). **outiller** 1 vt equip.

outrage /utraʒ/ nm (grave) insult.

outrance /utrɑ̃s/ nf **à ~** excessively. **outrancier, -ière** adj extreme.

outre /utr/ prép besides. ● adv **passer ~** pay no heed; **~ mesure** unduly; **en ~** in addition. **outre-mer** adv overseas.

outrepasser /utrəpase/ 1 vt exceed.

outrer /utre/ 1 vt exaggerate; (indigner) incense.

ouvert, ~e /uvɛr, -t/ adj open; (gaz, radio) on. ● →OUVRIR 21.

ouverture /uvɛrtyr/ nf opening; (Mus) overture; (Photo) aperture; **~s** (offres) overtures; **~ d'esprit** open-mindedness.

ouvrable /uvrabl/ adj **jour ~** working day; **aux heures ~s** during business hours.

ouvrage /uvraʒ/ nm (travail, livre) work; (couture) (piece of) needlework.

ouvre-boîtes /uvrəbwat/ nm inv tin-opener.

ouvre-bouteilles /uvrəbutɛj/ nm inv bottle-opener.

ouvreur, -euse /uvrœr, -øz/ nm, f usherette.

ouvrier, -ière /uvrije, -jɛr/ nm, f worker; **~ qualifié/spécialisé** skilled/unskilled worker. ● adj working-class; (conflit) industrial; **syndicat ~** trade union.

ouvrir /uvrir/ 21 vt open (up); (gaz, robinet) turn on. ● vi open (up). □ **s'~**

vpr open (up); **s'~ à qn** open one's heart to sb.

ovaire /ɔvɛr/ nm ovary.

ovale /ɔval/ adj & nm oval.

ovni /ɔvni/ abrév m (**objet volant non-identifié**) UFO.

ovule /ɔvyl/ nm (à féconder) ovum; (gynécologique) pessary.

oxygène /ɔksiʒɛn/ nm oxygen.

oxygéner (s') /(s)ɔksiʒene/ 14 vpr get some fresh air.

ozone /ozon/ nf ozone; **la couche d'~** the ozone layer.

. . . .

Pp

. . . .

pacifique /pasifik/ adj peaceful; (personne) peaceable; (Géog) Pacific. **P~** nm **le P~** the Pacific.

pacotille /pakotij/ nf junk, rubbish.

PACS abrév nm (**pacte de solidarité**) contract of civil union.

pacser (se) /səpakse/ 1 vpr sign a contract of civil union (PACS).

pagaie /pagɛ/ nf paddle.

pagaille /pagaj/ nf 1 mess, shambles (+ sg).

page /paʒ/ nf page; **mise en ~** layout; **tourner la ~** turn over a new leaf; **être à la ~** be up to date; **~ d'accueil** (Internet) home page.

paie /pɛ/ nf pay.

paiement /pɛmɑ̃/ nm payment.

païen, ~ne /pajɛ̃, -ɛn/ adj & nm, f pagan.

paillasson /pajasɔ̃/ nm doormat.

paille /paj/ nf straw. ● adj (cheveux) straw-coloured.

paillette /pajɛt/ nf (sur robe) sequin; (de savon) flake.

pain /pɛ̃/ nm bread; (miche) loaf (of bread); (de savon, cire) bar; **~ d'épices** gingerbread; **~ grillé** toast.

pair, ~e /pɛr/ adj (nombre) even. ● nm (personne) peer; **aller de ~** go together (**avec** with); **au ~** (jeune fille) au pair. **paire** nf pair.

paisible /pezibl/ adj peaceful.

paître /pɛtʀ/ [44] vi graze.

paix /pɛ/ nf peace; **fiche-moi la ~!** [1] leave me alone!

Pakistan /pakistɑ̃/ nm Pakistan.

palace /palas/ nm luxury hotel.

palais /palɛ/ nm palace; (Anat) palate; **~ de Justice** law courts; **~ des sports** sports stadium.

pâle /pɑl/ adj pale.

Palestine /palɛstin/ nf Palestine.

palier /palje/ nm (d'escalier) landing; (étape) stage.

pâlir /pɑliʀ/ [2] vt/i (turn) pale.

palissade /palisad/ nf fence.

pallier /palje/ [45] vt compensate for.

palmarès /palmaʀɛs/ nm list of prize-winners.

palme /palm/ nf palm leaf; (de nageur) flipper. **palmé, ~e** adj (patte) webbed.

palmier /palmje/ nm palm (tree).

palper /palpe/ [1] vt feel.

palpiter /palpite/ [1] vi (battre) pound; (frémir) quiver.

paludisme /palydism/ nm malaria.

pamplemousse /pɑ̃pləmus/ nm grapefruit.

panaché, ~e /panaʃe/ adj (bariolé, mélangé) motley; **glace ~e** mixed-flavour ice cream. ● nm shandy.

pancarte /pɑ̃kaʀt/ nf sign; (de manifestant) placard.

pané, ~e /pane/ adj breaded.

panier /panje/ nm basket; (de basket-ball) basket; **mettre au ~** [1] throw out; **~ à salade** salad shaker; (fourgon [1]) police van.

panique /panik/ nf panic. **paniquer** [1] vi panic.

panne /pan/ nf breakdown; **être en ~** have broken down; **être en ~ sèche** have run out of petrol; **~ d'électricité** ou **de courant** power failure.

panneau (pl ~x) /pano/ nm sign; (publicitaire) hoarding; (de porte) panel; (**~ d'affichage**) notice board; (**~ de signalisation**) road sign.

panoplie /panɔpli/ nf (jouet) outfit; (gamme) range.

pansement /pɑ̃smɑ̃/ nm dressing; **~ adhésif** plaster. **panser** [1] vt (plaie)

dress; (personne) dress the wound(s) of; (cheval) groom.

pantalon /pɑ̃talɔ̃/ nm trousers (+ pl).

panthère /pɑ̃tɛʀ/ nf panther.

pantin /pɑ̃tɛ̃/ nm puppet.

pantomime /pɑ̃tɔmim/ nf mime; (spectacle) mime show.

pantoufle /pɑ̃tufl/ nf slipper.

paon /pɑ̃/ nm peacock.

papa /papa/ nm dad(dy).

pape /pap/ nm pope.

paperasse /papʀas/ nf (péj) bumf.

papeterie /papɛtʀi/ nf (magasin) stationer's shop.

papier /papje/ nm paper; (formulaire) form; **~s (d'identité)** (identity) papers; **~ absorbant** kitchen paper; **~ aluminium** tin foil; **~ buvard** blotting paper; **~ cadeau** wrapping paper; **~ calque** tracing paper; **~ carbone** carbon paper; **~ collant** adhesive tape; **~ hygiénique** toilet paper; **~ journal** newspaper; **~ à lettres** writing paper; **~ mâché** papier mâché; **~ peint** wallpaper; **~ de verre** sandpaper.

papillon /papijɔ̃/ nm butterfly; (contravention [1]) parking-ticket; **~ de nuit** moth.

papoter /papɔte/ [1] vi [1] chatter.

paquebot /pakbo/ nm liner.

pâquerette /pɑkʀɛt/ nf daisy.

Pâques /pɑk/ nfpl & nm Easter.

paquet /pakɛ/ nm packet; (de cartes) pack; (colis) parcel; **un ~ de** (beaucoup [1]) a mass of.

par /paʀ/ prép by; (à travers) through; (motif) out of, from; (provenance) from; **commencer/finir ~ qch** begin/ end with sth; **commencer/finir ~ faire** begin by/ end up (by) doing; **~ an/mois** a ou per year/month; **~ jour** a day; **~ personne** each, per person; **~ avion** (lettre) (by) airmail; **~-ci**, **~-là** here and there; **~ contre** on the other hand; **~ ici/là** this/that way.

parachute /paʀaʃyt/ nm parachute. **parachutiste** nmf parachutist; (Mil) paratrooper.

parader /paʀade/ [1] vi show off.

paradis /paʀadi/ nm (Relig) heaven; (lieu idéal) paradise; **~ fiscal** tax haven.

paradoxal, ~e (*mpl* **-aux**) /paʀadɔksal, -o/ *adj* paradoxical.

paraffine /paʀafin/ *nf* paraffin wax.

parages /paʀaʒ/ *nmpl* **dans les ~** around.

paragraphe /paʀagʀaf/ *nm* paragraph.

paraître /paʀɛtʀ/ 🔢 *vi* (se montrer) appear; (sembler) seem, appear; (ouvrage) be published, come out; **faire ~** (ouvrage) bring out; **il paraît qu'ils...** apparently they...; **oui, il paraît** so I hear.

parallèle /paʀalɛl/ *adj* parallel; (illégal) unofficial. ● *nm* parallel; **faire le ~** make a connection. ● *nf* parallel (line).

paralyser /paʀalize/ 🔢 *vt* paralyse. **paralysie** *nf* paralysis.

paramètre /paʀamɛtʀ/ *nm* parameter.

parapente /paʀapɑ̃t/ *nm* paraglider; (activité) paragliding.

parapharmacie /paʀafaʀmasi/ *nf* toiletries and vitamins (pl.)

parapher /paʀafe/ 🔢 *vi* initial; (signer) sign.

parapluie /paʀaplɥi/ *nm* umbrella.

parasite /paʀazit/ *nm* parasite; **~s** (radio) interference (+ sg).

parasol /paʀasɔl/ *nm* sunshade.

paratonnerre /paʀatɔnɛʀ/ *nm* lightning conductor ou rod.

paravent /paʀavɑ̃/ *nm* screen.

parc /paʀk/ *nm* park; (de bétail) pen; (de bébé) play-pen; (entrepôt) depot; **~ de loisirs** theme park; **~ relais** park and ride; **~ de stationnement** car park.

parce que /paʀsk(ə)/ *conj* because.

parchemin /paʀʃəmɛ̃/ *nm* parchment.

parcmètre /paʀkmɛtʀ/ *nm* parking meter.

parcourir /paʀkuʀiʀ/ 🔢 *vt* travel ou go through; (distance) travel; (des yeux) glance at ou over.

parcours /paʀkuʀ/ *nm* route; (voyage) journey.

par-delà /paʀdəla/ *prép* beyond.

par-derrière /paʀdeʀjɛʀ/ *adv* (attaquer) from behind; (critiquer) behind sb's back.

par-dessous /paʀdəsu/ *prép & adv* under (neath).

pardessus /paʀdəsy/ *nm* overcoat.

par-dessus /paʀdəsy/ *prép & adv* over; **~ bord** overboard; **~ le marché** 🔲 into the bargain; **~ tout** above all.

par-devant /paʀdəvɑ̃/ *adv* (passer) by the front.

pardon /paʀdɔ̃/ *nm* forgiveness; **(je vous demande) ~!** (I am) sorry!; (pour demander qch) excuse me.

pardonner /paʀdɔne/ 🔢 *vt* forgive; **~ qch à qn** forgive sb for sth.

pare-brise /paʀbʀiz/ *nm inv* windscreen.

pare-chocs /paʀʃɔk/ *nm inv* bumper.

pareil, ~le /paʀɛj/ *adj* similar (à to); (tel) such (a); **c'est ~** it's the same; **ce n'est pas ~** it's not the same thing. ● *nm, f* equal. ● *adv* 🔲 the same.

parent, ~e /paʀɑ̃, -t/ *adj* related (de to). ● *nm, f* relative, relation; **~s** (père et mère) parents; **~ isolé** single parent; **réunion de ~s d'élèves** parents' evening.

parenté /paʀɑ̃te/ *nf* relationship.

parenthèse /paʀɑ̃tɛz/ *nf* bracket, parenthesis; (fig) digression.

parer /paʀe/ 🔢 *vt* (esquiver) parry; (orner) adorn. ● *vi* **~ à** deal with; **~ au plus pressé** tackle the most urgent things first.

paresse /paʀɛs/ *nf* laziness.

paresseux, -euse /paʀɛsø, -z/ *adj* lazy. ● *nm, f* lazy person.

parfait, ~e /paʀfɛ, -t/ *adj* perfect. **parfaitement** *adv* perfectly; (bien sûr) absolutely.

parfois /paʀfwa/ *adv* sometimes.

parfum /paʀfœ̃/ *nm* (senteur) scent; (substance) perfume, scent; (goût) flavour. **parfumé, ~e** *adj* fragrant; (savon) scented; (thé) flavoured.

parfumer /paʀfyme/ 🔢 *vt* (embaumer) scent; (gâteau) flavour. □ **se ~** *vpr* put on one's perfume. **parfumerie** *nf* (produits) perfumes; (boutique) perfume shop.

pari /paʀi/ *nm* bet.

Paris /paʀi/ *npr* Paris.

parisien, ~ne /paʀizjɛ̃, -ɛn/ *adj* Parisian; (banlieue) Paris. **P~, ~ne** *nm, f* Parisian.

parking /paʀkiŋ/ *nm* car park.

parlement /paʀləmɑ̃/ nm parliament.

parlementaire /paʀləmɑ̃tɛʀ/ adj parliamentary. ● nmf Member of Parliament.

parlementer /paʀləmɑ̃te/ **1** vi negotiate.

parler /paʀle/ **1** vi talk (à to); ~ de talk about; **tu parles d'un avantage!** call that a benefit!; **de quoi ça parle?** what is it about? ● vt (langue) speak; (politique, affaires) talk. □ **se** ~ vpr (personnes) talk (to each other); (langue) be spoken. ● nm speech; (dialecte) dialect.

parmi /paʀmi/ prép among(st).

paroi /paʀwa/ nf wall; ~ **rocheuse** rock face.

paroisse /paʀwas/ nf parish.

parole /paʀɔl/ nf (mot, promesse) word; (langage) speech; **demander la** ~ ask to speak; **prendre la** ~ (begin to) speak; **tenir** ~ keep one's word; **croire qn sur** ~ take sb's word for it.

parquet /paʀkɛ/ nm (parquet) floor; **lame de** ~ floorboard; **le** ~ (Jur) prosecution.

parrain /paʀɛ̃/ nm godfather; (fig) sponsor.

parsemer /paʀsəme/ **6** vt strew (de with).

part /paʀ/ nf share, part; **à** ~ (de côté) aside; (séparément) separate; (excepté) apart from; **d'une** ~ on the one hand; **d'autre** ~ on the other hand; (de plus) moreover; **de la** ~ **de** from; **de toutes** ~s from all sides; **de** ~ **et d'autre** on both sides; **faire** ~ **à qn** inform sb (de of); **faire la** ~ **des choses** make allowances; **prendre** ~ **à** take part in; (joie, douleur) share; **pour ma** ~ as for me.

partage /paʀtaʒ/ nm (division) dividing; (répartition) sharing out; **recevoir qch en** ~ be left sth in a will.

partager /paʀtaʒe/ **40** vt divide; (distribuer) share out; (avoir en commun) share. □ **se** ~ **qch** vpr share sth.

partenaire /paʀtənɛʀ/ nmf partner.

parterre /paʀtɛʀ/ nm flower bed; (Théât) stalls.

parti /paʀti/ nm (Pol) party; (décision) decision; (en mariage) match; ~ **pris** bias; **prendre** ~ get involved; **prendre** ~ **pour qn** side with sb; **j'en ai pris mon** ~ I've come to terms with that.

partial, ~e (mpl **-iaux**) /paʀsjal, -jo/ adj biased.

participe /paʀtisip/ nm (Gram) participle.

participant, ~e /paʀtisipɑ̃, -t/ nm, f participant (à in).

participation /paʀtisipasjɔ̃/ nf participation; (financière) contribution; (d'un artiste) appearance.

participer /paʀtisipe/ **1** vi ~ **à** take part in, participate in; (profits, frais) share.

particule /paʀtikyl/ nf particle.

particulier, -ière /paʀtikylje, -jɛʀ/ adj (spécifique) particular; (bizarre) unusual; (privé) private; **rien de** ~ nothing special. ● nm private individual; **en** ~ in particular, particularly. **particulièrement** adv particularly.

partie /paʀti/ nf part; (cartes, Sport) game; (Jur) party; **une** ~ **de pêche** a fishing trip; **en** ~ partly, in part; **en grande** ~ largely; **faire** ~ **de** be part of; (adhérer à) be a member of; **faire** ~ **intégrante de** be an integral part of.

partiel, ~le /paʀsjɛl/ adj partial. ● nm (Univ) exam based on a module.

partir /paʀtiʀ/ **46** vi (aux être) go; (quitter un lieu) leave, go; (tache) come out; (bouton) come off; (coup de feu) go off; (commencer) start; ~ **pour le Brésil** leave for Brazil; ~ **du principe que** work on the assumption that; **à** ~**de** from; **à** ~ **de maintenant** from now on.

partisan, ~e /paʀtizɑ̃, -an/ nm, f supporter. ● nm (Mil) partisan; **être** ~ **de** be in favour of.

partition /paʀtisjɔ̃/ nf (Mus) score.

partout /paʀtu/ adv everywhere; ~ **où** wherever.

paru /paʀy/ →**PARAÎTRE 18**.

parure /paʀyʀ/ nf finery; (bijoux) set of jewels; (de draps) set.

parution /paʀysjɔ̃/ nf publication.

parvenir /paʀvəniʀ/ **58** vi (aux être) ~ **à** reach; ~ **à faire** manage to do; **faire** ~ send.

parvenu, ~e /paʀvəny/ nm, f upstart.

pas¹ /pɑ/

> ➡ Pour les expressions comme **pas encore, pas mal**, etc. ➡**encore, mal** etc.

● *adverbe*

····▸ not; **ne ~** not; **je ne sais ~** I don't know; **je ne pense ~** I don't think so; **il a aimé, moi ~** he liked it, I didn't; **~ cher/poli** cheap/impolite.

····▸ **~ du tout** not at all; **~ de chance!** tough luck!

····▸ **on a bien ri, ~ vrai?** 🔢 we had a good laugh, didn't we?

> ❗ In spoken colloquial French **ne... pas** is often shortened to **pas**. You will hear **j'ai pas compris** instead of **je n'ai pas compris** (*I didn't understand*). NB This is not correct written French.

pas² /pɑ/ *nm* step; (*bruit*) footstep; (*trace*) footprint; (*vitesse*) pace; **à deux ~ (de)** a step away (from); **marcher au ~** march; **rouler au ~** move very slowly; **à ~ de loup** stealthily; **faire les cent ~** walk up and down; **faire le premier ~** make the first move; **~ de porte** doorstep; **~ de vis** (Tech) thread.

passage /pɑsaʒ/ *nm* (*traversée*) crossing; (*visite*) visit; (*chemin*) way, passage; (*d'une œuvre*) passage; **de ~** (*voyageur*) visiting; (*amant*) casual; **la tempête a tout emporté sur son ~** the storm swept everything away; **~ clouté** pedestrian crossing; **~ interdit** (*panneau*) no thoroughfare; **~ à niveau** level crossing; **~ souterrain** subway.

passager, -ère /pɑsaʒe, -ɛʀ/ *adj* temporary. ● *nm, f* passenger; **~ clandestin** stowaway.

passant, ~e /pɑsɑ̃, -t/ *adj* (*rue*) busy. ● *nm, f* passer-by. ● *nm* (*anneau*) loop.

passe /pɑs/ *nf* pass; **bonne/mauvaise ~** good/bad patch; **en ~ de** on the road to.

passé, ~e /pɑse/ *adj* (*révolu*) past; (*dernier*) last; (*fané*) faded; **~ de mode** out of fashion. ● *nm* past. ● *prép* after.

passe-partout /pɑspaʀtu/ *nm inv* master-key. ● *adj inv* for all occasions.

passeport /pɑspɔʀ/ *nm* passport.

passer /pɑse/ 🔢 *vi* (*aux être ou avoir*) go past, pass; (*aller*) go; (*venir*) come; (*temps, douleur*) pass; (*film*) be on; (*couleur*) fade; **laisser ~** let through; (*occasion*) miss; **~ devant** (à pied) walk past; (en voiture) drive past; **~ par** go through; **où est-il passé?** where did he get to?; **~ outre** take no notice; **passons!** let's forget about it!; **passons aux choses sérieuses** let's turn to serious matters; **~ dans la classe supérieure** go up a year; **~ pour un idiot** look a fool. ● *vt* (*aux avoir*) (*franchir*) pass, cross; (*donner*) pass, hand; (*temps*) spend; (*enfiler*) slip on; (*vidéo, disque*) put on; (*examen*) take, sit; (*commande*) place; (*faire*) **~ le temps** while away the time; **~ l'aspirateur** hoover; **~ un coup de fil à qn** give sb a ring; **je vous passe Mme X** (par le standard) I'll put you through to Mrs X; (en donnant l'appareil) I'll pass you over to Mrs X; **~ qch en fraude** smuggle sth. □ **se ~** *vpr* happen, take place; (*s'écouler*) go by; **se ~ de** go *ou* do without.

passerelle /pɑsʀɛl/ *nf* footbridge; (*de navire*) gangway; (*d'avion*) (passenger) footbridge; (*Internet*) gateway.

passe-temps /pɑstɑ̃/ *nm inv* pastime.

passif, -ive /pɑsif, -v/ *adj* passive. ● *nm* (Comm) liabilities.

passion /pɑsjɔ̃/ *nf* passion. **passionnant, ~e** *adj* fascinating.

passionné, ~e /pɑsjɔne/ *adj* passionate; **être ~ de** have a passion for.

passionner /pɑsjɔne/ 🔢 *vt* fascinate. □ **se ~ pour** *vpr* have a passion for.

passoire /pɑswaʀ/ *nf* (à thé) strainer; (à légumes) colander.

pastèque /pɑstɛk/ *nf* watermelon.

pasteur /pɑstœʀ/ *nm* (Relig) minister.

pastille /pɑstij/ *nf* (médicament) pastille, lozenge.

patate /patat/ *nf* 🔢 spud; **~ (douce)** sweet potato.

patauger /patoʒe/ 🔢 *vi* splash about.

pâte /pɑt/ *nf* paste; (à gâteau) dough; (à tarte) pastry; (à frire) batter; **~s (alimentaires)** pasta (+ *sg.*); **~ à modeler** Plasticine®; **~ d'amandes** marzipan.

pâté /pɑte/ nm (Culin) pâté; (d'encre) blot; (de sable) sandpie; ∼ **en croûte** ≈ pie; ∼ **de maisons** block (of houses).

pâtée /pɑte/ nf feed, mash.

patente /patɑ̃t/ nf trade licence.

paternel, ∼le /patɛʀnɛl/ adj paternal. **paternité** nf paternity.

pathétique /patetik/ adj moving.

patience /pasjɑ̃s/ nf patience. **patient, ∼e** adj & nm, f patient. **patienter** 🔟 vi wait.

patin /patɛ̃/ nm skate; ∼ **à roulettes** roller-skate.

patinage /patinaʒ/ nm skating. **patiner** 🔟 vi skate; (roue) spin. **patinoire** nf ice rink.

pâtisserie /pɑtisʀi/ nf cake shop; (gâteau) pastry; (secteur) cake making. **pâtissier, -ière** nm, f confectioner, pastry-cook.

patrie /patʀi/ nf homeland.

patrimoine /patʀimwan/ nm heritage.

patriote /patʀijɔt/ adj patriotic. ● nmf patriot.

patron, ∼ne /patʀɔ̃, -ɔn/ nm, f employer, boss; (propriétaire) owner, boss; (saint) patron saint. ● nm (couture) pattern. **patronal, ∼e** (mpl -aux) adj employers'. **patronat** nm employers (+ pl).

patrouille /patʀuj/ nf patrol.

patte /pat/ nf leg; (pied) foot; (de chat) paw; ∼s (favoris) sideburns; **marcher à quatre ∼s** walk on all fours; (bébé) crawl; ∼s **de derrière** hind legs.

paume /pom/ nf (de main) palm.

paumé, ∼e /pome/ nm, f 🔟 misfit.

paupière /popjɛʀ/ nf eyelid.

pause /poz/ nf pause; (halte) break.

pauvre /povʀ/ adj poor. ● nmf poor man, poor woman. **pauvreté** nf poverty.

pavé /pave/ nm cobblestone.

pavillon /pavijɔ̃/ nm (maison) house; (drapeau) flag.

payant, ∼e /pɛjɑ̃, -t/ adj (hôte) paying; **c'est ∼** you have to pay to get in.

payer /peje/ 🛐 vt/i pay; (service, travail) pay for; ∼ **qch à qn** buy sb sth; **faire ∼ qn** charge sb; **il me le paiera!** he'll pay for this. ▢ **se ∼** vpr ∼ **qch** buy oneself sth; **se ∼ la tête de** make fun of.

pays /pei/ nm country; (région) region; **du ∼** local.

paysage /peizaʒ/ nm landscape.

paysan, ∼ne /peizɑ̃, -an/ nm, f farmer, country person; (péj) peasant. ● adj (agricole) farming; (rural) country.

Pays-Bas /peibɑ/ nmpl **les ∼** the Netherlands.

PCV abrév m (**paiement contre vérification**) **téléphoner en ∼** reverse the charges.

PDG abrév m (**président-directeur général**) chairman and managing director.

péage /peaʒ/ nm toll; (lieu) tollgate.

peau (pl ∼x) /po/ nf skin; (cuir) hide; ∼ **de chamois** shammy (leather); ∼**de mouton** sheepskin; **être bien/ mal dans sa ∼** be/not be at ease with oneself.

pêche /pɛʃ/ nf (fruit) peach; (activité) fishing; (poissons) catch; ∼ **à la ligne** angling.

péché /peʃe/ nm sin.

pêcher /peʃe/ vt (poisson) catch; (dénicher 🔟) dig up. ● vi fish. **pêcheur** nm fisherman; (à la ligne) angler.

pécuniaire /pekynjɛʀ/ adj financial.

pédagogie /pedagɔʒi/ nf education.

pédale /pedal/ nf pedal.

pédalo ® /pedalo/ nm pedal boat.

pédant, ∼e /pedɑ̃, -t/ adj pedantic.

pédestre /pedɛstʀ/ adj **faire de la randonnée ∼** go walking ou hiking.

pédiatre /pedjatʀ/ nmf paediatrician.

pédicure /pedikyʀ/ nmf chiropodist.

peigne /pɛɲ/ nm comb.

peigner /peɲe/ 🔟 vt comb; (personne) comb the hair of. ▢ **se ∼** vpr comb one's hair.

peignoir /peɲwaʀ/ nm dressing gown.

peindre /pɛ̃dʀ/ 🟤 vt paint.

peine /pɛn/ nf sadness, sorrow; (effort, difficulté) trouble; (Jur) sentence; **avoir de la ∼** feel sad; **faire de la ∼ à** hurt; **ce n'est pas la ∼ de sonner** you don't need to ring the bell; **j'ai de la ∼ à le croire** I find it hard to believe; **se donner** ou **prendre la ∼ de faire** go to the trouble of doing; ∼ **de mort** death penalty. ● adv **à ∼** hardly.

peiner /pene/ 🔟 vi struggle. ● vt sadden.

peintre /pɛtʀ/ nm painter; ∼ **en bâti-ment** house painter.

peinture /pɛtyʀ/ nf painting; (matière) paint; ∼ **à l'huile** oil painting.

péjoratif, -ive /peʒɔʀatif, -v/ adj pejorative.

pelage /pəlaʒ/ nm coat, fur.

pêle-mêle /pɛlmɛl/ adv in a jumble.

peler /pəle/ 6 vt/i peel.

pèlerinage /pɛlʀinaʒ/ nm pilgrimage.

pelle /pɛl/ nf shovel; (d'enfant) spade.

pellicule /pelikyl/ nf film; ∼s (cheveux) dandruff.

pelote /pəlɔt/ nf (of wool) ball.

peloton /p(ə)lɔtɔ̃/ nm platoon; (Sport) pack; ∼ **d'exécution** firing squad.

pelotonner (se) /(sə)plɔtɔne/ 1 vpr curl up.

pelouse /p(ə)luz/ nf lawn.

peluche /p(ə)lyʃ/ nf (matière) plush; (jouet) cuddly toy; **en** ∼ (lapin, chien) fluffy.

pénal, ∼e (mpl -aux) /penal, -o/ adj penal. **pénaliser** 1 vt penalize. **pénalité** nf penalty.

penchant /pɑ̃ʃɑ̃/ nm inclination; (goût) liking (pour for).

pencher /pɑ̃ʃe/ 1 vt tilt; ∼ **pour** favour. ● vi lean (over), tilt. □ **se** ∼ vpr lean (forward); **se** ∼ **sur** (problème) examine.

pendaison /pɑ̃dɛzɔ̃/ nf hanging.

pendant[1] /pɑ̃dɑ̃/ prép (au cours de) during; (durée) for; ∼ **que** while.

pendant[2], ∼**e** /pɑ̃dɑ̃, -t/ adj hanging; **jambes** ∼**es** with one's legs dangling. ● nm (contrepartie) matching piece (de to); ∼ **d'oreille** drop earring.

pendentif /pɑ̃dɑ̃tif/ nm pendant.

penderie /pɑ̃dʀi/ nf wardrobe.

pendre /pɑ̃dʀ/ 3 vt/i hang. □ **se** ∼ vpr hang (à from); (se tuer) hang oneself.

pendule /pɑ̃dyl/ nf clock. ● nm pendulum.

pénétrer /penetre/ 14 vi ∼ **(dans)** enter; **faire** ∼ **une crème** rub a cream in. ● vt penetrate.

pénible /penibl/ adj (travail) hard; (nouvelle) painful; (enfant) tiresome.

péniche /peniʃ/ nf barge.

pénitence /penitɑ̃s/ nf (Relig) penance; (punition) punishment; **faire** ∼ repent.

pénitentiaire /penitɑ̃sjɛʀ/ adj (établissement) penal.

pénombre /penɔ̃bʀ/ nf half-light.

pensée /pɑ̃se/ nf (idée) thought; (fleur) pansy.

penser /pɑ̃se/ 1 vt/i think; ∼ **à** (réfléchir à) think about; (se souvenir de, prévoir) think of; ∼ **faire** think of doing; **faire** ∼ **à** remind one of.

pensif, -ive /pɑ̃sif, -v/ adj pensive.

pension /pɑ̃sjɔ̃/ nf (Scol) boarding school; (repas, somme) board; (allocation) pension; (∼ **de famille**) guest house; ∼ **alimentaire** (Jur) alimony. **pensionnaire** nmf (Scol) boarder; (d'hôtel) guest. **pensionnat** nm boarding school.

pente /pɑ̃t/ nf slope; **en** ∼ sloping.

Pentecôte /pɑ̃tkot/ nf **la** ∼ Whitsun.

pénurie /penyʀi/ nf shortage.

pépin /pepɛ̃/ nm (graine) pip; (ennui 🔟) hitch.

pépinière /pepinjɛʀ/ nf (tree) nursery.

perçant, -e /pɛʀsɑ̃, -t/ adj (cri) shrill; (regard) piercing.

perce-neige /pɛʀsənɛʒ/ nm or f inv snowdrop.

percepteur /pɛʀsɛptœʀ/ nm tax inspector.

percer /pɛʀse/ 10 vt pierce; (avec perceuse) drill; (mystère) penetrate. ● vi break through; (dent) come through. **perceuse** nf drill.

percevoir /pɛʀsəvwaʀ/ 52 vt perceive; (impôt) collect.

perche /pɛʀʃ/ nf (bâton) pole.

percher (se) /(sə)pɛʀʃe/ 1 vpr perch.

percolateur /pɛʀkɔlatœʀ/ nm coffee machine.

percuter /pɛʀkyte/ 1 vt (véhicule) crash into.

perdant, ∼e /pɛʀdɑ̃, -t/ adj losing. ● nm, f loser.

perdre /pɛʀdʀ/ 3 vt/i lose; (gaspiller) waste; ∼ **ses poils** (chat) moult. □ **se** ∼ vpr get lost; (rester inutilisé) go to waste.

perdrix /pɛʀdʀi/ nf partridge.

perdu, ∼e /pɛʀdy/ adj lost; (endroit) isolated; (balle) stray; **c'est du temps** ∼ it's a waste of time.

père /pɛʀ/ nm father; ∼ **de famille** father, family man; ∼ **spirituel** father figure; **le ~ Noël** Santa Claus.

perfection /pɛʀfɛksjɔ̃/ *nf* perfection.

perfectionner /pɛʀfɛksjɔne/ **1** *vt*
(*technique*) perfect; (*art*) refine. □ **se
~** *vpr* improve; **se ~ en anglais** improve one's English.

perforer /pɛʀfɔʀe/ **1** *vt* perforate;
(*billet, bande*) punch.

performance /pɛʀfɔʀmɑ̃s/ *nf* performance.

perfusion /pɛʀfyzjɔ̃/ *nf* drip; **sous ~**
on a drip.

péridurale /peʀidyʀal/ *nf* epidural.

péril /peʀil/ *nm* peril; **à tes risques et
~s** at your own risk.

périlleux, -euse /peʀijø, -z/ *adj*
perilous.

périmé, ~e /peʀime/ *adj* (*produit*)
past its use-by date; (*désuet*)
outdated.

période /peʀjɔd/ *nf* period.

périodique /peʀjɔdik/ *adj* periodic(al).
● *nm* (*journal*) periodical.

péripétie /peʀipesi/ *nf* (unexpected)
event, adventure.

périphérique /peʀifeʀik/ *adj* peripheral. ● *nm* (**boulevard**) ~ ring road.

périple /peʀipl/ *nm* journey.

périr /peʀiʀ/ **2** *vi* perish, die.

perle /pɛʀl/ *nf* (d'huître) pearl; (de
verre) bead.

permanence /pɛʀmanɑ̃s/ *nf* permanence; (Scol) study room; **de ~** on
duty; **en ~** permanently; **assurer une
~** keep the office open.

permanent, ~e /pɛʀmanɑ̃, -t/ *adj*
permanent; (*constant*) constant; **formation ~e** continuous education.
permanente *nf* (*coiffure*) perm.

permettre /pɛʀmɛtʀ/ **42** *vt* allow; **~ à
qn de** allow sb to. □ **se ~** *vpr* (*achat*)
afford; **se ~ de faire** take the liberty
of doing.

permis, ~e /pɛʀmi, -z/ *adj* allowed.
● *nm* licence, permit; **~ (de conduire)**
driving licence.

permission /pɛʀmisjɔ̃/ *nf* permission;
en ~ (Mil) on leave.

Pérou /peʀu/ *nm* Peru.

perpendiculaire /pɛʀpɑ̃dikylɛʀ/ *adj*
& *nf* perpendicular.

perpétuité /pɛʀpetɥite/ *nf* **à ~**
for life.

perplexe /pɛʀplɛks/ *adj* perplexed.

perquisition /pɛʀkizisjɔ̃/ *nf* (police)
search.

perron /pɛʀɔ̃/ *nm* (front) steps.

perroquet /pɛʀɔkɛ/ *nm* parrot.

perruche /pɛʀyʃ/ *nf* budgerigar.

perruque /peʀyk/ *nf* wig.

persécuter /pɛʀsekyte/ **1** *vt* persecute.

persévérance /pɛʀseveʀɑ̃s/ *nf* perseverance. **persévérer** **14** *vi* persevere.

persienne /pɛʀsjɛn/ *nf* (outside)
shutter.

persil /pɛʀsi/ *nm* parsley.

persistance /pɛʀsistɑ̃s/ *nf* persistence. **persistant, ~e** *adj* persistent;
(*feuillage*) evergreen.

persister /pɛʀsiste/ **1** *vi* persist (**à
faire** in doing).

personnage /pɛʀsɔnaʒ/ *nm* character;
(*personne célèbre*) personality.

personnalité /pɛʀsɔnalite/ *nf* personality.

personne /pɛʀsɔn/ *nf* person; **~s**
people. ● *pron* nobody, no-one; **je n'ai
vu ~** I didn't see anybody.

personnel, ~le /pɛʀsɔnɛl/ *adj* personal; (*égoïste*) selfish. ● *nm* staff.

perspective /pɛʀspɛktiv/ *nf* (art,
point de vue) perspective; (*vue*) view;
(*éventualité*) prospect.

perspicace /pɛʀspikas/ *adj* shrewd.
perspicacité *nf* shrewdness.

persuader /pɛʀsɥade/ **1** *vt* persuade
(**de faire** to do).

persuasif, -ive /pɛʀsɥazif, -v/ *adj* persuasive.

perte /pɛʀt/ *nf* loss; (ruine) ruin; **à ~
de vue** as far as the eye can see; **~
de** (*temps, argent*) waste of; **~ sèche**
total loss; **~s** (Méd) discharge.

pertinent, ~e /pɛʀtinɑ̃, -t/ *adj* pertinent.

perturbateur, -trice /pɛʀtyʀ- batœʀ,
-tʀis/ *nm, f* disruptive element. **perturbation** *nf* disruption. **perturber** **1**
vt disrupt; (*personne*) perturb.

pervers, ~e /pɛʀvɛʀ, -s/ *adj* (dépravé)
perverted; (méchant) wicked.

pervertir /pɛʀvɛʀtiʀ/ **2** *vt* pervert.

pesant, ~e /pəzɑ̃, -t/ *adj* heavy.

pesanteur /pəzɑ̃tœʀ/ *nf* heaviness; **la
~** (force) gravity.

pesée /pəze/ *nf* weighing; (effort) pressure.

pèse-personne (*pl* ~s) /pɛzpɛʀ- sɔn/ *nm* (bathroom) scales.

peser /pəze/ **6** *vt/i* weigh; ~ **sur** bear upon.

pessimiste /pesimist/ *adj* pessimistic. ● *nmf* pessimist.

peste /pɛst/ *nf* plague; (personne **🄵**) pest.

pet /pɛ/ *nm* **🄵** fart **🄵**.

pétale /petal/ *nm* petal.

Pétanque See ▷**Boules**.

pétard /petaʀ/ *nm* banger.

péter /pete/ **14** *vi* **🄵** fart **🄵**, go bang; (casser) snap.

pétillant, ~**e** /petijã, -t/ *adj* (*boisson*) sparkling; (*personne*) bubbly.

pétiller /petije/ **1** *vi* (*feu*) crackle; (*champagne, yeux*) sparkle; ~ **d'intelligence** sparkle with intelligence.

petit, ~**e** /p(ə)ti, -t/ *adj* small; (avec nuance affective) little; (*jeune*) young, small; (*défaut*) minor; (*mesquin*) petty; **en** ~ in miniature; ~ **à** ~ little by little; **un** ~ **peu** a little bit; ~ **ami** boyfriend; ~**e amie** girlfriend; ~**es annonces** small ads; ~**e cuillère** teaspoon; ~ **déjeuner** breakfast; ~ **pois** garden pea. ● *nm, f* little child; (Scol) junior; ~**s** (de chat) kittens; (de chien) pups. **petite-fille** (*pl* **petites-filles**) *nf* granddaughter. **petit-fils** (*pl* **petits-fils**) *nm* grandson.

pétition /petisjɔ̃/ *nf* petition.

petits-enfants /pətizɑ̃fɑ̃/ *nmpl* grandchildren.

pétrin /petʀɛ̃/ *nm* **dans le** ~ **🄵** in a fix **🄵**.

pétrir /petʀiʀ/ **2** *vt* knead.

pétrole /petʀɔl/ *nm* oil; ~ **brut** crude oil.

pétrolier, -ière /petʀɔlje, -jɛʀ/ *adj* oil. ● *nm* (navire) oil-tanker.

peu /pø/ *adv* (~ **de**) (quantité) little, not much; (nombre) few, not many; ~ **intéressant** not very interesting; **il mange** ~ he doesn't eat very much. ● *pron* few. ● *nm* little; **un** ~ **(de)** a little; **à** ~ **près** more or less; **de** ~ only just; ~ **à** ~ gradually; ~ **après/ avant** shortly after/before; ~ **de**

chose not much; ~ **nombreux** few; ~ **souvent** seldom; **pour** ~ **que** if.

peuple /pœpl/ *nm* people. **peupler** **1** *vt* populate.

peuplier /pøplije/ *nm* poplar.

peur /pœʀ/ *nf* fear; **avoir** ~ be afraid (de of); **de** ~ **de** for fear of; **faire** ~ **à** frighten. **peureux, -euse** *adj* fearful.

peut /pø/ ➙**POUVOIR 49**.

peut-être /pøtɛtʀ/ *adv* perhaps, maybe; ~ **qu'il viendra** he might come.

peux /pø/ ➙**POUVOIR 49**.

phare /faʀ/ *nm* (tour) lighthouse; (de véhicule) headlight; ~ **antibrouillard** fog lamp.

pharmacie /faʀmasi/ *nf* (magasin) chemist's (shop), pharmacy; (science) pharmacy; (armoire) medicine cabinet. **pharmacien,** ~**ne** *nm, f* chemist, pharmacist.

phénomène /fenɔmɛn/ *nm* phenomenon; (personne **🄵**) eccentric.

philosophe /filɔzɔf/ *nmf* philosopher. ● *adj* philosophical. **philosophie** *nf* philosophy. **philosophique** *adj* philosophical.

phobie /fɔbi/ *nf* phobia.

phonétique /fɔnetik/ *adj* phonetic. ● *nf* phonetics.

phoque /fɔk/ *nm* (animal) seal.

photo /fɔto/ *nf* photo; (art) photography; **prendre en** ~ take a photo of; ~ **d'identité** passport photograph.

photocopie /fɔtɔkɔpi/ *nf* photocopy. **photocopier** **45** *vt* photocopy.

photographe /fɔtɔɡʀaf/ *nmf* photographer. **photographie** *nf* photograph; (art) photography. **photographier** **45** *vt* take a photo of.

phrase /fʀɑz/ *nf* sentence.

physicien, ~**ne** /fizisjɛ̃, -ɛn/ *nm, f* physicist.

physique /fizik/ *adj* physical. ● *nm* physique; **au** ~ physically. ● *nf* physics (+ *sg.*).

piano /pjano/ *nm* piano.

pianoter /pjanɔte/ **1** *vi* tinkle; ~ **sur** (ordinateur) tap at.

PIB *abrév m* (**produit intérieur brut**) GDP.

pic /pik/ *nm* (outil) pickaxe; (sommet) peak; (oiseau) woodpecker; **à** ~ (fa-

laise) sheer; (*couler*) straight to the bottom; **tomber à ~ 🔢** come just at the right time.

pichet /piʃɛ/ *nm* jug.

picorer /pikɔʀe/ **🔢** *vt/i* peck.

picotement /pikɔtmɑ̃/ *nm* tingling. **picoter** **🔢** *vt* sting; (*yeux*) sting.

pie /pi/ *nf* magpie.

pièce /pjɛs/ *nf* (d'habitation) room; (de monnaie) coin; (Théât) play; (pour raccommoder) patch; (écrit) document; (morceau) piece; (~ **de théâtre**) play; **dix euros (la ~)** ten euros each; ~ **détachée** part; ~ **d'identité** identity paper; ~**s jointes** enclosures; (courrier électronique) attachments; ~**s justificatives** written proof; ~ **montée** tiered cake; ~ **de rechange** spare part; **un deux- ~s** a two-room flat.

pied /pje/ *nm* foot; (de meuble) leg; (de lampe) base; (de verre) stem; (d'appareil photo) stand; **être ~s nus** be barefoot; **à ~** on foot; **au ~ de la lettre** literally; **avoir ~** be able to touch the bottom; **jouer au tennis comme un 🔢** be hopeless at tennis; **mettre sur ~** set up; **sur un ~ d'égalité** on an equal footing; **mettre les ~s dans le plat 🔢** put one's foot in it; **c'est le ~ 🔢** it's great. **pied-bot** (*pl* **piedsbots**) *nm* club-foot.

piédestal /pjedɛstal/ *nm* pedestal.

piège /pjɛʒ/ *nm* trap.

piéger /pjeʒe/ **🔢 🔢** *vt* trap; **lettre/ voiture piégée** letter/car bomb.

piercing /piʀsiŋ/ *nm* body piercing.

pierre /pjɛʀ/ *nf* stone; ~ **précieuse** precious stone; ~ **tombale** tombstone.

piétiner /pjetine/ **🔢** *vi* (avancer lentement) shuffle along; (fig) make no headway; ~ **d'impatience** hop up and down with impatience. ● *vt* trample (on).

piéton /pjetɔ̃/ *nm* pedestrian.

pieu (*pl* ~**x**) /pjø/ *nm* post, stake.

pieuvre /pjœvʀ/ *nf* octopus.

pieux, -ieuse /pjø, -z/ *adj* pious.

pigeon /piʒɔ̃/ *nm* pigeon.

piger /piʒe/ **🔢** *vt/i* 🔢 understand, get (it).

pile /pil/ *nf* (tas) pile; (Électr) battery; ~ **ou face?** heads or tails? ● *adv* (s'ar-

rêter 🔢) dead; **à dix heures ~** 🔢 at ten on the dot.

pilier /pilje/ *nm* pillar.

pillage /pijaʒ/ *nm* looting. **pillard, ~e** *nm, f* looter. **piller** **🔢** *vt* loot.

pilote /pilɔt/ *nm* (Aviat, Naut) pilot; (Auto) driver. ● *adj* pilot. **piloter** **🔢** *vt* (Aviat, Naut) pilot; (Auto) drive.

pilule /pilyl/ *nf* pill; **la ~** the pill.

piment /pimɑ̃/ *nm* hot pepper; (fig) spice. **pimenté, ~e** *adj* spicy.

pin /pɛ̃/ *nm* pine.

pinard /pinaʀ/ *nm* 🔢 plonk 🔢, cheap wine.

pince /pɛ̃s/ *nf* (outil) pliers (+ *pl*); (levier) crowbar; (de crabe) pincer; (à sucre) tongs (+ *pl*); ~ **à épiler** tweezers (+ *pl*); ~ **à linge** clothes peg.

pinceau (*pl* ~**x**) /pɛ̃so/ *nm* paintbrush.

pincée /pɛ̃se/ *nf* pinch (**de** of).

pincer /pɛ̃se/ **🔢** *vt* pinch; (*attraper* 🔢) catch. □ **se ~** *vpr* catch oneself; **se le doigt** catch one's finger.

pince-sans-rire /pɛ̃ssɑ̃ʀiʀ/ *nmf inv* **c'est un ~** he has a deadpan sense of humour.

pingouin /pɛ̃gwɛ̃/ *nm* penguin.

pingre /pɛ̃gʀ/ *adj* 🔢 stingy.

pintade /pɛ̃tad/ *nf* guinea fowl.

piocher /pjɔʃe/ **🔢** *vt/i* dig; (étudier 🔢) study hard, slog away (at).

pion /pjɔ̃/ *nm* (de jeu) counter; (aux échecs) pawn; (Scol 🔢) supervisor.

pipe /pip/ *nf* pipe; **fumer la ~** smoke a pipe.

piquant, ~e /pikɑ̃, -t/ *adj* (barbe) prickly; (goût) pungent; (remarque) cutting. ● *nm* prickle.

pique /pik/ *nm* (aux cartes) spades.

-pique-nique (*pl* ~**s**) /piknik/ *nm* picnic.

piquer /pike/ **🔢** *vt* (épine) prick; (épice) burn, sting; (abeille, ortie) sting; (serpent, moustique) bite; (enfoncer) stick; (coudre) (machine-) stitch; (curiosité) excite; (voler 🔢) pinch. ● *vi* (avion) dive; (goût) be hot. □ **se ~** *vpr* prick oneself.

piquet /pikɛ/ *nm* stake; (de tente) peg; (de parasol) pole; ~ **de grève** (strike) picket.

piqûre /pikyʀ/ *nf* prick; (d'abeille) sting; (de serpent) bite; (point) stitch;

(Méd) injection, jab; **faire une ~ à qn** give sb an injection.

pirate /piʀat/ nm pirate; **~ informatique** computer hacker; **~ de l'air** hijacker.

pire /piʀ/ adj worse (que than); **les ~s mensonges** the most wicked lies.
● nm **le ~** the worst; **au ~** at worst.

pis /pi/ nm (de vache) udder. ● adj inv & adv worse; **aller de mal en ~** go from bad to worse.

piscine /pisin/ nf swimming pool; **~ couverte** indoor swimming-pool.

pissenlit /pisɑ̃li/ nm dandelion.

pistache /pistaʃ/ nf pistachio.

piste /pist/ nf track; (de personne, d'animal) track, trail; (Aviat) runway; (de cirque) ring; (de ski) slope; (de danse) floor; (Sport) racetrack; **~ cyclable** cycle lane.

pistolet /pistɔlɛ/ nm gun, pistol; (de peintre) spray-gun.

piteux, -euse /pitø, -z/ adj pitiful.

pitié /pitje/ nf pity; **il me fait ~** I feel sorry for him.

piton /pitɔ̃/ nm (à crochet) hook; (sommet pointu) peak.

pitoyable /pitwajabl/ adj pitiful.

pitre /pitʀ/ nm clown; **faire le ~** clown around.

pittoresque /pitɔʀɛsk/ adj picturesque.

pivot /pivo/ nm pivot. **pivoter** ⊞ vi revolve; (personne) swing round.

placard /plakaʀ/ nm cupboard; (affiche) poster. **placarder** ⊞ vt (affiche) post up; (mur) cover with posters.

place /plas/ nf place; (espace libre) room, space; (siège) seat, place; (prix d'un trajet) fare; (esplanade) square; (emploi) position; (de parking) space; **à la ~ de** instead of; **en ~, à sa ~** in its place; **faire ~ à** give way to; **sur ~ on the spot; remettre qn à sa ~** put sb in his place; **ça prend de la ~** it takes up a lot of room; **se mettre à la ~ de qn** put oneself in sb's shoes ou place.

placement /plasmɑ̃/ nm (d'argent) investment.

placer /plase/ ⑩ vt place; (invité, spectateur) seat; (argent) invest. ⊡ **se ~** vpr (personne) take up a position.

plafond /plafɔ̃/ nm ceiling.

plage /plaʒ/ nf beach; **~ horaire** time slot.

plagiat /plaʒja/ nm plagiarism.

plaider /plede/ ⊞ vt/i plead. **plaidoirie** nf (défence) speech. **plaidoyer** nm plea.

plaie /plɛ/ nf wound; (personne ⊞) nuisance.

plaignant, ~e /plɛɲɑ̃, -t/ nm, f plaintiff.

plaindre /plɛ̃dʀ/ ㉒ vt pity. ⊡ **se ~** vpr complain (de about); **se ~ de** (souffrir de) complain of.

plaine /plɛn/ nf plain.

plainte /plɛ̃t/ nf complaint; (gémissement) groan. **plaintif, -ive** adj plaintive.

plaire /plɛʀ/ ㊼ vi **~ à** please; **ça lui plaît** he likes it; **elle lui plaît** he likes her; **ça me plaît de faire** I like ou enjoy doing; **s'il vous plaît** please. ⊡ **se ~** vpr **il se plaît ici** he likes it here.

plaisance /plɛzɑ̃s/ nf **la (navigation de) ~** boating.

plaisant, ~e /plɛzɑ̃, -t/ adj pleasant; (drôle) amusing.

plaisanter /plɛzɑ̃te/ ⊞ vi joke. **plaisanterie** nf joke. **plaisantin** nm joker.

plaisir /pleziʀ/ nm pleasure; **faire ~ à** please; **pour le ~** for fun ou pleasure.

plan /plɑ̃/ nm plan; (de ville) map; (de livre) outline; **~ d'eau** artificial lake; **~ social** planned redundancy programme; **premier ~** foreground.

planche /plɑ̃ʃ/ nf board, plank; (gravure) plate; **~ à repasser** ironing-board; **~ à voile** windsurfing board; (Sport) windsurfing.

plancher /plɑ̃ʃe/ nm floor.

planer /plane/ ⊞ vi glide; **~ sur** (mystère, danger) hang over.

planète /planɛt/ nf planet.

planeur /planœʀ/ nm glider.

planifier /planifje/ ㊸ vt plan.

plant /plɑ̃/ nm seedling; (de légumes) patch.

plante /plɑ̃t/ nf plant; **~ d'appartement** houseplant; **~ des pieds** sole (of the foot).

planter /plɑ̃te/ ⊞ vt (plante) plant; (enfoncer) drive in; (tente) put up; rester **planté** ① stand still.

plaque /plak/ *nf* plate; (de marbre)
slab; (insigne) badge; ~ **chauffante**
hotplate; ~ **commémorative** plaque;
~ **minéralogique** numberplate; ~ **de
verglas** patch of ice.

plaquer /plake/ ❶ *vt* (*bois*) veneer;
(aplatir) flatten; (rugby) tackle; (abandonner ①) ditch ①; **tout** ~ chuck
it all.

plastique /plastik/ *adj & nm* plastic; **en**
~ plastic.

plastiquer /plastike/ ❶ *vt* blow up.

plat, ~**e** /pla, -t/ *adj* flat. ● *nm* (Culin)
dish; (partie de repas) course; (de la
main) flat. ● **à plat** *adv* (poser) flat;
(batterie, pneu) flat; **à** ~ **ventre** flat on
one's face.

platane /platan/ *nm* plane tree.

plateau (*pl* ~**x**) /plato/ *nm* tray; (de
cinéma) set; (de balance) pan; (Géog)
plateau; ~ **de fromages** cheeseboard;
~ **de fruits de mer** seafood platter.
plate-bande (*pl* **plates-bandes**) *nf*
flower bed.

platine /platin/ *nm* platinum. ● *nf*
(tourne-disque) turntable; ~ **laser**
compact disc player.

plâtre /plɑtʀ/ *nm* plaster; (Méd) (plaster) cast.

plein, ~**e** /plɛ̃, -ɛn/ *adj* full (**de** of);
(total) complete. ● *nm* **faire le** ~
(**d'essence**) fill up (the tank); **à** ~
fully; **à** ~ **temps** full-time; **en** ~ **air**
in the open air; **en** ~ **milieu**/**visage**
right in the middle/the face; **en** ~**e
nuit** in the middle of the night. ● *adv*
avoir des idées ~ **la tête** be full of
ideas. **pleinement** *adv* fully.

pleurer /plœʀe/ ❶ *vi* cry, weep (**sur**
over); (yeux) water. ● *vt* mourn.

pleurnicher /plœʀniʃe/ ❶ *vi* ①
snivel.

pleurs /plœʀ/ *nmpl* tears; **en** ~ in
tears.

pleuvoir /pløvwaʀ/ ❹ *vi* rain; (fig)
rain *ou* shower down; **il pleut** it is
raining; **il pleut à verse** *ou* **des
cordes** it is pouring.

pli /pli/ *nm* fold; (de jupe) pleat; (de
pantalon) crease; (lettre) letter; (habitude) habit; (**faux** ~) crease.

pliant, ~**e** /plijɑ̃, -t/ *adj* folding. ● *nm*
folding stool, camp-stool.

plier /plije/ ❹ *vt* fold; (courber) bend;
(soumettre) submit (**à** to). ● *vi* bend.
□ **se** ~ *vpr* fold; **se** ~ **à** submit to.

plinthe /plɛ̃t/ *nf* skirting-board.

plissé, ~**e** /plise/ *adj* (jupe) pleated.

plisser /plise/ ❶ *vt* crease; (yeux)
screw up.

plomb /plɔ̃/ *nm* lead; (fusible) fuse; ~**s**
(de chasse) lead shot; **de** *ou* **en** ~
lead. **plombage** *nm* filling.

plomberie /plɔ̃bʀi/ *nf* plumbing.
plombier *nm* plumber.

plongée /plɔ̃ʒe/ *nf* diving; **en** ~ (sous-
marin) submerged.

plongeoir /plɔ̃ʒwaʀ/ *nm* diving board.

plonger /plɔ̃ʒe/ ❹ *vi* dive; (route)
plunge. ● *vt* plunge. □ **se** ~ *vpr*
plunge into; **se** ~ **dans** (fig) (lecture)
bury oneself in. **plongeur**, -**euse** *nm, f*
diver; (de restaurant) dishwasher.

plu /ply/ ➡**PLAIRE** ㊼, **PLEUVOIR** ㊽.

pluie /plɥi/ *nf* rain; (averse) shower; ~
battante/**diluvienne** driving/torren-
tial rain.

plume /plym/ *nf* feather; (pointe) nib.

plumeau (*pl* ~**x**) /plymo/ *nm* feather
duster.

plumier /plymje/ *nm* pencil box.

plupart: **la** ~ /laplypaʀ/ *loc* **la** ~ **des**
(gens, cas) most; **la** ~ **du temps** most
of the time; **pour la** ~ for the
most part.

pluriel, ~**le** /plyʀjɛl/ *adj & nm* plural.

---

plus /ply, plys, plyz/
● *adverbe de comparaison*
┄┄➤ more (**que** than); ~ **âgé**/**tard** older/later; ~ **beau** more beautiful; ~ **j'y pense**... the more I think about it...; **deux fois** ~ twice as much; **deux fois** ~ **cher** twice as expensive.
┄┄➤ **le** ~ the most; **le** ~ **grand** the biggest; (de deux) the bigger.
┄┄➤ ~ **de** (pain) more; (dix jours) more than; **il est** ~ **de 8 heures** it is after 8 o'clock.
┄┄➤ **de** ~ more (**que** than); (en outre) moreover; **les enfants de** ~ **de 10 ans** children over 10 years old; **de** ~ **en** ~ more and more.
┄┄➤ **en** ~ on top of that; **c'est en**

~ it's extra; **en ~ de** in addition to.

····➤ **~ ou moins** more or less.

····➤ **au ~ tard** at the latest.

● *adverbe de négation*

····➤ **ne ~** (*temps*) no longer, not any more; **je n'y vais ~** I don't go there any longer *ou* any more.

····➤ **ne ~ de** (*quantité*) no more; **il n'y a ~ de pain** there is no more bread.

····➤ **~ que deux jours!** only two days left!

● *préposition & nom masculin*

····➤ (*maths*) plus.

plusieurs /plyzjœʀ/ *adj & pron* several.

plus-value (*pl* ~s) /plyvaly/ *nf* (bénéfice) profit.

plutôt /plyto/ *adv* rather (**que** than).

pluvieux, -ieuse /plyvjø, -z/ *adj* rainy.

PME *abrév f* (**petites et moyennes entreprises**) SME.

PNB *abrév m* (**produit national brut**) GNP.

pneu (*pl* ~s) /pnø/ *nm* tyre. **pneumatique** *adj* inflatable.

pneumonie /pnømɔni/ *nf* pneumonia; **~ atypique** severe acute respiratory syndrome.

poche /pɔʃ/ *nf* pocket; (sac) bag; ~s (sous les yeux) bags.

pocher /pɔʃe/ **1** *vt* (œuf) poach.

pochette /pɔʃɛt/ *nf* (de documents) folder; (sac) bag, pouch; (d'allumettes) book; (de disque) sleeve; (mouchoir) pocket handkerchief.

poêle /pwal/ *nf* (~ **à frire**) frying-pan. ● *nm* stove.

poème /pɔɛm/ *nm* poem. **poésie** *nf* poetry; (poème) poem. **poète** *nm* poet. **poétique** *adj* poetic.

poids /pwa/ *nm* weight; **~ coq/lourd/ plume** bantamweight/heavyweight/ featherweight; **~ lourd** (camion) lorry, juggernaut; (US) truck.

poignard /pwaɲaʀ/ *nm* dagger. **poignarder** **1** *vt* stab.

poigne /pwaɲ/ *nf* **avoir de la ~** have a strong grip.

poignée /pwaɲe/ *nf* (de porte) handle; (quantité) handful; **~ de main** handshake.

poignet /pwaɲɛ/ *nm* wrist; (de chemise) cuff.

poil /pwal/ *nm* hair; (pelage) fur; (de brosse) bristle; **~s** (de tapis) pile; **à ~** 🆇 naked; **~ à gratter** itching powder. **poilu, -e** *adj* hairy.

poinçon /pwɛ̃sɔ̃/ *nm* awl; (marque) hallmark. **poinçonner** **1** *vt* (billet) punch.

poing /pwɛ̃/ *nm* fist.

point /pwɛ̃/ *nm* (endroit, Sport) point; (marque visible) spot, dot; (de couture) stitch; (pour évaluer) mark; **enlever un ~ par faute** lose a mark off for each mistake; **à ~** (Culin) medium; (arriver) at the right time; **faire le ~** take stock; **mettre au ~** (photo) focus; (technique) develop; **mettre les choses au ~** get things clear; **Camille n'est pas encore au ~ pour ses examens** Camille is not ready for her exams; **sur le ~ de** about to; **au ~ que** to the extent that; (**~ final**) full stop, period; **deux ~s** colon; **~ d'interrogation/d'exclamation** question/exclamation mark; **~s de suspension** suspension points; **~ virgule** semicolon; **~ culminant** peak; **~ du jour** daybreak; **~ mort** (Auto) neutral; **~ de repère** landmark; **~ de suture** (Méd) stitch; **~ de vente** point of sale; **~ de vue** point of view. ● *adv* (**ne**) **~** not.

pointe /pwɛ̃t/ *nf* point, tip; (clou) tack; (de grille) spike; (fig) touch (**de** of); **de ~** (industrie) high-tech; **heure de ~** peak hour; **sur la ~ des pieds** on tiptoe.

pointer /pwɛ̃te/ **1** *vt* (cocher) tick off; (diriger) point, aim. ● *vi* (employé) (en arrivant) clock in; (en sortant) clock out. □ **se ~** *vpr* 🆇 turn up.

pointillé /pwɛ̃tije/ *nm* dotted line.

pointilleux, -euse /pwɛ̃tijø, -z/ *adj* fastidious, particular.

pointu, -e /pwɛ̃ty/ *adj* pointed; (aiguisé) sharp.

pointure /pwɛ̃tyʀ/ *nf* size.

poire /pwaʀ/ *nf* pear.

poireau (*pl* ~x) /pwaʀo/ *nm* leek.

poirier /pwaʀje/ *nm* pear tree.

pois /pwa/ *nm* pea; (motif) dot; **robe à ~** polka dot dress.

poison /pwazɔ̃/ *nm* poison.

poisseux, -euse /pwasø, -z/ adj sticky.
poisson /pwasɔ̃/ nm fish; ~ **rouge** goldfish; ~ **d'avril** April fool; **les P~s** Pisces. **poissonnerie** nf fish shop. **poissonnier, -ière** nm, f fishmonger.
poitrine /pwatʀin/ nf chest; (seins) bosom.
poivre /pwavʀ/ nm pepper. **poivré, ~e** adj peppery. **poivrière** nf pepper-pot.
poivron /pwavʀɔ̃/ nm sweet pepper.
polaire /polɛʀ/ adj polar. ● nf (veste) fleece.
pôle /pol/ nm pole.
polémique /polemik/ nf debate. ● adj controversial.
poli, ~e /poli/ adj (personne) polite.
police /polis/ nf (force) police (+ pl); (discipline) (law and) order; (d'assurance) policy.
policier, -ière /polisje, -jɛʀ/ adj police; (roman) detective. ● nm policeman.
polir /poliʀ/ **2** vt polish.
politesse /polites/ nf politeness; (parole) polite remark.
politicien, ~ne /politisjɛ̃, -ɛn/ nm, f (péj) politician.
politique /politik/ adj political; **homme ~** politician. ● nf politics; (ligne de conduite) policy.
pollen /polɛn/ nm pollen.
polluant, ~e /polɥɑ̃, -t/ adj polluting. ● nm pollutant.
polluer /polɥe/ **1** vt pollute. **pollution** nf pollution.
polo /polo/ nm (Sport) polo; (vêtement) polo shirt.
Pologne /polɔɲ/ nf Poland.
polonais, ~e /polonɛ, -z/ adj Polish. ● nm (Ling) Polish. **P~, ~e** nm, f Pole.
poltron, ~ne /poltʀɔ̃, -on/ adj cowardly. ● nm, f coward.
polygame /poligam/ nmf polygamist.
polyvalent, ~e /polivalɑ̃, -t/ adj varied; (personne) versatile.
pommade /pɔmad/ nf ointment.
pomme /pɔm/ nf apple; (d'arrosoir) rose; ~ **d'Adam** Adam's apple; ~ **de pin** pine cone; ~ **de terre** potato; ~**s frites** chips; (US) French fries; **tomber dans les ~s** 🗊 pass out.
pommette /pɔmɛt/ nf cheekbone.
pommier /pɔmje/ nm apple tree.

pompe /pɔ̃p/ nf pump; (splendeur) pomp; ~ **à incendie** fire engine; ~s **funèbres** undertaker's (+ sg).
pomper /pɔ̃pe/ **1** vt pump; (copier 🗊) copy, crib; ~ **l'air à qn** 🗊 get on sb's nerves.
pompier /pɔ̃pje/ nm fireman.
pomponner (se) /(sə)pɔ̃pɔne/ **1** vpr get dolled up.
poncer /pɔ̃se/ **10** vt sand.
ponctuation /pɔ̃ktɥasjɔ̃/ nf punctuation.
ponctuel, ~le /pɔ̃ktɥɛl/ adj punctual.
pondre /pɔ̃dʀ/ **3** vt/i lay.
poney /ponɛ/ nm pony.
pont /pɔ̃/ nm bridge; (de navire) deck; (de graissage) ramp; **faire le ~** get an extended weekend; ~ **aérien** airlift. **pont-levis** (pl **ponts-levis**) nm drawbridge.
populaire /popylɛʀ/ adj popular; (expression) colloquial; (quartier, origine) working-class. **popularité** nf popularity.
population /popylasjɔ̃/ nf population.
porc /pɔʀ/ nm pig; (viande) pork.
porcelaine /pɔʀsəlɛn/ nf china, porcelain.
porc-épic (pl **porcs-épics**) /pɔʀkepik/ nm porcupine.
porcherie /pɔʀʃəʀi/ nf pigsty.
pornographie /pɔʀnɔɡʀafi/ nf pornography.
port /pɔʀ/ nm port, harbour; **à bon ~** safely; ~ **maritime** seaport; (transport) carriage; (d'armes) carrying; (de barbe) wearing.
portable /pɔʀtabl/ nm (Ordinat) laptop (computer); (telephone) mobile (phone).
portail /pɔʀtaj/ nm gate.
portatif, -ive /pɔʀtatif, -v/ adj portable.
porte /pɔʀt/ nf door; (passage) doorway; (de jardin, d'embarquement) gate; **mettre à la ~** throw out; ~ **d'entrée** front door.
porté, ~e /pɔʀte/ adj ~ **à** inclined to; ~ **sur** keen on.
porte-avions /pɔʀtavjɔ̃/ nm inv aircraft carrier.
porte-bagages /pɔʀtbagaʒ/ nm inv (de vélo) carrier.

porte-bonheur /pɔrtbɔnœr/ nm inv lucky charm.

porte-clefs /pɔrtəkle/ nm inv key ring.

porte-documents /pɔrtdɔkymã/ nm inv briefcase.

portée /pɔrte/ nf (d'une arme) range; (de voûte) span; (d'animaux) litter; (impact) significance; (Mus) stave; **à ∼ de (la) main** within (arm's) reach; **hors de ∼ (de)** out of reach (of); **à la ∼ de qn** at sb's level.

porte-fenêtre (pl **portes-fenêtres**) /pɔrtfənɛtr/ nf French window.

portefeuille /pɔrtəfœj/ nm wallet; (de ministre) portfolio.

porte-jarretelles /pɔrtʒartɛl/ nm inv suspender belt.

portemanteau (pl **∼x**) /pɔrtmãto/ nm coat ou hat stand.

porte-monnaie /pɔrtmɔnɛ/ nm inv purse.

porte-parole /pɔrtparɔl/ nm inv spokesperson.

porter /pɔrte/ **1** vt carry; (vêtement, bague) wear; (fruits, responsabilité, nom) bear; (coup) strike; (amener) bring; (inscrire) enter. ● vi (bruit) carry; (coup) hit home; **∼ sur** rest on; (concerner) be about. □ **se ∼** vpr **bien se ∼** be ou feel well; **se ∼ candidat** stand as a candidate.

porteur, -euse /pɔrtœr, -øz/ nm, f (de nouvelles) bearer; (Méd) carrier. ● nm (Rail) porter.

portier /pɔrtje/ nm doorman.

portière /pɔrtjɛr/ nf door.

porto /pɔrto/ nm port (wine).

portrait /pɔrtrɛ/ nm portrait. **portrait-robot** (pl **portraits-robots**) nm identikit®, photofit®.

portuaire /pɔrtɥɛr/ adj port.

portugais, ∼e /pɔrtygɛ, -z/ adj Portuguese. ● nm (Ling) Portuguese. **P∼, ∼e** nm, f Portuguese.

Portugal /pɔrtygal/ nm Portugal.

pose /poz/ nf installation; (attitude) pose; (Photo) exposure.

posé, ∼e /poze/ adj calm, serious.

poser /poze/ **1** vt put (down); (installer) install, put in; (fondations) lay; (question) ask; (problème) pose; **∼ sa candidature** apply (à for). ● vi (modèle) pose. □ **se ∼** vpr (avion, oiseau) land; (regard) fall; (se présenter) arise.

positif, -ive /pozitif, -v/ adj positive.

position /pozisjã/ nf position; **prendre ∼** take a stand.

posologie /pozɔlɔʒi/ nf dosage.

posséder /pɔsede/ **14** vt (propriété) own, possess; (diplôme) have.

possessif, -ive /pɔsesif, -v/ adj possessive.

possession /pɔsesjã/ nf possession; **prendre ∼ de** take possession of.

possibilité /pɔsibilite/ nf possibility.

possible /pɔsibl/ adj possible; **dès que ∼** as soon as possible; **le plus tard ∼** as late as possible. ● nm **le ∼** what is possible; **faire son ∼** do one's utmost.

postal, ∼e (mpl **-aux**) /pɔstal, -o/ adj postal.

poste /pɔst/ nf (service) post; (bureau) post office; **∼ aérienne** airmail; **mettre à la ∼** post; **∼ restante** poste restante. ● nm (lieu, emploi) post; (de radio, télévision) set; (téléphone) extension (number); **∼ d'essence** petrol station; **∼ d'incendie** fire point; **∼ de pilotage** cockpit; **∼ de police** police station; **∼ de secours** first-aid post.

poster¹ /pɔste/ **1** vt (lettre, personne) post.

poster² /pɔstɛr/ nm poster.

postérieur, ∼e /pɔsterjœr/ adj later; (partie) back; **∼ à** after. ● nm **1** posterior.

posthume /pɔstym/ adj posthumous.

postiche /pɔstiʃ/ adj false.

postier, -ière /pɔstje, -jɛr/ nm, f postal worker.

post-scriptum /pɔstskriptɔm/ nm inv postscript.

postuler /pɔstyle/ **1** vt/i apply (à for); (principe) postulate.

pot /po/ nm pot; (en plastique) carton; (en verre) jar; (chance **1**) luck; (boisson **1**) drink; **∼ catalytique** catalytic converter; **∼ d'échappement** exhaust pipe.

potable /pɔtabl/ adj eau **∼** drinking water.

potage /pɔtaʒ/ nm soup.

potager, -ère /pɔtaʒe,.-ɛr/ adj vegetable. ● nm vegetable garden.

pot-au-feu /pɔtofø/ nm inv (plat) stew.

pot-de-vin (pl **pots-de-vin**) /pɔdvɛ̃/ nm bribe.

poteau (pl ~x) /pɔto/ nm post; (télégraphique) pole; ~ **indicateur** signpost.

potelé, ~e /pɔtle/ adj plump.

potentiel, ~le /pɔtɑ̃sjɛl/ adj & nm potential.

poterie /pɔtʀi/ nf pottery; (objet) piece of pottery. **potier** nm potter.

potins /pɔtɛ̃/ nmpl gossip (+ sg).

potiron /pɔtiʀɔ̃/ nm pumpkin.

pou (pl ~x) /pu/ nm louse.

poubelle /pubɛl/ nf dustbin.

pouce /pus/ nm thumb; (de pied) big toe; (mesure) inch.

poudre /pudʀ/ nf powder; (~ à canon) gunpowder; en ~ (lait) powdered; (chocolat) drinking.

poudrier /pudʀije/ nm (powder) compact.

pouf /puf/ nm pouffe.

poulailler /pulaje/ nm henhouse.

poulain /pulɛ̃/ nm foal; (protégé) protégé.

poule /pul/ nf hen; (Culin) fowl; (femme 🔲) tart.

poulet /pulɛ/ nm chicken.

pouliche /puliʃ/ nf filly.

poulie /puli/ nf pulley.

pouls /pu/ nm pulse.

poumon /pumɔ̃/ nm lung.

poupe /pup/ nf stern.

poupée /pupe/ nf doll.

pour /puʀ/ prép for; (envers) to; (à la place de) on behalf of; (comme) as; ~ **cela** for that reason; ~ **cent** per cent; ~ **de bon** for good; ~ **faire** (in order) to do; ~ **que** so that; ~ **moi** (à mon avis) as for me; **trop poli** ~ too polite to; ~ **ce qui est de** as for; **être** ~ be in favour. ● nm inv **le** ~ **et le contre** the pros and cons.

pourboire /puʀbwaʀ/ nm tip.

pourcentage /puʀsɑ̃taʒ/ nm percentage.

pourparlers /puʀpaʀle/ nmpl talks.

pourpre /puʀpʀ/ adj & nm crimson; (violet) purple.

pourquoi /puʀkwa/ conj & adv why. ● nm inv **le** ~ **et le comment** the why and the wherefore.

pourra, pourrait /puʀa, puʀɛ/ →**POUVOIR** 49.

pourri, ~e /puʀi/ adj rotten. **pourrir** 2 vt/i rot. **pourriture** nf rot.

poursuite /puʀsɥit/ nf pursuit (de of); ~s (Jur) legal action (+ sg).

poursuivre /puʀsɥivʀ/ 57 vt pursue; (continuer) continue (with); ~ **(en justice)** take to court; (droit civil) sue. ● vi continue. □ **se** ~ vpr continue.

pourtant /puʀtɑ̃/ adv yet.

pourvoir /puʀvwaʀ/ 63 vi ~ **à** provide for; **pourvu de** supplied with.

pourvu que /puʀvyk(ə)/ conj (condition) provided (that); (souhait) let us hope (that).

pousse /pus/ nf growth; (bourgeon) shoot.

poussé, ~e /puse/ adj (études) advanced; (enquête) thorough.

poussée /puse/ nf pressure; (coup) push; (de prix) upsurge; (Méd) attack.

pousser /puse/ 1 vt push; (cri) let out; (soupir) heave; (continuer) continue; (exhorter) urge (à to); (forcer) drive (à to). ● vi push; (grandir) grow; **faire** ~ (cheveux) let grow; (plante) grow. □ **se** ~ vpr move over ou up; **pousse-toi!** move over!

poussette /pusɛt/ nf pushchair.

poussière /pusjɛʀ/ nf dust. **poussiéreux, -euse** adj dusty.

poussin /pusɛ̃/ nm chick.

poutre /putʀ/ nf beam; (en métal) girder.

pouvoir /puvwaʀ/ 49 v aux (possibilité) can, be able; (permission, éventualité) may, can; **il peut/pouvait/pourrait venir** he can/could/might come; **je n'ai pas pu** I couldn't; **j'ai pu faire** (réussi à) I managed to do; **je n'en peux plus** I am exhausted; **il se peut que** it may be that. ● nm power; (gouvernement) government; **au** ~ **in** power; ~s **publics** authorities.

prairie /pʀeʀi/ nf meadow.

praticien, ~ne /pʀatisjɛ̃, -ɛn/ nm, f practitioner.

pratiquant, ~e /pʀatikɑ̃, -t/ adj practising. ● nm, f churchgoer.

pratique /pʀatik/ adj practical. ● nf practice; (expérience) experience; **la** ~ **du golf/du cheval** golfing/riding.

pratiquement adv (en pratique) in practice; (presque) practically.

pratiquer /pratike/ **1** vt/i practise; (Sport) play; (faire) make.

pré /pre/ nm meadow.

pré-affranchi, ~e /preafrɑ̃ʃi/ adj postage-paid.

préalable /prealabl/ adj preliminary, prior. ● nm precondition; **au ~** first.

préambule /preɑ̃byl/ nm preamble.

préavis /preavi/ nm notice.

précaire /preker/ adj precarious. **précarité** nf (d'emploi) insecurity.

précaution /prekosjɔ̃/ nf (mesure) precaution; (prudence) caution.

précédent, ~e /presedɑ̃, -t/ adj previous. ● nm precedent.

précéder /presede/ **14** vt/i precede.

précepteur, -trice /preseptœr, -tris/ nm, f (private) tutor.

prêcher /preʃe/ **1** vt/i preach.

précieux, -ieuse /presjø, -z/ adj precious.

précipitamment /presipitamɑ̃/ adv hastily. **précipitation** nf haste.

précipiter /presipite/ **1** vt throw, precipitate; (hâter) hasten. □ **se ~** vpr (se dépêcher) rush (**sur** at, on to); (se jeter) throw oneself; (s'accélérer) speed up.

précis, ~e /presi, -z/ adj precise, specific; (mécanisme) accurate; **dix heures ~es** ten o'clock sharp. ● nm summary.

préciser /presize/ **1** vt specify; **précisez votre pensée** could you be more specific. □ **se ~** vpr become clear(er). **précision** nf precision; (détail) detail.

précoce /prekɔs/ adj (enfant) precocious.

préconiser /prekɔnize/ **1** vt advocate.

précurseur /prekyrsœr/ nm forerunner.

prédicateur /predikatœr/ nm preacher.

prédilection /predilɛksjɔ̃/ nf preference.

prédire /predir/ **37** vt predict.

prédominer /predɔmine/ **1** vi predominate.

préface /prefas/ nf preface.

préfecture /prefɛktyr/ nf prefecture; **~ de police** police headquarters.

préféré, ~e /prefere/ adj & nm, f favourite.

préférence /preferɑ̃s/ nf preference; **de ~** preferably.

préférentiel, ~le /preferɑ̃sjɛl/ adj preferential.

préférer /prefere/ **14** vt prefer (**à** to); **~ faire** prefer to do; **je ne préfère pas** I'd rather not; **j'aurais préféré ne pas savoir** I wish I hadn't found out.

préfet /prefɛ/ nm prefect; **~ de police** prefect ou chief of police.

préfixe /prefiks/ nm prefix.

préhistorique /preistorik/ adj prehistoric.

préjudice /preʒydis/ nm harm, prejudice; **porter ~ à** harm.

préjugé /preʒyʒe/ nm prejudice; **être plein de ~s** be very prejudiced.

prélasser (se) /(sə)prelase/ **1** vpr loll (about).

prélèvement /prelɛvmɑ̃/ nm deduction; (de sang) sample. **prélever** **6** vt deduct (**sur** from); (sang) take.

préliminaire /preliminer/ adj & nm preliminary; **~s** (sexuels) foreplay.

prématuré, ~e /prematyre/ adj premature. ● nm premature baby.

premier, -ière /prəmje, -jɛr/ adj first; (rang) front, first; (enfance) early; (nécessité, souci) prime; (qualité) top, prime; **de ~ ordre** first-rate; **~ ministre** Prime Minister. ● nm, f first (one). ● nm (date) first; (étage) first floor; **en ~** first. **première** nf (Rail) first class; (exploit jamais vu) first; (cinéma, Théât) première; (Aut) (vitesse) first (gear). **premièrement** adv firstly.

prémunir /premynir/ **2** vt protect (**contre** against).

prenant, ~e /prənɑ̃, -t/ adj (activité) engrossing; (enfant) demanding.

prénatal, ~e (mpl ~s) /prenatal/ adj antenatal.

prendre /prɑ̃dr/ **50** vt take; (attraper) catch, get; (acheter) get; (repas) have; (engager, adopter) take on; (poids) put on; (chercher) pick up; **qu'est-ce qui te prend?** what's the matter with you? ● vi (liquide) set; (feu) catch; (vaccin) take. □ **se ~** vpr se **~ pour** think one is; **s'en ~ à** attack; (rendre responsable) blame; **s'y ~** set about (it).

preneur, -euse /pRənœR, -øz/ *nm, f* buyer; **être ~** be willing to buy; **trouver ~** find a buyer.

prénom /pRenɔ̃/ *nm* first name.

prénommer /pRenɔme/ **1** *vt* call. □ **se ~** *vpr* be called.

préoccupation /pReɔkypasjɔ̃/ *nf* (souci) worry; (idée fixe) preoccupation.

préoccuper /pReɔkype/ **1** *vt* worry; (absorber) preoccupy. □ **se ~ de** *vpr* think about.

préparation /pRepaRasjɔ̃/ *nf* preparation. **préparatoire** *adj* preparatory.

préparer /pRepaRe/ **1** *vt* prepare; (repas, café) make; **plats préparés** ready-cooked meals. □ **se ~** *vpr* prepare oneself (à for); (s'apprêter) get ready; (être proche) be brewing.

préposé, ~e /pRepoze/ *nm, f* employee; (des postes) postman, postwoman.

préposition /pRepozisjɔ̃/ *nf* preposition.

préretraite /pReRətRɛt/ *nf* early retirement.

près /pRɛ/ *adv* near, close; **~ de** near (to), close to; (presque) nearly; **à cela ~ except that; de ~** closely.

présage /pRezaʒ/ *nm* omen.

presbyte /pRɛsbit/ *adj* longsighted, far-sighted.

prescrire /pRɛskRiR/ **30** *vt* prescribe.

préséance /pReseãs/ *nf* precedence.

présence /pRezãs/ *nf* presence; (Scol) attendance.

présent, ~e /pRezã, -t/ *adj* present. ● *nm* (temps, cadeau) present; **à ~** now.

présentateur, -trice /pRezãta- tœR, -tRis/ *nm, f* presenter.

présentation /pRezãtasjɔ̃/ *nf* (de personne) introduction; (exposé) presentation.

présenter /pRezãte/ **1** *vt* present; (personne) introduce (à to); (montrer) show. ● *vi* **~ bien** have a pleasing appearance. □ **se ~** *vpr* introduce oneself (à to); (aller) go; (apparaître) appear; (candidat) come forward; (occasion) arise; **se ~ à** (examen) sit for; (élection) stand for; **se ~ bien** look good.

préservatif /pRezɛRvatif/ *nm* condom.

préserver /pRezɛRve/ **1** *vt* protect.

présidence /pRezidãs/ *nf* (d'État) presidency; (de société) chairmanship.

président, ~e /pRezidã, -t/ *nm, f* president; (de société, comité) chairman, chairwoman; **~-directeur général** managing director.

présidentiel, ~le /pRezidãsjɛl/ *adj* presidential.

présider /pRezide/ **1** *vt* preside.

présomptueux, -euse /pRezɔ̃p- tɥø, -z/ *adj* presumptuous.

presque /pRɛsk(ə)/ *adv* almost, nearly; **~ jamais** hardly ever; **~ rien** hardly anything; **~ pas (de)** hardly any.

presqu'île /pRɛskil/ *nf* peninsula.

pressant, ~e /pRɛsã, -t/ *adj* pressing, urgent.

presse /pRɛs/ *nf* (journaux, appareil) press.

pressentiment /pRɛsãtimã/ *nm* premonition. **pressentir** **46** *vt* have a premonition of.

pressé, ~e /pRese/ *adj* in a hurry; (orange, citron) freshly squeezed.

presser /pRese/ **1** *vt* squeeze, press; (appuyer sur, harceler) press; (hâter) hasten; (inciter) urge (de to). ● *vi* (temps) press; (affaire) be pressing. □ **se ~** *vpr* (se hâter) hurry; (se grouper) crowd.

pressing /pResiŋ/ *nm* (teinturerie) dry-cleaner's.

pression /pResjɔ̃/ *nf* pressure; (bouton) press-stud.

prestance /pRɛstãs/ *nf* (imposing) presence.

prestation /pRɛstasjɔ̃/ *nf* allowance; (d'artiste) performance.

prestidigitation /pRɛstidiʒita- sjɔ̃/ *nf* conjuring.

prestige /pRɛstiʒ/ *nm* prestige. **prestigieux, -ieuse** *adj* prestigious.

présumé, e /pRezyme/ *adj* alleged.

présumer /pRezyme/ **1** *vt* presume; **~ que** assume that; **~ de** overrate.

prêt, ~e /pRɛ, -t/ *adj* ready (à qch for sth, à faire to do). ● *nm* loan. **prêt-à-porter** *nm inv* ready-to-wear clothes.

prétendre /pRetãdR/ **3** *vt* claim (que that); (vouloir) intend; **on le prétend riche** he is said to be very rich. **prétendu, ~e** /pRetãdy/ *adj* so-called. **prétendument** *adv* supposedly, allegedly.

prétentieux, -ieuse /pʀetɑ̃sjø, -z/ adj pretentious.

prêter /pʀete/ **1** vt lend (à to); (attribuer) attribute; ~ **son aide à qn** give sb some help; ~ **attention** pay attention; ~ **serment** take an oath. ● vi ~ **à** lead to.

prêteur, -euse /pʀetœʀ, -øz/ nm, f (money-)lender; ~ **sur gages** pawnbroker.

prétexte /pʀetɛkst/ nm pretext, excuse.

prêtre /pʀɛtʀ/ nm priest.

preuve /pʀœv/ nf proof; **des** ~s evidence (+ sg); **faire** ~ **de** show; **faire ses** ~s prove oneself.

prévaloir /pʀevalwaʀ/ **60** vi prevail.

prévenant, ~**e** /pʀevnɑ̃, -t/ adj thoughtful.

prévenir /pʀevniʀ/ **58** vt (menacer) warn; (informer) tell; (médecin) call; (éviter, anticiper) prevent.

préventif, -ive /pʀevɑ̃tif, -v/ adj preventive.

prévention /pʀevɑ̃sjɔ̃/ nf prevention; **faire de la** ~ take preventive action; ~ **routière** road safety.

prévenu, ~**e** /pʀevny/ nm, f defendant.

prévisible /pʀevizibl/ adj predictable.

prévision nf prediction; (météorologique) forecast.

prévoir /pʀevwaʀ/ **63** vt foresee; (temps) forecast; (organiser) plan (for), provide for; (envisager) allow (for); **prévu pour** (jouet) designed for; **comme prévu** as planned.

prévoyance /pʀevwajɑ̃s/ nf foresight.

prévoyant, ~**e** adj farsighted.

prier /pʀije/ **45** vi pray. ● vt pray to; (demander à) ask (de to); **je vous en prie** please; (il n'y a pas de quoi) don't mention it.

prière /pʀijɛʀ/ nf prayer; (demande) request; ~ **de** (vous êtes prié de) will you please.

primaire /pʀimɛʀ/ adj primary.

prime /pʀim/ nf free gift; (d'employé) bonus; (subvention) subsidy; (d'assurance) premium.

primé, ~**e** /pʀime/ adj prizewinning.

primeurs /pʀimœʀ/ nfpl early fruit and vegetables.

primevère /pʀimvɛʀ/ nf primrose.

primitif, -ive /pʀimitif, -v/ adj primitive; (d'origine) original. ● nm, f primitive.

primordial, ~**e** (mpl **-iaux**) /pʀimɔʀdjal, -jo/ adj essential.

prince /pʀɛ̃s/ nm prince. **princesse** nf princess.

principal, ~**e** (mpl **-aux**) /pʀɛ̃sipal, -o/ adj main, principal. ● nm headmaster; (chose) main thing.

principe /pʀɛ̃sip/ nm principle; **en** ~ in theory; (d'habitude) as a rule.

printanier, -ière /pʀɛ̃tanje, -jɛʀ/ adj spring(-like).

printemps /pʀɛ̃tɑ̃/ nm spring.

prioritaire /pʀijɔʀitɛʀ/ adj priority; **être** ~ have priority. **priorité** nf priority; (Auto) right of way.

Priorité à droite Except at *i*
roundabouts, and unless there
are other indications or regulations
in force, French drivers must always
give way to traffic approaching from
the right.

---

pris, ~**e** /pʀi, -z/ adj (place) taken; (personne, journée) busy; (nez) stuffed up; ~ **de** (peur, fièvre) stricken with; ~ **de panique** panic-stricken. ● ⇒PRENDRE **50**.

prise /pʀiz/ nf hold, grip; (animal attrapé) catch; (Mil) capture; (~ **de courant**) (mâle) plug; (femelle) socket; ~ **multiple** multiplug adapter; **avoir** ~ **sur qn** have a hold over sb; **aux** ~s **avec** to grapple with; ~ **de conscience** awareness; ~ **de contact** first contact, initial meeting; ~ **de position** stand; ~ **de sang** blood test.

prisé, ~**e** /pʀize/ adj popular.

prison /pʀizɔ̃/ nf prison, jail; (réclusion) imprisonment. **prisonnier, -ière** nm, f prisoner.

privation /pʀivasjɔ̃/ nf deprivation; (sacrifice) hardship.

privatiser /pʀivatize/ **1** vt privatize.

privé /pʀive/ adj private. ● nm (Comm) private sector; (Scol) private schools (+ pl); **en** ~ in private.

priver /pʀive/ **1** vt ~ **de** deprive of. □ **se** ~ (**de**) vpr go without.

privilège /pʀivilɛʒ/ nm privilege. **privilégié,** ~**e** nm, f privileged person.

prix /pʀi/ nm price; (récompense) prize; à tout ~ at all costs; au ~ de (fig) at the expense of; ~ coûtant, ~ de revient cost price; à ~ fixe set price.

probabilité /pʀɔbabilite/ nf probability. **probable** adj probable, likely. **probablement** adv probably.

probant, ~e /pʀɔbɑ̃, -t/ adj convincing, conclusive.

problème /pʀɔblɛm/ nm problem.

procédé /pʀɔsede/ nm process; (manière d'agir) practice.

procéder /pʀɔsede/ 14 vi proceed; ~ à carry out.

procès /pʀɔsɛ/ nm (criminel) trial; (civil) lawsuit, proceedings (+ pl).

processus /pʀɔsesys/ nm process; ~ de paix peace process.

procès-verbal (pl procès-verbaux) /pʀɔsɛvɛʀbal, -o/ nm minutes (+ pl); (contravention) ticket.

prochain, ~e /pʀɔʃɛ̃, -ɛn/ adj (suivant) next; (proche) imminent; (avenir) near. ● nm fellow man. **prochainement** adv soon.

proche /pʀɔʃ/ adj near, close; (avoisinant) neighbouring; (parent, ami) close; ~ de close ou near to; de ~ en ~ gradually; dans un ~ avenir in the near future; être ~ (imminent) be approaching. ● nm close relative; (ami) close friend.

Proche-Orient /pʀɔʃɔʀjɑ̃/ nm Near East.

proclamation /pʀɔklamasjɔ̃/ nf declaration, proclamation. **proclamer** 1 vt declare, proclaim.

procuration /pʀɔkyʀasjɔ̃/ nf proxy.

procurer /pʀɔkyʀe/ 1 vt bring (à to). □ se ~ vpr obtain.

procureur /pʀɔkyʀœʀ/ nm public prosecutor.

prodige /pʀɔdiʒ/ nm (fait) marvel; (personne) prodigy; **enfant/musicien** ~ child/musical prodigy. **prodigieux, -ieuse** adj tremendous, prodigious.

prodigue /pʀɔdig/ adj wasteful; fils ~ prodigal son.

producteur, -trice /pʀɔdyktœʀ, -tʀis/ adj producing. ● nm, f producer. **productif, -ive** adj productive. **production** nf production; (produit) product. **productivité** nf productivity.

produire /pʀɔdɥiʀ/ 17 vt produce. □ se ~ vpr (survenir) happen; (acteur) perform.

produit /pʀɔdɥi/ nm product; ~s (de la terre) produce (+ sg) ; ~ chimique chemical; ~s alimentaires foodstuffs; ~ de consommation consumer goods; ~ intérieur brut gross domestic product; ~ national brut gross national product.

proéminent, ~e /pʀɔeminɑ̃, -t/ adj prominent.

profane /pʀɔfan/ adj secular. ● nmf lay person.

proférer /pʀɔfeʀe/ 14 vt utter.

professeur /pʀɔfesœʀ/ nm teacher; (Univ) lecturer; (avec chaire) professor.

profession /pʀɔfɛsjɔ̃/ nf occupation; ~ libérale profession.

professionnel, ~le /pʀɔfɛsjɔnɛl/ adj professional; (école) vocational. ● nm, f professional.

profil /pʀɔfil/ nm profile.

profit /pʀɔfi/ nm profit; au ~ de in aid of. **profitable** adj profitable.

profiter /pʀɔfite/ 1 vi ~ à benefit; ~ de take advantage of.

profond, ~e /pʀɔfɔ̃, -d/ adj deep; (sentiment, intérêt) profound; (causes) underlying; au plus ~ de in the depths of. **profondément** adv deeply; (différent, triste) profoundly; (dormir) soundly. **profondeur** nf depth.

progéniture /pʀɔʒenityʀ/ nf offspring.

progiciel /pʀɔʒisjɛl/ nm (Ordinat) package.

programmation /pʀɔgʀamasjɔ̃/ nf programming.

programme /pʀɔgʀam/ nm programme; (Scol) (d'une matière) syllabus; (général) curriculum; (Ordinat) program. **programmer** 1 vt (ordinateur, appareil) program; (émission) schedule. **programmeur, -euse** nm, f computer programmer.

progrès /pʀɔgʀɛ/ nm & nmpl progress; faire des ~ make progress. **progresser** 1 vi progress. **progressif, -ive** adj progressive. **progression** nf progression.

prohibitif, -ive /pʀɔibitif, -v/ adj prohibitive.

proie /pʀwa/ nf prey; **en ~ à** tormented by.

projecteur /pʀɔʒɛktœʀ/ nm floodlight; (Mil) searchlight; (cinéma) projector.

projectile /pʀɔʒɛktil/ nm missile.

projection /pʀɔʒɛksjɔ̃/ nf projection; (séance) show.

projet /pʀɔʒɛ/ nm plan; (ébauche) draft; **~ de loi** bill.

projeter /pʀɔʒte/ 38 vt (prévoir) plan **(de** to); (film) project, show; (jeter) hurl, project.

prolétaire /pʀɔletɛʀ/ nmf proletarian.

prologue /pʀɔlɔg/ nm prologue.

prolongation /pʀɔlɔ̃gasjɔ̃/ nf extension; **~s** (football) extra time.

prolonger /pʀɔlɔ̃ʒe/ 40 vt extend. □ **se ~** vpr go on.

promenade /pʀɔmnad/ nf walk; (à bicyclette, à cheval) ride; (en auto) drive, ride; **faire une ~** go for a walk.

promener /pʀɔmne/ 6 vt take for a walk; **~ son regard sur** cast an eye over. □ **se ~** vpr walk; **(aller) se ~** go for a walk. **promeneur, -euse** nm, f walker.

promesse /pʀɔmɛs/ nf promise.

prometteur, -euse /pʀɔmɛtœʀ, -øz/ adj promising.

promettre /pʀɔmɛtʀ/ 42 vt/i promise. ● vi be promising. □ **se ~ de** vpr resolve to.

promoteur /pʀɔmɔtœʀ/ nm (immobilier) property developer.

promotion /pʀɔmɔsjɔ̃/ nf promotion; (Univ) year; (Comm) special offer.

prompt, ~e /pʀɔ̃, -t/ adj swift.

promu, ~e /pʀɔmy/ adj **être ~** be promoted.

prôner /pʀone/ 1 vt extol.

pronom /pʀɔnɔ̃/ nm pronoun. **pronominal, ~e** (mpl **-aux**) adj pronominal.

prononcé, ~e /pʀɔnɔ̃se/ adj strong.

prononcer /pʀɔnɔ̃se/ 10 vt pronounce; (discours) make. □ **se ~** vpr (mot) be pronounced; (personne) make a decision (**pour** in favour of). **prononciation** nf pronunciation.

pronostic /pʀɔnɔstik/ nm forecast; (Méd) prognosis.

propagande /pʀɔpagɑ̃d/ nf propaganda.

propager /pʀɔpaʒe/ 40 vt spread. □ **se ~** vpr spread.

prophète /pʀɔfɛt/ nm prophet. **prophétie** nf prophecy.

propice /pʀɔpis/ adj favourable.

proportion /pʀɔpɔʀsjɔ̃/ nf proportion; (en mathématiques) ratio; **toutes ~s gardées** relatively speaking. **proportionné, ~e** adj proportionate (**à** to). **proportionnel, ~le** adj proportional. **proportionnellement** adv proportionately.

propos /pʀɔpo/ nm intention; (sujet) subject; **à ~** at the right time; (dans un dialogue) by the way; **à ~ de** about; **à tout ~** at every possible occasion. ● nmpl (paroles) remarks.

proposer /pʀɔpoze/ 1 vt suggest, propose; (offrir) offer. □ **se ~** vpr volunteer (**pour** to). **proposition** nf proposal; (affirmation) proposition; (Gram) clause.

propre /pʀɔpʀ/ adj (non sali) clean; (soigné) neat; (honnête) decent; (à soi) own; (sens) literal; **~ à** (qui convient) suited to; (spécifique) particular to. ● nm mettre **au ~** write out again neatly; **c'est du ~!** (ironique) well done!

proprement /pʀɔpʀəmɑ̃/ adv (avec soin) neatly; (au sens strict) strictly; **le bureau ~ dit** the office itself.

propreté /pʀɔpʀəte/ nf cleanliness.

propriétaire /pʀɔpʀijetɛʀ/ nmf owner; (Comm) proprietor; (qui loue) landlord, landlady.

propriété /pʀɔpʀijete/ nf property; (droit) ownership.

propulser /pʀɔpylse/ 1 vt propel.

proroger /pʀɔʀɔʒe/ 40 vt (contrat) defer; (passeport) extend.

proscrire /pʀɔskʀiʀ/ 30 vt proscribe.

proscrit, ~e /pʀɔskʀi, -t/ adj proscribed. ● nm, f (exilé) exile.

prose /pʀoz/ nf prose.

prospectus /pʀɔspɛktys/ nm leaflet.

prospère /pʀɔspɛʀ/ adj flourishing, thriving. **prospérer** 14 vi thrive, prosper. **prospérité** nf prosperity.

prosterner (se) /(sə)pʀɔstɛʀne/ 1 vpr prostrate oneself; **prosterné devant** prostrate before.

prostituée /pʀɔstitɥe/ nf prostitute. **prostitution** nf prostitution.

protecteur, -trice /pʀɔtɛktœʀ, -tʀis/ nm, f protector. ● adj protective.

protection /pʀɔtɛksjɔ̃/ nf protection.
protégé, ∼e /pʀɔteʒe/ nm, f protégé.
protéger /pʀɔteʒe/ 40 vt protect. □ **se ∼** vpr protect oneself.
protéine /pʀɔtein/ nf protein.
protestant, ∼e /pʀɔtɛstɑ̃, -t/ adj & nm, f Protestant.
protestation /pʀɔtɛstasjɔ̃/ nf protest. **protester** 1 vt/i protest.
protocole /pʀɔtɔkɔl/ nm protocol.
protubérant, ∼e /pʀɔtybeʀɑ̃/ adj protruding.
proue /pʀu/ nf bow, prow.
prouesse /pʀuɛs/ nf feat, exploit.
prouver /pʀuve/ 1 vt prove.
provenance /pʀɔvnɑs/ nf origin; **en ∼ de** from.
provençal, ∼e (mpl **-aux**) /pʀɔ- vɑsal, -o/ adj & nm, f Provençal.
provenir /pʀɔvniʀ/ 58 vi **∼ de** come from.
proverbe /pʀɔvɛʀb/ nm proverb.
province /pʀɔvɛ̃s/ nf province; **de ∼** provincial; **la ∼** the provinces (+ pl). **provincial, ∼e** (mpl **-iaux**) adj & nm, f provincial.
proviseur /pʀɔvizœʀ/ nm headmaster, principal.
provision /pʀɔvizjɔ̃/ nf supply, store; (sur un compte) credit (balance); (acompte) deposit; **∼s** (vivres) food shopping.
provisoire /pʀɔvizwaʀ/ adj provisional.
provocant, ∼e /pʀɔvɔkɑ̃, -t/ adj provocative. **provocation** nf provocation. **provoquer** 1 vt cause; (sexuellement) arouse; (défier) provoke.
proxénète /pʀɔksenet/ nm pimp, procurer.
proximité /pʀɔksimite/ nf proximity; **à ∼ de** close to.
prude /pʀyd/ adj prudish.
prudemment /pʀydamɑ̃/ adv (conduire) carefully; (attendre) cautiously. **prudence** nf caution. **prudent, ∼e** adj (au volant) careful; (à agir) cautious; (sage) wise.
prune /pʀyn/ nf plum.
pruneau (pl **∼x**) /pʀyno/ nm prune.
prunelle /pʀynɛl/ nf (pupille) pupil; (fruit) sloe.
prunier /pʀynje/ nm plum tree.

psaume /psom/ nm psalm.
pseudonyme /psødɔnim/ nm pseudonym.
psychanalyse /psikanaliz/ nf psychoanalysis. **psychanalyste** nmf psychoanalyst.
psychiatre /psikjatʀ/ nmf psychiatrist. **psychiatrie** nf psychiatry. **psychiatrique** adj psychiatric.
psychique /psiʃik/ adj mental, psychological.
psychologie /psikɔlɔʒi/ nf psychology. **psychologique** adj psychological. **psychologue** nmf psychologist.
pu /py/ →POUVOIR 49.
puant, ∼e /pyɑ̃, -t/ adj stinking.
pub /pyb/ nf 1 **la ∼** advertising; **une ∼** an advert.
puberté /pybɛʀte/ nf puberty.
public, -que /pyblik/ adj public. ● nm public; (assistance) audience; (Scol) state schools (+ pl); **en ∼** in public.
publication /pyblikasjɔ̃/ nf publication.
publicitaire /pyblisitɛʀ/ adj publicity. **publicité** nf publicity, advertising; (annonce) advertisement.
publier /pyblije/ 45 vt publish.
publiquement /pyblikmɑ̃/ adv publicly.
puce /pys/ nf flea; (électronique) chip; **marché aux ∼s** flea market.
pudeur /pydœʀ/ nf modesty.
pudibond, ∼e /pydibɔ̃, -d/ adj prudish.
pudique /pydik/ adj modest.
puer /pɥe/ 1 vi stink. ● vt stink of.
puéricultrice /pɥeʀikyltʀis/ nf pediatric nurse.
puéril, ∼e /pɥeʀil/ adj puerile.
puis /pɥi/ adv then.
puiser /pɥize/ 1 vt draw (**dans** from). ● vi **∼ dans qch** dip into sth.
puisque /pɥisk(ə)/ conj since, as.
puissance /pɥisɑ̃s/ nf power; **en ∼** potential.
puissant, ∼e /pɥisɑ̃, -t/ adj powerful.
puits /pɥi/ nm well; (de mine) shaft.
pull(-over) /pyl(ɔvɛʀ)/ nm pullover, jumper.
pulpe /pylp/ nf pulp.
pulsation /pylsasjɔ̃/ nf (heart-) beat.

pulvériser /pylveʀize/ **1** vt pulverize; (liquide) spray.

punaise /pynɛz/ nf (insecte) bug; (clou) drawing pin.

punch[1] /pɔ̃ʃ/ nm (boisson) punch.

punch[2] /pœnʃ/ nm **avoir du ~** have drive.

punir /pyniʀ/ **2** vt punish. **punition** nf punishment.

pupille /pypij/ nf (de l'œil) pupil. ● nmf (enfant) ward.

pupitre /pypitʀ/ nm (Scol) desk; **~ à musique** music stand.

pur /pyʀ/ adj pure; (whisky) neat.

purée /pyʀe/ nf purée; (de pommes de terre) mashed potatoes (+ pl).

pureté /pyʀte/ nf purity.

purgatoire /pyʀgatwaʀ/ nm purgatory.

purge /pyʀʒ/ nf purge. **purger 40** vt (Pol, Méd) purge; (peine: Jur) serve.

purifier /pyʀifje/ **45** vt purify.

puritain, **~e** /pyʀitɛ̃, -ɛn/ nm, f puritan. ● adj puritanical.

pur-sang /pyʀsɑ̃/ nm inv (cheval) thoroughbred.

pus /py/ nm pus.

putain /pytɛ̃/ nf p whore.

puzzle /pœzl/ nm jigsaw (puzzle).

P-V abrév m (**procès-verbal**) ticket, traffic fine.

pyjama /piʒama/ nm pyjamas (+ pl); **un ~** a pair of pyjamas.

pylône /pilon/ nm pylon.

Pyrénées /piʀene/ nfpl **les ~** the Pyrenees.

pyromane /piʀɔman/ nmf arsonist.

....

Qq

....

QG abrév m (**quartier général**) HQ.

QI abrév m (**quotient intellectuel**) IQ.

qu' /k/ ➡QUE.

quadriller /kadʀije/ **1** vt (armée) take control of; (police) spread one's net over; **papier quadrillé** squared paper.

quadrupède /kadʀypɛd/ nm quadruped.

quadruple /kadʀypl/ adj quadruple. ● nm **le ~ de** four times. **quadrupler 1** vt/i quadruple.

quai /ke/ nm (de gare) platform; (de port) quay; (de rivière) bank.

qualification /kalifikasjɔ̃/ nf qualification; (compétence pratique) skills (+ pl).

qualifié, **~e** /kalifje/ adj (diplômé) qualified; (main-d'œuvre) skilled.

qualifier /kalifje/ **45** vt qualify; (décrire) describe (**de** as). □ **se ~** vpr qualify (**pour** for).

qualité /kalite/ nf quality; (titre) occupation; (fonction) position; **en sa ~ de** in his ou her capacity as.

quand /kɑ̃/ adv when; **~ même** all the same. ● conj when; (toutes les fois que) whenever; **~ bien même** even if.

quant à /kɑ̃ta/ prép as for.

quantité /kɑ̃tite/ nf quantity; **une ~ de** a lot of; **des ~s (de)** masses ou lots (of).

quarantaine /kaʀɑ̃tɛn/ nf (Méd) quarantine; **une ~ (de)** about forty; **avoir la ~** be in one's forties.

quarante /kaʀɑ̃t/ adj & nm forty.

quart /kaʀ/ nm quarter; (Naut) watch; **onze heures moins le ~** quarter to eleven; **~ (de litre)** quarter litre; **~ de finale** quarter- final; **~ d'heure** quarter of an hour; **~ de tour** ninety-degree turn.

quartier /kaʀtje/ nm area, district; (zone ethnique) quarter; (de lune, pomme, bœuf) quarter; (d'une orange) segment; **~s** (Mil) quarters; **de ~, du ~** local; **~ général** headquarters; **avoir ~ libre** be free.

quasiment /kazimɑ̃/ adv almost, practically.

quatorze /katɔʀz/ adj & nm fourteen.

quatre /katʀ(ə)/ adj & nm four. **quatre-vingt(s)** adj & nm eighty. **quatre-vingt-dix** adj & nm ninety.

quatre-quatre /katʀkatʀ/ nm four-wheel drive.

quatrième /katʀijɛm/ adj & nmf fourth. ● nf (Auto) fourth gear.

quatuor /kwatɥɔʀ/ nm quartet.

que, qu' /kə, k/

qu' before vowel or mute h.

● *conjonction*
····➤ that; **je crains ~...** I'm worried that...
····➤ (souhait, volonté) **je veux ~ tu viennes** I want you to come; **~ tu viennes ou non** whether you come or not; **qu'il entre** let him come in.
····➤ (comparaison) than; **plus grand ~ toi** taller than you.
● *pronom interrogatif*
····➤ what; **~ voulez-vous manger?** what would you like to eat?
● *pronom relatif*
····➤ (personne) whom, that; **l'homme ~ j'ai rencontré** the man (whom) I met.
····➤ (chose) that, which; **le cheval ~ Nick m'a offert** the horse (which) Nick gave me.
● *adverbe*
····➤ **que c'est joli!** it's so pretty!; **~ de monde!** what a lot of people!

Québec /kebɛk/ *nm* Quebec.

quel, quelle (*pl* **quel(le)s**) /kɛl/
● *adjectif interrogatif*
····➤ which, what; **~ auteur a écrit...?** which writer wrote...?; **~ jour sommes-nous?** what day is it today?
● *adjectif exclamatif*
····➤ what; **~ idiot!** what an idiot!; **quelle horreur!** that's horrible!
● *adjectif relatif*
····➤ **~ que soit son âge** whatever his age; **quelles que soient tes raisons** whatever your reasons; **~ que soit le gagnant** whoever the winner is.

quelconque /kɛlkɔ̃k/ *adj* any, some; (banal) ordinary; (médiocre) poor, second rate.

quelque /kɛlkə/ *adj* some; **~s** a few, some. ● *adv* (environ) about, some; **et ~ 🛈** and a bit; **~ chose** something; (dans les phrases interrogatives) anything; **~ part** somewhere; **~ peu** somewhat.

quelquefois /kɛlkəfwa/ *adv* sometimes.

quelques-uns, -unes /kɛlkəzœ̃, -yn/ *pron* some, a few.

quelqu'un /kɛlkœ̃/ *pron* someone, somebody; (dans les phrases interrogatives) anyone, anybody.

querelle /kərɛl/ *nf* quarrel. **quereller (se) 🛈** *vpr* quarrel. **querelleur, -euse** *adj* quarrelsome.

question /kɛstjɔ̃/ *nf* question; (affaire) matter, question; **poser une ~** ask a question; **en ~** in question; **il est ~ de** (cela concerne) it is about; (on parle de) there is talk of; **il n'en est pas ~** it is out of the question; **pas ~!** no way!

questionnaire /kɛstjɔnɛʀ/ *nm* questionnaire.

questionner /kɛstjɔne/ 🛈 *vt* question.

quête /kɛt/ *nf* (Relig) collection; (recherche) search; **en ~ de** in search of.

queue /kø/ *nf* tail; (de poêle) handle; (de fruit) stalk; (de fleur) stem; (file) queue; (US) line; (de train) rear; **faire la ~** queue (up); (US) line up; **~ de cheval** ponytail; **faire une ~ de poisson à qn** (Auto) cut in front of sb.

qui /ki/
● *pronom interrogatif*
····➤ (sujet) who; **~ a fait ça?** who did that?
····➤ (complément) whom; **à ~ est ce livre?** whose book is this?
● *pronom relatif*
····➤ (personne sujet) who; **c'est Isabelle qui vient d'appeler** it's Isabelle who's just called.
····➤ (autres cas) that, which; **qu'est-ce ~ te prend?** what is the matter with you?; **invite ~ tu veux** invite whoever you want; **~ que ce soit** whoever it is, anybody.

quiche /kiʃ/ *nf* quiche.

quiconque /kikɔ̃k/ *pron* whoever; (n'importe qui) anyone.

quille /kij/ *nf* (de bateau) keel; (jouet) skittle.

quincaillerie /kɛ̃kɑjʀi/ *nf* hardware; (magasin) hardware shop. **quincaillier, -ière** *nm, f* hardware dealer.

quintal (pl **-aux**) /kɛ̃tal, -o/ nm quintal, one hundred kilos.

quinte /kɛ̃t/ nf ~ **de toux** coughing fit.

quintuple /kɛ̃typl/ adj quintuple. ● nm **le** ~ **de** five times. **quintupler** 1 vt/i quintuple, increase fivefold.

quinzaine /kɛ̃zɛn/ nf **une** ~ **(de)** about fifteen.

quinze /kɛ̃z/ adj & nm inv fifteen; ~ **jours** two weeks.

quiproquo /kipʀoko/ nm misunderstanding.

quittance /kitɑ̃s/ nf receipt.

quitte /kit/ adj quits (**envers** with); ~ **à faire** even if it means doing.

quitter /kite/ 1 vt leave; (vêtement) take off; **ne quittez pas!** hold the line, please! □ **se** ~ vpr part.

qui-vive /kiviv/ nm inv **être sur le** ~ be alert.

quoi /kwa/ pron what; (après une préposition) which; **de** ~ **vivre** (assez) enough to live on; **de** ~ **écrire** something to write with; ~ **qu'il dise** whatever he says; ~ **que ce soit** anything; **il n'y a pas de** ~ my pleasure; **il n'y a pas de** ~ **s'inquiéter** there's nothing to worry about.

quoique /kwak(ə)/ conj although, though.

quota /kɔta/ nm quota.

quote-part (pl **quotes-parts**) /kɔtpaʀ/ nf share.

quotidien, ~**ne** /kɔtidjɛ̃, -ɛn/ adj daily; (banal) everyday. ● nm daily (paper); (vie quotidienne) everyday life. **quotidiennement** adv daily.

. . . .

Rr

. . . .

rabâcher /ʀabaʃe/ 1 vt keep repeating.

rabais /ʀabɛ/ nm reduction, discount. **rabaisser** 1 vt (déprécier) belittle; (réduire) reduce.

rabat-joie /ʀabajwa/ nm inv killjoy.

rabattre /ʀabatʀ/ 11 vt (chapeau, visière) pull down; (refermer) shut; (diminuer) reduce; (déduire) take off;

(col, drap) turn down. □ **se** ~ vpr (se refermer) close; (véhicule) cut back in; **se** ~ **sur** make do with.

rabot /ʀabo/ nm plane.

rabougri, ~**e** /ʀabugʀi/ adj stunted.

racaille /ʀakɑj/ nf rabble.

raccommoder /ʀakɔmɔde/ 1 vt mend; (personnes 1) reconcile.

raccompagner /ʀakɔ̃paɲe/ 1 vt see ou take back (home).

raccord /ʀakɔʀ/ nm link; (de papier peint) join; (retouche) touch-up. **raccorder** 1 vt connect, join.

raccourci /ʀakuʀsi/ nm short cut; **en** ~ in short.

raccourcir /ʀakuʀsiʀ/ 2 vt shorten. ● vi get shorter.

raccrocher /ʀakʀɔʃe/ 1 vt hang back up; (passant) grab hold of; (relier) connect; ~ **le combiné** or **le téléphone** hang up. ● vi hang up. □ **se** ~ **à** vpr cling to; (se relier à) be connected to ou with.

race /ʀas/ nf race; (animale) breed; **de** ~ (chien) pedigree; (cheval) thoroughbred.

racheter /ʀaʃte/ 6 vt buy (back); (acheter encore) buy more; (nouvel objet) buy another; (société) buy out; ~ **des chaussettes** buy new socks. □ **se** ~ vpr make amends.

racial, ~**e** (mpl **-iaux**) /ʀasjal, -o/ adj racial.

racine /ʀasin/ nf root; ~ **carrée/ cubique** square/cube root.

racisme /ʀasism/ nm racism. **raciste** adj & nmf racist.

racket /ʀakɛt/ nm racketeering.

raclée /ʀakle/ nf 1 thrashing.

racler /ʀakle/ 1 vt scrape. □ **se** ~ vpr **se** ~ **la gorge** clear one's throat.

racolage /ʀakɔlaʒ/ nm soliciting.

raconter /ʀakɔ̃te/ 1 vt (histoire) tell; (vacances) grab about; (vie, épisode) describe; ~ **à qn que** tell sb that, say to sb that; **qu'est-ce que tu racontes?** what are you talking about?

radar /ʀadaʀ/ nm radar; (automatique) speed camera.

radeau (pl ~**x**) /ʀado/ nm raft.

radiateur /ʀadjatœʀ/ nm radiator; (électrique) heater.

radiation /ʀadjasjɔ̃/ nf radiation.

radical, ~e (*mpl* -**aux**) /ʀadikal, -o/ *adj* radical. ● *nm* (*pl* -**aux**) radical.

radieux, -ieuse /ʀadjø, -z/ *adj* radiant.

radin, ~e /ʀadɛ̃, -in/ *adj* 🔢 stingy 🔢.

radio /ʀadjo/ *nf* radio; **à la** ~ on the radio; (*radiographie*) X-ray.

radioactif, -ive /ʀadjoaktif, -v/ *adj* radioactive. **radioactivité** *nf* radioactivity.

radiocassette /ʀadjokasɛt/ *nf* radio cassette player.

radiodiffuser /ʀadjodifyze/ 🔢 *vt* broadcast.

radiographie /ʀadjogʀafi/ *nf* (*photographie*) X-ray.

radiomessageur /ʀadjomesa-ʒœʀ/ *nm* pager.

radis /ʀadi/ *nm* radish; **ne pas avoir un** ~ 🔢 be broke.

radoter /ʀadote/ 🔢 *vi* 🔢 talk drivel.

radoucir (se) /(sə)ʀadusiʀ/ 🔢 *vpr* (*humeur*) improve; (*temps*) become milder.

rafale /ʀafal/ *nf* (*de vent*) gust; (*de mitraillette*) burst.

raffermir /ʀafɛʀmiʀ/ 🔢 *vt* strengthen. □ **se** ~ *vpr* become stronger.

raffiné, ~e /ʀafine/ *adj* refined. **raffinement** *nm* refinement.

raffiner /ʀafine/ 🔢 *vt* refine. **raffinerie** *nf* refinery.

raffoler /ʀafole/ 🔢 *vt* 🔢 ~ **de** be crazy about.

raffut /ʀafy/ *nm* 🔢 din.

rafle /ʀafl/ *nf* (*police*) raid.

rafraîchir /ʀafʀeʃiʀ/ 🔢 *vt* cool (down); (*mur*) give a fresh coat of paint to; (*personne, mémoire*) refresh. □ **se** ~ *vpr* (*boire*) refresh oneself; (*temps*) get cooler. **rafraîchissant**, ~e *adj* refreshing.

rafraîchissement /ʀafʀeʃismã/ *nm* (*boisson*) cold drink; ~**s** refreshments.

ragaillardir /ʀagajaʀdiʀ/ 🔢 *vt* 🔢 cheer up.

rage /ʀaʒ/ *nf* rage; (*maladie*) rabies; **faire** ~ (*bataille, incendie*) rage; (*maladie*) be rife; ~ **de dents** raging toothache. **rageant**, ~e *adj* infuriating.

ragots /ʀago/ *nmpl* 🔢 gossip.

ragoût /ʀagu/ *nm* stew.

raid /ʀɛd/ *nm* (Mil) raid; (Sport) trek.

raide /ʀɛd/ *adj* stiff; (*côte*) steep; (*corde*) tight; (*cheveux*) straight. ● *adv* (monter, descendre) steeply. **raideur** *nf* stiffness; steepness.

raidir /ʀediʀ/ 🔢 *vt* (*corps*) tense. □ **se** ~ *vt* tense up; (*position*) harden; (*corde*) tighten.

raie /ʀɛ/ *nf* (*ligne*) line; (*bande*) strip; (*de cheveux*) parting; (*poisson*) skate.

raifort /ʀɛfoʀ/ *nm* horseradish.

rail /ʀɑj/ *nm* rail, track; **le** ~ (transport) rail.

raisin /ʀezɛ̃/ *nm* **le** ~ grapes; ~ **sec** raisin; **un grain de** ~ a grape.

raison /ʀezɔ̃/ *nf* reason; **à** ~ **de** at the rate of; **avec** ~ rightly; **avoir** ~ be right (**de faire** to do); **avoir** ~ **de qn** get the better of sb; **donner** ~ **à** prove right; **en** ~ **de** because of; ~ **de plus** all the more reason; **perdre la** ~ lose one's mind.

raisonnable /ʀezonabl/ *adj* reasonable, sensible.

raisonnement /ʀezonmã/ *nm* reasoning; (*propositions*) argument.

raisonner /ʀezone/ 🔢 *vi* think. ● *vt* (*personne*) reason with.

rajeunir /ʀaʒœniʀ/ 🔢 *vt* ~ **qn** make sb (look) younger; (*moderniser*) modernize; (Méd) rejuvenate. ● *vi* (*personne*) look younger.

rajuster /ʀaʒyste/ 🔢 *vt* straighten; (*salaires*) (re)adjust.

ralenti, ~e /ʀalãti/ *adj* slow. ● *nm* (au cinéma) slow motion; **tourner au** ~ tick over, idle.

ralentir /ʀalãtiʀ/ 🔢 *vt/i* slow down. □ **se** ~ *vpr* slow down.

ralentisseur /ʀalãtisœʀ/ *nm* speed ramp.

râler /ʀɑle/ 🔢 *vi* groan; (protester 🔢) moan.

rallier /ʀalje/ 🔢 *vt* rally; (rejoindre) rejoin. □ **se** ~ *vpr* rally; **se** ~ **à** (avis) come round to; (parti) join.

rallonge /ʀalɔ̃ʒ/ *nf* (de table) leaf; (de fil électrique) extension lead. **rallonger** 🔢 *vt* lengthen; (séjour, fil, table) extend.

rallumer /ʀalyme/ 🔢 *vt* (feu) relight; (lampe) switch on again; (ranimer: fig) revive.

rallye /ʀali/ *nm* rally.

ramassage /ʀamasaʒ/ nm (cueillette) gathering; (d'ordures) collection; ~ **scolaire** school bus service.

ramasser /ʀamase/ **1** vt pick up; (récolter) gather; (recueillir, rassembler) collect. □ **se** ~ vpr huddle up, curl up.

rame /ʀam/ nf (aviron) oar; (train) train.

ramener /ʀamne/ **1** vt (rapporter, faire revenir) bring back; (reconduire) take back; ~ **à** (réduire à) reduce to. □ **se** ~ vpr **1** turn up; **se** ~ **à** (problème) come down to.

ramer /ʀame/ **1** vi row.

ramollir /ʀamɔliʀ/ **2** vt soften. □ **se** ~ vpr become soft.

ramoneur /ʀamɔnœʀ/ nm (chimney) sweep.

rampe /ʀɑ̃p/ nf banisters; (pente) ramp; ~ **d'accès** (Auto) slip road; ~ **de lancement** launching pad.

ramper /ʀɑ̃pe/ **1** vi crawl.

rancard /ʀɑ̃kaʀ/ nm **1** date.

rancart /ʀɑ̃kaʀ/ nm **mettre** ou **jeter au** ~ **1** scrap.

rance /ʀɑ̃s/ adj rancid.

rancœur /ʀɑ̃kœʀ/ nf resentment.

rançon /ʀɑ̃sɔ̃/ nf ransom. **rançonner 1** vt rob, extort money from.

rancune /ʀɑ̃kyn/ nf grudge; **sans** ~**!** no hard feelings! **rancunier, -ière** adj vindictive.

randonnée /ʀɑ̃dɔne/ nf walk, ramble; **la** ~ **à cheval** pony trekking; **faire une** ~ go walking ou rambling.

rang /ʀɑ̃/ nm row; (hiérarchie, condition) rank; **se mettre en** ~ line up; **au premier** ~ in the first row; (fig) at the forefront; **de second** ~ (péj) second-rate.

rangée /ʀɑ̃ʒe/ nf row.

rangement /ʀɑ̃ʒmɑ̃/ nm (de pièce) tidying (up); (espace) storage space.

ranger /ʀɑ̃ʒe/ **40** vt put away; (chambre) tidy (up); (disposer) place. □ **se** ~ vpr (véhicule) park; (s'écarter) stand aside; (conducteur) pull over; (s'assagir) settle down; **se** ~ **à** (avis) accept.

ranimer /ʀanime/ **1** vt revive; (Méd) resuscitate. □ **se** ~ vpr come round.

rapace /ʀapas/ nm bird of prey. ● adj grasping.

rapatriement /ʀapatʀimɑ̃/ nm repatriation. **rapatrier** **45** vt repatriate.

rap /ʀap/ nm rap (music).

râpe /ʀɑp/ nf (Culin) grater; (lime) rasp.

râpé, ~e /ʀɑpe/ adj (vêtement) threadbare; (fromage) grated.

râper /ʀɑpe/ **1** vt grate; (bois) rasp.

rapide /ʀapid/ adj fast, rapid. ● nm (train) express (train); (cours d'eau) rapids (+ pl). **rapidement** adv fast, rapidly. **rapidité** nf speed.

rappel /ʀapɛl/ nm recall; (deuxième avis) reminder; (de salaire) back pay; (Méd) booster; (de diplomate) recall; (de réservistes) call-up; (Théât) curtain call.

rappeler /ʀaple/ **38** vt (par téléphone) call back; (réserviste) call up; (diplomate) recall; (évoquer) recall; ~ **qch à qn** remind sb of sth. □ **se** ~ vpr remember, recall.

rappeur, -euse /ʀapœɔeːʀ, -øz/ nmf rapper.

rapport /ʀapɔʀ/ nm connection; (compte-rendu) report; (profit) yield; ~**s** (relations) relations; **en** ~ **avec** (accord) in keeping with; **mettre/se mettre en** ~ **avec** put/get in touch with; **par** ~ **à** (comparé à) compared with; (vis-à-vis de) with regard to; ~**s** (sexuels) intercourse.

rapporter /ʀapɔʀte/ **1** vt (ici) bring back; (là-bas) take back, return; (profit) bring in; (dire, répéter) report. ● vi (Comm) bring in a good return; (moucharder **1**) tell tales. □ **se** ~ **à** vpr relate to.

rapporteur, -euse /ʀapɔʀtœʀ, -øz/ nm, f (mouchard) tell-tale. ● nm protractor.

rapprochement /ʀapʀɔʃmɑ̃/ nm reconciliation; (Pol) rapprochement; (rapport) connection; (comparaison) parallel.

rapprocher /ʀapʀɔʃe/ vt move closer (**de** to); (réconcilier) bring together; (comparer) compare; (date, rendezvous) bring forward. □ **se** ~ vpr get ou come closer (**de** to); (personnes, pays) come together; (s'apparenter) be close (**de** to).

rapt /ʀapt/ nm abduction.

raquette /ʀakɛt/ nf (de tennis) racket; (de ping-pong) bat.

rare /ʀaʀ/ adj rare; (insuffisant) scarce. **rarement** adv rarely, seldom. **rareté** nf rarity; scarcity.

ras, ~e /ʀɑ, ʀɑz/ adv **coupé** ~ **cut short.** ● adj (herbe, poil) short; **à** ~ **de terre** very close to the ground; **en avoir** ~ **le bol** 🔲 be really fed up; ~e **campagne** open country; **à** ~ **bord** to the brim.

raser /ʀɑze/ 🔳 vt shave; (cheveux, barbe) shave off; (frôler) skim; (abattre) raze. □ **se** ~ vpr shave.

rasoir /ʀɑzwaʀ/ nm razor. ● adj inv 🔲 boring.

rassasier /ʀɑsɑzje/ 🔳 vt satisfy, fill up; **être rassasié de** have had enough of.

rassemblement /ʀɑsɑ̃bləmɑ̃/ nm gathering; (manifestation) rally.

rassembler /ʀɑsɑ̃ble/ 🔳 vt gather; (forces, courage) summon up; (idées) collect. □ **se** ~ vpr gather.

rassis, ~e /ʀɑsi, -z/ adj (pain) stale.

rassurer /ʀɑsyʀe/ 🔳 vt reassure. □ **se** ~ vpr reassure oneself; **rassure-toi** don't worry.

rat /ʀa/ nm rat.

rate /ʀat/ nf spleen.

raté, ~e /ʀate/ nm, f (personne) failure. ● nm **avoir des** ~s (voiture) backfire.

râteau (pl ~x) /ʀɑto/ nm rake.

râtelier /ʀɑtəlje/ nm hayrack; (dentier 🔲) dentures.

rater /ʀate/ 🔳 vt (train, rendez-vous, cible) miss; (gâcher) make a mess of, spoil; (examen) fail. ● vi fail.

ratio /ʀasjo/ nm ratio.

rationaliser /ʀɑsjɔnalize/ 🔳 vt rationalize.

rationnel, ~le /ʀɑsjɔnɛl/ adj rational.

rationnement /ʀɑsjɔnmɑ̃/ nm rationing.

ratisser /ʀatise/ 🔳 vt rake; (fouiller) comb.

rattacher /ʀataʃe/ 🔳 vt (lacets) tie up again; (ceinture de sécurité, collier) refasten; (relier) link; (incorporer) join.

rattrapage /ʀatʀapaʒ/ nm (Comm) adjustment; **cours de** ~ remedial lesson.

rattraper /ʀatʀape/ 🔳 vt catch; (rejoindre) catch up with; (retard, erreur) make up for. □ **se** ~ vpr catch up; (se dédommager) make up for it; **se** ~ **à** catch hold of.

rature /ʀatyʀ/ nf deletion.

rauque /ʀok/ adj raucous, harsh.

ravager /ʀavaʒe/ 🔟 vt devastate, ravage.

ravages /ʀavaʒ/ nmpl **faire des** ~ wreak havoc.

ravaler /ʀavale/ 🔳 vt (façade) clean; (colère) swallow.

ravi, ~e /ʀavi/ adj delighted (que that).

ravin /ʀavɛ̃/ nm ravine.

ravir /ʀaviʀ/ 🔳 vt delight; ~ **qch à qn** rob sb of sth.

ravissant, ~e /ʀavisɑ̃, -t/ adj beautiful.

ravisseur, -euse /ʀavisœʀ, -øz/ nm, f kidnapper.

ravitaillement /ʀavitajmɑ̃/ nm provision of supplies (de to); (denrées) supplies; ~ **en essence** refuelling.

ravitailler /ʀavitaje/ 🔳 vt provide with supplies; (avion) refuel. □ **se** ~ vpr stock up.

raviver /ʀavive/ 🔳 vt revive; (feu, colère) rekindle.

rayé, ~e /ʀeje/ adj striped.

rayer /ʀeje/ 🔳 vt scratch; (biffer) cross out; **'**~ **la mention inutile'** 'delete as appropriate'.

rayon /ʀɛjɔ̃/ nm ray; (étagère) shelf; (de magasin) department; (de roue) spoke; (de cercle) radius; ~ **d'action** range; ~ **de miel** honeycomb; ~ X X-ray; **en connaître un** ~ 🔲 know one's stuff 🔲.

rayonnement /ʀɛjɔnmɑ̃/ nm (éclat) radiance; (influence) influence; (radiations) radiation. **rayonner** 🔳 vi radiate; (de joie) beam; (se déplacer) tour around (from a central point).

rayure /ʀɛjyʀ/ nf scratch; (dessin) stripe; **à** ~s striped.

raz-de-marée /ʀɑdmaʀe/ nm inv tidal wave; ~ **électoral** electoral landslide.

réacteur /ʀeaktœʀ/ nm jet engine; (nucléaire) reactor.

réaction /ʀeaksjɔ̃/ nf reaction; ~ **en chaîne** chain reaction; **moteur à** ~ jet engine.

réagir /ʀeaʒiʀ/ 🔳 vi react; ~ **sur** have an effect on.

réalisateur, -trice /ʀealizatœʀ, -tʀis/ nm, f (au cinéma) director; (TV) producer.

réalisation /ʀealizasjɔ̃/ nf (de rêve) fulfilment; (œuvre) achievement; (TV, cinéma) production; **projet en ~** project in progress.

réaliser /Realize/ **1** vt carry out; (effort, bénéfice, achat) make; (rêve) fulfil; (film) direct; (capital) realize; (se rendre compte de) realize. □ **se ~** vpr be fulfilled.

réalisme /Realism/ nm realism.

réaliste /Realist/ adj realistic. ● nmf realist.

réalité /Realite/ nf reality.

réanimation /Reanimasjɔ̃/ nf resuscitation; **service de ~** intensive care. **réanimer** **1** vt resuscitate.

réarmement /RearRməmã/ nm rearmament.

rébarbatif, -ive /RebaRbatif, -v/ adj forbidding, off-putting.

rebelle /Rabɛl/ adj rebellious; (soldat) rebel; **~ à** resistant to. ● nmf rebel.

rébellion /Rebeljɔ̃/ nf rebellion.

rebondir /Rəbɔ̃diR/ **2** vi bounce; rebound; (fig) get moving again.

rebondissement /Rəbɔ̃dismã/ nm (new) development.

rebord /RabɔR/ nm edge; **~ de la fenêtre** window ledge ou sill.

rebours: à ~ /aRabuR/ loc (compter, marcher) backwards.

rebrousse-poil: à ~ /aRabRuspwal/ loc the wrong way; (fig) **prendre qn à ~** rub sb up the wrong way.

rebrousser /RabRuse/ **1** vt **~ chemin** turn back.

rebut /Raby/ nm **mettre** ou **jeter au ~** scrap.

rebutant, ~e /Rabytã, -t/ adj off-putting.

recaler /Rakale/ **1** vt **1** fail; **se faire ~, être recalé** fail.

recel /Rasɛl/ nm receiving. **receler** **6** vt (objet volé) receive; (cacher) conceal.

récemment /Resamã/ adv recently.

recensement /Rasãsmã/ nm census; (inventaire) inventory. **recenser** **1** vt (population) take a census of; (objets) list.

récent, ~e /Resã, -t/ adj recent.

récépissé /Resepise/ nm receipt.

récepteur /ReseptœR/ nm receiver.

réception /Resɛpsjɔ̃/ nf reception; (de courrier) receipt. **réceptionniste** nmf receptionist.

récession /Resesjɔ̃/ nf recession.

recette /Rasɛt/ nf (Culin) recipe; (argent) takings; **~s** (Comm) receipts.

receveur, -euse /Ras(ə)vœR, -øz/ nm, f (de bus) conductor; **~ des contributions** tax collector.

recevoir /Ras(ə)vwaR/ **52** vt receive; get; (client, malade) see; (invités) welcome, receive; **être reçu à un examen** pass an exam.

rechange: de ~ /dəRaʃãʒ/ loc (roue, vêtements) spare; (solution) alternative.

réchapper /Reʃape/ **1** vt/i **~ de** come through, survive.

recharge /RəʃaRʒ/ nf (de stylo) refill.

réchaud /Reʃo/ nm stove.

réchauffement /Reʃofmã/ nm (de température) rise (de in); **le ~ de la planète** global warming.

réchauffer /Reʃofe/ **1** vt warm up. □ **se ~** vpr warm oneself up; (temps) get warmer.

rêche /Rɛʃ/ adj rough.

recherche /RəʃɛRʃ/ nf search (de for); (raffinement) meticulousness; **~(s)** (Univ) research; **~s** (enquête) investigations; **~ d'emploi** jobhunting.

recherché, ~e /RaʃɛRʃe/ adj in great demand; (style) original, recherché (péj); **~ pour meurtre** wanted for murder.

rechercher /RaʃɛRʃe/ **1** vt search for.

rechute /Raʃyt/ nf (Méd) relapse; **faire une ~** have a relapse.

récidiver /Residive/ **1** vi commit a second offence.

récif /Resif/ nm reef.

récipient /Resipjã/ nm container.

réciproque /ResipRɔk/ adj mutual, reciprocal.

réciproquement /ResipRɔkmã/ adv each other; **et ~** and vice versa.

récit /Resi/ nm (compte-rendu) account, story; (histoire) story.

réciter /Resite/ **1** vt recite.

réclamation /Reklamasjɔ̃/ nf complaint; (demande) claim.

réclame /Reklam/ nf advertisement; **faire de la ~** advertise; **en ~** on offer.

réclamer /Reklame/ **1** vt call for, demand. ● vi complain.

reclus, ~e /Rakly, -z/ nm, f recluse. ● adj reclusive.

réclusion /ʀeklyzjɔ̃/ *nf* imprisonment.

récolte /ʀekɔlt/ *nf* (action) harvest; (produits) crop, harvest; (fig) crop. **récolter** **1** *vt* harvest, gather; (fig) collect, get.

recommandation /ʀekɔmɑ̃dasjɔ̃/ *nf* recommendation.

recommandé /ʀəkɔmɑ̃de/ *nm* registered letter; **envoyer en ~** send by registered post.

recommander /ʀəkɔmɑ̃de/ **1** *vt* recommend.

recommencer /ʀəkɔmɑ̃se/ **10** *vt* (reprendre) begin *ou* start again; (refaire) repeat. ● *vi* start *ou* begin again; **ne recommence pas** don't do it again.

récompense /ʀekɔ̃pɑ̃s/ *nf* reward; (prix) award. **récompenser** **1** *vt* reward (**de** for).

réconcilier /ʀekɔ̃silje/ **45** *vt* reconcile. □ **se ~** *vpr* become reconciled (**avec** with).

reconduire /ʀəkɔ̃dɥiʀ/ **17** *vt* see home; (à la porte) show out; (renouveler) renew.

réconfort /ʀekɔ̃fɔʀ/ *nm* comfort.

reconnaissance /ʀekɔnɛsɑ̃s/ *nf* gratitude; (fait de reconnaître) recognition; (Mil) reconnaissance. **reconnaissant, ~e** *adj* grateful (**de** for).

reconnaître /ʀəkɔnɛtʀ/ **18** *vt* recognize; (admettre) admit (**que** that); (Mil) reconnoitre; (*enfant, tort*) acknowledge. □ **se ~** *vpr* (s'orienter) know where one is; (l'un l'autre) recognize each other.

reconstituer /ʀəkɔ̃stitɥe/ **1** *vt* reconstitute; (*crime*) reconstruct; (*époque*) recreate.

reconversion /ʀəkɔ̃vɛʀsjɔ̃/ *nf* (de main-d'œuvre) redeployment.

recopier /ʀəkɔpje/ **45** *vt* copy out.

record /ʀəkɔʀ/ *nm & a inv* record.

recouper /ʀəkupe/ **1** *vt* confirm. □ **se ~** *vpr* check, tally, match up.

recourbé, ~e /ʀəkuʀbe/ *adj* curved; (*nez*) hooked.

recourir /ʀəkuʀiʀ/ **20** *vi* **~ à** (*expédient, violence*) resort to; (*remède, méthode*) have recourse to.

recours /ʀəkuʀ/ *nm* resort; **avoir ~ à** have recourse to, resort to; **avoir ~ à qn** turn to sb.

recouvrer /ʀəkuvʀe/ **1** *vt* recover.

recouvrir /ʀəkuvʀiʀ/ **21** *vt* cover.

récréation /ʀekʀeasjɔ̃/ *nf* recreation; (Scol) break; (US) recess.

recroqueviller (se) /(sə)ʀəkʀɔkvije/ **1** *vpr* curl up.

recrudescence /ʀəkʀydesɑ̃s/ *nf* new outbreak.

recrue /ʀəkʀy/ *nf* recruit.

recrutement /ʀəkʀytmɑ̃/ *nm* recruitment. **recruter** **1** *vt* recruit.

rectangle /ʀɛktɑ̃gl/ *nm* rectangle. **rectangulaire** *adj* rectangular.

rectifier /ʀɛktifje/ **45** *vt* correct, rectify.

recto /ʀɛkto/ *nm* **au ~** on the front of the page.

reçu, ~e /ʀəsy/ *adj* accepted; (*candidat*) successful. ● *nm* receipt. ● ➡**RECEVOIR** **52**.

recueil /ʀəkœj/ *nm* collection.

recueillement /ʀəkœjmɑ̃/ *nm* meditation.

recueillir /ʀəkœjiʀ/ **25** *vt* collect; (prendre chez soi) take in. □ **se ~** *vpr* meditate.

recul /ʀəkyl/ *nm* retreat; (éloignement) distance; (déclin) decline; **avoir un mouvement de ~** recoil; **être en ~** be on the decline; **avec le ~** with hindsight.

reculé, ~e /ʀəkyle/ *adj* (*région*) remote.

reculer /ʀəkyle/ **1** *vt* move back; (*véhicule*) reverse; (différer) postpone. ● *vi* move back; (*voiture*) reverse; (*armée*) retreat; (régresser) fall; (céder) back down; **~ devant** (fig) shrink from. □ **se ~** *vpr* move back.

récupération /ʀekypeʀasjɔ̃/ *nf* (de l'organisme, de dette) recovery; (d'objets) salvage.

récupérer /ʀekypeʀe/ **14** *vt* recover; (*vieux objets*) salvage. ● *vi* recover.

récurer /ʀekyʀe/ **1** *vt* scour; **poudre à ~** scouring powder.

récuser /ʀekyze/ **1** *vt* challenge. □ **se ~** *vpr* state that one is not qualified to judge.

recyclage /ʀəsiklaʒ/ *nm* (de personnel) retraining; (de matériau) recycling.

recycler /ʀəsikle/ **1** *vt* (*personne*) retrain; (*chose*) recycle. □ **se ~** *vpr* retrain.

rédacteur, -trice /ʀedaktœʀ, -tʀis/ nm, f author, writer; (de journal, magazine) editor.

rédaction /ʀedaksjɔ̃/ nf writing; (Scol) essay, composition; (personnel) editorial staff.

redevable /ʀədvabl/ adj être ~ à qn de (argent) owe sb; (fig) be indebted to sb for.

redevance /ʀədvɑ̃s/ nf (de télévision) licence fee; (de téléphone) rental charge.

rédiger /ʀediʒe/ 40 vt write; (contrat) draw up.

redire /ʀədiʀ/ 27 vt repeat; **avoir** ou **trouver à ~ à** find fault with.

redondant, ~e /ʀədɔ̃dɑ̃, -t/ adj superfluous.

redonner /ʀədɔne/ 1 vt (rendre) give back; (donner davantage) give more; (donner de nouveau) give again.

redoubler /ʀəduble/ 1 vt increase; (classe) repeat; ~ **de prudence** be even more careful. ● vi (Scol) repeat a year; (s'intensifier) intensify.

redoutable /ʀədutabl/ adj formidable.

redouter /ʀədute/ 1 vt dread.

redressement /ʀədʀɛsmɑ̃/ nm (reprise) recovery; ~ **judiciaire** receivership.

redresser /ʀədʀese/ 1 vt straighten (out ou up); (situation) right, redress; (économie, entreprise) turn around. □ **se ~** vpr (personne) straighten (oneself) up; (se remettre debout) stand up; (pays, économie) recover.

réduction /ʀedyksjɔ̃/ nf reduction.

réduire /ʀeduiʀ/ 17 vt reduce (à to). □ **se ~** vpr be reduced ou cut; **se ~ à** (revenir à) come down to.

réduit, ~e /ʀedui, -t/ adj (objet) small-scale; (limité) limited. ● nm cubbyhole.

rééducation /ʀeedykasjɔ̃/ nf (de handicapé) rehabilitation; (Méd) physiotherapy. **rééduquer** 1 vt (personne) rehabilitate; (membre) restore normal movement to.

réel, ~le /ʀeɛl/ adj real. ● nm reality. **réellement** adv really.

réexpédier /ʀeɛkspedje/ 45 vt forward; (retourner) send back.

refaire /ʀəfɛʀ/ 33 vt do again; (erreur, voyage) make again; (réparer) do up, redo.

réfectoire /ʀefɛktwaʀ/ nm refectory.

référence /ʀefeʀɑ̃s/ nf reference.

référendum /ʀefeʀɛ̃dɔm/ nm referendum.

référer /ʀefeʀe/ 14 vi **en ~ à** consult. □ **se ~ à** vpr refer to, consult.

refermer /ʀəfɛʀme/ 1 vt close (again). □ **se ~** vpr close (again).

réfléchi, ~e /ʀeflefi/ adj (personne) thoughtful; (verbe) reflexive.

réfléchir /ʀeflefiʀ/ 2 vi think (à, sur about). ● vt reflect. □ **se ~** vpr be reflected.

reflet /ʀəflɛ/ nm reflection; (nuance) sheen.

refléter /ʀəflete/ 14 vt reflect. □ **se ~** vpr be reflected.

réflexe /ʀeflɛks/ adj reflex. ● nm reflex; (réaction) reaction.

réflexion /ʀeflɛksjɔ̃/ nf (pensée) thought, reflection; (remarque) remark, comment; **à la ~** on second thoughts.

refluer /ʀəflye/ 1 vi flow back; (foule) retreat; (inflation) go down.

reflux /ʀəfly/ nm (marée) ebb, tide.

réforme /ʀefɔʀm/ nf reform. **réformer** 1 vt reform; (soldat) invalid out.

refouler /ʀəfule/ 1 vt (larmes) hold back; (désir) repress; (souvenir) suppress.

refrain /ʀəfʀɛ̃/ nm chorus; **le même ~** the same old story.

refréner /ʀəfʀene/ 14 vt curb, check.

réfrigérateur /ʀefʀiʒeʀatœʀ/ nm refrigerator.

refroidir /ʀəfʀwadiʀ/ 2 vt/i cool (down). □ **se ~** vpr (personne, temps) get cold. **refroidissement** nm cooling; (rhume) chill.

refuge /ʀəfyʒ/ nm refuge; (chalet) mountain hut.

réfugié, ~e /ʀefyʒje/ nm, f refugee. **réfugier (se)** 45 vpr take refuge.

refus /ʀəfy/ nm refusal; **ce n'est pas de ~** 11 I wouldn't say no.

refuser /ʀəfyze/ 1 vt refuse (de to); (client, spectateur) turn away; (recaler) fail; (à un poste) turn down. □ **se ~ à** vpr (évidence) reject; **se ~ à faire** refuse to do.

regain /ʀəgɛ̃/ nm ~ **de** renewal ou revival of; (Comm) rise.

régal (*pl* ~s) /Regal/ *nm* treat, delight.

régaler /Regale/ **1** *vt* ~ **qn de** treat sb to. □ **se** ~ *vpr* (*de nourriture*) **je me régale** it's delicious.

regard /RəgaR/ *nm* (expression, coup d'œil) look; (vue) eye; (yeux) eyes; ~ **fixe** stare; **au** ~ **de** with regard to; **en** ~ **de** compared with.

regardant, -e /RəgaRdɑ̃, -t/ *adj* ~ **avec son argent** careful with money; **peu** ~ (**sur**) not fussy (about).

regarder /RəgaRde/ **1** *vt* look at; (observer) watch; (considérer) consider; (concerner) concern; ~ **fixement** stare at; ~ **à** think about, pay attention to. ● *vi* look. □ **se** ~ *vpr* (*soi-même*) look at oneself; (*personnes*) look at each other.

régate /Regat/ *nf* regatta.

régie /Reʒi/ *nf* ~ **d'État** public corporation; (radio, TV) control room; (au cinéma) production; (Théât) stage management.

régime /Reʒim/ *nm* (organisation) system; (Pol) regime; (Méd) diet; (de moteur) speed; (de bananes) bunch; **se mettre au** ~ go on a diet; **à ce** ~ at this rate.

régiment /Reʒimɑ̃/ *nm* regiment.

région /Reʒjɔ̃/ *nf* region. **régional, -e** (*mpl* **-aux**) *adj* regional.

> **Région** The largest administrative unit in France, consisting of a number of *départements*. Each has its own *Conseil régional* (regional council) which has responsibilities in education and economic planning. ▷**Département**.

régir /ReʒiR/ **2** *vt* govern.

régisseur /ReʒisœR/ *nm* (Théât) stage manager; ~ **de plateau** (TV) floor manager; (au cinéma) studio manager.

registre /RəʒistR/ *nm* register.

réglage /Reglaʒ/ *nm* adjustment; (de moteur) tuning.

règle /Regl/ *nf* rule; (instrument) ruler; ~**s** (de femme) period; **en** ~ in order.

réglé, -e /Regle/ *adj* (vie) ordered; (arrangé) settled; (papier) ruled.

règlement /Regləmɑ̃/ *nm* (règles) regulations; (solution) settlement; (paiement) payment. **réglementaire** *adj* (uniforme) regulation. **réglementa-**

tion *nf* regulation, rules. **réglementer** **1** *vt* regulate, control.

régler /Regle/ **14** *vt* settle; (machine) adjust; (programmer) set; (facture) settle; (personne) settle up with; ~ **son compte à** **1** settle a score with.

réglisse /Reglis/ *nf* liquorice.

règne /Rɛɲ/ *nm* reign; (végétal, animal, minéral) kingdom.

regret /RəgRɛ/ *nm* regret; **à** ~ with regret.

regretter /RəgRete/ **1** *vt* regret; (personne) miss; (pour s'excuser) be sorry.

regrouper /RəgRupe/ **1** *vt* group *ou* bring together. □ **se** ~ *vpr* gather *ou* group together.

régularité /RegylaRite/ *nf* regularity; (de rythme, progrès) steadiness; (de surface, écriture) evenness.

régulier, -ière /Regylje, -jɛR/ *adj* regular; (qualité, vitesse) steady, even; (ligne, paysage) even; (légal) legal; (honnête) honest.

rehausser /Rəose/ **1** *vt* raise; (faire valoir) enhance.

rein /Rɛ̃/ *nm* kidney; ~**s** (dos) small of the back.

reine /Rɛn/ *nf* queen.

réinsertion /Reɛ̃sɛRsjɔ̃/ *nf* reintegration.

réintégrer /Reɛ̃tegRe/ **14** *vt* (lieu) return to; (Jur) reinstate; (personne) reintegrate.

réitérer /ReiteRe/ **14** *vt* repeat.

rejaillir /RəʒajiR/ **2** *vi* ~ **sur** splash back onto; ~ **sur qn** (succès) reflect on sb.

rejet /Rəʒɛ/ *nm* rejection; ~**s** (déchets) waste.

rejeter /Rəʒte/ **38** *vt* throw back; (refuser) reject; (déverser) discharge; ~ **une faute sur qn** shift the blame for a mistake onto sb.

rejoindre /RəʒwɛdR/ **22** *vt* go back to, rejoin; (rattraper) catch up with; (rencontrer) join, meet up with. □ **se** ~ *vpr* (personnes) meet up; (routes) join, meet.

réjoui, -e /Reʒwi/ *adj* joyful.

réjouir /ReʒwiR/ **2** *vt* delight. □ **se** ~ *vpr* be delighted (**de** at). **réjouissances** *nfpl* festivities. **réjouissant, -e** *adj* cheering.

relâche /Rəlɑʃ/ nm (repos) break, rest; **faire ~** (Théât) be closed.

relâcher /Rəlɑʃe/ **1** vt slacken; (personne) release; (discipline) relax. □ **se ~** vpr slacken.

relais /Rəlɛ/ nm (Sport) relay; (hôtel) hotel; (intermédiaire) intermediary; **prendre le ~ de** take over from.

relancer /Rəlɑ̃se/ **10** vt boost, revive; (renvoyer) throw back.

relatif, -ive /Rəlatif, -v/ adj relative; **~ à** relating to.

relation /Rəlasjɔ̃/ nf relationship; (ami) acquaintance; (personne puissante) connection; **~s** relations; **~s extérieures** foreign affairs; **en ~ avec qn** in touch with sb.

relativement /Rəlativmɑ̃/ adv relatively; **~ à** in relation to.

relativité /Rəlativite/ nf relativity.

relax /Rəlaks/ adj inv **1** laid-back.

relaxer (se) /(sə)Rəlakse/ **1** vpr relax.

relayer /Rəleje/ **31** vt relieve; (émission) relay. □ **se ~** vpr take over from one another.

reléguer /Rəlege/ **14** vt relegate.

relent /Rəlɑ̃/ nm stink; (fig) whiff.

relève /Rəlɛv/ nf relief; **prendre ou assurer la ~** take over (de from).

relevé, -e /Rəlve/ adj spicy. ● nm (de compteur) reading; (facture) bill; **~ bancaire, ~ de compte** bank statement; **faire le ~ de** list.

relever /Rəlve/ **6** vt pick up; (personne tombée) help up; (remonter) raise; (col) turn up; (compteur) read; (défi) accept; (relayer) relieve; (remarquer, noter) note; (plat) spice up; (rebâtir) rebuild; **~ de** come within the competence of; (Méd) recover from. □ **se ~** vpr (personne) get up (again); (pays, économie) recover.

relief /Rəljɛf/ nm relief; **mettre en ~** highlight.

relier /Rəlje/ **45** vt link (up) (à to); (livre) bind.

religieux, -ieuse /Rəliʒjø, -z/ adj religious. ● nm, f monk, nun.

religion /Rəliʒjɔ̃/ nf religion.

reliure /RəljyR/ nf binding.

reluire /RəlɥiR/ **17** vi shine.

remaniement /Rəmanimɑ̃/ nm revision; **~ ministériel** cabinet reshuffle.

remarquable /Rəmarkabl/ adj remarkable.

remarque /Rəmark/ nf remark; (par écrit) comment.

remarquer /Rəmarke/ **1** vt notice; (dire) say; **faire ~** point out (à to); **se faire ~** draw attention to oneself; **remarque(z)** mind you.

remblai /Rɑ̃blɛ/ nm embankment.

remboursement /Rɑ̃buRsəmɑ̃/ nm (d'emprunt, dette) repayment; (Comm) refund.

rembourser /Rɑ̃buRse/ **1** vt (dette, emprunt) repay; (billet, frais) refund; (client) give a refund to; (ami) pay back.

remède /Rəmɛd/ nm remedy; (médicament) medicine.

remédier /Rəmedje/ **45** vi **~ à** remedy.

remerciements /RəmɛRsimɑ̃/ nmpl thanks. **remercier 45** vt thank (de for); (licencier) dismiss.

remettre /RəmɛtR/ **42** vt put back; (vêtement) put back on; (donner) hand over; (devoir, démission) hand in; (faire fonctionner) switch back on; (restituer) give back; (différer) put off; (ajouter) add; (se rappeler) remember; **~ en cause ou en question** call into question. □ **se ~** vpr (guérir) recover; **se ~ au tennis** take up tennis again; **se ~ au travail** get back to work; **se ~ à faire** start doing again; **s'en ~ à** leave it to.

remise /Rəmiz/ nf (abri) shed; (rabais) discount; (transmission) handing over; (ajournement) postponement; **~ en cause ou en question** calling into question; **~ des prix** prizegiving; **~ des médailles** medals ceremony; **~ de peine** remission.

remontant /Rəmɔ̃tɑ̃/ nm tonic.

remontée /Rəmɔ̃te/ nf ascent; (d'eau, de prix) rise; **~ mécanique** ski lift.

remonte-pente (pl **~s**) /Rəmɔ̃tpɑ̃t/ nm ski tow.

remonter /Rəmɔ̃te/ **1** vi go ou come (back) up; (prix, niveau) rise (again); (revenir) go back (up); **~ dans le temps** go back in time. ● vt (rue, escalier) go ou come (back) up; (relever) raise; (montre) wind up; (objet démonté) put together again; (personne) buck up.

remontoir /ʀəmɔ̃twaʀ/ nm winder.

remords /ʀəmɔʀ/ nm remorse; **avoir du** or **des** ~ feel remorse.

remorque /ʀəmɔʀk/ nf trailer; **en** ~ on tow. **remorquer** ◼ vt tow.

remous /ʀəmu/ nm eddy; (de bateau) backwash; (fig) turmoil.

rempart /ʀɑ̃paʀ/ nm rampart.

remplaçant, ~e /ʀɑ̃plasɑ̃, -t/ nm, f replacement; (joueur) reserve, substitute.

remplacement /ʀɑ̃plasmɑ̃/ nm replacement; **faire des** ~s do supply teaching. **remplacer** ◼◻ vt replace.

rempli, ~e /ʀɑ̃pli/ adj full (**de** of); (journée) busy.

remplir /ʀɑ̃pliʀ/ ◻ vt fill (up); (formulaire) fill in ou out; (condition) fulfil; (devoir, tâche, rôle) carry out. ◻ **se** ~ vpr fill (up). **remplissage** nm filling; (de texte) padding.

remporter /ʀɑ̃pɔʀte/ ◼ vt take back; (victoire) win.

remuant, ~e /ʀəmɥɑ̃, -t/ adj boisterous.

remue-ménage /ʀəmymenaʒ/ nm inv commotion, bustle.

remuer /ʀəmɥe/ ◼ vt move; (thé, café) stir; (passé) rake up. ● vi move; (gigoter) fidget. ◻ **se** ~ vpr move.

rémunération /ʀemyneʀasjɔ̃/ nf payment.

renaissance /ʀənɛsɑ̃s/ nf rebirth.

renard /ʀənaʀ/ nm fox.

renchérir /ʀɑ̃ʃeʀiʀ/ ◻ vi (dans une vente) raise the bidding; ~ **sur** go one better than. ● vt increase, put up.

rencontre /ʀɑ̃kɔ̃tʀ/ nf meeting; (de routes) junction; (Mil) encounter; (match) match; (US) game.

rencontrer /ʀɑ̃kɔ̃tʀe/ ◼ vt meet; (heurter) hit; (trouver) find. ◻ **se** ~ vpr meet.

rendement /ʀɑ̃dmɑ̃/ nm yield; (travail) output.

rendez-vous /ʀɑ̃devu/ nm appointment; (d'amoureux) date; (lieu) meeting-place; **prendre** ~ (**avec**) make an appointment (with).

rendormir (se) /(sə)ʀɑ̃dɔʀmiʀ/ ◻ vpr go back to sleep.

rendre /ʀɑ̃dʀ/ ◻ vt give back, return; (donner en retour) return; (monnaie) give; (justice) dispense; (jugement)

pronounce; ~ **heureux/possible** make happy/possible; (vomir ◻) vomit; ~ **compte de** report on; ~ **service (à)** help; ~ **visite à** visit. ● vi (terres) yield; (activité) be profitable. ◻ **se** ~ vpr (capituler) surrender; (aller) go (**à** to); **se** ~ **utile** make oneself useful.

rêne /ʀɛn/ nf rein.

renfermé, ~e /ʀɑ̃fɛʀme/ adj withdrawn. ● nm **sentir le** ~ smell musty.

renflé, ~e /ʀɑ̃fle/ adj bulging.

renforcer /ʀɑ̃fɔʀse/ ◻ vt reinforce.

renfort /ʀɑ̃fɔʀ/ nm reinforcement; **à grand** ~ **de** with a great deal of.

renier /ʀənje/ ◻ vt (personne, œuvre) disown; (foi) renounce.

renifler /ʀənifle/ ◼ vt/i sniff.

renne /ʀɛn/ nm reindeer.

renom /ʀənɔ̃/ nm renown; (réputation) reputation. **renommé,** ~e adj famous. **renommée** nf (célébrité) fame; (réputation) reputation.

renoncement /ʀənɔ̃smɑ̃/ nm renunciation.

renoncer /ʀənɔ̃se/ ◻ vi ~ **à** (habitude, ami) give up, renounce; (projet) abandon; ~ **à faire** abandon the idea of doing.

renouer /ʀənwe/ ◼ vt tie up (again); (amitié) renew; ~ **avec qn** get back in touch with sb; (après une dispute) make up with sb.

renouveau (pl ~x) /ʀənuvo/ nm revival.

renouveler /ʀənuvle/ ◼◼ vt renew; (réitérer) repeat; (remplacer) replace. ◻ **se** ~ vpr be renewed; (incident) recur, happen again.

renouvellement /ʀənuvɛlmɑ̃/ nm renewal.

rénovation /ʀenɔvasjɔ̃/ nf (d'édi- fice) renovation; (d'institution) reform.

renseignement /ʀɑ̃sɛɲ(ə)mɑ̃/ nm ~(s) information; (bureau des) ~s information desk; (service des) ~s **téléphoniques** directory enquiries.

renseigner /ʀɑ̃seɲe/ ◼ vt inform, give information to. ◻ **se** ~ vpr enquire, make enquiries, find out.

rentabilité /ʀɑ̃tabilite/ nf profitability. **rentable** adj profitable.

rente /ʀɑ̃t/ nf (private) income; (pension) annuity. **rentier, -ière** nm, f person of private means.

rentrée /ʀɑ̃tʀe/ nf return; (revenu) income; **la ∼ (des classes)** the start of the new school year; **faire sa ∼** make a comeback.

> **Rentrée** The start of the new school year at the beginning of September, used as a major marketing opportunity by stores and supermarkets. The concept of the *rentrée* also extends to literary, political and other activities which resume after the holiday period. *La rentrée parlementaire*, for example, signals the return of Parliament after the summer recess.

rentrer /ʀɑ̃tʀe/ **1** vi (aux être) go ou come back home, return home; (entrer) go ou come in; (entrer à nouveau) go ou come back in; (revenu) come in; (élèves) go back (to school); **∼ dans** (heurter) smash into; **tout est rentré dans l'ordre** everything is back to normal; **∼ dans ses frais** break even. ● vt (aux avoir) bring in; (griffes) draw in; (vêtement) tuck in.

renverser /ʀɑ̃vɛʀse/ **1** vt knock over ou down; (piéton) knock down; (liquide) upset, spill; (mettre à l'envers) turn upside down; (gouvernement) overthrow; (inverser) reverse. □ **se ∼** vpr (véhicule) overturn; (verre, vase) fall over.

renvoi /ʀɑ̃vwa/ nm return; (d'employé) dismissal; (d'élève) expulsion; (report) postponement; (dans un livre, fichier) cross-reference; (rot) burp.

renvoyer /ʀɑ̃vwaje/ **32** vt send back, return; (employé) dismiss; (élève) expel; (ajourner) postpone; (référer) refer; (réfléchir) reflect.

repaire /ʀəpɛʀ/ nm den.

répandre /ʀepɑ̃dʀ/ **3** vt (liquide) spill; (étendre, diffuser) spread; (odeur) give off. □ **se ∼** vpr spread; (liquide) spill; **se ∼ en injures** let out a stream of abuse.

répandu, **∼e** /ʀepɑ̃dy/ adj widespread.

réparateur, -trice /ʀepaʀatœʀ, -tʀis/ nm engineer. **réparation** nf repair; (compensation) compensation. **réparer** **1** vt repair, mend; (faute) make amends for; (remédier à) put right.

repartie /ʀəpaʀti/ nf retort; **avoir de la ∼** always have a ready reply.

repartir /ʀəpaʀtiʀ/ **46** vi start again; (voyageur) set off again; (s'en retourner) go back; (secteur économique) pick up again.

répartir /ʀepaʀtiʀ/ **2** vt distribute; (partager) share out; (étaler) spread. **répartition** nf distribution.

repas /ʀəpɑ/ nm meal.

repassage /ʀəpasaʒ/ nm ironing.

repasser /ʀəpase/ **1** vi come ou go back; **∼ devant qch** go past sth again. ● vt (linge) iron; (examen) retake, resist; (film) show again.

repêcher /ʀəpeʃe/ **1** vt recover, fish out; (candidat) allow to pass.

repentir¹ /ʀəpɑ̃tiʀ/ nm repentance.

repentir² (se) /(sə)ʀəpɑ̃tiʀ/ **2** vpr (Relig) repent (**de** of); **se ∼ de** (regretter) regret.

répercuter /ʀepɛʀkyte/ **1** vt (bruit) send back. □ **se ∼** vpr echo; **se ∼ sur** have repercussions on.

repère /ʀəpɛʀ/ nm mark; (jalon) marker; (événement) landmark; (référence) reference point.

repérer /ʀəpeʀe/ **14** vt locate, spot. □ **se ∼** vpr get one's bearings.

répertoire /ʀepɛʀtwaʀ/ nm (artistique) repertoire; (liste) directory; **∼ téléphonique** telephone directory; (personnel) telephone book. **répertorier** **45** vt index.

répéter /ʀepete/ **14** vt repeat; (Théât) rehearse. ● vi rehearse. □ **se ∼** vpr be repeated; (personne) repeat oneself.

répétition /ʀepetisjɔ̃/ nf repetition; (Théât) rehearsal.

répit /ʀepi/ nm respite, break.

replier /ʀəplije/ **45** vt fold (up); (ailes, jambes) tuck in. □ **se ∼** vpr withdraw (**sur soi-même** into oneself).

réplique /ʀeplik/ nf reply; (riposte) retort; (objection) objection; (Théât) line; (copie) replica. **répliquer** **1** vt/i reply; (riposter) retort; (objecter) answer back.

répondeur /ʀepɔ̃dœʀ/ nm answering machine.

répondre /ʀepɔ̃dʀ/ **3** vt (injure, bêtise) reply with; **∼ que** answer ou reply that; **∼ à** (être conforme à) answer; (affection, sourire) return; (avances, *appel, critique*) respond to; **~ de** answer for. ● *vi* answer, reply; (*être insolent*) answer back; (*réagir*) respond (à to).

réponse /ʀepɔ̃s/ *nf* answer, reply; (*fig*) response.

report /ʀəpɔʀ/ *nm* (transcription) transfer; (renvoi) postponement.

reportage /ʀəpɔʀtaʒ/ *nm* report; (par écrit) article.

reporter¹ /ʀəpɔʀte/ **1** *vt* take back; (ajourner) put off; (transcrire) transfer. □ **se ~ à** *vpr* refer to.

reporter² /ʀəpɔʀtɛʀ/ *nm* reporter.

repos /ʀəpo/ *nm* rest; (paix) peace. **reposant, ~e** *adj* restful.

reposer /ʀəpoze/ **1** *vt* put down again; (délasser) rest. ● *vi* rest (**sur** on); **laisser ~** (*pâte*) leave to stand. □ **se ~** *vpr* rest; **se ~ sur** rely on.

repousser /ʀəpuse/ **1** *vt* push back; (écarter) push away; (dégoûter) repel; (décliner) reject; (ajourner) postpone, put back. ● *vi* grow again.

reprendre /ʀəpʀɑ̃dʀ/ **50** *vt* take back; (*confiance, conscience*) regain; (souffle) get back; (évadé) recapture; (recommencer) resume; (redire) repeat; (modifier) alter; (blâmer) reprimand; **~ du pain** take some more bread; **on ne m'y reprendra pas** I won't be caught out again. ● *vi* (recommencer) resume; (*affaires*) pick up. □ **se ~** *vpr* (se ressaisir) pull oneself together; (se corriger) correct oneself.

représailles /ʀəpʀezaj/ *nfpl* reprisals.

représentant, ~e /ʀəpʀezɑ̃tɑ̃, -t/ *nm, f* representative.

représentation /ʀəpʀezɑ̃tasjɔ̃/ *nf* representation; (Théât) performance.

représenter /ʀəpʀezɑ̃te/ **1** *vt* represent; (figures) depict, show; (*pièce de théâtre*) perform. □ **se ~** *vpr* (s'imaginer) imagine.

répression /ʀepʀesjɔ̃/ *nf* repression; (d'élan) suppression.

réprimande /ʀepʀimɑ̃d/ *nf* reprimand.

réprimer /ʀepʀime/ **1** *vt* (peuple) repress; (sentiment) suppress; (fraude) crack down on.

reprise /ʀəpʀiz/ *nf* resumption; (Théât) revival; (TV) repeat; (de tissu) darn, mend; (essor) recovery; (Comm) part-exchange, trade-in; **à plusieurs ~s** on several occasions.

repriser /ʀəpʀize/ **1** *vt* darn, mend.

reproche /ʀəpʀɔʃ/ *nm* reproach; **faire des ~s à** to find fault with.

reprocher /ʀəpʀɔʃe/ **1** *vt* **~ qch à qn** reproach *ou* criticize sb for sth.

reproducteur, -trice /ʀəpʀɔdyktœʀ, -tʀis/ *adj* reproductive.

reproduire /ʀəpʀɔdɥiʀ/ **17** *vt* reproduce; (répéter) repeat. □ **se ~** *vpr* reproduce; (se répéter) recur.

reptile /ʀɛptil/ *nm* reptile.

repu, ~e /ʀəpy/ *adj* satiated, replete.

républicain, ~e /ʀepyblikɛ̃, -ɛn/ *adj & nm, f* republican.

république /ʀepyblik/ *nf* republic; **~ populaire** people's republic.

répudier /ʀepydje/ **45** *vt* repudiate; (droit) renounce.

répugnance /ʀepyɲɑ̃s/ *nf* repugnance; (hésitation) reluctance; **avoir de la ~ pour** loathe. **répugnant, ~e** *adj* repulsive.

répugner /ʀepyɲe/ **1** *vt* be repugnant to, disgust; **~ à** (*effort, violence*) be averse to; **~ à faire** be reluctant to do.

répulsion /ʀepylsjɔ̃/ *nf* repulsion.

réputation /ʀepytasjɔ̃/ *nf* reputation.

réputé, ~e /ʀepyte/ *adj* renowned (**pour** for); (*école, compagnie*) reputable; **~ pour être** reputed to be.

requérir /ʀəkeʀiʀ/ **7** *vt* require, demand.

requête /ʀəkɛt/ *nf* request; (Jur) petition.

requin /ʀəkɛ̃/ *nm* shark.

requis, ~e /ʀəki, -z/ *adj* (exigé) required; (nécessaire) necessary.

RER *abrév m* (**réseau express régional**) *Parisian rapid transit rail system.*

rescapé, ~e /ʀɛskape/ *nm, f* survivor. ● *adj* surviving.

rescousse /ʀɛskus/ *nf* **à la ~** to the rescue.

réseau (*pl ~x*) /ʀezo/ *nm* network; **~ local** local area network, LAN; **le ~ des ~x** (Ordinat) Internet.

réservation /ʀezɛʀvasjɔ̃/ *nf* reservation, booking.

réserve /ʀezɛʀv/ *nf* reserve; (restriction) reservation, reserve; (indienne) reservation; (entrepôt) store-room; **en ~ in reserve; les ~s** (Mil) the reserves.

réserver /Rezɛrve/ **1** vt reserve; (place) book, reserve. □ **se ~** vpr se **~ qch** save sth for oneself; **se ~ pour** save oneself for; **se ~ le droit de** reserve the right to.

réservoir /Rezɛrvwar/ nm tank; (lac) reservoir.

résidence /Rezidɑ̃s/ nf residence; **~ secondaire** second home; **~ universitaire** hall of residence.

résident, ~e /Rezidɑ̃, -t/ nm, f resident; (étranger) foreign resident.

résider /Rezide/ **1** vi reside; **~ dans qch** (difficulté) lie in.

résigner (se) /(sə)Rezine/ **1** vpr se **~ à faire** resign oneself to doing.

résilier /Rezilje/ **45** vt terminate.

résine /Rezin/ nf resin.

résistance /Rezistɑ̃s/ nf resistance; (fil électrique) element. **résistant, ~e** adj tough.

résister /Reziste/ **1** vi resist; **~ à** (agresseur, assaut, influence, tentation) resist; (corrosion, chaleur) withstand.

résolu, ~e /Rezɔly/ adj resolute; **~ à faire** determined to do. ● **→RÉSOUDRE 53**.

résolution /Rezɔlysjɔ̃/ nf (fermeté) resolution; (d'un problème) solving.

résonner /Rezɔne/ **1** vi resound.

résorber /Rezɔrbe/ **1** vt reduce. □ **se ~** vpr be reduced.

résoudre /Rezudr/ **53** vt solve; (crise, conflit) resolve. □ **se ~ à** vpr (se décider) resolve to; (se résigner) resign oneself to.

respect /Rɛspɛ/ nm respect. **respectabilité** nf respectability.

respecter /Rɛspɛkte/ **1** vt respect; **faire ~** (loi, décision) enforce.

respectueux, -euse /Rɛspɛktɥø, -z/ adj respectful; **~ de l'environnement** environmentally friendly.

respiration /Rɛspirasjɔ̃/ nf breathing; (haleine) breath. **respiratoire** adj respiratory, breathing.

respirer /Rɛspire/ **1** vi breathe; (se reposer) catch one's breath. ● vt breathe (in); (exprimer) radiate.

resplendir /Rɛsplɑ̃dir/ **2** vi shine (de with). **resplendissant, ~e** adj brilliant, radiant.

responsabilité /Rɛspɔ̃sabilite/ nf responsibility; (légale) liability.

responsable /Rɛspɔ̃sabl/ adj responsible (de for); **~ de** (chargé de) in charge of. ● nmf person in charge; (coupable) person responsible.

resquiller /Rɛskije/ **1** vi **1** (dans le train) fare-dodge; (au spectacle) get in without paying; (dans la queue) jump the queue.

ressaisir (se) /(sə)Rəsezir/ **2** vpr pull oneself together; (équipe sportive, valeurs boursières) make a recovery.

ressemblance /Rəsɑ̃blɑ̃s/ nf resemblance.

ressemblant, ~e /Rəsɑ̃blɑ̃, -t/ adj **être ~** (portrait) be a good likeness.

ressembler /Rəsɑ̃ble/ **1** vi **~ à** resemble, look like. □ **se ~** vpr be alike; (physiquement) look alike.

ressentiment /Rəsɑ̃timɑ̃/ nm resentment.

ressentir /Rəsɑ̃tir/ **46** vt feel. □ **se ~ de** vpr feel the effects of.

resserrer /Rəsere/ **1** vt tighten; (contracter) compress; (vêtement) take in. □ **se ~** vpr tighten; (route) narrow; (se regrouper) move closer together.

ressort /Rəsɔr/ nm (objet) spring; (fig) energy; **être du ~ de** be the province of; (Jur) be within the jurisdiction of; **en dernier ~** as a last resort.

ressortir /Rəsɔrtir/ **46** vi **go ou** come back out; (se voir) stand out; (film, disque) be re-released; **faire ~** bring out; **il ressort que** it emerges that. ● vt take out again; (redire) come out with again; (disque, film) re-release.

ressortissant, ~e /Rəsɔrtisɑ̃, -t/ nm, f national.

ressource /Rəsurs/ nf resource; **~s** resources; **à bout de ~** at one's wits' end.

ressusciter /Resysite/ **1** vi come back to life. ● vt bring back to life; (fig) revive.

restant, ~e /Rɛstɑ̃, -t/ adj remaining. ● nm remainder.

restaurant /Rɛstɔrɑ̃/ nm restaurant.

restauration /Rɛstɔrasjɔ̃/ nf restoration; (hôtellerie) catering.

restaurer /ʀɛstɔʀe/ **1** vt restore. □ se ~ vpr eat.

reste /ʀɛst/ nm rest; (d'une soustraction) remainder; ~s remains (de of); (nourriture) leftovers; **un ~ de poulet** some left-over chicken; **au ~, du ~** moreover, besides.

rester /ʀɛste/ **1** vi (aux être) stay, remain; (subsister) be left, remain; **il reste du pain** there is some bread left (over); **il me reste du pain** I have some bread left (over); **il me reste à** it remains for me to; **en ~ à** go no further than; **en ~ là** stop there.

restituer /ʀɛstitɥe/ **1** vt (rendre) return; (recréer) reproduce; (rétablir) reconstruct.

restreindre /ʀɛstʀɛ̃dʀ/ **22** vt restrict. □ se ~ vpr (dans les dépenses) cut back.

restriction /ʀɛstʀiksjɔ̃/ nf restriction.

résultat /ʀezylta/ nm result.

résulter /ʀezylte/ **1** vi ~ de result from, be the result of.

résumé /ʀezyme/ nm summary; **en ~** in short; (pour finir) to sum up. **résumer** **1** vt summarize.

résurrection /ʀezyʀɛksjɔ̃/ nf resurrection; (renouveau) revival.

rétablir /ʀetabliʀ/ **2** vt restore; (personne) restore to health. □ se ~ vpr (ordre, silence) be restored; (guérir) recover. **rétablissement** nm restoration; (de malade, monnaie) recovery.

retard /ʀətaʀ/ nm lateness; (sur un programme) delay; (infériorité) backwardness; **avoir du ~** be late; (montre) be slow; **en ~** late; (retardé) behind; **en ~ sur l'emploi du temps** behind schedule; **rattraper** ou **combler son ~** catch up; **prendre du ~** fall behind.

retardataire /ʀətaʀdatɛʀ/ nmf latecomer. ● adj late.

retarder /ʀətaʀde/ **1** vt ~ **qn/ qch** delay sb/sth, hold sb/sth up; (par rapport à une heure convenue) make sb/sth late; (montre) put back. ● vi (montre) be slow; (personne) be out of touch.

retenir /ʀətəniʀ/ **58** vt hold back; (souffle, attention, prisonnier) hold; (eau, chaleur) retain, hold; (larmes) hold back; (garder) keep; (retarder) detain, hold up; (réserver) book; (se rappeler)

remember; (déduire) deduct; (accepter) accept. □ se ~ vpr (se contenir) restrain oneself; **se ~ à** hold on to; **se ~ de faire** stop oneself from doing.

rétention /ʀetɑ̃sjɔ̃/ nf retention.

retentir /ʀətɑ̃tiʀ/ **2** vi ring out, resound; ~ **sur** have an impact on. **retentissant, ~e** adj resounding. **retentissement** nm (effet) effect.

retenue /ʀətny/ nf restraint; (somme) deduction; (Scol) detention.

réticent, ~e /ʀetisɑ̃, -t/ adj (hésitant) hesitating; (qui rechigne) reluctant; (réservé) reticent.

rétine /ʀetin/ nf retina.

retiré, ~e /ʀətiʀe/ adj (vie) secluded; (lieu) remote.

retirer /ʀətiʀe/ **1** vt (sortir) take out; (ôter) take off; (argent, offre, candidature) withdraw; (écarter) (main, pied) withdraw; (billet, bagages) collect, pick up; (avantage) derive; ~ **à qn** take away from sb. □ se ~ vpr withdraw, retire.

retombées /ʀətɔ̃be/ nfpl (conséquences) effects; ~ **radioactives** nuclear fall-out.

retomber /ʀətɔ̃be/ **1** vi (faire une chute) fall again; (retourner au sol) land, come down; ~ **dans** (erreur) fall back into.

retouche /ʀətuʃ/ nf alteration; (de photo, tableau) retouch.

retour /ʀətuʀ/ nm return; **être de ~** be back (de from); ~ **en arrière** flashback; **par ~ du courrier** by return of post; **en ~** in return.

retourner /ʀətuʀne/ **1** vt (aux avoir) turn over; (vêtement) turn inside out; (maison) turn upside down; (lettre, compliment) return; (émouvoir **1**) shake, upset. ● vi (aux être) go back, return. □ se ~ vpr turn round; (dans son lit) twist and turn; **s'en ~** go back; **se ~ contre** turn against.

retrait /ʀətʀɛ/ nm withdrawal; (des eaux) receding; **être (situé) en ~ (de)** be set back (from). ●

retraite /ʀətʀɛt/ nf retirement; (pension) (retirement) pension; (fuite, refuge) retreat; **mettre à la ~** pension off; **prendre sa ~** retire.

retraité, ~e /ʀətʀete/ adj retired. ● nm, f (old-age) pensioner.

retrancher /rətrɑ̃ʃe/ **1** vt remove; (soustraire) deduct, subtract. □ se ~ vpr (Mil) entrench oneself; se ~ derrière take refuge behind.

retransmettre /rətrɑ̃smɛtr/ **42** vt broadcast.

rétrécir /retresir/ **2** vt make narrower; (vêtement) take in. ● vi (tissu) shrink. □ se ~ vpr (rue) narrow.

rétribution /retribysjɔ̃/ nf payment.

rétroactif, -ive /retrɔaktif, -v/ adj retrospective; **augmentation à effet** ~ backdated pay rise.

retrousser /rətruse/ **1** vt pull up; (manche) roll up.

retrouvailles /rətruvaj/ nfpl reunion.

retrouver /rətruve/ **1** vt find (again); (rejoindre) meet (again); (forces, calme) regain; (lieu) be back in; (se rappeler) remember. □ se ~ vpr find oneself (back); (se réunir) meet (again); (être présent) be found; **s'y** ~ (s'orienter, comprendre) find one's way; (rentrer dans ses frais **1**) break even.

rétroviseur /retrɔvizœr/ nm (Auto) (rear-view) mirror.

réunion /reynjɔ̃/ nf meeting; (rencontre) gathering; (après une séparation) réunion; (d'objets) collection.

réunir /reynir/ **2** vt gather, collect; (rapprocher) bring together; (convoquer) call together; (raccorder) join; (qualités) combine. □ se ~ vpr meet.

réussi, ~e /reysi/ adj successful.

réussir /reysir/ **2** vi succeed, be successful; ~ **à faire** succeed in doing, manage to do; ~ **à un examen** pass an exam; ~ **à qn** (méthode) work well for sb; (climat, mode de vie) agree with sb. ● vt (vie) make a success of.

réussite /reysit/ nf success; (jeu) patience.

revaloir /rəvalwar/ **60** vt **je vous revaudrai cela** (en mal) I'll pay you back for this; (en bien) I'll repay you some day.

revanche /rəvɑ̃ʃ/ nf revenge; (Sport) return ou revenge match; **en** ~ on the other hand.

rêvasser /rɛvase/ **1** vi daydream.

rêve /rɛv/ nm dream; **faire un** ~ have a dream.

réveil /revɛj/ nm waking up, (fig) awakening; (pendule) alarm clock.

réveillé, ~e /reveje/ adj awake.

réveille-matin /revɛjmatɛ̃/ nm inv alarm clock.

réveiller /reveje/ **1** vt wake (up); (sentiment, souvenir) awaken; (curiosité) arouse. □ se ~ vpr wake up.

réveillon /revɛjɔ̃/ nm (Noël) Christmas Eve; (nouvel an) New Year's Eve. **réveillonner** **1** vi see Christmas ou the New Year in.

révéler /revele/ **14** vt reveal. □ se ~ vpr be revealed; se ~ **facile** turn out to be easy, prove easy.

revendeur, -euse /rəvɑ̃dœr, -øz/ nm, f dealer, stockist; ~ **de drogue** drug dealer.

revendication /rəvɑ̃dikasjɔ̃/ nf claim. **revendiquer** **1** vt claim.

revendre /rəvɑ̃dr/ **3** vt sell (again); **avoir de l'énergie à** ~ have energy to spare.

revenir /rəvnir/ **58** vi (aux être) come back, return (à to); ~ **à** (activité) go back to; (se résumer à) come down to; (échoir à) fall to; ~ **à 100 euros** cost 100 euros; ~ **de** (maladie, surprise) get over; ~ **sur ses pas** retrace one's steps; **faire** ~ (Culin) brown; **ça me revient!** now I remember!; **je n'en reviens pas! 1** I can't get over it!

revenu /rəvny/ nm income; (de l'État) revenue.

rêver /rɛve/ **1** vt/i dream (à of; de **faire** of doing).

réverbère /revɛrbɛr/ nm street lamp.

révérence /reverɑ̃s/ nf reverence; (salut d'homme) bow; (salut de femme) curtsy.

rêverie /rɛvri/ nf daydream; (activité) daydreaming.

revers /rəvɛr/ nm reverse; (de main) back; (d'étoffe) wrong side; (de veste) lapel; (de pantalon) turn-up; (de manche) cuff; (tennis) backhand; (fig) set-back.

revêtement /rəvɛtmɑ̃/ nm covering; (de route) surface; ~ **de sol** floor covering. **revêtir** **61** vt cover; (habit) put on; (prendre, avoir) assume.

rêveur, -euse /rɛvœr, -øz/ adj dreamy. ● nm, f dreamer.

réviser /ʀevize/ ◆ vt revise; (machine, véhicule) service. **révision** nf revision; service.

revivre /ʀəvivʀ/ ◆ vi come alive again. ● vt relive.

révocation /ʀevɔkasjɔ̃/ nf repeal; (d'un fonctionnaire) dismissal.

revoir[1] /ʀəvwaʀ/ ◆ vt see (again); (réviser) revise.

revoir[2] /ʀəvwaʀ/ nm **au ∼** goodbye.

révolte /ʀevɔlt/ nf revolt. **révolté, ∼e** nm, f rebel.

révolter /ʀevɔlte/ ◆ vt appal, revolt. □ **se ∼** vpr revolt.

révolu, ∼e /ʀevɔly/ adj past; **avoir 21 ans ∼s** be over 21 years of age.

révolution /ʀevɔlysjɔ̃/ nf revolution. **révolutionnaire** adj & nmf revolutionary. **révolutionner** ◆ vt revolutionize.

revolver /ʀevɔlvɛʀ/ nm revolver, gun.

révoquer /ʀevɔke/ ◆ vt repeal; (fonctionnaire) dismiss.

revue /ʀəvy/ nf (examen, défilé) review; (magazine) magazine; (spectacle) variety show.

rez-de-chaussée /ʀedʃose/ nm inv ground floor; (US) first floor.

RF abrév f **(République Française)** French Republic.

rhinocéros /ʀinɔseʀɔs/ nm rhinoceros.

rhubarbe /ʀybaʀb/ nf rhubarb.

rhum /ʀɔm/ nm rum.

rhumatisme /ʀymatism/ nm rheumatism.

rhume /ʀym/ nm cold; **∼ des foins** hay fever.

ri /ʀi/ ➡**RIRE** 54.

ricaner /ʀikane/ ◆ vi snigger.

riche /ʀiʃ/ adj rich (**en** in). ● nmf rich man, rich woman.

richesse /ʀiʃes/ nf wealth; (de sol, décor) richness; **∼s** wealth; (ressources) resources.

ride /ʀid/ nf wrinkle; (sur l'eau) ripple.

rideau (pl **∼x**) /ʀido/ nm curtain; (métallique) shutter; (fig) screen.

ridicule /ʀidikyl/ adj ridiculous. ● nm (d'une situation) absurdity; (le grotesque) **le ∼** ridicule. **ridiculiser** ◆ vt ridicule.

rien /ʀjɛ̃/ pron nothing; (quoi que ce soit) anything; **de ∼!** don't mention it!; **∼ de bon** nothing good; **elle n'a**

∼ dit she didn't say anything; **∼ d'autre/de plus** nothing else/more; **∼ du tout** nothing at all; **∼ que** (seulement) just, only; **trois fois ∼** next to nothing; **il n'y est pour ∼** he has nothing to do with it; **∼ à faire!** (c'est impossible) it's no good!; (refus) no way! ◆. ● nm **un ∼ de** a touch of; **être puni pour un ∼** be punished for the slightest thing; **se disputer pour un ∼** fight over nothing; **en un ∼ de temps** in next to no time.

rieur, -euse /ʀijœʀ, -øz/ adj cheerful; (yeux) laughing.

rigide /ʀiʒid/ adj rigid.

rigolade /ʀigɔlad/ nf fun.

rigoler /ʀigɔle/ ◆ vi laugh; (s'amuser) have some fun; (plaisanter) joke.

rigolo, ∼te /ʀigɔlo, -ɔt/ adj ◆ funny. ● nm, f ◆ joker.

rigoureux, -euse /ʀiguʀø, -z/ adj rigorous; (hiver) harsh; (sévère) strict; (travail, recherches) meticulous.

rigueur /ʀigœʀ/ nf rigour; **à la ∼** at a pinch; **être de ∼** be obligatory; **tenir ∼ à qn de qch** bear sb a grudge for sth.

rime /ʀim/ nf rhyme.

rimer /ʀime/ ◆ vi rhyme (**avec** with); **cela ne rime à rien** it makes no sense.

rinçage /ʀɛ̃saʒ/ nm rinse; (action) rinsing.

rincer /ʀɛ̃se/ ◆ vt rinse.

riposte /ʀipɔst/ nf retort.

riposter /ʀipɔste/ ◆ vi retaliate; **∼ à** (attaque) counter; (insulte) reply to. ● vt retort (**que** that).

rire /ʀiʀ/ ◆ vi laugh (**de** at); (plaisanter) joke; (s'amuser) have fun; **c'était pour ∼** it was a joke. ● nm laugh; **des ∼s** laughter.

risée /ʀize/ nf **la ∼ de** the laughing stock of.

risque /ʀisk/ nm risk. **risqué, ∼e** adj risky; (osé) daring.

risquer /ʀiske/ ◆ vt risk (**de faire** of doing); (être passible de) face; **il risque de pleuvoir** it might rain; **tu risques de te faire mal** you might hurt yourself. □ **se ∼ à/ dans** vpr venture to/into.

ristourne /ʀistuʀn/ nf discount.

rite /Rit/ nm rite; (habitude) ritual. **rituel, ∼le** adj & nm ritual.

rivage /Rivaʒ/ nm shore.

rival, ∼e (mpl **-aux**) /Rival, -o/ adj & nm, f rival. **rivaliser 1** vi compete (avec with). **rivalité** nf rivalry.

rive /Riv/ nf (de fleuve) bank; (de lac) shore.

riverain, ∼e /RivRɛ̃, -ɛn/ adj riverside. ● nm, f riverside resident; (d'une rue) resident.

rivière /RivjɛR/ nf river.

riz /Ri/ nm rice. **rizière** nf paddy field.

robe /Rɔb/ nf (de femme) dress; (de juge) robe; (de cheval) coat; ∼ **de chambre** dressing-gown.

robinet /Rɔbinɛ/ nm tap; (US) faucet.

robot /Rɔbo/ nm robot; ∼ **ménager** food processor.

robuste /Rɔbyst/ adj robust.

roche /Rɔʃ/ nf rock.

rocher /Rɔʃe/ nm rock.

rock /Rɔk/ nm (Mus) rock.

rodage /Rɔdaʒ/ nm en ∼ (Auto) running in.

roder /Rɔde/ 1 vt (Auto) run in; **être rodé** (personne) have got the hang of things.

rôder /Rode/ 1 vi roam; (suspect) prowl.

rogne /Rɔɲ/ nf 1 anger; **en** ∼ in a temper.

rogner /Rɔɲe/ 1 vt trim; ∼ **sur** cut down on.

rognon /Rɔɲɔ̃/ nm (Culin) kidney.

roi /Rwa/ nm king; **les R** ∼ **mages** the Magi; **la fête des R** ∼ Twelfth Night.

rôle /Rol/ nm role, part.

roller /RɔlɛR/ nm (patin) rollerblade®; (activité) rollerblading.

romain, ∼e /Rɔmɛ̃, -ɛn/ adj Roman. **R** ∼, ∼**e** nm, f Roman. **romaine** nf (laitue) cos.

roman /Rɔmɑ̃/ nm novel; (genre) fiction.

romance /Rɔmɑ̃s/ nf ballad.

romancier, -ière /Rɔmɑ̃sje, -jɛR/ nm, f novelist.

romanesque /Rɔmanɛsk/ adj romantic; (fantastique) fantastic; (récit) fictional; **œuvres** ∼**s** novels, fiction.

romantique /Rɔmɑ̃tik/ adj & nmf romantic. **romantisme** nm romanticism.

rompre /Rɔ̃pR/ **3** vt break; (relations) break off. ● vi (se séparer) break up; ∼ **avec** (fiancé) break up with; (parti) break away from; (tradition) break with. □ **se** ∼ vpr break.

ronce /Rɔ̃s/ nf bramble.

rond, ∼e /Rɔ̃, -d/ adj round; (gras) plump; (ivre 1) drunk. ● nm (cercle) ring; (tranche) slice; **en** ∼ in a circle; **il n'a pas un** ∼ 1 he hasn't got a penny.

ronde /Rɔ̃d/ nf (de policier) beat; (de soldat, gardien) watch; (Mus) semibreve.

rondelle /Rɔ̃dɛl/ nf (Tech) washer; (tranche) slice.

rondement /Rɔ̃dmɑ̃/ adv promptly; (franchement) frankly.

rondeur /Rɔ̃dœR/ nf roundness; (franchise) frankness; (embonpoint) plumpness.

rondin /Rɔ̃dɛ̃/ nm log.

rond-point (pl **ronds-points**) /Rɔ̃pwɛ̃/ nm roundabout; (US) traffic circle.

ronfler /Rɔ̃fle/ **1** vi snore; (moteur) purr.

ronger /Rɔ̃ʒe/ **40** vt gnaw (at); (vers, acide) eat into. □ **se** ∼ vpr **se** ∼ **les ongles** bite one's nails.

rongeur /Rɔ̃ʒœR/ nm rodent.

ronronner /RɔRɔne/ **1** vi purr.

rosbif /Rɔsbif/ nm roast beef.

rose /Roz/ nf rose. ● adj & nm pink.

rosé, ∼e /Roze/ adj pinkish. ● nm rosé.

roseau (pl ∼**x**) /Rozo/ nm reed.

rosée /Roze/ nf dew.

rosier /Rozje/ nm rose bush.

rossignol /Rɔsiɲɔl/ nm nightingale.

rotatif, -ive /Rɔtatif, -v/ adj rotary.

roter /Rɔte/ **1** vi 1 burp.

rôti /Roti/ nm joint; (cuit) roast; ∼ **de porc** roast pork.

rotin /Rɔtɛ̃/ nm (rattan) cane.

rôtir /RotiR/ **2** vt roast.

rôtissoire /RotiswaR/ nf roasting spit.

rotule /Rɔtyl/ nf kneecap.

rouage /Rwaʒ/ nm (Tech) wheel; **les** ∼**s** the works; (d'une organisation: fig) wheels.

roucouler /Rukule/ **1** vi coo.

roue /Ru/ nf wheel; ∼ **dentée** cog (wheel); ∼ **de secours** spare wheel.

rouer /ʀwe/ **1** vt ~ **de coups** thrash.

rouge /ʀuʒ/ adj red; (fer) red-hot. ● nm red; (vin) red wine; (fard) blusher; ~ **à lèvres** lipstick. ● nmf (Pol) red. **rouge-gorge** (pl **rouges-gorges**) nm robin.

rougeole /ʀuʒɔl/ nf measles (+ sg).
rouget /ʀuʒɛ/ nm red mullet.

rougeur /ʀuʒœʀ/ nf redness; (tache) red blotch.

rougir /ʀuʒiʀ/ **2** vi turn red; (de honte) blush.

rouille /ʀuj/ nf rust. **rouillé, ~e** adj rusty.

rouiller /ʀuje/ **1** vi rust. □ **se** ~ vpr get rusty.

rouleau (pl ~**x**) /ʀulo/ nm roll; (outil, vague) roller; ~ **à pâtisserie** rolling pin; ~ **compresseur** steamroller.

roulement /ʀulmɑ̃/ nm rotation; (bruit) rumble; (alternance) rotation; (de tambour) roll; ~ **à billes** ball-bearing; **travailler par** ~ work in shifts.

rouler /ʀule/ **1** vt roll; (ficelle, manches) roll up; (pâte) roll out; (duper **1**) cheat. ● vi (véhicule, train) go, travel; (conducteur) drive. □ **se** ~ **dans** vpr (herbe) roll in; (couverture) roll oneself up in.

roulette /ʀulɛt/ nf (de meuble) castor; (de dentiste) drill; (jeu) roulette; **comme sur des** ~**s** very smoothly.

roulotte /ʀulɔt/ nf caravan.

roumain, ~e /ʀumɛ̃, -ɛn/ adj Romanian. **R~, ~e** nm, f Romanian.

Roumanie /ʀumani/ nf Romania.

rouquin, ~e /ʀukɛ̃, -in/ **1** adj red-haired. ● nm, f redhead.

rouspéter /ʀuspete/ **14** vi **1** grumble, moan.

rousse /ʀus/ **→ROUX.**

roussir /ʀusiʀ/ **2** vt scorch. ● vi turn brown.

route /ʀut/ nf road; (Naut, Aviat) route; (direction) way; (voyage) journey; (chemin: fig) path; **en** ~ on the way; **en** ~**!** let's go!; **mettre en** ~ start; ~ **nationale** trunk road, main road; **se mettre en** ~ set out.

routier, -ière /ʀutje, -jɛʀ/ adj road. ● nm long-distance lorry ou truck driver; (restaurant) transport café; (US) truck stop.

routine /ʀutin/ nf routine.

roux, rousse /ʀu, ʀus/ adj red, russet; (personne) red-haired; (chat) ginger. ● nm, f redhead.

royal, ~e (mpl **-aux**) /ʀwajal, -jo/ adj royal; (cadeau) fit for a king.

royaume /ʀwajom/ nm kingdom.

Royaume-Uni /ʀwajomyni/ nm United Kingdom.

royauté /ʀwajote/ nf royalty.

RTT abrév f (**réduction du temps de travail**) reduction in working hours.

ruban /ʀybɑ̃/ nm ribbon; (de chapeau) band; ~ **adhésif** sticky tape; ~ **magnétique** magnetic tape.

rubéole /ʀybeɔl/ nf German measles (+ sg).

rubis /ʀybi/ nm ruby.

rubrique /ʀybʀik/ nf heading; (article) column.

ruche /ʀyʃ/ nf beehive.

rude /ʀyd/ adj (au toucher) rough; (pénible) tough; (grossier) coarse; (fameux **1**) tremendous.

rudement /ʀydmɑ̃/ adv (frapper) hard; (traiter) harshly; (très **1**) really.

rudimentaire /ʀydimɑ̃tɛʀ/ adj rudimentary.

rue /ʀy/ nf street.

ruée /ʀye/ nf rush.

ruer /ʀye/ **1** vi (cheval) buck. □ **se** ~ vpr rush (**dans** into; **vers** towards); **se** ~ **sur** pounce on.

rugby /ʀygbi/ nm rugby.

rugir /ʀyʒiʀ/ **2** vi roar.

rugueux, -euse /ʀygø, -z/ adj rough.

ruine /ʀɥin/ nf ruin; **en** (~**s**) in ruins. **ruiner** **1** vt ruin.

ruisseau (pl ~**x**) /ʀɥiso/ nm stream; (rigole) gutter.

rumeur /ʀymœʀ/ nf (nouvelle) rumour; (son) murmur, hum.

ruminer /ʀymine/ **1** vi (animal) ruminate; (méditer) meditate.

rupture /ʀyptyʀ/ nf break; (action) breaking; (de contrat) breach; (de pourparlers) breakdown; (de relations) breaking off; (de couple, coalition) break-up.

rural, ~e (mpl **-aux**) /ʀyʀal, -o/ adj rural.

ruse /ʀyz/ nf cunning; **une** ~ a trick, a ruse. **rusé, ~e** adj cunning.

russe /ʀys/ adj Russian. ● nm (Ling) Russian. **R~** nmf Russian.

Russie /ʀysi/ nf Russia.

rustique /ʀystik/ adj rustic.

rythme /ʀitm/ nm rhythm; (vitesse) rate; (de la vie) pace. **rythmique** adj rhythmical.

• •

Ss

• •

s' /s/ ➞SE.

sa /sa/ ➞SON¹.

SA abrév f (société anonyme) PLC.

sabbatique /sabatik/ adj (année) sabbatical year.

sable /sɑbl/ nm sand; **~s mouvants** quicksands. **sabler** vt **1** grit.

sablier /sɑblije/ nm (Culin) eggtimer.

sablonneux, -euse /sablɔnø, -z/ adj sandy.

sabot /sabo/ nm (de cheval) hoof; (chaussure) clog; (de frein) shoe; **~ de Denver®** (wheel) clamp.

saboter /sabɔte/ **1** vt sabotage; (bâcler) botch.

sac /sak/ nm bag; (grand, en toile) sack; **mettre à ~** (maison) ransack; (ville) sack; **~ à dos** rucksack; **~ à main** handbag; **~ de couchage** sleeping-bag; **mettre dans le même ~** lump together.

saccadé, ~e /sakade/ adj jerky.

saccager /sakaʒe/ **40** vt (abîmer) wreck; (maison) ransack; (ville, pays) sack.

saccharine /sakaʀin/ nf saccharin.

sachet /saʃɛ/ nm (small) bag; (d'aromates) sachet; **~ de thé** teabag.

sacoche /sakɔʃ/ nf bag; (de vélo) saddlebag.

sacre /sakʀ/ nm (de roi) coronation; (d'évêque) consecration. **sacré, ~e** adj sacred; (maudit **1**) damned. **sacrement** nm sacrament. **sacrer** **1** vt crown; consecrate.

sacrifice /sakʀifis/ nm sacrifice.

sacrifier /sakʀifje/ **45** vt sacrifice; **~ à** conform to. □ **se ~** vpr sacrifice oneself.

sacrilège /sakʀilɛʒ/ nm sacrilege. ● adj sacrilegious.

sadique /sadik/ adj sadistic. ● nmf sadist.

sage /saʒ/ adj wise; (docile) good, well behaved. ● nm wise man.

sage-femme (pl **sages-femmes**) /saʒfam/ nf midwife.

sagesse /saʒɛs/ nf wisdom.

Sagittaire /saʒitɛʀ/ nm **le ~** Sagittarius.

saignant, ~e /sɛɲɑ̃, -t/ adj (Culin) rare.

saigner /seɲe/ **1** vt/i bleed; **~ du nez** have a nosebleed.

saillant, ~e /sajɑ̃, -t/ adj prominent.

sain, ~e /sɛ̃, sɛn/ adj healthy; (moralement) sane; **~ et sauf** safe and sound.

saindoux /sɛ̃du/ nm lard.

saint, ~e /sɛ̃, -t/ adj holy; (bon, juste) saintly. ● nm, f saint. **Saint- Esprit** nm Holy Spirit. **sainteté** nf holiness; (d'un lieu) sanctity. **Sainte Vierge** nf Blessed Virgin. **Saint-Sylvestre** nf New Year's Eve.

sais /sɛ/ ➞SAVOIR **55**.

saisie /sezi/ nf (Jur) seizure; (Comput) keyboarding; **~ de données** data capture.

saisir /seziʀ/ **2** vt grab (hold of); (proie) seize; (occasion, biens) seize; (comprendre) grasp; (frapper) strike; (Ordinat) keyboard, capture; **saisi de** (peur) stricken by, overcome by. □ **se ~ de** vpr seize. **saisissant, ~e** adj (spectacle) gripping.

saison /sɛzɔ̃/ nf season; **la morte ~** the off season. **saisonnier, -ière** adj seasonal.

sait /sɛ/ ➞SAVOIR **55**.

salade /salad/ nf (plat) salad; (plante) lettuce. **saladier** nm salad bowl.

salaire /salɛʀ/ nm wages (+ pl), salary.

salarié, ~e /salaʀje/ adj wageearning. ● nm, f wage earner.

sale /sal/ adj dirty; (mauvais) nasty.

salé, ~e /sale/ adj (goût) salty; (plat) salted; (opposé à sucré) savoury; (grivois **1**) spicy; (excessif **1**) steep. **saler** **1** vt salt.

saleté /salte/ nf dirtiness; (crasse) dirt; (obscénité) obscenity; **~(s)** (camelote) rubbish; (détritus) mess.

salir /saliʀ/ 2 *vt* (make) dirty; (*réputation*) tarnish. □ **se ~** *vpr* get dirty. **salissant, ~e** *adj* dirty; (*étoffe*) easily dirtied.

salive /saliv/ *nf* saliva.

salle /sal/ *nf* room; (grande, publique) hall; (de restaurant) dining room; (Théât, cinéma) auditorium; **cinéma à trois ~** a three-screen cinema; **~ à manger** dining room; **~ d'attente** waiting room; **~ de bains** bathroom; **~ de causette** chatroom. **~ de séjour** living room; **~ de classe** classroom; **~ d'embarquement** departure lounge; **~ d'opération** operating theatre; **~ des ventes** saleroom.

salon /salɔ̃/ *nm* lounge; (de coiffure, beauté) salon; (exposition) show; **~ de thé** tea-room; **~ virtuel** chatroom.

salopette /salɔpɛt/ *nf* dungarees (+ *pl*); (d'ouvrier) overalls (+ *pl*).

saltimbanque /saltɛ̃bɑ̃k/ *nmf* (street) acrobat.

salubre /salybʀ/ *adj* healthy.

saluer /salɥe/ 1 *vt* greet; (en partant) take one's leave of; (de la tête) nod to; (de la main) wave to; (Mil) salute; (accueillir favorablement) welcome.

salut /saly/ *nm* greeting; (de la tête) nod; (de la main) wave; (Mil) salute; (rachat) salvation. ● *interj* (bonjour 🛈) hello; (au revoir 🛈) bye.

salutation /salytasjɔ̃/ *nf* greeting.

samedi /samdi/ *nm* Saturday.

SAMU /samy/ *abrév m* (**Service d'assistance médicale d'urgence**) ≈ mobile accident unit.

> **SAMU** A twenty-four hour ⓘ
> service coordinated by each
> *département* to send mobile medical
> services and staff, ambulances and
> helicopters to scenes of accidents
> and other emergencies.

---

sanction /sɑ̃ksjɔ̃/ *nf* sanction. **sanctionner** 1 *vt* sanction; (punir) punish.

sandale /sɑ̃dal/ *nf* sandal.

sang /sɑ̃/ *nm* blood; **se faire du mauvais ~ ou un ~ d'encre** be worried stiff. **sang-froid** *nm inv* self-control. **sanglant, ~e** *adj* bloody.

sangle /sɑ̃gl/ *nf* strap.

sanglier /sɑ̃glije/ *nm* wild boar.

sanglot /sɑ̃glo/ *nm* sob. **sangloter** 1 *vi* sob.

sanguin, ~e /sɑ̃gɛ̃, -in/ *adj* (groupe) blood.

sanguinaire /sɑ̃ginɛʀ/ *adj* bloodthirsty.

sanitaire /sanitɛʀ/ *adj* (directives) health; (conditions) sanitary; (appareils, installations) bathroom, sanitary. **sanitaires** *nmpl* bathroom.

sans /sɑ̃/ *prép* without; **~ ça, ~ quoi** otherwise; **~ arrêt** nonstop; **~ encombre/faute/tarder** without incident/fail/delay; **~ fin/goût/limite** endless/tasteless/limitless; **~ importance/pareil/précédent/travail** unimportant/unparalleled/unprecedented/unemployed; **j'ai aimé mais ~ plus** it was good, it wasn't great.

sans-abri /sɑ̃zabʀi/ *nmf inv* homeless person.

sans-gêne /sɑ̃ʒɛn/ *adj inv* inconsiderate, thoughtless. ● *nm inv* thoughtlessness.

sans-papiers /sɑ̃papje/ *nm inv* illegal immigrant.

santé /sɑ̃te/ *nf* health; **à ta ou votre ~!** cheers!

saoul, ~e /su, sul/ ➡SOUL.

sapin /sapɛ̃/ *nm* fir (tree); **~ de Noël** Christmas tree.

sarcasme /saʀkasm/ *nm* sarcasm. **sarcastique** *adj* sarcastic.

sardine /saʀdin/ *nf* sardine.

sas /sɑs/ *nm* (Naut, Aviat) airlock.

satané, ~e /satane/ *adj* 🛈 damned.

satellite /satelit/ *nm* satellite.

satin /satɛ̃/ *nm* satin.

satire /satiʀ/ *nf* satire.

satisfaction /satisfaksjɔ̃/ *nf* satisfaction.

satisfaire /satisfɛʀ/ 33 *vt* satisfy. ● *vi* **~ à** fulfil. **satisfaisant, ~e** *adj* (acceptable) satisfactory. **satisfait, ~e** *adj* satisfied (**de** with).

saturer /satyʀe/ 1 *vt* saturate.

sauce /sos/ *nf* sauce; **~ tartare** tartar sauce. **saucière** *nf* sauceboat.

saucisse /sosis/ *nf* sausage.

saucisson /sosisɔ̃/ *nm* (slicing) sausage.

sauf¹ /sof/ *prép* except; **~ erreur** if I'm not mistaken; **~ imprévu** unless anything unforeseen happens; ~ **avis contraire** unless otherwise stated.

sauf², -ve /sof, sov/ adj safe, unharmed.

sauge /soʒ/ nf (Culin) sage.

saule /sol/ nm willow; ~ **pleureur** weeping willow.

saumon /somɔ̃/ nm salmon. ● adj inv salmon-(pink).

sauna /sona/ nm sauna.

saupoudrer /sopudʀe/ **1** vt sprinkle (de with).

saut /so/ nm jump; **faire un ~ chez qn** pop round to sb's (place); **le ~** (Sport) jumping; ~ **en hauteur/ longueur** high/long jump; ~ **périlleux** somersault; **au ~ du lit** on getting up.

sauté, ~e /sote/ adj & nm (Culin) sauté.

saute-mouton /sotmutɔ̃/ nm inv leap-frog.

sauter /sote/ **1** vi jump; (exploser) blow up; (fusible) blow; (se détacher) come off; **faire ~** (détruire) blow up; (fusible) blow; (casser) break; ~ **à la corde** skip; ~ **aux yeux** be obvious; ~ **au cou de qn** fling one's arms round sb; ~ **sur une occasion** jump at an opportunity. ● vt jump (over); (page, classe) skip.

sauterelle /sotʀɛl/ nf grasshopper.

sautiller /sotije/ **1** vi hop.

sauvage /sovaʒ/ adj wild; (primitif, cruel) savage; (farouche) unsociable; (illégal) unauthorized. ● nmf unsociable person; (brute) savage.

sauve /sov/ ➡SAUF.²

sauvegarder /sovgaʀde/ **1** vt safeguard; (Ordinat) back up.

sauver /sove/ **1** vt save; (d'un danger) rescue, save; (matériel) salvage. □ **se ~** vpr (fuir) run away; (partir **1**) be off. **sauvetage** nm rescue. **sauveteur** nm rescuer. **sauveur** nm saviour.

savant, ~e /savɑ̃, -t/ adj learned; (habile) skilful. ● nm scientist.

saveur /savœʀ/ nf flavour; (fig) savour.

savoir /savwaʀ/ **55** vt know; **elle sait conduire/nager** she can drive/ swim; **faire ~ à qn que** inform sb that; **(pas) que je sache** (not) as far as I know; **à ~** namely. ● nm learning.

savon /savɔ̃/ nm soap; **passer un ~ à qn** **1** give sb a telling-off. **savonnette** nf bar of soap.

savourer /savuʀe/ **1** vt savour. **savoureux, -euse** adj tasty; (fig) spicy.

scandale /skɑ̃dal/ nm scandal; (tapage) uproar; (en public) noisy scene; **faire ~** shock people; **faire un ~** make a scene. **scandaleux, -euse** adj scandalous. **scandaliser** **1** vt scandalize, shock.

scander /skɑ̃de/ **1** vt (vers) scan; (slogan) chant.

scandinave /skɑ̃dinav/ adj Scandinavian. **S~** nmf Scandinavian.

Scandinavie /skɑ̃dinavi/ nf Scandinavia.

scarabée /skaʀabe/ nm beetle.

sceau (pl ~**x**) /so/ nm seal.

scélérat /seleʀa/ nm scoundrel.

sceller /sele/ **1** vt seal.

scène /sɛn/ nf scene; (estrade, art dramatique) stage; **mettre en ~** (pièce) stage; (film) direct; **mise en ~** direction; ~ **de ménage** domestic dispute.

scepticisme /sɛptisism/ nm scepticism.

sceptique /sɛptik/ adj sceptical. ● nmf sceptic.

schéma /ʃema/ nm diagram. **schématique** adj schematic; (sommaire) sketchy. **schématiser** **1** vt simplify.

schizophrène /skizofʀɛn/ adj & nmf schizophrenic.

sciatique /sjatik/ adj (nerf) sciatic. ● nf sciatica.

scie /si/ nf saw.

sciemment /sjamɑ̃/ adv knowingly.

science /sjɑ̃s/ nf science; (savoir) knowledge.

science-fiction /sjɑ̃sfiksjɔ̃/ nf science fiction.

scientifique /sjɑ̃tifik/ adj scientific. ● nmf scientist.

scier /sje/ **45** vt saw.

scintiller /sɛ̃tije/ **1** vi glitter; (étoile) twinkle.

scission /sisjɔ̃/ nf split.

sclérose /skleʀoz/ nf sclerosis; ~ **en plaques** multiple sclerosis.

scolaire /skɔlɛʀ/ adj school. **scolarisé, ~e** adj going to school. **scolarité** nf schooling.

score /skɔʀ/ nm score.

scorpion /skɔʀpjɔ̃/ nm scorpion; **le S~** Scorpio.

scotch /skɔtʃ/ nm (boisson) Scotch (whisky); (ruban adhésif)® Sellotape®.

scout, ~e /skut/ nm & adj scout.

scrupule /skʀypyl/ nm scruple. **scrupuleux, -euse** adj scrupulous.

scruter /skʀyte/ **1** vt examine, scrutinize.

scrutin /skʀytɛ̃/ nm (vote) ballot; (élections) polls (+ pl).

sculpter /skylte/ **1** vt sculpt, carve. **sculpteur** nm sculptor. **sculpture** nf sculpture.

SDF abrév m (**sans domicile fixe**) homeless person.

---

se, s' /sə, s/

s' before vowel or mute h.

● pronom

⋯▸ himself, (féminin) herself; (indéfini) oneself; (non humain) itself; (au pluriel) themselves; **~ laver les mains** wash one's hands; (réciproque) each other, one another; **ils se détestent** they hate each other.

! The translation of **se** will vary according to which verb it is associated with. You should therefore refer to the verb to find it. For example, **se promener**, **se taire** will be treated respectively under **promener** and **taire**.

---

séance /seɑ̃s/ nf session; (Théât, cinéma) show; **~ de pose** sitting; **~ tenante** forthwith.

seau (pl **~x**) /so/ nm bucket, pail.

sec, sèche /sɛk, sɛʃ/ adj dry; (fruits) dried; (coup, bruit) sharp; (cœur) hard; (whisky) neat. ● nm **à ~** (sans eau) dry; (sans argent) broke; **au ~** in a dry place.

sèche-cheveux /sɛʃʃəvø/ nm inv hairdrier.

sèchement /sɛʃmɑ̃/ adv drily.

sécher /seʃe/ **14** vt/i dry; (cours: **1**) skip; (ne pas savoir **1**) be stumped. □ **se ~** vpr dry oneself. **sécheresse** nf (de climat) dryness; (temps sec) drought. **séchoir** nm drier.

second, ~e /səgɔ̃, -d/ adj & nm, f second. ● nm (adjoint) second in command; (étage) second floor. **secondaire** adj secondary. **seconde** nf (instant) second; (vitesse) second gear.

seconder /səgɔ̃de/ **1** vt assist.

secouer /səkwe/ **1** vt shake; (poussière, torpeur) shake off. □ **se ~** vpr **1** (se dépêcher) get a move on; (réagir) shake oneself up.

secourir /səkuʀiʀ/ **20** vt assist, help. **secouriste** nmf first-aid worker.

secours /səkuʀ/ nm assistance, help; **au ~!** help!; **de ~** (sortie) emergency; (équipe, opération) rescue. ● nmpl (Méd) first aid.

secousse /səkus/ nf jolt, jerk; (séisme) tremor.

secret, -ète /səkʀɛ, -t/ adj secret. ● nm secret; (discrétion) secrecy; **le ~ professionnel** professional confidentiality; **~ de Polichinelle** open secret; **en ~** in secret, secretly.

secrétaire /səkʀetɛʀ/ nmf secretary; **~ de direction** personal assistant. ● nm (meuble) writing desk; **~ d'État** junior minister.

secrétariat /səkʀetaʀja/ nm secretarial work; (bureau) secretariat.

sectaire /sɛktɛʀ/ adj sectarian.

secte /sɛkt/ nf sect.

secteur /sɛktœʀ/ nm area; (Comm) sector; (circuit: Électr) mains (+ pl).

section /sɛksjɔ̃/ nf section; (Scol) stream; (Mil) platoon. **sectionner** **1** vt sever.

sécuriser /sekyʀize/ **1** vt reassure.

sécurisé, e /sekyʀize/ adj (Ordinat) secure; **une ligne ~e** a secure line.

sécurité /sekyʀite/ nf security; (absence de danger) safety; **en ~** safe, secure; **Sécurité sociale** nf social services, social security services; **~ des frontières** homeland security.

sédatif /sedatif/ nm sedative.

sédentaire /sedɑ̃tɛʀ/ adj sedentary.

séducteur, -trice /sedyktœʀ, -tʀis/ adj seductive. ● nm, f seducer. **séduction** nf seduction; (charme) charm.

séduire /sedɥiʀ/ **17** vt charm; (plaire à) appeal to; (sexuellement) seduce. **séduisant, ~e** adj attractive.

ségrégation /segʀegasjɔ̃/ nf segregation.

seigle /sɛgl/ nm rye.

seigneur /sɛɲœʀ/ nm lord; **le S~** the Lord.

sein /sɛ̃/ nm breast; **au ~ de** within.

séisme /seism/ nm earthquake.

seize /sɛz/ adj & nm sixteen.

séjour /seʒuʀ/ nm stay; (pièce) living room. **séjourner** ◼ vi stay.

sel /sɛl/ nm salt; (piquant) spice.

sélectif, -ive /selɛktif, -v/ adj selective.

sélection /selɛksjɔ̃/ nf selection. **sélectionner** ◼ vt select.

selle /sɛl/ nf saddle; **~s** (Méd) stools.

sellette /selɛt/ nf **sur la ~** (personne) in the hot seat.

selon /səlɔ̃/ prép according to; **~ que** depending on whether.

semaine /səmɛn/ nf week; **en ~** during the week.

sémantique /semɑ̃tik/ adj semantic. ● nf semantics.

semblable /sɑ̃blabl/ adj similar (à to). ● nm fellow (creature).

semblant /sɑ̃blɑ̃/ nm **faire ~ de** pretend to; **un ~ de** a semblance of.

sembler /sɑ̃ble/ ◼ vi seem (à to; que that); **il me semble que** it seems to me that.

semelle /səmɛl/ nf sole; **~ compensée** wedge heel.

semence /s(ə)mɑ̃s/ nf seed.

semer /s(ə)me/ ◢ vt (graine, doute) sow; (jeter, parsemer) strew; (personne ◼) lose; **~ la panique** spread panic.

semestre /səmɛstʀ/ nm half year; (Univ) semester. **semestriel, ~le** adj (revue) biannual; (examen) end-of-semester.

séminaire /seminɛʀ/ nm (Relig) seminary; (Univ) seminar.

semi-remorque /s(ə)miʀ(ə)mɔʀk/ nm articulated lorry.

semis /s(ə)mi/ nm seedling.

semoule /s(ə)mul/ nf semolina.

sénat /sena/ nm senate. **sénateur** nm senator.

sénile /senil/ adj senile.

senior /senjɔʀ/ adj (âgé) senior; (mode, publication) for senior citizens. ● nmf senior citizen.

sens /sɑ̃s/ nm (Méd) sense; (signification) meaning, sense; (direction) direction; **à mon ~** to my mind; **à ~**

unique (rue) one-way; **ça n'a pas de ~** it doesn't make sense; **~ commun** common sense; **~ giratoire** roundabout; **~ interdit** no-entry sign; (rue) one-way street; **dans le ~ des aiguilles d'une montre** clockwise; **dans le ~ inverse des aiguilles d'une montre** anticlockwise; **~ dessus dessous** upside down; **~ devant derrière** back to front.

sensation /sɑ̃sasjɔ̃/ nf feeling, sensation; **faire ~** create a sensation. **sensationnel, ~le** adj sensational.

sensé, ~e /sɑ̃se/ adj sensible.

sensibiliser /sɑ̃sibilize/ ◼ vt **~ l'opinion** increase people's awareness (à qch to sth).

sensibilité /sɑ̃sibilite/ nf sensitivity. **sensible** adj sensitive (à to); (appréciable) noticeable. **sensiblement** adv noticeably.

sensoriel, ~le /sɑ̃sɔʀjɛl/ adj sensory.

sensualité /sɑ̃sɥalite/ nf sensuousness; sensuality. **sensuel, ~le** adj sensual.

sentence /sɑ̃tɑ̃s/ nf sentence.

senteur /sɑ̃tœʀ/ nf scent.

sentier /sɑ̃tje/ nm path.

sentiment /sɑ̃timɑ̃/ nm feeling; **faire du ~** sentimentalize; **j'ai le ~ que...** I get the feeling that... **sentimental, ~e** (mpl **-aux**) adj sentimental.

sentir /sɑ̃tiʀ/ ◢◼ vt feel; (odeur) smell; (pressentir) sense; **~ la lavande** smell of lavender; **je ne peux pas le ~** ◼ I can't stand him. ● vi smell. □ **se ~** vpr **se ~ fier/mieux** feel proud/better.

séparation /separasjɔ̃/ nf separation.

séparatiste /separatist/ adj & nmf separatist.

séparé, ~e /separe/ adj separate; (conjoints) separated.

séparer /separe/ ◼ vt separate; (en deux) split. □ **se ~** vpr separate, part (de from); (se détacher) split; **se ~ de** (se défaire de) part with.

sept /sɛt/ adj & nm seven.

septante /sɛptɑ̃t/ adj & nm seventy.

septembre /sɛptɑ̃bʀ/ nm September.

septentrional, ~e (mpl **-aux**) /sɛptɑ̃tʀijɔnal, -o/ adj northern.

septième /sɛtjɛm/ adj & nmf seventh.

sépulture /sepyltyʀ/ nf burial; (lieu) burial place.

séquelles /sekɛl/ *nfpl* (maladie) after-effects; (fig) aftermath.

séquence /sekɑ̃s/ *nf* sequence.

séquestrer /sekɛstʀe/ **1** *vt* confine (illegally).

sera, serait /səʀa, səʀɛ/ ➡ÊTRE **4**.

serbe /sɛʀb/ *adj* Serbian. **S~** *nmf* Serbian.

Serbie /sɛʀbi/ *nf* Serbia.

serein, ~e /səʀɛ̃, -ɛn/ *adj* serene.

sérénité /seʀenite/ *nf* serenity.

sergent /sɛʀʒɑ̃/ *nm* sergeant.

série /seʀi/ *nf* series (+ *sg*) ; (d'objets) set; **de ~** (véhicule etc.) standard; **fabrication** *ou* **production en ~** mass production.

sérieusement /seʀjøzmɑ̃/ *adv* seriously.

sérieux, -ieuse /seʀjø, -z/ *adj* serious; (digne de confiance) reliable; (chances, raison) good. ● *nm* seriousness; **garder son ~** keep a straight face; **prendre au ~** take seriously.

serin /səʀɛ̃/ *nm* canary.

seringue /səʀɛ̃g/ *nf* syringe.

serment /sɛʀmɑ̃/ *nm* oath; (promesse) vow.

sermon /sɛʀmɔ̃/ *nm* sermon. **sermonner** **1** *vt* lecture.

séropositif, -ive /seʀɔpozitif, -v/ *adj* HIV positive.

serpent /sɛʀpɑ̃/ *nm* snake; **~ à son-nettes** rattlesnake.

serpillière /sɛʀpijɛʀ/ *nf* floorcloth.

serre /sɛʀ/ *nf* (de jardin) greenhouse; (griffe) claw.

serré, ~e /seʀe/ *adj* (habit, nœud, écrou) tight; (personnes) packed, crowded; (lutte, mailles) close; (écriture) cramped; (cœur) heavy.

serrer /seʀe/ **1** *vt* (saisir) grip; (presser) squeeze; (vis, corde, ceinture) tighten; (poing, dents) clench; **~ qn dans ses bras** hug sb; **~ les rangs** close ranks; **~ qn** (vêtement) be tight on sb; **~ qn de près** follow sb closely; **~ la main à** shake hands with. ● *vi* **~ à droite** keep over to the right. □ **se ~** *vpr* (se rapprocher) squeeze (up).

serrure /seʀyʀ/ *nf* lock. **serrurier** *nm* locksmith.

servante /sɛʀvɑ̃t/ *nf* (maid) servant.

serveur, -euse /sɛʀvœʀ, -øz/ *nm, f* (homme) waiter; (femme) waitress.

● *nm* (Ordinat) server.

serviable /sɛʀvjabl/ *adj* helpful.

service /sɛʀvis/ *nm* service; (fonction, temps de travail) duty; (pourboire) service (charge); (dans une société) department; (**~ non**) **compris** service (not) included; **être de ~** be on duty; **pendant le ~** (when) on duty; **rendre ~ à qn** be a help to sb; **~ à thé** tea set; **~ d'ordre** stewards (+ *pl*); **~ après-vente** after-sales service; **~ militaire** military service; **les ~s secrets** the secret service (+ *sg*).

serviette /sɛʀvjɛt/ *nf* (de toilette) towel; (cartable) briefcase; (**~ de table**) serviette, napkin; **~ hygiénique** sanitary towel.

servir /sɛʀviʀ/ **46** *vt/i* serve; (être utile) be of use, serve; **~ qn (à table)** wait on sb; **ça sert à** (outil, récipient) it is used for; **ça me sert à/de** I use it to/as; **ça ne sert à rien** (action) it's pointless; **~ de** serve as, be used as; **~ à qn de guide** act as a guide for sb. □ **se ~** *vpr* (à table) help oneself (**de** to); **se ~ de** use. **serviteur** *nm* servant.

ses /se/ ➡SON¹.

session /sesjɔ̃/ *nf* session.

seuil /sœj/ *nm* doorstep; (entrée) doorway; (fig) threshold.

seul, ~e /sœl/ *adj* alone, on one's own; (unique) only; **un ~ exemple** only one example; **pas un ~ ami** not a single friend; **lui ~ le sait** only he knows; **dans le ~ but de** with the sole aim of; **parler tout ~** talk to oneself; **faire qch tout ~** do sth on one's own. ● *nm, f* **le ~**, **la ~e** the only one. **seulement** *adv* only.

sève /sɛv/ *nf* sap.

sévère /sevɛʀ/ *adj* severe. **sévérité** *nf* severity.

sévices /sevis/ *nmpl* physical abuse.

sévir /seviʀ/ **2** *vi* (fléau) rage; **~ contre** punish.

sevrer /səvʀe/ **6** *vt* wean.

sexe /sɛks/ *nm* sex; (organes) genitals (+ *pl*). **sexiste** *adj* sexist. **sexualité** *nf* sexuality. **sexuel, ~le** *adj* sexual.

shampooing /ʃɑ̃pwɛ̃/ *nm* shampoo.

shérif /ʃeʀif/ *nm* sheriff.

short /ʃɔʀt/ *nm* shorts (+ *pl*).

si (s' | sinueux

si (**s'** *before il, ils*) /si, s/ *conj* if; (interrogation indirecte) if, whether; ~ **on allait se promener?** what about a walk?; **s'il vous** *ou* **te plaît** please; ~ **oui** if so; ~ **seulement** if only. ● *adv* (tellement) so; (oui) yes; **un ~ bon repas** such a good meal; ~ **habile qu'il soit** however skilful he may be; ~ **bien que** with the result that.

sida /sida/ *nm* (Méd) Aids.

sidérurgie /sideʀyʀʒi/ *nf* steel industry.

siècle /sjɛkl/ *nm* century; (époque) age.

siège /sjɛʒ/ *nm* seat; (Mil) siege; ~ **éjectable** ejector seat; ~ **social** head office, headquarters (+ *pl*). **siéger** 14 40 *vi* (assemblée) sit.

sien, ~**ne** /sjɛ̃, -ɛn/ *pron* **le** ~, **la** ~**ne**, **les** (~**ne**)**s** (homme) his; (femme) hers; (chose) its; **les** ~**s** (famille) one's family.

sieste /sjɛst/ *nf* nap, siesta.

sifflement /sifləmɑ̃/ *nm* whistling; **un** ~ a whistle.

siffler /sifle/ 1 *vi* whistle; (avec un sifflet) blow one's whistle; (serpent, gaz) hiss. ● *vt* (air) whistle; (chien) whistle to *ou* for; (acteur) hiss.

sifflet /siflɛ/ *nm* whistle; ~**s** (huées) boos.

sigle /sigl/ *nm* acronym.

signal (*pl* -**aux**) /siɲal, -o/ *nm* signal; ~ **sonore** (de répondeur) tone.

signalement /siɲalmɑ̃/ *nm* description.

signaler /siɲale/ 1 *vt* indicate; (par une sonnerie, un écriteau) signal; (dénoncer, mentionner) report; (faire remarquer) point out.

signalisation /siɲalizasjɔ̃/ *nf* signalling, signposting; (signaux) signals (+ *pl*).

signataire /siɲatɛʀ/ *nmf* signatory.

signature /siɲatyʀ/ *nf* signature; (action) signing; ~ **électronique** digital signature.

signe /siɲ/ *nm* sign; (de ponctuation) mark; **faire** ~ **à qn** wave at sb; (contacter) contact; **faire** ~ **à qn de** beckon sb to; **faire** ~ **que non** shake one's head; **faire** ~ **que oui** nod.

signer /siɲe/ 1 *vt* sign. □ **se** ~ *vpr* (Relig) cross oneself.

signet /siɲɛ/ *nm* (pour livre, Internet) bookmark; ~**s favoris** (Internet) hotlist.

significatif, -ive /siɲifikatif, -v/ *adj* significant.

signification /siɲifikasjɔ̃/ *nf* meaning. **signifier** 45 *vt* mean, signify; (faire connaître) make known (à to).

silence /silɑ̃s/ *nm* silence; (Mus) rest; **garder le** ~ keep silent.

silencieux, -ieuse /silɑ̃sjø, -z/ *adj* silent. ● *nm* silencer.

silex /silɛks/ *nm inv* flint.

silhouette /silwɛt/ *nf* outline, silhouette.

sillon /sijɔ̃/ *nm* furrow; (de disque) groove.

sillonner /sijone/ 1 *vt* crisscross.

similaire /similɛʀ/ *adj* similar. **similitude** *nf* similarity.

simple /sɛ̃pl/ *adj* simple; (non double) single. ● *nm* ~ **dames/messieurs** ladies'/men's singles (+ *pl*). **simple d'esprit** *nmf* simpleton. **simplement** *adv* simply. **simplicité** *nf* simplicity; (naïveté) simpleness.

simplification /sɛ̃plifikasjɔ̃/ *nf* simplification. **simplifier** 45 *vt* simplify.

simpliste /sɛ̃plist/ *adj* simplistic.

simulacre /simylakʀ/ *nm* pretence, sham.

simulation /simylasjɔ̃/ *nf* simulation. **simuler** 1 *vt* simulate.

simultané, ~e /simyltane/ *adj* simultaneous.

sincère /sɛ̃sɛʀ/ *adj* sincere. **sincérité** *nf* sincerity.

singe /sɛ̃ʒ/ *nm* monkey; (grand) ape. **singer** 40 *vt* mimic, ape.

singulier, -ière /sɛ̃gylje, -jɛʀ/ *adj* peculiar, remarkable; (Gram) singular. ● *nm* (Gram) singular.

sinistre /sinistʀ/ *adj* sinister. ● *nm* disaster; (incendie) blaze; (dommages) damage.

sinistré, ~e /sinistʀe/ *adj* stricken. ● *nm, f* disaster victim.

sinon /sinɔ̃/ *conj* (autrement) otherwise; (sauf) except (que that); **difficile** ~ **impossible** difficult if not impossible.

sinueux, -euse /sinɥø, -z/ *adj* winding; (fig) tortuous.

sirène /siʀɛn/ *nf* (appareil) siren; (femme) mermaid.

sirop /siʀo/ *nm* (de fruits, Méd) syrup; (boisson) cordial.

sismique /sismik/ *adj* seismic.

site /sit/ *nm* site; ~ **touristique** place of interest; ~ **Internet** *or* **Web** Web site.

sitôt /sito/ *adv* ~ **entré** immediately after coming in; ~ **que** as soon as; **pas de** ~ not for a while.

situation /situɑsjɔ̃/ *nf* situation; (emploi) job, position; ~ **de famille** marital status.

situé, ~e /situe/ *adj* situated.

situer /situe/ **1** *vt* situate, locate. □ **se** ~ *vpr* (se trouver) be situated.

six /sis/ (/si/ *before consonant*, /siz/ *before vowel*) *adj & nm* six. **sixième** *adj & nmf* sixth.

sketch (*pl* ~**es**) /skɛtʃ/ *nm* (Théât) sketch.

ski /ski/ *nm* (matériel) ski; (Sport) skiing; **faire du** ~ ski; ~ **de fond** cross-country skiing; ~ **nautique** water skiing. **skier** 45 *vi* ski.

slave /slav/ *adj* Slav; (Ling) Slavonic.

slip /slip/ *nm* (d'homme) underpants (+ *pl*); (de femme) knickers (+ *pl*); ~ **de bain** (swimming) trunks (+ *pl*); (du bikini) bikini bottom.

slogan /slɔgɑ̃/ *nm* slogan.

Slovaquie /slɔvaki/ *nf* Slovakia.

Slovénie /slɔveni/ *nf* Slovenia.

smoking /smɔkiŋ/ *nm* dinner jacket.

SNCF *abrév f* (**Société nationale des Chemins de fer français**) *French national railway company*.

snob /snɔb/ *nmf* snob. ● *adj* snobbish. **snobisme** *nm* snobbery.

sobre /sɔbʀ/ *adj* sober.

social, ~e (*mpl* **-iaux**) /sɔsjal, -jo/ *adj* social.

socialisme /sɔsjalism/ *nm* socialism. **socialiste** *nmf & a* socialist.

société /sɔsjete/ *nf* society; (entreprise) company; ~ **point com** dot-com.

socle /sɔkl/ *nm* (de colonne, statue) plinth; (de lampe) base.

socquette /sɔkɛt/ *nf* ankle sock.

soda /sɔda/ *nm* fizzy drink.

sœur /sœʀ/ *nf* sister.

soi /swa/ *pron* oneself; **derrière** ~ behind one; **en** ~ in itself; **aller de** ~ be obvious.

soi-disant /swadizɑ̃/ *adj inv* so-called. ● *adv* supposedly.

soie /swa/ *nf* silk.

soif /swaf/ *nf* thirst; **avoir** ~ be thirsty; **donner** ~ make one thirsty.

soigné, ~e /swaɲe/ *adj* (apparence) tidy, neat; (travail) carefully done.

soigner /swaɲe/ **1** *vt* (s'occuper de) look after, take care of; (tenue, style) take care over; (maladie) treat. □ **se** ~ *vpr* look after oneself.

soigneusement /swaɲøzmɑ̃/ *adv* carefully. **soigneux, -euse** *adj* careful (de about); (ordonné) tidy.

soi-même /swamɛm/ *pron* oneself.

soin /swɛ̃/ *nm* care; (ordre) tidiness; ~**s** care; (Méd) treatment; **avec** ~ carefully; **avoir** *ou* **prendre** ~ **de** take care of sb/to do; **premiers** ~**s** first aid (+ *sg*).

soir /swaʀ/ *nm* evening; **à ce** ~ see you tonight.

soirée /swaʀe/ *nf* evening; (réception) party.

soit /swa/ *conj* (à savoir) that is to say; ~... ~ either... or. ● →**ÊTRE** 4.

soixante /swasɑ̃t/ *adj & nm* sixty. **soixante-dix** *adj & nm* seventy.

soja /sɔʒa/ *nm* (graines) soya beans (+ *pl*); (plante) soya.

sol /sɔl/ *nm* ground; (de maison) floor; (terrain agricole) soil.

solaire /sɔlɛʀ/ *adj* solar; (huile, filtre) sun.

soldat /sɔlda/ *nm* soldier.

solde[1] /sɔld/ *nf* (salaire) pay.

solde[2] /sɔld/ *nm* (Comm) balance; **les** ~**s** the sales; ~**s** (écrit en vitrine) sale; **en** ~ (acheter) at sale price.

solder /sɔlde/ **1** *vt* sell off at sale price; (compte) settle. □ **se** ~ **par** *vpr* (aboutir à) end in.

sole /sɔl/ *nf* (poisson) sole.

soleil /sɔlɛj/ *nm* sun; (fleur) sunflower; **il y a du** ~ it's sunny.

solennel, ~le /sɔlanɛl/ *adj* solemn.

solfège /sɔlfɛʒ/ *nm* musical theory.

solidaire /sɔlidɛʀ/ *adj* (mécanismes) interdependent; (collègues) (mutually) supportive; **être** ~ **de qn** support sb.

solidarité /sɔlidaRite/ nf solidarity.

solide /sɔlid/ adj solid; (personne) strong. ● nm solid.

solidifier /sɔlidifje/ [45] vt solidify. □ se ~ vpr solidify.

solitaire /sɔlitɛR/ adj solitary. ● nmf (personne) loner. **solitude** nf solitude.

solliciter /sɔlisite/ [1] vt seek; (faire appel à) call upon; **être très sollicité** be very much in demand.

sollicitude /sɔlisityd/ nf concern.

solo /sɔlo/ nm & a inv (Mus) solo.

solution /sɔlysjɔ̃/ nf solution.

solvable /sɔlvabl/ adj solvent.

solvant /sɔlvã/ nm solvent.

sombre /sɔ̃bR/ adj dark; (triste) sombre.

sombrer /sɔ̃bRe/ [1] vi sink (dans into).

sommaire /sɔmɛR/ adj (exécution) summary; (description) rough. ● nm contents (+ pl); **au ~** on the programme.

sommation /sɔmasjɔ̃/ nf (Mil) warning; (Jur) notice.

somme /sɔm/ nf sum; **en ~, ~ toute** in short; **faire la ~ de** add (up), total (up). ● nm nap.

sommeil /sɔmɛj/ nm sleep; **avoir ~** be ou feel sleepy; **en ~** (projet) put on ice. **sommeiller** [1] vi doze; (fig) lie dormant.

sommelier /sɔməlje/ nm wine steward.

sommer /sɔme/ [1] vt summon.

sommes /sɔm/ ⇒ÊTRE [4].

sommet /sɔmɛ/ nm top; (de montagne) summit; (de triangle) apex; (gloire) height.

sommier /sɔmje/ nm bed base.

somnambule /sɔmnãbyl/ nm sleepwalker.

somnifère /sɔmnifɛR/ nm sleeping pill.

somnolent, ~e /sɔmnɔlã, -t/ adj drowsy. **somnoler** [1] vi doze.

somptueux, -euse /sɔ̃ptɥø, -z/ adj sumptuous.

son¹, sa (**son** before vowel or mute h) (pl **ses**) /sɔ̃, sa, sɔ̃n, se/ adj (homme) his; (femme) her; (chose) its; (indéfini) one's.

son² /sɔ̃/ nm (bruit) sound; (de blé) bran; **baisser le ~** turn the volume down.

sondage /sɔ̃daʒ/ nm ~ (**d'opinion**) (opinion) poll.

sonde /sɔ̃d/ nf (de forage) drill; (Méd) (d'évacuation) catheter; (d'examen) probe.

sonder /sɔ̃de/ [1] vt (population) poll; (explorer) sound; (terrain) drill; (intentions) sound out.

songe /sɔ̃ʒ/ nm dream.

songer /sɔ̃ʒe/ [40] vt ~ **que** think that; ~ **à** think about. **songeur, -euse** adj pensive.

sonné, ~e /sɔne/ adj (étourdi) groggy; [1] crazy.

sonner /sɔne/ [1] vt/i ring; (clairon, glas) sound; (heure) strike; (domestique) ring for; **midi sonné** well past noon; ~ **de** (clairon) sound, blow.

sonnerie /sɔnRi/ nf ringing; (de clairon) sounding; (sonnette) bell; (téléphone portable) ringtone.

sonnette /sɔnɛt/ nf bell.

sonore /sɔnɔR/ adj resonant; (onde, effets) sound; (rire) resounding.

sonorisation /sɔnɔRizasjɔ̃/ nf (matériel) public address system.

sonorité /sɔnɔRite/ nf resonance; (d'un instrument) tone.

sont /sɔ̃/ ⇒ÊTRE [4].

sophistiqué, ~e /sɔfistike/ adj sophisticated.

sorcellerie /sɔRsɛlRi/ nf witchcraft. **sorcier** nm (guérisseur) witch doctor; (maléfique) sorcerer. **sorcière** nf witch.

sordide /sɔRdid/ adj sordid; (lieu) squalid.

sort /sɔR/ nm (destin, hasard) fate; (condition) lot; (maléfice) spell; **tirer** (qch) **au ~** draw lots (for sth).

sortant, ~e /sɔRtã, -t/ adj (président etc.) outgoing.

sorte /sɔRt/ nf sort, kind; **de ~ que** so that; **en quelque ~** in a way; **de la ~** in this way; **faire en ~ que** make sure that.

sortie /sɔRti/ nf exit; (promenade, dîner) outing; (déclaration [1]) remark; (parution) publication; (de disque, film) release; (d'un ordinateur) output; ~**s** (argent) outgoings.

sortilège /sɔRtilɛʒ/ nm (magic) spell.

sortir /sɔrtir/ 46 *vi* (*aux être*) go out, leave; (*venir*) come out; (*aller au spectacle*) go out; (*livre, film*) come out; (*plante*) come up; ~ **de** (*pièce*) leave; (*milieu social*) come from; (*limites*) go beyond; ~ **du commun** *ou* **de l'ordinaire** be out of the ordinary. ● *vt* (*aux avoir*) take out; (*livre, modèle*) bring out; (*dire* 1) come out with; ~ **qn de** get sb out of; **être sorti d'affaire** be in the clear. ▫ **s'en** ~ *vpr* cope, manage.

sosie /sɔzi/ *nm* double.

sot, ~**te** /so, sɔt/ *adj* silly.

sottise /sɔtiz/ *nf* silliness; (action, remarque) foolish thing; **faire des** ~**s** be naughty.

sou /su/ *nm* 1 ~**s** money; **sans le** ~ without a penny; **près de ses** ~**s** tight-fisted.

soubresaut /subrəso/ *nm* (sudden) start.

souche /suʃ/ *nf* (d'arbre) stump; (de famille) stock; (de carnet) counterfoil.

souci /susi/ *nm* (inquiétude) worry; (préoccupation) concern; (plante) marigold; **se faire du** ~ worry.

soucier (se) /(sə)susje/ 45 *vpr* **se** ~ **de** care about. **soucieux, -ieuse** *adj* concerned (**de** about).

soucoupe /sukup/ *nf* saucer; ~ **volante** flying saucer.

soudain, ~**e** /sudɛ̃, -ɛn/ *adj* sudden. ● *adv* suddenly.

soude /sud/ *nf* soda.

souder /sude/ 1 *vt* weld, solder; **famille très soudée** close-knit family. ▫ **se** ~ *vpr* (os) knit (together).

soudoyer /sudwaje/ 31 *vt* bribe.

souffle /sufl/ *nm* (haleine) breath; (respiration) breathing; (explosion) blast; (vent) breath of air; **le** ~ **coupé** out of breath; **à couper le** ~ breathtaking.

souffler /sufle/ 1 *vi* blow; (haleter) puff. ● *vt* (bougie) blow out; (poussière, fumée) blow; (verre) blow; (par explosion) destroy; (chuchoter) whisper; ~ **la réplique à** prompt. **souffleur, -euse** *nm, f* (Théât) prompter.

souffrance /sufrɑ̃s/ *nf* suffering; **en** ~ (affaire) pending. **souffrant**, ~**e** *adj* unwell.

souffrir /sufrir/ 21 *vi* suffer (**de** from). ● *vt* (endurer) suffer; **il ne peut pas le** ~ he cannot stand *ou* bear him.

soufre /sufr/ *nm* sulphur.

souhait /swɛ/ *nm* wish; **à tes** ~**s!** bless you!; **paisible à** ~ incredibly peaceful. **souhaitable** *adj* desirable.

souhaiter /swete/ 1 *vt* ~ **qch à qn** wish sb sth; ~ **que/faire** hope that/to do; ~ **la bienvenue à qn** welcome sb.

soûl, ~**e** /su, sul/ *adj* drunk. ● *nm* **tout son** ~ as much as one can.

soulagement /sulaʒmɑ̃/ *nm* relief. **soulager** 40 *vt* relieve.

soûler /sule/ 1 *vt* make drunk. ▫ **se** ~ *vpr* get drunk.

soulèvement /sulɛvmɑ̃/ *nm* uprising.

soulever /sulve/ 6 *vt* lift, raise; (question, poussière) raise; (enthousiasme) arouse; (foule) stir up. ▫ **se** ~ *vpr* lift *ou* raise oneself up; (se révolter) rise up.

soulier /sulje/ *nm* shoe.

souligner /suliɲe/ 1 *vt* underline; (yeux) outline; (taille) emphasize.

soumettre /sumɛtr/ 42 *vt* (assujettir) subject (**à** to); (présenter) submit (**à** to). ▫ **se** ~ *vpr* submit (**à** to). **soumis**, ~**e** *adj* submissive. **soumission** *nf* submission.

soupape /supap/ *nf* valve.

soupçon /supsɔ̃/ *nm* suspicion; **un** ~ **de** (un peu de) a touch of. **soupçonner** 1 *vt* suspect. **soupçonneux, -euse** *adj* suspicious.

soupe /sup/ *nf* soup.

souper /supe/ 6 *vi* have supper. ● *nm* supper.

soupeser /supəze/ 1 *vt* judge the weight of; (fig) weigh up.

soupière /supjɛr/ *nf* (soup) tureen.

soupir /supir/ *nm* sigh; **pousser un** ~ heave a sigh.

soupirer /supire/ 1 *vi* sigh.

souple /supl/ *adj* supple; (règlement, caractère) flexible. **souplesse** *nf* suppleness; (de règlement) flexibility.

source /surs/ *nf* (de rivière, origine) source; (eau) spring; **prendre sa** ~ **à** rise in; **de** ~ **sûre** from a reliable source; ~ **thermale** hot spring.

sourcil /sursi/ *nm* eyebrow.

sourciller /sursije/ 1 *vi* **sans** ~ without batting an eyelid.

sourd, ~e /suʀ, -d/ adj deaf; (bruit, douleur) dull; **faire la ~e oreille** turn a deaf ear. ● nm, f deaf person.

sourd-muet (pl **sourds-muets**), **sourde-muette** (pl **sourdes-muettes**) /suʀmɥɛ, suʀdmɥɛt/ adj deaf and dumb. ● nm, f deafmute.

souricière /suʀisjɛʀ/ nf mousetrap; (fig) trap.

sourire /suʀiʀ/ 54 vi smile (à at); ~ à (fortune) smile on. ● nm smile; **garder le ~** keep smiling.

souris /suʀi/ nf mouse; des ~ mice.

sournois, ~e /suʀnwa, -z/ adj sly, underhand.

sous /su/ prép under, beneath; ~ **la main** handy; ~ **la pluie** in the rain; ~ **peu** shortly; ~ **terre** underground.

sous-alimenté, ~e /suzalimãte/ adj undernourished.

souscription /suskʀipsjɔ̃/ nf subscription. **souscrire** 80 vi ~ à subscribe to.

sous-entendre /suzãtãdʀ/ 3 vt imply. **sous-entendu** nm innuendo, insinuation.

sous-estimer /suzɛstime/ 1 vt underestimate.

sous-jacent, ~e /suʒasã, -t/ adj underlying.

sous-marin, ~e /sumaʀɛ̃, -in/ adj underwater; (plongée) deep-sea. ● nm submarine.

soussigné, ~e /susiɲe/ adj & nm, f undersigned.

sous-sol /susɔl/ nm (cave) basement.

sous-titre /sutitʀ/ nm subtitle.

soustraction /sustʀaksjɔ̃/ nf (déduction) subtraction.

soustraire /sustʀɛʀ/ 29 vt (déduire) subtract; (retirer) take away (à from). □ **se ~ à** vpr escape from.

sous-traitant /sutʀɛtã/ nm subcontractor.

sous-verre /suvɛʀ/ nm inv glass mount.

sous-vêtement /suvɛtmã/ nm underwear.

soute /sut/ nf (de bateau) hold; ~ **à charbon** coal-bunker.

soutenir /sutniʀ/ 59 vt support; (effort, rythme) sustain; (résister à) withstand; ~ **que** maintain that.

soutenu, ~e /sutny/ adj (constant) sustained; (style) formal.

souterrain, ~e /sutɛʀɛ̃, -ɛn/ adj underground. ● nm underground passage.

soutien /sutjɛ̃/ nm support.

soutien-gorge (pl **soutiensgorge**) /sutjɛ̃gɔʀʒ/ nm bra.

soutirer /sutiʀe/ 1 vt ~ **à qn** extract from sb.

souvenir¹ /suvniʀ/ nm memory, recollection; (objet) memento; (cadeau) souvenir; **en ~ de** in memory of.

souvenir² (se) /(sə)suvniʀ/ 59 vpr se ~ **de** remember; **se ~ que** remember that.

souvent /suvã/ adv often.

souverain, ~e /suvʀɛ̃, -ɛn/ adj sovereign. ● nm, f sovereign.

soviétique /sɔvjetik/ adj Soviet.

soyeux, -euse /swajø, -z/ adj silky.

spacieux, -ieuse /spasjø, -z/ adj spacious.

sparadrap /spaʀadʀa/ nm (sticking) plaster.

spatial, ~e (mpl **-iaux**) /spasjal, -jo/ adj space.

speaker, ~ine /spikœʀ, -kʀin/ nm, f announcer.

spécial, ~e (mpl **-iaux**) /spesjal, -jo/ adj special; (bizarre) odd. **spécialement** adv (exprès) specially; (très) especially.

spécialiser (se) /səspesjalize/ 1 vpr specialize (dans in). **spécialiste** nmf specialist. **spécialité** nf speciality; (US) specialty.

spécifier /spesifje/ 45 vt specify.

spécifique /spesifik/ adj specific.

spécimen /spesimɛn/ nm specimen.

spectacle /spɛktakl/ nm show; (vue) sight, spectacle.

spectaculaire /spɛktakylɛʀ/ adj spectacular.

spectateur, -trice /spɛktatœʀ, -tʀis/ nm, f (Sport) spectator; (témoin oculaire) onlooker; **les ~s** (Théât) the audience (+ sg).

spectre /spɛktʀ/ nm (revenant) spectre; (images) spectrum.

spéculateur, -trice /spekylatœʀ, -tʀis/ nm, f speculator. **spéculation** nf speculation. **spéculer** 1 vi speculate.

spéléologie /speleɔlɔʒi/ nf cave exploration, pot-holing.

spermatozoïde /spɛRmatɔzɔid/ *nm* spermatozoon. **sperme** *nm* sperm.

sphère /sfɛR/ *nf* sphere.

spirale /spiRal/ *nf* spiral.

spirituel, **~le** /spiRitɥɛl/ *adj* spiritual; (*amusant*) witty.

spiritueux /spiRitɥø/ *nm* (*alcool*) spirit.

splendeur /splɑ̃dœR/ *nf* splendour. **splendide** *adj* splendid.

sponsoriser /spɔ̃sɔRize/ **1** *vt* sponsor.

spontané, **~e** /spɔ̃tane/ *adj* spontaneous. **spontanéité** *nf* spontaneity.

sport /spɔR/ *adj inv* (*vêtements*) casual. ● *nm* sport; **veste/voiture de ~** sports jacket/car.

sportif, **-ive** /spɔRtif, -v/ *adj* (*personne*) sporty; (*physique*) athletic; (*résultats*) sports. ● *nm, f* sportsman, sportswoman.

spot /spɔt/ *nm* spotlight; (**~ publicitaire**) ad.

square /skwaR/ *nm* small public garden.

squatter /skwate/ **1** *vt* squat in.

squelette /skəlɛt/ *nm* skeleton. **squelettique** *adj* skeletal.

SRAS *abrév m* (**syndrome respiratoire aigu sévère**) SARS.

SSII *abrév f* (**société de services et d'ingénierie informatiques**) computer services company

stabiliser /stabilize/ **1** *vt* stabilize. **stable** *adj* stable.

stade /stad/ *nm* (Sport) stadium; (*phase*) stage.

stage /staʒ/ *nm* (*cours*) course; (*professionnel*) placement. **stagiaire** *nmf* course member; (*apprenti*) trainee.

stagner /stagne/ **1** *vi* stagnate.

stand /stɑ̃d/ *nm* stand; (*de fête foraine*) stall.

standard /stɑ̃daR/ *nm* switchboard. ● *adj inv* standard. **standardiser** **1** *vt* standardize.

standardiste /stɑ̃daRdist/ *nmf* switchboard operator.

standing /stɑ̃diŋ/ *nm* status, standing; **de ~** (*hôtel*) luxury.

starter /staRtɛR/ *nm* (Auto) choke.

station /stasjɔ̃/ *nf* station; (*halte*) stop; **~ debout** standing position; **~ de taxis** taxi rank; **~ balnéaire/ de ski**

seaside/ski resort; **~ thermale** spa.

stationnaire /stasjɔnɛR/ *adj* stationary.

stationnement /stasjɔnmɑ̃/ *nm* parking. **stationner** **1** *vi* park.

station-service (*pl* **stations-service**) /stasjɔ̃sɛRvis/ *nf* service station.

statique /statik/ *adj* static.

statistique /statistik/ *nf* statistic; (*science*) statistics (+ *sg.*) ● *adj* statistical.

statue /staty/ *nf* statue.

statuer /statɥe/ **1** *vi* **~ sur** give a ruling on.

statut /staty/ *nm* status. **statutaire** *adj* statutory.

sténo /steno/ *nf* (sténographie) shorthand. **sténodactylo** *nf* shorthand typist. **sténographie** *nf* shorthand.

stéréo /steReo/ *nf & adj inv* stereo.

stéréotype /steReɔtip/ *nm* stereotype.

stérile /steRil/ *adj* sterile.

stérilet /steRilɛ/ *nm* coil, IUD.

stérilisation /steRilizasjɔ̃/ *nf* sterilization. **stériliser** **1** *vt* sterilize.

stéroïde /steRɔid/ *adj & nm* steroid.

stimulant /stimylɑ̃/ *nm* stimulus; (*médicament*) stimulant.

stimulateur /stimylatœR/ *nm* **~ cardiaque** (Méd) pacemaker.

stimuler /stimyle/ **1** *vt* stimulate.

stipuler /stipyle/ **1** *vt* stipulate.

stock /stɔk/ *nm* stock. **stocker** **1** *vt* stock.

stoïque /stɔik/ *adj* stoical. ● *nmf* stoic.

stop /stɔp/ *interj* stop. ● *nm* stop sign; (*feu arrière*) brake light; **faire du ~** **1** hitch-hike. **stopper** **1** *vt/i* stop.

store /stɔR/ *nm* blind; (*de magasin*) awning.

strapontin /stRapɔ̃tɛ̃/ *nm* folding seat, jump seat.

stratégie /stRateʒi/ *nf* strategy. **stratégique** *adj* strategic.

stress /stRɛs/ *nm* stress. **stressant**, **~e** *adj* stressful. **stressé**, **~e** *adj* stressed. **stresser** **1** *vt* put under stress.

strict /stRikt/ *adj* strict; (*tenue, vérité*) plain; **le ~ minimum** the bare minimum. **strictement** *adv* strictly.

strident, **~e** /stRidɑ̃, -t/ *adj* shrill.

strophe /stRɔf/ *nf* stanza, verse.

structure /stʀyktyʀ/ nf structure.

studieux, -ieuse /stydjø, -z/ adj studious.

studio /stydjo/ nm (d'artiste, de télévision) studio; (logement) studio flat.

stupéfaction /stypefaksjɔ̃/ nf amazement. **stupéfait, ~e** adj amazed.

stupéfiant, ~e /stypefjɑ̃, -t/ adj astounding. ● nm drug, narcotic.

stupéfier /stypefje/ 45 vt amaze.

stupeur /stypœʀ/ nf amazement; (Méd) stupor.

stupide /stypid/ adj stupid. **stupidité** nf stupidity.

style /stil/ nm style.

styliste /stilist/ nmf fashion designer.

stylo /stilo/ nm pen; ~ (à) bille ball-point pen; ~ (à) encre fountain pen.

su /sy/ ➡SAVOIR 55.

suave /sɥav/ adj sweet.

subalterne /sybaltɛʀn/ adj & nmf subordinate.

subconscient /sypkɔ̃sjɑ̃/ nm subconscious.

subir /sybiʀ/ 2 vt be subjected to; (traitement, expériences) undergo.

subit, ~e /sybi, -t/ adj sudden.

subjectif, -ive /sybʒɛktif, -v/ adj subjective.

subjonctif /sybʒɔ̃ktif/ nm subjunctive.

subjuguer /sybʒyge/ 1 vt (charmer) captivate.

sublime /syblim/ adj sublime.

submerger /sybmɛʀʒe/ 40 vt submerge; (fig) overwhelm.

subordonné, ~e /sybɔʀdɔne/ adj & nm, f subordinate.

subside /sybzid/ nm grant.

subsidiaire /sybzidjɛʀ/ adj subsidiary; **question ~** tiebreaker.

subsistance /sybzistɑ̃s/ nf subsistence. **subsister** 1 vi subsist; (durer, persister) exist.

substance /sypstɑ̃s/ nf substance.

substantiel, ~le /sypstɑ̃sjɛl/ adj substantial.

substantif /sypstɑ̃tif/ nm noun.

substituer /sypstitɥe/ 1 vt substitute (à for). ◻ se ~ à vpr (remplacer) substitute for. **substitut** nm substitute; (Jur) deputy public prosecutor.

subtil, ~e /syptil/ adj subtle.

subtiliser /syptilize/ 1 vt ~ qch (à qn) steal sth (from sb).

subvenir /sybvəniʀ/ 59 vi ~ à provide for.

subvention /sybvɑ̃sjɔ̃/ nf subsidy. **subventionner** 1 vt subsidize.

subversif, -ive /sybvɛʀsif, -v/ adj subversive.

suc /syk/ nm juice.

succédané /syksedane/ nm substitute (de for).

succéder /syksede/ 14 vi ~ à succeed. ◻ se ~ vpr succeed one another.

succès /syksɛ/ nm success; à ~ (film, livre) successful; **avoir du ~** be a success.

successeur /syksesœʀ/ nm successor. **successif, -ive** adj successive. **succession** nf succession; (Jur) inheritance.

succinct, ~e /syksɛ̃, -t/ adj succinct.

succomber /sykɔ̃be/ 1 vi die; ~ à succumb to.

succulent, ~e /sykylɑ̃, -t/ adj delicious.

succursale /sykyʀsal/ nf (Comm) branch.

sucer /syse/ 10 vt suck.

sucette /sysɛt/ nf (bonbon) lollipop; (tétine) dummy; (US) pacifier.

sucre /sykʀ/ nm sugar; ~ d'orge barley sugar; ~ en poudre caster sugar; ~ glace icing sugar; ~ roux brown sugar.

sucré /sykʀe/ adj sweet; (additionné de sucre) sweetened. **sucrer** 1 vt sugar, sweeten. **sucreries** nfpl sweets.

sucrier, -ière /sykʀije, -jɛʀ/ adj sugar. ● nm (récipient) sugar-bowl.

sud /syd/ nm south. ● adj inv south; (partie) southern.

sud-est /sydɛst/ nm south-east.

sud-ouest /sydwɛst/ nm southwest.

Suède /sɥɛd/ nf Sweden.

suédois, ~e /sɥedwa, -z/ adj Swedish. ● nm (Ling) Swedish. **S~, ~e** nm, f Swede.

suer /sɥe/ 1 vt/i sweat; **faire ~ qn** 1 get on sb's nerves.

sueur /sɥœʀ/ nf sweat; **en ~** covered in sweat.

suffire /syfiʀ/ 57 vi be enough (à qn for sb); **il suffit de compter** all you have to do is count; **une goutte suffit** a drop is enough; ~ **à** (besoin) satisfy. □ **se** ~ vpr se ~ **à soi-même** be self-sufficient.

suffisamment /syfizamɑ̃/ adv sufficiently; ~ **de qch** enough of sth. **suffisance** nf (vanité) conceit. **suffisant, ~e** adj sufficient; (vaniteux) conceited.

suffixe /syfiks/ nm suffix.

suffoquer /syfɔke/ ◼ vt/i choke, suffocate.

suffrage /syfʀaʒ/ nm (voix: Pol) vote; (système) suffrage.

suggérer /sygʒeʀe/ ◼◼ vt suggest. **suggestion** nf suggestion.

suicidaire /sɥisidɛʀ/ adj suicidal. **suicide** nm suicide. **suicider (se)** ◼ vpr commit suicide.

suinter /sɥɛ̃te/ ◼ vi ooze.

suis /sɥi/ →ÊTRE ◼, →SUIVRE ◼◼.

Suisse /sɥis/ nf Switzerland. ● nmf Swiss. **suisse** adj Swiss.

suite /sɥit/ nf continuation, rest; (d'un film) sequel; (série) series; (appartement, escorte) suite; (résultat) conséquence; **à la ~, de ~** (successivement) in a row; **à la ~ de** (derrière) behind; **à la ~ de, par ~ de** (en conséquence) as a result of; **faire ~ (à)** follow; **par la ~** afterwards; ~ **à votre lettre du** further to your letter of the; **des ~s de** as a result of.

suivant[1], ~e /sɥivɑ̃, -t/ adj following, next. ● nm, f following ou next person.

suivant[2] /sɥivɑ̃/ prép (selon) according to.

suivi, ~e /sɥivi/ adj (effort) steady, sustained; (cohérent) consistent; **peu/très ~** (cours) poorly/well attended.

suivre /sɥivʀ/ ◼◼ vt/i follow; (comprendre) follow; **faire ~** (courrier) forward. □ **se** ~ vpr follow each other.

sujet, ~te /syʒɛ, -t/ adj ~ **à** liable ou subject to. ● nm (d'un royaume) subject; (question) subject; (motif) cause; (Gram) subject; **au** ~ **de** about.

super /sypɛʀ/ nm (essence) fourstar. ● adj inv ◼ (très) great. ● adv ◼ ultra, really.

superbe /sypɛʀb/ adj superb.

supérette /sypeʀɛt/ nf minimarket.

superficie /sypɛʀfisi/ nf area.

superficiel, ~le /sypɛʀfisjɛl/ adj superficial.

superflu /sypɛʀfly/ adj superfluous. ● nm (excédent) surplus.

supérieur, ~e /sypeʀjœʀ/ adj (plus haut) upper; (quantité, nombre) greater (à than); (études, principe) higher (à than); (meilleur, hautain) superior (à to). ● nm, f superior. **supériorité** nf superiority.

superlatif, -ive /sypɛʀlatif, -v/ adj & nm superlative.

supermarché /sypɛʀmaʀʃe/ nm supermarket.

superposer /sypɛʀpoze/ ◼ vt superimpose; **lits superposés** bunk beds.

superproduction /sypɛʀpʀɔdyksjɔ̃/ nf (film) blockbuster.

superpuissance /sypɛʀpɥisɑ̃s/ nf superpower.

superstitieux, -ieuse /sypɛʀstisjø, -z/ adj superstitious.

superviser /sypɛʀvize/ ◼ vt supervise.

suppléant, ~e /sypleɑ̃, -t/ nmf & adj (professeur ~) supply teacher; (juge) ~ deputy (judge).

suppléer /syplee/ ◼◼ vt (remplacer) fill in for. ● vi ~ **à** (compenser) make up for.

supplément /syplemɑ̃/ nm (argent) extra charge; (de frites, légumes) extra portion; **en** ~ extra; **un** ~ **de** (travail) additional; **payer un** ~ pay a supplement. **supplémentaire** adj extra, additional.

supplice /syplis/ nm torture.

supplier /syplije/ ◼◼ vt beg, beseech (de to).

support /sypɔʀ/ nm support; (Ordinat) medium.

supportable /sypɔʀtabl/ adj bearable.

supporter[1] /sypɔʀte/ ◼ vt (privations) bear; (personne) put up with; (structure: Ordinat) support; **il ne supporte pas les enfants/de perdre** he can't stand children/losing.

supporter[2] /sypɔʀtɛʀ/ nm (Sport) supporter.

supposer /sypoze/ ◼ vt suppose; (impliquer) imply; **à** ~ **que** supposing that.

suppression /sypʀesjɔ̃/ nf (de taxe) abolition; (de sanction) lifting; (de mot) deletion. **supprimer** ◼ vt (allocation) withdraw; (contrôle) lift; (train) cancel; (*preuve*) suppress.

suprématie /sypʀemasi/ *nf* supremacy.

suprême /sypʀɛm/ *adj* supreme.

sur /syʀ/ *prép* on, upon; (*pardessus*) over; (au sujet de) about, on; (proportion) out of; (mesure) by; ~ **la photo** in the photograph; **mettre/ jeter** ~ put/throw on to; ~ **mesure** made to measure; ~ **place** on the spot; ~ **ce, je pars** with that, I must go; ~ **le moment** at the time.

sûr /syʀ/ *adj* certain, sure; (sans danger) safe; (digne de confiance) reliable; (*main*) steady; (*jugement*) sound; **être** ~ **de soi** be self-confident; **j'en étais** ~**!** I knew it!

surabondance /syʀabɔ̃dɑ̃s/ *nf* overabundance.

surcharge /syʀʃaʀʒ/ *nf* overloading; (poids) excess load. **surcharger** 🔳 *vt* overload; (*texte*) alter.

surchauffer /syʀʃofe/ 🔳 *vt* overheat.

surcroît /syʀkʀwa/ *nm* increase (**de** in); **de** ~ in addition.

surdité /syʀdite/ *nf* deafness.

surélever /syʀelve/ 🔳 *vt* raise.

sûrement /syʀmɑ̃/ *adv* certainly; (sans danger) safely; **il a** ~ **oublié** he must have forgotten.

surenchère /syʀɑ̃ʃɛʀ/ *nf* higher bid. **surenchérir** 🔳 *vi* bid higher (**sur** than).

surestimer /syʀɛstime/ 🔳 *vt* overestimate.

sûreté /syʀte/ *nf* safety; (de pays) security; (d'un geste) steadiness; **être en** ~ be safe; **S~ (nationale)** police (+ *pl*).

surexcité, ~e /syʀɛksite/ *adj* very excited.

surf /sœʀf/ *nm* surfing.

surface /syʀfas/ *nf* surface; **faire** ~ (sous-marin, fig) surface; **en** ~ on the surface.

surfait, ~e /syʀfɛ, -t/ *adj* overrated.

surfer /syʀfe/ 🔳 *vi* go surfing; ~ **sur l'Internet** surf the Internet.

surgelé, ~e /syʀʒəle/ *adj* (deep-) frozen; **aliments** ~**s** frozen food.

surgir /syʀʒiʀ/ 🔳 *vi* appear (suddenly); (difficulté) crop up.

sur-le-champ /syʀləʃɑ̃/ *adv* right away.

surlendemain /syʀlɑ̃dmɛ̃/ *nm* le ~ two days later; le ~ **de** two days after.

surligneur /syʀliɲœʀ/ *nm* highlighter (pen).

surmenage /syʀmənaʒ/ *nm* overwork.

surmonter /syʀmɔ̃te/ 🔳 *vt* (vaincre) overcome, surmount; (être au-dessus de) surmount, top.

surnaturel, ~le /syʀnatyʀɛl/ *adj* supernatural.

surnom /syʀnɔ̃/ *nm* nickname. **surnommer** 🔳 *vt* nickname.

surpeuplé, ~e /syʀpœple/ *adj* overpopulated.

surplomber /syʀplɔ̃be/ 🔳 *vt/i* overhang.

surplus /syʀply/ *nm* surplus.

suprenant, ~e /syʀpʀənɑ̃, -t/ *adj* surprising. **surprendre** 🔳 *vt* (étonner) surprise; (prendre au dépourvu) catch, surprise; (entendre) overhear. **surpris, ~e** *adj* surprised (**de** at).

surprise /syʀpʀiz/ *nf* surprise.

surréaliste /syʀʀealist/ *adj & nmf* surrealist.

sursaut /syʀso/ *nm* start, jump; **en** ~ with a start; ~ **de** (regain) burst of. **sursauter** 🔳 *vi* start, jump.

sursis /syʀsi/ *nm* reprieve; (Mil) deferment; **deux ans (de prison) avec** ~ a two-year suspended sentence.

surtaxe /syʀtaks/ *nf* surcharge.

surtout /syʀtu/ *adv* especially; (avant tout) above all; ~ **pas** certainly not.

surveillance /syʀvejɑ̃s/ *nf* watch; (d'examen) supervision; (de la police) surveillance. **surveillant, ~e** *nm, f* (de prison) warder; (au lycée) supervisor (in charge of discipline). **surveiller** 🔳 *vt* watch; (travaux, élèves) supervise.

survenir /syʀvəniʀ/ 🔳 *vi* occur, take place; (personne) turn up.

survêtement /syʀvɛtmɑ̃/ *nm* (Sport) tracksuit.

survie /syʀvi/ *nf* survival.

survivant, ~e /syʀvivɑ̃, -t/ *adj* surviving. ● *nm, f* survivor.

survivre /syʀvivʀ/ 🔳 *vi* survive; ~ **à** (conflit) survive; (personne) outlive.

survoler /syʀvɔle/ 🔳 *vt* fly over; (livre) skim through.

sus: en ~ /ɑ̃sys/ *loc* in addition.

susceptible /sysɛptibl/ adj touchy; ~ de faire likely to do.

susciter /sysite/ **1** vt (éveiller) arouse; (occasionner) create.

suspect, ~e /syspɛ, -ɛkt/ adj (individu, faits) suspicious; (témoignage) suspect; ~ de suspected of. ● nm, f suspect. **suspecter** **1** vt suspect.

suspendre /syspɑ̃dʀ/ **3** vt (accrocher) hang (up); (interrompre, destituer) suspend; **suspendu à** hanging from. □ se ~ à vpr hang from.

suspens: en ~ /ɑ̃syspɑ̃/ loc (affaire) outstanding; (dans l'indécision) in suspense.

suspense /syspɛns/ nm suspense.

suture /sytyʀ/ nf **point de ~** stitch.

svelte /svɛlt/ adj slender.

S.V.P. abrév (s'il vous plaît) please.

syllabe /silab/ nf syllable.

symbole /sɛ̃bɔl/ nm symbol. **symboliser** **1** vt symbolize.

symétrie /simetʀi/ nf symmetry.

sympa /sɛ̃pa/ adj inv **E** nice; **sois ~** be a pal.

sympathie /sɛ̃pati/ nf (goût) liking; (compassion) sympathy; **avoir de la ~ pour** like. **sympathique** adj nice, pleasant. **sympathisant, ~e** nm, f sympathizer. **sympathiser** **1** vi get on well (avec with).

symphonie /sɛ̃fɔni/ nf symphony.

symptôme /sɛ̃ptom/ nm symptom.

synagogue /sinagɔg/ nf synagogue.

synchroniser /sɛ̃kʀɔnize/ **1** vt synchronize.

syncope /sɛ̃kɔp/ nf (Méd) blackout.

syndic /sɛ̃dik/ nm ~ **(d'immeuble)** property manager.

syndicaliste /sɛ̃dikalist/ nmf (trade-)unionist. ● adj (trade-) union.

syndicat /sɛ̃dika/ nm (trade) union; ~ **d'initiative** tourist office.

syndiqué, ~e /sɛ̃dike/ adj **être ~** be a (trade-)union member.

synonyme /sinɔnim/ adj synonymous. ● nm synonym.

syntaxe /sɛ̃taks/ nf syntax.

synthèse /sɛ̃tɛz/ nf synthesis. **synthétique** adj synthetic.

synthé(tiseur) /sɛ̃te(tizœʀ)/ nm synthesizer.

systématique /sistematik/ adj systematic.

système /sistɛm/ nm system; **le ~ D** **E** resourcefulness.

Tt

t' /t/ ➡TE.

ta /ta/ ➡TON[1].

tabac /taba/ nm tobacco; (magasin) tobacconist's shop.

table /tabl/ nf table; **à ~!** dinner is ready!; ~ **de nuit** bedside table; ~ **des matières** table of contents; ~ **à repasser** ironing board; ~ **roulante** (tea-)trolley; (US) serving cart.

tableau (pl ~x) /tablo/ nm picture; (peinture) painting; (panneau) board; (graphique) chart; (Scol) blackboard; ~ **d'affichage** notice-board; ~ **de bord** dashboard.

tablette /tablɛt/ nf shelf; ~ **de chocolat** bar of chocolate.

tableur /tablœʀ/ nm spreadsheet.

tablier /tablije/ nm apron; (de pont) platform; (de magasin) shutter.

tabou /tabu/ nm & adj taboo.

tabouret /tabuʀɛ/ nm stool.

tache /taʃ/ nf mark, spot; (salissure) stain; **faire ~ d'huile** spread; ~ **de rousseur** freckle.

tâche /taʃ/ nf task, job.

tacher /taʃe/ **1** vt stain. □ se ~ vpr (personne) get oneself dirty.

tâcher /taʃe/ **1** vi ~ **de faire** try to do.

tacheté, ~e /taʃte/ adj spotted.

tact /takt/ nm tact.

tactique /taktik/ adj tactical. ● nf (Mil) tactics; **une ~** a tactic.

taie /tɛ/ nf ~ **(d'oreiller)** pillowcase.

taille /tɑj/ nf (milieu du corps) waist; (hauteur) height; (grandeur) size; **de ~** sizeable; **être de ~ à faire** be up to doing.

taille-crayons /tajkʀɛjɔ̃/ nm inv pencil-sharpener.

tailler /taje/ **1** vt cut; (arbre) prune; (crayon) sharpen; (vêtement) cut out.

□ **se** ~ vpr 🔢 clear off.

tailleur /tajœʀ/ nm (costume) woman's suit; (couturier) tailor; **en** ~ cross-legged; ~ **de pierre** stonecutter.

taire /tɛʀ/ 47 vt not to reveal; **faire** ~ silence. □ **se** ~ vpr be silent ou quiet; (devenir silencieux) fall silent.

talc /talk/ nm talcum powder.

talent /talɑ̃/ nm talent. **talentueux, -euse** adj talented, gifted.

talon /talɔ̃/ nm heel; (de chèque) stub.

tambour /tɑ̃buʀ/ nm drum; (d'église) vestibule.

Tamise /tamiz/ nf Thames.

tampon /tɑ̃pɔ̃/ nm (de bureau) stamp; (ouate) wad, pad; (~ **hygiénique**) tampon.

tamponner /tɑ̃pɔne/ 🔢 vt (document) stamp; (véhicule) crash into; (plaie) swab.

tandem /tɑ̃dɛm/ nm (vélo) tandem; (personnes: fig) duo.

tandis que /tɑ̃dik(ə)/ conj while.

tanière /tanjɛʀ/ nf den.

tant /tɑ̃/ adv (travailler, manger) so much; ~ **de** (quantité) so much; (nombre) so many; ~ **que** as long as; **en** ~ **que** as; ~ **mieux!** all the better!; ~ **pis!** too bad!

tante /tɑ̃t/ nf aunt.

tantôt /tɑ̃to/ adv sometimes.

tapage /tapaʒ/ nm din.

tape /tap/ nf slap. **tape-à-l'œil** adj inv flashy, tawdry.

taper /tape/ 🔢 vt hit; (prendre 🔢) scrounge; ~ (**à la machine**) type. ● vi (cogner) bang; (soleil) beat down; ~ **dans** (puiser dans) dig into; ~ **sur** hit; ~ **sur l'épaule de qn** tap sb on the shoulder. □ **se** ~ vpr (corvée 🔢) get stuck with 🔢.

tapis /tapi/ nm carpet; (petit) rug; ~ **de bain** bathmat; ~ **roulant** (pour objets) conveyor belt; (pour piétons) moving walkway.

tapisser /tapise/ 🔢 vt (wall) paper; (fig) cover (**de** with). **tapisserie** nf tapestry; (papier peint) wallpaper.

taquin, ~e /takɛ̃, -in/ adj fond of teasing. ● nm, f tease(r).

tard /taʀ/ adv late; **au plus** ~ at the latest; **plus** ~ later; **sur le** ~ late in life.

tarder /taʀde/ 🔢 vi (être lent à venir) be a long time coming; ~ (**à faire**) take a long time (doing), delay (doing); **sans (plus)** ~ without (further) delay; **il me tarde de** I'm longing to.

tardif, -ive /taʀdif, -v/ adj late.

tare /taʀ/ nf (défaut) defect.

tarif /taʀif/ nm rate; (de train, taxi) fare; **plein** ~ full price.

tarir /taʀiʀ/ 2 vt/i dry up. □ **se** ~ vpr dry up.

tarte /taʀt/ nf tart. ● adj inv (ridicule 🔢) ridiculous.

tartine /taʀtin/ nf slice of bread; ~ **de beurre** slice of bread and butter. **tartiner** 🔢 vt spread.

tartre /taʀtʀ/ nm (de bouilloire) fur, scale; (sur les dents) tartar.

tas /tɑ/ nm pile, heap; **un** ou **des** ~ **de** 🔢 lots of.

tasse /tɑs/ nf cup; ~ **à thé** teacup.

tasser /tɑse/ 🔢 vt pack, squeeze; (terre) pack (down). □ **se** ~ vpr (terrain) sink; (se serrer) squeeze up.

tâter /tate/ 🔢 vt feel; (opinion: fig) sound out. ● vi ~ **de** try out.

tatillon, ~ne /tatijɔ̃, -jɔn/ adj finicky.

tâtonnements /tatɔnmɑ̃/ nmpl (essais) trial and error (+ sg). **tâtons: à** ~ /atatɔ̃/ loc **avancer à** ~ grope one's way along.

tatouage /tatwaʒ/ nm (dessin) tattoo.

taupe /top/ nf mole.

taureau (pl ~x) /tɔʀo/ nm bull; **le T~** Taurus.

taux /to/ nm rate.

taxe /taks/ nf tax.

taxi /taksi/ nm taxi(-cab); (personne 🔢) taxi driver.

taxiphone ® /taksifɔn/ nm pay phone.

Tchécoslovaquie /tʃekɔslɔvaki/ nf Czechoslovakia.

tchèque /tʃɛk/ adj Czech; **République** ~ Czech Republic. **T~** nmf Czech.

te, t' /tə, t/ pron you; (indirect) (to) you; (réfléchi) yourself.

technicien, ~ne /tɛknisjɛ̃, -ɛn/ nm, f technician.

technique /tɛknik/ adj technical. ● nf technique.

techno /tɛkno/ nf (Mus) techno.

technologie /tɛknɔlɔʒi/ nf technology.

teindre /tɛ̃dʀ/ [22] vt dye. □ se ~ vpr se ~ les cheveux dye one's hair.

teint /tɛ̃/ nm complexion.

teinte /tɛ̃t/ nf shade. **teinter** [1] vt (verre) tint; (bois) stain.

teinture /tɛ̃tyʀ/ nf (produit) dye.

teinturier, -ière /tɛ̃tyʀje, -jɛʀ/ nm, f dry-cleaner.

tel, ~le /tɛl/ adj such; **un ~ livre** such a book; **~ que** such as, like; (ainsi que) (just) as; **~ ou ~** such-and-such; **~ quel** (just) as it is.

télé /tele/ nf [1] TV; **~ réalité** nf reality TV.

télécharger /teleʃaʀʒe/ [40] vt (Ordinat) download.

télécommande /telekɔmɑ̃d/ nf remote control.

télécommunications /telekɔmynikasjɔ̃/ nfpl telecommunications.

téléconférence /telekɔ̃feʀɑ̃s/ nf teleconferencing.

télécopie /telekɔpi/ nf fax. **télécopieur** nm fax machine.

téléfilm /telefilm/ nm TV film.

télégramme /telegʀam/ nm telegram.

télégraphier /telegʀafje/ [45] vt/i ~ (à) cable.

téléguidé, ~e /telegide/ adj radio-controlled.

télématique /telematik/ nf telematics (+ sg).

téléphérique /teleferik/ nm cable car.

téléphone /telefɔn/ nm (tele-) phone; **~ à carte** cardphone. **téléphoner** [1] vt/i ~ (à) (tele)phone.

téléphonie /telefɔni/ nf telephony; **~ mobile** mobile telephony. **téléphonique** adj (tele)phone.

télé-réalité /telerealite/ nf reality TV.

téléserveur /teleseʀvœʀ/ nm (Internet) remote server.

télésiège /telesjɛʒ/ nm chairlift.

téléski /teleski/ nm ski tow.

téléspectateur, -trice /tele-spɛktatœʀ, -tʀis/ nm, f (tv) viewer.

télévente /televɑ̃t/ nf telesales (+ pl).

télévisé, ~e /televize/ adj (débat) televised; **émission ~e** television programme. **télévision** nf television.

télex /telɛks/ nm telex.

tellement /tɛlmɑ̃/ adv (tant) so much; (si) so; **~ de** (quantité) so much; (nombre) so many.

téméraire /temeʀɛʀ/ adj (personne) reckless.

témoignage /temwaɲaʒ/ nm testimony, evidence; (récit) account; **~ de** (marque) token of.

témoigner /temwaɲe/ [1] vi testify (de to). ● vt (montrer) show; **~ que** testify that.

témoin /temwɛ̃/ nm witness; (Sport) baton; **être ~ de** witness; **~ oculaire** eyewitness.

tempe /tɑ̃p/ nf (Anat) temple.

tempérament /tɑ̃peʀamɑ̃/ nm temperament, disposition.

température /tɑ̃peʀatyʀ/ nf temperature.

tempête /tɑ̃pɛt/ nf storm; **~ de neige** snowstorm.

temple /tɑ̃pl/ nm temple; (protestant) church.

temporaire /tɑ̃pɔʀɛʀ/ adj temporary.

temps /tɑ̃/ nm (notion) time; (Gram) tense; (étape) stage; **à ~ partiel/plein** part-/full-time; **ces derniers ~** lately; **dans le ~** at one time; **dans quelque ~** in a while; **de ~ en ~** from time to time; **d'arrêt** pause; **avoir tout son ~** have plenty of time; (météo) weather; **~ de chien** filthy weather; **quel ~ fait-il?** what's the weather like?

tenace /tənas/ adj stubborn.

tenaille /tənɑj/ nf pincers (+ pl).

tendance /tɑ̃dɑ̃s/ nf tendency; (évolution) trend; **avoir ~ à** tend to.

tendon /tɑ̃dɔ̃/ nm tendon.

tendre¹ /tɑ̃dʀ/ [3] vt stretch; (piège) set; (bras) stretch out; (main) hold out; (cou) crane; **~ qch à qn** hold sth out to sb; **~ l'oreille** prick up one's ears. ● vi **~ à** tend to.

tendre² /tɑ̃dʀ/ adj tender; (couleur, bois) soft. **tendresse** nf tenderness.

tendu, ~e /tɑ̃dy/ adj (corde) tight; (personne, situation) tense.

ténèbres /tenɛbʀ/ nfpl darkness.

teneur /tənœʀ/ nf content.

tenir /təniʀ/ [59] vt hold; (pari, promesse, hôtel) keep; (place) take up;

(*propos*) utter; (*rôle*) play; ~ de (avoir reçu de) have got from; ~ pour regard as; ~ chaud keep warm; ~ compte de take into account; ~ le coup hold out; ~ tête à stand up to. ● *vi* hold; ~ à be attached to; ~ à faire be anxious to do; ~ bon stand firm; ~ dans fit into; ~ de qn take after sb; tiens! (surprise) hey! □ se ~ *vpr* (debout) stand; (avoir lieu) be held; se ~ à hold on to; s'en ~ à (se limiter à) confine oneself to.

tennis /tenis/ *nm* tennis; ~ de table table tennis. ● *nmpl* (chaussures) sneakers.

ténor /tenɔʀ/ *nm* tenor.

tension /tɑ̃sjɔ̃/ *nf* tension; avoir de la ~ have high blood pressure.

tentation /tɑ̃tasjɔ̃/ *nf* temptation.

tentative /tɑ̃tativ/ *nf* attempt.

tente /tɑ̃t/ *nf* tent.

tenter /tɑ̃te/ **1** *vt* (allécher) tempt; (essayer) try (de faire to do).

tenture /tɑ̃tyʀ/ *nf* curtain; ~s draperies.

tenu, ~e /təny/ *adj* bien ~ well kept; ~ de required. ● →TENIR **58**.

tenue /təny/ *nf* (habillement) dress; (de maison) upkeep; (conduite) (good) behaviour; (maintien) posture; ~ de soirée evening dress.

Tergal ® /tɛʀgal/ *nm* Terylene®.

terme /tɛʀm/ *nm* (mot) term; (date limite) time-limit; (fin) end; né avant ~ premature; à long/court ~ long-/short-term; en bons ~s on good terms (avec with).

terminaison /tɛʀminɛzɔ̃/ *nf* (Gram) ending.

terminal, ~e (*mpl* -aux) /tɛʀmi- nal, -o/ *adj* terminal. ● *nm* terminal. **terminale** *nf* (Scol) ≈ sixth form; (US) twelfth grade.

terminer /tɛʀmine/ **1** *vt/i* finish; (*discours*) end, finish. □ se ~ *vpr* end (par with).

terne /tɛʀn/ *adj* dull, drab.

ternir /tɛʀniʀ/ **2** *vt/i* tarnish. □ se ~ *vpr* tarnish.

terrain /tɛʀɛ̃/ *nm* ground; (parcelle) piece of land; (à bâtir) plot; ~ d'aviation airfield; ~ de camping campsite; ~ de golf golf course; ~ de jeu playground; ~ vague waste ground.

terrasse /tɛʀas/ *nf* terrace; à la ~ (d'un café) outside (a café).

terrasser /tɛʀase/ **1** *vt* (adversaire) knock down; (maladie) strike down.

terre /tɛʀ/ *nf* (planète, matière) earth; (étendue, pays) land; (sol) ground; à ~ (Naut) ashore; par ~ (dehors) on the ground; (dedans) on the floor; ~ (cuite) terracotta; la ~ ferme dry land; ~ glaise clay. **terreau** (*pl* ~x) *nm* compost. **terre-plein** (*pl* terrespleins) *nm* platform; (de route) central reservation.

terrestre /tɛʀɛstʀ/ *adj* (animaux) land; (de notre planète) of the Earth.

terreur /tɛʀœʀ/ *nf* terror.

terrible /tɛʀibl/ *adj* terrible; (formidable **!**) terrific.

terrier /tɛʀje/ *nm* (trou) burrow; (chien) terrier.

terrifier /tɛʀifje/ **45** *vt* terrify.

territoire /tɛʀitwaʀ/ *nm* territory.

terroir /tɛʀwaʀ/ *nm* land; du ~ local.

terroriser /tɛʀɔʀize/ **1** *vt* terrorize.

terrorisme /tɛʀɔʀism/ *nm* terrorism. **terroriste** *nmf* terrorist.

tertiaire /tɛʀsjɛʀ/ *adj* (secteur) service.

tes /te/ →TON¹.

test /tɛst/ *nm* test.

testament /tɛstamɑ̃/ *nm* (Jur) will; (politique, artistique) testament; Ancien/Nouveau T~ Old/New Testament.

tétanos /tetanos/ *nm* tetanus.

têtard /tɛtaʀ/ *nm* tadpole.

tête /tɛt/ *nf* head; (visage) face; (cheveux) hair; à la ~ de at the head of; à ~ reposée at one's leisure; de ~ (calculer) in one's head; faire la ~ sulk; tenir ~ à qn stand up to sb; il n'en fait qu'à sa ~ he does just as he pleases; en ~ (Sport) in the lead; faire une ~ (au football) head the ball; une forte ~ a rebel; la ~ la première head first; de la ~ aux pieds from head to toe.

tête-à-tête /tɛtatɛt/ *nm inv* tête-à-tête; en ~ in private.

tétée /tete/ *nf* feed.

tétine /tetin/ *nf* (de biberon) teat; (sucette) dummy; (US) pacifier.

têtu, ~e /tety/ *adj* stubborn.

texte /tɛkst/ *nm* text; (de leçon) subject; (morceau choisi) passage.

texteur /tɛkstœʀ/ nm (Ordinat) word-processor.

textile /tɛkstil/ nm & adj textile.

texto /tɛksto/ nm ⚠ text message.

TGV abrév m (**train à grande vitesse**) TGV, high-speed train.

> **TGV** Abbreviation of *Train à grande vitesse*, the high-speed electric passenger train operated by the SNCF. It runs on special track and can reach speeds of up to 300 km/h (180 mph). Marseilles, for example, is now only three hours from Paris by *TGV*.

thé /te/ nm tea.

théâtre /teɑtʀ/ nm theatre; (d'un crime) scene; **faire du ~** act.

théière /tejɛʀ/ nf teapot.

thème /tɛm/ nm theme; (traduction: Scol) prose.

théorie /teɔʀi/ nf theory. **théorique** adj theoretical.

thérapie /teʀapi/ nf therapy.

thermique /tɛʀmik/ adj thermal.

thermomètre /tɛʀmɔmɛtʀ/ nm thermometer.

thermos® /tɛʀmos/ nm ou f Thermos® (flask).

thermostat /tɛʀmɔsta/ nm thermostat.

thèse /tɛz/ nf thesis.

thon /tɔ̃/ nm tuna.

thym /tɛ̃/ nm thyme.

tibia /tibja/ nm shinbone.

tic /tik/ nm (contraction) tic, twitch; (manie) habit.

ticket /tikɛ/ nm ticket.

tiède /tjɛd/ adj lukewarm; (nuit) warm.

tiédir /tjediʀ/ ② vt/i (faire) ~ warm up.

tien, ~ne /tjɛ̃, -ɛn/ pron le ~, la ~ne, les ~(ne)s yours; **à la ~ne!** cheers!

tiens, tient /tjɛ̃/ ➡ **TENIR** 59.

tiercé /tjɛʀse/ nm place-betting.

tiers, tierce /tjɛʀ, tjɛʀs/ adj third. ● nm (fraction) third; (personne) third party. **tiers-monde** nm Third World.

tige /tiʒ/ nf (Bot) stem, stalk; (en métal) shaft, rod.

tigre /tigʀ/ nm tiger.

tigresse /tigʀɛs/ nf tigress.

tilleul /tijœl/ nm lime tree.

timbre /tɛ̃bʀ/ nm stamp; (sonnette) bell; (de voix) tone. ~ **poste** (pl ~s poste) nm postage stamp. **timbrer** ⚠ vt stamp.

timide /timid/ adj shy, timid. **timidité** nf shyness.

timoré, ~e /timɔʀe/ adj timorous.

tintement /tɛ̃tmɑ̃/ nm (de sonnette) ringing; (de clés) jingling.

tique /tik/ nf tick.

tir /tiʀ/ nm (Sport) shooting; (action de tirer) firing; (feu, rafale) fire; ~ **à l'arc** archery; ~ **au pigeon** clay pigeon shooting.

tirage /tiʀaʒ/ nm (de photo) printing; (de journal) circulation; (de livre) edition; (Ordinat) hard copy; (de cheminée) draught; ~ **au sort** draw.

tire-bouchon (pl ~s) /tiʀbuʃɔ̃/ nm corkscrew.

tirelire /tiʀliʀ/ nf piggy bank.

tirer /tiʀe/ ① vt pull; (langue) stick out; (conclusion, trait, rideaux) draw; (coup de feu) fire; (gibier) shoot; (photo) print; ~ **de** (sortir) take ou get out of; (extraire) extract from; (plaisir, nom) derive from; ~ **parti de** take advantage of; ~ **profit de** profit from; **se faire ~ l'oreille** get told off. ● vi shoot, fire (sur at); ~ **sur** (corde) pull at; (couleur) verge on; **à sa fin** be drawing to a close; ~ **au clair** clarify; ~ **au sort** draw lots (for). □ **se ~** vpr ⚠ clear off; **se ~ de** get out of; **s'en ~** (en réchapper) pull through; (réussir ⚠) cope.

tiret /tiʀɛ/ nm dash.

tireur /tiʀœʀ/ nm gunman; ~ **d'élite** marksman; ~ **isolé** sniper.

tiroir /tiʀwaʀ/ nm drawer. **tiroircaisse** (pl **tiroirs-caisses**) nm till, cash register.

tisane /tizan/ nf herbal tea.

tissage /tisaʒ/ nm weaving. **tisser** ⚠ vt weave. **tisserand** nm weaver.

tissu /tisy/ nm fabric, material; (biologique) tissue; **un ~ de mensonges** (fig) a pack of lies. **tissu-éponge** (pl **tissus-éponge**) nm towelling.

titre /titʀ/ nm title; (diplôme) qualification; (Comm) bond; ~s (droits) claims; (gros) ~s headlines; **à ~ d'exemple** as an example; **à juste ~**

rightly; **à ~ privé** in a private capacity; **à double ~** on two accounts; **~ de propriété** title deed.

tituber /titybe/ **1** vi stagger.

titulaire /titylɛʀ/ adj **être ~** be a permanent staff member; **être ~ de** hold. ● nmf (de permis) holder. **titulariser** **1** vt give permanent status to.

toast /tost/ nm (pain) piece of toast; (canapé, allocution) toast.

toboggan /tɔbɔgɑ̃/ nm (de jeu) slide; (Auto) flyover.

toi /twa/ pron you; (réfléchi) yourself; **dépêche-~** hurry up.

toile /twal/ nf cloth; (tableau) canvas; **~ d'araignée** cobweb; **~ de fond** (fig) backdrop; **la ~** (Internet) the Web.

toilette /twalɛt/ nf (habillement) outfit; **~s** (cabinets) toilet(s); **de ~** (articles, savon) toilet; **faire sa ~** have a wash.

toi-même /twamɛm/ pron yourself.

toit /twa/ nm roof; **~ ouvrant** (Auto) sunroof.

toiture /twatyʀ/ nf roof.

tôle /tol/ nf (plaque) iron sheet; **~ ondulée** corrugated iron.

tolérant, ~e /tɔleʀɑ̃, -t/ adj tolerant. **tolérer** **14** vt tolerate.

tomate /tɔmat/ nf tomato.

tombe /tɔ̃b/ nf grave; (pierre) gravestone.

tombeau (pl **~x**) /tɔ̃bo/ nm tomb.

tomber /tɔ̃be/ **1** vi (aux être) fall; (fièvre, vent) drop; **faire ~** knock over; (gouvernement) bring down; **laisser ~** (objet, amoureux) drop; (collègue) let down; (activité) give up; **laisse ~!** forget it!; **~ à l'eau** (projet) fall through; **~ bien** ou **à point** come at the right time; **~ en panne** break down; **~ en syncope** faint; **~ sur** (trouver) run across.

tombola /tɔ̃bɔla/ nf tombola; (US) lottery.

tome /tɔm/ nm volume.

ton¹, ta (**ton** before vowel or mute h) (pl **tes**) /tɔ̃, ta, tɔ̃n, te/ adj your.

ton² /tɔ̃/ nm (hauteur de voix) pitch; **d'un ~ sec** drily; **de bon ~** in good taste.

tonalité /tɔnalite/ nf (Mus) key; (de téléphone) dialling tone; (US) dial tone.

tondeuse /tɔ̃døz/ nf (à moutons) shears (+ pl); (à cheveux) clippers (+ pl); **~ à gazon** lawn-mower. **tondre** **3** vt (herbe) mow; (mouton) shear; (cheveux) clip.

tonne /tɔn/ nf tonne.

tonneau (pl **~x**) /tɔno/ nm barrel; (en voiture) somersault.

tonnerre /tɔnɛʀ/ nm thunder.

tonton /tɔ̃tɔ̃/ nm **1** uncle.

tonus /tɔnys/ nm energy.

torche /tɔʀʃ/ nf torch.

torchon /tɔʀʃɔ̃/ nm (pour la vaisselle) tea towel.

tordre /tɔʀdʀ/ **3** vt twist. □ **se ~** vpr **se ~ la cheville** twist one's ankle; **se ~ de douleur** writhe in pain; **se ~ (de rire)** split one's sides.

tordu, ~e /tɔʀdy/ adj twisted, bent; (esprit) warped, twisted.

torpille /tɔʀpij/ nf torpedo.

torrent /tɔʀɑ̃/ nm torrent.

torride /tɔʀid/ adj torrid; (chaleur) scorching.

torse /tɔʀs/ nm chest; (Anat) torso.

tort /tɔʀ/ nm wrong; **avoir ~** be wrong (**de faire** to do); **donner ~ à** prove wrong; **être dans son ~** be in the wrong; **faire (du) ~ à** harm; **à ~** wrongly; **à ~ et à travers** without thinking.

torticolis /tɔʀtikɔli/ nm stiff neck.

tortiller /tɔʀtije/ **1** vt twist, twirl. □ **se ~** vpr wriggle.

tortionnaire /tɔʀsjɔnɛʀ/ nm torturer.

tortue /tɔʀty/ nf tortoise; (d'eau) turtle.

tortueux, -euse /tɔʀtɥø, -z/ adj (chemin) twisting; (explication) tortuous.

torture /tɔʀtyʀ/ nf torture. **torturer** **1** vt torture.

tôt /to/ adv early; **au plus ~** at the earliest; **le plus ~ possible** as soon as possible; **~ ou tard** sooner or later; **ce n'est pas trop ~!** it's about time!

total, ~e (mpl **-aux**) /tɔtal, -o/ adj total. ● nm (pl **-aux**) total; **au ~** all in all. **totalement** adv totally. **totaliser** **1** vt total. **totalitaire** adj totalitarian.

totalité /tɔtalite/ *nf* **la ∼ de** all of.

touche /tuʃ/ *nf* (de piano) key; (de peinture) touch; **(ligne de) ∼** (Sport) touchline.

toucher /tuʃe/ **1** *vt* touch; (émouvoir) move, touch; (contacter) get in touch with; (cible) hit; (argent) draw; (chèque) cash; (concerner) affect. ● *vi* **∼ à** touch; (question) touch on; (fin, but) approach; **je vais lui en ∼ deux mots** I'll talk to him about it. □ **se ∼** *vpr* (lignes) touch. ● *nm* (sens) touch.

touffe /tuf/ *nf* (de poils, d'herbe) tuft; (de plantes) clump.

toujours /tuʒuʀ/ *adv* always; (encore) still; (de toute façon) anyway; **pour ∼** for ever; **∼ est-il que** the fact remains that.

toupet /tupɛ/ *nm* (culot 🅸) cheek, nerve.

tour /tuʀ/ *nf* tower; (immeuble) tower block; (échecs) rook; **∼ de contrôle** control tower. ● *nm* (mouvement, succession, tournure) turn; (excursion) trip; (à pied) walk; (en auto) drive; (artifice) trick; (circonférence) circumference; (Tech) lathe; **∼ (de piste)** lap; **à ∼ de rôle** in turn; **à mon ∼** when it is my turn; **c'est mon ∼ de** it is my turn to; **faire le ∼ de** go round; (question) survey; **∼ d'horizon** overview; **∼ de potier** potter's wheel; **∼ de taille** waist measurement; (ligne) waistline.

> **Tour de France** The race for   🅸 professional cyclists held annually in July since 1903, when it was created by Henri Desgrange (1865-1940). Renowned for its mountain stages, it covers approximately 4,800 km (3,000 miles) over a three-week period, finishing triumphantly on the *Champs Élysées*. Throughout the *Tour*, the previous day's leader wears the coveted *maillot jaune* (yellow jersey).

tourbillon /tuʀbijɔ̃/ *nm* whirlwind; (d'eau) whirlpool; (fig) swirl.

tourisme /tuʀism/ *nm* tourism; **faire du ∼** do some sightseeing.

touriste /tuʀist/ *nmf* tourist. **touristique** *adj* tourist; (route) scenic.

tourmenter /tuʀmɑ̃te/ *vt* torment. □ **se ∼** *vpr* worry.

tournant, ∼e /tuʀnɑ̃, -t/ *adj* (qui pivote) revolving. ● *nm* bend; (fig) turning-point.

tourne-disque (*pl* ∼**s**) /tuʀnədisk/ *nm* record-player.

tournée /tuʀne/ *nf* (de facteur, au café) round; **c'est ma ∼** I'll buy this round; (d'artiste) tour.

tourner /tuʀne/ **1** *vt* turn; (film) shoot, make; **∼ le dos à** turn one's back on; **∼ en dérision** mock. ● *vi* turn; (toupie, tête) spin; (moteur, usine) run; **∼ autour de** go round; (personne, maison) hang around; (terre) revolve round; (question) centre on; **∼ de l'œil** 🅸 faint; **mal ∼** (affaire) turn out badly. □ **se ∼** *vpr* turn.

tournesol /tuʀnəsɔl/ *nm* sunflower.

tournevis /tuʀnəvis/ *nm* screwdriver.

tournoi /tuʀnwa/ *nm* tournament.

tourte /tuʀt/ *nf* pie.

tourterelle /tuʀtəʀɛl/ *nf* turtle dove.

Toussaint /tusɛ̃/ *nf* **la ∼** All Saints' Day.

tousser /tuse/ **1** *vi* cough.

tout, ∼e (*pl* **tous, toutes**) /tu, tut/ *nm* (ensemble) whole; **en ∼** in all; **pas du ∼!** not at all! ● *adj* all; (n'importe quel) any; **∼ le pays** the whole country, all the country; **∼e la nuit/ journée** the whole night/day; **∼ un paquet** a whole pack; **tous les jours** every day; **tous les deux ans** every two years; **∼ le monde** everyone; **tous les deux, toutes les deux** both of them; **tous les trois** all three (of them). ● *pron* everything; all; anything; **tous** /tus/, **toutes** all; **tous ensemble** all together; **prends ∼** take everything; **∼ ce que tu veux** everything you want. ● *adv* (très) very; (entièrement) all; **∼ au bout/début** right at the end/beginning; **∼ en marchant** while walking; **∼ à coup** all of a sudden; **∼ à fait** quite, completely; **∼ à l'heure** in a moment; (passé) a moment ago; **∼ au** *ou* **le long de** throughout; **∼ au plus/moins** at most/least; **∼ de même** all the same; **∼ de suite** straight away; **∼ entier** whole; **∼ neuf** brand new; **∼ nu** stark naked. **tout-à-l'égout** *nm inv* main drainage.

toutefois /tutfwa/ *adv* however.

tout(-)terrain /tuteʀɛ̃/ *adj inv* all terrain.

toux /tu/ *nf* cough.

toxicomane /tɔksikɔman/ *nmf* drug addict.

toxique /tɔksik/ *adj* toxic.

trac /tʀak/ *nm* **le ~** nerves; (Théât) stage fright.

tracas /tʀaka/ *nm* worry.

trace /tʀas/ *nf* (traînée, piste) trail; (d'animal, de pneu) tracks; **~s de pas** footprints.

tracer /tʀase/ 🔟 *vt* draw; (écrire) write; (route) open up.

trachée-artère /tʀaʃeaʀtɛʀ/ *nf* windpipe.

tracteur /tʀaktœʀ/ *nm* tractor.

tradition /tʀadisjɔ̃/ *nf* tradition. **traditionnel, ~le** *adj* traditional.

traducteur, -trice /tʀadyktœʀ, -tʀis/ *nm, f* translator. **traduction** *nf* translation.

traduire /tʀaduiʀ/ 🔢 *vt* translate; **~ en justice** take to court.

trafic /tʀafik/ *nm* (commerce, circulation) traffic.

trafiquant, ~e /tʀafikɑ̃, -t/ *nm, f* trafficker; (d'armes, de drogues) dealer.

trafiquer /tʀafike/ 🔟 *vi* traffic. ● *vt* 🔟 (moteur) fiddle with.

tragédie /tʀaʒedi/ *nf* tragedy. **tragique** *adj* tragic.

trahir /tʀaiʀ/ 🔢 *vt* betray. **trahison** *nf* betrayal; (Mil) treason.

train /tʀɛ̃/ *nm* (Rail) train; (allure) pace; **aller bon ~** walk briskly; **en ~ de faire** (busy) doing; **~ d'atterrissage** undercarriage; **~ électrique** (jouet) electric train set; **~ de vie** lifestyle.

traîne /tʀɛn/ *nf* (de robe) train; **à la ~** lagging behind.

traîneau (*pl* **~x**) /tʀɛno/ *nm* sleigh.

traînée /tʀɛne/ *nf* (trace) trail; (longue) streak; (femme: péj) slut.

traîner /tʀɛne/ 🔟 *vt* drag (along); **~ les pieds** drag one's feet. ● *vi* (pendre) trail; (rester en arrière) trail behind; (flâner) hang about; (papiers, affaires) lie around; **~ (en longueur)** drag on. □ **se ~** *vpr* (par terre) crawl.

traire /tʀɛʀ/ 🔢 *vt* milk.

trait /tʀɛ/ *nm* line; (en dessinant) stroke; (caractéristique) feature, trait;

~s (du visage) features; **avoir ~ à** relate to; **d'un ~** (boire) in one gulp; **~ d'union** hyphen; (fig) link.

traite /tʀɛt/ *nf* (de vache) milking; (Comm) draft; **d'une (seule) ~** in one go, at a stretch.

traité /tʀete/ *nm* (pacte) treaty; (ouvrage) treatise.

traitement /tʀɛtmɑ̃/ *nm* treatment; (salaire) salary; **~ de données** data processing; **~ de texte** word processing.

traiter /tʀete/ 🔟 *vt* treat; (affaire) deal with; (données, produit) process; **~ qn de lâche** call sb a coward. ● *vi* deal (avec with); **~ de** (sujet) deal with.

traiteur /tʀɛtœʀ/ *nm* caterer; (boutique) delicatessen.

traître, -esse /tʀɛtʀ, -ɛs/ *adj* treacherous. ● *nm, f* traitor.

trajectoire /tʀaʒɛktwaʀ/ *nf* path.

trajet /tʀaʒɛ/ *nm* (voyage) journey; (itinéraire) route.

trame /tʀam/ *nf* (de tissu) weft.

tramway /tʀamwɛ/ *nm* tram; (US) streetcar.

tranchant, ~e /tʀɑ̃ʃɑ̃, -t/ *adj* sharp; (fig) cutting. ● *nm* cutting edge; **à double ~** two-edged.

tranche /tʀɑ̃ʃ/ *nf* (rondelle) slice; (bord) edge; (d'âge, de revenu) bracket.

tranchée /tʀɑ̃ʃe/ *nf* trench.

trancher /tʀɑ̃ʃe/ 🔟 *vt* cut; (question) decide; (contraster) contrast (**sur** with).

tranquille /tʀɑ̃kil/ *adj* quiet; (esprit) at rest; (conscience) clear; **être/laisser ~** be/leave in peace; **tiens-toi ~!** be quiet! **tranquillisant** *nm* tranquillizer. **tranquilliser** 🔟 *vt* reassure. **tranquillité** *nf* (peace and) quiet; (d'esprit) peace of mind.

transcription /tʀɑ̃skʀipsjɔ̃/ *nf* transcription; (copie) transcript. **transcrire** 🔟 *vt* transcribe.

transe /tʀɑ̃s/ *nf* **en ~** in a trance.

transférer /tʀɑ̃sfeʀe/ 🔢 *vt* transfer.

transfert /tʀɑ̃sfɛʀ/ *nm* transfer; **~ d'appel** (au téléphone) call diversion.

transformation /tʀɑ̃sfɔʀmasjɔ̃/ *nf* change; transformation.

transformer /tʀɑ̃sfɔʀme/ 🔟 *vt* change; (radicalement) transform; (vê-

tement) alter. □ **se** ~ *vpr* change; (ra-dicalement) be transformed; (se) ~ **en** turn into.

transgénique /tʀɑ̃ʒenik/ *adj* genet-ically modified.

transiger /tʀɑ̃ziʒe/ ⁴⁰ *vi* compromise.

transiter /tʀɑ̃zite/ ❶ *vt/i* ~ **par** pass through.

transitif, -ive /tʀɑ̃zitif, -v/ *adj* tran-sitive.

translucide /tʀɑ̃slysid/ *adj* trans-lucent.

transmettre /tʀɑ̃smɛtʀ/ ⁴² *vt* (*savoir, maladie*) pass on; (*ondes*) transmit; (à la radio) broadcast. **transmission** *nf* transmission; (*radio*) broadcasting.

transparence /tʀɑ̃spaʀɑ̃s/ *nf* trans-parency. **transparent, ~e** *adj* trans-parent.

transpercer /tʀɑ̃spɛʀse/ ❿ *vt* pierce.

transpiration /tʀɑ̃spiʀasjɔ̃/ *nf* per-spiration. **transpirer** ❶ *vi* perspire.

transplanter /tʀɑ̃splɑ̃te/ ❶ *vt* (Bot, Méd) transplant.

transport /tʀɑ̃spɔʀ/ *nm* transport(a-tion); **durant le** ~ in transit; **les** ~**s** transport (+ *sg*); **les** ~**s en commun** public transport (+ *sg*). **transporter** /tʀɑ̃spɔʀte/ ❶ *vt* transport; (à la main) carry. **transporteur** *nm* haulier; (US) trucker.

transversal, ~e (*mpl* -**aux**) /tʀɑ̃svɛʀsal, -o/ *adj* cross, transverse.

trapu, ~e /tʀapy/ *adj* stocky.

traumatisant, ~e /tʀɔmatizɑ̃, -t/ *adj* traumatic. **traumatiser** *vt* ❶ trauma-tize. **traumatisme** *nm* trauma.

travail (*pl* -**aux**) /tʀavaj, -o/ *nm* work; (*emploi, tâche*) job; (*façonnage*) work-ing; **travaux** work (+ *sg*); (*routiers*) roadworks; ~ **à la chaîne** production line work; **travaux dirigés** (Scol) prac-tical; **travaux forcés** hard labour; **tra-vaux manuels** handicrafts; **travaux ménagers** housework.

travailler /tʀavaje/ ❶ *vi* work; (se dé-former) warp. ● *vt* (façonner) work; (étudier) work at *ou* on.

travailleur, -euse /tʀavajœʀ, -øz/ *nm, f* worker. ● *adj* hardworking.

travailliste /tʀavajist/ *adj* Labour. ● *nmf* Labour party member.

travers /tʀavɛʀ/ *nm* (défaut) failing; **à** ~ through; **au** ~ **(de)** through; **de** ~

(*chapeau, nez*) crooked; (*regarder*) askance; **j'ai avalé de** ~ it went down the wrong way; **en** ~ **(de)** across.

traversée /tʀavɛʀse/ *nf* crossing.

traverser /tʀavɛʀse/ ❶ *vt* cross; (transpercer) go (right) through; (*pé-riode, forêt*) go *ou* pass through.

traversin /tʀavɛʀsɛ̃/ *nm* bolster.

travesti /tʀavɛsti/ *nm* transvestite.

trébucher /tʀebyʃe/ ❶ *vi* stumble, trip (over); **faire** ~ trip (up).

trèfle /tʀɛfl/ *nm* (plante) clover; (car-tes) clubs.

treillis /tʀeji/ *nm* trellis; (en métal) wire mesh; (tenue militaire) combat uniform.

treize /tʀɛz/ *adj & nm* thirteen.

> **Treizième mois** An addition to an employee's salary, equal to his/her usual monthly payment, which some employees receive at the end of the calendar year.

tréma /tʀema/ *nm* diaeresis.

tremblement /tʀɑ̃bləmɑ̃/ *nm* shak-ing; ~ **de terre** earthquake. **trembler** ❶ *vi* shake, tremble; (lumière, voix) quiver.

tremper /tʀɑ̃pe/ ❶ *vt/i* soak; (plonger) dip; (acier) temper; **faire** ~ soak; ~ **dans** (fig) be mixed up. □ **se** ~ *vpr* (se baigner) have a dip.

tremplin /tʀɑ̃plɛ̃/ *nm* springboard.

trente /tʀɑ̃t/ *adj & nm* thirty; **se mettre sur son** ~ **et un** dress up; **tous les** ~-**six du mois** once in a blue moon.

trépied /tʀepje/ *nm* tripod.

très /tʀɛ/ *adv* very; ~ **aimé/estimé** much liked/esteemed.

trésor /tʀezɔʀ/ *nm* treasure; **le T** ~ **pu-blic** the revenue department.

trésorerie /tʀezɔʀʀi/ *nf* (bureaux) ac-counts department; (du Trésor public) revenue office; (argent) funds (+ *pl*); (gestion) accounts (+ *pl*). **trésorier, -ière** *nm, f* treasurer.

tressaillement /tʀesajmɑ̃/ *nm* quiver; start.

tresse /tʀɛs/ *nf* braid, plait.

trêve /tʀɛv/ *nf* truce; (fig) respite; ~ **de plaisanteries** that's enough joking.

tri /tʀi/ *nm* (classement) sorting; (sélec-tion) selection; **faire le** ~ **de** (classer) sort; (choisir) select; **centre de ~** sorting office.

triangle /tʀijɑ̃gl/ nm triangle.

tribal, ~e (mpl **-aux**) /tʀibal, -o/ adj tribal.

tribord /tʀibɔʀ/ nm starboard.

tribu /tʀiby/ nf tribe.

tribunal (mpl **-aux**) /tʀibynal, -o/ nm court.

tribune /tʀibyn/ nf (de stade) grandstand; (d'orateur) rostrum; (débat) forum; (d'église) gallery.

tribut /tʀiby/ nm tribute.

tributaire /tʀibytɛʀ/ adj ~ **de** dependent on.

tricher /tʀiʃe/ **1** vi cheat. **tricheur, -euse** nm, f cheat.

tricolore /tʀikɔlɔʀ/ adj three-coloured; (écharpe) red, white and blue; (équipe) French.

tricot /tʀiko/ nm (activité) knitting; (pull) sweater; **en ~** knitted; **~ de corps** vest; (US) undershirt. **tricoter** **1** vt/i knit.

trier /tʀije/ **45** vt (classer) sort; (choisir) select.

trimestre /tʀimɛstʀ/ nm quarter; (Scol) term. **trimestriel, ~le** adj quarterly; (bulletin) end-of-term.

tringle /tʀɛ̃gl/ nf rail.

trinquer /tʀɛ̃ke/ **1** vi clink glasses.

triomphant, ~e /tʀijɔ̃fɑ̃, -t/ adj triumphant. **triomphe** nm triumph. **triompher** **1** vi triumph (**de** over); (jubiler) be triumphant.

tripes /tʀip/ nfpl (mets) tripe (+ sg); (entrailles **1**) guts.

triple /tʀipl/ adj triple, treble. ● nm le **~** three times as much (**de** as). **triplés, -es** nm, fpl triplets.

tripot /tʀipo/ nm gambling den.

tripoter /tʀipɔte/ **1** vt **1** (personne) grope; (objet) fiddle with.

trisomique /tʀizɔmik/ adj être ~ have Down's syndrome.

triste /tʀist/ adj sad; (rue, temps, couleur) dreary; (lamentable) dreadful. **tristesse** nf sadness; dreariness.

trivial, ~e (mpl **-iaux**) /tʀivjal, -jo/ adj coarse.

troc /tʀɔk/ nm exchange; (Comm) barter.

trognon /tʀɔɲɔ̃/ nm (de fruit) core.

trois /tʀwa/ adj & nm three; **hôtel ~ étoiles** three-star hotel. **troisième** adj & nmf third.

trombone /tʀɔ̃bɔn/ nm (Mus) trombone; (agrafe) paperclip.

trompe /tʀɔ̃p/ nf (d'éléphant) trunk; (Mus) horn.

tromper /tʀɔ̃pe/ **1** vt deceive, mislead; (déjouer) elude. □ **se ~** vpr be mistaken; **se ~ de route/d'heure** take the wrong road/get the time wrong.

trompette /tʀɔ̃pɛt/ nf trumpet.

trompeur, -euse /tʀɔ̃pœʀ, -øz/ adj (apparence) deceptive.

tronc /tʀɔ̃/ nm trunk; (boîte) collection box.

tronçon /tʀɔ̃sɔ̃/ nm section.

tronçonneuse /tʀɔ̃sɔnøz/ nf chain saw.

trône /tʀon/ nm throne. **trôner** **1** vi (vase) have pride of place (**sur** on).

trop /tʀo/ adv (grand, loin) too; (boire, marcher) too much; **~ (de)** quantité) too much; (nombre) too many; **ce se-rait ~ beau** one should be so lucky; **de ~ en ~** too much; too many; **il a bu un verre de ~** he's had one too many; **se sentir de ~** feel one is in the way.

trophée /tʀɔfe/ nm trophy.

tropical, ~e (mpl **-aux**) /tʀɔpikal, -o/ adj tropical. **tropique** nm tropic.

trop-plein (pl **~s**) /tʀɔplɛ̃/ nm excess; (dispositif) overflow.

troquer /tʀɔke/ **1** vt exchange; (Comm) barter (**contre** for).

trot /tʀo/ nm trot; **aller au ~** trot. **trotter** **1** vi trot.

trotteuse /tʀɔtøz/ nf (de montre) second hand.

trottoir /tʀɔtwaʀ/ nm pavement; (US) sidewalk; **~ roulant** moving walkway.

trou /tʀu/ nm hole; (moment) gap; (lieu: péj) dump; **~ (de mémoire)** memory lapse; **~ de serrure** keyhole; **faire son ~** carve one's niche.

trouble /tʀubl/ adj (eau, image) unclear; (louche) shady. ● nm (émoi) emotion; **~s** (Pol) disturbances; (Méd) disorder (+ sg). **troubler** /tʀuble/ **1** vt disturb; (eau) make cloudy; (inquiéter) trouble. □ **se ~** vpr (personne) become flustered.

trouer /tRue/ **1** vt make a hole ou holes in; **mes chaussures sont trouées** my shoes have got holes in them.

troupe /tRup/ nf troop; (d'acteurs) company.

troupeau (pl ~x) /tRupo/ nm herd; (de moutons) flock.

trousse /tRus/ nf case, bag; **aux ~s de** hot on sb's heels; **~ de toilette** toilet bag.

trousseau (pl ~x) /tRuso/ nm (de clefs) bunch; (de mariée) trousseau.

trouver /tRuve/ **1** vt find; (penser) think; **il est venu me ~** he came to see me. **□ se ~** vpr (être) be; (se sentir) feel; **il se trouve que** it happens that; **si ça se trouve** maybe; **se ~ mal** faint.

truand /tRyã/ nm gangster.

truc /tRyk/ nm (moyen) way; (artifice) trick; (chose 🔢) thing. **trucage** nm (cinéma) special effect.

truffe /tRyf/ nf (champignon, chocolat) truffle; (de chien) nose.

truffer /tRyfe/ **1** vt (fig) fill, pack (**de** with).

truie /tRɥi/ nf (animal) sow.

truite /tRɥit/ nf trout.

truquer /tRyke/ **1** vt fix, rig; (photo) fake; (résultats) fiddle.

tsar /tsar/ nm tsar, czar.

tu /ty/ pron (parent, ami, enfant) you. **→TAIRE 47**

tuba /tyba/ nm (Mus) tuba; (Sport) snorkel.

tube /tyb/ nm tube.

tuberculose /tybɛRkyloz/ nf tuberculosis.

tuer /tɥe/ **1** vt kill; (d'une balle) shoot, kill; (épuiser) exhaust; **~ par balles** shoot dead. **□ se ~** vpr kill oneself; (accident) be killed.

tuerie /tyRi/ nf killing.

tue-tête: à ~ /atytɛt/ loc at the top of one's voice.

tuile /tɥil/ nf tile; (malchance 🔢) (stroke of) bad luck.

tulipe /tylip/ nf tulip.

tumeur /tymœR/ nf tumour.

tumulte /tymylt/ nm commotion; (désordre) turmoil.

tunique /tynik/ nf tunic.

Tunisie /tynizi/ nf Tunisia.

tunnel /tynɛl/ nm tunnel.

turbo /tyRbo/ adj turbo. ● nf (voiture) turbo.

turbulent, ~e /tyRbulã, -t/ adj boisterous, turbulent.

turc, -que /tyRk/ adj Turkish. ● nm (Ling) Turkish. **T~, -que** Turk.

turfiste /tyRfist/ nmf racegoer.

Turquie /tyRki/ nf Turkey.

tutelle /tytɛl/ nf (Jur) guardianship; (fig) protection.

tuteur, -trice /tytœR, -tRis/ nm, f (Jur) guardian. ● nm (bâton) stake.

tutoiement /tytwamã/ nm use of the 'tu' form. **tutoyer 31** vt address using the 'tu' form.

tuyau (pl ~x) /tɥijo/ nm pipe; (conseil 🔢) tip; **~ d'arrosage** hosepipe.

TVA abrév f (**taxe à la valeur ajoutée**) VAT.

tympan /tɛ̃pã/ nm ear-drum.

type /tip/ nm (genre, traits) type; (individu 🔢) bloke, guy; **le ~ même de a** classic example of. ● adj inv typical.

typique /tipik/ adj typical.

tyran /tiRã/ nm tyrant. **tyrannie** nf tyranny. **tyranniser** **1** vt oppress, tyrannize.

•••••••••••••••••••••••••••

Uu

•••••••••••••••••••••••••••

UE abrév f (**Union européenne**) European Union.

Ukraine /ykRɛn/ nf Ukraine.

ulcère /ylsɛR/ nm (Méd) ulcer.

ULM abrév m (**ultraléger motorisé**) microlight.

ultérieur, ~e /ylteRjœR/ adj later. **ultérieurement** adv later.

ultime /yltim/ adj final.

un, une /œ̃, yn/
● déterminant
••••➤ a; (devant voyelle) an; **~ animal** an animal; **~ jour** one day; **pas ~arbre** not a single tree; **il fait ~ froid!** it's so cold!

● *pronom*

····▸ one; **l'~ d'entre nous** one of us; **les ~s croient que...** some believe...

····▸ **la une** the front page.

····▸ **j'en veux une** I want one.

● *adjectif*

····▸ one, a, an; **j'ai ~ garçon et deux filles** I have a ou one boy and two girls; **il est une heure** it is one o'clock.

● *nom masculin & féminin*

····▸ **~ par ~** one by one.

unanime /ynanim/ *adj* unanimous.

unanimité /ynanimite/ *nf* unanimity; **à l'~** unanimously.

uni, **~e** /yni/ *adj* united; (*couple*) close; (*surface*) smooth; (*tissu*) plain.

unième /ynjɛm/ *adj* -first; **vingt et ~** twenty-first; **cent ~** one hundred and first.

unifier /ynifje/ 45 *vt* unify.

uniforme /ynifɔRm/ *nm* uniform. ● *adj* uniform. **uniformiser** 1 *vt* standardize. **uniformité** *nf* uniformity.

unilatéral, **~e** (*mpl* -**aux**) /ynilateRal, -o/ *adj* unilateral.

union /ynjɔ̃/ *nf* union; **l'U ~ européenne** the European Union.

unique /ynik/ *adj* (*seul*) only; (*prix, voie*) one; (*incomparable*) unique; **enfant ~** only child; **sens ~** oneway street. **uniquement** *adv* only, solely.

unir /yniR/ 2 *vt* unite. □ **s'~** *vpr* unite, join.

unité /ynite/ *nf* unit; (*harmonie*) unity; **~ centrale** (Ordinat) processor.

univers /yniveR/ *nm* universe.

universel, **~le** /yniveRsel/ *adj* universal.

universitaire /yniveRsiteR/ *adj* (*résidence*) university; (*niveau*) academic. ● *nmf* academic.

université /yniveRsite/ *nf* university.

uranium /yRanjɔm/ *nm* uranium.

urbain, **~e** /yRbɛ̃, -ɛn/ *adj* urban. **urbanisme** *nm* town planning.

urgence /yR3ɑ̃s/ *nf* (*cas*) emergency; (*de situation, tâche*) urgency; **d'~** (*mesure*) emergency; (*transporter*) urgently; **les ~s** casualty (+ *sg*). **urgent**, **~e** *adj* urgent.

urine /yRin/ *nf* urine. **urinoir** *nm* urinal.

urne /yRn/ *nf* (*électorale*) ballot box; (*vase*) urn; **aller aux ~s** go to the polls.

urticaire /yRtikeR/ *nf* hives (+ *pl*), urticar.

us /ys/ *nmpl* **les ~ et coutumes** habits and customs.

usage /yza3/ *nm* use; (*coutume*) custom; (*de langage*) usage; **à l'~** de for; **d'~** (*habituel*) customary; **faire ~ de** make use of.

usagé, **~e** /yza3e/ *adj* worn.

usager /yza3e/ *nm* user.

usé, **~e** /yze/ *adj* worn (out); (*banal*) trite.

user /yze/ 1 *vt* wear (out). ● *vi* **~ de** use. □ **s'~** *vpr* (*tissu*) wear (out).

usine /yzin/ *nf* factory, plant; **~ sidérurgique** ironworks (+ *pl*).

usité, **~e** /yzite/ *adj* common.

ustensile /ystãsil/ *nm* utensil.

usuel, **~le** /yzɥɛl/ *adj* ordinary, everyday.

usure /yzyR/ *nf* (*détérioration*) wear (and tear).

utérus /yteRys/ *nm* womb, uterus.

utile /ytil/ *adj* useful.

utilisable /ytilizabl/ *adj* usable. **utilisation** *nf* use. **utiliser** 1 *vt* use.

utopie /ytɔpi/ *nf* Utopia; (*idée*) Utopian idea. **utopique** *adj* Utopian.

UV[1] *abrév f* (**unité de valeur**) course unit.

UV[2] *abrév mpl* (**ultraviolets**) ultraviolet rays; **faire des ~** use a sunbed.

Vv

va /va/ ➡**ALLER** 8.

vacance /vakãs/ *nf* (*poste*) vacancy.

vacances /vakãs/ *nfpl* holiday(s); (US) vacation; **en ~** on holiday; **~ d'été**, **grandes ~** summer holidays. **vacancier**, **-ière** *nm*, *f* holidaymaker; (US) vacationer.

vacant, **~e** /vakã, -t/ *adj* vacant.

vacarme /vakaRm/ *nm* din.

vaccin /vaksɛ̃/ *nm* vaccine. **vacciner** 1 *vt* vaccinate.

vache /vaʃ/ *nf* cow. ● *adj* (méchant 🔲) nasty.

vaciller /vasije/ **1** *vi* sway, wobble; (*lumière*) flicker; (*hésiter*) falter; (*santé, mémoire*) fail.

vadrouiller /vadRuje/ **1** *vi* 🔲 wander about.

va-et-vient /vaevjɛ̃/ *nm inv* toing and froing; (*de personnes*) comings and goings; **faire le ∼** go to and fro; (interrupteur) two-way switch.

vagabond, ∼e /vagabɔ̃, -d/ *nm, f* vagrant.

vagin /vaʒɛ̃/ *nm* vagina.

vague /vag/ *adj* vague. ● *nm* **regarder dans le ∼** stare into space; **il est resté dans le ∼** he was vague about it. ● *nf* wave; **∼ de fond** ground swell; **∼ de froid** cold spell; **∼ de chaleur** heatwave.

vaillant, ∼e /vajɑ̃, -t/ *adj* brave; (vigoureux) strong.

vaille /vaj/ ➡VALOIR 🔲.

vain, ∼e /vɛ̃, vɛn/ *adj* vain, futile; **en ∼** in vain.

vaincre /vɛ̃kR/ 🔲 *vt* defeat; (surmonter) overcome. **vaincu, ∼e** *nm, f* (Sport) loser. **vainqueur** *nm* victor; (Sport) winner.

vais /vɛ/ ➡ALLER 🔲.

vaisseau (*pl* ∼**x**) /vɛso/ *nm* ship; (veine) vessel; **∼ spatial** spaceship.

vaisselle /vɛsɛl/ *nf* crockery; (à laver) dishes; **faire la ∼** do the washing-up, wash the dishes; **liquide ∼** washing-up liquid.

valable /valabl/ *adj* valid; (de qualité) worthwhile.

valet /valɛ/ *nm* (aux cartes) jack; (**∼ de chambre**) manservant.

valeur /valœR/ *nf* value; (mérite) worth, value; **∼s** (Comm) stocks and shares; **avoir de la ∼** be valuable; **prendre/perdre de la ∼** go up/down in value; **objets de ∼** valuables; **sans ∼** worthless.

valide /valid/ *adj* (personne) fit; (billet) valid. **valider** **1** *vt* validate.

valise /valiz/ *nf* (suit) case; **faire ses ∼s** pack (one's bags).

vallée /vale/ *nf* valley.

valoir /valwaR/ 🔲 *vi* (mériter) be worth; (égaler) be as good as; (être valable) (règle) apply; **faire ∼** (mérite,

qualité) emphasize; (terrain) cultivate; (droit) assert; **se faire ∼** put oneself forward; **∼ cher/100 euros** be worth a lot/100 euros; **que vaut ce vin?** what's this wine like?; **ne rien ∼** be useless *ou* no good; **ça ne me dit rien qui vaille** I don't like the sound of that; **∼ la peine** *or* **le coup** 🔲 be worth it; **il vaut/vaudrait mieux faire** it is worth/would be better to do. ● *vt* **∼ qch à qn** (éloges, critiques) earn sb sth; (admiration) win sb sth. □ **se ∼** *vpr* (être équivalents) be as good as each other; **ça se vaut** it's all the same.

valoriser /valɔRize/ **1** *vt* add value to; (produit) promote; (profession) make attractive; (région, ressources) develop.

valse /vals/ *nf* waltz.

vandale /vɑ̃dal/ *nmf* vandal.

vanille /vanij/ *nf* vanilla.

vanité /vanite/ *nf* vanity. **vaniteux, -euse** *adj* vain, conceited.

vanne /van/ *nf* (d'écluse) sluicegate; (propos 🔲) dig 🔲

vantard, ∼e /vɑ̃taR, -d/ *adj* boastful. ● *nm, f* boaster.

vanter /vɑ̃te/ **1** *vt* praise. □ **se ∼** *vpr* boast (**de** about); **se ∼ de faire** pride oneself on doing.

vapeur /vapœR/ *nf* (eau) steam; (brume, émanation) vapour; **∼s** fumes; **à ∼** (bateau, locomotive) steam; **faire cuire à la ∼** steam.

vaporisateur /vapɔRizatœR/ *nm* spray, atomizer. **vaporiser** **1** *vt* spray.

varappe /vaRap/ *nf* rock-climbing.

variable /vaRjabl/ *adj* variable; (temps) changeable.

varicelle /vaRisɛl/ *nf* chickenpox.

varié, ∼e /vaRje/ *adj* (non monotone, étendu) varied; (divers) various; **sandwichs ∼s** a selection of sandwiches.

varier /vaRje/ 🔲 *vt/i* vary.

variété /vaRjete/ *nf* variety; **spectacle de ∼s** variety show.

vase /vɑz/ *nm* vase. ● *nf* silt, mud.

vaseux, -euse /vɑzø, -z/ *adj* (confus 🔲) woolly, hazy.

vaste /vast/ *adj* vast, huge.

vaurien, ∼ne /voRjɛ̃, -ɛn/ *nm, f* good-for-nothing.

vautour /votuR/ *nm* vulture.

vautrer (se) /(sə)votʀe/ **1** *vpr* sprawl; **se ~ dans** (*vice, boue*) wallow in.

veau (*pl* **~x**) /vo/ *nm* calf; (*viande*) veal; (*cuir*) calfskin.

vécu, **~e** /veky/ *adj* (*réel*) true, real. ➡ VIVRE **82**.

vedette /vədɛt/ *nf* (*artiste*) star; **en ~** (*objet*) in a prominent position; (*personne*) in the limelight; **joueur ~** star player; (*bateau*) launch.

végétal (*mpl* **-aux**) /veʒetal, -o/ *adj* plant. ● *nm* (*pl* **-aux**) plant.

végétalien, **~ne** /veʒetaljɛ̃, -ɛn/ *adj* & *nm*, *f* vegan.

végétarien, **~ne** /veʒetaʀjɛ̃, -ɛn/ *adj* & *nm*, *f* vegetarian.

végétation /veʒetasjɔ̃/ *nf* vegetation; **~s** (Méd) adenoids.

véhicule /veikyl/ *nm* vehicle.

veille /vɛj/ *nf* (*état*) wakefulness; (*jour précédent*) **la ~ (de)** the day before; **la ~ de Noël** Christmas Eve; **à la ~ de** on the eve of; **la ~ au soir** the previous evening.

veillée /veje/ *nf* evening (gathering).

veiller /veje/ **1** *vi* stay up; (*monter la garde*) be on watch. ● *vt* (*malade*) watch over; **~ à** attend to; **~ sur** watch over.

veilleur /vɛjœʀ/ *nm* **~ de nuit** nightwatchman.

veilleuse /vɛjøz/ *nf* night light; (*de véhicule*) sidelight; (*de réchaud*) pilot light; **mettre qch en ~** put sth on the back burner.

veine /vɛn/ *nf* (Anat) vein; (*nervure, filon*) vein; (*chance* **1**) luck; **avoir de la ~** **1** be lucky.

véliplanchiste /veliplɑ̃ʃist/ *nmf* windsurfer.

vélo /velo/ *nm* bike; (*activité*) cycling; **faire du ~** go cycling; **~ tout terrain** mountain bike.

vélomoteur /velɔmɔtœʀ/ *nm* moped.

velours /v(ə)luʀ/ *nm* velvet; **~ côtelé** corduroy.

velouté, **~e** /vəlute/ *adj* smooth. ● *nm* (Culin) **~ d'asperges** cream of asparagus soup.

vendanges /vɑ̃dɑ̃ʒ/ *nfpl* grape harvest.

vendeur, **-euse** /vɑ̃dœʀ, -øz/ *nm*, *f* shop assistant; (*marchand*) salesman, saleswoman; (*jur*) vendor, seller.

vendre /vɑ̃dʀ/ **3** *vt* sell; **à ~** for sale. □ **se ~** *vpr* (être vendu) be sold; (trouver acquéreur) sell; **se ~ bien** sell well.

vendredi /vɑ̃dʀədi/ *nm* Friday; **V~ saint** Good Friday.

vénéneux, **-euse** /venenø, -z/ *adj* poisonous.

vénérer /veneʀe/ **14** *vt* revere.

vénérien, **~ne** /veneʀjɛ̃, -ɛn/ *adj* **maladie ~ne** venereal disease.

vengeance /vɑ̃ʒɑ̃s/ *nf* revenge, vengeance.

venger /vɑ̃ʒe/ **40** *vt* avenge. □ **se ~** *vpr* take *ou* get one's revenge (**de qch** for sth; **de qn** on sb).

vengeur, **-eresse** /vɑ̃ʒœʀ, -əʀɛs/ *adj* vengeful. ● *nm*, *f* avenger.

venimeux, **-euse** /vənimø, -z/ *adj* poisonous, venomous.

venin /vənɛ̃/ *nm* venom.

venir /vəniʀ/ **58** *vi* (*aux être*) come (**de** from); **faire ~ qn** send for sb, call sb; **en ~ à** come to; **en ~ aux mains** come to blows; **où veut-elle en ~?** what is she driving at?; **il m'est venu à l'esprit** *or* **à l'idée que** it occurred to me that; **s'il venait à pleuvoir** if it should rain; **dans les jours à ~** in the next few days. ● *v aux* **~ de faire** have just done; **il vient/venait d'arriver** he has/had just arrived; **~ faire** come to do; **viens voir** come and see.

vent /vɑ̃/ *nm* wind; **il fait du ~** it is windy; **être dans le ~** **1** be trendy.

vente /vɑ̃t/ *nf* sale; **~ (aux enchères)** auction; **en ~** on *ou* for sale; **mettre qch en ~** put sth up for sale; **~ de charité** (charity) bazaar; **~ au détail/ en gros** retailing/wholesaling; **équipe de ~** sales team.

ventilateur /vɑ̃tilatœʀ/ *nm* fan, ventilator. **ventiler** **1** *vt* ventilate.

ventouse /vɑ̃tuz/ *nf* suction pad; (pour déboucher) plunger.

ventre /vɑ̃tʀ/ *nm* stomach; (d'animal) belly; (utérus) womb; **avoir du ~** have a paunch.

venu, **~e** /vəny/ *adj* **bien ~** (à propos) apt, timely; **mal ~** badly timed; **il serait mal ~ de faire** it wouldn't be a good idea to do. ● ➡ VENIR **59**

venue /vəny/ *nf* coming.

ver /vɛʀ/ nm worm; (dans la nourriture) maggot; (du bois) woodworm; **~ lui-sant** glow-worm; **~ à soie** silkworm; **~ solitaire** tapeworm; **~ de terre** earthworm.

verbal, ~e (mpl **-aux**) /vɛʀbal, -o/ adj verbal.

verbe /vɛʀb/ nm verb.

verdir /vɛʀdiʀ/ **2** vi turn green.

véreux, -euse /vɛʀø, -z/ adj wormy; (malhonnête) shady.

verger /vɛʀʒe/ nm orchard.

verglas /vɛʀɡla/ nm black ice.

véridique /veʀidik/ adj true.

vérification /veʀifikasjɔ̃/ nf check-(ing), verification.

vérifier /veʀifje/ **45** vt check, verify; (confirmer) confirm.

véritable /veʀitabl/ adj true, real; (authentique) real.

vérité /veʀite/ nf truth; (de tableau, roman) realism; **en ~** in fact, actually.

> **Verlan** A form of French slang which reverses the order of syllables in many common words. The term itself is derived from the word *l'envers* the syllables of which are reversed to create *vers-l'en* (*verlan*) . Single syllable words are also converted so *femme* becomes *meuf*, *mec* becomes *keum*, etc.

---

vermine /vɛʀmin/ nf vermin.

verni, ~e /vɛʀni/ adj (chaussures) patent (leather); (chanceux 🔟) lucky.

vernir /vɛʀniʀ/ **2** vt varnish. □ **se ~** vpr **se ~ les ongles** apply nail polish.

vernis /vɛʀni/ nm varnish; (de poterie) glaze; **~ à ongles** nail polish.

verra, verrait /vɛʀa, vɛʀɛ/ ➡**VOIR 64**.

verre /vɛʀ/ nm glass; (de lunettes) lens; **~ à vin** wine glass; **prendre** ou **boire un ~** have a drink; **~ de contact** contact lens; **~ dépoli** frosted glass.

verrière /vɛʀjɛʀ/ nf (toit) glass roof; (paroi) glass wall.

verrou /vɛʀu/ nm bolt; **sous les ~s** behind bars.

verrouillage /vɛʀujaz/ nm **~ central** or **centralisé (des portes)** central locking.

verrue /vɛʀy/ nf wart; **~ plantaire** verruca.

vers¹ /vɛʀ/ prép towards; (aux environs de) (temps) about; (lieu) near, around; (période) towards; **~ le soir** towards evening.

vers² /vɛʀ/ nm (poésie) line of verse.

versatile /vɛʀsatil/ adj unpredictable, volatile.

verse: à ~ /avɛʀs/ loc in torrents.

Verseau /vɛʀso/ nm **le ~** Aquarius.

versement /vɛʀsəmɑ̃/ nm payment; (échelonné) instalment.

verser /vɛʀse/ **1** vt/i pour; (larmes, sang) shed; (payer) pay. ● vi pour; (voiture) overturn; **~ dans** (fig) lapse into.

version /vɛʀsjɔ̃/ nf version; (traduction) translation.

verso /vɛʀso/ nm back (of the page); **voir au ~** see overleaf.

vert, ~e /vɛʀ, -t/ adj green; (vieillard) sprightly. ● nm green; **les ~s** the Greens.

vertèbre /vɛʀtɛbʀ/ nf vertebra; **se déplacer une ~** slip a disc.

vertical, ~e (mpl **-aux**) /vɛʀtikal, -o/ adj vertical.

vertige /vɛʀtiʒ/ nm dizziness; **~s** dizzy spells; **avoir le ~** feel dizzy. **vertigineux, -euse** adj dizzy; (très grand) staggering.

vertu /vɛʀty/ nf virtue; **en ~ de** in accordance with. **vertueux, -euse** adj virtuous.

verveine /vɛʀvɛn/ nf verbena.

vessie /vesi/ nf bladder.

veste /vɛst/ nf jacket.

vestiaire /vɛstjɛʀ/ nm cloakroom; (Sport) changing-room; (US) locker-room.

vestibule /vɛstibyl/ nm hall; (Théât, d'hôtel) foyer.

vestige /vɛstiʒ/ nm (objet) relic; (trace) vestige.

veston /vɛstɔ̃/ nm jacket.

vêtement /vɛtmɑ̃/ nm article of clothing; **~s** clothes, clothing.

vétéran /veteʀɑ̃/ nm veteran.

vétérinaire /veteʀinɛʀ/ nmf vet, veterinary surgeon, (US) veterinarian.

vêtir /vetiʀ/ **61** vt dress. □ **se ~** vpr dress.

veto /veto/ nm inv veto.

vêtu, ~e /vety/ adj dressed (**de** in).

veuf, veuve /vœf, -vœf/ adj widowed. ● nm, f widower, widow.

veuille /vœj/ →VOULOIR 64.

veut, veux /vø/ →VOULOIR 64.

vexation /vɛksasjɔ̃/ nf humiliation.

vexer /vɛkse/ 1 vt upset, hurt. □ **se ~** vpr be upset, be hurt.

viable /vjabl/ adj viable; (projet) feasible.

viande /vjɑ̃d/ nf meat.

vibrer /vibʀe/ 1 vi vibrate; **faire ~** (âme, foules) stir.

vicaire /vikɛʀ/ nm curate.

vice /vis/ nm (moral) vice; (physique) defect.

vicier /visje/ 45 vt contaminate; (air) pollute.

vicieux, -ieuse /visjø, -z/ adj depraved. ● nm, f pervert.

victime /viktim/ nf victim; (d'un accident) casualty.

victoire /viktwaʀ/ nf victory; (Sport) win. **victorieux, -ieuse** adj victorious; (équipe) winning.

vidange /vidɑ̃ʒ/ nf emptying; (Auto) oil change; (tuyau) waste pipe ou outlet.

vide /vid/ adj empty. ● nm (absence, manque) vacuum, void; (espace) space; (trou) gap; (sans air) vacuum; **à ~** empty; **emballé sous ~** vacuum packed; **suspendu dans le ~** dangling in space.

vide-greniers /vidgʀənje/ nm inv bric-a-brac sale.

vidéo /video/ adj inv video; **jeu ~** video game. ● nf video.

vidéocassette nf video (tape).

vidéoclip nm music video.

vidéoconférence nf videoconferencing; (séance) videoconference. **vidéodisque** nm videodisc. **vidéophone** nm videophone.

vide-ordures /vidɔʀdyʀ/ nm inv rubbish chute.

vidéothèque /videotɛk/ nf video library.

vider /vide/ 1 vt empty; (poisson) gut; (expulser 1) throw out. □ **se ~** vpr empty.

vie /vi/ nf life; (durée) lifetime; **à ~, pour la ~** for life; **donner la ~ à** give birth to; **en ~** alive; **la ~ est chère** the cost of living is high.

vieil /vjɛj/ →VIEUX.

vieillard /vjɛjaʀ/ nm old man.

vieille /vjɛj/ →VIEUX.

vieillesse /vjɛjɛs/ nf old age.

vieillir /vjɛjiʀ/ 2 vi grow old, age; (mot, idée) become old-fashioned. ● vt age. **vieillissement** nm ageing.

viens, vient /vjɛ̃/ →VENIR 59.

vierge /vjɛʀʒ/ nf virgin; **la V~** Virgo. ● adj virgin; (feuille, cassette) blank; (cahier, pellicule) unused, new.

vieux (**vieil** before vowel or mute h), **vieille** (mpl **vieux**) /vjø, vjɛj/ adj old. ● nm, f old man, old woman; **petit ~** little old man; **les ~** old people; **vieille fille** (péj) spinster; **~ garçon** old bachelor. **vieux jeu** adj inv old-fashioned.

vif, vive /vif, viv/ adj (animé) lively; (émotion, vent) keen; (froid) biting; (lumière) bright; (douleur, contraste, parole) sharp; (souvenir, style, teint) vivid; (succès, impatience) great; **brûler/ enterrer ~** burn/bury alive; **de vive voix** personally. ● nm **à ~** (plaie) open; **avoir les nerfs à ~** be on edge; **blessé au ~** cut to the quick.

vigie /viʒi/ nf lookout.

vigilant, ~e /viʒilɑ̃, -t/ adj vigilant.

Vigipirate /viʒipiʀat/ nm government public security measures.

vigne /viɲ/ nf (plante) vine; (vignoble) vineyard. **vigneron, ~ne** nm, f wine-grower.

vignette /viɲɛt/ nf (étiquette) label; (Auto) road tax disc.

vignoble /viɲɔbl/ nm vineyard.

vigoureux, -euse /viguʀø, -z/ adj vigorous, sturdy.

vigueur /vigœʀ/ nf vigour; **être/ entrer en ~** (loi) be/come into force; **en ~** current.

VIH abrév m (**virus immunodéficitaire humain**) HIV.

vilain, ~e /vilɛ̃, -ɛn/ adj (mauvais) nasty; (laid) ugly. ● nm, f naughty boy, naughty girl.

villa /villa/ nf detached house.

village /vilaʒ/ nm village.

villageois, ~e /vilaʒwa, -z/ adj village. ● nm, f villager.

ville /vil/ nf town; (importante) city; ~ **d'eaux** spa.

vin /vɛ̃/ nm wine; ~ **d'honneur** reception.

vinaigre /vinɛɡʀ/ nm vinegar. **vinaigrette** nf oil and vinegar dressing, vinaigrette.

vingt /vɛ̃/ (/vɛ̃t/ before vowel and in numbers 22-29) adj & nm twenty.

vingtaine /vɛ̃tɛn/ nf **une** ~ **(de)** about twenty.

vingtième /vɛ̃tjɛm/ adj & nmf twentieth.

vinicole /vinikɔl/ adj wine(-producing).

viol /vjɔl/ nm (de femme) rape; (de lieu, loi) violation.

violemment /vjɔlamɑ̃/ adv violently.

violence /vjɔlɑ̃s/ nf violence; (acte) act of violence. **violent,** ~e adj violent.

violer /vjɔle/ **1** vt rape; (lieu, loi) violate.

violet, ~te /vjɔlɛ, -t/ adj purple. ● nm purple. **violette** nf violet.

violon /vjɔlɔ̃/ nm violin; ~ **d'Ingres** hobby.

violoncelle /vjɔlɔ̃sɛl/ nm cello.

vipère /vipɛʀ/ nf viper, adder.

virage /viʀaʒ/ nm bend; (en ski) turn; (changement d'attitude: fig) change of course.

virée /viʀe/ nf **1** trip, tour; (en voiture) drive; (à vélo) ride.

virement /viʀmɑ̃/ nm (Comm) (credit) transfer; ~ **automatique** standing order.

virer /viʀe/ **1** vi turn; ~ **de bord** tack; (fig) do a U-turn; ~ **au rouge** turn red. ● vt (argent) transfer; (expulser **1**) throw out; (élève) expel; (licencier **1**) fire.

virgule /viʀɡyl/ nf comma; (dans un nombre) (decimal) point.

viril, ~e /viʀil/ adj virile.

virtuel, ~le /viʀtɥɛl/ adj (potentiel) potential; (mémoire, réalité) virtual.

virulent, ~e /viʀylɑ̃, -t/ adj virulent.

virus /viʀys/ nm virus.

vis[1] /vi/ ➡VIVRE **62**, ➡VOIR **63**.

vis[2] /vis/ nf screw.

visa /viza/ nm visa.

visage /vizaʒ/ nm face.

vis-à-vis /vizavi/ prép ~ **de** (en face de) opposite; (à l'égard de) in relation to; (comparé à) compared to, beside. ● nm inv (personne) person opposite; **en** ~ opposite each other.

visée /vize/ nf aim; **avoir des** ~**s sur** have designs on.

viser /vize/ **1** vt (cible, centre) aim at; (poste, résultats) aim for; (concerner) be aimed at; (document) stamp; ~ **à** aim at; (mesure, propos) be aimed at; ~ **à faire** aim to do. ● vi aim.

viseur /vizœʀ/ nm (d'arme) sights (+ pl); (Photo) viewfinder.

visière /vizjɛʀ/ nf (de casquette) peak; (de casque) visor.

vision /vizjɔ̃/ nf vision.

visite /vizit/ nf visit; (pour inspecter) inspection; (personne) visitor; **heures de** ~ visiting hours; ~ **guidée** guided tour; ~ **médicale** medical; **rendre** ~ **à, faire une** ~ **à** pay a visit; **être en** ~ **(chez qn)** be visiting (sb); **avoir de la** ~ have visitors.

visiter /vizite/ **1** vt visit; (appartement) view. **visiteur, -euse** nm, f visitor.

visser /vise/ vt screw (on).

visuel, ~le /vizɥɛl/ adj visual. ● nm (Ordinat) visual display unit, VDU.

vit /vi/ ➡VIVRE **62**, ➡VOIR **63**.

vital, ~e (mpl -aux) /vital, -o/ adj vital.

vitamine /vitamin/ nf vitamin.

vite /vit/ adv fast, quickly; (tôt) soon; ~**!** quick!; **faire** ~ be quick; **au plus** ~, **le plus** ~ **possible** as quickly as possible.

vitesse /vitɛs/ nf speed; (régime: Auto) gear; **à toute** ~ at top speed; **en** ~ in a hurry, quickly; **boîte à cinq** ~**s** five-speed gearbox.

viticole /vitikɔl/ adj (industrie) wine; (région) wine-producing. **viticulteur** nm wine-grower.

vitrage /vitʀaʒ/ nm (vitres) windows; **double** ~ double glazing.

vitrail (pl -aux) /vitʀaj, -o/ nm stained-glass window.

vitre /vitʀ/ nf (window) pane; (de véhicule) window.

vitrine /vitʀin/ nf (shop) window; (meuble) display cabinet.

vivace /vivas/ adj (plante) perennial; (durable) enduring.

vivacité /vivasite/ nf liveliness; (agilité) quickness; (d'émotion, d'intelligence) keenness; (de souvenir, style, teint) vividness.

vivant, ~e /vivã, -t/ adj (example, symbole) living; (en vie) alive, living; (actif, vif) lively. ● nm un bon ~ a bon viveur; **de son ~** in his lifetime; **les ~s** the living.

vive[1] /viv/ →VIF.

vive[2] /viv/ interj ~ le roi! long live the king!

vivement /vivmã/ adv (fortement) strongly; (vite, sèchement) sharply; (avec éclat) vividly; (beaucoup) greatly; ~ la fin! I'll be glad when it's the end!

vivier /vivje/ nm fish pond; (arti- ficiel) fish tank.

vivifier /vivifje/ 45 vt invigorate.

vivre /vivʀ/ 63 vi live; ~ de (nourri- ture) live on; ~ encore be still alive; **faire ~** (famille) support. ● vt (vie) live; (période, aventure) live through.

vivres /vivʀ/ nmpl supplies.

VO abrév f (version originale) en ~ in the original language.

vocabulaire /vɔkabylɛʀ/ nm vo- cabulary.

vocal, ~e (mpl -aux) /vɔkal, -o/ adj vocal.

vœu (pl ~x) /vø/ nm (souhait) wish; (promesse) vow; **meilleurs ~x** best wishes.

vogue /vɔg/ nf fashion, vogue; **en ~** in fashion ou vogue.

voguer /vɔge/ 1 vi sail.

voici /vwasi/ prép here is, this is; (au pluriel) here are, these are; **me ~** here I am; ~ un an (temps passé) a year ago; ~ un an que it is a year since.

voie /vwa/ nf (route) road; (partie de route) lane; (chemin) way; (moyen) means, way; (rails) track; (quai) plat- form; **en ~ de** in the process of; **en ~ de développement** (pays) develop- ing; **espèce en ~ de disparition** en- dangered species; **par la ~ des airs** by air; **par ~ orale** orally; **sur la bonne/mauvaise ~** (fig) on the right/ wrong track; **montrer la ~** lead the

way; ~ **de dégagement** slip-road; ~ **ferrée** railway; (US) railroad; **V ~ lac- tée** Milky Way; ~ **navigable** water- way; ~ **publique** public highway; ~ **sans issue** (sur panneau) no through road; (fig) dead end.

voilà /vwala/ prép there is, that is; (au pluriel) there are, those are; (voici) here is, here are; **le** ~ there he is; ~! right!; (en offrant qch) there you are!; ~ **un an** (temps passé) a year ago; ~ **un an que** it is a year since; **tu en veux?** en ~ do you want some? here you are; **en** ~ **des histoires!** what a fuss!; **et** ~ **que** and then.

voilage /vwalaʒ/ nm net curtain.

voile /vwal/ nf (de bateau) sail; (Sport) sailing. ● nm veil; (tissu léger) net.

voilé, ~e /vwale/ adj (allusion, femme) veiled; (flou) hazy.

voiler /vwale/ 1 vt (dissimuler) veil; (déformer) buckle. □ se ~ vpr (devenir flou) become hazy; (se déformer) (roue) buckle.

voilier /vwalje/ nm sailing ship.

voir /vwaʀ/ 64 vt see; **faire** ~ qch à qn show sth to sb; **laisser** ~ show; **avoir quelque chose à** ~ **avec** have something to do with; **ça n'a rien à** ~ that's got nothing to do with it; **je ne peux pas le** ~ 1 I can't stand him. ● vi y ~ be able to see; **je n'y vois rien** I cannot see; ~ **trouble** have blurred vision; **voyons** let's see now; **voyons, soyez sages!** come on now, behave yourselves! □ se ~ vpr (dans la glace) see oneself; (être visi- ble) show; (se produire) be seen; (se trouver) find oneself; (se fréquenter, se rencontrer) see each other; (être vu) be seen.

voire /vwaʀ/ adv or even, not to say.

voirie /vwaʀi/ nf (service) highway maintenance.

voisin, ~e /vwazɛ̃, -in/ adj (de voisi- nage) neighbouring; (proche) nearby; (adjacent) next (de to); (semblable) similar (de to). ● nm, f neighbour; **le** ~ the man next door, the neighbour. **voisinage** nm neighbourhood; (proxi- mité) proximity.

voiture /vwatyʀ/ nf (motor) car; (wagon) coach, carriage; **en** ~! all aboard!; ~ **bélier** ramraiding car; ~ **à cheval** horse-drawn carriage; ~ **de**

course racing car; ~ **école** driving school car; ~ **d'enfant** pram; (US) baby carriage; ~ **de tourisme** saloon car.

voix /vwa/ *nf* voice; (*suffrage*) vote; **à** ~ **basse** in a whisper.

vol /vɔl/ *nm* (d'avion, d'oiseau) flight; (groupe d'oiseaux) flock, flight; (délit) theft; (hold-up) robbery; ~ **à l'étalage** shoplifting; ~ **à la tire** pickpocketing; **à** ~ **d'oiseau** as the crow flies; **de haut** ~ high-ranking; ~ **libre** hang-gliding; ~ **à voile** gliding.

volaille /vɔlaj/ *nf* **la** ~ (poules) poultry; **une** ~ **a** fowl.

volant /vɔlɑ̃/ *nm* (steering-)wheel; (de jupe) flounce; (de badminton) shuttlecock; **donner un coup de** ~ turn the wheel sharply.

volcan /vɔlkɑ̃/ *nm* volcano.

volée /vɔle/ *nf* flight; (oiseaux) flight, flock; (de coups, d'obus, au tennis) volley; **à toute** ~ hard; **à la** ~ in flight, in mid-air.

voler /vɔle/ **1** *vi* (*oiseau*) fly; (dérober) steal (**à** from). ● *vt* steal; ~ **qn** rob sb; **il ne l'a pas volé** he deserved it.

volet /vɔlɛ/ *nm* (de fenêtre) shutter; (de document) (folded *ou* tear-off) section; **trié sur le** ~ hand-picked.

voleur, -euse /vɔlœr, -øz/ *nm, f* thief; **au** ~**!** stop thief! ● *adj* thieving.

volley-ball /vɔlɛbol/ *nm* volleyball.

volontaire /vɔlɔ̃tɛr/ *adj* (délibéré) voluntary; (opiniâtre) determined. ● *nmf* volunteer. **volontairement** *adv* voluntarily; (exprès) intentionally.

volonté /vɔlɔ̃te/ *nf* (faculté, intention) will; (souhait) wish; (énergie) willpower; **à** ~ (comme on veut) as required; **du vin à** ~ unlimited wine; **bonne** ~ goodwill; **mauvaise** ~ ill will.

volontiers /vɔlɔ̃tje/ *adv* (de bon gré) with pleasure, willingly, gladly; (admettre) readily.

volt /vɔlt/ *nm* volt.

volte-face /vɔltəfas/ *nf inv* (fig) U-turn; **faire** ~ do a U-turn.

voltige /vɔltiʒ/ *nf* acrobatics (+ *pl*).

volume /vɔlym/ *nm* volume.

volumineux, -euse /vɔlyminø, -z/ *adj* bulky; (livre, dossier) thick.

volupté /vɔlypte/ *nf* voluptuousness.

vomi /vɔmi/ *nm* vomit.

vomir /vɔmir/ **2** *vt* vomit; (fig) belch out. ● *vi* be sick, vomit.

vomissement /vɔmismɑ̃/ *nm* vomiting; ~**s du matin** morning sickness.

vont /vɔ̃/ →**ALLER 8**.

vorace /vɔras/ *adj* voracious.

vos /vo/ →**VOTRE.**

votant, ~e /vɔtɑ̃, -t/ *nm, f* voter.

vote /vɔt/ *nm* (action) voting; (suffrage) vote; ~ **d'une loi** passing of a bill; ~ **par correspondance/procuration** postal/proxy vote.

voter /vɔte/ **1** *vi* vote. ● *vt* vote for; (adopter) pass; (crédits) vote.

votre (*pl* **vos**) /vɔtr, vo/ *adj* your.

vôtre /votr/ *pron* **le** ou **la** ~, **les** ~**s** yours.

vouer /vwe/ **1** *vt* (vie, temps) dedicate (**à** to); **voué à l'échec** doomed to failure.

vouloir /vulwar/ **64** *vt* (exiger) want (**faire** to do); (souhaiter) want; **que veux-tu boire?** what would you like to drink?; **je voudrais bien y aller** I'd really like to go; **je veux bien venir** I'm happy to come; **comme tu voudras** as you wish; (accepter) **veuillez vous asseoir** please sit down; **veuillez patienter** (au téléphone) please hold the line; (signifier) ~ **dire** mean; **qu'est-ce que cela veut dire?** what does that mean?; **en** ~ **à qn** bear a grudge against sb. □ **s'en** ~ *vpr* regret; **je m'en veux de lui avoir dit** I really regret having told her.

voulu, ~e /vuly/ *adj* (délibéré) intentional; (requis) required.

vous /vu/ *pron* (sujet, complément) you; (indirect) (to) you; (réfléchi) yourself; (pluriel) yourselves; (l'un l'autre) each other. **vous-même** *pron* yourself. **vous-mêmes** *pron* yourselves.

voûte /vut/ *nf* (plafond) vault; (porche) archway.

vouvoiement /vuvwamɑ̃/ *nm* use of the 'vous' form. **vouvoyer** **31** *vt* address using the 'vous' form.

voyage /vwajaʒ/ *nm* trip; (déplacement) journey; (par mer) voyage; ~**(s)** (action) travelling; ~ **d'affaires** business trip; ~ **d'études** study trip; ~ **de noces** honeymoon; ~ **organisé** (package) tour.

voyager /vwajaʒe/ 40 *vi* travel.

voyageur, -euse /vwajaʒœʀ, -øz/ *nm, f* traveller; (passager) passenger; **~ de commerce** travelling salesman.

voyant, ~e /vwajã, -t/ *adj* gaudy. ● *nm* (signal) (warning) light.

voyelle /vwajɛl/ *nf* vowel.

voyou /vwaju/ *nm* hooligan.

vrac: en ~ /ãvʀak/ *loc* (pêle-mêle) haphazardly; (sans emballage) loose; (en gros) in bulk.

vrai, ~e /vʀɛ/ *adj* true; (authentique) real. ● *nm* truth; **à ~ dire** to tell the truth; **pour de ~** for real. **vraiment** *adv* really.

vraisemblable /vʀɛsãblabl/ *adj* (probable) likely; (excuse, histoire) plausible. **vraisemblablement** *adv* probably. **vraisemblance** *nf* likelihood, plausibility.

vrombir /vʀɔ̃biʀ/ 2 *vi* roar.

VRP *abrév m* (**voyageur représentant placier**) rep, representative.

VTC *abrév m* (**vélo tous chemins**) hybrid bike.

VTT *abrév m* (**vélo tout terrain**) mountain bike.

vu, ~e /vy/ *adj* **bien ~** well thought of; **ce serait plutôt mal ~** it wouldn't go down well; **bien ~!** good point! ● *prép* in view of; **~ que** seeing that. ● →VOIR 64.

vue /vy/ *nf* (spectacle) sight; (vision) (eye) sight; (panorama, idée, image, photo) view; **avoir en ~** have in mind; **à ~** (tirer) on sight; (payable) at sight; **de ~** by sight; **perdre de ~** lose sight of; **en ~** (proche) in sight; (célèbre) in the public eye; **en ~ de faire** with a view to doing; **à ~ d'œil** visibly; **avoir des ~s sur** have designs on.

vulgaire /vylgɛʀ/ *adj* (grossier) vulgar; (ordinaire) common.

vulnérable /vylneʀabl/ *adj* vulnerable.

Ww

wagon /vagɔ̃/ *nm* (de voyageurs) carriage; (de marchandises) wagon. **wagon-lit** (*pl* **wagons-lits**) *nm* sleeper. **wagon-restaurant** (*pl* **wagons-restaurants**) *nm* restaurant car.

walkman® /wokman/ *nm* personal stereo, walkman®.

> ***i*** **Wallon** A regional Romance language spoken in southern Belgium (*Wallonie*) by approximately 600,000 *Wallons*. It belongs to the same linguistic family as the French language, and is sometimes considered a French dialect. *Wallon* should not be confused with Belgian French, which differs from the French of France in pronunciation and vocabulary only.

waters /watɛʀ/ *nmpl* toilets.

watt /wat/ *nm* watt.

wc /(dublə)vese/ *nmpl* toilet (+ *sg*).

Web /wɛb/ *nm* Web; **un site ~** a website; **une page ~** web page.

webcam /wɛbkam/ *nf* webcam.

webmestre /wɛbmɛstʀ/ *nm* webmaster.

week-end /wikɛnd/ *nm* weekend.

whisky (*pl* **-ies**) /wiski/ *nm* whisky.

Xx

xénophobe /gzenɔfɔb/ *adj* xenophobic. ● *nmf* xenophobe.

xérès /gzeʀɛs/ *nm* sherry.

xylophone /ksilɔfon/ *nm* xylophone.

Yy   Zz

 y /i/
● adverbe
····➤ there; (dessus) on it; (pluriel) on them; (dedans) in it; (pluriel) in them; **j'~ vais** I'm on my way; **n'~ va pas** don't go; **du lait? il n'~ en a pas** milk? there's none; **tu n'~ arriveras jamais** you'll never manage it.
● pronom
····➤ **s'~ habituer** get used to it.
····➤ **s'~ attendre** expect it.
····➤ **~ penser** think about it.
····➤ **~ être pour qch** have sth to do with it.

yaourt /'jauʀ(t) / nm yoghurt. **yaourtière** nf yoghurt-maker.
yard /'jaʀd/ nm yard (= 91,44 cm).
yen /'jɛn/ nm yen.
yeux /jø/ ➝**ŒIL.**
yoga /'jɔga/ nm yoga.
yougoslave /'jugɔslav/ adj Yugoslav. **Y~** nmf Yugoslav.
Yougoslavie /'jugɔslavi/ nf Yugoslavia.
yo-yo® /'jojo/ nm inv yo-yo®.

zapper /zape/ ❶ vi (à la télévision) channel-hop.
zèbre /zɛbʀ/ nm zebra.
zèle /zɛl/ nm zeal.
zéro /zeʀo/ nm nought, zero; (température) zero; (Sport) nil; (tennis) love; (personne) nonentity; **partir de ~** start from scratch; **repartir à ~** start all over again.
zeste /zɛst/ nm peel; **un ~ de** (fig) a touch of.
zézayer /zezeje/ ❸ vi lisp.
zigzag /zigzag/ nm zigzag; **en ~** winding.
zinc /zɛ̃g/ nm (métal) zinc; (comptoir ❶) bar.
zizanie /zizani/ nf discord; **semer la ~** put the cat among the pigeons.
zizi /zizi/ nm ❶ willy.
zodiaque /zɔdjak/ nm zodiac.
zona /zona/ nm (Méd) shingles (+ sg).
zone /zon/ nf zone, area; (banlieue pauvre) slums; **~ bleue** restricted parking zone; **~ euro** eurozone; **~ de saisie** input box.
zoo /zo(o) / nm zoo.
zoom /zum/ nm zoom lens.
zut /zyt/ interj ❶ damn ❶.

a /eɪ, ə/ *determiner*

> **an** avant voyelle ou h muet.

> ➡️ For expressions such as **make a noise, make a fortune** ➡️**noise, fortune.**

····▸ un/une. ~ **tree** un arbre; ~ **chair** une chaise.

····▸ (per) **two euros** ~ **kilo** deux euros le kilo; **three times** ~ **day** trois fois par jour.

> ❗ When talking about what people do or are, **a** is not translated into French: **she's a teacher** *elle est professeur*; **he's a widower** *il est veuf.*

aback /əˈbæk/ *adv* **taken** ~ déconcerté.

abandon /əˈbændən/ *vt* abandonner. ● *n* abandon *m.*

abate /əˈbeɪt/ *vi* (*flood, fever*) baisser; (*storm*) se calmer. ● *vt* diminuer.

abbey /ˈæbɪ/ *n* abbaye *f.*

abbot /ˈæbət/ *n* abbé *m.*

abbreviate /əˈbriːvɪeɪt/ *vt* abréger. **abbreviation** *n* abréviation *f.*

abdicate /ˈæbdɪkeɪt/ *vt/i* abdiquer.

abdomen /ˈæbdəmən/ *n* abdomen *m.*

abduct /əbˈdʌkt/ *vt* enlever. **abductor** *n* ravisseur/-euse *m/f.*

abhor /əbˈhɔː(r)/ *vt* (*pt* **abhorred**) exécrer.

abide /əˈbaɪd/ *vt* supporter; ~ **by** respecter.

ability /əˈbɪlətɪ/ *n* capacité *f* (**to do** à faire); (*talent*) talent *m.*

abject /ˈæbdʒekt/ *adj* (*state*) misérable; (*coward*) abject.

ablaze /əˈbleɪz/ *adj* en feu.

able /ˈeɪbl/ *adj* (*skilled*) compétent; **be** ~ **to do** pouvoir faire; (*know how to*) savoir faire. **ably** *adv* avec compétence.

abnormal /æbˈnɔːml/ *adj* anormal. **abnormality** *n* anomalie *f.*

aboard /əˈbɔːd/ *adv* à bord. ● *prep* à bord de.

abode /əˈbəʊd/ *n* demeure *f*; **of no fixed** ~ sans domicile fixe.

abolish /əˈbɒlɪʃ/ *vt* abolir.

Aborigine /æbəˈrɪdʒənɪ/ *n* aborigène *mf* (d'Australie).

abort /əˈbɔːt/ *vt* faire avorter; (*Comput*) abandonner. ● *vi* avorter.

abortion /əˈbɔːʃn/ *n* avortement *m*; **have an** ~ se faire avorter.

abortive /əˈbɔːtɪv/ *adj* (*attempt*) avorté; (*coup*) manqué.

about /əˈbaʊt/ *adv* (*approximately*) environ; ~ **the same** à peu près pareil; **there was no-one** ~ il n'y avait personne. ● *prep* **it's** ~ ... il s'agit de ...; **what I like** ~ **her is** ce que j'aime chez elle c'est; **to wander** ~ **the streets** errer dans les rues; **how/what** ~ **some tea?** et si on prenait un thé?; **what** ~ **you?** et toi? ● *adj* **be** ~ **to do** être sur le point de faire; **be up and** ~ être debout. ~**-face,** ~**-turn** *n* (*fig*) volte-face *f inv.*

above /əˈbʌv/ *prep* au-dessus de; **he is not** ~ **lying** il n'est pas incapable de mentir; ~ **all** surtout. ● *adv* **the apartment** ~ l'appartement du dessus; **see** ~ voir ci-dessus. ~**-board** *adj* honnête. ~**-mentioned** *adj* susmentionné.

abrasive /əˈbreɪsɪv/ *adj* abrasif; (*manner*) mordant. ● *n* abrasif *m.*

abreast /əˈbrest/ *adv* de front; **keep** ~ **of** se tenir au courant de.

abroad /əˈbrɔːd/ *adv* à l'étranger.

abrupt /əˈbrʌpt/ *adj* (*sudden, curt*) brusque; (*steep*) abrupt. **abruptly** *adv* (*suddenly*) brusquement; (*curtly*) avec brusquerie.

abscess /ˈæbses/ *n* abcès *m.*

abseil /ˈæbseɪl/ *vi* descendre en rappel.

absence /ˈæbsəns/ *n* absence *f*; (*lack*) manque *m*; **in the** ~ **of** faute de.

absent /ˈæbsənt/ *adj* absent.

absentee /æbsənˈtiː/ *n* absent/-e *m/f.*

absent-minded *adj* distrait.

absolute /ˈæbsəluːt/ *adj* (*monarch, majority*) absolu; (*chaos, idiot*) véritable. **absolutely** *adv* absolument.

241

absolve | achieve

absolve /əb'zɒlv/ vt ~ sb of sth décharger qn de qch.

absorb /əb'zɔːb/ vt absorber.

abstain /əb'steɪn/ vi s'abstenir (from de).

abstract[1] /'æbstrækt/ adj abstrait. ● n (summary) résumé m; **in the** ~ dans l'abstrait.

abstract[2] /əb'strækt/ vt tirer.

absurd /əb'sɜːd/ adj absurde.

abundance /ə'bʌndəns/ n abondance f. **abundant** adj abondant. **abundantly** adv (entirely) tout à fait.

abuse[1] /ə'bjuːz/ vt (position) abuser de; (person) maltraiter; (insult) injurier.

abuse[2] /ə'bjuːs/ n (misuse) abus m (of de); (cruelty) mauvais traitement m; (insults) injures fpl.

abusive /ə'bjuːsɪv/ adj (person) grossier; (language) injurieux.

abysmal /ə'bɪzml/ adj épouvantable.

abyss /ə'bɪs/ n abîme m.

academic /ækə'demɪk/ adj (career) universitaire; (year) académique; (scholarly) intellectuel; (theoretical) théorique. ● n universitaire mf.

academy /ə'kædəmɪ/ n (school) école f; (society) académie f.

accelerate /ək'seləreɪt/ vi (speed up) s'accélérer; (Auto) accélérer. **accelerator** n accélérateur m.

accent[1] /'æksent/ n accent m.

accent[2] /æk'sent/ vt accentuer.

accept /ək'sept/ vt accepter. **acceptable** adj acceptable. **acceptance** n (of offer) acceptation f; (of proposal) approbation f.

access /'ækses/ n accès m. **accessible** adj accessible.

accessory /ək'sesərɪ/ adj accessoire. ● n (Jur) complice mf (to de).

accident /'æksɪdənt/ n accident m; (chance) hasard m; **by** ~ par hasard. **accidental** (death) accidentel; (meeting) fortuit. **accidentally** adv accidentellement; (by chance) par hasard.

acclaim /ə'kleɪm/ vt applaudir. ● n louanges fpl.

acclimatize /ə'klaɪmətaɪz/ vt/i (s')acclimater (to à).

accommodate /ə'kɒmədeɪt/ vt loger; (adapt to) s'adapter à; (satisfy) satisfaire. **accommodating** adj accommo-

dant. **accommodation** n logement m.

accompaniment /ə'kʌmpənɪmənt/ n accompagnement m. **accompany** vt accompagner.

accomplice /ə'kʌmplɪs/ n complice mf (in, to de).

accomplish /ə'kʌmplɪʃ/ vt accomplir; (objective) réaliser. **accomplished** adj très compétent. **accomplishment** n (feat) réussite f; (talent) talent m.

accord /ə'kɔːd/ vi concorder (with avec). ● vt accorder (sb sth qch à qn). ● n accord m; **of my own** ~ de moi-même.

accordance /ə'kɔːdəns/ n **in** ~ **with** conformément à.

according /ə'kɔːdɪŋ/ adv ~ **to** (principle, law) selon; (person, book) d'après. **accordingly** adv en conséquence.

accordion /ə'kɔːdɪən/ n accordéon m.

accost /ə'kɒst/ vt aborder.

account /ə'kaʊnt/ n (Comm) compte m; (description) compte-rendu m; **on** ~ **of** à cause de; **on no** ~ en aucun cas; **take into** ~ tenir compte de; **it's of no** ~ peu importe. □ ~ **for** (explain) expliquer; (represent) représenter. **accountability** n responsabilité f. **accountable** adj responsable (for de; to envers).

accountancy /ə'kaʊntənsɪ/ n comptabilité f. **accountant** n comptable mf. **accounts** npl comptabilité f, comptes mpl.

accumulate /ə'kjuːmjʊleɪt/ vt/i (s')accumuler.

accuracy /'ækjərəsɪ/ n (of figures) justesse f; (of aim) précision f; (of forecast) exactitude f. **accurate** adj juste, précis. **accurately** adv exactement, précisément.

accusation /ækjuː'zeɪʃn/ n accusation f.

accuse /ə'kjuːz/ vt accuser; **the** ~**d** l'accusé/-e m/f.

accustomed /ə'kʌstəmd/ adj accoutumé; **become** ~ **to** s'accoutumer à.

ace /eɪs/ n (card, person) as m.

ache /eɪk/ n douleur f. ● vi (person) avoir mal; **my leg** ~**s** ma jambe me fait mal.

achieve /ə'tʃiːv/ vt (aim) atteindre; (result) obtenir; (ambition) réaliser.

achievement n (feat) réussite f; (fulfilment) réalisation f (**of** de).

acid /'æsɪd/ adj & n acide (m). **acidity** n acidité f. **~ rain** n pluies fpl acides.

acknowledge /ək'nɒlɪdʒ/ vt (error, authority) reconnaître. (letter) accuser réception de. **acknowledgement** n reconnaissance f.

acne /'æknɪ/ n acné f.

acorn /'eɪkɔːn/ n (Bot) gland m.

acoustic /ə'kuːstɪk/ adj acoustique. **acoustics** npl acoustique f.

acquaint /ə'kweɪnt/ vt **~ sb with sth** mettre qn au courant de qch; **be ~ed with** (person) connaître. (fact) savoir. **acquaintance** n connaissance f.

acquire /ə'kwaɪə(r)/ vt acquérir; (habit) prendre.

acquit /ə'kwɪt/ vt (pt **acquitted**) (Jur) acquitter. **acquittal** n acquittement m.

acre /'eɪkə(r)/ n acre f; ≈ demi-hectare m.

acrid /'ækrɪd/ adj âcre.

acrimonious /ækrɪ'məʊnɪəs/ adj acrimonieux.

acrobat /'ækrəbæt/ n acrobate mf. **acrobatics** npl acrobaties fpl.

acronym /'ækrənɪm/ n acronyme m.

across /ə'krɒs/ adv & prep (side to side) d'un côté à l'autre (de); (on other side) de l'autre côté (**from** de); **go or walk ~** traverser; **lie ~ the bed** se coucher en travers du lit; **~ the world** partout dans le monde.

act /ækt/ n acte m; (Jur, Pol) loi f; **put on an ~** jouer la comédie. ● vi agir; (Theat) jouer; **~ as** servir de. ● vt (part, role) jouer.

acting /'æktɪŋ/ n (Theat) jeu m. ● adj (temporary) intérimaire.

action /'ækʃn/ n action f; (Mil) combat m; **out of ~** hors service; **take ~** agir.

activate /'æktɪveɪt/ vt (machine) faire démarrer; (alarm) déclencher.

active /'æktɪv/ adj actif; (volcano) en activité; **take an ~ interest in** s'intéresser activement à. **activist** n activiste mf. **activity** n activité f.

actor /'æktə(r)/ n acteur m. **actress** n actrice f.

actual /'æktʃʊəl/ adj réel; **the ~ words** les mots exacts; **in the ~ house** (the house itself) dans la maison elle-même. **actuality** n réalité f.

actually adv (in fact) en fait; (really) vraiment.

acute /ə'kjuːt/ adj (anxiety) vif; (illness) aigu; (shortage) grave; (mind) pénétrant.

ad /æd/ n (TV) pub f 🗓; small **~** petite annonce f.

AD abbr (Anno Domini) ap. J.-C.

adamant /'ædəmənt/ adj catégorique.

adapt /ə'dæpt/ vt/i (s')adapter (**to** à). **adaptability** n adaptabilité f. **adaptable** adj souple. **adaptation** n adaptation f. **adaptor** n (Electr) adaptateur m.

add /æd/ vt/i ajouter (**to** à); (in maths) additionner. □ **~ up** (facts, figures) s'accorder; **~ sth up** additionner qch; **~ up to** s'élever à.

adder /'ædə(r)/ n vipère f.

addict /'ædɪkt/ n toxicomane mf; (fig) accro mf 🗓.

addicted /ə'dɪktɪd/ adj **be ~** avoir une dépendance (**to** à); (fig) être accro 🗓 (**to** à). **addiction** n (Med) dépendance f (**to** à); passion f (**to** pour). **addictive** adj qui crée une dépendance.

addition /ə'dɪʃn/ n (item) ajout m; (in maths) addition f; **in ~** en plus. **additional** adj supplémentaire.

additive /'ædɪtɪv/ n additif m.

address /ə'dres/ n adresse f; (speech) discours m. ● vt (letter) mettre l'adresse sur; (crowd) s'adresser à; **~ sth to** adresser qch à. **addressee** n destinataire mf.

adequate /'ædɪkwət/ adj suffisant; (satisfactory) satisfaisant.

adhere /əd'hɪə(r)/ vi (lit, fig) adhérer (**to** à); **~ to** (policy) observer.

adjacent /ə'dʒeɪsnt/ adj contigu; **~ to** attenant à.

adjective /'ædʒɪktɪv/ n adjectif m.

adjoin /ə'dʒɔɪn/ vt être contigu à. **adjoining** adj (room) voisin.

adjourn /ə'dʒɜːn/ vt (trial) ajourner; **the session was ~ed** la séance a été levée. ● vi s'arrêter; (Parliament) lever la séance; **~ to** passer à.

adjust /ə'dʒʌst/ vt (level, speed) régler; (price) ajuster; (clothes) rajuster. ● vt/i **~ (oneself) to** s'adapter à. **adjustable** adj réglable. **adjustment** n (of rates) rajustement m; (of control) réglage m; (of person) adaptation f.

ad lib /ˌæd ˈlɪb/ vt/i (pt **ad libbed**) improviser.

administer /ədˈmɪnɪstə(r)/ vt administrer.

administration /ədˌmɪnɪˈstreɪʃn/ n administration f. **administrative** adj administratif. **administrator** n administrateur/-trice m/f.

admiral /ˈædmərəl/ n amiral m.

admiration /ˌædməˈreɪʃn/ n admiration f. **admire** vt admirer. **admirer** n admirateur/-trice m/f.

admission /ədˈmɪʃn/ n (to a place) entrée f; (confession) aveu m.

admit /ədˈmɪt/ vt (pt **admitted**) (acknowledge) reconnaître, admettre. (crime) avouer; (new member) admettre; ~ **to** reconnaître. **admittance** n entrée f. **admittedly** adv il est vrai.

ado /əˈduː/ n **without more** ~ sans plus de cérémonie.

adolescence /ˌædəˈlesns/ n adolescence f. **adolescent** n & a adolescent/-e m/f.

adopt /əˈdɒpt/ vt adopter. **adopted** adj (child) adoptif. **adoption** n adoption f. **adoptive** adj adoptif.

adorable /əˈdɔːrəbl/ adj adorable. **adoration** n adoration f. **adore** vt adorer.

adorn /əˈdɔːn/ vt orner.

adrift /əˈdrɪft/ adj & adv à la dérive.

adult /ˈædʌlt/ adj & n adulte (m/f).

adultery /əˈdʌltərɪ/ n adultère m.

adulthood /ˈædʌlthʊd/ n âge m adulte.

advance /ədˈvɑːns/ vt (sum) avancer; (tape, career) faire avancer; (interests) servir. ● vi (lit) avancer; (progress) progresser. ● n avance f; (progress) progrès m; **in**~ à l'avance. **advanced** adj avancé; (studies) supérieur.

advantage /ədˈvɑːntɪdʒ/ n avantage m; **take** ~ **of** profiter de; (person) exploiter. **advantageous** adj avantageux.

adventure /ədˈventʃə(r)/ n aventure f.

adventurer /ədˈventʃərə(r)/ n aventurier-ière m/f. **adventurous** adj aventureux.

adverb /ˈædvɜːb/ n adverbe m.

adverse /ˈædvɜːs/ adj défavorable.

advert /ˈædvɜːt/ n annonce f; (TV) pub f 🔲.

advertise /ˈædvətaɪz/ vt faire de la publicité pour; (car, house, job) mettre une annonce pour. ● vi faire de la publicité; (for staff) passer une annonce.

advertisement n publicité f; (in newspaper) annonce f. **advertiser** n annonceur m. **advertising** n publicité f.

advice /ədˈvaɪs/ n conseils mpl; **some** ~, **a piece of** ~ un conseil.

advise /ədˈvaɪz/ vt conseiller; (inform) aviser; ~ **against** déconseiller. **adviser** n conseiller/-ère m/f. **advisory** adj consultatif.

advocate[1] /ˈædvəkət/ n (Jur) avocat m; (supporter) partisan m.

advocate[2] /ˈædvəkeɪt/ vt recommander.

aerial /ˈeərɪəl/ adj aérien. ● n antenne f.

aerobics /eəˈrəʊbɪks/ n aérobic m.

aeroplane /ˈeərəpleɪn/ n avion m.

aerosol /ˈeərəsɒl/ n bombe f aérosol.

aesthetic /iːsˈθetɪk/ adj esthétique.

afar /əˈfɑː(r)/ adv **from** ~ de loin.

affair /əˈfeə(r)/ n (matter) affaire f; (romance) liaison f.

affect /əˈfekt/ vt affecter.

affection /əˈfekʃn/ n affection f. **affectionate** adj affectueux.

affinity /əˈfɪnətɪ/ n affinité f.

afflict /əˈflɪkt/ vt affliger.

affluence /ˈæfluəns/ n richesse f.

afford /əˈfɔːd/ vt avoir les moyens d'acheter; (provide) fournir; **can you** ~ **the time?** avez-vous le temps?

afloat /əˈfləʊt/ adj & adv (boat) à flot.

afoot /əˈfʊt/ adv **sth is** ~ il se prépare qch.

afraid /əˈfreɪd/ adj **be** ~ (frightened) avoir peur (of, to de; that que); (worried) craindre (that que); **I'm** ~ **I can't come** je suis désolé mais je ne peux pas venir.

Africa /ˈæfrɪkə/ n Afrique f.

African /ˈæfrɪkən/ n Africain/-e m/f. ● adj africain.

after /ˈɑːftə(r)/ adv & prep après; **soon** ~ peu après; **be** ~ **sth** rechercher qch; ~ **all** après tout. ● conj après que; ~ **doing** après avoir fait.

aftermath /ˈɑːftəmæθ/ n conséquences fpl (of de).

afternoon /ˌɑːftəˈnuːn/ n après-midi m or f inv; **in the** ~ (dans) l'après-midi.

after: ~ **shave** n après-rasage m. ~ **thought** n pensée f après coup.

afterwards /'ɑːftəwədz/ adv après, par la suite.

again /ə'geɪn/ adv encore; ~ **and** ~ à plusieurs reprises; **start** ~ recommencer; **she never saw him** ~ elle ne l'a jamais revu.

against /ə'geɪnst/ prep contre; ~ **the law** illégal.

age /eɪdʒ/ n âge m; (era) ère f, époque f; **I've been waiting for** ~**s** j'attends depuis des heures. ● vt/i (pres p **ageing**) vieillir.

aged¹ /'eɪdʒd/ adj ~ **six** âgé de six ans.

aged² /'eɪdʒɪd/ adj âgé.

ageism /'eɪdʒɪzəm/ n discrimination f en raison de l'âge.

agency /'eɪdʒɪzsɪ/ n agence f.

agenda /ə'dʒendə/ n ordre m du jour; (fig) programme m.

agent /'eɪdʒənt/ n agent m.

aggravate /'ægrəveɪt/ vt (make worse) aggraver; (annoy) exaspérer. **aggravation** n (worsening) aggravation f; (annoyance) ennuis mpl.

aggression /ə'greʃn/ n agression f. **aggressive** adj agressif. **aggressiveness** n agressivité f. **aggressor** n agresseur m.

agitate /'ædʒɪteɪt/ vt agiter.

ago /ə'gəʊ/ adv il y a; **a month** ~ il y a un mois; **long** ~ il y a longtemps; **how long** ~**?** il y a combien de temps?

agonize /'ægənaɪz/ vi se tourmenter (over à propos de). **agonized** adj angoissé. **agonizing** adj déchirant. **agony** n douleur f atroce; (mental) angoisse f.

agree /ə'griː/ vi être d'accord (on sur; with avec); ~ **to** consentir à; ~ **with** (approve of) approuver. ● vt être d'accord (that sur le fait que); (admit) convenir (that que); (date, solution) se mettre d'accord sur.

agreeable /ə'griːəbl/ adj agréable; **be** ~ (willing) être d'accord.

agreed /ə'griːd/ adj (time, place) convenu; **we're** ~ nous sommes d'accord.

agreement /ə'griːmənt/ n accord m; **in** ~ d'accord.

agricultural /ægrɪ'kʌltʃərəl/ adj agricole. **agriculture** n agriculture f.

aground /ə'graʊnd/ adv **run** ~ (ship) s'échouer.

ahead /ə'hed/ adv (in front) en avant, devant; (in advance) à l'avance; **be 10 points** ~ avoir 10 points d'avance; ~ **of time** en avance; **go** ~! allez-y!

aid /eɪd/ vt aider. ● n aide f; **in** ~ **of** au profit de.

aide /eɪd/ n aide mf.

Aids /eɪdz/ n (Med) sida m.

aim /eɪm/ vt (gun) braquer (at sur); **be** ~ **ed at sb** (campaign, remark) viser qn. ● vi ~ **for/at sth** viser qch; ~ **to do** avoir l'intention de faire. ● n but m; **take** ~ viser. **aimless** adj sans but.

air /eə(r)/ n air m; **by** ~ par avion; **on the** ~ à l'antenne. ● vt aérer; (views) exprimer. ● adj (base, disaster) aérien; (pollution, pressure) atmosphérique. ~ **bed** n matelas m pneumatique. ~ **conditioning** n climatisation f. ~**craft** n inv avion m. ~**craft carrier** n porte-avions m inv. ~**field** n terrain m d'aviation. ~ **force** n armée f de l'air. ~ **freshener** n désodorisant m d'atmosphère. ~ **hostess** n hôtesse f de l'air. ~**lift** n transporter par pont aérien. ~**line** n compagnie f aérienne. ~**liner** n avion m de ligne. ~**lock** n (in pipe) bulle f d'air; (chamber) sas m. ~**mail** n (by) ~**mail** par avion. ~**plane** n (US) avion m. ~**port** n aéroport m. ~ **raid** n attaque f aérienne. ~**-tight** adj hermétique. ~ **traffic controller** n contrôleur/-euse m/f aérien/-ne. ~**waves** npl ondes fpl.

airy /'eərɪ/ adj (-ier, -iest) (room) clair et spacieux.

aisle /aɪl/ n (of church) allée f centrale; (in train) couloir m.

ajar /ə'dʒɑː(r)/ adv & adj entrouvert.

akin /ə'kɪn/ adj ~ **to** semblable à.

alarm /ə'lɑːm/ n alarme f; (clock) réveil m; (feeling) frayeur f. ● vt inquiéter. ~ **clock** n réveil m.

alas /ə'læs/ interj hélas.

Albania /æl'beɪnɪə/ n Albanie f.

album /'ælbəm/ n album m.

alcohol /'ælkəhɒl/ n alcool m.

alcoholic /ælkə'hɒlɪk/ adj alcoolique; (drink) alcoolisé. ● n alcoolique mf.

ale /eɪl/ n bière f.

alert /ə'lɜːt/ adj alerte; (watchful) vigilant. ● n alerte f; **on the** ~ sur le qui-vive. ● vt alerter; ~ **sb to** prévenir qn de. **alertness** n vivacité f, vigilance f.

A-level /'eɪlevl/ n ≈ baccalauréat m.

algebra /'ældʒɪbrə/ n algèbre f.

Algeria /æl'dʒɪərɪə/ n Algérie f.

alias /'eɪlɪəs/ n (pl ~**es**) faux nom m. ● prep alias.

alibi /'ælɪbaɪ/ n alibi m.

alien /'eɪlɪən/ n & a étranger/-ère (m/f) (to à).

alienate /'eɪlɪəneɪt/ vt éloigner.

alight /ə'laɪt/ adj en feu, allumé.

alike /ə'laɪk/ adj semblable. ● adv de la même façon; **look** ~ se ressembler.

alive /ə'laɪv/ adj vivant; ~ **to** conscient de; ~ **with** grouillant de.

---

all /ɔːl/

● pronoun

····▶ (everything) tout; **is that** ~? c'est tout?; **that was** ~ **(that) he said** c'est tout ce qu'il a dit; **I ate it** ~ j'ai tout mangé.

❗ Use the translation **tous** for a group of masculine or mixed gender people or objects and **toutes** for a group of feminine gender: **we were all delighted** nous étions tous ravis; '**where are the cups?**'—'**they're all in the kitchen**' 'où sont les tasses?'-'elles sont toutes dans la cuisine'.

● determiner

····▶ tout/toute/tous/toutes; ~ **the time** tout le temps; ~ **his life** toute sa vie; ~ **of us** nous tous; ~ **(the) women** toutes les femmes.

● adverb

····▶ (completely) tout; **they were** ~ **alone** ils étaient tout seuls; **tell me** ~ **about it** raconte-moi tout; ~ **for** tout à fait pour; **not** ~ **that well** pas si bien que ça; ~ **too** bien trop.

❗ When the adjective that follows is in the feminine and begins with a consonant, the translation is **toute/toutes**: **she was all alone** elle était toute seule.

---

allege /ə'ledʒ/ vt prétendre. ~**d** adj présumé; **allegedly** adv prétendument.

allergic /ə'lɜːdʒɪk/ adj allergique (**to** à). **allergy** n allergie f.

alleviate /ə'liːvɪeɪt/ vt alléger.

alley /'ælɪ/ n (street) ruelle f.

alliance /ə'laɪəns/ n alliance f.

allied /'ælaɪd/ adj allié.

alligator /'ælɪgeɪtə(r)/ n alligator m.

allocate /'æləkeɪt/ vt (funds) affecter; (time) accorder; (task) assigner.

allot /ə'lɒt/ vt (pt **allotted**) (money) attribuer; (task) assigner. **allotment** n attribution f; (land) parcelle f de terre.

all-out /'ɔːlaʊt/ adj (effort) acharné; (strike) total.

allow /ə'laʊ/ vt (authorize) autoriser à; (let) laisser; (enable) permettre; (concede) accorder; ~ **for** tenir compte de.

allowance /ə'laʊəns/ n allocation f; **make** ~**s for sth** tenir compte de qch; **make** ~**s for sb** essayer de comprendre qn.

alloy /'ælɔɪ/ n alliage m.

all right /ɔːl'raɪt/ adj (not bad) pas mal; **are you** ~? ça va?; **is it** ~ **if ...?** est-ce que ça va si ...? ● adv (see) bien; (function) comme il faut. ● interj d'accord.

ally¹ /'ælaɪ/ n allié/-e m/f.

ally² /ə'laɪ/ vt allier; ~ **oneself with** s'allier avec.

almighty /ɔːl'maɪtɪ/ adj tout-puissant; (very great) formidable.

almond /'ɑːmənd/ n amande f. ~ **tree** n amandier m.

almost /'ɔːlməʊst/ adv presque; **he** ~ **died** il a failli mourir.

alone /ə'ləʊn/ adj & adv seul.

along /ə'lɒŋ/ prep le long de; **walk** ~ **the beach** marcher sur la plage. ● adv **come** ~ venir; **walk** ~ marcher; **push/pull sth** ~ pousser/tirer qch; **all** ~ (time) depuis le début; ~ **with** avec.

alongside /ə'lɒŋsaɪd/ adv à côté; **come** ~ (Naut) accoster. ● prep (next to) à côté de; (all along) le long de.

aloof /ə'luːf/ adj distant.

aloud /ə'laʊd/ adv à haute voix.

alphabet /'ælfəbet/ n alphabet m. **alphabetical** adj alphabétique.

alpine /'ælpaɪn/ adj (landscape) alpestre; (climate) alpin.

already /ɔːl'redɪ/ adv déjà.

alright /ɔːl'raɪt/ a & adv →ALL RIGHT.

Alsatian /æl'seɪʃn/ n (dog) berger m allemand.

also /'ɔːlsəʊ/ adv aussi.

altar /'ɔːltə(r)/ n autel m.

alter /'ɔːltə(r)/ vt/i changer; (building) transformer; (garment) retoucher. **alteration** n changement m; (to building) transformation f; (to garment) retouche f.

alternate[1] /'ɔːltəneɪt/ vt/i alterner.

alternate[2] /ɔːl'tɜːnət/ adj en alternance; **on ~ days** un jour sur deux. **alternately** adv alternativement.

alternative /ɔːl'tɜːnətɪv/ adj autre; (solution) de rechange. ● n (specified option) alternative f; (possible option) choix m. **alternatively** adv sinon.

alternator /'ɔːltəneɪtə(r)/ n alternateur m.

although /ɔːl'ðəʊ/ conj bien que.

altitude /'æltɪtjuːd/ n altitude f.

altogether /ɔːltə'geðə(r)/ adv (completely) tout à fait; (on the whole) tout compte fait.

aluminium /æljʊ'mɪnjəm/ n aluminium m.

always /'ɔːlweɪz/ adv toujours.

am /æm/ →BE.

a.m. /eɪem/ adv du matin.

amalgamate /ə'mælgəmeɪt/ vt/i (merge) fusionner; (metals) (s')amalgamer.

amateur /'æmətə(r)/ n & adj amateur (m).

amaze /ə'meɪz/ vt stupéfaire. **amazed** adj stupéfait. **amazement** n stupéfaction f. **amazing** adj stupéfiant; (great) exceptionnel.

ambassador /æm'bæsədə(r)/ n ambassadeur m.

amber /'æmbə(r)/ n ambre m; (Auto) orange m.

ambiguity /æmbɪ'gjuːətɪ/ n ambiguïté f.

ambiguous /æm'bɪgjʊəs/ adj ambigu.

ambition /æm'bɪʃn/ n ambition f. **ambitious** adj ambitieux.

ambulance /'æmbjʊləns/ n ambulance f.

ambush /'æmbʊʃ/ n embuscade f. ● vt tendre une embuscade à.

amenable /ə'miːnəbl/ adj obligeant; **~ to** (responsive) sensible à.

amend /ə'mend/ vt modifier. **amendment** n (to rule) amendement m.

amends /ə'mendz/ npl **make ~** réparer son erreur.

amenities /ə'miːnətɪz/ npl équipements mpl.

America /ə'merɪkə/ n Amérique f.

American /ə'merɪkən/ n Américain/-e m/f. ● adj américain.

American dream Cette expression désigne un principe américain selon lequel la réussite, en particulier financière et sociale, est accessible à quiconque travaille avec acharnement. Pour les immigrants, s'y ajoute le rêve de liberté et d'égalité.

amiable /'eɪmɪəbl/ adj aimable.

amicable /'æmɪkəbl/ adj amical.

amid(st) /ə'mɪd(st)/ prep au milieu de.

amiss /ə'mɪs/ adj **there is something ~** il y a quelque chose qui ne va pas.

ammonia /ə'məʊnɪə/ n (gas) ammoniac m; (solution) ammoniaque f.

ammunition /æmjʊ'nɪʃn/ n munitions fpl.

amnesty /'æmnəstɪ/ n amnistie f.

among(st) /ə'mʌŋ(st)/ prep parmi; (affecting a group) chez; **be ~ the poorest** être un des plus pauvres; **be ~ the first** être dans les premiers.

amorous /'æmərəs/ adj amoureux.

amount /ə'maʊnt/ n quantité f; (total) montant m; (sum of money) somme f ● vi **~ to** (add up to) s'élever à; (be equivalent to) revenir à.

amp /æmp/ n ampère m.

amphibian /æm'fɪbɪən/ n amphibie m.

ample /'æmpl/ adj (resources) largement suffisant; (proportions) généreux.

amplifier /'æmplɪfaɪə(r)/ n amplificateur m.

amputate /'æmpjʊteɪt/ vt amputer.

amuse /ə'mjuːz/ vt amuser.

amusement /ə'mjuːzmənt/ n (mirth) amusement m; (diversion) distraction f. **~ arcade** n salle f de jeux.

an /æn, ən/ →A.

anaemia /əˈniːmɪə/ n anémie f.

anaesthetic /ænɪsˈθetɪk/ n anesthésique m.

analyse /ˈænəlaɪz/ vt analyser. **analysis** n (pl **-yses**) analyse f. **analyst** n analyste mf.

anarchist /ˈænəkɪst/ n anarchiste mf.

anatomical /ænəˈtɒmɪkl/ adj anatomique. **anatomy** n anatomie f.

ancestor /ˈænsestə(r)/ n ancêtre m.

anchor /ˈæŋkə(r)/ n ancre f. ● vt mettre à l'ancre. ● vi jeter l'ancre.

anchovy /ˈæntʃəvɪ/ n anchois m.

ancient /ˈeɪnʃənt/ adj ancien.

ancillary /ænˈsɪlərɪ/ adj auxiliaire.

and /ænd, ənd/ conj et; **two hundred ~ sixty** deux cent soixante; **go ~ see him** allez le voir; **richer ~ richer** de plus en plus riche.

anew /əˈnjuː/ adv (once more) encore, de nouveau; (in a new way) à nouveau.

angel /ˈeɪndʒl/ n ange m.

anger /ˈæŋɡə(r)/ n colère f. ● vt mettre en colère, fâcher.

angle /ˈæŋɡl/ n angle m. ● vi pêcher (à la ligne); **~ for** (fig) quêter. **angler** n pêcheur/-euse m/f.

Anglo-Saxon /æŋɡləʊˈsæksn/ adj anglo-saxon. ● n Anglo-Saxon/-ne m/f.

angry /ˈæŋɡrɪ/ adj (**-ier, -iest**) fâché, en colère; **get ~** se fâcher, se mettre en colère (**with** contre); **make sb ~** mettre qn en colère.

anguish /ˈæŋɡwɪʃ/ n angoisse f.

animal /ˈænɪml/ n & adj animal (m).

animate¹ /ˈænɪmət/ adj (person) vivant; (object) animé.

animate² /ˈænɪmeɪt/ vt animer.

aniseed /ˈænɪsiːd/ n anis m.

ankle /ˈæŋkl/ n cheville f. **~ sock** n socquette f.

annex /əˈneks/ vt annexer.

anniversary /ænɪˈvɜːsərɪ/ n anniversaire m.

announce /əˈnaʊns/ vt annoncer (**that** que). **announcement** n (spoken) annonce f; (written) avis m. **announcer** n (radio, TV) speaker/-ine m/f.

annoy /əˈnɔɪ/ vt agacer, ennuyer. **annoyance** n contrariété f. **annoyed** adj fâché (**with** contre); **get ~ed** se fâcher. **annoying** adj ennuyeux.

annual /ˈænjʊəl/ adj annuel. ● n publication f annuelle. **annually** adv (earn, produce) par an; (do, inspect) tous les ans.

annul /əˈnʌl/ vt (pt **annulled**) annuler.

anonymity /ænəˈnɪmətɪ/ n anonymat m. **anonymous** adj anonyme.

anorak /ˈænəræk/ n anorak m.

another /əˈnʌðə(r)/ det & pron un/-e autre; **~ coffee** (one more) encore un café; **~ ten minutes** encore dix minutes, dix minutes de plus; **can I have ~?** est-ce que je peux en avoir un autre?

answer /ˈɑːnsə(r)/ n réponse f; (solution) solution f; (phone) **there's no ~** ça ne répond pas. ● vt répondre à; (prayer) exaucer; **~ the door** ouvrir la porte. ● vi répondre. □ **~ back** répondre; **~ for** répondre de; **~ to** (superior) dépendre de; (description) répondre à. **answerable** adj responsable (**for** de; **to** devant). **answering machine** n répondeur m.

ant /ænt/ n fourmi f.

antagonism /ænˈtæɡənɪzəm/ n antagonisme m. **antagonize** vt provoquer l'hostilité de.

Antarctic /ænˈtɑːktɪk/ n **the ~** l'Antarctique m. ● adj antarctique.

antenatal /æntɪˈneɪtl/ adj prénatal.

antenna /ænˈtenə/ n (pl **-ae**) (of insect) antenne f; (pl **-as**; aerial: US) antenne f.

anthem /ˈænθəm/ n (Relig) motet m; (of country) hymne m national.

anthrax /ˈænθræks/ n charbon m.

antibiotic /æntɪbaɪˈɒtɪk/ n & adj antibiotique (m).

antibody /ˈæntɪbɒdɪ/ n anticorps m.

anticipate /ænˈtɪsɪpeɪt/ vt (foresee, expect) prévoir, s'attendre à.

anticipation /æntɪsɪˈpeɪʃn/ n attente f; **in ~ of** en prévision or attente de.

anticlimax /æntɪˈklaɪmæks/ n (letdown) déception f.

anticlockwise /æntɪˈklɒkwaɪz/ adv & adj dans le sens inverse des aiguilles d'une montre.

antics /ˈæntɪks/ npl pitreries fpl.

antifreeze /ˈæntɪfriːz/ n antigel m.

antiquated /ˈæntɪkweɪtɪd/ adj (idea) archaïque; (building) vétuste.

antique /ænˈtiːk/ adj (old) ancien; (old-style) à l'ancienne. ● n objet m ancien, antiquité f. ~ **dealer** n antiquaire mf. ~ **shop** n magasin m d'antiquités.

anti-Semitic /æntɪsɪˈmɪtɪk/ adj anti-sémite.

antiseptic /æntɪˈseptɪk/ adj & n antiseptique (m).

antisocial /æntɪˈsəʊʃl/ adj asocial, antisocial; (reclusive) sauvage.

antlers /ˈæntləz/ npl bois mpl.

anxiety /æŋˈzaɪətɪ/ n (worry) anxiété f; (eagerness) impatience f.

anxious /ˈæŋkʃəs/ adj (troubled) anxieux; (eager) impatient (**to** de).

any /ˈenɪ/ det (some) du, de l', de la, des; (after negative) de, d'; (every) tout; (no matter which) n'importe quel; **at** ~ **moment** à tout moment; **have you** ~ **water?** avez-vous de l'eau? ● pron (no matter which one) n'importe lequel; (any amount of it or them) en; **I do not have** ~ je n'en ai pas; **did you see** ~ **of them?** en avez-vous vu? ● adv (a little) un peu; **do you have** ~ **more?** en avez-vous encore?; **do you have** ~ **more tea?** avez-vous encore du thé?; **I don't do it** ~ **more** je ne le fais plus.

anybody /ˈenɪbɒdɪ/ pron (no matter who) n'importe qui; (somebody) quelqu'un; (after negative) personne; **he did not see** ~ il n'a vu personne.

anyhow /ˈenɪhaʊ/ adv (anyway) de toute façon; (carelessly) n'importe comment.

anyone /ˈenɪwʌn/ pron ➡ANYBODY.

anything /ˈenɪθɪŋ/ pron (no matter what) n'importe quoi; (something) quelque chose; (after negative) rien; **he did not see** ~ il n'a rien vu; ~ **but** nullement; ~ **you do** tout ce que tu fais.

anyway /ˈenɪweɪ/ adv de toute façon.

anywhere /ˈenɪweə(r)/ adv (no matter where) n'importe où; (somewhere) quelque part; (after negative) nulle part; **he does not go** ~ il ne va nulle part; ~ **you go** partout où tu vas, où que tu ailles; ~ **else** partout ailleurs.

apart /əˈpɑːt/ adv (on or to one side) à part; (separated) séparé; (into pieces) en pièces; ~ **from** à part, excepté; **ten metres** ~ à dix mètres l'un de l'autre; **come** ~ (break) tomber en morceaux; (machine) se démonter; **legs** ~ les jambes écartées; **keep** ~ séparer; **take** ~ démonter.

apartment /əˈpɑːtmənt/ n (US) appartement m.

ape /eɪp/ n singe m. ● vt singer.

aperitif /əˈperətɪf/ n apéritif m.

apex /ˈeɪpeks/ n sommet m.

apologetic /əpɒləˈdʒetɪk/ adj (tone) d'excuse; **be** ~ s'excuser. **apologetically** adv en s'excusant.

apologize /əˈpɒlədʒaɪz/ vi s'excuser (**for** de; **to** auprès de).

apology /əˈpɒlədʒɪ/ n excuses fpl.

apostrophe /əˈpɒstrəfɪ/ n apostrophe f.

appal /əˈpɔːl/ vt (pt **appalled**) horrifier. **appalling** adj épouvantable.

apparatus /æpəˈreɪtəs/ n appareil m.

apparent /əˈpærənt/ adj apparent. **apparently** adv apparemment.

appeal /əˈpiːl/ n appel m; (attractiveness) attrait m, charme m; ● vi faire appel; ~ **to sb** (beg) faire appel à qn; (attract) plaire à qn; ~ **to sb for sth** demander qch à qn. **appealing** adj (attractive) attirant.

appear /əˈpɪə(r)/ vi apparaître. (arrive) se présenter; (seem, be published) paraître. (Theat) jouer; ~ **on TV** passer à la télé. **appearance** n apparition f; (aspect) apparence f.

appease /əˈpiːz/ vt apaiser.

appendix /əˈpendɪks/ n (pl -**ices**) appendice m.

appetite /ˈæpɪtaɪt/ n appétit m.

appetizer /ˈæpɪtaɪzə(r)/ n (snack) amuse-gueule m inv; (drink) apéritif m.

appetizing /ˈæpɪtaɪzɪŋ/ adj appétissant.

applaud /əˈplɔːd/ vt/i applaudir; (decision) applaudir à. **applause** n applaudissements mpl.

apple /ˈæpl/ n pomme f; ~-**tree** n pommier m.

appliance /əˈplaɪəns/ n appareil m.

applicable /ˈæplɪkəbl/ adj valable; **if** ~ le cas échéant.

applicant /ˈæplɪkənt/ n candidat/-e m/f (**for** à).

application /æplɪˈkeɪʃn/ n application f; (request, form) demande f; (for job) candidature f.

apply /əˈplaɪ/ vt appliquer. ● vi ~ **to** (refer) s'appliquer à; (ask) s'adresser à; ~ **for** (job) postuler pour; (grant) demander; ~ **oneself to** s'appliquer à.

appoint /əˈpɔɪnt/ vt (to post) nommer; (fix) désigner; **well-~ed** bien équipé.

appointment /əˈpɔɪntmənt/ n nomination f; (meeting) rendez-vous m inv; (job) poste m; **make an** ~ prendre rendez-vous (**with** avec).

appraisal /əˈpreɪzl/ n évaluation f. **appraise** vt évaluer.

appreciate /əˈpriːʃɪeɪt/ vt (like) apprécier; (understand) comprendre; (be grateful for) être reconnaissant de. ● vi prendre de la valeur. **appreciation** n appréciation f; (gratitude) reconnaissance f; (rise) augmentation f. **appreciative** adj reconnaissant; (audience) enthousiaste.

apprehend /æprɪˈhend/ vt (arrest) appréhender; (understand) comprendre. **apprehension** n (arrest) appréhension f; (fear) crainte f.

apprehensive /æprɪˈhensɪv/ adj inquiet; **be** ~ **of** craindre.

apprentice /əˈprentɪs/ n apprenti m. ● vt mettre en apprentissage.

approach /əˈprəʊtʃ/ vt (s')approcher de; (accost) aborder; (with request) s'adresser à. ● vi (s')approcher. ● n approche f; **an** ~ **to** (problem) une façon d'aborder; (person) une démarche auprès de. **approachable** adj abordable.

appropriate¹ /əˈprəʊprɪeɪt/ vt s'approprier.

appropriate² /əˈprəʊprɪət/ adj approprié, propre. **appropriately** adv à propos.

approval /əˈpruːvl/ n approbation f; **on** ~ à or sous condition.

approve /əˈpruːv/ vt approuver. ● vi ~ **of** approuver. **approving** adj approbateur.

approximate¹ /əˈprɒksɪmeɪt/ vi ~ **to** se rapprocher de.

approximate² /əˈprɒksɪmət/ adj approximatif. **approximately** adv environ. **approximation** n approximation f.

apricot /ˈeɪprɪkɒt/ n abricot m.

April /ˈeɪprɪl/ n avril m. ~ **Fools Day** n le premier avril.

apron /ˈeɪprən/ n tablier m.

apt /æpt/ adj (suitable) approprié; **be** ~ **to** avoir tendance à.

aptitude /ˈæptɪtjuːd/ n aptitude f.

aptly /ˈæptlɪ/ adv à propos.

Aquarius /əˈkweərɪəs/ n Verseau m.

aquatic /əˈkwætɪk/ adj aquatique; (Sport) nautique.

Arab /ˈærəb/ n Arabe mf. ● adj arabe.

Arabian /əˈreɪbɪən/ adj d'Arabie.

Arabic /ˈærəbɪk/ adj & n (Ling) arabe (m).

arbitrary /ˈɑːbɪtrərɪ/ adj arbitraire.

arbitrate /ˈɑːbɪtreɪt/ vi arbitrer. **arbitration** n arbitrage m. **arbitrator** n médiateur/-trice m/f.

arcade /ɑːˈkeɪd/ n (shops) galerie f; (arches) arcades fpl.

arch /ɑːtʃ/ n arche f; (of foot) voûte f plantaire. ● vt/i (s')arquer. ● adj (playful) malicieux.

archaeological /ɑːkɪəˈlɒdʒɪkl/ adj archéologique. **archaeologist** n archéologue mf. **archaeology** n archéologie f.

archbishop /ɑːtʃˈbɪʃəp/ n archevêque m.

archery /ˈɑːtʃərɪ/ n tir m à l'arc.

architect /ˈɑːkɪtekt/ n architecte mf; (of plan) artisan m. **architectural** adj architectural. **architecture** n architecture f.

archives /ˈɑːkaɪvz/ npl archives fpl.

archway /ˈɑːtʃweɪ/ n voûte f.

Arctic /ˈɑːktɪk/ n **the** ~ l'Arctique m. ● adj (climate) arctique; (expedition) polaire; (conditions) glacial.

ardent /ˈɑːdnt/ adj ardent.

are /ɑː(r)/ ➡BE.

area /ˈeərɪə/ n (region) région f; (district) quartier m; (fig) domaine m; (in geometry) aire f; **parking/picnic** ~ aire f de parking/de pique-nique.

arena /əˈriːnə/ n arène f.

aren't /ɑː(r)nt/ ➡ARE NOT.

Argentina /ɑːdʒənˈtiːnə/ n Argentine f.

arguable /ˈɑːgjʊəbl/ adj discutable. **arguably** adv selon certains.

argue /ˈɑːgjuː/ vi (quarrel) se disputer; (reason) argumenter. ● vt (debate) discuter; ~ **that** alléguer que.

argument /ˈɑːgjʊmənt/ n dispute f; (reasoning) argument m; (discussion) débat m. **argumentative** adj ergoteur.

Aries /ˈeəriːz/ n Bélier m.

arise /əˈraɪz/ vi (pt **arose**; pp **arisen**) (*problem*) survenir; (*question*) se poser; ~ **from** résulter de.

aristocrat /ˈærɪstəkræt/ n aristocrate mf.

arithmetic /əˈrɪθmətɪk/ n arithmétique f.

ark /ɑːk/ n (Relig) arche f.

arm /ɑːm/ n bras m; ~ **in arm** bras dessus bras dessous. ● vt armer; ~**ed robbery** vol m à main armée.

armament /ˈɑːməmənt/ n armement m.

arm: /ɑːm/ ~**-band** n brassard m. ~**chair** n fauteuil m.

armour /ˈɑːmə(r)/ n armure f. **armoured** adj blindé. **armoury** n arsenal m.

armpit /ˈɑːmpɪt/ n aisselle f.

arms /ɑːmz/ npl (weapons) armes fpl. ~ **dealer** n trafiquant m d'armes.

army /ˈɑːmɪ/ n armée f.

aroma /əˈrəʊmə/ n arôme m. **aromatic** adj aromatique.

arose /əˈrəʊz/ ➡ARISE.

around /əˈraʊnd/ adv (tout) autour; (here and there) çà et là. ● prep autour de; ~ **here** par ici.

arouse /əˈraʊz/ vt (awaken, cause) éveiller; (excite) exciter.

arrange /əˈreɪndʒ/ vt arranger; (time, date) fixer; ~ **to** s'arranger pour.

arrangement /əˈreɪndʒmənt/ n arrangement m; (agreement) entente f; **make** ~**s** prendre des dispositions.

array /əˈreɪ/ n **an** ~ **of** (display) un étalage impressionnant de.

arrears /əˈrɪəz/ npl arriéré m; **in** ~ (rent) arriéré; **he is in** ~ il a des retards dans ses paiements.

arrest /əˈrest/ vt arrêter; (attention) retenir. ● n arrestation f; **under** ~ en état d'arrestation.

arrival /əˈraɪvl/ n arrivée f; **new** ~ nouveau venu m, nouvelle venue f.

arrive /əˈraɪv/ vi arriver; ~ **at** (destination) arriver à; (decision) parvenir à.

arrogance /ˈærəgəns/ n arrogance f.

arrow /ˈærəʊ/ n flèche f.

arse /ɑːs/ n 🚫 cul m 🚫.

arson /ˈɑːsn/ n incendie m criminel. **arsonist** n incendiaire mf.

art /ɑːt/ n art m; (fine arts) beaux-arts mpl.

artery /ˈɑːtərɪ/ n artère f.

art gallery n (public) musée m (d'art); (private) galerie f (d'art).

arthritis /ɑːˈθraɪtɪs/ n arthrite f.

artichoke /ˈɑːtɪtʃəʊk/ n artichaut m.

article /ˈɑːtɪkl/ n article m; ~ **of clothing** vêtement m.

articulate /ɑːˈtɪkjʊlət/ adj (person) capable de s'exprimer clairement; (speech) distinct.

articulated lorry n semiremorque m.

artificial /ɑːtɪˈfɪʃl/ adj artificiel.

artist /ˈɑːtɪst/ n artiste mf.

arts /ɑːts/ npl **the** ~ les arts mpl; (Univ) lettres fpl.

artwork /ˈɑːtwɜːk/ n (of book) illustrations fpl.

as /æz/, /əz/ conj comme; (while) pendant que; (over gradual period of time) au fur et à mesure que; ~ **she grew older** au fur et à mesure qu'elle vieillissait; **do** ~ **I say** fais ce que je dis; ~ **usual** comme d'habitude.
● prep ~ **a mother** en tant que mère; ~ **a gift** en cadeau; ~ **from Monday** à partir de lundi; ~ **for**, ~ **to** quant à; ~ **if** comme si; **you look** ~ **if you're tired** vous avez l'air (d'être) fatigué. ● adv ~ **tall** ~ aussi grand que; ~ **much** ~, ~ **many** ~ autant que; ~ **soon** ~ aussitôt que; ~ **well** ~ aussi bien que; ~ **wide** ~ **possible** aussi large que possible.

asbestos /æzˈbestɒs/ n amiante f.

ascend /əˈsend/ vt gravir. ● vi monter.

ascertain /æsəˈteɪn/ vt établir (that que).

ash /æʃ/ n cendre f; ~**(-tree)** frêne m.

ashamed /əˈʃeɪmd/ adj be ~ avoir honte (of de).

ashore /əˈʃɔː(r)/ adv à terre.

ashtray /ˈæʃtreɪ/ n cendrier m.

Asia /ˈeɪʃə/ n Asie f.

Asian /ˈeɪʃn/ n Asiatique mf. ● adj asiatique.

aside /əˈsaɪd/ adv de côté; ~ **from** à part. ● n aparté m.

ask /ɑːsk/ vt/i demander; (a question) poser; (invite) inviter; ~ **sb sth** demander qch à qn; ~ **sb to do** demander à qn de faire; ~ **about** (thing) se renseigner sur; (*person*) demander des nouvelles de; ∼ **for** demander.

asleep /ə'sliːp/ *adj* endormi; (numb) engourdi. ● *adv* **fall** ∼ s'endormir.

asparagus /ə'spærəgəs/ *n*(plant) asperge *f*; (Culin) asperges *fpl*.

aspect /'æspekt/ *n* aspect *m*; (direction) orientation *f*.

asphyxiate /əs'fɪksɪeɪt/ *vt/i* (s')asphyxier.

aspire /ə'spaɪə(r)/ *vi* aspirer (**to** à; **to do** à faire).

aspirin /'æspərɪn/ *n* aspirine® *f*.

ass /æs/ *n* âne *m*; (person Ⓤ) idiot/-e *m/f*.

assail /ə'seɪl/ *vt* attaquer. **assailant** *n* agresseur *m*.

assassin /ə'sæsɪn/ *n* assassin *m*. **assassinate** *vt* assassiner. **assassination** *n* assassinat *m*.

assault /ə'sɔːlt/ *n* (Mil) assaut *m*; (Jur) agression *f*. ● *vt* (*person*: Jur) agresser.

assemble /ə'sembl/ *vt*(construct) assembler; (gather) rassembler. ● *vi* se rassembler.

assembly /ə'semblɪ/ *n* assemblée *f*. ∼ **line** *n* chaîne *f* de montage.

assent /ə'sent/ *n* assentiment *m*. ● *vi* consentir.

assert /ə'sɜːt/ *vt* affirmer; (*rights*) revendiquer. **assertion** *n* affirmation *f*. **assertive** *adj* assuré.

assess /ə'ses/ *vt* évaluer; (*payment*) déterminer le montant de. **assessment** *n* évaluation *f*. **assessor** *n* (valuer) expert *m*.

asset /'æset/ *n* (advantage) atout *m*; (financial) bien *m*; ∼ **s** (Comm) actif *m*.

assign /ə'saɪn/ *vt* (allot) assigner; ∼ **sb to** (appoint) affecter qn à.

assignment /ə'saɪnmənt/ *n* (task) mission *f*; (diplomatic) poste *m*; (academic) devoir *m*.

assist /ə'sɪst/ *vt/i* aider. **assistance** *n* aide *f*.

assistant /ə'sɪstənt/ *n* aide *mf*; (in shop) vendeur/-euse *m/f*. ● *adj* (manager) adjoint.

associate¹ /ə'səʊʃɪət/ *n & adj* associé/-e (*m/f*).

associate² /ə'səʊʃɪeɪt/ *vt* associer. ● *vi* ∼ **with** fréquenter. **association** *n* association *f*.

assorted /ə'sɔːtɪd/ *adj* divers; (*foods*) assorti.

assortment /ə'sɔːtmənt/ *n* assortiment *m*; (of people) mélange *m*.

assume /ə'sjuːm/ *vt* supposer; (*power*, *attitude*) prendre; (*role*, *burden*) assumer.

assurance /ə'ʃɔːrəns/ *n* assurance *f*.

assure /ə'ʃɔː(r)/ *vt* assurer.

asterisk /'æstərɪsk/ *n* astérisque *m*.

asthma /'æsmə/ *n* asthme *m*.

astonish /ə'stɒnɪʃ/ *vt* étonner.

astound /ə'staʊnd/ *vt* stupéfier.

astray /ə'streɪ/ *adv* **go** ∼ s'égarer; **lead** ∼ égarer.

astride /ə'straɪd/ *adv & prep* à califourchon (sur).

astrologer /ə'strɒlədʒə(r)/ *n* astrologue *mf*. **astrology** *n* astrologie *f*.

astronaut /'æstrənɔːt/ *n* astronaute *mf*.

astronomer /ə'strɒnəmə(r)/ *n* astronome *mf*.

asylum /ə'saɪləm/ *n* asile *m*.

---

at /æt, ət/
● *preposition*

> ➡️ For expressions such as **laugh at**, **look at** ➡️**laugh**, **look**.

····▸ (in position or place) à; **he's** ∼ **his desk** il est à son bureau; **she's** ∼ **work/school** elle est au travail/ à l'école.

····▸ (at someone's house or business) chez; ∼**Mary's/the dentist's** chez Mary/le dentiste.

····▸ (in times, ages) à; ∼ **four o'clock** à quatre heures; ∼ **two years of age** à l'âge de deux ans.

····▸ (in email addresses) arobase *f*

---

ate &/eɪt/ ➡️**EAT**.

atheist /'eɪθɪɪst/ *n* athée *mf*.

athlete /'æθliːt/ *n* athlète *mf*. **athletic** *adj* athlétique. **athletics** *npl* athlétisme *m*; (US) sports *mpl*.

Atlantic /ət'læntɪk/ *adj* atlantique. ● *n* **the** ∼ **(Ocean)** l'Atlantique *m*.

atlas /'ætləs/ *n* atlas *m*.

atmosphere /'ætməsfɪə(r)/ *n* (air) atmosphère *f*; (mood) ambiance *f*. **at-**

mospheric *adj* atmosphérique; d'ambiance.

atom /'ætəm/ *n* atome *m*.

atrocious /ə'trəʊʃəs/ *adj* atroce.

atrocity /ə'trɒsəti/ *n* atrocité *f*.

attach /ə'tætʃ/ *vt/i* (s')attacher; (*letter*) joindre (**to** à).

attaché /ə'tæʃeɪ/ *n* (Pol) attaché/-e *m/f*. **~ case** *n* attaché-case *m*.

attached /ə'tætʃt/ *adj* be **~ to** (like) être attaché à; **the ~ letter** la lettre ci-jointe.

attachment /ə'tætʃmənt/ *n* (accessory) accessoire *m*; (affection) attachement *m*; (e-mail) pièces *fpl* jointes.

attack /ə'tæk/ *n* attaque *f*; (Med) crise *f*. ● *vt* attaquer.

attain /ə'teɪn/ *vt* atteindre (à); (gain) acquérir.

attempt /ə'tempt/ *vt* tenter. ● *n* tentative *f*; **an ~ on sb's life** un attentat contre qn.

attend /ə'tend/ *vt* assister à; (class) suivre; (school, church) aller à. ● *vi* assister; **~ (to)** (look after) s'occuper de. **attendance** *n* présence *f*; (people) assistance *f*.

attendant /ə'tendənt/ *n* employé/-e *m/f*. ● *adj* associé.

attention /ə'tenʃn/ *n* attention *f*; **~!** (Mil) garde-à-vous! **pay ~** faire *or* prêter attention (**to** à).

attentive /ə'tentɪv/ *adj* attentif; (considerate) attentionné. **attentively** *adv* attentivement. **attentiveness** *n* attention *f*.

attest /ə'test/ *vt/i* **~ (to)** attester.

attic /'ætɪk/ *n* grenier *m*.

attitude /'ætɪtjuːd/ *n* attitude *f*.

attorney /ə'tɜːnɪ/ *n* (US) avocat/-e *m/f*.

attract /ə'trækt/ *vt* attirer. **attraction** *n* attraction *f*; (charm) attrait *m*.

attractive /ə'træktɪv/ *adj* attrayant, séduisant. **attractively** *adv* agréablement. **attractiveness** *n* attrait *m*, beauté *f*.

attribute¹ /ə'trɪbjuːt/ *vt* **~ to** attribuer à.

attribute² /'ætrɪbjuːt/ *n* attribut *m*.

aubergine /'əʊbəʒiːn/ *n* aubergine *f*.

auction /'ɔːkʃn/ *n* vente *f* aux enchères. ● *vt* vendre aux enchères. **auctioneer** *n* commissaire priseur *m*.

audacious /ɔː'deɪʃəs/ *adj* audacieux.

audience /'ɔːdɪəns/ *n* (theatre, radio) public *m*; (interview) audience *f*.

audiovisual /ɔːdɪəʊ'vɪʒʊəl/ *adj* audiovisuel.

audit /'ɔːdɪt/ *n* vérification *f* des comptes. ● *vt* vérifier.

audition /ɔː'dɪʃn/ *n* audition *f*. ● *vt/i* auditionner (**for** pour).

auditor /'ɔːdɪtə(r)/ *n* commissaire *m* aux comptes.

August /'ɔːgəst/ *n* août *m*.

aunt /ɑːnt/ *n* tante *f*.

auspicious /ɔː'spɪʃəs/ *adj* favorable.

Australia /ɒ'streɪlɪə/ *n* Australie *f*.

Australian /ɒ'streɪlɪən/ *n* Australien/-ne *m/f*. ● *adj* australien.

Austria /'ɒstrɪə/ *n* Autriche *f*.

Austrian /'ɒstrɪən/ *n* Autrichien/-ne *m/f*. ● *adj* autrichien.

authentic /ɔː'θentɪk/ *adj* authentique.

author /'ɔːθə(r)/ *n* auteur *m*.

authoritarian /ɔːθɒrɪ'teərɪən/ *adj* autoritaire.

authoritative /ɔː'θɒrətətɪv/ *adj* (credible) qui fait autorité; (manner) autoritaire.

authority /ɔː'θɒrətɪ/ *n* autorité *f*; (permission) autorisation *f*.

authorization /ɔːθəraɪ'zeɪʃn/ *n* autorisation *f*. **authorize** *vt* autoriser.

autistic /ɔː'tɪstɪk/ *adj* (person) autiste; (response) autistique.

autograph /'ɔːtəgrɑːf/ *n* autographe *m*. ● *vt* signer, dédicacer.

automate /'ɔːtəmeɪt/ *vt* automatiser.

automatic /ɔːtə'mætɪk/ *adj* automatique. ● *n* (Auto) voiture *f* automatique.

automobile /'ɔːtəməbiːl/ *n* (US) auto(mobile) *f*.

autonomous /ɔː'tɒnəməs/ *adj* autonome.

autumn /'ɔːtəm/ *n* automne *m*.

auxiliary /ɔːg'zɪlɪərɪ/ *adj* & *n* auxiliaire (*mf*); **~ (verb)** auxiliaire *m*.

avail /ə'veɪl/ *vt* **~ oneself of** profiter de. ● *n* **of no ~** inutile; **to no ~** sans résultat.

availability /əveɪlə'bɪlətɪ/ *n* disponibilité *f*. **available** *adj* disponible.

avenge /ə'vendʒ/ *vt* venger; **~ oneself** se venger (**on** de).

avenue /ˈævənjuː/ n avenue f; (line of approach:fig) voie f.

average /ˈævərɪdʒ/ n moyenne f; **on ∼** en moyenne. ● adj moyen. ● vt faire la moyenne de; (produce, do) faire en moyenne.

aviary /ˈeɪvɪərɪ/ n volière f.

avocado /ævəˈkɑːdəʊ/ n avocat m.

avoid /əˈvɔɪd/ vt éviter. **avoidance** n (of injuries) prévention f; (of responsibility) refus m.

await /əˈweɪt/ vt attendre.

awake /əˈweɪk/ vt/i (pt **awoke**; pp **awoken**) (s')éveiller. ● adj be ∼ ne pas dormir, être (r)éveillé.

award /əˈwɔːd/ vt (grant) attribuer; (prize) décerner; (points) accorder. ● n récompense f;prix m; (scholarship) bourse f; **pay ∼** augmentation f (de salaire).

aware /əˈweə(r)/ adj (well-informed) averti; **be ∼ of** (danger) être conscient de; (fact) savoir; **become ∼ of** prendre conscience de. **awareness** n conscience f.

away /əˈweɪ/ adv (far) (au) loin; (absent) absent, parti; ∼ **from** loin de; **move ∼** s'écarter; (to new home) déménager; **six kilometres ∼** à six kilomètres (de distance); **take ∼** emporter; **he was snoring ∼** il ronflait. ● adj & n ∼ **(match)** match m à l'extérieur.

awe /ɔː/ n crainte f (révérencielle).

awe-inspiring /ˈɔːɪnspaɪərɪŋ/ adj impressionnant.

awesome /ˈɔːsəm/ adj redoutable.

awful /ˈɔːfl/ adj affreux. **awfully** adv (badly) affreusement; (very 🄸) rudement.

awkward /ˈɔːkwəd/ adj difficile (inconvenient) inopportun; (clumsy) maladroit; (embarrassing) gênant; (embarrassed) gêné. **awkwardly** adv maladroitement; avec gêne. **awkwardness** n maladresse f; (discomfort) gêne f.

awning /ˈɔːnɪŋ/ n auvent m; (of shop) store m.

awoke, **awoken** →AWAKE.

axe /æks/ n hache f. ● vt (pres p **axing**) réduire; (eliminate) supprimer; (employee) renvoyer.

axis /ˈæksɪs/ n (pl **axes**) axe m.

axle /ˈæksl/ n essieu m.

BA abbr →BACHELOR OF ARTS.

babble /ˈbæbl/ vi babiller; (stream) gazouiller. ● n babillage m.

baby /ˈbeɪbɪ/ n bébé m. ∼ **carriage** n (US) voiture f d'enfant. ∼**-sit** vi faire du babysitting, garder des enfants. ∼**-sitter** n baby-sitter mf.

bachelor /ˈbætʃələ(r)/ n célibataire m. **B∼ of Arts** licencié/-e m/f ès lettres.

back /bæk/ n (of person, hand, page, etc.) dos m; (of house) derrière m; (of vehicle) arrière m; (of room) fond m; (of chair) dossier m; (in football) arrière m; **at the ∼ of the book** à la fin du livre; **in ∼ of** (US) derrière. ● adj (leg, wheel) arrière inv; (door, gate) de derrière; (taxes) arriéré. ● adv en arrière; (returned) de retour, rentré; **come ∼** revenir; **give ∼** rendre; **take ∼** reprendre; **I want it ∼** je veux le récupérer. ● vt (support) appuyer; (bet on) miser sur; (vehicle) faire reculer. ● vi (of person, vehicle) reculer. ∼ **down** céder; ∼**out** se désister; (Auto) sortir en marche arrière; ∼ **up** (support) appuyer. ∼**ache** n mal m de dos. ∼**-bencher** n (Pol) député m. ∼**bone** n colonne f vertébrale. ∼**date** vt antidater. ∼**fire** vi (Auto) pétarader; (fig) mal tourner. ∼**gammon** n trictrac m.

background /ˈbækgraʊnd/ n fond m, arrièreplan m; (context) contexte m; (environment) milieu m; (experience) formation f. ● adj (music, noise) de fond.

backhand /ˈbækhænd/ n revers m. **backhander** n (bribe) pot-de-vin m.

backing /ˈbækɪŋ/ n soutien m.

back: ∼**lash** n retour m de bâton; réaction f violente (**against** contre). ∼**log** n retard m. ∼ **number** n vieux numéro m. ∼**pack** n sac m à dos. ∼**side** n (buttocks 🄸) derrière m. ∼**stage** adj & adv dans les coulisses. ∼**stroke** n dos m crawlé. ∼**track** vi rebrousser chemin; (change one's opinion) faire marche arrière.

backup /'bækʌp/ n soutien m; (Comput) sauvegarde f. ● adj de secours; (Comput) de sauvegarde.

backward /'bækwəd/ adj (step etc.) en arrière; (retarded) arriéré.

backwards /'bækwəd/ adv en arrière; (walk) à reculons; (read) à l'envers; go ~ and forwards aller et venir.

bacon /'beikən/ n lard m; (in rashers) bacon m.

bacteria /bæk'tɪərɪə/ npl bactéries fpl.

bad /bæd/ adj (worse, worst) mauvais; (wicked) méchant; (ill) malade; (accident) grave; (food) gâté; feel ~ se sentir mal; go ~ se gâter; ~ language gros mots mpl; too ~! tant pis!; (I'm sorry) dommage!

badge /bædʒ/ n badge m; (coat of arms) insigne m.

badger /'bædʒə(r)/•n blaireau m. ● vt harceler.

badly /'bædlɪ/ adv mal; (hurt) gravement; want ~ avoir grande envie de.

badminton /'bædmɪntn/ n badminton m.

bad-tempered adj irritable.

baffle /'bæfl/ vt déconcerter.

bag /bæg/ n sac m; ~s (luggage) bagages mpl; (under eyes 🔲) valises fpl; ~s of plein de.

baggage /'bægɪdʒ/ n bagages mpl; ~ reclaim réception f des bagages.

baggy /'bægɪ/ adj large.

bagpipes /'bægpaɪps/ npl cornemuse f.

bail /beɪl/ n caution f; on ~ sous caution; (cricket) bâtonnet m. ● vt mettre en liberté provisoire.

bailiff /'beɪlɪf/ n huissier m.

bait /beɪt/ n appât m. ● vt appâter; (fig) tourmenter.

bake /beɪk/ vt faire cuire au four; ~ a cake faire un gâteau. ● vi cuire; (person) faire du pain. **baked beans** npl haricots mpl blancs à la tomate. **baked potato** n pomme f de terre en robe des champs. **baker** n boulanger/-ère m/f. **bakery** n boulangerie f.

balance /'bæləns/ n équilibre m; (scales) balance f; (outstanding sum: Comm) solde m; (of payments, of trade) balance f; (remainder) restant m. ● vt mettre en équilibre; (weigh up also Comm) balancer; (budget) équilibrer; (to compensate) contrebalancer.

● vi être en équilibre.

balcony /'bælkənɪ/ n balcon m.

bald /bɔːld/ adj chauve; (tyre) lisse; (fig) simple.

balk /bɔːk/ vt contrecarrer. ● vi ~ at reculer devant.

ball /bɔːl/ n (golf, tennis, etc.) balle f; (football) ballon m; (billiards) bille f; (of wool) pelote f; (sphere) boule f; (dance) bal m.

ballet /'bæleɪ/ n ballet m.

balloon /bə'luːn/ n ballon m.

ballot /'bælət/ n scrutin m. ● vt consulter par vote (on sur). ~ box n urne f. ~ paper n bulletin m de vote.

ballpoint pen n stylo m (à) bille.

ban /bæn/ vt (pt banned) interdire; ~ sb from exclure qn de; ~ sb from doing interdire à qn de faire. ● n interdiction f (on de).

banal /bə'nɑːl/ adj banal.

banana /bə'nɑːnə/ n banane f.

band /bænd/ n (strip, group of people) bande f; (pop group) groupe m; (brass band) fanfare f. ● vi ~ together se réunir.

bandage /'bændɪdʒ/ n bandage m. ● vt bander.

B and B abbr ➥BED AND BREAKFAST.

bandit /'bændɪt/ n bandit m.

bandstand /'bændstənd/ n kiosque m à musique.

bang /bæŋ/ n (blow, noise) coup m; (explosion) détonation f; (of door) claquement m. ● vt/i taper; (door) claquer; ~ one's head se cogner la tête. ● interj vlan. ● adv 🔲 ~ in the middle en plein milieu; ~ on time à l'heure pile.

banger /'bæŋə(r)/ n (firework) pétard m; (Culin) saucisse f; (old) ~ (car 🔲) guimbarde f.

banish /'bænɪʃ/ vt bannir.

banister /'bænɪstə(r)/ n rampe f d'escalier.

bank /bæŋk/ n (Comm) banque f; (of river) rive f; (of sand) banc m. ● vt mettre en banque. ● vi (Aviat) virer; ~ with avoir un compte à; ~ on compter sur. ~ account n compte m en banque. ~ card n carte f bancaire. ~ holiday n jour m férié.

banking /'bæŋkɪŋ/ n opérations fpl bancaires; (as career) la banque.

Bank holiday Jour chômé où les banques sont fermées au Royaume-Uni, en général à l'occasion d'une fête religieuse ou civile (*Christmas Day, Easter Monday, May Day*, etc.). La plupart tombe un lundi: par exemple, le *spring bank holiday*, qui coïncide avec la Pentecôte, tombe le dernier lundi de mai ou le premier lundi de juin.

banknote /ˈbæŋknəʊt/ n billet m de banque.

bankrupt /ˈbæŋkrʌpt/ adj be ~ être en faillite; go ~ faire faillite. ● n failli/-e m/f. ● vt mettre en faillite. **bankruptcy** n faillite f.

bank statement n relevé m de compte.

banner /ˈbænə(r)/ n bannière f.

baptism /ˈbæptɪzəm/ n baptême m. **baptize** vt baptiser.

bar /bɑː(r)/ n (of metal) barre f; (on window, cage) barreau m; (of chocolate) tablette f; (pub) bar m; (counter) comptoir m; (Mus) mesure f; (fig) obstacle m; ~ **of soap** savonnette f; **the** ~ (Jur) le barreau. ● vt (pt **barred**) (obstruct) barrer; (prohibit) interdire; (exclude) exclure. ● prep sauf.

barbecue /ˈbɑːbɪkjuː/ n barbecue m. ● vt faire au barbecue.

barbed wire n fil m de fer barbelé.

barber /ˈbɑːbə(r)/ n coiffeur m (*pour hommes*).

bar code n code m (à) barres.

bare /beə(r)/ adj nu; (cupboard) vide. ● vt mettre à nu. ~**foot** adj nu-pieds inv, pieds nus. **barely** adv à peine.

bargain /ˈbɑːgɪn/ n (deal) marché m; (cheap thing) occasion f. ● vi négocier; (haggle) marchander; **not** ~ **for** ne pas s'attendre à.

barge /bɑːdʒ/ n péniche f. ● vi ~ **in** interrompre; (into room) faire irruption.

bark /bɑːk/ n (of tree) écorce f; (of dog) aboiement m. ● vi aboyer.

barley /ˈbɑːlɪ/ n orge f.

bar: ~**maid** n serveuse f. ~**man** n (pl -**men**) barman m.

barn /bɑːn/ n grange f.

barracks /ˈbærəks/ npl caserne f.

barrel /ˈbærəl/ n tonneau m; (of oil) baril m; (of gun) canon m.

barren /ˈbærən/ adj stérile.

barricade /ˈbærɪkeɪd/ n barricade f. ● vt barricader.

barrier /ˈbærɪə(r)/ n barrière f; **ticket** ~ guichet m.

barrister /ˈbærɪstə(r)/ n avocat m.

bartender /ˈbɑːtendə(r)/ n (US) barman m.

barter /ˈbɑːtə(r)/ n troc m. ● vt troquer (**for** contre).

base /beɪs/ n base f. ● vt baser (**on** sur; **in** à). ● adj ignoble. **baseball** n baseball m.

basement /ˈbeɪsmənt/ n sous-sol m.

bash /bæʃ/ 🗊 vt cogner; ~**ed in** enfoncé. ● n coup m violent; **have a** ~ **at** s'essayer à.

basic /ˈbeɪsɪk/ adj fondamental, élémentaire; **the** ~**s** l'essentiel m. **basically** adv au fond.

basil /ˈbæzl/ n basilic m.

basin /ˈbeɪsn/ n (for liquids) cuvette f; (for food) bol m; (for washing) lavabo m; (of river) bassin m.

basis /ˈbeɪsɪs/ n (pl **bases**) base f.

bask /bɑːsk/ vi se prélasser (**in** à).

basket /ˈbɑːskɪt/ n corbeille f; (with handle) panier m. **basketball** n basket(- ball) m.

Basque /bæsk/ n (person) Basque mf; (Ling) basque m. ● adj basque.

bass¹ /beɪs/ adj (voice, part) de basse; (sound, note) grave. ● n (pl **basses**) basse f.

bass² /bæs/ n inv (freshwater fish) perche f; (sea) bar m.

bassoon /bəˈsuːn/ n basson m.

bastard /ˈbɑːstəd/ n (illegitimate) bâtard/-e m/f; (insult 🗷) salaud m 🗷.

bat /bæt/ n (cricket etc.) batte f; (table tennis) raquette f; (animal) chauve-souris f. ● vt (pt **batted**) (ball) frapper; **not** ~ **an eyelid** ne pas sourciller.

batch /bætʃ/ n (of cakes, people) fournée f; (of goods, text *also* Comput) lot m.

bath /bɑːθ/ n (pl -**s**) bain m; (tub) baignoire f; **have a** ~ prendre un bain; (**swimming**) ~**s** piscine f. ● vt donner un bain à.

bathe /beɪð/ vt baigner. ● vi se baigner; (US) prendre un bain.

bathing /'beɪðɪŋ/ n baignade f. ~**-costume** n maillot m de bain.

bath: ~**robe** n (US) robe f de chambre. ~**room** n salle f de bains.

baton /'bætn/ n (policeman's) matraque f; (Mus) baguette f.

batter /'bætə(r)/ vt battre. ● n (Culin) pâte f (à frire).

battery /'bætəri/ n (Mil, Auto) batterie f; (of torch, radio) pile f.

battle /'bætl/ n bataille f; (fig) lutte f. ● vi se battre. ~**field** n champ m de bataille.

baulk /bɔːk/ vt/i ➡BALK.

bay /beɪ/ n (Bot) laurier m; (Geog, Archit) baie f; (area) aire f; (bark) aboiement m; **keep** or **hold at** ~ tenir à distance. ● vi aboyer. ~**-leaf** n feuille f de laurier. ~ **window** n fenêtre f en saillie.

bazaar /bə'zɑː(r)/ n (shop, market) bazar m; (sale) vente f.

BC abbr (**before Christ**) avant J.-C.

BBS abbr (**Bulletin Board System**) (Internet) babillard m électronique, BBS m.

---

be /biː/

present **am, is, are;** past **was, were;** past participle **been.**

● intransitive verb

····➤ être; **I am tired** je suis fatigué; **it's me** c'est moi.

····➤ (feelings) avoir; **I am hot** j'ai chaud; **he is hungry/thirsty** il a faim/soif; **her hands are cold** elle a froid aux mains.

····➤ (age) avoir; **I am 15** j'ai 15 ans.

····➤ (weather) faire; **it's warm** il fait chaud; **it's 25°** il fait 25°.

····➤ (health) aller; **how are you?** comment allez-vous or comment vas-tu?

····➤ (visit) aller; **I've never been to Italy** je ne suis jamais allé en Italie.

● auxiliary verb

····➤ (in tenses) **I am working** je travaille; **he was writing to his mother** il écrivait à sa mère; **she is to do it at once** (obligation) elle doit le faire tout de suite.

····➤ (in passives) **he was killed** il a été tué; **the window has been fixed** on a réparé la fenêtre.

····➤ (in tag questions) **their house is lovely, isn't it?** leur maison est très jolie, n'est-ce pas?

····➤ (in short answers) **'I am a painter'—'are you?'** je suis peintre'—'ah oui?'; **'are you a doctor?'—'yes, I am'** 'êtes-vous médecin?'—'oui'; **'you're not going out'—'yes I am'** 'tu ne sors pas'—'si'.

---

beach /biːtʃ/ n plage f.

beacon /'biːkən/ n (lighthouse) phare m; (marker) balise f.

bead /biːd/ n perle f.

beak /biːk/ n bec m.

beaker /'biːkə(r)/ n gobelet m.

beam /biːm/ n (timber) poutre f; (of light) rayon m; (of torch) faisceau m. ● vi rayonner. ● vt (broadcast) transmettre.

bean /biːn/ n haricot m.

bear /beə(r)/ n ours m. ● vt (pt **bore**; pp **borne**) (carry, show, feel) porter; (endure, sustain) supporter; (child) mettre au monde. ● vi ~ **left** (go) prendre à gauche; ~ **in mind** tenir compte de. ~ **out** confirmer; ~ **up** tenir le coup. **bearable** adj supportable.

beard /bɪəd/ n barbe f.

bearer /'beərə(r)/ n porteur-euse m/f.

bearing /'beərɪŋ/ n (behaviour) maintien m; (relevance) rapport m; **get one's** ~**s** s'orienter.

beast /biːst/ n bête f; (person) brute f.

beat /biːt/ vt/i (pt **beat**; pp **beaten**) battre; ~ **a retreat** battre en retraite; ~ **it!** dégage! 🆒; **it** ~**s me** 🆒 ça me dépasse. ● n (of drum, heart) battement m; (Mus) mesure f; (of policeman) ronde f. ~ **off** repousser; ~ **up** tabasser. **beating** n raclée f.

beautiful /'bjuːtɪfl/ adj beau.

beauty /'bjuːtɪ/ n beauté f. ~**parlour** n institut m de beauté. ~**spot** n grain m de beauté; (place) site m pittoresque.

beaver /'biːvə(r)/ n castor m.

became /bɪ'keɪm/ ➡BECOME.

because /bɪ'kɒz/ conj parce que; ~ of à cause de.

become /bɪ'kʌm/ vt/i (pt **became**; pp **become**) devenir; (befit) convenir à; **what has** ~ **of her?** qu'est-ce qu'elle est devenue?

bed /bed/ n lit m; (layer) couche f; (of sea) fond m; (of flowers) parterre m; **go to** ~ (aller) se coucher. ● vi (pt **bedded**) ~ **down** se coucher. **bed and breakfast** n chambre f avec petit déjeuner, chambre f d'hôte. ~ **bug** n punaise f. ~**clothes** npl couvertures fpl.

bedding /'bedɪŋ/ n literie f.

bed: ~**ridden** adj cloué au lit. ~**room** n chambre f (à coucher). ~**side** n chevet m. ~**sit**, ~**sitter** n chambre f meublée, studio m. ~**spread** n dessus m de lit. ~**time** n heure f du coucher.

bee /biː/ n abeille f; **make a** ~**-line for** aller tout droit vers.

beech /biːtʃ/ n hêtre m.

beef /biːf/ n bœuf m. ~**burger** n hamburger m.

beehive /'biːhaɪv/ n ruche f.

been /biːn/ ➡ **BE**.

beer /bɪə(r)/ n bière f.

beetle /'biːtl/ n scarabée m.

beetroot /'biːtruːt/ n inv betterave f.

before /bɪ'fɔː(r)/ prep (time) avant; (place) devant; **the day** ~ **yesterday** avant-hier. ● adv avant; (already) déjà; **the day** ~ la veille. ● conj ~ **leaving** avant de partir; ~ **I forget** avant que j'oublie. **beforehand** adv à l'avance.

beg /beg/ vt (pt **begged**) (food, money, favour) demander (**from** à); ~ **sb to do** supplier qn de faire. ● vi mendier; **it is going** ~**ging** personne n'en veut.

began /bɪ'gæn/ ➡ **BEGIN**.

beggar /'begə(r)/ n mendiant/-e m/f.

begin /bɪ'gɪn/ vt/i (pt **began**, pp **begun**, pres p **beginning**) commencer (**to do** à faire). **beginner** n débutant/-e m/f. **beginning** n commencement m, début m.

begun /bɪ'gʌn/ ➡ **BEGIN**.

behalf /bɪ'hɑːf/ n on ~ **of** (act, speak, campaign) pour; (phone, write) de la part de.

behave /bɪ'heɪv/ vi se conduire; (**oneself**) se conduire bien.

behaviour /bɪ'heɪvjə(r)/, (US) **behavior** n comportement m (**towards** envers).

behead /bɪ'hed/ vt décapiter.

behind /bɪ'haɪnd/ prep derrière; (in time) en retard sur. ● adv derrière; (late) en retard; **leave** ~ oublier. ● n (buttocks 🄸) derrière m 🄸.

beige /beɪʒ/ adj & n beige (m).

being /'biːɪŋ/ n (person) être m.

belch /beltʃ/ vi avoir un renvoi. ● vt ~ **out** (smoke) s'échapper. ● n renvoi m.

Belgian /'beldʒən/ n Belge mf. ● adj belge. **Belgium** n Belgique f.

belief /bɪ'liːf/ n conviction f; (trust) confiance f; (faith: Relig) foi f.

believe /bɪ'liːv/ vt/i croire; ~ **in** croire à; (deity) croire en. **believer** n croyant/-e m/f.

bell /bel/ n cloche f; (small) clochette f; (on door) sonnette f.

belly /'belɪ/ n ventre m. ~ **button** n nombril m.

belong /bɪ'lɒŋ/ vi ~ **to** appartenir à; (club) être membre de.

belongings /bɪ'lɒŋɪŋz/ npl affaires fpl.

beloved /bɪ'lʌvɪd/ adj & n bien-aimé/-e (m/f).

below /bɪ'ləʊ/ prep sous, au-dessous de; (fig) indigne de. ● adv en dessous; (on page) ci-dessous.

belt /belt/ n ceinture f; (Tech) courroie f; (fig) zone f. ● vt (hit 🄸) rosser. ● vi (rush 🄸) ~ **in/out** entrer/sortir à toute vitesse.

beltway /'beltweɪ/ n (US) périphérique m.

bemused /bɪ'mjuːzd/ adj perplexe.

bench /bentʃ/ n banc m; **the** ~ (Jur) la magistrature (assise).

bend /bend/ vt (pt **bent**) (knee, arm, wire) plier; (head, back) courber. ● vi (road) tourner; (person) ~ **down/over** se pencher. ● n courbe f; (in road) virage m; (of arm, knee) pli m.

beneath /bɪ'niːθ/ prep sous, au-dessous de; (fig) indigne de. ● adv en dessous.

benefactor /'benɪfæktə(r)/ n bienfaiteur/-trice m/f.

beneficial /benɪ'fɪʃl/ adj bénéfique.

benefit /'benɪfɪt/ n avantage m; (allowance) allocation f. ● vt (be useful to) profiter à; (do good to) faire du bien à. ● *vi* profiter; ~ **from** tirer profit de.

benign /bɪˈnaɪn/ *adj* (kindly) bienveillant; (Med) bénin.

bent /bent/ →**BEND**. ● *n* (talent) aptitude *f*; (inclination) penchant *m*. ● *adj* tordu; ⊠ corrompu; ~ **on doing** décidé à faire.

bequest /bɪˈkwest/ *n* legs *m*.

bereaved /bɪˈriːvd/ *adj* endeuillé; **the** ~ la famille endeuillée. **bereavement** *n* deuil *m*.

berry /ˈberɪ/ *n* baie *f*.

berserk /bəˈsɜːk/ *adj* fou furieux.

berth /bɜːθ/ *n* (in train, ship) couchette *f*; (anchorage) mouillage *m*; **give a wide** ~ **to** éviter. ● *vi* mouiller.

beside /bɪˈsaɪd/ *prep* à côté de; ~ **oneself** hors de soi; ~ **the point** sans rapport.

besides /bɪˈsaɪdz/ *prep* en plus de. ● *adv* en plus.

besiege /bɪˈsiːdʒ/ *vt* assiéger.

best /best/ *adj* meilleur; **the** ~ **book** le meilleur livre; **the** ~ **part of** la plus grande partie de; **the** ~ **thing is to** le mieux est de. ● *adv* (**the**) ~ (*behave, play*) le mieux. ● *n* **the** ~ le meilleur, la meilleure; **do one's** ~ faire de son mieux; **make the** ~ **of** s'accommoder de. ~ **man** *n* témoin. ~**seller** *n* best-seller *m*, livre *m* à succès.

bet /bet/ *n* pari *m*. ● *vt/i* (*pt* **bet** or **betted**, *pres p* **betting**) parier (**on** sur).

betray /bɪˈtreɪ/ *vt* trahir.

better /ˈbetə(r)/ *adj* meilleur; **the** ~ **part of** la plus grande partie de; **get** ~ s'améliorer; (*recover*) se remettre. ● *adv* mieux; **I had** ~ **go** je ferais mieux de partir. ● *vt* (*improve*) améliorer; (*do better than*) surpasser. ● *n* **get the** ~ **of** l'emporter sur; **so much the** ~ tant mieux. ~ **off** *adj* (richer) plus riche; **he is/would be** ~ **off at home** il est/serait mieux chez lui.

betting shop *n* bureau *m* du PMU.

between /bɪˈtwiːn/ *prep* entre. ● *adv* **in** ~ au milieu.

beverage /ˈbevərɪdʒ/ *n* boisson *f*.

beware /bɪˈweə(r)/ *vi* prendre garde (**of** à).

bewilder /bɪˈwɪldə(r)/ *vt* déconcerter.

beyond /bɪˈjɒnd/ *prep* au-delà de; (control, reach) hors de; (besides) excepté. ● *adv* au-delà; **it is** ~ **me** ça me dépasse.

bias /ˈbaɪəs/ *n* (inclination) tendance *f*; (prejudice) parti *m* pris. ● *vt* (*pt* **biased**) influer sur. **biased** *adj* partial.

bib /bɪb/ *n* bavoir *m*.

Bible /ˈbaɪbl/ *n* Bible *f*.

biceps /ˈbaɪseps/ *n* biceps *m*.

bicycle /ˈbaɪsɪkl/ *n* vélo *m*, bicyclette *f*. ● *adj* (bell, chain) de vélo; (pump, clip) à vélo.

bid /bɪd/ *n* (at auction) enchère *f*; (attempt) tentative *f*. ● *vt/i* (*pt* **bade**, *pp* **bidden** or **bid**, *pres p* **bidding**) (offer) offrir, mettre une enchère (de) (**for** pour); ~ **sb good morning** dire bonjour à qn; ~ **sb farewell** faire ses adieux à qn.

bidding /ˈbɪdɪŋ/ *n* (at auction) enchères *fpl*; **he did my** ~ il a fait ce que je lui ai dit.

bifocals /baɪˈfəʊklz/ *npl* verres *mpl* à double foyer.

big /bɪg/ *adj* (**bigger, biggest**) grand; (in bulk) gros.

bike /baɪk/ *n* vélo *m*.

bikini /bɪˈkiːnɪ/ *n* bikini *m*.

bilberry /ˈbɪlbrɪ/ *n* myrtille *f*.

bilingual /baɪˈlɪŋgwəl/ *adj* bilingue.

bill /bɪl/ *n* (invoice) facture *f*; (in hotel, for gas) note *f*; (in restaurant) addition *f*; (of sale) acte *m*; (Pol) projet *m* de loi; (banknote: US) billet *m* de banque; (Theat) **on the** ~ à l'affiche; (of bird) bec *m*. ● *vt* (person: Comm) envoyer la facture à. ~**board** *n* panneau *m* d'affichage.

billet /ˈbɪlɪt/ *n* cantonnement *m*. ● *vt* (*pt* **billeted**) cantonner (**on** chez).

billiards /ˈbɪljədz/ *n* billard *m*.

billion /ˈbɪlɪən/ *n* billion *m*; (US) milliard *m*.

bin /bɪn/ *n* (for rubbish) poubelle *f*; (for storage) casier *m*.

bind /baɪnd/ *vt* (*pt* **bound**) attacher; (book) relier; **be bound by** être tenu par. ● *n* (bore) corvée *f*.

binding /ˈbaɪndɪŋ/ *n* reliure *f*. ● *adj* (agreement, contract) qui lie.

binge /bɪndʒ/ *n* (drinking) beuverie *f*; (eating) gueuleton *m*.

binoculars /bɪˈnɒkjʊləz/ *npl* jumelles *fpl*.

biochemistry /baɪəʊ'kemɪstrɪ/ n biochimie f.

biodegradable /baɪəʊdɪ'greɪdəbl/ adj biodégradable.

biographer /baɪ'ɒgrəfə(r)/ n biographe mf. **biography** n biographie f.

biological /baɪə'lɒdʒɪkl/ adj biologique.

biologist /baɪ'ɒlədʒɪst/ n biologiste mf.

biology /baɪ'ɒlədʒɪ/ n biologie f.

bioterrorism /baɪə'terərɪzm/ n bioterrorisme m.

birch /bɜːtʃ/ n (tree) bouleau m; (whip) fouet m.

bird /bɜːd/ n oiseau m; (girl 🔲) nana f.

Biro® /'baɪrəʊ/ n stylo m à bille, bic® m.

birth /bɜːθ/ n naissance f; give ~ accoucher. ~ **certificate** n acte m de naissance. ~**-control** n contraception f. ~**day** n anniversaire m. ~**mark** n tache f de naissance. ~**-rate** n taux m de natalité.

biscuit /'bɪskɪt/ n biscuit m; (US) petit pain m (au lait).

bishop /'bɪʃəp/ n évêque m.

bit /bɪt/ ➡BITE. ● n morceau m; (of horse) mors m; (of tool) mèche f; **a** ~ (a little) un peu; (Comput) bit m.

bitch /bɪtʃ/ n chienne f; (woman 🔲) garce f 🔲. ● vi dire du mal (about de).

bite /baɪt/ vt/i (pt bit; pp bitten) mordre; ~ **one's nails** se ronger les ongles. ● n morsure f; (by insect) piqûre f; (mouthful) bouchée f; **have a** ~ manger un morceau.

bitter /'bɪtə(r)/ adj amer; (weather) glacial. ● n bière f. **bitterly** adv amèrement; **it is** ~**ly cold** il fait un temps glacial.

bizarre /bɪ'zɑː(r)/ adj bizarre.

black /blæk/ adj noir; ~ **and blue** couvert de bleus. ● n (colour) noir m; **B**~ (person) Noir/-e m/f. ● vt noircir; (goods) boycotter. ~**berry** n mûre f. ~**bird** n merle m. ~**board** n tableau m noir. ~**currant** n cassis m.

blacken /'blækən/ vt/i noircir.

black: ~ **eye** n œil m poché. ~**head** n point m noir. ~ **ice** n verglas m. ~**leg** n jaune m.

blacklist /'blæklɪst/ n liste f noire. ● vt mettre à l'index.

blackmail /'blækmeɪl/ n chantage m. ● vt faire chanter. **blackmailer** n maître-chanteur m.

black: ~ **market** n marché m noir. ~**out** n panne f de courant; (Med) syncope f. ~ **pudding** n boudin m. ~ **sheep** n brebis f galeuse. ~**smith** n forgeron m. ~ **spot** n point m noir.

bladder /'blædə(r)/ n vessie f.

blade /bleɪd/ n (of knife) lame f; (of propeller, oar) pale f; ~ **of grass** brin m d'herbe.

blame /bleɪm/ vt accuser; ~ **sb for sth** reprocher qch à qn; **he is to** ~ il est responsable (for de). ● n responsabilité f (for de).

bland /blænd/ adj (insipid) fade.

blank /blæŋk/ adj (page) blanc; (screen) vide; (cheque) en blanc; **to look** ~ avoir l'air ébahi. ● n blanc m; ~ (cartridge) cartouche f à blanc.

blanket /'blæŋkɪt/ n couverture f; (layer) couche f.

blasphemous /'blæsfəməs/ adj blasphématoire; (person) blasphémateur.

blast /blɑːst/ n explosion f; (wave of air) souffle m; (of wind) rafale f; (noise from siren etc.) coup m. ● vt (blow up) faire sauter. ~ **off** décoller. ~ **furnace** n haut-fourneau m. ~ **off** n lancement m.

blatant /'bleɪtnt/ adj (obvious) flagrant; (shameless) éhonté.

blaze /bleɪz/ n feu m; (accident) incendie m. ● vt ~ **a trail** faire œuvre de pionnier. ● vi (fire) brûler; (sky, eyes) flamboyer.

bleach /bliːtʃ/ n (for cleaning) eau f de Javel; (for hair, fabric) décolorant m. ● vt/i blanchir; (hair) décolorer.

bleak /bliːk/ adj (landscape) désolé; (outlook, future) sombre.

bleed /bliːd/ vt/i (pt bled) saigner.

bleep /bliːp/ n bip m.

blemish /'blemɪʃ/ n imperfection f; (on fruit, reputation) tache f. ● vt entacher.

blend /blend/ vt mélanger. ● vi se fondre ensemble; **to** ~ **with** se marier à. ● n mélange m. **blender** n mixeur n, mixer n.

bless /bles/ vt bénir; **be** ~**ed with** jouir de; ~ **you!** à vos souhaits! **blessed** adj (holy) saint; (damned 🔲) sacré. **blessing** n bénédiction f; (benefit) avantage *m*; (stroke of luck) chance *f.*

blew /blu:/ →**BLOW.**

blight /blaɪt/ *n* (disease: Bot) rouille *f*; (fig) plaie *f.*

blind /blaɪnd/ *adj* aveugle (**to** à;) (*corner, bend*) sans visibilité. ● *vt* aveugler. ● *n* (on window) store *m*; **the ~** les aveugles *mpl.*

blindfold /'blaɪndfəʊld/ *adj* **be ~** avoir les yeux bandés. ● *adv* les yeux bandés. ● *n* bandeau *m.* ● *vt* bander les yeux à.

blindness /'blaɪndnɪs/ *n* (Med) cécité *f*; (fig) aveuglement *m.*

blind spot *n* (Auto) angle *m* mort.

blink /blɪŋk/ *vi* cligner des yeux; (*light*) clignoter.

bliss /blɪs/ *n* délice *m.* **blissful** *adj* délicieux.

blister /'blɪstə(r)/ *n* ampoule *f*; (on paint) cloque *f.* ● *vi* cloquer.

blitz /blɪts/ *n* (Aviat) raid *m* éclair. ● *vt* bombarder.

blob /blɒb/ *n* (drop) (grosse) goutte *f*; (stain) tache *f.*

block /blɒk/ *n* bloc *m*; (buildings) pâté *m* de maisons; (in pipe) obstruction *f*; **~ (of flats)** immeuble *m*; **~ letters** majuscules *fpl.* ● *vt* bloquer.

blockade /blɒ'keɪd/ *n* blocus *m.* ● *vt* bloquer.

blockage /'blɒkɪdʒ/ *n* obstruction *f.*

blockbuster *n* gros succès *m.*

bloke /bləʊk/ *n* 🔲 type *m.*

blond /blɒnd/ *adj & n* blond (*m*).

blonde /blɒnd/ *adj & n* blonde (*f*).

blood /blʌd/ *n* sang *m.* ● *adj* (donor, bath) de sang; (bank, poisoning) du sang; (group, vessel) sanguin. **~-pressure** *n* tension *f* artérielle. **~shed** *n* effusion *f* de sang. **~shot** *adj* injecté de sang. **~stream** *n* sang *m.* **~ test** *n* prise *f* de sang.

bloody /'blʌdɪ/ *adj* (**-ier, -iest**) sanglant; 🔲 sacré. ● *adv* 🔲 vachement 🔲. **~-minded** *adj* 🔲 hargneux, obstiné.

bloom /blu:m/ *n* fleur *f.* ● *vi* fleurir; (person) s'épanouir.

blossom /'blɒsəm/ *n* fleur(s) *f* (*pl*). ● *vi* fleurir; (person) s'épanouir.

blot /blɒt/ *n* tache *f.* ● *vt* (*pt* **blotted**) tacher; (dry) sécher; **~ out** effacer.

blotch /blɒtʃ/ *n* tache *f.*

blouse /blaʊz/ *n* chemisier *m.*

blow /bləʊ/ *vt/i* (*pt* **blew**; *pp* **blown**) souffler; (*fuse*) (faire) sauter; (*squander* 🔲) claquer; (*opportunity*) rater; **~ one's nose** se moucher; **~ a whistle** siffler. ● *n* coup *m.* □ **~ away** or **off** emporter; **~ out** souffler; **~ over** passer; **~ up** (faire) sauter; (*tyre*) gonfler; (Photo) agrandir.

blow-dry *n* brushing *m.* ● *vt* faire un brushing à.

blown /bləʊn/ →**BLOW.**

bludgeon /'blʌdʒən/ *n* matraque *f.* ● *vt* matraquer.

blue /blu:/ *adj* bleu; (*movie*) porno. ● *n* bleu *m*; **come out of the ~** être inattendu; **have the ~s** avoir le cafard. **~bell** *n* jacinthe *f* des bois. **~print** *n* projet *m.*

bluff /blʌf/ *vt/i* bluffer. ● *n* bluff *m*; **call sb's ~** dire chiche à qn. ● *adj* (*person*) carré.

blunder /'blʌndə(r)/ *vi* faire une bourde; (move) avancer à tâtons. ● *n* gaffe *f.*

blunt /blʌnt/ *adj* (*knife*) émoussé; (person) brusque. ● *vt* émousser. **bluntly** *adv* carrément.

blur /blɜ:(r)/ *n* image *f* floue. ● *vt* (*pt* **blurred**) brouiller.

blurb /blɜ:b/ *n* résumé *m* publicitaire.

blush /blʌʃ/ *vi* rougir. ● *n* rougeur *f.* **blusher** *n* fard *m* à joues.

blustery /'blʌstərɪ/ *adj* **~ wind** bourrasque *f.*

BMI *abbr* (**body mass index**) IMC *f.*

boar /bɔ:(r)/ *n* sanglier *m.*

board /bɔ:d/ *n* planche *f*; (for notices) tableau *m*; (food) pension *f*; **full ~** pension *f* complète; **half ~** demi-pension *f*; (committee) conseil *m*; **~ of directors** conseil *m* d'administration; **go by the ~** tomber à l'eau; **on ~** à bord. ● *vt/i* (bus, train) monter dans; (Naut) monter à bord (de); **~ with** être en pension chez.

boarding-school *n* école *f* privée avec internat.

boast /bəʊst/ *vi* se vanter (**about** de). ● *vt* s'enorgueillir de. ● *n* vantardise *f.*

boat /bəʊt/ *n* bateau *m*; (small) canot *m*; **in the same ~** logé à la même enseigne.

bode /bəʊd/ vi ~ **well**/**ill** être de bon/ mauvais augure.

bodily /ˈbɒdɪlɪ/ adj (need, well-being) physique; (injury) corporel. ● adv physiquement; (in person) en personne.

body /ˈbɒdɪ/ n corps m; (mass) masse f; (organization) organisme m; ~ **part** n partie f de corps; ~**(work)** (Auto) carrosserie f; **the main** ~ **of** le gros de. ~**-building** n culturisme m. ~**guard** n garde m du corps.

bog /bɒg/ n marais m. ● vt (pt **bogged**) **get** ~**ged down** s'enliser dans.

bogus /ˈbəʊgəs/ adj faux.

boil /bɔɪl/ n furoncle m; **bring to the** ~ porter à ébullition. ● vt/i bouillir. ~ **down to** se ramener à; ~ **over** déborder. **boiled** adj (egg) à la coque; (potatoes) à l'eau.

boiler /ˈbɔɪlə(r)/ n chaudière f; ~ **suit** bleu m (de travail).

boisterous /ˈbɔɪstərəs/ adj tapageur; (child) turbulent.

bold /bəʊld/ adj hardi; (cheeky) effronté; (type) gras.

Bolivia /bəˈlɪvɪə/ n Bolivie f.

bollard /ˈbɒlɑːd/ n (on road) balise f.

bolt /bəʊlt/ n (on door) verrou m; (for nut) boulon m; (lightning) éclair m. ● vt (door) verrouiller; (food) engouffrer. ● vi s'emballer.

bomb /bɒm/ n bombe f; ~ **scare** alerte f à la bombe. ● vt bombarder.

bomber /ˈbɒmə(r)/ n (aircraft) bombardier m; (person) plastiqueur m.

bond /bɒnd/ n (agreement) engagement m; (link) lien m; (Comm) obligation f, bon m; **in** ~ (entreposé) en douane.

bone /bəʊn/ n os m; (of fish) arête f. ● vt désosser. ~**-dry** adj tout à fait sec.

bonfire /ˈbɒnfaɪə(r)/ n feu m; (for celebration) feu m de joie.

bonnet /ˈbɒnɪt/ n (hat) bonnet m; (of vehicle) capot m.

bonus /ˈbəʊnəs/ n prime f.

bony /ˈbəʊnɪ/ adj (**-ier**, **-iest**) (thin) osseux; (fish) plein d'arêtes.

boo /buː/ interj hou. ● vt/i huer. ● n huée f.

booby trap /ˈbuːbɪtræp/ n mécanisme m piégé. ● vt (pt **-trapped**) piéger.

book /bʊk/ n livre m; (exercise) cahier m; (of tickets etc.) carnet m; ~**s** (Comm) comptes mpl. ● vt (reserve) réserver; (driver) dresser un PV à; (player) prendre le nom de; (write down) inscrire. ● vi retenir des places; (fully) ~**ed** complet. ~**case** n bibliothèque f. **booking-office** n guichet m. ~**keeping** n comptabilité f. **booklet** n brochure f. ~**maker** n bookmaker m. ~**mark** n (for book, Internet) signet m. ~**seller** n libraire mf. ~**shop** n librairie f. ~**stall** n kiosque m (à journaux).

boom /buːm/ vi (gun, wind, etc.) gronder; (trade) prospérer. ● n grondement m; (Comm) boom m, prospérité f.

boost /buːst/ vt stimuler; (morale) remonter; (price) augmenter; (publicize) faire de la réclame pour.

boot /buːt/ n (knee-length) botte f; (anklelength) chaussure f (montante); (for walking) chaussure f de marche; (Sport) chaussure f de sport; (of vehicle) coffre m; **get the** ~ se faire virer. ● vt/i ~ **up** (Comput) amorcer.

booth /buːð/ n (for telephone) cabine f; (at fair) baraque f.

booze /buːz/ vi 🔲 boire (beaucoup). ● n 🔲 alcool m.

border /ˈbɔːdə(r)/ n (edge) bord m; (frontier) frontière f; (in garden) bordure f. ● vi ~ **on** être voisin de, avoisiner.

bore /bɔː(r)/ vt ennuyer; **be** ~**d** s'ennuyer; ➡**BEAR**. ● vi (Tech) forer. ● n raseur-euse m/f; (thing) ennui m. **boredom** n ennui m. **boring** adj ennuyeux.

born /bɔːn/ adj né; **be** ~ naître.

borne /bɔːn/ ➡**BEAR**.

borough /ˈbʌrə/ n municipalité f.

borrow /ˈbɒrəʊ/ vt emprunter (**from** à).

Bosnia /ˈbɒznɪə/ n Bosnie f.

Bosnian /ˈbɒznɪən/ adj bosniaque. ● n Bosniaque.

bosom /ˈbʊzəm/ n poitrine f; ~ **friend** ami/-e m/f intime.

boss /bɒs/ n 🔲 patron/-ne m/f. ● vt ~ (**about**) 🔲 mener par le bout du nez.

bossy /ˈbɒsɪ/ adj autoritaire.

botch /bɒtʃ/ vt bâcler, saboter.

both /bəʊθ/ *det* les deux; ~ **the books** les deux livres. ● *pron* tous/toutes (les) deux, l'un/-e et l'autre; **we ~ agree** nous sommes tous les deux d'accord; **I bought ~ (of them)** j'ai acheté les deux; **I saw ~ of you** je vous ai vus tous les deux; **~ Paul and Anne** (et) Paul et Anne. ● *adv* à la fois.

bother /'bɒðə(r)/ *vt* (annoy, worry) ennuyer; (disturb) déranger. ● *vi* se déranger; **don't ~ (calling)** ce n'est pas la peine (d'appeler); **don't ~ about us** ne t'inquiète pas pour nous; **I can't be ~ed** j'ai la flemme 🔲. ● *n* ennui *m*; (effort) peine *f*; **it's no ~** ce n'est rien.

bottle /'bɒtl/ *n* bouteille *f*; (for baby) biberon *m*. ● *vt* mettre en bouteille. ~ **up** contenir. ~ **bank** *n* collecteur *m* (de verre usagé). ~**neck** *n* (traffic jam) embouteillage *m*. ~**-opener** *n* ouvre-bouteilles *m inv*.

bottom /'bɒtəm/ *n* fond *m*; (of hill, page, etc.) bas *m*; (buttocks) derrière *m* 🔲. ● *adj* inférieur(e), du bas.

bought /bɔːt/ ➡BUY.

bounce /baʊns/ *vi* rebondir; (person) faire des bonds, bondir; (cheques 🔲) être refusé. ● *vt* faire rebondir. ● *n* rebond *m*.

bound /baʊnd/ *vi* (leap) bondir; ~**ed by** limité par; ➡BIND. ● *n* bond *m*. ● *adj* **be ~ for** être en route pour, aller vers; ~ **to** (obliged) obligé de; (certain) sûr de.

boundary /'baʊndrɪ/ *n* limite *f*.

bounds /baʊndz/ *npl* limites *fpl*; **out of ~** être interdit d'accès.

bout /baʊt/ *n* période *f*; (Med) accès *m*; (boxing) combat *m*.

bow¹ /bəʊ/ *n* (weapon) arc *m*; (of violin) archet *m*; (knot) nœud *m*.

bow² /baʊ/ *n* salut *m*; (of ship) proue *f*. ● *vt/i* (s')incliner.

bowels /'baʊəlz/ *npl* intestins *mpl*; (fig) profondeurs *fpl*.

bowl /bəʊl/ *n* (for washing) cuvette *f*; (for food) bol *m*; (for soup) assiette *f* creuse. ● *vt/i* (cricket) lancer; ~ **over** bouleverser.

bowler /'bəʊlə(r)/ *n* (cricket) lanceur *m*; ~ **(hat)** (chapeau) melon *m*.

bowling /'bəʊlɪŋ/ *n* (ten-pin) bowling *m*; (on grass) jeu *m* de boules. ~**-alley** *n* bowling *m*.

bow tie *n* nœud *m* papillon.

box /bɒks/ *n* boîte *f*; (cardboard) carton *m*; (Theat) loge *f*; **the ~** 🔲 la télé. ● *vt* mettre en boîte; (Sport) boxer; ~ **sb's ears** gifler qn; ~ **in** enfermer.

boxing /'bɒksɪŋ/ *n* boxe *f*. ● *adj* de boxe. **B~ Day** *n* le lendemain de Noël.

box office *n* guichet *m*.

boy /bɔɪ/ *n* garçon *m*; ~ **band** boys band *m*.

boycott /'bɔɪkɒt/ *vt* boycotter. ● *n* boycottage *m*.

boyfriend /'bɔɪfrend/ *n* (petit) ami *m*.

bra /brɑː/ *n* soutien-gorge *m*.

brace /breɪs/ *n* (fastener) attache *f*; (dental) appareil *m*; (tool) vilbrequin *m*; ~**s** (for trousers) bretelles *fpl*. ● *vt* soutenir; ~ **oneself** rassembler ses forces.

bracket /'brækɪt/ *n* (for shelf etc.) tasseau *m*, support *m*; (group) tranche *f*; **in ~s** entre parenthèses. ● *vt* mettre entre parenthèses or crochets.

braid /breɪd/ *n* (trimming) galon *m*; (of hair) tresse *f*.

brain /breɪn/ *n* cerveau *m*; ~**s** (fig) intelligence *f*. ● *vt* assommer. **brainless** *adj* stupide. ~**wash** *vt* faire subir un lavage de cerveau à. ~**wave** *n* idée *f* géniale, trouvaille *f*. **brainy** *adj* (-ier, -iest) doué.

brake /breɪk/ *n* (Auto also fig) frein *m*. ● *vt/i* freiner. ~ **light** *n* feu *m* stop.

bran /bræn/ *n* son *m*.

branch /brɑːntʃ/ *n* (of tree) branche *f*; (of road) embranchement *m*; (Comm) succursale *f*; (of bank) agence *f*. ● *vi* ~ **(off)** bifurquer.

brand /brænd/ *n* marque *f*. ● *vt* ~ **sb as sth** désigner qn comme qch.

brand-new /brænd'njuː/ *adj* tout neuf.

brandy /'brændɪ/ *n* cognac *m*.

brass /brɑːs/ *n* cuivre *m*; **get down to ~ tacks** en venir aux choses sérieuses; **the ~** (Mus) les cuivres *mpl*; **top ~** 🔲 galonnés *mpl*.

brat /bræt/ *n* 🔲 môme *mf* 🔲.

brave /breɪv/ *adj* courageux, (smile) brave. ● *n* (American Indian) brave *m*. ● *vt* braver. **bravery** *n* courage *m*.

brawl /brɔːl/ *n* bagarre *f*. ● *vi* se bagarrer.

Brazil /brə'zɪl/ *n* Brésil *m*.

breach /briːtʃ/ n (of copyright, privilege) violation f; (in relationship) rupture f; (gap) brèche f. ● vt ouvrir une brèche dans.

bread /bred/ n pain m; ~ **and butter** tartine f. ~**-bin,** (US) ~**-box** boîte f à pain. ~**crumbs** npl chapelure f.

breadth /bretθ/ n largeur f.

bread-winner /ˈbredwɪnə(r)/ n soutien m de famille.

break /breɪk/ vt (pt **broke,** pp **broken**) casser; (smash into pieces) briser; (vow, silence, rank, etc.) rompre; (law) violer; (a record) battre; (news) révéler; (journey) interrompre; (heart, strike, ice) briser; ~ **one's arm** se casser le bras. ● vi (se) casser; se briser. ● n cassure f, rupture f; (in relationship, continuity) rupture f; (interval) interruption f; (at school) récréation f, récré f; (for coffee) pause f; (luck 🄸) chance f. ~ **away from** se détacher; ~ **down** vi (collapse) s'effondrer; (negotiations) échouer; (machine) tomber en panne; vt (door) enfoncer; (analyse) analyser; ~ **even** rentrer dans ses frais; ~ **into** cambrioler; ~ **off** (se) détacher; (suspend) rompre; (stop talking) s'interrompre; ~ **out** (fire, war, etc.) éclater; ~ **up** (end) (faire) cesser; (couple) rompre; (marriage) (se) briser; (crowd) (se) disperser; (schools) être en vacances. **breakable** adj fragile. **breakage** n casse f.

breakdown /ˈbreɪkdaʊn/ n (Tech) panne f; (Med) dépression f; (of figures) analyse f. ● adj (Auto) de dépannage.

breakfast /ˈbrekfəst/ n petit déjeuner m.

break /breɪk/: ~**-in** n cambriolage m. ~**through** n percée f.

breast /brest/ n sein m; (chest) poitrine f. ~**-feed** vt (pt **-fed**) allaiter. ~**-stroke** n brasse f.

breath /breθ/ n souffle m, haleine f; **out of** ~ à bout de souffle; **under one's** ~ tout bas.

breathalyser® /ˈbreθəlaɪzə(r)/ n alcootest m.

breathe /briːð/ vt/i respirer. ~ **in** inspirer; ~ **out** expirer.

breathless /ˈbreθlɪs/ adj à bout de souffle.

breathtaking /ˈbreθteɪkɪŋ/ adj à vous couper le souffle.

bred /bred/ ➞BREED.

breed /briːd/ vt (pt **bred**) élever; (give rise to) engendrer. ● vi se reproduire. ● n race f.

breeze /briːz/ n brise f.

brew /bruː/ vt (beer) brasser; (tea) faire infuser. ● vi (beer) fermenter; (tea) infuser; (fig) se préparer. ● n décoction f. **brewer** n brasseur m. **brewery** n brasserie f.

bribe /braɪb/ n pot-de-vin m. ● vt soudoyer. **bribery** n corruption f.

brick /brɪk/ n brique f. ~**layer** n maçon m.

bridal /ˈbraɪdl/ adj (dress) de mariée; (car, chamber) des mariés.

bride /braɪd/ n mariée f. ~**groom** n marié m. ~**smaid** n demoiselle f d'honneur.

bridge /brɪdʒ/ n pont m; (Naut) passerelle f; (of nose) arête f; (card game) bridge m. ● vt ~ **a gap** combler une lacune.

bridle /ˈbraɪdl/ n bride f. ● vt brider. ~**-path** n piste f cavalière.

brief /briːf/ adj bref. ● n instructions fpl; (Jur) dossier m. ● vt donner des instructions à.

briefcase /ˈbriːfkeɪs/ n serviette f.

briefs /briːfs/ npl slip m.

bright /braɪt/ adj brillant, vif; (day, room) clair; (cheerful) gai; (clever) intelligent.

brighten /ˈbraɪtn/ vt égayer. ● vi (weather) s'éclaircir; (face) s'éclairer.

brilliant /ˈbrɪlɪənt/ adj (student, career) brillant; (light) éclatant; (very good 🄸) super.

brim /brɪm/ n bord m. ● vi (pt **brimmed**); ~ **over** déborder (with de).

bring /brɪŋ/ vt (pt **brought**) (thing) apporter; (person, vehicle) amener; ~ **to bear** (pressure etc.) exercer. ~ **about** provoquer; ~ **back** (return with) rapporter; (colour, shine) redonner; ~ **down** faire tomber; (shoot down, knock down) abattre; ~ **forward** avancer; ~ **off** réussir; ~ **out** (take out) sortir; (show) faire ressortir; (book) publier; ~ **round** faire revenir à soi; ~ **up** (*child*) élever; (Med) vomir; (*question*) aborder.

brink /brɪŋk/ n bord m.

brisk /brɪsk/ adj vif.

bristle /'brɪsl/ n poil m. ● vi se hérisser; **bristling with** hérissé de.

Britain /'brɪtn/ n Grande-Bretagne f.

British /'brɪtɪʃ/ adj britannique; **the** ~ les Britanniques mpl.

Briton /'brɪtn/ n Britannique mf.

Brittany /'brɪtənɪ/ n Bretagne f.

brittle /'brɪtl/ adj fragile.

broad /brɔːd/ adj large; (*choice, range*) grand. ~ **bean** n fève f.

broadband /'brɔːdbænd/adj à haut débit. ● n ADSL m haut débit m.

broadcast /'brɔːdkɑːst/ vt/i (pt **broadcast**) diffuser; (*person*) parler à la television or à la radio. ● n émission f.

broadly /'brɔːdlɪ/ adv en gros.

broad-minded /brɔːd'maɪndɪd/ adj large d'esprit.

broccoli /'brɒkəlɪ/ n inv brocoli m.

brochure /'brəʊʃə(r)/ n brochure f.

broke /brəʊk/ ➡BREAK. ● adj (penniless 🔲) fauché.

broken /'brəʊkən/ ➡BREAK. ● adj ~ **English** mauvais anglais m.

bronchitis /brɒŋ'kaɪtɪs/ n bronchite f.

bronze /brɒnz/ n bronze m.

brooch /brəʊtʃ/ n broche f.

brood /bruːd/ n nichée f, couvée f. ● vi méditer tristement.

broom /bruːm/ n balai m.

broth /brɒθ/ n bouillon m.

brothel /'brɒθl/ n maison f close.

brother /'brʌðə(r)/ n frère m. ~**hood** n fraternité f. ~**-in-law** n (pl ~**s-in-law**) beau-frère m.

brought /brɔːt/ ➡BRING.

brow /braʊ/ n front m; (of hill) sommet m.

brown /braʊn/ adj (*object*) marron; (*hair*) brun; ~ **bread** pain m complet; ~ **sugar** sucre m roux. ● n marron m; brun m. ● vt/i brunir; (Culin) (faire) dorer.

Brownie /'braʊnɪ/ n jeannette f.

browse /braʊz/ vi flâner; (*animal*) brouter. ● vt (Comput) naviguer.

browser n (Comput) navigateur m.

bruise /bruːz/ n bleu m. ● vt (*knee, arm* etc.) faire un bleu à; (*fruit*) abîmer.

brush /brʌʃ/ n brosse f; (skirmish) accrochage m; (bushes) broussailles fpl. ● vt brosser. ~ **against** frôler; ~ **aside** (dismiss) repousser; (move) écarter; ~ **up (on)** se remettre à.

Brussels /'brʌslz/ n Bruxelles. ~ **sprouts** npl choux mpl de Bruxelles.

brutal /'bruːtl/ adj brutal.

brute /bruːt/ n brute f; **by** ~ **force** par la force.

BSE abbr (Bovine Spongiform Encephalopathy) encéphalopathie f spongiforme bovine, ESB f.

bubble /'bʌbl/ n bulle f; **blow** ~**s** faire des bulles. ● vi bouillonner; ~ **over** déborder. ~ **bath** n bain m moussant.

buck /bʌk/ n mâle m; (US, 🔲) dollar m; **pass the** ~ rejeter la responsabilité (to sur). ● vi (*horse*) ruer; ~ **up** 🔲 prendre courage; (hurry 🔲) se grouiller 🔲.

bucket /'bʌkɪt/ n seau m (**of** de).

buckle /'bʌkl/ n boucle f. ● vt/i (fasten) (se) boucler; (bend) voiler.

bud /bʌd/ n bourgeon m. ● vi (pt **budded**) bourgeonner.

Buddhism /'bʊdɪzəm/ n bouddhisme m.

budding /'bʌdɪŋ/ adj (talent) naissant; (athlete) en herbe.

budge /bʌdʒ/ vt/i (faire) bouger.

budgerigar /'bʌdʒərɪgɑː(r)/ n perruche f.

budget /'bʌdʒɪt/ n budget m. ● vi ~ **for** prévoir (dans son budget).

buff /bʌf/ n (colour) chamois m; 🔲 fanatique mf.

buffalo /'bʌfələʊ/ n (pl **-oes** or **-o** buffle m; (US) bison m.

buffer /'bʌfə(r)/ n tampon m; ~ **zone** zone f tampon.

buffet¹ /'bʊfeɪ/ n (meal, counter) buffet m; ~ **car** buffet m.

buffet² /'bʌfɪt/ n (blow) soufflet m. ● vt (pt **buffeted**) souffleter.

bug /bʌg/ n (bedbug) punaise f; (any small insect) bestiole f; (germ) microbe m; (stomachache 🔲) ennuis mpl

gastriques; (device) micro m; (defect)
défaut m; (Comput) bogue f, bug m.
● vt (pt **bugged**) mettre des micros
dans; 🗵 embêter.

buggy /'bʌgɪ/ n poussette f.

build /bɪld/ vt/i (pt **built**) bâtir, construire. ● n carrure f. ~ **up** (increase)
augmenter, monter; (accumulate)
(s')accumuler. **builder** n entrepreneur
m en bâtiment; (workman) ouvrier m
du bâtiment.

building /'bɪldɪŋ/ n (structure) bâtiment m; (dwelling) immeuble m. ~
society n caisse f d'épargne.

build-up /'bɪldʌp/ n accumulation f;
(fig) publicité f.

built /bɪlt/ ➡BUILD.

built-in /bɪlt'ɪn/ adj encastré.

built-up area n agglomération f, zone
f urbanisée.

bulb /bʌlb/ n (Bot) bulbe m; (Electr)
ampoule f.

Bulgaria /bʌl'geərɪə/ n Bulgarie f.

Bulgarian /bʌl'geərɪən/ n (person)
Bulgare mf; (Ling) bulgare m. ● adj
bulgare.

bulge /bʌldʒ/ n renflement m. ● vi se
renfler, être renflé; **be bulging with**
être gonflé or bourré de.

bulimia /bjuː'lɪmɪə/ n boulimie f.

bulk /bʌlk/ n volume f; **in** ~ (buy, sell)
en gros; (transport) en vrac; **the** ~ **of**
la majeure partie de.

bull /bʊl/ n taureau m. ~**dog** n bouledogue m. ~**doze** vt raser au bulldozer.

bullet /'bʊlɪt/ n balle f.

bulletin /'bʊlətɪn/ n bulletin m.

bullet-proof /'bʊlɪtpruːf/ adj (vest)
pare-balles inv; (vehicle) blindé.

bullion /'bʊlɪən/ n or m or argent m en
lingots.

bullring /'bʊlrɪŋ/ n arène f.

bull's-eye /'bʊlzaɪ/ n mille m.

bully /'bʊlɪ/ n (child) petite brute f;
(adult) tyran m. ● vt maltraiter.

bum /bʌm/ n 🗵 derrière m 🗓; (US, 🗵)
vagabond/-e m/f.

bumble-bee /'bʌmblbiː/ n bourdon m.

bump /bʌmp/ n (swelling) bosse f; (on
road) bosse f. ● vt/i cogner, heurter. ~

along cahoter; ~ **into** (hit) rentrer
dans; (meet) tomber sur.

bumper /'bʌmpə(r)/ n pare-chocs m
inv. ● adj exceptionnel.

bumpy /'bʌmpɪ/ adj (road) accidenté.

bun /bʌn/ n (cake) petit pain m; (hair)
chignon m.

bunch /bʌntʃ/ n (of flowers) bouquet
m; (of keys) trousseau m; (of people)
groupe m; (of bananas) régime m; ~
of grapes grappe f de raisin.

bundle /'bʌndl/ n paquet m. ● vt mettre en paquet; (push) fourrer.

bung /bʌŋ/ n bouchon m. ● vt (stop
up) boucher; (throw 🗵) flanquer 🗓.

bunion /'bʌnjən/ n (Med) oignon m.

bunk /bʌŋk/ n (on ship, train) couchette f. ~**beds** npl lits mpl superposés.

buoy /bɔɪ/ n bouée f. ● vt ~ **up**
(hearten) soutenir, encourager.

buoyancy /'bɔɪənsɪ/ n (of floating object) flottabilité f; (cheerfulness)
gaieté f.

burden /'bɜːdn/ n fardeau m. ● vt ennuyer (**with** de).

bureau /'bjʊərəʊ/ n (pl -**eaux**) bureau m.

bureaucracy /bjʊə'rɒkrəsɪ/ n bureaucratie f.

burglar /'bɜːglə(r)/ n cambrioleur m;
~ **alarm** alarme f. **burglarize** vt (US)
cambrioler. **burglary** n cambriolage m.
burgle vt cambrioler.

Burgundy /'bɜːgəndɪ/ n (wine) bourgogne m.

burial /'berɪəl/ n enterrement m.

burn /bɜːn/ vt/i (pt **burned** or **burnt**)
brûler. ● n brûlure f. ~ **down** être réduit en cendres. **burner** n (on cooker)
brûleur m; (on computer) graveur m.
burning adj en flammes; (fig) brûlant.

burnt /bɜːnt/ ➡BURN.

burp /bɜːp/ n 🗓 rot m. ● vi 🗓 roter.

burrow /'bʌrəʊ/ n terrier m. ● vt
creuser.

bursar /'bɜːsə(r)/ n intendant/-e m/f.
bursary n bourse f.

burst /bɜːst/ vt/i (pt **burst** (balloon,
bubble) crever; (pipe) (faire) éclater.
● n explosion f; (of laughter) éclat m;
(surge) élan m. ~ **into** (room) faire in-

terruption dans; ~ **into tears** fondre en larmes; ~ **out** ~ **out laughing** éclater de rire; ~ **with be** ~**ing with** déborder de.

bury /'berɪ/ vt (person etc.) enterrer; (hide, cover) enfouir; (engross, thrust) plonger.

bus /bʌs/ n (pl **buses**) (auto)bus m. ● vt transporter en bus. ● vi (pt **bussed**) prendre l'autobus.

bush /bʊʃ/ n (shrub) buisson m; (land) brousse f.

business /'bɪznɪs/ n (task, concern) affaire f; (commerce) affaires fpl; (line of work) métier m; (shop) commerce m; **he has no** ~ **to** il n'a pas le droit de; **mean** ~ être sérieux; **that's none of your** ~**!** ça ne vous regarde pas! ~**like** adj sérieux. ~**man** n homme m d'affaires.

busker /'bʌskə(r)/ n musicien/-ne m/f des rues.

bus-stop n arrêt m d'autobus.

bust /bʌst/ n (statue) buste m; (bosom) poitrine f. ● vt/i (pt **busted** or **bust**) (burst 🔲) crever; (break 🔲) (se) casser. ● adj (broken, finished 🔲) fichu; **go** ~ 🔲 faire faillite.

bustle /'bʌsl/ vi s'affairer. ● n affairement m, remue-ménage m.

busy /'bɪzɪ/ adj (**-ier, -iest**) (person) occupé; (street) animé; (day) chargé. ● vt ~ **oneself with** s'occuper à.

but /bʌt/ conj mais. ● prep sauf; ~ **for** sans; **nobody** ~ personne d'autre que; **nothing** ~ rien que. ● adv (only) seulement.

butcher /'bʊtʃə(r)/ n boucher m. ● vt massacrer.

butler /'bʌtlə(r)/ n maître m d'hôtel.

butt /bʌt/ n (of gun) crosse f; (of cigarette) mégot m; (of joke) cible f; (barrel) tonneau m; (US, 🔲) derrière m 🔲. ● vi ~ **in** interrompre.

butter /'bʌtə(r)/ n beurre m. ● vt beurrer. ~**bean** n haricot m blanc. ~**cup** n bouton-d'or m.

butterfly /'bʌtəflaɪ/ n papillon m.

buttock /'bʌtək/ n fesse f.

button /'bʌtn/ n bouton m. ● vt/i ~ **(up)** (se) boutonner.

buttonhole /'bʌtnhəʊl/ n boutonnière f. ● vt accrocher.

buy /baɪ/ vt (pt **bought**) acheter (**from** à); ~ **sth for sb** acheter qch à qn, prendre qch pour qn; (believe 🔲) croire, avaler.

buzz /bʌz/ n bourdonnement m. ● vi bourdonner. **buzzer** n sonnerie f.

by /baɪ/ prep par, de; (near) à côté de; (before) avant; (means) en, à, par; ~ **bike** à vélo; ~ **car** en auto; ~ **day** de jour; ~ **the kilo** au kilo; ~ **running** en courant; ~ **sea** par mer; ~ **that time** à ce moment-là; ~ **the way** à propos; ~ **oneself** tout seul. ● adv **close** ~ tout près; ~ **and large** dans l'ensemble.

bye(-bye) /'baɪbaɪ/ interj 🔲 au revoir, salut 🔲.

by-election n élection f partielle.

Byelorussia /bjeləʊ'rʊʃə/ n Biélorussie f.

by-law /'baɪlɔː/ n arrêté m municipal.

bypass /'baɪpɑːs/ n (Auto) rocade f; (Med) pontage m. ● vt contourner.

by-product n dérivé m; (fig) conséquence f.

byte /baɪt/ n octet m.

Cc

cab /kæb/ n taxi m; (of lorry, train) cabine f.

cabbage /'kæbɪdʒ/ n chou m.

cabin /'kæbɪn/ n (hut) cabane f; (in ship, aircraft) cabine f.

cabinet /'kæbɪnɪt/ n petit placard m; (glassfronted) vitrine f; (Pol) cabinet m.

cable /'keɪbl/ n câble m. ● vt câbler. ~**-car** n téléphérique m. ~ **television** n télévision f par câble.

cache /kæʃ/ n (hoard) cache f; (place) cachette f.

cackle /'kækl/ n (of hen) caquet m; (laugh) ricanement m. ● vi caqueter; (laugh) ricaner.

cactus /'kæktəs/ n (pl **-ti** or ~**es**) cactus m.

cadet /kə'det/ n élève m officier.

Caesarean /sɪ'zeərɪən/ adj ~ **(section)** césarienne f.

café /'kæfeɪ/ n café m, snack-bar m.

caffeine /'kæfiːn/ n caféine f.

cage /keɪdʒ/ n cage f. ● vt mettre en cage.

cagey /'keɪdʒɪ/ adj réticent.

cagoule /kə'guːl/ n K-way® m.

cajole /kə'dʒəʊl/ vt ~ sb into doing sth amener qn à faire qch par la cajolerie.

cake /keɪk/ n gâteau m; (of soap) pain m. ● vi former une croûte (on sur).

calculate /'kælkjʊleɪt/ vt calculer; (estimate) évaluer. **calculated** adj délibéré; (risk) calculé. **calculating** adj calculateur. **calculation** n calcul m. **calculator** n calculatrice f.

calculus /'kælkjʊləs/ n (pl -li or ~es) calcul m.

calendar /'kælɪndə(r)/ n calendrier m.

calf /kɑːf/ n (pl calves) (young cow or bull) veau m; (of leg) mollet m.

calibre /'kælɪbə(r)/ n calibre m.

call /kɔːl/ vt/i appeler; (loudly) crier; **he's ~ed John** il s'appelle John; ~ **sb stupid** traiter qn d'imbécile. ● n appel m; (of bird) cri m; (visit) visite f; **make/pay a ~ on** rendre visite à; **be on ~** être de garde; ~ **box** cabine f téléphonique. ~ **centre** n centre m d'appels. ~ **back** rappeler; (visit) repasser; ~ **for** (help) appeler à; (demand) demander; (require) exiger; (collect) passer prendre; ~ **in** passer. ~ **off** annuler. ~ **on** (visit) rendre visite à; (urge) demander à (**to do** de faire). ~ **out** (**to**) appeler. ~ **round** venir. ~ **up** appeler.

calling /'kɔːlɪŋ/ n vocation f.

callous /'kæləs/ adj inhumain.

calm /kɑːm/ adj calme. ● n calme m. ● vt/i ~ (**down**) (se) calmer.

calorie /'kælərɪ/ n calorie f.

camcorder /'kæmkɔːdə(r)/ n camé-scope® m.

came /keɪm/ ⇒COME.

camel /'kæml/ n chameau m.

camera /'kæmərə/ n appareil(-photo) m; (TV, cinema) caméra f; **in** ~ à huis clos. ~**man** n (pl -**men**) cadreur m, cameraman m.

camouflage /'kæməflɑːʒ/ n camouflage m. ● vt camoufler.

camp /kæmp/ n camp m. ● vi camper.

campaign /kæm'peɪn/ n campagne f. ● vi faire campagne.

camper /'kæmpə(r)/ n campeur/-euse m/f. ~ (**-van**) n camping-car m.

camping /'kæmpɪŋ/ n camping m; **go** ~ faire du camping.

campsite /'kæmpsaɪt/ n camping m.

campus /'kæmpəsɪz/ n (pl ~es) campus m.

---

can¹ /kæn, kən/

> infinitive **be able to**; present **can**; present negative **can't**, **cannot** (formal); past **could**; past participle **been able to**

● auxiliary verb

⋯▸ pouvoir; **where** ~ **I buy stamps?** où est-ce que je peux acheter des timbres?; **she can't come** elle ne peut pas venir.

⋯▸ (be allowed to) pouvoir; ~ **I smoke?** est-ce que je peux fumer?

⋯▸ (know how to) savoir; **she** ~ **swim** elle sait nager; **he can't drive** il ne sait pas conduire.

⋯▸ (with verbs of perception) **I** ~ **hear you** je t'entends; ~ **they see us?** est-ce qu'ils nous voient?

---

can² /kæn/ n (for food) boîte f; (of petrol) bidon m. ● vt (pt **canned**) mettre en conserve.

Canada /'kænədə/ n Canada m.

Canadian /kə'neɪdɪən/ n Canadien/-ne m/f. ● adj canadien.

canal /kə'næl/ n canal m.

canary /kə'neərɪ/ n canari m.

cancel /'kænsl/ vt/i (pt **cancelled**) (call off, revoke) annuler; (a stamp) oblitérer; ~ **out** (se) neutraliser. **cancellation** n annulation f.

cancer /'kænsə(r)/ n cancer m; **have** ~ avoir un cancer.

Cancer /'kænsə(r)/ n Cancer m.

cancerous /'kænsərəs/ adj cancéreux.

candid /'kændɪd/ adj franc.

candidate /'kændɪdət/ n candidat/-e m/f.

candle /'kændl/ n bougie f; (in church) cierge m. ~**stick** n bougeoir m.

candy /'kændɪ/ n (US) bonbon(s) m(pl).
~-**floss** n barbe f à papa.

cane /keɪn/ n canne f; (for baskets)
rotin m; (for punishment) badine f. ● vt
donner des coups de badine à.

canister /'kænɪstə(r)/ n boîte f.

cannabis /'kænəbɪs/ n cannabis m.

cannibal /'kænɪbl/ n cannibale mf.

cannon /'kænən/ n (pl ~ or ~s)
canon m. ~-**ball** n boulet m de canon.

cannot →CAN NOT.

canoe /kə'nuː/ n canoë m. ● vi faire du
canoë. **canoeist** n canoéiste mf.

canon /'kænən/ n (clergyman) cha-
noine m; (rule) canon m.

can-opener n ouvre-boîtes m inv.

canopy /'kænəpɪ/ n dais m; (for bed)
baldaquin m.

can't →CAN NOT.

canteen /kæn'tiːn/ n (restaurant) cantine f; (flask) bidon m.

canter /'kæntə(r)/ n petit galop m. ● vi
aller au petit galop.

canvas /'kænvəs/ n toile f.

canvass /'kænvəs/ vt/i (Comm, Pol)
faire du démarchage (auprès de); ~
opinion sonder l'opinion.

canyon /'kænjən/ n cañon m.

cap /kæp/ n (hat) casquette f; (of bottle, tube) bouchon m; (of beer or milk
bottle) capsule f; (of pen) capuchon m;
(for toy gun) amorce f. ● vt (pt
capped) couronner.

capability /keɪpə'bɪlətɪ/ n capacité f.

capable /'keɪpəbl/ adj (person) compétent; ~ **of doing** capable de faire.

capacity /kə'pæsətɪ/ n capacité f; **in
my ~ as a doctor** en ma qualité de
médecin.

cape /keɪp/ n (cloak) cape f; (Geog)
cap m.

caper /'keɪpə(r)/ vi gambader. ● n
(leap) cabriole f; (funny film) comédie
f; (Culin) câpre f.

capital /'kæpɪtl/ adj (letter) majuscule;
(offence) capital. ● n (town) capitale f;
(money) capital m; ~ (**letter**) majuscule f.

capitalism /'kæpɪtəlɪzəm/ n capitalisme m.

capitalize /'kæpɪtəlaɪz/ vi ~ **on** tirer
parti de.

capitulate /kə'pɪtʃʊleɪt/ vi capituler.

Capricorn /'kæprɪkɔːn/ n Capricorne m.

capsize /kæp'saɪz/ vt/i (faire) chavirer.

capsule /'kæpsjuːl/ n capsule f.

captain /'kæptɪn/ n capitaine m.

caption /'kæpʃn/ n (under photo) légende f; (subtitle) sous-titre m.

captivate /'kæptɪveɪt/ vt captiver.

captive /'kæptɪv/ adj & n captif/-ive
(m/f). **captivity** n captivité f.

capture /'kæptʃə(r)/ vt (person, animal) capturer; (moment, likeness) saisir. ● n capture f.

car /kɑː(r)/ n voiture f. ● adj (industry)
automobile; (accident) de voiture;
(journey) en voiture.

caravan /'kærəvæn/ n caravane f.

carbohydrate /kɑːbə'haɪdreɪt/ n hy-
drate m de carbone.

carbon /'kɑːbən/ n carbone m. ~ **footprint** empreinte f écologique.

carburettor /'kɑːrbəreɪtər/ n carburateur m.

card /kɑːd/ n carte f.

cardboard /'kɑːdbɔːd/ n carton m.

cardiac /'kɑːdɪæk/ adj cardiaque; ~ **arrest** arrêt m du cœur.

cardigan /'kɑːdɪgən/ n cardigan m.

carer /'keərə(r)/ n (relative) personne
ayant un parent handicapé ou un
malade à charge; (professional) aide f à
la domicile.

cardinal /'keərə(r)/ adj (sin) capital;
(rule) fondamental; (number) cardinal.
● n cardinal m.

card index n fichier m.

care /keə(r)/ n (attention) soin m, attention f; (worry) souci m; (looking
after) soins mpl; **take ~ of** (deal with)
s'occuper de; (be careful with) prendre soin de; **take ~ to do sth** faire

bien attention à faire qch. ● *vi* ~
about s'intéresser à; ~ **for** s'occuper
de; (*invalid*) soigner; ~ **to do** vouloir
faire; **I don't** ~ ça m'est égal.

career /kə'rɪə(r)/ *n* carrière *f.* ● *vi* ~
in/out entrer/sortir à toute vitesse.

carefree /'keəfriː/ *adj* insouciant.

careful /'keəfl/ *adj* prudent; (*research,
study*) méticuleux; **(be)** ~! (fais) attention! **carefully** *adv* avec soin; (cautiously) prudemment.

careless /'keəlɪs/ *adj* négligent; (work)
bâclé.

caress /kə'res/ *n* caresse *f.* ● *vt* caresser.

caretaker /'keəteɪkə(r)/ *n* concierge
mf. ● *adj* (*president*) par intérim.

car ferry *n* ferry *m.*

cargo /'kɑːgəʊ/ *n* (*pl* ~**es**) chargement
m; (Naut) cargaison *f.*

Caribbean /kærɪ'biːən/ *adj* des Caraïbes, des Antilles. ● *n* **the** ~ (sea) la
mer des Antilles; (islands) les Antilles *fpl.*

caring /'keərɪŋ/ *adj* affectueux.

carnation /kɑː'neɪʃn/ *n* œillet *m.*

carnival /'kɑːnɪvl/ *n* carnaval *m.*

carol /'kærəl/ *n* chant *m* de Noël.

carp /kɑːp/ *n inv* carpe *f.* ● *vi* maugréer.

car-park *n* parc *m* de stationnement,
parking *m.*

carpenter /'kɑːpəntə(r)/ *n* (joiner) menuisier *m;* (builder) charpentier *m.* **carpentry** *n* menuiserie *f;* (structural)
charpenterie *f.*

carpet /'kɑːpɪt/ *n* (fitted) moquette *f;*
(loose) tapis *m.* ● *vt* (*pt* **carpeted**)
mettre de la moquette dans.

carriage /'kærɪdʒ/ *n* (rail) wagon *m;*
(ceremonial) carrosse *m;* (of goods)
transport *m;* (cost) port *m.*

carriageway /'kærɪdʒweɪ/ *n*
chaussée *f.*

carrier /'kærɪə(r)/ *n* transporteur *m;*
(Med) porteur/-euse *m/f;* ~ **(bag)** sac
m en plastique.

carrot /'kærət/ *n* carotte *f.*

carry /'kærɪ/ *vt/i* porter; (goods) transporter; (involve) comporter; (motion)
voter; **be carried away** s'emballer.
□ ~ **off** emporter; (prize) remporter;
~ **on** (continue) continuer; (business)
conduire; (conversation) mener; ~ **out**
(order, plan) exécuter; (duty) remplir;

(experiment, operation, repair) effectuer. ~**-cot** *n* portebébé *m.*

car sharing *n* covoiturage *m.*

cart /kɑːt/ *n* charrette *f.* ● *vt* (heavy bag
🄸) trimballer 🄸.

carton /'kɑːtn/ *n* (box) boîte *f;* (of yoghurt, cream) pot *m;* (of cigarettes) cartouche *f.*

cartoon /kɑː'tuːn/ *n* dessin *m* humoristique; (cinema) dessin *m* animé; (strip
cartoon) bande *f* dessinée.

cartridge /'kɑːtrɪdʒ/ *n* cartouche *f.*

carve /kɑːv/ *vt* tailler; (meat) découper.

car-wash *n* lavage *m* automatique.

cascade /kæ'skeɪd/ *n* cascade *f.* ● *vi*
tomber en cascade.

case /keɪs/ *n* cas *m;* (Jur) affaire *f;* (suitcase) valise *f;* (crate) caisse *f;* (for spectacles) étui *m;* **(just) in** ~ au cas où;
in ~ **he comes** au cas où il viendrait;
in ~ **of fire** en cas d'incendie; **in any**
~ de toute façon; **the** ~ **for sth** les
arguments *mpl* en faveur de qch; **the**
~ **for the defence** la défense.

cash /kæʃ/ *n* espèces *fpl,* argent *m;* **in**
~ en espèces. ● *adj* (price) comptant.
● *vt* encaisser; ~ **in (on)** profiter (de).
~**-back** *n* retrait *m* d'argent à la
caisse. ~ **desk** *n* caisse *f.* ~ **dispenser** *n* distributeur *m* de billets.

cashew /'kæʃuː/ *n* cajou *m.*

cash flow *n* marge *f* brute d'auto-
financement.

cashier /kæ'ʃɪə(r)/ *n* caissier/-ière *m/f.*

cashmere /kæʃ'mɪə(r)/ *n* cache-
mire *m.*

cash: ~**point** *n* distributeur *m* de
billets. ~ **point card** *n* carte *f* de retrait. ~ **register** *n* caisse *f* enregistreuse.

casino /kə'siːnəʊ/ *n* casino *m.*

casket /'kɑːskɪt/ *n* (box) coffret *m;*
(coffin) cercueil *m.*

casserole /'kæsərəʊl/ *n* (pan) daubière
f; (food) ragoût *m.*

cassette /kə'set/ *n* cassette *f.*

cast /kɑːst/ *vt* (*pt* **cast**) (object, glance)
jeter; (shadow) projeter; (metal) cou-
ler; ~ **(off)** (shed) se dépouiller de; ~
one's vote voter; ~ **iron** fonte *f.* ● *n*
(cinema, Theat, TV) distribution *f;*
(Med) plâtre *m.*

castaway /'kɑːstəweɪ/ *n* naufragé/-
e *m/f.*

cast-iron adj de fonte; (fig) en béton.

castle /'kɑːsl/ n château m; (chess) tour f.

cast-offs npl vieux vêtements mpl.

castor /'kɑːstə(r)/ n (wheel) roulette f.

castrate /kæ'streɪt/ vt châtrer.

casual /'kæʒʊəl/ adj (informal) décontracté; (remark) désinvolte; (acquaintance) de passage; (work) temporaire. **casually** adv (remark) d'un air détaché; (dress) simplement.

casualty /'kæʒʊəltɪ/ n victime f; (part of hospital) urgences fpl.

cat /kæt/ n chat m; (feline) félin m.

catalogue /'kætəlɒg/ n catalogue m. ● vt dresser un catalogue de.

catalyst /'kætəlɪst/ n catalyseur m.

catalytic /kætə'lɪtɪk/ adj ~ **converter** pot m catalytique.

catapult /'kætəpʌlt/ n lance-pierres m inv. ● vt projeter.

cataract /'kætərækt/ n (Med, Geog) cataracte f.

catarrh /kə'tɑː(r)/ n catarrhe m.

catastrophe /kə'tæstrəfɪ/ n catastrophe f.

catch /kætʃ/ vt (pt **caught**) attraper; (bus, plane) prendre; (understand) saisir; ~ **sb doing** surprendre qn en train de faire; ~ **fire** prendre feu; ~ **sight of** apercevoir; ~ **sb's attention/eye** attirer l'attention de qn. ● vi (get stuck) se prendre (**in** dans); (start to burn) prendre. ● n (fastening) fermeture f; (drawback) piège m; (in sport) prise f. ~ **on** devenir populaire. ~ **out** prendre de court. ~ **up** rattraper son retard; ~ **up with sb** rattraper qn.

catching /'kætʃɪŋ/ adj contagieux.

catchment /'kætʃmənt/ n ~ **area** (School) secteur m.

catch-phrase n formule f favorite.

catchy /'kætʃɪ/ adj entraînant.

category /'kætəgərɪ/ n catégorie f.

cater /'keɪtə(r)/ vi organiser des réceptions; ~ **for/to** (guests) accueillir; (needs) pourvoir à; (reader) s'adresser à. **caterer** n traiteur m.

caterpillar /'kætəpɪlə(r)/ n chenille f.

cathedral /kə'θiːdrəl/ n cathédrale f.

catholic /'kæθəlɪk/ adj éclectique. **Catholic** adj & n catholique (mf). **Cath-**

olicism n catholicisme m.

Catseye® n plot m rétroréfléchissant.

cattle /'kætl/ npl bétail m.

caught /kɔːt/ ➡CATCH.

cauliflower /'kɒlɪflaʊə(r)/ n chou-fleur m.

cause /kɔːz/ n cause f; (reason) raison f, motif m. ● vt causer; ~ **sth to grow/move** faire pousser/bouger qch.

causeway /'kɔːzweɪ/ n chaussée f.

caution /'kɔːʃn/ n prudence f; (warning) avertissement m. ● vt avertir. **cautious** adj prudent. **cautiously** adv prudemment.

cave /keɪv/ n grotte f. ● vi ~ **in** s'effondrer; (agree) céder. ~**man** n (pl -men) homme m des cavernes.

cavern /'kævən/ n caverne f.

caviare /'kævɪɑː(r)/ n caviar m.

caving /'keɪvɪŋ/ n spéléologie f.

CCTV abbr (closed circuit television) télévision f en circuit fermé.

CD abbr (**compact disc**) disque m compact, CD m.

CD-ROM /siːdiː'rɒm/ n disque m optique compact, CD-ROM m.

cease /siːs/ vt/i cesser. ~**-fire** n cessez-le-feu m inv.

cedar /'siːdə(r)/ n cèdre m.

cedilla /sɪ'dɪlə/ n cédille f.

ceiling /'siːlɪŋ/ n plafond m.

celebrate /'selɪbreɪt/ vt (occasion) fêter; (Easter, mass) célébrer. ● vi faire la fête. **celebrated** adj célèbre. **celebration** n fête f.

celebrity /sɪ'lebrətɪ/ n célébrité f.

celery /'selərɪ/ n céleri m.

cell /sel/ n cellule f; (Electr) élément m.

cellar /'selə(r)/ n cave f.

cellist /'tʃelɪst/ n violoncelliste mf. **cello** n violoncelle m.

cellphone /'selfəʊn/ n (téléphone m) portable.

Celt /kelt/ n Celte mf.

cement /sɪ'ment/ n ciment m. ● vt cimenter. ~**-mixer** n bétonnière f.

cemetery /'semətrɪ/ n cimetière m.

censor /'sensə(r)/ n censeur m. ● vt censurer.

censure /'senʃə(r)/ n censure f. ● vt critiquer.

census /'sensəs/ n recensement m.

cent /sent/ n cent m.

centenary /sen'tiːnərɪ/ n centenaire m.

centigrade /'sentɪgreɪd/ adj centigrade.

centilitre, (US) **centiliter** /'sentɪliːtə(r)/ n centilitre m.

centimetre, (US) **centimeter** /'sentɪmiːtə(r)/ n centimètre m.

centipede /'sentɪpiːd/ n millepattes m inv.

central /'sentrəl/ adj central; ~ **heating** chauffage m central; ~ **locking** fermeture f centralisée des portes. **centralize** vt centraliser. **centrally** adv (situated) au centre.

centre /'sentə(r)/, (US) **center** n centre m. ● vt (pt **centred**) centrer. ● vi ~ **on** tourner autour de.

century /'sentʃərɪ/ n siècle m.

ceramic /sɪ'ræmɪk/ adj (art) céramique; (object) en céramique.

cereal /'sɪərɪəl/ n céréale f.

ceremonial /serɪ'məʊnɪəl/ adj (dress) de cérémonie. ● n cérémonial m. **ceremony** n cérémonie f.

certain /'sɜːtn/ adj certain; for ~ avec certitude; **make** ~ **of** s'assurer de. **certainly** adv certainement. **certainty** n certitude f.

certificate /sə'tɪfɪkət/ n certificat m.

certify /'sɜːtɪfaɪ/ vt certifier.

cesspit, cesspool /'sespɪt, 'sespuːl/ n fosse f d'aisances.

chafe /tʃeɪf/ vt/i frotter (contre).

chagrin /'ʃægrɪn/ n dépit m.

chain /tʃeɪn/ n chaîne f; ~ **reaction** réaction f en chaîne; ~ **store** magasin m à succursales multiples. ● vt enchaîner. ~**-smoke** vi fumer sans arrêt.

chair /tʃeə(r)/ n chaise f; (armchair) fauteuil m; (Univ) chaire f; (chairperson) président/-e m/f. ● vt (preside over) présider. ~**man** n (pl **-men**) président/-e m/f. ~**woman** n (pl **-women**) présidente f.

chalk /tʃɔːk/ n craie f.

challenge /'tʃælɪndʒ/ n défi m; (opportunity) challenge m. ● vt (summon) défier (**to do** de faire); (question truth of) contester. **challenger** n (Sport) challenger m. **challenging** adj stimulant.

chamber /'tʃeɪmbə(r)/ n (old use) chambre f. ~**maid** n femme f de

chambre. ~ **music** n musique f de chambre. ~**-pot** n pot m de chambre.

champagne /ʃæm'peɪn/ n champagne m.

champion /'tʃæmpɪən/ n champion/-ne m/f. ● vt défendre. **championship** n championnat m.

chance /tʃɑːns/ n (luck) hasard m; (opportunity) occasion f; (likelihood) chances fpl; (risk) risque m; **by** ~ par hasard; **by any** ~ par hasard; ~**s are that** il est probable que. ● adj fortuit. ● vt ~ **doing** prendre le risque de faire; ~ **it** tenter sa chance.

chancellor /'tʃɑːnsələ(r)/ n chancelier m; **C~ of the Exchequer** Chancelier de l'échiquier.

chandelier /ʃændə'lɪə(r)/ n lustre m.

change /tʃeɪndʒ/ vt (alter) changer; (exchange) échanger (**for** contre). (money) changer; ~ **trains/one's dress** changer de train/de robe; ~ **one's mind** changer d'avis. ● vi changer; (change clothes) se changer; ~ **into** se transformer en; ~ **over** passer (**to** à). ● n changement m; (money) monnaie f; **a** ~ **for the better** une amélioration; **a** ~ **for the worse** un changement en pire; **a** ~ **of clothes** des vêtements de rechange; **for a** ~ pour changer. **changeable** adj changeant. **changing room** n (in shop) cabine f d'essayage; (Sport) vestiaire m.

channel /'tʃænl/ n (for liquid, information) canal m; (TV) chaîne f; (groove) rainure f. ● vt (pt **channelled**) canaliser. **C~** n **the (English) C~** la Manche; **the C~ tunnel** le tunnel sous la Manche; **the C~ Islands** les îles fpl Anglo-Normandes

chant /tʃɑːnt/ n (Relig) mélopée f; (of demonstrators) chant m scandé. ● vt/i scander; (Relig) psalmodier.

chaos /'keɪɒs/ n chaos m.

chap /tʃæp/ n (man Ⅱ) type m Ⅱ

chapel /'tʃæpl/ n chapelle f.

chaplain /'tʃæplɪn/ n aumônier m.

chapped /tʃæpt/ adj gercé.

chapter /'tʃæptə(r)/ n chapitre m.

char /tʃɑː(r)/ vt (pt **charred**) carboniser.

character /'kærəktə(r)/ n caractère m; (in novel, play) personnage m; **of good** ~ de bonne réputation.

characteristic /kærəktə'rıstık/ adj & n caractéristique (f).

charcoal /'tʃɑːkəʊl/ n charbon m de bois; (art) fusain m.

charge /tʃɑːdʒ/ n (fee) frais mpl; (Mil) charge f; (Jur) inculpation f; (task, custody) charge f; **in ~ of** responsable de; **take ~ of** prendre en charge, se charger de. ● vt (customer) faire payer; (enemy, gun) charger; (Jur) inculper (**with** de); **~ £20 an hour** prendre 20 livres de l'heure; **~ card** carte f d'achat. ● vi faire payer; (bull) foncer; (person) se précipiter.

charisma /kə'rızmə/ n charisme m. **charismatic** adj charismatique.

charitable /'tʃærıtəbl/ adj charitable. **charity** n charité f; (organization) organisation f caritative.

charm /tʃɑːm/ n charme m; (trinket) amulette f. ● vt charmer. **charming** adj charmant.

chart /tʃɑːt/ n (graph) graphique m; (table) tableau m; (map) carte f. ● vt (route) porter sur la carte.

charter /'tʃɑːtə(r)/ n charte f; **~ (flight)** charter m. ● vt affréter; **~ed accountant** expert-comptable m.

chase /tʃeıs/ vt poursuivre; **~ away** or **off** chasser. ● vi courir (**after** après). ● n chasse f.

chassis /'ʃæsı/ n châssis m.

chastise /tʃæ'staız/ vt châtier.

chat /tʃæt/ n conversation f; (on Internet) causette f, bavardage m; **have a ~** bavarder; **~ show** talk-show m. **~room** n salle f de causette, salle f de bavardage. ● vi (pt **chatted**) bavarder. **~ up** 🄸 draguer 🄸.

chatter /'tʃætə(r)/ n bavardage m. ● vi bavarder; **his teeth are ~ing** il claque des dents. **~box** n bavard/-e m/f.

chatty /'tʃætı/ adj bavard.

chauffeur /'ʃəʊfə(r)/ n chauffeur m.

chauvinist /'ʃəʊvınıst/ n chauvin/-e m/f; macho m.

cheap /tʃiːp/ adj bon marché inv; (fare, rate) réduit; (joke, gimmick) facile; **~er** meilleur marché inv. **cheapen** vt déprécier. **cheaply** adv à bas prix.

cheat /tʃiːt/ vi tricher. ● vt tromper. ● n tricheur/-euse m/f.

check /tʃek/ vt/i vérifier; (tickets, rises, inflation) contrôler; (stop) arrêter; (tick

off; US) cocher. ● n contrôle m; (curb) frein m; (chess) échec m; (pattern) carreaux mpl; (bill; US) addition f; (cheque; US) chèque m. **~ in** remplir la fiche; (at airport) enregistrer; **~ out** partir; **~ sth out** vérifier qch. **~ up** vérifier. **~ up on** (story) vérifier; (person) faire une enquête sur.

check: ~-in n enregistrement m. **checking account** n (US) compte m courant. **~-list** n liste f de contrôle. **~mate** n échec m et mat. **~-out** n caisse f. **~-point** n contrôle m. **~-up** n examen m médical.

cheek /tʃiːk/ n joue f; (impudence) culot m 🄸. **cheeky** adj effronté.

cheer /'tʃıə(r)/ n gaieté f; **~s** acclamations fpl; (when drinking) à la vôtre. ● vt/i applaudir; **~ (up)** (gladden) remonter le moral à qn; **~ up** prendre courage. **cheerful** adj joyeux. **cheerfulness** n gaieté f.

cheerio /tʃıərı'əʊ/ interj 🄸 salut 🄸.

cheese /tʃiːz/ n fromage m.

cheetah /'tʃiːtə/ n guépard m.

chef /ʃef/ n chef m.

chemical /'kemıkl/ adj chimique. ● n produit m chimique.

chemist /'kemıst/ n pharmacien/-ne m/f; (scientist) chimiste mf; **~'s (shop)** pharmacie f. **chemistry** n chimie f.

cheque /tʃek/ n chèque m. **~-book** n chéquier m. **~ card** n carte f bancaire.

chequered /'tʃekəd/ adj (pattern) à damiers; (fig) en dents de scie.

cherish /'tʃerıʃ/ vt chérir; (hope) caresser.

cherry /'tʃerı/ n cerise f; (tree, wood) cerisier m.

chess /tʃes/ n échecs mpl. **~-board** n échiquier m.

chest /tʃest/ n (Anat) poitrine f; (box) coffre m; **~ of drawers** commode f.

chestnut /'tʃesnʌt/ n (nut) marron m, châtaigne f; (tree) marronnier m; (sweet) châtaignier m.

chew /tʃuː/ vt mâcher.

chic /ʃiːk/ adj chic inv.

chick /tʃık/ n poussin m.

chicken /'tʃıkın/ n poulet m. ● adj 🅭 froussard. ● vi **~ out** 🅭 se dégonfler. **~-pox** n varicelle f.

chick-pea /'tʃıkpiː/n pois m chiche.

chicory /'tʃɪkərɪ/ n (for salad) endive f; (in coffee) chicorée f.

chief /tʃiːf/ n chef m. ● adj principal. **chiefly** adv principalement.

chilblain /'tʃɪlbleɪn/ n engelure f.

child /tʃaɪld/ n (pl **children**) enfant mf. ∼**birth** n accouchement m. **childhood** n enfance f. **childish** adj puéril. **childless** adj sans enfants. **childlike** adj enfantin. ∼**-minder** n nourrice f.

Chile /'tʃɪlɪən/ n Chili m.

chill /tʃɪl/ n froid m; (Med) refroidissement m. ● adj froid. ● vt (person) faire frissonner; (wine) rafraîchir; (food) mettre à refroidir.

chilli /'tʃɪlɪ/ n (pl ∼**es**) piment m.

chilly /'tʃɪlɪ/ adj froid; **it's** ∼ il fait froid.

chime /tʃaɪm/ n carillon m. ● vt/i carillonner.

chimney /'tʃɪmnɪ/ n cheminée f. ∼**sweep** n ramoneur m.

chimpanzee /tʃɪmpən'ziː/ n chimpanzé m.

chin /tʃɪn/ n menton m.

china /'tʃaɪnə/ n porcelaine f.

China /'tʃaɪnə/ n Chine f.

Chinese /tʃaɪ'niːz/ n (person) Chinois/e m/f; (Ling) chinois m. ● adj chinois.

chip /tʃɪp/ n (on plate) ébréchure f; (piece) éclat m; (of wood) copeau m; (Culin) frite f; (Comput) puce f; (potato) ∼s (US) chips fpl. ● vt/i (pt **chipped**) (s')ébrécher; ∼ **in** 🄸 dire son mot; (with money) contribuer.

chiropodist /kɪ'rɒpədɪst/ n pédicure mf.

chirp /tʃɜːp/ n pépiement m. ● vi pépier. **chirpy** adj gai.

chisel /'tʃɪzl/ n ciseau m. ● vt (pt **chiselled**) ciseler.

chit /tʃɪt/ n note f; (voucher) bon m.

chitchat /'tʃɪttʃæt/ n 🄸 bavardage m.

chivalrous /'ʃɪvəlrəs/ adj galant.

chives /tʃaɪvz/ npl ciboulette f.

chlorine /'klɔːriːn/ n chlore m.

choc ice /'tʃɒkaɪs/ n esquimau m.

chock-a-block /tʃɒkə'blɒk/ adj plein à craquer.

chocolate /'tʃɒklət/ n chocolat m.

choice /tʃɔɪs/ n choix m. ● adj de choix.

choir /'kwaɪə(r)/ n chœur m. ∼**boy** n jeune choriste m.

choke /tʃəʊk/ vt/i (s')étrangler; ∼ **(up)** boucher. ● n starter m.

cholesterol /kə'lestərɒl/ n cholestérol m.

choose /tʃuːz/ vt/i (pt **chose**. pp **chosen**) choisir; ∼ **to do** décider de faire. **choosy** adj difficile.

chop /tʃɒp/ vt/i (pt **chopped**) (wood) couper; (food) hacher; **chopping board** planche f à découper; ∼ **down** abattre. ● n (meat) côtelette f. **chopper** n hachoir m. 🄸 hélico m 🄸.

choppy /'tʃɒpɪ/ adj (sea) agité.

chopstick /'tʃɒpstɪk/ n baguette f (chinoise).

chord /kɔːd/ n (Mus) accord m.

chore /tʃɔː(r)/ n (routine) tâche f; (unpleasant) corvée f.

chortle /'tʃɔːtl/ n gloussement m. ● vi glousser.

chorus /'kɔːrəs/ n chœur m; (of song) refrain m.

chose, chosen /tʃəʊz, 'tʃəʊzən/ ➡CHOOSE.

Christ /kraɪst/ n le Christ.

christen /'krɪsn/ vt baptiser. **christening** n baptême m.

Christian /'krɪstʃən/ adj & n chrétien/ne (m/f). ∼ **name** nom m de baptême. **Christianity** n christianisme m.

Christmas /'krɪsməs/ n Noël m; ∼ **Day/Eve** le jour/la veille de Noël. ● adj (card, tree) de Noël.

chronic /'krɒnɪk/ adj (situation, disease) chronique; (bad 🄸) nul.

chronicle /'krɒnɪkl/ n chronique f.

chronological /krɒnə'lɒdʒɪkl/ adj chronologique.

chrysanthemum /krɪ'sænθəməm/ n chrysanthème m.

chubby /'tʃʌbɪ/ adj (-ier, -iest) potelé.

chuck /tʃʌk/ vt 🄸 lancer; ∼ **away** or **out** 🄸 balancer.

chuckle /'tʃʌkl/ n gloussement m. ● vi glousser.

chuffed /tʃʌft/ adj 🄸 vachement content 🄸.

chunk /tʃʌŋk/ n morceau m. **chunky** adj (sweater, jewellery) gros; (person) costaud.

church /tʃɜːtʃ/ n église f. ∼ **goer** n pratiquant/-e m/f. ∼**yard** n cimetière m.

churn /tʃɜːn/ n baratte f; (milk-can) bidon m. ● vt baratter; ~ **out** produire en série.

chute /ʃuːt/ n toboggan m; (for rubbish) vide-ordures m inv.

chutney /'tʃʌtnɪ/ n condiment m aigredoux.

cider /'saɪdə(r)/ n cidre m.

cigar /sɪ'gɑː(r)/ n cigare m.

cigarette /sɪgə'ret/ n cigarette f; ~ **end** mégot m.

cinder /'sɪndə(r)/ n cendre f.

cinema /'sɪnəmə/ n cinéma m.

cinnamon /'sɪnəmən/ n cannelle f.

circle /'sɜːkl/ n cercle m; (Theat) balcon m. ● vt (go round) tourner autour de; (word, error) encercler. ● vi tourner en rond.

circuit /'sɜːkɪt/ n circuit m. ~ **board** n carte f de circuit imprimé. ~**-breaker** n disjoncteur m.

circuitous /sɜː'kjuːɪtəs/ adj indirect.

circular /'sɜːkjʊlə(r)/ adj & n circulaire (f).

circulate /'sɜːkjʊleɪt/ vt/i (faire) circuler. **circulation** n circulation f; (of newspaper) tirage m.

circumcise /'sɜːkəmsaɪz/ vt circoncire.

circumference /sə'kʌmfərəns/ n circonférence f.

circumflex /'sɜːkəmfleks/ n circonflexe m.

circumstance /'sɜːkəmstəns/ n circonstance f; ~s (financial) situation f; **under no** ~s en aucun cas.

circus /'sɜːkəs/ n cirque m.

cistern /'sɪstən/ n réservoir m.

citizen /'sɪtɪzn/ n citoyen/-ne m/f; (of town) habitant/-e m/f. **citizenship** n nationalité f.

citrus /'sɪtrəs/ adj ~ **fruit(s)** agrumes mpl; ~ **tree** citrus m.

city /'sɪtɪ/ n (grande) ville f.

The City Quartier londonien des affaires et de la finance, la City est le siège des grandes banques, des compagnies d'assurance et de la plupart des sociétés d'agents de change. 500 000 personnes viennent y travailler chaque jour.

civic /'sɪvɪk/ adj (official) municipal; (pride, duty) civique.

civil /'sɪvl/ adj civil. ~ **disobedience** n résistance f passive. ~ **engineer** n ingénieur m des travaux publics.

civilian /sɪ'vɪlɪən/ adj & n civil/-e (m/f).

civilization /sɪvəlaɪ'zeɪʃn/ n civilisation f. **civilize** vt civiliser.

civil: ~ **law** n droit m civil. ~ **liberties** npl libertés fpl individuelles. ~ **rights** npl droits mpl civils. ~ **servant** n fonctionnaire mf. ~ **service** n fonction f publique. ~ **war** n guerre f civile.

claim /kleɪm/ vt (demand) revendiquer; (assert) prétendre. ● n revendication f; (assertion) affirmation f; (for insurance) réclamation f; (right) droit m. **claimant** n (of benefits) demandeur/-euse m/f.

clairvoyant /kleə'vɔɪənt/ n voyant/-e m/f.

clam /klæm/ n palourde f.

clamber /'klæmbə(r)/ vi grimper.

clammy /'klæmɪ/ adj (-ier, -iest) moite.

clamour /'klæmə(r)/ n clameur f. ● vi ~ **for** réclamer.

clamp /klæmp/ n valet m; (Med) pince f; (wheel) ~ sabot m de Denver. ● vt cramponner; (jaw) serrer; (car) mettre un sabot de Denver à; ~ **down on** faire de la répression contre.

clan /klæn/ n clan m.

clang /'klæŋ/ n son m métallique.

clap /klæp/ vt/i (pt **clapped**) applaudir; (put forcibly) mettre; ~ **one's hands** frapper dans ses mains. ● n applaudissement m; (of thunder) coup m.

claret /'klærət/ n bordeaux m rouge.

clarification /klærɪfɪ'keɪʃn/ n clarification f. **clarify** vt/i (se) clarifier.

clarinet /klærə'net/ n clarinette f.

clarity /'klærətɪ/ n clarté f.

clash /klæʃ/ n choc m; (fig) conflit m. ● vi (metal objects) s'entrechoquer; (armies) s'affronter; (meetings) avoir lieu en même temps; (colours) jurer.

clasp /klɑːsp/ n (fastener) fermoir m. ● vt serrer.

class /klɑːs/ n classe f. ● vt classer; ~ **sb/sth as** assimiler qn/qch à.

classic /'klæsɪk/ adj & n classique (m). ~**s** (Univ) lettres fpl classiques. **classical** adj classique.

classified /'klæsɪfaɪd/ adj (information) secret; ~ **(ad)** petite annonce f.

classroom /'klɑːsrʊm/ *n* salle *f* de classe.

clatter /'klætə(r)/ *n* cliquetis *m.* ● *vi* cliqueter.

clause /klɔːz/ *n* clause *f*; (Gram) proposition *f.*

claw /klɔː/ *n* (of animal, small bird) griffe *f*; (of bird of prey) serre *f*; (of lobster) pince *f.* ● *vt* griffer.

clay /kleɪ/ *n* argile *f.*

clean /kliːn/ *adj* propre; (shape, stroke) net. ● *adv* complètement. ● *vt* nettoyer; ~ **one's teeth** se brosser les dents. ● *vi* ~ **up** faire le nettoyage. **cleaner** *n* (at home) femme *f* de ménage; (industrial) agent *m* de nettoyage; (of clothes) teinturier/-ière *m/f.* **cleanliness** *n* propreté *f.* **cleanly** *adv* proprement; (sharply) nettement.

cleanse /klenz/ *vt* nettoyer; (fig) purifier.

clean-shaven *adj* glabre.

clear /klɪə(r)/ *adj* (explanation) clair; (need, sign) évident; (glass) transparent; (profit) net; (road) dégagé; **make sth** ~ être très clair sur qch; ~ **of** (away from) à l'écart de. ● *adv* complètement; **stand** ~ of s'éloigner de. ● *vt* (free) dégager (**of** de). (table) débarrasser; (building) évacuer; (cheque) compenser; (jump over) franchir; (debt) liquider; (Jur) disculper. ● *vi* (fog) se dissiper; (cheque) être compensé. ~ **away** or **off** (remove) enlever. ~ **off** or **out** [T] décamper. ~ **out** (clean) nettoyer. ~ **up** (tidy) ranger; (weather) s'éclaircir.

clearance /'klɪərəns/ *n* (permission) autorisation *f*; (space) espace *m*; ~ **sale** liquidation *f.*

clear-cut *adj* net.

clearing /'klɪərɪŋ/ *n* clairière *f.*

clearly /'klɪəlɪ/ *adv* clairement.

clef /klef/ *n* (Mus) clé *f.*

cleft /kleft/ *n* fissure *f.*

clench /klentʃ/ *vt* serrer.

clergy /'klɜːdʒɪ/ *n* clergé *m.* ~**man** *n* (*pl* -**men**) ecclésiastique *m.*

cleric /'klerɪk/ *n* clerc *m.* **clerical** *adj* (Relig) clérical; (staff, work) de bureau.

clerk /klɑːk/ *n* employé/-e *m/f* de bureau; (US) **(sales)** ~ vendeur/-euse *m/f.*

clever /'klevə(r)/ *adj* intelligent; (skilful) habile.

click /klɪk/ *n* déclic *m;* (Comput) clic *m.* ● *vi* faire un déclic; (people [T]) sympathiser; (Comput) cliquer (**on** sur.) ● *vt* (heels, tongue) faire claquer.

client /'klaɪənt/ *n* client/-e *m/f.*

clientele /kliːənˈtel/ *n* clientèle *f.*

cliff /klɪf/ *n* falaise *f.*

climate /'klaɪmɪt/ *n* climat *m.* ~ **change** changement *m* climatique.

climax /'klaɪmæks/ *n* (of story, contest) point *m* culminant; (sexual) orgasme *m.*

climb /klaɪm/ *vt* grimper; (steps) monter; (tree, ladder) grimper à; (mountain) faire l'ascension de. ● *vi* grimper; ~ **into** (car) monter dans; ~ **into bed** se mettre au lit. ● *n* (of mountain) escalade *f*; (steep hill, rise) montée *f.* ~ **down** (fig) reculer. **climber** *n* (Sport) alpiniste *mf.*

clinch /klɪntʃ/ *vt* (deal) conclure; (victory, order) décrocher.

cling /klɪŋ/ *vi* (*pt* **clung**) se cramponner (**to** à.) (stick) coller. ~**-film** *n* scellofrais® *m.*

clinic /'klɪnɪk/ *n* centre *m* médical; (private) clinique *f.* **clinical** *adj* clinique.

clink /klɪŋk/ *n* tintement *m.* ● *vt/i* (faire) tinter.

clip /klɪp/ *n* (for paper) trombone *m;* (for hair) barrette *f*; (for tube) collier *m;* (of film) extrait *m.* ● *vt* (*pt* **clipped**) (fasten) attacher (**to** à.) cut) couper.

clippers /'klɪpəz/ *npl* tondeuse *f*; (for nails) coupe-ongles *m inv.*

clipping /'klɪpɪŋ/ *n* (from press) coupure *f* de presse.

cloak /kləʊk/ *n* cape *f*; (man's) houppelande *f.* ~**room** *n* vestiaire *m*; (toilet) toilettes *fpl.*

clobber /'klɒbə(r)/ *n* [T] attirail *m.* ● *vt* (hit [T]) tabasser [T].

clock /klɒk/ *n* pendule *f*; (large) horloge *f.* ● *vi* ~ **on/in** or **off/out** pointer; ~ **up** (miles) faire. ~**-tower** *n* beffroi *m.* ~**wise** *adj & adv* dans le sens des aiguilles d'une montre.

clockwork /'klɒkwɜːk/ *n* mécanisme *m.* ● *adj* mécanique.

clog /klɒg/ *n* sabot *m.* ● *vt/i* (*pt* **clogged**) (se) boucher.

cloister /'klɔɪstə(r)/ *n* cloître *m.*

clone /kləʊn/ n clone m. ● vt cloner.

close¹ /kləʊs/ adj (friend) proche (**to** de). (link) étroit; (examination) minutieux; (match) serré; (weather) lourd; ~ **together** (crowded) serrés; ~ **by**, ~ **at hand** tout près; **have a** ~ **shave** l'échapper belle; **keep a** ~ **watch on** surveiller de près. ● adv près. ● n (street) impasse f.

close² /kləʊz/ vt fermer; (meeting, case) mettre fin à. ● vi se fermer; (shop) fermer; (meeting, play) prendre fin. ● n fin f.

closely /ˈkləʊslɪ/ adv (follow) de près. **closeness** n proximité f.

closet /ˈklɒzɪt/ n (US) placard m.

close-up n gros plan m.

closure /ˈkləʊʒə(r)/ n fermeture f.

clot /klɒt/ n (of blood) caillot m; (in sauce) grumeau m. ● vt/i (pt **clotted**) (se) coaguler.

cloth /klɒθ/ n (fabric) tissu m; (duster) chiffon m; (table-cloth) nappe f.

clothe /kləʊð/ vt vêtir.

clothes /kləʊðz/ npl vêtements mpl. ~-**hanger** n cintre m. ~-**line** n corde f à linge.

clothing /ˈkləʊðɪŋ/ n vêtements mpl.

cloud /klaʊd/ n nuage m. ● vi ~ **over** se couvrir (de nuages); (face) s'assombrir. **cloudy** adj (sky) couvert; (liquid) trouble.

clout /klaʊt/ n (blow) coup m de poing; (power) influence f. ● vt frapper.

clove /kləʊv/ n clou m de girofle; ~ **of garlic** gousse f d'ail.

clover /ˈkləʊvə(r)/ n trèfle m.

clown /klaʊn/ n clown m. ● vi faire le clown.

club /klʌb/ n (group) club m; (weapon) massue f; (golf) ~ club m (de golf); ~**s** (cards) trèfle m. ● vt/i (pt **clubbed**) matraquer. ~ **together** cotiser.

cluck /klʌk/ vi glousser.

clue /kluː/ n indice m; (in crossword) définition f; **I haven't a** ~ 🔢 je n'en ai pas la moindre idée.

clump /klʌmp/ n massif m.

clumsy /ˈklʌmzɪ/ adj (-ier, -iest) maladroit; (tool) peu commode.

clung /klʌŋ/ vi →CLING.

cluster /ˈklʌstə(r)/ n (of people, islands) groupe m; (of flowers, berries) grappe f. ● vi se grouper.

clutch /klʌtʃ/ vt (hold) serrer fort; (grasp) saisir. ● vi ~ **at** (try to grasp) essayer de saisir. ● n (Auto) embrayage m; (of eggs) couvée f; (of people) groupe m.

clutter /ˈklʌtə(r)/ n désordre m. ● vt ~ (**up**) encombrer.

coach /kəʊtʃ/ n autocar m; (of train) wagon m; (horse-drawn) carrosse m; (Sport) entraîneur/-euse m/f. ● vt (team) entraîner; (pupil) donner des leçons particulières à.

coal /kəʊl/ n charbon m. ~**field** n bassin m houiller. ~-**mine** n mine f de charbon.

coarse /kɔːs/ adj grossier.

coast /kəʊst/ n côte f. ● vi (car, bicycle) descendre en roue libre. **coastal** adj côtier.

coast: ~**guard** n (person) gardecôte m; (organization) gendarmerie f maritime. ~**line** n littoral m.

coat /kəʊt/ n manteau m; (of animal) pelage m; (of paint) couche f; ~ **of arms** armoiries fpl. ● vt enduire, couvrir; (with chocolate) enrober (**with** de). **coating** n couche f.

coax /kəʊks/ vt cajoler.

cob /kɒb/ n (of corn) épi m.

cobbler /ˈkɒblə(r)/ n cordonnier m.

cobblestones /ˈkɒblstəʊnz/ npl pavés mpl.

cobweb /ˈkɒbweb/ n toile f d'araignée.

cocaine /kəʊˈkeɪn/ n cocaïne f.

cock /kɒk/ n (rooster) coq m. (oiseau) mâle m. ● vt (gun) armer; (ears) dresser.

cockerel /ˈkɒkrəl/ n jeune coq m.

cockle /ˈkɒkl/ n (Culin) coque f.

cock: ~**pit** n poste m de pilotage. ~**roach** n cafard m. ~**tail** n cocktail m.

cocky /ˈkɒkɪ/ adj (-ier, -iest) trop sûr de soi.

cocoa /ˈkəʊkəʊ/ n cacao m.

coconut /ˈkəʊkənʌt/ n noix f de coco.

COD abbr (**cash on delivery**) envoi m contre remboursement.

cod /ˈkɒd/ n inv morue f; ~-**liver oil** huile f de foie de morue.

code /kəʊd/ n code m. ● vt coder.

coerce /kəʊˈɜːs/ vt contraindre.

coexist /kəʊɪgˈzɪst/ vi coexister.

coffee /ˈkɒfɪ/ n café m. ~ **bar** n café m. ~ **bean** n grain m de café. ~-**pot** n cafetière f. ~-**table** n table f basse.

coffin /ˈkɒfɪn/ n cercueil m.

cog /kɒg/ n pignon m; (fig) rouage m.

cognac /ˈkɒnjæk/ n cognac m.

coil /kɔɪl/ vt/i (s')enrouler. ● n (of rope) rouleau m; (of snake) anneau m; (contraceptive) stérilet m.

coin /kɔɪn/ n pièce f (de monnaie). ● vt (word) inventer.

coincide /kəʊɪnˈsaɪd/ vi coïncider. **coincidence** n coïncidence f. **coincidental** adj dû à une coïncidence.

colander /ˈkʌləndə(r)/ n passoire f.

cold /kəʊld/ adj froid; (person) be or feel ~ avoir froid; **it is** ~ il fait froid; **get** ~ **feet** avoir les jetons 🔢; ~-**blooded** (lit) à sang froid; (fig) sans pitié. ● n froid m; (Med) rhume m; ~ **sore** bouton m de fièvre. **coldness** n froideur f.

coleslaw /ˈkəʊlslɔː/ n salade f de chou cru.

colic /ˈkɒlɪk/ n coliques fpl.

collaborate /kəˈlæbəreɪt/ vi collaborer.

collapse /kəˈlæps/ vi s'effondrer; (person) s'écrouler; (fold) se plier. ● n effondrement m.

collar /ˈkɒlə(r)/ n col m; (of dog) collier m. ~-**bone** n clavicule f.

collateral /kəˈlætərəl/ n nantissement m.

colleague /ˈkɒliːg/ n collègue mf.

collect /kəˈlekt/ vt rassembler; (pick up) ramasser; (call for) passer prendre; (money, fare) encaisser; (taxes, rent) percevoir; (as hobby) collectionner. ● vi se rassembler; (dust) s'amasser. ● adv call ~ (US) appeler en PCV. **collection** n collection f; (of money) collecte f; (in church) quête f; (of mail) levée f.

collective /kəˈlektɪv/ adj collectif.

collector /kəˈlektə(r)/ n (as hobby) collectionneur/-euse m/f; (of taxes) percepteur m; (of rent, debt) encaisseur m.

college /ˈkɒlɪdʒ/ n (for higher education) établissement m d'enseignement supérieur; (within university) collège m; **be at** ~ faire des études supérieures.

collide /kəˈlaɪd/ vi entrer en collision (with avec).

colliery /ˈkɒlɪərɪ/ n houillère f.

collision /kəˈlɪʒn/ n collision f.

colloquial /kəˈləʊkwɪəl/ adj familier. **colloquialism** n expression f familière.

Colombia /kəˈlɒmbɪə/ n Colombie f.

colon /ˈkəʊlən/ n (Gram) deux-points m inv; (Anat) côlon m.

colonel /ˈkɜːnl/ n colonel m.

colonial /kəˈləʊnɪəl/ adj & n colonial/-e (m/f).

colour, (US) **color** /ˈkʌlə(r)/ n couleur f; ~-**blind** daltonien. ● adj (photo) en couleur; (TV set) couleur inv. ● vt colorer; (with crayon) colorier. **coloured** adj de couleur. **colourful** adj aux couleurs vives; (fig) haut en couleur. **colouring** n (of skin) teint m; (in food) colorant m.

colt /kəʊlt/ n poulain m.

column /ˈkɒləm/ n colonne f.

coma /ˈkəʊmə/ n coma m.

comb /kəʊm/ n peigne m. ● vt peigner; ~ **one's hair** se peigner; ~ **a place** passer un lieu au peigne fin.

combat /ˈkɒmbæt/ n combat m. ● vt (pt **combated**) combattre.

combination /kɒmbɪˈneɪʃn/ n combinaison f.

combine¹ /kəmˈbaɪn/ vt/i (se) combiner, (s')unir.

combine² /ˈkɒmbaɪn/ n (Comm) groupe m; ~ **harvester** moissonneuse-batteuse f.

come /kʌm/ vi (pt **came**. pp **come**) venir; (bus, letter) arriver; (postman) passer; ~ **and look!** viens voir!; ~ **in** (size, colour) exister en; **when it** ~**s to** lorsqu'il s'agit de. ~ **about** survenir. ~ **across** (meaning) passer; ~ **across** sth tomber sur qch. ~ **away** (leave) partir; (come off) se détacher. ~ **back** revenir. ~ **by** obtenir. ~ **down** descendre; (price) baisser; ~ **forward** se présenter. ~ **in** entrer; ~ **in useful** être utile. ~ **in for** recevoir. ~ **into** (money) hériter de. ~ **off** (succeed) réussir; (fare) s'en tirer; (detach) se détacher. ~ **on** (actor) entrer en scène; (light) s'allumer; (improve) faire des progrès; ~ **on!** allez!. ~ **out** sortir. **~ round** reprendre connaissance; (change mind) changer d'avis; **~ through** s'en tirer. **~ to** reprendre connaissance; **~ to sth** (*amount*) revenir à qch; (*decision, conclusion*) arriver à qch. **~ up** (*problem*) être soulevé; (*opportunity*) se présenter; (*sun*) se lever; **~ up against** se heurter à. **~ up with** trouver.

comedian /kə'miːdɪən/ *n* comique *m*.

comedy /'kɒmədɪ/ *n* comédie *f*.

comfort /'kʌmfət/ *n* confort *m*; (consolation) réconfort *m*. ● *vt* consoler. **comfortable** *adj* (*chair, car*) confortable; (*person*) à l'aise; (*wealthy*) aisé.

comfortably /'kʌmftəblɪ/ *adv* confortablement; **~ off** aisé.

comfy /'kʌmfɪ/ *adj* **I** ➡COMFORTABLE.

comic /'kɒmɪk/ *adj* comique. ● *n* (person) comique *m*; **~ (book)**, **~ strip** bande *f* dessinée.

coming /'kʌmɪŋ/ *n* arrivée *f*; **~s and goings** allées et venues *fpl*. ● *adj* à venir.

comma /'kɒmə/ *n* virgule *f*.

command /kə'mɑːnd/ *n* (authority) commandement *m*; (order) ordre *m*; (mastery) maîtrise *f*. ● *vt* ordonner à (**to do** de faire); (be able to use) disposer de; (respect) inspirer. **commandeer** *vt* réquisitionner. **commander** *n* commandant *m*. **commanding** *adj* imposant. **commandment** *n* commandement *m*.

commando /kə'mɑːndəʊ/ *n* commando *m*.

commemorate /kə'meməreɪt/ *vt* commémorer.

commence /kə'mens/ *vt/i* commencer.

commend /kə'mend/ *vt* (praise) louer; (entrust) confier.

commensurate /kə'menʃərət/ *adj* proportionné.

comment /'kɒment/ *n* commentaire *m*. ● *vi* faire des commentaires; **~ on** commenter. **commentary** *n* commentaire *m*; (radio, TV) reportage *m*. **commentate** *vi* faire un reportage. **commentator** *n* commentateur/-trice *m/f*.

commerce /'kɒmɜːs/ *n* commerce *m*.

commercial /kə'mɜːʃl/ *adj* commercial; (*traveller*) de commerce. ● *n* publicité *f*.

commiserate /kə'mɪzəreɪt/ *vi* compatir (**with avec**).

commission /kə'mɪʃn/ *n* commission *f*; (order for work) commande *f*; **out of ~** hors service. ● *vt* (order) commander; (Mil) nommer officier; **~ to do** charger de faire. **commissioner** *n* préfet *m* (de police); (in EU) membre *m* de la Commission européenne.

commit /kə'mɪt/ *vt* (*pt* **committed**) commettre; (entrust) confier; **~ oneself** s'engager; **~ perjury** se parjurer; **~ suicide** se suicider; **~ to memory** apprendre par cœur. **commitment** *n* engagement *m*.

committee /kə'mɪtɪ/ *n* comité *m*.

commodity /kə'mɒdətɪ/ *n* article *m*.

common /'kɒmən/ *adj* (shared by all) commun (**to** à); (usual) courant; (vulgar) vulgaire, commun; **in ~** en commun; **~ people** le peuple; **~ sense** bon sens *m*. ● *n* terrain *m* communal; **the C~s** Chambre *f* des Communes. **commoner** /'kɒmənə(r)/ *n* roturier/-ière *m/f*.

common law *n* droit *m* coutumier.

commonly /'kɒmənlɪ/ *adv* communément.

commonplace /'kɒmənpleɪs/ *adj* banal. ● *n* banalité *f*.

common-room *n* salle *f* de détente.

Commonwealth /'kɒmənwelθ/ *n* **the ~** le Commonwealth *m*.

Commonwealth of Nations
Association de nations ayant pour la plupart fait partie de l'empire britannique et qui maintiennent une coopération avec la Grande-Bretagne en matière d'économie, de culture et d'éducation. Des championnats d'athlétisme, les *Commonwealth Games* ont lieu tous les quatre ans. Le mot *Commonwealth* figure dans le nom officiel de quelques États américains (*Kentucky, Virginia, Pennsylvania, Massachusetts*).

commotion /kə'məʊʃn/ *n* (noise) vacarme *m*; (disturbance) agitation *f*.

communal /'kɒmjʊnl/ *adj* (shared) commun; (life) collectif.

commune /'kɒmjuːn/ *n* (group) communauté *f*.

communicate /kə'mju:nɪkeɪt/ vt/i communiquer. **communication** n communication f. **communicative** adj communicatif.

communion /kə'mju:nɪən/ n communion f.

Communism /'kɒmjʊnɪzəm/ n communisme m. **Communist** adj & n communiste (mf).

community /kə'mju:nətɪ/ n communauté f.

commute /kə'mju:t/ vi faire la navette. ● vt (Jur) commuer. **commuter** n navetteur/-euse m/f.

compact /kəm'pækt/ adj compact; (lady's case) poudrier m.

compact disc n disque m compact. ~ **player** n platine f laser.

companion /kəm'pænɪən/ n compagnon/-agne m/f. **companionship** n camaraderie f.

company /'kʌmpənɪ/ n (companionship, firm) compagnie f; (guests) invités/-es m/fpl.

comparative /kəm'pærətɪv/ adj (study, form) comparatif; (comfort) relatif.

compare /kəm'peə(r)/ vt comparer (**with, to** à). ~**d with** par rapport à. ● vi être comparable. **comparison** n comparaison f.

compartment /kəm'pɑ:tmənt/ n compartiment m.

compass /'kʌmpəs/ n (for direction) boussole f; (scope) portée f; **a pair of** ~**es** un compas.

compassionate /kəm'pæʃənət/ adj compatissant.

compatible /kəm'pætəbl/ adj compatible.

compel /kəm'pel/ vt (pt **compelled**) contraindre. **compelling** adj irrésistible.

compensate /'kɒmpenseɪt/ vt/i (financially) dédommager (**for** de). ~ **for sth** compenser qch. **compensation** n compensation f; (financial) dédommagement m.

compete /kəm'pi:t/ vi concourir; ~ **with** rivaliser avec.

competent /'kɒmpɪtənt/ adj compétent.

competition /kɒmpə'tɪʃn/ n (contest) concours m; (Sport) compétition f;

(Comm) concurrence f.

competitive /kəm'petɪtɪv/ adj (prices) compétitif; (person) qui a l'esprit de compétition.

competitor /kəm'petɪtə(r)/ n concurrent/-e m/f.

compile /kəm'paɪl/ vt (list) dresser; (book) rédiger.

complacency /kəm'pleɪsnsɪ/ n suffisance f.

complain /kəm'pleɪn/ vi se plaindre (**about, of** de). **complaint** n plainte f; (official) réclamation f; (illness) maladie f.

complement /'kɒmplɪmənt/ n complément m. ● vt compléter. **complementary** adj complémentaire.

complete /kəm'pli:t/ adj complet; (finished) achevé; (downright) parfait. ● vt achever; (a form) remplir. **completely** adv complètement. **completion** n achèvement m.

complex /'kɒmpleks/ adj complexe. ● n (Psych) complexe m.

complexion /kəm'plekʃn/ n (of face) teint m; (fig) caractère m.

compliance /kəm'plaɪəns/ n (agreement) conformité f.

complicate /'kɒmplɪkeɪt/ vt compliquer. **complicated** adj compliqué. **complication** n complication f.

compliment /'kɒmplɪmənt/ n compliment m. ● vt complimenter. **complimentary** adj (offert) à titre gracieux; (praising) flatteur.

comply /kəm'plaɪ/ vi ~ **with** se conformer à, obéir à.

component /kəm'pəʊnənt/ n (of machine) pièce f; (chemical substance) composant m; (element: fig) composante f. ● adj constituant.

compose /kəm'pəʊz/ vt composer; ~ **oneself** se calmer. **composed** adj calme. **composer** n (Mus) compositeur m. **composition** n composition f.

composure /kəm'pəʊzə(r)/ n calme m.

compound /'kɒmpaʊnd/ n (substance, word) composé m; (enclosure) enclos m. ● adj composé.

comprehend /kɒmprɪ'hend/ vt comprendre. **comprehension** n compréhension f.

comprehensive /ˌkɒmprɪˈhensɪv/ adj étendu, complet; (insurance) tous risques inv. ~ **school** n collège m d'enseignement secondaire.

compress /kəmˈpres/ vt comprimer.

comprise /kəmˈpraɪz/ vt comprendre, inclure.

compromise /ˈkɒmprəmaɪz/ n compromis m. ● vt compromettre. ● vi transiger, arriver à un compromis.

compulsive /kəmˈpʌlsɪv/ adj (Psych) compulsif; (liar, smoker) invétéré.

compulsory /kəmˈpʌlsərɪ/ adj obligatoire.

compute /kəmˈpjuːt/ vt calculer.

computer /kəmˈpjuːt/ n ordinateur m; ~ **science** informatique f. **computerize** vt informatiser.

comrade /ˈkɒmreɪd/ n camarade mf.

con¹ /kɒn/ vt (pt **conned** ☒) rouler ☒, escroquer (**out of** de.) ● n ☒ escroquerie f.

con² /kɒn/ ➡**PRO**.

conceal /kənˈsiːl/ vt dissimuler (**from** à.)

concede /kənˈsiːd/ vt concéder. ● vi céder.

conceited /kənˈsiːtɪd/ adj vaniteux.

conceive /kənˈsiːv/ vt/i concevoir; ~ **of** concevoir.

concentrate /ˈkɒnsntreɪt/ vt/i (se) concentrer. **concentration** n concentration f.

concept /ˈkɒnsept/ n concept m.

conception /kənˈsepʃn/ n conception f.

concern /kənˈsɜːn/ n (interest, business) affaire f; (worry) inquiétude f; (firm: Comm) entreprise f, affaire f. ● vt concerner; ~ **oneself with**, be ~**ed with** s'occuper de. **concerned** adj inquiet. **concerning** prep en ce qui concerne.

concert /ˈkɒnsət/ n concert m.

concession /kənˈseʃn/ n concession f.

conciliation /kənsɪlɪˈeɪʃn/ n conciliation f.

concise /kənˈsaɪs/ adj concis.

conclude /kənˈkluːd/ vt conclure. ● vi se terminer. **conclusion** n conclusion f. **conclusive** adj concluant.

concoct /kənˈkɒkt/ vt confectionner; (invent: fig) fabriquer. **concoction** n mélange m.

concourse /ˈkɒŋkɔːs/ n (Rail) hall m.

concrete /ˈkɒŋkriːt/ n béton m. ● adj de béton; (fig) concret. ● vt bétonner.

concur /kənˈkɜː(r)/ vi (pt **concurred**) être d'accord.

concurrently /kənˈkʌrəntlɪ/ adv simultanément.

concussion /kənˈkʌʃn/ n commotion f (cérébrale).

condemn /kənˈdem/ vt condamner.

condensation /kɒndenˈseɪʃn/ n (on walls) condensation f; (on windows) buée f. **condense** vt/i (se) condenser.

condition /kənˈdɪʃn/ n condition f; **on** ~ **that** à condition que. ● vt conditionner. **conditional** adj conditionnel.

conditioner /kənˈdɪʃənə(r)/ n après-shampooing m.

condolences /kənˈdəʊlənsɪz/ npl condoléances fpl.

condom /ˈkɒndɒm/ n préservatif m.

condone /kənˈdəʊn/ vt pardonner, fermer les yeux sur.

conducive /kənˈdjuːsɪv/ adj ~ **to** favorable à.

conduct¹ /ˈkɒndʌkt/ n conduite f.

conduct² /kənˈdʌkt/ vt conduire; (orchestra) diriger. **conductor** n chef m d'orchestre; (of bus) receveur m; (on train: US) chef m de train; (Electr) conducteur m. **conductress** n receveuse f.

cone /kəʊn/ n cône m. (of ice-cream) cornet m.

confectioner /kənˈfekʃənə(r)/ n confiseur/-euse m/f. **confectionery** n confiserie f.

confer /kənˈfɜː(r)/ vt/i (pt **conferred**) conférer.

conference /ˈkɒnfərəns/ n conférence f.

confess /kənˈfes/ vt/i avouer; (Relig) (se) confesser. **confession** n confession f; (of crime) aveu m.

confide /kənˈfaɪd/ vt confier. ● vi ~ **in** se confier à.

confidence /ˈkɒnfɪdəns/ n (trust) confiance f; (boldness) confiance f en soi; (secret) confidence f; **in** ~ en confidence. **confident** adj sûr.

confidential /kɒnfɪˈdenʃl/ adj confidentiel.

configuration /kənfɪgəˈreɪʃn/ n configuration f. ● **configure** vt configurer.

confine /kən'faɪn/ vt enfermer; (limit) limiter; ~d space espace m réduit; ~d to limité à.

confirm /kən'fɜːm/ vt confirmer. **confirmed** adj (bachelor) endurci; (smoker) invétéré.

confiscate /'kɒnfɪskeɪt/ vt confisquer.

conflict[1] /'kɒnflɪkt/ n conflit m.

conflict[2] /kən'flɪkt/ vi (statements, views) être en contradiction (with avec.) (appointments) tomber en même temps (with que). **conflicting** adj contradictoire.

conform /kən'fɔːm/ vt/i (se) conformer.

confound /kən'faʊnd/ vt confondre.

confront /kən'frʌnt/ vt affronter; ~ with confronter avec.

confuse /kən'fjuːz/ vt (bewilder) troubler; (mistake, confound) confondre; **become ~d** s'embrouiller; **I am ~d** je m'y perds. **confusing** adj déroutant. **confusion** n confusion f.

congeal /kən'dʒiːl/ vt/i (se) figer.

congested /kən'dʒestɪd/ adj (road) embouteillé; (passage) encombré; (Med) congestionné. **congestion** n (traffic) encombrement(s) m(pl); (Med) congestion f.

congratulate /kən'grætʃʊleɪt/ vt féliciter (on de). **congratulations** npl félicitations fpl.

congregate /'kɒŋgrɪgeɪt/ vi se rassembler. **congregation** n assemblée f.

congress /'kɒŋgres/ n congrès m. C ~ (US) le Congrès.

> **Congress** Le Congrès est le corps législatif des États-Unis composé de la Chambre des représentants (House of Representatives) qui compte 435 membres, et du Sénat (Senate) qui compte 100 sénateurs, deux par État. Pour devenir loi, un projet de loi doit être approuvé par les deux chambres, et ratifié par le président. ▷CAPITOL.

conjugate /'kɒndʒʊgeɪt/ vt conjuguer. **conjugation** n conjugaison f.

conjunction /kən'dʒʌŋkʃn/ n (Ling) conjonction f. **in ~with** conjointement avec.

conjunctivitis /kəndʒʌŋktɪ'vaɪtɪs/ n conjonctivite f.

conjure /'kʌndʒə(r)/ vi faire des tours de passe-passe. ● vt ~ up faire apparaître. **conjuror** n prestidigitateur/-trice m/f.

con man n ▣ escroc m.

connect /kə'nekt/ vt/i (se) relier; (in mind) faire le rapport entre; (install, wire up to mains) brancher; ~ with (of train) assurer la correspondance avec; ~ed (idea, event) lié; **be ~ed with** avoir rapport à.

connection /kə'nekʃn/ n rapport m. (Rail) correspondance f; (phone call) communication f; (Electr) contact m; (joining piece) raccord m; ~s (Comm) relations fpl.

connive /kə'naɪv/ vi ~ at se faire le complice de.

conquer /'kɒŋkə(r)/ vt vaincre; (country) conquérir. **conqueror** n conquérant m.

conquest /'kɒŋkwest/ n conquête f.

conscience /'kɒnʃəns/ n conscience f. **conscientious** adj consciencieux.

conscious /'kɒnʃəs/ adj conscient; (deliberate) voulu. **consciously** adv consciemment. **consciousness** n conscience f; (Med) connaissance f.

conscript /'kɒnskrɪpt/ n appelé m.

consecutive /kən'sekjʊtɪv/ adj consécutif.

consensus /kən'sensəs/ n consensus m.

consent /kən'sent/ vi consentir (to à). ● n consentement m.

consequence /'kɒnsɪkwəns/ n conséquence f. **consequently** adv par conséquent.

conservation /kɒnsə'veɪʃn/ n préservation f. ~ area zone f protégée. **conservationist** n défenseur m de l'environnement.

conservative /kən'sɜːvətɪv/ adj conservateur; (estimate) minimal.

Conservative Party n parti m conservateur.

conservatory /kən'sɜːvətrɪ/ n (greenhouse) serre f; (room) véranda f.

conserve /kən'sɜːv/ vt conserver; (energy) économiser.

consider /kən'sɪdə(r)/ vt considérer; (allow for) tenir compte de; (possibility) envisager (**doing** de faire).

considerable /kən'sɪdərəbl/ adj considérable; (much) beaucoup de.

considerate /kən'sɪdərət/ adj prévenant, attentionné. **consideration** n considération f. (respect) égard(s) m(pl)

considering /kən'sɪdərɪŋ/ prep compte tenu de.

consignment /kən'saɪnmənt/ n envoi m.

consist /kən'sɪst/ vi consister (of en; in doing à faire).

consistency /kən'sɪstənsɪ/ n (of liquids) consistance f. (of argument) cohérence f.

consistent /kən'sɪstənt/ adj cohérent; ~ with conforme à.

consolation /kɒnsə'leɪʃn/ n consolation f.

consolidate /kən'sɒlɪdeɪt/ vt/i (se) consolider.

consonant /'kɒnsənənt/ n consonne f.

conspicuous /kən'spɪkjʊəs/ adj (easily seen) en évidence; (showy) voyant; (noteworthy) remarquable.

conspiracy /kən'spɪrəsɪ/ n conspiration f.

constable /'kʌnstəbl/ n agent m de police, gendarme m.

constant /'kɒnstənt/ adj (questions) incessant; (unchanging) constant; (friend) fidèle. ● n constante f. **constantly** adv constamment.

constellation /kɒnstə'leɪʃn/ n constellation f.

constipation /kɒnstɪ'peɪʃn/ n constipation f.

constituency /kən'stɪtjʊənsɪ/ n circonscription f électorale.

constituent /kən'stɪtjʊənt/ adj constitutif. ● n élément m constitutif; (Pol) électeur/-trice m/f.

constitution /kɒnstɪ'tjuːʃn/ n constitution f.

constrain /kən'streɪn/ vt contraindre. **constraint** n contrainte f.

constrict /kən'strɪkt/ vt (flow) comprimer; (movement) gêner.

construct /kən'strʌkt/ vt construire. **construction** n construction f. **constructive** adj constructif.

consulate /'kɒnsjʊlət/ n consulat m.

consult /kən'sʌlt/ vt consulter. ● vi ~ with conférer avec. **consultant** n

conseiller/-ère m/f. (Med) spécialiste m/f. **consultation** n consultation f.

consume /kən'sjuːm/ vt consommer; (destroy) consumer. **consumer** n consommateur/-trice m/f.

consummate /'kɒnsəmeɪt/ vt consommer.

consumption /kən'sʌmpʃn/ n consommation f; (Med) phtisie f.

contact /'kɒntækt/ n contact m; (person) relation f. ● vt contacter. ~ **lenses** npl lentilles fpl (de contact).

contagious /kən'teɪdʒəs/ adj contagieux.

contain /kən'teɪn/ vt contenir; ~ oneself se contenir. **container** n récipient m. (for transport) container m.

contaminate /kən'tæmɪneɪt/ vt contaminer.

contemplate /'kɒntəmpleɪt/ vt (gaze at) contempler; (think about) envisager.

contemporary /kən'temprərɪ/ adj & n contemporain/-e (m/f).

contempt /kən'tempt/ n mépris m. **contemptible** adj méprisable. **contemptuous** adj méprisant.

contend /kən'tend/ vt soutenir. ● vi ~ with (compete) rivaliser avec; (face) faire face à. **contender** n adversaire m/f.

content[1] /'kɒntent/ n (of letter) contenu m. (amount) teneur f; ~s contenu m.

content[2] /kən'tent/ adj satisfait. ● vt contenter. **contented** adj satisfait. **contentment** n contentement m.

contest[1] /'kɒntest/ n (competition) concours m. (struggle) lutte f.

contest[2] /kən'test/ vt contester; (compete for or in) disputer. **contestant** n concurrent/-e m/f.

context /'kɒntekst/ n contexte m.

continent /'kɒntɪnənt/ n continent m; **the C** ~ l'Europe f (continentale). **continental** adj continental, européen. **continental quilt** n couette f.

contingency /kən'tɪndʒənsɪ/ n éventualité f. ~ **plan** plan m d'urgence.

continual /kən'tɪnjʊəl/ adj continuel.

continuation /kəntɪnjʊ'eɪʃn/ n continuation f. (after interruption) reprise f; (new episode) suite f.

continue /kən'tɪnjuː/ vt/i continuer; (resume) reprendre. **continued** adj continu.

continuous /kən'tɪnjʊəs/ adj continu. **continuously** adv (without a break) sans interruption; (repeatedly) continuellement.

contort /kən'tɔːt/ vt tordre; ∼ **oneself** se contorsionner.

contour /'kɒntʊə(r)/ n contour m.

contraband /'kɒntrəbænd/ n contrebande f.

contraception /kɒntrə'sepʃn/ n contraception f. **contraceptive** adj & n contraceptif (m).

contract¹ /'kɒntrækt/ n contrat m.

contract² /kən'trækt/ vt/i (se) contracter. **contraction** n contraction f.

contractor /kən'træktə(r)/ n entrepreneur/-euse m/f.

contradict /kɒntrə'dɪkt/ vt contredire. **contradictory** adj contradictoire.

contrary¹ /'kɒntrərɪ/ adj contraire (to à). ● n contraire m. **on the** ∼ au contraire. ● adv ∼ **to** contrairement à.

contrary² /kən'treərɪ/ adj entêté.

contrast¹ /'kɒntrɑːst/ n contraste m.

contrast² /kən'trɑːst/ vt/i contraster.

contravention /kɒntrə'venʃn/ n infraction f.

contribute /kən'trɪbjuːt/ vt donner. ● vi ∼ **to** contribuer à; (take part) participer à; (newspaper) collaborer à. **contribution** n contribution f. **contributor** n collaborateur/-trice m/f.

contrive /kən'traɪv/ vt imaginer; ∼ **to do** trouver moyen de faire.

control /kən'trəʊl/ vt (pt controlled) (firm) diriger; (check) contrôler; (restrain) maîtriser. ● n contrôle m. (mastery) maîtrise f. ∼**s** commandes fpl. (knobs) boutons mpl; **have under** ∼ (event) avoir en main; **in** ∼ **of** maître de. ∼ **tower** n tour f de contrôle.

controversial /kɒntrə'vɜːʃl/ adj discutable, discuté. **controversy** n controverse f.

conurbation /kɒnɜː'beɪʃn/ n agglomération f, conurbation f.

convalesce /kɒnvə'les/ vi être en convalescence.

convene /kən'viːn/ vt convoquer. ● vi se réunir.

convenience /kən'viːnɪəns/ n commodité f. ∼**s** toilettes fpl. **all modern** ∼**s** tout le confort moderne; **at your** ∼ quand cela vous conviendra, à votre convenance. ∼ **foods** npl plats mpl tout préparés.

convenient /kən'viːnɪənt/ adj commode, pratique; (time) bien choisi; **be** ∼ **for** convenir à.

convent /'kɒnvənt/ n couvent m.

convention /kən'venʃn/ n (assembly, agreement) convention f. (custom) usage m. **conventional** adj conventionnel.

conversation /kɒnvə'seɪʃn/ n conversation f. **conversational** adj (tone) de la conversation; (French) de tous les jours.

converse¹ /kən'vɜːs/ vi s'entretenir, converser (**with** avec).

converse² /'kɒnvɜːs/ adj & n inverse (m). **conversely** adv inversement.

conversion /kən'vɜːʃn/ n conversion f.

convert¹ /kən'vɜːt/ vt convertir; (house) aménager. ● vi ∼ **into** se transformer en.

convert² /'kɒnvɜːt/ n converti/-e m/f.

convertible /kən'vɜːtəbl/ adj convertible. ● n (car) décapotable f.

convey /kən'veɪ/ vt (wishes, order) transmettre; (goods, people) transporter; (idea, feeling) communiquer. **conveyor belt** n tapis m roulant.

convict¹ /kən'vɪkt/ vt déclarer coupable.

convict² /'kɒnvɪkt/ n prisonnier/-ière m/f.

conviction /kən'vɪkʃn/ n (Jur) condamnation f. (opinion) conviction f.

convince /kən'vɪns/ vt convaincre.

convoke /kən'vəʊk/ vt convoquer.

convoy /'kɒnvɔɪ/ n convoi m.

convulse /kən'vʌls/ vt convulser; (fig) bouleverser; **be** ∼**d with laughter** se tordre de rire.

cook /kʊk/ vt/i (faire) cuire; (of person) faire la cuisine; ∼ **up** 🄸 fabriquer. ● n cuisinier/-ière m/f. **cooker** n (stove) cuisinière f. **cookery** n cuisine f.

cookie /'kʊkɪ/ n (US) biscuit m.

cooking /'kʊkɪŋ/ n cuisine f. ● adj de cuisine.

cool /kuːl/ adj frais; (calm) calme; (unfriendly) froid. ● n fraîcheur f. (calmness 🔀 sang-froid *m*; **in the ~** au frais. ● *vt/i* rafraîchir. **~ box** *n* glacière *f.*

coolly /'ku:llɪ/ *adv* calmement, froidement.

coop /ku:p/ *n* poulailler *m.* ● *vt* **~ up** enfermer.

cooperate /kəʊˈɒpəreɪt/ *vi* coopérer. **co-operation** *n* coopération *f.*

cooperative /kəʊˈɒpərətɪv/ *adj* coopératif. ● *n* coopérative *f.*

coordinate /kəʊˈɔːdɪnət/ *vt* coordonner.

cop /kɒp/ *vt* (*pt* **copped**) 🔀 piquer. ● *n* (*policeman*) 🔀 flic *m.* **~ out** 🔀 se dérober.

cope /kəʊp/ *vi* s'en sortir 🔀, se débrouiller; **~ with** (*problem*) faire face à.

copper /'kɒpə(r)/ *n* cuivre *m.* (*coin*) sou *m*; 🔀 flic *m.* ● *adj* de cuivre.

copulate /'kɒpjʊleɪt/ *vi* s'accoupler.

copy /'kɒpɪ/ *n* copie *f.* (*of book, newspaper*) exemplaire *m*; (print: Photo) épreuve *f.* ● *vt/i* copier.

copyright /'kɒpɪraɪt/ *n* droit *m* d'auteur, copyright *m.*

copy-writer *n* rédacteur-concepteur *m*, rédactrice-conceptrice *f.*

cord /kɔːd/ *n* (petite) corde *f*; (*of curtain, pyjamas*) cordon *m*; (Electr) cordon *m* électrique; (*fabric*) velours *m* côtelé.

cordial /'kɔːdɪəl/ *adj* cordial. ● *n* (*drink*) sirop *m.*

corduroy /'kɔːdərɔɪ/ *n* velours *m* côtelé.

core /kɔː(r)/ *n* (*of apple*) trognon *m*; (*of problem*) cœur *m*; (*Tech*) noyau *m.* ● *vt* (*apple*) évider.

cork /kɔːk/ *n* liège *m.* (*for bottle*) bouchon *m.* ● *vt* boucher. **corkscrew** *n* tire-bouchon *m.*

corn /kɔːn/ *n* blé *m.* (maize: US) maïs *m*; (*seed*) grain *m*; (hard skin) cor *m.*

cornea /'kɔːnɪə/ *n* cornée *f.*

corner /'kɔːnə(r)/ *n* coin *m*; (bend in road) virage *m*; (football) corner *m.* ● *vt* coincer, acculer; (*market*) accaparer. ● *vi* prendre un virage.

cornflour /'kɔːnflaʊə(r)/ *n* farine *f* de maïs.

cornice /'kɔːnɪs/ *n* corniche *f.*

corny /'kɔːnɪ/ *adj* (**-ier, -iest**) (*joke*) éculé.

corollary /kəˈrɒlərɪ/ *n* corollaire *m.*

coronary /'kɒrənrɪ/ *n* infarctus *m.*

coronation /kɒrəˈneɪʃn/ *n* couronnement *m.*

corporal /'kɔːpərəl/ *n* caporal *m.* **~punishment** *n* châtiment *m* corporel.

corporate /'kɔːpərət/ *adj* (*ownership*) en commun; (*body*) constitué.

corporation /kɔːpəˈreɪʃn/ *n* (Comm) société *f.*

corpse /kɔːps/ *n* cadavre *m.*

corpuscle /'kɔːpʌsl/ *n* globule *m.*

correct /kəˈrekt/ *adj* (right) exact, juste, correct; (*proper*) correct; **you are ~** vous avez raison. ● *vt* corriger.

correction /kəˈrekʃn/ *n* correction *f.*

correlate /'kɒrəleɪt/ *vt/i* (faire) correspondre.

correspond /kɒrɪˈspɒnd/ *vi* correspondre. **correspondence** *n* correspondance *f.*

corridor /'kɒrɪdɔː(r)/ *n* couloir *m.*

corrode /kəˈrəʊd/ *vt/i* (se) corroder.

corrugated /'kɒrəgeɪtɪd/ *adj* ondulé; **~ iron** tôle *f* ondulée.

corrupt /kəˈrʌpt/ *adj* corrompu. ● *vt* corrompre. **corruption** *n* corruption *f.*

Corsica /'kɔːsɪkə/ *n* Corse *f.*

cosh /kɒʃ/ *n* matraque *f.* ● *vt* matraquer.

cosmetic /kɒzˈmetɪk/ *n* produit *m* de beauté. ● *adj* cosmétique; (fig, pej) superficiel. **~ surgery** *n* chirurgie *f* esthétique.

cosmopolitan /kɒzməˈpɒlɪtn/ *adj & n* cosmopolite (*mf*).

cosmos /'kɒzmɒs/ *n* cosmos *m.*

cost /kɒst/ *vt* (*pt* **cost**) coûter. (*pt* **costed**) établir le prix de. ● *n* coût *m.* **~s** (Jur) dépens *mpl.* **at all ~s** à tout prix; **to one's ~** à ses dépens; **~ price** prix *m* de revient; **~ of living** coût *m* de la vie. **~-effective** *adj* rentable.

costly /'kɒstlɪ/ *adj* (**-ier, -iest**) coûteux; (*valuable*) précieux.

costume /'kɒstjuːm/ *n* costume *m.* (for swimming) maillot *m.* **~ jewellery** *npl* bijoux *mpl* de fantaisie.

cosy /'kəʊzɪ/ *adj* (**-ier, -iest**) confortable, intime.

cot /kɒt/ n lit m d'enfant; (camp-bed: US) lit m de camp.

cottage /'kɒtɪdʒ/ n petite maison f de campagne; (thatched) chaumière f. ~ **pie** n hachis m Parmentier.

cotton /'kɒtn/ n coton m. (for sewing) fil m (à coudre). ● vi ~ **on** 🔲 piger. ~ **wool** n coton m hydrophile.

couch /kaʊtʃ/ n canapé m. ● vt (express) formuler.

cough /kɒf/ vi tousser. ● n toux f. ~ **up** 🔲 cracher, payer.

could /kʊd/ →**CAN**¹.

couldn't →**COULD NOT**.

council /'kaʊnsl/ n conseil m. ~ **house** n maison f louée par la municipalité, ≈ H.L.M. m or f.

councillor /'kaʊnsələ(r)/ n conseiller/-ère m/f municipal/-e.

counsel /'kaʊnsl/ n conseil m. ● n inv (Jur) avocat/-e m/f. **counsellor** n conseiller/-ère m/f.

count /kaʊnt/ vt/i compter. ● n (numerical record) décompte m. (nobleman) comte m. ~ **on** compter sur.

counter /'kaʊntə(r)/ n comptoir m. (in bank) guichet m; (token) jeton m. ● adv ~ **to** à l'encontre de. ● adj opposé. ● vt opposer; (blow) parer. ● vi riposter.

counteract /kaʊntə'rækt/ vt neutraliser.

counterbalance /'kaʊntəbæləns/ n contrepoids m. ● vt contrebalancer.

counterfeit /'kaʊntəfɪt/ adj & n faux (m). ● vt contrefaire.

counterfoil /'kaʊntəfɔɪl/ n souche f.

counter-productive /kaʊntəprə'dʌktɪv/ adj qui produit l'effet contraire.

countess /'kaʊntɪs/ n comtesse f.

countless /'kaʊntlɪs/ adj innombrable.

country /'kʌntrɪ/ n (land, region) pays m. (homeland) patrie f; (countryside) campagne f.

countryman /'kʌntrɪmən/ n (pl -men) campagnard m; (fellow citizen) compatriote m.

countryside /'kʌntrɪsaɪd/ n campagne f.

county /'kaʊntɪ/ n comté m.

coup /ku:/ n (achievement) joli coup m. (Pol) coup m d'état.

couple /'kʌpl/ n (people, animals) couple m. **a** ~ **of** (two or three) deux ou trois. ● vt/i (s')accoupler.

coupon /'ku:pɒn/ n coupon m; (for shopping) bon m or coupon m de réduction.

courage /'kʌrɪdʒ/ n courage m.

courgette /kʊə'ʒet/ n courgette f.

courier /'kʊrɪə(r)/ n messager/-ère m/f; (for tourists) guide m.

course /kɔ:s/ n cours m; (for training) stage m; (series) série f; (Culin) plat m; (for golf) terrain m; (at sea) itinéraire m. **change** ~ changer de cap; ~ **(of action)** façon f de faire; **during the** ~ **of** pendant; **in due** ~ en temps utile; **of** ~ bien sûr.

court /kɔ:t/ n cour f; (tennis) court m; **go to** ~ aller devant les tribunaux. ● vt faire la cour à; (danger) rechercher.

courteous /'kɜ:tɪəs/ adj courtois.

courtesy /'kɜ:təsɪ/ n courtoisie f; **by** ~ **of** avec la permission de.

courthouse /'kɔ:thaʊs/ n (US) palais m de justice.

court-martial vt (pt -martialled) faire passer en conseil de guerre. ● n cour f martiale.

court: ~**room** n salle f de tribunal. ~**shoe** n escarpin m. ~**yard** n cour f.

cousin /'kʌzn/ n cousin/-e m/f. **first** ~ cousin/-e m/f germain/-e.

cove /kəʊv/ n anse f, crique f.

covenant /'kʌvənənt/ n convention f.

cover /'kʌvə(r)/ vt couvrir. ● n (for bed, book) couverture f. (lid) couvercle m; (for furniture) housse f; (shelter) abri m; **take** ~ se mettre à l'abri. ~ **up** cacher; (crime) couvrir; ~**up for** couvrir.

coverage /'kʌvərɪdʒ/ n reportage m.

covering /'kʌvərɪŋ/ n enveloppe f. ~ **letter** lettre f d'accompagnement.

covert /'kʌvət/ adj (activity) secret; (threat) voilé; (look) dérobé.

cover-up n opération f de camouflage.

cow /kaʊ/ n vache f.

coward /'kaʊəd/ n lâche mf.

cowboy /'kaʊbɔɪ/ n cow-boy m.

cowshed /'kaʊʃed/ n étable f.

coy /kɔɪ/ adj (faussement) timide, qui fait le or la timide.

cozy US →cosy.

crab /kræb/ n crabe m. ~-apple n pomme f sauvage.

crack /kræk/ n fente f; (in glass) fêlure f; (noise) craquement m; (joke ▣) plaisanterie f. ● adj ▣ d'élite. ● vt/i (break partially) (se) fêler; (split) (se) fendre; (nut) casser; (joke) raconter; (problem) résoudre; **get ~ing** ▣ s'y mettre. ~ **down on** ▣ sévir contre. ~ **up** ▣ craquer.

cracker /'krækə(r)/ n (Culin) biscuit m (salé); (for Christmas) diablotin f.

crackle /'krækl/ vi crépiter. ● n crépitement m.

cradle /'kreɪdl/ n berceau m. ● vt bercer.

craft /krɑːft/ n métier m artisanal; (technique) art m; (boat) bateau m. **craftsman** n (pl -men) artisan m. **craftsmanship** n art m.

crafty /'krɑːftɪ/ adj (-ier, -iest) rusé.

crag /kræg/ n rocher m à pic.

cram /kræm/ vt/i (pt crammed). (for an exam) bachoter (**for** pour;) ~ **into** (pack) (s')entasser dans; ~ **with** (fill) bourrer de.

cramp /kræmp/ n crampe f.

cramped /kræmpt/ adj à l'étroit.

cranberry /'krænbərɪ/ n canneberge f.

crane /kreɪn/ n grue f. ● vt (neck) tendre.

crank /kræŋk/ n excentrique mf. (Tech) manivelle f.

crap /kræp/ n (nonsense ▣) conneries fpl ▣; (faeces ▣) merde f ▣.

crash /kræʃ/ n accident m; (noise) fracas m; (of thunder) coup m; (of firm) faillite f. ● vt/i avoir un accident (avec); (of plane) s'écraser; (two vehicles) se percuter; ~ **into** rentrer dans. ~ **course** n cours m intensif. ~-**helmet** n casque m (anti-choc). ~-**land** vi atterrir en catastrophe.

crate /kreɪt/ n cageot m.

cravat /krə'væt/ n foulard m.

crave /kreɪv/ vt/i ~ **for** désirer ardemment. **craving** n envie f irrésistible.

crawl /krɔːl/ vi (insect) ramper; (vehicle) se traîner; **be ~ing with** grouiller de. ● n (pace) pas m. (swimming) crawl m.

crayfish /'kreɪfɪʃ/ n inv écrevisse f.

crayon /'kreɪən/ n craie f grasse.

craze /kreɪz/ n engouement m.

crazy /'kreɪzɪ/ adj (-ier, -iest) fou; ~ **about** (person) fou de; (thing) fana or fou de.

creak /kriːk/ n grincement m. ● vi grincer.

cream /kriːm/ n crème f. ● adj crème inv. ● vt écrémer.

crease /kriːs/ n pli m. ● vt/i (se) froisser.

create /kriː'eɪt/ vt créer. **creation** n création f. **creative** adj (person) créatif; (process) créateur. **creator** n créateur/-trice m/f.

creature /'kriːtʃə(r)/ n créature f.

crèche /kreʃ/ n garderie f.

credentials /krɪ'denʃlz/ npl (identity) pièces fpl d'identité; (competence) références fpl.

credibility /kredə'bɪlətɪ/ n crédibilité f.

credit /'kredɪt/ n (credence) crédit m. (honour) honneur m; **in** ~ créditeur; ~s (cinema) générique m. ● adj (balance) créditeur. ● vt croire; (Comm) créditer; ~ **sb with** attribuer à qn. ~ **card** n carte f de crédit. ~ **note** n avoir m.

creditor /'kredɪtə(r)/ n créancier/-ière m/f.

creditworthy /'kredɪtwɜːðɪ/ adj solvable.

creed /kriːd/ n credo m.

creek /kriːk/ n (US) ruisseau m. **up the** ~ ▣ dans le pétrin ▣.

creep /kriːp/ vi (pt crept) (insect, cat) ramper; (fig) se glisser. ● n (person ▣) pauvre type m ▣. **give sb the** ~s faire frissonner qn. **creeper** n liane f.

cremate /krɪ'meɪt/ vt incinérer. **cremation** n incinération f. **crematorium** n (pl -ia) crématorium m.

crêpe /kreɪp/ n crêpe m. ~ **paper** n papier m crépon.

crept /krept/ →CREEP.

crescent /'kresnt/ n croissant m; (of houses) rue f en demi-lune.

cress /kres/ n cresson m.

crest /krest/ n crête f. (coat of arms) armoiries fpl.

cretin /'kretɪn/ n crétin/-e m/f.

crevice /'krevɪs/ n fente f.

crew /kru:/ n (of plane, ship) équipage m; (gang) équipe f. **~ cut** n coupe f en brosse. **~ neck** n (col) ras du cou m.

crib /krɪb/ n lit m d'enfant. ● vt/i (pt **cribbed**) copier.

cricket /'krɪkɪt/ n (Sport) cricket m. (insect) grillon m.

crime /kraɪm/ n crime m; (minor) délit m; (acts) criminalité f.

criminal /'krɪmɪnl/ adj & n criminel/-le (m/f).

crimson /'krɪmzn/ adj & n cramoisi (m).

cringe /krɪndʒ/ vi reculer; (fig) s'humilier.

crinkle /'krɪŋkl/ vt/i (cloth) (se) froisser. ● n pli m.

cripple /'krɪpl/ n infirme mf. ● vt estropier; (fig) paralyser.

crisis /'kraɪsɪs/ n (pl **crises**) crise f.

crisp /krɪsp/ adj (Culin) croquant; (air, reply) vif. **crisps** npl chips fpl.

criss-cross /'krɪskrɒs/ adj entrecroisé. ● vt/i (s')entrecroiser.

criterion /kraɪ'tɪərɪən/ n (pl **-ia**) critère m.

critic /'krɪtɪk/ n critique m. **critical** adj critique. **critically** adv d'une manière critique; (ill) gravement.

criticism /'krɪtɪsɪzəm/ n critique f.

criticize /'krɪtɪsaɪz/ vt/i critiquer.

croak /krəʊk/ n (bird) croassement m; (frog) coassement m. ● vi croasser; coasser.

Croatia /krəʊ'eɪʃə/ n Croatie f.

Croatian /krəʊ'eɪʃn/ n Croate mf. ● adj Croate.

crochet /'krəʊʃeɪ/ n crochet m. ● vt faire du crochet.

crockery /'krɒkərɪ/ n vaisselle f.

crocodile /'krɒkədaɪl/ n crocodile m.

crook /krʊk/ n (criminal 🆙) escroc m; (stick) houlette f.

crooked /'krʊkɪd/ adj tordu; (winding) tortueux; (askew) de travers; (dishonest: fig) malhonnête.

crop /krɒp/ n récolte f; (fig) quantité f. ● vt (pt **cropped**) couper. ● vi **~ up** se présenter.

cross /krɒs/ n croix f; (hybrid) hybride m. ● vt/i traverser; (legs, animals) croiser; (cheque) barrer; (paths) se croiser; **~ sb's mind** venir à l'esprit de qn.

● adj en colère, fâché (**with** contre). **talk at ~ purposes** parler sans se comprendre. □ ● **off** or **out** rayer.

~-check vt vérifier (pour confirmer).

~-country (running) n cross m.

~-examine vt faire subir un contre-interrogatoire à. **~-eyed** adj **be ~-eyed** loucher. **~fire** n feux mpl croisés.

crossing /'krɒsɪŋ/ n (by boat) traversée f; (on road) passage m clouté.

crossly /'krɒslɪ/ adv avec colère.

cross: ~-reference n renvoi m. **~roads** n carrefour m. **~word** n mots mpl croisés.

crotch /krɒtʃ/ n (of garment) entre-jambes m inv.

crouch /kraʊtʃ/ vi s'accroupir.

crow /krəʊ/ n corbeau m; **as the ~ flies** à vol d'oiseau. ● vi (of cock) chanter; (fig) jubiler. **~bar** n pied-de-biche m.

crowd /kraʊd/ n foule f. **crowded** adj plein.

crown /kraʊn/ n couronne f; (top part) sommet m. ● vt couronner.

Crown Court n Cour f d'assises.

crucial /'kru:ʃl/ adj crucial.

crucifix /'kru:sɪfɪks/ n crucifix m.

crucify /'kru:sɪfaɪ/ vt crucifier.

crude /kru:d/ adj (raw) brut; (rough, vulgar) grossier.

cruel /'krʊəl/ adj (**crueller, cruellest**) cruel.

cruise /kru:z/ n croisière f. ● vi (ship) croiser; (tourists) faire une croisière; (vehicle) rouler; **cruising speed** vitesse f de croisière.

crumb /krʌm/ n miette f.

crumble /'krʌmbl/ vt/i (s')effriter; (bread) (s')émietter; (collapse) s'écrouler.

crumple /'krʌmpl/ vt/i (se) froisser.

crunch /krʌntʃ/ vt croquer. ● n (event) moment m critique; **when it comes to the ~** quand ça devient sérieux.

crusade /kru:'seɪd/ n croisade f. **crusader** n (knight) croisé m; (fig) militant/-e m/f.

crush /krʌʃ/ vt écraser; (clothes) froisser. ● n (crowd) presse f; **a ~ on** 🆇 le béguin pour.

crust /krʌst/ n croûte f. **crusty** adj croustillant.

crutch /krʌtʃ/ n béquille f; (crotch) entrejambes m inv.

crux /krʌks/ n the ~ of (problem) le point crucial de.

cry /kraɪ/ n cri m. ● vi (weep) pleurer; (call out) crier. □ ~ off se décommander.

crying /'kraɪɪŋ/ adj (need) urgent; a ~ shame une vraie honte. ● n pleurs mpl.

cryptic /'krɪptɪk/ adj énigmatique.

crystal /'krɪstl/ n cristal m. ~-clear adj parfaitement clair.

cub /kʌb/ n petit m; Cub (Scout) louveteau m.

Cuba /'kju:bə/ n Cuba f.

cube /kju:b/ n cube m. **cubic** adj cubique; (metre) cube.

cubicle /'kju:bɪkl/ n (in room, hospital) box m; (at swimming-pool) cabine f.

cuckoo /'kʊku:/ n coucou m.

cucumber /'kju:kʌmbə(r)/ n concombre m.

cuddle /'kʌdl/ vt câliner. ● vi (kiss and) ~ s'embrasser. ● n caresse f. **cuddly** adj câlin; **cuddly toy** peluche f.

cue /kju:/ n signal m; (Theat) réplique f; (billiards) queue f.

cuff /kʌf/ n manchette f; (US: on trousers) revers m; **off the** ~ impromptu. ● vt gifler. ~-link n bouton m de manchette.

cul-de-sac /'kʌldəsæk/ n (pl **culs-de-sac**) impasse f.

cull /kʌl/ vt (select) choisir; (kill) massacrer.

culminate /'kʌlmɪneɪt/ vi ~ in se terminer par. **culmination** n point m culminant.

culprit /'kʌlprɪt/ n coupable mf.

cult /kʌlt/ n culte m.

cultivate /'kʌltɪveɪt/ vt cultiver. **cultivation** n culture f.

cultural /'kʌltʃərəl/ adj culturel.

culture /'kʌltʃə(r)/ n culture f. **cultured** adj cultivé.

cumbersome /'kʌmbəsəm/ adj encombrant.

cunning /'kʌnɪŋ/ adj rusé. ● n astuce f, ruse f.

cup /kʌp/ n tasse f; (prize) coupe f; **Cup final** finale f de la coupe.

cupboard /'kʌbəd/ n placard m.

cup-tie n match m de coupe.

curate /'kjʊərət/ n vicaire m.

curator /kjʊə'reɪtə(r)/ n (of museum) conservateur m.

curb /kɜ:b/ n (restraint) frein m; (of path) (US) bord m du trottoir. ● vt (desires) refréner; (price increase) freiner.

cure /'kjʊə(r)/ vt guérir; (fig) éliminer; (Culin) fumer; (in brine) saler. ● n (recovery) guérison f; (remedy) remède m.

curfew /'kɜ:fju:/ n couvre-feu m.

curiosity /kjʊərɪ'ɒsəti/ n curiosité f. **curious** adj curieux.

curl /kɜ:l/ vt/i (hair) boucler. ● n boucle f. □ ~up se pelotonner; (shrivel) se racornir.

curler /'kɜ:lə(r)/ n bigoudi m.

curly /'kɜ:li/ adj (-ier, -iest) bouclé.

currant /'kʌrənt/ n raisin m de Corinthe.

currency /'kʌrənsi/ n (money) monnaie f; (of word) fréquence f; **foreign** ~ devises fpl étrangères.

current /'kʌrənt/ adj (term, word) usité; (topical) actuel; (year) en cours. ● n courant m. ~ **account** n compte m courant. ~ **events** npl l'actualité f.

currently /'kʌrəntli/ adv actuellement.

curriculum /kə'rɪkjʊləm/ n (pl **-la**) programme m scolaire. ~ **vitae** n curriculum vitae m.

curry /'kʌri/ n curry m. ● vt ~ **favour with** chercher à plaire à.

curse /kɜ:s/ n (spell) malédiction f; (swearword) juron m. ● vt maudire. ● vi (swear) jurer.

cursor /'kɜ:sə(r)/ n curseur m.

curt /kɜ:t/ adj brusque.

curtain /'kɜ:tn/ n rideau m.

curve /kɜ:v/ n courbe f. ● vi (line) s'incurver; (edge) se recourber; (road) faire une courbe. ● vt courber.

cushion /'kʊʃn/ n coussin m. ● vt (a blow) amortir; (fig) protéger.

custard /'kʌstəd/ n crème f anglaise; (set) flan m.

custody /'kʌstədi/ n (of child) garde f; (Jur) détention f préventive.

custom /'kʌstəm/ n coutume f; (patronage: Comm) clientèle f. **customary** adj habituel.

customer /'kʌstəmə(r)/ n client/-e m/f; (person **I**) type m.

customize /'kʌstəmaɪz/ vt personnaliser.

custom-made adj fait sur mesure.

customs /'kʌstəmz/ npl douane f. ● adj douanier. **~ officer** n douanier m.

cut /kʌt/ vt/i (pt cut. pres p **cutting**) vt couper; (hedge) tailler; (prices) réduire. ● vi couper. ● n (wound) coupure f; (of clothes) coupe f; (in surgery) incision f; (share) part f; (in prices) réduction f. □ **~ back** vi faire des économies. vt réduire. **~ down (on)** réduire. **~ in** (in conversation) intervenir. **~ off** couper; (tide, army) isoler; **~ out** vt découper; (leave out) supprimer; vi (engine) s'arrêter. **~ short** (visit) écourter. **~ up** couper; (carve) découper.

cutback /'kʌtbæk/ n réduction f.

cute /kju:t/ adj **I** mignon.

cutlery /'kʌtlərɪ/ n couverts mpl.

cutlet /'kʌtlɪt/ n côtelette f.

cut-price adj à prix réduit.

cutting /'kʌtɪŋ/ adj cinglant. ● n (from newspaper) coupure f; (plant) bouture f.

CV abbr →CURRICULUM VITAE.

cyanide /'saɪənaɪd/ n cyanure m.

cyberspace /'saɪbəspeɪs/ n cyberspace m.

cycle /'saɪbəspeɪs/ n cycle m; (bicycle) vélo m. ● vi aller à vélo.

cycling /'saɪklɪŋ/ n cyclisme m. **~ shorts** npl cycliste m.

cyclist /'saɪklɪst/ n cycliste mf.

cylinder /'sɪlɪndə(r)/ n cylindre m.

cymbal /'sɪmbl/ n cymbale f.

cynic /'sɪnɪk/ n cynique mf. **cynical** adj cynique. **cynicism** n cynisme m.

cypress /'saɪprəs/ n cyprès m.

Cypriot /'sɪprɪət/ n Cypriote mf. ● adj cypriote.

Cyprus /'saɪprəs/ n Chypre f.

cyst /sɪst/ n kyste m.

czar /zɑː(r)/ n tsar m.

Czech /tʃek/ n (person) Tchèque mf; (Ling) tchèque m. **~ Republic** n République f tchèque.

Dd

dab /dæb/ vt (pt **dabbed**) tamponner; **~ sth on** appliquer qch par petites touches. ● n touche f.

dabble /'dæbl/ vi **~ in sth** faire qch en amateur.

dad /dæd/ n **I** papa m. **daddy** n **I** papa m.

daffodil /'dæfədɪl/ n jonquille f.

daft /dɑːft/ adj bête.

dagger /'dægə(r)/ n poignard m.

> **Dáil Éireann** Ces mots de gaélique irlandais, que l'on prononce /dɔɪl ˈɜː(ə)n/ désignent la Chambre des représentants au parlement de la République d'Irlande. Les 166 députés qui la composent représentent 42 circonscriptions électorales et sont élus par un système de scrutin à la représentation proportionnelle pour cinq ans.

daily /'deɪlɪ/ adj quotidien. ● adv tous les jours. ● n (newspaper) quotidien m.

dainty /'deɪntɪ/ adj (**-ier, -iest**) (lace, food) délicat; (shoe, hand) mignon.

dairy /'deərɪ/ n (on farm) laiterie f; (shop) crémerie f. ● adj (farm, cow, product) laitier; (butter) fermier.

daisy /'deɪzɪ/ n pâquerette f.

dam /dæm/ n barrage m.

damage /'dæmɪdʒ/ n (to property) dégâts mpl; (Med) lésions fpl; **to do sth ~** (cause, trade) porter atteinte à; **~s** (Jur) dommages-intérêts mpl. ● vt (property) endommager; (health) nuire à; (reputation) porter atteinte à. **damaging** adj (to health) nuisible; (to reputation) préjudiciable.

damn /dæm/ vt (Relig) damner; (condemn: fig) condamner. ● interj **I** zut **I**, merde **X**. ● n **not give/care a ~ about** se ficher de **I**. ● adj fichu **I**. ● adv franchement.

damp /dæmp/ n humidité f. ● adj humide. **dampen** vt (lit) humecter; (fig) refroidir. **dampness** n humidité f.

dance /dɑːns/ vt/i danser. ● n danse f; (gathering) bal m; **~ hall** dancing m.

dancer n danseur/-euse m/f.

dandelion /'dændɪlaɪən/ n pissenlit m.

dandruff /'dændrʌf/ n pellicules fpl.

Dane /deɪn/ n Danois/-e m/f.

danger /'deɪndʒə(r)/ n danger m; (risk) risque m; **be in ~ of** risquer de. **dangerous** adj dangereux.

dangle /'dæŋgl/ vt (object) balancer; (legs) laisser pendre. ● vi (object) se balancer (from à).

Danish /'deɪnɪʃ/ n (Ling) danois m. ● adj danois.

dare /deə(r)/ vt oser ((to) do faire). ~ **sb to do** défier qn de faire. ● n défi m. **daring** adj audacieux.

dark /dɑːk/ adj (day, colour, suit, mood, warning) sombre; (hair, eyes, skin) brun; (secret, thought) noir. ● n noir m; (nightfall) tombée f de la nuit; **in the ~** (fig) dans le noir. **darken** vt/i (sky) (s')obscurcir; (mood) (s')assombrir. **darkness** n obscurité f. **~-room** n chambre f noire.

darling /'dɑːlɪŋ/ adj & n chéri/-e (m/f).

dart /dɑːt/ n fléchette f; **~s** (game) fléchettes fpl. ● vi ~ **in/away** entrer/filer comme une flèche.

dash /dæʃ/ vi se précipiter; ~ **off** se sauver. ● vt (hope) anéantir; ~ **sth against** projeter qch contre. ● n course f folle; (of liquid) goutte f; (of colour) touche f; (in punctuation) tiret m.

dashboard /'dæʃbɔːd/ n tableau m de bord.

data /'deɪtə/ npl données fpl. ~**base** n base f de données. ~ **capture** n saisie f de données. ~ **processing** n traitement m des données. ~ **protection** n protection f de l'information.

date /deɪt/ n date f; (meeting) rendez-vous m; (fruit) datte f; **out of ~** (old-fashioned) démodé; (passport) périmé; **to ~** à ce jour; **up to ~** (modern) moderne; (list) à jour. ● vt/i dater; (go out with) sortir avec; ~ **from** dater de. **dated** adj démodé.

daughter /'dɔːtə(r)/ n fille f. ~-**in-law** n (pl ~**s-in-law**) belle-fille f.

daunt /dɔːnt/ vt décourager.

dawdle /'dɔːdl/ vi flâner, traînasser Ⅱ.

dawn /dɔːn/ n aube f. ● vi (day) se lever; **it ~ed on me that** je me suis rendu compte que.

day /deɪ/ n jour m; (whole day) journée f; (period) époque f; **the ~ before** la veille; **the following** or **next ~** le lendemain. ~**break** n aube f.

daydream /'deɪdriːm/ n rêves mpl. ● vi rêvasser (about de).

day: ~**light** n jour m. ~**time** n journée f. ~ **trader** spéculateur m à la journée, scalpeur m.

daze /deɪz/ n **in a ~** (from blow) étourdi; (from drug) hébété. **dazed** adj (by blow) abasourdi; (by news) ahuri.

dazzle /'dæzl/ vt éblouir.

dead /ded/ adj mort; (numb) engourdi. ● adv complètement; **in ~ centre** au beau milieu; **stop ~** s'arrêter net. ● n **in the ~ of** au cœur de; **the ~** les morts. **deaden** vt (sound, blow) amortir; (pain) calmer. ~ **end** n impasse f. ~**line** n date f limite. ~**lock** n impasse f.

deadly /'dedlɪ/ adj (-ier, -iest) mortel; (weapon) meurtrier.

deaf /def/ adj sourd. **deafen** vt assourdir. **deafness** n surdité f.

deal /diːl/ vt (pt dealt) donner; (blow) porter. ● vi (trade) être en activité; ~ **in** être dans le commerce de. ~ n affaire f; (cards) donne f; **a great** or **good ~** beaucoup (of de). □ ~ **with** (handle, manage) s'occuper de; (be about) traiter de. **dealer** n marchand/-e m/f; (agent) concessionnaire mf. **dealings** npl relations fpl.

dear /dɪə(r)/ adj cher; ~ **Sir/Madam** Monsieur/Madame. ● n (my) ~ mon chéri/ma chérie m/f. ● adv cher. ● interj **oh ~!** oh mon Dieu!

death /deθ/ n mort f; ~ **penalty** peine f de mort.

debatable /dɪ'beɪtəbl/ adj discutable.

debate /dɪ'beɪt/ n (formal) débat m; (informal) discussion f. ● vt (formally) débattre de; (informally) discuter.

debit /'debɪt/ n débit m. ● adj (balance) débiteur. ● vt (pt debited) débiter.

debris /'debriː/ n débris mpl; (rubbish) déchets mpl.

debt /det/ n dette f; **be in ~** avoir des dettes.

debug /diː'bʌg/ vt (Comput) déboguer.

decade /'dekeɪd/ n décennie f.

decadent /'dekədənt/ adj décadent.

decaffeinated | deference

decaffeinated /diːˈkæfɪneɪtɪd/ adj décaféiné.

decay /dɪˈkeɪ/ vi (vegetation) pourrir; (tooth) se carier; (fig) décliner. ● n pourriture f; (of tooth) carie f; (fig) déclin m.

deceased /dɪˈsiːst/ adj décédé. ● n défunt/-e m/f.

deceit /dɪˈsiːt/ n tromperie f. **deceitful** adj trompeur.

deceive /dɪˈsiːv/ vt tromper.

December /dɪˈsembə(r)/ n décembre m.

decent /ˈdiːsnt/ adj (respectable) comme il faut; (adequate) convenable; (good) bon; (kind) gentil; (not indecent) décent. **decently** adv convenablement.

deception /dɪˈsepʃn/ n tromperie f. **deceptive** adj trompeur.

decide /dɪˈsaɪd/ vt/i décider (**to do** faire); (question) régler; ~ **on** se décider pour. **decided** adj (firm) résolu; (clear) net. **decidedly** adv nettement.

decimal /ˈdesɪml/ adj décimal. ● n décimale f; ~ **point** virgule f.

decipher /dɪˈsaɪfə(r)/ vt déchiffrer.

decision /dɪˈsɪʒn/ n décision f.

decisive /dɪˈsaɪsɪv/ adj (conclusive) décisif; (firm) décidé.

deck /dek/ n pont m; (of cards: US) jeu m; (of bus) étage m. ~**-chair** n chaise f longue.

declaration /deklaˈreɪʃn/ n déclaration f. **declare** vt déclarer.

decline /dɪˈklaɪn/ vt/i refuser; (fall) baisser. ● n (waning) déclin m; (drop) baisse f; **in** ~ sur le déclin.

decode /diːˈkəʊd/ vt décoder.

decommission /diːkəˈmɪʃn/ vt (arms) mettre hors service; (reactor) démanteler.

decompose /diːkəmˈpəʊz/ vt/i (se) décomposer.

decor /ˈdeɪkɔː(r)/ n décor m.

decorate /ˈdekəreɪt/ vt décorer; (room) refaire, peindre. **decoration** n décoration f. **decorative** adj décoratif.

decorator /ˈdekəreɪtə(r)/ n peintre m; (interior) ~ décorateur/-trice m/f.

decoy /ˈdiːkɔɪ/ n (person, vehicle) leurre m; (for hunting) appeau m.

decrease[1] /dɪˈkriːs/ vt/i diminuer.

decrease[2] /ˈdiːkriːs/ n diminution f.

decree /dɪˈkriː/ n (Pol, Relig) décret m; (Jur) jugement m. ● vt (pt **decreed**) décréter.

decrepit /dɪˈkrepɪt/ adj (building) délabré; (person) décrépit.

dedicate /ˈdedɪkeɪt/ vt dédier; ~ **oneself to** se consacrer à.

dedicated /ˈdedɪkeɪtɪd/ adj dévoué; ~ **line** (Internet) ligne f spécialisée.

dedication /dedɪˈkeɪʃn/ n dévouement m; (in book) dédicace f.

deduce /dɪˈdjuːs/ vt déduire.

deduct /dɪˈdʌkt/ vt déduire; (from wages) retenir.

deed /diːd/ n acte m.

deem /diːm/ vt considérer.

deep /diːp/ adj profond; (mud, carpet) épais. ● adv profondément; ~ **in thought** absorbé dans ses pensées. **deepen** vt/i (admiration, concern) augmenter.

deep-freeze n congélateur m. ● vt congeler.

deep vein thrombosis n thrombose f veineuse profonde.

deer /dɪə(r)/ n inv cerf m; (doe) biche f.

deface /dɪˈfeɪs/ vt dégrader.

default /dɪˈfɔːlt/ vi (Jur) ~ **(on payments)** ne pas régler ses échéances. ● n (on payments) non-remboursement m; **by** ~ par défaut; **win by** ~ gagner par forfait. ● adj (Comput) par défaut.

defeat /dɪˈfiːt/ vt vaincre; (thwart) faire échouer. ● n défaite f.

defect[1] /ˈdiːfekt/ n défaut m.

defect[2] /dɪˈfekt/ vi faire défection; ~ **to** passer à.

defective /dɪˈfektɪv/ adj défectueux.

defector /dɪˈfektə(r)/ n transfuge mf.

defence /dɪˈfens/ n défense f.

defend /dɪˈfend/ vt défendre. **defendant** n (Jur) accusé/-e m/f. **defender** n défenseur m.

defensive /dɪˈfensɪv/ adj défensif. ● n défensive f.

defer /dɪˈfɜː(r)/ vt (pt **deferred**) (postpone) reporter; (judgement) suspendre; (payment) différer.

deference /ˈdefərəns/ n déférence f. **deferential** adj déférent.

defiance /dɪˈfaɪəns/ n défi m; **in ~ of** contre. **defiant** adj rebelle. **defiantly** adv avec défi.

deficiency /dɪˈfɪʃənsɪ/ n insuffisance f; (fault) défaut m.

deficient /dɪˈfɪʃnt/ adj insuffisant; **be ~ in** manquer de.

deficit /ˈdefɪsɪt/ n déficit m.

define /dɪˈfaɪn/ vt définir.

definite /ˈdefɪnɪt/ adj (exact) précis; (obvious) net; (firm) ferme; (certain) certain. **definitely** adv certainement; (clearly) nettement.

definition /defɪˈnɪʃn/ n définition f.

deflate /dɪˈfleɪt/ vt dégonfler.

deflect /dɪˈflekt/ vt (missile) dévier; (criticism) détourner.

deforestation /diːfɒrɪˈsteɪʃn/ n déforestation f.

deform /dɪˈfɔːm/ vt déformer.

defraud /dɪˈfrɔːd/ vt (client, employer) escroquer; (state, customs) frauder; **~ sb of sth** escroquer qch à qn.

defrost /diːˈfrɒst/ vt dégivrer.

deft /deft/ adj adroit.

defunct /dɪˈfʌŋkt/ adj défunt.

defuse /diːˈfjuːz/ vt désamorcer.

defy /dɪˈfaɪ/ vt défier; (attempts) résister à.

degenerate¹ /dɪˈdʒenəreɪt/ vi dégénérer (**into** en).

degenerate² /dɪˈdʒenərət/ adj & n dégénéré/-e (m/f).

degrade /dɪˈgreɪd/ vt (humiliate) humilier; (damage) dégrader.

degree /dɪˈgriː/ n degré m; (Univ) diplôme m universitaire; (Bachelor's degree) licence f; **to such a ~ that** à tel point que.

dehydrate /diːˈhaɪdreɪt/ vt/i (se) déshydrater.

deign /deɪn/ vt **~ to do** daigner faire.

dejected /dɪˈdʒektɪd/ adj découragé.

delay /dɪˈleɪ/ vt (flight) retarder; (decision) différer; **~ doing** attendre pour faire. ● n (of plane, post) retard m; (time lapse) délai m.

delegate¹ /ˈdelɪgət/ n délégué/-e m/f.

delegate² /ˈdelɪgeɪt/ vt déléguer. **delegation** n délégation f.

delete /dɪˈliːt/ vt supprimer; (Comput) effacer; (with pen) barrer. **deletion** n suppression f; (with line) rature f.

deliberate¹ /dɪˈlɪbəreɪt/ vi délibérer.

deliberate² /dɪˈlɪbərət/ adj délibéré; (steps, manner) mesuré. **deliberately** adv (do, say) exprès; (sarcastically, provocatively) délibérément.

delicacy /ˈdelɪkəsɪ/ n délicatesse f; (food) mets m raffiné.

delicate /ˈdelɪkət/ adj délicat.

delicatessen /delɪkəˈtesn/ n épicerie f fine.

delicious /dɪˈlɪʃəs/ adj délicieux.

delight /dɪˈlaɪt/ n joie f, plaisir m. ● vt ravir. ● vi **~ in** prendre plaisir à. **delighted** adj ravi. **delightful** adj charmant/-e.

delinquent /dɪˈlɪŋkwənt/ adj & n délinquant/-e (m/f).

delirious /dɪˈlɪrɪəs/ adj délirant.

deliver /dɪˈlɪvə(r)/ vt (message) remettre; (goods) livrer; (speech) faire; (baby) mettre au monde; (rescue) délivrer. **delivery** n (of goods) livraison f; (of mail) distribution f; (of baby) accouchement m.

delude /dɪˈluːd/ vt tromper; **~ oneself** se faire des illusions.

deluge /ˈdeljuːdʒ/ n déluge m. ● vt submerger (**with** de).

delusion /dɪˈluːʒn/ n illusion f.

delve /delv/ vi fouiller.

demand /dɪˈmɑːnd/ vt (request, require) demander; (forcefully) exiger. ● n (request) demande f; (pressure) exigence f; **in ~** très demandé; **on ~** à la demande. **demanding** adj exigeant.

demean /dɪˈmiːn/ vt **~ oneself** s'abaisser.

demeanour, (US)**demeanor** /dɪˈmiːnə(r)/ n comportement m.

demented /dɪˈmentɪd/ adj fou.

demise /dɪˈmaɪz/ n disparition f.

demo /ˈdeməʊ/ n (demonstration 🔢) manif f 🔢.

democracy /dɪˈmɒkrəsɪ/ n démocratie f.

democrat /ˈdeməkræt/ n démocrate mf. **democratic** adj démocratique.

demolish /dɪˈmɒlɪʃ/ vt démolir.

demon /ˈdiːmən/ n démon m.

demonstrate /ˈdemənstreɪt/ vt démontrer; (concern, skill) manifester. ● vi (Pol) manifester. **demonstration**

n démonstration *f*; (Pol) manifestation *f*. **demonstrative** *adj* démonstratif. **demonstrator** *n* manifestant/-e *m/f*.

demoralize /dɪˈmɒrəlaɪz/ *vt* démoraliser.

demote /diːˈməʊt/ *vt* rétrograder.

den /den/ *n* (of lion) antre *m*; (room) tanière *f*.

denial /dɪˈnaɪəl/ *n* (of rumour) démenti *m*; (of rights) négation *f*; (of request) rejet *m*.

denim /ˈdenɪm/ *n* jean *m*; ~s (jeans) jean *m*.

Denmark /ˈdenmɑːk/ *n* Danemark *m*.

denomination /dɪnɒmɪˈneɪʃn/ *n* (Relig) confession *f*; (money) valeur *f*.

denounce /dɪˈnaʊns/ *vt* dénoncer.

dense /dens/ *adj* dense. **densely** *adv* (packed) très. **density** *n* densité *f*.

dent /dent/ *n* bosse *f*. ● *vt* cabosser.

dental /ˈdentl/ *adj* dentaire; ~ **floss** fil *m* dentaire; ~ **surgeon** chirurgiendentiste *m*.

dentist /ˈdentɪst/ *n* dentiste *mf*. **dentistry** *n* médecine *f* dentaire.

dentures /ˈdentʃəz/ *npl* dentier *m*.

deny /dɪˈnaɪ/ *vt* nier (**that** que); (rumour) démentir; ~ **sb sth** refuser qch à qn.

deodorant /diːˈəʊdərənt/ *n* déodorant *m*.

depart /dɪˈpɑːt/ *vi* partir; ~ **from** (deviate) s'éloigner de.

department /dɪˈpɑːtmənt/ *n* (in shop) rayon *m*; (in hospital, office) service *m*; (Univ) département *m*; **D**~ **of Health** ministère *m* de la Santé; ~ **store** grand magasin *m*.

departure /dɪˈpɑːtʃə(r)/ *n* départ *m*; **a** ~ **from** (custom, truth) une entorse à.

depend /dɪˈpend/ *vi* dépendre (**on** de). ~ **on** (rely on) compter sur; **it** (all) ~s ça dépend; ~ing **on the season** suivant la saison. **dependable** *adj* (person) digne de confiance. **dependant** *n* personne *f* à charge. **dependence** *n* dépendance *f*.

dependent /dɪˈpendənt/ *adj* dépendant; **be** ~ **on** dépendre de.

depict /dɪˈpɪkt/ *vt* (describe) dépeindre; (in picture) représenter.

deplete /dɪˈpliːt/ *vt* réduire.

deport /dɪˈpɔːt/ *vt* expulser.

depose /dɪˈpəʊz/ *vt* déposer.

deposit /dɪˈpɒzɪt/ *vt* (pt **deposited**) déposer. ● *n* (in bank) dépôt *m*; (on house) versement *m* initial; (on holiday) acompte *m*; (against damage) caution *f*; (on bottle) consigne *f*; (of mineral) gisement *m*; ~ **account** compte *m* de dépôt. **depositor** *n* (Comm) déposant/-e *m/f*.

depot /ˈdepəʊ/ *n* dépôt *m*; (US) gare *f*.

depreciate /dɪˈpriːʃɪeɪt/ *vt/i* (se) déprécier.

depress /dɪˈpres/ *vt* déprimer. **depressing** *adj* déprimant. **depression** *n* dépression *f*; (Econ) récession *f*.

deprivation /deprɪˈveɪʃn/ *n* privation *f*.

deprive /dɪˈpraɪv/ *vt* ~ **of** priver de. **deprived** *adj* démuni.

depth /depθ/ *n* profondeur *f*; (of knowledge, ignorance) étendue *f*; (of colour, emotion) intensité *f*.

deputize /ˈdepjʊtaɪz/ *vi* ~ **for** remplacer.

deputy /ˈdepjʊtɪ/ *n* adjoint/-e *m/f*. ● *adj* adjoint; ~ **chairman** vice-président *m*.

derail /dɪˈreɪl/ *vt* faire dérailler. **derailment** *n* déraillement *m*.

deranged /dɪˈreɪndʒd/ *adj* dérangé.

derelict /ˈderəlɪkt/ *adj* abandonné.

deride /dɪˈraɪd/ *vt* ridiculiser. **derision** *n* moqueries *fpl*. **derisory** *adj* dérisoire.

derivative /dəˈrɪvətɪv/ *adj* & *n* dérivé (*m*).

derive /dɪˈraɪv/ *vt* ~ **sth from** tirer qch de. ● *vi* ~ **from** découler de.

derogatory /dɪˈrɒɡətrɪ/ *adj* (word) péjoratif; (remark) désobligeant.

descend /dɪˈsend/ *vt/i* descendre; **be** ~**ed from** descendre de. **descendant** *n* descendant/-e *m/f*. **descent** *n* descente *f*; (lineage) origine *f*.

describe /dɪˈskraɪb/ *vt* décrire; ~ **sb as sth** qualifier qn de qch. **description** *n* description *f*. **descriptive** *adj* descriptif.

desert¹ /ˈdezət/ *n* désert *m*.

desert² /dɪˈzɜːt/ *vt/i* abandonner; (cause) déserter. **deserted** *adj* désert. **deserter** *n* déserteur *m*.

deserts /dɪˈzɜːts/ *npl* **get one's** ~ avoir ce qu'on mérite.

deserve /dɪˈzɜːv/ *vt* mériter (**to** de). **deservedly** *adv* à juste titre. **deserv-**

ing adj (person) méritant; (action) louable.

design /dɪˈzaɪn/ n (sketch) plan m; (idea) conception f; (pattern) motif m; (art of designing) design m; (aim) dessein m. ● vt (sketch) dessiner; (devise, intend) concevoir.

designate /ˈdezɪɡneɪt/ vt désigner.

designer /dɪˈzaɪnə(r)/ n concepteur/-trice m/f; (of fashion, furniture) créateur/-trice m/f. ● adj (clothes) de haute couture; (sunglasses, drink) de dernière mode.

desirable /dɪˈzaɪərəbl/ adj (outcome) souhaitable; (person) désirable.

desire /dɪˈzaɪə(r)/ n désir m. ● vt désirer.

desk /desk/ n bureau m; (of pupil) pupitre m; (in hotel) réception f; (in bank) caisse f.

desolate /ˈdesələt/ adj (place) désolé; (person) affligé.

despair /dɪˈspeə(r)/ n désespoir m. ● vi désespérer (of de).

desperate /ˈdespərət/ adj désespéré; (criminal) prêt à tout; be ~ for avoir désespérément besoin de. **desperately** adv désespérément; (worried) terriblement; (ill) gravement.

desperation /despəˈreɪʃn/ n désespoir m; in ~ en désespoir de cause.

despicable /dɪˈspɪkəbl/ adj méprisable.

despise /dɪˈspaɪz/ vt mépriser.

despite /dɪˈspaɪt/ prep malgré.

despondent /dɪˈspɒndənt/ adj découragé.

dessert /dɪˈzɜːt/ n dessert m. ~**spoon** n cuillère f à dessert.

destination /destɪˈneɪʃn/ n destination f.

destiny /ˈdestɪnɪ/ n destin m.

destitute /ˈdestɪtjuːt/ adj sans ressources.

destroy /dɪˈstrɔɪ/ vt détruire; (animal) abattre. **destroyer** n (warship) contretorpilleur m.

destruction /dɪˈstrʌkʃn/ n destruction f. **destructive** adj destructeur.

detach /dɪˈtætʃ/ vt détacher; ~**ed house** maison f (individuelle).

detail /ˈdiːteɪl/ n détail m; go into ~ entrer dans les détails. ● vt (plans) exposer en détail.

detain /dɪˈteɪn/ vt retenir; (in prison) placer en détention. **detainee** n détenu/-e m/f.

detect /dɪˈtekt/ vt (error, trace) déceler; (crime, mine, sound) détecter. **detection** n détection f. **detective** n inspecteur/-trice m/f; (private) détective m.

detention /dɪˈtenʃn/ n détention f; (School) retenue f.

deter /dɪˈtɜː(r)/ vt (pt deterred) dissuader (from de).

detergent /dɪˈtɜːdʒənt/ adj & n détergent (m).

deteriorate /dɪˈtɪərɪəreɪt/ vi se détériorer.

determine /dɪˈtɜːmɪn/ vt déterminer; ~ to do résoudre de faire. **determined** adj (person) décidé; (air) résolu.

deterrent /dɪˈterənt/ n moyen m de dissuasion. ● adj (effect) dissuasif.

detest /dɪˈtest/ vt détester.

detonate /ˈdetəneɪt/ vt/i (faire) détoner. **detonation** n détonation f. **detonator** n détonateur m.

detour /ˈdiːtʊə(r)/ n détour m.

detract /dɪˈtrækt/ vi ~ from (success, value) porter atteinte à; (pleasure) diminuer.

detriment /ˈdetrɪmənt/ n to the ~ of au détriment de. **detrimental** adj nuisible (to à).

devalue /diːˈvæljuː/ vt dévaluer.

devastate /ˈdevəsteɪt/ vt (place) ravager; (person) accabler.

develop /dɪˈveləp/ vt (plan) élaborer; (mind, body) développer; (land) mettre en valeur; (illness) attraper; (habit) prendre. ● vi (child, country, plot, business) se développer; (hole, crack) se former.

development /dɪˈveləpmənt/ n développement m; (housing) ~ lotissement m; (new) ~ fait m nouveau.

deviate /ˈdiːvɪeɪt/ vi dévier; ~ from (norm) s'écarter de.

device /dɪˈvaɪs/ n appareil m; (means) moyen m; (bomb) engin m explosif.

devil /ˈdevl/ n diable m.

devious /ˈdiːvɪəs/ adj (person) retors.

devise /dɪˈvaɪz/ vt (scheme) concevoir; (product) inventer.

devoid /dɪˈvɔɪd/ adj ~ of dépourvu de.

devolution /di:vəˈluːʃn/ n (Pol) régionalisation f.

devote /dɪˈvəʊt/ vt consacrer (**to** à). **devoted** adj dévoué. **devotion** n dévouement m; (Relig) dévotion f.

devour /dɪˈvaʊə(r)/ vt dévorer.

devout /dɪˈvaʊt/ adj fervent.

dew /djuː/ n rosée f.

diabetes /daɪəˈbiːtiːz/ n diabète m.

diabolical /daɪəˈbɒlɪkl/ adj diabolique; (bad 🔲) atroce.

diagnose /ˈdaɪəgnəʊz/ vt diagnostiquer. **diagnosis** n (pl **-oses**) diagnostic m.

diagonal /daɪˈægənl/ adj diagonal. ● n diagonale f.

diagram /ˈdaɪəgræm/ n schéma m.

dial /ˈdaɪəl/ n cadran m. ● vt (pt **dialled**) (number) faire; (person) appeler; **dialling code** indicatif m; **dialling tone** tonalité f.

dialect /ˈdaɪəlekt/ n dialecte m.

dialogue /ˈdaɪəlɒg/ n dialogue m.

diameter /daɪˈæmɪtə(r)/ n diamètre m.

diamond /ˈdaɪəmənd/ n diamant m; (shape) losange m; (baseball) terrain m; ∼**s** (cards) carreau m.

diaper /ˈdaɪəpə(r)/ n (US) couche f.

diaphragm /ˈdaɪəfræm/ n diaphragme m.

diarrhoea, (US) **diarrhea** /daɪəˈrɪə/ n diarrhée f.

diary /ˈdaɪərɪ/ n (for appointments) agenda m; (journal) journal m intime.

dice /daɪs/ n inv dé m. ● vt (food) couper en dés.

dictate /dɪkˈteɪt/ vt/i dicter.

dictation /dɪkˈteɪʃn/ n dictée f.

dictator /dɪkˈteɪtə(r)/ n dictateur m. **dictatorship** n dictature f.

dictionary /ˈdɪkʃənrɪ/ n dictionnaire m.

did /dɪd/ ➡DO.

didn't ➡DID NOT.

die /daɪ/ vi (pres p **dying**) mourir; (plant) crever; **be dying to do** mourir d'envie de faire. ◻ ∼ **down** diminuer. ∼ **out** disparaître.

diesel /ˈdiːzl/ n gazole m; ∼ **engine** moteur m diesel.

diet /ˈdaɪət/ n (usual food) alimentation f; (restricted) régime m. ● vi être au régime. **dietary** adj alimentaire. **diet-**

ician n diététicien/-ne m/f.

differ /ˈdɪfə(r)/ vi différer (**from** de).

difference /ˈdɪfrəns/ n différence f; (disagreement) différend m. **different** adj différent (**from, to** de).

differentiate /dɪfəˈrenʃɪeɪt/ vt différencier. ● vi faire la différence (**between** entre).

differently /ˈdɪfrəntlɪ/ adv différemment (**from** de).

difficult /ˈdɪfɪkəlt/ adj difficile. **difficulty** n difficulté f.

diffuse[1] /dɪˈfjuːs/ adj diffus.

diffuse[2] /dɪˈfjuːz/ vt diffuser.

dig /dɪg/ vt/i (pt **dug**; pres p **digging**) (excavate) creuser; (in garden) bêcher. ● n (poke) coup m de coude; (remark) pique f 🔲; (Archeol) fouilles fpl. ◻ ∼ **up** déterrer.

digest /daɪˈdʒest/ vt/i digérer. **digestible** adj digestible. **digestion** n digestion f.

digger /ˈdɪgə(r)/ n excavateur m.

digit /ˈdɪdʒɪt/ n chiffre m. ● **digitize** vt numériser.

digital /ˈdɪdʒɪtl/ adj (clock) à affichage numérique; (display, recording) numérique. ∼ **audio tape** n cassette f audionumérique. ∼ **camera** n appareil m photo numérique.

dignified /ˈdɪgnɪfaɪd/ adj digne.

dignitary /ˈdɪgnɪtərɪ/ n dignitaire m.

dignity /ˈdɪgnətɪ/ n dignité f.

digress /daɪˈgres/ vi faire une digression.

dilapidated /dɪˈlæpɪdeɪtɪd/ adj délabré.

dilate /daɪˈleɪt/ vt/i (se) dilater.

dilemma /daɪˈlemə/ n dilemme m.

diligent /ˈdɪlɪdʒənt/ adj appliqué.

dilute /daɪˈljuːt/ vt diluer.

dim /dɪm/ adj (**dimmer, dimmest**) (weak) faible; (dark) sombre; (indistinct) vague; 🔲 stupide. ● vt/i (pt **dimmed**) (light) baisser.

dime /daɪm/ n (US) (pièce f de) dix cents.

dimension /dɪˈmenʃn/ n dimension f.

diminish /dɪˈmɪnɪʃ/ vt/i diminuer.

dimple /ˈdɪmpl/ n fossette f.

din /dɪn/ n vacarme m.

dine /daɪn/ vi dîner. **diner** n dîneur/-euse m/f; (US) restaurant m à service rapide.

dinghy /'dɪŋɡɪ/ n dériveur m.

dingy /'dɪndʒɪ/ adj (**-ier, -iest**) minable.

dining room /'daɪnɪŋrʊm/n salle f à manger.

dinner /'dɪnə(r)/ n (evening meal) dîner m; (lunch) déjeuner m; **have ~** dîner. **~-jacket** n smoking m. **~ party** n dîner m.

dinosaur /'daɪnəsɔː(r)/ n dinosaure m.

dip /dɪp/ vt/i (pt **dipped**) plonger; **~ into** (book) feuilleter; (savings) puiser dans; **~ one's headlights** se mettre en code. ● n (slope) déclivité f; (in sea) bain m rapide.

diploma /dɪ'pləʊmə/ n diplôme m (**in** en).

diplomacy /dɪp'ləʊməsɪ/ n diplomatie f. **diplomat** n diplomate mf. **diplomatic** adj (Pol) diplomatique; (tactful) diplomate.

dire /'daɪə(r)/ adj affreux; (need, poverty) extrême.

direct /daɪ'rekt/ adj direct. ● adv directement. ● vt diriger; (letter, remark) adresser; (a play) mettre en scène; **~ sb to** indiquer à qn le chemin de; (order) signifier à qn de.

direction /daɪ'rekʃn/ n direction f; (Theat) mise f en scène; **~s** indications fpl; **ask ~s** demander le chemin; **~s for use** mode m d'emploi.

directly /daɪ'rektlɪ/ adv directement; (at once) tout de suite. ● conj dès que.

director /daɪ'rektə(r)/ n directeur/-trice m/f; (Theat) metteur m en scène.

directory /daɪ'rektərɪ/ n (phone book) annuaire m. **~ enquiries** npl renseignements npl téléphoniques.

dirt /dɜːt/ n saleté f; (earth) terre f; **~ cheap** ⌧ très bon marché inv. **~-track** n (Sport) cendrée f.

dirty /dɜːtɪ/ adj (**-ier, -iest**) sale; (word) grossier; **get ~** se salir. ● vt/i (se) salir.

disability /dɪsə'bɪlətɪ/ n handicap m.

disable /dɪs'eɪbl/ vt rendre infirme. **disabled** adj handicapé.

disadvantage /dɪsəd'vɑːntɪdʒ/ n désavantage m. **disadvantaged** adj défavorisé.

disagree /dɪsə'ɡriː/ vi ne pas être d'accord (**with** avec). **~ with sb** (food, climate) ne pas convenir à qn. **disagreement** n désaccord m; (quarrel) différend m.

disappear /dɪsə'pɪə(r)/ vi disparaître. **disappearance** n disparition f (**of** de).

disappoint /dɪsə'pɔɪnt/ vt décevoir. **disappointment** n déception f.

disapproval /dɪsə'pruːvl/ n désapprobation f (**of** de).

disapprove /dɪsə'pruːv/ vi **~ (of)** désapprouver.

disarm /dɪs'ɑːm/ vt/i désarmer. **disarmament** n désarmement m.

disarray /dɪsə'reɪ/ n désordre m.

disaster /dɪ'zɑːstə(r)/ n désastre m. **disastrous** adj désastreux.

disband /dɪs'bænd/ vi disperser. ● vt dissoudre.

disbelief /dɪsbɪ'liːf/ n incrédulité f.

disc /dɪsk/ n disque m; (Comput) ➡DISK.

discard /dɪs'kɑːd/ vt se débarrasser de; (beliefs) abandonner.

discharge /dɪs'tʃɑːdʒ/ vt (unload) décharger; (liquid) déverser; (duty) remplir; (dismiss) renvoyer; (prisoner) libérer. ● vi (of pus) s'écouler.

disciple /dɪ'saɪpl/ n disciple m.

disciplinary /'dɪsɪplɪnərɪ/ adj disciplinaire.

discipline /'dɪsɪplɪn/ n discipline f. ● vt discipliner; (punish) punir.

disc jockey n disc-jockey m, animateur m.

disclaimer /dɪs'kleɪmə(r)/ n démenti m.

disclose /dɪs'kləʊz/ vt révéler. **disclosure** n révélation f (**of** de).

disco /'dɪskəʊ/ n (club Ⅰ) discothèque f; (event) soirée f disco.

discolour /dɪs'kʌlə(r)/ vt/i (se) décolorer.

discomfort /dɪs'kʌmfət/ n gêne f.

disconcert /dɪskən'sɜːt/ vt déconcerter.

disconnect /dɪskə'nekt/ vt détacher; (unplug) débrancher; (cut off) couper.

discontent /dɪskən'tent/ n mécontentement m.

discontinue /dɪskən'tɪnjuː/ vt (service) supprimer; (production) arrêter.

discord /'dɪskɔːd/ n discorde f; (Mus) discordance f.

discount¹ /'dɪskaʊnt/ n remise f; (on minor purchase) rabais m.

discount² /dɪs'kaʊnt/ vt (advice) ne pas tenir compte de; (possibility) écarter.

discourage /dɪs'kʌrɪdʒ/ vt décourager.

discourse /'dɪskɔːs/ n discours m.

discourteous /dɪs'kɜːtɪəs/ adj peu courtois.

discover /dɪs'kʌvə(r)/ vt découvrir. **discovery** n découverte f.

discreet /dɪ'skriːt/ adj discret.

discrepancy /dɪs'krepənsɪ/ n divergence f.

discretion /dɪ'skreʃn/ n discrétion f.

discriminate /dɪ'skrɪmɪneɪt/ vt/i distinguer; ~ **against** faire de la discrimination contre. **discriminating** adj qui a du discernement. **discrimination** n discernement m; (bias) discrimination f.

discus /'dɪskəs/ n disque m.

discuss /dɪs'kʌs/ vt (talk about) discuter de; (in writing) examiner. **discussion** n discussion f.

disdain /dɪs'deɪn/ n dédain m.

disease /dɪ'ziːz/ n maladie f.

disembark /dɪsɪm'bɑːk/ vt/i débarquer.

disenchanted /dɪsɪn'tʃɑːntɪd/ adj désabusé.

disentangle /dɪsɪn'tæŋgl/ vt démêler.

disfigure /dɪs'fɪgə(r)/ vt défigurer.

disgrace /dɪs'greɪs/ n (shame) honte f; (disfavour) disgrâce f. ● vt déshonorer. **disgraced** adj (in disfavour) disgracié. **disgraceful** adj honteux.

disgruntled /dɪs'grʌntld/ adj mécontent.

disguise /dɪs'gaɪz/ vt déguiser. ● n déguisement m; in ~ déguisé.

disgust /dɪs'gʌst/ n dégoût m. ● vt dégoûter.

dish /dɪʃ/ n plat m; the ~es (crockery) la vaisselle. ● vt ~ **out** ⊞ distribuer; ~ **up** servir.

dishcloth /'dɪʃklɒθ/ n lavette f; (for drying) torchon m.

dishearten /dɪs'hɑːtn/ vt décourager.

dishevelled /dɪ'ʃevld/ adj échevelé.

dishonest /dɪs'ɒnɪst/ adj malhonnête.

dishonour, (US) **dishonor** /dɪs'ɒnə(r)/ n déshonneur m.

dishwasher /'dɪʃwɒʃə(r)/ n lave-vaisselle m inv.

disillusion /dɪsɪ'luːʒn/ vt désabuser. **disillusionment** n désillusion f.

disincentive /dɪsɪn'sentɪv/ n be a ~ to décourager.

disinclined /dɪsɪn'klaɪnd/ adj ~ **to** peu disposé à.

disinfect /dɪsɪn'fekt/ vt désinfecter. **disinfectant** n désinfectant m.

disintegrate /dɪs'ɪntɪgreɪt/ vt/i (se) désintégrer.

disinterested /dɪs'ɪntrəstɪd/ adj désintéressé.

disjointed /dɪs'dʒɔɪntɪd/ adj (talk) décousu.

disk /dɪsk/ n (US) ➡**DISC**; (Comput) disque m. ~ **drive** n drive m, lecteur m de disquettes.

diskette /dɪ'sket/ n disquette f.

dislike /dɪs'laɪk/ n aversion f. ● vt ne pas aimer.

dislocate /'dɪsləkeɪt/ vt (limb) disloquer.

dislodge /dɪs'lɒdʒ/ vt (move) déplacer; (drive out) déloger.

disloyal /dɪs'lɔɪəl/ adj déloyal (**to** envers).

dismal /'dɪzməl/ adj morne, triste.

dismantle /dɪs'mæntl/ vt démonter, défaire.

dismay /dɪs'meɪ/ n consternation f (at devant). ● vt consterner.

dismiss /dɪs'mɪs/ vt renvoyer; (appeal) rejeter; (from mind) écarter. **dismissal** n renvoi m.

dismount /dɪs'maʊnt/ vi descendre, mettre pied à terre.

disobedient /dɪsə'biːdɪənt/ adj désobéissant.

disobey /dɪsə'beɪ/ vt désobéir à. ● vi désobéir.

disorder /dɪs'ɔːdə(r)/ n désordre m; (ailment) trouble(s) m(pl). **disorderly** adj désordonné.

disorganized /dɪs'ɔːgənaɪzd/ adj désorganisé.

disown /dɪs'əʊn/ vt renier.

disparaging /dɪ'spærɪdʒɪŋ/ adj désobligeant.

dispassionate /dɪˈspæʃənət/ adj impartial; (unemotional) calme.

dispatch /dɪˈspætʃ/ vt (send, complete) expédier; (troops) envoyer. ● n expédition f; envoi m; (report) dépêche f.

dispel /dɪˈspel/ vt (pt **dispelled**) dissiper.

dispensary /dɪˈspensərɪ/ n (in hospital) pharmacie f; (in pharmacy) officine f.

dispense /dɪˈspens/ vt distribuer; (medicine) préparer. ● vi ~ **with** se passer de. **dispenser** n (container) distributeur m.

disperse /dɪˈspɜːs/ vt/i (se) disperser.

display /dɪˈspleɪ/ vt montrer, exposer; (feelings) manifester. ● n exposition f; manifestation f; (Comm) étalage m; (of computer) visuel m.

displeased /dɪsˈpliːzd/ adj mécontent (with de).

disposable /dɪˈspəʊzəbl/ adj jetable.

disposal /dɪˈspəʊzl/ n (of waste) évacuation f; at sb's ~ à la disposition de qn.

dispose /dɪˈspəʊz/ vt disposer. ● vi ~ **of** se débarrasser de; well ~d **to** bien disposé envers.

disposition /dɪspəˈzɪʃn/ n disposition f; (character) naturel m.

disprove /dɪsˈpruːv/ vt réfuter.

dispute /dɪˈspjuːt/ vt contester. ● n discussion f; (Pol) conflit m; in ~ contesté.

disqualify /dɪsˈkwɒlɪfaɪ/ vt rendre inapte; (Sport) disqualifier; ~ **from driving** retirer le permis à.

disquiet /dɪsˈkwaɪət/ n inquiétude f. **disquieting** adj inquiétant.

disregard /dɪsrɪˈɡɑːd/ vt ne pas tenir compte de. ● n indifférence f (for à).

disrepair /dɪsrɪˈpeə(r)/ n délabrement m.

disreputable /dɪsˈrepjʊtəbl/ adj peu recommendable.

disrepute /dɪsrɪˈpjuːt/ n discrédit m.

disrespect /dɪsrɪˈspekt/ n manque m de respect. **disrespectful** adj irrespectueux.

disrupt /dɪsˈrʌpt/ vt (disturb, break up) perturber; (plans) déranger. **disruption** n perturbation f. **disruptive** adj perturbateur.

dissatisfied /dɪˈsætɪsfaɪd/ adj mécontent.

dissect /dɪˈsekt/ vt disséquer.

disseminate /dɪˈsemɪneɪt/ vt diffuser.

dissent /dɪˈsent/ vi différer (from de). ● n dissentiment m.

dissertation /dɪsəˈteɪʃn/ n mémoire m.

disservice /dɪsˈsɜːvɪs/ n **do a ~ to sb** rendre un mauvais service à qn.

dissident /ˈdɪsɪdənt/ adj & n dissident/-e (m/f).

dissimilar /dɪˈsɪmɪlə(r)/ adj dissemblable, différent.

dissipate /ˈdɪsɪpeɪt/ vt/i (se) dissiper. **dissipated** adj (person) dissolu.

dissolve /dɪˈzɒlv/ vt/i (se) dissoudre.

dissuade /dɪˈsweɪd/ vt dissuader.

distance /ˈdɪstəns/ n distance f; **from a ~** de loin; **in the ~** au loin. **distant** adj éloigné, lointain; (relative) éloigné; (aloof) distant.

distaste /dɪsˈteɪst/ n dégoût m. **distasteful** adj désagréable.

distil /dɪˈstɪl/ vt (pt **distilled**) distiller.

distinct /dɪˈstɪŋkt/ adj distinct; (definite) net; **as ~ from** par opposition à. **distinction** n distinction f; (in exam) mention f très bien. **distinctive** adj distinctif.

distinguish /dɪˈstɪŋɡwɪʃ/ vt/i distinguer.

distort /dɪˈstɔːt/ vt déformer. **distortion** n distorsion f; (of facts) déformation f.

distract /dɪˈstrækt/ vt distraire. **distracted** adj (distraught) éperdu. **distracting** adj gênant. **distraction** n (lack of attention, entertainment) distraction f.

distraught /dɪˈstrɔːt/ adj éperdu.

distress /dɪˈstres/ n douleur f; (poverty, danger) détresse f. ● vt peiner. **distressing** adj pénible.

distribute /dɪˈstrɪbjuːt/ vt distribuer.

district /ˈdɪstrɪkt/ n région f; (of town) quartier m.

distrust /dɪsˈtrʌst/ n méfiance f. ● vt se méfier de.

disturb /dɪˈstɜːb/ vt déranger; (alarm, worry) troubler. **disturbance** n dérangement m (of de); (noise) tapage m. **disturbances** npl (Pol) troubles mpl.

disturbed *adj* troublé; (psychologically) perturbé. **disturbing** *adj* troublant.

disused /dɪsˈjuːzd/ *adj* désaffecté.

ditch /dɪtʃ/ *n* fossé *m*. ● *vt* ▣ abandonner.

ditto /ˈdɪtəʊ/ *adv* idem.

dive /daɪv/ *vi* plonger; (rush) se précipiter. ● *n* plongeon *m*; (of plane) piqué *m*; (place ▣) bouge *m*. **diver** *n* plongeur/-euse *m/f.*

diverge /daɪˈvɜːdʒ/ *vi* diverger. **divergent** *adj* divergent.

diverse /daɪˈvɜːs/ *adj* divers.

diversion /daɪˈvɜːʃn/ *n* détournement *m*; (distraction) diversion *f*; (of traffic) déviation *f*. **divert** *vt* détourner; (traffic) dévier.

divide /dɪˈvaɪd/ *vt/i* (se) diviser.

dividend /ˈdɪvɪdend/ *n* dividende *m.*

divine /dɪˈvaɪn/ *adj* divin.

diving: **~-board** *n* plongeoir *m.* **~-suit** *n* scaphandre *m.*

division /dɪˈvɪʒn/ *n* division *f.*

divorce /dɪˈvɔːs/ *n* divorce *m* (**from** avec). ● *vt/i* divorcer (d'avec).

divulge /daɪˈvʌldʒ/ *vt* divulguer.

DIY *abbr* ➡ DO-IT-YOURSELF.

dizziness /ˈdɪzɪnɪs/ *n* vertige *m.*

dizzy /ˈdɪzɪ/ *adj* (**-ier, -iest**) vertigineux; **be** or **feel ~** avoir le vertige.

---

do /duː/

present do, does; present negative don't, do not; past did; past participle done

● *transitive and intransitive verb*

····▶ faire; **she is doing her homework** elle fait ses devoirs.

····▶ (progress, be suitable) aller; **how are you doing?** comment ça va?

····▶ (be enough) suffire; **will five dollars ~?** cinq dollars, ça suffira?

● *auxiliary verb*

····▶ (in questions) **~ you like Mozart?** aimes-tu Mozart?, est-ce que tu aimes Mozart?; **did your sister phone?** est-ce que ta sœur a téléphoné?, ta sœur a-t-elle téléphoné?

····▶ (in negatives) **I don't like Mozart** je n'aime pas Mozart.

····▶ (emphatic uses) **I ~ like your dress** j'aime beaucoup ta robe; **I ~ think you should go** je pense vraiment que tu devrais y aller.

····▶ (referring back to another verb) **I live in Orford and so does Lily** j'habite à Orford et Lily aussi; **she gets paid more than I ~** elle est payée plus que moi; **'I don't like carrots'—'neither ~ I'** 'je n'aime pas les carottes'—'moi non plus'.

····▶ (imperatives) **don't shut the door** ne ferme pas la porte; **~ be quiet** tais-toi!

····▶ (short questions and answers) **you like fish, don't you?** tu aimes le poisson, n'est-ce pas?; **Lola didn't phone, did she?** Lola n'a pas téléphoné par hasard?; **'does he play tennis?'—'no he doesn't/yes he does'** 'est-ce qu'il joue au tennis?'—'non/oui'; **'Marion didn't say that'—'yes she did'** 'Marion n'a pas dit ça'—'si'.

□ **do away with** supprimer. **do up** (fasten) fermer; (house) refaire; **do with it's to ~ with** c'est à propos de; **it's nothing to ~ with** ça n'a rien à voir avec. **do without** se passer de.

---

docile /ˈdəʊsaɪl/ *adj* docile.

dock /dɒk/ *n* (Jur) banc *m* des accusés; dock *m*. ● *vi* arriver au port. ● *vt* mettre à quai; (wages) faire une retenue sur.

doctor /ˈdɒktə(r)/ *n* médecin *m*, docteur *m*; (Univ) docteur *m*. ● *vt* (cat) châtrer; (fig) altérer.

doctorate /ˈdɒktərət/ *n* doctorat *m.*

document /ˈdɒkjʊmənt/ *n* document *m*. **documentary** *adj* & *n* documentaire (*m*). **documentation** *n* documentation *f.*

dodge /dɒdʒ/ *vt* esquiver. ● *vi* faire un saut de côté. ● *n* mouvement *m* de côté.

dodgems /ˈdɒdʒəmz/ *npl* autos *fpl* tamponneuses.

dodgy /ˈdɒdʒɪ/ *adj* (**-ier, -iest**) (▣: difficult) épineux, délicat; (untrustworthy) louche ▣.

doe /dəʊ/ n (deer) biche f.

does /dʌz/ →DO.

doesn't →DOES NOT.

dog /dɒg/ n chien m. ● vt (pt **dogged**) poursuivre. ~**-collar** n col m romain. ~**-eared** adj écorné.

dogged /ˈdɒgɪd/ adj obstiné.

dogma /ˈdɒgmə/ n dogme m. **dogmatic** adj dogmatique.

dogsbody /ˈdɒgzbɒdɪ/ n bonne f à tout faire.

do-it-yourself /duːɪtjɔːˈself/ n bricolage m.

doldrums /ˈdɒldrəmz/ npl be in the ~ (person) avoir le cafard.

dole /dəʊl/ vt ~ **out** distribuer. ● n Ⓔ indemnité f de chômage; **on the** ~ Ⓔ au chômage.

doll /ˈdɒl/ n poupée f. ● vt ~ **up** Ⓔ bichonner.

dollar /ˈdɒlə(r)/ n dollar m.

dollop /ˈdɒləp/ n (of food Ⓔ) gros morceau m.

dolphin /ˈdɒlfɪn/ n dauphin m.

domain /dəʊˈmeɪn/ n domaine m.

dome /dəʊm/ n dôme m.

domestic /dəˈmestɪk/ adj familial; (trade, flights) intérieur; (animal) domestique. **domesticated** adj (animal) domestiqué.

domestic science n arts mpl ménagers.

dominant /ˈdɒmɪnənt/ adj dominant.

dominate /ˈdɒmɪneɪt/ vt/i dominer. **domination** n domination f.

domineering /dɒmɪˈnɪərɪŋ/ adj dominateur.

domino /ˈdɒmɪnəʊ/ n (pl ~**es**) domino m; ~**es** (game) dominos mpl.

donate /dəʊˈneɪt/ vt faire don de. **donation** n don m.

done /dʌn/ →DO.

donkey /ˈdɒŋkɪ/ n âne m. ~ **work** n travail m pénible.

donor /ˈdəʊnə(r)/ n donateur/-trice m/f; (of blood) donneur/-euse m/f.

don't →DO NOT.

doodle /ˈduːdl/ vi griffonner.

doom /duːm/ n (ruin) ruine f; (fate) destin m. ● vt **be** ~**ed to** être destiné or condamné à; ~**ed (to failure)** voué à l'échec.

door /dɔː(r)/ n porte f; (of vehicle) portière f, porte f. ~**bell** n sonnette f. ~**man** n (pl **-men**) portier m. ~**mat** n paillasson m. ~**step** n pas m de (la) porte, seuil m. ~**way** n porte f.

dope /dəʊp/ n Ⓔ cannabis m; (idiot Ⓧ) imbécile mf. ● vt doper. **dopey** adj (foolish Ⓧ) imbécile.

dormant /ˈdɔːmənt/ adj en sommeil.

dormitory /ˈdɔːmɪtrɪ/ n dortoir m; (Univ, US) résidence f.

dosage /ˈdəʊsɪdʒ/ n dose f; (on label) posologie f.

dose /dəʊs/ n dose f.

dot /dɒt/ n point m; **on the** ~ Ⓔ à l'heure pile.

dot-com /dɒtˈkɒm/ n (société) point com f; ~ **millionaire** n millionaire mf de l'Internet. ~ **shares** npl actions fpl des sociétés point com.

dote /dəʊt/ vi ~ **on** adorer.

dotted /ˈdɒtɪd/ adj (fabric) à pois; ~ **line** pointillé m; ~ **with** parsemé de.

double /ˈdʌbl/ adj double; (room, bed) pour deux personnes; ~ **the size** deux fois plus grand. ● adv deux fois; **pay** ~ payer le double. ● n double m; (stuntman) doublure f; ~**s** (tennis) double m; **at** or **on the** ~ au pas de course. ● vt/i doubler; (fold) plier en deux. ~**-bass** n (Mus) contrebasse f. ~**-check** vt revérifier. ~ **chin** n double menton m. ~**-cross** vt tromper. ~**-decker** n autobus m à impériale.

doubt /daʊt/ n doute m. ● vt douter de; ~ **if** or **that** douter que. **doubtful** adj incertain, douteux; (person) qui a des doutes. **doubtless** adv sans doute.

dough /dəʊ/ n pâte f; (money Ⓧ) fric m Ⓔ.

doughnut /ˈdəʊnʌt/ n beignet m.

douse /daʊs/ vt arroser; (light, fire) éteindre.

dove /dʌv/ n colombe f.

Dover /ˈdəʊvə(r)/ n Douvres.

dowdy /ˈdaʊdɪ/ adj (**-ier, -iest**) (clothes) sans chic, monotone; (person) sans élégance.

down /daʊn/ adv en bas; (of sun) couché; (lower) plus bas; **come** or **go** ~ descendre; **go** ~ **to the post office** aller à la poste; ~ **under** aux antipodes; ~ **with** à bas. ● prep en bas de; (along) le long de. ● vt (knock down, shoot down) abattre; (drink) vider. ● *n* (fluff) duvet *m*.

down: ~**-and-out** *n* clochard/-e *m/f*. ~**cast** *adj* démoralisé. ~**fall** *n* chute *f*. ~**grade** *vt* déclasser. ~**-hearted** *adj* découragé.

downhill /daʊn'hɪl/ *adv* go ~ descendre; (pej) baisser.

down: ~**load** *n* (Comput) télécharger. ~**-market** *adj* bas de gamme. ~ **payment** *n* acompte *m*. ~**pour** *n* grosse averse *f*.

downright /'daʊnraɪt/ *adj* (utter) véritable; (honest) franc. ● *adv* carrément.

downstairs /daʊn'steəz/ *adv* en bas. ● *adj* d'en bas.

down: ~**stream** *adv* en aval. ~**-to-earth** *adj* pratique.

Downing Street Célèbre rue de Londres où se trouvent la résidence officielle du Premier ministre au n°10 et celle du Chancelier de l'Échiquier au n°11. Les médias emploient souvent *Number 10 Downing Street* ou *Downing Street* pour désigner le Premier ministre ou le gouvernement britannique.

downtown /'daʊntaʊn/ *adj* (US) du centre-ville; ~ **Boston** le centre de Boston.

downward /'daʊnwəd/ *adj & adv*, **downwards** *adv* vers le bas.

doze /dəʊz/ *vi* somnoler; ~ **off** s'assoupir. ● *n* somme *m*.

dozen /'dʌzn/ *n* douzaine *f*; **a** ~ **eggs** une douzaine d'œufs; ~**s of** ⊞ des dizaines de.

Dr *abbr* (**Doctor**) Docteur.

drab /dræb/ *adj* terne.

draft /drɑːft/ *n* (outline) brouillon *m*; (Comm) traite *f*; **the** ~ (Mil, US) la conscription; **a** ~ **treaty** un projet de traité; (US) ➡**DRAUGHT**. ● *vt* faire le brouillon de; (draw up) rédiger.

drag /dræg/ *vt/i* (*pt* **dragged**) traîner; (river) draguer; (pull away) arracher; ~ **on** s'éterniser. ● *n* (task ⊞) corvée *f*; (person ⊞) raseur/-euse *m/f*; **in** ~ en travesti.

dragon /'drægən/ *n* dragon *m*.

drain /dreɪn/ *vt* (land) drainer; (vegetables) égoutter; (tank, glass) vider;

(use up) épuiser; ~ **(off)** (liquid) faire écouler. ● *vi* ~ **(off)** (of liquid) s'écouler. ● *n* (sewer) égout *m*; ~**(-pipe)** tuyau *m* d'écoulement; **a** ~ **on** une ponction sur. **draining-board** *n* égouttoir *m*.

drama /'drɑːmə/ *n* art *m* dramatique, théâtre *m*; (play, event) drame *m*. **dramatic** *adj* (situation) dramatique; (increase) spectaculaire. **dramatist** *n* dramaturge *m*. **dramatize** *vt* adapter pour la scène; (fig) dramatiser.

drank /dræŋk/ ➡**DRINK**.

drape /dreɪp/ *vt* draper. **drapes** *npl* (US) rideaux *mpl*.

drastic /'dræstɪk/ *adj* sévère.

draught /drɑːft/ *n* courant *m* d'air; ~**s** (game) dames *fpl*. ~ **beer** *n* bière *f* pression.

draughty /'drɑːftɪ/ *adj* plein de courants d'air.

draw /drɔː/ *vt* (*pt* **drew**; *pp* **drawn**) (picture) dessiner; (line) tracer; (pull) tirer; (attract) attirer. ● *vi* dessiner; (Sport) faire match nul; (come, move) venir. ● *n* (Sport) match *m* nul; (in lottery) tirage *m* au sort. □ ~ **back** reculer. ~ **near** (s')approcher (**to** de). ~ **out** (money) retirer. ~ **up** *vi* (stop) s'arrêter; *vt* (document) dresser; (chair) approcher.

drawback /'drɔːbæk/ *n* inconvénient *m*.

drawbridge /'drɔːbrɪdʒ/ *n* pont-levis *m*.

drawer /'drɔː(r)/ *n* tiroir *m*.

drawing /'drɔːɪŋ/ *n* dessin *m*. ~**-board** *n* planche *f* à dessin. ~**-pin** *n* punaise *f*. ~**-room** *n* salon *m*.

drawl /drɔːl/ *n* voix *f* traînante.

drawn /drɔːn/ ➡**DRAW**. ● *adj* (features) tiré; (match) nul.

dread /dred/ *n* terreur *f*, crainte *f*. ● *vt* redouter. **dreadful** *adj* épouvantable, affreux. **dreadfully** *adv* terriblement.

dream /driːm/ *n* rêve *m*. ● *vt/i* (*pt* **dreamed** or **dreamt**) rêver; ~ **up** imaginer. ● *adj* (ideal) de ses rêves.

dreary /'drɪərɪ/ *adj* (**-ier**, **-iest**) triste; (boring) monotone.

dredge /dredʒ/ *vt* (river) draguer; ~ **sth up** (fig) exhumer.

dregs /dregz/ *npl* lie *f*.

drench /drentʃ/ vt tremper.

dress /dres/ n robe f; (clothing) tenue f. ● vt/i (s')habiller; (food) assaisonner; (wound) panser; ~ **up as** se déguiser en; **get** ~**ed** s'habiller. ~ **circle** n premier balcon m.

dresser /'dresə(r)/ n (furniture) buffet m; **be a stylish** ~ s'habiller avec chic.

dressing /'dresɪŋ/ n (sauce) assaisonnement m; (bandage) pansement m. ~**-gown** n robe f de chambre. ~**-room** n (Sport) vestiaire m; (Theat) loge f. ~**-table** n coiffeuse f.

dressmaker /'dresmeɪkə(r)/ n couturière f. **dressmaking** n couture f.

dress rehearsal n répétition f générale.

dressy /'dresɪ/ adj (-ier, -iest) chic inv.

drew /druː/ →DRAW .

dribble /'drɪbl/ vi (liquid) dégouliner; (person) baver; (football) dribbler.

dried /draɪd/ adj (fruit) sec.

drier /'draɪə(r)/ n séchoir m.

drift /drɪft/ vi aller à la dérive; (pile up) s'amonceler; ~ **towards** glisser vers. ● n dérive f. amoncellement m; (of events) tournure f; (meaning) sens m; **snow** ~ congère f. **driftwood** n bois m flotté.

drill /drɪl/ n (tool) perceuse f; (for teeth) roulette f; (training) exercice m; (procedure Ⅰ) marche f à suivre; (pneumatic) ~ marteau m piqueur. ● vt percer; (train) entraîner. ● vi être à l'exercice.

drink /drɪŋk/ vt/i (pt **drank**; pp **drunk**) boire. ● n (liquid) boisson f; (glass of alcohol) verre m; **a** ~ **of water** un verre d'eau. **drinking water** n eau f potable.

drip /drɪp/ vi (pt **dripped**) (é)goutter; (washing) s'égoutter. ● n goutte f; (person 🔟) lavette f.

drip-dry vt laisser égoutter. ● adj sans essorage.

drive /draɪv/ vt (pt **drove**; pp **driven**) (vehicle) conduire; (sb somewhere) chasser, pousser; (machine) actionner; ~ **mad** rendre fou. ● vi conduire. ● n promenade f en voiture; (private road) allée f; (fig) énergie f; (Psych) instinct m; (Pol) campagne f; (Auto) traction f; (golf, Comput) drive m; **it's a two-**

hour ~ il y a deux heures de route; **lefthand** ~ conduite f à gauche. □ ~ **at** en venir à.

drivel /'drɪvl/ n bêtises fpl.

driver /'draɪvə(r)/ n conducteur/-trice m/f. chauffeur m. ~**'s license** n (US) permis m de conduire.

driving /'draɪvɪŋ/ n conduite f; **take one's** ~ **test** passer son permis. ● adj (rain) battant; (wind) cinglant. ~ **licence** n permis m de conduire. ~ **school** n auto-école f.

drizzle /'drɪzl/ n bruine f. ● vi bruiner.

drone /drəʊn/ n (of engine) ronronnement m; (of insects) bourdonnement m. ● vi ronronner; bourdonner.

drool /druːl/ vi baver (over sur).

droop /druːp/ vi pencher, tomber.

drop /drɒp/ n goutte f; (fall, lowering) chute f. ● vt/i (pt **dropped**) (laisser) tomber; (decrease, lower) baisser; ~ **(off)** (person from car) déposer; ~ **a line** écrire un mot (to à). □ ~ **in** passer (on chez). ~ **off** (doze) s'assoupir. ~ **out** se retirer (of de); (of student) abandonner.

dropout /'drɒpaʊt/ n marginal/-e m/f, raté/-e m/f.

droppings /'drɒpɪŋz/ npl crottes fpl.

drought /draʊt/ n sécheresse f.

drove /drəʊv/ →DRIVE.

droves /drəʊvz/ npl foules fpl.

drown /draʊn/ vt/i (se) noyer.

drowsy /'draʊzɪ/ adj somnolent; **be** or **feel** ~ avoir envie de dormir.

drug /drʌg/ n drogue f; (Med) médicament m. ● vt (pt **drugged**) droguer. ~ **addict** n drogué/-e m/f. **drugstore** n (US) drugstore m.

drum /drʌm/ n tambour m; (for oil) bidon m; ~**s** batterie f. ● vi (pt **drummed**) tambouriner. ● vt ~ **into sb** répéter sans cesse à qn; ~ **up** (support) susciter; (business) créer. **drummer** n tambour m; (in pop group) batteur m.

drumstick /'drʌmstɪk/ n baguette f de tambour; (of chicken) pilon m.

drunk /drʌŋk/ →DRINK. ● adj ivre; **get** ~ s'enivrer. ● n ivrogne/-esse m/f. **drunkard** n ivrogne/-esse m/f. **drunken** adj ivre. **drunkenness** n ivresse f.

dry /draɪ/ *adj* (**drier, driest**) sec; (*day*) sans pluie; **be** *or* **feel** ~ avoir soif. ● *vt/i* (faire) sécher; ~ **up** (dry dishes) essuyer la vaisselle; (of supplies) (se) tarir; (be silent 🔲) se taire. ~**-clean** *vt* nettoyer à sec. ~**-cleaner** *n* teinturier *m*. ~ **run** *n* galop *m* d'essai.

DTD *abbr* (Document Type Definition) DTD *f*.

dual /'dju:əl/ *adj* double. ~ **carriageway** *n* route *f* à quatre voies. ~**-purpose** *adj* qui fait double emploi.

dub /dʌb/ *vt* (*pt* **dubbed**) (film) doubler (**into** en); (nickname) surnommer.

dubious /'dju:bɪəs/ *adj* (pej) douteux; **be** ~ **about** avoir des doutes sur.

duck /dʌk/ *n* canard *m*. ● *vi* se baisser subitement. ● *vt* (head) baisser; (person) plonger dans l'eau.

duct /'dʌkt/ *n* conduit *m*.

dud /dʌd/ *adj* (tool 🔲) mal fichu; (coin 🔲) faux; (cheque 🔲) sans provision. ● *n* **be a** ~ (not work 🔲) ne pas marcher.

due /dju:/ *adj* (owing) dû; (expected) attendu; (proper) qui convient; ~ **to** à cause de; (caused by) dû à; **she's** ~ **to leave now** il est prévu qu'elle parte maintenant; **in** ~ **course** (at the right time) en temps voulu; (later) plus tard. ● *adv* ~ **east** droit vers l'est. ● *n* dû *m*; ~**s** droits *mpl*; (of club) cotisation *f*.

duel /'dju:əl/ *n* duel *m*.

duet /dju:'et/ *n* duo *m*.

dug /dʌg/ ➡DIG.

duke /dju:k/ *n* duc *m*.

dull /dʌl/ *adj* ennuyeux; (colour) terne; (weather) maussade; (sound) sourd. ● *vt* (pain) atténuer; (shine) ternir.

duly /'dju:lɪ/ *adv* comme il convient; (as expected) comme prévu.

dumb /dʌm/ *adj* muet; (stupid 🔲) bête. □ ~ **down** (course, TV coverage) baisser le niveau intellectuel de.

dumbfound /dʌm'faʊnd/ *vt* sidérer, ahurir.

dummy /'dʌmɪ/ *n* (of tailor) mannequin *m*; (of baby) sucette *f*. ● *adj* factice. ~ **run** *n* galop *m* d'essai.

dump /dʌmp/ *vt* déposer; (get rid of 🔲) se débarrasser de. ● *n* tas *m* d'ordures; (refuse tip) décharge *f*; (Mil) dépôt *m*; (dull place 🔲) trou *m* 🔲; **be**

in the ~**s** 🔲 avoir le cafard.

dune /dju:n/ *n* dune *f*.

dung /dʌŋ/ *n* (excrement) bouse *f*, crotte *f*; (manure) fumier *m*.

dungarees /dʌŋgə'ri:z/ *npl* salopette *f*.

dungeon /'dʌndʒən/ *n* cachot *m*.

duplicate[1] /'dju:plɪkət/ *n* double *m*. ● *adj* identique.

duplicate[2] /'dju:plɪkeɪt/ *vt* faire un double de; (on machine) polycopier.

durable /'djʊərəbl/ *adj* (tough) résistant; (enduring) durable.

duration /djʊ'reɪʃn/ *n* durée *f*.

during /'djʊərɪŋ/ *prep* pendant.

dusk /dʌsk/ *n* crépuscule *m*.

dusky /'dʌskɪ/ *adj* (**-ier, -iest**) foncé.

dust /dʌst/ *n* poussière *f*. ● *vt/i* épousseter; (sprinkle) saupoudrer (**with** de). ~**bin** *n* poubelle *f*.

duster /'dʌstə(r)/ *n* chiffon *m*.

dust: ~**man** *n* (*pl* **-men**) éboueur *m*. ~**pan** *n* pelle *f* (à poussière).

dusty /'dʌstɪ/ *adj* (**-ier, -iest**) poussiéreux.

Dutch /dʌtʃ/ *adj* néerlandais; **go** ~ partager les frais. ● *n* (Ling) néerlandais *m*. ~**man** *n* Néerlandais *m*. ~**woman** *n* Néerlandaise *f*.

dutiful /'dju:tɪfl/ *adj* obéissant.

duty /'dju:tɪ/ *n* devoir *m*; (tax) droit *m*; (of official) fonction *f*; **on** ~ de service. ~**-free** *adj* hors-taxe.

duvet /'du:veɪ/ *n* couette *f*.

DVD *abbr* (**digital versatile disc**) DVD *m*.

dwarf /dwɔ:f/ *n* nain/-e *m/f*. ● *vt* rapetisser.

dwell /dwel/ *vi* (*pt* **dwelt**) demeurer; ~ **on** s'étendre sur. **dweller** *n* habitant/-e *m/f*. **dwelling** *n* habitation *f*.

dwindle /'dwɪndl/ *vi* diminuer.

dye /daɪ/ *vt* teindre. ● *n* teinture *f*.

dying /'daɪɪŋ/ *adj* mourant; (art) qui se perd.

dynamic /daɪ'næmɪk/ *adj* dynamique.

dynamite /'daɪnəmaɪt/ *n* dynamite *f*.

dysentery /'dɪsəntrɪ/ *n* dysenterie *f*.

dyslexia /dɪs'leksɪə/ *n* dyslexie *f*. **dyslexic** *adj* & *n* dyslexique (*mf*).

Ee

each /iːtʃ/ det chaque inv; ~ **one** chacun/-e m/f. ● pron chacun/-e m/f; **oranges at 30p** ~ des oranges à 30 pence pièce.

each other pron l'un/l'une l'autre, les uns/les unes les autres; **know** ~ se connaître; **love** ~ s'aimer.

eager /ˈiːgə(r)/ adj impatient (**to** de); (person, acceptance) enthousiaste; ~ **for** avide de.

eagle /ˈiːgl/ n aigle m.

ear /ɪə(r)/ n oreille f; (of corn) épi m. ~**ache** n mal à l'oreille. ~**-drum** n tympan m.

earl /ɜːl/ n comte m.

early /ˈɜːlɪ/ (**-ier, -iest**) adv tôt, de bonne heure; (ahead of time) en avance; **as I said earlier** comme je l'ai déjà dit. ● adj (attempt, years) premier; (hour) matinal; (fruit) précoce; (retirement) anticipé; **have an** ~ **dinner** dîner tôt; **in** ~ **summer** au début de l'été; **at the earliest** au plus tôt.

earmark /ˈɪəmɑːk/ vt désigner (**for** pour).

earn /ɜːn/ vt gagner; (interest: Comm) rapporter.

earnest /ˈɜːnɪst/ adj sérieux; **in** ~ sérieusement.

earnings /ˈɜːnɪŋz/ npl salaire m; (profits) gains mpl.

ear: ~**phones** npl casque m. ~**-ring** n boucle f d'oreille. ~**shot** n **within/in** ~**shot** à portée de voix.

earth /ɜːθ/ n terre f; **why/how/where on** ~**...?** pourquoi/comment/où diable...? ● vt (Electr) mettre à la terre. **earthenware** n faïence f. ~**quake** n tremblement m de terre.

ease /iːz/ n facilité f; (comfort) bien-être m; **at** ~ à l'aise; (Mil) au repos; **with** ~ facilement. ● vt (pain, pressure) atténuer; (congestion) réduire; (transition) faciliter. ● vi (pain, pressure) s'atténuer; (congestion, rain) diminuer.

easel /ˈiːzl/ n chevalet m.

east /iːst/ n est m; **the E**~ (Orient) l'Orient m. ● adj (side, coast) est; (wind) d'est. ● adv à l'est.

Easter /ˈiːstə(r)/ n Pâques m; ~ **egg** œuf m de Pâques.

easterly /ˈiːstəlɪ/ adj (wind) d'est; (direction) de l'est.

eastern de l'est; ~ **France** l'est de la France.

eastward /ˈiːstwəd/ adj (side) est inv; (journey) vers l'est.

easy /ˈiːzɪ/ adj (**-ier, -iest**) facile; **go** ~ **with** 🔟 y aller doucement avec; **take it** ~ ne te fatigue pas. ~**going** adj accommodant.

eat /iːt/ vt/i (pt **ate**; pp **eaten**) manger; ~ **into** ronger.

eavesdrop /ˈiːvzdrɒp/ vi (pt **-dropped**) écouter aux portes.

ebb /eb/ n reflux m. ● vi descendre; (fig) décliner.

EC abbr (**European Commission**) CE f.

eccentric /ɪkˈsentrɪk/ adj & n excentrique (mf).

echo /ˈekəʊ/ n (pl **-oes**) écho m. ● vt répercuter; (idea, opinion) reprendre. ● vi retentir, résonner (**to, with** de).

eclipse /ɪˈklɪps/ n éclipse f. ● vt éclipser.

ecological /iːkəˈlɒdʒɪkl/ adj écologique.

ecology /ɪˈkɒlədʒɪ/ n écologie f.

e-commerce /ˈiːkɒmɜːs/ n commerce m électronique, commerce m en ligne.

economic /iːkəˈnɒmɪk/ adj économique; (profitable) rentable; ~ **refugee** réfugié/-e m/f économique. **economical** adj économique; (person) économe. **economics** n économie f, sciences fpl économiques. **economist** n économiste mf.

economize /ɪˈkɒnəmaɪz/ vi ~ (**on**) économiser.

economy /ɪˈkɒnəmɪ/ n économie f. ~**-class syndrome** n syndrome m de la classe économique.

ecosystem /ˈiːkəʊsɪstəm/ n écosystème m.

ecstasy /ˈekstəsɪ/ n extase f; (drug) ecstasy m.

edge /edʒ/ n bord m; (of town) abords mpl; (of knife) tranchant m; **have the** ~ **on** 🔟 l'emporter sur; **on** ~ énervé. ● vt (trim) border. ● vi ~ **forward**

avancer doucement.

edgeways /'edʒweɪz/ adv **I can't get a word in** ~ je n'arrive pas à placer un mot.

edible /'edɪbl/ adj comestible.

Edinburgh Festival Festival international des Arts qui se déroule tous les étés à Édimbourg (Écosse) depuis 1947. Pendant trois semaines, au programme du festival institutionnel et du festival parallèle (*Fringe festival*), se côtoient les plus grands noms de la musique, de la danse, du théâtre, les artistes d'avant-garde et les nouveaux talents.

---

edit /'edɪt/ vt (pt **edited**) (*newspaper, page*) être le rédacteur/la rédactrice de; (*check*) réviser; (*cut*) couper; (TV, cinema) monter.

edition /ɪ'dɪʃn/ n édition f.

editor /'edɪtə(r)/ n (*writer*) rédacteur/-trice m/f; (*of works, anthology*) éditeur/-trice m/f; (TV, cinema) monteur/-teuse m/f; **the** ~ (**in chief**) le rédacteur en chef.

editorial /edɪ'tɔːrɪəl/ adj de la rédaction. ● n éditorial m.

educate /'edʒʊkeɪt/ vt instruire; (*mind*) éduquer. **educated** adj instruit. **education** n éducation f; (*schooling*) études fpl. **educational** adj éducatif; (*method*) d'enseignement.

eel /iːl/ n anguille f.

eerie /'ɪərɪ/ adj (**-ier, -iest**) sinistre.

effect /ɪ'fekt/ n effet m; **come into** ~ entrer en vigueur; **in** ~ effectivement; **take** ~ agir. ● vt effectuer.

effective /ɪ'fektɪv/ adj efficace; (*actual*) effectif. **effectively** adv efficacement; (*in effect*) en réalité. **effectiveness** n efficacité f.

effeminate /ɪ'femɪnət/ adj efféminé.

effervescent /efə'vesnt/ adj effervescent.

efficiency /ɪ'fɪʃnsɪ/ n efficacité f; (*of machine*) rendement m. **efficient** adj efficace. **efficiently** adv efficacement.

effort /'efət/ n efforts mpl; **make an** ~ faire un effort; **be worth the** ~ en valoir la peine. **effortless** adj facile.

effusive /ɪ'fjuːsɪv/ adj expansif.

e.g. /ɪː'dʒiː/ abbr par ex.

egg /eg/ n œuf m. ● vt ~ **on** pousser. ~**-cup** n coquetier m. ~**-plant** n (US) aubergine f. ~**shell** n coquille f d'œuf.

ego /'iːgəʊ/ n amour-propre m; (Psych) moi m. **egotism** n égotisme m. **egotist** n égotiste mf.

Egypt /'iːdʒɪpt/ n Égypte f.

EHIC abbr (**European Health Insurance Card**) CEAM f.

eiderdown /'aɪdədaʊn/ n édredon m.

eight /eɪt/ adj & n huit (m). **eighteen** adj & n dix-huit (m). **eighth** adj & n huitième (mf). **eighty** adj & n quatre-vingts (m).

either /'aɪðər/ det & pron l'un/une ou l'autre; (*with negative*) ni l'un/une ni l'autre; **you can take** ~ tu peux prendre n'importe lequel/laquelle. ● adv non plus. ● conj ~**...or** ou (bien)...ou (bien); (*with negative*) ni...ni.

eject /ɪ'dʒekt/ vt (*troublemaker*) expulser; (*waste*) rejeter.

elaborate[1] /ɪ'læbərət/ adj compliqué.

elaborate[2] /ɪ'læbəreɪt/ vt élaborer. ● vi préciser; ~ **on** s'étendre sur.

elastic /ɪ'læstɪk/ adj & n élastique (m); ~ **band** élastique m. **elasticity** n élasticité f.

elated /ɪ'leɪtɪd/ adj transporté de joie.

elbow /'elbəʊ/ n coude m; ~ **room** espace m vital.

elder /'eldə(r)/ adj & n aîné/-e (m/f); (*tree*) sureau m.

elderly /'eldəlɪ/ adj âgé; **the** ~ les personnes fpl âgées.

eldest /'eldɪst/ adj & n aîné/-e (m/f).

elect /ɪ'lekt/ vt élire; ~ **to do** choisir de faire. ● adj (*president etc.*) futur. **election** n élection f. **elector** n électeur/-trice m/f. **electoral** adj électoral. **electorate** n électorat m.

electric /ɪ'lektrɪk/ adj électrique; ~ **blanket** couverture f chauffante. **electrical** adj électrique. **electrician** n électricien/-ne m/f. **electricity** n électricité f. **electrify** vt électrifier; (*excite*) électriser. **electrocute** vt électrocuter.

electronic /ɪlek'trɒnɪk/ adj électronique. ~ **publishing** n édutique f. **electronics** n électronique f.

elegance /'elɪgəns/ n élégance f.

element /'elɪmənt/ n élément m; (*of heater etc.*) résistance f. **elementary** adj élémentaire.

elephant /'elɪfənt/ n éléphant m.

elevate /'elɪveɪt/ vt élever. **elevation** n élévation f. **elevator** n (US) ascenseur m.

eleven /ɪ'levn/ adj & n onze (m). **eleventh** adj & n onzième (mf).

elicit /ɪ'lɪsɪt/ vt obtenir (from de).

eligible /'elɪdʒəbl/ adj admissible (for à); **be ~ for** (entitled to) avoir droit à.

eliminate /ɪ'lɪmɪneɪt/ vt éliminer.

elm /elm/ n orme m.

elongate /'iːlɒŋgeɪt/ vt allonger.

elope /ɪ'ləʊp/ vi s'enfuir (with avec). **elopement** n fugue f (amoureuse).

eloquence /'eləkwəns/ n éloquence f.

else /els/ adv d'autre; **somebody/nothing ~** quelqu'un/rien d'autre; **everybody ~** tous les autres; **somewhere/something ~** autre part/chose; **or ~** ou bien. **elsewhere** adv ailleurs.

elude /ɪ'luːd/ vt échapper à.

elusive /ɪ'luːsɪv/ adj insaisissable.

email /'iːmeɪl/ n (medium) courrier m électronique; (item) e-mail m, mél m; **~ sb** envoyer un e-mail à qn; **~ sth** envoyer qch par courrier électronique.

emancipate /ɪ'mænsɪpeɪt/ vt émanciper.

embankment /ɪm'bæŋkmənt/ n (of river) quai m; (of railway) remblai m.

embark /ɪm'bɑːk/ vt embarquer. ● vi (Naut) embarquer; **~ on** (journey) entreprendre; (campaign, career) se lancer dans.

embarrass /ɪm'bærəs/ vt plonger dans l'embarras; **be/feel ~ed** être/se sentir gêné. **embarrassment** n confusion f, gêne f.

embassy /'embəsɪ/ n ambassade f.

embed /ɪm'bed/ vt (pt **embedded**) enfoncer (in dans).

embellish /ɪm'belɪʃ/ vt embellir.

embers /'embəz/ npl braises fpl.

embezzle /ɪm'bezl/ vt détourner (from de). **embezzlement** n détournement m de fonds.

emblem /'embləm/ n emblème m.

embodiment /ɪm'bɒdɪmənt/ n incarnation f. **embody** vt incarner; (legally) incorporer.

emboss /ɪm'bɒs/ vt (metal) repousser; (paper) gaufrer.

embrace /ɪm'breɪs/ vt (person) étreindre; (religion) embrasser; (include) comprendre. ● n étreinte f.

embroider /ɪm'brɔɪdə(r)/ vt broder. **embroidery** n broderie f.

embryo /'embrɪəʊ/ n embryon m.

emerald /'emərəld/ n émeraude f.

emerge /ɪ'mɜːdʒ/ vi (person) sortir (from de); **it ~d that** il est apparu que. **emergence** n apparition f.

emergency /ɪ'mɜːdʒənsɪ/ n (crisis) crise f; (urgent case: Med) urgence f; **in an ~** en cas d'urgence. ● adj d'urgence. **~ exit** n sortie f de secours; **~ landing** n atterrissage m forcé. **~ room** (US) salle f des urgences.

emigrant /'emɪgrənt/ n émigrant/-e m/f. **emigrate** vi émigrer.

eminence /'emɪnəns/ n éminence f. **eminent** adj éminent.

emission /ɪ'mɪʃn/ n émission f.

emit /ɪ'mɪt/ vt (pt **emitted**) émettre.

emotion /ɪ'məʊʃn/ n émotion f. **emotional** adj (development) émotif; (reaction) émotionel; (film, scene) émouvant.

emotive /ɪ'məʊtɪv/ adj qui soulève les passions.

emperor /'empərə(r)/ n empereur m.

emphasis /'emfəsɪs/ n accent m; **lay ~ on** mettre l'accent sur. **emphasize** vt mettre l'accent sur. **emphatic** adj catégorique; (manner) énergique.

empire /'empaɪə(r)/ n empire m.

employ /ɪm'plɔɪ/ vt employer. **employee** n employé/-e m/f. **employer** n employeur/-euse m/f.

employment /ɪm'plɔɪmənt/ n emploi m; **find ~** trouver du travail.

empower /ɪm'paʊə(r)/ vt autoriser (to do à faire).

empty /'emptɪ/ adj (-ier, -iest) vide; (street) désert; (promise) vain; **on an ~ stomach** à jeun. ● vt/i (se) vider. **~-handed** adj les mains vides.

emulate /'emjʊleɪt/ vt imiter.

enable /ɪ'neɪbl/ vt **~ sb to** permettre à qn de.

enamel /ɪ'næml/ n émail m. ● vt (pt **enamelled**) émailler.

encase /ɪn'keɪs/ vt revêtir, recouvrir (in de).

enchant /ɪn'tʃɑːnt/ vt enchanter.

enclose /ɪn'kləʊz/ vt entourer; (land) clôturer; (with letter) joindre. **enclosed** adj (space) clos; (with letter) ci-joint. **enclosure** n enceinte f; (with letter) pièce f jointe.

encompass /ɪn'kʌmpəs/ vt inclure.

encore /'ɒŋkɔː(r)/ interj & n bis (m).

encounter /ɪn'kaʊntə(r)/ vt rencontrer. ● n rencontre f.

encourage /ɪn'kʌrɪdʒ/ vt encourager.

encroach /ɪn'krəʊtʃ/ vi ~ **upon** empiéter sur.

encyclopedia /ɪnsaɪklə'piːdɪə/ n encyclopédie f. **encyclopaedic** adj encyclopédique.

end /end/ n fin f; (farthest part) bout m; **come to an ~** prendre fin; **~-product** m fini; **in the ~** finalement; **no ~ of** 🆃 énormément de; **on ~** (upright) debout; (in a row) de suite; **put an ~to** mettre fin à. ● vt (marriage) mettre fin à; ~ **one's days** finir ses jours. ● vi se terminer; ~ **up doing** finir par faire.

endanger /ɪn'deɪndʒə(r)/ vt mettre en danger.

endearing /ɪn'dɪərɪŋ/ adj attachant.

endeavour, (US) **endeavor** /ɪn'devə(r)/ n (attempt) tentative f; (hard work) effort m. ● vi faire tout son possible (**to do** pour faire).

ending /'endɪŋ/ n fin f.

endive /'endɪv/ n chicorée f.

endless /'endlɪs/ adj interminable; (supply) inépuisable; (patience) infini.

endorse /ɪn'dɔːs/ vt (candidate, decision) appuyer; (product, claim) approuver; (cheque) endosser.

endurance /ɪn'djʊərəns/ n endurance f.

endure /ɪn'djʊə(r)/ vt supporter. ● vi durer. **enduring** adj durable.

enemy /'enəmɪ/ n & adj ennemi/-e (m/f).

energetic /enə'dʒetɪk/ adj énergique. **energy** n énergie f.

enforce /ɪn'fɔːs/ vt (rule, law) appliquer, faire respecter; (silence, discipline) imposer (**on** à); ~**d** forcé.

engage /ɪn'geɪdʒ/ vt (staff) engager; (attention) retenir; **be ~d in** se livrer à. ● vi ~ **in** se livrer à. **engaged** adj fiancé; (busy) occupé; **get ~d** se fiancer. **engagement** n fiançailles fpl;

(meeting) rendezvous m; (undertaking) engagement m.

engaging /ɪn'geɪdʒɪŋ/ adj attachant, engageant.

engine /'endʒɪn/ n moteur m; (of train) locomotive f; (of ship) machines fpl. ~**-driver** n mécanicien m.

engineer /endʒɪ'nɪə(r)/ n ingénieur m; (repairman) technicien m; (on ship) mécanicien m. ● vt (contrive) manigancer.

engineering /endʒɪ'nɪərɪŋ/ n ingénierie f; (industry) mécanique f; **civil ~** génie m civil.

England /'ɪŋglənd/ n Angleterre f.

English /'ɪŋglɪʃ/ adj anglais. ● n (Ling) anglais m; **the ~** les Anglais mpl. ~**man** n Anglais m. ~**-speaking** adj anglophone. ~**woman** n Anglaise f.

engrave /ɪn'greɪv/ vt graver.

engrossed /ɪn'grəʊst/ adj absorbé (**in** dans).

engulf /ɪn'gʌlf/ vt engouffrer.

enhance /ɪn'hɑːns/ vt (prospects, status) améliorer; (price, value) augmenter.

enjoy /ɪn'dʒɔɪ/ vt aimer (**doing** faire); (benefit from) jouir de; ~ **oneself** s'amuser; ~ **your meal!** bon appétit! **enjoyable** adj agréable. **enjoyment** n plaisir m.

enlarge /ɪn'lɑːdʒ/ vt agrandir. ● vi s'agrandir; (pupil) se dilater; ~ **on** s'étendre sur. **enlargement** n agrandissement m.

enlighten /ɪn'laɪtn/ vt éclairer (**on** sur). **enlightenment** n instruction f; (information) éclaircissement m.

enlist /ɪn'lɪst/ vt (person) recruter; (fig) obtenir. ● vi s'engager.

enmity /'enmɪtɪ/ n inimitié f.

enormous /ɪ'nɔːməs/ adj énorme. **enormously** adv énormément.

enough /ɪ'nʌf/ adv & n assez; **have ~ of** en avoir assez de. ● det assez de; ~ **glasses/time** assez de verres/de temps.

enquire →INQUIRE. **enquiry** →INQUIRY.

enrage /ɪn'reɪdʒ/ vt mettre en rage, rendre furieux.

enrol /ɪn'rəʊl/ vt/i (pt **enrolled**) (s')inscrire. **enrolment** n inscription f.

ensure /ɪnˈʃɔː(r)/ *vt* garantir; ∼ **that** (ascertain) s'assurer que.

entail /ɪnˈteɪl/ *vt* entraîner.

entangle /ɪnˈtæŋgl/ *vt* emmêler.

enter /ˈentə(r)/ *vt* (*room, club, phase*) entrer dans; (note down, register) inscrire; (data) entrer, saisir. ● *vi* entrer (**into** dans); ∼ **for** s'inscrire à.

enterprise /ˈentəpraɪz/ *n* entreprise *f*; (*boldness*) initiative *f*. **enterprising** *adj* entreprenant.

entertain /entəˈteɪn/ *vt* amuser, divertir; (guests) recevoir; (ideas) considérer. **entertainer** *n* artiste *mf*. **entertaining** *adj* divertissant. **entertainment** *n* divertissement *m*; (performance) spectacle *m*.

enthral /ɪnˈθrɔːl/ *vt* (*pt* **enthralled**) captiver.

enthusiasm /ɪnˈθjuːzɪæzəm/ *n* enthousiasme *m* (**for** pour).

enthusiast /ɪnˈθjuːzɪæst/ *n* passionné/-e *m/f* (**for** de). **enthusiastic** *adj* (supporter) enthousiaste; **be** ∼**ic about** être enthousiasmé par. **enthusiastically** *adv* avec enthousiasme.

entice /ɪnˈtaɪs/ *vt* attirer; ∼ **sb to do** entraîner qn à faire.

entire /ɪnˈtaɪə(r)/ *adj* entier. **entirely** *adv* entièrement. **entirety** *n* **in its** ∼**ty** en entier.

entitle /ɪnˈtaɪtl/ *vt* donner droit à (**to sth** à qch; **to do** de faire); ∼**d** (book) intitulé; **be** ∼**d to sth** avoir droit à qch.

entrance[1] /ˈentrəns/ *n* (entering, way in) entrée *f* (**to** de); (right to enter) admission *f*. ● *adj* (charge, exam) d'entrée.

entrance[2] /ɪnˈtrɑːns/ *vt* transporter.

entrant /ˈentrənt/ *n* (Sport) concurrent/-e *m/f*; (in exam) candidat/-e *m/f*.

entrenched /ɪnˈtrentʃt/ *adj* (opinion) inébranlable; (Mil) retranché.

entrepreneur /ɒntrəprəˈnɜː(r)/ *n* entrepreneur/-euse *m/f*.

entrust /ɪnˈtrʌst/ *vt* confier; ∼ **sb with sth** confier qch à qn.

entry /ˈentrɪ/ *n* entrée *f*; ∼**-form** fiche *f* d'inscription.

envelop /ɪnˈveləp/ *vt* (*pt* **enveloped**) envelopper.

envelope /ˈenvələup/ *n* enveloppe *f*.

envious /ˈenvɪəs/ *adj* envieux (**of** de).

environment /ɪnˈvaɪərənmənt/ *n* (ecological) environnement *m*; (social) milieu *m*. **environmental** *adj* du milieu; de l'environnement. **environmentalist** *n* écologiste *mf*.

envisage /ɪnˈvɪzɪdʒ/ *vt* prévoir (**doing** de faire).

envoy /ˈenvɔɪ/ *n* envoyé/-e *m/f*.

envy /ˈenvɪ/ *n* envie *f*. ● *vt* envier; ∼ **sb sth** envier qch à qn.

epic /ˈepɪk/ *n* épopée *f*. ● *adj* épique.

epidemic /epɪˈdemɪk/ *n* épidémie *f*.

epilepsy /ˈepɪlepsɪ/ *n* épilepsie *f*.

episode /ˈepɪsəʊd/ *n* épisode *m*.

epitome /ɪˈpɪtəmɪ/ *n* modèle *m*. **epitomize** *vt* incarner.

equal /ˈiːkwəl/ *adj* & *n* égal/-e (*m/f*); ∼ **opportunities/rights** égalité *f* des chances/droits; ∼ **to** (task) à la hauteur de. ● *vt* (*pt* **equalled**) égaler. **equality** *n* égalité *f*. **equalize** *vt/i* égaliser. **equalizer** *n* (goal) but *m* égalisateur. **equally** *adv* (divide) en parts égales; (just as) tout aussi.

equanimity /ekwəˈnɪmətɪ/ *n* sérénité *f*.

equate /ɪˈkweɪt/ *vt* assimiler (**with** à). **equation** *n* équation *f*.

equator /ɪˈkweɪtə(r)/ *n* équateur *m*.

equilibrium /iːkwɪˈlɪbrɪəm/ *n* équilibre *m*.

equip /ɪˈkwɪp/ *vt* (*pt* **equipped**) équiper (**with** de). **equipment** *n* équipement *m*.

equity /ˈekwətɪ/ *n* équité *f*.

equivalence /ɪˈkwɪvələns/ *n* équivalence *f*.

era /ˈɪərə/ *n* ère *f*, époque *f*.

eradicate /ɪˈrædɪkeɪt/ *vt* éliminer; (disease) éradiquer.

erase /ɪˈreɪz/ *vt* effacer. **eraser** *n* (rubber) gomme *f*.

erect /ɪˈrekt/ *adj* droit. ● *vt* ériger. **erection** *n* érection *f*.

erode /ɪˈrəʊd/ *vt* éroder; (fig) saper. **erosion** *n* érosion *f*.

erotic /ɪˈrɒtɪk/ *adj* érotique.

errand /ˈerənd/ *n* commission *f*, course *f*.

erratic /ɪˈrætɪk/ *adj* (behaviour, person) imprévisible; (performance) inégal.

error /ˈerə(r)/ *n* erreur *f*.

erupt /ɪ'rʌpt/ vi (volcano) entrer en éruption; (fig) éclater.

escalate /'eskəleɪt/ vt intensifier. ● vi (conflict) s'intensifier. **escalation** n intensification f. **escalator** n escalier m mécanique, escalator® m.

escapade /'eskəpeɪd/ n frasque f.

escape /ɪ'skeɪp/ vt échapper à. ● vi s'enfuir, s'évader; (gas) fuir. ● n fuite f, évasion f; (of gas etc.) fuite f; **have a lucky** or **narrow** ~ l'échapper belle.

escapism /ɪ'skeɪpɪzəm/ n évasion f (du réel).

escort¹ /'eskɔːt/ n (guard) escorte f; (companion) compagnon/compagne m/f.

escort² /ɪ'skɔːt/ vt escorter.

Eskimo /'eskɪməʊ/ n Esquimau/-de m/f.

especially /ɪ'speʃəlɪ/ adv en particulier.

espionage /'espɪɑːnɑːʒ/ n espionnage m.

espresso /e'spresəʊ/ n (café) express m.

essay /'eseɪ/ n (in literature) essai m; (School) rédaction f; (Univ) dissertation f.

essence /'esns/ n essence f.

essential /ɪ'senʃl/ adj essentiel; **the** ~**s** l'essentiel m. **essentially** adv essentiellement.

establish /ɪ'stæblɪʃ/ vt établir; (business) fonder.

establishment /ɪ'stæblɪʃmənt/ n (process) instauration f; (institution) établissement m; **the E**~ l'ordre m établi.

estate /ɪ'steɪt/ n (house and land) domaine m; (possessions) biens mpl; (housing estate) cité f; ~ **agent** n agent m immobilier. ~ **car** n break m.

esteem /ɪ'stiːm/ n estime f.

esthetic /es'θetɪk/ adj (US) ➡AES-THETIC.

estimate¹ /'estɪmət/ n (calculation) estimation f; (Comm) devis m.

estimate² /'estɪmeɪt/ vt évaluer; ~ **that** estimer que. **estimation** n (esteem) estime f; (judgment) opinion f.

Estonia /ɪ'stəʊnɪə/ n Estonie f.

estuary /'estʃʊərɪ/ n estuaire m.

eternal /ɪ'tɜːnl/ adj éternel.

eternity /ɪ'tɜːnətɪ/ n éternité f.

ethic /'eθɪk/ n éthique f; ~**s** moralité f. **ethical** adj éthique.

ethnic /'eθnɪk/ adj ethnique. ~ **cleansing** nettoyage m ethnique.

EU abbr **European Union** UE f, Union f européenne.

euphoria /juː'fɔːrɪə/ n euphorie f.

euro /'jʊərəʊ/ n euro m. ~ **zone** zone f euro.

Europe /'jʊərəp/ n Europe f.

European /jʊərə'pɪən/ adj & n européen/-ne (m/f); ~ **Community** Communauté f européenne.

eurosceptic /'jʊərəuskeptɪk/ n eurosceptique mf.

euthanasia /'jʊərəuskeptɪk/ n euthanasie f.

evacuate /ɪ'vækjʊeɪt/ vt évacuer.

evade /ɪ'veɪd/ vt (blow) esquiver; (question) éluder.

evaluation /ɪvæljʊ'eɪʃn/ n évaluation f.

evaporate /ɪvæljʊ'eɪʃn/ vi s'évaporer; ~**d milk** lait m condensé.

evasion /ɪ'veɪʒn/ n fuite f (of devant); (excuse) faux-fuyant m; **tax** ~ évasion f fiscale. **evasive** adj évasif.

eve /iːv/ n veille f (of de).

even /'iːvn/ adj (surface, voice, contest) égal; (teeth, hem) régulier; (number) pair; **get** ~**with** se venger de. ● adv même; ~ **better**/etc. (still) encore mieux/etc.; ~ **so** quand même. □ ~ **out** (differences) s'atténuer; ~ **sth out** (inequalities) réduire qch; ~ **up** équilibrer.

evening /'iːvnɪŋ/ n soir m; (whole evening, event) soirée f.

evenly /'iːvnlɪ/ adv (spread, apply) uniformément; (breathe) régulièrement; (equally) en parts égales.

event /ɪ'vent/ n événement m; (Sport) épreuve f; **in the** ~ **of** en cas de. **eventful** adj mouvementé.

eventual /ɪ'ventʃʊəl/ adj (outcome, decision) final; (aim) à long terme. **eventuality** n éventualité f. **eventually** adv finalement; (in future) un jour ou l'autre.

ever /'evə(r)/ adv jamais; (at all times) toujours.

evergreen /'evəgriːn/ n arbre m à feuilles persistantes.

everlasting /evə'lɑːstɪŋ/ adj éternel.

ever since *prep & adv* depuis.

every /'evrɪ/ *adj* ~ **house/window** toutes les maisons/les fenêtres; ~ **time/minute** chaque fois/minute; ~ **day** tous les jours; ~ **other day** tous les deux jours. **everybody** *pron* tout le monde. **everyday** *adj* quotidien. **everyone** *pron* tout le monde. **everything** *pron* tout. **everywhere** *adv* partout; ~**where he goes** partout où il va.

evict /ɪ'vɪkt/ *vt* expulser (**from** de).

evidence /'evɪdəns/ *n* (proof) preuves *fpl* (**that** que; **of, for** de); (testimony) témoignage *m*; (traces) trace *f* (**of** de); **give** ~ témoigner; **be in** ~ être visible. **evident** *adj* manifeste. **evidently** *adv* (apparently) apparemment; (obviously) manifestement.

evil /'iːvl/ *adj* malfaisant. ● *n* mal *m*.

evoke /ɪ'vəʊk/ *vt* évoquer.

evolution /iːvə'luːʃn/ *n* évolution *f*.

evolve /ɪ'vɒlv/ *vi* évoluer. ● *vt* élaborer.

ewe /juː/ *n* brebis *f*.

ex- /eks/ *pref* ex-, ancien.

exact /ɪg'zækt/ *adj* exact; **the** ~ **opposite** exactement le contraire. ● *vt* exiger (**from** de). **exactly** *adv* exactement.

exaggerate /ɪg'zædʒəreɪt/ *vt/i* exagérer.

exalted /ɪg'zɔːltɪd/ *adj* élevé.

exam /ɪg'zæm/ *n* 🆇 examen *m*.

examination /ɪgzæmɪ'neɪʃn/ *n* examen *m*.

examine /ɪg'zæmɪn/ *vt* examiner; (witness) interroger. **examiner** *n* examinateur/-trice *m/f*.

example /ɪg'zɑːmpl/ *n* exemple *m*; **for** ~ par exemple; **make an** ~ **of** punir pour l'exemple.

exasperate /ɪg'zæspəreɪt/ *vt* exaspérer.

excavate /'ekskəveɪt/ *vt* fouiller. **excavations** *npl* fouilles *fpl*.

exceed /ɪk'siːd/ *vt* dépasser. **exceedingly** *adv* extrêmement.

excel /ɪk'sel/ *vi* (*pt* **excelled**) exceller (**at, in** en; **at doing** à faire). ● *vt* surpasser.

excellence /'eksələns/ *n* excellence *f*. **excellent** *adj* excellent.

except /ɪk'sept/ *prep* sauf, excepté; ~ **for** à part. ● *vt* excepter. **excepting** *prep* sauf, excepté.

exception /ɪk'sepʃn/ *n* exception *f*; **take** ~ **to** s'offusquer de. **exceptional** *adj* exceptionnel.

excerpt /'eksɜːpt/ *n* extrait *m*.

excess¹ /ɪk'ses/ *n* excès *m*.

excess² /'ekses/ *adj* ~ **weight** excès *m* de poids; ~ **baggage** excédent *m* de bagages.

excessive /ɪk'sesɪv/ *adj* excessif.

exchange /ɪks'tʃeɪndʒ/ *vt* échanger (**for** contre). ● *n* échange *m*; (between currencies) change *m*; ~ **rate** taux *m* de change; **telephone** ~ central *m* téléphonique.

Exchequer /ɪks'tʃekə(r)/ *n* (Pol) ministère *m* britannique des finances.

excise /'eksaɪz/ *n* excise *f*, taxe *f*.

excite /ɪk'saɪt/ *vt* exciter; (enthuse) enthousiasmer. **excited** *adj* excité; **get** ~**d** s'exciter. **excitement** *n* excitation *f*. **exciting** *adj* passionnant.

exclaim /ɪk'skleɪm/ *vt* s'exclamer.

exclamation /eksklə'meɪʃn/ *n* exclamation *f*; ~ **mark** or **point** (US) point *m* d'exclamation.

exclude /ɪk'skluːd/ *vt* exclure.

exclusive /ɪk'skluːsɪv/ *adj* (club) fermé; (rights) exclusif; (news item) en exclusivité; ~ **of meals** repas non compris. **exclusively** *adv* exclusivement.

excruciating /ɪk'skruːʃɪeɪtɪŋ/ *adj* atroce.

excursion /ɪk'skɜːʃn/ *n* excursion *f*.

excuse¹ /ɪk'skjuːz/ *vt* excuser; ~ **from** (exempt) dispenser de; ~ **me!** excusez-moi!, pardon!

excuse² /ɪk'skjuːs/ *n* (reason) excuse *f*; (pretext) prétexte *m* (**for sth** à qch; **for doing** pour faire).

ex-directory /eksdaɪ'rektərɪ/ *adj* sur liste rouge.

execute /'eksɪkjuːt/ *vt* exécuter. **executioner** *n* bourreau *m*.

executive /ɪg'zekjʊtɪv/ *n* (person) cadre *m*; (committee) exécutif *m*. ● *adj* exécutif.

exemplary /ɪg'zemplərɪ/ *adj* exemplaire.

exemplify /ɪg'zemplɪfaɪ/ *vt* illustrer.

exempt /ɪg'zempt/ adj exempt (**from** de). ● vt exempter.

exercise /'eksəsaɪz/ n exercice m; ~ **book** cahier m. ● vt exercer; (restraint, patience) faire preuve de. ● vi faire de l'exercice.

exert /ɪg'zɜːt/ vt exercer; ~ **oneself** se fatiguer. **exertion** n effort m.

exhaust /ɪg'zɔːst/ vt épuiser. ● n (Auto) pot m d'échappement.

exhaustive /ɪg'zɔːstɪv/ adj exhaustif.

exhibit /ɪg'zɪbɪt/ vt exposer; (fig) manifester. ● n objet m exposé.

exhibition /eksɪ'bɪʃn/ n exposition f; (of skill) démonstration f. **exhibitionist** n exhibitionniste mf.

exhibitor /ɪg'zɪbɪtə(r)/ n exposant/-e m/f.

exhilarate /ɪg'zɪləreɪt/ vt griser.

exile /'eksaɪl/ n exil m; (person) exilé/-e m/f. ● vt exiler.

exist /ɪg'zɪst/ vi exister. **existence** n existence f; **be in ~ence** exister. **existing** adj actuel.

exit /'eksɪt/ n sortie f. ● vt/i (also Comput) sortir (de).

exodus /'eksədəs/ n exode m.

exonerate /ɪg'zɒnəreɪt/ vt disculper.

exotic /ɪg'zɒtɪk/ adj exotique.

expand /ɪk'spænd/ vt développer; (workforce) accroître. ● vi se développer; (population) s'accroître; (metal) se dilater.

expanse /ɪk'spæns/ n étendue f.

expansion /ɪk'spænʃn/ n développement m; (Pol, Comm) expansion f.

expatriate /eks'pætrɪət/ adj & n expatrié/-e (m/f).

expect /ɪk'spekt/ vt s'attendre à; (suppose) supposer; (demand) exiger; (baby) attendre.

expectancy /ɪk'spektənsɪ/ n attente f.

expectant /ɪk'spektənt/ adj ~ **mother** future maman f.

expectation /ekspek'teɪʃn/ n (assumption) prévision f; (hope) aspiration f; (demand) exigence f.

expedient /ɪk'spiːdɪənt/ adj opportun. ● n expédient m.

expedition /ekspɪ'dɪʃn/ n expédition f.

expel /ɪk'spel/ vt (pt **expelled**) expulser; (pupil) renvoyer.

expend /ɪk'spend/ vt consacrer.

expenditure /ɪk'spendɪtʃə(r)/ n dépenses fpl.

expense /ɪk'spens/ n frais mpl; **at sb's** ~ aux frais de qn; ~ **account** frais mpl de représentation. **expensive** adj cher; (tastes) de luxe. **expensively** adv luxueusement.

experience /ɪk'spɪərɪəns/ n expérience f. ● vt (undergo) connaître; (feel) éprouver; ~**d** expérimenté.

experiment /ɪk'sperɪmənt/ n expérience f. ● vi expérimenter, faire des essais.

expert /'ekspɜːt/ n spécialiste mf. ● adj spécialisé, expert. **expertise** n compétence f. **expertly** adv de manière experte.

expire /ɪk'spaɪə(r)/ vi expirer; ~**d** périmé. **expiry** n expiration f.

explain /ɪk'spleɪn/ vt expliquer. **explanation** n explication f. **explanatory** adj explicatif.

explicit /ɪk'splɪsɪt/ adj explicite.

explode /ɪk'spləʊd/ vt/i (faire) exploser.

exploit¹ /'eksplɔɪt/ n exploit m.

exploit² /ɪk'splɔɪt/ vt exploiter.

exploration /eksplə'reɪʃn/ n exploration f. **exploratory** adj (talks) exploratoire. **explore** vt explorer; (fig) étudier. **explorer** n explorateur/-trice m/f.

explosion /ɪk'spləʊʒn/ n explosion f. **explosive** adj & n explosif (m).

exponent /ɪk'spəʊnənt/ n avocat/-e m/f (of de).

export¹ /ɪk'spɔːt/ vt exporter.

export² /'ekspɔːt/ n (process) exportation f; (product) produit m d'exportation.

expose /ɪk'spəʊz/ vt exposer; (disclose) révéler.

exposure /ɪk'spəʊʒə(r)/ n révélation f; (Photo) pose f; **die of** ~ mourir de froid.

express /ɪk'spres/ vt exprimer. ● adj exprès. ● adv **send sth** ~ envoyer qch en exprès. ● n (train) rapide m. **expression** n expression f. **expressive** adj expressif. **expressly** adv expressément.

exquisite /'ekskwɪzɪt/ adj exquis.

extend /ɪk'stend/ vt (visit) prolonger; (house) agrandir; (range) élargir; (arm, leg) étendre. ● vi (stretch) s'étendre;

(in time) se prolonger. **extension** n (of line, road) prolongement m; (of visa, loan) prorogation f; (building) addition f; (phone number) poste m; (cable) rallonge f.

extensive /ɪk'stensɪv/ adj vaste; (study) approfondi; (damage) considérable. **extensively** adv (much) beaucoup; (very) très.

extent /ɪk'stent/ n (size, scope) étendue f; (degree) mesure f; **to some ∼** dans une certaine mesure; **to such an ∼ that** à tel point que.

extenuating /ɪk'stenjʊeɪtɪŋ/ adj atténuant.

exterior /ɪk'stɪərɪə(r)/ adj & n extérieur (m).

exterminate /ɪk'stɜːmɪneɪt/ vt exterminer.

external /ɪk'stɜːnl/ adj extérieur; (cause, medical use) externe.

extinct /ɪk'stɪŋkt/ adj (species) disparu; (volcano, passion) éteint.

extinguish /ɪk'stɪŋgwɪʃ/ vt éteindre. **extinguisher** n extincteur m.

extol /ɪk'stəʊl/ vt (pt **extolled**) louer, chanter les louanges de.

extort /ɪk'stɔːt/ vt extorquer (**from** à). **extortion** n (Jur) extorsion f. **extortionate** adj exorbitant.

extra /'ekstrə/ adj supplémentaire; **∼ charge** supplément m; **∼ time** (football) prolongation f; **∼ strong** extra-fort. ● adv encore; plus. ● n supplément m; (cinema) figurant/-e m/f.

extract[1] /ɪk'strækt/ vt sortir (**from** de); (tooth) extraire; (promise) arracher.

extract[2] /'ekstrækt/ n extrait m.

extra-curricular /ekstrəkə 'rɪkjʊlə(r)/ adj parascolaire.

extradite /'ekstrədaɪt/ vt extrader.

extramarital /ekstrə'mærɪtl/ adj extraconjugal.

extramural /ekstrə'mjʊərəl/ adj (Univ) hors faculté.

extraordinary /ɪk'strɔːdnrɪ/ adj extraordinaire.

extravagance /ɪk'strævəgəns/ n prodigalité f. **extravagant** adj (person) dépensier; (claim) extravagant.

extreme /ɪk'striːm/ adj & n extrême (m). **extremely** adv extrêmement. **ex-**

tremist n extrémiste mf. **extremity** n extrémité f.

extricate /'ekstrɪkeɪt/ vt dégager.

extrovert /'ekstrəvɜːt/ n extraverti/-e m/f.

exuberance /ɪg'zjuːbərəns/ n exubérance f.

exude /ɪg'zjuːd/ vt (charm) respirer; (smell) exhaler.

eye /aɪ/ n œil m (pl yeux); **keep an ∼ on** surveiller. ● vt (pt **eyed**; pres p **eyeing**) regarder. **∼ball** n globe m oculaire. **∼brow** n sourcil m. **∼-catching** adj attrayant. **∼lash** n cil m. **∼lid** n paupière f. **∼-opener** n révélation f. **∼-shadow** n ombre f à paupières. **∼sight** n vue f. **∼sore** n horreur f. **∼witness** n témoin m oculaire.

• •

Ff

• •

fable /'feɪbl/ n fable f.

fabric /'fæbrɪk/ n (cloth) tissu m.

fabulous /'fæbjʊləs/ adj fabuleux; (marvellous 🇬🇧) formidable.

face /feɪs/ n visage m, figure f; (expression) air m; (appearance, dignity) face f; (of clock) cadran m; (Geol) face f; (of rock) paroi f; **in the ∼ of** face à; **make a (funny) ∼** faire la grimace; **∼ to ∼** face à face. ● vt être en face de; (risk) devoir affronter; (confront) faire face à; (deal with) **I can't ∼ him** je n'ai pas le courage de le voir. ● vi (person) regarder; (chair) être tourné vers; (window) donner sur; **∼ up to** faire face à; **∼d with** face à.

facelift /'feɪslɪft/ n lifting m; **give a ∼ to** donner un coup de neuf à.

face value n valeur f nominale; **take sth at∼** prendre qch au pied de la lettre.

facial /'feɪʃl/ adj (hair) du visage; (injury) au visage. ● n soin m du visage.

facility /fə'sɪlətɪ/ n (building) complexe m; (feature) fonction f; **facilities** (equipment) équipements mpl.

facsimile /fæk'sɪmǝlɪ/ n fac-similé m.

fact /fækt/ n fait m; **as a matter of ∼, in ∼** en fait; **know for a ∼ that** savoir de source sûre que; **owing/due to the ~ that** étant donné que.

factor /'fæktə(r)/ n facteur m.

factory /'fæktərɪ/ n usine f.

factual /'fæktʃʊəl/ adj (account, description) basé sur les faits; (evidence) factuel.

faculty /'fækltɪ/ n faculté f.

fade /feɪd/ vi (sound) s'affaiblir; (memory) s'effacer; (flower) se faner; (material) se décolorer; (colour) passer.

fail /feɪl/ vi échouer; (grow weak) (s'af)faiblir; (run short) manquer; (engine) tomber en panne. ● vt (exam) échouer à; **~ to do** (not do) ne pas faire; (not be able) ne pas réussir à faire; **without ~** à coup sûr.

failing /'feɪlɪŋ/ n défaut m; **~ that/this** sinon.

failure /'feɪljə(r)/ n échec m; (person) raté/-e m/f; (breakdown) panne f; **~ to do** (inability) incapacité f de faire.

faint /feɪnt/ adj léger, faible; **feel ~** (ill) se sentir mal; **I haven't the ~est idea** je n'en ai pas la moindre idée. ● vi s'évanouir. ● n évanouissement m; **~-hearted** adj timide.

fair /feə(r)/ n foire f. ● adj (hair) blond; (skin) clair; (weather) beau; (amount) raisonnable; (just) juste, équitable. ● adv (play) loyalement. **~ trade** commerce m équitable.

fairground n champ m de foire.

fairly /'feəlɪ/ adv (justly) équitablement; (rather) assez.

fairness /'feənɪs/ n justice f.

fairy /'feərɪ/ n fée f. **~ story**, **~-tale** n conte m de fées.

faith /feɪθ/ n (belief) foi f; (confidence) confiance f.

faithful /'feɪθfl/ adj fidèle.

fake /feɪk/ n (forgery) faux m; (person) imposteur m; **it is a ~** c'est un faux. ● adj faux. ● vt (signature) contrefaire; (results) falsifier; (illness) feindre.

falcon /'fɔːlkən/ n faucon m.

fall /fɔːl/ vi (pt **fell**; pp **fallen**) tomber; **~ short** être insuffisant. ● n chute f; (autumn: US) automne m; **Niagara F~s** chutes fpl du Niagara. □ **~ back on** se rabattre sur. **~ behind** prendre du retard. **~ down** or **off** tomber. **~ for** (person 🔲) tomber amoureux de; (a trick 🔲) se laisser prendre à. **~ in**

(Mil) se mettre en rangs. **~ off** (decrease) diminuer. **~ out** se brouiller (with avec). **~ over** tomber (par terre). **~ through** (plans) tomber à l'eau.

fallacy /'fæləsɪ/ n erreur f.

false /fɔːls/ adj faux. **~ teeth** npl dentier m.

falter /'fɔːltə(r)/ vi (courage) faiblir; (when speaking) bafouiller 🔲.

fame /feɪm/ n renommée f. **famed** adj célèbre (for pour).

familiar /fə'mɪlɪə(r)/ adj familier; **be ~ with** connaître.

family /'fæməlɪ/ n famille f.

famine /'fæmɪn/ n famine f.

famished /'fæmɪʃt/ adj affamé.

famous /'feɪməs/ adj célèbre (for pour).

fan /fæn/ n (mechanical) ventilateur m; (hand-held) éventail m; (of person) fan mf 🔲, admirateur/-trice m/f; (enthusiast) fervent/-e m/f, passionné/-e m/f. ● vt (pt **fanned**) (face) éventer; (fig) attiser. ● vi **~ out** se déployer en éventail.

fanatic /fə'nætɪk/ n fanatique mf.

fan belt n courroie f de ventilateur.

fancy /'fænsɪ/ n (whim, fantasy) fantaisie f; **take a ~to sb** se prendre d'affection pour qn; **it took my ~** ça m'a plu. ● adj (buttons etc.) fantaisie inv; (prices) extravagant; (impressive) impressionnant. ● vt s'imaginer; (want 🔲) avoir envie de; (like 🔲) aimer. **~ dress** n déguisement m.

fang /fæŋ/ n (of dog) croc m; (of snake) crochet m.

fantasize /'fæntəsaɪz/ vi fantasmer.

fantastic /fæn'tæstɪk/ adj fantastique.

fantasy /'fæntəsɪ/ n fantaisie f; (daydream) fantasme m.

fanzine /'fænziːn/ n magazine m des fans, fanzine m.

FAQ abbr (**Frequently Asked Questions**) (Internet) FAQ f, foire f aux questions.

far /fɑː(r)/ adv loin; (much) beaucoup; (very) très; **~ away**, **~ off** au loin; **as ~ as** (up to) jusqu'à; **as ~as I know** autant que je sache; **by ~** de loin; **~ from** loin de. ● adj lointain; (end, side) autre. **~away** adj lointain.

farce /fɑːs/ n farce f.

fare /feə(r)/ n (prix du) billet m; (food) nourriture f. ● vi (progress) aller; (manage) se débrouiller.

Far East n Extrême-Orient m.

farewell /feə'wel/ interj & n adieu (m).

farm /fɑːm/ n ferme f. ● vt cultiver; ~ **out** céder en sous-traitance. ● vi être fermier. **farmer** n fermier m. ~**house** n ferme f. **farming** n agriculture f. ~**yard** n basse-cour f.

fart /fɑːt/ ⊞ vi péter ⊞. ● n pet m ⊞.

farther /'fɑːðə(r)/ adv plus loin. ● adj plus éloigné.

farthest /'fɑːðɪst/ adv le plus loin. ● adj le plus éloigné.

fascinate /'fæsɪneɪt/ vt fasciner.

Fascism /'fæʃɪzəm/ n fascisme m.

fashion /'fæʃn/ n (current style) mode f; (manner) façon f; **in** ~ à la mode; **out of** ~ démodé. ● vt façonner. **fashionable** adj à la mode.

fast /fɑːst/ adj rapide; (colour) grand teint inv; (firm) fixe, solide; **be** ~ (of a clock) avancer. ● adv vite; (firmly) ferme; **be** ~ **asleep** dormir d'un sommeil profond. ● vi jeûner. ● n jeûne m.

fasten /'fɑːsn/ vt/i (s')attacher. **fastener**, **fastening** n attache f, fermeture f.

fast food n fast-food m. restauration f rapide.

fat /fæt/ n graisse f; (on meat) gras m. ● adj (**fatter, fattest**) gros, gras; (meat) gras; (profit) gros; **a** ~ **lot** ⊞ bien peu (**of** de).

fatal /'feɪtl/ adj mortel; (fateful, disastrous) fatal. **fatality** n mort m. **fatally** adv mortellement.

fate /feɪt/ n sort m. **fateful** adj fatidique.

father /'fɑːðə(r)/ n père m. ~**hood** n paternité f. ~**-in-law** n (pl ~**s-inlaw**) beau-père m.

fathom /'fæðəm/ n brasse f (= 1.8 m). ● vt ~**(out)** comprendre.

fatigue /fə'tiːg/ n épuisement m; (Tech) fatigue f. ● vt fatiguer.

fatten /'fætn/ vt/i engraisser. **fattening** adj qui fait grossir.

fatty /'fætɪ/ adj (food) gras; (tissue) adipeux.

faucet /'fɔːsɪt/ n (US) robinet m.

fault /fɔːlt/ n (defect, failing) défaut m; (blame) faute f; (Geol) faille f; **at** ~ fautif; **find** ~ **with** critiquer. ● vt ~ **sth/sb** prendre en défaut qn/qch. **faulty** adj défectueux.

favour, (US) **favor** /'feɪvə(r)/ n faveur f; **do sb a** ~ rendre service à qn; **in** ~ **of** pour. ● vt favoriser; (support) être en faveur de; (prefer) préférer. **favourable** adj favorable.

favourite /'feɪvərɪt/ adj & n favori/-te (m/f).

fawn /fɔːn/ n (animal) faon m; (colour) beige m foncé. ● vi ~ **on** flagorner.

fax /fæks/ n fax m, télécopie f. ● vt faxer, envoyer par télécopie. ~ **machine** n fax m. télécopieur m; (for public use) Publifax® m.

FBI abbr (**Federal Bureau of Investigation**) (US) Police f judiciaire fédérale.

fear /fɪə(r)/ n crainte f, peur f; (fig) risque m; **for** ~ **of/that** de peur de/que. ● vt craindre.

feasible /'fiːzəbl/ adj faisable; (likely) plausible.

feast /fiːst/ n festin m; (Relig) fête f. ● vi festoyer. ● vt régaler (**on** de).

feat /fiːt/ n exploit m.

feather /'feðə(r)/ n plume f. ● vt ~ **one's nest** s'enrichir.

feature /'fiːtʃə(r)/ n caractéristique f; (of person, face) trait m; (film) long métrage m; (article) article m de fond. ● vt (advert) représenter; (give prominence to) mettre en vedette. ● vi figurer (**in** dans).

February /'februərɪ/ n février m.

fed /fed/ ➡**FEED**. ● adj **be** ~ **up** ⊞ en avoir marre ⊞ (**with** de).

federal /'fedərəl/ adj fédéral.

fee /fiː/ n (for entrance) prix m; ~**(s)** (of doctor) honoraires mpl; (of actor, artist) cachet m; (for tuition) frais mpl; (for enrolment) droits mpl.

feeble /'fiːbl/ adj faible.

feed /fiːd/ vt (pt **fed**) nourrir, donner à manger à; (suckle) allaiter; (supply) alimenter. ● vi se nourrir (**on** de). ~ **in information** rentrer des données. ● n nourriture f; (of baby) tétée f.

feedback /'fiːdbæk/ n réaction (s) f(pl); (Med, Tech) feed-back m.

feel /fiːl/ vt (pt **felt**) (touch) tâter; (be conscious of) sentir; (emotion) ressentir; (experience) éprouver; (think) estimer. ● vi (tired, lonely) se sentir; ~

hot/thirsty avoir chaud/soif; ∼ **as if** avoir l'impression que; ∼ **awful** (ill) se sentir malade; ∼ **like** (want 🎵) avoir envie de.

feeler /'fiːlə(r)/ n antenne f; **put out** ∼s tâter le terrain.

feeling /'fiːlɪŋ/ n (emotion) sentiment m; (physical) sensation f; (impression) impression f.

feet /fiːt/ →**FOOT**.

feign /feɪn/ vt feindre.

fell /fel/ →**FALL**. ● vt (cut down) abattre.

fellow /'feləʊ/ n compagnon m, camarade m; (of society) membre m; (man 🎵) type m 🎵. ∼**-countryman** n compatriote m. ∼**-passenger** n compagnon m de voyage.

fellowship /'feləʊʃɪp/ n camaraderie f; (group) association f.

felony /'feləni/ n crime m.

felt /felt/ →**FEEL**. ● n feutre m. ∼**-tip** n feutre m.

female /'fiːmeɪl/ adj (animal) femelle; (voice, sex) féminin. ● n femme f; (animal) femelle f.

feminine /'femənɪn/ adj & n féminin (m). **femininity** n féminité f. **feminist** n féministe mf.

fence /fens/ n barrière f; **sit on the** ∼ ne pas prendre position. ● vt ∼ (**in**) clôturer. ● vi (Sport) faire de l'escrime. **fencing** n escrime f.

fend /fend/ vi ∼ **for oneself** se débrouiller tout seul. ● vt ∼ **off** (blow, attack) parer.

fender /'fendə(r)/ n (for fireplace) garde-cendre m; (mudguard: US) garde-boue m inv.

ferment[1] /'fɜːment/ n ferment m; (excitement: fig) agitation f.

ferment[2] /fə'ment/ vt/i (faire) fermenter.

fern /fɜːn/ n fougère f.

ferocious /fə'rəʊʃəs/ adj féroce.

ferret /'ferɪt/ n (animal) furet m. ● vi ∼ **about** fureter. ● vt ∼ **out** dénicher.

ferry /'feri/ n (long-distance) ferry m; (short-distance) bac m. ● vt transporter.

fertile /'fɜːtaɪl/ adj fertile; (person, animal) fécond. **fertilizer** n engrais m.

festival /'festɪvl/ n festival m; (Relig) fête f.

festive /'festɪv/ adj de fête, gai; ∼ **season** période f des fêtes. **festivity** n réjouissances fpl.

fetch /fetʃ/ vt (go for) aller chercher; (bring person) amener; (bring thing) apporter; (be sold for) rapporter.

fête /feɪt/ n fête f; (church) kermesse f. ● vt fêter.

fetish /'fetɪʃ/ n (object) fétiche m; (Psych) obsession f.

feud /fjuːd/ n querelle f.

fever /'fiːvə(r)/ n fièvre f. **feverish** adj fiévreux.

few /fjuː/ det peu de; **a** ∼ **houses** quelques maisons; **quite a** ∼ **people** un bon nombre de personnes. ● pron quelques-uns/quelques-unes.

fewer /'fjuːə(r)/ det moins de; **be** ∼ être moins nombreux (**than** que). **fewest** det le moins de.

fiancé /fɪ'ɒseɪ/ n fiancé m. **fiancée** n fiancée f.

fibre, (US) **fiber** /'faɪbə(r)/ n fibre f. ∼**glass** n fibre f de verre.

fiction /'fɪkʃn/ n fiction f; (works of) ∼ romans mpl. **fictional** adj fictif.

fiddle /'fɪdl/ n 🎵 violon m; (swindle 🎵) combine f. ● vi ⊠ frauder. ● vt 🎵 falsifier; ∼ **with** 🎵 tripoter 🎵.

fidget /'fɪdʒɪt/ vi gigoter sans cesse.

field /fiːld/ n champ m; (Sport) terrain m; (fig) domaine m. ● vt (ball: cricket) bloquer.

fierce /fɪəs/ adj féroce; (storm, attack) violent.

fiery /'faɪəri/ adj (**-ier, -iest**) (hot) ardent; (spirited) fougueux.

fifteen /fɪf'tiːn/ adj & n quinze (m).

fifth /fɪfθ/ adj & n cinquième (mf).

fifty /'fɪfti/ adj & n cinquante (m).

fig /fɪɡ/ n figue f.

fight /faɪt/ vi (pt **fought**) se battre; (struggle: fig) lutter; (quarrel) se disputer. ● vt se battre avec; (evil: fig) lutter contre. ● n (struggle) lutte f; (quarrel) dispute f; (brawl) bagarre f; (Mil) combat m. ☐ ∼ **back** se défendre (**against** contre). ∼**off** surmonter. ∼**over** se disputer qch. **fighter** n (determined person) lutteur/-euse m/f; (plane) avion m de chasse. **fighting** n combats mpl.

figment /'fɪɡmənt/ n **a** ∼ **of the imagination** un produit de l'imagination.

figure /ˈfɪgə(r)/ n (number) chiffre m; (diagram) figure f; (shape) forme f; (body) ligne f; ~s arithmétique f. ● vt s'imaginer. ● vi (appear) figurer; **that ~s** (US, 🔲) c'est logique; ~ **out** comprendre; ~ **of speech** n façon f de parler.

file /faɪl/ n (tool) lime f. dossier m, classeur m; (Comput) fichier m; (row) file f. ● vt limer; (papers) classer; (Jur) déposer. ❏ ~ **in** entrer en file. ~ **past** défiler devant.

filing cabinet n classeur m.

fill /fɪl/ vt/i (se) remplir. ● n **have had one's ~** en avoir assez. ❏ ~ **in** (form) remplir. ~ **out** prendre du poids. ~ **up** (Auto) faire le plein (de carburant); (bath, theatre) (se) remplir.

fillet /ˈfɪlɪt/ n filet m. ● vt découper en filets.

filling /ˈfɪlɪŋ/ n (of tooth) plombage m; (of sandwich) garniture f. ~ **station** n station-service f.

film /fɪlm/ n film m; (Photo) pellicule f. ● vt filmer. ~**-goer** n cinéphile mf. ~**star** n vedette f de cinéma.

filter /ˈfɪltə(r)/ n filtre m; (traffic signal) flèche f. ● vt/i filtrer; (of traffic) suivre la flèche. ~ **coffee** n café m filtre.

filth /fɪlθ/ n crasse f. **filthy** adj crasseux.

fin /fɪn/ n (of fish, seal) nageoire f; (of shark) aileron m.

final /ˈfaɪnl/ adj dernier; (conclusive) définitif. ● n (Sport) finale f.

finale /fɪˈnɑːlɪ/ n (Mus) finale m.

finalize /ˈfaɪnəlaɪz/ vt mettre au point, fixer.

finally /ˈfaɪnəlɪ/ adv (lastly, at last) enfin, finalement; (once and for all) définitivement.

finance /ˈfaɪnæns/ n finance f. ● adj financier. ● vt financer. **financial** adj financier.

find /faɪnd/ vt (pt **found**) trouver; (sth lost) retrouver. ● n trouvaille f; ~ **out** vt découvrir; vi se renseigner (**about** sur). **findings** npl conclusions fpl.

fine /faɪn/ adj fin; (excellent) beau; ~ **arts** beaux-arts mpl. ● n amende f. ● vt condamner à une amende.

finger /ˈfɪŋgə(r)/ n doigt m. ● vt palper. ~**-nail** n ongle m. ~**print** n empreinte f digitale. ~**tip** n bout m du doigt.

finish /ˈfɪnɪʃ/ vt/i finir; ~ **doing** finir de faire; ~ **up doing** finir par faire; ~ **up in** se retrouver à. ● n fin f; (of race) arrivée f; (appearance) finition f.

finite /ˈfaɪnaɪt/ adj fini.

Finland /ˈfɪnlənd/ n Finlande f. **Finn** n Finlandais/-e m/f.

Finnish /ˈfɪnɪʃ/ adj finlandais. ● n (Ling) finnois m.

fir /fɜː(r)/ n sapin m.

fire /ˈfaɪə(r)/ n (element) feu m; (blaze) incendie m; (heater) radiateur m; **set ~ to** mettre le feu à. ● vt (bullet) tirer; (dismiss) renvoyer; (fig) enflammer. ● vi tirer (**at** sur). ~ **a gun** tirer un coup de revolver/de fusil. ~ **alarm** n alarme f incendie. ~**arm** n arme f à feu. ~ **brigade** n pompiers mpl. ~ **engine** n voiture f de pompiers. ~ **escape** n escalier m de secours. ~ **extinguisher** n extincteur m. ~ **man** n (pl **-men**) pompier m. ~**place** n cheminée f. ~ **station** n caserne f de pompiers. ~**wall** n mur m coupe-feu; (Internet) pare-feu m inv. ~**wood** n bois m de chauffage. ~**work** n feu m d'artifice.

firing squad n peloton m d'exécution.

firm /fɜːm/ n entreprise f, société f. ● adj ferme; (belief) solide.

first /fɜːst/ adj premier; **at ~ hand** de première main; **at ~ sight** à première vue; ~ **of all** tout d'abord. ● n premier/-ière m/f. ● adv d'abord, premièrement; (arrive) le premier, la première; **at ~** d'abord. ~ **aid** n premiers soins mpl. ~**-class** adj de première classe. ~ **floor** n premier étage m; (US) rez-de-chaussée m inv. ~ **gear** n première (vitesse) f. **F~ Lady** n (US) épouse f du Président.

firstly /ˈfɜːstlɪ/ adv premièrement.

first name n prénom m.

fish /fɪʃ/ n poisson m; ~ **shop** poissonnerie f. ● vi pêcher; ~ **for** (cod) pêcher; ~ **out** (from water) repêcher; (take out 🔲) sortir. **fisherman** n (pl **-men**) n pêcheur m.

fishing /ˈfɪʃɪŋ/ n pêche f; **go ~** aller à la pêche. ~ **rod** n canne f à pêche.

fishmonger /ˈfɪʃmʌŋgə(r)/ n poissonnier/-ière m/f.

fist /fɪst/ n poing m.

fit /fɪt/ n accès m, crise f; **be a good ~** (dress) être à la bonne taille. ● adj (fit-

ter, fittest) en bonne santé; (proper) convenable; (good enough) bon; (able) capable; **in no ~ state to do** pas en état de faire. ● vt/i (pt **fitted**) (into space) aller; (install) poser. **~ in** vt caser; vi (newcomer) s'intégrer. **~ out, ~ up** équiper.

fitness /'fɪtnɪs/ n forme f; (of remark) justesse f.

fitted /'fɪtɪd/ adj (wardrobe) encastré. **~ carpet** n moquette f.

fitting /'fɪtɪŋ/ adj approprié. ● n essayage m. **~ room** n cabine f d'essayage.

five /faɪv/ adj & n cinq (m).

fix /fɪks/ vt (make firm, attach, decide) fixer; (mend) réparer; (deal with) arranger; **~ sb up with sth** trouver qch à qn.

fixture /'fɪkstʃə(r)/ n (Sport) match m; **~s** (in house) installations fpl.

fizz /fɪz/ vi pétiller. ● n pétillement m. **fizzy** adj gazeux.

flabbergast /'flæbəgɑːst/ vt sidérer.

flabby /'flæbi/ adj flasque.

flag /flæg/ n drapeau m; (Naut) pavillon m. ● vt (pt **flagged**) **~ (down)** faire signe de s'arrêter à. ● vi (weaken) faiblir; (sick person) s'affaiblir. **~-pole** n mât m. **~stone** n dalle f.

flake /fleɪk/ n flocon m; (of paint, metal) écaille f. ● vi s'écailler.

flamboyant /flæm'bɔɪənt/ adj (colour) éclatant; (manner) extravagant.

flame /fleɪm/ n flamme f; **burst into ~s** exploser; **go up in ~s** brûler. ● vi flamber.

flamingo /flə'mɪŋgəʊ/ n flamant m (rose).

flammable /'flæməbl/ adj inflammable.

flan /flæn/ n tarte f; (custard tart) flan m.

flank /flæŋk/ n flanc m. ● vt flanquer.

flannel /'flænl/ n (material) flannelle f; (for face) gant m de toilette.

flap /flæp/ vi (pt **flapped**) battre. ● vt **~ its wings** battre des ailes. ● n (of pocket) rabat m; (of table) abattant m.

flare /fleə(r)/ vi **~ up** (fighting) éclater. ● n flamboiement m; (Mil) fusée f éclairante; (in skirt) évasement m. **flared** adj évasé.

flash /flæʃ/ vi briller; (on and off) clignoter; **~ past** passer à toute vitesse. ● vt faire briller; (aim torch) diriger (at sur); (flaunt) étaler; **~ one's headlights** faire un appel de phares. ● n (of news, camera) flash m; **in a ~** en un éclair. **~back** n retour m en arrière. **~light** n lampe f de poche.

flask /flɑːsk/ n (for chemicals) flacon m; (for drinks) thermos® m or f inv.

flat /flæt/ adj (**flatter, flattest**) plat; (tyre) à plat; (refusal) catégorique. (fare, rate) fixe. ● adv (say) carrément. ● n (rooms) appartement m; (tyre 🇺🇸) crevaison f; (Mus) bémol m.

flat out adv (drive) à toute vitesse; (work) d'arrache-pied.

flatten /'flætn/ vt/i (s')aplatir.

flatter /'flætə(r)/ vt flatter.

flaunt /flɔːnt/ vt étaler, afficher.

flavour, (US) **flavor** /'fleɪvə(r)/ n goût m; (of ice-cream) parfum m. ● vt parfumer (**with** à), assaisonner (**with** de). **flavouring** n arôme m artificiel.

flaw /flɔː/ n défaut m.

flea /fliː/ n puce f. **~ market** n marché m aux puces.

fleck /flek/ n petite tache f.

fled /fled/ ➡FLEE.

flee /fliː/ vt/i (pt **fled**) fuir.

fleece /fliːs/ n toison f; (garment) polaire f. ● vt plumer.

fleet /fliːt/ n (Naut, Aviat) flotte f; **a ~ of vehicles** (in reserve) parc m; (on road) convoi m.

fleeting /'fliːtɪŋ/ adj très bref.

Flemish /'flemɪʃ/ adj flamand. ● n (Ling) flamand m.

flesh /fleʃ/ n chair f; **one's (own) ~ and blood** la chair de sa chair.

flew /fluː/ ➡FLY.

flex /fleks/ vt (knee) fléchir; (muscle) faire jouer. ● n (Electr) fil m.

flexible /'fleksəbl/ adj flexible.

flexitime /'fleksɪtaɪm/ n horaire m variable.

flick /flɪk/ n petit coup m. ● vt donner un petit coup à; **~ through** feuilleter.

flight /flaɪt/ n (of bird, plane) vol m; **~ of stairs** escalier m; (fleeing) fuite f; **take ~** prendre la fuite. **~-deck** n poste m de pilotage.

flimsy /'flɪmzi/ adj (**-ier, -iest**) (pej) mince, peu solide.

flinch /flɪntʃ/ vi (wince) broncher; (draw back) reculer.

fling /flɪŋ/ vt (pt **flung**) jeter.

flint /flɪnt/ n (rock) silex m.

flip /flɪp/ vt (pt **flipped**) donner un petit coup à; ~ **through** feuilleter. ● n chiquenaude f.

flippant /'flɪpənt/ adj désinvolte.

flipper /'flɪpə(r)/ n (of seal) nageoire f; (of swimmer) palme f.

flirt /flɜːt/ vi flirter. ● n flirteur/-euse m/f.

float /fləʊt/ vt/i (faire) flotter. ● n flotteur m; (cart) char m.

flock /flɒk/ n (of sheep) troupeau m; (of people) foule f. ● vi affluer.

flog /flɒg/ vt (pt **flogged**) (beat) fouetter; (sell 🔲) vendre.

flood /flʌd/ n inondation f; (fig) flot m. ● vt inonder. ● vi (building) être inondé; (river) déborder; (people: fig) affluer.

floodlight /'flʌdlaɪt/ n projecteur m. ● vt (pt **floodlit**) illuminer.

floor /flɔː(r)/ n sol m, plancher m; (for dancing) piste f; (storey) étage m. ● vt (knock down) terrasser; (baffle) stupéfier. ~**board** n planche f.

flop /flɒp/ vi (pt **flopped**) (drop) s'affaler; (fail 🔲) échouer; (head) tomber. ● n 🔲 échec m, fiasco m.

floppy /'flɒpɪ/ adj lâche, flasque. ~ **(disk)** n disquette f.

florist /'flɒrɪst/ n fleuriste mf.

flounder /'flaʊndə(r)/ vi (animal, person) se débattre (**in** dans); (economy) stagner. ● n flet m; (US) poisson m plat.

flour /'flaʊə(r)/ n farine f.

flourish /'flʌrɪʃ/ vi prospérer. ● vt brandir. ● n geste m élégant.

flout /flaʊt/ vt se moquer de.

flow /fləʊ/ vi couler; (circulate) circuler; (traffic) s'écouler; (hang loosely) flotter; ~ **in** affluer; ~ **into** (of river) se jeter dans. ● n (of liquid, traffic) écoulement m; (of tide) flux m; (of orders, words: fig) flot m. ~ **chart** n organigramme m.

flower /'flaʊə(r)/ n fleur f. ● vi fleurir.

flown /fləʊn/ ➡FLY.

flu /fluː/ n grippe f.

fluctuate /'flʌktjʊeɪt/ vi varier.

fluent /'fluːənt/ adj (style) aisé; **be** ~ **(in a language)** parler (une langue) couramment.

fluff /flʌf/ n peluche(s) f(pl). (down) duvet m.

fluid /'fluːɪd/ adj & n fluide (m).

fluke /fluːk/ n coup m de chance.

flung /flʌŋ/ ➡FLING.

fluoride /'flɔːraɪd/ n fluor m.

flush /flʌʃ/ vi rougir. ● vt nettoyer à grande eau; ~ **the toilet** tirer la chasse d'eau. ● n (blush) rougeur f; (fig) excitation f. ● adj ~ **with** (level with) au ras de. ◻ ~ **out** chasser.

fluster /'flʌstə(r)/ vt énerver.

flute /fluːt/ n flûte f.

flutter /'flʌtə(r)/ vi voleter; (of wings) battre. ● n (wings) battement m; (fig) agitation f; (bet 🔲) pari m.

flux /flʌks/ n changement m continuel.

fly /flaɪ/ n mouche f; (of trousers) braguette f. ● vi (pt **flew**; pp **flown**) voler; (passengers) voyager en avion; (flag) flotter; (rush) filer. ● vt (aircraft) piloter; (passengers, goods) transporter par avion; (flag) arborer. ◻ ~ **off** s'envoler.

flyer /'flaɪə(r)/ n (person) aviateur m; (circular) prospectus m.

flying /'flaɪɪŋ/ adj (saucer) volant; **with** ~ **colours** haut la main; ~ **start** excellent départ m; ~ **visit** visite f éclair (adj inv). ● n (activity) aviation f.

flyover /'flaɪəʊvə(r)/ n pont m (routier).

foal /fəʊl/ n poulain m.

foam /fəʊm/ n écume f, mousse f; ~ **(rubber)** caoutchouc m mousse. ● vi écumer, mousser.

focus /'fəʊkəs/ n (pl ~**es** or -**ci**) foyer m; (fig) centre m; **be in/out of** ~être/ ne pas être au point. ● vt/i (faire) converger; (instrument) mettre au point; (with camera) faire la mise au point (**on** sur); (fig) (se) concentrer. ~ **group** groupe m de discussion.

fodder /'fɒdə(r)/ n fourrage m.

foe /fəʊ/ n ennemi/-e m/f.

foetus /'fiːtəs/ n fœtus m.

fog /fɒg/ n brouillard m. ● vt/i (pt **fogged**) (window) (s')embuer.

foggy /'fɒgɪ/ adj brumeux; **it is ~** il fait du brouillard.

foil /fɔɪl/ n (tin foil) papier m d'aluminium; (deterrent) repoussoir m. ● vt (thwart) déjouer.

fold /fəʊld/ vt/i (paper, clothes) (se) plier; (arms) croiser; (fail) s'effondrer. ● n pli m; (for sheep) parc m à moutons; (Relig) bercail m. **folder** n (file) chemise f; (leaflet) dépliant m. **folding** adj pliant.

foliage /'fəʊlɪɪdʒ/ n feuillage m.

folk /fəʊk/ n gens mpl; **~s** parents mpl. ● adj (dance) folklorique; (music) folk.

folklore /'fəʊklɔː(r)/ n folklore m.

follow /'fɒləʊ/ vt/i suivre; **it ~s that** il s'ensuit que; **~ suit** en faire autant; **~ up** (letter) donner suite à. **follower** n partisan m.

following /'fɒləʊwɪŋ/ n partisans mpl. ● adj suivant; **~ day** lendemain. ● prep à la suite de.

fond /fɒnd/ adj (loving) affectueux; (hope) cher; **be ~ of** aimer.

fondle /'fɒndl/ vt caresser.

fondness /'fɒndnɪs/ n affection f; (for things) attachement m.

food /fuːd/ n nourriture f; **French ~** la cuisine française. ● adj alimentaire. **~ processor** n robot m (ménager).

fool /fuːl/ n idiot/-e m/f. ● vt duper. ● vi **~ around** faire l'idiot; **foolish** adj idiot.

foot /fʊt/ n (pl feet) pied m; (measure) pied m (=30.48 cm); (of stairs, page) bas m; **on ~** à pied; **on** or **to one's feet** debout; **under sb's feet** dans les jambes de qn. ● vt (bill) payer.

foot-and-mouth disease n fièvre f aphteuse.

football /'fʊtbɔːl/ n (ball) ballon m; (game) football m. **footballer** n footballeur m.

foot: ~-bridge n passerelle f; **~hold** n prise f.

footing /'fʊtɪŋ/ n **on an equal ~** sur un pied d'égalité; **be on a friendly ~ with sb** avoir des rapports amicaux avec qn; **lose one's ~** perdre pied.

foot: ~note n note f (en bas de la page). **~path** n (in countryside) sentier m; (in town) chemin m. **~print** n empreinte f (de pied). **~step** n pas m. **~wear** n chaussures fpl.

---

for /fɔː(r)/

● preposition

⋯▸ pour; **~ me** pour moi; **music ~ dancing** de la musique pour danser; **what is it ~?** ça sert à quoi?

⋯▸ (with a time period that is still continuing) depuis; **I've been waiting ~ two hours** j'attends depuis deux heures; **I haven't seen him ~ ten years** je ne l'ai pas vu depuis dix ans.

⋯▸ (with a time period that has ended) pendant; **I waited ~ two hours** j'ai attendu pendant deux heures.

⋯▸ (with a future time period) pour; **I'm going to Paris ~ six weeks** je vais à Paris pour six semaines.

⋯▸ (with distances) pendant; **I drove ~ 50 kilometres** j'ai roulé pendant 50 kilomètres.

---

forbid /fə'bɪd/ vt (pt **forbade**. pp **forbidden**) interdire, défendre (**sb to do sth** à qn de faire). **~ sb sth** interdire or défendre qch à qn; **you are forbidden to leave** il vous est interdit de partir. **forbidding** adj menaçant.

force /fɔːs/ n force f; **come into ~** entrer en vigueur; **the ~s** les forces fpl armées. ● vt forcer. □ **~ into** faire entrer de force. **~ on** imposer à. **forced** adj forcé.

force-feed vt (pt **-fed**) (person) nourrir de force; (animal) gaver.

forceful /'fɔːsfl/ adj énergique.

ford /fɔːd/ n gué m. ● vt passer à gué.

forearm /'fɔːrɑːm/ n avant-bras m inv.

forecast /'fɔːkɑːst/ vt (pt **forecast**) prévoir. ● n weather **~** météo f.

forecourt /'fɔːkɔːt/ n (of garage) devant m; (of station) cour f.

forefinger /'fɔːfɪŋgə(r)/ n index m.

forefront /'fɔːfrʌnt/ n **at/in the ~ of** à la pointe de.

foregone /'fɔːgɒn/ adj **it's a ~ conclusion** c'est couru d'avance.

foreground /'fɔːgraʊnd/ n premier plan m.

forehead /'fɒrɪd/ n front m.

foreign /'fɒrən/ adj étranger; (trade) extérieur; (travel) à l'étranger. **for-**

eigner n étranger/-ère m/f.

foreman /'fɔːmən/ n (pl **-men**) contremaître m.

foremost /'fɔːməʊst/ adj le plus éminent. ● adv first and ~ tout d'abord.

forensic /fə'rensɪk/ adj médico-légal; ~ **medicine** médecine f légale.

foresee /fɔː'siː/ vt (pt **-saw**. pp **-seen**) prévoir.

forest /'fɒrɪst/ n forêt f. **forestry** n sylviculture f.

foretaste /'fɔːteɪst/ n avant-goût m.

forever /fə'revə(r)/ adv toujours.

foreword /'fɔːwɜːd/ n avant-propos m inv.

forfeit /'fɔːfɪt/ n (penalty) peine f; (in game) gage m. ● vt perdre.

forgave /fə'geɪv/ →**FORGIVE**.

forge /fɔːdʒ/ n forge f. ● vt (metal, friendship) forger; (copy) contrefaire, falsifier. ● vi ~ **ahead** aller de l'avant, avancer. **forger** n faussaire m. **forgery** n faux m, contrefaçon f.

forget /fə'get/ vt/i (pt **forgot**. pp **forgotten**) oublier; ~ **oneself** s'oublier. **forgetful** adj distrait. ~**-me-not** n myosotis m.

forgive /fə'gɪv/ vt (pt **forgave**. pp **forgiven**) pardonner (**sb for sth** qch à qn).

fork /fɔːk/ n fourchette f; (for digging) fourche f; (in road) bifurcation f. ● vi (road) bifurquer; ~ **out** ▣ payer. **forked** adj fourchu. ~**-lift truck** n chariot m élévateur.

form /fɔːm/ n forme f; (document) formulaire m; (School) classe f; **on** ~ en forme. ● vt/i (se) former.

formal /'fɔːml/ adj officiel, en bonne et due forme; (person) compassé, cérémonieux; (dress) de cérémonie; (denial, grammar) formel; (language) soutenu. **formality** n cérémonial m; (requirement) formalité f.

format /'fɔːmæt/ n format m. ● vt (pt **formatted**) (disk) formater.

former /'fɔːmə(r)/ adj ancien; (first of two) premier. ● n **the** ~ celui-là, celle-là. **formerly** adv autrefois.

formula /'fɔːmjʊlə/ n (pl **-ae** or **-as**) formule f. **formulate** vt formuler.

fort /fɔːt/ n (Mil) fort m; **to hold the** ~ s'occuper de tout.

forth /fɔːθ/ adv from this day ~ à partir d'aujourd'hui; **and so** ~ et ainsi de suite; **go back and** ~ aller et venir.

forthcoming /fɔːθ'kʌmɪŋ/ adj à venir, prochain; (sociable ▣) communicatif.

forthright /'fɔːθraɪt/ adj direct.

forthwith /fɔːθ'wɪθ/ adv sur-le-champ.

fortnight /'fɔːtnaɪt/ n quinze jours mpl, quinzaine f.

fortnightly /'fɔːtnaɪtlɪ/ adj bimensuel. ● adv tous les quinze jours.

fortunate /'fɔːtʃənət/ adj heureux; **be** ~ avoir de la chance. **fortunately** adv heureusement.

fortune /'fɔːtʃuːn/ n fortune f; **make a** ~ faire fortune; **have the good** ~ **to** avoir la chance de. ~**-teller** n diseur/-euse m/f de bonne aventure.

forty /'fɔːtɪ/ adj & n quarante (m). ~ **winks** un petit somme.

forward /'fɔːwəd/ adj en avant; (advanced) précoce; (bold) effronté. ● n (Sport) avant m. ● adv en avant; **come** ~ se présenter; **go** ~ avancer. ● vt (letter, e-mail) faire suivre; (goods) expédier; (fig) favoriser. **forwardness** n précocité f. **forwards** adv en avant.

fossil /'fɒsl/ n & adj fossile (m).

foster /'fɒstə(r)/ vt (promote) encourager; (child) élever. ● adj (child, parent) adoptif; (family, home) de placement.

fought /fɔːt/ →**FIGHT**.

foul /faʊl/ adj (smell, weather) infect; (place, action) immonde; (language) ordurier. ● n (football) faute f. ● vt souiller, encrasser; ~ **up** ▣ gâcher. ~**-mouthed** adj grossier.

found /faʊnd/ →**FIND**. ● vt fonder. **foundation** n fondation f; (basis) fondement m; (make-up) fond m de teint. **founder** n fondateur/-trice m/f.

fountain /'faʊntɪn/ n fontaine f; ~**-pen** n stylo m à encre.

four /fɔː(r)/ adj & n quatre (m).

fourteen /fɔː'tiːn/ adj & n quatorze (m).

fourth /fɔːθ/ adj & n quatrième (mf).

four-wheel drive n (car) quatre-quatre m.

fowl /faʊl/ n (one bird) poulet m; (group) volaille f.

fox /fɒks/ n renard m. ● vt (baffle) mystifier; (deceive) tromper.

fraction /'frækʃn/ n fraction f.

fracture /'fræktʃə(r)/ n fracture f. ● vt/i (se) fracturer.

fragile /'frædʒaɪl/ adj fragile.

fragment /'frægmənt/ n fragment m.

fragrance /'freɪgrəns/ n parfum m.

frail /freɪl/ adj frêle.

frame /freɪm/ n (of building, boat) charpente f; (of picture) cadre m; (of window) châssis m; (of spectacles) monture f; ~ **of mind** humeur f. ● vt encadrer; (fig) formuler; (Jur, 🔢) monter un coup contre. ~**work** n structure f; (context) cadre m.

France /frɑːns/ n France f.

franchise /'fræntʃaɪz/ n (Pol) droit m de vote; (Comm) franchise f.

frank /fræŋk/ adj franc. ● vt affranchir. **frankly** adv franchement.

frantic /'fræntɪk/ adj frénétique. ~ **with** fou de.

fraternity /frə'tɜːnətɪ/ n (bond) fraternité f; (group, club) confrérie f.

fraud /frɔːd/ n (deception) fraude f; (person) imposteur m. **fraudulent** adj frauduleux.

fray /freɪ/ n the ~ la bataille. ● vt/i (s')effilocher.

freckle /'frekl/ n tache f de rousseur.

free /friː/ adj libre; (gratis) gratuit; (lavish) généreux; ~ **(of charge)** gratuit(ement); **a** ~ **hand** carte f blanche. ● vt (pt **freed**) libérer; (clear) dégager.

freedom /'friːdəm/ n liberté f.

free: ~ **enterprise** n la libre entreprise. ~ **kick** n coup m franc. ~**lance** adj & n free-lance (mf), indépendant/-e (m/f).

freely /'friːlɪ/ adv librement.

Freemason /'friːmeɪsn/ n francmaçon m.

Freenet /'friːnet/ n (Comput) Libertel m.

free: ~**phone**, ~ **number** n numéro m vert. ~**-range** adj (eggs) de ferme.

Freeware /'friːweə(r)/ n (Comput) Gratuiciel m.

freeway /'friːweɪ/ n (US) autoroute f.

freeze /friːz/ vt/i (pt **froze**, pp **frozen**) geler; (Culin) (se) congeler; (wages) bloquer. ● n gel m, blocage m; ~**-dried** adj lyophilisé.

freezer /'friːzə(r)/ n congélateur m.

freezing /'friːzɪŋ/ adj glacial; **below** ~ au-dessous de zéro.

freight /freɪt/ n fret m.

French /frentʃ/ adj français. ● n (Ling) français m; **the** ~ les Français mpl; ~ **bean** n haricot m vert; ~ **fries** npl frites fpl; ~**man** n Français m; ~**-speaking** adj francophone; ~ **window** n porte-fenêtre f; ~**woman** n Française f.

frenzied /'frenzɪd/ adj frénétique. **frenzy** n frénésie f.

frequent[1] /'friːkwənt/ adj fréquent.

frequent[2] /frɪ'kwent/ vt fréquenter.

fresco /'freskəʊ/ n fresque f.

fresh /freʃ/ adj frais; (different, additional) nouveau; (cheeky 🔢) culotté.

freshen /'freʃn/ vi (weather) fraîchir. ~ **up** (person) se rafraîchir.

freshly /'freʃlɪ/ adv nouvellement.

freshness /'freʃnɪs/ n fraîcheur f.

freshwater /'freʃwɔːtə(r)/ adj d'eau douce.

friction /'frɪkʃn/ n friction f.

Friday /'fraɪdɪ/ n vendredi m.

fridge /frɪdʒ/ n frigo m.

fried /fraɪd/ ➡**FRY.** ● adj frit; ~ **eggs** œufs mpl sur le plat.

friend /frend/ n ami/-e m/f. **friendly** adj (-**ier**, -**iest**) amical, gentil. **friendship** n amitié f.

frieze /friːz/ n frise f.

fright /fraɪt/ n peur f; (person, thing) horreur f.

frighten /'fraɪtn/ vt effrayer; ~ **off** faire fuir. **frightened** adj effrayé; **be** ~**ed** avoir peur (**of** de). **frightening** adj effrayant.

frill /frɪl/ n (trimming) fanfreluche f; **with no** ~**s** très simple.

fringe /frɪndʒ/ n (edging, hair) frange f; (of area) bordure f; (of society) marge f. ~ **benefits** npl avantages mpl sociaux.

frisk /frɪsk/ vt (search) fouiller.

fritter /'frɪtə(r)/ n beignet m. ● vt ~ **away** gaspiller.

frivolity /frɪ'vɒlətɪ/ n frivolité f.

frizzy /'frɪzɪ/ adj crépu.

fro ➡**TO AND FRO.**

frog /frɒg/ n grenouille f; **a** ~ **in one's throat** un chat dans la gorge.

frolic /'frɒlɪk/ vi (pt **frolicked**) s'ébattre. ● n ébats mpl.

from /frɒm/ prep de; (with time, prices) à partir de, de; (habit, conviction) par; (according to) d'après; **take ~ sb** prendre à qn; **take ~ one's pocket** prendre dans sa poche.

front /frʌnt/ n (of car, train) avant m; (of garment, building) devant m; (Mil, Pol) front m; (of book, pamphlet) début m; (appearance: fig) façade f. ● adj de devant, avant inv; (first) premier; **~ door** porte f d'entrée; **in ~ (of)** devant. **frontage** n façade f.

frontier /frʌntɪə(r)/ n frontière f.

frost /frɒst/ n gel m, gelée f; (on glass) givre m. ● vt/i (se) givrer. **~bite** n gelure f.

frosty /ˈfrɒstɪ/ adj (weather, welcome) glacial; (window) givré.

froth /frɒθ/ n (on beer) mousse f; (on water) écume f. ● vi mousser, écumer.

frown /fraʊn/ vi froncer les sourcils; **~ on** désapprouver. ● n froncement m de sourcils.

froze /frəʊz/ ➡FREEZE.

frozen /ˈfrəʊzn/ ➡FREEZE. ● adj congelé.

fruit /fruːt/ n fruit m; (collectively) fruits mpl. **fruitful** adj (discussions) fructueux. **~ machine** n machine f à sous.

frustrate /frʌˈstreɪt/ vt (plan) faire échouer; (person: Psych) frustrer; (upset 🄸) exaspérer. **frustration** n (Psych) frustration f; (disappointment) déception f.

fry /fraɪ/ vt/i (pt **fried**) (faire) frire. **frying-pan** n poêle f (à frire).

FTP abbr (**File Transfer Protocol**) (Internet) protocole m FTP.

fudge /fʌdʒ/ n caramel m mou. ● vt (issue) esquiver.

fuel /ˈfjuːəl/ n combustible m; (for car engine) carburant m. ● vt (pt **fuelled**) alimenter en combustible.

fugitive /ˈfjuːdʒətɪv/ n & a fugitif/-ive (m/f).

fulfil /fʊlˈfɪl/ vt (pt **fulfilled**) accomplir, réaliser; (condition) remplir; **~ oneself** s'épanouir. **fulfilling** adj satisfaisant. **fulfilment** n réalisation f. épanouissement m.

full /fʊl/ adj plein (of de); (bus, hotel) complet; (programme) chargé; (skirt) ample; **be ~ (up)** n'avoir plus faim; **at**

~ speed à toute vitesse. ● n in ~ intégralement; **to the ~** complètement. **~ back** n (Sport) arrière m. **~ moon** n pleine lune f. **~ name** n nom m et prénom m. **~-scale** adj (drawing etc.) grandeur nature inv; (fig) de grande envergure. **~ stop** n point m. **~-time** adj & adv à plein temps.

fully /ˈfʊlɪ/ adv complètement; **~ fledged** (member, citizen) à part entière.

fume /fjuːm/ vi rager. **fumes** npl émanations fpl, vapeurs fpl.

fun /fʌn/ n amusement m; **be ~** être chouette; **for ~** pour rire; **make ~ of** se moquer de.

function /ˈfʌŋkʃn/ n (purpose, duty) fonction f; (event) réception f. ● vi fonctionner.

fund /fʌnd/ n fonds m. ● vt fournir les fonds pour.

fundamental /fʌndəˈmentl/ adj fondamental. **fundamentalist** n intégriste mf.

funeral /ˈfjuːnərəl/ n enterrement m. ● adj funèbre.

funfair /ˈfʌnfeə(r)/ n fête f foraine.

fungus /ˈfʌŋɡəs/ n (pl **-gi**) (plant) champignon m; (mould) moisissure f.

funnel /ˈfʌnl/ n (for pouring) entonnoir m; (of ship) cheminée f.

funny /ˈfʌnɪ/ adj (**-ier, -iest**) drôle; (odd) bizarre.

fur /fɜː(r)/ n (for garment) fourrure f; (on animal) poils mpl; (in kettle) tartre m.

furious /ˈfjʊərɪəs/ adj furieux.

furnace /ˈfɜːnɪs/ n fourneau m.

furnish /ˈfɜːnɪʃ/ vt (room) meubler; (supply) fournir. **furnishings** npl ameublement m.

furniture /ˈfɜːnɪtʃə(r)/ n meubles mpl, mobilier m.

furry /ˈfɜːrɪ/ adj (animal) à fourrure; (toy) en peluche.

further /ˈfɜːðə(r)/ adj plus éloigné; (additional) supplémentaire. ● adv plus loin; (more) davantage. ● vt avancer. **~ education** n formation f continue.

furthermore /fɜːðəˈmɔː(r)/ adv en outre, de plus.

furthest /ˈfɜːðɪst/ adj le plus éloigné. ● adv le plus loin.

fury /ˈfjʊərɪ/ n fureur f.

fuse | gather

fuse /fju:z/ vt/i (melt) fondre; (unite: fig) fusionner; ~ **the lights** faire sauter les plombs. ● n (of plug) fusible m; (of bomb) amorce f.

fuss /fʌs/ n (when upset) histoire(s) f(pl); (when excited) agitation f; **make a** ~ faire des histoires. s'agiter; (about food) faire des chichis; **make a** ~ **of** faire grand cas de. ● vi s'agiter.
fussy adj (finicky) tatillon; (hard to please) difficile.

future /'fju:tʃə(r)/ adj futur. ● n avenir m; (Gram) futur m; **in** ~ à l'avenir.

fuzzy /'fʌzɪ/ adj (hair) crépu; (photograph) flou; (person 🔢) à l'esprit confus.

Gg

Gaelic /'geɪlɪk/ n gaélique m.

gag /gæg/ n (on mouth) bâillon m; (joke) blague f. ● vt (pt **gagged**) bâillonner.

gain /geɪn/ vt (respect, support) gagner; (speed, weight) prendre. ● vi (of clock) avancer. ● n (increase) augmentation f (in de); (profit) gain m.

galaxy /'gæləksɪ/ n galaxie f.

gale /geɪl/ n tempête f.

gallery /'gælərɪ/ n galerie f; (art) ~ musée m.

Gallic /'gælɪk/ adj français.

gallon /'gælən/ n gallon m (imperial = 4.546 litres; Amer. = 3.785 litres).

gallop /'gæləp/ n galop m. ● vi (pt **galloped**) galoper.

galore /gə'lɔː(r)/ adv (prizes, bargains) en abondance; (drinks, sandwiches) à gogo 🔢.

gamble /'gæmbl/ vt/i jouer. ~ **on** miser sur. ● n (venture) entreprise f risquée; (bet) pari m; (risk) risque m. **gambling** n jeu m.

game /geɪm/ n jeu m; (football) match m; (tennis) partie f; (animals, birds) gibier m. ● adj (brave) courageux. ~ **for** prêt à. ~**keeper** n gardechasse m.

gammon /'gæmən/ n jambon m.

gang /gæŋ/ n (of youths) bande f; (of workmen) équipe f. ● vi ~ **up** se li-

guer (**on**, **against** contre).

gangmaster n gangmaster m, chef m d'équipe (d'ouvriers saisonniers).

gangway /'gæŋweɪ/ n passage m; (aisle) allée f; (of ship) passerelle f.

gaol /dʒeɪl/ n & vt ➡**JAIL**.

Gap Year La prise d'une année sabbatique est une pratique répandue chez les jeunes britanniques avant d'entrer à l'université. Certains trouvent un stage dans une entreprise et en profitent pour mettre de l'argent de côté pour leurs études, mais beaucoup partent travailler ou étudier à l'étranger ou faire le tour du monde.

gap /gæp/ n trou m, vide m; (in time) intervalle m; (in education) lacune f; (difference) écart m.

gape /geɪp/ vi rester bouche bée. **gaping** adj béant.

garage /'gærɑːʒ/ n garage m. ● vt mettre au garage.

garbage /'gɑːbɪdʒ/ n (US) ordures fpl.

garden /'gɑːdn/ n jardin m. ● vi jardiner. **gardener** n jardinier/-ière m/f. **gardening** n jardinage m.

gargle /'gɑːgl/ vi se gargariser.

garish /'geərɪʃ/ adj (clothes) tape-à-l'œil.

garland /'gɑːlənd/ n guirlande f.

garlic /'gɑːlɪk/ n ail m.

garment /'gɑːmənt/ n vêtement m.

garnish /'gɑːnɪʃ/ vt garnir (**with** de). ● n garniture f.

garter /'gɑːtə(r)/ n jarretière f.

gas /gæs/ n (pl ~**es**) gaz m; (Med) anesthésie m; (petrol: US) essence f. ● adj (mask, pipe) à gaz. ● vt asphyxier; (Mil) gazer.

gash /gæʃ/ n entaille f. ● vt entailler.

gasoline /'gæsəliːn/ n (petrol: US) essence f.

gasp /gɑːsp/ vi haleter; (in surprise: fig) avoir le souffle coupé. ● n halètement m.

gate /geɪt/ n (in garden, airport) porte f; (of field, level crossing) barrière f. ~**way** n porte f; (Internet) passerelle f.

gather /'gæðə(r)/ vt (people, objects) rassembler; (pick up) ramasser; (flowers) cueillir; (fig) comprendre; ~

speed prendre de la vitesse; (sewing) froncer. ● vi (people) se rassembler; (pile up) s'accumuler. **gathering** n réunion m.

gauge /geɪdʒ/ n jauge f, indicateur m. ● vt (speed, distance) jauger; (reaction, mood) évaluer.

gaunt /gɔːnt/ adj décharné.

gauze /gɔːz/ n gaze f.

gave /geɪv/ ➡GIVE.

gay /geɪ/ adj (joyful) gai; (homosexual) gay inv. ● n gay mf.

gaze /geɪz/ vi ~ (at) regarder (fixement). ● n regard m (fixe).

GB abbr ➡GREAT BRITAIN.

gear /gɪə(r)/ n (equipment) matériel m; (Tech) engrenage m; (Auto) vitesse f; **in** ~ en prise. **out of** ~ au point mort. ● vt **to be geared to** s'adresser à. ~**box** n (Auto) boîte f de vitesses. ~**-lever**, (US) ~**-shift** n levier m de vitesse.

geese /giːs/ ➡GOOSE.

gel /dʒel/ n (for hair) gel m.

gem /dʒem/ n pierre f précieuse.

Gemini /'dʒemɪnaɪ/ n Gémeaux mpl.

gender /'dʒendə(r)/ n (Ling) genre m; (of person) sexe m.

gene /dʒiːn/ n gène m. ~ **library** n génothèque f.

general /'dʒenrəl/ adj général. ● n général m; **in** ~ en général.

general election n élections fpl législatives.

generalization /dʒenrəlaɪˈzeɪʃn/ n généralisation f. **generalize** vt/i généraliser.

general practitioner n (Med) généraliste m.

generate /'dʒenəreɪt/ vt produire.

generation /dʒenəˈreɪʃn/ n génération f.

generator /'dʒenəreɪtə(r)/ n (Electr) groupe m électrogène.

generosity /dʒenəˈrɒsətɪ/ n générosité f. **generous** adj généreux; (plentiful) copieux.

genetics /dʒɪˈnetɪks/ n génétique f.

Geneva /dʒɪˈniːvə/ n Genève.

genial /'dʒiːnɪəl/ adj affable, sympathique.

genitals /'dʒenɪtlz/ npl organes mpl génitaux.

genius /'dʒiːnɪəs/ n (pl ~es) génie m.

genome /'dʒiːnəʊm/ n génome m.

gentle /'dʒiːnəʊm/ adj (mild, kind) doux; (pressure, breeze) léger; (reminder, hint) discret.

gentleman /'dʒentlmən/ n (pl -men) (man) monsieur m; (well-bred) gentleman m.

gently /'dʒentlɪ/ adv doucement.

gents /dʒents/ npl (toilets) toilettes fpl; (on sign) 'Messieurs'.

genuine /'dʒenjʊɪn/ adj (reason, motive) vrai; (jewel, substance) véritable; (person, belief) sincère.

geography /dʒɪˈɒɡrəfɪ/ n géographie f.

geology /dʒɪˈɒlədʒɪ/ n géologie f.

geometry /dʒɪˈɒmətrɪ/ n géométrie f.

geriatric /dʒerɪˈætrɪk/ adj gériatrique.

germ /dʒɜːm/ n (Med) microbe m.

German /'dʒɜːmən/ n (person) Allemand/-e m/f; (Ling) allemand m. ● adj allemand.

German measles n rubéole f.

Germany /'dʒɜːmənɪ/ n Allemagne f.

gesture /'dʒestʃə(r)/ n geste m.

---

get /get/

past **got**; past participle **got**, **gotten** (US); present participle **getting**

● transitive verb

····▸ recevoir. **we got a letter** nous avons reçu une lettre.

····▸ (obtain) **I got a job in Paris** j'ai trouvé un travail à Paris. **I'll** ~ **sth to eat at the airport** je mangerai qch à l'aéroport.

····▸ (buy) acheter. ~ **sb a present** acheter un cadeau à qn.

····▸ (achieve) obtenir. **he got it right** il a obtenu le bon résultat. ~ **good grades** avoir de bonnes notes.

····▸ (fetch) chercher. **go and** ~ **a chair** va chercher une chaise.

····▸ (transport) prendre. **we can** ~ **the bus** on peut prendre le bus.

····▸ (understand Ⅱ) comprendre. **now let me** ~ **this right** alors si je comprends bien...

····➤ (experience) ~ **a surprise** être surpris. ~ **a shock** avoir un choc.

····➤ (illness) ~ **measles** attraper la rougeole. ~ **a cold** s'enrhumer.

····➤ (ask or persuade) ~ **him to call me** dis-lui de m'appeler. **I'll ~ her to help me** je lui demanderai de m'aider.

····➤ (cause to be done) ~ **a TV repaired** faire réparer une télévision. ~ **one's hair cut** se faire couper les cheveux.

● *intransitive verb*

····➤ devenir. **he's getting old** il vieillit; **it's getting late** il se fait tard.

····➤ (in passives) ~ **married** se marier. ~ **hurt** être blessé.

····➤ (arrive) arriver. ~ **to the airport** arriver à l'aéroport. □ ~ **about** (*person*) se déplacer. ~ **along** (manage) se débrouiller; (*progress*) avancer. ~ **along with** s'entendre avec. ~ **at** (reach) atteindre; (*imply*) vouloir dire. ~ **away** partir; (escape) s'échapper. ~ **back** vi revenir. ● vt récupérer. ~ **by** vi (manage) se débrouiller. ● vt (pass) passer. ~ **down** vt/i descendre. ● vt (depress) déprimer. ~ **in** entrer. ~ **into** (*car*) monter dans; (*dress*) mettre. ~ **off** vt (bus) descendre; (remove) enlever. ● vi (from bus) descendre; (leave) partir; (Jur) être acquitté. ~ **on** vi (to bus) monter; (succeed) réussir. ● vt (bus) monter. ~ **on with** (*person*) s'entendre avec; (*job*) attaquer. ~ **out** sortir. ~ **out of** (fig) se soustraire. ~ **over** (illness) se remettre de. ~ **round** (rule) contourner; (*person*) entortiller. ~ **through** vi passer; (on phone) ~ **through to sb** avoir qn. ● vt traverser. ~ **up** se lever. ~ **up to** faire.

getaway /ˈgetəweɪ/ n fuite f.
ghastly /ˈgɑːstlɪ/ adj (**-ier, -iest**) affreux.
gherkin /ˈgɜːkɪn/ n cornichon m.
ghetto /ˈgetəʊ/ n ghetto m.
ghost /gəʊst/ n fantôme m.
giant /ˈdʒaɪənt/ n & adj géant (m).

gibberish /ˈdʒɪbərɪʃ/ n baragouin m, charabia m.
giblets /ˈdʒɪblɪts/ npl abats mpl.
giddy /ˈgɪdɪ/ adj (**-ier, -iest**) vertigineux. **be** or **feel ~** avoir le vertige.
gift /gɪft/ n (present) cadeau m; (ability) don m.
gifted /ˈgɪftɪd/ adj doué.
gift wrap n papier m cadeau.
gigantic /dʒaɪˈgæntɪk/ adj gigantesque.
giggle /ˈgɪgl/ vi ricaner (sottement), glousser. ● n ricanement m; **the ~s** le fou rire.
gimmick /ˈgɪmɪk/ n truc m.
gin /dʒɪn/ n gin m.
ginger /ˈdʒɪndʒə(r)/ n gingembre m. ● adj (hair) roux. ~ **beer** n boisson f gazeuse au gingembre. ~**bread** n pain m d'épices.
gingerly /ˈdʒɪndʒəlɪ/ adv avec précaution.
giraffe /dʒɪˈrɑːf/ n girafe f.
girl /gɜːl/ n (child) (petite) fille f; (young woman) (jeune) fille f. ~ **band** n girls band m. ~**friend** n amie f; (of boy) petite amie f.
giro /ˈdʒaɪrəʊ/ n virement m bancaire; (cheque) mandat m.
gist /dʒɪst/ n essentiel m.
give /gɪv/ vt (pt **gave**; pp **given**) donner; (gesture) faire; (laugh, sigh) pousser; ~ **sb sth** donner qch à qn. ● vi donner; (yield) céder; (stretch) se détendre. ● n élasticité f. □ ~ **away** donner; (secret) trahir; ~ **back** rendre. ~ **in** (yield) céder (**to** à). ~ **off** (heat, fumes) dégager; (signal, scent) émettre. ~ **out** vt distribuer. ~ **over** (devote) consacrer; (stop 🄸) cesser; ~ **up** vt/i (renounce) renoncer (à); (yield) céder. ~ **oneself up** se rendre. ~ **way** céder; (collapse) s'effondrer.
given /ˈgɪvn/ ➡ GIVE. ● adj donné. ~ **name** n prénom m.
glad /glæd/ adj content. **gladly** adv avec plaisir.
glamorous /ˈglæmərəs/ adj séduisant, ensorcelant.
glamour, (US) **glamor** /ˈglæmə(r)/ n enchantement m, séduction f.
glance /glɑːns/ n coup m d'œil. ● vi ~ **at** jeter un coup d'œil à.
gland /glænd/ n glande f.

glare /gleə(r)/ vi briller très fort. ~ **at** regarder d'un air furieux. ● n (of lights) éclat m (aveuglant); (stare: fig) regard m furieux. **glaring** adj (dazzling) éblouissant; (obvious) flagrant.

glass /glɑːs/ n verre m. **glasses** npl (spectacles) lunettes fpl.

glaze /gleɪz/ vt (door) vitrer; (pottery) vernisser. ● n vernis m.

gleam /gliːm/ n lueur f. ● vi luire.

glide /glaɪd/ vi glisser; (of plane) planer. **glider** n planeur m.

glimpse /glɪmps/ n (insight) aperçu m; **catch a** ~ **of** entrevoir.

glitter /'glɪtə(r)/ vi scintiller. ● n scintillement m.

global /'gləʊbl/ adj (world-wide) mondial; (allembracing) global. ~ **warming** n réchauffement m de la planète.

globalization /gləʊbəlaɪˈzeɪʃən/ n globalisation f.

globe /gləʊbəlaɪˈzeɪʃən/ n globe m.

gloom /gluːm/ n obscurité f; (sadness: fig) tristesse f. **gloomy** adj triste; (pessimistic) pessimiste.

glorious /'glɔːrɪəs/ adj splendide; (deed, hero) glorieux.

glory /'glɔːrɪ/ n gloire f; (beauty) splendeur f. ● vi ~ **in** être très fier de.

gloss /glɒs/ n lustre m, brillant m. ● adj brillant. ● vi ~ **over** (make light of) glisser sur; (cover up) dissimuler.

glossary /'glɒsərɪ/ n glossaire m.

glossy /'glɒsɪ/ adj brillant.

glove /glʌv/ n gant m. ~ **compartment** n (Auto) boîte f à gants.

glow /gləʊ/ vi (fire) rougeoyer; (person, eyes) rayonner. ● n rougeoiement m, éclat m. **glowing** adj (report) enthousiaste.

glucose /'gluːkəʊs/ n glucose m.

glue /gluː/ n colle f. ● vt (pres p **gluing**) coller.

GM abbr (genetically modified) transgénique.

gnaw /glɪf/ vt/i ronger.

GNP abbr (**Gross National Product**) produit m national brut, PNB m.

go /gəʊ/
present go, goes; past went; past participle gone

● intransitive verb

····➤ aller; ~ **to school/town/market** aller à l'école/en ville/au marché. ~ **for a swim/walk** aller nager/se promener.

····➤ (leave) s'en aller. **I must be** ~**ing** il faut que je m'en aille.

····➤ (vanish) **the money's gone** il n'y a plus d'argent. **my bike's gone** mon vélo n'est plus là.

····➤ (work, function) marcher. **is the car** ~**ing?** est-ce que la voiture marche?

····➤ (become) devenir. ~ **blind** devenir aveugle. ~ **pale/red** pâlir/rougir.

····➤ (turn out, progress) aller. **how's it going?** comment ça va? **how did the exam** ~ ? comment s'est passé l'examen?

····➤ (in future tenses) **be** ~**ing to do** aller faire.

● noun

····➤ (turn) tour m; (try) essai m; **have a** ~! essaie!; **full of** ~ 🄸 dynamique.

□ **go across** traverser. **go after** poursuivre. **go away** partir. ~ **away!** va-t-en!, allez-vous-en! **go back** retourner. ~ **back in** rentrer. ~ **back to work** reprendre le travail. **go down** (quality, price) baisser; (person) descendre; (sun) se coucher. **go in** entrer. **go in for** (exam) se présenter à. **go off** (leave) partir; (bomb) exploser; (alarm clock) sonner; (milk) tourner; (light) s'éteindre. **go on** (continue) continuer; (light) s'allumer; ~ **on doing** continuer à faire. **what's** ~**ing on?** qu'est-ce qui se passe? **go out** sortir; (light, fire) s'éteindre. **go over** vérifier. **go round** (be enough) être assez. ~ **round to see sb** passer voir qn. **go through** (check) examiner; (search) fouiller; ~ **through a difficult time** traverser une période difficile. **go together** aller ensemble. **go under** (sink) couler; (fail) échouer. **go up** (person) monter; (price, salary) augmenter. **go without** se passer de.

go-ahead /ˈɡəʊəhed/ n feu m vert.
● adj dynamique.

goal /ɡəʊl/ n but m. **~keeper** n gardien m de but. **~-post** n poteau m de but.

goat /ɡəʊt/ n chèvre f.

gobble /ˈɡɒbl/ vt engouffrer.

go-between /ˈɡəʊbɪtwiːn/ n intermédiaire mf.

god /ɡɒd/ n dieu m. **~child** n (pl **-children**) filleul/-e m/f. **~daughter** n filleule f.

goddess /ˈɡɒdɪs/ n déesse f.

god: ~father n parrain m. **~mother** n marraine f. **~send** n aubaine f. **~son** n filleul m.

goggles /ˈɡɒɡlz/ npl lunettes fpl (protectrices).

going /ˈɡəʊɪŋ/ n **it is slow/hard ~** c'est lent/difficile. ● adj (price, rate) actuel.

go-kart /ˈɡəʊkɑːt/ n kart m.

gold /ɡəʊld/ n or m. ● adj en or, d'or.

golden /ˈɡəʊldən/ adj en or, d'or; (in colour) doré; (opportunity) unique.

gold: ~fish n poisson m rouge. **~-plated** adj plaqué or. **~smith** n orfèvre m.

golf /ɡɒlf/ n golf m. **~-course** n terrain m de golf.

gone /ɡɒn/ ➡GO. ● adj parti. **~ six o'clock** six heures passées. **the butter's all ~** il n'y a plus de beurre.

good /ɡʊd/ adj (better, best) bon; (weather) beau; (well-behaved) sage; **as ~ as** (almost) pratiquement. **that's ~ of you** c'est gentil (de ta part). **be ~ with** savoir s'y prendre avec. **feel ~** se sentir bien. **it is ~ for you** ça vous fait du bien. ● n bien m; **do ~** faire du bien. **is it any ~?** est-ce que c'est bien?. **it's no ~** ça ne vaut rien. **it is no ~ shouting** ça ne sert à rien de crier. **for ~** pour toujours. **~ afternoon** interj bonjour. **~bye** interj & n au revoir (m inv). **~ evening** interj bonsoir. **G~ Friday** n Vendredi m saint. **~-looking** adj beau. **~ morning** interj bonjour. **~-natured** adj gentil.

goodness /ˈɡʊdnɪs/ n bonté f; **my ~!** mon Dieu!

goodnight interj bonsoir, bonne nuit.

goods /ɡʊdz/ npl marchandises fpl.

goodwill /ɡʊdˈwɪl/ n bonne volonté f.

google® /ˈɡuːɡl/vt/i chercher sur (le moteur de recherche) Google®, googler.

goose /ɡuːs/ n (pl **geese**) oie f. **gooseberry** n groseille f à maquereau. **~-pimples** npl chair f de poule.

gorge /ɡɔːdʒ/ n (Geog) gorge f. ● vt **~ oneself** se gaver (**on** de).

gorgeous /ˈɡɔːdʒəs/ adj magnifique, splendide, formidable.

gorilla /ɡəˈrɪlə/ n gorille m.

gory /ˈɡɔːrɪ/ adj (-ier, -iest) sanglant; (horrific: fig) horrible.

gospel /ˈɡɒspl/ n évangile m; **the G~** l'Évangile m.

gossip /ˈɡɒsɪp/ n bavardages mpl, commérages mpl; (person) bavard/-e m/f. ● vi bavarder.

got /ɡɒt/ ➡GET. ● **have ~** avoir. **have ~ to do** devoir faire.

govern /ˈɡʌvn/ vt/i gouverner. **governess** n gouvernante f. **government** n gouvernement m. **governor** n gouverneur m.

gown /ɡaʊn/ n robe f; (of judge, teacher) toge f.

GP abbr ➡GENERAL PRACTITIONER.

GPS abbr (Global Positioning System) GPS m.

grab /ɡrɑː/ vt (pt **grabbed**) saisir.

grace /ɡreɪs/ n grâce f. ● vt (honour) honorer; (adorn) orner. **graceful** adj gracieux.

gracious /ˈɡreɪʃəs/ adj (kind) bienveillant; (elegant) élégant.

grade /ɡreɪd/ n catégorie f; (of goods) qualité f; (on scale) grade m; (school mark) note f; (class: US) classe f. ● vt classer; (school work) noter. **~ school** n (US) école f primaire.

gradual /ˈɡrædʒʊəl/ adj progressif, graduel. **gradually** adv progressivement, peu à peu.

graduate¹ /ˈɡrædʒʊət/ n (Univ) diplômé/-e m/f.

graduate² /ˈɡrædjʊeɪt/ vi obtenir son diplôme. ● vt graduer. **graduation** n remise f des diplômes.

graffiti /ɡrəˈfiːtɪ/ npl graffiti mpl.

graft /ɡrɑːft/ n (Med, Bot) greffe f; (work) boulot m. ● vt greffer (**on to** sur); (work) trimer.

grain /greɪn/ n (seed, quantity, texture) grain m; (in wood) fibre f.

gram /græm/ n gramme m.

grammar /'græmə(r)/ n grammaire f.

grand /grænd/ adj magnifique; (duke, chorus) grand.

grandad /'grændæd/ n [T] papy m.

grand: ~**child** n (girl) petite-fille f; (boy) petit-fils m; **her** ~**children** ses petits-enfants mpl. ~**daughter** n petite-fille f. ~**father** n grand-père m. ~**ma** →GRANNY. ~**mother** n grandmère f. ~**parents** npl grandsparents mpl. ~**piano** n piano m à queue. ~**son** n petit-fils m. ~**stand** n tribune f.

granny /'grænɪ/ n [T] mémé f, mamie f.

grant /grɑːnt/ vt (permission) accorder; (request) accéder à; (admit) admettre (**that** que); **take sth for** ~**ed** considérer qch comme une chose acquise. ● n subvention f; (Univ) bourse f.

granule /'grænjuːl/ n (of sugar, salt) grain m; (of coffee) granulé m.

grape /greɪp/ n grain m de raisin. ~**s** raisin(s) m (pl).

grapefruit /'greɪpfruːt/ n inv pamplemousse m.

graph /grɑːf/ n graphique m.

graphic /'græfɪk/ adj (arts) graphique; (fig) vivant, explicite. **graphics** npl (Comput) graphiques mpl.

grasp /grɑːsp/ vt saisir. ● n (hold) prise f; (strength of hand) poigne f; (reach) portée f; (fig) compréhension f.

grass /grɑːs/ n herbe f. ~**hopper** n sauterelle f. ~**land** n prairie f.

grass roots npl peuple m. ● adj (movement) populaire; (support) de base.

grate /greɪt/ n (hearth) âtre m; (fire basket) grille f. ● vt râper. ● vi grincer.

grateful /'greɪtfl/ adj reconnaissant.

grater /'greɪtə(r)/ n râpe f.

gratified /'grætɪfaɪd/ adj très heureux. **gratify** vt faire plaisir à.

grating /'greɪtɪŋ/ n (bars) grille f; (noise) grincement m.

gratitude /'grætɪtjuːd/ n reconnaissance f.

gratuity /grə'tjuːətɪ/ n (tip) pourboire m; (bounty) Mil) prime f.

grave¹ /greɪv/ n tombe f. ● adj (serious) grave.

grave² /grɑːv/ adj ~ **accent** accent m grave.

gravel /'grævl/ n graviers mpl.

grave: ~**stone** n pierre f tombale. ~**yard** n cimetière m.

gravity /'grævətɪ/ n (seriousness) gravité f; (force) pesanteur f.

gravy /'greɪvɪ/ n jus m (de viande).

gray /greɪ/ n (US) adj & n →GREY.

graze /greɪz/ vi (eat) paître. ● vt (touch) frôler; (scrape) écorcher. ● n écorchure f.

grease /griːs/ n graisse f. ● vt graisser. **greasy** adj graisseux.

great /greɪt/ adj grand; (very good [T]) génial [T], formidable [T], (grandfather, grandmother) arrière.

Great Britain n Grande-Bretagne f.

greatly /'greɪtlɪ/ adv (very) très; (much) beaucoup.

Greece /griːs/ n Grèce f.

greed /griːd/ n avidité f; (for food) gourmandise f. **greedy** adj avide; gourmand.

Greek /griːk/ n (person) Grec/-que m/f; (Ling) grec m. ● adj grec.

green /griːn/ adj vert; (fig) naïf. ● n vert m; (grass) pelouse f; (golf) green m; ~**s** légumes mpl verts. ~ **grocer** n marchand/-e m/f de fruits et légumes.

Green Card Document qui permet à un étranger de vivre et de travailler aux États-Unis, et qui lui donne les mêmes droits que ceux d'un citoyen américain, à l'exception du droit de vote. Les services d'immigration américains distribuent 50 000 green cards par an au moyen d'une loterie à laquelle participent des millions de candidats.

---

greenhouse n serre f; ~ **effect** effet m de serre.

greet /griːt/ vt (welcome) accueillir; (address politely) saluer. **greeting** n accueil m.

greetings /'griːtɪŋz/ interj salutations [T] ● npl (Christmas) vœux mpl. ~ **card** n carte f de vœux.

grew /gruː/ →GROW.

grey /greɪ/ adj gris; (fig) triste; **go** ~ (hair, person) grisonner. ● n gris m. ~**hound** n lévrier m.

grid /grɪd/ n grille f; (network: Electr) réseau m.

grief /griːf/ n chagrin m; **come to ～** (person) avoir un malheur; (fail) tourner mal.

grievance /ˈgriːvns/ n griefs mpl.

grieve /griːv/ vt/i (s')affliger; **～ for** pleurer.

grill /grɪl/ n (cooking device) gril m; (food) grillade f; (Auto) calandre f. ● vt/i (faire) griller; (interrogate) mettre sur la sellette.

grim /grɪm/ adj sinistre.

grimace /grɪˈmeɪs/ n grimace f. ● vi grimacer.

grime /graɪm/ n crasse f.

grin /grɪn/ vi (pt grinned) sourire. ● n (large) sourire m.

grind /graɪnd/ vt (pt ground) (grain) écraser; (coffee) moudre; (sharpen) aiguiser; **～ one's teeth** grincer des dents. ● vi **～ to a halt** s'immobiliser. ● n corvée f.

grip /grɪp/ vt (pt gripped) saisir; (interest) passionner. ● n prise f; (strength of hand) poigne f; **come to ～s with** en venir aux prises avec.

grisly /ˈgrɪzlɪ/ adj (-ier, -iest) (remains) macabre; (sight) horrible.

gristle /ˈgrɪsl/ n cartilage m.

grit /grɪt/ n (for roads) sable m; (fig) courage m. ● vt (pt gritted) (road) sabler; (teeth) serrer.

groan /grəʊn/ vi gémir. ● n gémissement m.

grocer /ˈgrəʊsə(r)/ n (person) épicier/-ière m/f; (shop) épicerie f. **groceries** npl (shopping) courses fpl; (goods) épicerie f. **grocery** n (shop) épicerie f.

groin /grɔɪn/ n aine f.

groom /gruːm/ n marié m; (for horses) palefrenier/-ière /m/f. ● vt (horse) panser; (fig) préparer.

groove /gruːv/ n (for door etc.) rainure f; (in record) sillon m.

grope /grəʊp/ vi tâtonner. **～ for** chercher à tâtons.

gross /grəʊs/ adj (behaviour) vulgaire; (Comm) brut. ● n inv grosse f.

grotto /ˈgrɒtəʊ/ n (pl **～es**) grotte f.

grouch /graʊtʃ/ vi (grumble 🗊) rouspéter, râler.

ground[1] /graʊnd/ n terre f, sol m; (area) terrain m; (reason) raison f; (Electr, US) masse f; **～s** terres fpl, parc m; (of coffee) marc m; **on the ～** par terre. **lose ～** perdre du terrain. ● vt/i (Naut) échouer; (aircraft) retenir au sol.

ground[2] /graʊnd/ ➡GRIND. ● adj **～ beef** (US) bifteck m haché.

ground: ～ floor n rez-de-chaussée m inv. **～work** n travail m préparatoire.

group /gruːp/ n groupe m. ● vt/i (se) grouper. **～ware** n (Comput) logiciel m de groupe.

grovel /ˈgrɒvl/ vi (pt grovelled) ramper.

grow /grəʊ/ vi (pt grew; pp grown) (person) grandir; (plant) pousser; (become) devenir; (crime) augmenter. ● vt cultiver; **～ up** devenir adulte, grandir. **grower** n cultivateur/-trice m/f.

growl /graʊl/ vi (dog) gronder; (person) grogner. ● n grognement m.

grown /grəʊn/ ➡GROW. ● adj adulte. **～-up** adj & n adulte (mf).

growth /grəʊθ/ n (of person, plant) croissance f; (in numbers) accroissement m; (of hair, tooth) pousse f; (Med) grosseur f, tumeur f.

grudge /grʌdʒ/ vt **～ doing** faire à contrecœur. **～ sb sth** (success, wealth) en vouloir à qn de qch. ● n rancune f; **have a ～ against** en vouloir à.

grumble /ˈgrʌmbl/ vi ronchonner, grogner (at après).

grumpy /ˈgrʌmpɪ/ adj (-ier, -iest) grincheux, grognon.

grunt /grʌnt/ vi grogner. ● n grognement m.

guarantee /gærənˈtiː/ n garantie f. ● vt garantir.

guard /gɑːd/ vt protéger; (watch) surveiller. ● vi **～ against** se protéger contre. ● n (Mil) garde f; (person) garde m; (on train) chef m de train.

guardian /ˈgɑːdɪən/ n gardien/-ne m/f; (of orphan) tuteur/-trice m/f.

guess /ges/ vt/i deviner; (suppose) penser. ● n conjecture f.

guest /gest/ n invité/-e m/f; (in hotel) client/-e m/f. **～-house** n pension f. **～-room** n chambre f d'amis.

guidance /'gaɪdns/ n (advice) conseils mpl; (information) information f.

guide /gaɪd/ n (person, book) guide m; (girl) guide f. ● vt guider. ~**book** n guide m. ~ **dog** n chien m d'aveugle. ~**line** n indication f; (advice) conseils mpl.

guillotine /'gɪləti:n/ n (for execution) guillotine f; (for paper) massicot m.

guilt /gɪlt/ n culpabilité f. **guilty** adj coupable.

guinea-pig /'gɪnɪpɪg/ n (animal) cochon m d'Inde; (fig) cobaye m.

guitar /gɪ'tɑ:(r)/ n guitare f.

gulf /gʌlf/ n (part of sea) golfe m; (hollow) gouffre m.

gull /gʌl/ n mouette f, (larger) goéland m.

gullible /'gʌləbl/ adj crédule.

gully /'gʌlɪ/ n (ravine) ravin m; (drain) rigole f.

gulp /gʌlp/ vt ~ (**down**) avaler en vitesse. ● vi (from fear etc.) avoir la gorge serrée. ● n gorgée f.

gum /gʌm/ n (Anat) gencive f; (glue) colle f; (for chewing) chewing-gum m. ● vt (pt **gummed**) gommer.

gun /gʌn/ n (pistol) revolver m; (rifle) fusil m; (large) canon m. ● vt (pt **gunned**) ~ **down** abattre. ~ **fire** n fusillade f. ~**powder** n poudre f à canon. ~**shot** n coup m de feu.

gurgle /'gɜ:gl/ n (of water) gargouillement m; (of baby) gazouillis m. ● vi (water) gargouiller; (baby) gazouiller.

gush /gʌʃ/ vi ~ (**out**) jaillir. ● n jaillissement m.

gust /gʌst/ n rafale f; (of smoke) bouffée f.

gut /gʌt/ n (belly 🔢) ventre m. ● vt (pt **gutted**) (fish) vider; (of fire) dévaster. **gutted** adj 🔢 abattu.

guts /gʌts/ npl 🔢 (insides of human) tripes fpl 🔢; (insides of animal, building) entrailles fpl; (courage) cran m 🔢.

gutter /'gʌtə(r)/ n (on roof) gouttière f; (in street) caniveau m.

guy /gaɪ/ n (man 🔢) type m.

gym /dʒɪm/ n (place) gymnase m; (activity) gym(nastique) f.

gymnasium /dʒɪm'neɪzɪəm/ n gymnase m.

gymnastics /dʒɪm'næstɪks/ npl gymnastique f.

gynaecologist /gaɪnə'kɒlədʒɪst/ n gynécologue mf.

gypsy /'dʒɪpsɪ/ n bohémien/-ne m/f.

Hh

habit /'hæbɪt/ n habitude f; (costume: Relig) habit m; **be in/get into the** ~ **of** avoir/prendre l'habitude de.

habitual /hə'bɪtʃʊəl/ adj (usual) habituel; (smoker, liar) invétéré.

hack /hæk/ n (writer) écrivaillon m. ● vi (Comput) pirater; ~ **into** s'introduire dans. ● vt tailler. **hacker** n (Comput) pirate m informatique.

hackneyed /'hæknɪd/ adj rebattu.

had /hæd/ →HAVE.

haddock /'hædək/ n inv églefin m.

haemorrhage /'hemərɪdʒ/ n hémorragie f.

haggard /'hægəd/ adj (person) exténué; (face, look) défait.

haggle /'hægl/ vi marchander; ~ **over** sth discuter du prix de qch.

hail /heɪl/ n grêle f. ● vt (greet) saluer; (taxi) héler. ● vi grêler; ~ **from** venir de. ~**stone** n grêlon m.

hair /heə(r)/ n (on head) cheveux mpl; (on body, of animal) poils mpl; (single strand on head) cheveu m; (on body) poil m. ~**brush** n brosse f à cheveux. ~**cut** n coupe f de cheveux. ~**do** n 🔢 coiffure f. ~**dresser** n coiffeur/-euse m/f. ~**-drier** n séchoir m (à cheveux). ~**pin** n épingle f à cheveux. ~ **remover** n dépilatoire m. ~**-style** n coiffure f.

hairy /'heərɪ/ adj (-ier, -iest) poilu; (terrifying) 🔢 horrifiant.

half /hɑ:f/ n (pl **halves**) (part) moitié f; (fraction) demi m; ~ **a dozen** une demi-douzaine; ~ **an hour** une demi-heure; **four and a** ~ quatre et demi; **an hour and a** ~ une heure et demie; ~ **and half** moitié moitié; **in** ~ en deux. ● adj demi; ~ **price** à moitié prix. ● adv à moitié. ~**-back** n (Sport) demi m. ~**-hearted** adj tiède.

~**-mast** n at ~**-mast** en berne.

~**-term** n vacances fpl de demi-trimestre. ~**-time** n mi-temps f.

~**way** adv à mi-chemin. ~**wit** n imbécile mf.

hall /hɔːl/ n (in house) entrée f; (corridor) couloir m; (in airport) hall m; (for events) salle f; ~ **of residence** résidence f universitaire.

hallmark /'hɔːlmɑːk/ n (on gold) poinçon m; (fig) caractéristique f.

hallo →HELLO.

Hallowe'en /hæləʊ'iːn/ n la veille de la Toussaint.

halt /hɔːlt/ n arrêt m; (temporary) suspension f; (Mil) halte f. ● vt (proceedings) interrompre; (arms sales, experiments) mettre fin à. ● vi (vehicle) s'arrêter; (army) faire halte.

halve /hɑːv/ vt (time) réduire de moitié; (fruit) couper en deux.

ham /hæm/ n jambon m.

hamburger /'hæmbɜːgə(r)/ n hamburger m.

hammer /'hæmə(r)/ n marteau m. ● vt/i marteler; ~ **sth into sth** enfoncer qch dans qch; ~ **sth out** (agreement) parvenir à qch.

hammock /'hæmək/ n hamac m.

hamper /'hæmpə(r)/ n panier m. ● vt gêner.

hamster /'hæmstə(r)/ n hamster m.

hand /hænd/ n main f; (of clock) aiguille f; (writing) écriture f; (worker) ouvrier/-ière m/f; (cards) jeu m; **give sb a** ~ donner un coup de main à qn; **at** ~ proche; **on** ~ disponible; **on the one** ~...**on the other** ~ d'une part...d'autre part; **to** ~ à portée de la main. ● vt ~ **sb sth**, ~**sth to sb** donner qch à qn. □ ~**in** or **over** remettre; ~ **out** distribuer. ~**bag** n sac m à main. ~**baggage** n bagages mpl à main. ~**book** n manuel m. ~**brake** n frein m à main. ~**cuffs** npl menottes fpl.

handicap /'hændɪkæp/ n handicap m. ● vt (pt **handicapped**) handicaper.

handkerchief /'hæŋkətʃɪf/ n (pl ~s) mouchoir m.

handle /'hændl/ n (of door, bag) poignée f; (of implement) manche m; (of cup, bucket) anse f; (of frying pan)

queue f. ● vt (manage) manier; (deal with) traiter; (touch) manipuler.

handout /'hændaʊt/ n document m; (leaflet) prospectus m; (money) aumône f.

hands-free kit n kit m mains libres conducteur.

handshake /'hændʃeɪk/ n poignée f de main.

handsome /'hænsəm/ adj (good looking) beau; (generous) généreux.

handwriting /'hændraɪtɪŋ/ n écriture f.

handy /'hændɪ/ adj (-ier, -iest) (book, skill) utile; (size, shape, tool) pratique; (person) doué. ~**man** n (pl -men) bricoleur m.

hang /hæŋ/ vt (pt **hung**) (from hook, hanger) accrocher; (from rope) suspendre; (pt **hanged**) (person) pendre. ● vi (from hook) être accroché; (from rope) être suspendu; (person) être pendu. ● n get the ~ of doing ⒤ piger comment faire ⒤. □ ~ **about** traîner; ~ **on** ⒤ hold out) tenir; (wait) attendre; ~ **on to sth** s'agripper à qch; ~ **out** vi ⒤ (live) crécher ⒤; (spend time) passer son temps; vt (washing) étendre; ~ **up** (telephone) raccrocher.

hanger /'hæŋə(r)/ n (for clothes) cintre m.

hang-gliding /'hæŋglaɪdɪŋ/ n vol m libre.

hangover /'hæŋəʊvə(r)/ n gueule f de bois ⒤.

hang-up /'hæŋʌp/ n ⒤ complexe m.

haphazard /hæp'hæzəd/ adj peu méthodique.

happen /'hæpən/ vi arriver, se passer; ~ **to sb** arriver à qn; **it so** ~**s that** il se trouve que.

happily /'hæpɪlɪ/ adv joyeusement; (fortunately) heureusement.

happiness /'hæpɪnɪs/ n bonheur m.

happy /'hæpɪ/ adj (-ier, -iest) heureux; **I'm not** ~ je ne suis pas content; ~ **with sth** satisfait de qch; ~ **medium** juste milieu m.

harass /hə'ræs/ vt harceler. **harassment** n harcèlement m.

harbour, (US) **harbor** /'hɑːbə(r)/ n port m. ● vt (shelter) héberger.

hard /hɑːd/ adj dur; (difficult) difficile, dur; (evidence, fact) solide; **find it ~to do** avoir du mal à faire; **~ on sb** dur envers qn. ● adv (work) dur; (pull, hit, cry) fort; (think, study) sérieusement. **~board** n aggloméré m. **~ copy** n (Comput) tirage m. **~ disk** n disque m dur.

hardly /'hɑːdlɪ/ adv à peine; (expect, hope) difficilement; **~ ever** presque jamais.

hardship /'hɑːdʃɪp/ n (poverty) privations fpl; (ordeal) épreuve f.

hard: **~ shoulder** n bande f d'arrêt d'urgence. **~ up** adj 🄶 fauché 🄶. **~ware** n (Comput) matériel m, hardware m; (goods) quincaillerie f. **~-working** adj travailleur.

hardy /'hɑːdɪ/ adj (-ier, -iest) résistant.

hare /heə(r)/ n lièvre m.

harm /hɑːm/ n mal m; **there is no ~ in** il n'y a pas de mal à. ● vt (person) faire du mal à; (object) endommager. **harmful** adj nuisible. **harmless** adj inoffensif.

harmony /'hɑːmənɪ/ n harmonie f.

harness /'hɑːnɪs/ n harnais m. ● vt (horse) harnacher; (use) exploiter.

harp /hɑːp/ n harpe f. ● vi **~ on (about)** rabâcher.

harrowing /'hærəʊɪŋ/ adj (experience) atroce; (story) déchirant.

harsh /hɑːʃ/ adj (punishment) sévère; (person) dur; (light) cru; (voice) rude; (chemical) corrosif. **harshness** n dureté f.

harvest /'hɑːvɪst/ n récolte f; **the wine ~** les vendanges fpl. ● vt (corn) moissonner; (vegetables) récolter.

has /hæz/ ➡HAVE.

hassle /'hæsl/ n complications fpl. ● vt 🄶 talonner (about à propos de); (worry) stresser.

haste /heɪst/ n hâte f; **in ~** à la hâte; **make ~** se dépêcher.

hasty /'heɪstɪ/ adj (-ier, -iest) précipité.

hat /hæt/ n chapeau m.

hatch /hætʃ/ n (Aviat) panneau m mobile; (Naut) écoutille f; (for food) passeplats m inv. ● vt/i (eggs) (faire) éclore.

hate /heɪt/ n haine f. ● vt détester; (violently) haïr; (sport, food) avoir horreur de.

hatred /'heɪtrɪd/ n haine f.

haughty /'hɔːtɪ/ adj (-ier, -iest) hautain.

haul /hɔːl/ vt tirer. ● n (by thieves) butin m; (by customs) saisie f; **it will be a long ~** l'étape sera longue; **long/short ~** (transport) long/court courrier m. **haulage** n transport m routier. **haulier** n (firm) société f de transports routiers.

haunt /hɔːnt/ vt hanter. ● n lieu m de prédilection.

---

have /hæv/

- *present* have, has;
- *past* had;
- *past participle* had

● *transitive verb*

····▸ (possess) avoir; **I ~ (got) a car** j'ai une voiture; **they ~ (got) problems** ils ont des problèmes.

····▸ (do sth) **~ a try** essayer; **~ a bath** prendre un bain.

····▸ **~ sth done** faire faire qch; **~ your hair cut** se faire couper les cheveux.

● *auxiliary verb*

····▸ (in perfect tenses) avoir; être; **I ~ seen him** je l'ai vu; **she had fallen** elle était tombée.

····▸ (in tag questions) **you've seen her, haven't you?** tu l'as vue, n'est-ce pas?; **you haven't seen her, ~you?** tu ne l'as pas vue, par hasard?

····▸ (in short answers) **'you've never met him'**—**'yes I ~'** 'tu ne l'as jamais rencontré'—'mais si!'

····▸ (must) **~ to** devoir; **I ~ to go** je dois partir; **you don't ~ to do it** tu n'es pas obligé de le faire.

➡ For expressions such as **have a walk, have dinner** ➡walk, dinner.

---

haven /'heɪvn/ n refuge m; (fig) havre m.

havoc /'hævək/ n dévastation f.

hawk /hɔːk/ n faucon m.

hay /heɪ/ n foin m; **~ fever** rhume m des foins.

haywire /ˈheɪwaɪə(r)/ adj go ~ (plans) dérailler; (machine) se détraquer.

hazard /ˈhæzəd/ n risque m; ~ (warning) **lights** feux mpl de détresse. ● vt hasarder.

haze /heɪz/ n brume f.

hazel /ˈheɪzl/ n (bush) noisetier m. ~**nut** n noisette f.

hazy /ˈheɪzɪ/ adj (-ier, -iest) (misty) brumeux; (fig) vague.

he /hiː/ pron il; (emphatic) lui; **here ~ is** le voici.

head /hed/ n tête f; (leader) chef m; (of beer) mousse f; ~**s or tails?** pile ou face? ● vt (list) être en tête de; (team) être à la tête de; (chapter) intituler; ~ **the ball** faire une tête. ● vi ~ **for** se diriger vers.

headache /ˈhedeɪk/ n mal m de tête; **have a ~** avoir mal à la tête.

heading /ˈhedɪŋ/ n titre m; (subject category) rubrique f.

head: ~**lamp,** ~**light** n phare m. ~**line** n gros titre m. ~**master** n directeur m. ~**mistress** n directrice f. ~ **office** n siège m social. ~**on** adj & adv de front. ~**phones** npl casque m. ~**quarters** npl siège m social; (Mil) quartier m général. ~ **rest** n (Auto) repose-tête m inv. ~**strong** adj têtu.

heal /hiːl/ vt/i guérir.

health /helθ/ n santé f. ~ **centre** n centre m médico-social. ~ **food** n produits mpl diététiques. ~ **insurance** n assurance f maladie.

healthy /ˈhelθɪ/ adj (person, plant, skin, diet) sain; (air) salutaire.

heap /hiːp/ n tas m; ~**s of** 🄸 un tas de. ● vt ~ **(up)** entasser.

hear /hɪə(r)/ vt (pt heard) entendre; (news, rumour) apprendre; (lecture, broadcast) écouter. ● vi entendre; ~ **from** recevoir des nouvelles de; ~ **of** or **about** entendre parler de.

hearing /ˈhɪərɪŋ/ n ouïe f; (of case) audience f; **give sb a ~** écouter qn. ~**aid** n prothèse f auditive.

hearse /hɜːs/ n corbillard m.

heart /hɑːt/ n cœur m; ~**s** (cards) cœur m; **at ~** au fond; **by ~** par cœur; **be ~broken** avoir le cœur brisé; **lose ~** perdre courage. ~ **attack** n crise f cardiaque. ~**burn** n brû-

lures fpl d'estomac. ~**felt** adj sincère.

hearth /hɑːθ/ n foyer m.

heartily /ˈhɑːtɪlɪ/ adv (greet) chaleureusement; (laugh, eat) de bon cœur.

hearty /ˈhɑːtɪ/ adj (-ier, -iest) (sincere) chaleureux; (meal) solide.

heat /hiːt/ n chaleur f; (contest) épreuve f éliminatoire. ● vt (house) chauffer; ~ **(up)** (food) faire chauffer; (reheat) réchauffer. **heated** adj (fig) passionné; (lit) (pool) chauffé. **heater** n appareil m de chauffage.

heather /ˈheðə(r)/ n bruyère f.

heating /ˈhiːtɪŋ/ n chauffage m.

heave /hiːv/ vt (lift) hisser; (pull) traîner péniblement; **a sigh** pousser un soupir. ● vi (pull) tirer de toutes ses forces; (retch) avoir un haut-le-cœur.

heaven /ˈhevn/ n ciel m.

heavily /ˈhevɪlɪ/ adv lourdement; (smoke, drink) beaucoup.

heavy /ˈhevɪ/ adj (-ier, -iest) lourd; (cold, work) gros; (traffic) dense. ~ **goods vehicle** n poids m lourd. ~**-handed** adj maladroit. ~**weight** n poids m lourd.

Hebrew /ˈhiːbruː/ n (person) Hébreu m; (Ling) hébreu m. ● adj hébreu; (Ling) hébraïque.

hectic /ˈhektɪk/ adj (activity) intense; (period, day) mouvementé.

hedge /hedʒ/ n haie f. ● vi (in answering) se dérober.

hedgehog /ˈhedʒhɒg/ n hérisson m.

heel /hiːl/ n talon m.

hefty /ˈheftɪ/ adj (-ier, -iest) (person) costaud 🄸; (object) pesant.

height /haɪt/ n hauteur f; (of person) taille f; (of plane, mountain) altitude f; (of fame, glory) apogée m; (of joy, folly, pain) comble m.

heir /eə(r)/ n héritier/-ière m/f. **heiress** n héritière f. **heirloom** n objet m de famille.

held /held/ ➡HOLD.

helicopter /ˈhelɪkɒptə(r)/ n hélicoptère m.

hell /hel/ n enfer m.

hello /həˈləʊ/ interj bonjour!; (on phone) allô!

helmet /ˈhelmɪt/ n casque m.

help /help/ vt/i aider (**to do** à faire); ~ **(sb) with a bag/the housework** aider qn à porter un sac/à faire le ménage; **~ oneself** se servir; **he can't ~ it** ce n'est pas de sa faute. ● *n* aide *f.* ● *interj* au secours! **helper** *n* aide *mf.* **helpful** *adj* utile; (*person*) serviable. **helping** *n* portion *f.* **helpless** *adj* impuissant.

hem /hem/ *n* ourlet *m.* ● *vt* (*pt* **hemmed**) faire un ourlet à; **~ in** cerner.

hen /hen/ *n* poule *f.*

hence /hens/ *adv* (for this reason) d'où; (from now) d'ici. **henceforth** *adv* désormais.

hepatitis /hepəˈtaɪtɪs/ *n* hépatite *f.*

her /hɜː(r)/ *pron* la, l'; (indirect object) lui; **it's ~** c'est elle; **for ~** pour elle. ● *adj* son, sa; *pl* ses.

herb /hɜːb/ *n* herbe *f;* **~s** (Culin) fines herbes *fpl.*

herd /hɜːd/ *n* troupeau *m.*

here /hɪə(r)/ *adv* ici; **~!** (take this) tiens!; tenez!; **~ is, ~ are** voici; **I'm ~** je suis là. **hereabouts** *adv* par ici. **hereafter** *adv* après; (in book) ci-après. **hereby** *adv* par le présent acte; (in letter) par la présente.

herewith /hɪəwɪð/ *adv* ci-joint.

heritage /ˈherɪtɪdʒ/ *n* patrimoine *m.* **~ tourism** *n* tourisme *m* culturel.

hernia /ˈhɜːnɪə/ *n* hernie *f.*

hero /ˈhɪərəʊ/ *n* (*pl* **~es**) héros *m.*

heroic /hɪˈrəʊɪk/ *adj* héroïque.

heroin /ˈherəʊɪn/ *n* héroïne *f.*

heroine /ˈherəʊɪn/ *n* héroïne *f.*

heron /ˈherən/ *n* héron *m.*

herring /ˈherɪŋ/ *n* hareng *m.*

hers /hɜːz/ *pron* le sien, la sienne, les sien(ne)s; **it is ~** c'est à elle *or* le sien *or* la sienne.

herself /hɜːˈself/ *pron* (emphatic) elle-même; (reflexive) se; **proud of ~** fière d'elle; **by ~** toute seule.

hesitate /ˈhezɪteɪt/ *vi* hésiter. **hesitation** *n* hésitation *f.*

heterosexual /hetərəˈsekʃʊəl/ *adj & n* hétérosexuel/-le (*m/f*).

hexagon /ˈheksəgən/ *n* hexagone *m.*

heyday /ˈheɪdeɪ/ *n* apogée *m.*

HGV *abbr* ➔**HEAVY GOODS VEHICLE.**

hi /haɪ/ *interj* 🔲 salut! 🔲.

hiccup /ˈhɪkʌp/ *n* hoquet *m;* **(the) ~s** le hoquet. ● *vi* hoqueter.

hide /haɪd/ *vt* (*pt* **hid;** *pp* **hidden**) cacher (**from** à). ● *vi* se cacher (**from** de); **go into hiding** se cacher. ● *n* (skin) peau *f.*

hideous /ˈhɪdɪəs/ *adj* (*monster, object*) hideux; (*noise*) affreux.

hiding /ˈhaɪdɪŋ/ *n* **go into ~** se cacher; **give sb a ~** administrer une correction à qn.

hierarchy /ˈhaɪərɑːkɪ/ *n* hiérarchie *f.*

hi-fi /ˈhaɪfaɪ/ *n* (chaîne *f*) hi-fi *f inv.*

high /haɪ/ *adj* haut; (*price, number*) élevé; (*priest, speed*) grand; (*voice*) aigu; **in the ~ season** en pleine saison. ● *n* **a (new) ~** un niveau record. ● *adv* haut. **~brow** *adj & n* intellectuel/-le (*m/f*). **~ chair** *n* chaise *f* haute. **~ court** *n* cour *f* suprême. **higher education** *n* enseignement *m* supérieur. **~-jump** *n* saut *m* en hauteur. **~-level** *adj* à haut niveau.

highlight /ˈhaɪlaɪt/ *n* (best moment) point *m* fort; **~s** (in hair) reflet *m;* (artificial) mèches *fpl;* (Sport) résumé *m.* ● *vt* (emphasize) souligner.

highly /ˈhaɪlɪ/ *adv* extrêmement; (paid) très bien; **speak/think ~ of** dire/penser beaucoup de bien de.

Highness /ˈhaɪnɪs/ *n* Altesse *f.*

high: ~-rise (building) *n* tour *f.* **~ school** *n* lycée *m.* **~-speed** *adj* (train) à grande vitesse; (film) ultrarapide. **~ street** *n* rue *f* principale. **~-tech** *adj* de pointe.

High School Établissement d'enseignement secondaire aux États-Unis, souvent subdivisé en *Junior high school* (12-14 ans) et *Senior high school* (15-17 ans) où les élèves passent un examen pour être admis dans un *College* (établissement d'enseignement supérieur). *i*

---

highway /ˈhaɪweɪ/ *n* route *f* nationale; (US) autoroute *f;* **~ code** code *m* de la route.

hijack /ˈhaɪdʒæk/ *vt* détourner. ● *n* détournement *m.* **hijacker** *n* pirate *m* (de l'air).

hike /haɪk/ *n* randonnée *f;* **price ~** hausse *f* de prix. ● *vi* faire de la randonnée.

hilarious /hɪˈleərɪəs/ adj désopilant.

hill /hɪl/ n colline f; (slope) côte f. **hilly** adj vallonné.

him /hɪm/ pron le, l'; (indirect object) lui; **it's** ~ c'est lui; **for** ~ pour lui.

himself /hɪmˈself/ pron (emphatic) lui-même; (reflexive) se; **proud of** ~ fier de lui; **by** ~ tout seul.

hind /haɪnd/ adj de derrière.

hinder /ˈhɪndə(r)/ vt (hamper) gêner; (prevent) empêcher. **hindrance** n obstacle m, gêne f.

hindsight /ˈhaɪndsaɪt/ n **with** ~ rétrospectivement.

Hindu /hɪnˈduː/ n Hindou/-e m/f. ● adj hindou.

hinge /hɪndʒ/ n charnière f. ● vi ~ **on** dépendre de.

hint /hɪnt/ n allusion f; (of spice, accent) pointe f; (of colour) touche f; (advice) conseil m. ● vt laisser entendre. ● vi ~ **at** faire allusion à.

hip /hɪp/ n hanche f.

hippopotamus /hɪpəˈpɒtəməs/ n (pl ~es) hippopotame m.

hire /ˈhaɪə(r)/ vt (thing) louer; (person) engager. ● n location f. ~**-car** n voiture f de location. ~**-purchase** n achat m à crédit.

his /hɪz/ adj son, sa, pl ses. ● pron le sien, la sienne, les sien(ne)s; **it is** ~ c'est à lui or le sien or la sienne.

hiss /hɪs/ n sifflement m. ● vt/i siffler.

history /ˈhɪstrɪ/ n histoire f; **make** ~ entrer dans l'histoire.

hit /hɪt/ vt (pt **hit**; pres p **hitting**) frapper; (collide with) heurter; (find) trouver; (affect, reach) toucher. ● vi ~ **on** (find) tomber sur; ~ **it off** s'entendre bien (with avec). ● n (blow) coup m; (fig) succès m; (song) tube m 🄸; (on Internet) visite f, accès m; (result) page f trouvée, résultat m.

hitch /hɪtʃ/ vt (fasten) accrocher; ~ **up** remonter. ● n (snag) anicroche f. ~**-hike** vi faire du stop 🄸. ~**-hiker** n auto-stoppeur/-euse m/f.

hi-tech /ˈhɪtʃhaɪk/ adj de pointe.

HIV abbr (**human immunodeficiency virus**) VIH m.

hive /haɪv/ n ruche f. ● vt ~ **off** séparer; (industry) céder.

HIV-positive adj séropositif.

hoard /hɔːd/ vt amasser; (supplies) stocker. ● n trésor m; (of provisions) provisions fpl.

hoarse /hɔːs/ adj enroué.

hoax /həʊks/ n canular m.

hobby /ˈhɒbɪ/ n passe-temps m inv.

hockey /ˈhɒkɪ/ n hockey m.

hog /hɒɡ/ n cochon m. ● vt (pt **hogged**) 🄸 monopoliser.

hold /həʊld/ vt (pt **held**) tenir; (contain) contenir; (conversation, opinion) avoir; (shares, record, person) détenir; ~ **(the line), please** ne quittez pas. ● vi (rope, weather) tenir. ● n prise f; **get** ~ **of** attraper; (ticket) se procurer; (person) (by phone) joindre; **on** ~ en attente. ▫ ~ **back** (contain) retenir; (hide) cacher; ~ **down** (job) garder; (person) tenir; (costs) limiter; ~ **on** (stand firm) tenir bon; (wait) attendre; ~ **on to** (keep) garder; (cling to) se cramponner à; ~ **out** vt (offer) offrir; vi (resist) tenir le coup; ~ **up** (support) soutenir; (delay) retarder; (rob) attaquer.

holder /ˈhəʊldə(r)/ n détenteur/-trice m/f; (of passport, post) titulaire mf; (for object) support m.

holding /ˈhəʊldɪŋ/ n participation f.

hold-up /ˈhəʊldʌp/ n retard m; (of traffic) embouteillage m; (robbery) hold-up m inv.

hole /həʊl/ n trou m.

holiday /ˈhɒlədeɪ/ n vacances fpl; (public) jour m férié; (time off) congé m. ● vi passer les vacances. ● adj de vacances. ~**-maker** n vacancier/-ière m/f.

Holland /ˈhɒlənd/ n Hollande f.

hollow /ˈhɒləʊ/ adj creux; (fig) faux. ● n creux m. ● vt creuser.

holly /ˈhɒlɪ/ n houx m.

holy /ˈhəʊlɪ/ adj (-**ier**, -**iest**) saint; (water) bénit; **H**~ **Ghost**, **H**~ **Spirit** Saint-Esprit m.

homage /ˈhɒmɪdʒ/ n hommage m.

home /həʊm/ n (place to live) logement m; maison f; (institution) maison f; (family base) foyer m; (country) pays m. ● adj de la maison, du foyer; (of family) de famille; (Pol) intérieur; (match, visit) à domicile. ● adv (at) ~ à la maison, chez soi; **come** or **go** ~ rentrer; (from abroad) rentrer dans son pays; **feel at ~ with** être à l'aise avec. **~ computer** n ordinateur m, PC m.

homeland /'həʊmlənd/n patrief; **~ security** n sécurité f des frontières.

homeless /'həʊmlɪs/ adj sans abri. ● n **the ~** les sans-abri mpl.

homely /'həʊmlɪ/ adj (**-ier, -iest**) (cosy) accueillant; (simple) sans prétention; (person: US) sans attraits.

home: ~-made adj (fait) maison. **H~ Office** n ministère m de l'Intérieur. **~ page** n (Internet) page f d'accueil. **H~ Secretary** n Ministre m de l'Intérieur. **~sick** adj be **~sick** avoir le mal du pays. **~work** n devoirs mpl.

homosexual /hɒmə'sekʃʊəl/ adj & n homosexuel/-le (m/f).

honest /'ɒnɪst/ adj (truthful) intègre; (trustworthy) honnête; (sincere) franc. **honestly** adv honnêtement; franchement. **honesty** n honnêteté f.

honey /'hʌnɪ/ n miel m; (person 🔲) chéri/-e m/f. **~moon** n voyage m de noces; (fig) lune f de miel.

honk /hɒŋk/ vi klaxonner.

honorary /'ɒnərərɪ/ adj (person) honoraire; (degree) honorifique.

honour, (US) **honor** /'ɒnə(r)/ n honneur m. ● vt honorer.

hood /hʊd/ n capuchon m; (on car, pram) capote f; (car engine cover: US) capot m.

hoof /huːf/ n (pl **~s**) sabot m.

hook /hʊk/ n crochet m; (on garment) agrafe f; (for fishing) hameçon m; **off the ~** tiré d'affaire; (phone) décroché. ● vt accrocher.

hoot /huːt/ n (of owl) (h)ululement m; (of car) coup m de klaxon. ● vi (owl) (h)ululer; (car) klaxonner; (jeer) huer.

hoover /'huːvə(r)/ vt **~ a room** passer l'aspirateur dans une pièce.

Hoover® /'huːvə(r)/ n aspirateur m.

hop /hɒp/ vi (pt **hopped**) sauter (à cloche-pied); **~ in!** 🔲 vas-y, monte! ● n bond m; **~s** houblon m.

hope /həʊp/ n espoir m. ● vt/i espérer; **~ for** espérer avoir; **I ~ so** je l'espère.

hopeful /'həʊpfl/ adj (news, sign) encourageant; (person) plein d'espoir; (mood) optimiste. **hopefully** adv (with luck) avec un peu de chance; (with hope) avec optimisme.

hopeless /'həʊplɪs/ adj désespéré; (useless: fig) nul 🔲.

horizon /hə'raɪzn/ n horizon m.

horizontal /hɒrɪ'zɒntl/ adj horizontal.

hormone /'hɔːməʊn/ n hormone f.

horn /hɔːn/ n corne f; (of car) klaxon® m; (Mus) cor m.

horoscope /'hɒrəskəʊp/ n horoscope m.

horrible /'hɒrɪbl/ adj horrible.

horrid /'hɒrɪd/ adj horrible.

horrific /hə'rɪfɪk/ adj horrifiant.

horrify /'hɒrɪfaɪ/ vt horrifier.

horror /'hɒrə(r)/ n horreur f. ● adj (film, story) d'épouvante.

horse /hɔːs/ n cheval m. **~back** n on **~back** à cheval. **~-chestnut** n marron m (d'Inde). **~-man** n (pl **-men**) cavalier m. **~power** n puissance f (en chevaux). **~-race** n course f de chevaux. **~-radish** n raifort m. **~shoe** n fer m à cheval. **~ show** n concours m hippique.

hose /həʊz/ n tuyau m. ● vt arroser. **~-pipe** n tuyau m.

hospitable /hɒ'spɪtəbl/ adj hospitalier.

hospital /'hɒspɪtl/ n hôpital m.

host /həʊst/ n (to guests) hôte m; (on TV) animateur m; (Internet) ordinateur m hôte; **a ~ of** une foule de; (Relig) hostie f.

hostage /'hɒstɪdʒ/ n otage m; **hold sb ~** garder qn en otage.

hostel /'hɒstl/ n foyer m; (**youth**) **~** auberge f (de jeunesse).

hostess /'həʊstɪs/ n hôtesse f.

hostile /'hɒstaɪl/ adj hostile.

hot /hɒt/ adj (**hotter, hottest**) chaud; (Culin) épicé; **be** or **feel ~** avoir chaud; **it is ~** il fait chaud; **in ~ water** 🔲 dans le pétrin. ● vt/i (pt **hotted**) **~ up** 🔲 chauffer. **~ air balloon** n montgolfière f. **~ dog** n hot-dog m.

hotel /həʊ'tel/ n hôtel m.

hot: ~headed adj impétueux. **~ list** n (Internet) signets mpl favoris. **~plate** n plaque f chauffante. **~ water bottle** n bouillotte f.

hound /haʊnd/ n chien m de chasse. ● vt poursuivre.

hour /auə(r)/ n heure f.

hourly /'auəlɪ/ adj horaire; **on an ~ basis** à l'heure. ● adv toutes les heures.

house¹ /haus/ n maison f; (Pol) Chambre f; **on the ~** aux frais de la maison.

house² /hauz/ vt loger; (of building) abriter.

household /'haushəuld/ n (house, family) ménage m. ● adj ménager.

house: **~keeper** n gouvernante f. **~-proud** adj méticuleux. **~-warming** n pendaison f de crémaillère. **~wife** n (pl **-wives**) ménagère f. **~work** n travaux mpl ménagers.

housing /'hauzɪŋ/ n logement m; **~ association** service m de logement; **~ development** cité f; (smaller) lotissement m.

hover /'hɒvə(r)/ vi (bird) voleter; (vacillate) vaciller. **hovercraft** n aéroglisseur m.

how /hau/ adv comment; **~ are you?** comment allez-vous?; **~ long/tall is...?** quelle est la longueur/hauteur de...?; **~ many?, ~ much?** combien?; **~ pretty!** comme or que c'est joli!; **~ about a walk?** si on faisait une promenade?; **~ do you do?** (greeting) enchanté.

however /hau'evə(r)/ adv (nevertheless) cependant; **~ hard I try** j'ai beau essayer; **~ much it costs** quel que soit le prix; **~ young/poor he is** si jeune/pauvre soit-il; **~ you like** comme tu veux.

howl /haul/ n hurlement m. ● vi hurler.

HP abbr ➡HIRE-PURCHASE.

hp abbr ➡HORSEPOWER.

HQ abbr ➡HEADQUARTERS.

hub /hʌb/ n moyeu m; (fig) centre m.

hug /hʌg/ vt (pt **hugged**) serrer dans ses bras. ● n étreinte f; **give sb a ~** serrer qn dans ses bras.

huge /hju:dʒ/ adj énorme.

hull /hʌl/ n (of ship) coque f.

hum /hʌm/ vt/i (pt **hummed**) (person) fredonner; (insect) bourdonner; (engine) ronronner. ● n bourdonnement m; ronronnement m.

human /'hju:mən/ adj humain. ● n humain m. **~ being** n être m humain.

humane /hju:'meɪn/ adj (person) humain; (act) d'humanité; (killing) sans cruauté.

humanitarian /hju:mænɪ'teərɪən/ adj humanitaire.

humanity /hju:'mænətɪ/ n humanité f.

humble /'hʌmbl/ adj humble.

humid /'hju:mɪd/ adj humide.

humiliate /hju:'mɪlɪeɪt/ vt humilier.

humorous /'hju:mərəs/ adj humoristique; (person) plein d'humour.

humour, (US) **humor** /'hju:mə(r)/ n humour m; (mood) humeur f. ● vt amadouer.

hump /hʌmp/ n bosse f. ● vt 🔲 porter.

hunchback /'hʌntʃbæk/ n bossu/-e m/f.

hundred /'hʌndrəd/ adj & n cent (m); **two ~ and one** deux cent un; **~s of** des centaines de. **hundredth** adj & n centième (mf).

hung /hʌŋ/ ➡HANG.

Hungarian /hʌŋ'geərɪən/ n (person) Hongrois/-e m/f; (Ling) hongrois m. ● adj hongrois. **Hungary** n Hongrie f.

hunger /'hʌŋgə(r)/ n faim f. ● vi **~ for** avoir faim de.

hungry /'hʌŋgrɪ/ adj (**-ier, -iest**) affamé; **be ~** avoir faim.

hunt /hʌnt/ vt/i chasser; **~ for** chercher. ● n chasse f. **hunter** n chasseur m. **hunting** n chasse f.

hurdle /'hɜ:dl/ n (Sport) haie f; (fig) obstacle m.

hurricane /'hʌrɪkən/ n ouragan m.

hurry /'hʌrɪ/ vi se dépêcher; **~ out** sortir précipitamment. ● vt (work) terminer à la hâte; (person) bousculer. ● n hâte f; **in a ~** pressé.

hurt /hɜ:t/ vt/i (pt **hurt**) faire mal (à); (injure, offend) blesser. ● adj blessé. ● n blessure f.

hurtle /'hɜ:tl/ vi **~ down** dévaler; **~ along a road** foncer sur une route.

husband /'hʌzbənd/ n mari m.

hush /hʌʃ/ vt faire taire; **~ up** (news) étouffer. ● n silence m. ● interj chut!

husky /'hʌskɪ/ adj (**-ier, -iest**) enroué. ● n husky m.

hustle /'hʌsl/ vt (push, rush) bousculer. ● vi (hurry) se dépêcher; (work: US) se démener. ● n **~ and bustle** agitation f.

hut /hʌt/ n cabane f.

hyacinth /'haɪəsɪnθ/ n jacinthe f.

hydrant /'haɪdrənt/ n (**fire**) ~ bouche f d'incendie.

hydraulic /haɪ'drɔːlɪk/ adj hydraulique.

hydroelectric /haɪdrəʊɪ'lektrɪk/ adj hydroélectrique.

hydrogen /'haɪdrədʒən/ n hydrogène m; ~ **bomb** bombe f à hydrogène.

hyena /haɪ'iːnə/ n hyène f.

hygiene /'haɪdʒiːn/ n hygiène f. **hygienic** adj hygiénique.

hymn /hɪm/ n cantique m; (fig) hymne m.

hype /haɪp/ n ① battage m publicitaire. ● vt ~ (**up**) (film, book) faire du battage pour.

hyperactive /haɪpər'æktɪv/ adj hyperactif.

hyperlink /'haɪpəlɪŋk/ n hyperlien m.

hypermarket /'haɪpəmɑːkɪt/ n hypermarché m.

hypertext /'haɪpətekst/ n hypertexte m.

hyphen /'haɪfn/ n trait m d'union.

hypnosis /hɪp'nəʊsɪs/ n hypnose f.

hypocrisy /hɪ'pɒkrəsɪ/ n hypocrisie f. **hypocrite** n hypocrite mf. **hypocritical** adj hypocrite.

hypothesis /haɪ'pɒθəsɪs/ n (pl **-ses**) hypothèse f.

hysteria /hɪ'stɪərɪə/ n hystérie f. **hysterical** adj hystérique.

hysterics /hɪ'sterɪks/ npl crise f de nerfs; **be in** ~ rire aux larmes.

I i

I /aɪ/ pron je, j'; (stressed) moi.

ice /aɪs/ n glace f; (on road) verglas m. ● vt (cake) glacer. ● vi ~ (**up**) (window) se givrer; (river) geler. ~**box** n (US) réfrigérateur m. ~**-cream** n glace f. ~**-cube** n glaçon m. ~ **hockey** n hockey m sur glace.

Iceland /'aɪslənd/ n Islande f. **Icelander** n Islandais/-e m/f. **Icelandic** adj & n islandais (m).

ice: ~ **lolly** n glace f (sur bâtonnet). ~ **rink** n patinoire f. ~ **skate** n patin m à glace.

icicle /'aɪsɪkl/ n stalactite f (de glace).

icing /'aɪsɪŋ/ n (sugar) glaçage m.

icy /'aɪsɪ/ adj (**-ier, -iest**) (hands, wind) glacé; (road) verglacé; (manner, welcome) glacial.

ID /ɪd/ n pièce f d'identité; ~ **card** carte f d'identité.

idea /aɪ'dɪə/ n idée f.

ideal /aɪ'diːəl/ adj idéal. ● n idéal m.

identical /aɪ'dentɪkl/ adj identique.

identification /aɪdentɪfɪ'keɪʃn/ n identification f; (papers) pièce f d'identité.

identify /aɪ'dentɪfaɪ/ vt identifier. ● vi ~ **with** s'identifier à.

identikit /aɪ'dentɪkɪt/ n ~ **picture** portraitrobot m.

identity /aɪ'dentətɪ/ n identité f; ~ **theft** vol m d'identité.

ideological /aɪdɪə'lɒdʒɪkl/ adj idéologique.

idiom /'ɪdɪəm/ n (phrase) idiome m; (language) parler m, langue f. **idiomatic** adj idiomatique.

idiosyncrasy /ɪdɪə'sɪŋkrəsɪ/ n particularité f.

idiot /'ɪdɪət/ n idiot/-e m/f. **idiotic** adj idiot.

idle /'aɪdl/ adj (lazy) paresseux; (doing nothing) oisif; (boast, threat) vain. ● vi (engine) tourner au ralenti. ● vt ~ **away** gaspiller.

idol /'aɪdl/ n idole f. **idolize** vt idolâtrer.

idyllic /ɪ'dɪlɪk/ adj idyllique.

i.e. abbr c-à-d, c'est-à-dire.

if /ɪf/ conj si.

ignite /ɪg'naɪt/ vt/i (s')enflammer.

ignition /ɪg'nɪʃn/ n (Auto) allumage m; ~ (**switch**) contact m; ~ **key** clé f de contact.

ignorance /'ɪgnərəns/ n ignorance f. **ignorant** adj ignorant (**of** de). **ignorantly** adv par ignorance.

ignore /ɪg'nɔː(r)/ vt (person) ignorer; (mistake, remark) ne pas relever; (feeling, fact) ne pas tenir compte de.

ill /ɪl/ adj malade. ● adv mal. ● n mal m. ~**-advised** adj malavisé. ~ **at ease** adj mal à l'aise. ~**-bred** adj mal élevé.

illegal /ɪ'liːgl/ adj illégal.

illegible /ɪˈledʒəbl/ adj illisible.

illegitimate /ɪlɪˈdʒɪtɪmət/ adj illégitime.

ill: ~-**fated** adj malheureux. ~ **feeling** n ressentiment m.

illiterate /ɪˈlɪtərət/ adj & n analphabète (mf).

illness /ˈɪlnɪs/ n maladie f.

ill-treat vt maltraiter.

illuminate /ɪˈluːmɪneɪt/ vt éclairer; (decorate with lights) illuminer. **illumination** n éclairage m. illumination f.

illusion /ɪˈluːʒn/ n illusion f.

illustrate /ˈɪləstreɪt/ vt illustrer. **illustration** n illustration f. **illustrative** adj qui illustre.

image /ˈɪmɪdʒ/ n image f; (of firm, person) image f de marque. **imagery** n images fpl.

imaginable /ɪˈmædʒɪnəbl/ adj imaginable. **imaginary** adj imaginaire. **imagination** n imagination f. **imaginative** adj plein d'imagination.

imagine /ɪˈmædʒɪn/ vt (s')imaginer (that que); ~ **being rich** s'imaginer riche.

imbalance /ɪmˈbæləns/ n déséquilibre m.

imitate /ˈɪmɪteɪt/ vt imiter.

immaculate /ɪˈmækjʊlət/ adj impeccable.

immaterial /ɪməˈtɪərɪəl/ adj sans importance (to pour; that que).

immature /ɪməˈtjʊə(r)/ adj (person) immature; (plant) qui n'est pas arrivé à maturité.

immediate /ɪˈmiːdɪət/ adj immédiat.

immediately /ɪˈmiːdɪətlɪ/ adv immédiatement. ● conj dès que.

immense /ɪˈmens/ adj immense. **immensely** adv extrêmement, immensément. **immensity** n immensité f.

immerse /ɪˈmɜːs/ vt plonger (in dans). **immersion** n immersion f; **immersion heater** chauffe-eau m inv électrique.

immigrant /ˈɪmɪgrənt/ n & adj immigré/-e (m/f). (newly-arrived) immigrant/-e (m/f). **immigrate** vi immigrer. **immigration** n immigration f.

imminent /ˈɪmɪnənt/ adj imminent.

immobilizer /ɪˈməʊbɪlaɪzə(r)/ n système m antidémarrage.

immoral /ɪˈmɒbɪlaɪzə(r)/ adj immoral.

immortal /ɪˈmɔːtl/ adj immortel.

immune /ɪˈmjuːn/ adj immunisé (from, to contre); (reaction, system) immunitaire. **immunity** n immunité f. **immunization** n immunisation f. **immunize** vt immuniser.

impact /ˈɪmpækt/ n impact m.

impair /ɪmˈpeə(r)/ vt (performance) affecter; (ability) affaiblir.

impart /ɪmˈpɑːt/ vt communiquer, transmettre.

impartial /ɪmˈpɑːʃl/ adj impartial.

impassable /ɪmˈpɑːsəbl/ adj (barrier) infranchissable; (road) impraticable.

impassive /ɪmˈpæsɪv/ adj impassible.

impatience /ɪmˈpeɪʃns/ n impatience f. **impatient** adj impatient; **get impatient** s'impatienter. **impatiently** adv impatiemment.

impeccable /ɪmˈpekəbl/ adj impeccable.

impede /ɪmˈpiːd/ vt entraver.

impediment /ɪmˈpedɪmənt/ n entrave f; **speech** ~ défaut m d'élocution.

impending /ɪmˈpendɪŋ/ adj imminent.

imperative /ɪmˈperətɪv/ adj urgent. ● n impératif m.

imperfect /ɪmˈpɜːfɪkt/ adj incomplet; (faulty) défectueux. ● n (Gram) imparfait m. **imperfection** n imperfection f.

imperial /ɪmˈpɪərɪəl/ adj impérial; (measure) conforme aux normes britanniques. **imperialism** n impérialisme m.

impersonal /ɪmˈpɜːsənl/ adj impersonnel.

impersonate /ɪmˈpɜːsəneɪt/ vt se faire passer pour; (mimic) imiter.

impertinent /ɪmˈpɜːtɪnənt/ adj impertinent.

impervious /ɪmˈpɜːvɪəs/ adj imperméable (to à).

impetuous /ɪmˈpetʃʊəs/ adj impétueux.

impetus /ˈɪmpɪtəs/ n impulsion f.

impinge /ɪmˈpɪndʒ/ vi ~ **on** affecter; (encroach) empiéter sur.

implement /ˈɪmplɪmənt/ n instrument m; (tool) outil m. ● vt exécuter, mettre en application; (software) implanter. **implementation** n mise f en application.

implicit /ɪmˈplɪsɪt/ adj (implied) implicite (in dans); (unquestioning) absolu.

imply /ɪm'plaɪ/ vt (assume, mean) impliquer; (insinuate) laisser entendre.

impolite /ɪmpə'laɪt/ adj impoli.

import¹ /ɪm'pɔːt/ vt importer.

import² /'ɪmpɔːt/ n (article) importation f; (meaning) signification f.

importance /ɪm'pɔːtns/ n importance f. **important** adj important.

impose /ɪm'pəʊz/ vt imposer (**on sb** à qn; **on sth** sur qch). ● vi s'imposer; ~ **on sb** abuser de la bienveillance de qn. **imposing** adj imposant.

impossible /ɪm'pɒsəbl/ adj impossible. ● n the ~ l'impossible m.

impotent /'ɪmpətənt/ adj impuissant.

impound /ɪm'paʊnd/ vt confisquer, saisir.

impoverish /ɪm'pɒvərɪʃ/ vt appauvrir.

impractical /ɪm'præktɪkl/ adj peu réaliste.

impregnable /ɪm'pregnəbl/ adj imprenable.

impress /ɪm'pres/ vt impressionner; ~ **sth on sb** faire bien comprendre qch à qn. **impression** n impression f. **impressionable** adj impressionnable. **impressive** adj impressionnant.

imprint¹ /'ɪmprɪnt/ n empreinte f.

imprint² /ɪm'prɪnt/ vt (fix) graver (**on** dans); (print) imprimer.

imprison /ɪm'prɪzn/ vt emprisonner.

improbable /ɪm'prɒbəbl/ adj (not likely) improbable; (incredible) invraisemblable.

improper /ɪm'prɒpə(r)/ adj (unseemly) malséant; (dishonest) irrégulier.

improve /ɪm'pruːv/ vt/i (s')améliorer. **improvement** n amélioration f.

improvise /'ɪmprəvaɪz/ vt/i improviser.

impudent /'ɪmpjʊdənt/ adj impudent.

impulse /'ɪmpʌls/ n impulsion f; **on** ~ sur un coup de tête. **impulsive** adj impulsif. **impulsively** adv par impulsion.

impurity /ɪm'pjʊərətɪ/ n impureté f.

in /ɪn/ prep (inside, within) dans; (expressing place, position) à, en; (expressing time) en, dans; ~ **the box/garden** dans la boîte/le jardin; ~ **Paris/school** à Paris/l'école; ~ **town** en ville; ~ **the country** à la campagne; ~ **English** en anglais; ~ **India**

en Inde; ~ **Japan** au Japon; ~ **winter** en hiver; ~ **spring** au printemps; ~ **an hour** (at end of) au bout d'une heure; ~ **an hour('s time)** dans une heure; ~ **(the space of) an hour** en une heure; ~ **doing** en faisant; ~ **the evening** le soir; **one** ~ **ten** un sur dix; ~ **between** entre les deux; (time) entretemps; ~ **a firm voice** d'une voix ferme; ~ **blue** en bleu; ~ **ink** à l'encre; ~ **uniform** en uniforme; ~ **a skirt** en jupe; ~ **a whisper** en chuchotant; ~ **a loud voice** d'une voix forte; **the best** ~ le meilleur de; **we are** ~ **for** on va avoir; **have it** ~ **for sb** 🅸 avoir qn dans le collimateur. ● adv (inside) dedans; (at home) là, à la maison; (in fashion) à la mode; **come** ~ entrer; **run** ~ entrer en courant.

inability /ɪnə'bɪlətɪ/ n incapacité f (**to do** de faire).

inaccessible /ɪnæk'sesəbl/ adj inaccessible.

inaccurate /ɪn'ækjʊrət/ adj inexact.

inactive /ɪn'æktɪv/ adj inactif. **inactivity** n inaction f.

inadequate /ɪn'ædɪkwət/ adj insuffisant.

inadvertently /ɪnəd'vɜːtəntlɪ/ adv par mégarde.

inadvisable /ɪnəd'vaɪzəbl/ adj inopportun, à déconseiller.

inane /ɪ'neɪn/ adj idiot, débile.

inanimate /ɪn'ænɪmət/ adj inanimé.

inappropriate /ɪnə'prəʊprɪət/ adj inopportun; (term) inapproprié.

inarticulate /ɪnɑː'tɪkjʊlət/ adj qui a du mal à s'exprimer.

inasmuch as /ɪnəz'mʌtʃəz/ adv dans la mesure où; (because) vu que.

inaugurate /ɪ'nɔːgjʊreɪt/ vt (open, begin) inaugurer; (person) investir.

inborn /'ɪnbɔːn/ adj inné.

inbred /ɪn'bred/ adj (inborn) inné.

Inc. abbr (**Incorporated**) S.A.

incapable /ɪn'keɪpəbl/ adj incapable (**of doing** de faire).

incapacitate /ɪnkə'pæsɪteɪt/ vt immobiliser.

incense¹ /'ɪnsens/ n encens m.

incense² /ɪn'sens/ vt mettre en fureur.

incentive /ɪn'sentɪv/ n motivation f; (payment) prime f.

incessant /ɪnˈsesnt/ adj incessant. **incessantly** adv sans cesse.

incest /ˈɪnsest/ n inceste m. **incestuous** adj incestueux.

inch /ɪntʃ/ n pouce m (=2.54 cm.). ● vi ~ **towards** se diriger petit à petit vers.

incidence /ˈɪnsɪdəns/ n fréquence f.

incident /ˈɪnsɪdənt/ n incident m. **incidental** adj secondaire. **incidentally** adv à propos; (by chance) par la même occasion.

incinerate /ɪnˈsɪnəreɪt/ vt incinérer. **incinerator** n incinérateur m.

incite /ɪnˈsaɪt/ vt inciter, pousser.

inclination /ɪŋklɪˈneɪʃn/ n (tendency) tendance f; (desire) envie f.

incline[1] /ɪnˈklaɪn/ vt/i (s')incliner; be ~d to avoir tendance à.

incline[2] /ˈɪnklaɪn/ n pente f.

include /ɪnˈkluːd/ vt comprendre, inclure. **including** prep (y) compris. **inclusion** n inclusion f.

inclusive /ɪnˈkluːsɪv/ adj & adv inclus; ~ **of delivery** livraison comprise.

income /ˈɪnkʌm/ n revenus mpl; ~ **tax** impôt m sur le revenu.

incoming /ˈɪnkʌmɪŋ/ adj (tide) montant; (tenant, government) nouveau; (call) qui vient de l'extérieur.

incompatible /ɪnkəmˈpætɪbl/ adj incompatible.

incompetent /ɪnˈkɒmpɪtənt/ adj incompétent.

incomplete /ɪnkəmˈpliːt/ adj incomplet.

incomprehensible /ɪnkɒmprɪˈhensəbl/ adj incompréhensible.

inconceivable /ɪnkənˈsiːvəbl/ adj inconcevable.

inconclusive /ɪnkənˈkluːsɪv/ adj peu concluant.

incongruous /ɪnˈkɒŋgruəs/ adj déconcertant, surprenant.

inconsiderate /ɪnkənˈsɪdərət/ adj (person) peu attentif à autrui; (act) maladroit.

inconsistent /ɪnkənˈsɪstənt/ adj (argument) incohérent; (performance) inégal; (behaviour) changeant; ~ **with** en contradiction avec.

inconspicuous /ɪnkənˈspɪkjuəs/ adj qui passe inaperçu.

incontinent /ɪnˈkɒntɪnənt/ adj incontinent.

inconvenience /ɪnkənˈviːnɪəns/ n dérangement m; (drawback) inconvénient m. ● vt déranger. **inconvenient** adj incommode; **if it's not inconvenient for you** si cela ne vous dérange pas.

incorporate /ɪnˈkɔːpəreɪt/ vt incorporer (into dans); (contain) comporter.

incorrect /ɪnkəˈrekt/ adj incorrect.

increase[1] /ˈɪnkriːs/ n augmentation f (in, of de). be on the ~ être en progression.

increase[2] /ɪnˈkriːs/ vt/i augmenter. **increasing** adj croissant. **increasingly** adv de plus en plus.

incredible /ɪnˈkredəbl/ adj incroyable.

incriminate /ɪnˈkrɪmɪneɪt/ vt incriminer. **incriminating** adj compromettant.

incubate /ˈɪŋkjubeɪt/ vt (eggs) couver. **incubation** n incubation f. **incubator** n couveuse f.

incur /ɪnˈkɜː(r)/ vt (pt **incurred**) (penalty, anger) encourir; (debts) contracter.

indebted /ɪnˈdetɪd/ adj ~ **to sb** redevable à qn (for de); (grateful) reconnaissant à qn.

indecent /ɪnˈdiːsnt/ adj indécent.

indecisive /ɪndɪˈsaɪsɪv/ adj indécis; (ending) peu concluant.

indeed /ɪnˈdiːd/ adv en effet; (emphatic) vraiment.

indefinite /ɪnˈdefɪnət/ adj vague; (period, delay) illimité. **indefinitely** adv indéfiniment.

indelible /ɪnˈdeləbl/ adj indélébile.

indemnity /ɪnˈdemnətɪ/ n (protection) assurance f; (payment) indemnité f.

indent /ɪnˈdent/ vt (text) renfoncer. **indentation** n (dent) marque f.

independence /ɪndɪˈpendəns/ n indépendance f. **independent** adj indépendant. **independently** adv de façon indépendante; **independently of** indépendamment de.

index /ˈɪndeks/ n (pl ~es) (in book) index m; (in library) catalogue m; (in economy) indice m; ~ **card** fiche f; ~ (**finger**) index m. ● vt classer. ~-**linked** adj indexé.

India /ˈɪndɪə/ n Inde f.

Indian /'ɪndɪən/ n Indien/-ne m/f. ● adj indien.

indicate /'ɪndɪkeɪt/ vt indiquer. **indication** n indication f.

indicative /ɪn'dɪkətɪv/ adj & n indicatif (m).

indicator /'ɪndɪkeɪtə(r)/ n (pointer) aiguille f; (on vehicle) clignotant m; (board) tableau m.

indict /ɪn'daɪt/ vt inculper. **indictment** n accusation f.

indifferent /ɪn'dɪfrənt/ adj indifférent; (not good) médiocre.

indigenous /ɪn'dɪdʒɪnəs/ adj indigène.

indigestible /ɪndɪ'dʒestəbl/ adj indigeste. **indigestion** n indigestion f.

indignant /ɪn'dɪgnənt/ adj indigné.

indirect /ɪndɪ'rekt/ adj indirect. **indirectly** adv indirectement.

indiscreet /ɪndɪ'skriːt/ adj indiscret. **indiscretion** n indiscrétion f.

indiscriminate /ɪndɪ'skrɪmɪnət/ adj sans distinction. **indiscriminately** adv sans distinction.

indisputable /ɪndɪ'spjuːtəbl/ adj indiscutable.

individual /ɪndɪ'vɪdʒʊəl/ adj individuel; (tuition) particulier. ● n individu m. **individualist** n individualiste mf. **individuality** n individualité f. **individually** adv individuellement.

indoctrinate /ɪn'dɒktrɪneɪt/ vt endoctriner. **indoctrination** n endoctrinement m.

indolent /'ɪndələnt/ adj indolent.

Indonesia /ɪndəʊ'niːzjə/ n Indonésie f.

indoor /ɪn'dɔː(r)/ adj (clothes) d'intérieur; (pool, court) couvert. **indoors** adv à l'intérieur.

induce /ɪn'djuːs/ vt (influence) persuader; (stronger) inciter (**to do** à faire). **inducement** n (financial) récompense f; (incentive) motivation f.

induction /ɪn'dʌkʃn/ n (Electr) induction f; (inauguration) installation f.

indulge /ɪn'dʌldʒ/ vt (person, whim) céder à; (child) gâter. ● vi **~ in** se livrer à. **indulgence** n indulgence f; (treat) plaisir m. **indulgent** adj indulgent.

industrial /ɪn'dʌstrɪəl/ adj industriel; (accident) du travail; **~ action** grève f; **~ dispute** conflit m social. **industrialist** n industriel/-le m/f. **industrialized** adj industrialisé.

industrious /ɪn'dʌstrɪəs/ adj diligent.

industry /'ɪndəstrɪ/ n industrie f; (zeal) zèle m.

inebriated /ɪ'niːbrɪeɪtɪd/ adj ivre.

inedible /ɪn'edɪbl/ adj immangeable.

ineffective /ɪnɪ'fektɪv/ adj inefficace.

inefficient /ɪnɪ'fɪʃnt/ adj inefficace; (person) incompétent.

ineligible /ɪn'elɪdʒəbl/ adj inéligible; be **~ for** ne pas avoir droit à.

inept /ɪ'nept/ adj incompétent; (tactless) maladroit.

inequality /ɪnɪ'kwɒlətɪ/ n inégalité f.

inescapable /ɪnɪ'skeɪpəbl/ adj indéniable.

inevitable /ɪn'evɪtəbl/ adj inévitable.

inexcusable /ɪnɪk'skjuːzəbl/ adj inexcusable.

inexhaustible /ɪnɪg'zɔːstəbl/ adj inépuisable.

inexpensive /ɪnɪk'spensɪv/ adj pas cher.

inexperience /ɪnɪk'spɪərɪəns/ n inexpérience f. **inexperienced** adj inexpérimenté.

infallible /ɪn'fæləbl/ adj infaillible.

infamous /'ɪnfəməs/ adj (person) tristement célèbre; (deed) infâme.

infancy /'ɪnfənsɪ/ n petite enfance f; **in its ~** (fig) à ses débuts mpl. **infant** n (baby) bébé m; (at school) enfant m. **infantile** adj infantile.

infatuated /ɪn'fætʃʊeɪtɪd/ adj **~ with** entiché de. **infatuation** n engouement m.

infect /ɪn'fekt/ vt contaminer; **~ sb with sth** transmettre qch à qn. **infection** n infection f. **infectious** adj contagieux.

infer /ɪn'fɜː(r)/ vt (pt **inferred**) (deduce) déduire.

inferior /ɪn'fɪərɪə(r)/ adj inférieur (**to** à). (work, product) de qualité inférieure. ● n inférieur/-e m/f. **inferiority** n infériorité f.

inferno /ɪn'fɜːnəʊ/ n (hell) enfer m; (blaze) brasier m.

infertile /ɪn'fɜːtaɪl/ adj infertile.

infest /ɪn'fest/ vt infester (**with** de).

infidelity /ɪnfɪ'delətɪ/ n infidélité f

infighting /'ɪnfaɪtɪŋ/ n conflits mpl internes.

infinite /'ɪnfɪnət/ adj infini. **infinitely** adv infiniment. **infinitive** n infinitif m. **infinity** n infinité f.

infirm /ɪn'fɜːm/ adj infirme. **infirmary** n hôpital m; (sick-bay) infirmerie f. **infirmity** n infirmité f.

inflame /ɪn'fleɪm/ vt enflammer. **inflammable** adj inflammable. **inflammation** n inflammation f. **inflammatory** adj incendiaire.

inflatable /ɪn'fleɪtəbl/ adj gonflable. **inflate** vt (lit, fig) gonfler.

inflation /ɪn'fleɪʃn/ n inflation f.

inflection /ɪn'flekʃn/ n (of word root) flexion f; (of vowel, voice) inflexion f.

inflict /ɪn'flɪkt/ vt infliger (**on** à).

influence /'ɪnfluəns/ n influence f; **under the** 🄳 éméché. ● vt (person) influencer; (choice) influer sur. **influential** adj (powerful) influent; (theory, artist) très suivi.

influenza /ɪnflʊ'enzə/ n grippe f.

influx /'ɪnflʌks/ n afflux m.

inform /ɪn'fɔːm/ vt informer (**of** de). **keep ~ed** tenir au courant.

informal /ɪn'fɔːml/ adj (simple) simple, sans façons; (unofficial) officieux; (colloquial) familier. **informality** n simplicité f. **informally** adv (dress) en tenue décontractée; (speak) en toute simplicité.

informant /ɪn'fɔːmənt/ n indicateur/-trice m/f.

information /ɪnfə'meɪʃn/ n renseignements mpl, informations fpl; **some ~** un renseignement. **~ superhighway** n autoroute f de l'information. **~ technology** n informatique f.

informative /ɪn'fɔːmətɪv/ adj (book) riche en renseignements; (visit) instructif.

informer /ɪn'fɔːmə(r)/ n indicateur/-trice m/f.

infrequent /ɪn'friːkwənt/ adj rare.

infringe /ɪn'frɪndʒ/ vt (rule) enfreindre; (rights) ne pas respecter. **infringement** n infraction f.

infuriate /ɪn'fjʊərɪeɪt/ vt exaspérer.

ingenuity /ɪndʒɪ'njuːətɪ/ n ingéniosité f.

ingot /'ɪŋgət/ n lingot m.

ingrained /ɪn'greɪnd/ adj (hatred) enraciné; (dirt) bien incrusté.

ingratiate /ɪn'greɪʃɪeɪt/ vt **~ oneself with** se faire bien voir de.

ingredient /ɪn'griːdɪənt/ n ingrédient m.

inhabit /ɪn'hæbɪt/ vt habiter. **inhabitable** adj habitable. **inhabitant** n habitant/-e m/f.

inhale /ɪn'heɪl/ vt inhaler; (smoke) avaler. **inhaler** n inhalateur m.

inherent /ɪn'hɪərənt/ adj inhérent (**in** à). **inherently** adv en soi, par sa nature.

inherit /ɪn'herɪt/ vt hériter de; **~ sth from sb** hériter qch de qn. **inheritance** n héritage m.

inhibit /ɪn'hɪbɪt/ vt (restrain) inhiber; (prevent) entraver.

inhospitable /ɪnhɒ'spɪtəbl/ adj inhospitalier.

inhuman /ɪn'hjuːmən/ adj inhumain.

initial /ɪ'nɪʃl/ n initiale f. ● vt (pt **initialled**) parapher. ● adj initial.

initiate /ɪ'nɪʃɪeɪt/ vt (project) mettre en œuvre; (talks) amorcer; (person) initier (**into** à). **initiation** n initiation f; (start) amorce f.

initiative /ɪ'nɪʃətɪv/ n initiative f.

inject /ɪn'dʒekt/ vt injecter (**into** dans). (new element: fig) insuffler (**into** à). **injection** n injection f, piqûre f.

injure /'ɪndʒə(r)/ vt blesser; (damage) nuire à. **injury** n blessure f.

injustice /ɪn'dʒʌstɪs/ n injustice f.

ink /ɪŋk/ n encre f.

inkling /'ɪŋklɪŋ/ n petite idée f.

inland /'ɪnlənd/ adj intérieur; **I~ Revenue** service m des impôts britannique.

in-laws /'ɪnlɔːz/ npl (parents) beaux-parents mpl; (family) belle-famille f.

inlay¹ /ɪn'leɪ/ vt (pt **inlaid**) incruster (**with** de); (on wood) marqueter.

inlay² /'ɪnleɪ/ n incrustation f; (on wood) marqueterie f.

inlet /'ɪnlet/ n bras m de mer; (Tech) arrivée f.

inmate /'ɪnmeɪt/ n (of asylum) interné/-e m/f; (of prison) détenu/-e m/f.

inn /ɪn/ n auberge f.

innate /ɪ'neɪt/ adj inné.

inner /'mə(r)/ adj intérieur; ~ **city** quartiers mpl déshérités; ~ **tube** chambre f à air.

innocent /'məsnt/ adj & n innocent/-e (m/f).

innocuous /ı'nɒkjʊəs/ adj inoffensif.

innovate /'məveıt/ vi innover.

innuendo /mju:'endəʊ/ n (pl ~**es**) insinuations fpl; (sexual) allusions fpl grivoises.

innumerable /ı'nju:mərəbl/ adj innombrable.

inoculate /ı'nɒkjʊleıt/ vt vacciner (**against** contre).

inopportune /m'ɒpətju:n/ adj inopportun.

in-patient /'mpeıʃnt/ n malade mf hospitalisé/-e.

input /'mpʊt/ n (of energy) alimentation f (**of** en); (contribution) contribution f; (data) données fpl; (computer process) saisie f des données. ● vt (data) saisir.

inquest /'mkwest/ n enquête f.

inquire /m'kwaıə(r)/ vi se renseigner (**about, into** sur). ● vt demander.

inquiry /m'kwaıərı/ n demande f de renseignements; (inquest) enquête f.

inquisitive /m'kwızətıv/ adj curieux.

inroad /'mrəʊd/ n make ~**s into** faire une avancée sur.

insane /m'seın/ adj fou; (Jur) aliéné. **insanity** n folie f; (Jur) aliénation f mentale.

inscribe /m'skraıb/ vt inscrire. **inscription** n inscription f.

inscrutable /m'skru:təbl/ adj énigmatique.

insect /'msekt/ n insecte m. **insecticide** n insecticide m.

insecure /msı'kjʊə(r)/ adj (person) qui manque d'assurance; (job) précaire; (lock, property) peu sûr. **insecurity** n (of person) manque m d'assurance; (of situation) insécurité f.

insensitive /m'sensətıv/ adj insensible; (remark) indélicat.

inseparable /m'seprəbl/ adj inséparable (**from** de).

insert /m'sɜ:t/ vt insérer (**in** dans).

in-service /'msɜ:rvıs/ adj (training) continu.

inshore /m'ʃɔ:(r)/ adj côtier.

inside /m'saıd/ n intérieur m; ~**s** 🄸 entrailles fpl. ● adj intérieur. ● adv à l'intérieur; **go** ~ entrer. ● prep à l'intérieur de; (of time) en moins de; ~ **out** à l'envers; (thoroughly) à fond.

insight /'msaıt/ n (perception) perspicacité f; (idea) aperçu m.

insignia /m'sıgnıə/ npl insigne m.

insignificant /msıg'nıfıkənt/ adj (cost, difference) négligeable; (person) insignifiant.

insincere /msm'sıə(r)/ adj peu sincère.

insinuate /m'sınjʊeıt/ vt insinuer.

insist /m'sıst/ vt/i insister (**that** pour que). ~ **on** exiger; ~ **on doing** vouloir à tout prix faire. **insistence** n insistance f. **insistent** adj insistant. **insistently** adv avec insistance.

insofar as /msəʊ'fa:əz/ adv dans la mesure où.

insolent /'msələnt/ adj insolent.

insolvent /m'sɒlvənt/ adj insolvable.

insomnia /m'sɒmnıə/ n insomnie f. **insomniac** n insomniaque mf.

inspect /m'spekt/ vt (school, machinery) inspecter; (tickets) contrôler. **inspection** n inspection f; (of passport, ticket) contrôle m. **inspector** n inspecteur/-trice m/f; (on bus) contrôleur/-euse m/f.

inspiration /mspə'reıʃn/ n inspiration f. **inspire** vt inspirer.

install /m'stɔ:l/ vt installer.

instalment /m'stɔ:lmənt/ n (payment) versement m; (of serial) épisode m.

instance /'mstəns/ n exemple m; (case) cas m; **for** ~ par exemple; **in the first** ~ en premier lieu.

instant /'mstənt/ adj immédiat; (food) instantané. ● n instant m. **instantaneous** adj instantané. **instantly** adv immédiatement.

instead /m'sted/ adv plutôt; ~ **of doing** au lieu de faire; ~ **of sb** à la place de qn.

instep /'mstep/ n cou-de-pied m.

instigate /'mstıgeıt/ vt (attack) lancer; (proceedings) engager.

instil /m'stıl/ vt (pt instilled) inculquer; (fear) insuffler.

instinct /'mstıŋkt/ n instinct m. **instinctive** adj instinctif.

institute /'mstıtju:t/ n institut m. ● vt instituer; (proceedings) engager. **insti-**

tution n institution f; (school, hospital) établissement m.

instruct /ɪnˈstrʌkt/ vt (teach) instruire; (order) ordonner; ~ **sb in sth** enseigner qch à qn; ~ **sb to do** donner l'ordre à qn de faire. **instruction** n instruction f; **instructions** npl (for use) mode m d'emploi. **instructive** adj instructif. **instructor** n (skiing, driving) moniteur/-trice m/f.

instrument /ˈɪnstrʊmənt/ n instrument m.

instrumental /ɪnstrʊˈmentl/ adj instrumental; **be** ~ **in** contribuer à. **instrumentalist** n instrumentaliste mf.

insubordinate /ɪnsəˈbɔːdɪnət/ adj insubordonné.

insufficient /ɪnsəˈfɪʃnt/ adj insuffisant.

insular /ˈɪnsjʊlə(r)/ adj (Geog) insulaire; (mind, person: fig) borné.

insulate /ˈɪnsjʊleɪt/ vt (room, wire) isoler.

insulin /ˈɪnsjʊlɪn/ n insuline f.

insult¹ /ɪnˈsʌlt/ vt insulter.

insult² /ˈɪnsʌlt/ n insulte f.

insurance /ɪnˈʃɔːrəns/ n assurance f (**against** contre).

insure /ɪnˈʃɔː(r)/ vt assurer; ~ **that** (US) s'assurer que.

intact /ɪnˈtækt/ adj intact.

intake /ˈɪnteɪk/ n (of food) consommation f; (School, Univ) admissions fpl.

integral /ˈɪntɪgrəl/ adj intégral (**to** à).

integrate /ˈɪntɪgreɪt/ vt/i (s')intégrer (**with** à; **into** dans).

integrity /ɪnˈtegrətɪ/ n intégrité f.

intellect /ˈɪntəlekt/ n intelligence f. **intellectual** adj & n intellectuel/-le (m/f).

intelligence /ɪnˈtelɪdʒəns/ n intelligence f; (Mil) renseignements mpl. **intelligent** adj intelligent. **intelligently** adv intelligemment.

intend /ɪnˈtend/ vt (outcome) vouloir; ~ **to do** avoir l'intention de faire. **intended** adj (result) voulu; (visit) projeté.

intense /ɪnˈtens/ adj intense; (person) sérieux. **intensely** adv (very) extrêmement.

intensify /ɪnˈtensɪfaɪ/ vt/i (s')intensifier.

intensive /ɪnˈtensɪv/ adj intensif; **in** ~ **care** en réanimation.

intent /ɪnˈtent/ n intention f. ● adj absorbé; ~ **on doing** résolu à faire.

intention /ɪnˈtenʃn/ n intention f. **intentional** adj intentionnel.

intently /ɪnˈtentlɪ/ adv attentivement.

interact /ɪntərˈækt/ vi (factors) agir l'un sur l'autre; (people) communiquer. **interactive** adj (TV, video) interactif.

intercept /ɪntəˈsept/ vt intercepter.

interchange /ˈɪntətʃeɪndʒ/ n (road junction) échangeur m; (exchange) échange m.

interchangeable /ɪntəˈtʃeɪndʒəbl/ adj interchangeable.

intercom /ˈɪntəkɒm/ n interphone® m.

interconnected /ɪntəkəˈnektɪd/ adj (parts) raccordé; (problems) lié.

intercourse /ˈɪntəkɔːs/ n rapports mpl.

interest /ˈɪntrəst/ n intérêt m; ~ **rate** taux m d'intérêt. ● vt intéresser (**in** à). **interested** adj intéressé; **be** ~**ed in** s'intéresser à. **interesting** adj intéressant.

interface /ˈɪntəfeɪs/ n interface f.

interfere /ɪntəˈfɪə(r)/ vi se mêler des affaires des autres; ~ **in** se mêler de; ~ **with** (freedom) empiéter sur; (tamper with) toucher. **interference** n ingérence f; (sound, light waves) brouillage m; (radio) parasites mpl.

interim /ˈɪntərɪm/ n **in the** ~ entre-temps. ● adj (government) provisoire; (payment) intermédiaire.

interior /ɪnˈtɪərɪə(r)/ n intérieur m. ● adj intérieur.

interjection /ɪntəˈdʒekʃn/ n interjection f.

interlock /ɪntəˈlɒk/ vt/i (Tech) (s')emboîter, (s')enclencher.

interlude /ˈɪntəluːd/ n intervalle m; (Theat, Mus) intermède m.

intermediary /ɪntəˈmiːdɪərɪ/ adj & n intermédiaire (mf).

intermediate /ɪntəˈmiːdɪət/ adj intermédiaire; (exam, level) moyen.

intermission /ɪntəˈmɪʃn/ n (Theat) entracte m.

intermittent /ɪntəˈmɪtənt/ adj intermittent.

intern¹ /ɪnˈtɜːn/ vt interner.

intern² /ˈɪntɜːn/ n (US) stagiaire mf; (Med) interne mf.

internal /ɪnˈtɜːnl/ adj interne; (domestic: Pol) intérieur; **I~ Revenue** (US) service m des impôts américain.

international /ɪntəˈnæʃnəl/ adj international.

Internet /ˈɪntənet/ n Internet m; **on the ~** sur Internet; **~ access** accès à Internet; **~ service provider** fournisseur m d'accès Internet.

interpret /ɪnˈtɜːprɪt/ vt interpréter (**as** comme). ● vi faire l'interprète. **interpretation** n interprétation f. **interpreter** n interprète mf.

interrelated /ɪntərɪˈleɪtɪd/ adj interdépendant, lié.

interrogate /ɪnˈterəgeɪt/ vt interroger. **interrogative** adj & n (Ling) interrogatif (m).

interrupt /ɪntəˈrʌpt/ vt/i interrompre. **interruption** n interruption f.

intersect /ɪntəˈsekt/ vt/i (lines, roads) (se) croiser. **intersection** n intersection f.

interspersed /ɪntəˈspɜːst/ adj parsemé (**with** de).

intertwine /ɪntəˈtwaɪn/ vt/i (s')entrelacer.

interval /ˈɪntəvl/ n intervalle m; (Theat) entracte m.

intervene /ɪntəˈviːn/ vi intervenir; (of time) s'écouler (**between** entre); (happen) arriver.

interview /ˈɪntəvjuː/ n (for job) entretien m; (by a journalist) interview f. ● vt (candidate) faire passer un entretien à; (celebrity) interviewer.

intestine /ɪnˈtestɪn/ n intestin m.

intimacy /ˈɪntɪməsɪ/ n intimité f.

intimate¹ /ˈɪntɪmeɪt/ vt (state) annoncer; (hint) laisser entendre.

intimate² /ˈɪntɪmət/ adj intime. **intimately** adv intimement.

intimidate /ɪnˈtɪmɪdeɪt/ vt intimider.

into /ˈɪntuː/, /ˈɪntə/ prep (put, go, fall) dans; (divide, translate, change) en; be **~ jazz** être fana du jazz Ⅱ; **8 ~ 24 is 3** 24 divisé par 8 égale 3.

intolerant /ɪnˈtɒlərənt/ adj intolérant.

intonation /ɪntəˈneɪʃn/ n intonation f.

intoxicate /ɪnˈtɒksɪkeɪt/ vt enivrer. **intoxicated** adj ivre. **intoxication** n ivresse f.

intractable /ɪnˈtræktəbl/ adj (person) intraitable; (problem) rebelle.

intranet /ˈɪntrənet/ n (Comput) intranet m.

intransitive /ɪnˈtrænsətɪv/ adj intransitif.

intravenous /ɪntrəˈviːnəs/ adj (Med) intraveineux.

intricate /ˈɪntrɪkət/ adj complexe.

intrigue /ɪnˈtriːg/ vt intriguer. ● n intrigue f. **intriguing** adj fascinant; (curious) curieux.

intrinsic /ɪnˈtrɪnzɪk/ adj intrinsèque (**to** à).

introduce /ɪntrəˈdjuːs/ vt (person, idea, programme) présenter; (object, law) introduire (**into** dans). **introduction** n introduction f; (of person) présentation f. **introductory** adj (words) préliminaire.

introvert /ˈɪntrəvɜːt/ n introverti/-e m/f.

intrude /ɪnˈtruːd/ vi (person) s'imposer (**on** sb à qn), déranger. **intruder** n intrus/-e m/f. **intrusion** n intrusion f.

intuition /ɪntjuːˈɪʃn/ n intuition f. **intuitive** adj intuitif.

inundate /ˈɪnʌndeɪt/ vt inonder (**with** de).

invade /ɪnˈveɪd/ vt envahir.

invalid¹ /ˈɪnvəliːd/ n malade mf; (disabled) infirme mf.

invalid² /ɪnˈvælɪd/ adj (passport) pas valable; (claim) sans fondement. **invalidate** vt (argument) infirmer; (claim) annuler.

invaluable /ɪnˈvæljʊəbl/ adj inestimable.

invariable /ɪnˈveərɪəbl/ adj invariable. **invariably** adv invariablement.

invasion /ɪnˈveɪʒn/ n invasion f.

invent /ɪnˈvent/ vt inventer. **invention** n invention f. **inventive** adj inventif. **inventor** n inventeur/-trice m/f.

inventory /ˈɪnvəntrɪ/ n inventaire m.

invert /ɪnˈvɜːt/ vt (order) intervertir; (image, values) renverser; **~ed commas** guillemets mpl.

invest /ɪnˈvest/ vt investir; (time, effort) consacrer. ● vi faire un investissement; **~ in** (buy) s'acheter.

investigate /ɪnˈvestɪgeɪt/ vt examiner; (crime) enquêter sur. **investigation** n investigation f. **investigator** n (police) enquêteur/-euse m/f.

investment /ɪnˈvestmənt/ n investissement m; **emotional ~** engagement m personnel. **investor** n investisseur/-euse m/f; (in shares) actionnaire mf.

invigilate /ɪnˈvɪdʒɪleɪt/ vi (exam) surveiller. **invigilator** n surveillant/-e m/f.

invigorate /ɪnˈvɪgəreɪt/ vt revigorer.

invisible /ɪnˈvɪzəbl/ adj invisible.

invitation /ɪnvɪˈteɪʃn/ n invitation f. **invite** vt inviter; (ask for) demander. **inviting** adj engageant.

invoice /ˈɪnvɔɪs/ n facture f. ● vt facturer.

involuntary /ɪnˈvɒləntrɪ/ adj involontaire.

involve /ɪnˈvɒlv/ vt impliquer; (person) faire participer (**in** à). **involved** adj (complex) compliqué; (at stake) en jeu; **be ~d in** (work) participer à; (crime) être mêlé à. **involvement** n participation f (**in** à).

inward /ˈɪnwəd/ adj (feeling) intérieur. **inwardly** adv intérieurement. **inwards** adv vers l'intérieur.

iodine /ˈaɪədiːn/ n iode m; (antiseptic) teinture f d'iode.

iota /aɪˈəʊtə/ n iota m; **not one ~ of** pas un grain de.

IOU abbr (**I owe you**) reconnaissance f de dette.

IQ abbr (**intelligence quotient**) QI m.

Iran /ɪˈrɑːn/ n Iran m.

Iraq /ɪˈrɑːk/ n Irak m.

irate /aɪˈreɪt/ adj furieux.

IRC abbrev (**Internet Relay Chat**) (Internet) conversation f IRC.

Ireland /ˈaɪələnd/ n Irlande f.

Irish /ˈaɪərɪʃ/ n & adj irlandais (m). **~man** n Irlandais m. **~woman** n Irlandaise f.

iron /ˈaɪən/ n fer m; (appliance) fer m (à repasser). ● adj (will) de fer; (bar) en fer. ● vt repasser.

ironic /aɪˈrɒnɪk/ adj ironique.

iron: ironing-board n planche f à repasser. **~monger** n quincaillier m.

irony /ˈaɪrənɪ/ n ironie f.

irrational /ɪˈræʃənl/ adj irrationnel; (person) pas raisonnable.

irregular /ɪˈregjʊlə(r)/ adj irrégulier.

irrelevant /ɪˈreləvnt/ adj hors de propos.

irreplaceable /ɪrɪˈpleɪsəbl/ adj irremplaçable.

irresistible /ɪrɪˈzɪstəbl/ adj irrésistible.

irrespective /ɪrɪˈspektɪv/ adj **~ of** sans tenir compte de.

irresponsible /ɪrɪˈspɒnsəbl/ adj irresponsable.

irreverent /ɪˈrevərənt/ adj irrévérencieux.

irrigate /ˈɪrɪgeɪt/ vt irriguer.

irritable /ˈɪrɪtəbl/ adj irritable.

irritate /ˈɪrɪteɪt/ vt irriter. **irritating** adj irritant.

is /ɪz/ ⇒BE.

ISDN abbr (**integrated services digital network**) RNIS n, réseau m numérique à intégration de services.

Islam /ɪzˈlɑːm/ n (faith) islam m; (Muslims) Islam m. **Islamic** adj islamique.

island /ˈaɪlənd/ n île f.

isle /aɪl/ n île f.

isolate /ˈaɪsəleɪt/ vt isoler. **isolation** n isolement m.

Israel /ˈɪzreɪl/ n Israël m.

Israeli /ɪzˈreɪlɪ/ n Israélien-ne m/f. ● adj israélien.

issue /ˈɪsjuː/ n question f; (outcome) résultat m; (of magazine) numéro m; (of stamps) émission f; (offspring) descendance f; **at ~** en cause. ● vt distribuer; (stamps) émettre; (book) publier; (order) délivrer. ● vi **~ from** provenir de.

---

it /ɪt/

● pronoun

····▸ (subject) il, elle; **'where's the book/chair?'— '~'s in the kitchen'** 'où est le livre/la chaise?'—'il/elle est dans la cuisine'.

····▸ (object) le, la, l'; **~'s my book and I want ~** c'est mon livre et je le veux; **I liked his shirt, did you notice ~?** sa chemise m'a plu, l'as-tu remarquée?; **give ~ to me** donne-le-moi.

····▸ (with preposition) **we talked a lot about ~** on en a beaucoup parlé; **Elliott went to ~** Elliott y est allé.

····▸ (impersonal) il; **~'s raining** il pleut; **~ will snow** il va neiger.

IT *abbr* →INFORMATION TECHNOLOGY.

Italian /ɪ'tæljən/ *n* (person) Italien/-ne *m/f;* (Ling) italien *m.* ● *adj* italien.

italics /ɪ'tælɪks/ *npl* italique *m.*

Italy /'ɪtəlɪ/ *n* Italie *f.*

itch /ɪtʃ/ *n* démangeaison *f.* ● *vi* démanger; **my arm ~es** j'ai le bras qui me démange; **be ~ing to do** mourir d'envie de faire.

item /'aɪtəm/ *n* article *m;* (on agenda) point *m.*

itemize /'aɪtəmaɪz/ *vt* détailler; **~d bill** facture *f* détaillée.

itinerary /aɪ'tɪnərərɪ/ *n* itinéraire *m.*

its /ɪts/ *det* son, sa; *pl* ses.

it's →IT IS, IT HAS.

itself /ɪt'self/ *pron* lui-même, elle-même; (reflexive) se.

ivory /'aɪvərɪ/ *n* ivoire *m;* **~ tower** tour *f* d'ivoire.

ivy /'aɪvɪ/ *n* lierre *m.*

i **The Ivy League** Ce terme désigne la huit universités les plus prestigieuses de la côte est des États-Unis (Harvard, Yale, Columbia, Cornell, Dartmouth, Brown, Princeton, Pennsylvania). Elles doivent ce nom au lierre qui pousse sur les bâtiments des plus anciennes d'entre elles. Ces universités sont réputées tant dans les domaines académiques que sportifs.

Jj

jab /dʒæb/ *vt* (*pt* **jabbed**) **~ sth into sth** planter qch dans qch. ● *n* coup *m;* (injection) piqûre *f.*

jack /dʒæk/ *n* (Auto) cric *m;* (cards) valet *m;* (Electr) jack *m.* ● *vt* **~ up** soulever avec un cric.

jacket /'dʒækɪt/ *n* veste *f,* veston *m;* (of book) jaquette *f.*

jackknife /'dʒæknaɪf/ *n* couteau *m* pliant. ● *vi* (lorry) se mettre en portefeuille.

jackpot /'dʒækpɒt/ *n* gros lot *m;* **hit the ~** gagner le gros lot.

jade /dʒeɪd/ *n* (stone) jade *m.*

jaded /'dʒeɪdɪd/ *adj* (tired) fatigué; (bored) blasé.

jagged /'dʒægɪd/ *adj* (rock) déchiqueté; (knife) dentelé.

jail /dʒeɪl/ *n* prison *f.* ● *vt* mettre en prison.

jam /dʒæm/ *n* confiture *f;* **(traffic) ~** embouteillage *m.* ● *vt/i* (*pt* **jammed**) (wedge) (se) coincer; (cram) (s')entasser; (street) encombrer; (radio) brouiller.

Jamaica /dʒə'meɪkə/ *n* Jamaïque *f.*

jam-packed *adj* 🄸 bondé; **~ with** bourré de.

jangle /'dʒæŋgl/ *n* tintement *m.* ● *vt/i* (faire) tinter.

janitor /'dʒænɪtə(r)/ *n* (US) gardien *m.*

January /'dʒænjʊərɪ/ *n* janvier *m.*

Japan /dʒə'pæn/ *n* Japon *m.*

Japanese /dʒæpə'niːz/ *n* (person) Japonais/-e *m/f;* (Ling) japonais *m.* ● *adj* japonais.

jar /dʒɑː(r)/ *n* pot *m,* bocal *m.* ● *vi* (*pt* **jarred**) rendre un son discordant; (colours) détonner. ● *vt* ébranler.

jargon /'dʒɑːgən/ *n* jargon *m.*

jaundice /'dʒɔːndɪs/ *n* jaunisse *f.*

javelin /'dʒævlɪn/ *n* javelot *m.*

jaw /dʒɔː/ *n* mâchoire *f.*

jay /dʒeɪ/ *n* geai *m.*

jazz /dʒæz/ *n* jazz *m.* ● *vt* **~ up** (dress) rajeunir; (event) ranimer.

jealous /'dʒeləs/ *adj* jaloux. **jealousy** *n* jalousie *f.*

jeans /dʒiːnz/ *npl* jean *m.*

jeer /dʒɪə(r)/ *vt/i* **~ (at)** huer. ● *n* huée *f.*

jelly /'dʒelɪ/ *n* gelée *f.* **~fish** *n* méduse *f.*

jeopardize /'dʒepədaɪz/ *vt* (career, chance) compromettre; (lives) mettre en péril.

jerk /dʒɜːk/ *n* secousse *f;* (fool 🄴) crétin *m* 🄸. ● *vt* tirer brusquement. ● *vi* tressaillir. **jerky** *adj* saccadé.

jersey /'dʒɜːzɪ/ *n* (garment) pull-over *m;* (fabric) jersey *m.*

jet /dʒet/ *n* (plane, stream) jet *m;* (mineral) jais *m;* **~ lag** décalage *m* horaire.

jettison /'dʒetɪsn/ *vt* jeter par-dessus bord; (Aviat) larguer; (fig) rejeter.

jetty /'dʒetɪ/ *n* jetée *f.*

Jew /dʒuː/ n juif/juive m/f.

jewel /'dʒuːəl/ n bijou m. **jeweller** n bijoutier/-ière m/f. **jeweller('s)** n (shop) bijouterie f. **jewellery** n bijoux mpl.

Jewish /'dʒuːɪʃ/ adj juif.

jibe /dʒaɪb/ n moquerie f.

jigsaw /'dʒɪgsɔː/ n puzzle m.

jingle /'dʒɪŋgl/ vt/i (faire) tinter. ● n tintement m; (advertising) refrain m publicitaire, sonal m.

jinx /dʒɪŋks/ n (person) porte-malheur m inv; (curse) sort m.

jitters /'dʒɪtəz/ npl **have the ~** 🄣 être nerveux. **jittery** adj nerveux.

job /dʒɒb/ n emploi m; (post) poste m; **out of a ~** sans emploi; **it is a good ~ that** heureusement que; **just the ~** tout à fait ce qu'il faut. **~ centre** n bureau m des services nationaux de l'emploi. **jobless** adj sans emploi.

jockey /'dʒɒkɪ/ n jockey m.

jog /dʒɒg/ n **go for a ~** aller faire un jogging. ● vt (pt **jogged**) heurter; (memory) rafraîchir. ● vi faire du jogging. **jogging** n jogging m.

join /dʒɔɪn/ vt (attach) réunir, joindre; (club) devenir membre de; (company) entrer dans; (army) s'engager dans; (queue) se mettre dans; **~ sb** (in activity) se joindre à qn; (meet) rejoindre qn. ● vi (become member) adhérer; (pieces) se joindre; (roads) se rejoindre. □ **~ in** participer; **~ in sth** participer à qch; **~ up** (Mil) s'engager; **~ sth up** relier qch. **joiner** n menuisier/-ière m/f.

joint /dʒɔɪnt/ adj (action) collectif; (measures, venture) commun; (winner) ex aequo inv; (account) joint; **~ author** coauteur m. ● n (join) joint m; (Anat) articulation f; (Culin) rôti m; **out of ~** déboîté.

joke /dʒəʊk/ n plaisanterie f; (trick) farce f; **it's no ~** ce n'est pas drôle. ● vi plaisanter. **joker** n blagueur/-euse m/f; (cards) joker m.

jolly /'dʒɒlɪ/ adj (-ier, -iest) (person) enjoué; (tune) joyeux. ● adv 🄣 drôlement.

jolt /dʒəʊlt/ vt secouer. ● vi cahoter. ● n secousse f; (shock) choc m.

jostle /'dʒɒsl/ vt/i (se) bousculer.

jot /dʒɒt/ vt (pt **jotted**) **~ (down)** noter.

journal /'dʒɜːnl/ n journal m. **journalism** n journalisme m. **journalist** n journaliste mf.

journey /'dʒɜːnɪ/ n (trip) voyage m; (short or habitual) trajet m. ● vi voyager.

joy /dʒɔɪ/ n joie f. **joyful** adj joyeux.

joy: **~riding** n rodéo m à la voiture volée. **~stick** n (Comput) manette f; (Aviat) manche m à balai.

jubilant /'dʒuːbɪlənt/ adj (person) exultant; (mood) réjoui.

Judaism /'dʒuːdeɪɪzəm/ n judaïsme m.

judge /dʒʌdʒ/ n juge m. ● vt juger; (distance) estimer; **judging by/from** à en juger par. **judg(e)ment** n jugement m.

judicial /dʒuːˈdɪʃl/ adj judiciaire. **judiciary** n magistrature f.

judo /'dʒuːdəʊ/ n judo m.

jug /dʒʌg/ n (glass) carafe f; (pottery) pichet m.

juggernaut /'dʒʌgənɔːt/ n (lorry) poids m lourd.

juggle /'dʒʌgl/ vt/i jongler (avec). **juggler** n jongleur/-euse m/f.

juice /dʒuːs/ n jus m. **juicy** adj juteux; (details 🄣) croustillant.

jukebox /'dʒuːkbɒks/ n juke-box m.

July /dʒuːˈlaɪ/ n juillet m.

jumble /'dʒʌmbl/ vt mélanger. ● n (of objects) tas m; (of ideas) fouillis m; **~ sale** vente f de charité.

jumbo /'dʒʌmbəʊ/ n (also **~ jet**) grosporteur m.

jump /dʒʌmp/ vt sauter; **~ the lights** passer au feu rouge; **~ the queue** passer devant tout le monde. ● vi sauter; (in surprise) sursauter; (price) monter en flèche; **~ at** (opportunity) sauter sur. ● n saut m, bond m; (increase) bond m.

jumper /'dʒʌmpə(r)/ n pull(-over) m; (dress: US) robe f chasuble.

jump-leads npl câbles mpl de démarrage.

jumpy /'dʒʌmpɪ/ adj nerveux.

junction /'dʒʌŋkʃn/ n (of roads) carrefour m; (on motorway) échangeur m.

June /dʒuːn/ n juin m.

jungle /'dʒʌŋgl/ n jungle f.

junior /'dʒuːnɪə(r)/ adj (young) jeune; (in rank) subalterne; (school) primaire.

● *n* cadet/-te *m/f;* (School) élève *mf* du primaire.

junk /dʒʌŋk/ *n* bric-à-brac *m inv;* (poor quality) camelote *f;* ~ **food** nourriture *f* industrielle.

junkie /'dʒʌŋkɪ/ *n* ⊠ drogué/-e *m/f.*

junk: ~ **mail** *n* prospectus *mpl.* ~**-shop** *n* boutique *f* de bric-à-brac.

jurisdiction /dʒʊərɪs'dɪkʃn/ *n* compétence *f;* (Jur) juridiction *f.*

juror /'dʒʊərə(r)/ *n* juré *m.*

jury /'dʒʊərɪ/ *n* jury *m.*

just /dʒʌst/ *adj* (fair) juste. ● *adv* (immediately, slightly) juste; (simply) tout simplement; (exactly) exactement; **he has/had ~ left** il vient/venait de partir; **have ~ missed** avoir manqué de peu; **I'm ~ leaving** je suis sur le point de partir; **it's ~ a cold** ce n'est qu'un rhume; **~ as tall/well as** tout aussi grand/bien que; **~ listen!** écoutez donc!; **it's ~ ridiculous** c'est vraiment ridicule.

justice /'dʒʌstɪs/ *n* justice *f;* **J~ of the Peace** juge *m* de paix.

justification /dʒʌstɪfɪ'keɪʃn/ *n* justification *f.* **justify** *vt* justifier.

jut /dʒʌt/ *vi* (*pt* **jutted**) ~ **(out)** s'avancer en saillie.

juvenile /'dʒuːvənaɪl/ *adj* (childish) puéril; (*offender*) mineur; (*delinquent*) jeune. ● *n* jeune *mf;* (Jur) mineur/-e *m/f.*

juxtapose /dʒʌkstə'pəʊz/ *vt* juxtaposer.

Kk

kangaroo /kæŋgə'ruː/ *n* kangourou *m.*

karate /kə'rɑːtɪ/ *n* karaté *m.*

kebab /kɪ'bæb/ *n* brochette *f.*

keel /kiːl/ *n* (of ship) quille *f.* ● *vi* ~ **over** (*bateau*) chavirer; (*person*) s'écrouler.

keen /kiːn/ *adj* (*interest, wind, feeling*) vif; (*mind, analysis*) pénétrant; (*edge, appetite*) aiguisé; (*eager*) enthousiaste; **be ~ on** être passionné de; **be ~ to do** *or* **on doing** tenir beaucoup à

faire. **keenly** *adv* vivement. **keenness** *n* enthousiasme *m.*

keep /kiːp/ *vt* (*pt* **kept**) garder; (*promise, shop, diary*) tenir; (*family*) faire vivre; (*animals*) élever; (*rule*) respecter; (*celebrate*) célébrer; (*delay*) retenir; ~ **sth clean/warm** garder qch propre/au chaud; ~ **sb in/out** empêcher qn de sortir/d'entrer; ~ **sb from doing** empêcher qn de faire. ● *vi* (*food*) se conserver; ~ **(on)** continuer (**doing** à faire). ● *n* pension *f;* (of castle) donjon *m.* □ ~ **down** rester allongé; ~ **sth down** limiter qch; ~ **your voice down!** baisse la voix!; ~ **to** (*road*) ne pas s'écarter de; (*rules*) respecter; ~ **up** (*car, runner*) suivre; (*rain*) continuer; ~ **up with sb** (in speed) aller aussi vite que; (*class, inflation, fashion, news*) suivre.

keeper /'kiːpə(r)/ *n* gardien/-ne *m/f.*

keepsake /'kiːpseɪk/ *n* souvenir *m.*

kennel /'kenl/ *n* niche *f.*

kept /kept/ →**KEEP.**

kerb /kɜːb/ *n* bord *m* du trottoir.

kernel /'kɜːnl/ *n* amande *f;* ~ **of truth** fond *m* de vérité.

kettle /'ketl/ *n* bouilloire *f.*

key /kiː/ *n* clé *f;* (of computer, piano) touche *f.* ● *adj* (*industry, figure*) clé (*inv*). ● *vt* ~ **(in)** saisir. ~**board** *n* clavier *m.* ~**hole** *n* trou *m* de serrure. ~**-pad** *n* (of telephone) clavier *m* numérique. ~**-ring** *n* porte-clés *m inv.* ~**stroke** *n* (Comput) frappe *f.*

khaki /'kɑːkɪ/ *adj* kaki *inv.*

kick /kɪk/ *vt/i* donner un coup de pied (à); (*horse*) botter. ● *n* coup *m* de pied; (of gun) recul *m;* **get a ~ out of doing** ⊡ prendre plaisir à faire. □ ~ **out** ⊡ virer ⊡.

kick-off *n* coup *m* d'envoi.

kid /kɪd/ *n* (goat, leather) chevreau *m;* (child ⊡) gosse *mf* ⊡. ● *vt/i* (*pt* **kidded**) blaguer.

kidnap /'kɪdnæp/ *vt* (*pt* **kidnapped**) enlever. **kidnapping** *n* enlèvement *m.*

kidney /'kɪdnɪ/ *n* rein *m;* (Culin) rognon *m.*

kill /kɪl/ *vt* tuer; (*rumour:* fig) arrêter. ● *n* mise *f* à mort. **killer** *n* tueur/-euse *m/f.* **killing** *n* meurtre *m.*

kiln /kɪln/ *n* four *m.*

kilo /'kiːləʊ/ *n* kilo *m.*

kilobyte /ˈkɪləbaɪt/ n kilo-octet m.

kilogram /ˈkɪləɡræm/ n kilo-gramme m.

kilometre, (US) **kilometer** /ˈkɪləmiːtə(r)/ n kilomètre m.

kilowatt /ˈkɪləwɒt/ n kilowatt m.

kin /kɪn/ n parents mpl.

kind /kaɪnd/ n genre m, sorte f; in ~ en nature; ~ of (somewhat 🗆) assez. ● adj gentil, bon.

kindergarten /ˈkɪndəɡɑːtn/ n jardin m d'enfants.

kindle /ˈkɪndl/ vt/i (s')allumer.

kindly /ˈkaɪndlɪ/ adj (**-ler**, **-iest**) (person) gentil; (interest) bienveillant. ● adv avec gentillesse; **would you ~ do** auriez-vous l'amabilité de faire.

kindness /ˈkaɪndnɪs/ n bonté f.

king /kɪŋ/ n roi m. **kingdom** n royaume m; (Bot) règne m. **~fisher** n martin-pêcheur m. **~-size(d)** adj géant.

kiosk /ˈkiːɒsk/ n kiosque m; **telephone ~** cabine f téléphonique; (Internet) borne f interactive, kiosque m.

kiss /kɪs/ n baiser m. ● vt/i (s')embrasser.

kit /kɪt/ n (clothing) affaires fpl; (set of tools) trousse f; (for assembly) kit m. ● vt (pt **kitted**) ~ **out** équiper.

kitchen /ˈkɪtʃɪn/ n cuisine f.

kite /kaɪt/ n (toy) cerf-volant m; (bird) milan m.

kitten /ˈkɪtn/ n chaton m.

kitty /ˈkɪtɪ/ n (fund) cagnotte f.

knack /næk/ n tour m de main (**of doing** pour faire).

knead /niːd/ vt pétrir.

knee /niː/ n genou m. **~cap** n rotule f.

kneel /niːl/ vi (pt **knelt**) ~ **(down)** se mettre à genoux; (in prayer) s'agenouiller.

knew /njuː/ ➡KNOW.

knickers /ˈnɪkəz/ npl petite culotte f, slip m.

knife /naɪf/ n (pl **knives**) couteau m. ● vt poignarder.

knight /naɪt/ n chevalier m; (chess) cavalier m. ● vt anoblir. **~hood** n titre m de chevalier.

knit /nɪt/ vt/i (pt **knitted** or **knit**) tricoter; (bones) (se) souder. **knitting** n tricot m. **knitwear** n tricots mpl.

knob /nɒb/ n bouton m.

knock /nɒk/ vt/i cogner; (criticize 🗆) critiquer; ~ **sth off/out** faire tomber qch. ● n coup m. □ ~ **down** (chair, pedestrian) renverser; (demolish) abattre; (reduce) baisser; ~ **off** (stop work 🗆) arrêter de travailler; ~ **£ 10 off** faire une réduction de 10 livres; ~ **it off!** 🗆 ça suffit!; ~ **out** assommer; ~ **over** renverser; ~ **up** (meal) préparer en vitesse.

knockout /ˈnɒkaʊt/ n (boxing) knock-out m.

knot /nɒt/ n nœud m. ● vt (pt **knotted**) nouer.

know /nəʊ/ vt/i (pt **knew**; pp **known**) (answer, reason, language) savoir (**that** que); (person, place, name, rule, situation) connaître; (recognize) reconnaître; ~ **how to do** savoir faire; ~ **about** (event) être au courant de; (subject) s'y connaître en; ~ **of** (from experience) connaître; (from information) avoir entendu parler de. **~-how** n savoir-faire m inv.

knowingly /ˈnəʊɪŋlɪ/ adv (intentionally) délibérément; (meaningfully) d'un air entendu.

knowledge /ˈnɒlɪdʒ/ n connaissance f; (learning) connaissances fpl. **knowledgeable** adj savant.

knuckle /ˈnʌkl/ n jointure f, articulation f.

Koran /kəˈrɑːn/ n Coran m.

Korea /kəˈrɪə/ n Corée f.

kosher /ˈkəʊʃə(r)/ adj casher inv.

lab /læb/ n 🗆 labo m.

label /ˈleɪbl/ n étiquette f. ● vt (pt **labelled**) étiqueter.

laboratory /ləˈbɒrətrɪ/ n laboratoire m.

laborious /ləˈbɔːrɪəs/ adj laborieux.

labour, (US) **labor** /ˈleɪbə(r)/ n travail m; (workers) main-d'œuvre f; **in ~** en train d'accoucher. ● vi peiner (**to do** à faire). ● vt trop insister sur.

Labour /'leɪbə(r)/ n le parti travailliste.
● adj travailliste.

laboured /'leɪbəd/ adj laborieux.

labourer /'leɪbərə(r)/ n ouvrier/-ière m/f; (on farm) ouvrier/-ière m/f agricole.

lace /leɪs/ n dentelle f; (of shoe) lacet m. ● vt (shoe) lacer; (drink) arroser.

lacerate /'læsəreɪt/ vt lacérer.

lack /læk/ n manque m; **for ~ of** faute de. ● vt manquer de; **be ~ing** manquer (**in** de).

lad /læd/ n garçon m, gars m.

ladder /'lædə(r)/ n échelle f; (in stocking) maille f filée. ● vt/i (stocking) filer.

laden /'leɪdn/ adj chargé (**with** de).

ladle /'leɪdl/ n louche f.

lady /'leɪdɪ/ n (pl **ladies**) dame f; **ladies and gentlemen** mesdames et messieurs; **young ~** jeune femme or fille f. **~bird** n coccinelle f.

ladylike /'leɪdɪlaɪk/ adj distingué.

lag /læg/ vi (pt **lagged**) traîner. ● vt (pipes) calorifuger. ● n (interval) décalage m.

lager /'lɑːgə(r)/ n bière f blonde.

lagoon /lə'guːn/ n lagune f.

laid /leɪd/ ➡LAY¹. **~ back** adj décontracté.

lain /leɪn/ ➡LIE².

lake /leɪk/ n lac m.

lamb /læm/ n agneau m; **leg of ~** gigot m d'agneau.

lame /leɪm/ adj boiteux.

lament /lə'ment/ n lamentation f. ● vt/i se lamenter (sur).

laminated /'læmɪneɪtɪd/ adj laminé.

lamp /læmp/ n lampe f. **~post** n réverbère m. **~shade** n abat-jour m inv.

lance /lɑːns/ vt (Med) inciser.

land /lænd/ n terre f; (plot) terrain m; (country) pays m. ● adj terrestre; (policy, reform) agraire. ● vt/i débarquer; (aircraft) (se) poser, (faire) atterrir; (fall) tomber; (obtain) décrocher; (a blow) porter; **~ up** se retrouver.

landing /'lændɪŋ/ n débarquement m; (Aviat) atterrissage m; (top of stairs) palier m. **~-stage** n débarcadère m.

land: **~lady** n propriétaire f; (of pub) patronne f. **~lord** n propriétaire m; (of pub) patron m. **~mark** n (point de) repère m. **~mine** n mine f terrestre.

landscape /'lænskeɪp/ n paysage m.
● vt aménager.

landslide /'lænslaɪd/ n glissement m de terrain; (Pol) raz-de-marée m inv (électoral).

lane /leɪn/ n (path, road) chemin m; (strip of road) voie f; (of traffic) file f; (Aviat) couloir m.

language /'læŋgwɪdʒ/ n langue f; (speech, style) langage m. **~ engineering** n ingénierie f des langues. **~ laboratory** n laboratoire m de langue.

lank /læŋk/ adj (hair) plat.

lanky /'læŋkɪ/ adj (**-ier, -iest**) grand et maigre.

lantern /'læntən/ n lanterne f.

lap /læp/ n genoux mpl; (Sport) tour m (de piste). ● vi (pt **lapped**) (waves) clapoter. □ **~ up** laper.

lapel /lə'pel/ n revers m.

lapse /læps/ vi (decline) se dégrader; (expire) se périmer; **~ into** retomber dans. ● n défaillance f, erreur f; (of time) intervalle m.

laptop /'læptɒp/ n (Comput) portable m.

lard /lɑːd/ n saindoux m.

larder /'lɑːdə(r)/ n garde-manger m inv.

large /lɑːdʒ/ adj grand, gros; **at ~** en liberté; **by and ~** en général. **largely** adv en grande mesure.

lark /lɑːk/ n (bird) alouette f; (bit of fun **Ⅰ**) rigolade f. ● vi **Ⅰ** rigoler.

larva /'lɑːvə/ n (pl **-vae**) larve f.

laryngitis /lærɪn'dʒaɪtɪs/ n laryngite f.

laser /'leɪzə(r)/ n laser m. **~ printer** n imprimante f laser. **~ treatment** n (Med) laserothérapie f.

lash /læʃ/ vt fouetter. ● n coup m de fouet; (eyelash) cil m. □ **~ out** (spend) dépenser follement; **~ out against** attaquer.

lass /læs/ n jeune fille f.

lasso /læ'suː/ n lasso m.

last /lɑːst/ adj dernier; **the ~ straw** le comble; **the ~ word** le mot de la fin; **on its ~ legs** sur le point de rendre l'âme; **~ night** hier soir. ● adv en dernier; (most recently) la dernière fois. ● n dernier/-ière m/f; (remainder) reste m; **at (long) ~** enfin. ● vi durer. **~-ditch** adj ultime. **lasting** adj durable. **lastly** adv en dernier lieu. **~-minute** adj de dernière minute.

latch /lætʃ/ n loquet m.

late /leɪt/ adj (not on time) en retard; (former) ancien; (hour, fruit) tardif; **the ~ Mrs X** feu Mme X. ● adv (not early) tard; (not on time) en retard; **in ~ July** fin juillet; **of ~** dernièrement. **lately** adv dernièrement. **latest** adj ➡LATE; (last) dernier.

lathe /leɪð/ n tour m.

lather /'lɑːðə(r)/ n mousse f. ● vt savonner. ● vi mousser.

Latin /'lætɪn/ n (Ling) latin m. ● adj latin. **~ America** n Amérique f latine.

latitude /'lætɪtjuːd/ n latitude f.

latter /'lætə(r)/ adj dernier. ● n **the ~** celui-ci, celle-ci.

Latvia /'lætvɪə/ n Lettonie f.

laudable /'lɔːdəbl/ adj louable.

laugh /lɑːf/ vi rire (**at** de). ● n rire m. **laughable** adj ridicule.

laughing stock n risée f.

laughter /'lɑːftə(r)/ n (act) rire m; (sound of laughs) rires mpl.

launch /lɔːntʃ/ vt (rocket) lancer; (boat) mettre à l'eau; **~ (out) into** se lancer dans. ● n lancement m; (boat) vedette f. **launching pad** n aire f de lancement.

launderette /'lɔːndrəmæt/ n laverie f automatique.

laundry /'lɔːndrɪ/ n (place) blanchisserie f; (clothes) linge m.

laurel /'lɒrəl/ n laurier m.

lava /'lɑːvə/ n lave f.

lavatory /'lævətrɪ/ n toilettes fpl.

lavender /'lævəndə(r)/ n lavande f.

lavish /'lævɪʃ/ adj (person) généreux; (lush) somptueux. ● vt prodiguer (**on** à). **lavishly** adv luxueusement.

law /lɔː/ n loi f; (profession, subject of study) droit m; **~ and order** l'ordre public. **~-abiding** adj respectueux des lois. **~court** n tribunal m.

lawful /'lɔːfl/ adj légal.

lawn /lɔːn/ n pelouse f, gazon m. **~-mower** n tondeuse f à gazon.

lawsuit /'lɔːsuːt/ n procès m.

lawyer /'lɔːjə(r)/ n avocat m.

lax /læks/ adj (government) laxiste; (security) relâché.

laxative /'læksətɪv/ n laxatif m.

lay¹ /leɪ/ adj (non-clerical) laïque; (worker) non-initié. ● vt (pt **laid**) poser, mettre; (trap) tendre; (table) mettre; (plan) former; (eggs) pondre. ● vi pondre; **~ waste** ravager. □ **~ aside** mettre de côté; **~ down** (dé)poser; (condition) (im-)poser; **~ off** vt (worker) licencier; vi ⊞ arrêter; **~ on** (provide) fournir; **~ out** (design) dessiner; (display) disposer; (money) dépenser.

lay² /leɪ/ ➡LIE².

lay-by /'leɪbaɪ/ n (pl **~s**) aire f de repos.

layer /'leɪə(r)/ n couche f.

layman /'leɪmən/ n (pl **-men**) profane m.

layout /'leɪaʊt/ n disposition f.

laze /leɪz/ vi paresser. **laziness** n paresse f. **lazy** adj (**-ier, -iest**) paresseux.

lead¹ /liːd/ vt/i (pt **led**) mener; (team) diriger; (life) mener; (induce) amener; **~ to** conduire à, mener à. ● n avance f; (clue) indice m; (leash) laisse f; (Theat) premier rôle m; (wire) fil m; **in the ~** en tête. □ **~ away** emmener; **~ up to** (come to) en venir à; (precede) précéder.

lead² /led/ n plomb m; (of pencil) mine f.

leader /'liːdə(r)/ n chef m; (of country, club) dirigeant/-e m/f; (leading article) éditorial m. **leadership** n direction f.

lead-free adj (petrol) sans plomb.

leading /'liːdɪŋ/ adj principal.

leaf /liːf/ n (pl **leaves**) feuille f; (of table) rallonge f. ● vi **~ through** feuilleter.

leaflet /'liːflɪt/ n prospectus m.

leafy /'liːfɪ/ adj feuillu.

league /liːg/ n ligue f; (Sport) championnat m; **in ~ with** de mèche avec.

leak /liːk/ n fuite f. ● vi fuir; (news: fig) s'ébruiter. ● vt répandre; (fig) divulguer.

lean¹ /liːn/ adj maigre. ● n (of meat) maigre m.

lean² /liːn/ vt/i (pt **leaned** or **leant**) (rest) (s')appuyer; (slope) pencher. □ **~ out** se pencher à l'extérieur; **~ over** (of person) se pencher.

leaning /'liːnɪŋ/ adj penché. ● n tendance f.

leap /liːp/ vi (pt **leaped** or **leapt**) bondir. ● n bond m. **~ year** n année f bissextile.

learn /lɜːn/ vt/i (pt **learned** or **learnt**)
apprendre (**to do** à faire). **learned** adj
érudit. **learner** n débutant/-e m/f.
learning curve n courbe f d'apprentissage.

lease /liːs/ n bail m. ● vt louer à bail.

leash /liːʃ/ n laisse f.

least /liːst/ adj **the ~** (smallest amount
of) le moins de; (slightest) le or la
moindre. ● n le moins. ● adv le moins;
(with adjective) le or la moins; **at ~**
au moins.

leather /ˈleðə(r)/ n cuir m.

leave /liːv/ vt (pt **left**) laisser; (depart
from) quitter; (person) laisser tranquille; **be left (over)** rester. ● n (holiday) congé m; (consent) permission f;
take one's ~ prendre congé (of de);
on ~ (Mil) en permission. □ **~ alone**
(thing) ne pas toucher; (person) laisser
tranquille; **~ behind** laisser; **~ out**
omettre.

Lebanon /ˈlebənən/ n Liban m.

lecture /ˈlektʃə(r)/ n cours m, conférence f; (rebuke) réprimande f. ● vt/i
faire un cours or une conférence (à);
(rebuke) réprimander. **lecturer** n
conférencier/-ière m/f; (Univ)
enseignant/-e m/f.

led /led/ ⇒LEAD[1].

ledge /ledʒ/ n (window) rebord m;
(rock) saillie f.

ledger /ˈledʒə(r)/ n grand livre m.

leech /liːtʃ/ n sangsue f.

leek /liːk/ n poireau m.

leer /lɪə(r)/ vi **~ (at)** lorgner. ● n regard m sournois.

leeway /ˈliːweɪ/ n (fig) liberté f d'action; (Naut) dérive f.

left /left/ ⇒LEAVE. ● adj gauche. ● adv
à gauche. ● n gauche f. **~-hand** adj à
or de gauche. **~-handed** adj gaucher.

left luggage (office) n consigne f.

left-overs npl restes mpl.

left-wing adj de gauche.

leg /leg/ n jambe f; (of animal) patte f;
(of table) pied m; (of chicken) cuisse f;
(of lamb) gigot m; (of journey) étape f.

legacy /ˈlegəsɪ/ n legs m.

legal /ˈliːgl/ adj légal; (affairs) juridique.

legend /ˈledʒənd/ n légende f.

leggings /ˈlegɪŋz/ npl (for woman) caleçon m.

legible /ˈledʒəbl/ adj lisible.

legionnaire /liːdʒəˈneə(r)/ n légion-
naire m.

legislation /ledʒɪsˈleɪʃn/ n (body of
laws) législation f; (law) loi f. **legisla-
ture** n corps m législatif.

legitimate /lɪˈdʒɪtɪmət/ adj légitime.

leisure /ˈleʒə(r)/ n loisirs mpl; **at one's
~** à tête reposée. ● adj (centre) de
loisirs.

leisurely /ˈleʒəlɪ/ adj lent. ● adv sans
se presser.

lemon /ˈlemən/ n citron m.

lemonade /leməˈneɪd/ n (fizzy) limonade f; (still) citronnade f.

lend /lend/ vt (pt **lent**) prêter; (credibility) conférer; **~ itself to** se prêter à.

length /leŋθ/ n longueur f; (in time)
durée f; (section) morceau m; **at ~** (at
last) enfin; **at (great) ~** longuement.

lengthen /ˈleŋθən/ vt/i (s')allonger.

lengthways /ˈleŋθweɪz/ adv dans le
sens de la longueur.

lengthy /ˈleŋθɪ/ adj long.

lenient /ˈliːnɪənt/ adj indulgent.

lens /lenz/ n lentille f; (of spectacles)
verre m; (Photo) objectif m.

lent /lent/ ⇒LEND.

Lent /lent/ n Carême m.

lentil /ˈlentl/ n lentille f.

Leo /ˈliːəʊ/ n Lion m.

leopard /ˈlepəd/ n léopard m.

leotard /ˈliːətɑːd/ n body m.

leprosy /ˈleprəsɪ/ n lèpre f.

lesbian /ˈlezbɪən/ n lesbienne f. ● adj
lesbien.

less /les/ adj (in quantity) moins de
(**than** que). ● adv, n & prep moins; **~
than** (with numbers) moins de; **work
~ than** travailler moins que; **ten
pounds ~** dix livres de moins; **~ and
~** de moins en moins. **lessen** vt/i diminuer. **lesser** adj moindre.

lesson /ˈlesn/ n leçon f.

let /let/ vt (pt **let**; pres p **letting**) laisser;
(lease) louer. ● v aux **~ us do, ~'s do**
faisons; **~ him do** qu'il fasse; **~ me
know the results** informe-moi des résultats. ● n location f. □ **~ down**
baisser; (deflate) dégonfler; (fig) décevoir; **~ go** vt lâcher; vi lâcher prise; **~
sb in/out** laisser or faire entrer/sortir
qn; **~ a dress out** élargir une robe; **~**

oneself in for (*task*) s'engager à; (*trouble*) s'attirer; ~ **off** (explode, fire) faire éclater *or* partir; (*excuse*) dispenser; (not punish) ne pas punir; ~ **up** 🔲 s'arrêter.

let-down *n* déception *f.*

lethal /'li:θl/ *adj* mortel; (weapon) meurtrier.

letter /'letə(r)/ *n* lettre *f.* ~**-bomb** *n* lettre *f* piégée. ~**-box** *n* boîte *f* à *or* aux lettres.

lettering /'letərɪŋ/ *n* (letters) caractères *mpl.*

lettuce /'letɪs/ *n* laitue *f,* salade *f.*

let-up /'letʌp/ *n* répit *m.*

leukaemia /lu:'ki:mɪə/ *n* leucémie *f.*

level /'levl/ *adj* plat, uni; (on surface) horizontal; (in height) au même niveau (**with** que); (in score) à égalité. ● *n* niveau *m*; (spirit) ~ niveau *m* à bulle; **be on the** ~ 🔲 être franc. ● *vt* (*pt* **levelled**) niveler; (aim) diriger. ~ **crossing** *n* passage *m* à niveau. ~**-headed** *adj* équilibré.

lever /'li:və(r)/ *n* levier *m.* ● *vt* soulever au moyen d'un levier.

leverage /'li:vərɪdʒ/ *n* influence *f.*

levy /'levɪ/ *vt* (*tax*) prélever. ● *n* impôt *m.*

lexicon /'leksɪkən/ *n* lexique *m.*

liability /laɪə'bɪlətɪ/ *n* responsabilité *f*; 🔲 handicap *m*; **liabilities** (debts) dettes *fpl.*

liable /'laɪəbl/ *adj* be ~ **to do** avoir tendance à faire, pouvoir faire; ~ **to** (illness) sujet à; (fine) passible de; ~ **for** responsable de.

liaise /lɪ'eɪz/ *vi* 🔲 faire la liaison. **liaison** *n* liaison *f.*

liar /'laɪə(r)/ *n* menteur/-euse *m/f.*

libel /'laɪbl/ *n* diffamation *f.* ● *vt* (*pt* **libelled**) diffamer.

liberal /'lɪbərəl/ *adj* libéral; (generous) généreux, libéral.

Liberal /'lɪbərəl/ *adj & n* (Pol) libéral/-e (*m/f*).

liberate /'lɪbəreɪt/ *vt* libérer.

liberty /'lɪbətɪ/ *n* liberté *f*; **at** ~ **to** libre de; **take liberties** prendre des libertés.

Libra /'li:brə/ *n* Balance *f.*

librarian /laɪ'breərɪən/ *n* bibliothécaire *mf.*

library /'laɪbrərɪ/ *n* bibliothèque *f.*

libretto /lɪ'bretəʊ/ *n* livret *m.*

lice /laɪs/ ➡LOUSE.

licence, (US) **license** /'laɪsns/ *n* permis *m*; (for television) redevance *f*; (Comm) licence *f*; (liberty: fig) licence *f.* ~ **plate** *n* plaque *f* minéralogique.

license /'laɪsns/ *vt* accorder un permis à, autoriser.

lick /lɪk/ *vt* lécher; (defeat 🔲) rosser; (fig) **a** ~ **of paint** un petit coup de peinture. ● *n* coup *m* de langue.

lid /lɪd/ *n* couvercle *m.*

lie[1] /laɪ/ *n* mensonge *m.* ● *vi* (*pt* **lied**; *pres p* **lying**) mentir.

lie[2] /laɪ/ *vi* (*pt* **lay**; *pp* **lain**; *pres p* **lying**) s'allonger; (remain) rester; (be) se trouver, être; (in grave) reposer; **be lying** être allongé. □ ~ **down** s'allonger; ~ **in** faire la grasse matinée; ~ **low** se cacher.

lieutenant /lef'tenənt/ *n* lieutenant *m.*

life /laɪf/ *n* (*pl* **lives**) vie *f.* ~**belt** *n* bouée *f* de sauvetage. ~**boat** *n* canot *m* de sauvetage. ~**buoy** *n* bouée *f* de sauvetage. ~ **coach** *n* conseiller/ère *m/f* en développement personnel. ~ **cycle** *n* cycle *m* de vie. ~**-guard** *n* sauveteur *m.* ~ **insurance** *n* assurance-vie *f.* ~**-jacket** *n* gilet *m* de sauvetage.

lifeless /'laɪflɪs/ *adj* inanimé.

lifelike /'laɪflaɪk/ *adj* très ressemblant.

life: ~**long** *adj* de toute la vie. ~ **sentence** *n* condamnation *f* à perpétuité. ~**-size(d)** *adj* grandeur nature *inv.* ~ **story** *n* vie *f.* ~**-style** *n* style *m* de vie. ~ **support machine** *n* appareil *m* de respiration artificielle.

lifetime /'laɪftaɪm/ *n* vie *f*; **in one's** ~ de son vivant.

lift /lɪft/ *vt* lever; (steal 🔲) voler. ● *vi* (of fog) se lever. ● *n* (in building) ascenseur *m*; **give a** ~ **to** emmener (en voiture). ~**-off** *n* (Aviat) décollage *m.*

light /laɪt/ *n* lumière *f*; (lamp) lampe *f*; (for fire, on vehicle) feu *m*; (headlight) phare *m*; **bring to** ~ révéler; **come to** ~ être révélé; **have you got a** ~**?** vous avez du feu? ● *adj* (not dark) clair; (not heavy) léger. ● *vt* (*pt* **lit** *or* **lighted**) allumer; (room) éclairer; (*match*) frotter. □ ~ **up** *vi* s'allumer; *vt* (room) éclairer. ~ **bulb** *n* ampoule *f.*

lighten /'laɪtn/ vt (give light to) éclairer; (make brighter) éclaircir; (make less heavy) alléger.

lighter /'laɪtə(r)/ n briquet m; (for stove) allume-gaz m inv.

light: ~**-headed** adj (dizzy) qui a un vertige; (frivolous) étourdi. ~**-hearted** adj gai. ~**house** n phare m.

lighting /'laɪtɪŋ/ n éclairage m.

lightly /'laɪtlɪ/ adv légèrement.

lightning /'laɪtnɪŋ/ n éclair m, foudre f. ● adj.(visit) éclair inv.

lightweight /'laɪtweɪt/ adj léger. ● n (boxing) poids m léger.

light year n année f lumière.

like¹ /laɪk/ adj semblable, pareil; **be ~-minded** avoir les mêmes sentiments. ● prep comme. ● conj ⊡ comme. ● n pareil m; **the ~s of you** les gens comme vous.

like² /laɪk/ vt aimer (bien); **I should ~** je voudrais, j'aimerais; **would you ~?** voudriez-vous?, voudrais-tu?; ~**s** goûts mpl. **likeable** adj sympathique.

likelihood /'laɪklɪhʊd/ n probabilité f.

likely /'laɪklɪ/ adj (**-ier, -iest**) probable. ● adv probablement; **he is ~ to do it** fera probablement; **not ~!** ⊡ pas question!

likeness /'laɪknɪs/ n ressemblance f.

likewise /'laɪkwaɪz/ adv également.

liking /'laɪkɪŋ/ n (for thing) penchant m; (for person) affection f.

lilac /'laɪlək/ n lilas m. ● adj lilas inv.

Lilo® /'laɪləʊ/ n matelas m pneumatique.

lily /'lɪlɪ/ n lis m, lys m.

limb /lɪm/ n membre m.

limber /'lɪmbə(r)/ vi ~ **up** faire des exercices d'assouplissement.

limbo /'lɪmbəʊ/ n **be in ~** (forgotten) être tombé dans l'oubli.

lime /laɪm/ n (fruit) citron m vert; ~**(-tree)** tilleul m.

limelight /'laɪmlaɪt/ n **in the ~** en vedette.

limestone /'laɪmstəʊn/ n calcaire m.

limit /'lɪmɪt/ n limite f. ● vt limiter.

limited company n société f anonyme.

limp /lɪmp/ vi boiter. ● n **have a ~** boiter. ● adj mou.

line /laɪn/ n ligne f; (track) voie f; (wrinkle) ride f; (row) rangée f, file f; (of poem) vers m; (rope) corde f; (of goods) gamme f; (queue: US) queue f; **be in ~ for** avoir de bonnes chances de; **hold the ~** ne quittez pas; **in ~ with** en accord avec; **stand in ~** faire la queue. ● vt (paper) régler; (streets) border; (garment) doubler; (fill) remplir, garnir. □ ~ **up** (s')aligner; (in queue) faire la queue; ~ **sth up** prévoir qch. ~ **dancing** danse f en ligne.

linen /'lɪnɪn/ n (sheets) linge m; (material) lin m.

liner /'laɪnə(r)/ n paquebot m.

linesman /'laɪnzmən/ n (football) juge m de touche; (tennis) juge m de ligne.

linger /'lɪŋgə(r)/ vi s'attarder; (smells) persister.

linguist /'lɪŋgwɪst/ n linguiste mf. **linguistics** n linguistique f.

lining /'laɪnɪŋ/ n doublure f.

link /lɪŋk/ n lien m; (of chain) maillon m. ● vt relier; (relate) (re)lier; ~ **up** (of roads) se rejoindre. **linkage** n lien m. **links** n inv terrain m de golf. ~**-up** n liaison f.

lino /'laɪnəʊ/ n lino m.

lion /'laɪən/ n lion m. **lioness** n lionne f.

lip /lɪp/ n lèvre f; (edge) rebord m; **pay ~-service to** n'approuver que pour la forme. ~**-read** vt/i lire sur les lèvres. ~**salve** n baume m pour les lèvres. ~**stick** n rouge m (à lèvres).

liquid /'lɪkwɪd/ n & adj liquide (m).

liquidation /lɪkwɪ'deɪʃn/ n liquidation f; **go into ~** déposer son bilan.

liquidize /'lɪkwɪdaɪz/ vt passer au mixeur. **liquidizer** n mixeur m.

liquor /'lɪkə(r)/ n alcool m.

liquorice /'lɪkərɪs/ n réglisse f.

lisp /lɪsp/ n zézaiement m; **with a ~** en zézayant. ● vi zézayer.

list /lɪst/ n liste f. ● vt dresser la liste de. ● vi (ship) gîter.

listen /'lɪsn/ vi écouter; ~ **to,** ~ **in (to)** écouter. **listener** n auditeur/-trice m/f.

listless /'lɪstlɪs/ adj apathique.

lit /lɪt/ ⇒LIGHT.

liter ⇒LITRE.

literal /'lɪtərəl/ adj (meaning) littéral; (translation) mot à mot. **literally** adv littéralement; mot à mot.

literary /'lɪtərərɪ/ adj littéraire.

literate /'lɪtərət/ adj qui sait lire et écrire.

literature /'lɪtrətʃə(r)/ n littérature f; (brochures) documentation f.

Lithuania /lɪθju:'eɪnɪə/ n Lituanie f.

litigation /lɪtɪ'geɪʃn/ n litiges mpl.

litre, (US) **liter** /'li:tə(r)/ n litre m.

litter /'lɪtə(r)/ n (rubbish) détritus mpl, papiers mpl; (animals) portée f. ● vt éparpiller; (make untidy) laisser des détritus dans; ~ed with jonché de. ~-bin n poubelle f.

little /'lɪtl/ adj petit; (not much) peu de. ● n peu m; a ~ un peu (de). ● adv peu.

live[1] /laɪv/ adj vivant; (wire) sous tension; (broadcast) en direct; **be a** ~ **wire** être très dynamique.

live[2] /lɪv/ vt/i vivre; (reside) habiter, vivre; ~ **it up** mener la belle vie. □ ~ **down** faire oublier; ~ **on** (feed oneself on) vivre de; (continue) survivre; ~ **up to** se montrer à la hauteur de.

livelihood /'laɪvlɪhʊd/ n moyens mpl d'existence.

lively /'laɪvlɪ/ adj (-ier, -iest) vif, vivant.

liven /'laɪvn/ vt/i ~ **up** (s')animer; (cheer up) (s')égayer.

liver /'lɪvə(r)/ n foie m.

livestock /'laɪvstɒk/ n bétail m.

livid /'lɪvɪd/ adj livide; (angry) furieux.

living /'lɪvɪŋ/ adj vivant. ● n vie f; **make a** ~ gagner sa vie; ~ **conditions** conditions fpl de vie. ~-**room** n salle f de séjour.

lizard /'lɪzəd/ n lézard m.

load /ləʊd/ n charge f; (loaded goods) chargement m, charge f; (weight, strain) poids m; ~**s of** 🔳 des tas de 🔳. ● vt charger.

loaf /ləʊf/ n (pl **loaves**) pain m. ● vi ~ (about) fainéanter.

loan /ləʊn/ n prêt m; (money borrowed) emprunt m. ● vt prêter.

loathe /ləʊð/ vt détester (doing faire). **loathing** n dégoût m.

lobby /'lɒbɪ/ n entrée f, vestibule m; (Pol) lobby m, groupe m de pression. ● vt faire pression sur.

lobster /'lɒbstə(r)/ n homard m.

local /'ləʊkl/ adj local; (shops) du quartier; ~ **government** administration f

locale. ● n personne f du coin; (pub 🔳) pub m du coin.

localization /ləʊklaɪ'zeɪʃn/n localisation f.

locally /'ləʊklɪ/ adv localement; (nearby) dans les environs.

locate /ləʊ'keɪt/ vt (situate) situer; (find) repérer.

location /ləʊ'keɪʃn/ n emplacement m; **on** ~ (cinema) en extérieur.

lock /lɒk/ n (of door) serrure f; (on canal) écluse f; (of hair) mèche f. ● vt/i fermer à clef; (Auto) (se) bloquer. □ ~ **in** or **up** (person) enfermer; ~ **out** (by mistake) enfermer dehors.

locker /'lɒkə(r)/ n casier m.

locket /'lɒkɪt/ n médaillon m.

locksmith /'lɒksmɪθ/ n serrurier m.

locum /'ləʊkəm/ n (doctor) remplaçant/-e m/f.

lodge /lɒdʒ/ n (house) pavillon m (de gardien or de chasse); (of porter) loge f. ● vt (accommodate) loger; (money, complaint) déposer. ● vi être logé (with chez); (become fixed) se loger. **lodger** n locataire mf, pensionnaire mf. **lodgings** n logement m.

loft /lɒft/ n grenier m.

lofty /'lɒftɪ/ adj (-ier, -iest) (tall, noble) élevé; (haughty) hautain.

log /lɒg/ n (of wood) bûche f; ~ (~**book**) (Naut) journal m de bord; (Auto) ≈ carte f grise. ● vt (pt **logged**) noter; (distance) parcourir. □ ~ **on** (Comput) se connecter; ~ **off** (Comput) se déconnecter.

logic /'lɒdʒɪk/ adj logique. **logical** adj logique.

logistics /lə'dʒɪstɪks/ n logistique f.

loin /lɔɪn/ n (Culin) filet m; ~**s** reins mpl.

loiter /'lɔɪtə(r)/ vi traîner.

loll /lɒl/ vi se prélasser.

lollipop /'lɒlɪpɒp/ n sucette f.

London /'lʌndən/ n Londres. **Londoner** n Londonien/-ne m/f.

lone /ləʊn/ adj solitaire.

lonely (-ier, -iest) solitaire; (person) seul, solitaire.

long /lɒŋ/ adj long; **how** ~ **is?** quelle est la longueur de?; (in time) quelle est la durée de?; **how** ~**?** combien de temps?; **a** ~ **time** longtemps. ● adv longtemps; **he will not be** ~ il n'en a pas pour longtemps; **as** or **so ~ as** pourvu que; **before ~** avant peu; **I no ~er do** je ne fais plus. ● vi avoir bien or très envie **(for, to** de); **~ for sb** (pine for) se languir de qn.

~-distance adj (flight) sur long parcours; (phone call) interurbain; (runner) de fond. **~ face** n grimace f. **~hand** n écriture f courante.

longing /'lɒŋɪŋ/ n envie f (**for** de); (nostalgia) nostalgie f (**for** de).

longitude /'lɒndʒɪtjuːd/ n longitude f.

long: ~ jump n saut m en longueur. **~-range** adj (missile) à longue portée; (forecast) à long terme. **~-sighted** adj presbyte. **~-standing** adj de longue date. **~-term** adj à long terme. **~ wave** n grandes ondes fpl. **~-winded** adj verbeux.

loo /luː/ n 🔲 toilettes fpl.

look /lʊk/ vi regarder; (seem) avoir l'air; **~ like** ressembler à, avoir l'air de. ● n regard m; (appearance) air m, aspect m; **(good) ~s** beauté f. **~ after** s'occuper de, soigner; **~ at** regarder; **~ back on** repenser à; **~ down on** mépriser; **~ for** chercher; **~ forward to** attendre avec impatience; **~ in on** passer voir; **~ into** examiner; **~ out** faire attention; **~ out for** (person) guetter; (symptoms) guetter l'apparition de; **~ round** se retourner; **~ up** (word) chercher; (visit) passer voir; **~ up to** respecter.

lookout /'lʊkaʊt/ n (Mil) poste m de guet; (person) guetteur m; **be on the ~ for** rechercher.

loom /luːm/ vi surgir; (war) menacer; (interview) être imminent. ● n métier m à tisser.

loony /'luːnɪ/ n & adj 🔲 fou, folle (mf).

loop /luːp/ n boucle f. ● vt boucler. **~hole** n lacune f.

loose /luːs/ adj (knot) desserré; (page) détaché; (clothes) ample, lâche; (tooth) qui bouge; (lax) relâché; (not packed) en vrac; (inexact) vague; (pej) immoral; **at a ~ end** désœuvré; **come ~** bouger. **loosely** adv sans serrer; (roughly) vaguement. **loosen** vt (slacken) desserrer; (untie) défaire.

loot /luːt/ n butin m. ● vt piller.

lord /lɔːd/ n seigneur m; (British title) lord m; **the L~** le Seigneur; **(good) L~!** mon Dieu!

lorry /'lɒrɪ/ n camion m.

lose /luːz/ vt/i (pt **lost**) perdre; **get lost** se perdre. **loser** n perdant/-e m/f.

loss /lɒs/ n perte f; **be at a ~** être perplexe; **be at a ~ to** être incapable de; **heat ~** déperdition f de chaleur.

lost /lɒst/ →LOSE. ● adj perdu. **~ property** n objets mpl trouvés.

lot /lɒt/ n **the ~** (le) tout m; (people) tous mpl, toutes fpl; **a ~ (of)**, **~s (of)** 🔲 beaucoup (de); **quite a ~ (of)** 🔲 pas mal (de); (fate) sort m; (at auction) lot m; (land) lotissement m.

lotion /'ləʊʃn/ n lotion f.

lottery /'lɒtərɪ/ n loterie f.

loud /laʊd/ adj bruyant, fort. ● adv fort; **out ~** tout haut. **loudly** adv fort. **~speaker** n haut-parleur m.

lounge /laʊndʒ/ vi paresser. ● n salon m.

louse /laʊs/ n (pl **lice**) pou m.

lousy /'laʊzɪ/ adj (-ier, -iest) 🔲 infect.

lout /laʊt/ n rustre m.

lovable /'lʌvəbl/ adj adorable.

love /lʌv/ n amour m; (tennis) zéro m; **in ~** amoureux (**with** de); **make ~** faire l'amour. ● vt (person) aimer; (like greatly) aimer (beaucoup) (**to do** faire). **~ affair** n liaison f amoureuse. **~ life** n vie f amoureuse.

lovely /'lʌvlɪ/ adj (-ier, -iest) joli; (delightful 🔲) très agréable.

lover /'lʌvə(r)/ n (male) amant m; (female) maîtresse f; (devotee) amateur m (**of** de).

loving /'lʌvɪŋ/ adj affectueux.

low /ləʊ/ adj & adv bas; **~ in sth** à faible teneur en qch. ● n (low pressure) dépression f; **reach a (new) ~** atteindre son niveau le plus bas. ● vi meugler. **~-calorie** adj basses-calories. **~-cut** adj décolleté.

lower /'ləʊə(r)/ adj & adv →LOW. ● vt baisser; **~ oneself** s'abaisser.

low: ~-fat adj (diet) sans matières grasses; (cheese) allégé. **~-key** adj modéré; (discreet) discret. **~-lands** npl plaine(s) f(pl). **~-lying** adj à faible altitude.

loyal /'lɔɪəl/ adj loyal (**to** envers).

loyalty /'lɔɪəltɪ/ n fidélité f. **~ card** n carte f de fidélité.

lozenge /'lɒzəndʒ/ n (shape) losange m; (tablet) pastille f.

LP *n* (disque *m*) 33 tours *m*.

Ltd. *abbr* (**Limited**) SA.

lubricant /ˈluːbrɪkənt/ *n* lubrifiant *m*. **lubricate** *vt* lubrifier.

luck /lʌk/ *n* chance *f*; **bad** ∼ malchance *f*; **good** ∼**!** bonne chance!

luckily /ˈlʌkɪlɪ/ *adv* heureusement.

lucky /ˈlʌkɪ/ *adj* (**-ier, -iest**) qui a de la chance, heureux; (event) heureux; (number) qui porte bonheur; **it's** ∼ **that** heureusement que.

ludicrous /ˈluːdɪkrəs/ *adj* ridicule.

lug /lʌg/ *vt* (*pt* **lugged**) traîner.

luggage /ˈlʌgɪdʒ/ *n* bagages *mpl*. ∼**-rack** *n* porte-bagages *m inv*.

lukewarm /luːkˈwɔːm/ *adj* tiède.

lull /lʌl/ *vt* **he** ∼**ed them into thinking that** il leur a fait croire que. ● *n* accalmie *f*.

lullaby /ˈlʌləbaɪ/ *n* berceuse *f*.

lumber /ˈlʌmbə(r)/ *n* bois *m* de charpente. ● *vt* □ ∼ **sb with** (*chore*) coller à qn □. ∼**jack** *n* bûcheron *m*.

luminous /ˈluːmɪnəs/ *adj* lumineux.

lump /lʌmp/ *n* morceau *m*; (swelling on body) grosseur *f*; (in liquid) grumeau *m*. ● *vt* ∼ **together** réunir. ∼ **sum** *n* somme *f* globale.

lunacy /ˈluːnəsɪ/ *n* folie *f*.

lunar /ˈluːnə(r)/ *adj* lunaire.

lunatic /ˈluːnətɪk/ *n* fou/folle *m/f*.

lunch /lʌntʃ/ *n* déjeuner *m*. ● *vi* déjeuner.

luncheon /ˈlʌntʃən/ *n* déjeuner *m*. ∼ **voucher** *n* chèque-repas *m*.

lung /lʌŋ/ *n* poumon *m*.

lunge /lʌndʒ/ *vi* bondir (at sur; **forward** en avant).

lurch /lɜːtʃ/ *n* **leave in the** ∼ planter là, laisser en plan. ● *vi* (*person*) tituber.

lure /lʊə(r)/ *vt* appâter, attirer. ● *n* (attraction) attrait *m*, appât *m*.

lurid /ˈlʊərɪd/ *adj* choquant, affreux; (gaudy) voyant.

lurk /lɜːk/ *vi* se cacher; (in ambush) s'embusquer; (prowl) rôder; (suspicion, danger) menacer.

luscious /ˈlʌʃəs/ *adj* appétissant.

lush /lʌʃ/ *adj* luxuriant.

lust /lʌst/ *n* luxure *f*.

Luxemburg /ˈlʌksəmbɜːg/ *n* Luxembourg *m*.

luxurious /lʌgˈzjʊərɪəs/ *adj* luxueux.

luxury /ˈlʌkʃərɪ/ *n* luxe *m*. ● *adj* de luxe.

lying /ˈlaɪɪŋ/ ⇒LIE[1], ⇒LIE[2]. ● *n* mensonges *mpl*.

lyric /ˈlɪrɪk/ *adj* lyrique. **lyrical** *adj* lyrique. **lyrics** *npl* paroles *fpl*.

Mm

MA *abbr* ⇒MASTER OF ARTS.

mac /mæk/ *n* □ imper *m*.

machine /məˈʃiːn/ *n* machine *f*. ● *vt* (sew) coudre à la machine; (Tech) usiner. ∼**-gun** *n* mitrailleuse *f*.

mackerel /ˈmækrəl/ *n inv* maquereau *m*.

mackintosh /ˈmækɪntɒʃ/ *n* imperméable *m*.

mad /mæd/ *adj* (**madder, maddest**) fou; (foolish) insensé; (dog) enragé; (angry □) furieux; **be** ∼ **about** se passionner pour; (person) être fou de; **drive sb** ∼ exaspérer qn; **like** ∼ comme un fou. ∼ **cow disease** *n* maladie *f* de la vache folle.

madam /ˈmædəm/ *n* madame *f*; (unmarried) mademoiselle *f*.

made /meɪd/ ⇒MAKE.

madly /ˈmædlɪ/ *adv* (interested, in love) follement; (frantically) comme un fou.

madman /ˈmædmən/ *n* (*pl* **-men**) fou *m*.

madness /ˈmædnɪs/ *n* folie *f*.

magazine /mægəˈziːn/ *n* revue *f*, magazine *m*; (of gun) magasin *m*.

maggot /ˈmægət/ *n* (in fruit) ver *m*, (for fishing) asticot *m*.

magic /ˈmædʒɪk/ *n* magie *f*. ● *adj* magique.

magician /məˈdʒɪʃn/ *n* magicien/-ne *m/f*.

magistrate /ˈmædʒɪstreɪt/ *n* magistrat *m*.

magnet /ˈmægnɪt/ *n* aimant *m*. **magnetic** *adj* magnétique.

magnificent /mæg'nɪfɪsnt/ adj magnifique.

magnify /'mægnɪfaɪ/ vt grossir; (sound) amplifier; (fig) exagérer. **magnifying glass** n loupe f.

magpie /'mægpaɪ/ n pie f.

mahogany /mə'hɒgənɪ/ n acajou m.

maid /meɪd/ n (servant) bonne f; (in hotel) femme f de chambre.

maiden /'meɪdn/ n (old use) jeune fille f. ● adj (aunt) célibataire; (voyage) premier. ~ **name** n nom m de jeune fille.

mail /meɪl/ n (postal service) poste f; (letters) courrier m; (armour) cotte f de mailles. ● adj (bag, van) postal. ● vt envoyer par la poste. ~ **box** n boîte f aux lettres; (Comput) boîte f aux lettres électronique. **mailing list** n liste f d'adresses. ~**man** n (pl -**men**) (US) facteur m. ~ **order** n vente f par correspondance. ~ **shot** n publipostage m.

main /meɪn/ adj principal; **a ~ road** une grande route. ● n (water/gas) ~ conduite f d'eau/de gaz; **the ~s** (Electr) le secteur; **in the ~** en général. ~**frame** n unité f centrale. ~**land** n continent m. ~**stream** n tendance f principale, ligne f.

maintain /meɪn'teɪn/ vt (continue, keep, assert) maintenir; (house, machine, family) entretenir; (rights) soutenir.

maintenance /'meɪntənəns/ n (care) entretien m; (continuation) maintien m; (allowance) pension f alimentaire.

maisonette /meɪzə'net/ n duplex m.

maize /meɪz/ n maïs m.

majestic /mə'dʒestɪk/ adj majestueux.

majesty /'mædʒəstɪ/ n majesté f.

major /'meɪdʒə(r)/ adj majeur. ● n commandant m. ● vi ~ **in** (Univ, US) se spécialiser en.

majority /mə'dʒɒrətɪ/ n majorité f; **the ~ of people** la plupart des gens. ● adj majoritaire.

make /meɪk/ vt/i (pt made) faire; (manufacture) fabriquer; (friends) se faire; (money) gagner; (decision) prendre; (place, position) arriver à; (cause to be) rendre; ~ **sb do sth** faire faire qch à qn; (force) obliger qn à faire qch; **be made of** être fait de; ~ **one-**
self at home se mettre à l'aise; ~ **sb happy** rendre qn heureux; ~ **it** arriver; (succeed) réussir; **I ~ it two o'clock** j'ai deux heures; **I ~ it 150** d'après moi, ça fait 150; **I cannot ~ anything of it** je n'y comprends rien; **can you ~ Friday?** vendredi, c'est possible?; ~ **as if to** faire mine de. ● n (brand) marque f. □ ~ **do** (manage) se débrouiller (**with** avec); ~ **for** se diriger vers; (cause) tendre à créer; ~ **good** vi réussir; vt compenser; (repair) réparer; ~ **off** filer (**with** avec); ~ **out** distinguer; (understand) comprendre; (draw up) faire; (assert) prétendre; ~ **up** vt faire, former; (story) inventer; (deficit) combler; vi se réconcilier; ~ **up for** compenser; (time) rattraper; ~ **up one's mind** se décider.

make-believe adj feint, illusoire. ● n fantaisie f.

maker /'meɪkə(r)/ n fabricant m.

makeshift /'meɪkʃɪft/ adj improvisé.

make-up /'meɪkʌp/ n maquillage m; (of object) constitution f; (Psych) caractère m.

malaria /mə'leərɪə/ n paludisme m.

Malaysia /mə'leɪzɪə/ n Malaisie f.

male /meɪl/ adj (voice, sex) masculin; (Bot, Tech) mâle. ● n mâle m.

malfunction /mæl'fʌŋkʃn/ n mauvais fonctionnement m. ● vi mal fonctionner.

malice /'mælɪs/ n méchanceté f. **malicious** adj méchant.

malignant /mə'lɪgnənt/ adj malveillant; (tumour) malin.

mall /mɔːl/ n (shopping) ~ (in suburbs) centre m commercial; (in town) galerie f marchande.

malnutrition /mælnjuː'trɪʃn/ n sous-alimentation f.

Malta /'mɔːltə/ n Malte f.

mammal /'mæml/ n mammifère m.

mammoth /'mæməθ/ n mammouth m. ● adj (task) gigantesque; (organization) géant.

man /mæn/ n (pl men) homme m; (in sports team) joueur m; (chess) pièce f; ~ **to man** d'homme à homme. ● vt (pt manned) (desk) tenir; (ship) armer; (guns) servir; (be on duty at) être de service à.

manage /'mænɪdʒ/ vt (project, organization) diriger; (shop, affairs) gérer; (handle) manier; **I could ~ another drink** 🅸 je prendrais bien encore un verre; **can you ~ Friday?** vendredi, c'est possible? ● vi se débrouiller; **~ to do** réussir à faire. **manageable** adj (tool, size, person) maniable; (job) faisable.

management /'mænɪdʒmənt/ n (managers) direction f; (of shop) gestion f.

manager /'mænɪdʒə(r)/ n directeur/-trice m/f; (of shop) gérant/-e m/f; (of actor) impresario m.

mandate /'mændeɪt/ n mandat m.

mandatory /'mændətərɪ/ adj obligatoire.

mane /meɪn/ n crinière f.

mango /'mæŋgəʊ/ n (pl ~es) mangue f.

manhandle /'mænhændl/ vt maltraiter, malmener.

man: ~hole n regard m. **~hood** n âge m d'homme; (quality) virilité f.

maniac /'meɪnɪæk/ n maniaque mf, fou m, folle f.

manicure /'mænɪkjʊə(r)/ n manucure f. ● vt soigner, manucurer.

manifest /'mænɪfest/ adj manifeste. ● vt manifester.

manipulate /mə'nɪpjʊleɪt/ vt (tool, person) manipuler.

mankind /mæn'kaɪnd/ n genre m humain.

manly /'mænlɪ/ adj viril.

man-made adj (fibre) synthétique; (pond) artificiel; (disaster) d'origine humaine.

manned // adj (spacecraft) habité.

manner /'mænə(r)/ n manière f; (attitude) attitude f; (kind) sorte f; **~s** (social behaviour) manières fpl.

mannerism /'mænərɪzəm/ n particularité f; (quirk) manie f.

manoeuvre /mə'nu:və(r)/ n manœuvre f. ● vt/i manœuvrer.

manor /'mænə(r)/ n manoir m.

manpower /'mænpaʊə(r)/ n main-d'œuvre f.

mansion /'mænʃn/ n (in countryside) demeure f; (in town) hôtel m particulier.

manslaughter /'mænslɔ:tə(r)/ n homicide m involontaire.

mantelpiece /'mæntlʃelf/ n (manteau m de) cheminée.

manual /'mænjʊəl/ adj (labour) manuel; (typewriter) mécanique. ● n (handbook) manuel m.

manufacture /mænjʊ'fæktʃə(r)/ vt fabriquer. ● n fabrication f.

manure /mə'njʊə(r)/ n fumier m.

many /'menɪ/ adj & n beaucoup (de); **a great** or **good ~** un grand nombre (de); **~ a** bien des.

map /mæp/ n carte f; (of streets) plan m. ● vt (pt **mapped**) faire la carte de; **~ out** (route) tracer; (arrange) organiser.

mar /mɑ:(r)/ vt (pt **marred**) gâcher.

marble /'mɑ:bl/ n marbre m; (for game) bille f.

March /mɑ:tʃ/ n mars m.

march /mɑ:tʃ/ vi (Mil) marcher (au pas). ● vt **~ off** (lead away) emmener. ● n marche f.

margin /'mɑ:dʒɪn/ n marge f.

marginal /'mɑ:dʒɪnl/ adj marginal; (increase) léger, faible; (seat: Pol) disputé.

marinate /'mærɪneɪt/ vt faire mariner (in dans).

marine /mə'ri:n/ adj marin. ● n (shipping) marine f; (sailor) fusilier m marin.

marital /'mærɪtl/ adj conjugal. **~ status** n situation f de famille.

mark /mɑ:k/ n (currency) mark m; (stain) tache f; (trace) marque f; (School) note f; (target) but m. ● vt marquer; (exam) corriger; **~ out** délimiter; (person) désigner; **~ time** marquer le pas.

marker /'mɑ:kə(r)/ n (pen) marqueur m; (tag) repère m; (School, Univ) examinateur/-trice m/f.

market /'mɑ:kɪt/ n marché m; **on the ~** en vente. ● vt (sell) vendre; (launch) commercialiser. **~ research** n étude f de marché.

marmalade /'mɑ:məleɪd/ n confiture f d'oranges.

maroon /mə'ru:n/ n bordeaux m inv. ● adj bordeaux inv.

marooned /mə'ru:nd/ adj abandonné; (snowbound) bloqué.

marquee /mɑːˈkiː/ n grande tente f; (of circus) chapiteau m; (awning: US) auvent m.

marriage /ˈmærɪdʒ/ n mariage m (to avec).

married /ˈmærɪd/ adj marié (to à); (life) conjugal; **get ~** se marier (to avec).

marrow /ˈmærəʊ/ n (of bone) moelle f; (vegetable) courge f.

marry /ˈmærɪ/ vt épouser; (give or unite in marriage) marier. ● vi se marier.

marsh /mɑːʃ/ n marais m.

marshal /ˈmɑːʃl/ n maréchal m; (at event) membre m du service d'ordre. ● vt (pt **marshalled**) rassembler.

martyr /ˈmɑːtə(r)/ n martyr/-e m/f. ● vt martyriser.

marvel /ˈmɑːvl/ n merveille f. ● vi (pt **marvelled**) s'émerveiller (at de).

marvellous /ˈmɑːvələs/ adj merveilleux.

marzipan /ˈmɑːzɪpæn/ n pâte f d'amandes.

masculine /ˈmæskjʊlɪn/ adj & n masculin (m).

mash /mæʃ/ n (potatoes **US**) purée f. ● vt écraser. **mashed potatoes** npl purée f (de pommes de terre).

mask /mɑːsk/ n masque m. ● vt masquer.

Mason /ˈmeɪsn/ n franc-maçon m.

masonry /ˈmeɪsənrɪ/ n maçonnerie f.

mass /mæs/ n (Relig) messe f; masse f; **the ~es** les masses fpl. ● vt/i (se) masser.

massacre /ˈmæsəkə(r)/ n massacre m. ● vt massacrer.

massage /ˈmæsɑːʒ/ n massage m. ● vt masser.

massive /ˈmæsɪv/ adj (large) énorme; (heavy) massif.

mass media n médias mpl.

mass-produce vt fabriquer en série.

mast /mɑːst/ n (on ship) mât m; (for radio, TV) pylône m.

master /ˈmɑːstə(r)/ n maître m; (in secondary school) professeur m; M~ of Arts titulaire mf d'une maîtrise ès lettres. ● vt maîtriser.

masterpiece /ˈmɑːstəpiːs/ n chef-d'œuvre m.

mastery /ˈmɑːstərɪ/ n maîtrise f.

mat /mæt/ n (petit) tapis m; (at door) paillasson m.

match /mætʃ/ n (for lighting fire) allumette f; (Sport) match m; (equal) égal/-e m/f; (marriage) mariage m; (sb to marry) parti m; **be a ~** for pouvoir tenir tête à. ● vt opposer; (go with) aller avec; (cups) assortir; (equal) égaler. ● vi (be alike) être assorti. **matchbox** n boîte f à allumettes.

matching /ˈmætʃɪŋ/ adj assorti.

mate /meɪt/ n camarade mf; (of animal) compagnon m, compagne f; (assistant) aide mf; (chess) mat m. ● vt/i (s')accoupler (with avec).

material /məˈtɪərɪəl/ n matière f; (fabric) tissu m; (documents, for building) matériau(x) m(pl); ~s (equipment) matériel m. ● adj matériel; (fig) important. **materialistic** adj matérialiste.

materialize /məˈtɪərɪəlaɪz/ vi se matérialiser, se réaliser.

maternal /məˈtɜːnl/ adj maternel.

maternity /məˈtɜːnətɪ/ n maternité f. ● adj (clothes) de grossesse. **~ hospital** n maternité f. **~ leave** n congé m maternité.

mathematics /mæθəˈmætɪks/ n & npl mathématiques fpl.

maths, (US) **math** /mæθs/ n maths fpl.

mating /ˈmeɪtɪŋ/ n accouplement m.

matrimony /ˈmætrɪmənɪ/ n mariage m.

matron /ˈmeɪtrən/ n (married, elderly) dame f âgée; (in hospital) infirmière f en chef.

matt /mæt/ adj mat.

matter /ˈmætə(r)/ n (substance) matière f; (affair) affaire f; **as a ~ of fact** en fait; **what is the ~?** qu'est-ce qu'il y a? ● vi importer; **it does not ~** ça ne fait rien; **no ~ what happens** quoi qu'il arrive.

mattress /ˈmætrɪs/ n matelas m.

mature /məˈtjʊə(r)/ adj (psychologically) mûr; (plant) adulte. ● vt/i (se) mûrir. **maturity** n maturité f.

mauve /məʊv/ adj & n mauve (m).

maverick /ˈmævərɪk/ n non-conformiste mf.

maximize /ˈmæksɪmaɪz/ vt porter au maximum.

maximum /'mæksɪməm/ adj & n (pl **-ima**) maximum (m).

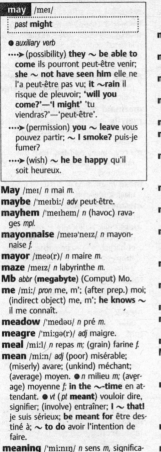

may /meɪ/

past **might**

● auxiliary verb

····▸ (possibility) **they ~ be able to come** ils pourront peut-être venir; **she ~ not have seen him** elle ne l'a peut-être pas vu; **it ~rain** il risque de pleuvoir; **'will you come?'—'I might'** 'tu viendras?'—'peut-être'.

····▸ (permission) **you ~ leave** vous pouvez partir; **~ I smoke?** puis-je fumer?

····▸ (wish) **~ he be happy** qu'il soit heureux.

May /meɪ/ n mai m.

maybe /'meɪbi:/ adv peut-être.

mayhem /'meɪhem/ n (havoc) ravages mpl.

mayonnaise /meɪə'neɪz/ n mayonnaise f.

mayor /meə(r)/ n maire m.

maze /meɪz/ n labyrinthe m.

Mb abbr (**megabyte**) (Comput) Mo.

me /mi:/ pron me, m'; (after prep.) moi; (indirect object) me, m'; **he knows ~** il me connaît.

meadow /'medəʊ/ n pré m.

meagre /'mi:gə(r)/ adj maigre.

meal /mi:l/ n repas m; (grain) farine f.

mean /mi:n/ adj (poor) misérable; (miserly) avare; (unkind) méchant; (average) moyen. ● n milieu m; (average) moyenne f; **in the ~-time** en attendant. ● vt (pt **meant**) vouloir dire, signifier; (involve) entraîner; **I ~ that!** je suis sérieux; **be meant for** être destiné à; **~ to do** avoir l'intention de faire.

meaning /'mi:nɪŋ/ n sens m, signification f. **meaningful** adj significatif. **meaningless** adj dénué de sens.

means /mi:nz/ n moyen(s) m (pl;) **by ~ of sth** au moyen de qch. ● npl (wealth) moyens mpl financiers; **by all ~** certainement; **by no ~** nullement.

meant /ment/ ➡MEAN.

meantime /'mi:ntaɪm/, **meanwhile** adv en attendant.

measles /'mi:zlz/ n rougeole f.

measure /'meʒə(r)/ n mesure f; (ruler) règle f. ● vt/i mesurer; **~up to** être à la hauteur de. **measurement** n mesures fpl.

meat /mi:t/ n viande f. **meaty** adj de viande; (fig) substantiel.

mechanic /mɪ'kænɪk/ n mécanicien/-ne m/f.

mechanical /mɪ'kænɪkl/ adj mécanique.

mechanism /'mekənɪzəm/ n mécanisme m.

medal /'medl/ n médaille f.

meddle /'medl/ vi (interfere) se mêler (in de); (tinker) toucher (with à).

media /'mi:dɪə/ n ➡MEDIUM. ● npl **the~** les média mpl; **talk to the ~** parler à la presse.

median /'mi:dɪən/ adj médian. ● n médiane f.

mediate /'mi:dɪeɪt/ vi servir d'intermédiaire.

medical /'medɪkl/ adj médical; (student) en médecine. ● n visite f médicale.

medication /medɪ'keɪʃn/ n médicaments mpl.

medicine /'medsn/ n (science) médecine f; (substance) médicament m.

medieval /medɪ'i:vl/ adj médiéval.

mediocre /mi:dɪ'əʊkə(r)/ adj médiocre.

meditate /'medɪteɪt/ vt/i méditer.

Mediterranean /medɪtə'reɪnɪən/ adj méditerranéen. ● n the **~** la Méditerranée f.

medium /'mi:dɪəm/ n (pl **media**) (mid-point) milieu m; (for transmitting data) support m; (pl **mediums**) (person) médium m. ● adj moyen.

medley /'medlɪ/ n mélange m; (Mus) potpourri m.

meet /mi:t/ vt (pt **met**) rencontrer; (see again) retrouver; (be introduced to) faire la connaissance de; (face) faire face à; (requirement) satisfaire. ● vi se rencontrer; (see each other again) se retrouver; (in session) se réunir.

meeting /'mi:tɪŋ/ n réunion f; (between two people) rencontre f.

megabyte /'megəbaɪt/ n (Comput) mégaoctet m.

melancholy /'melənkəlɪ/ n mélancolie
f. ● adj mélancolique.

mellow /'meləʊ/ adj (fruit) mûr;
(sound, colour) moelleux, doux; (person) mûri. ● vt/i (mature) mûrir;
(soften) (s')adoucir.

melody /'melədɪ/ n mélodie f.

melon /'melən/ n melon m.

melt /melt/ vt/i (faire) fondre.

member /'membə(r)/ n membre m.
M~ of Parliament n député m.
membership n adhésion f; (members)
membres mpl; (fee) cotisation f.

memento /mɪ'mentəʊ/ n (pl ~es)
(object) souvenir m.

memo /'meməʊ/ n note f.

memoir /'memwɑ:(r)/ n (record,
essay) mémoire m.

memorandum /memə'rændəm/ n
note f.

memorial /mə'mɔ:rɪəl/ n monument
m. ● adj commémoratif.

memorize /'meməraɪz/ vt apprendre
par cœur.

memory /'memərɪ/ n (mind, in computer) mémoire f; (thing remembered)
souvenir m; **from ~** de mémoire; **in
~ of** à la mémoire de.

men /men/ →MAN.

menace /'menəs/ n menace f; (nuisance) peste f. ● vt menacer.

mend /mend/ vt réparer; (darn) raccommoder; **~ one's ways** s'amender.
● n raccommodage m; **on the ~** en
voie de guérison.

meningitis /menɪn'dʒaɪtɪs/ n méningite f.

menopause /'menəpɔ:z/ n méno-
pause f.

mental /'mentl/ adj mental; (hospital)
psychiatrique.

mentality /men'tælətɪ/ n mentalité f.

mention /'menʃn/ vt mentionner;
don't ~it! il n'y a pas de quoi, je
vous en prie! ● n mention f.

menu /'menju:/ n (food, on computer)
menu m; (list) carte f.

MEP abbr (**Member of the European
Parliament**) député m au Parlement
européen.

mercenary /'mɜ:sɪnərɪ/ adj & n mercenaire (m.)

merchandise /'mɜ:tʃəndaɪz/ n marchandises fpl.

merchant /'mɜ:tʃənt/ n marchand m.
● adj (ship, navy) marchand. **~ bank** n
banque f de commerce.

merciful /'mɜ:sɪfl/ adj miséricordieux.

mercury /'mɜ:kjʊrɪ/ n mercure m.

mercy /'mɜ:sɪ/ n pitié f; **at the ~ of** à
la merci de.

mere /mɪə(r)/ adj simple. **merest** adj
moindre.

merge /mɜ:dʒ/ vt/i (se) mêler (**with** à)
(companies: Comm) fusionner. **merger**
n fusion f.

mermaid /'mɜ:meɪd/ n sirène f.

merrily /'merɪlɪ/ adv (happily) joyeusement; (unconcernedly) avec insouciance.

merry /'merɪ/ adj (-ier, -iest) gai;
make ~ faire la fête. **~-go-round** n
manège m.

mesh /meʃ/ n maille f; (fabric) tissu m à
mailles; (network) réseau m.

mesmerize /'mezməraɪz/ vt hypnotiser.

mess /mes/ n désordre m, gâchis m;
(dirt) saleté f; (Mil) mess m; **make a ~
of** gâcher. ● vt **~ up** gâcher.; vi **~
about** s'amuser; (dawdle) traîner; **~
with** (tinker with) tripoter.

message /'mesɪdʒ/ n message m.

messenger /'mesɪndʒə(r)/ n
messager/-ère m/f.

messy /'mesɪ/ adj (-ier, -iest) en désordre; (dirty) sale.

met /met/ →MEET.

metal /'metl/ n métal m. ● adj de
métal. **metallic** adj métallique; (paint,
colour) métallisé.

metallurgy /mɪ'tælədʒɪ/ n métallurgie f.

metaphor /'metəfɔ:(r)/ n métaphore f.

meteor /'mi:tɪə(r)/ n météore m.

meteorite /'mi:tɪəraɪt/ n météorite m.

meteorology /mi:tɪə'rɒlədʒɪ/ n météorologie f.

meter /'mi:tə(r)/ n compteur m; (US)
→METRE.

method /'meθəd/ n méthode f.

methylated spirit(s) /'meθəleɪtɪd
'spɪrɪt(s)/ n alcool m à brûler.

meticulous /mɪ'tɪkjʊləs/ adj méticuleux.

metre, (US) **meter** /'mi:tə(r)/ n
mètre m.

metric /'metrɪk/ adj métrique.

metropolis /mə'trɒpəlɪs/ n métropole f. **metropolitan** adj métropolitain.

mew /mju:/ n miaulement m. ● vi miauler.

mews /mju:z/ npl appartements mpl chic aménagés dans d'anciennes écuries.

Mexico /'meksɪkəʊ/ n Mexique m.

miaow /mi:'aʊ/ n & vi ⇒MEW.

mice /maɪs/ ⇒MOUSE.

mickey /'mɪkɪ/ n take the ~ out of 🔟 se moquer de.

microchip /'maɪkrəʊtʃɪp/ n puce f; circuit m intégré.

microlight /'maɪkrəʊlaɪt/ n ULM m.

microprocessor /'maɪkrəʊprəʊsesə(r)/ n microprocesseur m.

microscope /'maɪkrəskəʊp/ n microscope m.

microwave /'maɪkrəweɪv/ n microonde f; ~ (oven) four m à microondes. ● vt passer au four à microondes.

mid /mɪd/ adj in ~ air en plein ciel; in ~ March à la mi-mars; ~ afternoon milieu m de l'après-midi; he's in his ~ twenties il a environ vingt-cinq ans.

midday /mɪd'deɪ/ n midi m.

middle /'mɪdl/ adj (door, shelf) du milieu; (size) moyen. ● n milieu m; in the ~ of au milieu de. ~-aged adj d'âge mûr. M~ Ages n Moyen Âge m. ~ class n classe f moyenne. M~ East n Moyen-Orient m.

midge /mɪdʒ/ n moucheron m.

midget /'mɪdʒɪt/ n nain/-e m/f. ● adj minuscule.

midnight /'mɪdnaɪt/ n minuit f; it's ~ il est minuit.

midst /mɪdst/ n in the ~ of au beau milieu de; in our ~ parmi nous.

midsummer /mɪd'sʌmə(r)/ n milieu m de l'été; (solstice) solstice m d'été.

midway /mɪd'weɪ/ adv ~ between/ along à mi-chemin entre/le long de.

midwife /'mɪdwaɪf/ n (pl -wives) sagefemme f.

might¹ /maɪt/ v aux I ~ have been killed! j'aurais pu être tué; you ~ try doing sth vous pourriez faire qch; ⇒MAY.

might² /maɪt/ n puissance f.

mighty /'maɪtɪ/ adj puissant; (huge 🔟) énorme. ● adv 🔟 vachement 🔟.

migrant /'maɪgrənt/ adj & n (bird) migrateur (m); (worker) migrant/-e (m/f).

migrate /maɪ'greɪt/ vi émigrer. **migration** n migration f.

mild /maɪld/ adj (surprise, taste, tobacco, attack) léger; (weather, cheese, soap, person) doux; (case, infection) bénin.

mile /maɪl/ n mile m (= 1,6 km); walk for ~s marcher pendant des kilomètres; ~s better 🔟 bien meilleur. **mileage** n nombre m de miles, kilométrage m.

milestone /'maɪlstəʊn/ n (lit) borne f; (fig) étape f importante.

military /'mɪlɪtrɪ/ adj militaire.

militia /mɪ'lɪʃə/ n milice f.

milk /mɪlk/ n lait m. ● vt (cow) traire; (fig) pomper.

milkman /'mɪlkmən/ n (pl -men) laitier m.

milky /'mɪlkɪ/ adj (skin, colour) laiteux; (tea) au lait; M~ Way Voie f lactée.

mill /mɪl/ n moulin m; (factory) usine f. ● vt moudre. ● vi ~ around grouiller.

millennium /mɪ'lenɪəm/ n (pl ~s) millénaire m.

millimetre, (US) **millimeter** /'mɪlɪmi:tə(r)/ n millimètre m.

million /'mɪljən/ n million m; a ~ pounds un million de livres. **millionaire** n millionnaire m.

millstone /'mɪlstəʊn/ n meule f; (fig) boulet m.

mime /maɪm/ n (actor) mime mf; (art) mime m. ● vt/i mimer.

mimic /'mɪmɪk/ vt (pt mimicked) imiter. ● n imitateur/-trice m/f.

mince /mɪns/ vt hacher; not to ~ matters ne pas mâcher ses mots. ● n viande f hachée.

mind /maɪnd/ n esprit m; (sanity) raison f; (opinion) avis m; be on sb's ~ préoccuper qn; bear that in ~ ne l'oubliez pas; change one's ~ changer d'avis; make up one's ~ se décider (to à). ● vt (have charge of) s'occuper de; (heed) faire attention à; I do not ~ the noise le bruit ne me dérange pas; **I don't ~** ça m'est égal; **would you ~ checking?** je peux vous demander de vérifier?

minder /'maɪndə(r)/ n (bodyguard) garde m de corps; **(child) ~** nourrice f.

mindless /'maɪndlɪs/ adj (programme) bête; (work) abrutissant; (vandalism) gratuit.

mine /maɪn/ n mine f. • vt extraire; (Mil) miner. • pron le mien, la mienne, les mien(ne)s; **the blue car is ~** la voiture bleue est la mienne or à moi.

minefield /'maɪnfiːld/ n (lit) champ m de mines; (fig) terrain m miné.

miner /'maɪnə(r)/ n mineur m.

mineral /'mɪnərəl/ n & adj minéral (m); **~ water** eau f minérale.

minesweeper /'maɪnswiːpə(r)/ n (ship) dragueur m de mines.

mingle /'mɪŋgl/ vt/i (se) mêler (with à).

minibus /'mɪnɪbʌs/ n minibus m.

minicab /'mɪnɪkæb/ n taxi m (non agréé).

minimal /'mɪnɪml/ adj minimal.

minimize /'mɪnɪmaɪz/ vt minimiser; (Comput) réduire.

minimum /'mɪnɪməm/ adj & n (pl) **-ima** minimum (m).

minister /'mɪnɪstə(r)/ n ministre m. **ministerial** adj ministériel. **ministry** n ministère m.

mink /mɪŋk/ n vison m.

minor /'maɪnə(r)/ adj (change, surgery) mineur; (injury, burn) léger; (road) secondaire. • n (Jur) mineur/-e m/f.

minority /maɪ'nɒrəti/ n minorité f; **in the ~** en minorité. • adj minoritaire.

mint /mɪnt/ n (Bot, Culin) menthe f; (sweet) bonbon m à la menthe; (fortune 🔟) fortune f. • vt frapper; **in ~ condition** à l'état neuf.

minus /'maɪnəs/ prep moins; (without 🔟) sans. • n moins m; (drawback) inconvénient m.

minute¹ /'mɪnɪt/ n minute f; **~s** (of meeting) compte-rendu m.

minute² /maɪ'njuːt/ adj (object) minuscule; (risk, variation) minime.

miracle /'mɪrəkl/ n miracle m.

mirror /'mɪrə(r)/ n miroir m, glace f; (Auto) rétroviseur m. • vt refléter.

misbehave /mɪsbɪ'heɪv/ vi se conduire mal.

miscalculation /mɪskælkjʊ'leɪʃn/ n (lit) erreur f de calcul; (fig) mauvais calcul m.

miscarriage /'mɪskærɪdʒ/ n fausse couche f; **~ of justice** erreur f judiciaire.

miscellaneous /mɪsə'leɪnɪəs/ adj divers.

mischief /'mɪstʃɪf/ n (playfulness) espièglerie f; (by children) bêtises fpl.
mischievous adj espiègle; (malicious) méchant.

misconduct /mɪs'kɒndʌkt/ n mauvaise conduite f.

misconstrue /mɪskən'struː/ vt mal interpréter.

misdemeanour, (US) **misdemeanor** /mɪsdɪ'miːnə(r)/ n (Jur) délit m.

miser /'maɪzə(r)/ n avare mf.

miserable /'mɪzrəbl/ adj (sad) malheureux; (wretched) misérable; (performance, result) lamentable.

misery /'mɪzəri/ n (unhappiness) souffrance f; (misfortune) misère f; (person 🔟) rabat-joie mf inv.

misfit /'mɪsfɪt/ n inadapté/-e m/f.

misfortune /mɪs'fɔːtʃuːn/ n malheur m.

misgiving /mɪs'gɪvɪŋ/ n (doubt) doute m; (apprehension) crainte f.

misguided /mɪs'gaɪdɪd/ adj (foolish) imprudent; (mistaken) erroné; **be ~** (person) se tromper.

mishap /'mɪshæp/ n incident m.

misjudge /mɪs'dʒʌdʒ/ vt (distance, speed) mal évaluer; (person) mal juger.

mislay /mɪs'leɪ/ vt (pt **mislaid**) égarer.

mislead /mɪs'liːd/ vt (pt) **misled** tromper. **misleading** adj trompeur.

misplace /mɪs'pleɪs/ vt mal ranger; (lose) égarer. **misplaced** adj (fear, criticism) déplacé.

misprint /'mɪsprɪnt/ n coquille f, faute f typographique.

misread /mɪs'riːd/ vt (pt) **misread** mal lire; (intentions) mal interpréter.

miss /mɪs/ vt/i manquer; (bus) rater; **he ~es her/Paris** elle/Paris lui manque; **you're ~ing the point** tu n'as rien compris; **~ sth out** omettre qch; **~ out on sth** laisser passer qch. • n coup *m* manqué; **it was a near ~** on l'a échappé belle.

Miss /mɪs/ *n* Mademoiselle *f*; **~ Smith** (written) Mlle Smith.

misshapen /mɪsˈʃeɪpən/ *adj* difforme.

missile /ˈmɪsaɪl/ *n* (Mil) missile *m*; (thrown) projectile *m*.

mission /ˈmɪʃn/ *n* mission *f*. **missionary** *n* missionnaire *mf*.

misspell /mɪsˈspel/ *vt* (*pt* **misspelt** or **misspelled**) mal écrire.

mist /mɪst/ *n* brume *f*; (on window) buée *f*. ● *vt/i* (s')embuer.

mistake /mɪˈsteɪk/ *n* erreur *f*; **by ~** par erreur; **make a ~** faire une erreur. ● *vt* (*pt* **mistook**; *pp* **mistaken**) (*meaning*) mal interpréter; **~ for** prendre pour.

mistaken /mɪˈsteɪkən/ *adj* (*enthusiasm*) mal placé; **be ~** avoir tort.

mistletoe /ˈmɪsltəʊ/ *n* gui *m*.

mistreat /mɪsˈtriːt/ *vt* maltraiter.

mistress /ˈmɪstrɪs/ *n* maîtresse *f*.

misty /ˈmɪsti/ *adj* (**-ier, -iest**) brumeux; (*window*) embué.

misunderstanding /mɪsʌndəˈstændɪŋ/ *n* malentendu *m*.

misuse /mɪsˈjuːz/ *vt* (*word*) mal employer; (*power*) abuser de; (*equipment*) faire mauvais usage de.

mitten /ˈmɪtn/ *n* moufle *f*.

mix /mɪks/ *n* mélange *m*. ● *vt* mélanger; (*drink*) préparer; (*cement*) malaxer. ● *vi* se mélanger (**with** avec, à); (socially) être sociable; **~ with sb** fréquenter qn. □ **~ up** (confuse) confondre; (jumble up) mélanger; **get ~ed up in** se trouver mêlé à.

mixed /mɪkst/ *adj* (*school*) mixte; (*collection, diet*) varié; (*nuts, sweets*) assorti.

mixer /ˈmɪksə(r)/ *n* (Culin) batteur *m* électrique; **be a good ~** être sociable; **~ tap** mélangeur *m*.

mixture /ˈmɪkstʃə(r)/ *n* mélange *m*.

mix-up /ˈmɪksʌp/ *n* confusion *f* (over sur).

moan /məʊn/ *n* gémissement *m*. ● *vi* gémir; (complain 🔢) râler 🔢.

mob /mɒb/ *n* (crowd) foule *f*; (gang) gang *m*; **the M~** la Mafia. ● *vt* (*pt* **mobbed**) assaillir.

mobile /ˈməʊbaɪl/ *adj* mobile; **~ phone** téléphone *m* portable. ● *n* mobile *m*.

mobilize /ˈməʊbɪlaɪz/ *vt/i* mobiliser.

mock /mɒk/ *vt/i* se moquer (de). ● *adj* faux.

mockery /ˈmɒkəri/ *n* moquerie *f*; **a ~ of** une parodie de.

mock-up *n* maquette *f*.

mode /məʊd/ *n* mode *m*.

model /ˈmɒdl/ *n* (Comput, Auto) modèle *m*; (scale representation) maquette *f*; (person showing clothes) mannequin *m*. ● *adj* modèle; (*car*) modèle réduit *inv*; (*railway*) miniature. ● *vt* (*pt* **modelled**) modeler; (*clothes*) présenter. ● *vi* être mannequin; (pose) poser. **modelling** *n* métier *m* de mannequin.

modem /ˈməʊdem/ *n* modem *m*.

moderate /ˈmɒdərət/ *adj* & *n* modéré/-e (*m/f*).

moderation /mɒdəˈreɪʃn/ *n* modération *f*; **in ~** avec modération.

modern /ˈmɒdn/ *adj* moderne; **~ languages** langues *fpl* vivantes. **modernize** *vt* moderniser.

modest /ˈmɒdɪst/ *adj* modeste. **modesty** *n* modestie *f*.

modification /mɒdɪfɪˈkeɪʃn/ *n* modification *f*. **modify** *vt* modifier.

module /ˈmɒdjuːl/ *n* module *m*.

moist /mɔɪst/ *adj* (*soil*) humide; (*skin, palms*) moite; (*cake*) moelleux. **moisten** *vt* humecter. **moisture** *n* humidité *f*. **moisturizer** *n* crème *f* hydratante.

molar /ˈməʊlə(r)/ *n* molaire *f*.

mold (US) →**MOULD**.

mole /məʊl/ *n* grain *m* de beauté; (animal) taupe *f*.

molecule /ˈmɒlɪkjuːl/ *n* molécule *f*.

molest /məˈlest/ *vt* (pester) importuner; (sexually) agresser sexuellement.

moment /ˈməʊmənt/ *n* (short time) instant *m*; (point in time) moment *m*. **momentarily** *adv* momentanément; (soon: US) très bientôt. **momentary** *adj* momentané.

momentum /məˈmentəm/ *n* élan *m*.

monarch /ˈmɒnək/ *n* monarque *m*. **monarchy** *n* monarchie *f*.

Monday /ˈmʌndeɪ/ *n* lundi *m*.

monetary /ˈmʌnɪtri/ *adj* monétaire.

money /'mʌnɪ/ n argent m; **make ~** (person) gagner de l'argent; (business) rapporter de l'argent. **~-box** n tirelire f. **~ order** n mandat m postal.

monitor /'mɒnɪtə(r)/ n dispositif m de surveillance; (Comput) moniteur m. ● vt surveiller; (broadcast) être à l'écoute de.

monk /mʌŋk/ n moine m.

monkey /'mʌŋkɪ/ n singe m.

monopolize /mə'nɒpəlaɪz/ vt monopoliser. **monopoly** n monopole m.

monotonous /mə'nɒtənəs/ adj monotone. **monotony** n monotonie f.

monsoon /mɒn'suːn/ n mousson f.

monster /'mɒnstə(r)/ n monstre m. **monstrous** adj monstrueux.

month /mʌnθ/ n mois m.

monthly /'mʌnθlɪ/ adj mensuel. ● adv (pay) au mois; (publish) tous les mois. ● n (periodical) mensuel m.

monument /'mɒnjʊmənt/ n monument m.

moo /muː/ vi meugler.

mood /muːd/ n humeur f; **in a good/bad ~** de bonne/mauvaise humeur. **moody** adj d'humeur changeante.

moon /muːn/ n lune f.

moonlight /'muːnlaɪt/ n clair m de lune. **moonlighting** n 🔲 travail m au noir.

moor /mɔː(r)/ n lande f. ● vt amarrer.

mop /mɒp/ n balai m à franges; **~ of hair** crinière f 🔲. ● vt (pt **mopped**) **~ (up)** éponger.

moped /'məʊped/ n vélomoteur m.

moral /'mɒrəl/ adj moral. ● n morale f; **~s** moralité f.

morale /mə'rɑːl/ n moral m.

morbid /'mɔːbɪd/ adj morbide.

more /mɔː(r)/ adv plus; **~ serious** plus sérieux; **work ~** travailler plus; **sleep ~ and ~** dormir de plus en plus; **once ~** une fois de plus; **I don't go there any ~** je n'y vais plus; **~ or less** plus ou moins. ● det plus de; **a little ~ wine** un peu plus de vin; **~ bread** encore un peu de pain; **there's no ~ bread** il n'y a plus de pain; **nothing ~** rien de plus. ● pron plus; **cost ~ than** coûter plus cher que; **I need ~ of it** il m'en faut davantage.

moreover /mɔː'rəʊvə(r)/ adv de plus.

morning /'mɔːnɪŋ/ n matin m; (whole morning) matinée f.

Morocco /mə'rɒkəʊ/ n Maroc m.

morsel /'mɔːsl/ n morceau m.

mortal /'mɔːtl/ adj & n mortel/-le (m/f).

mortgage /'mɔːgɪdʒ/ n emprunt-logement m. ● vt hypothéquer.

mortuary /'mɔːtʃərɪ/ n morgue f.

mosaic /məʊ'zeɪk/ n mosaïque f.

mosque /mɒsk/ n mosquée f.

mosquito /məs'kiːtəʊ/ n (pl **~es**) moustique m.

moss /mɒs/ n mousse f.

most /məʊst/ det (nearly all) la plupart de; **~ people** la plupart des gens; **the ~ votes/money** le plus de voix/d'argent. ● n le plus. ● pron la plupart; **~ of us** la plupart d'entre nous; **~ of the money** la plus grande partie de l'argent; **the ~ I can do is ...** tout ce que je peux faire c'est ...; **the ~ beautiful house/hotel in Oxford** la maison la plus belle/l'hôtel le plus beau d'Oxford; **~ interesting** très intéressant; **what I like ~ (of all) is** ce que j'aime le plus c'est. **mostly** adv surtout.

moth /mɒθ/ n papillon m de nuit; (in cloth) mite f.

mother /'mʌðə(r)/ n mère f. ● vt (lit) materner; (fig) dorloter. **motherhood** n maternité f. **~-in-law** (pl **~s-in-law**) belle-mère f. **~-of-pearl** n nacre f. **M~'s Day** n la fête des mères. **~-to-be** n future maman f. **~ tongue** n langue f maternelle.

motion /'məʊʃn/ n mouvement m; (proposal) motion f; **~ picture** (US) film m. ● vt/i **~ (to) sb** to faire signe à qn de. **motionless** adj immobile.

motivate /'məʊtɪveɪt/ vt motiver.

motive /'məʊtɪv/ n motif m; (Jur) mobile m.

motor /'məʊtə(r)/ n moteur m; (car) auto f. ● adj (industry, insurance, vehicle) automobile; (activity, disorder: Med) moteur. **~bike** n moto f. **~ car** n auto f. **~-cyclist** n motocycliste mf. **~ home** n autocaravane f.

motorist /'məʊtərɪst/ n automobiliste mf.

motorway /'məʊtəweɪ/ n autoroute f.

mottled /'mɒtld/ adj tacheté.

motto /'mɒtəʊ/ n (pl **~es**) devise f.

mould /məʊld/ n (shape) moule m; (fungus) moisissure f. ● vt mouler; (influence) former. **moulding** n moulure f. **mouldy** adj moisi.

mount /maʊnt/ n (hill) mont m; (horse) monture f. ● vt (stairs) gravir; (platform, horse, bike) monter sur; (jewel, picture, campaign, exhibit) monter. ● vi monter; (number, toll) augmenter; (concern) grandir.

mountain /'maʊntɪn/ n montagne f; ∼ **bike** (vélo) tout terrain m, VTT m. **mountaineer** n alpiniste mf.

mourn /mɔːn/ vt/i ∼ (for) pleurer. **mournful** adj mélancolique. **mourning** n deuil m.

mouse /maʊs/ n (pl mice) souris f. ∼**trap** n souricière f.

mouth /maʊθ/ n bouche f; (of dog, cat) gueule f; (of cave, tunnel) entrée f. **mouthful** n bouchée f. ∼**wash** n eau f dentifrice. ∼**watering** adj appétissant.

move /muːv/ vt (object) déplacer; (limb, head) bouger; (emotionally) émouvoir; ∼ **house** déménager. ● vi bouger; (vehicle) rouler; (change address) déménager; (act) agir. ● n mouvement m; (in game) coup m; (player's turn) tour m; (step, act) manœuvre f; (house change) déménagement m; **on the** ∼ en mouvement. □ ∼ **back** reculer; ∼ **in with** s'installer avec; ∼ **on** (person) se mettre en route; (vehicle) repartir; (time) passer; ∼ **sth on** faire avancer qch; ∼ **sb on** faire circuler qn; ∼ **over** or **up** se pousser.

movement /'muːvmənt/ n mouvement m.

movie /'muːvɪ/ n (US) film m; **the** ∼**s** le cinéma.

moving /'muːvɪŋ/ adj (vehicle) en marche; (part, target) mobile; (staircase) roulant; (touching) émouvant.

mow /məʊ/ vt (pp mowed or mown) (lawn) tondre; (hay) couper; ∼ **down** faucher. **mower** n tondeuse f.

MP abbr ➡ MEMBER OF PARLIAMENT.

Mr /'mɪstə(r)/ n (pl Messrs) ∼ Smith Monsieur or M. Smith; ∼ **President** Monsieur le Président.

Mrs /'mɪsɪz/ n (pl Mrs) ∼ Smith Madame or Mme Smith.

Ms /məz/ n Mme.

much /mʌtʃ/ adv beaucoup; **too** ∼ trop; **very** ∼ beaucoup; **I like them as** ∼ **as you (do)** je les aime autant que toi. ● pron beaucoup; **not** ∼ pas grand-chose; **he didn't say** ∼ il n'a pas dit grand-chose; **I ate so** ∼ **that** j'ai tellement mangé que. ● det beaucoup de; **too** ∼ **money** trop d'argent; **how** ∼ **time is left?** combien de temps reste-t-il?

muck /mʌk/ n saletés fpl; (manure) fumier m. □ ∼ **about** 🄸 faire l'imbécile. **mucky** adj sale.

mud /mʌd/ n boue f.

muddle /'mʌdl/ n (mix-up) malentendu m; (mess) pagaille f 🄸; **get into a** ∼ s'embrouiller. □ ∼ **through** se débrouiller; ∼ **up** embrouiller.

muddy /'mʌdɪ/ adj couvert de boue.

muffle /'mʌfl/ vt emmitoufler; (bell) assourdir; (voice) étouffer.

mug /mʌg/ n grande tasse f; (for beer) chope f; (face 🄸) gueule f 🄽; (fool 🄸) poire f 🄸. ● vt (pt **mugged**) agresser. **mugger** n agresseur m.

muggy /'mʌgɪ/ adj lourd.

mule /mjuːl/ n mulet m.

multicoloured /mʌltɪ'kʌləd/ adj multicolore.

multiple /'mʌltɪpl/ adj & n multiple (m); ∼ **sclerosis** sclérose f en plaques.

multiplication /mʌltɪplɪ'keɪʃn/ n multiplication f. **multiply** vt/i (se) multiplier.

multistorey /mʌltɪ'stɔːrɪ/ adj (car park) à niveaux multiples.

mum /mʌm/ n 🄸 maman f.

mumble /'mʌmbl/ vt/i marmonner.

mummy /'mʌmɪ/ n (mother 🄸) maman f; (embalmed body) momie f.

mumps /mʌmps/ n oreillons mpl.

munch /mʌntʃ/ vt mâcher.

mundane /mʌn'deɪn/ adj terre-à-terre.

municipal /mjuː'nɪsɪpl/ adj municipal.

mural /'mjʊərəl/ adj mural. ● n peinture f murale.

murder /'mɜːdə(r)/ n meurtre m. ● vt assassiner. **murderer** n meurtrier m, assassin m.

murky /'mɜːkɪ/ adj (-ier, -iest) (water) glauque; (past) trouble.

murmur /'mɜːmə(r)/ n murmure m.
● vt/i murmurer.

muscle /'mʌsl/ n muscle m. ● vi ~ **in**
Ⓣ s'imposer (**on** dans).

muscular /'mʌskjʊlə(r)/ adj (tissue,
disease) musculaire; (body, person)
musclé.

museum /mjuː'zɪəm/ n musée m.

mushroom /'mʌʃrʊm/ n champignon
m. ● vi (town) proliférer; (demand)
s'accroître rapidement.

music /'mjuːzɪk/ n musique f.

musical /'mjuːzɪkl/ adj (person) musicien; (voice) mélodieux; (accompaniment) musical; (instrument) de musique. ● n comédie f musicale.

musician /mjuː'zɪʃn/ n musicien/-
ne m/f.

Muslim /'mʊzlɪm/ n Musulman/-e m/f.
● adj musulman.

mussel /'mʌsl/ n moule f.

must /mʌst/v aux devoir; **you ~ go**
vous devez partir, il faut que vous par-
tiez; **she ~ be consulted** il faut la
consulter; **he ~ be old** il doit être
vieux; **I ~ have done it** j'ai dû le
faire. ● n **be a ~** Ⓣ être indispensable.

mustard /'mʌstəd/ n moutarde f.

musty /'mʌstɪ/ adj (-ier, -iest) (room)
qui sent le renfermé; (smell) de moisi.

mute /mjuːt/ adj & n muet/-te (m/f).
muted adj (colour) sourd; (response)
tiède; (celebration) mitigé.

mutilate /'mjuːtɪleɪt/ vt mutiler.

mutter /'mʌtə(r)/ vt/i marmonner.

mutton /'mʌtn/ n mouton m.

mutual /'mjuːtʃʊəl/ adj (reciprocal) réciproque; (common) commun; (con-
sent) mutuel. **mutually** adv mutuellement.

muzzle /'mʌzl/ n (snout) museau m;
(device) muselière f; (of gun) canon m.
● vt museler.

my /maɪ/ adj mon, ma, pl mes.

myself /maɪ'self/ pron (reflexive) me,
m'; **I've hurt ~** je me suis fait mal;
(emphatic) moi-même; **I did it ~** je
l'ai fait moi-même; (after preposition)
moi, moi-même; **I am proud of ~** je
suis fier de moi.

mysterious /mɪ'stɪərɪəs/ adj mystérieux.

mystery /'mɪstərɪ/ n mystère m.

mystic /'mɪstɪk/ adj & n mystique (mf).
mystical adj mystique.

myth /mɪθ/ n mythe m. **mythical** adj
mythique. **mythology** n mythologie f.

Nn

nag /næg/ vt/i (pt **nagged**) critiquer;
(pester) harceler. **nagging** adj persistant.

nail /neɪl/ n clou m; (of finger, toe)
ongle m; **on the ~** sans tarder, tout
de suite. ● vt clouer. ~ **polish** n vernis m à ongles.

naïve /naɪ'iːv/ adj naïf.

naked /'neɪkɪd/ adj nu; **to the ~ eye** à
l'œil nu.

name /neɪm/ n nom m; (fig) réputation
f. ● vt nommer; (terms) fixer; **be ~d**
after porter le nom de.

namely /'neɪmlɪ/ adv à savoir.

nanny /'nænɪ/ n nurse f.

nap /næp/ n somme m.

nape /neɪp/ n nuque f.

napkin /'næpkɪn/ n serviette f.

nappy /'næpɪ/ n couche f.

narcotic /nɑː'kɒtɪk/ adj & n narcotique (m).

narrative /'nærətɪv/ n récit m. **narra-
tor** n narrateur/-trice m/f.

narrow /'nærəʊ/ adj étroit. ● vt/i (se)
rétrécir; (limit) (se) limiter; ~ **down**
the choices limiter les choix.
~-**minded** adj à l'esprit étroit; (ideas)
étroit.

nasal /'neɪzl/ adj nasal.

nasty /'nɑːstɪ/ adj (-ier, -iest) mauvais,
désagréable; (malicious) méchant.

nation /'neɪʃn/ n nation f.

national /'næʃənl/ adj national. ● n
ressortissant/-e m/f.

nationality /næʃə'nælətɪ/ n nationalité f.

nationalize /'næʃnəlaɪz/ vt nationaliser.

nationally /'næʃnəlɪ/ adv à l'échelle
nationale.

National Trust Association *i*
caritative britannique fondée
en 1895 pour assurer la protection
de certains édifices ou parties de littoral menacés par l'industrialisation.
Cette association est aujourd'hui le
premier propriétaire foncier britannique car elle a acquis ou reçu en
dons depuis sa création de nombreux sites et bâtiments; la plupart
sont ouverts au public.

native /'neɪtɪv/ n (local inhabitant) autochtone mf; (non-European) indigène
mf; **be a ~ of** être originaire de. ● adj
indigène; (country) natal; (inborn)
inné; **~ language** langue f maternelle;
~ speaker of French personne f de
langue maternelle française.

natural /'nætʃrəl/ adj naturel.

naturally /'nætʃrəlɪ/ adv (normally, of
course) naturellement; (by nature) de
nature.

nature /'neɪtʃə(r)/ n nature f.

naughty /'nɔːtɪ/ adj (-ier, -iest) vilain,
méchant; (indecent) grivois.

nausea /'nɔːsɪə/ n nausée f. **nauseous**
adj (smell) écœurant.

nautical /'nɔːtɪkl/ adj nautique.

naval /'neɪvl/ adj (battle) naval; (officer)
de marine.

navel /'neɪvl/ n nombril m.

navigate /'nævɪɡeɪt/ vt (sea) naviguer
sur; (ship) piloter. ● vi naviguer. **navigation** n navigation f.

navy /'neɪvɪ/ n marine f. ● adj ~ (blue)
bleu inv marine.

near /nɪə(r)/ adv près; **draw ~** (s')ap-
procher (to de). ● prep près de. ● adj
proche; **~ to** près de. ● vt approcher de.

nearby /nɪə'baɪ/ adj proche. ● adv à
proximité.

nearly /'nɪəlɪ/ adv presque; **I ~ forgot**
j'ai failli oublier; **not ~ as pretty as**
loin d'être aussi joli que.

nearness /'nɪənɪs/ n proximité f.

nearside /'nɪəsaɪd/ adj (Auto) du côté
du passager.

neat /niːt/ adj soigné, net; (room) bien
rangé; (clever) habile; (drink) sec.
neatly adv avec soin; habilement.

necessarily /nesə'serəlɪ/ adv nécessai-
rement.

necessary /'nesəsərɪ/ adj nécessaire.

necessitate /nɪ'sesɪteɪt/ vt nécessiter.

necessity /nɪ'sesətɪ/ n nécessité f;
(thing) chose f indispensable.

neck /nek/ n cou m; (of dress) encolure
f. **~ and neck** adj à égalité. **~lace** n
collier m. **~line** n encolure f. **~tie** n
cravate f.

nectarine /'nektərɪn/ n brugnon m,
nectarine f.

need /niːd/ n besoin m. ● vt avoir besoin de; (demand) demander; **you ~
not come** vous n'êtes pas obligé de
venir.

needle /'niːdl/ n aiguille f.

needless /'niːdlɪs/ adj inutile.

needlework /'niːdlwɜːk/ n couture f;
(object) ouvrage m (à l'aiguille).

needy /'niːdɪ/ adj (-ier, -iest) nécessi-
teux. ● the ~ les indigents.

negative /'neɡətɪv/ adj négatif. ● n (of
photograph) négatif m; (word: Gram)
négation f; **in the ~** (answer) par la
négative; (Gram) à la forme négative.

neglect /nɪ'ɡlekt/ vt négliger, laisser à
l'abandon; **~ to do** négliger de faire.
● n manque m de soins; **(state of) ~**
abandon m.

negligent /'neɡlɪdʒənt/ adj négligent.

negotiate /nɪ'ɡəʊʃɪeɪt/ vt/i négocier.
negotiation n négociation f.

neigh /neɪ/ n hennissement m. ● vi
hennir.

neighbour, (US) **neighbor** /'neɪbə(r)/
n voisin/-e m/f. **neighbourhood** n voisinage m, quartier m; **in the ~hood of**
aux alentours de. **neighbouring** adj
voisin. **neighbourly** adj amical.

neither /'naɪðə(r)/ adj & pron aucun/-e
des deux, ni l'un/-e ni l'autre. ● adv ni;
~ big nor small ni grand ni petit.
● conj (ne) non plus; **~ am I coming**
je ne viendrai pas non plus.

nephew /'nefjuː/ n neveu m.

nerve /nɜːv/ n nerf m; (courage) courage m; (calm) sang-froid m; (impudence 🔢) culot m; **~s** (before exams)
trac m. **~-racking** adj éprouvant.

nervous /'nɜːvəs/ adj nerveux; **be** or
feel ~ (afraid) avoir peur; **~ breakdown** dépression f nerveuse. **nervousness** n nervosité f; (fear) crainte f.

nest /nest/ n nid m. ● vi nicher. **~-egg**
n pécule m.

nestle /'nesl/ *vi* se blottir.

net /net/ *n* filet *m*; (Comput) net *m*, Internet *m*. ● *vt* (*pt* **netted**) prendre au filet. ● *adj* (weight) net. **~ball** *n* netball *m*.

Netherlands /'neðələndz/ *n* the ~ les Pays-Bas *mpl*.

netiquette /'netɪket/ *n* nétiquette *f*.

Netsurfer /'netɪket/ *n* Internaute *mf*.

nettle /'netl/ *n* ortie *f*.

network /'netwɜːk/ *n* réseau *m*.

neurotic /njʊə'rɒtɪk/ *adj & n* névrosé/-e (*m/f*).

neuter /'njuːtə(r)/ *adj & n* neutre (*m*). ● *vt* (castrate) castrer.

neutral /'njuːtrəl/ *adj* neutre; ~ **(gear)** (Auto) point *m* mort.

never /'nevə(r)/ *adv* (ne) jamais; **he ~ refuses** il ne refuse jamais; **I ~ saw him** 🔲 je ne l'ai pas vu; ~ **again** plus jamais; ~ **mind** (don't worry) ne vous en faites pas; (it doesn't matter) peu importe.

nevertheless /nevəðə'les/ *adv* néanmoins, toutefois.

new /njuː/ *adj* nouveau; (brand-new) neuf. **~-born** *adj* nouveau-né. **~comer** *n* nouveau venu *m*, nouvelle venue *f*.

newly /'njuːlɪ/ *adv* nouvellement. **~-weds** *npl* jeunes mariés *mpl*.

news /njuːz/ *n* nouvelle(s) *f(pl)*; (radio, press) informations *fpl*; (TV) actualités *fpl*, informations *fpl*. ~ **agency** *n* agence *f* de presse. **~agent** *n* marchand/-e *m/f* de journaux. **~caster** *n* présentateur/-trice *m/f*. **~group** *n* (Internet) forum *m* de discussion. **~letter** *n* bulletin *m*. **~paper** *n* journal *m*.

new year *n* nouvel an *m*. **New Year's Day** *n* le jour de l'an. **New Year's Eve** *n* la Saint-Sylvestre.

New Zealand /njuː'ziːlənd/ *n* Nouvelle-Zélande *f*.

next /nekst/ *adj* prochain; (adjoining) voisin; (following) suivant; ~ **to** à côté de; ~ **door** à côté (**to** de). ● *adv* la prochaine fois; (afterwards) ensuite. ● *n* suivant/-e *m/f*; (e-mail) message *m* suivant. **~-door** *adj* d'à côté. ~ **of kin** *n* parent *m* le plus proche.

nib /nɪb/ *n* plume *f*.

nibble /'nɪbl/ *vt/i* grignoter.

nice /naɪs/ *adj* agréable, bon; (kind) gentil; (pretty) joli; (respectable) bien *inv*; (subtle) délicat. **nicely** *adv* agréablement; gentiment; (well) bien.

nicety /'naɪsətɪ/ *n* subtilité *f*.

niche /niːʃ/ *n* (recess) niche *f*; (fig) place *f*, situation *f*.

nick /nɪk/ *n* petite entaille *f*; **be in good/bad** ~ 🔲 être en bon/mauvais état. ● *vt* (steal, arrest 🔲) piquer.

nickel /'nɪkl/ *n* (metal) nickel *m*; (US) pièce *f* de cinq cents.

nickname /'nɪkneɪm/ *n* surnom *m*. ● *vt* surnommer.

nicotine /'nɪkətiːn/ *n* nicotine *f*.

niece /niːs/ *n* nièce *f*.

niggling /'nɪglɪŋ/ *adj* (person) tatillon; (detail) insignifiant.

night /naɪt/ *n* nuit *f*; (evening) soir *m*. ● *adj* de nuit. **~cap** *n* boisson *f* (avant d'aller se coucher). **~club** *n* boîte *f* de nuit. **~-dress** *n* chemise *f* de nuit. **~fall** *n* tombée *f* de la nuit. **nightie** *n* chemise *f* de nuit.

nightingale /'naɪtɪŋgeɪl/ *n* rossignol *m*.

nightly /'naɪtlɪ/ *adj & adv* (de) chaque nuit *or* soir.

night /naɪt/: **~mare** *n* cauchemar *m*. **~-time** *n* nuit *f*.

nil /nɪl/ *n* (Sport) zéro *m*. ● *adj* (chances, risk) nul.

nimble /'nɪmbl/ *adj* agile.

nine /naɪn/ *adj & n* neuf (*m*).

nineteen /naɪn'tiːn/ *adj & n* dix-neuf (*m*).

ninety /'naɪntɪ/ *adj & n* quatre-vingt-dix (*m*).

ninth /naɪnθ/ *adj & n* neuvième (*mf*).

nip /nɪp/ *vt/i* (*pt* **nipped**) (pinch) pincer; (rush 🔲) courir; ~ **out/back** sortir/rentrer rapidement. ● *n* pincement *m*.

nipple /'nɪpl/ *n* mamelon *m*; (of baby's bottle) tétine *f*.

nippy /'nɪpɪ/ *adj* (**-ier, -iest**) (air) piquant; (car) rapide.

nitrogen /'naɪtrədʒən/ *n* azote *m*.

no /nəʊ/ *det* aucun/-e; pas de; ~ **man** aucun homme; ~ **money/time** pas d'argent/de temps; ~ **one →NOBODY**; ~ **smoking/entry** défense de fumer/d'entrer; ~ **way!** 🔲 pas question! ● *adv* non. ● *n* (*pl* **noes**) non *m inv*.

nobility /nəʊˈbɪlətɪ/ n noblesse f.

noble /ˈnəʊbl/ adj noble. **~man** n (pl **-men**) noble m.

nobody /ˈnəʊbədɪ/ pron (ne) personne; **he knows ~** il ne connaît personne. ● n nullité f.

nocturnal /nɒkˈtɜːnl/ adj nocturne.

nod /nɒd/ vt/i (pt nodded); **~ (one's head)** faire un signe de tête; **~ off** s'endormir. ● n signe m de tête.

noise /nɔɪz/ n bruit m; **make a ~** faire du bruit. **noisily** adv bruyamment. **noisy** adj (-ier, -iest) bruyant.

no man's land n no man's land m.

nominal /ˈnɒmɪnl/ adj symbolique, nominal; (value) nominal.

nominate /ˈnɒmɪneɪt/ vt nommer; (put forward) proposer.

none /nʌn/ pron aucun/-e; **~ of us** aucun/-e de nous; **I have ~** je n'en ai pas.

non-existent /nɒnɪgˈzɪstənt/ adj inexistant.

nonplussed /nɒnˈplʌst/ adj perplexe.

nonsense /ˈnɒnsns/ n absurdités fpl.

non-smoker /nɒnˈsməʊkə(r)/ n nonfumeur m.

non-stick adj antiadhésif.

non-stop /nɒnˈstɒp/ adj (train, flight) direct. ● adv sans arrêt.

noodles /ˈnuːdlz/ npl nouilles fpl.

noon /nuːn/ n midi m.

nor /nɔː(r)/ adv ni. ● conj (ne) non plus; **~ shall I come** je ne viendrai pas non plus.

norm /nɔːm/ n norme f.

normal /ˈnɔːml/ adj normal.

Norman /ˈnɔːmən/ n Normand/-e m/f. ● adj (village) normand; (arch) roman.

north /nɔːθ/ n nord m. ● adj nord inv, du nord. ● adv vers le nord.

North America n Amérique f du Nord.

north-east /nɔːθˈiːst/ n nord-est m.

northerly /ˈnɔːðəlɪ/ adj (wind, area) du nord; (point) au nord.

northern /ˈnɔːðən/ adj (accent) du nord; (coast) nord. **northerner** n habitant/-e m/f du nord.

northward /ˈnɔːθwəd/ adj (side) nord inv; (journey) vers le nord.

north-west /nɔːθˈwest/ n nordouest m.

Norway /ˈnɔːweɪ/ n Norvège f.

Norwegian /nɔːˈwiːdʒən/ n (person) Norvégien/-ne m/f; (language) norvégien m. ● adj norvégien.

nose /nəʊz/ n nez m. ● vi **~ about** fouiner.

nosedive /ˈnəʊzdaɪv/ n piqué m. ● vi descendre en piqué.

nostalgia /nɒˈstældʒə/ n nostalgie f.

nostril /ˈnɒstrɪl/ n narine f; (of horse) naseau m.

nosy /ˈnəʊzɪ/ adj (-ier, -iest) 🆃 curieux, indiscret.

not /nɒt/ adv (ne) pas; **I do ~ know** je ne sais pas; **~ at all** pas du tout; **~ yet** pas encore; **I suppose ~** je suppose que non.

notably /ˈnəʊtəblɪ/ adv notamment.

notch /nɒtʃ/ n entaille f. ● vt **~ up** (score) marquer.

note /nəʊt/ n note f; (banknote) billet m; (short letter) mot m. ● vt noter; (notice) remarquer. **~book** n carnet m.

nothing /ˈnʌθɪŋ/ pron (ne) rien; **he eats ~** il ne mange rien; **~ else** rien d'autre; **~ much** pas grand-chose; **for ~** pour rien, gratis. ● n rien m; (person) nullité f. ● adv nullement.

notice /ˈnəʊtɪs/ n avis m, annonce f; (poster) affiche f; **(advance) ~** préavis m; **at short ~** dans des délais très brefs; **give in one's ~** donner sa démission; **take ~** faire attention (of à). ● vt remarquer, observer. **noticeable** adj visible. **~-board** n tableau m d'affichage.

notify /ˈnəʊtɪfaɪ/ vt (inform) aviser; (make known) notifier.

notion /ˈnəʊʃn/ n idée f, notion f.

notorious /nəʊˈtɔːrɪəs/ adj (criminal) notoire; (district) mal famé; (case) tristement célèbre.

notwithstanding /nɒtwɪθˈstændɪŋ/ prep malgré. ● adv néanmoins.

nought /nɔːt/ n zéro m.

noun /naʊn/ n nom m.

nourish /ˈnʌrɪʃ/ vt nourrir. **nourishing** adj nourrissant. **nourishment** n nourriture f.

novel /'nɒvl/ n roman m. ● adj nouveau. **novelist** n romancier/-ière m/f. **novelty** n nouveauté f.

November /nə'vembə(r)/ n novembre m.

now /naʊ/ adv maintenant. ● conj maintenant que; **just ~** maintenant; (a moment ago) tout à l'heure; **~ and again, ~ and then** de temps à autre.

nowadays /'naʊədeɪz/ adv de nos jours.

nowhere /'nəʊweə(r)/ adv nulle part.

nozzle /'nɒzl/ n (tip) embout m; (of hose) jet m.

nuclear /'njuːklɪə(r)/ adj nucléaire.

nude /njuːd/ adj nu. ● n nu/-e m/f; **in the ~** tout nu.

nudge /nʌdʒ/ vt pousser du coude. ● n coup m de coude.

nudism /'njuːdɪzəm/ n nudisme. **nudity** n nudité f.

nuisance /'njuːsns/ n (thing, event) ennui m; (person) peste f; **be a ~** être embêtant.

null /nʌl/ adj nul.

numb /nʌm/ adj engourdi (**with** par). ● vt engourdir.

number /'nʌmbə(r)/ n nombre m; (of ticket, house, page) numéro m; (written figure) chiffre m; **a ~ of people** plusieurs personnes. ● vt numéroter; (count, include) compter. **~-plate** n plaque f d'immatriculation.

numeral /'njuːmərəl/ n chiffre m.

numerate /'njuːmərət/ adj qui sait compter.

numerical /njuː'merɪkl/ adj numérique.

numerous /'njuːmərəs/ adj nombreux.

nun /nʌn/ n religieuse f.

nurse /nɜːs/ n infirmier/-ière m/f; (nanny) nurse f. ● vt soigner; (hope) nourrir.

nursery /'nɜːsərɪ/ n (room) chambre f d'enfants; (for plants) pépinière f; **(day) ~** crèche f. **~ rhyme** n comptine f. **~ school** n (école) maternelle f.

nursing home n maison f de retraite.

nut /nʌt/ n (walnut, Brazil nut) noix f; (hazelnut) noisette f; (peanut) cacahuète f; (Tech) écrou m. **~crackers** npl casse-noix m inv.

nutmeg /'nʌtmeg/ n muscade f.

nutrient /'njuːtrɪənt/ n substance f nutritive.

nutritious /njuː'trɪʃəs/ adj nutritif.

nuts /nʌts/ adj (crazy 🔲) cinglé.

nutshell /'nʌtʃel/ n coquille f de noix; **in a ~** en un mot.

nylon /'naɪlɒn/ n nylon m.

Oo

oak·/əʊk/ n chêne m.

OAP abbr **old-age pensioner** retraité/-e m/f.

oar /ɔː(r)/ n rame f.

oath /əʊθ/ n (promise) serment m; (swearword) juron m.

oats /əʊts/ npl avoine f.

obedience /ə'biːdɪəns/ n obéissance f. **obedient** adj obéissant. **obediently** adv docilement.

obese /əʊ'biːs/ adj obèse.

obey /ə'beɪ/ vt/i obéir (à).

object¹ /'ɒbdʒɪkt/ n (thing) objet m; (aim) but m; (Gram) complément m d'objet; **money is no ~** l'argent n'est pas un problème.

object² /əb'dʒekt/ vi protester. ● vt **~ that** objecter que; **~ to** (behaviour) désapprouver; (plan) protester contre. **objection** n objection f; (drawback) inconvénient m.

objective /əb'dʒektɪv/ adj & n objectif (m)

obligation /ɒblɪ'geɪʃn/ n devoir m.

obligatory /ə'blɪgətrɪ/ adj obligatoire.

oblige /ə'blaɪdʒ/ vt obliger (**to do** faire).

oblivion /ə'blɪvɪən/ n oubli m. **oblivious** adj inconscient (**to, of** de).

oblong /'ɒblɒŋ/ adj oblong. ● n rectangle m.

obnoxious /əb'nɒkʃəs/ adj odieux.

oboe /'əʊbəʊ/ n hautbois m.

obscene /əb'siːn/ adj obscène.

obscure /əb'skjʊə(r)/ adj obscur. ● vt obscurcir; (conceal) cacher.

observance /əbˈzɜːvəns/ n (of law) respect m; (of sabbath) observance f. **observant** adj observateur.

observation /ˌɒbzəˈveɪʃn/ n observation f.

observe /əbˈzɜːv/ vt observer; (remark) remarquer.

obsess /əbˈses/ vt obséder. **obsession** n obsession f. **obsessive** adj (person) maniaque; (thought) obsédant; (illness) obsessionnel.

obsolete /ˈɒbsəliːt/ adj dépassé.

obstacle /ˈɒbstəkl/ n obstacle m.

obstinate /ˈɒbstənət/ adj obstiné.

obstruct /əbˈstrʌkt/ vt (road) bloquer; (view) cacher; (progress) gêner. **obstruction** n (act) obstruction f; (thing) obstacle m; (in traffic) encombrement m.

obtain /əbˈteɪn/ vt obtenir. ● vi avoir cours. **obtainable** adj disponible.

obvious /ˈɒbvɪəs/ adj évident. **obviously** adv manifestement.

occasion /əˈkeɪʒn/ n occasion f; (big event) événement m; **on ~** à l'occasion.

occasional /əˈkeɪʒənl/ adj (event) qui a lieu de temps en temps; **the ~ letter** une lettre de temps en temps. **occasionally** adv de temps à autre.

occupation /ˌɒkjʊˈpeɪʃn/ n (activity) occupation f; (job) métier m, profession f. **occupational therapy** n ergothérapie f.

occupier /ˈɒkjʊpaɪə(r)/ n occupant/-e m/f.

occupy /ˈɒkjʊpaɪ/ vi occuper.

occur /əˈkɜː(r)/ vi (pt occurred) se produire; (arise) se présenter; **~ to sb** venir à l'esprit de qn.

occurrence /əˈkʌrəns/ n (event) fait m; (instance) occurrence f.

ocean /ˈəʊʃn/ n océan m.

Oceania /ˌəʊʃɪˈeɪnɪə/ n Océanie f.

o'clock /əˈklɒk/ adv **it is six ~** il est six heures; **at one ~** à une heure.

October /ɒkˈtəʊbə(r)/ n octobre m.

octopus /ˈɒktəpəs/ n (pl ~es) pieuvre f.

odd /ɒd/ adj bizarre; (number) impair; (left over) qui reste; (sock) dépareillé; **write the ~ article** écrire un article de temps en temps; **~ jobs** menus travaux mpl; **twenty ~** vingt et quelques. **oddity** n bizarrerie f.

odds /ɒdz/ npl chances fpl; (in betting) cote f (on de); **at ~** en désaccord; **it makes no ~** ça ne fait rien; **~ and ends** des petites choses.

odour, (US) **odor** /ˈəʊdə(r)/ n odeur f. **odourless** adj inodore.

of /ɒv/

⇒ For expressions such as **of course, consist of** ⇒**course, consist.**

● preposition
····▸ de; **a photo ~ the dog** une photo du chien; **the king ~ the beasts** le roi des animaux; **(made) ~ gold** en or; **it's kind ~ you** c'est très gentil de votre part; **some ~ us** quelques-uns d'entre nous; **~ it/them** en; **have you heard ~ it?** est-ce que tu en as entendu parler?

off /ɒf/ adv be **~** partir, s'en aller; **I'm ~** je m'en vais; **30 metres ~** à 30 mètres; **a month ~** dans un mois. ● adj (gas, water) coupé; (tap) fermé; (light, TV) éteint; (party, match) annulé; (bad) (food) avarié; (milk) tourné; **Friday is my day ~** je ne travaille pas le vendredi; **25% ~** 25% de remise. ● prep **3 metres ~ the ground** 3 mètres (au-dessus) du sol; **just ~ the kitchen** juste à côté de la cuisine; **that is ~ the point** là n'est pas la question.

offal /ˈɒfl/ n abats mpl.

offence /əˈfens/ n (Jur) infraction f; **give ~ to** offenser; **take ~** s'offenser (at de).

offend /əˈfend/ vt offenser; **be ~ed** s'offenser (at de). ● vi (Jur) commettre une infraction. **offender** n délinquant/-e m/f.

offensive /əˈfensɪv/ adj (remark) injurieux; (language) grossier; (smell) repoussant; (weapon) offensif. ● n offensive f.

offer /ˈɒfə(r)/ vt (pt offered) offrir. ● n offre f; **on ~** en promotion.

offhand /ɒfˈhænd/ adj désinvolte. ● adv à l'improviste.

office /'ɒfɪs/ n bureau m; (duty) fonction f; **in ~** au pouvoir. ● adj de bureau.

officer /'ɒfɪsə(r)/ n (army) officier m; (**police ~**) policier m; (**government ~**) fonctionnaire mf.

official /ə'fɪʃl/ adj officiel. ● n (civil servant) fonctionnaire mf; (of party, union) officiel/-le m/f; (of police, customs) agent m.

off: ~licence n magasin m de vins et spiritueux. **~line** adj autonome; (switched off) déconnecté; (Comput) hors connexion. **~load** vt (stock) écouler; (Comput) décharger. **~peak** adj (call) au tarif réduit; (travel) en période creuse. **~putting** adj rebutant. **~-set** vt (pt **-set**. pres p **-setting**) compenser. **~shore** adj (out to sea) au large, en mer; (towards the sea) de terre; **an ~ breeze** une brise de terre. ● adv (funds) hors-lieu inv. **~side** adj (Sport) hors jeu inv; (Auto) du côté du conducteur. **~spring** n inv progéniture f.

Off-licence On trouve ces magasins de vins et spiritueux dans tous les quartiers commerçants des villes britanniques. Les gens y achètent surtout de l'alcool à emporter, mais on y vend aussi des boissons non alcoolisées, des friandises ou du tabac et on peut même y louer des verres pour une fête. ▷**PUB.**

often /'ɒfn/ adv souvent; **how ~ do you meet?** vous vous voyez tous les combien?; **every so ~** de temps en temps.

oil /ɔɪl/ n (for lubrication, cooking) huile f; (for fuel) pétrole m; (for heating) mazout m. ● vt huiler. **~ field** n gisement m pétrolifère. **~-painting** n peinture f à l'huile. **~ skins** npl ciré m. **~-tanker** n pétrolier m.

oily /'ɔɪlɪ/ adj graisseux.

ointment /'ɔɪntmənt/ n pommade f.

OK, okay /əʊ'keɪ/ adj d'accord; **is it ~ if…?** ça va si…?; **feel ~** aller bien.

old /əʊld/ adj vieux; (person) vieux, âgé; (former) ancien; **how ~ is he?** quel âge a-t-il?; **he is eight years ~** il a huit ans; **~er, ~est** aîné. **~ age** n vieillesse f. **~-age pensioner** n

retraité/-e m/f. **~-fashioned** adj démodé; (person) vieux jeu inv. **~ man** n vieillard m, vieux m. **~ woman** n vieille f.

olive /'ɒlɪv/ n olive f; **~ oil** huile f d'olive. ● adj olive inv.

Olympic /ə'lɪmpɪk/ adj olympique. **~ Games** npl Jeux mpl olympiques.

omelette /'ɒmlɪt/ n omelette f.

omen /'əʊmən/ n augure m.

ominous /'ɒmɪnəs/ adj (presence, cloud) menaçant; (sign) de mauvais augure.

omission /ə'mɪʃn/ n omission f. **omit** vt (pt **omitted**) omettre.

on /ɒn/ prep sur; **~ the table** sur la table; **put the key ~ it** mets la clé dessus; **~ 22 March** le 22 mars; **~ Monday** lundi; **~ TV** à la télé; **~ video** en vidéo; **be ~ steroids** prendre des stéroïdes; **~ arriving** en arrivant. ● adj (TV, oven, light) allumé; (dishwasher, radio) en marche; (tap) ouvert; (lid) mis; **the match is still ~** le match aura lieu quand même; **the news is ~ in 10 minutes** les informations sont dans 10 minutes. ● adv **have sth ~** porter qch; **20 years ~** 20 ans plus tard; **from that day ~** à partir de ce jour-là; **further ~** plus loin; **~ and off** (occasionally) de temps en temps; **go ~ and ~** (person) parler pendant des heures.

once /wʌns/ adv une fois; (formerly) autrefois. ● conj une fois que; **all at ~** tout d'un coup.

oncoming /'ɒnkʌmɪŋ/ adj (vehicle) qui approche.

one /wʌn/ det & n un/-e (m/f). ● pron un/-e m/f; (impersonal) on; **~ (and only)** seul (et unique); **a big ~** un grand/une grande; **this/that ~** celui-ci/-là, celle-ci/-là; **~ another** l'un/-e l'autre. **~-off** adj ⚹ unique, exceptionnel. **~self** pron soi-même; (reflexive) se. **~-way** adj (street) à sens unique; (ticket) simple.

ongoing /'ɒngəʊɪŋ/ adj (process) continu; **be ~** être en cours.

onion /'ʌnɪən/ n oignon m.

on-line /ɒn'laɪn/ adj & adv en ligne.

onlooker /'ɒnlʊkə(r)/ n spectateur/-trice m/f.

only /'əʊnlɪ/ adj seul; **~ son** fils unique. ● adv & conj seulement; **he is ~**

six il n'a que six ans.

onset /'ɒnset/ n début m.

onward(s) /'ɒnwəd(z)/ adv en avant.

open /'əupən/ adj ouvert; (view) dégagé; (free to all) public; (undisguised) manifeste; (question) en attente; **in the ∼ air** en plein air. ● vt/i (door) (s')ouvrir; (shop, play) ouvrir; **∼ out** or **up** (s')ouvrir. **∼-ended** adj (stay) de durée indéterminée; (debate, question) ouvert. **∼-heart** adj (surgery) à cœur ouvert.

opening /'əupnɪŋ/ n (of book) début m; (of exhibition, shop) ouverture f; (of film) première f; (in market) débouché m; (job) poste m (disponible).

open: **∼-minded** adj be **∼-minded** avoir l'esprit ouvert. **∼-plan** adj paysagé.

Open University Organisme britannique d'enseignement universitaire à distance. Les étudiants de tous âges travaillent chez eux et suivent les cours à la télévision ou sur Internet; ils envoient leurs travaux à leur directeur d'études (tutor) qu'ils peuvent rencontrer lors de stages en été. Les diplômes obtenus ont la même valeur que ceux délivrés par les universités traditionnelles.

opera /'ɒprə/ n opéra m.

operate /'ɒpəreɪt/ vt/i opérer; (Tech) (faire) fonctionner; **∼ on** (Med) opérer; **operating theatre** salle f d'opération.

operation /ɒpə'reɪʃn/ n opération f; **have an ∼** se faire opérer; **in ∼** (plan) en vigueur; (mine) en service.

operative /'ɒpərətɪv/ n employé/-e m/f. ● adj (law) en vigueur.

operator /'ɒpəreɪtə(r)/ n opérateur/-trice m/f; (telephonist) standardiste mf.

opinion /ə'pɪnɪən/ n opinion f, avis m.
opinionated adj qui a des avis sur tout.

opponent /ə'pəunənt/ n adversaire mf.

opportunity /ɒpə'tjuːnətɪ/ n occasion f (**to do** de faire).

oppose /ə'pəuz/ vt s'opposer à; **as ∼d to** par opposition à. **opposing** adj opposé.

opposite /'ɒpəzɪt/ adj (direction, side) opposé; (building) d'en face. ● n contraire m. ● adv en face. ● prep **∼ (to)** en face de.

opposition /ɒpə'zɪʃn/ n opposition f.

oppress /ə'pres/ vt opprimer. **oppressive** adj (cruel) oppressif; (heat) oppressant.

opt /ɒpt/ vi **∼ for** opter pour; **∼ out** refuser de participer (**of** à); **∼ to do** choisir de faire.

optical /'ɒptɪkl/ adj optique. **∼ illusion** n illusion f d'optique. **∼ scanner** n lecteur m optique.

optician /ɒp'tɪʃn/ n opticien/-ne m/f.

optimism /'ɒptɪmɪzəm/ n optimisme m. **optimist** n optimiste mf. **optimistic** adj optimiste.

option /'ɒpʃn/ n option f; (choice) choix m.

optional /'ɒpʃənl/ adj facultatif; **∼ extras** accessoires mpl en option.

or /ɔː(r)/ conj ou; (with negative) ni.

oral /'ɔːrəl/ n & adj oral (m).

orange /'ɒrɪndʒ/ n (fruit) orange f; (colour) orange m. ● adj (colour) orange inv.

orbit /'ɔːbɪt/ n orbite f. ● vt décrire une orbite autour de.

orchard /'ɔːtʃəd/ n verger m.

orchestra /'ɔːkɪstrə/ n orchestre m.

orchid /'ɔːkɪd/ n orchidée f.

ordeal /ɔː'diːl/ n épreuve f.

order /'ɔːdə(r)/ n ordre m; (Comm) commande f; **in ∼** (tidy) en ordre; (document) en règle; **in ∼ that** pour que; **in ∼ to** pour. ● vt ordonner; (goods) commander; **∼ sb to** ordonner à qn de.

orderly /'ɔːdəlɪ/ adj (tidy) ordonné; (not unruly) discipliné. ● n (Mil) planton m; (Med) aide-soignant/-e m/f.

ordinary /'ɔːdənrɪ/ adj (usual) ordinaire; (average) moyen.

ore /ɔː(r)/ n minerai m.

organ /'ɔːgən/ n organe m; (Mus) orgue m.

organic /ɔː'gænɪk/ adj organique; (produce) biologique.

organization /ɔːgənaɪ'zeɪʃn/ n organisation f.

organize /'ɔːgənaɪz/ vt organiser.

organizer /'ɔːgənaɪzə(r)/ n organisateur/-trice m/f; **electronic ∼**

agenda *m* électronique.

orgasm /ˈɔːgæzəm/ *n* orgasme *m*.

Orient /ˈɔːrɪənt/ *n* **the** ~ l'Orient *m*. **oriental** *adj* oriental.

origin /ˈɒrɪdʒɪn/ *n* origine *f*.

original /əˈrɪdʒənl/ *adj* original; (*inhabitant*) premier; (*member*) originaire. **originality** *n* originalité *f*. **originally** *adv* (at the outset) à l'origine.

originate /əˈrɪdʒɪneɪt/ *vi* (plan) prendre naissance; ~ **from** provenir de; (person) venir de. ● *vt* être l'auteur de. **originator** *n* (of idea) auteur *m*; (of invention) créateur/-trice *m/f*.

ornament /ˈɔːnəmənt/ *n* (decoration) ornement *m*; (object) objet *m* décoratif.

orphan /ˈɔːfn/ *n* orphelin/-e *m/f*. ● *vt* rendre orphelin. **orphanage** *n* orphelinat *m*.

orthopaedic /ɔːθəˈpiːdɪk/ *adj* orthopédique.

ostentatious /ɒstenˈteɪʃəs/ *adj* tape-à-l'œil *inv*.

osteopath /ˈɒstɪəpæθ/ *n* ostéopathe *mf*.

ostrich /ˈɒstrɪtʃ/ *n* autruche *f*.

other /ˈʌðə(r)/ *adj* autre; **the** ~ **one** l'autre *mf*. ● *n* & *pron* autre *mf*; (some) ~**s** d'autres. ● *adv* ~ **than** (apart from) à part; (otherwise than) autrement que. **otherwise** *adv* autrement.

otter /ˈɒtə(r)/ *n* loutre *f*.

ouch /aʊtʃ/ *interj* aïe!

ought /ɔːt/ *v aux* devoir; **you** ~ **to stay** vous devriez rester; **he** ~ **to succeed** il devrait réussir; **I** ~ **to have done it** j'aurais dû le faire.

ounce /aʊns/ *n* once *f* (= 28.35 g).

our /ˈaʊə(r)/ *adj* notre, *pl* nos.

ours /ˈaʊəz/ *poss* le *or* la nôtre, les nôtres.

ourselves /aʊəˈselvz/ *pron* (reflexive) nous; (emphatic) nous-mêmes; (after preposition) **for** ~ pour nous, pour nous-mêmes.

out /aʊt/ *adv* dehors; **he's** ~ il est sorti; **further** ~ plus loin; **be** ~ (book) être publié; (light) être éteint; (sun) briller; (flower) être épanoui; (tide) être bas; (player) être éliminé; ~ **of hors de**; **go/walk/get** ~ sortir de; ~ **of pity** par pitié; **made** ~ **of** fait de; **5** ~ **of 6** 5 sur 6. ~**break** *n*

(of war) déclenchement *m*; (of violence, boils) éruption *f*. ~**burst** *n* explosion *f*. ~**cast** *n* paria *m*. ~**class** *vt* surclasser. ~**come** *n* résultat *m*. ~**cry** *n* tollé *m*. ~**dated** *adj* démodé. ~**door** *adj* (activity) de plein air; (pool) en plein air. ~**doors** *adv* dehors.

outer /ˈaʊtə(r)/ *adj* extérieur; ~ **space** espace *m* extra-atmosphérique.

outfit /ˈaʊtfɪt/ *n* (clothes) tenue *f*.

outgoing /ˈaʊtgəʊɪŋ/ *adj* (minister, tenant) sortant; (sociable) ouvert. **outgoings** *npl* dépenses *fpl*.

outgrow /aʊtˈgrəʊ/ *vt* (*pt* -**grew**. *pp* -**grown**) (clothes) devenir trop grand pour; (habit) dépasser.

outing /ˈaʊtɪŋ/ *n* sortie *f*.

outlaw /ˈaʊtlɔː/ *n* hors-la-loi *m inv*. ● *vt* déclarer illégal.

outlet /ˈaʊtlet/ *n* (for water, gas) tuyau *m* de sortie; (for goods) débouché *m*; (for feelings) exutoire *m*.

outline /ˈaʊtlaɪn/ *n* contour *m*; (of plan) grandes lignes *fpl*; (of essay) plan *m*. ● *vt* tracer le contour de; (summarize) exposer brièvement.

out: ~**live** *vt* survivre à. ~**look** *n* perspective *f*. ~**number** *vt* surpasser en nombre. ~ **of date** *adj* démodé; (expired) périmé. ~ **of hand** *adj* incontrôlable. ~ **of order** *adj* en panne. ~ **of work** *adj* sans travail. ~**patient** *n* malade *mf* externe.

output /ˈaʊtpʊt/ *n* rendement *m*; (Comput) sortie *f*. ● *vt/i* (Comput) sortir.

outrage /ˈaʊtreɪdʒ/ *n* (anger) indignation *f*; (atrocity) attentat *m*; (scandal) outrage *m*. ● *vt* (morals) outrager; (person) scandaliser. **outrageous** *adj* scandaleux.

outright /ˈaʊtraɪt/ *adv* (completely) catégoriquement; (killed) sur le coup. ● *adj* (majority) absolu; (ban) catégorique; (hostility) pur et simple.

outset /ˈaʊtset/ *n* début *m*.

outside /aʊtˈsaɪd/ *n* extérieur *m*. ● *adv* dehors. ● *prep* en dehors de; (in front of) devant. ● *adj* extérieur. **outsider** *n* étranger/-ère *m/f*; (Sport) outsider *m*.

out: ~ **skirts** *npl* périphérie *f*. ~**spoken** *adj* franc. ~**standing** *adj* exceptionnel; (not settled) en suspens.

outward /'autwəd/ *adj & adv* vers l'extérieur; (*sign*) extérieur. (*journey*) d'aller. **outwards** *adv* vers l'extérieur.

oval /'əuvl/ *n & adj* ovale (*m*).

Oval Office Symbole même de la présidence américaine, le bureau ovale du président des États-Unis est situé dans l'aile ouest de la Maison-Blanche et a été inauguré en 1909. Le goût des pièces de forme ovale remonte à la présidence de George Washington (1789-1797) qui donnait des réceptions à son domicile de Philadelphie dans un salon ovale.

ovary /'əuvərɪ/ *n* ovaire *m*.

oven /'ʌvn/ *n* four *m*.

over /'əuvə(r)/ *prep* (across) par-dessus; (above) au-dessus de; (covering) sur; (more than) plus de; **it's ~ the road** c'est de l'autre côté de la rue; **~ here/there** par ici/là; **children ~ six** les enfants de plus de six ans; **~ the weekend** pendant le weekend; **all ~ the house** partout dans la maison. ● *adj, adv* (term) terminé; (war) fini; **get sth ~ with** en finir avec qch; **ask sb ~** inviter qn; **~ and ~ (again)** à plusieurs reprises; **five times ~** cinq fois de suite.

overall /əuvər'ɔ:l/ *adj* global, d'ensemble; (*length*) total. ● *adv* globalement.

overalls /'əuvərɔ:ls/*npl* combinaison *f*.

over /'əuvə(r)/ **~board** *adv* par-dessus bord. **~cast** *adj* couvert. **~charge** *vt* faire payer trop cher à. **~coat** *n* pardessus *m*.

overcome /əuvə'kʌm/ *vt* (*pt* **-came**. *pp* **-come**) (*enemy*) vaincre; (*difficulty, fear*) surmonter; **~by** accablé de.

overcrowded /əuvə'kraudɪd/ *adj* bondé; (*country*) surpeuplé.

overdo /əuvə'du:/ *vt* (*pt* **-did**. *pp* **-done**) (Culin) trop cuire; **~ it** (overwork) en faire trop.

over: **~ dose** *n* surdose *f*, overdose *f*. **~ draft** *n* découvert *m*. **~ draw** *vt* (*pt* **-drew**. *pp* **-drawn**) faire un découvert sur. **~ due** *adj* en retard; (*bill*) impayé.

overflow¹ /əuvə'fləu/ *vi* déborder.

overflow² /'əuvəfləu/ *n* (outlet) trop-plein *m*. **~ car park** *n* parking *m* de délestage.

overhaul /əuvə'hɔ:l/ *vt* réviser.

overhead¹ /əuvə'hed/ *adv* au-dessus; (in sky) dans le ciel.

overhead² /'əuvəhed/ *adj* aérien; **~ projector** rétroprojecteur *m*. **overheads** *npl* frais *mpl* généraux.

over: **~hear** *vt* (*pt* **-heard**) entendre par hasard. **~lap** *vt/i* (*pt* **-lapped**) (se) chevaucher. **~leaf** *adv* au verso. **~load** *vt* surcharger. **~look** *vt* (*window*) donner sur; (miss) ne pas voir.

overnight¹ /əuvə'naɪt/ *adv* dans la nuit; (instantly: fig) du jour au lendemain.

overnight² /'əuvənaɪt/ *adj* (train) de nuit; (stay) d'une nuit; (fig) soudain.

over: **~power** *vt* (thief) maîtriser; (army) vaincre; (fig) accabler. **~-priced** *adj* trop cher. **~rate** *vt* surestimer. **~react** *vi* réagir de façon excessive. **~riding** *adj* (consideration) numéro un; (importance) primordial. **~rule** *vt* (decision) annuler.

overrun /əuvə'rʌn/ *vt* (*pt* **-ran**. *pp* **-run**; *pres p* **-running**) (country) envahir; (budget) dépasser. ● *vi* (meeting) durer plus longtemps que prévu.

overseas /əuvə'si:z/ *adj* étranger. ● *adv* outre-mer, à l'étranger.

over: **~see** *vt* (*pt* **-saw**. *pp* **-seen**) surveiller. **~sight** *n* omission *f*. **~sleep** *vi* (*pt* **-slept**) se réveiller trop tard. **~take** *vt/i* (*pt* **-took**. *pp* **-taken**) dépasser; (fig) frapper. **~time** *n* heures *fpl* supplémentaires. **~turn** *vt/i* (se) renverser. **~weight** *adj* trop gros.

overwhelm /əuvə'welm/ *vt* (enemy) écraser; (shame) accabler. **overwhelmed** *adj* (with offers, calls) submergé (**with**, **by** de); (with shame, work) accablé; (by sight) ébloui. **overwhelming** *adj* (heat, grief) accablant; (defeat, victory) écrasant; (urge) irrésistible.

overwork /əuvə'wɜ:k/ *vt/i* (se) surmener. ● *n* surmenage *m*.

owe /əu/ *vt* devoir. **owing** *adj* dû; **owing to** en raison de.

owl /aul/ *n* hibou *m*.

own /əun/ *adj* propre. ● *pron* **my ~** le mien, la mienne; **a house of one's ~** sa propre maison; **on one's ~** tout seul. ● *vt* posséder; **~ up (to)** [1] avouer. **owner** *n* propriétaire *mf*. **own-**

ership n propriété f; (of land) possession f.

Oxbridge Formé de la combinaison de Oxford et Cambridge, ce mot-valise est fréquemment employé pour désigner les universités de ces deux villes, en particulier quand on veut les distinguer des autres universités britanniques, car ce sont les plus prestigieuses.

oxygen /'ɒksɪdʒən/ n oxygène m.

oyster /'ɔɪstə(r)/ n huître f.

ozone /'əʊzəʊn/ n ozone m; ~ **layer** couche f d'ozone.

Pp

PA abbr ⟶ PERSONAL ASSISTANT.

pace /peɪs/ n pas m; (speed) allure f; **keep ~ with** suivre. ● vt (room) arpenter. ● vi ~ **(up and down)** faire les cent pas.

Pacific /pə'sɪfɪk/ n ~ **(Ocean)** océan m Pacifique.

pack /pæk/ n paquet m; (Mil) sac m; (of hounds) meute f; (of thieves) bande f; (of lies) tissu m. ● vt (into case) mettre dans une valise; (into box, crate) emballer; (for sale) conditionner; (crowd) remplir complètement; ~ **one's suitcase** faire sa valise. ● vi faire ses valises; ~ **into** (cram) s'entasser dans; ~ **off** expédier; **send ~ing** envoyer promener.

package /'pækɪdʒ/ n paquet m; (Comput) progiciel m; ~ **deal** offre f globale. ~ **holiday** voyage m organisé. ● vt empaqueter.

packed /pækt/ adj (crowded) bondé; ~ **lunch** repas m froid.

packet /'pækɪt/ n paquet m.

packing /'pækɪŋ/ n (action, material) emballage m.

pad /pæd/ n (of paper) bloc m; (to protect) protection f; (for ink) tampon m; (launch) rampe f de lancement. ● vt (pt **padded**) rembourrer; (text: fig) délayer. ● vi (pt **padded**) (walk) marcher à pas feutrés. **padding** n rembourrage m.

paddle /'pædl/ n pagaie f. ● vt ~ **a canoe** pagayer. ● vi patauger.

padlock /'pædlɒk/ n cadenas m. ● vt cadenasser.

paediatrician /piːdjə'trɪʃən/ n pédiatre mf.

pagan /'peɪgən/ adj & n païen/-ne (m/f).

page /peɪdʒ/ n (of book) page f. ● vt (on pager) rechercher; (over speaker) faire appeler. **pager** n radiomessageur m.

pain /peɪn/ n douleur f; ~s efforts mpl; **be in ~** souffrir; **take ~s to** se donner du mal pour. ● vt (grieve) peiner. **painful** adj douloureux; (laborious) pénible. ~-**killer** n analgésique m. **painless** adj (operation) indolore; (death) sans souffrance; (trouble-free) sans peine. **painstaking** adj minutieux.

paint /peɪnt/ n peinture f; ~s (in tube, box) couleurs fpl. ● vt/i peindre. ~ **brush** n pinceau m. **painter** n peintre m. **painting** n peinture f. ~**work** n peintures fpl.

pair /peə(r)/ n paire f; (of people) couple m; **a ~ of trousers** un pantalon. ● vi ~ **off** former un couple.

pajamas /pə'dʒɑːməz/ npl (US) ⟶ PYJAMAS.

Pakistan /pɑːkɪ'stɑːn/ n Pakistan m.

palace /'pælɪs/ n palais m.

palatable /'pælətəbl/ adj (food) savoureux; (solution) acceptable. **palate** n palais m.

pale /peɪl/ adj pâle. ● vi pâlir.

Palestine /'pælɪstaɪn/ n Palestine f.

pallid /'pælɪd/ adj pâle.

palm /pɑːm/ n (of hand) paume f; (tree) palmier m; (symbol) palme f. □ ~ **off** ① | ~ **sth off as** faire passer qch pour; ~ **sth off on sb** refiler qch à qn ①.

palpitate /'pælpɪteɪt/ vi palpiter.

paltry /'pɔːltrɪ/ adj (-**ier**, -**iest**) dérisoire, piètre.

pamper /'pæmpə(r)/ vt choyer.

pamphlet /'pæmflɪt/ n brochure f.

pan /pæn/ n casserole f; (for frying) poêle f.

pancake /'pæŋkeɪk/ n crêpe f.

pandemonium /pændr'məʊnɪəm/ n tohu-bohu m.

pander /'pændə(r)/ vi ~ **to** (person, taste) flatter bassement.

pane /peɪn/ n carreau m, vitre f.

panel /'pænl/ n (of door) panneau m; (of experts, judges) commission f; (on discussion programme) invités mpl; **(instrument)** ~ tableau m de bord.

pang /pæŋ/ n serrement m au cœur; ~**s of conscience** remords mpl.

panic /'pænɪk/ n panique f. ● vt/i (pt **panicked**) (s')affoler. ~**-stricken** adj pris de panique, affolé.

pansy /'pænzɪ/ n (Bot) pensée f.

pant /pænt/ vi haleter.

panther /'pænθə(r)/ n panthère f.

pantomime /'pæntəmaɪm/ n (show) spectacle m de Noël; (mime) mime m.

pantry /'pæntrɪ/ n garde-manger m inv.

pants /pænts/ npl (underwear) slip m; (trousers: US) pantalon m.

paper /'peɪpə(r)/ n papier m; (news-paper) journal m; (exam) épreuve f; (essay) exposé m; (wallpaper) papier m peint; (identity) ~**s** papiers mpl (d'identité); **on** ~ par écrit. ● vt (room) tapisser. ~**back** n livre m de poche. ~**-clip** n trombone m. ~ **feed tray** n (Comput) bac m d'alimentation en papier. ~ **work** n (work) travail m administratif; (documentation) documents mpl.

par /pɑː(r)/ n **be below** ~ ne pas être en forme; **on a** ~ **with** (performance) comparable à; (person) l'égal de; (golf) par m.

parachute /'pærəʃuːt/ n parachute m. ● vi descendre en parachute.

parade /pə'reɪd/ n (procession) parade f; (Mil) défilé m. ● vi défiler. ● vt faire étalage de.

paradise /'pærədaɪs/ n paradis m.

paradox /'pærədɒks/ n paradoxe m.

paraffin /'pærəfɪn/ n pétrole m (lampant); (wax) paraffine f.

paragliding /'pærəglaɪdɪŋ/ n parapente m.

paragon /'pærəgən/ n modèle m.

paragraph /'pærəgrɑːf/ n paragraphe m.

parallel /'pærəlel/ adj parallèle. ● n parallèle m; (maths) parallèle f.

Paralympics /pærə'lɪmpɪks/ npl the ~ les jeux paralympiques.

paralyse /'pærəlaɪz/ vt paralyser. **paralysis** n paralysie f.

paramedic /pærə'medɪk/ n auxiliaire mf médical/-e.

parameter /pə'ræmɪtə(r)/ n paramètre m.

paramount /'pærəmaʊnt/ adj suprême.

paranoia /pærə'nɔɪə/ n paranoïa f. **paranoid** adj paranoïaque; (Psych) paranoïde.

paraphernalia /pærəfə'neɪlɪə/ n attirail m.

parasol /'pærəsɒl/ n ombrelle f; (on table, at beach) parasol m.

paratrooper /'pærətruːpə(r)/ n (Mil) parachutiste mf.

parcel /'pɑːsl/ n paquet m.

parchment /'pɑːtʃmənt/ n parchemin m.

pardon /'pɑːdn/ n pardon m; (Jur) grâce f; **I beg your** ~ je vous demande pardon. ● vt (pt **pardoned**) pardonner (**sb for sth** qch à qn); (Jur) gracier.

parent /'peərənt/ n parent m.

parenthesis /pə'renθəsɪs/ n (pl -**theses**) parenthèse f.

parenthood /'peərənthʊd/ n (fatherhood) paternité f; (motherhood) maternité f.

Paris /'pærɪs/ n Paris.

parish /'pærɪʃ/ n (Relig) paroisse f; (municipal) commune f.

park /pɑːk/ n parc m. ● vt/i (se) garer; (remain parked) stationner. ~ **and ride** n parc m relais.

parking /'pɑːkɪŋ/ n stationnement m; **no** ~ stationnement interdit. ~ **lot** n (US) parking m. ~ **meter** n parcmètre m. ~ **ticket** n (fine) contravention f, PV m[1].

parliament /'pɑːləmənt/ n parlement m. **parliamentary** adj parlementaire.

Parliament Corps législatif britannique composé de la Chambre des communes (House of Commons) et de la Chambre des lords (House of Lords) qui siègent au Palais de Westminster. Le souverain convoque et dissout le Parlement,

ouvre chaque session parlementaire
et signe les textes de lois. ▷**Scot-**
tish Parliament, ▷**Welsh Assem-**
bly, ▷**Dáil**.

parlour, (US) **parlor** /'pɑːlə(r)/ n
salon m.

parody /'pærədɪ/ n parodie f. ● vt parodier.

parole /pə'rəʊl/ n **on ~** en liberté
conditionnelle.

parrot /'pærət/ n perroquet m.

parry /'pærɪ/ vt (Sport) parer; (question) éluder. ● n parade f.

parsley /'pɑːslɪ/ n persil m.

parsnip /'pɑːsnɪp/ n panais m.

part /pɑːt/ n partie f; (of serial) épisode
m; (of machine) pièce f; (Theat) rôle m;
(side in dispute) parti m; **in ~** en partie; **on the ~ of** de la part de; **take**
~ in participer à. ● adj partiel. ● adv
en partie. ● vt/i (separate) (se) séparer; **~ with** se séparer de.

part-exchange n reprise f; **take sth**
in ~ reprendre qch.

partial /'pɑːʃl/ adj partiel; (biased) partial; **be ~ to** avoir un faible pour.

participant /pɑː'tɪsɪpənt/ n
participant/-e m/f. **participate** vi participer (**in** à). **participation** n participation f.

participle /'pɑːtɪsɪpl/ n participe m.

particular /pə'tɪkjʊlə(r)/ n détail m;
~s détails mpl; **in ~** en particulier.
● adj particulier; (fussy) difficile; (careful) méticuleux; **that ~ man** cet
homme-là. **particularly** adv particulièrement.

parting /'pɑːtɪŋ/ n séparation f; (in
hair) raie f. ● adj d'adieu.

partition /pɑː'tɪʃn/ n (of room) cloison
f; (Pol) partition f. ● vt (room) cloison-
ner; (country) partager.

partly /'pɑːtlɪ/ adv en partie.

partner /'pɑːtnə(r)/ n (professional)
associé/-e m/f; (economic, sporting)
partenaire mf; (spouse) époux/-se m/f;
(unmarried) partenaire mf. **partner-**
ship n association f.

partridge /'pɑːtrɪdʒ/ n perdrix f.

part-time adj & adv à temps partiel.

party /'pɑːtɪ/ n fête f; (formal) réception f; (group) groupe m; (Pol) parti m;
(Jur) partie f.

pass /pɑːs/ vt/i (pt **passed**) passer;
(overtake) dépasser; (in exam) réussir;
(approve) (candidate) admettre; (invoice) approuver; (remark) faire;
(judgement) prononcer; (law, bill)
adopter; **~ (by)** (building) passer devant; (person) croiser. ● n (permit)
laisser-passer m inv; (ticket) carte f d'a-
bonnement; (Geog) col m; (Sport)
passe f; **~ (mark)** (in exam) moyenne
f. ▫ **~ away** mourir; **~ out** (faint)
s'évanouir; **~ sth out** distribuer qch;
~ over (overlook) délaisser; **~ up**
(forego) laisser passer.

passage /'pæsɪdʒ/ n (way through,
text) passage m; (voyage) traversée f;
(corridor) couloir m.

passenger /'pæsɪndʒə(r)/ n (in car,
plane, ship) passager/-ère m/f; (in
train, bus, tube) voyageur/-euse m/f.

passer-by /pɑːsə'baɪ/ n (pl **passers-**
by) passant/-e m/f.

passing /'pɑːsɪŋ/ adj (motorist) qui
passe; (whim) passager; (reference) en
passant.

passion /'pæʃn/ n passion f. **passion-**
ate adj passionné.

passive /'pæsɪv/ adj passif.

passport /'pɑːspɔːt/ n passeport m.

password /'pɑːswɜːd/ n mot m de
passe.

past /pɑːst/ adj (times, problems) passé;
(president) ancien; **the ~ months** ces
derniers mois. ● n passé m. ● prep (beyond) après; **walk/go ~ sth** passer
devant qch; **10 ~ 6** six heures dix; **it's**
~ 11 il est 11 heures passées. ● adv
go/walk ~ passer.

pasta /'pæstə/ n pâtes fpl (alimentaires).

paste /peɪst/ n (glue) colle f; (dough)
pâte f; (of fish, meat) pâté m; (jewellery) strass m. ● vt coller.

pasteurize /'pɑːstʃəraɪz/ vt pas-
teuriser.

pastime /'pɑːstaɪm/ n passe-temps
m inv.

pastry /'peɪstrɪ/ n (dough) pâte f;
(tart) pâtisserie f.

pat /pæt/ vt (pt **patted**) tapoter. ● n
petite tape f.

patch /pætʃ/ n pièce f; (over eye) bandeau m; (spot) tache f; (of snow, ice)
plaque f; (of vegetables) carré m; **bad**

~ période f difficile. □ ~ **up** (trousers) rapiécer; (quarrel) résoudre.

patent /'pætnt/ adj (obvious) manifeste; (patented) breveté; ~ **leather** cuir m verni. ● n brevet m. ● vt faire breveter.

path /pɑ:θ/ n (pl -s) sentier m, chemin m; (in park) allée f; (of rocket) trajectoire f.

pathetic /pə'θetɪk/ adj misérable; (bad 🄸) lamentable.

patience /'peɪʃns/ n patience f.

patient /'peɪʃnt/ adj patient. ● n patient/-e m/f. **patiently** adv patiemment.

patriotic /pætrɪ'ɒtɪk/ adj patriotique; (person) patriote.

patrol /pə'trəʊl/ n patrouille f; ~ **car** voiture f de police. ● vt/i patrouiller (dans).

patron /'peɪtrən/ n (of the arts) mécène m; (customer) client/-e m/f. **patronage** n clientèle f; (support) patronage m. **patronize** vt (person) traiter avec condescendance; (establishment) fréquenter.

patter /'pætə(r)/ n (of steps) bruit m; (of rain) crépitement m.

pattern /'pætn/ n motif m, dessin m; (for sewing) patron m; (for knitting) modèle m.

paunch /pɔ:ntʃ/ n ventre m.

pause /pɔ:z/ n pause f. ● vi faire une pause; (hesitate) hésiter.

pave /peɪv/ vt paver; ~ **the way** ouvrir la voie (**for** à).

pavement /'peɪvmənt/ n trottoir m; (US) chaussée f.

paving stone n pavé m.

paw /pɔ:/ n patte f. ● vt (animal) donner des coups de patte à; (touch 🄸) peloter 🄸.

pawn /pɔ:n/ n pion m. ● vt mettre en gage. ~**broker** n prêteur/-euse m/f sur gages. ~**-shop** n mont-de-piété m.

pay /peɪ/ vt (pt **paid**) payer; (interest) rapporter; (compliment, attention) faire; (visit, homage) rendre. ● vi payer; (business) rapporter; ~ **for sth** payer qch. ● n salaire m; ~ **rise** augmentation f (de salaire). ~ **back** rembourser; ~ **in** déposer; ~ **off** (loan) rembourser; (worker) congédier; (succeed) être payant; ~ **out** payer, débourser.

payable /'peɪəbl/ adj payable; ~ **to** (cheque) à l'ordre de.

payment /'peɪmənt/ n paiement m; (regular) versement m; (reward) récompense f.

payroll /'peɪrəʊl/ n fichier m des salaires; **be on the** ~ **of** être employé par.

PC abbr →PERSONAL COMPUTER.

PDA abbr (personal digital assistant) assistant m personnel numérique.

PE abbr (**physical education**) éducation f physique, EPS f.

pea /pi:/ n (petit) pois m.

peace /pi:s/ n paix f; ~ **of mind** tranquillité f d'esprit. **peaceful** adj (tranquil) paisible; (peaceable) pacifique.

peach /pi:tʃ/ n pêche f.

peacock /'pi:kɒk/ n paon m.

peak /pi:k/ n (of mountain) pic m; (of cap) visière f; (maximum) maximum m; (on graph) sommet m; (of career) apogée m; (of fitness) meilleur m; ~ **hours** heures fpl de pointe.

peal /pi:l/ n (of bells) carillon m; (of laughter) éclat m.

peanut /'pi:nʌt/ n cacahuète f; ~**s** (money) 🄸 clopinettes fpl 🄸.

pear /peə(r)/ n poire f.

pearl /pɜ:l/ n perle f.

peasant /'peznt/ n paysan/-ne m/f.

peat /pi:t/ n tourbe f.

pebble /'pebl/ n caillou m; (on beach) galet m.

peck /pek/ vt/i (food) picorer; (attack) donner des coups de bec (à). ● n coup m de bec; **a** ~ **on the cheek** une bise.

peckish /'pekɪʃ/ adj **be** ~ 🄸 avoir faim.

peculiar /pɪ'kju:lɪə(r)/ adj (odd) bizarre; (special) particulier (**to** à). **peculiarity** n bizarrerie f.

pedal /'pedl/ n pédale f. ● vi pédaler.

pedantic /pɪ'dæntɪk/ adj pédant.

peddle /'pedl/ vt colporter; (drugs) faire du trafic de.

pedestrian /pɪ'destrɪən/ n piéton m. ● adj (precinct, street) piétonnier; (fig) prosaïque; ~ **crossing** passage m pour piétons.

pedigree /'pedɪgri:/ n (of animal) pedigree m; (of person) ascendance f. ● adj (dog) de pure race.

pee /pi:/ vi 🔳 faire pipi 🔳.

peek /pi:k/ vi & n →PEEP.

peel /pi:l/ n (on fruit) peau m; (removed) épluchures fpl. ● vt (fruit, vegetables) éplucher; (prawn) décortiquer. ● vi (of skin) peler; (of paint) s'écailler.

peep /pi:p/ vi jeter un coup d'œil (furtif) (at à). ● n coup m d'œil (furtif). ~hole n judas m.

peer /pɪə(r)/ vi ~ (at) regarder fixement. ● n (equal, noble) pair m. peerage n pairie f.

peg /peg/ n (for clothes) pince f à linge; (to hang coats) patère f; (for tent) piquet m. ● vt (pt pegged) (clothes) accrocher avec des pinces; (prices) indexer.

pejorative /pɪˈdʒɒrətɪv/ adj péjoratif.

pelican /ˈpelɪkən/ n pélican m; ~ crossing passage m pour piétons.

pellet /ˈpelɪt/ n (round mass) boulette f; (for gun) plomb m.

pelt /pelt/ vt bombarder (with de). ● n (skin) peau f.

pelvis /ˈpelvɪs/ n (Anat) bassin m.

pen /pen/ n stylo m; (for sheep) enclos m; (for baby, cattle) parc m.

penal /ˈpi:nl/ adj pénal. **penalize** vt pénaliser.

penalty /ˈpenltɪ/ n peine f; (fine) amende f; (in football) penalty m.

penance /ˈpenəns/ n pénitence f.

pence /pens/ →PENNY.

pencil /ˈpensl/ n crayon m. ● vt (pt pencilled) crayonner; ~ in noter provisoirement. ~-sharpener n taille-crayons m inv.

pending /ˈpendɪŋ/ adj (matter) en souffrance; (Jur) en instance. ● prep (until) en attendant.

penetrate /ˈpenɪtreɪt/ vt pénétrer; (silence, defences) percer; (organization) infiltrer. ● vi pénétrer. **penetrating** adj pénétrant.

pen-friend n correspondant/-e m/f.

penguin /ˈpeŋgwɪn/ n manchot m, pingouin m.

pen: ~knife n (pl -knives) canif m. ~-name n pseudonyme m.

penniless /ˈpenɪlɪs/ adj sans le sou.

penny /ˈpenɪ/ n (pl pennies or pence) (unit of currency) penny m; (small amount) centime m.

pension /ˈpenʃn/ n (from state) pension f; (from employer) retraite f; ~ scheme plan m de retraite. ● vt ~ off mettre à la retraite. **pensioner** n retraité/-e m/f.

pensive /ˈpensɪv/ adj songeur.

penthouse /ˈpenthaʊs/ n appartement m de luxe (au dernier étage).

penultimate /penˈʌltɪmət/ adj avant-dernier.

people /ˈpi:pl/ npl gens mpl, personnes fpl; English ~ les Anglais mpl; ~ say on dit. ● n peuple m. ● vt peupler. ~ carrier n monospace m.

pepper /ˈpepə(r)/ n poivre m; (vegetable) poivron m. ● vt (Culin) poivrer.

peppermint /ˈpepəmɪnt/ n (plant) menthe f poivrée; (sweet) bonbon m à la menthe.

per /pɜ:(r)/ prep par; ~ annum par an; ~ cent pour cent; ~ kilo le kilo; ten km ~ hour dix km à l'heure.

percentage /pəˈsentɪdʒ/ n pourcentage m.

perception /pəˈsepʃn/ n perception f. **perceptive** adj perspicace.

perch /pɜ:tʃ/ n (of bird) perchoir m. ● vi (se) percher.

perennial /pəˈrenɪəl/ adj perpétuel; (plant) vivace.

perfect[1] /pəˈfekt/ vt perfectionner.

perfect[2] /ˈpɜ:fɪkt/ adj parfait. ● n (Ling) parfait m. **perfectly** adv parfaitement.

perfection /pəˈfekʃn/ n perfection f; to ~ à la perfection.

perforate /ˈpɜ:fəreɪt/ vt perforer.

perform /pəˈfɔ:m/ vt (task) exécuter; (function) remplir; (operation) procéder à; (play) jouer; (song) chanter. ● vi (actor, musician, team) jouer; ~ well/ badly (candidate, business) avoir de bons/de mauvais résultats. **performance** n interprétation f; (of car, team) performance f; (show) représentation f; (fuss) histoire f. **performer** n artiste mf.

perfume /ˈpɜ:fju:m/ n parfum m.

perhaps /pəˈhæps/ adv peut-être.

peril /ˈperəl/ n péril m. **perilous** adj périlleux.

perimeter /pəˈrɪmɪtə(r)/ n périmètre m.

period /'pɪərɪəd/ n période f; (era) époque f; (lesson) cours m; (Gram) point m; (Med) règles fpl. ● adj d'époque.
periodical n périodique m.

peripheral /pə'rɪfərəl/ adj (vision, suburb) périphérique; (issue) annexe. ● n (Comput) périphérique m.

perish /'perɪʃ/ vi périr; (rubber) se détériorer.

perjury /'pɜːdʒərɪ/ n faux témoignage m.

perk /pɜːk/ n ⊞ avantage m. ● vt/i ~ up ⊞ (se) remonter. **perky** adj ⊞ gai.

perm /pɜːm/ n permanente f. ● vt **have one's hair** ~ed se faire faire une permanente.

permanent /'pɜːmənənt/ adj permanent. **permanently** adv (happy) en permanence; (employed) de façon permanente.

permissible /pə'mɪsɪbl/ adj permis.

permission /pə'mɪʃn/ n permission f.

permissive /pə'mɪsɪv/ adj libéral; (pej) permissif.

permit¹ /pə'mɪt/ vt (pt **permitted**) permettre (**sb to** à qn de), autoriser (**sb to** qn à).

permit² /'pɜːmɪt/ n permis m.

perpendicular /pɜːpən'dɪkjʊlə(r)/ adj perpendiculaire.

perpetrator /'pɜːpɪtreɪtə(r)/ n auteur m.

perpetuate /pə'petjʊeɪt/ vt perpétuer.

perplexed /pə'plekst/ adj perplexe.

persecute /'pɜːsɪkjuːt/ vt persécuter.

perseverance /pɜːsɪ'vɪərəns/ n persévérance f. **persevere** vi persévérer.

persist /pə'sɪst/ vi persister (**in doing** à faire). **persistence** n persistance f. **persistent** adj (cough, snow) persistant; (obstinate) obstiné; (noise, pressure) continuel.

person /'pɜːsn/ n personne f; **in** ~ en personne.

personal /'pɜːsənl/ adj (life, problem, opinion) personnel; (safety, freedom, insurance) individuel. ~ **ad** n petite annonce f. ~ **assistant** n secrétaire mf de direction. ~ **computer** n ordinateur m (personnel), microordinateur m.

personality /pɜːsə'nælətɪ/ n personnalité f; (star) vedette f.

personal: ~ **organizer** n agenda m. ~ **stereo** n baladeur m.

personnel /pɜːsə'nel/ n personnel m.

perspiration /pɜːspɪ'reɪʃn/ n (sweat) sueur f; (sweating) transpiration f. **perspire** vi transpirer.

persuade /pə'sweɪd/ vt persuader (**to de**). **persuasion** n persuasion f. **persuasive** adj persuasif.

pertinent /'pɜːtɪnənt/ adj pertinent.

perturb /pə'tɜːb/ vt troubler.

Peru /pə'ruː/ n Pérou m.

pervasive /pə'veɪsɪv/ adj (smell) pénétrant; (feeling) envahissant.

perverse /pə'vɜːs/ adj (desire) pervers; (refusal, attitude) illogique. **perversion** n perversion f.

pervert¹ /pə'vɜːt/ vt (truth) travestir; (values) fausser; (justice) entraver.

pervert² /'pɜːvɜːt/ n pervers/-e m/f.

pessimist /'pesɪmɪst/ n pessimiste mf. **pessimistic** adj pessimiste.

pest /pest/ n (insect) insecte m nuisible; (animal) animal m nuisible; (person ⊞) enquiquineur/-euse m/f ⊞.

pester /'pestə(r)/ vt harceler.

pet /pet/ n animal m de compagnie; (favourite) chouchou/-te m/f. ● adj (theory, charity) favori; ~ **hate** bête f noire; ~ **name** petit nom m. ● vt (pt **petted**) caresser; (spoil) chouchouter ⊞.

petal /'petl/ n pétale m.

peter /'piːtə(r)/ vi ~ **out** (conversation) tarir; (supplies) s'épuiser.

petite /pə'tiːt/ adj (woman) menue.

petition /pə'tɪʃn/ n pétition f. ● vt adresser une pétition à.

petrol /'petrəl/ n essence f. ~ **bomb** n cocktail m molotov. ~ **station** n station-service f. ~ **tank** n réservoir m d'essence.

petticoat /'petɪkəʊt/ n jupon m.

petty /'petɪ/ adj (-ier, -iest) (minor) petit; (mean) mesquin; ~ **cash** petite caisse f.

pew /pjuː/ n banc m (d'église).

pharmacist /'fɑːməsɪst/ n pharmacien/-ne m/f. **pharmacy** n pharmacie f.

phase /feɪz/ n phase f. ● vt ~ **in/out** introduire/supprimer peu à peu.

PhD abbr (**Doctor of Philosophy**) doctorat m.

pheasant /'feznt/ n faisan/-e m/f.

phenomenon /fə'nɒmɪnən/ n (pl -ena) phénomène m.

phew /fjuː/ interj ouf.

philosopher /fɪ'lɒsəfə(r)/ n philosophe mf. **philosophical** adj philosophique; (resigned) philosophe. **philosophy** n philosophie f.

phlegm /flem/ n (Med) mucosité f.

phobia /'fəʊbɪə/ n phobie f.

phone /fəʊn/ n téléphone m; **on the ~** au téléphone. ● vt (person) téléphoner à; **~ England** téléphoner en Angleterre. ● vi téléphoner; **~ back** rappeler. **~ book** n annuaire m. **~ booth**, **~ box** n cabine f téléphonique. **~ call** n coup m de fil 🔲. **~card** n télécarte f. **~-in** n émission f à ligne ouverte. **~ number** n numéro m de téléphone.

phonetic /fə'netɪk/ adj phonétique.

phoney /'fəʊnɪ/ adj (-ier, -iest) 🔲 faux. ● n (person) charlatan m; **it's a ~** c'est un faux.

photocopier /'fəʊtəʊkɒpɪə(r)/ n photocopieuse f.

photocopy /'fəʊtəʊkɒpɪ/ n photocopie f. ● vt photocopier.

photograph /'fəʊtəgrɑːf/ n photographie f. ● vt photographier. **photographer** n photographe mf.

phrase /freɪz/ n expression f; (idiom) locution f. ● vt exprimer, formuler. **~-book** n guide m de conversation.

physical /'fɪzɪkl/ adj physique.

physicist /'fɪzɪsɪst/ n physicien-ne m/f.

physics /'fɪzɪks/ n physique f.

physiotherapist /fɪzɪəʊ'θerəpɪst/ n kinésithérapeute mf. **physiotherapy** n kinésithérapie f.

physique /fɪ'ziːk/ n physique m.

piano /pɪ'ænəʊ/ n piano m.

pick /pɪk/ n choix m; (best) meilleur-e m/f; (tool) pioche f. ● vt choisir; (flower) cueillir; (lock) crocheter; **~ a quarrel with** chercher querelle à; **~ one's nose** se curer le nez. ☐ **~ on** harceler; **~ out** choisir; (identify) distinguer; **~ up** vt ramasser; (sth fallen) relever; (weight) soulever; (habit, passenger, speed) prendre; (learn) apprendre; vi s'améliorer.

pickaxe /'pɪkæks/ n pioche f.

picket /'pɪkɪt/ n (striker) gréviste mf; (stake) piquet m; **~ (line)** piquet m de grève. ● vt (pt **picketed**) installer un piquet de grève devant.

pickle /'pɪkl/ n conserves fpl au vinaigre; (gherkin) cornichon m. ● vt conserver dans du vinaigre.

pick-up /'pɪkʌp/ n (stylus-holder) lecteur m; (on guitar) capteur m; (collection) ramassage m; (improvement) reprise f.

picnic /'pɪknɪk/ n pique-nique m. ● vi (pt **picnicked**) pique-niquer.

pictorial /pɪk'tɔːrɪəl/ adj (magazine) illustré; (record) graphique.

picture /'pɪktʃə(r)/ n image f; (painting) tableau m; (photograph) photo f; (drawing) dessin m; (film) film m; (fig) description f; **the ~s** le cinéma. ● vt s'imaginer; **be ~d** (shown) être représenté.

picturesque /pɪktʃə'resk/ adj pittoresque.

pie /paɪ/ n (sweet) tarte f; (savoury) tourte f.

piece /piːs/ n morceau m; (of string, ribbon) bout m; (of currency, machine) pièce f; **a ~ of advice/furniture** un conseil/meuble; **go to ~s** (fig) s'effondrer; **take to ~s** démonter.

pier /pɪə(r)/ n jetée f.

pierce /pɪəs/ vt percer.

pig /pɪg/ n porc m, cochon m.

pigeon /'pɪdʒɪn/ n pigeon m. **~-hole** n casier m.

pig-headed adj entêté.

pigsty /'pɪgstaɪ/ n porcherie f.

pigtail /'pɪgteɪl/ n natte f.

pike /paɪk/ n inv (fish) brochet m.

pile /paɪl/ n (heap) tas m; (stack) pile f; (of carpet) poil m; **~s of** 🔲 un tas de 🔲. ● vt **~ (up)** entasser. ● vi **~ into** s'engouffrer dans; **~ up** (snow, leaves) s'entasser; (debts, work) s'accumuler. **~-up** n (Auto) carambolage m.

pilgrim /'pɪlgrɪm/ n pèlerin m. **pilgrimage** n pèlerinage m.

pill /pɪl/ n pilule f.

pillar /'pɪlə(r)/ n pilier m. **~-box** n boîte f aux lettres.

pillion /'pɪlɪən/ n siège m de passager; **ride ~** monter en croupe.

pillow /'pɪləʊ/ n oreiller m. **~case** n taie f d'oreiller.

pilot /ˈpaɪlət/ n pilote m. ● adj pilote. ● vt (pt **piloted**) piloter. ∼-**light** n veilleuse f.

pimple /ˈpɪmpl/ n bouton m.

pin /pɪn/ n épingle f; (of plug) fiche f; (for wood, metal) goujon m; (in surgery) broche f; **have** ∼**s and needles** avoir des fourmis. ● vt (pt **pinned**) épingler, attacher; (trap) coincer; ∼ **sb down** (fig) forcer qn à se décider; ∼ **up** accrocher.

pinafore /ˈpɪnəfɔː(r)/ n tablier m.

pincers /ˈpɪnsəz/ npl tenailles fpl.

pinch /pɪntʃ/ vt pincer; (steal 🄵) piquer. ● vi (be too tight) serrer. ● n (mark) pinçon m; (of salt) pincée f; **at a** ∼ à la rigueur.

pine /paɪn/ n (tree) pin m. ● vi ∼ (**away**) dépérir; ∼ **for** languir après.

pineapple /ˈpaɪnæpl/ n ananas m.

pinecone /ˈpaɪnkəʊn/ n pomme f de pin.

pink /pɪŋk/ adj & n rose (m).

pinpoint /ˈpɪnpɔɪnt/ vt (problem, cause, location) indiquer; (time) déterminer.

pint /paɪnt/ n pinte f (GB = 0.57 litre; US = 0.47 litre).

pin-up /ˈpɪnʌp/ n 🄵 pin-up f inv. 🄵

pioneer /paɪəˈnɪə(r)/ n pionnier m. ● vt ∼ **the use of** être le premier à utiliser.

pious /ˈpaɪəs/ adj pieux.

pip /pɪp/ n (seed) pépin m; (sound) top m.

pipe /paɪp/ n tuyau m; (to smoke) pipe f; (Mus) chalumeau m; ∼**s** cornemuse f. ● vt transporter par tuyau. □ ∼ **down** se taire.

pipeline /ˈpaɪplaɪn/ n oléoduc m; **in the** ∼ en cours.

piping /ˈpaɪpɪŋ/ n tuyauterie f; ∼ **hot** fumant.

pirate /ˈpaɪərət/ n pirate m. ● vt pirater.

Pisces /ˈpaɪsiːz/ n Poissons mpl.

pistol /ˈpɪstl/ n pistolet m.

pit /pɪt/ n fosse f; (mine) puits m; (quarry) carrière f; (for orchestra) fosse f; (of stomach) creux m; (of cherry: US) noyau m. ● vt (pt **pitted**) marquer; (fig) opposer; ∼ **oneself against** se mesurer à.

pitch /pɪtʃ/ n (Sport) terrain m; (of voice, note) hauteur f; (degree) degré m; (Mus) ton m; (tar) brai m. ● vt jeter; (tent) planter. ● vi (ship) tanguer. □ ∼ **in** 🄴 contribuer.

pitfall /ˈpɪtfɔːl/ n écueil m.

pitiful /ˈpɪtɪfl/ adj pitoyable. **pitless** adj impitoyable.

pit stop n arrêt m mécanique.

pittance /ˈpɪtns/ n **earn a** ∼ gagner trois fois rien.

pity /ˈpɪtɪ/ n pitié f; (regrettable fact) dommage m; **take** ∼ **on** avoir pitié de; **what a** ∼**!** quel dommage! ● vt avoir pitié de.

pivot /ˈpɪvət/ n pivot m. ● vi (pt **pivoted**) pivoter.

placard /ˈplækɑːd/ n affiche f.

place /pleɪs/ n endroit m, lieu m; (house) maison f; (seat, rank) place f; **at** or **to my** ∼ chez moi; **change** ∼**s** changer de place; **in the first** ∼ d'abord; **out of** ∼ déplacé; **take** ∼ avoir lieu. ● vt placer; (order) passer; (remember) situer; **be** ∼**d** (in race) se placer. ∼-**mat** n set m.

placid /ˈplæsɪd/ adj placide.

plagiarism /ˈpleɪdʒərɪzəm/ n plagiat m. **plagiarize** vt/i plagier.

plague /pleɪg/ n (bubonic) peste f; (epidemic) épidémie f; (of ants, locusts) invasion f. ● vt harceler.

plaice /pleɪs/ n inv carrelet m.

plain /pleɪn/ adj (obvious) clair; (candid) franc; (simple) simple; (not pretty) sans beauté; (not patterned) uni; ∼ **chocolate** chocolat m noir; **in** ∼ **clothes** en civil. ● adv franchement. ● n plaine f. **plainly** adv clairement; franchement; simplement.

plaintiff /ˈpleɪntɪf/ n (Jur) plaignant/-e m/f.

plaintive /ˈpleɪntɪv/ adj plaintif.

plait /plæt/ vt tresser. ● n natte f.

plan /plæn/ n projet m, plan m; (diagram) plan m. ● vt (pt **planned**) projeter (**to do** de faire); (timetable, day) organiser; (economy, work) planifier. ● vi prévoir; ∼ **on** s'attendre à.

plane /pleɪn/ n (level) plan m; (aeroplane) avion m; (tool) rabot m. ● adj plan. ● vt raboter.

planet /ˈplænɪt/ n planète f.

plank /plæŋk/ n planche f.

planning /ˈplænɪŋ/ n (of economy, work) planification f; (of holiday, party) organisation f; (of town) urbanisme m; **family** ~ planning m familial; ~ **permission** permis m de construire.

plant /plɑːnt/ n plante f; (Tech) matériel m; (factory) usine f. ● vt planter; (bomb) placer.

plaster /'plɑːstə(r)/ n plâtre m; (adhesive) sparadrap m. ● vt plâtrer; (cover) couvrir (**with** de).

plastic /'plæstɪk/ adj en plastique; (art, substance) plastique; ~ **surgery** chirurgie f esthétique. ● n plastique m.

plate /pleɪt/ n assiette f; (of metal) plaque f; (silverware) argenterie f; (in book) gravure f. ● vt (metal) plaquer.

plateau /'plætəu/ n (pl ~x) plateau m; (fig) palier m.

platform /'plætfɔːm/ n (stage) estrade f; (for speaking) tribune f; (Rail) quai m; (Pol) plate-forme f.

platoon /plə'tuːn/ n (Mil) section f.

play /pleɪ/ vt/i jouer de; (record) mettre; (game) jouer à; (opponent) jouer contre; (match) disputer; ~ **safe** ne pas prendre de risques. ● n jeu m; (Theat) pièce f. □ ~ **down** minimiser; ~**on** (fears) exploiter; ~ **up** 🔢 commencer à faire des siennes 🔢; ~ **up sth** mettre l'accent sur qch.

playful /'pleɪfl/ adj (remark) taquin; (child) joueur.

play: ~**ground** n cour f de récréation. ~**-group,** ~**-school** n garderie f.

playing /'pleɪɪŋ/ n (Sport) jeu m; (Theat) interprétation f. ~**-card** n carte f à jouer. ~**-field** n terrain m de sport.

play: ~**-pen** n parc m (pour bébé). ~**wright** n auteur m dramatique.

plc abbr (**public limited company**) SA.

plea /pliː/ n (for mercy, tolerance) appel m; (for food, money) demande f; (reason) excuse f; **make a** ~ **of guilty** plaider coupable.

plead /pliːd/ vt/i supplier; (Jur) plaider.

pleasant /'pleznt/ adj agréable.

please /pliːz/ vt/i plaire (à), faire plaisir (à); ~ **oneself, do as one** ~**s** faire ce qu'on veut. ● adv s'il vous or te plaît. **pleased** adj content (**with** de). **pleasing** adj agréable.

pleasure /'pleʒə(r)/ n plaisir m; **with** ~ avec plaisir; **my** ~ je vous en prie.

pleat /pliːt/ n pli m. ● vt plisser.

pledge /pledʒ/ n (token) gage m; (promise) promesse f. ● vt promettre; (pawn) mettre en gage.

plentiful /'plentɪfl/ adj abondant.

plenty /'plentɪ/ n abondance f; ~ (**of**) (a great deal) beaucoup (de); (enough) assez (de).

pliers /'plaɪəz/ npl pinces fpl.

plight /plaɪt/ n détresse f.

plinth /plɪnθ/ n socle m.

plod /plɒd/ vi (pt **plodded**) avancer péniblement.

plonk /plɒŋk/ n 🔢 pinard m 🔢.

plot /plɒt/ n (conspiracy) complot m; (of novel) intrigue f; ~ (**of land**) terrain m. ● vt/i (pt **plotted**) (plan) comploter; (mark out) tracer.

plough /plau/ n charrue f. ● vt/i labourer. □ ~ **back** réinvestir; ~ **through** avancer péniblement dans.

plow /plau/ n & vt/i (US) →PLOUGH.

ploy /plɔɪ/ n stratagème m.

pluck /plʌk/ vt (flower, fruit) cueillir; (bird) plumer; (eyebrows) épiler; (strings: Mus) pincer; ~ **up courage** prendre son courage à deux mains. **plucky** adj courageux.

plug /plʌg/ n (for sink) bonde f; (Electr) fiche f, prise f. ● vt (pt **plugged**) (hole) boucher; (publicize 🔢) faire du battage autour de. □ ~ **in** brancher. ~**-hole** n bonde f.

plum /plʌm/ n prune f; ~ **pudding** (plum-)pudding m.

plumber /'plʌmə(r)/ n plombier m.

plume /pluːm/ n (of feathers) panache m.

plummet /'plʌmɪt/ vi tomber, plonger.

plump /plʌmp/ adj potelé, dodu.

plunge /plʌndʒ/ vt/i (dive, thrust) plonger; (fall) tomber. ● n plongeon m; (fall) chute f; **take the** ~ se jeter à l'eau. **plunger** n (for sink) ventouse f.

plural /'pluərəl/ adj pluriel; (noun) au pluriel; (ending) du pluriel. ● n pluriel m.

plus /plʌs/ prep plus; **ten** ~ plus de dix. ● adj (Electr & fig) positif. ● n signe m plus; (fig) atout m.

ply /plaɪ/ vt (tool) manier; (trade) exercer. ● vi faire la navette; ~ **sb with drink** offrir continuellement à boire à qn.

plywood /'plaɪwʊd/ n contreplaqué m.

p.m. /piː'em/ adv de l'après-midi or du soir.

pneumatic drill /njuː'mætɪk drɪl/ n marteaupiqueur m.

pneumonia /njuː'məʊnɪə/ n pneumonie f.

PO abbr ➡POST OFFICE.

poach /pəʊtʃ/ vt/i (game) braconner; (staff) débaucher; (Culin) pocher.

PO Box n boîte f postale.

pocket /'pɒkɪt/ n poche f; **be out of ~** avoir perdu de l'argent. ● adj de poche. ● vt empocher. **~-book** n (notebook) carnet m; (wallet: US) portefeuille m; (handbag: US) sac m à main. **~-money** n argent m de poche.

pod /pɒd/ n (peas) cosse f; (vanilla) gousse f.

podgy /'pɒdʒɪ/ adj (-ier, -iest) dodu.

poem /'pəʊɪm/ n poème m. **poet** n poète m. **poetic** adj poétique. **poetry** n poésie f.

point /pɔɪnt/ n (position) point m; (tip) pointe f; (decimal point) virgule f; (remark) remarque f; **good ~s** qualités fpl; **on the ~ of** sur le point de; **~ in time** moment m; **~ of view** point m de vue; **to the ~** pertinent; **what is the ~?** à quoi bon? ● vt (aim) braquer; (show) indiquer; **~ out** signaler. ● vi indiquer du doigt; **~ out that, make the ~ that** faire remarquer que. **~-blank** adj & adv à bout portant.

pointed /'pɔɪntɪd/ adj (sharp) pointu; (window) en pointe; (remark) lourd de sens.

pointless /'pɔɪntlɪs/ adj inutile.

poise /pɔɪz/ n (confidence) assurance f; (physical elegance) aisance f.

poison /'pɔɪzn/ n poison m. ● vt empoisonner. **poisonous** adj (substance) toxique; (plant) vénéneux; (snake) venimeux.

poke /pəʊk/ vt/i (push) pousser; (fire) tisonner; (thrust) fourrer; **~ fun at** se moquer de. ● n (petit) coup m. ▫**~out** (head) sortir.

poker /'pəʊkə(r)/ n (for fire) tisonnier m; (cards) poker m.

Poland /'pəʊlənd/ n Pologne f.

polar /'pəʊlə(r)/ adj polaire.

pole /pəʊl/ n (stick) perche f; (for flag) mât m; (Geog) pôle m.

Pole /pəʊl/ n Polonais/-e m/f.

pole-vault n saut m à la perche.

police /pə'liːs/ n police f. ● vt faire la police dans. **~ constable** n agent m de police. **~man** n (pl -men) agent m de police. **~ station** n commissariat m de police. **~woman** n (pl -women) femme-agent f.

policy /'pɒləsɪ/ n politique f; (insurance) police f (d'assurance).

polish /'pɒlɪʃ/ vt polir; (shoes, floor) cirer. ● n (for shoes) cirage m; (for floor) encaustique f; (for nails) vernis m; (shine) poli m; (fig) raffinement m. ▫ **~ off** finir en vitesse; **~ up** (language) perfectionner.

Polish /'pəʊlɪʃ/ adj polonais. ● n (Ling) polonais m.

polished /'pɒlɪʃt/ adj raffiné.

polite /pə'laɪt/ adj poli.

political /pə'lɪtɪkl/ adj politique.

politician /pɒlɪ'tɪʃn/ n homme m politique, femme f politique.

politics /'pɒlətɪks/ n politique f.

poll /pəʊl/ n (vote casting) scrutin m; (survey) sondage m; **go to the ~s** aller aux urnes. ● vt (votes) obtenir.

pollen /'pɒlən/ n pollen m.

polling booth n isoloir m.

polling station n bureau m de vote.

pollution /pə'luːʃn/ n pollution f.

polo /'pəʊləʊ/ n polo m. **~ neck** n col m roulé.

pomegranate /'pɒmɪgrænɪt/ n grenade f.

pomp /pɒmp/ n pompe f.

pompous /'pɒmpəs/ adj pompeux.

pond /pɒnd/ n étang m; (artificial) bassin m; (stagnant) mare f.

ponder /'pɒndə(r)/ vt/i réfléchir (à), méditer (sur).

pong /pɒŋ/ n (stink 🅰) puanteur f. ● vi 🅰 puer.

pony /'pəʊnɪ/ n poney m. **~tail** n queue f de cheval.

poodle /'puːdl/ n caniche m.

pool /puːl/ n (puddle) flaque f; (pond) étang m; (of blood) mare f; (for swimming) piscine f; (fund) fonds m commun; (of ideas) réservoir m; (snooker) billard m américain; **~s** pari m mutuel sur le football. ● vt mettre en commun.

poor /pɔː(r)/ adj (not wealthy) pauvre; (not good) médiocre, mauvais.

poorly /'pɔːlɪ/ adj malade. ● adv mal.

pop /pɒp/ n (noise) pan m; (music) pop m. ● adj pop inv. ● vt/i (pt **popped**) (burst) crever; (put) mettre; ~ **in/out/off** entrer/sortir/partir. □ ~ **up** surgir. ~-**up** fenêtre f pop-up.

pope /pəʊp/ n pape m.

poppy /'pɒpɪ/ n pavot m; (wild) coquelicot m.

popular /'pɒpjʊlə(r)/ adj populaire; (in fashion) en vogue; **be** ~ **with** plaire à.

population /pɒpjʊ'leɪʃn/ n population f.

porcelain /'pɔːsəlɪn/ n porcelaine f.

porcupine /'pɔːkjʊpaɪn/ n porc-épic m.

pork /pɔːk/ n porc m.

pornography /pɔː'nɒɡrəfɪ/ n pornographie f.

port /pɔːt/ n (harbour) port m; (left: Naut) bâbord m; ~ **of call** escale f; (wine) porto m.

portable /'pɔːtəbl/ adj portable.

porter /'pɔːtə(r)/ n (carrier) porteur m; (doorkeeper) portier m.

portfolio /pɔːt'fəʊlɪəʊ/ n (Pol, Comm) portefeuille m.

portion /'pɔːʃn/ n (at meal) portion f; (part) partie f.

portrait /'pɔːtreɪt/ n portrait m.

portray /pɔː'treɪ/ vt représenter.

Portugal /'pɔːtʃʊɡl/ n Portugal m.

Portuguese /pɔːtʃʊ'ɡiːz/ n (Ling) portugais m; (person) Portugais/-e m/f. ● adj portugais.

pose /pəʊz/ vt/i poser; ~ **as** (expert) se poser en. ● n pose f.

poser /'pəʊzə(r)/ n (person) frimeur/-euse m/f; (puzzle) colle f.

posh /pɒʃ/ adj 🆨 chic inv.

position /pə'zɪʃn/ n position f; (job, state) situation f. ● vt placer.

positive /'pɒzətɪv/ adj positif; (sure) sûr, certain; (real) réel, vrai.

possess /pə'zes/ vt posséder.

possession /pə'zeʃn/ n possession f; **take** ~ **of** prendre possession de.

possessive /pə'zesɪv/ adj possessif.

possible /'pɒsəbl/ adj possible.

possibly /'pɒsəblɪ/ adv peut-être; **if I** ~ **can** si cela m'est possible; **I cannot**

~ **leave** il m'est impossible de partir.

post /pəʊst/ n (pole) poteau m; (station, job) poste m; (mail service) poste f; (letters) courrier m. ● adj postal. ● vt (letter) poster; **keep** ~**ed** tenir au courant; ~ **(up)** (a notice) afficher; (appoint) affecter.

postage /'pəʊstɪdʒ/ n affranchissement m; tarif m postal.

postal /'pəʊstl/ adj postal. ~ **order** n mandat m.

post: ~**box** n boîte f aux lettres. ~**card** n carte f postale. ~ **code** n code m postal.

poster /'pəʊstə(r)/ n (for information) affiche f; (for decoration) poster m.

postgraduate /pəʊst'ɡrædʒʊət/ n étudiant/-e m/f de troisième cycle.

posthumous /'pɒstjʊməs/ adj posthume.

post: ~**man** n (pl -**men**) facteur m. ~**mark** n cachet m de la poste.

post-mortem /pəʊst'mɔːtəm/ n autopsie f.

post office n poste f.

postpone /pə'spəʊn/ vt remettre.

postscript /'pəʊsskrɪpt/ n (to letter) postscriptum m inv.

posture /'pɒstʃə(r)/ n posture f. ● vi prendre des poses.

pot /pɒt/ n pot m; (drug 🆨) hasch m; **go to** ~ 🆨 aller à la ruine; **take** ~ **luck** tenter sa chance. ● vt (plants) mettre en pot.

potato /pə'teɪtəʊ/ n (pl ~**es**) pomme f de terre.

pot-belly n bedaine f.

potential /pə'tenʃl/ adj & n potentiel (m).

pothole /'pɒthəʊl/ n (in rock) caverne f; (in road) nid m de poule. **pot-holing** n spéléologie f.

potter /'pɒtə(r)/ n potier m. ● vi bricoler. **pottery** n (art) poterie f; (objects) poteries fpl.

potty /'pɒtɪ/ adj (-**ier**, -**iest**) (crazy 🆨) toqué. ● n pot m.

pouch /paʊtʃ/ n poche f; (for tobacco) blague f.

poultry /'pəʊltrɪ/ n volailles fpl.

pounce /paʊns/ vi bondir (**on** sur). ● n bond m.

pound /paʊnd/ n (weight) livre f (= 454 g); (money) livre f; (for dogs, cars) fourrière f. ● vt (crush) piler; (bombard) pilonner. ● vi frapper fort; (of heart) battre fort; (walk) marcher à pas lourds.

pour /pɔː(r)/ vt verser. ● vi couler, ruisseler (**from** de); (rain) pleuvoir à torrents. ◻ ~ **in/out** (people) arriver/ sortir en masse; ~ **off** or **out** vider. **pouring rain** n pluie f torrentielle.

pout /paʊt/ vi faire la moue.

poverty /'pɒvətɪ/ n misère f, pauvreté f.

powder /'paʊdə(r)/ n poudre f. ● vt poudrer.

power /'paʊə(r)/ n (strength) puissance f; (control) pouvoir m; (energy) énergie f; (Electr) courant m. ● vt (engine) faire marcher; (plane) propulser; ~**ed by** (engine) propulsé par; (generator) alimenté par. ~ **cut** n coupure f de courant.

powerful /'paʊəfl/ adj puissant.

powerless /'paʊəlɪs/ adj impuissant.

power: ~**point** n prise f de courant. ~**-station** n centrale f électrique.

practical /'præktɪkl/ adj pratique. ~ **joke** n farce f.

practice /'præktɪs/ n (procedure) pratique f; (of profession) exercice m; (Sport) entraînement m; **in** ~ (in fact) en pratique; (well-trained) en forme; **out of** ~ rouillé; **put into** ~ mettre en pratique.

practise /'præktɪs/ vt/i (musician, typist) s'exercer (à); (Sport) s'entraîner (à); (put into practice) pratiquer; (profession) exercer.

practitioner /præk'tɪʃənə(r)/ n praticien/-ienne m/f; **dental** ~ dentiste mf.

praise /preɪz/ vt faire l'éloge de; (God) louer. ● n éloges mpl, louanges fpl.

pram /præm/ n landau m.

prance /prɑːns/ vi caracoler.

prawn /prɔːn/ n crevette f rose.

pray /preɪ/ vi prier. **prayer** n prière f.

preach /priːtʃ/ vt/i prêcher; ~ **at** or **to** prêcher.

precarious /prɪ'keərɪəs/ adj précaire.

precaution /prɪ'kɔːʃn/ n précaution f.

precede /prɪ'siːd/ vt précéder.

precedence /'presɪdəns/ n (in importance) priorité f; (in rank) préséance f.

precedent /'presɪdənt/ n précédent m.

precinct /'priːsɪŋkt/ n quartier m commerçant; (pedestrian area) zone f piétonne; (district: US) circonscription f.

precious /'preʃəs/ adj précieux.

precipitate /prɪ'sɪpɪteɪt/ vt (person, event, chemical) précipiter.

précis /'preɪsiː/ n résumé m.

precise /prɪ'saɪs/ adj précis; (careful) méticuleux. **precision** n précision f.

precocious /prɪ'kəʊʃəs/ adj précoce.

preconceived /priːkən'siːvd/ adj préconçu.

predator /'predətə(r)/ n prédateur m.

predicament /prɪ'dɪkəmənt/ n situation f difficile.

predict /prɪ'dɪkt/ vt prédire. **predictable** adj prévisible. **prediction** n prédiction f.

predispose /priːdɪ'spəʊz/ vt prédisposer (**to do** à faire).

predominant /prɪ'dɒmɪnənt/ adj prédominant.

pre-empt /priː'empt/ vt (anticipate) anticiper; (person) devancer.

preface /'prefɪs/ n (to book) préface f; (to speech) préambule m.

prefect /'priːfekt/ n (pupil) élève m/f chargé/-e de la discipline; (official) préfet m.

prefer /prɪ'fɜː(r)/ vt (pt **preferred**) préférer (**to do** faire). **preferably** adv de préférence. **preference** n préférence f. **preferential** adj préférentiel.

prefix /'priːfɪks/ n préfixe m.

pregnancy /'pregnənsɪ/ n grossesse f. **pregnant** adj (woman) enceinte; (animal) pleine; (pause) éloquent.

prehistoric /priːhɪ'stɒrɪk/ adj préhistorique.

prejudge /priː'dʒʌdʒ/ vt (issue) préjuger de; (person) juger d'avance.

prejudice /'predʒʊdɪs/ n préjugé(s) m(pl); (harm) préjudice m. ● vt (claim) porter préjudice à; (person) léser. **prejudiced** adj partial; (person) qui a des préjugés.

premature /'premətjʊə(r)/ adj prématuré.

premeditated /priː'medɪteɪtɪd/ adj prémédité.

premises /'premɪsɪz/ npl locaux mpl; **on the** ~ sur les lieux.

premium /'priːmɪəm/ n (insurance) prime f; **be at a** ~ être précieux.

preoccupied /priːˈɒkjʊpaɪd/ adj préoccupé.

preparation /prepəˈreɪʃn/ n préparation f; ~s préparatifs mpl.

preparatory /prɪˈpærətrɪ/ adj préparatoire. ~ **school** n école f primaire privée; (US) école f secondaire privée.

prepare /prɪˈpeə(r)/ vt/i (se) préparer (for à); **be ~d for** (expect) s'attendre à; ~**d to** prêt à.

preposition /prepəˈzɪʃn/ n préposition f.

preposterous /prɪˈpɒstərəs/ adj absurde, ridicule.

prep school n →**PREPARATORY SCHOOL**.

prerequisite /priːˈrekwɪzɪt/ n condition f préalable.

prescribe /prɪˈskraɪb/ vt prescrire.

prescription /prɪˈskrɪpʃn/ n (Med) ordonnance f.

presence /ˈprezns/ n présence f; ~ **of mind** présence f d'esprit.

present[1] /ˈpreznt/ adj présent. ● n présent m; (gift) cadeau m; **at** ~ à présent; **for the** ~ pour le moment.

present[2] /prɪˈzent/ vt présenter; (film, concert) donner; ~ **sb with** offrir à qn. **presentation** n présentation f. **presenter** n présentateur/-trice m/f.

preservation /prezəˈveɪʃn/ n (of food) conservation f; (of wildlife) préservation f.

preservative /prɪˈzɜːvətɪv/ n (Culin) agent m de conservation.

preserve /prɪˈzɜːv/ vt préserver; (Culin) conserver. ● n réserve f; (fig) domaine m; (jam) confiture f.

presidency /ˈprezɪdənsɪ/ n présidence f.

president /ˈprezɪdənt/ n président/-e m/f.

press /pres/ vt/i (button) appuyer (sur); (squeeze) presser; (iron) repasser; (pursue) poursuivre; **be ~ed for** (time) manquer de; ~ **for sth** faire pression pour avoir qch; ~ **sb to do sth** pousser qn à faire qch; ~ **on** continuer (**with sth** qch). ● n (newspapers, machine) presse f; (for wine) pressoir m. ~ **cutting** n coupure f de presse.

pressing /ˈpresɪŋ/ adj pressant.

press: ~ **release** n communiqué m de presse. ~-**stud** n bouton-pression m. ~-**up** n pompe f.

pressure /ˈpreʃə(r)/ n pression f. ● vt faire pression sur. ~-**cooker** n cocotte-minute f. ~ **group** n groupe m de pression.

pressurize /ˈpreʃəraɪz/ vt (cabin) pressuriser; (person) faire pression sur.

prestige /preˈstiːʒ/ n prestige m.

presumably /prɪˈzjuːməblɪ/ adv vraisemblablement.

presume /prɪˈzjuːm/ vt (suppose) présumer.

pretence, (US) **pretense** /prɪˈtens/ n feinte f, simulation f; (claim) prétention f; (pretext) prétexte m.

pretend /prɪˈtend/ vt/i faire semblant (**to do** de faire); ~ **to** (lay claim to) prétendre à.

pretentious /prɪˈtenʃəs/ adj prétentieux.

pretext /ˈpriːtekst/ n prétexte m.

pretty /ˈprɪtɪ/ adj (-ier, -iest) joli. ● adv assez; ~ **much** presque.

prevail /prɪˈveɪl/ vi (be usual) prédominer; (win) prévaloir; ~ **on** persuader (**to do** de faire). **prevailing** adj actuel; (wind) dominant.

prevalent /ˈprevələnt/ adj répandu.

prevent /prɪˈvent/ vt empêcher (**from doing** de faire). **prevention** n prévention f. **preventive** adj préventif.

preview /ˈpriːvjuː/ n avant-première f; (fig) aperçu m.

previous /ˈpriːvɪəs/ adj précédent, antérieur; ~ **to** avant. **previously** adv auparavant.

prey /preɪ/ n proie f; **bird of** ~ rapace m. ● vi ~ **on** faire sa proie de; (worry) préoccuper.

price /praɪs/ n prix m. ● vt fixer le prix de. **priceless** adj inestimable; (amusing 🔲) impayable 🔲.

prick /prɪk/ vt (with pin) piquer; ~ **up one's ears** dresser l'oreille. ● n piqûre f.

prickle /ˈprɪkl/ n piquant m.

pride /praɪd/ n orgueil m; (satisfaction) fierté f; ~ **of place** place f d'honneur. ● vpr ~ **oneself on** s'enorgueillir de.

priest /priːst/ n prêtre m.

prim /prɪm/ adj (**primmer, primmest**) guindé, méticuleux.

primarily /'praɪmərəlɪ/ adv essentiellement.

primary /'praɪmərɪ/ adj (school, elections) primaire; (chief, basic) premier, fondamental. ● n (Pol: US) primaire f.

prime /praɪm/ adj principal, premier; (first-rate) excellent. ● vt (pump, gun) amorcer; (surface) apprêter. **P~ Minister** n Premier Ministre m.

primitive /'prɪmɪtɪv/ adj primitif.

primrose /'prɪmrəʊz/ n primevère f (jaune).

prince /prɪns/ n prince m. **princess** n princesse f.

principal /'prɪnsəpl/ adj principal. ● n (of school) directeur/-trice m/f.

principle /'prɪnsəpl/ n principe m; **in/on ~** en/par principe.

print /prɪnt/ vt imprimer; (write in capitals) écrire en majuscules; **~ed matter** imprimés mpl. ● n (of foot) empreinte f; (letters) caractères mpl; (photograph) épreuve f; (engraving) gravure f; **in ~** disponible; **out of ~** épuisé. **printer** n (person) imprimeur m; (Comput) imprimante f.

prion /'priːɒn/ n prion m.

prior /'praɪə(r)/ adj précédent. ● n (Relig) prieur m. **~ to** prep avant (de).

priority /praɪˈɒrətɪ/ n priorité f; **take ~** avoir la priorité (**over** sur).

prise /praɪz/ vt forcer; **~ open** ouvrir en forçant.

prison /'prɪzn/ n prison f. **prisoner** n prisonnier/-ière m/f. **~ officer** n gardien/-ne m/f de prison.

pristine /'prɪstiːn/ adj be **in ~ condition** être comme neuf.

privacy /'prɪvəsɪ/ n intimité f, solitude f.

private /'praɪvɪt/ adj privé; (confidential) personnel; (lessons, house) particulier; (ceremony) intime; **in ~** en privé; (of ceremony) dans l'intimité. ● n (soldier) simple soldat m. **privately** adv en privé; dans l'intimité; (inwardly) intérieurement.

privilege /'prɪvəlɪdʒ/ n privilège m. **privileged** adj privilégié; **be ~d to** avoir le privilège de.

prize /praɪz/ n prix m. ● vt (value) priser.

pro /prəʊ/ n **the ~s and cons** le pour et le contre.

probable /'prɒbəbl/ adj probable. **probably** adv probablement.

probation /prəˈbeɪʃn/ n (testing) essai m; (Jur) liberté f surveillée.

probe /prəʊb/ n (device) sonde f; (fig) enquête f. ● vt sonder. ● vi **~ into** sonder.

problem /'prɒbləm/ n problème m. ● adj difficile. **problematic** adj problématique.

procedure /prəˈsiːdʒə(r)/ n procédure f; (way of doing sth) démarche f à suivre.

proceed /prəˈsiːd/ vi (go) aller, avancer; (pass) passer (**to** à); (act) procéder; **~ (with)** continuer; **~ to do** se mettre à faire.

proceedings /prəˈsiːdɪŋz/ npl (discussions) débats mpl; (meeting) réunion f; (report) actes mpl; (Jur) poursuites fpl.

proceeds /'prəʊsiːdz/ npl (profits) produit m, bénéfices mpl.

process /'prəʊses/ n processus m; (method) procédé m; **in ~** en cours; **in the ~ of doing** en train de faire. **~or** n (Culin) robot m (ménager); (Comput) unité f centrale. ● vt (material, data) traiter.

procession /prəˈseʃn/ n défilé m.

procrastinate /prəʊˈkræstɪneɪt/ vi différer, tergiverser.

procure /prəˈkjʊə(r)/ vt obtenir.

prod /prɒd/ vt/i (pt **prodded**) pousser doucement. ● n petit coup m.

prodigy /'prɒdɪdʒɪ/ n prodige m.

produce[1] /'prɒdjuːs/ n produits mpl.

produce[2] /prəˈdjuːs/ vt/i produire; (bring out) sortir; (show) présenter; (cause) provoquer; (Theat, TV), mettre en scène; (radio) réaliser; (cinema) produire. **producer** n metteur m en scène; réalisateur m; producteur m.

product /'prɒdʌkt/ n produit m.

production /prəˈdʌkʃn/ n production f; (Theat, TV) mise f en scène; (radio) réalisation f.

productive /prəˈdʌktɪv/ adj productif. **productivity** n productivité f.

profession /prəˈfeʃn/ n profession f.

professional /prəˈfeʃənl/ adj professionnel; (of high quality) de professionnel; (person) qui exerce une pro-

fession libérale. ● *n*
professionnel/-le *m/f.*

professor /prə'fesə(r)/ *n* professeur *m*
(*titulaire d'une chaire*).

proficient /prə'fɪʃnt/ *adj* compétent.

profile /'prəʊfaɪl/ *n* (of face) profil *m*;
(of body, mountain) silhouette *f*; (by
journalist) portrait *m*.

profit /'prɒfɪt/ *n* profit *m*, bénéfice *m*.
● *vi* ~ **by** tirer profit de. **profitable**
adj rentable.

profound /prə'faʊnd/ *adj* profond.

profusely /prə'fjuːslɪ/ *adv* (bleed)
abondamment; (*apologize*) avec effusion. **profusion** *n* profusion *f.*

program /'prəʊɡræm/ *n* (US) ➡**PRO-
GRAMME**; **(computer)** ~ programme
m. ● *vt* (*pt* **programmed**) programmer.

programme /'prəʊɡræm/ *n* programme *m*; (broadcast) émission *f.*

programmer /'prəʊɡræmə(r)/ *n*
programmeur/-euse *m/f.*

programming /'prəʊɡræmɪŋ/ *n*
(Comput) programmation *f.*

progress[1] /'prəʊɡres/ *n* progrès *m* (*pl*)
(in ~) en cours; **make** ~ faire des
progrès; ~ **report** compte-rendu *m.*

progress[2] /prə'ɡres/ *vi* (advance, improve) progresser.

progressive /prə'ɡresɪv/ *adj* progressif; (reforming) progressiste.

prohibit /prə'hɪbɪt/ *vt* interdire (**sb
from doing** à qn de faire).

project[1] /prə'dʒekt/ *vt* projeter. ● *vi*
(jut out) être en saillie.

project[2] /'prɒdʒekt/ *n* (plan) projet *m*;
(undertaking) entreprise *f*; (School)
dossier *m.*

projection /prə'dʒekʃn/ *n* projection *f*
; saillie *f*; (estimate) prévision *f.*

projector /prə'dʒektə(r)/ *n* projecteur *m.*

proliferate /prə'lɪfəreɪt/ *vi* proliférer.

prolong /prə'lɒŋ/ *vt* prolonger.

prominent /'prɒmɪnənt/ *adj* (project-
ing) proéminent; (conspicuous) bien
en vue; (fig) important.

promiscuous /prə'mɪskjʊəs/ *adj* de
mœurs faciles.

promise /'prɒmɪs/ *n* promesse *f.* ● *vt/i*
promettre. **promising** *adj* prometteur;

(person) qui promet.

promote /prə'məʊt/ *vt* promouvoir;
(advertise) faire la promotion de. **promotion** *n* promotion *f.*

prompt /prɒmpt/ *adj* rapide; (punctual) à l'heure, ponctuel. ● *adv* (on the
dot) pile. ● *vt* inciter; (cause) provoquer; (Theat) souffler à. ● *n* (Comput)
message *m* guide-opérateur. **prompter** *n* souffleur/-euse *m/f.* **promptly**
adv rapidement; ponctuellement.

Proms Festival annuel de musique classique qui se déroule
au Royal Albert Hall à Londres.
Proms est l'abréviation de *promenade concerts*, car une partie des au-
diteurs reste debout. Aux États-Unis,
prom (*night*) est un bal très habillé
qui marque la fin des études secon-
daires.

prone /prəʊn/ *adj* ~ **to** sujet à.

pronoun /'prəʊnaʊn/ *n* pronom *m.*

pronounce /prə'naʊns/ *vt* prononcer.
pronunciation *n* prononciation *f.*

proof /pruːf/ *n* (evidence) preuve *f*;
(test, trial copy) épreuve *f*; (of alcohol)
teneur *f* en alcool. ● *adj* ~ **against** à
l'épreuve de.

prop /prɒp/ *n* support *m*; (Theat) accessoire *m.* ● *vt* (*pt* **propped**) ~ **(up)**
(support) étayer; (lean) appuyer.

propaganda /prɒpə'ɡændə/ *n* propagande *f.*

propel /prə'pel/ *vt* (*pt* **propelled**) (vehicle, ship) propulser; (person) pousser.

propeller /prə'pelə(r)/ *n* hélice *f.*

proper /'prɒpə(r)/ *adj* correct, bon;
(adequate) convenable; (real) vrai;
(thorough **II**) parfait. **properly** *adv*
correctement, comme il faut; (ad-
equately) convenablement.

proper noun *n* nom *m* propre.

property /'prɒpətɪ/ *n* (house) propriété *f*; (things owned) biens *mpl*, propriété *f.* ● *adj* immobilier, foncier.

prophecy /'prɒfəsɪ/ *n* prophétie *f.*

prophet /'prɒfɪt/ *n* prophète *m.*

proportion /prə'pɔːʃn/ *n* (ratio, dimension) proportion *f*; (amount) partie *f.*

proposal /prə'pəʊzl/ *n* proposition *f*;
(of marriage) demande *f* en mariage.

propose /prə'pəʊz/ vt proposer. ● vi faire une demande en mariage; ~ **to do** se proposer de faire.

proposition /prɒpə'zɪʃn/ n proposition f; (matter Ⅰ) affaire f. ● vt Ⅰ faire des propositions malhonnêtes à.

proprietor /prə'praɪətə(r)/ n propriétaire mf.

propriety /prə'praɪətɪ/ n (correct behaviour) bienséance f.

prose /prəʊz/ n prose f; (translation) thème m.

prosecute /'prɒsɪkjuːt/ vt poursuivre en justice. **prosecution** n poursuites fpl. **prosecutor** n procureur m.

prospect[1] /'prɒspekt/ n (outlook) perspective f; (chance) espoir m.

prospect[2] /prə'spekt/ vt/i prospecter.

prospective /prə'spektɪv/ adj (future) futur; (possible) éventuel.

prospectus /prə'spektəs/ n brochure f; (Univ) livret m de l'étudiant.

prosperity /prɒ'sperətɪ/ n prospérité f. **prosperous** adj prospère.

prostitute /'prɒstɪtjuːt/ n prostituée f.

prostrate /'prɒstreɪt/ adj (prone) à plat ventre; (exhausted) prostré.

protect /prə'tekt/ vt protéger. **protection** n protection f. **protective** adj protecteur; (clothes) de protection.

protein /'prəʊtiːn/ n protéine f.

protest[1] /'prəʊtest/ n protestation f; under~ en protestant.

protest[2] /prə'test/ vt/i protester.

Protestant /'prɒtɪstənt/ adj & n protestant/-e (m/f).

protester /prə'testə(r)/ n manifestant/-e m/f.

protocol /'prəʊtəkɒl/ n protocole m.

protrude /prə'truːd/ vi dépasser.

proud /praʊd/ adj fier, orgueilleux.

prove /pruːv/ vt prouver. ● vi (~ **to be**) easy se révéler facile; ~ **oneself** faire ses preuves. **proven** adj éprouvé.

proverb /'prɒvɜːb/ n proverbe m.

provide /prə'vaɪd/ vt fournir (**sb with sth** qch à qn). ● vi ~ **for** (allow for) prévoir; (guard against) parer à; (person) pourvoir aux besoins de.

provided /prə'vaɪdɪd/ conj ~ **that** à condition que.

providing /prə'vaɪdɪŋ/ conj ➡**PROVIDED.**

province /'prɒvɪns/ n province f; (fig) compétence f.

provision /prə'vɪʒn/ n (stock) provision f; (supplying) fourniture f; (stipulation) dispositions fpl; ~**s** (food) provisions fpl.

provisional /prə'vɪʒənl/ adj provisoire.

provocative /prə'vɒkətɪv/ adj provocant.

provoke /prə'vəʊk/ vt provoquer.

prow /praʊ/ n proue f.

prowess /'praʊɪs/ n prouesses fpl.

prowl /praʊl/ vi rôder.

proxy /'prɒksɪ/ n **by ~** par procuration.

prudish /'pruːdɪʃ/ adj pudibond, prude.

prune /pruːn/ n pruneau m. ● vt (cut) tailler.

pry /praɪ/ vi ~ **into** mettre son nez dans.

psalm /sɑːm/ n psaume m.

pseudonym /'sjuːdənɪm/ n pseudonyme m.

psychiatric /saɪkɪ'ætrɪk/ adj psychiatrique. **psychiatrist** n psychiatre mf. **psychiatry** n psychiatrie f.

psychic /'saɪkɪk/ adj (phenomenon) métapsychique; (person) doué de télépathie.

psychoanalyse /saɪkəʊ'ænəlaɪz/ vt psychanalyser.

psychological /saɪkə'lɒdʒɪkl/ adj psychologique. **psychologist** n psychologue mf. **psychology** n psychologie f.

PTO abbr (please turn over) TSVP.

pub /pʌb/ n pub m.

> **Pub** Au Royaume-Uni, établissement où l'on sert des boissons (alcoolisées ou non) et parfois des repas légers. Certains appartiennent à une marque de bière alors que les free houses sont indépendants. C'est un lieu convivial où l'on vient passer un bon moment (fléchettes, billard, jeux de groupes). Aujourd'hui, la loi leur permet d'ouvrir de 11h à 23h.

puberty /'pjuːbətɪ/ n puberté f.

public /'pʌblɪk/ adj public; (library) municipal; **in ~** en public.

publican /'pʌblɪkən/ n patron/-ne m/f de pub.

publication /pʌblɪ'keɪʃn/ n publication f.

public house n pub m.

publicity /pʌb'lɪsɪtɪ/ n publicité f.

publicize /'pʌblɪsaɪz/ vt faire connaître au public.

public: ~ relations n relations fpl publiques. **~ school** n école f privée; (US) école f publique. **~ transport** n transports mpl en commun.

> **Public schools** Mis à part l'Écosse où ce terme désigne souvent une école publique, les *public schools* britanniques sont en réalité des écoles privées qui fonctionnent souvent sur le mode de l'internat et dont les frais de scolarité sont très élevés. Ces écoles accordent cependant des bourses aux élèves brillants mais peu fortunés. Les *public schools* américaines sont des écoles publiques et la scolarité y est gratuite. ▷ STATE SCHOOL.

publish /'pʌblɪʃ/ vt publier. **publisher** n éditeur m. **publishing** n édition f.

pudding /'pʊdɪŋ/ n dessert m; (steamed) pudding m.

puddle /'pʌdl/ n flaque f d'eau.

puff /pʌf/ n (of smoke) bouffée f; (of breath) souffle m. ● vt/i souffler. **~ at** (cigar) tirer sur. **~ out** (swell) (se) gonfler.

pull /pʊl/ vt/i tirer; (muscle) se froisser; **~ a face** faire une grimace; **~ one's weight** faire sa part du travail; **~ sb's leg** faire marcher qn. ● n traction f; (fig) attraction f; (influence) influence f; **give a ~** tirer. **~ away** (Auto) démarrer; **~ back** or **out** (withdraw) (se) retirer; **~ down** (building) démolir; **~ in** (enter) entrer; (stop) s'arrêter; **~ off** enlever; (fig) réussir; **~ out** (from bag) sortir; (extract) arracher; (Auto) déboîter; **~ over** (Auto) se ranger (sur le côté); **~ through** s'en tirer; **~ oneself together** se ressaisir.

pull-down menu n (Comput) menu m déroulant.

pulley /'pʊlɪ/ n poulie f.

pullover /'pʊləʊvə(r)/ n pull(-over) m.

pulp /pʌlp/ n (of fruit) pulpe f; (for paper) pâte f à papier.

pulpit /'pʊlpɪt/ n chaire f.

pulsate /pʌl'seɪt/ vi battre.

pulse /pʌls/ n (Med) pouls m.

pump /pʌmp/ n pompe f; (plimsoll) chaussure f de sport. ● vt/i pomper; (person) soutirer des renseignements à; **~ up** gonfler.

pumpkin /'pʌmpkɪn/ n citrouille f.

pun /pʌn/ n jeu m de mots.

punch /pʌntʃ/ vt donner un coup de poing à; (ticket) poinçonner. ● n coup m de poing; (vigour 🔲) punch m; (device) poinçonneuse f; (drink) punch m. **~-line** n chute f.

punctual /'pʌŋktʃʊəl/ adj à l'heure; (habitually) ponctuel.

punctuation /pʌŋktʃʊ'eɪʃn/ n ponctuation f.

puncture /'pʌŋktʃə(r)/ n crevaison f. ● vt/i crever.

pungent /'pʌndʒənt/ adj âcre.

punish /'pʌnɪʃ/ vt punir (for sth de qch). **punishment** n punition f.

punk /pʌŋk/ n (music, fan) punk m; (US: 🔲) voyou m.

punt /pʌnt/ n (boat) barque f; (Hist) (Irish pound) livre f irlandaise.

puny /'pju:nɪ/ adj **-ier, -iest** chétif.

pupil /'pju:pɪl/ n (person) élève mf; (of eye) pupille f.

puppet /'pʌpɪt/ n marionnette f.

puppy /'pʌpɪ/ n chiot m.

purchase /'pɜ:tʃəs/ vt acheter (from sb à qn). ● n achat m.

pure /pjʊə(r)/ adj pur.

purgatory /'pɜ:gətrɪ/ n purgatoire m.

purge /pɜ:dʒ/ vt purger (of de). ● n purge f.

purification /pjʊərɪfɪ'keɪʃn/ n (of water, air) épuration f; (Relig) purification f. **purify** vt épurer; purifier.

puritan /'pjʊərɪtən/ n puritain/-e m/f.

purity /'pjʊərətɪ/ n pureté f.

purple /'pɜ:pl/ adj & n violet (m).

purpose /'pɜ:pəs/ n but m; (determination) résolution f; **on ~** exprès; **to no ~** sans résultat.

purr /pɜ:(r)/ n ronronnement m. ● vi ronronner.

purse /pɜːs/ n porte-monnaie m inv; (handbag: US) sac m à main. ● vt (lips) pincer.

pursue /pəˈsjuː/ vt poursuivre.

pursuit /pəˈsjuːt/ n poursuite f; (hobby) activité f, occupation f.

pus /pʌs/ n pus m.

push /pʊʃ/ vt/i pousser; (button) appuyer sur; (thrust) enfoncer; (recommend 🆒) proposer avec insistance; **be ~ed for** (time) manquer de; **be ~ing thirty** 🆒 friser la trentaine; **~ sb around** bousculer qn. ● n poussée f; (effort) gros effort m; (drive) dynamisme m; **give the ~ to** 🆒 flanquer à la porte 🆒. □ **~ in** resquiller; **~ on** continuer; **~ up** (lift) relever; (prices) faire monter.

pushchair /ˈpʊʃtʃeə(r)/ n poussette f.

pusher /ˈpʊʃə(r)/ n revendeur/-euse m/f (de drogue).

push-up n pompe f.

put /pʊt/ vt/i (pt put; pres p putting) mettre, placer, poser; (question) poser; **~ the damage at a million** estimer les dégâts à un million; **~ sth tactfully** dire qch avec tact. □ **~ across** communiquer; **~ away** ranger; (in hospital, prison) enfermer; **~ back** (postpone) remettre; (delay) retarder; **~ down** (dé)poser; (write) inscrire; (pay) verser; (suppress) réprimer; **~ forward** (plan) soumettre; **~ in** (insert) introduire; (fit) installer; (submit) soumettre; **~ in for** faire une demande de; **~ off** (postpone) renvoyer à plus tard; (disconcert) déconcerter; (displease) rebuter; **~ sb off sth** dégoûter qn de qch; **~ on** (clothes, radio) mettre; (light) allumer; (accent, weight) prendre; **~ out** sortir; (stretch) (é)tendre; (extinguish) éteindre; (disconcert) déconcerter; (inconvenience) déranger; **~ up** lever, remonter; (building) construire; (notice) mettre; (price) augmenter; (guest) héberger; (offer) offrir; **~ up with** supporter.

putt /pʌt/ vi putter. ● n putt m.

putty /pʌt/ n mastic m.

puzzle /ˈpʌzl/ n énigme f; (game) casse-tête m inv; (jigsaw) puzzle m. ● vt rendre perplexe. ● vi se creuser la tête.

pyjamas /pəˈdʒɑːməz/ npl pyjama m.

pylon /ˈpaɪlən/ n pylône m.

quack /kwæk/ n (of duck) coin-coin m inv; (doctor) charlatan m.

quadrangle /ˈkwɒdræŋgl/ (of college) n cour f.

quadruple /ˈkwɒdrʊpl/ adj & n quadruple (m). ● vt/i quadrupler.

quail /kweɪl/ n (bird) caille f.

quaint /kweɪnt/ adj pittoresque; (old) vieillot; (odd) bizarre.

qualification /kwɒlɪfɪˈkeɪʃn/ n diplôme m; (ability) compétence f; (fig) réserve f, restriction f.

qualified /ˈkwɒlɪfaɪd/ adj diplômé; (able) qualifié (**to do** pour faire); (fig) conditionnel.

qualify /ˈkwɒlɪfaɪ/ vt qualifier; (modify) mettre des réserves à; (statement) nuancer. ● vi obtenir son diplôme (**as** de); (Sport) se qualifier; **~ for** remplir les conditions requises pour.

quality /ˈkwɒlətɪ/ n qualité f.

qualm /kwɑːm/ n scrupule m.

quantity /ˈkwɒntətɪ/ n quantité f.

quarantine /ˈkwɒrəntiːn/ n quarantaine f.

quarrel /ˈkwɒrəl/ n dispute f, querelle f. ● vi (pt **quarrelled**) se disputer.

quarry /ˈkwɒrɪ/ n (excavation) carrière f; (prey) proie f. ● vt extraire.

quart /kwɔːt/ n ≈ litre m.

quarter /ˈkwɔːtə(r)/ n quart m; (of year) trimestre m; (25 cents: US) quart m de dollar; (district) quartier m; **~s** logement m; **from all ~s** de toutes parts. ● vt diviser en quatre; (troops) cantonner.

quarterly /ˈkwɔːtəlɪ/ adj trimestriel. ● adv tous les trois mois.

quartet /kwɔːˈtet/ n quatuor m.

quartz /kwɔːts/ n quartz m. ● adj (watch) à quartz.

quash /kwɒʃ/ vt (suppress) étouffer; (Jur) annuler.

quaver /ˈkweɪvə(r)/ vi trembler, chevroter. ● n (Mus) croche f.

quay /kiː/ n (Naut) quai m.

queasy /ˈkwiːzɪ/ adj feel ∼ avoir mal au cœur.

queen /kwiːn/ n reine f; (cards) dame f.

queer /kwɪə(r)/ adj étrange; (dubious) louche; ▣ homosexuel.

quench /kwentʃ/ vt éteindre; (thirst) étancher; (desire) étouffer.

query /ˈkwɪərɪ/ n question f. ● vt mettre en question.

quest /kwest/ n recherche f.

question /ˈkwestʃən/ n question f; in ∼ en question; out of the ∼ hors de question. ● vt interroger; (doubt) mettre en question, douter de. ∼ mark n point m d'interrogation.

questionnaire /kwestʃəˈneə(r)/ n questionnaire m.

queue /kjuː/ n queue f. ● vi (pres p queuing) faire la queue.

quibble /ˈkwɪbl/ vi ergoter.

quick /kwɪk/ adj rapide; (clever) vif/vive; be ∼ (hurry) se dépêcher. ● adv vite. ● n cut to the ∼ piquer au vif. **quicken** vt/i (s')accélérer. **quickly** adv rapidement, vite. ∼sand n sables mpl mouvants.

quid /kwɪd/ n inv ▣ livre f sterling.

quiet /ˈkwaɪət/ adj (calm, still) tranquille; (silent) silencieux; (gentle) doux; (discreet) discret; keep ∼ se taire. ● n tranquillité f; on the ∼ en cachette. **quieten** vt/i (se) calmer. **quietly** adv (speak) doucement; (sit) en silence.

quilt /kwɪlt/ n édredon m; (continental) ∼ couette f.

quirk /kwɜːk/ n bizarrerie f.

quit /kwɪt/ vt (pt quitted) quitter; (smoking) arrêter de. ● vi abandonner; (resign) démissionner; ∼ doing (US) cesser de faire.

quite /kwaɪt/ adv tout à fait, vraiment; (rather) assez; ∼ a few un bon nombre (de).

quits /kwɪts/ adj quitte (with envers); call it ∼ en rester là.

quiver /ˈkwɪvə(r)/ vi trembler.

quiz /kwɪz/ n (pl quizzes) test m; (game) jeu-concours m. ● vt (pt quizzed) questionner.

quotation /kwəʊˈteɪʃn/ n citation f; (price) devis m; (stock exchange) cotation f; ∼ marks guillemets mpl.

quote /kwəʊt/ vt citer; (reference, number) rappeler; (price) indiquer; (share price) coter. ● vi ∼ for faire un devis pour; ∼ from citer. ● n (quotation) citation f; (estimate) devis m; in ∼s ▣ entre guillemets.

Rr

rabbi /ˈræbaɪ/ n rabbin m.

rabbit /ˈræbɪt/ n lapin m.

rabies /ˈreɪbiːz/ n (disease) rage f.

race /reɪs/ n (contest) course f; (group) race f. ● adj racial; ∼ relations relations fpl inter-raciales. ● vt (compete with) faire la course avec; (horse) faire courir. ● vi courir; (pulse) battre précipitamment; (engine) s'emballer. ∼course n champ m de courses. ∼horse n cheval m de course. ∼-track n piste f; (for horses) champ m de courses.

racing /ˈreɪsɪŋ/ n courses fpl; ∼ car voiture f de course.

racism /ˈreɪsɪzəm/ n racisme m. **racist** adj & n raciste (mf).

rack /ræk/ n (shelf) étagère f; (for clothes) portant m; (for luggage) compartiment m à bagages; (for dishes) égouttoir m. ● vt ∼ one's brains se creuser la cervelle.

racket /ˈrækɪt/ n (Sport) raquette f; (noise) vacarme m; (swindle) escroquerie f; (crime) trafic m.

radar /ˈreɪdɑː(r)/ n & adj radar (m).

radial /ˈreɪdɪəl/ n ∼ (tyre) pneu m radial.

radiate /ˈreɪdɪeɪt/ vt (happiness) rayonner de; (heat) émettre. ● vi rayonner (from de). **radiation** n (radioactivity) radiation f. **radiator** n radiateur m.

radical /ˈrædɪkl/ n & a radical/-e (m/f).

radio /ˈreɪdɪəʊ/ n radio f; on the ∼ à la radio. ● vt (message) envoyer par radio; (person) appeler par radio.

radioactive /reɪdɪəʊˈæktɪv/ adj radioactif.

radiographer /reɪdɪˈɒɡrəfə(r)/ n manipulateur/-trice m/f radiographe.

radish /ˈrædɪʃ/ n radis m.

radius /'reɪdɪəs/ n (pl **-dii**) rayon m.

raffle /'ræfl/ n tombola f.

rag /ræg/ n chiffon m; ~**s** loques fpl.

rage /reɪdʒ/ n rage f, colère f; **be all the** ~ faire fureur. ● vi (person) tempêter; (storm, battle) faire rage.

ragged /'rægɪd/ adj (clothes) en loques; (person) dépenaillé.

raid /reɪd/ n (Mil, on stock market) raid m; (by police) rafle f; (by criminals) hold-up m inv. ● vt faire un raid or une rafle or un hold-up dans. **raider** n (thief) pillard m; (Mil) commando m; (corporate) raider m.

rail /reɪl/ n (on balcony) balustrade f; (stairs) rampe f; (for train) rail m; (for curtain) tringle f; **by** ~ par chemin de fer.

railing /'reɪlɪŋ/ n (also ~**s**) grille f.

railway, (US) **railroad** n chemin m de fer. ~ **line** n voie f ferrée. ~ **station** n gare f.

rain /reɪn/ n pluie f. ● vi pleuvoir. ~**bow** n arc-en-ciel m. ~**coat** n imperméable m. ~**fall** n précipitation f. ~ **forest** n forêt f tropicale.

rainy /'reɪnɪ/ adj (**-ier, -iest**) pluvieux; (season) des pluies.

raise /reɪz/ vt (barrier, curtain) lever; (child, cattle) élever; (question) soulever; (price, salary) augmenter. ● n (US) augmentation f.

raisin /'reɪzn/ n raisin m sec.

rake /reɪk/ n râteau m. ● vt (garden) ratisser; (search) fouiller dans. □ ~ **in** (money) amasser; ~ **up** (past) remuer.

rally /'rælɪ/ vt/i (se) rallier; (strength) reprendre; (after illness) aller mieux; ~ **round** venir en aide. ● n rassemblement m; (Auto) rallye m; (tennis) échange m.

ram /ræm/ n bélier m. ● vt (pt **rammed**) (thrust) enfoncer; (crash into) rentrer dans.

RAM abbr (**random access memory**) RAM f.

ramble /'ræmbl/ n randonnée f. ● vi faire une randonnée. □ ~ **on** discourir.

ramp /ræmp/ n (slope) rampe f; (in garage) pont m de graissage.

rampage¹ /ræm'peɪdʒ/ vi se déchaîner (**through** dans).

rampage² /'ræmpeɪdʒ/ n **go on the** ~ tout saccager.

ran /ræn/ →**RUN**.

rancid /'rænsɪd/ adj rance.

random /'rændəm/ adj (fait) au hasard. ● n **at** ~ au hasard.

rang /ræŋ/ →**RING²**.

range /reɪndʒ/ n (of prices, products) gamme f; (of people, beliefs) variété f; (of radar, weapon) portée f; (of aircraft) autonomie f; (of mountains) chaîne f. ● vi aller; (vary) varier.

rank /ræŋk/ n rang m; (Mil) grade m. ● vt/i ~ **among** (se) classer parmi.

ransack /'rænsæk/ vt (search) fouiller; (pillage) mettre à sac.

ransom /'rænsəm/ n rançon f.

rap /ræp/ n coup m sec; (Mus) rap m. ● vi (pt **rapped**) donner des coups secs (**on** sur).

rape /reɪp/ vt violer. ● n viol m.

rapid /'ræpɪd/ adj rapide.

rapist /'reɪpɪst/ n violeur m.

rapturous /'ræptʃərəs/ adj (delight) extasié; (welcome) enthousiaste.

rare /reə(r)/ adj rare; (Culin) saignant. **rarely** adv rarement.

rascal /'rɑːskl/ n coquin/-e m/f.

rash /ræʃ/ n (Med) rougeurs fpl. ● adj irréfléchi.

raspberry /'rɑːzbrɪ/ n framboise f.

rat /ræt/ n rat m. ● vi (pt **ratted**) ~ **on** (desert) lâcher; (inform on) dénoncer.

rate /reɪt/ n (ratio, level) taux m; (speed) rythme m; (price) tarif m; (of exchange) taux m; **at any** ~ en tout cas. ● vt (value) estimer; (deserve) mériter; ~ **sth highly** admirer beaucoup qch. ● vi ~ **as** être considéré comme.

rather /'rɑːðə(r)/ adv (by preference) plutôt; (fairly) assez, plutôt; (a little) un peu; **I would** ~ **go** j'aimerais mieux partir; ~ **than go** plutôt que de partir.

rating /'reɪtɪŋ/ n (score, value) cote f; **the** ~**s** (TV) l'indice m d'écoute, l'audimat® m.

ratio /'reɪʃɪəʊ/ n proportion f.

ration /'ræʃn/ n ration f. ● vt rationner.

rational /'ræʃənl/ adj rationnel; (person) sensé.

rationalize /'ræʃnəlaɪz/ vt justifier; (organize) rationaliser.

rattle /'rætl/ vi (bottles, chains) s'entre-choquer; (window) vibrer. ● vt (bottles, chains) faire s'entrechoquer; (fig, 🔲) énerver. ● n cliquetis m; (toy) hochet m. ~**snake** n serpent m à sonnette, crotale m.

rave /reɪv/ vi (enthuse) s'emballer; (in fever) délirer; (in anger) tempêter.

raven /'reɪvn/ n corbeau m.

ravenous /'rævənəs/ adj be ~ avoir une faim de loup.

ravine /rə'viːn/ n ravin m.

raving /'reɪvɪŋ/ adj ~ **lunatic** fou m furieux, folle f furieuse.

ravishing /'rævɪʃɪŋ/ adj ravissant.

raw /rɔː/ adj cru; (not processed) brut; (wound) à vif; (immature) inexpérimenté; **get a ~ deal** être mal traité; ~ **material** matière f première.

ray /reɪ/ n (of light) rayon m; ~ **of hope** lueur f d'espoir.

razor /'reɪzə(r)/ n rasoir m. ~**-blade** n lame f de rasoir.

re /riː/ prep au sujet de; (at top of letter) objet.

reach /riːtʃ/ vt (place, level) atteindre; (decision) arriver à; (contact) joindre; (audience, market) toucher. ● vi ~ **up/down** lever/baisser le bras; ~ **across** étendre le bras. ● n portée f; **within ~ of** à portée de; (close to) à proximité de.

react /rɪ'ækt/ vi réagir. **reaction** n réaction f. **reactor** n réacteur m.

read /riːd/ vt/i (pt read) lire; (study) étudier; (instrument) indiquer; ~ **about sb** lire quelque chose sur qn; ~ **out** lire à haute voix. **reader** n lecteur/-trice m/f. **reading** n lecture f; (measurement) indication f; (interpretation) interprétation f.

readjust /riːə'dʒʌst/ vt rajuster. ● vi se réadapter (to à).

read-only memory, ROM n mémoire f morte.

ready /'redɪ/ adj (-ier, -iest) prêt; (quick) prompt. ~**-made** adj tout fait. ~**-to-wear** adj prêt-à-porter.

real /rɪəl/ adj (not imaginary) véritable, réel; (not artificial) vrai; **it's a ~ shame** c'est vraiment dommage. ~ **estate** n biens mpl immobiliers.

realism /'rɪəlɪzəm/ n réalisme m. **realistic** adj réaliste.

reality /rɪ'ælətɪ/ n réalité f. ~ **TV** n télé-réalité f.

reasonable /'riːznəbl/ adj raisonnable.

realize /'rɪəlaɪz/ vt se rendre compte de, comprendre; (fulfil, turn into cash) réaliser; (price) atteindre.

really /'rɪəlɪ/ adv vraiment.

reap /riːp/ vt (crop) recueillir; (benefits) récolter.

reappear /riːə'pɪə(r)/ vi reparaître.

rear /rɪə(r)/ n arrière m; (of person) derrière m. 🔲 ● adj (seat) arrière inv; (entrance) de derrière. ● vt élever. ● vi (horse) se cabrer. ~**-view mirror** n rétroviseur m.

reason /'riːzn/ n raison f (**to do, for doing** de faire); **within ~** dans la limite du raisonnable.

reassurance /riːə'ʃɔːrəns/ n réconfort m. **reassure** vt rassurer.

rebate /'riːbeɪt/ n (refund) remboursement m; (discount) remise f.

rebel¹ /'rebl/ n & adj rebelle (mf).

rebel² /rɪ'bel/ vi (pt **rebelled**) se rebeller. **rebellion** n rébellion f.

rebound¹ /rɪ'baʊnd/ vi rebondir; ~ **on** (backfire) se retourner contre.

rebound² /'riːbaʊnd/ n rebond m.

rebuke /rɪ'bjuːk/ vt réprimander. ● n réprimande f.

recall /rɪ'kɔːl/ vt (remember) se souvenir de; (call back) rappeler. ● n (memory) mémoire f; (Comput, Mil) rappel m.

recap /riː'kæp/ vt/i (pt **recapped**) récapituler. ● n récapitulation f.

recede /rɪ'siːd/ vi s'éloigner; **his hair is receding** son front se dégarnit.

receipt /rɪ'siːt/ n (written) reçu m; (of letter) réception f; ~**s** (Comm) recettes fpl.

receive /rɪ'siːv/ vt recevoir; (stolen goods) receler. **receiver** n (telephone) combiné m; (TV) récepteur m.

recent /'riːsnt/ adj récent. **recently** adv récemment.

receptacle /rɪ'septəkl/ n récipient m.

reception /rɪ'sepʃn/ n réception f; **give sb a warm ~** donner un accueil chaleureux à qn.

recess /rɪ'ses/ n (alcove) alcôve m; (for door) embrasure f; (Jur, Pol) vacances fpl; (School, US) récréation f.

recession /rɪ'seʃn/ *n* récession *f.*

recharge /riː'tʃɑːdʒ/ *vt* recharger.

recipe /'resəpɪ/ *n* recette *f.*

recipient /rɪ'sɪpɪənt/ *n* (of honour) récipiendaire *mf;* (of letter) destinataire *mf.*

reciprocate /rɪ'sɪprəkeɪt/ *vt* (compliment) retourner; (kindness) payer de retour. ● *vi* en faire autant.

recite /rɪ'saɪt/ *vi* réciter.

reckless /'reklɪs/ *adj* imprudent.

reckon /'rekən/ *vt/i* calculer; (judge) considérer; (think) penser; ∼ **on/with** compter sur/avec. **reckoning** *n* (guess) estimation *f;* (calculation) calculs *mpl.*

reclaim /rɪ'kleɪm/ *vt* récupérer; (flooded land) assécher.

recline /rɪ'klaɪm/ *vi* s'allonger; (seat) s'incliner.

recluse /rɪ'kluːs/ *n* reclus/-e *m/f.*

recognition /rekəg'nɪʃn/ *n* reconnaissance *f;* **beyond** ∼ méconnaissable; **gain** ∼ être reconnu.

recognize /'rekəgnaɪz/ *vt* reconnaître.

recollect /rekə'lekt/ *vt* se souvenir de, se rappeler. **recollection** *n* souvenir *m.*

recommend /rekə'mend/ *vt* recommander. **recommendation** *n* recommandation *f.*

reconcile /'rekənsaɪl/ *vt* (people) réconcilier; (facts) concilier; ∼ **oneself to** se résigner à.

recondition /riː'kən'dɪʃn/ *vt* remettre à neuf.

reconsider /riː'kən'sɪdə(r)/ *vt* réexaminer. ● *vi* réfléchir.

reconstruct /riː'kən'strʌkt/ *vt* reconstruire; (crime) faire une reconstitution de.

record[1] /rɪ'kɔːd/ *vt/i* (in register, on tape) enregistrer; (in diary) noter; ∼**that** rapporter que.

record[2] /'rekɔːd/ *n* (of events) compte-rendu *m;* (official) procès-verbal *m;* (personal, administrative) dossier *m;* (historical) archives *fpl;* (past history) réputation *f;* (Mus) disque *m;* (Sport) record *m;* **(criminal)** ∼ casier *m* judiciaire; **off the** ∼ officieusement. ● *adj* record *inv.*

recorder /rɪ'kɔːdə(r)/ *n* (Mus) flûte *f* à bec.

recording /rɪ'kɔːdɪŋ/ *n* enregistrement *m.*

record-player *n* tourne-disque *m.*

recover /rɪ'kʌvə(r)/ *vt* récupérer. ● *vi* se remettre; (economy) se redresser. **recovery** *n* (Med) rétablissement *m;* (of economy) relance *f.*

recreation /rekrɪ'eɪʃn/ *n* récréation *f.*

recruit /rɪ'kruːt/ *n* recrue *f.* ● *vt* recruter. **recruitment** *n* recrutement *m.*

rectangle /'rektæŋgl/ *n* rectangle *m.*

rectify /'rektɪfaɪ/ *vt* rectifier.

recuperate /rɪ'kuːpəreɪt/ *vt* récupérer. ● *vi* se rétablir.

recur /rɪ'kɜː(r)/ *vi* (pt **recurred**) se reproduire.

recycle /riː'saɪkl/ *vt* recycler.

red /red/ *adj* (**redder, reddest**) rouge; (hair) roux. ● *n* rouge *m;* **in the** ∼ en déficit. **R**∼ **Cross** *n* Croix- Rouge *f.* ∼**currant** *n* groseille *f.*

redecorate /riː'dekəreɪt/ *vt* repeindre, refaire.

redeploy /riː'dɪ'plɔɪ/ *vt* réorganiser; (troops) répartir.

red: ∼**-handed** *adj* en flagrant délit. ∼**-hot** *adj* brûlant.

redirect /riː'dɪ'rekt/ *vt* (traffic) dévier; (letter) faire suivre.

redness /'rednɪs/ *n* rougeur *f.*

redo /riː'duː/ *vt* (pt **-did**; pp **-done**) refaire.

redress /rɪ'dres/ *vt* (wrong) redresser; (balance) rétablir. ● *n* réparation *f.*

reduce /rɪ'djuːs/ *vt* réduire; (temperature) faire baisser. **reduction** *n* réduction *f.*

redundancy /rɪ'dʌndənsɪ/ *n* licenciement *m.*

redundant /rɪ'dʌndənt/ *adj* superflu; (worker) licencié; **make** ∼ licencier.

reed /riːd/ *n* (plant) roseau *m.*

reef /riːf/ *n* récif *m,* écueil *m.*

reel /riːl/ *n* (of thread) bobine *f;* (of film) bande *f;* (winding device) dévidoir *m.* ● *vi* chanceler. ● *vt* ∼ **off** réciter.

refectory /rɪ'fektrɪ/ *n* réfectoire *m.*

refer /rɪ'fɜː(r)/ *vt/i* (pt **referred**) ∼ **to** (allude to) faire allusion à; (concern) s'appliquer à; (consult) consulter; (direct) renvoyer à.

referee /refə'riː/ n (Sport) arbitre m. ● vt (pt **refereed**) arbitrer.

reference /'refərəns/ n référence f; (mention) allusion f; (person) personne f pouvant fournir des références; **in** or **with ~ to** en ce qui concerne; (Comm) suite à.

referendum /refə'rendəm/ n (pl **~s**) référendum m.

refill[1] /riː'fɪl/ vt (glass) remplir à nouveau; (pen) recharger.

refill[2] /'riːfɪl/ n recharge f.

refine /rɪ'faɪn/ vt raffiner.

reflect /rɪ'flekt/ vt refléter; (heat, light) renvoyer. ● vi réfléchir (on à); **~ well/badly on sb** faire honneur/du tort à qn.

reflection /rɪ'flekʃn/ n réflexion f; (image) reflet m; **on ~** à la réflexion.

reflective /rɪ'flektɪv/ adj (surface) réfléchissant; (person) réfléchi.

reflector /rɪ'flektə(r)/ n (on car) catadioptre m.

reflex /'riːfleks/ adj & n réflexe (m).

reflexive /rɪ'fleksɪv/ adj (Gram) réfléchi.

reform /rɪ'fɔːm/ vt réformer. ● vi (person) s'amender. ● n réforme f.

refrain /rɪ'freɪn/ n refrain m. ● vi s'abstenir (from de).

refresh /rɪ'freʃ/ vt (drink) rafraîchir; (rest) reposer. **refreshments** npl rafraîchissements mpl.

refrigerate /rɪ'frɪdʒəreɪt/ vt réfrigérer. **refrigerator** n réfrigérateur m.

refuel /riː'fjuːəl/ vt/i (pt **refuelled**) (se) ravitailler.

refuge /'refjuːdʒ/ n refuge m; **take ~** se réfugier. **refugee** n réfugié/-e m/f.

refund[1] /riː'fʌnd/ vt rembourser.

refund[2] /'riːfʌnd/ n remboursement m.

refurbish /riː'fɜːbɪʃ/ vt remettre à neuf.

refuse[1] /rɪ'fjuːz/ vt/i refuser.

refuse[2] /'refjuːs/ n ordures fpl.

regain /rɪ'geɪn/ vt retrouver; (lost ground) regagner.

regard /rɪ'gɑːd/ vt considérer; **as ~s** en ce qui concerne. ● n égard m, estime f; **in this ~** à cet égard; **~s** amitiés fpl. **regarding** prep en ce qui concerne.

regardless /rɪ'gɑːdlɪs/ adv malgré tout; **~ of** sans tenir compte de.

regime /'reʒiːm/ n régime m.

regiment /'redʒɪmənt/ n régiment m.

region /'riːdʒən/ n région f; **in the ~ of** environ.

register /'redʒɪstə(r)/ n registre m. ● vt (record) enregistrer; (vehicle) faire immatriculer; (birth) déclarer; (letter) recommander; (indicate) indiquer; (express) exprimer. ● vi (enrol) s'inscrire; (at hotel) se présenter; (fig) être compris.

registrar /redʒɪ'strɑː(r)/ n officier m de l'état civil; (Univ) responsable m du bureau de la scolarité.

registration /redʒɪ'streɪʃn/ n (of voter, student) inscription f; (of birth) déclaration f; **~ (number)** (Auto) numéro m d'immatriculation.

registry office n bureau m de l'état civil.

regret /rɪ'gret/ n regret m. ● vt (pt **regretted**) regretter (**to do** de faire). **regretfully** adv à regret.

regular /'regjʊlə(r)/ adj régulier; (usual) habituel. ● n habitué/-e m/f. **regularity** n régularité f. **regularly** adv régulièrement.

regulate /'regjʊleɪt/ vt régler. **regulation** n (rule) règlement m; (process) réglementation f.

rehabilitate /riːə'bɪlɪteɪt/ vt (in public esteem) réhabiliter; (prisoner) réinsérer.

rehearsal /rɪ'hɜːsl/ n répétition f. **rehearse** vt/i répéter.

reign /reɪn/ n règne m. ● vi régner (over sur).

reimburse /riːɪm'bɜːs/ vt rembourser.

reindeer /'reɪndɪə(r)/ n inv renne m.

reinforce /riːɪn'fɔːs/ vt renforcer. **reinforcement** n renforcement m; **~s** renforts mpl.

reinstate /riːɪn'steɪt/ vt (person) réintégrer; (law) rétablir.

reject[1] /'riːdʒekt/ n marchandise f de deuxième choix.

reject[2] /rɪ'dʒekt/ vt (offer, plea) rejeter; (goods) refuser. **rejection** n (personal) rejet m; (of candidate, work) refus m.

rejoice /rɪ'dʒɔɪs/ vi se réjouir.

relapse /'riːlæps/ n rechute f. ● vi rechuter; **~ into** retomber dans.

relate /rɪ'leɪt/ vt raconter; (associate) associer. ● vi **~ to** se rapporter à; (get on with) s'entendre avec. **related** *adj* (*ideas*) lié; **we are ~d** nous sommes parents.

relation /rɪˈleɪʃn/ *n* rapport *m*; (person) parent/-e *m/f*. **relationship** *n* relations *fpl*; (link) rapport *m*.

relative /ˈrelətɪv/ *n* parent/-e *m/f*. ● *adj* relatif; (respective) respectif.

relax /rɪˈlæks/ *vt* (*grip*) relâcher; (*muscle*) décontracter; (*discipline*) assouplir. ● *vi* (*person*) se détendre; (*grip*) se relâcher. **relaxation** *n* détente *f*. **relaxing** *adj* délassant.

relay[1] /ˈriːleɪ/ *n* (also **~ race**) course *f* de relais.

relay[2] /ˈriːleɪ/ *vt* relayer.

release /rɪˈliːs/ *vt* (*prisoner*) libérer; (*fastening*) faire jouer; (*object, hand*) lâcher; (*film*) faire sortir; (*news*) publier. ● *n* libération *f*; (of film) sortie *f*; (new record, film) nouveauté *f*.

relevance /ˈreləvəns/ *n* pertinence *f*, intérêt *m*.

relevant /ˈreləvənt/ *adj* pertinent; **be ~ to** avoir rapport à.

reliability /rɪlaɪəˈbɪlətɪ/ *n* (of firm) sérieux *m*; (of car) fiabilité *f*; (of person) honnêteté *f*. **reliable** *adj* (*firm*) sérieux; (*person, machine*) fiable.

reliance /rɪˈlaɪəns/ *n* dépendance *f*.

relic /ˈrelɪk/ *n* vestige *m*; (object) relique *f*.

relief /rɪˈliːf/ *n* soulagement *m* (from à); (assistance) secours *m*; (outline) relief *m*; **~ road** route *f* de délestage.

relieve /rɪˈliːv/ *vt* soulager; (help) secourir; (take over from) relayer.

religion /rɪˈlɪdʒən/ *n* religion *f*. **religious** *adj* religieux.

relish /ˈrelɪʃ/ *n* plaisir *m*; (Culin) condiment *m*. ● *vt* (*food*) savourer; (*idea*) se réjouir de.

relocate /riːləʊˈkeɪt/ *vt* muter. ● *vi* (*company*) déménager; (*worker*) être muté. **relocation** *n* délocalisation *f*.

reluctance /rɪˈlʌktəns/ *n* répugnance *f*.

reluctant /rɪˈlʌktənt/ *adj* (*person*) peu enthousiaste; (*consent*) accordé à contrecœur; **~ to** peu disposé à. **reluctantly** *adv* à contrecœur.

rely /rɪˈlaɪ/ *vi* **~ on** (count) compter sur; (be dependent) dépendre de.

remain /rɪˈmeɪn/ *vi* rester. **remainder** *n* reste *m*.

remand /rɪˈmɑːnd/ *vt* mettre en détention provisoire. ● *n* **on ~** en détention provisoire.

remark /rɪˈmɑːk/ *n* remarque *f*. ● *vt* remarquer. ● *vi* **~ on** faire des remarques sur. **remarkable** *adj* remarquable.

remedy /ˈremədɪ/ *n* remède *m*. ● *vt* remédier à.

remember /rɪˈmembə(r)/ *vt* se souvenir de, se rappeler; **~ to do** ne pas oublier de faire. **remembrance** *n* souvenir *m*.

remind /rɪˈmaɪnd/ *vt* rappeler (**sb of sth** qch à qn); **~ sb to do** rappeler à qn de faire. **reminder** *n* rappel *m*.

reminisce /remɪˈnɪs/ *vi* évoquer ses souvenirs.

remission /rɪˈmɪʃn/ *n* (Med) rémission *f*; (Jur) remise *f*.

remnant /ˈremnənt/ *n* reste *m*; (trace) vestige *m*; (of cloth) coupon *m*.

remodel /riːˈmɒdl/ *vt* (*pt* **remodelled**) remodeler.

remorse /rɪˈmɔːs/ *n* remords *m*.

remote /rɪˈməʊt/ *adj* (*place, time*) lointain; (*person*) distant; (*slight*) vague; **~ control** télécommande *f*.

removable /rɪˈmuːvəbl/ *adj* amovible.

removal /rɪˈmuːvl/ *n* (of employee) renvoi *m*; (of threat) suppression *f*; (of troops) retrait *m*; (of stain) détachage *m*; (from house) déménagement *m*; **~ men** déménageurs *mpl*.

remove /rɪˈmuːv/ *vt* enlever; (dismiss) renvoyer; (do away with) supprimer; (Comput) effacer.

remunerate /rɪˈmjuːnəreɪt/ *vt* rémunérer. **remuneration** *n* rémunération *f*.

render /ˈrendə(r)/ *vt* rendre.

renegade /ˈrenɪgeɪd/ *n* renégat/-e *m/f*.

renew /rɪˈnjuː/ *vt* renouveler; (resume) reprendre. **renewable** *adj* renouvelable.

renounce /rɪˈnaʊns/ *vt* renoncer à; (disown) renier.

renovate /ˈrenəveɪt/ *vt* rénover.

renown /rɪˈnaʊn/ *n* renommée *f*.

rent /rent/ *n* loyer *m*. ● *vt* louer; **for ~** à louer. **rental** *n* prix *m* de location.

reopen /riːˈəʊpən/ *vt/i* rouvrir.

reorganize / riː'ɔːgənaɪz/ vt réorganiser.

rep /rep/ n (Comm) représentant/-e m/f.

repair /rɪ'peə(r)/ vt réparer. ● n réparation f; **in good/bad ~** en bon/mauvais état.

repatriate /riː'pætrɪeɪt/ vt rapatrier. **repatriation** n rapatriement m.

repay /rɪ'peɪ/ vt (pt **repaid**) rembourser; (reward) récompenser. **repayment** n remboursement m.

repeal /rɪ'piːl/ vt abroger. ● n abrogation f.

repeat /rɪ'piːt/ vt/i répéter; (renew) renouveler; **~ itself**, **~ oneself** se répéter. ● n répétition f; (broadcast) reprise f.

repel /rɪ'pel/ vt (pt **repelled**) repousser.

repent /rɪ'pent/ vi se repentir (**of** de).

repercussion /riːpə'kʌʃn/ n répercussion f.

repetition /repɪ'tɪʃn/ n répétition f.

replace /rɪ'pleɪs/ vt (put back) remettre; (take the place of) remplacer. **replacement** n remplacement m (**of** de); (person) remplaçant/-e m/f; (new part) pièce f de rechange.

replay /'riːpleɪ/ n (Sport) match m rejoué; (recording) répétition f immédiate.

replenish /rɪ'plenɪʃ/ vt (refill) remplir; (renew) renouveler.

replica /'replɪkə/ n copie f exacte.

reply /rɪ'plaɪ/ vt/i répondre. ● n réponse f.

report /rɪ'pɔːt/ vt rapporter, annoncer (**that** que); (notify) signaler; (denounce) dénoncer. ● vi faire un rapport; **~ (on)** (news item) faire un reportage sur; **~ to** (go) se présenter chez. ● n rapport m; (in press) reportage m; (School) bulletin m. **reporter** n reporter m.

repossess /riːpə'zes/ vt reprendre.

represent /reprɪ'zent/ vt représenter.

representation /reprɪzen'teɪʃn/ n représentation f; **make ~s to** protester auprès de.

representative /reprɪ'zentətɪv/ adj représentatif, typique (**of** de). ● n représentant/-e m/f.

repress /rɪ'pres/ vt réprimer.

reprieve /rɪ'priːv/ n (delay) sursis m; (pardon) grâce f. ● vt accorder un sursis à; gracier.

reprimand /'reprɪmɑːnd/ vt réprimander. ● n réprimande f.

reprisals /rɪ'praɪzlz/ npl représailles fpl.

reproach /rɪ'prəʊtʃ/ vt reprocher (**sb for sth** qch à qn). ● n reproche m.

reproduce /riːprə'djuːs/ vt/i (se) reproduire. **reproduction** n reproduction f. **reproductive** adj reproducteur.

reptile /'reptaɪl/ n reptile m.

republic /rɪ'pʌblɪk/ n république f. **republican** adj & n républicain/-e (m/f).

repudiate /rɪ'pjuːdɪeɪt/ vt répudier; (contract) refuser d'honorer.

reputable /'repjʊtəbl/ adj honorable, de bonne réputation.

reputation /repjʊ'teɪʃn/ n réputation f.

repute /rɪ'pjuːt/ n réputation f.

request /rɪ'kwest/ n demande f. ● vt demander (**of**, **from** à).

require /rɪ'kwaɪə(r)/ vt (of thing) demander; (of person) avoir besoin de; (demand, order) exiger. **required** adj requis. **requirement** n exigence f; (condition) condition f (requise).

rescue /'reskjuː/ vt sauver. ● n sauvetage m (**of** de); (help) secours m.

research /rɪ'sɜːtʃ/ n recherche(s) f(pl). ● vt/i faire des recherches (sur). **researcher** n chercheur/-euse m/f.

resemblance /rɪ'zembləns/ n ressemblance f. **resemble** vt ressembler à.

resent /rɪ'zent/ vt être indigné de, s'offenser de. **resentment** n ressentiment m.

reservation /rezə'veɪʃn/ n (doubt) réserve f; (booking) réservation f; (US) réserve f (indienne); **make a ~** réserver.

reserve /rɪ'zɜːv/ vt réserver. ● n (stock, land) réserve f; (Sport) remplaçant/-e m/f; **in ~** en réserve; **the ~s** (Mil) les réserves fpl. **reserved** adj (person, room) réservé.

reshuffle /riː'ʃʌfl/ vt (Pol) remanier. ● n (Pol) remaniement m (ministériel).

residence /'rezɪdəns/ n résidence f; (of students) foyer m; **in ~** (doctor) résidant.

resident /'rezɪdənt/ adj résidant; **be ~** résider. ● n habitant/-e m/f; (foreigner) résident/-e *m/f*; (in hotel) pensionnaire *m/f*. **residential** *adj* résidentiel.

resign /rɪˈzaɪn/ *vt* abandonner; (*job*) démissionner de. ● *vi* démissionner; ~ oneself to se résigner à. **resignation** *n* résignation *f*; (from job) démission *f*. **resigned** *adj* résigné.

resilience /rɪˈzɪlɪəns/ *n* élasticité *f*; ressort *m*.

resin /ˈrezɪn/ *n* résine *f*.

resist /rɪˈzɪst/ *vt/i* résister (à). **resistance** *n* résistance *f*. **resistant** *adj* (Med) rebelle; (*metal*) résistant.

resolution /rezəˈluːʃn/ *n* résolution *f*.

resolve /rɪˈzɒlv/ *vt* résoudre (**to do** faire). ● *n* résolution *f*.

resort /rɪˈzɔːt/ *vi* ~ to avoir recours à. ● *n* (recourse) recours *m*; (place) station *f*; **in the last** ~ en dernier ressort.

resource /rɪˈsɔːs/ *n* ressource *f*; ~s (wealth) ressources *fpl*. **resourceful** *adj* ingénieux.

respect /rɪˈspekt/ *n* respect *m*; (aspect) égard *m*; **with** ~ **to** à l'égard de, relativement à. ● *vt* respecter.

respectability /rɪspektəˈbɪlətɪ/ *n* respectabilité *f*. **respectable** *adj* respectable.

respectful /rɪˈspektfl/ *adj* respectueux.

respective /rɪˈspektɪv/ *adj* respectif.

respite /ˈrespaɪt/ *n* répit *m*.

respond /rɪˈspɒnd/ *vi* répondre (**to** à); ~ **to** (react to) réagir à. **response** *n* réponse *f*.

responsibility /rɪspɒnsəˈbɪlətɪ/ *n* responsabilité *f*. **responsible** *adj* responsable; (*job*) qui comporte des responsabilités.

responsive /rɪˈspɒnsɪv/ *adj* réceptif.

rest /rest/ *vt/i* (se) reposer; (lean) (s')appuyer (**on** sur); (be buried, lie) reposer; (remain) demeurer. ● *n* repos *m*; (support) support *m*; **have a** ~ se reposer; **the** ~ (remainder) le reste (**of** de); (other people) les autres.

restaurant /ˈrestrɒnt/ *n* restaurant *m*.

restless /ˈrestlɪs/ *adj* agité.

restoration /restəˈreɪʃn/ *n* rétablissement *m*; restauration *f*.

restore /rɪˈstɔː(r)/ *vt* rétablir; (*building*) restaurer; ~ **sth to sb** restituer qch à qn.

restrain /rɪˈstreɪn/ *vt* contenir; ~ **sb from** retenir qn de. **restrained** *adj* (moderate) mesuré; (in control of self) maître de soi.

restrict /rɪˈstrɪkt/ *vt* restreindre. **restriction** *n* restriction *f*.

rest room *n* (US) toilettes *fpl*.

result /rɪˈzʌlt/ *n* résultat *m*. ● *vi* résulter; ~ **in** aboutir à.

resume /rɪˈzjuːm/ *vt/i* reprendre.

résumé /ˈrezjuːmeɪ/ *n* résumé *m*; (of career: US) CV *m*, curriculum vitae *m*.

resurrect /rezəˈrekt/ *vt* ressusciter.

resuscitate /rɪˈsʌsɪteɪt/ *vt* réanimer.

retail /ˈriːteɪl/ *n* détail *m*. ● *adj & adv* au détail. ● *vt/i* (se) vendre (au détail). **retailer** *n* détaillant/-e *m/f*.

retain /rɪˈteɪn/ *vt* (hold back, remember) retenir; (keep) conserver.

retaliate /rɪˈtælɪeɪt/ *vi* riposter. **retaliation** *n* représailles *fpl*.

retch /retʃ/ *vi* avoir un haut-le-cœur.

retire /rɪˈtaɪə(r)/ *vi* (from work) prendre sa retraite; (withdraw) se retirer; (go to bed) se coucher. **retired** *adj* retraité. **retirement** *n* retraite *f*.

retort /rɪˈtɔːt/ *vt/i* répliquer. ● *n* réplique *f*.

retrace /riːˈtreɪs/ *vt* ~ **one's steps** revenir sur ses pas.

retract /rɪˈtrækt/ *vt/i* (se) rétracter.

retrain /riːˈtreɪn/ *vt/i* (se) recycler.

retreat /rɪˈtriːt/ *vi* (Mil) battre en retraite. ● *n* retraite *f*.

retrieval /rɪˈtriːvl/ *n* (Comput) extraction *f*. **retrieve** *vt* (*object*) récupérer; (*situation*) redresser; (*data*) extraire.

retrospect /ˈretrəʊspekt/ *n* **in** ~ rétrospectivement.

return /rɪˈtɜːn/ *vi* (come back) revenir; (go back) retourner; (go home) rentrer. ● *vt* (give back) rendre; (bring back) rapporter; (send back) renvoyer; (put back) remettre. ● *n* retour *m*; (yield) rapport *m*; ~s (Comm) bénéfices *mpl*; **in** ~ **for** en échange de. ~ **ticket** *n* allerretour *m*.

reunion /riːˈjuːnɪən/ *n* réunion *f*.

reunite /riːjuːˈnaɪt/ *vt* réunir.

rev /rev/ *n* (Auto Ⅱ) tour *m*. ● *vt/i* (*pt* **revved**) ~ (**up**) (engine Ⅱ) (s')emballer.

reveal /rɪˈviːl/ *vt* révéler; (allow to appear) laisser voir.

revelation /revə'leɪʃn/ n révélation f.

revenge /rɪ'vendʒ/ n vengeance f. ● vt venger.

revenue /'revənjuː/ n revenu m.

reverberate /rɪ'vɜːbəreɪt/ vi (sound, light) se répercuter.

reverend /'revərənd/ adj révérend.

reversal /rɪ'vɜːsl/ n renversement m; (of view) revirement m.

reverse /rɪ'vɜːs/ adj contraire, inverse. ● n contraire m; (back) revers m, envers m; (gear) marche f arrière. ● vt (situation, bracket) renverser; (order) inverser; (decision) annuler; ~ the charges appeler en PCV. ● vi (Auto) faire marche arrière.

review /rɪ'vjuː/ n (inspection, magazine) revue f; (of book) critique f. ● vt passer en revue; (situation) réexaminer; faire la critique de. **reviewer** n critique m.

revise /rɪ'vaɪz/ vt réviser; (text) revoir. **revision** n révision f.

revival /rɪ'vaɪvl/ n (of economy) reprise f; (of interest) regain m.

revive /rɪ'vaɪv/ vt (person, hopes) ranimer; (custom) rétablir. ● vi se ranimer.

revoke /rɪ'vəʊk/ vt révoquer.

revolt /rɪ'vəʊlt/ vt/i (se) révolter. ● n révolte f. **revolting** adj dégoûtant.

revolution /revə'luːʃn/ n révolution f.

revolve /rɪ'vɒlv/ vi tourner.

revolver /rɪ'vɒlvə(r)/ n revolver m.

revolving door n porte f à tambour.

reward /rɪ'wɔːd/ n récompense f. ● vt récompenser (for de). **rewarding** adj rémunérateur; (worthwhile) qui (en) vaut la peine.

rewind /riː'waɪnd/ vt (pt rewound) rembobiner.

rewire /riː'waɪə(r)/ vt refaire l'installation électrique de.

rhetorical /rɪ'tɒrɪkl/ adj (de) rhétorique; (question) de pure forme.

rheumatism /'ruːmətɪzəm/ n rhumatisme m.

rhinoceros /raɪ'nɒsərəs/ n (pl ~ es) rhinocéros m.

rhubarb /'ruːbɑːb/ n rhubarbe f.

rhyme /raɪm/ n rime f; (poem) vers mpl. ● vt/i (faire) rimer.

rhythm /'rɪðəm/ n rythme m. **rhythmic-(al)** adj rythmique.

rib /rɪb/ n côte f.

ribbon /'rɪbən/ n ruban m; **in ~s** en lambeaux.

rice /raɪs/ n riz m. **~ pudding** n riz m au lait.

rich /rɪtʃ/ adj riche.

rid /rɪd/ vt (pt rid; pres p ridding) débarrasser (of de); **get ~ of** se débarrasser de.

ridden /'rɪdn/ →RIDE.

riddle /'rɪdl/ n énigme f. ● vt ~ with (bullets) cribler de; (mistakes) bourrer de.

ride /raɪd/ vi (pt rode; pp ridden) aller (à bicyclette, à cheval); (in car) rouler; (on a horse as sport) monter à cheval. ● vt (a particular horse) monter; (distance) parcourir. ● n promenade f, tour m; (distance) trajet m; **give sb a ~** (US) prendre qn en voiture; **go for a ~** aller faire un tour (à bicyclette, à cheval). **rider** n cavalier/-ière m/f; (in horse race) jockey m; (cyclist) cycliste m/f; (motorcyclist) motocycliste m/f.

ridge /rɪdʒ/ n arête f, crête f.

ridiculous /rɪ'dɪkjʊləs/ adj ridicule.

riding /'raɪdɪŋ/ n équitation f.

rifle /'raɪfl/ n fusil m. ● vt (rob) dévaliser.

rift /rɪft/ n (crack) fissure f; (between people) désaccord m.

rig /rɪg/ vt (pt rigged) (equip) équiper; (election, match) truquer. ● n (for oil) derrick m. □ ~ out habiller; ~ up (arrange) arranger.

right /raɪt/ adj (morally) bon; (fair) juste; (best) bon, qu'il faut; (not left) droit; **be ~** (person) avoir raison (to de); (calculation, watch) être exact; **put ~** arranger, rectifier. ● n (entitlement) droit m; (not left) droite f; (not evil) le bien; **be in the ~** avoir raison; **on the ~** à droite. ● vt (a wrong, sth fallen) redresser. ● adv (not left) à droite; (directly) tout droit; (exactly) bien, juste; (completely) tout à fait; **~ away** tout de suite; **~ now** (at once) tout de suite; (at present) en ce moment.

righteous /'raɪtʃəs/ adj vertueux.

rightful /'raɪtfl/ adj légitime.

right-handed adj droitier.

rightly /'raɪtlɪ/ adv correctement; (with reason) à juste titre.

right of way n (Auto) priorité f.

right wing adj de droite.

rigid /ˈrɪdʒɪd/ adj rigide.

rigorous /ˈrɪɡərəs/ adj rigoureux.

rim /rɪm/ n bord m.

rind /raɪnd/ n (on cheese) croûte f; (on bacon) couenne f; (on fruit) écorce f.

ring[1] /rɪŋ/ n (hoop) anneau m; (jewellery) bague f; (circle) cercle m; (boxing) ring m; **(wedding)** ~ alliance f. ● vt entourer; (word in text) entourer d'un cercle.

ring[2] /rɪŋ/ vt/i (pt **rang**; pp **rung**) sonner; (of words) retentir; ~ **the bell** sonner. ● n sonnerie f; **give sb a** ~ donner un coup de fil à qn. □ ~ **back** rappeler; ~ **off** raccrocher; ~ **up** téléphoner (à). ~**tone** sonnerie f.

ring road n périphérique m.

rink /rɪŋk/ n patinoire f.

rinse /rɪns/ vt rincer; ~ **out** rincer. ● n rinçage m.

riot /ˈraɪət/ n émeute f; (of colours) profusion f; **run** ~ se déchaîner. ● vi faire une émeute.

rip /rɪp/ vt/i (pt **ripped**) (se) déchirer; **let** ~ (not check) laisser courir; ~ **off** 🅇 rouler. ● n déchirure f.

ripe /raɪp/ adj mûr. **ripen** vt/i mûrir.

rip-off n 🅇 vol m; arnaque f 🅇.

ripple /ˈrɪpl/ n ride f, ondulation f. ● vt/i (water) (se) rider.

rise /raɪz/ vi (pt **rose**; pp **risen**) (increase) monter, s'élever; (stand up, get up) se lever; (rebel) se soulever; (sun) se lever; (water) monter; ~ **up** se soulever. ● n (slope) pente f; (increase) hausse f; (in pay) augmentation f; (progress, boom) essor m; **give** ~ **to** donner lieu à.

risk /rɪsk/ n risque m; **at** ~ menacé. ● vt risquer; ~ **doing** (venture) se risquer à faire. **risky** adj risqué.

rite /raɪt/ n rite m; **last** ~**s** derniers sacrements mpl.

rival /ˈraɪvl/ n rival/-e m/f. ● adj rival; (claim) opposé. ● vt (pt **rivalled**) rivaliser avec.

river /ˈrɪvə(r)/ n rivière f; (flowing into sea) fleuve m. ● adj (fishing, traffic) fluvial.

rivet /ˈrɪvɪt/ n (bolt) rivet m. ● vt (pt **riveted**) river, riveter.

Riviera /rɪvɪˈeərə/ n **the (French)** ~ la Côte d'Azur.

road /rəʊd/ n route f; (in town) rue f; (small) chemin m; **the** ~ **to** (glory: fig) le chemin de. ● adj (sign, safety) routier. ~**-map** n carte f routière. ~ **rage** n violence f au volant. ~**worthy** adj en état de marche.

roam /rəʊm/ vi errer. ● vt (streets, seas) parcourir.

roar /rɔː(r)/ n hurlement m; (of lion, wind) rugissement m; (of lorry, thunder) grondement m. ● vt/i hurler; (lion, wind) rugir; (lorry, thunder) gronder; ~ **with laughter** rire aux éclats.

roast /rəʊst/ vt/i rôtir. ● n (meat) rôti m. ● adj rôti. ~ **beef** n rôti m de bœuf.

rob /rɒb/ vt (pt **robbed**) voler (**sb of sth** qch à qn); (bank, house) dévaliser; (deprive) priver (**of** de). **robber** n voleur/-euse m/f. **robbery** n vol m.

robe /rəʊb/ n (of judge) robe f; (dressinggown) peignoir m.

robin /ˈrɒbɪn/ n rouge-gorge m.

robot /ˈrəʊbɒt/ n robot m.

robust /rəʊˈbʌst/ adj robuste.

rock /rɒk/ n roche f; (rock face, boulder) rocher m; (hurled stone) pierre f; (sweet) sucre m d'orge; (Mus) rock m; **on the** ~**s** (drink) avec des glaçons; (marriage) en crise. ● vt/i (se) balancer; (shake) (faire) trembler; (child) bercer. ~**-climbing** n varappe f.

rocket /ˈrɒkɪt/ n fusée f.

rocking-chair n fauteuil m à bascule.

rocky /ˈrɒkɪ/ adj (**-ier, -iest**) (ground) rocailleux; (hill) rocheux; (shaky: fig) branlant.

rod /rɒd/ n (metal) tige f; (wooden) baguette f; (for fishing) canne f à pêche.

rode /rəʊd/ ➡**RIDE**.

roe /rəʊ/ n œufs mpl de poisson.

rogue /rəʊg/ n (dishonest) bandit m; (mischievous) coquin/-e m/f.

role /rəʊl/ n rôle m.

roll /rəʊl/ vt/i rouler; ~ **(about)** (child, dog) se rouler; **be** ~**ing (in money)** 🅇 rouler sur l'or. ● n rouleau m; (list) liste f; (bread) petit pain m; (of drum, thunder) roulement m; (of ship) roulis m. □ ~ **out** étendre; ~ **over** se retourner; ~ **up** (sleeves) retrousser.

roll-call n appel m.

roller /ˈrəʊlə(r)/ n rouleau m. ~ **blade** n patin m en ligne, roller m. ~**-coaster** n montagnes fpl russes. ~**-skate** n patin m à roulettes.

ROM abbr (**read-only memory**) mémoire f morte.

Roman /ˈrəʊmən/ adj & n romain/-e (m/f). ~ **Catholic** adj & n catholique (mf).

romance /rəʊˈmæns/ n (novel) roman m d'amour; (love) amour m; (affair) idylle f; (fig) poésie f.

Romania /rəʊˈmeɪnɪə/ n Roumanie f.

Romanian /rəʊˈmeɪnɪən/ adj roumain. ● n (person) Roumain/-e m/f; (language) roumain m.

romantic /rəʊˈmæntɪk/ adj (love) romantique; (of the imagination) romanesque.

roof /ruːf/ n toit m; (of mouth) palais m. ● vt recouvrir. ~**-rack** n galerie f. ~**-top** n toit m.

room /ruːm/ n pièce f; (bedroom) chambre f; (large hall) salle f; (space) place f; ~ **for manoeuvre** marge f de manœuvre. ~**-mate** n camarade mf de chambre.

roomy /ˈruːmɪ/ adj spacieux; (clothes) ample.

root /ruːt/ n racine f; (source) origine f; **take** ~ prendre racine. ● vt/i (s')enraciner. □ ~ **about** fouiller; ~ **for** (US 🄸) encourager; ~ **out** extirper.

rope /rəʊp/ n corde f; **know the** ~**s** être au courant. ● vt attacher; ~ **in** (person) enrôler.

rose¹ /rəʊz/ n rose f. ● →RISE.

rosé /ˈrəʊzeɪ/ n rosé m.

rosy /ˈrəʊzɪ/ adj (**-ier, -iest**) rose; (hopeful) plein d'espoir.

rot /rɒt/ vt/i (pt **rotted**) pourrir.

rota /ˈrəʊtə/ n liste f (de service).

rotary /ˈrəʊtərɪ/ adj rotatif.

rotate /rəʊˈteɪt/ vt/i (faire) tourner; (change round) alterner.

rotten /ˈrɒtn/ adj pourri; (tooth) gâté; (bad 🄸) mauvais, sale.

rough /rʌf/ adj (manners) rude; (to touch) rugueux; (ground) accidenté; (violent) brutal; (bad) mauvais; (estimate) approximatif. ● adv (live) à la dure.

roughage /ˈrʌfɪdʒ/ n fibres fpl.

roughly /ˈrʌflɪ/ adv rudement; (approximately) à peu près.

round /raʊnd/ adj rond. ● n (circle) rond m; (slice) tranche f; (of visits, drinks) tournée f; (competition) partie f, manche f; (boxing) round m; (of talks) série f; ~ **of applause** applaudissements mpl; **go the** ~**s** circuler. ● prep autour de; **she lives** ~ **here** elle habite par ici; ~ **the clock** vingt-quatre heures sur vingt-quatre. ● adv autour; ~ **about** (nearby) par ici; (fig) à peu près; **go** or **come** ~ (to a friend) passer chez; **enough to go** ~ assez pour tout le monde. ● vt (object) arrondir; (corner) tourner. □ ~ **off** terminer; ~ **up** rassembler.

roundabout /ˈraʊndəbaʊt/ n (in fairground) manège m; (for traffic) rondpoint m (à sens giratoire). ● adj indirect.

round trip n voyage m aller-retour.

round-up n rassemblement m; (of suspects) rafle f.

route /ruːt/ n itinéraire m, parcours m; (Naut, Aviat) route f.

routine /ruːˈtiːn/ n routine f. ● adj de routine.

row¹ /rəʊ/ n rangée f, rang m; **in a** ~ (consecutive) consécutif. ● vi ramer; (Sport) faire de l'aviron. ● vt ~ **a boat up the river** remonter la rivière à la rame.

row² /raʊ/ n (noise 🄸) tapage m; (quarrel 🄸) dispute f. ● vi 🄸 se disputer.

rowdy /ˈraʊdɪ/ adj (**-ier, -iest**) tapageur.

rowing /ˈrəʊɪŋ/ n aviron m. ~**-boat** n bateau m à rames.

royal /ˈrɔɪəl/ adj royal. **royalty** n famille f royale; **royalties** droits mpl d'auteur.

RSI abbr (repetitive strain injury) TMS m, trouble m musculo-squelettique.

rub /rʌb/ vt/i (pt **rubbed**) frotter; ~ **it in** insister, en rajouter. ● n friction f. □ ~ **out** (s')effacer.

rubber /ˈrʌbə(r)/ n caoutchouc m; (eraser) gomme f. ~ **band** n élastique m. ~ **stamp** n tampon m.

rubbish /ˈrʌbɪʃ/ n (refuse) ordures fpl; (junk) saletés fpl; (fig) bêtises fpl.

rubble /ˈrʌbl/ n décombres mpl.

ruby /'ru:bɪ/ n rubis m.

rucksack /'rʌksæk/ n sac m à dos.

rude /ru:d/ adj impoli, grossier; (improper) indécent; (blow) brutal.

ruffle /'rʌfl/ vt (hair) ébouriffer; (clothes) froisser; (person) contrarier. ● n (frill) ruche f.

rug /rʌg/ n petit tapis m.

rugby /'rʌgbɪ/ n rugby m.

rugged /'rʌgɪd/ adj (surface) rude, rugueux; (ground) accidenté; (character, features) rude.

ruin /'ru:ɪn/ n ruine f. ● vt (destroy) ruiner; (damage) abîmer; (spoil) gâter.

rule /ru:l/ n règle f; (regulation) règlement m; (Pol) gouvernement m; **as a ~** en règle générale. ● vt gouverner; (master) dominer; (decide) décider; **~ out** exclure. ● vi régner. **ruler** n dirigeant/-e m/f, gouvernant m; (measure) règle f.

ruling /'ru:lɪŋ/ adj (class) dirigeant; (party) au pouvoir. ● n décision f.

rum /rʌm/ n rhum m.

rumble /'rʌmbl/ vi gronder; (stomach) gargouiller. ● n grondement m; gargouillement m.

rumour, (US) **rumor** /'ru:mə(r)/ n bruit m, rumeur f; **there's a ~ that** le bruit court que.

rump /rʌmp/ n (of animal) croupe f; (of bird) croupion m; (steak) romsteck m.

run /rʌn/ vi (pt **ran**; pp **run**; pres p **running**) courir; (flow) couler; (pass) passer; (function) marcher; (melt) fondre; (extend) s'étendre; (of bus) circuler; (of play) se jouer; (last) durer; (of colour in washing) déteindre; (in election) être candidat. ● vt (manage) diriger; (event) organiser; (risk, race) courir; (house) tenir; (temperature, errand) faire; (Comput) exécuter. ● n course f; (journey) parcours m; (outing) promenade f; (rush) ruée f; (series) série f; (for chickens) enclos m; (in cricket) point m; **in the long ~** avec le temps; **on the ~** en fuite. □ **~ across** rencontrer par hasard; **~ away** s'enfuir; **~ down** descendre en courant; (of vehicle) renverser; (production) réduire progressivement; (belittle) dénigrer; **~ into** (hit) heurter; **~ off** (copies) tirer; **~ out** (be used up) s'épuiser; (of lease) expirer; **~ out of** manquer de;

~ over (of vehicle) écraser; (details) revoir; **~ through** regarder qch rapidement; **~ sth through sth** passer qch à travers qch; **~ up** (bill) accumuler.

runaway /'rʌnəweɪ/ n fugitif/-ive m/f. ● adj fugitif; (horse, vehicle) fou; (inflation) galopant.

rung /rʌŋ/ →RING². ● n (of ladder) barreau m.

runner /'rʌnə(r)/ n coureur/-euse m/f. **~ bean** n haricot m d'Espagne. **~-up** n second/-e m/f.

running /'rʌnɪŋ/ n course f à pied; (of business) gestion f; (of machine) marche f; **be in the ~ for** être sur les rangs pour. ● adj (commentary) suivi; (water) courant; **four days ~** quatre jours de suite.

runway /'rʌnweɪ/ n piste f.

rural /'rʊərəl/ adj rural.

rush /rʌʃ/ vi (move) se précipiter; (be in a hurry) se dépêcher. ● vt (person) bousculer; (Mil) prendre d'assaut; **~ to** envoyer d'urgence à. ● n ruée f; (haste) bousculade f; (plant) jonc m; **in a ~** pressé. **~-hour** n heure f de pointe.

Russia /'rʌʃə/ n Russie f.

Russian /'rʌʃn/ adj russe. ● n (person) Russe mf; (language) russe.

rust /rʌst/ n rouille f. ● vt/i rouiller.

rustle /'rʌsl/ vt/i (papers) froisser.

rusty /'rʌstɪ/ adj rouillé.

ruthless /'ru:θlɪs/ adj impitoyable.

rye /raɪ/ n seigle m.

Ss

sabbath /'sæbəθ/ n (Jewish) sabbat m; (Christian) jour m du seigneur.

sabbatical /sə'bætɪkl/ adj (Univ) sabbatique.

sabotage /'sæbətɑːʒ/ n sabotage m. ● vt saboter.

saccharin /'sækərɪn/ n saccharine f.

sack /sæk/ n (bag) sac m; **get the ~** être renvoyé. ● vt 🔢 renvoyer; (plunder) saccager. **sacking** n (cloth) toile f à sac; (dismissal 🔢) renvoi m.

sacrament /'sækrəmənt/ n sacrement m.

sacred /'seɪkrɪd/ adj sacré.

sacrifice /'sækrɪfaɪs/ n sacrifice m. ● vt sacrifier.

sad /sæd/ adj (**sadder, saddest**) triste.

saddle /'sædl/ n selle f. ● vt (horse) seller.

sadist /'seɪdɪst/ n sadique mf. **sadistic** adj sadique.

sadly /'sædlɪ/ adv tristement; (unfortunately) malheureusement.

sadness /'sædnɪs/ n tristesse f.

safe /seɪf/ adj (not dangerous) sans danger; (reliable) sûr; (out of danger) en sécurité; (after accident) sain et sauf; ~ **from** à l'abri de. ● n coffre-fort m.

safeguard /'seɪfgɑːd/ n sauvegarde f. ● vt sauvegarder.

safely /'seɪflɪ/ adv sans danger; (in safe place) en sûreté.

safety /'seɪftɪ/ n sécurité f. ~**-belt** n ceinture f de sécurité. ~**-pin** n épingle f de sûreté. ~**-valve** n soupape f de sûreté.

saffron /'sæfrən/ n safran m.

sag /sæg/ vi (pt **sagged**) (beam, mattress) s'affaisser; (flesh) être flasque.

sage /seɪdʒ/ n (herb) sauge f.

Sagittarius /sædʒɪ'teərɪəs/ n Sagittaire m.

said /sed/ →SAY.

sail /seɪl/ n voile f; (journey) tour m en bateau. ● vi (person) voyager en bateau; (as sport) faire de la voile; (set off) prendre la mer; ~ **across** traverser. ● vt (boat) piloter; (sea) traverser. **sailing-boat, sailing-ship** n voilier m.

sailor /'seɪlə(r)/ n marin m.

saint /seɪnt/ n saint/-e m/f.

sake /seɪk/ n **for the** ~ **of** pour.

salad /'sæləd/ n salade f.

salaried /'sælərɪd/ adj salarié.

salary /'sælərɪ/ n salaire m.

sale /seɪl/ n vente f; **for** ~ à vendre; **on** ~ en vente; (reduced) en solde; ~**s** (reductions) soldes mpl; ~**s assistant**, (US) ~**s clerk** vendeur/-euse m/f.

salesman /'seɪlzmən/ n (pl **-men**) (in shop) vendeur m; (traveller) représentant m.

saline /'seɪlaɪn/ adj salin. ● n sérum m physiologique.

saliva /sə'laɪvə/ n salive f.

salmon /'sæmən/ n inv saumon m.

salon /'sælɒn/ n salon m.

saloon /sə'luːn/ n (on ship) salon m; ~ **(car)** berline f.

salt /sɔːlt/ n sel m. ● vt saler. **salty** adj salé.

salutary /'sæljʊtrɪ/ adj salutaire.

salute /sə'luːt/ n salut m. ● vt saluer. ● vi faire un salut.

salvage /'sælvɪdʒ/ n sauvetage m; (of waste) récupération f. ● vt sauver; (for re-use) récupérer.

same /seɪm/ adj même (as que). ● pron **the** ~ le même, la même, les mêmes; **at the** ~ **time** en même temps; **the** ~ **(thing)** la même chose.

sample /'sɑːmpl/ n échantillon m; (of blood) prélèvement m. ● vt essayer; (food) goûter.

sanctimonious /sæŋktɪ'məʊnɪəs/ adj (pej) supérieur.

sanction /'sæŋkʃn/ n sanction f. ● vt sanctionner.

sanctity /'sæŋktətɪ/ n sainteté f.

sanctuary /'sæŋktʃʊərɪ/ n (safe place) refuge m; (Relig) sanctuaire m; (for animals) réserve f.

sand /sænd/ n sable m; ~**s** (beach) plage f.

sandal /'sændl/ n sandale f.

sandpaper /'sændpeɪpə(r)/ n papier m de verre. ● vt poncer.

sandpit /'sændpɪt/ n bac m à sable.

sandwich /'sænwɪdʒ/ n sandwich m; ~ **course** cours m avec stage pratique.

sandy /'sændɪ/ adj (beach) de sable; (soil) sablonneux; (hair) blond roux inv.

sane /seɪn/ adj (view) sensé; (person) sain d'esprit.

sang /sæŋ/ →SING.

sanitary /'sænɪtrɪ/ adj (clean) hygiénique; (system) sanitaire; ~ **towel** serviette f hygiénique.

sanitation /sænɪ'teɪʃn/ n installations fpl sanitaires.

sanity /'sænətɪ/ n équilibre m mental; (sense) bon sens m.

sank /sæŋk/ →SINK.

Santa (Claus) /'sæntə (klɔːz)/ n le père Noël.

sapphire /'sæfaɪə(r)/ n saphir m.

sarcasm /'sɑːkæzəm/ n sarcasme m. **sarcastic** adj sarcastique.

sash /sæʃ/ n (on uniform) écharpe f; (on dress) ceinture f.

sat /sæt/ →SIT.

satchel /'sætʃəl/ n cartable m.

satellite /'sætəlaɪt/ n & adj satellite (m); ~ **dish** antenne f parabolique.

satire /'sætaɪə(r)/ n satire f. **satirical** adj satirique.

satisfaction /sætɪs'fækʃn/ n satisfaction f.

satisfactory /sætɪs'fæktərɪ/ adj satisfaisant.

satisfy /'sætɪsfaɪ/ vt satisfaire; (convince) convaincre.

satphone /'sætfəʊn/ n téléphone m satellite.

saturate /'sætʃəreɪt/ vt saturer. **saturated** adj (wet) trempé.

Saturday /'sætədeɪ/ n samedi m.

sauce /sɔːs/ n sauce f.

saucepan /'sɔːspən/ n casserole f.

saucer /'sɔːsə(r)/ n soucoupe f.

Saudi Arabia /saʊdɪ ə'reɪbɪə/ n Arabie f saoudite.

sausage /'sɒsɪdʒ/ n (for cooking) saucisse f; (ready to eat) saucisson m.

savage /'sævɪdʒ/ adj (blow, temper) violent; (attack) sauvage. ● n sauvage mf. ● vt attaquer sauvagement.

save /seɪv/ vt sauver; (money) économiser; (time) gagner; (keep) garder; ~ **(sb) doing sth** éviter (à qn) de faire qch. ● n (football) arrêt m. **saver** n épargnant/-e m/f. **saving** n économie f. **savings** npl économies fpl.

saviour, (US) **savior** /'seɪvɪə(r)/ n sauveur m.

savour, (US) **savor** /'seɪvə(r)/ n saveur f. ● vt savourer. **savoury** adj (tasty) savoureux; (Culin) salé.

saw /sɔː/ →SEE. ● n scie f. ● vt (pt sawed; pp sawn or sawed) scier.

sawdust /'sɔːdʌst/ n sciure f.

saxophone /'sæksəfəʊn/ n saxophone m.

say /seɪ/ vt/i (pt said) dire; (prayer) faire. ● n have a ~ dire son mot; (in decision) avoir voix au chapitre. **saying** n proverbe m.

scab /skæb/ n croûte f.

scaffolding /'skæfəldɪŋ/ n échafaudage m.

scald /skɔːld/ vt (injure, cleanse) ébouillanter. ● n brûlure f.

scale /skeɪl/ n (for measuring) échelle f; (extent) étendue f; (Mus) gamme f; (on fish) écaille f; **on a small ~** sur une petite échelle; ~ **model** maquette f. ● vt (climb) escalader; ~ **down** réduire. **scales** npl (for weighing) balance f.

scallop /'skɒləp/ n coquille f Saint-Jacques.

scalp /skælp/ n cuir m chevelu.

scampi /'skæmpɪ/ npl (fresh) langoustines fpl; (breaded) scampi mpl.

scan /skæn/ vt (pt scanned) scruter; (quickly) parcourir. ● n (ultrasound) échographie f; (CAT) scanner m.

scandal /'skændl/ n scandale m; (gossip) potins mpl 🔟.

Scandinavia /skændɪ'neɪvɪə/ n Scandinavie f.

scanty /'skæntɪ/ adj (-ier, -iest) maigre; (clothing) minuscule.

scapegoat /'skeɪpgəʊt/ n bouc m émissaire.

scar /skɑː(r)/ n cicatrice f. ● vt (pt scarred) marquer.

scarce /skeəs/ adj rare. **scarcely** adv à peine.

scare /skeə(r)/ vt faire peur à; **be ~d** avoir peur. ● n peur f; **bomb ~** alerte f à la bombe. **scarecrow** n épouvantail m.

scarf /skɑːf/ n (pl scarves) écharpe f; (over head) foulard m.

scarlet /'skɑːlət/ adj écarlate; ~ **fever** scarlatine f.

scary /'skeərɪ/ adj (-ier, -iest) 🔟 qui fait peur.

scathing /'skeɪðɪŋ/ adj cinglant.

scatter /'skætə(r)/ vt (throw) éparpiller, répandre; (disperse) disperser. ● vi se disperser.

scavenge /'skævɪndʒ/ vi fouiller (dans les ordures). **scavenger** n (animal) charognard m.

scene /siːn/ n scène f; (of accident, crime) lieu m; (sight) spectacle m; **behind the ~s** en coulisse. **scenery** n paysage m; (Theat) décors mpl. **scenic** adj panoramique.

scent /sent/ n (perfume) parfum m; (trail) piste f. ● vt flairer; (make fragrant) parfumer.

sceptic /'skeptɪk/ n sceptique mf. **sceptical** adj sceptique. **scepticism** n scepticisme m.

schedule /'ʃedjuːl/, /'skedʒʊl/ n horaire m; (for job) planning m; **behind ~** en retard; **on ~** dans les temps. ● vt prévoir; **~d flight** vol m régulier.

scheme /skiːm/ n projet m; (dishonest) combine f; **pension ~** plan m de retraite. ● vi comploter.

schizophrenic /skɪtsəʊ'frenɪk/ adj & n schizophrène (mf).

scholar /'skɒlə(r)/ n érudit/-e m/f.

school /skuːl/ n école f; **go to ~** aller à l'école. ● adj (age, year, holidays) scolaire. **~boy** n élève m. **~girl** n élève f. **schooling** n scolarité f. **~teacher** n (primary) instituteur/-trice m/f; (secondary) professeur m.

science /'saɪəns/ n science f; **teach ~** enseigner les sciences. **scientific** adj scientifique. **scientist** n scientifique mf.

scissors /'sɪzəz/ npl ciseaux mpl.

scold /skəʊld/ vt gronder.

scoop /skuːp/ n (shovel) pelle f; (measure) mesure f; (for ice cream) cuillère f à glace; (news) exclusivité f.

scooter /'skuːtə(r)/ n (child's) trottinette f; (motor cycle) scooter m.

scope /skəʊp/ n étendue f; (competence) compétence f; (opportunity) possibilité f.

scorch /skɔːtʃ/ vt brûler; (iron) roussir.

score /skɔː(r)/ n score m; (Mus) partition f; **on that ~** à cet égard. ● vt marquer; (success) remporter. ● vi marquer un point; (football) marquer un but; (keep score) marquer les points. **scorer** n (Sport) marqueur m.

scorn /skɔːn/ n mépris m. ● vt mépriser.

Scorpio /'skɔːpɪəʊ/ n Scorpion m.

Scot /skɒt/ n écossais/-e m/f.

Scotland /'skɒtlənd/ n écosse f.

Scottish /'skɒtɪʃ/ adj écossais.

scoundrel /'skaʊndrəl/ n gredin m.

scour /'skaʊə(r)/ vt (pan) récurer; (search) parcourir. **scourer** n tampon m à récurer.

scourge /skɜːdʒ/ n fléau m.

scout /skaʊt/ n éclaireur m. ● vi ~ **around for** rechercher.

scowl /skaʊl/ n air m renfrogné. ● vi prendre un air renfrogné.

scramble /'skræmbl/ vi (clamber) grimper. ● vt (eggs) brouiller. ● n (rush) course f.

scrap /skræp/ n petit morceau m; **~s** (of metal, fabric) déchets mpl; (of food) restes mpl; (fight 🔢) bagarre f. ● vt (pt **scrapped**) abandonner; (car) détruire.

scrape /skreɪp/ vt gratter; (damage) érafler. ● vi ~ **against** érafler. □ ~ **through** réussir de justesse.

scrap: ~paper n papier m brouillon. **~yard** n casse f.

scratch /skrætʃ/ vt/i (se) gratter; (with claw, nail) griffer; (graze) érafler; (mark) rayer. ● n (on body) égratignure f; (on surface) éraflure f; **start from ~** partir de zéro; **up to ~** à la hauteur. ~ **card** n jeu m de grattage.

scrawl /skrɔːl/ n gribouillage m. ● vt/i gribouiller.

scrawny /'skrɔːnɪ/ adj (**-ier, -iest**) décharné.

scream /skriːm/ vt/i crier. ● n cri m (perçant).

screech /skriːtʃ/ vi (scream) hurler; (tyres) crisser. ● n cri m strident; (of tyres) crissement m.

screen /skriːn/ n écran m; (folding) paravent m. ● vt masquer; (protect) protéger; (film) projeter; (candidates) filtrer; (Med) faire subir un test de dépistage. **screening** n (cinema) projection f; (Med) dépistage m.

screen: ~**play** n scénario m. ~ **saver** n protecteur m d'écran.

screw /skruː/ n vis f. ● vt visser; ~ **up** (eyes) plisser; (ruin 🄸) cafouiller 🄸. ~**driver** n tournevis m.

scribble /'skrɪbl/ vt/i griffonner. ● n griffonnage m.

script /skrɪpt/ n script m; (of play) texte m.

scroll /skrəʊl/ n rouleau m. ● vt/i (Comput) (faire) défiler. ~ **bar** n barre f de défilement.

scrounge /skraʊndʒ/ 🄸 vt (favour) quémander; (cigarette) piquer 🄸; ~ **money from sb** taper de l'argent à qn. ● vi ~ **off sb** vivre sur le dos de qn.

scrub /skrʌb/ n (land) broussailles fpl. ● vt/i (pt **scrubbed**) nettoyer (à la brosse), frotter.

scruffy /'skrʌfɪ/ adj (-**ier**, -**iest**) 🄸 dépenaillé.

scrum /skrʌm/ n (rugby) mêlée f.

scruple /'skruːpl/ n scrupule m.

scrutinize /'skruːtɪnaɪz/ vt scruter. **scrutiny** n examen m minutieux.

scuba-diving /'skuːbədaɪvɪŋ/ n plongée f sousmarine.

scuffle /'skʌfl/ n bagarre f.

sculpt /skʌlpt/ vt/i sculpter. **sculptor** n sculpteur m.

sculpture /'skʌlptʃə(r)/ n sculpture f.

scum /skʌm/ n (on liquid) mousse f; (people: pej) racaille f.

scurry /'skʌrɪ/ vi se précipiter, courir (**for** pour chercher); ~ **off** se sauver.

sea /siː/ n mer f; **at** ~ en mer; **by** ~ par mer. ● adj (air) marin; (bird) de mer; (voyage) par mer. ~**food** n fruits mpl de mer. ~**gull** n mouette f.

seal /siːl/ n (animal) phoque m; (insignia) sceau m; (with wax) cachet m. ● vt sceller; cacheter; (stick down) coller. □ ~ **off** (area) boucler.

seam /siːm/ n (in cloth) couture f; (of coal) veine f.

search /sɜːtʃ/ vt/i (examine) fouiller; (seek) chercher; (study) examiner; (Comput) rechercher. ● n fouille f; (quest) recherches fpl; (Comput) recherche f; **in** ~ **of** à la recherche de. ~ **engine** n (Internet) moteur m de

recherche. ~**light** n projecteur m. ~-**warrant** n mandat m de perquisition.

sea: ~**shell** n coquillage m. ~**shore** n (coast) littoral m; (beach) plage f.

seasick /'siːsɪk/ adj **be** ~ avoir le mal de mer.

seaside /'siːsaɪd/ n bord m de la mer.

season /'siːzn/ n saison f; ~ **ticket** carte f d'abonnement. ● vt assaisonner. **seasonal** adj saisonnier. **seasoning** n assaisonnement m.

seat /siːt/ n siège m; (place) place f; (of trousers) fond m; **take a** ~ asseyez-vous. ● vt (put) placer; **the room** ~**s 30** la salle peut accueillir 30 personnes. ~-**belt** n ceinture f (de sécurité)

seaweed /'siːwiːd/ n algue f marine.

secluded /sɪ'kluːdɪd/ adj retiré.

seclusion /sɪ'kluːʒn/ n isolement m.

second¹ /'sekənd/ adj deuxième, second; **a** ~ **chance** une nouvelle chance; **have** ~ **thoughts** avoir des doutes. ● n deuxième m/f, second/-e m/f; (unit of time) seconde f; ~ **s** (food) rab m. 🄸 ● adv (in race) deuxième; (secondly) deuxièmement. ● vt (proposal) appuyer.

second² /sɪ'kɒnd/ vt (transfer) détacher (**to** à).

secondary /'sekəndrɪ/ adj secondaire; ~**school** n lycée m, école f secondaire.

second-best n pis-aller m.

second-class adj (Rail) de deuxième classe; (post) au tarif lent.

second hand n (on clock) trotteuse f.

second-hand adj & adv (article) d'occasion; (information) de seconde main.

secondly /'sekəndlɪ/ adv deuxièmement.

second-rate adj médiocre.

secrecy /'siːkrəsɪ/ n secret m.

secret /'siːkrɪt/ adj secret. ● n secret m; **in** ~ en secret.

secretarial /sekrə'teərɪəl/ adj (work) de secrétaire.

secretary /'sekrətrɪ/ n secrétaire mf; S ~ **of State** ministre m; (US) ministre m des Affaires étrangères.

secrete /sɪ'kriːt/ vt (Med) sécréter; (hide) cacher.

secretive /'siːkrətɪv/ adj secret. **secretly** adv secrètement.

sect /sekt/ n secte f. **sectarian** adj sectaire.

section /'sekʃn/ n partie f; (in store) rayon m; (of newspaper) rubrique f; (of book) passage m.

sector /'sektə(r)/ n secteur m.

secular /'sekjʊlə(r)/ adj (school) laïque; (art, music) profane.

secure /sɪ'kjʊə(r)/ adj (safe) sûr; (job, marriage) stable; (knot, lock) solide; (window) bien fermé; (feeling) de sécurité; (person) sécurisé. ● vt attacher; (obtain) s'assurer; (ensure) assurer.

security /sɪ'kjʊərətɪ/ n (safety) sécurité f; (for loan) caution f; **~ guard** vigile m.

sedate /sɪ'deɪt/ adj calme. ● vt donner un sédatif à. **sedative** n sédatif m.

seduce /sɪ'djuːs/ vt séduire. **seducer** n séducteur/-trice m/f. **seduction** f. **seductive** adj séduisant.

see /siː/ vt/i (pt saw; pp seen) voir; see **you (soon)!** à bientôt!; **~ing that** vu que. □ **~ out** (person) raccompagner à la porte; **~ through** (deception) déceler; (person) percer à jour; **~ sth through** mener qch à bonne fin; **~ to** s'occuper de; **~ to it that** veiller à ce que.

seed /siːd/ n graine f; (collectively) graines fpl; (origin: fig) germe m; (tennis) tête f de série. **seedling** n plant m.

seek /siːk/ vt (pt sought) chercher.

seem /siːm/ vi sembler; he **~s to think** il a l'air de croire.

seen /siːn/ ➡SEE.

seep /siːp/ vi suinter; **~ into** s'infiltrer dans.

see-saw /'siːsɔː/ n tapecul m. ● vt osciller.

seethe /siːð/ vi **~ with** (anger) bouillir de; (people) grouiller de.

segment /'segmənt/ n segment m; (of orange) quartier m.

segregate /'segrɪgeɪt/ vt séparer.

seize /siːz/ vt saisir; (territory, prisoner) s'emparer de. ● vi **~ on** (chance) saisir; **~ up** (engine) se gripper.

seizure /'siːʒə(r)/ n (Med) crise f.

seldom /'seldəm/ adv rarement.

select /sɪ'lekt/ vt sélectionner. ● adj privilégié. **selection** n sélection f. **selective** adj sélectif.

self /self/ n (pl **selves**) moi m; (on cheque) moi-même. **~-assured** adj plein d'assurance. **~-catering** adj (holiday) en location. **~-centred**, (US) **~-centered** adj égocentrique. **~-confident** adj sûr de soi. **~-conscious** adj timide. **~-contained** adj (flat) indépendant. **~-control** n sangfroid m. **~-defence** n autodéfense f; (Jur) légitime défense f. **~-employed** adj qui travaille à son compte. **~-esteem** n amour-propre m. **~-governing** adj autonome. **~-indulgent** adj complaisant. **~-interest** n intérêt m personnel.

selfish /'selfɪʃ/ adj égoïste.

selfless /'selflɪs/ adj désintéressé.

self: ~-portrait n autoportrait m. **~-reliant** adj autosuffisant. **~-respect** n respect m de soi. **~-righteous** adj satisfait de soi. **~-sacrifice** n abnégation f. **~-satisfied** adj satisfait de soi. **~-seeking** adj égoïste. **~-service** n & adj libre-service (m).

sell /sel/ vt/i (pt sold) vendre; **~ well** se vendre bien. □ **~ off** liquider; **~ out** (items) se vendre; **have sold out** avoir tout vendu.

Sellotape® /'seləʊteɪp/ n scotch® m.

sell-out n (betrayal) ▣ revirement m; **be a ~** (show) afficher complet.

semester /sɪ'mestə(r)/ n (Univ) semestre m.

semicircle /'semɪsɜːkl/ n demi-cercle m.

semicolon /semɪ'kəʊlən/ n point-virgule m.

semi-detached /semɪdɪ'tætʃt/ adj **~ house** maison f jumelée.

semifinal /semɪ'faɪnl/ n demi-finale f.

seminar /'semɪnɑː(r)/ n séminaire m.

semolina /semə'liːnə/ n semoule f.

senate /'senɪt/ n sénat m. **senator** n sénateur m.

send /send/ vt/i (pt sent) envoyer. □ **~ away** (dismiss) renvoyer; **~ (away or off) for** commander (par la poste); **~ back** renvoyer; **~ for** (person, help) envoyer chercher; **~ up** ▣ parodier.

senile /'siːnaɪl/ adj sénile.

senior /'siːnɪə(r)/ adj plus âgé (to que); (in rank) haut placé; **be ~ to sb** être le supérieur de qn. ● n aîné/-e m/f. **~**

citizen *n* personne *f* âgée. ~ **school** *n* lycée *m*.

sensation /sen'seɪʃn/ *n* sensation *f*. **sensational** *adj* sensationnel.

sense /sens/ *n* sens *m*; (*mental impression*) sentiment *m*; (*common sense*) bon sens *m*; ~**s** (*mind*) raison *f*; **there's no ~ in doing** cela ne sert à rien de faire; **make ~** avoir un sens; **make ~ of** comprendre. ● *vt* (pres-)sentir. **senseless** *adj* insensé; (Med) sans connaissance.

sensible /'sensəbl/ *adj* raisonnable; (*clothing*) pratique.

sensitive /'sensətɪv/ *adj* sensible (**to** à); (*issue*) difficile.

sensory /'sensərɪ/ *adj* sensoriel.

sensual /'senʃʊəl/ *adj* sensuel. **sensuality** *n* sensualité *f*.

sensuous /'senʃʊəs/ *adj* sensuel.

sent /sent/ ➡**SEND**.

sentence /'sentəns/ *n* phrase *f*; (*punishment*; Jur) peine *f*. ● *vt* ~ **to** condamner à.

sentiment /'sentɪmənt/ *n* sentiment *m*. **sentimental** *adj* sentimental.

sentry /'sentrɪ/ *n* sentinelle *f*.

separate¹ /'sepərət/ *adj* (*piece*) à part; (*issue*) autre; (*sections*) différent; (*organizations*) distinct.

separate² /'sepəreɪt/ *vt/i* (se) séparer.

separately /'sepərətlɪ/ *adv* séparément.

separation /sepə'reɪʃn/ *n* séparation *f*.

September /sep'tembə(r)/ *n* septembre *m*.

septic /'septɪk/ *adj* (*wound*) infecté; ~ **tank** fosse *f* septique.

sequel /'si:kwəl/ *n* suite *f*.

sequence /'si:kwəns/ *n* (*order*) ordre *m*; (*series*) suite *f*; (*in film*) séquence *f*.

Serb /sɜ:b/ *adj* serbe. ● *n* (*person*) Serbe *mf*; (Ling) serbe *m*.

Serbia /'sɜ:bɪə/ *n* Serbie *f*.

sergeant /'sɑ:dʒənt/ *n* (Mil) sergent *m*; (*policeman*) brigadier *m*.

serial /'sɪərɪəl/ *n* feuilleton *m*. ● *adj* (Comput) série *inv*.

series /'sɪəri:z/ *n inv* série *f*.

serious /'sɪərɪəs/ *adj* sérieux *f*; (*accident*, *crime*) grave.

seriously /'sɪərɪəslɪ/ *adv* sérieusement; (*ill*) gravement; **take ~** prendre au sérieux.

sermon /'sɜ:mən/ *n* sermon *m*.

serpent /'sɜ:pənt/ *n* serpent *m*.

serrated /sɪ'reɪtɪd/ *adj* dentelé.

serum /'sɪərəm/ *n* sérum *m*.

servant /'sɜ:vənt/ *n* domestique *mf*.

serve /sɜ:v/ *vt/i* servir; faire; (*transport*, *hospital*) desservir; ~ **as/to** servir de/à; ~ **a purpose** être utile; ~ **a sentence** (Jur) purger une peine. ● *n* (tennis) service *m*.

server /'sɜ:və(r)/ *n* serveur *m*; **remote ~** téléserveur *m*.

service /'sɜ:vɪs/ *n* service *m*; (*maintenance*) révision *f*; (Relig) office *m*; ~**s** (Mil) forces *fpl* armées. ● *vt* (*car*) réviser. ~**area** *n* (Auto) aire *f* de services. ~ **charge** *n* service *m*. ~ **station** *n* station-service *f*.

session /'seʃn/ *n* séance *f*; **be in ~** (Jur) tenir séance.

set /set/ *vt* (*pt*) **set**; *pres p* **setting** placer; (*table*) mettre; (*limit*) fixer; (*clock*) mettre à l'heure; (*example*, *task*) donner; (TV), (cinema) situer; ~ **fire to** mettre le feu à; ~ **free** libérer; ~ **to music** mettre en musique. ● *vi* (*sun*) se coucher; (*jelly*) prendre; ~ **sail** partir. ● *n* (*of chairs*, *stamps*) série *f*; (*of knives*, *keys*) jeu *m*; (*of people*) groupe *m*; (TV), (radio) poste *m*; (Theat) décor *m*; (tennis) set *m*; (mathematics) ensemble *m*. ● *adj* (*time*, *price*) fixe; (*procedure*) bien determiné; (*meal*) à prix fixe; (*book*) au programme; ~ **against sth** opposé à; **be ~ on doing** tenir absolument à faire. □ ~ **about** se mettre à; ~ **back** (*delay*) retarder; (*cost* 🔢) coûter; ~ **in** (take hold) s'installer, commencer; ~ **off** *or* **out** partir; ~ **off** (*panic*, *riot*) déclencher; (*bomb*) faire exploser; ~ **out** (*state*) présenter; (*arrange*) disposer; ~ **out to do sth** chercher à faire qch; ~ **up** (*stall*) monter; (*equipment*) assembler; (*experiment*) préparer; (*company*) créer; (*meeting*) organiser. ~**-back** *n* revers *m*.

settee /se'ti:/ *n* canapé *m*.

setting /'setɪŋ/ *n* cadre *m*; (*on dial*) position *f*.

settle /'setl/ *vt* (arrange, pay) régler; (*date*) fixer; (*nerves*) calmer. ● *vi* (come to rest) (*bird*) se poser; (*dust*) se déposer; (*live*) s'installer. □ ~ **down** se calmer; (*marry etc.*) se ranger; ~ **for** accepter; ~ **in** s'installer; ~ **up** (**with**) régler.

settlement /'setlmənt/ *n* règlement *m* (*of* de); (*agreement*) accord *m*; (*place*) colonie *f.*

settler /'setlə(r)/ *n* colon *m.*

seven /'sevn/ *adj & n* sept (*m*).

seventeen /sevn'ti:n/ *adj & n* dix-sept (*m*).

seventh /'sevnθ/ *adj & n* septième (*mf*).

seventy /'sevntɪ/ *adj & n* soixante-dix (*m*).

sever /'sevə(r)/ *vt* (*cut*) couper; (*relations*) rompre.

several /'sevrəl/ *adj & pron* plusieurs; ~ **of us** plusieurs d'entre nous.

severe /sɪ'vɪə(r)/ *adj* (*harsh*) sévère; (*serious*) grave.

sew /səʊ/ *vt/i* (*pt* **sewed**; *pp* **sewn** or **sewed**) coudre.

sewage /'su:ɪdʒ/ *n* eaux *fpl* usées.

sewer /'su:ə(r)/ *n* égout *m.*

sewing /'səʊɪŋ/ *n* couture *f.*
~**-machine** *n* machine *f* à coudre.

sewn /səʊn/ ⇒**SEW.**

sex /seks/ *n* sexe *m*; **have** ~ avoir des rapports (sexuels). ● *adj* sexuel. **sexist** *adj & n* sexiste (*mf*). **sexual** *adj* sexuel.

shabby /'ʃæbɪ/ *adj* (**-ier, -iest**) (*place, object*) miteux; (*person*) habillé de façon miteuse; (*treatment*) mesquin.

shack /ʃæk/ *n* cabane *f.*

shade /ʃeɪd/ *n* ombre *f*; (*of colour, opinion*) nuance *f*; (*for lamp*) abat-jour *m inv*; **a** ~ **bigger** légèrement plus grand. ● *vt* (*tree*) ombrager; (*hat*) projeter une ombre sur.

shadow /'ʃædəʊ/ *n* ombre *f.* ● *vt* (*follow*) filer. **S**~ **Cabinet** *n* cabinet *m* fantôme.

shady /'ʃeɪdɪ/ *adj* (**-ier, -iest**) ombragé; (*dubious*) véreux.

shaft /ʃɑːft/ *n* (*of tool*) manche *m*; (*of arrow*) tige *f*; (*in machine*) axe *m*; (*of mine*) puits *m*; (*of light*) rayon *m.*

shake /ʃeɪk/ *vt* (*pt* **shook**; *pp* **shaken**) secouer; (*bottle*) agiter; (*belief*) ébranler; ~ **hands with** serrer la main à; ~ **one's head** dire non de la tête. ● *vi* trembler. ● *n* secousse *f*; **give sth a** ~ secouer qch. □ ~ **off** se débarrasser

de. ~**-up** *n* (Pol) remaniement *m.*

shaky /'ʃeɪkɪ/ *adj* (**-ier, -iest**) (*hand, voice*) tremblant; (*ladder*) branlant; (*weak*: fig) instable.

shall /ʃæl/ *v aux* **I** ~ **do** je ferai; **we** ~ **see** nous verrons; ~ **we go. . . ?** si on allait . . . ?

shallow /'ʃæləʊ/ *adj* peu profond; (fig) superficiel.

shame /ʃeɪm/ *n* honte *f*; **it's a** ~ c'est dommage. ● *vt* faire honte à.

shampoo /ʃæm'pu:/ *n* shampooing *m.*
● *vt* faire un shampooing à.

shandy /'ʃændɪgæf/ *n* panaché *m.*

shan't ⇒**SHALL NOT.**

shanty /'ʃæntɪ/ *n* (*shack*) baraque *f*; ~ **town** bidonville *m.*

shape /ʃeɪp/ *n* forme *f.* ● *vt* (*clay*) modeler; (*rock*) façonner; (*future*: fig) déterminer; ~ **sth into balls** faire des boules avec qch. ● *vi* ~ **up** (*plan*) prendre tournure; (*person*) faire des progrès.

share /ʃeə(r)/ *n* part *f*; (Comm) action *f.* ● *vt/i* partager; (*feature*) avoir en commun. ~**holder** *n* actionnaire *mf.*
~**ware** *n* (Comput) logiciel *m* contributif.

shark /ʃɑːk/ *n* requin *m.*

sharp /ʃɑːp/ *adj* (*knife*) tranchant; (*pin*) pointu; (*point, angle, cry*) aigu; (*person, mind*) vif; (*tone*) acerbe. ● *adv* (*stop*) net; (*sing, play*) trop haut; **six o'clock** ~ six heures pile. ● *n* (Mus) dièse *m.*

sharpen /'ʃɑːpən/ *vt* aiguiser; (*pencil*) tailler.

shatter /'ʃætə(r)/ *vt* (*glass*) fracasser; (*hope*) briser. ● *vi* (*glass*) voler en éclats.

shave /ʃeɪv/ *vt/i* (se) raser. ● *n* **have a** ~ se raser. **shaver** *n* rasoir *m* électrique.

shaving /'ʃeɪvɪŋ/ *n* (*of wood*) copeau *m.* ● *adj* (*cream, foam, gel*) à raser.

shawl /ʃɔːl/ *n* châle *m.*

she /ʃiː/ *pron* elle. ● *n* (*animal*) femelle *f.*

shear /ʃɪə(r)/ *vt* (*pp* **shorn** or **sheared**) (*sheep*) tondre; ~ **off** se détacher.

shears /ʃɪəz/ *npl* cisaille *f.*

shed /ʃed/ *n* remise *f.* ● *vt* (*pt* **shed**; *pres p* **shedding**) perdre; (*light, tears*) répandre.

sheen /ʃiːn/ *n* lustre *m.*

sheep /ʃiːp/ n inv mouton m. **~-dog** n chien m de berger.

sheepish /ˈʃiːpɪʃ/ adj penaud.

sheepskin /ˈʃiːpskɪn/ n peau f de mouton.

sheer /ʃɪə(r)/ adj pur; (steep) à pic; (fabric) très fin. ● adv à pic.

sheet /ʃiːt/ n drap m; (of paper) feuille f; (of glass, ice) plaque f.

shelf /ʃelf/ n (pl **shelves**) étagère f; (in shop, fridge) rayon m; (in oven) plaque f.

shell /ʃel/ n coquille f; (on beach) coquillage m; (of building) carcasse f; (explosive) obus m. ● vt (nut) décortiquer; (peas) écosser; (Mil) bombarder.

shellfish /ˈʃelfɪʃ/ npl (lobster etc.) crustacés mpl; (mollusc) coquillages mpl.

shelter /ˈʃeltə(r)/ n abri m. ● vt/i (s')abriter; (give lodging to) donner asile à.

shelve /ʃelv/ vt (plan) mettre en suspens.

shepherd /ˈʃepəd/ n berger m; **~'s pie** hachis m Parmentier. ● vt (people) guider.

sherry /ˈʃerɪ/ n xérès m.

shield /ʃiːld/ n bouclier m; (screen) écran m. ● vt protéger.

shift /ʃɪft/ vt/i (se) déplacer, bouger; (exchange, alter) changer de. ● n changement m; (workers) équipe f; (work) poste m; **~ work** travail m posté, travail m par roulement.

shifty /ˈʃɪftɪ/ adj (**-ier, -iest**) louche.

shimmer /ˈʃɪmə(r)/ vi chatoyer. ● n chatoiement m.

shin /ʃɪn/ n tibia m.

shine /ʃaɪn/ vt (pt **shone**) (torch) braquer (on sur). ● vi (light, sun, hair) briller; (brass) reluire. ● n lustre m.

shingle /ˈʃɪŋɡl/ n (pebbles) galets mpl; (on roof) bardeau m.

shingles /ˈʃɪŋɡlz/ npl (Med) zona m.

shiny /ˈʃaɪnɪ/ adj (**-ier, -iest**) brillant.

ship /ʃɪp/ n bateau m, navire m. ● vt (pt **shipped**) transporter. **shipment** n (by sea) cargaison f; (by air, land) chargement m. **shipping** n (ships) navigation f. **~wreck** n épave f; (event) naufrage m.

shirt /ʃɜːt/ n chemise f; (woman's) chemisier m.

shiver /ˈʃɪvə(r)/ vi frissonner. ● n frisson m.

shock /ʃɒk/ n choc m; (Electr) décharge f; **in ~** en état de choc; **~ absorber** amortisseur m. ● adj (result) choc inv; (tactics) de choc. ● vt choquer.

shoddy /ˈʃɒdɪ/ adj (**-ier, -iest**) mal fait; (behaviour) mesquin.

shoe /ʃuː/ n chaussure f; (of horse) fer m; (brake) ~ sabot m (de frein). ● vt (pt **shod**; pres p **shoeing**) (horse) ferrer. **~lace** n lacet m. **~ size** n pointure f.

shone /ʃɒn/ ➡SHINE.

shook /ʃʊk/ ➡SHAKE.

shoot /ʃuːt/ vt (pt **shot**) (gun) tirer un coup de; (bullet) tirer; (missile, glance) lancer; (person) tirer sur; (kill) abattre; (execute) fusiller; (film) tourner. ● vi tirer (at sur). ● n (Bot) pousse f. □ **~ down** abattre; **~ out** (rush) sortir en vitesse; **~ up** (spurt) jaillir; (grow) pousser vite.

shooting /ˈʃuːtɪŋ/ n (killing) meurtre m (par arme à feu) **hear ~** entendre des coups de feu.

shop /ʃɒp/ n magasin m; (small) boutique f; (workshop) atelier m. ● vi (pt **shopped**) faire ses courses; **~ around** comparer les prix. **~ assistant** n vendeur/-euse m/f. **~-floor** n (workers) ouvriers mpl. **~keeper** n commerçant/-e m/f. **~lifter** n voleur/-euse m/f à l'étalage.

shopper /ˈʃɒpə(r)/ n acheteur/-euse m/f.

shopping /ˈʃɒpɪŋ/ n (goods) achats mpl; **go ~** (for food) faire les courses; (for clothes etc.) faire les magasins. **~ bag** n sac m à provisions. **~ centre**, (US) **~ center** n centre m commercial.

shop window n vitrine f.

shore /ʃɔː(r)/ n côte f, rivage m; **on ~** à terre.

short /ʃɔːt/ adj court; (person) petit; (brief) court, bref; (curt) brusque; **be ~ (of)** manquer (de); **everything ~ of** tout sauf; **nothing ~ of** rien de moins que; **cut ~** écourter; **cut sb ~** interrompre qn; **fall ~ of** ne pas arriver à; **he is called Tom for ~** son diminutif est Tom; **in ~** en bref. ● adv (stop) net. ● n (Electr) court-circuit m; (film) courtmétrage m; **~s** (trousers) short m.

shortage /ˈʃɔːtɪdʒ/ n manque m.

short: ~**bread** n sablé m. ~**-change**
vt (cheat) rouler 🔲. ~ **circuit** n court-
circuit m. ~**coming** n défaut m. ~ **cut**
n raccourci m.

shorten /'ʃɔːtn/ vt raccourcir.

shortfall /'ʃɔːfɔːl/ n déficit m.

shorthand /'ʃɔːthænd/ n sténographie
f; ~ **typist** sténodactylo f.

short: ~ **list** n liste f des candidats
choisis. ~**lived** adj de courte durée.

shortly /'ʃɔːtlɪ/ adv bientôt.

short: ~**-sighted** adj myope.
~**-staffed** adj à court de personnel;
~ **story** n nouvelle f. ~**-term** adj à
court terme.

shot /ʃɒt/ ➡SHOOT. ● n (firing, attempt) coup m de feu; (person) tireur
m; (bullet) balle f; (photograph) photo
f; (injection) piqûre f; **like a** ~ sans
hésiter. ~**gun** n fusil m de chasse.

should /ʃʊd/ v aux devoir; **you** ~ **help**
me vous devriez m'aider; **I** ~ **have**
stayed j'aurais dû rester; **I** ~ **like to**
j'aimerais bien; **if he** ~ **come** s'il
venait.

shoulder /'ʃəʊldə(r)/ n épaule f. ● vt
(responsibility) endosser; (burden) se
charger de. ~ **bag** n sac m à bandoulière. ~ **blade** n omoplate f.

shout /ʃaʊt/ n cri m. ● vt/i crier (at
après); ~ **sth out** lancer qch à
haute voix.

shove /ʃʌv/ n give sth a ~ pousser
qch. ● vt/i pousser; ~ **off!** 🔲 tire-
toi! 🔲.

shovel /'ʃʌvl/ n pelle f. ● vt (pt shov-
elled) pelleter.

show /ʃəʊ/ vt (pt showed; pp shown)
montrer; (dial, needle) indiquer; (put
on display) exposer; (film) donner;
(conduct) conduire; ~ **sb in/out** faire
entrer/sortir qn. ● vi (be visible) se
voir. ● n (exhibition) exposition f, salon
m; (Theat) spectacle m; (cinema)
séance f; **for** ~ pour l'effet; **on** ~ exposé.
□ ~ **off** faire le fier/la fière; ~ **sth/sb**
off exhiber qch/qn; ~ **up** se voir; (appear) se montrer; ~ **sb up** 🔲 faire
honte à qn.

shower /'ʃaʊə(r)/ n douche f; (of rain)
averse f. ● vt ~ **with** couvrir de. ● vi
se doucher.

showing /'ʃəʊɪŋ/ n performance f;
(cinema) séance f.

show-jumping n concours m
hippique.

shown /ʃəʊn/ ➡SHOW.

show: ~**-off** n m'as-tu-vu mf inv. 🔲
~**room** n salle f d'exposition.

shrank /ʃræŋk/ ➡SHRINK.

shrapnel /'ʃræpnl/ n éclats mpl d'obus.

shred /ʃred/ n lambeau m; (least
amount: fig) parcelle f. ● vt (pt **shred-**
ded) déchiqueter; (Culin) râper.

shrewd /ʃruːd/ adj (person) habile;
(move) astucieux.

shriek /ʃriːk/ n hurlement m. ● vt/i
hurler.

shrill /ʃrɪl/ adj (voice) perçant; (tone)
strident.

shrimp /ʃrɪmp/ n crevette f.

shrine /ʃraɪn/ n (place) lieu m de pèlerinage.

shrink /ʃrɪŋk/ vt/i (pt shrank; pp
shrunk) rétrécir; (lessen) diminuer; ~
from reculer devant.

shrivel /'ʃrɪvl/ vt/i (pt shrivelled) (se)
ratatiner.

shroud /ʃraʊd/ n linceul m. ● vt (veil)
envelopper.

Shrove Tuesday n mardi m gras.

shrub /ʃrʌb/ n arbuste m.

shrug /ʃrʌg/ vt (pt shrugged) ~ **one's**
shoulders hausser les épaules; ~ **sth**
off ignorer qch.

shrunk /ʃrʌŋk/ ➡SHRINK.

shudder /'ʃʌdə(r)/ vi frémir. ● n fré-
missement m.

shuffle /'ʃʌfl/ vt (feet) traîner; (cards)
battre. ● vi traîner les pieds.

shun /ʃʌn/ vt (pt shunned) fuir.

shut /ʃʌt/ vt (pt shut; pres p shutting)
fermer. ● vi (door) se fermer; (shop)
fermer. □ ~ **in** or **up** enfermer; ~ **up**
🔲 se taire; ~ **sb up** faire taire qn.

shutter /'ʃʌtə(r)/ n volet m; (Photo)
obturateur m.

shuttle /'ʃʌtl/ n (bus) navette f; ~ **ser-**
vice navette f. ● vi faire la navette.
● vt transporter.

shuttlecock /'ʃʌtlkɒk/ n (badminton)
volant m.

shy /ʃaɪ/ adj timide. ● vi ~ **away from**
se tenir à l'écart de.

sibling /'sɪblɪŋ/ n frère/sœur m/f.

sick /sɪk/ adj malade; (humour) macabre; (mind) malsain; **be** ~ (vomit)

vomir; **be ~ of** ⊤ en avoir assez or marre de ⊤; **feel ~** avoir mal au cœur. **~leave** n congé m de maladie.

sickly /'sɪklɪ/ adj (**-ier,-iest**) (person) maladif; (taste, smell) écœurant.

sickness /'sɪknɪs/ n maladie f.

sick-pay n indemnité f de maladie.

side /saɪd/ n côté m; (of road, river) bord m; (of hill, body) flanc m; (Sport) équipe f; (TV ⊤) chaîne f; **~ by ~** côte à côte. ● adj latéral. ● vi **~ with** se ranger du côté de. **~ board** n buffet m. **~effect** n effet m secondaire. **~light** n (Auto) feu m de position. **~line** n activité f secondaire. **~show** n attraction f. **~step** vt (pt) **-stepped** éviter. **~street** n rue f latérale. **~track** vt fourvoyer. **~ walk** n (US) trottoir m.

sideways /'saɪdweɪz/ adj (look) de travers. ● adv (move) latéralement; (look at) de travers.

siding /'saɪdɪŋ/ n voie f de garage.

sidle /'saɪdl/ vi s'avancer furtivement (up to vers).

siege /siːdʒ/ n siège m.

siesta /sɪ'estə/ n sieste f.

sieve /sɪv/ n tamis m; (for liquids) passoire f. ● vt tamiser.

sift /sɪft/ vt tamiser. ● vi **~ through** examiner.

sigh /saɪ/ n soupir m. ● vt/i soupirer.

sight /saɪt/ n vue f; (scene) spectacle m; (on gun) mire f; **at** or **on ~** à vue; **catch ~ of** apercevoir; **in ~** visible; **lose ~ of** perdre de vue. ● vt apercevoir.

sightseeing /'saɪtsiːɪŋ/ n tourisme m.

sign /saɪn/ n signe m; (notice) panneau m. ● vt/i signer. ◻ **~ on** (as unemployed) pointer au chômage; **~ up** (s')engager.

signal /'sɪɡnl/ n signal m. ● vt (pt) **signalled** (gesture) faire signe (**that** que); (indicate) indiquer.

signatory /'sɪɡnətrɪ/ n signataire mf.

signature /'sɪɡnətʃə(r)/ n signature f; **~ tune** indicatif m.

significance /sɪɡ'nɪfɪkəns/ n importance f; (meaning) signification f. **significant** adj important; (meaningful) significatif. **significantly** adv (much) sensiblement.

signify /'sɪɡnɪfaɪ/ vt signifier.

signpost /'saɪnpəʊst/ n panneau m indicateur.

silence /'saɪləns/ n silence m. ● vt faire taire.

silent /'saɪlənt/ adj silencieux; (film) muet. **silently** adv silencieusement.

silhouette /sɪluː'et/ n silhouette f. ● vt **be ~d against** se profiler contre.

silicon /'sɪlɪkən/ n silicium m; **~ chip** puce f électronique.

silk /sɪlk/ n soie f.

silly /'sɪlɪ/ adj (**-ier, -iest**) bête.

silver /'sɪlvə(r)/ n argent m; (silverware) argenterie f. ● adj en argent.

SIM card /'sɪmkɑːd/ n carte f SIM.

similar /'sɪmɪlə(r)/ adj semblable (**to** à). **similarity** n ressemblance f. **similarly** adv de même.

simile /'sɪmɪlɪ/ n comparaison f.

simmer /'sɪmə(r)/ vt/i (soup) mijoter; (water) (laisser) frémir.

simple /'sɪmpl/ adj simple.

simplicity /sɪm'plɪsətɪ/ n simplicité f.

simplify /'sɪmplɪfaɪ/ vt simplifier.

simplistic /sɪm'plɪstɪk/ adj simpliste.

simply /'sɪmplɪ/ adv simplement; (absolutely) absolument.

simulate /'sɪmjʊleɪt/ vt simuler.

simultaneous /sɪml'teɪnɪəs/ adj simultané.

sin /sɪn/ n péché m. ● vi (pt **sinned**) pécher.

---

since /sɪns/

● preposition

····▸ depuis; **I haven't seen him ~ Monday** je ne l'ai pas vu depuis lundi; **I've been waiting ~ yesterday** j'attends depuis hier; **she had been living in Paris ~ 1985** elle habitait Paris depuis 1985.

● conjunction

····▸ (in time expressions) depuis que; **~ she's been working here** depuis qu'elle travaille ici; **~ she left** depuis qu'elle est partie or depuis son départ.

····▸ (because) comme; **~ he was ill, he couldn't go** comme il était malade, il ne pouvait pas y aller.

● adverb

····▸ depuis; **he hasn't been seen ~ on** ne l'a pas vu depuis.

sincere /sɪnˈsɪə(r)/ adj sincère. **sincerely** adv sincèrement. **sincerity** n sincérité f.

sinful /ˈsɪnfl/ adj immoral; ~ **man** pécheur m.

sing /sɪŋ/ vt/i (pt **sang**; pp **sung**) chanter.

singe /sɪndʒ/ vt (pres p **singeing**) brûler légèrement; (with iron) roussir.

singer /ˈsɪŋə(r)/ n chanteur/-euse m/f.

single /ˈsɪŋgl/ adj seul; (not double) simple; (unmarried) célibataire; (room, bed) pour une personne; (ticket) simple; **in** ~ **file** en file indienne. ● n (ticket) aller simple m; (record) 45 tours m inv; ~**s** (tennis) simple m. ● vt ~ **out** choisir. ~**-handed** adj tout seul. ~**-minded** adj tenace. ~ **parent** n parent m isolé.

singular /ˈsɪŋgjʊlə(r)/ n singulier m. ● adj (strange) singulier; (noun) au singulier.

sinister /ˈsɪnɪstə(r)/ adj sinistre.

sink /sɪŋk/ vt (pt **sank**; pp **sunk**) (boat) couler; (well) forer; (post) enfoncer. ● vi (boat) couler; (sun, level) baisser; (wall) s'effondrer. ● n (in kitchen) évier m; (wash-basin) lavabo m. □ ~ **in** (news) faire son chemin.

sinner /ˈsɪnə(r)/ n pécheur/-eresse m/f.

sip /sɪp/ n petite gorgée f. ● vt (pt **sipped**) boire à petites gorgées.

siphon /ˈsaɪfn/ n siphon m. ● vt ~ **off** siphonner.

sir /sɜː(r)/ n Monsieur m; Sir (title) Sir m.

siren /ˈsaɪərən/ n sirène f.

sirloin /ˈsɜːlɔɪn/ n aloyau m.

sister /ˈsɪstə(r)/ n sœur f; (nurse) infirmière f en chef. ~**-in-law** n (pl ~**s-in-law**) belle-sœur f.

sit /sɪt/ vt/i (pt **sat**; pres p **sitting**) (s')asseoir; (committee) siéger; ~ **(for)** (exam) se présenter à; **be** ~**ting** être assis. □ ~ **around** ne rien faire; ~ **down** s'asseoir.

site /saɪt/ n emplacement m; **(building)** ~ chantier m. ● vt construire.

sitting /ˈsɪtɪŋ/ n séance f; (in restaurant) service m. ~**-room** n salon m.

situate /ˈsɪtjʊeɪt/ vt situer; **be** ~**d** être situé. **situation** n situation f.

six /sɪks/ adj & n six (m).

sixteen /sɪkˈstiːn/ adj & n seize (m).

sixth /sɪksθ/ adj & n sixième (mf).

sixty /ˈsɪkstɪ/ adj & n soixante (m).

size /saɪz/ n dimension f; (of person, garment) taille f; (of shoes) pointure f; (of sum, salary) montant m; (extent) ampleur f. □ ~ **up** (person) se faire une opinion de; (situation) évaluer. **sizeable** adj assez grand.

skate /skeɪt/ n patin m; (fish) raie f. ● vi patiner.

skateboard /ˈskeɪtbɔːd/ n skateboard m, planche f à roulettes. ● vi faire du skateboard.

skating /ˈskeɪtbɔːd/ n patinage m.

skeleton /ˈskelɪtn/ n squelette m; ~ **staff** effectifs mpl minimums.

sketch /sketʃ/ n esquisse f; (hasty) croquis m; (Theat) sketch m. ● vt faire une esquisse ou un croquis de. ● vi faire des esquisses.

sketchy /ˈsketʃɪ/ adj (**-ier, -iest**) (details) insuffisant; (memory) vague.

skewer /ˈskjuːə(r)/ n brochette f.

ski /skiː/ n ski m. ● adj de ski. ● vi (pt **ski'd** or **skied**; pres p **skiing**) skier; (go skiing) faire du ski.

skid /skɪd/ vi (pt **skidded**) déraper. ● n dérapage m.

skier /ˈskiːə(r)/ n skieur/-euse m/f.

skiing /ˈskiːɪŋ/ n ski m.

ski jump n saut m à ski.

skilful /ˈskɪlfl/ adj habile.

ski lift n remontée f mécanique.

skill /skɪl/ n habileté f; (craft) compétence f; ~**s** connaissances fpl. **skilled** adj (worker) qualifié; (talented) consommé.

skim /skɪm/ vt (pt **skimmed**) écumer; (milk) écrémer; (pass over) effleurer. ● vi ~ **through** parcourir.

skimpy /ˈskɪmpɪ/ adj (clothes) étriqué.

skin /skɪn/ n peau f. ● vt (pt **skinned**) (animal) écorcher; (fruit) éplucher.

skinny /ˈskɪnɪ/ adj (**-ier, -iest**) 🔲 maigre.

skip /skɪp/ vi (pt **skipped**) sautiller; (with rope) sauter à la corde. ● vt (page, class) sauter. ● n petit saut m; (container) benne f.

skipper /ˈskɪpə(r)/ n capitaine m.

skirmish /ˈskɜːmɪʃ/ n escarmouche f.

skirt /skɜːt/ n jupe f. ● vt contourner. **skirting-board** n plinthe f.

skittle /'skɪtl/ n quille f.

skull /skʌl/ n crâne m.

sky /skaɪ/ n ciel m. ~-**blue** adj & n bleu ciel m inv. ~ **marshal** n garde m armé (à bord d'un avion.) ~**scraper** n gratte-ciel m inv.

slab /slæb/ n (of stone) dalle f.

slack /slæk/ adj (not tight) détendu; (person) négligent; (period) creux. ● n (in rope) mou m. ● vi se relâcher.

slacken /'slækən/ vt (rope) donner du mou à; (grip) relâcher; (pace) réduire. ● vi (grip, rope) se relâcher; (activity) ralentir; (rain) se calmer.

slam /slæm/ vt/i (pt **slammed**) (door) claquer; (throw) flanquer; (criticize 🆄) critiquer. ● n (noise) claquement m.

slander /'slɑːndə(r)/ n (offence) diffamation f; (statement) calomnie f. ● vt calomnier; (Jur) diffamer. **slanderous** adj diffamatoire.

slang /slæŋ/ n argot m.

slant /slɑːnt/ vt/i (faire) pencher; (news) présenter sous un certain jour. ● n inclinaison f; (bias) angle m. **slanted** adj (biased) orienté; (sloping) en pente.

slap /slæp/ vt (pt **slapped**) (strike) donner une tape à; (face) gifler; (put) flanquer 🆄. ● n claque f; (on face) gifle f. ● adv tout droit.

slapdash /'slæpdæʃ/ adj (person) brouillon 🆄; (work) bâclé 🆄.

slash /slæʃ/ vt (picture, tyre) taillader; (face) balafrer; (throat) couper; (fig) réduire (radicalement). ● n lacération f.

slat /slæt/ n (in blind) lamelle f; (on bed) latte f.

slate /sleɪt/ n ardoise f. ● vt 🆄 taper sur 🆄.

slaughter /'slɔːtə(r)/ vt massacrer; (animal) abattre. ● n massacre m; abattage m.

slave /sleɪv/ n esclave mf. ● vi trimer 🆄. **slavery** n esclavage m.

sleazy /'sliːzɪ/ adj (-ier, -iest) 🆄 (story) scabreux; (club) louche.

sledge /sledʒ/ n luge f; (horse-drawn) traîneau m.

sleek /sliːk/ adj (hair) lisse, brillant; (shape) élégant.

sleep /sliːp/ n sommeil m; **go to** ~ s'endormir. ● vi (pt **slept**) dormir; (spend the night) coucher; ~ **in** faire

la grasse matinée. ● vt loger.

sleeper /'sliːpə(r)/ n (Rail) (berth) couchette f; (on track) traverse f.

sleeping-bag n sac m de couchage.

sleeping-pill n somnifère m.

sleep-walker n somnambule mf.

sleepy /'sliːpɪ/ adj (-ier, -iest) somnolent; **be** ~ avoir sommeil.

sleet /sliːt/ n neige f fondue.

sleeve /sliːv/ n manche f; (of record) pochette f; **up one's** ~ en réserve.

sleigh /sleɪ/ n traîneau m.

slender /'slendə(r)/ adj (person) mince; (majority) faible.

slept /slept/ →SLEEP.

slice /slaɪs/ n tranche f. ● vt couper (en tranches).

slick /slɪk/ adj (adept) habile; (insincere) roublard 🆄. ● n (oil) ~ marée f noire.

slide /slaɪd/ vt/i (pt **slid**) glisser; ~ **into** (go silently) se glisser dans. ● n glissade f; (fall: fig) baisse f; (in playground) toboggan m; (for hair) barrette f; (Photo) diapositive f.

sliding /'slaɪdɪŋ/ adj (door) coulissant; ~ **scale** échelle f mobile.

slight /slaɪt/ adj petit, léger; (slender) mince; (frail) frêle. ● vt (insult) offenser. ● n affront m. **slightest** adj moindre. **slightly** adv légèrement, un peu.

slim /slɪm/ adj (**slimmer, slimmest**) mince. ● vi (pt **slimmed**) maigrir.

slime /slaɪm/ n dépôt m gluant; (on riverbed) vase f. **slimy** adj visqueux; (fig) servile.

sling /slɪŋ/ n (weapon, toy) fronde f; (bandage) écharpe f. ● vt (pt **slung**) jeter, lancer.

slip /slɪp/ vt/i (pt **slipped**) glisser; ~**ped disc** hernie f discale; ~ **sb's mind** échapper à qn. ● n (mistake) erreur f; (petticoat) combinaison f; (paper) bout m de papier; ~ **of the tongue** lapsus m. ▢ ~ **away** s'esquiver; ▢ **into** (go) se glisser dans; (clothes) mettre; ▢ **up** 🆄 faire une gaffe 🆄.

slipper /'slɪpə(r)/ n pantoufle f.

slippery /'slɪpərɪ/ adj glissant.

slip road n bretelle f.

slit /slɪt/ n fente f. ● vt (pt **slit**; pres p **slitting**) déchirer; ~ **sth open** ouvrir qch; ~ **sb's throat** égorger qn.

slither /ˈslɪðə(r)/ vi glisser.

sliver /ˈslɪvə(r)/ n (of glass) éclat m; (of soap) reste m.

slobber /ˈslɒbə(r)/ vi 🔲 baver.

slog /slɒg/ 🔲 vt (pt slogged) (hit) frapper dur. ● vi (work) bosser 🔲. ● n (work) travail m dur.

slogan /ˈsləʊgən/ n slogan m.

slope /sləʊp/ vi être en pente; (handwriting) pencher. ● n pente f; (of mountain) flanc m.

sloppy /ˈslɒpɪ/ adj (-ier, -iest) (food) liquide; (work) négligé; (person) négligent.

slosh /slɒʃ/ vt 🔲 répandre; (hit 🔲) frapper. ● vi clapoter.

slot /slɒt/ n fente f. ● vt/i (pt slotted) (s')insérer.

sloth /sləʊθ/ n paresse f.

slot-machine n distributeur m automatique; (for gambling) machine f à sous.

slouch /slaʊtʃ/ vi être avachi.

Slovakia /sləˈvækɪə/ n Slovaquie f.

Slovenia /sləˈviːnɪə/ n Slovénie f.

slovenly /ˈslʌvnlɪ/ adj débraillé.

slow /sləʊ/ adj lent; be ~ (clock) retarder; in ~ motion au ralenti. ● adv lentement. ● vt/i ralentir. slowly adv lentement. slowness n lenteur f.

sludge /slʌdʒ/ n vase f.

slug /slʌg/ n (mollusc) limace f; (bullet 🔲) balle f; (blow 🔲) coup m.

sluggish /ˈslʌgɪʃ/ adj (person) léthargique; (circulation) lent.

slum /slʌm/ n taudis m.

slump /slʌmp/ n (Econ) effondrement m; (in support) baisse f. ● vi (demand, trade) chuter; (economy) s'effondrer; (person) s'affaler.

slung slʌŋ// ➡SLING.

slur /slɜː(r)/ vt/i (pt slurred) (words) mal articuler. ● n calomnie f (on sur).

slush /slʌʃ/ n (snow) neige f fondue. ~ fund n caisse f noire.

sly /slaɪ/ adj (crafty) rusé; (secretive) sournois. ● n on the ~ en cachette.

smack /smæk/ n tape f; (on face) gifle f. ● vt donner une tape à; gifler. ● vi ~ of sth sentir qch. ● adv 🔲 tout droit.

small /smɔːl/ adj petit. ● n ~ of the back creux m des reins. ● adv (cut) menu. ~ ad n petite annonce f. ~

business n petite entreprise f. ~ **change** n petite monnaie f. ~**pox** n variole f. ~ **print** n petits caractères mpl. ~ **talk** n banalités fpl.

smart /smɑːt/ adj élégant; (clever 🔲) malin, habile; (restaurant) chic inv; (Comput) intelligent. ● vi (wound) brûler.

smarten /ˈsmɑːtn/ vt/i ~ (up) embellir; ~ (oneself) up s'arranger.

smash /smæʃ/ vt/i (se) briser, (se) fracasser; (opponent, record) pulvériser. ● n (noise) fracas m; (blow) coup m; (car crash) collision f; (hit record 🔲) tube m. 🔲

smashing /ˈsmæʃɪŋ/ adj 🔲 épatant.

SME abbr (small and medium enterprises) PME.

smear /smɪə(r)/ vt (stain) tacher; (coat) enduire; (discredit: fig) diffamer. ● n tache f; (effort to discredit) propos m diffamatoire; ~ (test) frottis m.

smell /smel/ n odeur f; (sense) odorat m. ● vt/i (pt smelt or smelled) sentir; ~ of sentir. smelly adj qui sent mauvais.

smelt /smelt/ ➡SMELL.

smile /smaɪl/ n sourire m. ● vi sourire.

smiley /ˈsmaɪlɪ/ n (Internet) binette f.

smirk /smɜːk/ n petit sourire m satisfait.

smitten /ˈsmɪtn/ adj (in love) fou d'amour.

smog /smɒg/ n smog m.

smoke /sməʊk/ n fumée f; have a ~ fumer. ● vt/i fumer. **smoked** adj fumé. **smokeless** adj (fuel) non polluant. **smoker** n fumeur/-euse m/f. **smoky** adj (air) enfumé.

smooth /smuːð/ adj lisse; (movement) aisé; (manners) onctueux; (flight) sans heurts. ● vt lisser; (process) faciliter.

smoothly /ˈsmuːðlɪ/ adv (move, flow) doucement; (brake, start) en douceur; go ~ marcher bien.

smother /ˈsmʌðə(r)/ vt (stifle) étouffer; (cover) couvrir.

smoulder /ˈsməʊldə(r)/ vi (lit) se consumer; (fig) couver.

smudge /smʌdʒ/ n trace f. ● vt/i (ink) (s')étaler.

smug /smʌg/ adj (smugger, smuggest) suffisant.

smuggle /ˈsmʌɡl/ vt passer (en contrebande). **smuggler** n contrebandier/-ière m/f. **smuggling** n contrebande f.

smutty /ˈsmʌtɪ/ adj grivois.

snack /snæk/ n casse-croûte m inv.

snag /snæɡ/ n inconvénient m; (in cloth) accroc m.

snail /sneɪl/ n escargot m.

snake /sneɪk/ n serpent m.

snap /snæp/ vt/i (pt **snapped**) (whip, fingers) (faire) claquer; (break) (se) casser net; (say) dire sèchement. ● n claquement m; (Photo) photo f. ● adj soudain. □ ~ **up** (buy) sauter sur.

snapshot /ˈsnæpʃɒt/ n photo f.

snare /sneə(r)/ n piège m.

snarl /snɑːl/ vi gronder (en montrant les dents). ● n grondement m. ~-**up** n embouteillage m.

snatch /snætʃ/ vt (grab) attraper; (steal) voler; (opportunity) saisir; ~ sth from sb arracher qch à qn. ● n (theft) vol m; (short part) fragment m.

sneak /sniːk/ vi aller furtivement. ● n 🄸 rapporteur/-euse m/f.

sneer /snɪə(r)/ n sourire m méprisant. ● vi sourire avec mépris.

sneeze /sniːz/ n éternuement m. ● vi éternuer.

snide /snaɪd/ adj narquois.

sniff /snɪf/ vt/i renifler. ● n reniflement m.

snigger /ˈsnɪɡə(r)/ n ricanement m. ● vi ricaner.

snip /snɪp/ vt (pt **snipped**) couper.

sniper /ˈsnaɪpə(r)/ n tireur m embusqué.

snippet /ˈsnɪpɪt/ n bribe f.

snivel /ˈsnɪvl/ vi (pt **snivelled**) pleurnicher.

snob /snɒb/ n snob mf.

snooker /ˈsnuːkə(r)/ n snooker m.

snoop /snuːp/ vi 🄸 fourrer son nez partout.

snooty /ˈsnuːtɪ/ adj (-ier, -iest) 🄸 snob inv, hautain.

snooze /snuːz/ n petit somme m. ● vi sommeiller.

snore /snɔː(r)/ n ronflement m. ● vi ronfler.

snorkel /ˈsnɔːkl/ n tuba m.

snort /snɔːt/ n grognement m. ● vi (person) grogner; (horse) s'ébrouer.

snout /snaʊt/ n museau m.

snow /snəʊ/ n neige f. ● vi neiger; be ~ed under with être submergé de.

snowball /ˈsnəʊbɔːl/ n boule f de neige. ● vi faire boule de neige.

snow: ~**board** n snowboard m. ~**boarding** n surf m des neiges. ~-**bound** adj bloqué par la neige. ~**drift** n congère f. ~**drop** n perce-neige m or f inv. ~**flake** n flocon m de neige. ~**man** n (pl -**men**) bonhomme m de neige. ~-**plough** n chasse-neige m inv.

snub /snʌb/ vt (pt **snubbed**) rembarrer. ● n rebuffade f.

snuffle /ˈsnʌfl/ vi renifler.

snug /snʌɡ/ adj (**snugger, snuggest**) (cosy) confortable; (tight) bien ajusté.

snuggle /ˈsnʌɡl/ vi se pelotonner.

so /səʊ/ adv si, tellement; (thus) ainsi; ~ am I moi aussi; ~ good as aussi bon que; **that is** ~ c'est ça; **I think** ~ je pense que oui; **five or** ~ environ cinq; ~ **as to** de manière à; ~ **far** jusqu'ici; ~ **long!** 🄸 à bientôt!; ~ **many,** ~ **much** tant (de); ~ **that** pour que. ● conj donc, alors.

soak /səʊk/ vt/i (faire) tremper (**in** dans). □ ~ **in** pénétrer; ~ **up** absorber. **soaking** adj trempé.

soap /səʊp/ n savon m. ● vt savonner. ~ **opera** n feuilleton m. ~ **powder** n lessive f.

soar /sɔː(r)/ vi monter (en flèche).

sob /sɒb/ n sanglot m. ● vi (pt **sobbed**) sangloter.

sober /ˈsəʊbə(r)/ adj qui n'a pas bu d'alcool; (serious) sérieux. ● vi ~ **up** dessoûler.

soccer /ˈsɒkə(r)/ n football m.

sociable /ˈsəʊʃəbl/ adj sociable.

social /ˈsəʊʃl/ adj social. ● n réunion f (amicale), fête f.

socialism /ˈsəʊʃəlɪzəm/ n socialisme m. **socialist** adj & n socialiste (mf).

socialize /ˈsəʊʃəlaɪz/ vi se mêler aux autres; ~ **with** fréquenter.

socially /ˈsəʊʃəlɪ/ adv socialement; (meet) en société.

social: ~ **security** n aide f sociale. ~ **worker** n travailleur/-euse m/f social/-e.

society /sə'saɪətɪ/ n société f.

sociological /səusɪə'lɒdʒɪkl/ adj socio-
logique. **sociologist** n sociologue mf.
sociology n sociologie f.

sock /sɒk/ n chaussette f. ● vt (hit 🄸)
flanquer un coup (de poing) à.

socket /'sɒkɪt/ n (for lamp) douille f;
(Electr) prise f (de courant); (of eye)
orbite f.

soda /'səudə/ n soude f; **~(-water)** eau
f de Seltz.

sodden /'sɒdn/ adj détrempé.

sofa /'səufə/ n canapé m. **~ bed** n
canapé-lit m.

soft /sɒft/ adj (gentle, lenient) doux;
(not hard) doux, mou; (heart, wood)
tendre; (silly) ramolli. **~ drink** n boisson f non alcoolisée.

soften /'sɒfn/ vt/i (se) ramollir; (tone
down, lessen) (s')adoucir.

soft spot n to have a **~ for sb** avoir
un faible pour qn.

software /'sɒftweə(r)/ n logiciel m.

soggy /'sɒgɪ/ adj (-ier, -iest) (ground)
détrempé; (food) ramolli.

soil /sɔɪl/ n sol m, terre f. ● vt/i (se)
salir.

sold /səuld/ ⇒SELL. ● adj **~ out**
épuisé.

solder /'səuldə(r)/ n soudure f. ● vt
souder.

soldier /'səuldʒə(r)/ n soldat m. ● vi **~
on** 🄸 persévérer.

sole /səul/ n (of foot) plante f; (of shoe)
semelle f; (fish) sole f. ● adj unique,
seul. **solely** adv uniquement.

solemn /'sɒləm/ adj solennel.

solicitor /sə'lɪsɪtə(r)/ n notaire m; (for
court and police work) ≈ avocat/-
e m/f.

solid /'sɒlɪd/ adj solide; (not hollow)
plein; (gold) massif; (mass) compact;
(meal) substantiel. ● n solide m; **~s**
(food) aliments mpl solides.

solidarity /sɒlɪ'dærətɪ/ n solidarité f.

solidify /sə'lɪdɪfaɪ/ vt/i (se) solidifier.

solitary /'sɒlɪtrɪ/ adj (alone) solitaire;
(only) seul.

solo /'səuləu/ n solo m. ● adj (Mus) solo
inv; (flight) en solitaire.

soluble /'sɒljubl/ adj soluble.

solution /sə'luːʃn/ n solution f.

solve /sɒlv/ vt résoudre.

solvent /'sɒlvənt/ adj (Comm) solvable. ● n (dis)solvant m.

---

some /sʌm, səm/

● determiner

····▸ (unspecified amount) du/de
l'/de la/des; **I have to buy ~
bread** je dois acheter du pain;
have ~ water prenez de l'eau; **~
sweets** des bonbons.

····▸ (certain) certains/certaines; **~
people say that** certains disent que.

····▸ (unknown) un/une; **~ man
came to the house** un homme
est venu à la maison.

····▸ (considerable amount) **we
stayed there for ~ time** nous
sommes restés là assez longtemps; **it will take ~ doing** ça
ne va pas être facile à faire.

➡ In front of a plural adjective des changes to de:
some pretty dresses de jolies
robes.

● pronoun

····▸ en; **he wants ~** il en veut;
have ~ more reprenez-en.

····▸ (certain) certains/certaines; **~
are expensive** certains sont chers.

● adverb

····▸ environ; **~ 20 people** environ
20 personnes.

---

somebody /'sʌmbədɪ/ pron quelqu'un.
● n be a **~** être quelqu'un.

somehow /'sʌmhau/ adv d'une manière ou d'une autre; (for some reason) je ne sais pas pourquoi.

someone /'sʌmwʌn/ pron & n
⇒SOMEBODY.

someplace /'sʌmpleɪs/ adv (US)
⇒SOMEWHERE.

somersault /'sʌməsɒlt/ n roulade f.
● vi faire une roulade.

something /'sʌmθɪŋ/ pron & n quelque
chose (m); **~ good** quelque chose de
bon; **~ like** un peu comme.

sometime /'sʌmtaɪm/ adv un jour; **~
in june** en juin. ● adj (former) ancien.

sometimes /'sʌmtaɪmz/ adv quelquefois, parfois.

somewhat /'sʌmwɒt/ adv quelque peu, un peu.

somewhere /'sʌmweə(r)/ adv quelque part.

son /sʌn/ n fils m.

song /sɒŋ/ n chanson f; (of bird) chant m.

son-in-law /'sʌnɪnlɔː/ n (pl **sons-in-law**) gendre m.

soon /suːn/ adv bientôt; (early) tôt; I would ∼er stay j'aimerais mieux rester; ∼ after peu après; ∼er or later tôt ou tard.

soot /sʊt/ n suie f.

soothe /suːð/ vt calmer.

sophisticated /sə'fɪstɪkeɪtɪd/ adj raffiné; (machine) sophistiqué.

sopping /'sɒpɪŋ/ adj trempé.

soppy /'sɒpɪ/ adj (-ier, -iest) Ⓘ sentimental.

sorcerer /'sɔːsərə(r)/ n sorcier m.

sordid /'sɔːdɪd/ adj sordide.

sore /sɔː(r)/ adj douloureux; (vexed) en rogne (**at, with** contre). ● n plaie f.

sorely /'sɔːlɪ/ adv fortement.

sorrow /'sɒrəʊ/ n chagrin m.

sorry /'sɒrɪ/ adj (-ier, -iest) (regretful) désolé (**to** de; **that** que); (wretched) triste; **feel** ∼ **for** plaindre; ∼! pardon!

sort /sɔːt/ n genre m, sorte f, espèce f; (person Ⓘ) type m; **what** ∼ **of?** quel genre de?; **be out of** ∼s ne pas être dans son assiette. ● vt ∼ (**out**) (classify) trier; ∼ **out** (tidy) ranger; (arrange) arranger; (problem) régler.

so-so /'səʊsəʊ/ adj & adv comme ci comme ça.

sought /sɔːt/⇒**SEEK.**

soul /səʊl/ n âme f.

sound /saʊnd/ n son m, bruit m. ● adj solide; (healthy) sain; (sensible) sensé. ● vt/i sonner; (seem) sembler (**as if** que); (test) sonder; ∼ **out** sonder; ∼ **a horn** klaxonner; ∼ **like** sembler être. ∼ **asleep** adj profondément endormi. ∼ **barrier** n mur m du son.

soundly /'saʊndlɪ/ adv (sleep) à poings fermés; (built) solidement.

sound-proof /'saʊndpruːf/ adj insonorisé. ● vt insonoriser.

sound-track /'saʊndtræk/ n bande f sonore.

soup /suːp/ n soupe f, potage m.

sour /'saʊə(r)/ adj aigre. ● vt/i (s')aigrir.

source /sɔːs/ n source f.

south /saʊθ/ n sud m. ● adj sud inv, du sud. ● adv vers le sud.

South Africa n Afrique f du Sud.

South America n Amérique f du Sud.

south-east n sud-est m.

southern /'sʌðən/ adj du sud. **southerner** n habitant/-e m/f du sud.

southward /'saʊθwəd/ adj (side) sud inv; (journey) vers le sud.

south-west n sud-ouest m.

souvenir /suːvə'nɪə(r)/ n souvenir m.

sovereign /'sɒvrɪn/ n & a souverain/-e (m/f).

sow[1] /səʊ/ vt (pt **sowed**; pp **sowed** or **sown**) (seed) semer; (land) ensemencer.

sow[2] /saʊ/ n (pig) truie f.

soya /'sɔɪə/ n soja m. ∼ **sauce** n sauce f soja.

spa /spɑː/ n station f thermale.

space /speɪs/ n espace m; (room) place f; (period) période f. ● adj (research) spatial. ● vt ∼ (**out**) espacer. ∼**craft** n inv, ∼**ship** n engin m spatial. ∼**suit** n combinaison f spatiale.

spacious /'speɪʃəs/ adj spacieux.

spade /speɪd/ n (for garden) bêche f; (child's) pelle f; (cards) pique m. ∼**work** n (fig) travail m préparatoire.

spaghetti /spə'getɪ/ n spaghetti mpl.

spam /spæm/ n (Comput) multipostage m abusif.

Spain /speɪn/ n Espagne f.

span /spæn/ n (of arch) portée f; (of wings) envergure f; (of time) durée f. ● vt (pt **spanned**) enjamber; (in time) embrasser.

Spaniard /'spænjəd/ n Espagnol/-e m/f.

spaniel /'spænjəl/ n épagneul m.

Spanish /'spænɪʃ/ adj espagnol. ● n (Ling) espagnol m.

spank /spæŋk/ vt donner une fessée à.

spanner /'spænə(r)/ n (tool) clé f (plate); (adjustable) clé f à molette.

spare /speə(r)/ vt (treat leniently) épargner; (do without) se passer de; (afford to give) donner, accorder. ● adj en réserve; (surplus) de trop; (tyre, shoes) de rechange; (room, bed) d'ami; **are there any** ∼ **tickets?** y a-t-il encore des places? ● n ∼ (**part**) pièce f

de rechange. ~ **time** n loisirs mpl.
sparing /ˈspeərɪŋ/ adj frugal. **sparingly** adv en petite quantité.
spark /spɑːk/ n étincelle f. ● vt ~ **off** (initiate) provoquer.
sparkle /ˈspɑːkl/ vi étinceler. ● n étincellement m. **sparkling** adj (wine) mousseux; (eyes) brillant.
spark-plug n bougie f.
sparrow /ˈspærəʊ/ n moineau m.
sparse /spɑːs/ adj clairsemé. **sparsely** adv (furnished) peu.
spasm /ˈspæzəm/ n (of muscle) spasme m; (of coughing, anger) accès m.
spat /spæt/ →SPIT.
spate /speɪt/ n a ~ **of** (letters) une avalanche de.
spatter /ˈspætə(r)/ vt éclabousser (with de).
spawn /spɔːn/ n frai m, œufs mpl. ● vt pondre. ● vi frayer.
speak /spiːk/ vi (pt spoke; pp spoken) parler. ● vt (say) dire; (language) parler. □ ~ **up** parler plus fort.
speaker /ˈspiːkə(r)/ n (in public) orateur m; (Pol) président m; (loudspeaker) baffle m; **be a French/a good** ~ parler français/bien.
spear /ˈspɪə(r)/ n lance f.
spearmint /ˈspɪəmɪnt/ n menthe f verte.
special /ˈspeʃl/ adj spécial; (exceptional) exceptionnel.
specialist /ˈspeʃəlɪst/ n spécialiste mf.
speciality, **specialty** /speʃɪˈælətɪ/ n spécialité f.
specialize /ˈspeʃəlaɪz/ vi se spécialiser (in en).
specially /ˈspeʃəlɪ/ adv spécialement.
species /ˈspiːʃiːz/ n inv espèce f.
specific /spəˈsɪfɪk/ adj précis, explicite.
specification /spesɪfɪˈkeɪʃn/ n (of design) spécification f; (of car equipment) caractéristiques fpl. **specify** vt spécifier.
specimen /ˈspesɪmən/ n spécimen m, échantillon m.
speck /spek/ n (stain) (petite) tache f; (particle) grain m.
specs /speks/ npl 🔲 lunettes fpl.
spectacle /ˈspektəkl/ n spectacle m. **spectacles** n lunettes fpl. **spectacular** adj spectaculaire.

spectator /spekˈteɪtə(r)/ n spectateur/-trice m/f.
spectrum /ˈspektrəm/ n (pl **-tra**) spectre m; (of ideas) gamme f.
speculate /ˈspekjʊleɪt/ vi s'interroger (**about** sur); (Comm) spéculer. **speculation** n conjectures fpl; (Comm) spéculation f. **speculator** n spéculateur/-trice m/f.
speech /spiːtʃ/ n (faculty) parole f; (diction) élocution f; (dialect) langage m; (address) discours m. **speechless** adj muet (**with** de).
speed /spiːd/ n (of movement) vitesse f; (swiftness) rapidité f. ~ **camera** n radar m. ~ **dating®** n rencontres fpl rapides, speed dating m. ● vi (pt sped) aller vite; (pt speeded) (drive too fast) aller trop vite. □ ~ **up** accélérer; (of pace) s'accélérer.
speedboat /ˈspiːdbəʊt/ n vedette f.
speeding /ˈspiːdɪŋ/ n excès m de vitesse.
speed limit n limitation f de vitesse.
speedometer /spɪˈdɒmɪtə(r)/ n compteur m (de vitesse).
spell /spel/ n (magic) charme m, sortilège m; (curse) sort m; (of time) (courte) période f. ● vt/i (pt spelled or spelt) écrire; (mean) signifier. ~ **out** épeler; (explain) expliquer. ~**checker** n correcteur m orthographique.
spelling /ˈspelɪŋ/ n orthographe f. ● adj (mistake) d'orthographe.
spend /spend/ vt (pt spent) (money) dépenser (**on** pour); (time, holiday) passer; (energy) consacrer (**on** à). ● vi dépenser.
spent /spent/ →SPEND. ● adj (used) utilisé; (person) épuisé.
sperm /spɜːm/ n (pl sperms or sperm) sperme m.
sphere /sfɪə(r)/ n sphère f.
spice /spaɪs/ n épice f; (fig) piquant m.
spick-and-span adj impeccable.
spicy /ˈspaɪsɪ/ adj épicé; piquant.
spider /ˈspaɪdə(r)/ n araignée f.
spike /spaɪk/ n pointe f.
spill /spɪl/ vt (pt spilled or spilt) renverser, répandre. ● vi se répandre; ~ **over** déborder.
spin /spɪn/ vt/i (pt spun; pres p **spinning**) (wool, web) filer; (turn) (faire) tourner; (story) débiter; ~ **out** faire

durer. ● *n* (movement, excursion) tour *m*.

spinach /'spɪnɪdʒ/ *n* épinards *mpl*.

spinal /'spaɪnl/ *adj* vertébral. ∼ **cord** *n* moelle *f* épinière.

spin-drier *n* essoreuse *f*.

spine /spaɪn/ *n* colonne *f* vertébrale; (prickle) piquant *m*.

spin-off *n* avantage *m* accessoire; (by-product) dérivé *m*.

spinster /'spɪnstə(r)/ *n* célibataire *f*; (pej) vieille fille *f*.

spiral /'spaɪərəl/ *adj* en spirale; (staircase) en colimaçon. ● *n* spirale *f*. ● *vi* (*pt* **spiralled**) (prices) monter (en flèche).

spire /'spaɪə(r)/ *n* flèche *f*.

spirit /'spɪrɪt/ *n* esprit *m*; (boldness) courage *m*; ∼**s** (morale) moral *m*; (drink) spiritueux *mpl*. ● *vt* ∼ **away** faire disparaître. **spirited** *adj* fougueux. ∼**-level** *n* niveau *m* à bulle.

spiritual /'spɪrɪtʃʊəl/ *adj* spirituel.

spit /spɪt/ *vt/i* (*pt* **spat** or **spit**; *pres p* **spitting**) cracher; (of rain) crachiner; ∼ **out** cracher; **the** ∼**ting image of** le portrait craché *or* vivant de. ● *n* crachat(s) *m*(*pl*); (for meat) broche *f*.

spite /spaɪt/ *n* rancune *f*; **in** ∼ **of** malgré. ● *vt* contrarier.

splash /splæʃ/ *vt* éclabousser. ● *vi* faire des éclaboussures; ∼ **(about)** patauger. ● *n* (act, mark) éclaboussure *f*; (sound) plouf *m*; (of colour) tache *f*.

spleen /spliːn/ *n* (Anat) rate *f*.

splendid /'splendɪd/ *adj* magnifique, splendide.

splint /splɪnt/ *n* (Med) attelle *f*.

splinter /'splɪntə(r)/ *n* éclat *m*; (in finger) écharde *f*. ∼ **group** *n* groupe *m* dissident.

split /splɪt/ *vt/i* (*pt* **split**; *pres p* **splitting**) (se) fendre; (tear) (se) déchirer; (divide) (se) diviser; (share) partager; ∼ **one's sides** se tordre (de rire). ● *n* fente *f*; déchirure *f*; (share 🅣) part *f*, partage *m*; (quarrel) rupture *f*; (Pol) scission *f*. □ ∼ **up** (couple) rompre. ∼ **second** *n* fraction *f* de seconde.

splutter /'splʌtə(r)/ *vi* crachoter; (stammer) bafouiller; (engine) tousser.

spoil /spɔɪl/ *vt* (*pt* **spoilt** *or* **spoiled**) (pamper) gâter; (ruin) abîmer; (mar) gâcher, gâter. ● *n* ∼**(s)** butin *m*.

∼**-sport** *n* trouble-fête *mf* *inv*.

spoke[1] /spəʊk/ *n* rayon *m*.

spoke[2], **spoken** ➡**SPEAK**.

spokesman /'spəʊksmən/ *n* (*pl* **-men**) porteparole *m* *inv*.

sponge /spʌndʒ/ *n* éponge *f*. ● *vt* éponger. ● *vi* ∼ **on** vivre aux crochets de. ∼**-bag** *n* trousse *f* de toilette. ∼**-cake** *n* génoise *f*.

sponsor /'spɒnsə(r)/ *n* (of concert) parrain *m*, sponsor *m*; (surety) garant *m*; (for membership) parrain *m*, marraine *f*. ● *vt* parrainer, sponsoriser; (member) parrainer. **sponsorship** *n* patronage *m*; parrainage *m*.

spontaneous /spɒn'teɪnɪəs/ *adj* spontané.

spoof /spuːf/ *n* 🅣 parodie *f*.

spoon /spuːn/ *n* cuiller *f*, cuillère *f*.

spoonful /'spuːnfʊl/ *n* (*pl* ∼**s**) cuillerée *f*.

sport /spɔːt/ *n* sport *m*; **(good)** ∼ (person 🅣) chic type *m*; ∼**s car/coat** voiture/veste *f* de sport. ● *vt* (display) exhiber, arborer.

sporting /'spɔːtɪŋ/ *adj* sportif; **a** ∼ **chance** une assez bonne chance.

sportsman /'spɔːtsmən/ *n* (*pl* **-men**) sportif *m*.

sporty /'spɔːtɪ/ *adj* 🅣 sportif.

spot /spɒt/ *n* (mark, stain) tache *f*; (dot) point *m*; (in pattern) pois *m*; (drop) goutte *f*; (place) endroit *m*; (pimple) bouton *m*; **a** ∼ **of** 🅣 un peu de; **on the** ∼ sur place; (without delay) sur le coup. ● *vt* (*pt* **spotted**) 🅣 apercevoir. ∼ **check** *n* contrôle *m* surprise.

spotless /'spɒtlɪs/ *adj* impeccable.

spotlight /'spɒtlaɪt/ *n* (lamp) projecteur *m*, spot *m*.

spotty /'spɒtɪ/ *adj* (skin) boutonneux.

spouse /spaʊz/ *n* époux *m*, épouse *f*.

spout /spaʊt/ *n* (of teapot) bec *m*; (of liquid) jet *m*; **up the** ∼ (ruined 🅣) fichu. ● *vi* jaillir.

sprain /spreɪn/ *n* entorse *f*, foulure *f*. ● *vt* ∼ **one's wrist** se fouler le poignet.

sprang /spræŋ/ ➡**SPRING**.

sprawl /sprɔːl/ *vi* (town, person) s'étaler. ● *n* étalement *m*.

spray /spreɪ/ *n* (of flowers) gerbe *f*; (water) gerbe *f* d'eau; (from sea) embruns *mpl*; (device) bombe *f*, atomiseur *m*. ● *vt* (*surface, insecticide, plant*) vaporiser; (*person*) asperger; (*crops*) traiter.

spread /spred/ *vt/i* (*pt* **spread**) (stretch, extend) (s')étendre; (*news, fear*) (se) répandre; (*illness*) (se) propager; (*butter*) (s')étaler. ● *n* propagation *f*; (of population) distribution *f*; (paste) pâte *f* à tartiner; (food) belle table *f*. ~**-eagled** *adj* bras et jambes écartés. ~**sheet** *n* tableur *m*.

spree /spriː/ *n* **go on a** ~ (have fun 🔢) faire la noce.

sprig /sprɪg/ *n* petite branche *f*.

sprightly /'spraɪtlɪ/ *adj* (**-ier, -iest**) alerte, vif.

spring /sprɪŋ/ *vi* (*pt* **sprang**, *pp* **sprung**) bondir. ● *vt* ~ **sth on sb** annoncer qch de but en blanc à qn. ● *n* bond *m*; (device) ressort *m*; (season) printemps *m*; (of water) source *f*. ~ **from** provenir de; ~ **up** surgir. ~**board** *n* tremplin *m*. ~ **onion** *n* oignon *m* blanc.

springy /'sprɪŋɪ/ *adj* (**-ier, -iest**) élastique.

sprinkle /'sprɪŋkl/ *vt* (with liquid) arroser (**with** de); (with salt, flour) saupoudrer (**with** de); (sand) répandre. **sprinkler** *n* (in garden) arroseur *m*; (for fires) extincteur *m* (à déclenchement) automatique.

sprint /sprɪnt/ *vi* (Sport) sprinter. ● *n* sprint *m*.

sprout /spraʊt/ *vt/i* pousser. ● *n* (on plant) pousse *f*. (**Brussels**) ~**s** choux *mpl* de Bruxelles.

spruce /spruːs/ *adj* pimpant. ● *vt* ~ **oneself up** se faire beau. ● *n* (tree) épicéa *m*.

sprung /sprʌŋ/ ➡**SPRING**.

spud /spʌd/ *n* 🔢 patate *f*.

spun /spʌn/ ➡**SPIN**.

spur /spɜː(r)/ *n* (of rider) éperon *m*; (stimulus) aiguillon *m*; **on the** ~ **of the moment** sous l'impulsion du moment. ● *vt* (*pt* **spurred**) éperonner.

spurious /'spjʊərɪəs/ *adj* faux.

spurn /spɜːn/ *vt* repousser.

spurt /spɜːt/ *vi* jaillir; (fig) accélérer. ● *n* jet *m*; (of energy) sursaut *m*.

spy /spaɪ/ *n* espion/-ne *m/f*. ● *vi* espionner. ● *vt* apercevoir.

squabble /'skwɒbl/ *vi* se chamailler. ● *n* chamaillerie *f*.

squad /skwɒd/ *n* (of soldiers) escouade *f*; (Sport) équipe *f*.

squadron /'skwɒdrən/ *n* (Mil) escadron *m*; (Aviat) escadrille *f*.

squalid /'skwɒlɪd/ *adj* sordide.

squander /'skwɒndə(r)/ *vt* (money, time) gaspiller.

square /skweə(r)/ *n* carré *m*; (open space in town) place *f*. ● *adj* carré; (honest) honnête; (meal) solide; (boring 🔢) ringard; (**all**) ~ (quits) quitte; ~ **metre** mètre *m* carré. ● *vt* (settle) régler; ~ **up to** faire face à.

squash /skwɒʃ/ *vt* écraser; (crowd) serrer. ● *n* (game) squash *m*; (marrow: US) courge *f*; **lemon** ~ citronnade *f*; **orange** ~ orangeade *f*.

squat /skwɒt/ *vi* (*pt* **squatted**) s'accroupir; ~ **in a house** squatteriser une maison. ● *adj* (dumpy) trapu. **squatter** *n* squatter *m*.

squawk /skwɔːk/ *n* cri *m* rauque. ● *vi* pousser un cri rauque.

squeak /skwiːk/ *n* petit cri *m*; (of door) grincement *m*. ● *vi* crier; grincer.

squeal /skwiːl/ *n* cri *m* aigu. ● *vi* pousser un cri aigu; ~ **on** (inform on 🔢) dénoncer.

squeamish /'skwiːmɪʃ/ *adj* (trop) délicat.

squeeze /skwiːz/ *vt* presser; (hand, arm) serrer; (extract) exprimer (**from** de); (extort) soutirer (**from** à). ● *vi* (force one's way) se glisser. ● *n* pression *f*; (Comm) restrictions *fpl* de crédit.

squid /skwɪd/ *n* calmar *m*.

squint /skwɪnt/ *vi* loucher; (with half-shut eyes) plisser les yeux. ● *n* (Med) strabisme *m*.

squirm /skwɜːm/ *vi* se tortiller.

squirrel /'skwɪrəl/ *n* écureuil *m*.

squirt /skwɜːt/ *vt/i* (faire) jaillir. ● *n* jet *m*.

stab /stæb/ *vt* (*pt* **stabbed**) (with knife) poignarder. ● *n* coup *m* (de couteau); **have a** ~ **at sth** essayer de faire qch.

stability /stə'bɪlətɪ/ *n* stabilité *f*. **stabilize** *vt* stabiliser.

stable /'steɪbl/ *adj* stable. ● *n* écurie *f*. ~**-boy** *n* lad *m*.

stack /stæk/ n tas m. ● vt (~ **up**) entasser, empiler.

stadium /'steɪdɪəm/ n stade m.

staff /stɑːf/ n personnel m; (in school) professeurs mpl; (Mil) état-major m; (stick) bâton m. ● vt pourvoir en personnel.

stag /stæg/ n cerf m.

stage /steɪdʒ/ n (Theat) scène f; (phase) stade m, étape f; (platform in hall) estrade f; **go on the ~** faire du théâtre. ● vt mettre en scène; (fig) organiser. ~ **door** n entrée f des artistes. ~ **fright** n trac m.

stagger /'stægə(r)/ vi chanceler. ● vt (shock) stupéfier; (payments) échelonner. **staggering** adj stupéfiant.

stagnate /stæg'neɪt/ vi stagner.

stag night n soirée f pour enterrer une vie de garçon.

staid /steɪd/ adj sérieux.

stain /steɪn/ vt tacher; (wood) colorer. ● n tache f; (colouring) colorant m. **stained glass window** n vitrail m.

stainless steel n acier m inoxydable.

stain remover n détachant m.

stair /steə(r)/ n marche f; **the ~s** l'escalier m. ~**case**, ~**way** n escalier m.

stake /steɪk/ n (post) pieu m; (wager) enjeu m; **at ~** en jeu. ● vt (area) jalonner; (wager) jouer; ~ **a claim to** revendiquer.

stale /steɪl/ adj pas frais; (bread) rassis; (smell) de renfermé.

stalk /stɔːk/ n (of plant) tige f. ● vi marcher de façon guindée. ● vt (hunter) chasser; (murderer) suivre.

stall /stɔːl/ n (in stable) stalle f; (in market) éventaire m; ~**s** (Theat) orchestre m. ● vt/i (Auto) caler; ~ **(for time)** temporiser.

stallion /'stælɪən/ n étalon m.

stamina /'stæmɪnə/ n résistance f.

stammer /'stæmə(r)/ vt/i bégayer. ● n bégaiement m.

stamp /stæmp/ vt/i ~ **(one's foot)** taper du pied. ● vt (letter) timbrer. ● n (for postage, marking) timbre m; (mark: fig) sceau m. ~ **out** supprimer. ~-**collecting** n philatélie f.

stampede /stæm'piːd/ n fuite f désordonnée; (rush: fig) ruée f. ● vi s'enfuir en désordre; se ruer.

stand /stænd/ vi (pt **stood**) être or se tenir (debout); (rise) se lever; (be situated) se trouver; (Pol) être candidat (for à); ~ **in line** (US) faire la queue; ~ **to reason** être logique. ● vt mettre (debout); (tolerate) supporter; ~ **a chance** avoir une chance. ● n (stance) position f; (Mil) résistance f; (for lamp) support m; (at fair) stand m; (in street) kiosque m; (for spectators) tribune f; (Jur, US) barre f; **make a ~** prendre position. ~ **back** reculer; ~ **by** or **around** ne rien faire; ~ **by** (be ready) se tenir prêt; (promise, person) rester fidèle à; ~ **down** se désister; ~ **for** représenter; Ⓘ supporter; ~ **in for** remplacer; ~ **out** ressortir; ~ **up** se lever; ~ **up for** défendre; ~ **up to** résister à.

standard /'stændəd/ n norme f; (level) niveau m (voulu); (flag) étendard m; ~ **of living** niveau m de vie; ~**s** (morals) principes mpl. ● adj ordinaire.

standard of living n niveau m de vie.

standby /'stændbaɪ/ adj de réserve. ● n be a ~ être de réserve.

stand-in /'stændɪn/ n remplaçant/-e m/f.

standing /'stændɪŋ/ adj debout inv. ● n réputation f; (duration) durée f. ~ **order** n prélèvement m bancaire.

standpoint /'stændpɔɪnt/ n point m de vue.

standstill /'stændstɪl/ n **at a ~** immobile; **bring/come to a ~** (s')immobiliser.

stank /stæŋk/ ➡STINK.

staple /'steɪpl/ n agrafe f. ● vt agrafer. ● adj principal, de base. **stapler** n agrafeuse f.

star /stɑː(r)/ n étoile f; (person) vedette f. ● vt (pt **starred**) (film) avoir pour vedette. ● vi ~ **in** être la vedette de.

starch /stɑːtʃ/ n amidon m; (in food) fécule f. ● vt amidonner.

stardom /'stɑːdəm/ n célébrité f.

stare /steə(r)/ vi ~ **at** regarder fixement. ● n regard m fixe.

starfish /'stɑːfɪʃ/ n étoile f de mer.

stark /stɑːk/ adj (desolate) désolé; (severe) austère; (utter) complet; (fact) brutal. ● adv complètement.

starling /'stɑːlɪŋ/ n étourneau m.

start /stɑːt/ vt/i commencer; (se) mettre en marche; (fashion) lancer; (cause) provoquer; (jump) sursauter; (of vehicle) démarrer; ~ **to do** commencer or se mettre à faire; ~**ing tomorrow** à partir de demain. ● n commencement m, début m; (of race) départ m; (lead) avance f; (jump) sursaut m. □ ~ **off** commencer (**doing** par faire); ~ **out** partir; ~ **up** (business) lancer. **starter** n (Auto) démarreur m; (runner) partant m; (Culin) entrée f.

starting point n point m de départ.

startle /'stɑːtl/ vt (make jump) faire tressaillir; (shock) alarmer.

starvation /stɑːˈveɪʃn/ n faim f.

starve /stɑːv/ vi mourir de faim. ● vt affamer; (deprive) priver.

stash /stæʃ/ vt cacher.

state /steɪt/ n état m; (pomp) apparat m; S~ état m; **the S~s** les États-Unis; **get into a** ~ s'affoler. ● adj d'état, de l'état; (school) public. ● vt affirmer (**that** que); (views) exprimer; (fix) fixer.

> **State school** Environ 90% des élèves britanniques font leur scolarité dans une *state school* (école publique). L'enseignement y est gratuit et suit le programme scolaire national établi par le gouvernement. À l'entrée dans le secondaire, les élèves intègrent normalement une *comprehensive school*, ou, à l'issue d'un examen d'entrée, une *grammar school*. ▷**PUBLIC SCHOOLS**.

stately /'steɪtlɪ/ adj (**-ier**, **-iest**) majestueux. ~ **home** n château m.

statement /'steɪtmənt/ n déclaration f; (of account) relevé m.

statesman /'steɪtsmən/ n (pl **-men**) homme m d'état.

static /'stætɪk/ adj statique. ● n (radio, TV) parasites mpl.

station /'steɪʃn/ n (Rail) gare f; (TV) chaîne f; (Mil) poste m; (rank) condition f. ● vt poster, placer; ~**ed at** or **in** (Mil) en garnison à.

stationary /'steɪʃənrɪ/ adj immobile, stationnaire; (vehicle) à l'arrêt.

stationery /'steɪʃənrɪ/ n papeterie f.

station wagon n (US) break m.

statistic /stəˈtɪstɪk/ n statistique f; ~**s** statistique f.

statue /'stætʃuː/ n statue f.

status /'steɪtəs/ n (pl ~**es**) situation f, statut m; (prestige) standing m.

statute /'stætʃuːt/ n loi f; ~**s** (rules) statuts mpl. **statutory** adj statutaire; (holiday) légal.

staunch /stɔːntʃ/ adj (friend) loyal, fidèle.

stave /steɪv/ n (Mus) portée f. ● vt ~ **off** éviter, conjurer.

stay /steɪ/ vi rester; (spend time) séjourner; (reside) loger. ● vt (hunger) tromper. ● n séjour m. □ ~ **away from** (school) ne pas aller à; ~ **behind** or ~ **on** rester; ~ **in** rester à la maison; ~ **up** veiller, se coucher tard.

stead /sted/ n **stand sb in good** ~ être utile à qn.

steadfast /'stedfɑːst/ adj ferme.

steady /'stedɪ/ adj (**-ier**, **-iest**) stable; (hand, voice) ferme; (regular) régulier; (staid) sérieux. ● vt maintenir, assurer; (calm) calmer.

steak /steɪk/ n steak m, bifteck m; (of fish) darne f.

steal /stiːl/ vt/i (pt **stole**; pp **stolen**) voler (**from sb** à qn).

steam /stiːm/ n vapeur f; (on glass) buée f. ● vt (cook) cuire à la vapeur. ● vi fumer. ~-**engine** n locomotive f à vapeur

steamer /'stiːmə(r)/ n (Culin) cuit-vapeur m; (boat) (bateau à) vapeur m.

steel /stiːl/ n acier m; ~ **industry** sidérurgie f. ● vpr ~ **oneself** s'endurcir, se cuirasser.

steep /stiːp/ adj raide, rapide; (price: 🄸) excessif. ● vt (soak) tremper; ~**ed in** (fig) imprégné de.

steeple /'stiːpl/ n clocher m.

steer /stɪə(r)/ vt diriger; (ship) gouverner; (fig) guider. ● vi (in ship) gouverner; ~ **clear of** éviter.

steering-wheel n volant m.

stem /stem/ n tige f; (of glass) pied m. ● vi (pt **stemmed**) ~ **from** provenir de. ● vt (pt **stemmed**) (check, stop) endiguer, contenir. ~ **cell** n cellule f souche.

stench /stentʃ/ n puanteur f.

stencil /'stensɪl/ n pochoir m. ● vt (pt **stencilled**) décorer au pochoir.

step /step/ vi (pt **stepped**) marcher, aller. ● n pas m; (stair) marche f; (of train) marchepied m; (action) mesure f; ~s (ladder) escabeau m; **in** ~ au pas; (fig) conforme (with à). ~ **down** (resign) démissionner; (from ladder) descendre; ~ **forward** faire un pas en avant; ~ **in** (intervene) intervenir; ~ **up** (pressure) augmenter. ~**brother** n demifrère m. ~**daughter** n belle-fille f. ~**father** n beau-père m. ~**ladder** n escabeau m. ~**mother** n belle-mère f. **stepping-stone** n (fig) tremplin m. ~**sister** n demi-sœur f. ~**son** n beau-fils m.

stereo /ˈsteriəʊ/ n stéréo f; (record-player) chaîne f stéréo. ● adj stéréo inv.

stereotype /ˈsteriətaip/ n stéréotype m.

sterile /ˈsterail/ adj stérile. **sterility** n stérilité f.

sterilize /ˈsterəlaiz/ vt stériliser.

sterling /ˈstɜːlɪŋ/ n livre(s) f (pl) sterling. ● adj sterling inv; (silver) fin; (fig) excellent.

stern /stɜːn/ adj sévère. ● n (of ship) arrière m.

steroid /ˈstɪərɔid/ n stéroïde m.

stew /stjuː/ vt/i cuire à la casserole; ~**ed fruit** compote f; ~**ed tea** thé m trop infusé. ● n ragoût m.

steward /stjʊəd/ n (of club) intendant m; (on ship) steward m. **stewardess** n hôtesse f.

stick /stik/ vt (pt **stuck**) (glue) coller; (put 🄸) mettre; (endure 🄸) supporter. ● vi (adhere) coller, adhérer; (to pan) attacher; (remain 🄸) rester; (be jammed) être coincé; **be stuck with sb** 🄸 se farcir qn. ● n bâton m; (for walking) canne f. ~ **at** persévérer dans; ~ **out** vt (head) sortir; (tongue) tirer; vi (protrude) dépasser; ~ **to** (promise) rester fidèle à; ~ **up for** 🄸 défendre.

sticker /ˈstikə(r)/ n autocollant m.

sticky /ˈstiki/ adj **-ier, -iest** poisseux; (label, tape) adhésif.

stiff /stif/ adj raide; (limb, joint) ankylosé; (tough) dur; (drink) fort; (price) élevé; (manner) guindé; ~ **neck** torticolis m.

stifle /ˈstaifl/ vt/i étouffer.

stiletto /stɪˈletəʊ/ adj & n ~**s, ~ heels** talons mpl aiguille.

still /stil/ adj immobile; (quiet) calme, tranquille; **keep ~!** arrête de bouger! ● n silence m. ● adv encore, toujours; (even) encore; (nevertheless) tout de même.

stillborn /ˈstilbɔːn/ adj mort-né.

still life n nature f morte.

stimulate /ˈstimjʊleit/ vt stimuler. **stimulation** n stimulation f.

stimulus /ˈstimjʊləs/ n (pl **-li**) (spur) stimulant m.

sting /stiŋ/ n piqûre f; (of insect) aiguillon m. ● vt/i (pt **stung**) piquer.

stingy /ˈstindʒi/ adj (**-ier, -iest**) avare (with de).

stink /stiŋk/ n puanteur f. ● vi (pt **stank** or **stunk**; pp **stunk**) ~ (of) puer.

stipulate /ˈstipjʊleit/ vt stipuler.

stir /stɜː(r)/ vt/i (pt **stirred**) (move) remuer; (excite) exciter; ~ **up** (trouble) provoquer. ● n agitation f.

stirrup /ˈstirəp/ n étrier m.

stitch /stitʃ/ n point m; (in knitting) maille f; (Med) point m de suture; (muscle pain) point m de côté; **be in** ~**es** 🄸 avoir le fou rire. ● vt coudre.

stock /stɒk/ n réserve f; (Comm) stock m; (financial) valeurs fpl; (family) souche f; (soup) bouillon m; **we're out of** ~ il n'y en a plus; **take** ~ (fig) faire le point; **in** ~ en stock. ● adj (goods) courant. ● vt (shop) approvisionner; (sell) vendre. ● vi ~ **up** s'approvisionner (with de). ~**broker** n agent m de change. ~ **cube** n bouillon-cube m. **S~ Exchange** n Bourse f.

stocking /ˈstɒkɪŋ/ n bas m.

stock market n Bourse f.

stockpile /ˈstɒkpail/ n stock m. ● vt stocker; (arms) amasser.

stock-taking n (Comm) inventaire m.

stocky /ˈstɒki/ adj (**-ier, -iest**) trapu.

stodgy /ˈstɒdʒi/ adj lourd.

stole, stolen →**STEAL.**

stomach /ˈstʌmək/ n estomac m; (abdomen) ventre m. ● vt (put up with) supporter. ~**-ache** n mal m à l'estomac or au ventre.

stone /stəʊn/ n pierre f; (pebble) caillou m; (in fruit) noyau m; (weight) 6,350 kg. ● adj de pierre; ~**-cold/-deaf** complètement froid/sourd. ● vt (throw stones) lapider; (*fruit*) dénoyauter.

stony /'stəʊnɪ/ *adj* pierreux.

stood /stʊd/ ⟶STAND.

stool /stu:l/ *n* tabouret *m*.

stoop /stu:p/ *vi* (bend) se baisser; (condescend) s'abaisser. ● *n* have a ~ être voûté.

stop /stɒp/ *vt/i* (*pt* **stopped**) arrêter (**doing** de faire); (*moving, talking*) s'arrêter; (prevent) empêcher (**from** de); (*hole, leak*) boucher; (*pain, noise*) cesser; (stay Ⅱ) rester. ● *n* arrêt *m*; (full stop) point *m*;~ (-over) halte *f*; (port of call) escale *f*. ~ **off** s'arrêter; ~ **up** boucher.

stopgap /'stɒpgæp/ *n* bouche-trou *m*. ● *adj* intérimaire.

stoppage /'stɒpɪdʒ/ *n* arrêt *m*; (of work) arrêt *m* de travail; (of pay) retenue *f*.

stopper /'stɒpə(r)/ *n* bouchon *m*.

stop-watch *n* chronomètre *m*.

storage /'stɔ:rɪdʒ/ *n* (of goods, food) emmagasinage *m*. ~ **heater** *n* radiateur *m* électrique à accumulation.

store /stɔ:(r)/ *n* réserve *f*; (warehouse) entrepôt *m*; (shop) grand magasin *m*; (US) magasin *m*; **have in** ~ **for** réserver à; **set** ~ **by** attacher du prix à. ● *vt* (for future) mettre en réserve; (in warehouse, mind) emmagasiner. ~**-room** *n* réserve *f*.

storey /'stɔ:rɪ/ *n* étage *m*.

stork /stɔ:k/ *n* cigogne *f*.

storm /stɔ:m/ *n* tempête *f*, orage *m*. ● *vt* prendre d'assaut. ● *vi* (rage) tempêter.

story /'stɔ:rɪ/ *n* histoire *f*; (in press) article *m*; (storey: US) étage *m*. ~**-teller** *n* conteur/-euse *m/f*.

stout /staʊt/ *adj* corpulent; (strong) solide. ● *n* bière *f* brune.

stove /stəʊv/ *n* cuisinière *f*.

stow /stəʊ/ *vt* ~ **away** (put away) ranger; (hide) cacher. ● *vi* voyager clandestinement.

straddle /'strædl/ *vt* être à cheval sur, enjamber.

straggler /'stræglə(r)/ *n* traînard/-e *m/f*.

straight /streɪt/ *adj* droit; (tidy) en ordre; (frank) franc; ~ **face** visage *m* sérieux; **get sth** ~ mettre qch au

clair. ● *adv* (in straight line) droit; (direct) tout droit; ~ **ahead** *or* **on** tout droit; ~ **away** tout de suite; ~ **off** Ⅱ sans hésiter. ● *n* (Sport) ligne *f* droite.

straighten /'streɪtn/ *vt* (nail, situation) redresser; (tidy) arranger.

straightforward /streɪt'fɔ:wəd/ *adj* honnête; (easy) simple.

straight off *adv* Ⅱ sans hésiter.

strain /streɪn/ *vt* (rope, ears) tendre; (limb) fouler; (eyes) fatiguer; (muscle) froisser; (filter) passer; (vegetables) égoutter; (fig) mettre à l'épreuve. ● *vi* fournir des efforts. ● *n* tension *f*; (fig) effort *m*; (breed) race *f*; (of virus) variété *f*; ~**s** (tune: Mus) accents *mpl*.

strained *adj* forcé; (relations) tendu.

strainer *n* passoire *f*.

strait /streɪt/ *n* détroit *m*; ~**s** détroit *m*; **be in dire** ~**s** être aux abois. ~**-jacket** *n* camisole *f* de force.

strand /strænd/ *n* (thread) fil *m*, brin *m*; (of hair) mèche *f*.

stranded /'strændɪd/ *adj* (person) en rade; (ship) échoué.

strange /streɪndʒ/ *adj* étrange; (unknown) inconnu. **stranger** *n* inconnu/-e *m/f*.

strangle /'stræŋgl/ *vt* étrangler.

stranglehold /'stræŋglhəʊld/ *n* **have a** ~ **on** tenir à la gorge.

strap /stræp/ *n* (of leather) courroie *f*; (of dress) bretelle *f*; (of watch) bracelet *m*. ● *vt* (*pt* **strapped**) attacher.

strategic /strə'ti:dʒɪk/ *adj* stratégique. **strategy** *n* stratégie *f*.

straw /strɔ:/ *n* paille *f*; **the last** ~ le comble.

strawberry /'strɔ:brɪ/ *n* fraise *f*.

stray /streɪ/ *vi* s'égarer; (deviate) s'écarter. ● *adj* perdu; (isolated) isolé. ● *n* animal *m* perdu.

streak /stri:k/ *n* raie *f*, bande *f*; (trace) trace *f*; (period) période *f*; (tendency) tendance *f*. ● *vt* (mark) strier. ● *vi* filer à toute allure.

stream /stri:m/ *n* ruisseau *m*; (current) courant *m*; (flow) flot *m*; (in school) classe *f* (de niveau). ● *vi* ruisseler (**with** de); (eyes, nose) couler.

streamline /'stri:mlaɪn/ *vt* rationaliser. **streamlined** *adj* (shape) aérodynamique.

street /striːt/ n rue f; ~**car** n (US) tramway m. ~ **lamp** n réverbère m. ~ **map** n indicateur m des rues.

strength /streŋθ/ n force f; (of wall, fabric) solidité f; **on the ~ of** en vertu de. **strengthen** vt renforcer, fortifier.

strenuous /ˈstrenjʊəs/ adj (exercise) énergique; (work) ardu.

stress /stres/ n (emphasis) accent m; (pressure) pression f; (Med) stress m. ● vt souligner, insister sur.

stretch /stretʃ/ vt (pull taut) tendre; (arm, leg) étendre; (neck) tendre; (clothes) étirer; (truth) forcer; ~ **one's legs** se dégourdir les jambes. ● vi s'étendre; (person) s'étirer; (clothes) se déformer. ● n étendue f; (period) période f; (of road) tronçon m; **at a ~** d'affilée. ● adj (fabric) extensible.

stretcher /ˈstretʃə(r)/ n brancard m.

strew /struː/ vt (pt **strewed**; pp **strewed** or **strewn**) (scatter) répandre; (cover) joncher.

strict /strɪkt/ adj strict.

stride /straɪd/ vi (pt **strode**; pp **stridden**) faire de grands pas. ● n grand pas m.

strife /straɪf/ n conflit(s) m(pl).

strike /straɪk/ vt (pt **struck**) frapper; (blow) donner; (match) frotter; (gold) trouver. ● vi faire grève; (attack) attaquer; (clock) sonner. ● n (of workers) grève f; (Mil) attaque f; (find) découverte f; **on ~** en grève. □ ~ **off** or **out** rayer; ~ **up** (a friendship) lier amitié (**with** avec). **striker** n gréviste mf; (football) attaquant/-e m/f. **striking** adj frappant.

string /strɪŋ/ n ficelle f; (of violin, racket) corde f; (of pearls) collier m; (of lies) chapelet m; **the ~s** (Mus) les cordes; **pull ~s** faire jouer ses relations. ● vt pt **strung** (thread) enfiler. **stringed** adj (instrument) à cordes.

stringent /ˈstrɪndʒənt/ adj rigoureux, strict.

stringy /ˈstrɪŋɪ/ adj filandreux.

strip /strɪp/ vt/i (pt **stripped**) (undress) (se) déshabiller; (deprive) dépouiller. ● n bande f.

stripe /straɪp/ n rayure f, raie f. **striped** adj rayé.

strip light n néon m.

stripper /ˈstrɪpə(r)/ n strip-teaseur/-euse m/f; (solvent) décapant.

strip-tease n strip-tease m.

strive /straɪv/ vi (pt **strove**; pp **striven**) s'efforcer (**to** de).

strode /strəʊd/ ➡STRIDE.

stroke /strəʊk/ vt (with hand) caresser. ● n coup m; (of pen) trait m; (swimming) nage f; (Med) attaque f, congestion f; **at a~** d'un seul coup.

stroll /strəʊl/ vi flâner; ~ **in** entrer tranquillement. ● n petit tour m. **stroller** n (US) poussette f.

strong /strɒŋ/ adj fort; (shoes, fabric) solide; **be fifty ~** être fort de cinquante personnes. ~**hold** n bastion m.

strongly /ˈstrɒŋlɪ/ adv (greatly) fortement; (with energy) avec force; (deeply) profondément.

strove /strəʊv/ ➡STRIVE.

struck /strʌk/ ➡STRIKE.

structure /ˈstrʌktʃə(r)/ n (of cell, poem) structure f; (building) construction f.

struggle /ˈstrʌgl/ vi lutter, se battre. ● n lutte f; (effort) effort m; **have a ~ to** avoir du mal à.

strum /strʌm/ vt (pt **strummed**) gratter de.

strung /strʌŋ/ ➡STRING. ● adj ~ **up** (tense) nerveux.

strut /strʌt/ n (support) étai m. ● vi (pt **strutted**) se pavaner.

stub /stʌb/ n bout m; (counterfoil) talon m. ● vt (pt **stubbed**) ~ **one's toe** se cogner le doigt de pied. □ ~ **out** écraser.

stubble /ˈstʌbl/ n (on chin) barbe f de plusieurs jours; (remains of wheat) chaume m.

stubborn /ˈstʌbən/ adj obstiné.

stuck /stʌk/ ➡STICK. ● adj (jammed) coincé; **I'm ~** (for answer) je sèche. ~**-up** adj 🄸 prétentieux.

stud /stʌd/ n (on jacket) clou m; (for collar) bouton m; (stallion) étalon m; (horse farm) haras m. ● vt (pt **studded**) clouter.

student /ˈstjuːdnt/ n (Univ) étudiant/-e m/f; (School) élève mf. ● adj (restaurant, life) universitaire.

studio /ˈstjuːdɪəʊ/ n studio m.

studious /ˈstjuːdɪəs/ adj (person) studieux; (deliberate) étudié.

study /'stʌdɪ/ n étude f; (office) bureau m. ● vt/i étudier.

stuff /stʌf/ n substance f; 🔲 chose (s) f (pl). ● vt rembourrer; (animal) empailler; (cram) bourrer; (Culin) farcir; (block up) boucher; (put) fourrer. **stuffing** n bourre f; (Culin) farce f.

stuffy /'stʌfɪ/ adj (-ier, -iest) mal aéré; (dull 🔲) vieux jeu inv.

stumble /'stʌmbl/ vi trébucher; ~ **across** or **on** tomber sur. **stumbling block** n obstacle m.

stump /stʌmp/ n (of tree) souche f; (of limb) moignon m; (of pencil) bout m.

stumped /stʌmpt/ adj embarrassé.

stun /stʌn/ vt (pt **stunned**) étourdir; (bewilder) stupéfier.

stung /stʌŋ/ ➡STING.

stunk /stʌŋk/ ➡STINK.

stunning /'stʌnɪŋ/ adj (delightful 🔲) sensationnel.

stunt /stʌnt/ vt (growth) retarder. ● n (feat 🔲) tour m de force; (trick 🔲) truc m; (dangerous) cascade f.

stupid /'stjuːpɪd/ adj stupide, bête. **stupidity** n stupidité f.

sturdy /'stɜːdɪ/ adj (-ier, -iest) robuste.

stutter /'stʌtə(r)/ vi bégayer. ● n bégaiement m.

sty /staɪ/ n (pigsty) porcherie f; (on eye) orgelet m.

style /staɪl/ n style m; (fashion) mode f; (sort) genre m; (pattern) modèle m; **do sth in** ~ faire qch avec classe. ● vt (design) créer; ~ **sb's hair** coiffer qn.

stylish /'staɪlɪʃ/ adj élégant.

stylist /'staɪlɪst/ n (of hair) coiffeur/-euse m/f.

suave /swɑːv/ adj (urbane) courtois; (smooth: pej) doucereux.

subconscious /sʌb'kɒnʃəs/ adj & n inconscient (m), subconscient (m.)

subcontract /sʌbkən'trækt/ vt soustraiter.

subdue /səb'djuː/ vt (feeling) maîtriser; (country) subjuguer. **subdued** adj (person, mood) morose; (light) tamisé; (criticism) contenu.

subject¹ /'sʌbdʒɪkt/ adj (state) soumis; ~ **to** soumis à; (liable to, dependent on) sujet à. ● n sujet m; (focus) objet m; (School,Univ) matière f; (citizen) ressortissant/-e m/f, sujet/-te m/f.

subject² /səb'dʒekt/ vt soumettre.

subjective /səb'dʒektɪv/ adj subjectif.

subject-matter n contenu m.

subjunctive /səb'dʒʌŋktɪv/ adj & n subjonctif (m.)

sublet /sʌb'let/ vt sous-louer.

submarine /sʌbmə'riːn/ n sous-marin m.

submerge /səb'mɜːdʒ/ vt submerger. ● vi plonger.

submissive /səb'mɪsɪv/ adj soumis.

submit /səb'mɪt/ vt/i (pt **submitted**) (se) soumettre (**to** à).

subordinate /sə'bɔːdɪnət/ adj subalterne; (Gram) subordonné. ● n subordonné/-e m/f.

subpoena /sə'piːnə/ n (Jur) citation f, assignation f.

subscribe /səb'skraɪb/ vt/i verser (de l'argent) (**to** à); ~ **to** (loan, theory) souscrire à; (newspaper) s'abonner à, être abonné à. **subscriber** n abonné/-e m/f. **subscription** n abonnement m; (membership dues) cotisation f.

subsequent /'sʌbsɪkwənt/ adj (later) ultérieur; (next) suivant. **subsequently** adv par la suite.

subside /səb'saɪd/ vi (land) s'affaisser; (flood, wind) baisser.

subsidiary /səb'sɪdɪərɪ/ adj accessoire. ● n (Comm) filiale f.

subsidize /'sʌbsɪdaɪz/ vt subventionner. **subsidy** n subvention f.

substance /'sʌbstəns/ n substance f.

substandard /sʌb'stændəd/ adj de qualité inférieure.

substantial /səb'stænʃl/ adj considérable; (meal) substantiel.

substitute /'sʌbstɪtjuːt/ n succédané m; (person) remplaçant/-e m/f. ● vt substituer (**for** à).

subtitle /'sʌbtaɪtl/ n sous-titre m.

subtle /'sʌtl/ adj subtil.

subtract /səb'trækt/ vt soustraire.

suburb /'sʌbɜːb/ n faubourg m, banlieue f; ~**s** banlieue f. **suburban** adj de banlieue. **suburbia** n la banlieue.

subway /'sʌbweɪ/ n passage m souterrain; (US) métro m.

succeed /sək'siːd/ vi réussir (**in doing** à faire). ● vt (follow) succéder à.

success /sək'ses/ n succès m, réussite f.

successful /sək'sesfl/ adj réussi, couronné de succès; (favourable) heureux;

(in exam) reçu; **be ～ in doing** réussir à faire.

succession /səkˈseʃn/ n succession f; **in ～** de suite.

successive /səkˈsesɪv/ adj successif; **six ～ days** six jours consécutifs.

successor /səkˈsesə(r)/ n successeur m.

such /sʌtʃ/ det & pron tel(le), tel(le)s; (so much) tant(de). ● adv si; **～ a book** un tel livre; **～ books** de tels livres; **～ courage** tant de courage; **～ a big house** une si grande maison; **～ as** comme, tel que; **as ～** en tant que tel; **there's no ～ thing** ça n'existe pas. **～-and-～** adj tel ou tel.

suck /sʌk/ vt sucer. □ **～ in** or **up** aspirer. **sucker** n (rubber pad) ventouse f; (person Ⓘ) dupe f.

suction /ˈsʌkʃn/ n succion f.

sudden /ˈsʌdn/ adj soudain, subit; **all of a ～** tout à coup. **suddenly** adv subitement, brusquement.

sue /suː/ vt (pres p) **suing** poursuivre (en justice).

suede /sweɪd/ n daim m.

suffer /ˈsʌfə(r)/ vt/i souffrir; (loss, attack) subir. **sufferer** n victime f, malade mf. **suffering** n souffrance(s) f(pl).

sufficient /səˈfɪʃnt/ adj (enough) suffisamment de; (big enough) suffisant m.

suffix /ˈsʌfɪks/ n suffixe m.

suffocate /ˈsʌfəkeɪt/ vt/i suffoquer.

sugar /ˈʃʊgə(r)/ n sucre m. ● vt sucrer.

suggest /səˈdʒest/ vt suggérer. **suggestion** n suggestion f.

suicidal /suːɪˈsaɪdl/ adj suicidaire.

suicide /ˈsuːɪsaɪd/ n suicide m; **commit ～** se suicider.

suit /suːt/ n (man's) costume m; (woman's) tailleur m; (cards) couleur f. ● vt convenir à; (garment, style) aller à; (adapt) adapter.

suitable /ˈsuːtəbl/ adj qui convient (**for** à), convenable. **suitably** adv convenablement.

suitcase /ˈsuːtkeɪs/ n valise f.

suite /swiːt/ n (rooms) suite f; (furniture) mobilier m.

suited /ˈsuːtɪd/ adj (**well**) **～** (matched) bien assorti; **～ to** fait pour, apte à.

sulk /sʌlk/ vi bouder.

sullen /ˈsʌlən/ adj maussade.

sultana /sʌlˈtɑːnə/ n raisin m de Smyrne, raisin m sec.

sultry /ˈsʌltrɪ/ adj (**-ier, -iest**) étouffant, lourd; (fig) sensuel.

sum /sʌm/ n somme f; (in arithmetic) calcul m. ● vt/i (pt **summed**) **～ up** résumer, récapituler; (assess) évaluer.

summarize /ˈsʌməraɪz/ vt résumer.

summary /ˈsʌmərɪ/ n résumé m. ● adj sommaire.

summer /ˈsʌmə(r)/ n été m. ● adj d'été. **～time** n (season) été m.

Summer camps Les camps de vacances sont une composante importante des vacances d'été des jeunes Américains. Souvent situés dans des parc nationaux, ces camps proposent de multiples activités de plein air (canoë, escalade, équitation, natation, ski nautique, tennis, randonnée, etc.). Des milliers d'étudiants y sont recrutés chaque année en tant que moniteurs.

summery /ˈsʌmərɪ/ adj estival.

summit /ˈsʌmɪt/ n sommet m; **～ (conference)** (Pol) (conférence f au) sommet m.

summon /ˈsʌmən/ vt appeler; **～ sb to a meeting** convoquer qn à une réunion; **～ up** (strength, courage) rassembler.

summons /ˈsʌmənz/ n (Jur) assignation f. ● vt assigner.

sun /sʌn/ n soleil m. ● vt (pt **sunned**) **～ oneself** se chauffer au soleil. **～burn** n coup m de soleil.

Sunday /ˈsʌndeɪ/ n dimanche m. **～ school** n catéchisme m.

sundry /ˈsʌndrɪ/ adj divers; **sundries** articles mpl divers; **all and ～** tout le monde.

sunflower /ˈsʌnflaʊə(r)/ n tournesol m.

sung /sʌŋ/ **➡SING**.

sun-glasses npl lunettes fpl de soleil.

sunk /sʌŋk/ **➡SINK**.

sunken /ˈsʌŋkən/ adj (ship) submergé; (eyes) creux.

sunlight /ˈsʌnlaɪt/ n soleil m.

sunny /ˈsʌnɪ/ adj (**-ier, -iest**) ensoleillé.

sun: ～rise n lever m du soleil. **～-roof** n toit m ouvrant. **～ screen** n filtre m solaire. **～set** n coucher m du soleil.

~**shine** n soleil m. ~**stroke** n insolation f.

sun-tan /'sʌntæn/ n bronzage m. ~ **lotion** n lotion f solaire. ~ **oil** n huile f solaire.

super /'suːpə(r)/ adj 🔟 formidable.

superb /suːˈpɜːb/ adj superbe.

superficial /suːpəˈfɪʃl/ adj superficiel.

superfluous /suːˈpɜːfluəs/ adj superflu.

superimpose /suːpərɪmˈpəʊz/ vt superposer (**on** à).

superintendent /suːpərɪnˈtendənt/ n directeur/-trice m/f; (of police) commissaire m.

superior /suːˈpɪərɪə(r)/ adj & n supérieur/-e (m /f).

superlative /suːˈpɜːlətɪv/ adj suprême. ● n (Gram) superlatif m.

supermarket /'suːpəmɑːkɪt/ n supermarché m.

supersede /suːpəˈsiːd/ vt remplacer, supplanter.

superstition /suːpəˈstɪʃn/ n superstition f. **superstitious** adj superstitieux.

superstore /'suːpəstɔː(r)/ n hypermarché m.

supervise /'suːpəvaɪz/ vt surveiller, diriger. **supervision** n surveillance f. **supervisor** n surveillant/-e m/f; (shop) chef m de rayon; (firm) chef m de service.

supper /'sʌpə(r)/ n dîner m; (late at night) souper m.

supple /'sʌpl/ adj souple.

supplement[1] /'sʌplɪmənt/ n supplément m. **supplementary** adj supplémentaire.

supplement[2] /'sʌplɪmənt/ vt compléter.

supplier /səˈplaɪə(r)/ n fournisseur m.

supply /səˈplaɪ/ vt fournir; (equip) pourvoir; (feed) alimenter (**with** en). ● n provision f; (of gas) alimentation f; **supplies** (food) vivres mpl; (material) fournitures fpl.

support /səˈpɔːt/ vt soutenir; (family) assurer la subsistance de. ● n soutien m, appui m; (Tech) support m. **supporter** n partisan/-e m/f; (Sport) supporter m. **supportive** adj qui soutient et encourage.

suppose /səˈpəʊz/ vt/i supposer; **be ~d to do** être censé faire, devoir

faire; **supposing he comes** supposons qu'il vienne. **supposedly** adv soi-disant, prétendument.

suppress /səˈpres/ vt (put an end to) supprimer; (restrain) réprimer; (stifle) étouffer.

supreme /suːˈpriːm/ adj suprême.

surcharge /'sɜːtʃɑːdʒ/ n supplément m; (tax) surtaxe f.

sure /ʃɔː(r)/ adj sûr; **make ~ of** s'assurer de; **make ~ that** vérifier que. ● adv (US 🔟) pour sûr. **surely** adv sûrement.

surf /sɜːf/ n ressac m. ● vi faire du surf; (Internet) surfer.

surface /'sɜːfɪs/ n surface f. ● adj superficiel. ● vt revêtir. ● vi faire surface; (fig) réapparaître.

surfer /'sɜːfə(r)/ n surfeur/-euse m/f; (Internet) internaute mf.

surge /sɜːdʒ/ vi (waves, crowd) déferler; (increase) monter. ● n (wave) vague f; (rise) montée f.

surgeon /'sɜːdʒən/ n chirurgien m.

surgery /'sɜːdʒərɪ/ n chirurgie f; (office) cabinet m; (session) consultation f; **need ~** devoir être opéré.

surgical /'sɜːdʒɪkl/ adj chirurgical. ~ **spirit** n alcool m à 90 degrés.

surly /'sɜːlɪ/ adj (**-ier, -iest**) bourru.

surname /'sɜːneɪm/ n nom m de famille.

surplus /'sɜːpləs/ n surplus m. ● adj en surplus.

surprise /səˈpraɪz/ n surprise f. ● vt surprendre. **surprised** adj surpris (**at** de). **surprising** adj surprenant.

surrender /səˈrendə(r)/ vi se rendre. ● vt (hand over) remettre; (Mil) rendre. ● n (Mil) reddition f; (of passport) remise f.

surround /səˈraʊnd/ vt entourer; (Mil) encercler. **surrounding** adj environnant. **surroundings** npl environs mpl; (setting) cadre m.

surveillance /sɜːˈveɪləns/ n surveillance f.

survey[1] /səˈveɪ/ vt (review) passer en revue; (inquire into) enquêter sur; (building) inspecter.

survey[2] /'sɜːveɪ/ n (inquiry) enquête f; inspection f; (general view) vue f d'ensemble.

surveyor /sə'veɪə(r)/ n expert m (géomètre).

survival /sə'vaɪvl/ n survie f.

survive /sə'vaɪv/ vt/i survivre (à). **survivor** n survivant/-e m/f.

susceptible /sə'septəbl/ adj sensible (**to** à); ~ **to** (prone to) prédisposé à.

suspect¹ /sə'spekt/ vt soupçonner; (doubt) douter de.

suspect² /'sʌspekt/ n & adj suspect/-e (m/f).

suspend /sə'spend/ vt (hang, stop) suspendre; (licence) retirer provisoirement. **suspended sentence** n condamnation f avec sursis.

suspender /sə'spendə(r)/ n jarretelle f; ~**s** (braces: US) bretelles fpl. ~ **belt** n porte-jarretelles m.

suspension /sə'spenʃn/ n suspension f; retrait m provisoire.

suspicion /sə'spɪʃn/ n soupçon m; (distrust) méfiance f.

suspicious /sə'spɪʃəs/ adj soupçonneux; (causing suspicion) suspect; **be** ~ **of** se méfier de. **suspiciously** adv de façon suspecte.

sustain /sə'steɪn/ vt supporter; (effort) soutenir; (suffer) subir.

sustenance /'sʌstməns/ n (food) nourriture f; (nourishment) valeur f nutritive.

swallow /'swɒləʊ/ vt/i avaler; ~ **up** (absorb, engulf) engloutir. ● n hirondelle f.

swam /swæm/ ⇒SWIM.

swamp /swɒmp/ n marais m. ● vt (flood, overwhelm) submerger.

swan /swɒn/ n cygne m.

swap /swɒp/ vt/i (pt **swapped**) 🆃 échanger. ● n 🆃 échange m.

swarm /swɔːm/ n essaim m. ● vi fourmiller; ~ **into** or **round** (crowd) envahir.

swat /swɒt/ vt (pt **swatted**) (fly) écraser.

sway /sweɪ/ vt/i (se) balancer; (influence) influencer. ● n balancement m; (rule) empire m.

swear /sweə(r)/ vt/i (pt **swore**; pp **sworn**) jurer (**to sth** de qch); ~ **at** injurier; ~ **by sth** 🆃 ne jurer que par qch. ~ **-word** n juron m.

sweat /swet/ n sueur f. ● vi suer.

sweater /'swetə(r)/ n pull-over m.

sweat-shirt n sweat-shirt m.

swede /swiːd/ n rutabaga m.

Swede /swiːd/ n Suédois/-e m/f. **Sweden** n Suède f.

Swedish /'swiːdɪʃ/ adj suédois. ● n (Ling) suédois m.

sweep /swiːp/ vt/i (pt **swept**) (floor) balayer; (carry away) emporter, entraîner; (chimney) ramoner. ● n coup m de balai; (curve) courbe f; (movement) geste m, mouvement m; (for chimneys) ramoneur m. ~ **by** passer rapidement or majestueusement.

sweeper n (for carpet) balai m mécanique; (football) libero m.

sweet /swiːt/ adj (not sour, pleasant) doux; (not savoury) sucré; (charming 🆃) gentil; **have a** ~ **tooth** aimer les sucreries. ● n bonbon m; (dish) dessert m. ~**corn** n maïs m.

sweeten /'swiːtn/ vt sucrer; (fig) adoucir. **sweetener** n édulcorant m.

sweetheart /'swiːthɑːt/ n petit/-e ami/-e m/f; (term of endearment) chéri/-e m/f.

sweetly /'swiːtlɪ/ adv gentiment.

sweetness /'swiːtnɪs/ n douceur f; goût m sucré.

sweet pea n pois m de senteur.

swell /swel/ vt/i (pt **swelled**; pp **swollen** or **swelled**) (increase) grossir; (expand) (se) gonfler; (hand, face) enfler. ● n (of sea) houle f. **swelling** n (Med) enflure f.

sweltering /'sweltərɪŋ/ adj étouffant.

swept /swept/ ⇒SWEEP.

swerve /swɜːv/ vi faire un écart.

swift /swɪft/ adj rapide. ● n (bird) martinet m.

swim /swɪm/ vi (pt **swam**; pp **swum**; pres p **swimming**) nager; (be dizzy) tourner. ● vt traverser à la nage; (distance) nager. ● n baignade f; **go for a** ~ aller se baigner. **swimmer** n nageur/-euse m/f. **swimming** n natation f.

swimming pool n piscine f.

swimsuit /'swɪmsuːt/ n maillot m (de bain).

swindle /'swɪndl/ vt escroquer. ● n escroquerie f.

swine /swaɪn/ *npl* (pigs) pourceaux *mpl.* ● *n inv* (person 🔒) salaud *m.*

swing /swɪŋ/ *vt/i* (*pt* **swung**) (se) balancer; (turn round) tourner; (*pendulum*) osciller. ● *n* balancement *m;* (seat) balançoire *f;* (of opinion) revirement *m* (**towards** en faveur de); (Mus) rythme *m;* **be in full ~** battre son plein. □ **~ round** (*person*) se retourner.

swipe /swaɪp/ *vt* (hit 🔒) frapper; (steal 🔒) piquer. **~ card** *n* carte *f* magnétique, badge *m.*

swirl /swɜːl/ *vi* tourbillonner. ● *n* tourbillon *m.*

Swiss /swɪs/ *adj* suisse. ● *n inv* Suisse *mf.*

switch /swɪtʃ/ *n* bouton *m* (électrique), interrupteur *m;* (shift) changement *m,* revirement *m.* ● *vt* (transfer) transférer; (exchange) échanger (**for** contre); (reverse positions of) changer de place; **~ trains** (change) changer de train. ● *vi* changer. □ **~ off** éteindre; **~ on** mettre, allumer.

switchboard /'swɪtʃbɔːd/ *n* standard *m.*

Switzerland /'swɪtsələnd/ *n* Suisse *f.*

swivel /'swɪvl/ *vt/i* (*pt* **swivelled**) (faire) pivoter.

swollen /'swəʊlən/ ➡**SWELL.**

swoop /swuːp/ *vi* (bird) fondre; (*police*) faire une descente, foncer. ● *n* (police raid) descente *f.*

sword /sɔːd/ *n* épée *f.*

swore /swɔː(r)/ ➡**SWEAR.**

sworn /swɔːn/ ➡**SWEAR.** ● *adj* (enemy) juré; (ally) dévoué.

swot /swɒt/ *vt/i* (*pt* **swotted**) (study 🔒) bûcher 🔒. ● *n* 🔒 bûcheur/-euse *m/f*🔒.

swum /swʌm/ ➡**SWIM.**

swung /swʌŋ/ ➡**SWING.**

syllabus /'sɪləbəs/ *n* (*pl* **~es**) (School, Univ) programme *m.*

symbol /'sɪmbl/ *n* symbole *m.* **symbolic (al)** *adj* symbolique. **symbolize** *vt* symboliser.

symmetrical /sɪ'metrɪkəl/ *adj* symétrique.

sympathetic /sɪmpə'θetɪk/ *adj* compatissant; (fig) compréhensif.

sympathize /'sɪmpəθaɪz/ *vi* **~ with** (pity) plaindre; (fig) comprendre les sentiments de. **sympathizer** *n* sympathisant/-e *m/f.*

sympathy /'sɪmpəθɪ/ *n* (pity) compassion *f;* (fig) compréhension *f;* (solidarity) solidarité *f;* (condolences) condoléances *fpl;* (affinity) affinité *f;* **be in ~ with** comprendre, être en accord avec.

symptom /'sɪmptəm/ *n* symptôme *m.*

synagogue /'sɪnəgɒg/ *n* synagogue *f.*

synonym /'sɪnənɪm/ *n* synonyme *m.*

synopsis /sɪ'nɒpsɪs/ *n* (*pl* **-opses**) résumé *m.*

syntax /'sɪntæks/ *n* syntaxe *f.*

synthesis /'sɪnθəsɪs/ *n* (*pl* **-theses**) synthèse *f.*

synthetic /sɪn'θetɪk/ *adj* synthétique.

syringe /sɪ'rɪndʒ/ *n* seringue *f.*

syrup /'sɪrəp/ *n* (liquid) sirop *m;* (treacle) mélasse *f* raffinée.

system /'sɪstəm/ *n* système *m;* (body) organisme *m;* (order) méthode *f.* **systematic** *adj* systématique.

systems analyst *n* analysteprogrammeur/- euse *m/f.*

· ·

Tt

· ·

tab /tæb/ *n* (on can) languette *f;* (on garment) patte *f;* (label) étiquette *f;* (US 🔒) addition *f;* (Comput) tabulatrice *f;* (setting) tabulation *f.*

table /'teɪbl/ *n* table *f;* **at (the) ~** à table; **lay** or **set the ~** mettre la table. ● *vt* (*motion*) présenter. **~-cloth** *n* nappe *f.* **~-mat** *n* set *m* de table. **~spoon** *n* cuillère *f* de service.

tablet /'tæblɪt/ *n* (of stone) plaque *f;* (drug) comprimé *m.*

table tennis *n* tennis *m* de table; ping-pong® *m.*

taboo /tə'buː/ *n & a* tabou (*m*).

tacit /'tæsɪt/ *adj* tacite.

tack /tæk/ *n* (nail) clou *m;* (stitch) point *m* de bâti; (course of action) voie *f.* ● *vt* (nail) clouer; (stitch) bâtir; (add) ajouter. ● *vi* (Naut) louvoyer.

tackle /'tækl/ *n* équipement *m*; (in soccer) tacle *m*; (in rugby) plaquage *m*. ● *vt* (*problem*) s'attaquer à; (*player*) tacler, plaquer.

tact /tækt/ *n* tact *m*. **tactful** *adj* plein de tact.

tactics /'tæktɪks/ *npl* tactique *f*.

tadpole /'tædpəʊl/ *n* têtard *m*.

tag /tæg/ *n* (label) étiquette *f*. ● *vt* (*pt* **tagged**) (label) étiqueter. ● *vi* ~ **along** Ⅱ suivre.

tail /teɪl/ *n* queue *f*; ~s (coat) habit *m*; ~s! (on coin) pile! ● *vt* (follow) filer. ● *vi* ~ **away** or **off** diminuer. ~-**back** *n* bouchon *m*. ~-**gate** *n* hayon *m*.

tailor /'teɪlə(r)/ *n* tailleur *m*. ● *vt* (*garment*) façonner; (fig) adapter. ~-**made** *adj* fait sur mesure.

take /teɪk/ *vt/i* (*pt* **took**; *pp* **taken**) prendre (**from sb** à qn); (carry) emporter, porter (**to** à); (escort) emmener; (contain) contenir; (tolerate) supporter; (accept) accepter; (*prize*) remporter; (*exam*) passer; (*precedence*) avoir; (*view*) adopter; ~ **sb home** ramener qn chez lui; **be taken by** or **with** être impressionné par; **be taken ill** tomber malade; **it** ~s **time** il faut du temps pour. ◻ ~ **after** tenir de; ~ **apart** démonter; (fig) descendre en flammes Ⅱ; ~ **away** (object) enlever; (*person*) emmener; (*pain*) supprimer; ~ **back** reprendre; (return) rendre; (accompany) raccompagner; (*statement*) retirer; ~ **down** (object) descendre; (notes) prendre; ~ **in** (object) rentrer; (include) inclure; (cheat) tromper; ~ **off** (Aviat) décoller; ~ **sth off** enlever qch; ~ **sb off** imiter qn; ~ **on** (task, staff, passenger) prendre; (challenger) relever le défi de; ~ **out** sortir; (stain) enlever; ~ **over** *vt* (country, firm) prendre le contrôle de; *vi* prendre le pouvoir; ~ **over from** remplacer; ~ **part** participer (**in** à); ~ **place** avoir lieu; ~ **to** se prendre d'amitié pour; (*activity*) prendre goût à; ~ **to doing** se mettre à faire; ~ **up** (object) monter; (hobby) se mettre à; (occupy) prendre; (resume) reprendre; ~ **up with** se lier avec. ~-**away** *n* (meal) repas *m* à emporter. ~-**off** *n* (Aviat) décollage *m*. ~-**over** *n* (Pol) prise *f* de pouvoir; (Comm) rachat *m*.

tale /teɪl/ *n* conte *m*; (report) récit *m*; (lie) histoire *f*.

talent /'tælənt/ *n* talent *m*. **talented** *adj* doué.

talk /tɔːk/ *vt/i* parler; (chat) bavarder; ~ **sb into doing** persuader qn de faire; ~ **sth over** discuter de qch. ● *n* (talking) propos *mpl*; (conversation) conversation *f*; (lecture) exposé *m*.

talkative /'tɔːkətɪv/ *adj* bavard.

tall /tɔːl/ *adj* (high) haut; (*person*) grand.

tame /teɪm/ *adj* apprivoisé; (dull) insipide. ● *vt* apprivoiser; (lion) dompter.

tamper /'tæmpə(r)/ *vi* ~ **with** (lock, machine) tripoter; (accounts, evidence) trafiquer.

tan /tæn/ *vt/i* (*pt* **tanned**) bronzer; (hide) tanner. ● *n* bronzage *m*.

tangerine /'tændʒəriːn/ *n* mandarine *f*.

tangle /'tæŋgl/ *vt/i* ~ **(up)** s'emmêler. ● *n* enchevêtrement *m*.

tank /tæŋk/ *n* réservoir *m*; (vat) cuve *f*; (for fish) aquarium *m*; (Mil) char *m* (de combat).

tanker /'tæŋkə(r)/ *n* (lorry) camion-citerne *m*; (ship) navire-citerne *m*; **oil/petrol** ~ pétrolier *m*.

tantrum /'tæntrəm/ *n* crise *f* (de colère).

tap /tæp/ *n* (for water) robinet *m*; (knock) petit coup *m*; **on** ~ disponible. ● *vt* (*pt* **tapped**) (knock) taper (doucement); (*resources*) exploiter; (*phone*) mettre sur écoute.

tape /teɪp/ *n* bande *f* (magnétique); (cassette) cassette *f*; (video) cassette *f* vidéo; (fabric) ruban *m*; (sticky) scotch (r) *m*. ● *vt* (record) enregistrer; ~ **sth to sth** coller qch à qch. ~-**measure** *n* mètre *m* ruban. ~ **recorder** *n* magnétophone *m*.

tapestry /'tæpəstrɪ/ *n* tapisserie *f*.

tar /tɑː(r)/ *n* goudron *m*. ● *vt* (*pt* **tarred**) goudronner.

target /'tɑːgɪt/ *n* cible *f*; (objective) objectif *m*. ● *vt* (city) prendre pour cible; (weapon) diriger; (in marketing) viser.

tariff /'tærɪf/ *n* (price list) tarif *m*; (on imports) droit *m* de douane.

tarmac, Tarmac® /'tɑːmæk/ *n* macadam *m*; (runway) piste *f*.

tarpaulin /tɑːˈpɔːlɪn/ *n* bâche *f*.

tarragon /'tærəgən/ n estragon m.

tart /tɑːt/ n tarte f. ● adj aigrelet.

task /tɑːsk/ n tâche f.

taste /teɪst/ n goût m; (experience) aperçu m. ● vt (eat, enjoy) goûter à; (try) goûter; (perceive taste of) sentir (le goût de). ● vi ~ of or like avoir un goût de. **tasteful** adj de bon goût.

tattoo /tə'tuː/ vt tatouer. ● n tatouage m.

tatty /'tætɪ/ adj (-ier, -iest) 🗊 miteux.

taught /tɔːt/ ➞TEACH.

taunt /tɔːnt/ vt railler. ● n raillerie f.

Taurus /'tɔːrəs/ n Taureau m.

tax /tæks/ n (on goods, services) taxe f; (on income) impôt m. ● vt imposer; (put to test: fig) mettre à l'épreuve. **taxable** adj imposable. **taxation** n imposition f; (taxes) impôts mpl.

tax: ~ **collector** n percepteur m. ~**-deductible** adj déductible des impôts. ~ **disc** n vignette f. ~**-free** adj exempt d'impôts. ~ **haven** n paradis m fiscal.

taxi /'tæksɪ/ n taxi m. ~ **rank** n station f de taxi.

tax: ~**payer** n contribuable mf. ~ **relief** n dégrèvement m fiscal. ~ **return** n déclaration f d'impôts.

tea /tiː/ n (drink, meal) thé m; (children's snack) goûter m; ~ **bag** sachet m de thé.

teach /tiːtʃ/ vt (pt taught) apprendre (sb sth qch à qn); (in school) enseigner (sb sth qch à qn). ● vi enseigner. **teacher** n enseignant/-e m/f; (secondary) professeur m; (primary) instituteur/-trice m/f.

team /tiːm/ n équipe f; (of animals) attelage m. ● vi ~ up faire équipe (with avec).

teapot /'tiːpɒt/ n théière f.

tear¹ /teə(r)/ vt/i (pt tore; pp torn) (se) déchirer; (snatch) arracher (from à); (rush) aller à toute vitesse. ● n déchirure f.

tear² /tɪə(r)/ n larme f; in ~s en larmes. ~**-gas** n gaz m lacrymogène.

tease /tiːz/ vt taquiner. ● n taquin/-e m/f.

tea: ~ **shop** n salon m de thé. ~**spoon** n petite cuillère f.

teat /tiːt/ n tétine f.

tea-towel n torchon m.

technical /'teknɪkl/ adj technique.

technician /tek'nɪʃn/ n technicien/-ne m/f.

technique /tek'niːk/ n technique f.

techno /'teknəʊ/ n (Mus) techno f.

technology /tek'nɒlədʒɪ/ n technologie f.

technophobe /teknɒ'fəʊb/ n technophobe mf.

teddy /'tedɪ/ adj ~ **bear** ours m en peluche.

tedious /'tiːdɪəs/ adj ennuyeux.

tee /tiː/ n (golf) tee m.

teenage /'tiːneɪdʒ/ adj (girl, boy) adolescent; (fashion) des adolescents. **teenager** n jeune mf, adolescent/-e m/f.

teens /tiːnz/ npl in one's ~ adolescent.

teeth /tiːθ/ ➞TOOTH.

teethe /tiːð/ vi faire ses dents.

teetotaller /tiː'təʊtələ(r)/ n personne f qui ne boit pas d'alcool.

telecommunications /telɪkəmjuːnɪ'keɪʃnz/ npl télécommunications fpl.

telecommuting /telɪkə'mjuːtɪŋ/ n télétravail m.

teleconferencing /telɪ'kɒnfərənsɪŋ/ n téléconférence f.

telegram /'telɪɡræm/ n télégramme m.

telegraph /'telɪɡrɑːf/ n télégraphe m. ● adj télégraphique.

telephone /'telɪfəʊn/ n téléphone m. ● vt (person) téléphoner à; (message) téléphoner. ● vi téléphoner. ~ **book** annuaire m. ~ **booth**, ~ **box** n cabine f téléphonique. ~ **call** n coup m de téléphone. ~ **number** n numéro m de téléphone.

telephoto /telɪ'fəʊtəʊ/ adj ~ **lens** téléobjectif m.

telescope /'telɪskəʊp/ n télescope m. ● vt/i (se) télescoper.

teletext /'telɪtekst/ n télétexte m.

televise /'telɪvaɪz/ vt téléviser.

television /'telɪvɪʒn/ n télévision f; ~ **set** poste m de télévision, téléviseur m.

teleworking /'telɪwɜːkɪŋ/ n télétravail m.

telex /'teleks/ n télex m. ● vt envoyer par télex.

tell /tel/ vt (pt told) dire (sb sth qch à qn); (story) raconter; (distinguish) distinguer; ~ **sb to do sth** dire à qn de faire qch; ~ **sth from sth** voir la différence entre qch et qch. ● *vi* (*show*) avoir un effet; (*know*) savoir. □ ~ **off** 🇬🇧 gronder.

temp /temp/ *n* intérimaire *mf.* ● *vi* faire de l'intérim.

temper /'tempə(r)/ *n* humeur *f;* (*anger*) colère *f;* **lose one's** ~ se mettre en colère.

temperament /'temprəmənt/ *n* tempérament *m.* **temperamental** *adj* capricieux.

temperature /'temprətʃə(r)/ *n* température *f;* **have a** ~ avoir de la fièvre or de la température.

temple /'templ/ *n* temple *m;* (*of head*) tempe *f.*

temporary /'temprəri/ *adj* temporaire, provisoire.

tempt /tempt/ *vt* tenter; ~ **sb to do** donner envie à qn de faire.

ten /ten/ *adj* & *n* dix (*m*).

tenacious /tɪ'neɪʃəs/ *adj* tenace.

tenancy /'tenənsɪ/ *n* location *f.* **tenant** *n* locataire *mf.*

tend /tend/ *vt* s'occuper de. ● *vi* ~ **to** (*be apt to*) avoir tendance à; (*look after*) s'occuper de. **tendency** *n* tendance *f.*

tender /'tendə(r)/ *adj* tendre; (*sore, painful*) sensible. ● *vt* offrir, donner. ● *vi* faire une soumission. ● *n* (Comm) soumission *f;* **be legal** ~ (*money*) avoir cours.

tendon /'tendən/ *n* tendon *m.*

tennis /'tenɪs/ *n* tennis *m.* ● *adj* (*court, match*) de tennis.

tenor /'tenə(r)/ *n* (*meaning*) sens *m* général; (*Mus*) ténor *m.*

tense /tens/ *n* (Gram) temps *m.* ● *adj* tendu. ● *vt* (*muscles*) tendre, raidir. ● *vi* (*face*) se crisper.

tension /'tenʃn/ *n* tension *f.*

tent /tent/ *n* tente *f.*

tentative /'tentətɪv/ *adj* provisoire; (*hesitant*) timide.

tenth /tenθ/ *adj* & *n* dixième (*mf*).

tepid /'tepɪd/ *adj* tiède.

term /tɜːm/ *n* (*word, limit*) terme *m;* (*of imprisonment*) temps *m;* (School) trimestre *m;* ~**s** conditions *fpl;* **on good/bad** ~**s** en bons/mauvais termes; **in the short/long** ~ à court/long terme;

come to ~**s with sth** accepter qch; ~ **of office** (Pol) mandat *m.* ● *vt* appeler.

terminal /'tɜːmɪnl/ *adj* (*point*) terminal; (*illness*) incurable. ● *n* (oil, computer) terminal *m;* (Rail) terminus *m;* (Electr) borne *f;* **air** ~ aérogare *f.*

terminate /'tɜːmɪneɪt/ *vt* mettre fin à. ● *vi* prendre fin.

terminus /'tɜːmɪnəs/ *n* (*pl* -**ni**) (station) terminus *m.*

terrace /'terəs/ *n* terrasse *f;* (*houses*) rangée *f* de maisons contiguës; **the** ~**s** (Sport) les gradins *mpl.*

terracotta /terə'kɒtə/ *n* terre *f* cuite.

terrible /'terəbl/ *adj* affreux, atroce.

terrific /tə'rɪfɪk/ *adj* (*huge*) énorme; (*great* 🇬🇧) formidable.

terrify /'terɪfaɪ/ *vt* terrifier; **be terrified of** avoir très peur de.

territory /'terətrɪ/ *n* territoire *m.*

terror /'terə(r)/ *n* terreur *f.*

terrorism /'terərɪzəm/ *n* terrorisme *m.* **terrorist** *n* terroriste *mf.*

test /test/ *n* épreuve *f;* (written exam) contrôle *m;* (of machine, product) essai *m;* (of sample) analyse *f;* **driving** ~ examen *m* du permis de conduire. ● *vt* évaluer; (School) contrôler; (*machine, product*) essayer; (*sample*) analyser; (*patience, strength*) mettre à l'épreuve. ● *vi* ~ **for** faire une recherche de.

testament /'testəmənt/ *n* testament *m;* **Old/New T**~ Ancien/Nouveau Testament *m.*

testicle /'testɪkl/ *n* testicule *m.*

testify /'testɪfaɪ/ *vt/i* témoigner (**to** de; **that** que).

testimony /'testɪmənɪ/ *n* témoignage *m.*

test tube *n* éprouvette *f.*

tetanus /'tetənəs/ *n* tétanos *m.*

text /tekst/ *n* texte *m.* ● *vt* ~ **sb** envoyer un texto à qn. ~**book** *n* manuel *m.* ~ **message** *n* texto *m.*

texture /'tekstʃə(r)/ *n* (of paper) grain *m;* (of fabric) texture *f.*

than /ðæn/, /ðən/ *conj* que, qu'; (with numbers) de; **more/less** ~ **ten** plus/moins de dix.

thank /θæŋk/ *vt* remercier; ~ **you!**, ~**s!** merci! **thankful** *adj* reconnaissant

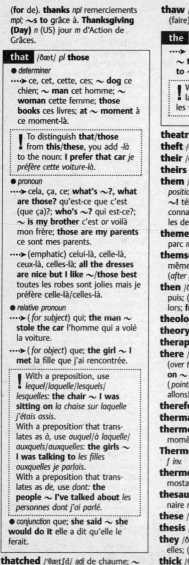

(for de). **thanks** *npl* remerciements *mpl;* **~s to** grâce à. **Thanksgiving (Day)** *n* (US) jour *m* d'Action de Grâces.

that /ðæt/ *pl* **those**

● *determiner*

····➤ ce, cet, cette, ces; **~ dog** ce chien; **~ man** cet homme; **~ woman** cette femme; **those books** ces livres; **at ~ moment** à ce moment-là.

❗ To distinguish **that/those** from **this/these**, you add *-là* to the noun: **I prefer that car** *je préfère cette voiture-là.*

● *pronoun*

····➤ cela, ça, ce; **what's ~?, what are those?** qu'est-ce que c'est (que ça?); **who's ~?** qui est-ce?; **~ is my brother** c'est *or* voilà mon frère; **those are my parents** ce sont mes parents.

····➤ (emphatic) celui-là, celle-là, ceux-là, celles-là; **all the dresses are nice but I like ~/those best** toutes les robes sont jolies mais je préfère celle-là/celles-là.

● *relative pronoun*

····➤ (*for subject*) qui; **the man ~ stole the car** l'homme qui a volé la voiture.

····➤ (*for object*) que; **the girl ~ I met** la fille que j'ai rencontrée.

❗ With a preposition, use *lequel/laquelle/lesquels/lesquelles:* **the chair ~ I was sitting on** *la chaise sur laquelle j'étais assis.*
With a preposition that translates as *à,* use *auquel/à laquelle/ auxquels/auxquelles:* **the girls ~ I was talking to** *les filles auxquelles je parlais.*
With a preposition that translates as *de,* use *dont:* **the people ~ I've talked about** *les personnes dont j'ai parlé.*

● *conjunction* que; **she said ~ she would do it** elle a dit qu'elle le ferait.

thatched /'θætʃd/ *adj* de chaume; **~ cottage** chaumière *f.*

thaw /θɔː/ *vt/i* (faire) dégeler; (*snow*) (faire) fondre. ● *n* dégel *m.*

the /ðə, ði:/ *determiner*

····➤ le, l', la, les; **~ dog** le chien; **~ tree** l'arbre; **~ chair** la chaise; **to ~ shops** aux magasins.

❗ With a preposition that translates as à: à + le = au and à + les = aux.

theatre /'θɪətə(r)/ *n* théâtre *m.*

theft /θeft/ *n* vol *m.*

their /ðeə(r)/ *adj* leur, *pl* leurs.

theirs /ðeəz/ *pron* le or la leur, les leurs.

them /ðem/, /ðəm/ *pron* les; (*after preposition*) eux, elles; **(to) ~** leur; **phone ~!** téléphone-leur!; **I know ~** je les connais; **both of ~** tous/toutes les deux.

theme /θiːm/ *n* thème *m.* **~ park** *n* parc *m* de loisirs (à thème).

themselves /ðem'selvz/ *pron* eux-mêmes, elles-mêmes; (*reflexive*) se; (*after preposition*) eux, elles.

then /ðen/ *adv* alors; (*next*) ensuite, puis; (*therefore*) alors, donc. ● *adj* d'alors; **from ~ on** dès lors.

theology /θɪ'ɒlədʒɪ/ *n* théologie *f.*

theory /'θɪərɪ/ *n* théorie *f.*

therapy /'θerəpɪ/ *n* thérapie *f.*

there /ðeə(r)/ *adv* là; (*with verb*) y; (*over there*) là-bas; **he goes ~** il y va; **on ~** là-dessus; **~ is, ~ are** il y a; (*pointing*) voilà. ● *interj* **~, ~!** allons, allons!

therefore /'ðeəfɔː(r)/ *adv* donc.

thermal /'θɜːml/ *adj* thermique.

thermometer /θə'mɒmɪtə(r)/ *n* thermomètre *m.*

Thermos® /'θɜːməs/ *n* thermos ® *m or f inv.*

thermostat /'θɜːməstæt/ *n* thermostat *m.*

thesaurus /θɪ'sɔːrəs/ *n* (*pl* **-ri**) dictionnaire *m* de synonymes.

these /ðiːz/ →THIS.

thesis /'θiːsɪs/ *n* (*pl* **theses**) thèse *f.*

they /ðeɪ/ *pron* ils, elles; (*emphatic*) eux, elles; (*people in general*) on.

thick /θɪk/ *adj* épais; (*stupid*) bête; **be 6 cm ~** avoir 6 cm d'épaisseur.

thief /θiːf/ n (pl **thieves**) voleur/-euse m/f.

thigh /θaɪ/ n cuisse f.

thin /θɪn/ adj (**thinner, thinnest**) mince; (person) maigre, mince; (sparse) clairsemé; (fine) fin. ● vt/i (pt **thinned**) ~ (**down**) (paint) diluer; (soup) allonger.

thing /θɪŋ/ n chose f; ~s (belongings) affaires fpl; **the best** ~ **is** to le mieux est de; **the (right)** ~ ce qu'il faut (**for sb** à qn).

think /θɪŋk/ vt/i (pt **thought**) penser (**about, of** à); (carefully) réfléchir (**about, of** à); (believe) croire; **I** ~ **so** je crois que oui; ~ **of doing** envisager de faire. □ ~ **over** bien réfléchir à; □ ~ **up** inventer.

third /θɜːd/ adj troisième. ● n troisième mf; (fraction) tiers m. **T**~ **World** n tiers-monde m.

thirst /θɜːst/ n soif f.

thirsty /'θɜːstɪ/ adj **be** ~ avoir soif; **make** ~ donner soif à.

thirteen /θɜː'tiːn/ adj & n treize (m).

thirty /'θɜːtɪ/ adj & n trente (m).

---

this /ðɪs/ pl **these**

● determiner

····▸ ce/cet/cette/ces; ~ **dog** ce chien; ~ **man** cet homme; ~ **woman** cette femme; **these books** ces livres.

! To distinguish from **that** and **those**, you need to add -ci after the noun: **I prefer this car** je préfère cette voiture-ci.

● pronoun

····▸ ce; **what's** ~?, **what are these?** qu'est-ce que c'est?; **who is** ~? qui est-ce?; ~ **is the kitchen** voici la cuisine; ~ **is Sophie** je te or vous présente Sophie; **these are your things** ce sont tes affaires.

····▸ (emphatic) celui-ci/celle-ci/ceux-ci/celles-ci; **all the dresses are nice but I like** ~/**these best** toutes les robes sont jolies mais je préfère celle-ci/celles-ci.

---

thistle /'θɪsl/ n chardon m.

thorn /θɔːn/ n épine f.

thorough /'θʌrə/ adj (detailed) approfondi; (meticulous) minutieux. **thoroughly** adv (clean, study) à fond; (very) tout à fait.

those /ðəʊz/ ➡THAT.

though /ðəʊ/ conj bien que. ● adv quand même.

thought /θɔːt/ ➡THINK. ● n pensée f, idée f. **thoughtful** adj pensif; (kind) prévenant.

thousand /'θaʊznd/ adj & n mille (m inv); ~**s of** des milliers de. **thousandth** adj & n millième (mf).

thread /θred/ n (yarn & fig) fil m; (of screw) pas m. ● vt enfiler; ~ **one's way** se faufiler.

threat /θret/ n menace f. **threaten** vt/i menacer (**with** de).

three /θriː/ adj & n trois (m).

threw /θruː/ ➡THROW.

thrill /θrɪl/ n frisson m; (pleasure) plaisir m. ● vt transporter (de joie); **be** ~**ed** être ravi. ● vi frissonner (de joie).

thrive /θraɪv/ vi (pt **thrived** or **throve**;pp **thrived** or **thriven**) prospérer; **he** ~**s on it** cela lui réussit.

throat /θrəʊt/ n gorge f; **have a sore** ~ avoir mal à la gorge.

throb /θrɒb/ vi (pt **throbbed**) (heart) battre; (engine) vibrer. ● n (pain) élancement m; (of engine) vibration f. **throbbing** adj (pain) lancinant.

throne /θrəʊn/ n trône m.

through /θruː/ prep à travers; (during) pendant; (by means or way of, out of) par; (by reason of) grâce à, à cause de. ● adv à travers; (entirely) jusqu'au bout. ● adj (train) direct; **be** ~ (finished) avoir fini; **come** or **go** ~ (cross, pierce) traverser; **I'm putting you** ~ je vous passe votre correspondant.

throughout /θruː'aʊt/ prep ~ **the country** dans tout le pays; ~ **the day** pendant toute la journée. ● adv (place) partout; (time) tout le temps.

throw /θrəʊ/ vt (pt **threw**; pp **thrown**) jeter, lancer; (baffle) déconcerter; ~ **a party** faire une fête. ● n jet m; (of dice) coup m. □ **away** jeter; ~ **off** (get rid of) se débarrasser de; ~ **out** jeter; (person) expulser; (reject) rejeter; ~ **up** (arms) lever; (vomit 🔲) vomir.

thrust /θrʌst/ vt (pt **thrust**) pousser. ● n poussée f.

thud /θʌd/ n bruit m sourd.

thug /θʌg/ n voyou m.

thumb /θʌm/ n pouce m. ● vt (book) feuilleter; ~ **a lift** faire de l'autostop. ~**-index** n répertoire m à onglets.

thump /θʌmp/ vt/i cogner (sur); (heart) battre fort. ● n coup m.

thunder /'θʌndə(r)/ n tonnerre m. ● vi (weather, person) tonner. ~**storm** n orage m.

Thursday /'θɜːzdeɪ/ n jeudi m.

thus /ðʌs/ adv ainsi.

thwart /θwɔːt/ vt contrecarrer.

thyme /taɪm/ n thym m.

tick /tɪk/ n (sound) tic-tac m; (mark) coche f; (moment ⏱) instant m; (insect) tique f. ● vi faire tic-tac. ● vt (~ **off**) cocher. □ ~ **over** tourner au ralenti.

ticket /'tɪkɪt/ n billet m; (for bus, cloakroom) ticket m; (label) étiquette f. ~**-collector** n contrôleur/-euse m/f. ~**-office** n guichet m.

tickle /'tɪkl/ vt chatouiller; (amuse: fig) amuser. ● n chatouillement m.

tidal /'taɪdl/ adj (river) à marées; ~ **wave** raz-de-marée m inv.

tide /taɪd/ n marée f; (of events) cours m.

tidy /'taɪdɪ/ adj (-ier, -iest) (room) bien rangé; (appearance, work) soigné; (methodical) ordonné; (amount ⏱) joli. ● vt/i ~ (**up**) faire du rangement; ~ **sth** (**up**) ranger qch; ~ **oneself up** s'arranger.

tie /taɪ/ vt (pres p **tying**) attacher; (knot) faire; (scarf) nouer; (link) lier. ● vi (in football) faire match nul; (in race) être ex aequo. ● n (necktie) cravate f; (fastener) attache f; (link) lien m; (draw) match m nul. ~ **down** attacher; ~ **in with** être lié à; ~ **up** attacher; (money) immobiliser; (occupy) occuper.

tier /tɪə(r)/ n étage m, niveau m; (in stadium) gradin m.

tiger /'taɪgə(r)/ n tigre m.

tight /taɪt/ adj (clothes, budget) serré; (grip) ferme; (rope) tendu; (security) strict; (angle) aigu. ● adv (hold, sleep) bien; (squeeze) fort.

tighten /'taɪtn/ vt/i (se) tendre; (bolt) (se) resserrer; (control) renforcer.

tights /taɪts/ npl collant m.

tile /taɪl/ n (on wall, floor) carreau m; (on roof) tuile f. ● vt carreler; couvrir de tuiles.

till /tɪl/ n caisse f (enregistreuse). ● vt (land) cultiver. ● prep & conj ➡UNTIL.

timber /'tɪmbə(r)/ n bois m (de construction); (trees) arbres mpl.

time /taɪm/ n temps m; (moment) moment m; (epoch) époque f; (by clock) heure f; (occasion) fois f; (rhythm) mesure f; ~**s** (multiplying) fois fpl; **any** ~ n'importe quand; **for the** ~ **being** pour le moment; **from** ~ **to** ~ de temps en temps; **have a good** ~ s'amuser; **in no** ~ en un rien de temps; **in** ~ à temps; (eventually) avec le temps; **a long** ~ longtemps; **on** ~ à l'heure; **what's the** ~? quelle heure est-il?; ~ **off** du temps libre. ● vt choisir le moment de; (measure) minuter; (Sport) chronométrer. ~ **limit** n délai m.

timer /'taɪmə(r)/ n minuterie f; (for cooker) minuteur m.

time: ~**-scale** n délais mpl. ~**table** n horaire m. ~ **zone** n fuseau m horaire.

timid /'tɪmɪd/ adj timide; (fearful) peureux.

tin /tɪn/ n étain m; (container) boîte f; ~(**plate**) fer-blanc m. ● vt (pt **tinned**) mettre en boîte. ~**foil** n papier m d'aluminium.

tingle /'tɪŋgl/ vi picoter. ● n picotement m.

tin-opener n ouvre-boîtes m inv.

tint /tɪnt/ n teinte f; (for hair) shampooing m colorant. ● vt teinter.

tiny /'taɪnɪ/ adj (-ier, -iest) tout petit.

tip /tɪp/ n (of stick, pen, shoe, ski) pointe f; (of nose, finger, wing) bout m; (gratuity) pourboire m; (advice) tuyau m; (for rubbish) décharge f. ● vt/i (pt **tipped**) (tilt) pencher; (overturn) (faire) basculer; (pour) verser; (empty) déverser; (give money) donner un pourboire à. □ ~ **off** prévenir.

tiptoe /'tɪptəʊ/ n **on** ~ sur la pointe des pieds.

tire /'taɪə(r)/ vt/i (se) fatiguer; ~ **of** se lasser de. ● n (US) pneu m.

tired /'taɪəd/ adj fatigué; **be** ~ **of** en avoir assez de.

tiring /'taɪərɪŋ/ adj fatigant.

tissue /'tɪʃuː/ n tissu m; (handkerchief) mouchoir m en papier; ~ **(paper)** papier m de soie.

tit /tɪt/ n (bird) mésange f; **give ~ for tat** rendre coup pour coup.

title /'taɪtl/ n titre m. ~ **deed** n titre m de propriété.

---

to /tuː, tə/
● preposition

····▸ à; ~ **Paris** à Paris; **give the book ~ Jane** donne le livre à Jane; ~ **the office** au bureau; ~ **the shops** aux magasins.

····▸ (with feminine countries) en; ~ **France** en France.

····▸ (to + personal pronoun) me/te/lui/nous/vous/leur; **she gave it ~ them** elle le leur a donné; **I'll say it ~ her** je vais le lui dire.

> ! à + le = au
> à + les = aux.

● in an infinitive

to is not translated (**to go** aller; **to sing** chanter)

····▸ (in order to) pour; **he's gone into town ~ buy a shirt** il est parti en ville pour acheter une chemise.

····▸ (after adjectives) à; de; **be easy/difficult ~ read** être facile/difficile à lire; **it's easy/difficult to read her writing** c'est facile/difficile de lire son écriture.

> ➡ For verbal expressions using the infinitive 'to' such as **to tell sb to do sth, to help sb to do sth** ➡**tell, help.**

---

toad /təʊd/ n crapaud m.

toast /təʊst/ n pain m grillé, toast m; (drink) toast m. ● vt (bread) faire griller; (drink to) porter un toast à. **toaster** n grille-pain m inv.

tobacco /tə'bækəʊ/ n tabac m.

tobacconist /tə'bækənɪst/ n marchand/-e m/f de tabac; ~**'s (shop)** tabac m.

toboggan /tə'bɒgən/ n toboggan m, luge f.

today /tə'deɪ/ n & adv aujourd'hui (m).

toddler /'tɒdlə(r)/ n bébé m (qui fait ses premiers pas).

toe /təʊ/ n orteil m; (of shoe) bout m; **on one's ~s** vigilant. ● vt ~ **the line** se conformer.

together /tə'geðə(r)/ adv ensemble; (at same time) à la fois; ~ **with** avec.

toilet /'tɔɪlɪt/ n toilettes fpl.

toiletries /'tɔɪlɪtrɪz/ npl articles mpl de toilette.

token /'təʊkən/ n (symbol) témoignage m; (voucher) bon m; (coin) jeton m. ● adj symbolique.

told /təʊld/ ➡TELL.

tolerance /'tɒlərəns/ n tolérance f.

tolerate /'tɒləreɪt/ vt tolérer.

toll /təʊl/ n péage m; **death ~** nombre m de morts; **take its ~** faire des ravages. ● vi (bell) sonner.

tomato /tə'mɑːtəʊ/ n (pl ~**es**) tomate f.

tomb /tuːm/ n tombeau m.

tomorrow /tə'mɒrəʊ/ n & adv demain (m); ~ **morning/night** demain matin/soir; **the day after ~** après-demain.

ton /tʌn/ n tonne f (= 1016 kg); (metric) ~ tonne f (= 1000 kg); ~**s of** 🄸 des masses de.

tone /təʊn/ n ton m; (of radio, telephone) tonalité f. ● vt ~ **down** atténuer. ● vi ~ **(in)** s'harmoniser (**with** avec).

tongs /tɒŋz/ npl (for coal) pincettes fpl; (for sugar) pince f; (for hair) fer m.

tongue /tʌŋ/ n langue f.

tonic /'tɒnɪk/ n (Med) tonique m. ● adj (effect, accent) tonique; ~ **(water)** tonic m, Schweppes® m.

tonight /tə'naɪt/ n & adv (evening) ce soir; (night) cette nuit.

tonsil /'tɒnsl/ n amygdale f.

too /tuː/ adv trop; (also) aussi; ~ **many people** trop de gens; **I've got ~much/many** j'en ai trop; **me ~** moi aussi.

took➡TAKE.

tool /tuːl/ n outil m. ~**bar** n barre f d'outils. ~-**box** n boîte f à outils.

toot /tuːt/ n coup m de klaxon®. ● vt/i ~ **(the horn)** klaxonner.

tooth /tuːθ/ n (pl **teeth**) dent f. ~**ache** n mal m de dents. ~**brush** n brosse f à dents. ~**paste** n dentifrice m.

~**pick** n cure-dents m inv.

top /tɒp/ n (highest point) sommet m; (upper part) haut m; (upper surface) dessus m; (lid) couvercle m; (of bottle, tube) bouchon m; (of beer bottle) capsule f; (of list) tête f; **on ~ of** sur; (fig) en plus de. ● adj (shelf) du haut; (step, floor) dernier; (in rank) premier; (best) meilleur; (distinguished) éminent; (maximum) maximum. ● vt (pt **topped**) (exceed) dépasser; (list) venir en tête de; **~ up** remplir; **~ped with** (dome) surmonté de; (cream) recouvert de.

topic /'tɒpɪk/ n sujet m.

topless /'tɒplɪs/ adj aux seins nus.

torch /tɔːtʃ/ n (electric) lampe f de poche; (flaming) torche f.

tore /tɔː(r)/ ➞TEAR¹.

torment /'tɔːment/ vt tourmenter.

torn /tɔːn/ ➞TEAR¹.

torrent /'tɒrənt/ n torrent m.

tortoise /'tɔːtəs/ n tortue f. **~shell** n écaille f.

torture /'tɔːtʃə(r)/ n torture f; (fig) supplice m. ● vt torturer.

Tory /'tɔːrɪ/ n & a tory (mf), conservateur/-trice (m/f).

toss /tɒs/ vt lancer; (salad) tourner; (pancake) faire sauter. ● vi se retourner; **~ a coin**, **~ up** tirer à pile ou face (**for** pour).

tot /tɒt/ n petit/-e enfant m/f; (drink) petit verre m.

total /'təʊtl/ n & a total (m). ● vt (pt **totalled**) (add up) additionner; (amount to) se monter à.

touch /tʌtʃ/ vt toucher; (tamper with) toucher à. ● vi se toucher. ● n (sense) toucher m; (contact) contact m; (of artist, writer) touche f; **a ~of** (small amount) un petit peu de; **get in ~ with** se mettre en contact avec; **out of ~** with déconnecté de. □ **~ down** (Aviat) atterrir; **~ up** retoucher. **~down** n atterrissage m; (Sport) essai m. **~ line** n ligne f de touche. **~tone** adj (phone) à touches.

tough /tʌf/ adj (negotiator) coriace; (law) sévère; (time) difficile; (robust) robuste.

tour /tʊə(r)/ n voyage m; (visit) visite f; (by team) tournée f; **on ~** en tournée. ● vt visiter.

tourist /'tʊərɪst/ n touriste mf. ● adj touristique. **~ office** n syndicat m d'initiative.

tournament /'tɔːnəmənt/ n tournoi m.

tout /taʊt/ vi **~ (for)** racoler 🔢. ● vt (sell) revendre. ● n racoleur/-euse m/f; revendeur/-euse m/f.

tow /təʊ/ vt remorquer. ● n remorque f; **on ~** en remorque.

toward(s) /tə'wɔːd(z)/ prep vers; (of attitude) envers.

towel /'taʊəl/ n serviette f.

tower /'taʊə(r)/ n tour f. ● vi **~ above** dominer.

town /taʊn/ n ville f; **in ~** en ville. **~ council** n conseil m municipal. **~ hall** n mairie f.

tow: ~ path n chemin m de halage. **~ truck** n dépanneuse f.

toxic /'tɒksɪk/ adj toxique.

toy /tɔɪ/ n jouet m. ● vi **~ with** (object) jouer avec; (idea) caresser.

trace /treɪs/ n trace f. ● vt (person) retrouver; (cause) déterminer; (life) retracer; (draw) tracer; (with tracing paper) décalquer.

track /træk/ n (of person, car) traces fpl; (of missile) trajectoire f; (path) sentier m; (Sport) piste f; (Rail) voie f; (on disc) morceau m; **keep ~ of** suivre. ● vt suivre la trace or la trajectoire de. □ **~ down** retrouver. **~ suit** n survêtement m.

tractor /'træktə(r)/ n tracteur m.

trade /treɪd/ n commerce m; (job) métier m; (swap) échange m. ● vi faire du commerce; **~on** exploiter. ● vt échanger. ● adj (route, deficit) commercial. **~-in** n reprise f. **~ mark** n marque f (de fabrique); (registered) marque f déposée.

trader /'treɪdə(r)/ n commerçant/-e m/f; (on stockmarket) opérateur/-trice m/f.

trade union n syndicat m.

trading /'treɪdɪŋ/ n commerce m; (on stockmarket) transactions fpl (boursières).

tradition /trə'dɪʃn/ n tradition f.

traffic /'træfɪk/ n trafic m; (on road) circulation f. ● vi (pt **trafficked**) faire du trafic (**in** de). **~ jam** n embouteillage m. **~-lights** npl feux mpl (de circulation). ~ **warden** contractuel/-le *m/f.*

trail /treɪl/ *vt/i* traîner; (*plant*) ramper; (*track*) suivre; ~ **behind** traîner. ● *n* (of powder) traînée *f;* (*track*) piste *f;* (*path*) sentier *m.*

trailer /'treɪlə(r)/ *n* remorque *f;* (caravan) caravane *f;* (*film*) bande-annonce *f.*

train /treɪn/ *n* (Rail) train *m;* (underground) rame *f;* (procession) file *f;* (of dress) traîne *f.* ● *vt* (instruct, develop) former; (*sportsman*) entraîner; (*animal*) dresser; (*ear*) exercer; (*aim*) braquer. ● *vi* être formé, étudier; (Sport) s'entraîner. **trained** *adj* (skilled) qualifié; (*doctor*) diplômé. **trainee** *n* stagiaire *mf.* **trainer** *n* (Sport) entraîneur/-euse *m/f.* **trainers** *npl* (shoes) chaussures *fpl* de sport. **training** *n* formation *f;* (Sport) entraînement *m.*

tram /træm/ *n* tram(way) *m.*

tramp /træmp/ *vi* marcher (d'un pas lourd). ● *vt* parcourir. ● *n* (vagrant) clochard/-e *m/f;* (sound) bruit *m.*

trample /'træmpl/ *vt/i* ~ **(on)** piétiner; (fig) fouler aux pieds.

tranquil /'træŋkwɪl/ *adj* tranquille. **tranquillizer** *n* tranquillisant *m.*

transact /træn'zækt/ *vt* négocier. **transaction** *n* transaction *f.*

transcript /'trænskrɪpt/ *n* transcription *f.*

transfer¹ /træns'fɜ:(r)/ *vt* (*pt* **transferred**) transférer; (*power*) céder; (*employee*) muter. ● *vi* être transféré; (*employee*) être muté.

transfer² /'trænsfɜ:(r)/ *n* transfert *m;* (of employee) mutation *f;* (image) décalcomanie *f.*

transform /træns'fɔ:m/ *vt* transformer.

transitive /'trænzətɪv/ *adj* transitif.

translate /trænz'leɪt/ *vt* traduire. **translation** *n* traduction *f.* **translator** *n* traducteur/-trice *m/f.*

transmit /trænz'mɪt/ *vt* (*pt* **transmitted**) transmettre. **transmitter** *n* émetteur *m.*

transparency /træns'pærənsɪ/ *n* transparence *f;* (Photo) diapositive *f.*

transplant /træns'plɑ:nt/ *n* transplantation *f;* (Med) greffe *f.*

transport¹ /træns'pɔ:t/ *vt* transporter.

transport² /'trænspɔ:t/ *n* transport *m.*

trap /træp/ *n* piège *m.* ● *vt pt* **trapped** (jam, pin down) coincer; (cut off) bloquer; (snare) prendre au piège.

trash /træʃ/ *n* (refuse) ordures *fpl;* (nonsense) idioties *fpl.* ~**-can** *n* (US) poubelle *f.*

trauma /'trɔːmə/ *n* traumatisme *m.* **traumatic** *adj* traumatisant.

travel /'trævl/ *vi* (*pt* **travelled**, US **traveled**) voyager; (*vehicle, bullet*) aller. ● *vt* parcourir. ● *n* voyages *mpl.* ~ **agency** *n* agence *f* de voyages.

traveller, (US) **traveler** /'trævlə(r)/ *n* voyageur/-euse *m/f.* ~**'s cheque** chèque *m* de voyage.

trawler /'trɔːlə(r)/ *n* chalutier *m.*

tray /treɪ/ *n* plateau *m;* (on office desk) corbeille *f.*

treacle /'triːkl/ *n* mélasse *f.*

tread /tred/ *vi* (*pt* **trod;** *pp* **trodden**) marcher (**on** sur). ● *vt* fouler. ● *n* (sound) pas *m;* (of tyre) chape *f.*

treasure /'treʒə(r)/ *n* trésor *m.* ● *vt* (*gift, memory*) chérir; (*friendship, possession*) tenir beaucoup à.

treasury /'treʒərɪ/ *n* trésorerie *f;* **the** T~ le ministère des Finances.

treat /triːt/ *vt* traiter; ~ **sb to sth** offrir qch à qn. ● *n* (pleasure) plaisir *m;* (food) gâterie *f.* **treatment** *n* traitement *m.*

treaty /'triːtɪ/ *n* traité *m.*

treble /'trebl/ *adj* triple; ~ **clef** clé *f* de sol. ● *vt/i* tripler. ● *n* (voice) soprano *m.*

tree /triː/ *n* arbre *m.*

trek /trek/ *n* randonnée *f.* ● *vi* (*pt* **trekked**) ~ **across/through** traverser péniblement; **go** ~**king** faire de la randonnée.

tremble /'trembl/ *vi* trembler.

tremendous /trɪ'mendəs/ *adj* énorme; (excellent) formidable.

tremor /'tremə(r)/ *n* tremblement *m;* (**earth**) ~ secousse *f.*

trench /trentʃ/ *n* tranchée *f.*

trend /trend/ *n* tendance *f;* (fashion) mode *f.* **trendy** *adj* 🔲 branché 🔲.

trespass /'trespəs/ *vi* s'introduire illégalement (**on** dans). **trespasser** *n* intrus/-e *m/f.*

trial /'traɪəl/ *n* (Jur) procès *m;* (test) essai *m;* (ordeal) épreuve *f;* **go on** ~

passer en jugement; **by ~ and error** par expérience.

triangle /'traɪæŋgl/ n triangle m.

tribe /traɪb/ n tribu f.

tribunal /traɪ'bjuːnl/ n tribunal m.

tributary /'trɪbjʊtərɪ/ n affluent m.

tribute /'trɪbjuːt/ n tribut m; **pay ~ to** rendre hommage à.

trick /trɪk/ n tour m; (dishonest) combine f; (knack) astuce f; **do the ~** ⊡ faire l'affaire. ● vt tromper. **trickery** n ruse f.

trickle /'trɪkl/ vi dégouliner; **~ in/out** arriver or partir en petit nombre. ● n filet m; (fig) petit nombre m.

tricky /'trɪkɪ/ adj (task) difficile; (question) épineux; (person) malin.

trifle /'traɪfl/ n bagatelle f; (cake) diplomate m; **a ~** (small amount) un peu. ● vi **~ with** jouer avec.

trigger /'trɪgə(r)/ n (of gun) gâchette f; (of machine) manette f. ● vt **~ (off)** (initiate) déclencher.

trim /trɪm/ adj (**trimmer, trimmest**) soigné; (figure) svelte. ● vt (pt **trimmed**) (hair, grass) couper; (budget) réduire; (decorate) décorer. ● n (cut) coupe f d'entretien; (decoration) garniture f; **in ~** en forme.

trinket /'trɪŋkɪt/ n babiole f.

trip /trɪp/ vt/i (pt **tripped**) (faire) trébucher. ● n (journey) voyage m; (outing) excursion f.

triple /'trɪpl/ adj triple. ● vt/i tripler. **triplets** npl triplés/-es m/fpl.

tripod /'traɪpɒd/ n trépied m.

trite /traɪt/ adj banal.

triumph /'traɪʌmf/ n triomphe m. ● vi triompher (**over** de).

trivial /'trɪvɪəl/ adj insignifiant.

trod, **trodden** /trɒd(ən)/ →TREAD.

trolley /'trɒlɪ/ n chariot m.

trombone /trɒm'bəʊn/ n (Mus) trombone m.

troop /truːp/ n bande f; **~s** (Mil) troupes fpl. ● vi **~ in/out** entrer/sortir en bande.

trophy /'trəʊfɪ/ n trophée m.

tropic /'trɒpɪk/ n tropique m; **~s** tropiques mpl.

trot /trɒt/ n trot m; **on the ~** ⊡ coup sur coup. ● vi (pt **trotted**) trotter.

trouble /'trʌbl/ n problèmes mpl; ennuis mpl; (pains, effort) peine f; **be in ~** avoir des ennuis; **go to a lot of ~** se donner du mal; **what's the ~?** quel est le problème? ● vt (bother) déranger; (worry) tracasser. ● vi **~ (oneself) to do** se donner la peine de faire. **~maker** n provocateur/-trice m/f. **~shooter** n conciliateur/-trice m/f; (Tech) expert m.

troublesome /'trʌblsəm/ adj ennuyeux.

trousers /'traʊzəz/ npl pantalon m; **short ~** short m.

trout /traʊt/ n inv truite f.

trowel /'traʊəl/ n (garden) déplantoir m; (for mortar) truelle f.

truant /'truːənt/ n (School) élève mf qui fait l'école buissonnière; **play ~** sécher les cours.

truce /truːs/ n trève f.

truck /trʌk/ n (lorry) camion m; (cart) chariot m; (Rail) wagon m de marchandises. **~driver** n routier m.

true /truː/ adj vrai; (accurate) exact; (faithful) fidèle.

truffle /'trʌfl/ n truffe f.

truly /'truːlɪ/ adv vraiment; (faithfully) fidèlement; (truthfully) sincèrement.

trumpet /'trʌmpɪt/ n trompette f.

trunk /trʌŋk/ n (of tree, body) tronc m; (of elephant) trompe f; (box) malle f; (Auto, US) coffre m; **~s** (for swimming) slip m de bain.

trust /trʌst/ n confiance f; (association) trust m; **in ~** en dépôt. ● vt avoir confiance en; **~ sb with** confier à qn. ● vi **~ in** or **to** s'en remettre à. **trustee** n administrateur/-trice m/f. **trustworthy** adj digne de confiance.

truth /truːθ/ n (pl **-s**) vérité f. **truthful** adj (account) véridique; (person) qui dit la vérité.

try /traɪ/ vt/i (pt **tried**) essayer; (be a strain on) éprouver; (Jur) juger; **~ on** or **out** essayer; **~ to do** essayer de faire. ● n (attempt) essai m; (rugby) essai m.

T-shirt /'tiːʃɜːt/ n tee-shirt m.

tub /tʌb/ n (for flowers) bac m; (of ice cream) pot m; (bath) baignoire f.

tube /tjuːb/ n tube m; **the ~** ⊡ le métro.

tuberculosis /tjuːbɜːkjʊˈləʊsɪs/ n tuberculose f.

tuck /tʌk/ n pli m. ● vt (put away, place) ranger; (hide) cacher. ● vi ~ **in** or **into** Ⅰ attaquer; ~ **in** (shirt) rentrer; (blanket, person) border.

Tuesday /ˈtjuːzdeɪ/ n mardi m.

tug /tʌɡ/ vt (pt **tugged**) tirer. ● vi ~ **at/on** tirer sur. ● n (boat) remorqueur m.

tuition /tjuːˈɪʃn/ n cours mpl; (fee) frais mpl pédagogiques.

tulip /ˈtjuːlɪp/ n tulipe f.

tumble /ˈtʌmbl/ vi (fall) dégringoler. ● n chute f. ~**-drier** n sèche-linge m inv.

tumbler /ˈtʌmblə(r)/ n verre m droit.

tummy /ˈtʌmɪ/ n Ⅰ ventre m.

tumour /ˈtjuːmə(r)/ n tumeur f.

tuna /ˈtjuːnə/ n inv thon m.

tune /tjuːn/ n air m; **be in ~/out of ~** (instrument) être/ne pas être en accord; (singer) chanter juste/faux. ● vt (engine) régler; (Mus) accorder. ● vi ~ **in (to)** (radio),TV écouter. □ ~ **up** s'accorder.

Tunisia /tjuːˈnɪzɪə/ n Tunisie f.

tunnel /ˈtʌnl/ n tunnel m; (in mine) galerie f. ● vi (pt **tunnelled**) creuser un tunnel (**into** dans).

turf /tɜːf/ n (pl **turf** or **turves**) gazon m; **the ~** (racing) le turf. ● vt ~ **out** Ⅰ jeter dehors.

Turk /tɜːk/ n Turc m, Turque f. **Turkey** n Turquie f.

turkey /ˈtɜːkɪ/ n dinde f.

Turkish /ˈtɜːkɪʃ/ adj turc. ● n (Ling) turc m.

turn /tɜːn/ vt/i tourner; (person) se tourner; (to other side) retourner; (change) (se) transformer (**into** en); (become) devenir; (deflect) détourner; (milk) tourner. ● n tour m; (in road) tournant m; (of mind, events) tournure f; **do a good ~** rendre service; **in ~** à tour de rôle; **take ~s** se relayer. □ ~ **against** vi se retourner contre; ~ **away** vi se détourner; vt (avert) détourner; (refuse) refuser; (send back) renvoyer; ~ **back** vi (return) retourner; (vehicle) faire demi-tour; vt (fold) rabattre; ~ **down** refuser; (fold) rabattre; (reduce) baisser; ~ **off** (light) éteindre; (engine) arrêter; (tap) fermer; (of driver) tour-ner; ~ **on** (light) allumer; (engine) allumer; (tap) ouvrir; ~ **out** vt (light) éteindre; (empty) vider; (produce) produire; vi **it ~s out that** il se trouve que; ~ **out well/badly** bien/mal se terminer; ~ **over** (se) retourner; ~ **round** (person) se retourner; ~ **up** vi arriver; (be found) se retrouver; vt (find) déterrer; (collar) remonter.

turning /ˈtɜːnɪŋ/ n rue f; (bend) virage m.

turnip /ˈtɜːnɪp/ n navet m.

turn- ~**out** n assistance f. ~**over** n (pie) chausson m; (money) chiffre m d'affaires. ~**table** n (for record) platine f.

turquoise /ˈtɜːkwɔɪz/ adj turquoise inv.

turtle /ˈtɜːtl/ n tortue f (de mer). ~**-neck** n col m montant.

tutor /ˈtjuːtə(r)/ n (private) professeur m particulier; (Univ) (GB) chargé/-e m/f de travaux dirigés.

tutorial /tjuːˈtɔːrɪəl/ n (Univ) classe f de travaux dirigés.

tuxedo /tʌkˈsiːdəʊ/ n (US) smoking m.

TV /tiːˈviː/ n télé f.

tweezers /ˈtwiːzəz/ npl pince f (à épiler).

twelfth /twelfθ/ adj & n douzième (mf).

twelve /twelv/ adj & n douze (m); ~ (**o'clock**) midi m or minuit m.

twentieth /ˈtwentɪəθ/ adj & n vingtième (mf).

twenty /ˈtwentɪ/ adj & n vingt (m).

twice /twaɪs/ adv deux fois.

twig /twɪɡ/ n brindille f.

twilight /ˈtwaɪlaɪt/ n crépuscule m. ● adj crépusculaire.

twin /twɪn/ n & a jumeau/-elle (m/f). ● vt (pt **twinned**) jumeler.

twinge /twɪndʒ/ n (of pain) élancement m; (of conscience, doubt) accès m.

twinkle /ˈtwɪŋkl/ vi (star) scintiller; (eye) pétiller. ● n scintillement m; pétillement m.

twinning /ˈtwɪnɪŋ/ n jumelage m.

twist /twɪst/ vt tordre; (weave together) entortiller; (roll) enrouler; (distort) déformer. ● vi (rope) s'entortiller; (road) zigzaguer. ● n torsion f; (in rope) tortillon m; (in road) tournant m; (in play, story) coup m de théâtre.

twitch /twɪtʃ/ vi (person) trembloter; (mouth) trembler; (string) vibrer.● n (tic) tic m; (jerk) secousse f.

two /tuː/ adj & n deux (m); in ~s par deux; **break in** ~ casser en deux.

tycoon /taɪˈkuːn/ n magnat m.

type /taɪp/ n type m, genre m; (print) caractères mpl. ● vt/i (write) taper (à la machine). **~face** n police f (de caractères). **~writer** n machine f à écrire.

typical /ˈtɪpɪkl/ adj typique.

typist /ˈtaɪpɪst/ n dactylo mf.

tyrant /ˈtaɪərənt/ n tyran m.

tyre /ˈtaɪə(r)/ n pneu m.

....

Uu

....

udder /ˈʌdə(r)/ n pis m, mamelle f.

UFO /ˈjuːfəʊ/ n OVNI m inv.

UHT abbr **ultra heat treated** ~ **milk** lait m longue conservation.

ugly /ˈʌɡlɪ/ adj (-ier, -iest) laid.

UK abbr ➡UNITED KINGDOM.

Ukraine /juːˈkreɪn/ n Ukraine f.

ulcer /ˈʌlsə(r)/ n ulcère m.

ulterior /ʌlˈtɪərɪə(r)/ adj ultérieur; ~ **motive** arrière-pensée f.

ultimate /ˈʌltɪmət/ adj dernier, ultime; (definitive) définitif; (basic) fondamental.

ultrasound /ˈʌltrəsaʊnd/ n ultrason m.

umbilical cord /ʌmˈbɪlɪkl kɔːd/ n cordon m ombilical.

umbrella /ʌmˈbrelə/ n parapluie m.

umpire /ˈʌmpaɪə(r)/ n arbitre m. ● vt arbitrer.

umpteenth /ʌmpˈtiːnθ/ adj 🇮 énième.

UN abbr (**United Nations**) ONU f.

unable /ʌnˈeɪbl/ adj incapable; (through circumstances) dans l'impossibilité (**to do** de faire).

unacceptable /ʌnəkˈseptəbl/ adj (suggestion) inacceptable; (behaviour) inadmissible.

unanimous /juːˈnænɪməs/ adj unanime. **unanimously** adv à l'unanimité.

unattended /ʌnəˈtendɪd/ adj sans surveillance.

unattractive /ʌnəˈtræktɪv/ adj (idea) peu attrayant; (person) peu attirant.

unauthorized /ʌnˈɔːθəraɪzd/ adj non autorisé.

unavoidable /ʌnəˈvɔɪdəbl/ adj inévitable.

unbearable /ʌnˈbeərəbl/ adj insupportable.

unbelievable /ʌnbrˈliːvəbl/ adj incroyable.

unbiased /ʌnˈbaɪəst/ adj impartial.

unblock /ʌnˈblɒk/ vt déboucher.

unborn /ʌnˈbɔːn/ adj (child) à naître; (generation) à venir.

uncalled-for /ʌnˈkɔːldfɔː(r)/ adj injustifié, déplacé.

uncanny /ʌnˈkænɪ/ adj (-ier, -iest) étrange, troublant.

uncivilized /ʌnˈsɪvɪlaɪzd/ adj barbare.

uncle /ˈʌŋkl/ n oncle m.

Uncle Sam Interprétation plaisante des initiales U.S.Am. (United States of America). Personnification du gouvernement ou du peuple des États-Unis représentés par un grand homme maigre avec une barbiche, habillé aux couleurs du drapeau américain. C'est à lui que l'on a recours pour faire appel au patriotisme de la population, mais aussi pour caricaturer les États-Unis.

uncomfortable /ʌnˈkʌmftəbl/ adj (chair) inconfortable; (feeling) pénible; **feel** or **be** ~ (person) être mal à l'aise.

uncommon /ʌnˈkɒmən/ adj rare.

unconscious /ʌnˈkɒnʃəs/ adj sans connaissance, inanimé; (not aware) inconscient (**of** de). ● n inconscient m.

unconventional /ʌnkənˈvenʃənl/ adj peu conventionnel.

uncouth /ʌnˈkuːθ/ adj grossier.

uncover /ʌnˈkʌvə(r)/ vt découvrir.

undecided /ʌndrˈsaɪdɪd/ adj indécis.

under /ˈʌndə(r)/ prep sous; (less than) moins de; (according to) selon. ● adv au-dessous; ~ **it/there** là-dessous. ~ **age** adj mineur. ~ **cover** adj secret. **~cut** vt (pt **-cut**; pres p **-cutting**) (Comm) vendre moins cher que. **~dog** n (Pol) opprimé/-e m/f; (socially) déshérité/-e m/f. **~done** adj pas assez cuit. **~-estimate** vt sous-estimer. **~fed** adj sous-alimenté. **~go** vt (pt **-went**; pp **-gone**) subir. **~graduate** n étudiant/-e m/f (qui prépare la licence).

underground /'ʌndəgraʊnd/ adj souterrain; (secret) clandestin. ● adv sous terre. ● n (rail) métro m.

under: **~line** vt souligner. **~mine** vt saper.

underneath /ʌndə'niːθ/ prep sous. ● adv (en) dessous.

under: **~pants** npl slip m. **~rate** vt sous-estimer.

understand /ʌndə'stænd/ vt/i (pt **-stood**) comprendre.

understanding /ʌndə'stændɪŋ/ adj compréhensif. ● n compréhension f; (agreement) entente f.

undertake /ʌndə'teɪk/ vt (pt **-took**; pp **-taken**) entreprendre. **~taker** n entrepreneur m de pompes funèbres. **~taking** n (task) entreprise f; (promise) promesse f.

underwater /ʌndə'wɔːtə(r)/ adj sousmarin. ● adv sous l'eau.

under: **~wear** n sous-vêtements mpl. **~world** n (of crime) milieu m, pègre f.

undo /ʌn'duː/ vt (pt **-did**; pp **-done**) défaire, détacher; (wrong) réparer; (Comput) annuler.

undress /ʌn'dres/ vt/i (se) déshabiller; **get ~ed** se déshabiller.

undue /ʌn'djuː/ adj excessif.

unearth /ʌn'ɜːθ/ vt déterrer.

uneasy /ʌn'iːzɪ/ adj (ill at ease) mal à l'aise; (worried) inquiet; (situation) difficile.

uneducated /ʌn'edʒʊkeɪtɪd/ adj (person) inculte; (speech) populaire.

unemployed /ʌnɪm'plɔɪd/ adj en chômage. ● npl **the ~** les chômeurs mpl.

unemployment /ʌnɪm'plɔɪmənt/ n chômage m; **~ benefit** allocations fpl de chômage.

uneven /ʌn'iːvn/ adj inégal.

unexpected /ʌnɪk'spektɪd/ adj inattendu, imprévu. **unexpectedly** adv (arrive) à l'improviste; (small, fast) étonnamment.

unfair /ʌn'feə(r)/ adj injuste.

unfaithful /ʌn'feɪθfl/ adj infidèle.

unfit /ʌn'fɪt/ adj (Med) pas en forme; (ill) malade; (unsuitable) impropre (for

à); **~ to** (unable) pas en état de.

unfold /ʌn'fəʊld/ vt déplier; (expose) exposer. ● vi se dérouler.

unforeseen /ʌnfɔː'siːn/ adj imprévu.

unforgettable /ʌnfə'getəbl/ adj inoubliable.

unfortunate /ʌn'fɔːtʃənət/ adj malheureux; (event) fâcheux.

ungrateful /ʌn'greɪtfl/ adj ingrat.

unhappy /ʌn'hæpɪ/ adj (**-ier, -iest**) (person) malheureux; (face) triste; (not pleased) mécontent (**with** de).

unharmed /ʌn'hɑːmd/ adj indemne, sain et sauf.

unhealthy /ʌn'helθɪ/ adj (**-ier, -iest**) (climate) malsain; (person) en mauvaise santé.

unheard-of /ʌn'hɜːdɒv/ adj inouï.

unhurt /ʌn'hɜːt/ adj indemne.

uniform /'juːnɪfɔːm/ n uniforme m. ● adj uniforme.

unify /'juːnɪfaɪ/ vt unifier.

unintentional /ʌnɪn'tenʃənl/ adj involontaire.

uninterested /ʌn'ɪntrəstɪd/ adj indifférent (**in** à).

union /'juːnɪən/ n union f; (trade union) syndicat m; **U~ Jack** drapeau m du Royaume-Uni.

unique /juːˈniːk/ adj unique.

unit /'juːnɪt/ n unité f; (of furniture) élément m; **~ trust** ≃ SICAV f.

unite /juːˈnaɪt/ vt/i (s')unir.

United Kingdom n Royaume-Uni m.

United Nations npl Nations fpl Unies.

United States (of America) npl états-Unis mpl (d'Amérique).

unity /'juːnətɪ/ n unité f.

universal /juːnɪ'vɜːsl/ adj universel.

universe /'juːnɪvɜːs/ n univers m.

university /juːnɪ'vɜːsətɪ/ n université f. ● adj universitaire; (student, teacher) d'université.

unkind /ʌn'kaɪnd/ adj pas gentil, méchant.

unknown /ʌn'nəʊn/ adj inconnu. ● n **the ~** l'inconnu m.

unleaded /ʌn'ledɪd/ adj sans plomb.

unless /ən'les/ conj à moins que.

unlike /ʌn'laɪk/ adj différent. ● prep contrairement à; (different from) différent de.

unlikely /ʌnˈlaɪklɪ/ *adj* improbable.

unload /ʌnˈləʊd/ *vt* décharger.

unlock /ʌnˈlɒk/ *vt* ouvrir.

unlucky /ʌnˈlʌkɪ/ *adj* **-ier, -iest** malheureux; (*number*) qui porte malheur.

unmarried /ʌnˈmærɪd/ *adj* célibataire.

unnatural /ʌnˈnætʃrəl/ *adj* pas naturel, anormal.

unnecessary /ʌnˈnesəsrɪ/ *adj* inutile.

unnoticed /ʌnˈnəʊtɪst/ *adj* inaperçu.

unofficial /ʌnəˈfɪʃl/ *adj* officieux.

unpack /ʌnˈpæk/ *vt* (*suitcase*) défaire; (*contents*) déballer. ● *vi* défaire sa valise.

unpleasant /ʌnˈpleznt/ *adj* désagréable (**to** avec).

unplug /ʌnˈplʌg/ *vt* débrancher.

unpopular /ʌnˈpɒpjʊlə(r)/ *adj* impopulaire; ~ **with** mal vu de.

unprofessional /ʌnprəˈfeʃənl/ *adj* peu professionnel.

unqualified /ʌnˈkwɒlɪfaɪd/ *adj* non diplômé; (*success*) total; **be** ~ **to** ne pas être qualifié pour.

unravel /ʌnˈrævl/ *vt* (*pt* **unravelled**) démêler.

unreasonable /ʌnˈriːznəbl/ *adj* irréaliste.

unrelated /ʌnrɪˈleɪtɪd/ *adj* sans rapport (**to** avec).

unreliable /ʌnrɪˈlaɪəbl/ *adj* peu sérieux; (*machine*) peu fiable.

unrest /ʌnˈrest/ *n* troubles *mpl*.

unroll /ʌnˈrəʊl/ *vt* dérouler.

unruly /ʌnˈruːlɪ/ *adj* indiscipliné.

unsafe /ʌnˈseɪf/ *adj* (*dangerous*) dangereux; (*person*) en danger.

unscheduled /ʌnˈʃedjuːld/ *adj* pas prévu.

unscrupulous /ʌnˈskruːpjʊləs/ *adj* sans scrupules, malhonnête.

unsettled /ʌnˈsetld/ *adj* instable.

unsightly /ʌnˈsaɪtlɪ/ *adj* laid.

unskilled /ʌnˈskɪld/ *adj* (*worker*) non qualifié.

unsound /ʌnˈsaʊnd/ *adj* (*roof*) en mauvais état; (*investment*) douteux.

unsteady /ʌnˈstedɪ/ *adj* (*step*) chancelant; (*ladder*) instable; (*hand*) mal assuré.

unsuccessful /ʌnsəkˈsesfl/ *adj* (*result, candidate*) malheureux; (*attempt*) in-

fructueux; **be** ~ ne pas réussir (**in doing** à faire).

unsuitable /ʌnˈsuːtəbl/ *adj* inapproprié; **be** ~ ne pas convenir.

unsure /ʌnˈʃɔː(r)/ *adj* incertain.

untidy /ʌnˈtaɪdɪ/ *adj* (**-ier, -iest**) (*person*) désordonné; (*room*) en désordre; (*work*) mal soigné.

untie /ʌnˈtaɪ/ *vt* (*knot, parcel*) défaire; (*person*) détacher.

until /ənˈtɪl/ *prep* jusqu'à; **not** ~ pas avant. ● *conj* jusqu'à ce que; **not** ~ pas avant que.

untrue /ʌnˈtruː/ *adj* faux.

unused /ʌnˈjuːst/ *adj* (new) neuf; (not in use) inutilisé.

unusual /ʌnˈjuːʒl/ *adj* exceptionnel; (*strange*) insolite, étrange.

unwanted /ʌnˈwɒntɪd/ *adj* (*useless*) superflu; (*child*) non désiré.

unwelcome /ʌnˈwelkəm/ *adj* fâcheux; (*guest*) importun.

unwell /ʌnˈwel/ *adj* souffrant.

unwilling /ʌnˈwɪlɪŋ/ *adj* peu disposé (**to** à); (*accomplice*) malgré soi.

unwind /ʌnˈwaɪnd/ *vt/i* (*pt* **unwound**) (se) dérouler; (relax ▣) se détendre.

unwise /ʌnˈwaɪz/ *adj* imprudent.

unwrap /ʌnˈræp/ *vt* déballer.

up /ʌp/ *adv* en haut, en l'air; (*sun, curtain*) levé; (*out of bed*) levé, debout; (*finished*) fini; **be** ~ (*level, price*) avoir monté. ● *prep* (a hill) en haut de; (a tree) dans; (a ladder) sur; **come** or **go** ~ monter; ~ **in the bedroom** là-haut dans la chambre; ~ **there** là-haut; ~ **to** jusqu'à; (*task*) à la hauteur de; **it is** ~ **to you** ça dépend de vous (**to** de); **be** ~ **to sth** (*able*) être capable de qch; (*plot*) préparer qch; **be** ~ **to** (in book) en être à; **be** ~ **against** faire face à; ~ **to date** moderne; (*news*) récent. ● *n* ~**s and downs** les hauts et les bas *mpl*.

up-and-coming *adj* prometteur.

upbringing /ˈʌpbrɪŋɪŋ/ *n* éducation *f.*

update /ʌpˈdeɪt/ *vt* mettre à jour.

upgrade /ʌpˈgreɪd/ *vt* améliorer; (*person*) promouvoir.

upheaval /ʌpˈhiːvl/ *n* bouleversement *m.*

uphill /ʌpˈhɪl/ *adj* qui monte; (fig) difficile. ● *adv* **go** ~ monter.

upholstery /ʌp'həʊlstərɪ/ n rembourrage m; (in vehicle) garniture f.

upkeep /'ʌpkiːp/ n entretien m.

up-market adj haut-de-gamme.

upon /ə'pɒn/ prep sur.

upper /'ʌpə(r)/ adj supérieur; **have the ~ hand** avoir le dessus. ● n (of shoe) empeigne f. **~ class** n aristocratie f. **~most** adj (highest) le plus haut.

upright /'ʌpraɪt/ adj droit. ● n (post) montant m.

uprising /'ʌpraɪzɪŋ/ n soulèvement m.

uproar /'ʌprɔː(r)/ n tumulte m.

uproot /ʌp'ruːt/ vt déraciner.

upset¹ /ʌp'set/ vt (pt upset; pres p upsetting) (overturn) renverser; (plan, stomach) déranger; (person) contrarier, affliger. ● adj peiné.

upset² /'ʌpset/ n dérangement m; (distress) chagrin m.

upside-down /ʌpsaɪd 'daʊn/ adv (lit) à l'envers; (fig) sens dessus dessous.

upstairs /ʌp'steəz/ adv en haut. ● adj (flat) du haut.

uptight /ʌp'taɪt/ adj 🅘 tendu, coincé 🅘.

up-to-date adj à la mode; (records) à jour.

upward /'ʌpwəd/ adj & adv, **upwards** adv vers le haut.

urban /'ɜːbən/ adj urbain.

urge /ɜːdʒ/ vt conseiller vivement (**to do** de faire); **~ on** encourager. ● n forte envie f.

urgency /'ɜːdʒənsɪ/ n urgence f; (of request, tone) insistance f. **urgent** adj urgent; (request) pressant.

urinal /jʊə'raɪnl/ n urinoir m.

urine /'jʊərɪn/ n urine f.

us /ʌs, əs/ pron nous; (to) **~** nous; **both of ~** tous/toutes les deux.

US abbr ➡UNITED STATES.

USA abbr ➡UNITED STATES OF AMERICA.

use¹ /juːz/ vt se servir de, utiliser. (consume) consommer; **~ up** épuiser.

use² /juːs/ n usage m, emploi m; **in ~** en usage; **it is no ~ doing** ça ne sert à rien de faire; **make ~ of** se servir de; **of ~** utile.

used¹ /juːzd/ adj (car) d'occasion.

used² /juːst/ v aux **he ~ to smoke** il fumait (autrefois). ● adj **~ to** habitué à.

useful /'juːsfl/ adj utile.

useless /'juːslɪs/ adj inutile; (person) incompétent.

user /'juːzə(r)/ n (of road, service) usager m; (of product) utilisateur/-trice m/f. **~-friendly** adj facile d'emploi; (Comput) convivial. **~name** nom m d'utilisateur.

usual /'juːʒl/ adj habituel, normal; **as ~** comme d'habitude. **usually** adv d'habitude.

utility /juː'tɪlətɪ/ n utilité f; **(public) ~** service m public.

utmost /'ʌtməʊst/ adj (furthest, most intense) extrême; **the ~ care** le plus grand soin. ● n **do one's ~** faire tout son possible.

utter /'ʌtə(r)/ adj complet, absolu. ● vt prononcer.

U-turn /'juːtɜːn/ n demi-tour m; (fig) volteface f inv.

Vv

vacancy /'veɪkənsɪ/ n (post) poste m vacant; (room) chambre f disponible.

vacant /'veɪkənt/ adj (post) vacant; (seat) libre; (look) vague.

vacate /və'keɪt/ vt quitter.

vacation /və'keɪʃn/ n vacances fpl.

vaccinate /'væksɪneɪt/ vt vacciner.

vacuum /'vækjʊəm/ n vide m. **~ cleaner** n aspirateur m. **~-packed** adj emballé sous vide.

vagina /və'dʒaɪnə/ n vagin m.

vagrant /'veɪgrənt/ n vagabond/-e m/f.

vague /veɪg/ adj vague; (outline) flou; **be ~ about** ne pas préciser.

vain /veɪn/ adj (conceited) vaniteux; (useless) vain; **in ~** en vain.

valentine /'væləntaɪn/ n **~ (card)** carte f de la Saint-Valentin.

valid /'vælɪd/ adj (argument, ticket) valable; (passport) valide.

valley /'vælɪ/ n vallée f.

valuable /'væljʊəbl/ adj (object) de valeur; (help) précieux. **valuables** npl objets mpl de valeur.

valuation /ˌvæljʊˈeɪʃn/ n (of painting) expertise f; (of house) évaluation f.

value /ˈvæljuː/ n valeur f; ~ **added tax** taxe f à la valeur ajoutée, TVA f. ● vt (appraise) évaluer; (cherish) attacher de la valeur à.

valve /vælv/ n (Tech) soupape f; (of tyre) valve f; (Med) valvule f.

van /væn/ n camionnette f.

vandal /ˈvændl/ n vandale mf.

vanguard /ˈvænɡɑːd/ n in the ~ of à l'avantgarde f de.

vanilla /vəˈnɪlə/ n vanille f.

vanish /ˈvænɪʃ/ vi disparaître.

vapour /ˈveɪpə(r)/ n vapeur f.

variable /ˈveərɪəbl/ adj variable.

varicose /ˈværɪkəʊs/ adj ~ **veins** varices fpl.

varied /ˈveərɪd/ adj varié.

variety /vəˈraɪətɪ/ n variété f; (entertainment) variétés fpl.

various /ˈveərɪəs/ adj divers.

varnish /ˈvɑːnɪʃ/ n vernis m. ● vt vernir.

vary /ˈveərɪ/ vt/i varier.

vase /vɑːz/ n vase m.

vast /vɑːst/ adj (space) vaste; (in quantity) énorme.

vat /væt/ n cuve f.

VAT abbr (**value added tax**) TVA f.

vault /vɔːlt/ n (roof) voûte f; (in bank) chambre f forte; (tomb) caveau m; (jump) saut m. ● vt/i sauter.

VCR abbr →VIDEO CASSETTE RECORDER.

VDU abbr →VISUAL DISPLAY UNIT.

veal /viːl/ n veau m.

vegan /ˈviːɡən/ adj & n végétalien/-ne (m/f).

vegetable /ˈvedʒtəbl/ n légume m. ● adj végétal.

vegetarian /ˌvedʒɪˈteərɪən/ adj & n végétarien/-ne (m/f).

vehicle /ˈviːɪkl/ n véhicule m.

veil /veɪl/ n voile m.

vein /veɪn/ n (in body, rock) veine f; (on leaf) nervure f.

velvet /ˈvelvɪt/ n velours m.

vending-machine /ˈvendɪŋ məˈʃiːn/ n distributeur m automatique.

veneer /vɪˈnɪə(r)/ n (on wood) placage m; (fig) vernis m.

venereal /vəˈnɪərɪəl/ adj vénérien.

venetian /vɪˈniːʃn/ adj ~ **blind** jalousie f.

vengeance /ˈvendʒəns/ n vengeance f; **with a** ~ de plus belle.

venison /ˈvenɪsn/ n venaison f.

venom /ˈvenəm/ n venin m.

vent /vent/ n bouche f, conduit m; (in coat) fente f. ● vt (anger) décharger (on sur).

ventilate /ˈventɪleɪt/ vt ventiler. **ventilator** n ventilateur m.

venture /ˈventʃə(r)/ n entreprise f. ● vt/i (se) risquer.

venue /ˈvenjuː/ n lieu m.

verb /vɜːb/ n verbe m.

verbal /ˈvɜːbl/ adj verbal.

verdict /ˈvɜːdɪkt/ n verdict m.

verge /vɜːdʒ/ n bord m; **on the** ~ **of doing** sur le point de faire. ● vi ~ **on** friser, frôler.

verify /ˈverɪfaɪ/ vt vérifier.

vermin /ˈvɜːmɪn/ n vermine f.

versatile /ˈvɜːsətaɪl/ adj (person) aux talents variés; (mind) souple.

verse /vɜːs/ n strophe f; (of Bible) verset m; (poetry) vers mpl.

version /ˈvɜːʃn/ n version f.

versus /ˈvɜːsəs/ prep contre.

vertebra /ˈvɜːtɪbrə/ n (pl -**brae**) vertèbre f.

vertical /ˈvɜːtɪkl/ adj vertical.

vertigo /ˈvɜːtɪɡəʊ/ n vertige m.

very /ˈverɪ/ adv très. ● adj (actual) même; **the** ~ **day** le jour même; **at the** ~ **end** tout à la fin; **the** ~ **first** le tout premier; ~ **much** beaucoup.

vessel /ˈvesl/ n vaisseau m.

vest /vest/ n maillot m de corps; (waistcoat: US) gilet m.

vet /vet/ n vétérinaire mf. ● vt (pt **vetted**) (candidate) examiner (de près).

veteran /ˈvetərən/ n vétéran m; **war** ~ ancien combattant m.

veterinary /ˈvetrɪnrɪ/ adj vétérinaire; ~ **surgeon** vétérinaire mf.

veto /ˈviːtəʊ/ n (pl ~**es**) veto m; (right) droit m de veto. ● vt mettre son veto à.

vibrate /vaɪˈbreɪt/ vt/i (faire) vibrer.

vicar /ˈvɪkə(r)/ n pasteur m.

vice /vaɪs/ n (depravity) vice m; (Tech) étau m.

vicinity /vɪˈsɪnətɪ/ n environs mpl; **in the ~ of** à proximité de.

vicious /ˈvɪʃəs/ adj (spiteful) méchant; (violent) brutal; **~ circle** cercle m vicieux.

victim /ˈvɪktɪm/ n victime f.

victor /ˈvɪktə(r)/ n vainqueur m. **victory** n victoire f.

video /ˈvɪdɪəʊ/ adj (game, camera) vidéo inv. ● n (recorder) magnétoscope m; (film) vidéo f; **~ (cassette)** cassette f vidéo. **~ game** n jeu m vidéo. **~phone** n vidéophone m. ● vt enregistrer.

videotape /ˈvɪdɪəʊteɪp/ n bande f vidéo. ● vt (programme) enregistrer; (wedding) filmer avec une caméra vidéo.

view /vjuː/ n vue f; **in my ~** à mon avis; **in ~ of** compte tenu de; **on ~** exposé; **with a ~ to** dans le but de. ● vt (watch) regarder; (consider) considérer (as comme); (house) visiter. **viewer** n (TV) téléspectateur/-trice m/f.

view: ~finder n viseur m. **~point** n point m de vue.

vigilant /ˈvɪdʒɪlənt/ adj vigilant.

vigour, (US) **vigor** /ˈvɪgə(r)/ n vigueur f.

vile /vaɪl/ adj (base) vil; (bad) abominable.

villa /ˈvɪlə/ n pavillon m; (for holiday) villa f.

village /ˈvɪlɪdʒ/ n village m.

villain /ˈvɪlən/ n scélérat m, bandit m; (in story) méchant m.

vindictive /vɪnˈdɪktɪv/ adj vindicatif.

vine /vaɪn/ n vigne f.

vinegar /ˈvɪnɪgə(r)/ n vinaigre m.

vineyard /ˈvɪnjəd/ n vignoble m.

vintage /ˈvɪntɪdʒ/ n (year) année f, millésime m. ● adj (wine) de grand cru; (car) d'époque.

viola /vɪˈəʊlə/ n (Mus) alto m.

violate /ˈvaɪəleɪt/ vt violer.

violence /ˈvaɪələns/ n violence f. **violent** adj violent.

violet /ˈvaɪələt/ n (Bot) violette f; (colour) violet m.

violin /vaɪəˈlɪn/ n violon m.

VIP abbr (**very important person**) personnalité f, VIP m.

virgin /ˈvɜːdʒɪn/ n (woman) vierge f.

Virgo /ˈvɜːgəʊ/ n Vierge f.

virtual /ˈvɜːtʃʊəl/ adj quasi-total; (Comput) virtuel. **virtually** adv pratiquement.

virtue /ˈvɜːtʃuː/ n vertu f; (advantage) mérite m; **by ~ of** en raison de.

virus /ˈvaɪərəs/ n virus m.

visa /ˈviːzə/ n visa m.

visibility /vɪzəˈbɪlətɪ/ n visibilité f. **visible** adj visible.

vision /ˈvɪʒn/ n vision f.

visit /ˈvɪzɪt/ vt (pt **visited**) (person) rendre visite à; (place) visiter. ● vi être en visite. ● n (tour, call) visite f; (stay) séjour m. **visitor** n visiteur/-euse m/f; (guest) invité/-e m/f.

visual /ˈvɪʒʊəl/ adj visuel. **~ display unit** n visuel m, console f de visualisation.

visualize /ˈvɪʒʊəlaɪz/ vt se représenter; (foresee) envisager.

vital /ˈvaɪtl/ adj vital.

vitamin /ˈvɪtəmɪn/ n vitamine f.

vivacious /vɪˈveɪʃəs/ adj plein de vivacité.

vivid /ˈvɪvɪd/ adj (colour, imagination) vif; (description, dream) frappant.

vivisection /vɪvɪˈsekʃn/ n vivisection f.

vocabulary /vəˈkæbjʊlərɪ/ n vocabulaire m.

vocal /ˈvəʊkl/ adj vocal; (person) qui s'exprime franchement. **~ cords** npl cordes fpl vocales.

vocation /vəʊˈkeɪʃn/ n vocation f. **vocational** adj professionnel.

voice /vɔɪs/ n voix f. ● vt (express) formuler. **~ mail** n messagerie f vocale.

void /vɔɪd/ adj vide (of de); (not valid) nul. ● n vide m.

volatile /ˈvɒlətaɪl/ adj (person) versatile; (situation) explosif.

volcano /vɒlˈkeɪnəʊ/ n (pl **~es**) volcan m.

volley /ˈvɒlɪ/ n (of blows, in tennis) volée f; (of gunfire) salve f.

volt /vəʊlt/ n (Electr) volt m. **voltage** n tension f.

volume /'vɒljuːm/ n volume m.

voluntary /'vɒləntrɪ/ adj volontaire; (unpaid) bénévole.

volunteer /vɒlən'tɪə(r)/ n volontaire mf. ● vi s'offrir (**to do** pour faire); (Mil) s'engager comme volontaire. ● vt offrir.

vomit /'vɒmɪt/ vt/i (pt **vomited**) vomir. ● n vomi m.

vote /vəʊt/ n vote m; (right) droit m de vote. ● vt/i voter; ∼ **sb in** élire qn. **voter** n électeur/-trice m/f. **voting** n vote m (**of** de); (poll) scrutin m.

vouch /vaʊtʃ/ vi ∼ **for** se porter garant de.

voucher /'vaʊtʃə(r)/ n bon m.

vowel /'vaʊəl/ n voyelle f.

voyage /'vɔɪɪdʒ/ n voyage m (en mer).

vulgar /'vʌlgə(r)/ adj vulgaire.

vulnerable /'vʌlnərəbl/ adj vulnérable.

Ww

wad /wɒd/ n (pad) tampon m; (bundle) liasse f.

wade /weɪd/ vi ∼ **through** (mud) patauger dans. (book: fig) avancer péniblement dans.

wafer /'weɪfə(r)/ n (biscuit) gaufrette f.

waffle /'wɒfl/ n (talk 🔲) verbiage m; (cake) gaufre f. ● vi 🔲 divaguer.

wag /wæg/ vt/i (pt **wagged**) (tail) remuer.

wage /weɪdʒ/ vt (campaign) mener; ∼ **war** faire la guerre. ● n (weekly, daily) salaire m; ∼s salaire m. ∼**-earner** n salarié/-e m/f.

wagon /'wægən/ n (horse-drawn) chariot m; (Rail) wagon m (de marchandises).

wail /weɪl/ vi gémir. ● n gémissement m.

waist /weɪst/ n taille f. ∼**coat** n gilet m.

wait /weɪt/ vt/i attendre; **I can't** ∼ **to start** j'ai hâte de commencer; **let's** ∼ **and see** attendons voir; ∼ **for** attendre; ∼ **on** servir. ● n attente f.

waiter /'weɪtə(r)/ n garçon m, serveur m.

waiting-list n liste f d'attente.

waiting-room n salle f d'attente.

waitress /'weɪtrɪs/ n serveuse f.

waive /weɪv/ vt renoncer à.

wake /weɪk/ vt/i (pt **woke**; pp **woken**) ∼ **(up)** (se) réveiller. ● n (track) sillage m; **in the** ∼ **of** (after) à la suite de. ∼ **up call** n réveil m téléphoné.

Wales /weɪlz/ n pays m de Galles.

walk /wɔːk/ vi marcher; (not ride) aller à pied; (stroll) se promener. ● vt (streets) parcourir; (distance) faire à pied; (dog) promener. ● n promenade f, tour m; (gait) démarche f; (pace) marche f, pas m; (path) allée f; **have a** ∼ faire une promenade. □ ∼ **out** (go away) partir; (worker) faire grève; ∼ **out on** abandonner.

walkie-talkie /wɔːkɪ'tɔːkɪ/ n talkie-walkie m.

walking /'wɔːkɪŋ/ n marche f (à pied). ● adj (corpse, dictionary: fig) ambulant.

walkman® /'wɔːkmən/ n walkman® m, baladeur m.

walk: ∼**-out** n grève f surprise. ∼**-over** n victoire f facile.

wall /wɔːl/ n mur m; (of tunnel, stomach) paroi f. ● adj mural. **walled** adj (city) fortifié.

> **Wall Street** Cette petite rue new yorkaise est le centre de la finance et des affaires aux États-Unis. Wall Street est souvent employé pour désigner la Bourse de New York, également située dans cette rue. ⓘ

wallet /'wɒlɪt/ n portefeuille m.

wallpaper /'wɔːlpeɪpə(r)/ n papier m peint. ● vt tapisser.

walnut /'wɔːlnʌt/ n (nut) noix f; (tree) noyer m.

waltz /wɔːls/ n valse f. ● vi valser.

wander /'wɒndə(r)/ vi errer; (stroll) flâner; (digress) s'écarter du sujet; (in mind) divaguer.

wane /weɪn/ vi décroître.

want /wɒnt/ vt vouloir (**to do** faire); (need) avoir besoin de (**doing** d'être fait); (ask for) demander; **I** ∼ **you to**

do it je veux que vous le fassiez. ● *vi* ~ **for** manquer de. ● *n* (*need, poverty*) besoin *m*; (*desire*) désir *m*; (*lack*) manque *m*; **for** ~ **of** faute de. **wanted** *adj* (*criminal*) recherché par la police.

war /wɔː(r)/ *n* guerre *f*; **at** ~ en guerre; **on the** ~**path** sur le sentier de la guerre.

ward /wɔːd/ *n* (*in hospital*) salle *f*; (*minor: Jur*) pupille *mf*; (*Pol*) division *f* électorale. ● *vt* ~ **off** (*danger*) prévenir.

warden /'wɔːdn/ *n* directeur/-trice *m/f*; (*of park*) gardien/-ne *m/f*; (**traffic** ~) contractuel/-le *m/f*.

wardrobe /'wɔːdrəʊb/ *n* (*furniture*) armoire *f*; (*clothes*) garde-robe *f*.

warehouse /'weəhaʊs/ *n* entrepôt *m*.

wares /weəz/ *npl* marchandises *fpl*.

warfare /'wɔːfeə(r)/ *n* guerre *f*.

warm /wɔːm/ *adj* chaud; (*hearty*) chaleureux; **be** or **feel** ~ avoir chaud; **it is** ~ il fait chaud. ● *vt/i* ~ (**up**) (se) réchauffer; (*food*) chauffer; (*liven up*) (s')animer; (*exercise*) s'échauffer.

warmth /wɔːmθ/ *n* chaleur *f*.

warn /wɔːn/ *vt* avertir, prévenir; ~ **sb off sth** (*advise against*) mettre qn en garde contre qch; (*forbid*) interdire qch à qn.

warning /'wɔːnɪŋ/ *n* avertissement *m*; (*notice*) avis *m*; **without** ~ sans prévenir. ~ **light** *n* voyant *m*. ~ **triangle** *n* triangle *m* de sécurité.

warp /wɔːp/ *vt/i* (*wood*) (se) voiler; (*pervert*) pervertir; (*judgment*) fausser.

warrant /'wɒrənt/ *n* (*for arrest*) mandat *m* (d'arrêt); (*Comm*) autorisation *f*. ● *vt* justifier.

warranty /'wɒrəntɪ/ *n* garantie *f*.

wart /wɔːt/ *n* verrue *f*.

wartime /'wɔːtaɪm/ *n* **in** ~ en temps de guerre.

wary /'weərɪ/ *adj* (**-ier, -iest**) prudent.

was /wɒz, wəz/ ➡**BE**.

wash /wɒʃ/ *vt/i* (se) laver. (*flow over*) baigner; ~ **one's hands of** se laver les mains de. ● *n* lavage *m*; (*clothes*) lessive *f*; **have a** ~ se laver. ~ **up** faire la vaisselle; (US) se laver. ~**-basin** *n* lavabo *m*.

washer /'wɒʃə(r)/ *n* rondelle *f*.

washing /'wɒʃɪŋ/ *n* lessive *f*.
~**-machine** *n* machine *f* à laver.
~**-powder** *n* lessive *f*.

washing-up *n* vaisselle *f*. ~ **liquid** *n* liquide *m* vaisselle.

wash: ~**-out** *n* ⊞ fiasco *m*. ~**-room** *n* (US) toilettes *fpl*.

wasp /wɒsp/ *n* guêpe *f*.

wastage /'weɪstɪdʒ/ *n* gaspillage *m*.

waste /weɪst/ *vt* gaspiller; (*time*) perdre. ● *vi* ~ **away** dépérir. ● *adj* superflu; ~ **products** or **matter** déchets *mpl*. ● *n* gaspillage *m*; (*of time*) perte *f*; (*rubbish*) déchets *mpl*; **lay** ~ dévaster. **wasteful** *adj* peu économique; (*person*) gaspilleur.

waste: ~**land** *n* (*desolate*) terre *f* désolée; (*unused*) terre *f* inculte; (*in town*) terrain *m* vague. ~ **paper** *n* vieux papiers *mpl*. ~**-paper basket** *n* corbeille *f* (à papier).

watch /wɒtʃ/ *vt/i* (*television*) regarder; (*observe*) observer; (*guard, spy on*) surveiller; (*be careful about*) faire attention à. ● *n* (*for telling time*) montre *f*; (Naut) quart *m*; **be on the** ~ guetter; **keep** ~ **on** surveiller. ~ **out** (*take care*) faire attention (**for** à); ~ **out for** (*keep watch*) guetter.

water /'wɔːtə(r)/ *n* eau *f*; **by** ~ en bateau. ● *vt* arroser. ● *vi* (*eyes*) larmoyer; **my/his mouth** ~**s** l'eau me/lui vient à la bouche. □ ~ **down** couper (d'eau); (*tone down*) édulcorer.
~**-colour** *n* (*painting*) aquarelle *f*.
~**cress** *n* cresson *m* (de fontaine).
~**fall** *n* chute *f* d'eau, cascade *f*. ~ **heater** *n* chauffe-eau *m*. **watering-can** *n* arrosoir *m*. ~**-lily** *n* nénuphar *m*.
~**-melon** *n* pastèque *f*. ~**proof** *adj* (*material*) imperméable. ~ **shed** *n* (*in affairs*) tournant *m* décisif. ~**-skiing** *n* ski *m* nautique. ~**tight** *adj* étanche.
~**-way** *n* voie *f* navigable.

watery /'wɔːtərɪ/ *adj* (*colour*) délavé; (*eyes*) humide; (*soup*) trop liquide.

wave /weɪv/ *n* vague *f*; (*in hair*) ondulation *f*; (*radio*) onde *f*; (*sign*) signe *m*. ● *vt* agiter. ● *vi* faire signe (de la main); (*move in wind*) flotter.

waver /'weɪvə(r)/ *vi* vaciller.

wavy /'weɪvɪ/ *adj* (*line*) onduleux; (*hair*) ondulé.

wax /wæks/ *n* cire *f*; (*for skis*) fart *m*. ● *vt* cirer; farter; (*car*) lustrer.

way /weɪ/ n (road, path) chemin m (**to** de); (distance) distance f; (direction) direction f; (manner) façon f; (means) moyen m; ∼**s** (habits) habitudes fpl; **be in the** ∼ bloquer le passage; (hindrance: fig) gêner (qn); **be on one's** or **the** ∼ être sur son or le chemin; **by the** ∼ à propos; **by the** ∼**side** au bord de la route; **by** ∼ **of** comme; (via) par; **go out of one's** ∼ se donner du mal; **in a** ∼ dans un sens; **make one's** ∼ **somewhere** se rendre quelque part; **push one's** ∼ **through** se frayer un passage; **that** ∼ par là; **this** ∼ par ici; ∼ **in** entrée f; ∼ **out** sortie f. ● adv 🔢 loin.

we /wiː/ pron nous.

weak /wiːk/ adj faible; (delicate) fragile.

weakness /ˈwiːknɪs/ n faiblesse f; (fault) point m faible; **a** ∼ **for** (liking) un faible pour.

wealth /welθ/ n richesse f; (riches, resources) richesses fpl; (quantity) profusion f.

wealthy /ˈwelθɪ/ adj (**-ier, -iest**) riche. ● n the ∼ les riches mpl.

weapon /ˈwepən/ n arme f; ∼**s of mass destruction** armes fpl de destruction massive.

wear /weə(r)/ vt (pt **wore**; pp **worn**) porter; (put on) mettre; (expression) avoir. ● vi (last) durer; ∼ (**out**) (s')user. ● n (use) usage m; (damage) usure f. ∼ **down** user; ∼ **off** (colour, pain) passer; ∼ **out** (exhaust) épuiser.

weary /ˈwɪərɪ/ adj (**-ier, -iest**) fatigué, las. ● vi ∼ **of** se lasser de.

weather /ˈweðə(r)/ n temps m; **under the** ∼ patraque. ● adj météorologique. ● vt (survive) réchapper de or à. ∼ **forecast** n météo f.

weave /wiːv/ vt/i (pt **wove**; pp **woven**) tisser; (basket) tresser; (move) se faufiler. ● n (style) tissage m.

web /web/ n (of spider) toile f; (on foot) palmure f.

Web /web/ n (Comput) Web m. ∼**cam** n webcam f. ∼**master** n administrateur m de site Internet. ∼ **page** n page f Web. ∼ **search** n recherche f sur le Web. ∼**site** n site m Internet.

wedding /ˈwedɪŋ/ n mariage m. ∼**-ring** n alliance f.

wedge /wedʒ/ n (of wood) coin m; (under wheel) cale f. ● vt caler; (push) enfoncer; (crowd) coincer.

Wednesday /ˈwenzdɪ/ n mercredi m.

weed /wiːd/ n mauvaise herbe f. ● vt/i désherber; ∼ **out** extirper.

week /wiːk/ n semaine f; **a** ∼ **today/ tomorrow** aujourd'hui/demain en huit. ∼**day** n jour m de semaine. ∼**end** n week-end m, fin f de semaine.

weekly /ˈwiːklɪ/ adv toutes les semaines. ● adj & n (periodical) hebdomadaire (m).

weep /wiːp/ vt/i (pt **wept**) pleurer (**for sb** qn).

weigh /weɪ/ vt/i peser; ∼ **anchor** lever l'ancre. ∼ **down** lester (avec un poids); (bend) faire plier; (fig) accabler; ∼ **up** calculer.

weight /weɪt/ n poids m; **lose/put on** ∼ perdre/prendre du poids. ∼**-lifting** n haltérophilie f. ∼ **training** n musculation f en salle.

weird /wɪəd/ adj bizarre.

welcome /ˈwelkəm/ adj agréable; (timely) opportun; **be** ∼ être le or la bienvenu(e), être les bienvenu(e)s; **you're** ∼**!** il n'y a pas de quoi; ∼ **to do** libre de faire. ● interj soyez le or la bienvenu(e), soyez les bienvenu(e)s. ● n accueil m. ● vt accueillir; (as greeting) souhaiter la bienvenue à; (fig) se réjouir de.

weld /weld/ vt souder. ● n soudure f.

welfare /ˈwelfeə(r)/ n bien-être m; (aid) aide f sociale. **W**∼ **State** n état-providence m.

well¹ /wel/ n puits m.

well² /wel/ adv (**better, best**) bien; **do** ∼ (succeed) réussir; ∼ **done!** bravo! ● adj bien inv; **as** ∼ aussi; **be** ∼ (healthy) aller bien. ● interj eh bien; (surprise) tiens.

well: ∼**-behaved** adj sage. ∼**-being** n bien-être m inv.

wellington /ˈwelɪŋtən/ n (boot) botte f de caoutchouc.

well: ∼**-known** adj (bien) connu. ∼**-meaning** adj bien intentionné. ∼ **off** aisé, riche. ∼**-read** adj instruit. ∼**-to-do** adj riche. ∼**-wisher** n admirateur/-trice m/f.

Welsh /welʃ/ adj gallois. ● n (Ling) gallois m.

Welsh Assembly L'Assemblée du Pays de Galles a été établie à Cardiff en 1999, à l'issue d'un référendum auprès de la population galloise. À la différence du parlement écossais, elle n'a pas de réel pouvoir législatif, mais ses 60 membres peuvent aménager les lois nationales en fonction des besoins spécifiques des Gallois. ▷**Scottish Parliament**.

went /went/ ➡**GO**.

wept /wept/ ➡**WEEP**.

were /wɜ:(r)/ ➡**BE**.

west /west/ n ouest m; **the W~** (Pol) l'Occident m. ● adj d'ouest. ● adv vers l'ouest.

western /'westən/ adj de l'ouest; (Pol) occidental. ● n (film) western m. **westerner** n occidental/-e m/f.

West Indies /west 'ɪndi:z/ n Antilles fpl.

westward /'westwəd/ adj (side) ouest inv; (journey) vers l'ouest.

wet /wet/ adj (**wetter, wettest**) mouillé; (damp, rainy) humide; (paint) frais; **get ~** se mouiller. ● vt (pt **wetted**) mouiller. ● n the ~ l'humidité f; (rain) la pluie f. **~suit** n combinaison f de plongée.

whale /weɪl/ n baleine f.

wharf /wɔ:f/ n quai m.

what /wɒt/
● pronoun
⋯➤ (in questions as object pronoun) qu'est-ce que?; **~ are we going to do?** qu'est-ce que nous allons faire?
⋯➤ (in questions as subject pronoun) qu'est-ce qui?; **~ happened?** qu'est-ce qui s'est passé?
⋯➤ (introducing clause as object) ce que; **I don't know ~ he wants** je ne sais pas ce qu'il veut.
⋯➤ (introducing clause as subject) ce qui; **tell me ~ happened** raconte moi ce qui s'est passé.
⋯➤ (with prepositions) quoi; **~ are you thinking about?** à quoi penses-tu?

● determiner
⋯➤ quel/quelle/quels/quelles; **~ train did you catch?** quel train as-tu pris?; **~ time is it?** quelle heure est-il?

whatever /wɒt'evə(r)/ adj **~ book** quel que soit le livre. ● pron (no matter what) quoi que, quoi qu'; (anything that) tout ce qui; (object) tout ce que or qu'; **~ happens** quoi qu'il arrive; **~ happened?** qu'est-ce qui est arrivé?; **~ the problems** quels que soient les problèmes; **~ you want** tout ce que vous voulez; **nothing ~** rien du tout.

whatsoever /wɒtsəʊ'evə(r)/ adj & pron ➡**WHATEVER**.

wheat /wi:t/ n blé m, froment m.

wheel /wi:l/ n roue f; **at the ~** (of vehicle) au volant; (helm) au gouvernail. ● vt pousser. ● vi tourner; **~ and deal** faire des combines. **~barrow** n brouette f. **~chair** n fauteuil m roulant.

when /wen/ adv & pron quand. ● conj quand, lorsque; **the day/moment ~** le jour/moment où.

whenever /wen'evə(r)/ conj & adv (at whatever time) quand; (every time that) chaque fois que.

where /weə(r)/ adv, conj & pron où; (whereas) alors que; (the place that) là où.

whereabouts /weərə'baʊts/ adv (à peu près) où. ● n sb's ~ l'endroit où se trouve qn.

whereas /weər'æz/ conj alors que.

wherever /weər'evə(r)/ conj & adv où que; (everywhere) partout où; (anywhere) (là) où; (emphatic where) où donc.

whether /'weðə(r)/ conj si; **not know ~** ne pas savoir si; **~ I go or not** que j'aille ou non.

which /wɪtʃ/
● pronoun
⋯➤ (in questions) lequel/laquelle/lesquels/lesquelles; **there are three peaches, ~ do you want?** il y a trois pêches, laquelle veux-tu?

····➤ (in questions with superlative adjective) quel/quelle/quels/ quelles; ~ **(apple) is the biggest?** quelle est la plus grosse?

····➤ (in relative clauses as subject) qui; **the book ~ is on the table** le livre qui est sur la table.

····➤ (in relative clauses as object) que; **the book ~ Tina is reading** le livre que lit Tina.

● determiner

····➤ quel/quelle/quels/quelles; ~ **car did you choose?** quelle voiture as-tu choisie?

whichever /wɪtʃˈevə(r)/ adj ~ **book** quel que soit le livre que or qui; **take ~ book you wish** prenez le livre que vous voulez. ● pron celui/celle/ceux/ celles qui or que.

while /waɪl/ n moment m. ● conj (when) pendant que; (although) bien que; (as long as) tant que. ● vt ~ **away** (time) passer.

whilst /waɪlst/ conj ➡WHILE.

whim /wɪm/ n caprice m.

whine /waɪn/ vi gémir, se plaindre. ● n gémissement m.

whip /wɪp/ n fouet m. ● vt (pt **whipped**) fouetter; (Culin) fouetter, battre; (seize) enlever brusquement. ● vi (move) aller en vitesse. □ ~ **up** exciter; (cause) provoquer; (meal 🇮) préparer.

whirl /wɜːl/ vt/i (faire) tourbillonner. ● n tourbillon m. ~**pool** n tourbillon m. ~**wind** n tourbillon m (de vent).

whisk /wɪsk/ vt (snatch) enlever or emmener brusquement; (Culin) fouetter. ● n (Culin) fouet m.

whiskers /ˈwɪskə(r)s/ npl (of animal) moustaches fpl; (of man) favoris mpl.

whisper /ˈwɪspə(r)/ vt/i chuchoter. ● n chuchotement m; (rumour: fig) rumeur f, bruit m.

whistle /ˈwɪsl/ n sifflement m; (instrument) sifflet m. ● vt/i siffler; ~ **at** or **for** siffler.

white /waɪt/ adj blanc. ● n blanc m; (person) blanc/-che m/f. ● ~ **coffee** n café m au lait. ~-**collar worker** n employé/-e m/f de bureau. ~ **elephant** n projet m coûteux et peu rentable. ~ **lie** n pieux mensonge m.

W~ Paper n livre m blanc.

whitewash /ˈwaɪtwɒʃ/ n blanc m de chaux. ● vt blanchir à la chaux; (person: fig) blanchir.

Whitsun /ˈwɪtsn/ n la Pentecôte.

whiz /wɪz/ vi (pt **whizzed**) (through air) fendre l'air; (hiss) siffler; (rush) aller à toute vitesse. ~-**kid** n jeune prodige m.

who /huː/ pron qui.

whoever /huːˈevə(r)/ pron (no matter who) qui que ce soit qui or que; (the one who) quiconque; **tell ~ you want** dites-le à qui vous voulez.

whole /həʊl/ adj entier; (intact) intact; **the ~ house** toute la maison. ● n totalité f; (unit) tout m; **on the ~** dans l'ensemble. ~**foods** npl aliments mpl naturels et diététiques. ~-**hearted** adj sans réserve. ~**meal** adj complet.

wholesale /ˈhəʊlseɪl/ adj (firm) de gros; (fig) systématique. ● adv (in large quantities) en gros; (fig) en masse.

wholesome /ˈhəʊlsəm/ adj sain.

wholly /ˈhəʊlɪ/ adv entièrement.

whom /huːm/ pron (that) que, qu'; (after prepositions & in questions) qui; **of ~** dont; **with ~** avec qui.

whooping cough /ˈhuːpɪŋ kɒf/ n coqueluche f.

whose /huːz/ pron & a à qui, de qui; ~ **hat is this?**, ~ **is this hat?** à qui est ce chapeau?; ~ **son are you?** de qui êtes-vous le fils?; **the man ~ hat I see** l'homme dont je vois le chapeau.

why /waɪ/ adv pourquoi; **the reason ~** la raison pour laquelle.

wicked /ˈwɪkɪd/ adj méchant, mauvais, vilain.

wide /waɪd/ adj large; (ocean) vaste. ● adv (fall) loin du but; **open ~** ouvrir tout grand; ~ **open** grand ouvert; ~ **awake** éveillé. **widely** adv (spread, spaced) largement; (travel) beaucoup; (generally) généralement; (extremely) extrêmement.

widespread /ˈwaɪdspred/ adj très répandu.

widow /ˈwɪdəʊ/ n veuve f. **widowed** adj (man) veuf; (woman) veuve. **widower** n veuf m.

width /wɪdθ/ n largeur f.

wield /wi:ld/ vt (axe) manier; (power: fig) exercer.

wife /waɪf/ n (pl **wives**) femme f, épouse f.

wig /wɪg/ n perruque f.

wiggle /'wɪgl/ vt/i remuer; (hips) tortiller; (worm) se tortiller.

wild /waɪld/ adj sauvage; (sea, enthusiasm) déchaîné; (mad) fou; (angry) furieux. ● adv (grow) à l'état sauvage.

wildlife /'waɪldlaɪf/ n faune f.

---

will¹ /wɪl/

present **will**; present negative **won't, will not**; past **would**

● auxiliary verb

····▸ (in future tense) **he'll come** il viendra; **it ~ be sunny tomorrow** il va faire du soleil demain.

····▸ (inviting and requesting) **~ you have some coffee?** est-ce que vous voulez du café?

····▸ (making assumptions) **they won't know what's happened** ils ne doivent pas savoir ce qui s'est passé.

····▸ (in short questions and answers) **you'll come again, won't you?** tu reviendras, n'est-ce pas?; **'they won't forget'—'yes they ~'** ils n'oublieront pas'—'si'.

····▸ (capacity) **the lift ~ hold 12** l'ascenseur peut transporter 12 personnes.

····▸ (ability) **the car won't start** la voiture ne veut pas démarrer.

● transitive verb **~ sb's death** souhaiter ardemment la mort de qn.

---

will² /wɪl/ n volonté f; (document) testament m; **at ~** quand or comme on veut.

willing /'wɪlɪŋ/ adj (help, offer) spontané; (helper) bien disposé; **~ to** disposé à. **willingly** adv (with pleasure) volontiers; (not forced) volontairement. **willingness** n empressement m (**to do** à faire).

willow /'wɪləʊ/ n saule m.

will-power /'wɪlpaʊə(r)/ n volonté f.

win /wɪn/ vt/i (pt **won**; pres p **winning**) gagner; (prize) remporter; (fame) ac-

quérir, trouver; **~ round** convaincre. ● n victoire f.

winch /wɪntʃ/ n treuil m. ● vt hisser au treuil.

wind¹ /wɪnd/ n vent m; (breath) souffle m; **get ~ of** avoir vent de; **in the ~** dans l'air. ● vt essouffler. **~ farm** n ferme f d'éoliennes. **~ turbine** moteur m éolien.

wind² /waɪnd/ vt/i (pt **wound**) (s')enrouler; (of path, river) serpenter; **~ (up)** (clock) remonter; **~ up** (end) (se) terminer; **~ up in hospital** finir à l'hôpital.

windmill /'wɪndmɪl/ n moulin m à vent.

window /'wɪndəʊ/ n fenêtre f; (glass pane) vitre f; (in vehicle, train) vitre f; (in shop) vitrine f; (counter) guichet m; (Comput) fenêtre f. **~-box** n jardinière f. **~-cleaner** n laveur m de carreaux. **~-dresser** n étalagiste mf. **~-ledge** n rebord m de (la) fenêtre. **~-shopping** n lèche-vitrines m. **~-sill** n (inside) appui m de (la) fenêtre; (outside) rebord m de (la) fenêtre.

windscreen /'wɪndskri:n/ n parebrise m inv. **~ wiper** n essuie-glace m.

windshield /'wɪndʃi:ld/ n (US) ➡WINDSCREEN.

windsurfing /'wɪndsɜ:fɪŋ/ n planche f à voile.

windy /'wɪndɪ/ adj (-ier, -iest) venteux; **it is ~** il y a du vent.

wine /waɪn/ n vin m. **~-cellar** n cave f (à vin). **~glass** n verre m à vin. **~-grower** n viticulteur m. **~ list** n carte f des vins. **~-tasting** n dégustation f de vins.

wing /wɪŋ/ n aile f; **~s** (Theat) coulisses fpl; **under one's ~** sous son aile. **~ mirror** n rétroviseur m extérieur.

wink /wɪŋk/ vi faire un clin d'œil; (light, star) clignoter. ● n clin m d'œil; clignotement m.

winner /'wɪnə(r)/ n (of game) gagnant/-e m/f; (of fight) vainqueur m.

winning /'wɪnɪŋ/ ➡WIN. ● adj (number, horse) gagnant; (team) victorieux; (smile) engageant. **winnings** npl gains mpl.

winter /'wɪntə(r)/ n hiver m.

wipe /waɪp/ vt essuyer. ● vi **~ up** essuyer la vaisselle. ● n coup m de torchon or d'éponge. □ ~ **out** (destroy) anéantir; (remove) effacer.

wire /'waɪə(r)/ n fil m; (US) télégramme m.

wiring /'waɪərɪŋ/ n (Electr) installation f électrique.

wisdom /'wɪzdəm/ n sagesse f.

wise /waɪz/ adj prudent, sage; (look) averti.

wish /wɪʃ/ n (specific) souhait m, vœu m; (general) désir m; best ~es (in letter) amitiés fpl; (on greeting card) meilleurs vœux mpl. ● vt souhaiter, vouloir, désirer (**to do** faire); (bid) souhaiter. ● vi ~ **for** souhaiter; **I ~ he'd leave** je voudrais bien qu'il parte.

wishful /'wɪʃfl/ adj it's ~ **thinking** c'est prendre ses désirs pour des réalités.

wistful /'wɪstfl/ adj mélancolique.

wit /wɪt/ n intelligence f; (humour) esprit m; (person) homme m d'esprit, femme f d'esprit.

witch /wɪtʃ/ n sorcière f.

with /'wɪð/ prep avec; (having) à; (because of) de; (at house of) chez; **the man ~ the beard** l'homme à la barbe; **fill ~ pleased/shaking** ~ content/frémissant de.

withdraw /wɪð'drɔː/ vt/i (pt **withdrew**; pp **withdrawn**) (se) retirer. **withdrawal** n retrait m.

wither /'wɪðə(r)/ vt/i (se) flétrir.

withhold /wɪð'həʊld/ vt (pt **withheld**) refuser (de donner); (retain) retenir; (conceal) cacher (**from** à).

within /wɪ'ðɪn/ prep & adv à l'intérieur (de); (in distances) à moins de; ~ **a month** (before) avant un mois; ~ **sight** en vue.

without /wɪ'ðaʊt/ prep sans; ~ **my knowing** sans que je sache.

withstand /wɪð'stænd/ vt (pt **withstood**) résister à.

witness /'wɪtnɪs/ n témoin m; (evidence) témoignage m; **bear** ~ **to** témoigner de. ● vt être le témoin de, voir. ~ **box**, ~ **stand** n barre f des témoins.

witty /'wɪtɪ/ adj (**-ier, -iest**) spirituel.

wives /waɪvz/ ➡WIFE.

wizard /'wɪzəd/ n magicien m; (genius: fig) génie m.

WMD abbr (weapon of mass destruction) ADM f.

woke, woken ➡WAKE.

wolf /wʊlf/ n (pl **wolves**) loup m. ● vt (food) engloutir.

woman /'wʊmən/ n (pl **women**) femme f; ~ **doctor** femme f médecin; ~ **driver** femme f au volant.

women /'wɪmɪn/ ➡WOMAN.

won /wʌn/➡WIN.

wonder /'wʌndə(r)/ n émerveillement m; (thing) merveille f; **it is no** ~ ce or il n'est pas étonnant (**that** que). ● vt se demander (**if** si). ● vi s'étonner (**at** de); (reflect) songer (**about** à).

wonderful /'wʌndəfl/ adj merveilleux.

won't /wəʊnt/ ➡WILL NOT.

wood /wʊd/ n bois m.

wooden /'wʊdn/ adj en or de bois. (stiff: fig) raide, comme du bois.

wood: ~**wind** n (Mus) bois mpl. ~**work** n (craft, objects) menuiserie f.

wool /wʊl/ n laine f. **woollen** adj de laine. **woollens** npl lainages mpl.

woolly /'wʊlɪ/ adj laineux; (vague) nébuleux. ● n (garment 🔲) lainage m.

word /wɜːd/ n mot m; (spoken) parole f, mot m; (promise) parole f; (news) nouvelles fpl; **by** ~ **of mouth** de vive voix; **give/keep one's** ~ donner/tenir sa parole; **have a** ~ **with** parler à; **in other** ~**s** autrement dit. ● vt rédiger. **wording** n termes mpl.

word processing n traitement m de texte. **word processor** n machine f à traitement de texte.

wore /wɔː(r)/ ➡WEAR.

work /wɜːk/ n travail m; (product, book) œuvre f, ouvrage m; (building work) travaux mpl; ~**s** (Tech) mécanisme m; (factory) usine f. ● vi (person) travailler; (drug) agir; (Tech) fonctionner, marcher. ● vt (Tech) faire fonctionner, faire marcher; (land, mine) exploiter; (shape, hammer) travailler; ~ **sb** (make work) faire travailler qn. □ ~ **out** vt (solve) résoudre; (calculate) calculer; (elaborate) élaborer; vi (succeed) marcher; (Sport) s'entraîner; ~ **up** vt développer; vi (to climax) monter vers; ~**ed up** (person) énervé.

workaholic /wɜːkə'hɒlɪk/ n 🔲 bourreau m de travail.

worker /'wɜːkə(r)/ n travailleur/-euse m/f; (manual) ouvrier/-ière m/f.

work-force n main-d'œuvre f.

working /'wɜːkɪŋ/ adj (day, lunch) de travail; ~s mécanisme m; **in ~ order** en état de marche.

working class n classe f ouvrière. ● adj ouvrier.

workman /'wɜːkmən/ n (pl **-men**) ouvrier m.

work: ~out n séance f de mise en forme. **~shop** n atelier m. **~-station** n poste m de travail.

world /wɜːld/ n monde m; **best in the ~** meilleur au monde. ● adj (power) mondial; (record) du monde.

world-wide adj universel.

World Wide Web, **WWW** n World Wide Web m, réseau m des réseaux.

worm /wɜːm/ n ver m. ● vt ~ **one's way into** s'insinuer dans.

worn /wɔːn/ →WEAR. ● adj usé. **~-out** adj (thing) complètement usé; (person) épuisé.

worried /'wʌrɪd/ adj inquiet.

worry /'wʌrɪ/ vt/i (s')inquiéter. ● n souci m.

worse /wɜːs/ adj pire, plus mauvais; **be ~ off** perdre. ● adv plus mal. ● n pire m. **worsen** vt/i empirer.

worship /'wɜːʃɪp/ n (adoration) culte m. ● vt (pt **worshipped**) adorer. ● vi faire ses dévotions.

worst /wɜːst/ adj pire, plus mauvais. ● adv (the) ~ (sing) le plus mal. ● n **the ~ (one)** (person, object) le or la pire; **the ~ (thing)** le pire.

worth /wɜːθ/ adj **be ~** valoir; **it is ~ waiting** ça vaut la peine d'attendre; **it is ~ (one's) while** ça (en) vaut la peine. ● n valeur f; **ten pence ~ of** (pour) dix pence de. **worthless** adj qui ne vaut rien. **worthwhile** adj qui (en) vaut la peine.

worthy /'wɜːðɪ/ adj (**-ier**, **-iest**) digne (of de); (laudable) louable.

would /wʊd/ v aux **he ~ do/you ~ sing** (conditional tense) il ferait/tu chanterais; **he ~ have done** il aurait fait; **I ~ come every day** (used to) je venais chaque jour; **I ~ like some tea** je voudrais du thé; **~ you come here?** voulez-vous venir ici?; **he**

wouldn't come il a refusé de venir. **~-be** adj soidisant.

wound¹ /wuːnd/ n blessure f. ● vt blesser; **the ~ed** les blessés mpl.

wound² /waʊnd/ →WIND².

wove, woven /wəʊv, 'wəʊvn/ →WEAVE.

wrap /ræp/ vt (pt **wrapped**) ~ **(up)** envelopper. ● vi ~ **up** (dress warmly) se couvrir; **~ped up in** (engrossed) absorbé dans.

wrapping /'ræpɪŋ/ n emballage m.

wreak /riːk/ vt ~ **havoc** faire des ravages.

wreath /riːθ/ n (of flowers, leaves) couronne f.

wreck /rek/ n (sinking) naufrage m; (ship, remains, person) épave f; (vehicle) voiture f accidentée or délabrée. ● vt détruire; (ship) provoquer le naufrage de. **wreckage** n (pieces) débris mpl; (wrecked building) décombres mpl.

wrestle /'resl/ vi lutter, se débattre (with contre).

wrestling /'reslɪŋ/ n lutte f; **(all-in) ~ catch** m.

wriggle /'rɪgl/ vt/i (se) tortiller.

wring /rɪŋ/ vt (pt **wrung**) (twist) tordre; (clothes) essorer; ~ **out of** (obtain from) arracher à.

wrinkle /'rɪŋkl/ n (crease) pli m; (on skin) ride f. ● vt/i (se) rider.

wrist /rɪst/ n poignet m.

write /raɪt/ vt/i (pt **wrote**, pp **written**) écrire. □ ~ **back** répondre; ~ **down** noter; ~ **off** (debt) passer aux profits et pertes; (vehicle) considérer bon pour la casse; ~ **up** (from notes) rédiger.

write-off /'raɪtɒf/ n perte f totale.

writer /'raɪtə(r)/ n auteur m, écrivain m; ~ **of** auteur de.

write-up /'raɪtʌp/ n compte-rendu m.

writing /'raɪtɪŋ/ n écriture f; **~(s)** (works) écrits mpl; **in ~** par écrit. **~-paper** n papier m à lettres.

written →WRITE.

wrong /rɒŋ/ adj (incorrect, mistaken) faux, mauvais. (unfair) injuste; (amiss) qui ne va pas; (clock) pas à l'heure; **be ~** (person) avoir tort (to de); (be mistaken) se tromper; **go ~** (err) se tromper; (turn out badly) mal tourner;

it is ~ to (morally) c'est mal de; **what's ~ with you?** qu'est-ce qui ne va pas?; **what is ~ with you?** qu'est-ce que vous avez? ● *adv* mal. ● *n* injustice *f*; (evil) mal *m*; **be in the ~** avoir tort. ● *vt* faire (du) tort à. **wrongful** *adj* injustifié, injuste. **wrongfully** *adv* à tort. **wrongly** *adv* mal; (*blame*) à tort.

wrote /rəʊt/ ➡WRITE.

wrought iron /rɔːt 'aɪən/ *n* fer *m* forgé.

wrung /rʌŋ/ ➡WRING.

Xx

Xmas /'krɪsməs/ *n* Noël *m*.

X-ray /'eksreɪ/ *n* rayon *m* X; (photograph) radio (graphie) *f*. ● *vt* radiographier.

Yy

yank /jæŋk/ *vt* tirer brusquement. ● *n* coup *m* brusque.

yard /jɑːd/ *n* (measure) yard *m* (= *0.9144 metre*). (of house) cour *f*; (garden: US) jardin *m*; (for storage) chantier *m*, dépôt *m*. **~stick** *n* mesure *f*.

yawn /jɔːn/ *vi* bâiller. ● *n* bâillement *m*.

yeah /jeə/ *adv* 🄸 ouais.

year /jɪə(r)/ *n* an *m*, année *f*; **school/ tax ~** année scolaire/fiscale; **be ten ~s old** avoir dix ans.

yearly /'jɪəlɪ/ *adj* annuel. ● *adv* annuellement.

yearn /jɜːn/ *vi* avoir bien *or* très envie **(for, to** de).

yeast /jiːst/ *n* levure *f*.

yell /jel/ *vt/i* hurler. ● *n* hurlement *m*.

yellow /'jeləʊ/ *adj* jaune; (cowardly 🄸) froussard. ● *n* jaune *m*.

yes /jes/ *adv* oui; (as answer to negative question) si. ● *n* oui *m inv*.

yesterday /'jestədeɪ/ *n & adv* hier (*m*).

yet /jet/ *adv* encore; (already) déjà. ● *conj* pourtant, néanmoins.

yew /juː/ *n* if *m*.

yield /jiːld/ *vt* (produce) produire, rendre; (*profit*) rapporter; (surrender) céder. ● *n* rendement *m*.

yoga /'jəʊɡə/ *n* yoga *m*.

yoghurt /'jɒɡət/ *n* yaourt *m*.

yolk /jəʊk/ *n* jaune *m* (d'œuf).

you /juː/ *pron* (familiar form) tu, *pl* vous; (polite form) vous; (object) te, t', *pl* vous; (polite) vous; (after prep.) toi, *pl* vous; (polite) vous; (indefinite) on; (object) vous; **(to) ~** te, t', *pl* vous; (polite) vous; **I gave ~ a pen** je vous ai donné un stylo; **I know ~** je te connais *or* je vous connais.

young /jʌŋ/ *adj* jeune. ● *n* (people) jeunes *mpl*; (of animals) petits *mpl*.

your /jɔː(r)/ *adj* (familiar form) ton, ta, *pl* tes; (polite form, & familiar form pl.) votre, *pl* vos.

yours /jɔːz/ *pron* (familiar form) le tien, la tienne, les tien(ne)s; (polite form, & familiar form pl.) le *or* la vôtre, les vôtres; **~ faithfully/sincerely** je vous prie d'agréer mes salutations les meilleures.

yourself /jɔːˈself/ *pron* (familiar form) toimême; (polite form) vous-même; (reflexive & after prepositions) te, t'; vous; **proud of ~** fier de toi. **yourselves** *pron* vous-mêmes; (reflexive) vous.

youth /juːθ/ *n* jeunesse *f*; (young man) jeune *m*. **~ hostel** *n* auberge *f* de jeunesse.

Yugoslav /'juːɡəʊslɑːv/ *adj* yougoslave. ● *n* Yougoslave *mf*.

Yugoslavia /juːɡəʊˈslɑːvɪə/ *n* Yougoslavie *f*.

Zz

zap /zæp/ *vt* 🄸 (kill) descendre; (Comput) enlever.

zeal /ziːl/ *n* zèle *m*.

zebra /'zebrə/ *n* zèbre *m*. **~ crossing** *n* passage *m* pour piétons.

zero /ˈzɪərəʊ/ n zéro m.

zest /zest/ n (gusto) entrain m; (spice: fig) piment m; (of orange or lemon peel) zeste m.

zip /zɪp/ n (vigour) allant m; ∼(**-fastener**) fermeture f éclair(r). ● vt (pt **zipped**) fermer avec une fermeture éclair(r); (Comput) compresser. **Zip code** (US) n code m postal.

zodiac /ˈzəʊdɪæk/ n zodiaque m.

zone /zəʊn/ n zone f.

zoo /zuː/ n zoo m.

zoom /zuːm/ vi (rush) se précipiter. □ ∼ **off** or **past** filer (comme une flèche). ∼ **lens** n zoom m.

zucchini /zuːˈkiːnɪ/ n inv (US) courgette f.

French Verbs

1 chanter

Present indicative

je	chante
tu	chantes
il	chante
nous	chantons
vous	chantez
ils	chantent

Present subjunctive

(que)	je	chante
(que)	tu	chantes
(qu')	il	chante
(que)	nous	chantions
(que)	vous	chantiez
(qu')	ils	chantent

Future indicative

je	chanterai
tu	chanteras
il	chantera
nous	chanterons
vous	chanterez
ils	chanteront

Present conditional

je	chanterais
tu	chanterais
il	chanterait
nous	chanterions
vous	chanteriez
ils	chanteraient

Imperfect indicative

je	chantais
tu	chantais
il	chantait
nous	chantions
vous	chantiez
ils	chantaient

Past participle

chanté/chantée

Pluperfect indicative

j'	avais	chanté
tu	avais	chanté
il	avait	chanté
elle	avait	chanté
nous	avions	chanté
vous	aviez	chanté
ils	avaient	chanté
elles	avaient	chanté

Perfect indicative

j'	ai	chanté
tu	as	chanté
il	a	chanté
elle	a	chanté
nous	avons	chanté
vous	avez	chanté
ils	ont	chanté
elles	ont	chanté

2 finir

Present indicative

je	finis
tu	finis
il	finit
nous	finissons
vous	finissez
ils	finissent

Present subjunctive

(que)	je	finisse
(que)	tu	finisses
(qu')	il	finisse
(que)	nous	finissions
(que)	vous	finissiez
(qu')	ils	finissent

Future indicative

je	finirai
tu	finiras
il	finira
nous	finirons
vous	finirez
ils	finiront

Present conditional

je	finirais
tu	finirais
il	finirait
nous	finirions
vous	finiriez
ils	finiraient

Imperfect indicative

je	finissais
tu	finissais
il	finissait
nous	finissions
vous	finissiez
ils	finissaient

Past participle

fini/finie

Pluperfect indicative

j'	avais	fini
tu	avais	fini
il	avait	fini
elle	avait	fini
nous	avions	fini
vous	aviez	fini
ils	avaient	fini
elles	avaient	fini

Perfect indicative

j'	ai	fini
tu	as	fini
il	a	fini
elles	a	fini
nous	avons	fini
vous	avez	fini
ils	ont	fini
elles	ont	fini

3 attendre

Present indicative

j'	attends
tu	attends
il	attend
nous	attendons
vous	attendez
ils	attendent

Present subjunctive

(que)	j'	attende
(que)	tu	attendes
(qu')	il	attende
(que)	nous	attendions
(que)	vous	attendiez
(qu')	ils	attendent

Future indicative

j'	attendrai
tu	attendras
il	attendra
nous	attendrons
vous	attendrez
ils	attendront

Present conditional

j'	attendrais
tu	attendrais
il	attendrait
nous	attendrions
vous	attendriez
ils	attendraient

Imperfect indicative

j'	attendais
tu	attendais
il	attendait
nous	attendions
vous	attendiez
ils	attendaient

Past participle

attendu/attendue

Pluperfect indicative

j'	avais	attendu
tu	avais	attendu
il	avait	attendu
elle	avait	attendu
nous	avions	attendu
vous	aviez	attendu
ils	avaient	attendu
elles	avaient	attendu

Perfect indicative

j'	ai	attendu
tu	as	attendu
il	a	attendu
elle	a	attendu
nous	avons	attendu
vous	avez	attendu
ils	ont	attendu
elles	ont	attendu

4 être

Present indicative

je	suis
tu	es
il	est
nous	sommes
vous	êtes
ils	sont

Future indicative

je	serai
tu	seras
il	sera
nous	serons
vous	serez
ils	seront

Imperfect indicative

j'	étais
tu	étais
il	était
nous	étions
vous	étiez
ils	étaient

Perfect indicative

j'	ai	été
tu	as	été
il	a	été
elle	a	été
nous	avons	été
vous	avez	été
ils	ont	été
elles	ont	été

Present subjunctive

(que)	je	sois
(que)	tu	sois
(qu')	il	soit
(que)	nous	soyons
(que)	vous	soyez
(qu')	ils	soient

Present conditional

je	serais
tu	serais
il	serait
nous	serions
vous	seriez
ils	seraient

Past participle

été (*invariable*)

Pluperfect indicative

j'	avais	été
tu	avais	été
il	avait	été
elle	avait	été
nous	avions	été
vous	aviez	été
ils	avaient	été
elles	avaient	été

5 avoir

Present indicative

j'	ai
tu	as
il	a
nous	avons
vous	avez
ils	ont

Present subjunctive

(que)	j'	aie
(que)	tu	aies
(qu')	il	ait
(que)	nous	ayons
(que)	vous	ayez
(qu')	ils	aient

Future indicative

j'	aurai
tu	auras
il	aura
nous	aurons
vous	aurez
ils	auront

Present conditional

j'	aurais
tu	aurais
il	aurait
nous	aurions
vous	auriez
ils	auraient

Imperfect indicative

j'	avais
tu	avais
il	avait
nous	avions
vous	aviez
ils	avaient

Past participle

eu/eue

Pluperfect indicative

j'	avais	eu
tu	avais	eu
il	avait	eu
elle	avait	eu
nous	avions	eu
vous	aviez	eu
ils	avaient	eu
elles	avaient	eu

Perfect indicative

j'	ai	eu
tu	as	eu
il	a	eu
elle	a	eu
nous	avons	eu
vous	avez	eu
ils	ont	eu
elles	ont	eu

[6] acheter

1 j'achète 2 j'achèterai 3 j'achetais
4 que j'achète 5 acheté

[7] acquérir

1 j'acquiers, nous acquérons,
ils acquièrent 2 j'acquerrai
3 j'acquérais 4 que j'acquière
5 acquis

[8] aller

1 je vais, tu vas, il va, nous allons,
vous allez, ils vont 2 j'irai 3 j'allais
4 que j'aille, que nous allions, qu'ils
aillent 5 allé

[9] asseoir

1 j'assois, tu assois, il assoit, nous
assoyons, vous assoyez, ils assoient
2 j'assoirai 3 j'assoyais 4 que
j'assoie, que nous assoyions, qu'ils
assoient 5 assis

[10] avancer

1 nous avançons 3 j'avançais

[11] battre

1 je bats, il bat, nous battons
2 je battrai 3 je battais 4 que je
batte 5 battu

[12] boire

1 je bois, il boit, nous buvons,
ils boivent 2 je boirai 3 je buvais
4 que je boive 5 bu

[13] bouillir

1 je bous, il bout, nous bouillons,
ils bouillent 2 je bouillirai

3 je bouillais 4 que je bouille
5 bouilli

[14] céder

1 je cède, nous cédons, ils cèdent
2 je céderai 3 je cédais 4 que je
cède 5 cédé

[15] créer

1 je crée, nous créons 2 je créerai
3 je créais 4 que je crée 5 créé

[16] conclure

1 je conclus, il conclut, nous
concluons, ils concluent 2 je
conclurai 3 je concluais 4 que je
conclue 5 conclu (*but* inclus)

[17] conduire

1 je conduis, nous conduisons,
2 je conduirai 3 je conduisais
4 que je conduise 5 conduit (*but* lui,
nui)

[18] connaître

1 je connais, il connaît, nous
connaissons 2 je connaîtrai
3 je connaissais 4 que je connaisse
5 connu

[19] coudre

1 je couds, il coud, nous cousons,
ils cousent 2 je coudrai 3 je cousais
4 que je couse 5 cousu

[20] courir

1 je cours, il court, nous courons,
ils courent 2 je courrai 3 je courais
4 que je coure 5 couru

---

1 Present Indicative   2 Future Indicative   3 Imperfect Indicative
4 Present Subjunctive   5 Past Participle

[21] couvrir

1 je couvre 2 je couvrirai 3 je couvrais 4 que je couvre 5 couvert

[22] craindre

1 je crains, il craint, nous craignons, ils craignent 2 je craindrai 3 je craignais 4 que je craigne 5 craint

[23] croire

1 je crois, il croit, nous croyons, ils croient 2 je croirai 3 je croyais, nous croyions 4 que je croie, que nous croyions 5 cru

[24] croître

1 je croîs, il croît, nous croissons 2 je croîtrai 3 je croissais 4 que je croisse 5 crû/crue (*but* accru, décru)

[25] cueillir

1 je cueille 2 je cueillerai 3 je cueillais 4 que je cueille 5 cueilli

[26] devoir

1 je dois, il doit, nous devons, ils doivent 2 je devrai 3 je devais 4 que je doive, que nous devions 5 dû/due

[27] dire

1 je dis, il dit, nous disons, vous dites, ils disent 2 je dirai 3 je disais 4 que je dise 5 dit

[28] dissoudre

1 je dissous, il dissout, nous dissolvons, ils dissolvent 2 je dissoudrai 3 je dissolvais 4 que je dissolve 5 dissous/dissoute

[29] distraire

1 je distrais, il distrait, nous distrayons 2 je distrairai 3 je distrayais 4 que je distraie 5 distrait

[30] écrire

1 j'écris, il écrit, nous écrivons 2 j'écrirai 3 j'écrivais 4 que j'écrive 5 écrit

[31] employer

1 j'emploie, nous employons, ils emploient 2 j'emploierai 3 j'employais, nous employions 4 que j'emploie, que nous employions 5 employé

[32] envoyer

1 j'envoie, nous envoyons, ils envoient 2 j'enverrai 3 j'envoyais, nous envoyions 4 que j'envoie, que nous envoyions 5 envoyé

[33] faire

1 je fais, nous faisons (*say* /fəzɔ̃/), vous faites, ils font 2 je ferai 3 je faisais (*say* /fəzɛ/) 4 que je fasse, que nous fassions 5 fait

[34] falloir (*impersonal*)

1 il faut 2 il faudra 3 il fallait 4 qu'il faille 5 fallu

[35] fuir

1 je fuis, nous fuyons 2 je fuirai 3 je fuyais, nous fuyions 4 que je fuie, que nous fuyions 5 fui

---

1 Present Indicative   2 Future Indicative   3 Imperfect Indicative
4 Present Subjunctive   5 Past Participle

[36] haïr

1 je hais, il hait, nous haïssons, ils haïssent **2** je haïrai **3** je haïssais **4** que je haïsse **5** haï

[37] interdire

1 j'interdis, vous interdisez **2** j'interdirai **3** j'interdisais **4** que j'interdise **5** interdit

[38] jeter

1 je jette, nous jetons, ils jettent **2** je jetterai **3** je jetais **4** que je jette **5** jeté

[39] lire

1 je lis, il lit, nous lisons **2** je lirai **3** je lisais **4** que je lise **5** lu

[40] manger

1 je mange, nous mangeons **2** je mangerai **3** je mangeais **4** que je mange, que nous mangions **5** mangé

[41] maudire

1 je maudis, il maudit, nous maudissons **2** je maudirai **3** je maudissais **4** que je maudisse **5** maudit

[42] mettre

1 je mets, tu mets, nous mettons **2** je mettrai **3** je mettais **4** que je mette **5** mis

[43] mourir

1 je meurs, il meurt, nous mourons **2** je mourrai **3** je mourais **4** que je meure **5** mort

[44] naître

1 je nais, il naît, nous naissons **2** je naîtrai **3** je naissais **4** que je naisse **5** né

[45] oublier

1 j'oublie, nous oublions, ils oublient **2** j'oublierai **3** j'oubliais, nous oubliions, vous oubliiez **4** que nous oubliions, que vous oubliiez **5** oublié

[46] partir

1 je pars, nous partons **2** je partirai **3** je partais **4** que je parte **5** parti

[47] plaire

1 je plais, il plaît (*but* il tait), nous plaisons **2** je plairai **3** je plaisais **4** que je plaise **5** plu

[48] pleuvoir (*impersonal*)

1 il pleut **2** il pleuvra **3** il pleuvait **4** qu'il pleuve **5** plu

[49] pouvoir

1 je peux, il peut, nous pouvons, ils peuvent **2** je pourrai **3** je pouvais **4** que je puisse, que nous puissions **5** pu

[50] prendre

1 je prends, il prend, nous prenons **2** je prendrai **3** je prenais **4** que je prenne **5** pris

---

1 Present Indicative   **2** Future Indicative   **3** Imperfect Indicative
4 Present Subjunctive   **5** Past Participle

[51] prévoir

1 je prévois, il prévoit, nous prévoyons, ils prévoient
2 je prévoirai 3 je prévoyais, nous prévoyions 4 que je prévoie, que nous prévoyions 5 prévu

[52] recevoir

1 je reçois, il reçoit, nous recevons, ils reçoivent 2 je recevrai
3 je recevais 4 que je reçoive, que nous recevions 5 reçu

[53] résoudre

1 je résous, il résout, nous résolvons, ils résolvent 2 je résoudrai 3 je résolvais 4 que je résolve 5 résolu

[54] rire

1 je ris, nous rions, ils rient
2 je rirai 3 je riais, nous riions
4 que je rie, que nous riions 5 ri

[55] savoir

1 je sais, il sait, nous savons, ils savent 2 je saurai 3 je savais
4 que je sache, que nous sachions 5 su

[56] suffire

1 il suffit, ils suffisent 2 il suffira
3 il suffisait 4 qu'il suffise 5 suffi (*but* frit)

[57] suivre

1 je suis, il suit, nous suivons
2 je suivrai 3 je suivais 4 que je suive 5 suivi

[58] tenir

1 je tiens, il tient, nous tenons, ils tiennent 2 je tiendrai 3 je tenais
4 que je tienne, que nous tenions
5 tenu

[59] vaincre

1 je vaincs, il vainc, nous vainquons, ils vainquent 2 je vaincrai
3 je vainquais 4 que je vainque
5 vaincu

[60] valoir

1 je vaux, il vaut, nous valons
2 je vaudrai 3 je valais 4 que je vaille, que nous valions 5 valu

[61] vêtir

1 je vêts, il vêt, nous vêtons
2 je vêtirai 3 je vêtais 4 que je vête
5 vêtu

[62] vivre

1 je vis, il vit, nous vivons, ils vivent
2 je vivrai 3 je vivais 4 que je vive
5 vécu

[63] voir

1 je vois, nous voyons, ils voient
2 je verrai 3 je voyais, nous voyions
4 que je voie, que nous voyions
5 vu

[64] vouloir

1 je veux, il veut, nous voulons, ils veulent 2 je voudrai 3 je voulais
4 que je veuille, que nous voulions
5 voulu

---

1 Present Indicative 2 Future Indicative 3 Imperfect Indicative
4 Present Subjunctive 5 Past Participle

What are the equivalent tenses in English

Present indicative
je chante = I sing, I'm singing

Future indicative
je chanterai = I will sing

Imperfect indicative
je chantais = I was singing

Perfect indicative
j'ai chanté = I sang, I have sung

Pluperfect indicative
j'avais chanté = I had sung

Present subjunctive
bien que je chante = although I sing

Present conditional
si je pouvais, je chanterais
= if I could, I would sing

Past participle
chanté/chantée = sung

How to conjugate a reflexive verb

Present indicative and other simple tenses

je me lave
tu te laves
il se lave
elle se lave
nous nous lavons
vous vous lavez
ils se lavent
elles se lavent

Perfect indicative and other compound tenses
(always with auxiliary être)

je me suis lavé
tu t'es lavé
il s'est lavé
elle s'est lavée
nous nous sommes lavés
vous vous êtes lavés
ils se sont lavés
elles se sont lavées

in the negative form

je ne me lave pas
tu ne te laves pas
il ne se lave pas
elle ne se lave pas
nous ne nous lavons pas
vous ne vous lavez pas
ils ne se lavent pas
elles ne se lavent pas

in the negative form

je ne me suis pas lavé
tu ne t'es pas lavé
il ne s'est pas lavé
elle ne s'est pas lavée
nous ne nous sommes pas lavés
vous ne vous êtes pas lavés
ils ne se sont pas lavés
elles ne se sont pas lavées

Verbes irréguliers anglais

Infinitif	Prétérit	Participe passé	Infinitif	Prétérit	Participe passé
be	was	been	drive	drove	driven
bear	bore	borne	eat	ate	eaten
beat	beat	beaten	fall	fell	fallen
become	became	become	feed	fed	fed
begin	began	begun	feel	felt	felt
bend	bent	bent	fight	fought	fought
bet	bet, betted	bet, betted	find	found	found
			flee	fled	fled
bid	bade, bid	bidden, bid	fly	flew	flown
bind	bound	bound	freeze	froze	frozen
bite	bit	bitten	get	got	got, gotten US
bleed	bled	bled	give	gave	given
blow	blew	blown	go	went	gone
break	broke	broken	grow	grew	grown
breed	bred	bred	hang	hung, hanged	hung, hanged
bring	brought	brought			
build	built	built	have	had	had
burn	burnt, burned	burnt, burned	hear	heard	heard
			hide	hid	hidden
burst	burst	burst	hit	hit	hit
buy	bought	bought	hold	held	held
catch	caught	caught	hurt	hurt	hurt
choose	chose	chosen	keep	kept	kept
cling	clung	clung	kneel	knelt	knelt
come	came	come	know	knew	known
cost	cost, costed (vt)	cost, costed	lay	laid	laid
			lead	led	led
cut	cut	cut	lean	leaned, leant	leaned, leant
deal	dealt	dealt			
dig	dug	dug	learn	learnt, learned	learnt, learned
do	did	done			
draw	drew	drawn	leave	left	left
dream	dreamt, dreamed	dreamt, dreamed	lend	lent	lent
			let	let	let
drink	drank	drunk	lie	lay	lain

Infinitif	Prétérit	Participe passé	Infinitif	Prétérit	Participe passé
lose	lost	lost	**spend**	spent	spent
make	made	made	**spit**	spat	spat
mean	meant	meant	**spoil**	spoilt, spoiled	spoilt, spoiled
meet	met	met			
pay	paid	paid	**spread**	spread	spread
put	put	put	**spring**	sprang	sprung
read	read	read	**stand**	stood	stood
ride	rode	ridden	**steal**	stole	stolen
ring	rang	rung	**stick**	stuck	stuck
rise	rose	risen	**sting**	stung	stung
run	ran	run	**stride**	strode	stridden
say	said	said	**strike**	struck	struck
see	saw	seen	**swear**	swore	sworn
seek	sought	sought	**sweep**	swept	swept
sell	sold	sold	**swell**	swelled	swollen, swelled
send	sent	sent			
set	set	set	**swim**	swam	swum
sew	sewed	sewn, sewed	**swing**	swung	swung
shake	shook	shaken	**take**	took	taken
shine	shone	shone	**teach**	taught	taught
shoe	shod	shod	**tear**	tore	torn
shoot	shot	shot	**tell**	told	told
show	showed	shown	**think**	thought	thought
shut	shut	shut	**throw**	threw	thrown
sing	sang	sung	**thrust**	thrust	thrust
sink	sank	sunk	**tread**	trod	trodden
sit	sat	sat	**under-stand**	under-stood	understood
sleep	slept	slept			
sling	slung	slung	**wake**	woke	woken
smell	smelt, smelled	smelt, smelled	**wear**	wore	worn
			win	won	won
speak	spoke	spoken	**write**	wrote	written
spell	spelled, spelt	spelled, spelt			

Numbers/Les nombres

Cardinal numbers/ Les nombres cardinaux

0	zero	**zéro**
1	one	**un**
2	two	**deux**
3	three	**trois**
4	four	**quatre**
5	five	**cinq**
6	six	**six**
7	seven	**sept**
8	eight	**huit**
9	nine	**neuf**
10	ten	**dix**
11	eleven	**onze**
12	twelve	**douze**
13	thirteen	**treize**
14	fourteen	**quatorze**
15	fifteen	**quinze**
16	sixteen	**seize**
17	seventeen	**dix-sept**
18	eighteen	**dix-huit**
19	nineteen	**dix-neuf**
20	twenty	**vingt**
21	twenty-one	**vingt et un**
22	twenty-two	**vingt-deux**
30	thirty	**trente**
40	forty	**quarante**
50	fifty	**cinquante**
60	sixty	**soixante**
70	seventy	**soixante-dix**
80	eighty	**quatre-vingt**
90	ninety	**quatre-vingt-dix**

100	a hundred	**cent**
101	a hundred and one	**cent un**
110	a hundred and ten	**cent dix**
200	two hundred	**deux cents**
250	two hundred and fifty	**deux cent cinquante**
1,000	one thousand	**mille**
1,001	one thousand and one	**mille un**
2,000	two thousand	**deux mille**
10,000	ten thousand	**dix mille**
100,000	a hundred thousand	**cent mille**
1,000,000	a million	**un million**

Ordinal numbers/ Les nombres ordinaux

1st	first	**premier**
2nd	second	**deuxième**
3rd	third	**troisième**
4th	fourth	**quatrième**
5th	fifth	**cinquième**
6th	sixth	**sixième**
7th	seventh	**septième**
8th	eighth	**huitième**
9th	ninth	**neuvième**
10th	tenth	**dixième**
11th	eleventh	**onzième**
12th	twelfth	**douzième**
13th	thirteenth	**treizième**
14th	fourteenth	**quatorzième**
15th	fifteenth	**quinzième**

16th	sixteenth	**seizième**
17th	seventeenth	**dix-septième**
18th	eighteenth	**dix-huitième**
19th	nineteenth	**dix-neuvième**
20th	twentieth	**vingtième**
21st	twenty-first	**vingt et unième**
22nd	twenty-second	**vingt-deuxième**
30th	thirtieth	**trentième**
40th	fortieth	**quarantième**
50th	fiftieth	**cinquantième**
60th	sixtieth	**soixantième**
70th	seventieth	**soixante-dixième**
80th	eightieth	**quatre-vingtième**
90th	ninetieth	**quatre-vingt-dixième**
100th	hundredth	**centième**
101st	hundred and first	**cent unième**
110th	hundred and tenth	**cent dixième**
200th	two hundredth	**deux centième**
250th	two hundred and fiftieth	**deux cent cinquantième**
1,000th	thousandth	**millième**
1,001st	thousand and first	**mille et unième**
2,000th	two thousandth	**deux millième**
10,000th	ten thousandth	**dix millième**
100,000th	hundred thousandth	**cent millième**
1,000,000th	millionth	**millionième**

Fractions/Les fractions

½	a half	**un demi**
⅓	a third	**un tiers**
¼	a quarter	**un quart**
¹⁄₁₀	a tenth	**un dixième**
⅔	two-thirds	**deux tiers**
⅝	five-eighths	**cinq huitièmes**
¹⁄₁₀₀	one hundredth	**un centième**
1½	one and a half	**un et demi**
2¼	two and a quarter	**deux et un quart**

Decimals/Les décimaux

0.1	point one	**zéro virgule un**
0.25	point two five	**zéro virgule vingt-cinq**
1.2	one point two	**un virgule deux**
1.46	one point four six	**un virgule quarante-six**

Percentages/Pourcentages

25%	twenty-five per cent	**vingt-cinq pour cent**
50%	fifty per cent	**cinquante pour cent**
100%	a hundred per cent	**cent pour cent**
365%	three hundred and sixty-five per cent	**trois cent soixante-cinq pour cent**
4.25%	four point two five per cent	**quatre virgule vingt-cinq pour cent**